**CADOGAN** *guides*

Dana Facaros & Michael Pauls

# ITALY

P9-CCQ-814

*MARZO 1994*

*MEMO: SABEMOS QUE EN TU FUTURO SE ENCUENTRA UN VIAJE A ITALIA Y POR ESTA RAZÓN TE DAMOS ÉSTE LIBRO PARA QUE LO PLANEES SUERTE!*

*Cony Gisel.*

*Michell*

**Cadogan Books plc**
London House, Parkgate Road, London SW11 4NQ, UK

Distributed in North America by
**The Globe Pequot Press**
6 Business Park Road, PO Box 833, Old Saybrook,
Connecticut 06475–0833

Copyright © Dana Facaros and Michael Pauls 1994
Illustrations © Horatio Monteverde 1994

Reprinted 1996
Book and cover design by Animage
Cover illustrations by Animage
Maps © Cadogan Guides, drawn by Thames Cartographic Ltd

Series Editors: Rachel Fielding and Vicki Ingle

Managing Editor: Vicki Ingle
Editing: Nick Ryder, Amelia Maiden and Linda McQueen
Updating: Sam Cole, Adam Coulter, Josh Lacey, Clare Pedrick,
    Rupert Scott, Jane Shaw, Lindsay Hunt and Tom Parsons
Proofreading: Stephanie Maury, Annabel Hall and Linda McQueen
Indexing: Jane Wregg
Production: Rupert Wheeler Book Production Services

A catalogue record for this book is available from the British Library
US Library of Congress Cataloging-in-Publication-Data available

ISBN 0–94–7754–61–X

Output by Bookworm, Manchester
Printed and bound in Finland by Werner Söderström Oy on Kymexcote

## About the Authors

Dana Facaros and Michael Pauls are professional travel writers. To research this book, they spent three years based in a small Umbrian village, where they suffered massive overdoses of art, food and wine, and enjoyed every minute of it. The success of the original version of their Italy led to a series of highly popular regional and city guides. Though now acclaimed as the authorities on Italy for travellers, Dana and Michael have pretty much covered it completely; they regret there isn't more of it. But for consolation they have moved to a leaky-roofed farmhouse in the Lot valley. From there they have already cranked out three books in the Cadogan Guides France series.

## Please help us keep this guide up to date

We have done our best to ensure that the information in this guide is correct at the time of going to press. But places and facilities are constantly changing, and standards and prices in hotels and restaurants fluctuate. We would be delighted to receive any comments concerning existing entries or omissions. Significant contributions will be acknowledged in the next edition, and authors of the best letters will receive a copy of the Cadogan Guide of their choice.

# Contents

## Art and Architecture · 66–76

## Topics · 77–86

## Italian Culture · 87–94

## Piedmont, Valle d'Aosta and Liguria · 95–212

## Lombardy and the Lakes       213–330

## Venetia       331–500

## Emilia-Romagna       501–576

# Acknowledgements

**For the first edition,** we would like to thank the Italian National Tourist Office, and all the local and municipal tourist boards who so kindly answered our questions that had answers and loaded us down with enough information to write several more volumes about Italy. Also, we would like to extend our warmest gratitude to Michael Davidson and Brian Walsh, whose unfailing good humour helped us through the darkest corners of Italy; to Mario, Fiorella, Alessandra and Sara who never minded having a couple of extra children in their happy home; to Anna and Tito Illuminati, who guided us through the intricacies of life in Rosciano and always let us use their phone; to Bruce Johnston, for his innumerable suggestions and his Deux Chevaux; to longtime residents Clare Pedrick, Anne and Santino, for their invaluable insights into the Italian miasma; to Carolyn Steiner and Chris Malumphy, who crossed the Atlantic to cheer us up; and especially to Rachel Fielding and Janey Dalrymple.

**For this second edition** we are grateful to our updaters Sam Cole, Adam Coulter, Josh Lacey, Clare Pedrick, Rupert Scott and Jane Shaw for their tireless practical research, and to Amelia Maiden and Nick Ryder for editing this rather large book; and a big hug and thanks to Linda McQueen for tying up the loose ends, and to Vicki Ingle for masterminding the whole project.

**Extract from** Petrarch and corresponding English translation on p.94 from *Some Love Songs of Petrarch*, translated and annotated and with a biographical introduction by William Dudley Foulke LL.D (Humphrey Milford, OUP 1915), included by permission of Oxford University Press.

# Introduction

Italy dangles from the centre of western Europe like a Christmas stocking, stuffed to the brim with marvels, some as soaring and grand as a Verdi opera or Brunelleschi's dome over Florence Cathedral, some as weird and unexpected as the pagan tombs buried underneath St Peter's in Rome, or Galileo's erect middle finger, carefully, significantly preserved in a reliquary in Florence's science museum. Even first-time visitors, with eyes and brains spinning, soon become uneasily aware that for every Italian cliché, every Mount Vesuvius, St Mark's Basilica and Leonardo's *Last Supper*, Italy has a hundred other natural wonders and artistic showpieces that any other nation would die for. Someone once tried to count up all the works of art, and concluded that there were three per inhabitant, no less. This national patrimony is echoed by even the most ephemeral arts, whether cranked out by the fashion and design workshops or simmered in the kitchen: for every Italian dish or wine you've been craving to try on its home turf, expect a hundred other delights you've never heard of before.

Even the common, everyday Italy that co-exists next to the overflow of museums, art cities, ruins and rivieras is an extravagant, daunting place to digest, and as the latest headlines confirm (the advent of Berlusconi's Forza Italia, the Mafia trials, the Tangentopoli bribery scandals), it is a country that operates on rules entirely unlike those in force back home, full of contradictions and paradoxes, depths and shallows. As an Umbrian friend of ours told us, you cry twice in Italy: when you first arrive and when you have to leave. In the meantime, pack your intellect, gird your senses and watch out, not only for pickpockets but for a country that might just pick your heart.

**NOTE:** this book covers only the Italian mainland—and it's long enough at that. We have tried to say a little bit about the islands close to the mainland, however, and which ferries will take you there.

## A Little Geography

This is not a complex subject; there are tall mountains, and there are not-so-tall mountains. From the Alps down through the Apennines, the Italians are often at a loss to find enough level ground to plant a football field. In all Italy, you'll find only three substantial flatlands: the broad valley of the Po, separating the Alps and Apennines, offering forgettable scenery but Italy's richest farmlands and a score of her most interesting cities; the coastal plain that includes the Maremma of southern Tuscany and Lazio, and the thoroughly flat *tavoliere* stretching across Apulia. Most of the really impressive mountains are in the Alps (Mont Blanc, the Matterhorn and other great peaks form part of Italy's northern boundaries) but the tallest completely within Italy is the Gran Sasso d'Italia (the 'Big Rock of Italy'), centre of a mighty patch of snow-clad peaks in the northwestern Abruzzo.

Not counting the islands, there are about 260,000 square km of Italy, roughly the size of the island of Britain (Americans can think of it as a New York, a Pennsylvania, and most of a New Jersey). Even with some 55 million Italians, busily tending the world's 5th or 6th most opulent economy, the country never seems too crowded. Some large patches of urban sprawl exist—in the Po valley, for example, or around the Bay of Naples—but the Italians enjoy each other's company, and generally live in tightly packed cities, hill towns and villages, with plenty of good green countryside in between. It is about 1,000 km, as the crow flies, from Mont Blanc to the furthest corner of Apulia, the 'heel' of the Italian boot (1,400 km if you're driving), and the long peninsula is in most places 150–250 km across.

There are very few easy routes across the Apennines between the Adriatic and the Tyrrhenian; now as in ancient times the main highways parallel the coast or converge on Rome from all points. The long coastline is unevenly blessed; at one extreme there is the delicious Amalfi coast, the Riviera, the Gargano in Apulia and a few isolated lovely expanses (on Calabria's Tyrrhenian coast, Monte Conero near Ancona, near Terracina and Gaeta in Lazio). Most of the rest is surprisingly dull—much of Tuscany and Lazio, and the greater part of the Adriatic and Ionian coasts.

## Some Features of the Landscape

**In the north:** the beautiful, oddly shaped Dolomites, partially made of million-year-old coral; the 'seven seas', a string of lagoons from Venice to Ravenna along the Adriatic; the caves and underground streams of the karst topography around Trieste and the Friuli; the lakes region, formed by Alpine rivers that can't reach the sea, large enough to form a small pocket of Mediterranean climate on the edge of the Alps; the Ligurian Alps, blocking off the Italian Riviera from the rest of the continent and giving it the mildest winter weather north of Calabria.

**Central Italy:** the Apennines flanked by the rolling hills of Tuscany, Umbria and the Marches; in Umbria and Lazio, a string of large lakes, mostly of volcanic origin, of which the

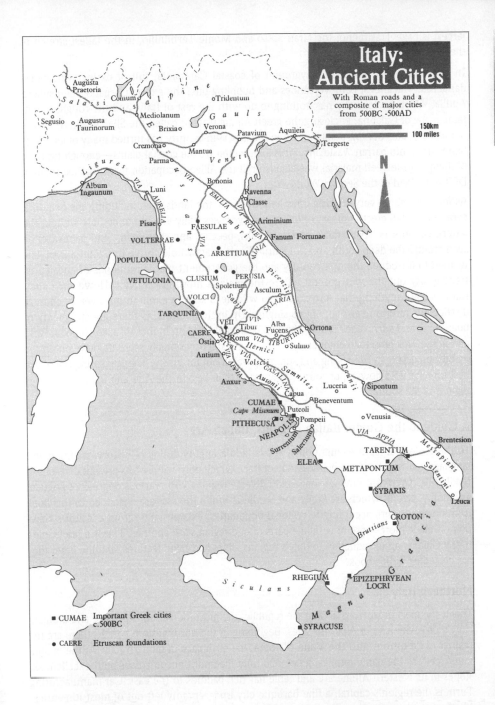

# Italy: Ancient Cities

With Roman roads and a composite of major cities from 500BC -500AD

150km
100 miles

N

- ■ CUMAE — Important Greek cities c.500BC
- ● CAERE — Etruscan foundations

largest is Lake Trasimeno; the Gran Sasso and Monte Terminillo, in the tallest stretch of the Apennines.

**In the south**: the volcanic playground of coastal Campania, full of extinct volcanoes, dangerous volcanoes, baby volcanoes and bubbling pits; the exotic Gargano Peninsula in Apulia, which geologically has nothing to do with the rest of Italy; and the rough, mountainous toe of Calabria, enclosing the green Alpine plateau called the Sila. Southern Italy is hot and dry, and wanton deforestation in the late 19th century has turned many of its mountain regions into barren wastelands. It is a bit wetter on the coastal plains—enough for most of them to have been malarial wastelands until the Allied occupation forces bathed them in DDT at the end of the Second World War.

As for trees, some very striking ones help decorate the landscape, including the beautiful parasol pine, tall erect Lombardy poplars and cypresses (Italy would not be Italy without the latter). Old forests have large numbers of oaks, beeches and evergreens, and palms can be seen around the deep south and in Liguria. Koala bears would thrive in Calabria if anyone wanted to introduce them; a century ago the government planted millions of eucalyptus trees to dry out the wet ground where the malaria mosquitoes lived. However, Italian hunters blast anything that moves, and so wildlife is kept to a minimum. Even in country districts it's rare to hear many birds singing. Up in the mountains there are still plenty of boar, foxes and such. The famous Abruzzo bears still hang on in the Abruzzo National Park, and in the Alps mountain chamois and wolves are still occasionally seen. If you're out in the woods, especially in late spring and summer, watch out for vipers. The late spring is also the best time for wild flowers, of course; they are at their best in the Alps and the mountainous regions in the south.

## A Guide to the Guide: Italian Regions, Italian Art

To the geological features mentioned above, add a mighty dollop of history, tradition and language, and you have the political map of Italy, which only acquired its present divisions in the 1960s. There are now 21 amazingly diverse regions with various degrees of political autonomy, two of which are Sicily and Sardinia, while the rest are described in this book from north to south according to regional boundaries, except where from a visitor's viewpoint it made more sense to combine parts of one region with another. This is a brief Guide to the Guide—an introduction to Italy's regions, cities and main features, and the order they are presented in this book.

## Northern Italy

This is the most prosperous area of the republic, the most industrial, expensive and dramatically scenic, the land of Alps and lakes. Beginning in the northwestern corner, there are the regions of **Piedmont and the Valle d'Aosta**, the birthplace of modern Italy. At the 'mountains' feet', as the name implies, green and hilly Piedmont encompasses both excellent ski slopes in its western Alpine arc and table-flat rice paddies to the east. Car-manufacturing Turin is the region's capital, a fine Baroque city undeservedly left out of most itineraries. Much of southern Piedmont, around Asti and Alba, is given over to the cultivation of Italy's greatest wines. The proximity of France has had an excellent influence on the Piedmontese kitchen; white truffles are the speciality in the autumn.

The northwest's most spectacular scenery, however, is contained in the small, autonomous, bilingual (French and Italian) region of the Valle d'Aosta. The Aosta valleys are one of Italy's great holiday playgrounds, with Courmayeur, Breuil-Cervinia, and other stunning Alpine resorts on the southern slopes of giants like Mont Blanc (Monte Bianco) and the Matterhorn (Cervino), near legendary Alpine passes like the Great St Bernard, and in lovely Gran Paradiso National Park. Aosta, the fine little capital, is nicknamed the 'Rome of the Alps' for its extensive ruins.

Over the lush Maritime Alps lies Italy's smallest region, **Liguria**, a beautiful arch of coast that is better known abroad as the Italian Riviera. In the centre lies Genoa, Italy's greatest seaport, while on either side are famous resorts like San Remo, Alassio, Rapallo, Portofino, Portovenere, and the magnificent Cinque Terre. The climate is especially mild; palms, olives, flowers, and vines grow in profusion. The seafood and the dishes with *pesto* sauce are superb.

East of Piedmont lies the relatively large region of **Lombardy**, which is treated together with the whole area covered by the Italian Lakes in one chapter in this book. First is a section on Milan and southern Lombardy, which encompasses both Italy's second city and the three jewels of Lombardy's Po plain: medieval Pavia, violin-making Cremona, and the Renaissance art city of Mantua. Lombardy's capital, Milan, adopted city of Leonardo da Vinci, centre of fashion and finance, home of one of Europe's greatest cathedrals and opera houses, throbs with life and excitement, a vision of the new Italy.

Northern Lombardy, and a piece of eastern Piedmont and western Veneto, all form part of the **Italian Lakes**, that lovely and legendary district beloved of poets since Roman times. Westernmost is little Lake Orta and the famous Simplon Tunnel near Domodossola; nearby Lake Maggiore has its Borromean isles and the world-famous resort of Stresa. Then comes zig-zagging Lake Lugano, which Italy shares with Switzerland, and then lovely Lake Como, with resorts deeply ingraved in the English traveller's Romantic memory—Bellagio, Cernobbio, Tremezzo, and Menaggio. From the northeast bank of Como extends the Valtellina, surrounded by Lombardy's rugged Alps, stretching all the way to Bormio and the western confines of Stelvio National Park. To the south of the Valtellina are more lakes—Iseo and tiny Idro, and two excellent art cities, Bergamo and Brescia. Westernmost is Lake Garda, nicknamed the 'Riviera of the Dolomites' for its dramatic surroundings. Sirmione, Gardone, Limone, and Riva are its most famous resorts; famous wines grow between its eastern shore and Verona.

The next three regions to the east, for centuries part of the Most Serene Republic of Venice, are traditionally known altogether as **Venetia**. The main attraction of the **Veneto**, the region east of Lake Garda, is of course Venice itself, one of the world's most extraordinary visions; but there are three other lovely cities—St Anthony's Padua, Palladio's Vicenza, and Romeo and Juliet's Verona. Magnificent villas, built for Venetian patricians, dot the landscape, especially around the Brenta Canal between Padua and Venice, and in enchanting districts like the Eugaean Hills near Padua, and Bassano del Grappa, Asolo and Treviso in the foothills of the Dolomites; wines like Bardolino, Soave and Valpolicella are produced around Verona. To the south lie the haunting flatlands of the river Po and its Delta.

Rising up in northern Venetia, the **Dolomites** are a majestic range of strange and fabulous peaks, a paradise for summer and winter sports. The Dolomites cross over two regions: the eastern half, still part of the Veneto, includes the famous Olympic resort of Cortina d'Ampezzo, while to the west is the partly autonomous region known as Trentino-Alto Adige. Trent, the capital of Trentino, is a fine old town associated with the great 16th-century Counter-Reformation council; nearby are the rugged Brenta Dolomites, valleys of apple orchards, castles, and vineyards. Alto Adige, on the Austrian border, is a bilingual region that prefers to be known as Süd Tirol—an intriguing mix of strudel and pasta, fairytale castles and resorts, vineyards and spas. Bolzano is its capital, but its most celebrated watering-hole, Merano, is better known. Much of the western portion of Alto Adige is occupied by Stelvio National Park, Italy's largest, with glaciers that permit year-round skiing.

East of Venice lies the third Venetia, **Friuli-Venezia Giulia**, occupying the corner between Austria and Yugoslavia, with the neoclassical city and seaport of Trieste as its capital. There are popular resorts on the coast like Grado and Lignano, pretty towns like Udine and Cividale, and more Alps in the north. Friuli is famous for its white wines; its ethnic mix of Slavic, Germanic, and Friulian cultures give it a unique twist.

Separating Northern Italy from Central, **Emilia-Romagna** almost crosses the entire peninsula, occupying the plain south of the Po and the northernmost section of the Apennines. Many people associate it with Italy's finest cuisine, but there are splendid cities to visit: the historic capital and medieval university town of Bologna; stately Parma, city of cheese and ham; Modena, home of Ferraris and Lambrusco; Busseto, the home of Verdi; Ferrara, the Renaissance city of the Este dynasty; Faenza, city of ceramics, and Ravenna, with dazzling Byzantine mosaics unique in Italy. Here, too, the string of Adriatic resorts begins—with Rimini, biggest and brashest of them all, yet secreting a Renaissance pearl in its heart. Just a short ride from Rimini, up in the mountains you'll find San Marino, the world's smallest and oldest republic, where tourists are more than welcome.

## Central Italy

Here, for many, lies the archetypical image of Italy—those rolling hills, faded ochre farmhouses and stone villas, the cypresses, the hill towns, the pines of Rome—the background to a thousand Renaissance paintings.

The first chapter, however, begins where Emilia-Romagna left off, in one of the lesser known corners of Central Italy, **The Marches**, where the landscapes are often similar to those of Tuscany. The Marches have two fine towns: Urbino, built around Duke Federico's perfect Renaissance palace, and lovely, medieval Ascoli Piceno. In between come a score of pleasant, seldom-visited hill towns and an almost continuous string of modest resorts, on either side of the salty old port city of Ancona.

South of the Marches are two even less familiar regions, **Abruzzo and Molise**. Abruzzo, containing the other loftiest peaks in the Apennines, is Rome's mountain playground, with winter sports at the Gran Sasso and summertime exploring in the National Park of the

Abruzzi, the home of the Abruzzo bear and other fauna. The coast is fairly nondescript, lined with family resorts; inland there's the interesting capital of L'Aquila and a fascinating collection of unspoiled medieval villages and churches. With the highest villages in the Apennines, Molise is a small mountain-bound region tucked in south of Abruzzo, utterly obscure, quiet, and charmingly unprepared for 20th-century tourism.

Back on the western, or Tyrrhenian coast, **Tuscany** probably needs no introduction. There's more to it, however, than just the charmed trio of Medieval and Renaissance art cities, Florence, Siena, and Pisa. Lucca, Pistoia, Prato and Arezzo have also accumulated more than their share of notable art and architecture, and the rolling, civilized landscape will take you to beautiful hill towns in every direction: San Gimignano with its medieval 'skyscrapers', brooding Etruscan Volterra, the Renaissance planned city of Pienza, Montepulciano, and dozens more.

Landlocked, vaguely other-worldly **Umbria** is in many ways a more rustic version of Tuscany, spangled with historic hill towns like Perugia, the capital and cultural centre; Orvieto with its famous cathedral; Spoleto, synonymous with Italy's most important arts festival; medieval Gubbio; and Assisi, the city of St Francis, as well as a dozen others, set in the emerald valleys and hills.

**Lazio**, ancient *Latium*, includes Rome and a good deal more; despite being right at the centre of things Lazio's attractions are not well known. Northern Lazio, an area of large lakes and hills, was the homeland of the ancient Etruscans, containing fascinating archaeological sites such as those at Tarquinia and Cerveteri. There is a lot to see in towns like Viterbo and Anagni, two places that contributed much to the history of the Popes in the Middle Ages, important Renaissance villas and gardens (as at Caprarola, Tivoli and Bomarzo), major Roman ruins at Ostia Antica and Tivoli—not to mention Rome itself—and a pretty stretch of coast between Cape Circeo and Formia.

## Southern Italy

The four regions of Italy's *Mezzogiorno* often seem an entirely different country from the green and tidy north. Not many visitors ever make it further south than **Campania**, where Naples and its famous bay make up the south's prime attraction—including Pompeii, Vesuvius, Capri, Sorrento, the infernal volcanic Phlegraean fields, dozens of Roman ruins and much more. The wonderful Amalfi Drive between Sorrento and Salerno covers the most spectacular bit of coastline in Italy, passing the truly unique towns of Positano, Amalfi and Ravello. Naples itself, famous for its pizza and animated *Italianità*, is also the south's art capital, with many surprises from the Middle Ages and Baroque period. The rest of Campania includes venerable and interesting towns like Salerno, Caserta, Capua and Benevento, the well-preserved Greek temples at Paestum, and the pleasant, unspoiled Cilento coast.

Lovers of fine Italian art and cuisine will not find them in **Calabria and the Basilicata**, once the most backward corners of the nation and now struggling gamely to catch up. The west coast from Maratea to Reggio Calabria, the 'Calabrian Riviera', offers some clean beaches and beautiful scenery (especially around Maratea and Cape Vaticano) and the heavily forested mountain plateau west of Cosenza called the Sila attracts hikers and nature-lovers. Of the once-mighty Greek cities of the Ionian coast, there's little left but the great museum at Reggio and some scanty ruins at Metaponto. The bare, eroded hills of the inland Basilicata are not particularly inviting, unless you want to see the famous *sassi* (cave-dwellers' quarters) of Matera.

**Apulia** for many will be the real find in the south. The flat *tavoliere*, covered with fields of corn, covers most of the region, but the rugged limestone Gargano Peninsula offers scenery unique in Italy, along with growing but still enjoyable resorts like Vieste. Apulia was doing quite well in the Middle Ages, seen in the fine Apulian Romanesque cathedrals in so many towns on the *tavoliere*, including that of Bari, the south's prosperous second city and the burial place of Santa Claus. This plain also grows some of Italy's most robust wines; on it Emperor Frederick II built his mysterious Castel del Monte. Táranto, founded by the ancient Greeks, has a museum full of Greek vases, great seafood and a wonderful maritime atmosphere. You won't see anything in Italy like the *trulli*, the whitewashed houses with conical stone roofs that turn the areas around Alberobello into a fairytale landscape; if you press on further south into Italy's 'heel', the Salentine Peninsula, you can visit Baroque Lecce, the south's most beautiful city.

# Travel

### By Air

### from the UK

Flying is obviously the quickest and most painless way of getting to Italy from the UK. There are direct flights to over 20 destinations from over half a dozen British airports. Rome, Milan, Pisa and Venice have the greatest choice of year-round services, though there are plenty of regular flights to the business cities of Genoa, Bologna and Turin too; coastal or island resort destinations may be much more seasonal. Florence has more limited air links with Britain, but is well connected by rail to Pisa, Milan, etc. Scheduled services have fewer booking restrictions, but are usually more expensive than charters. To sweeten the bill, promotional perks like rental cars, discounts on domestic flights, accommodation, tours and so forth may be included, though fly-drive deals are surprisingly expensive in Italy.

Most scheduled flights are operated either by the Italian state airline **Alitalia**, ✆ (0171) 602 7111, or **British Airways**, ✆ (0181) 897 4000. A few services are operated by **Air UK**, ✆ (0345) 666777 and **Meridiana**, ✆ (0171) 839 2222. Return fares vary greatly, depending on the season. The best-value deals are usually **Apex** or **SuperApex** fares, which you must book seven days ahead, and stay a Saturday night in Italy—no alterations or refunds are possible without high penalties. Return scheduled fares range typically from around £200 off-season (midsummer fares will probably be well over £250). Early birds get the best seats in the airline business, so think well ahead when booking. If you're prepared to be flexible (and philosophical), last-minute stand-bys can be a snip. Children, young people or bona fide students, and senior citizens may travel for reduced fares.

### from mainland Europe

Air travel between Italy and other parts of Europe can be relatively expensive, especially for short hops, so check overland options unless you're in a great hurry. You may need to shop around a little for the best deals, and perhaps choose a less prestigious carrier. Some airlines (**Alitalia, Qantas, Air France**, etc.) offer excellent rates on the European stages of intercontinental flights, and Italy is an important touchdown for many long-haul services to the Middle or Far East. Many of these may have inconvenient departure times and booking restrictions. Amsterdam, Paris and Athens are good centres for finding cheap flights, e.g. a Rome–Paris fare with Air India or Kenya Airways could cost you under £150 return.

### from the USA and Canada

The main Italian air gateways for direct flights from North America are Rome and Milan, though, if you're doing a grand tour, check fares to other European destinations (Paris or Amsterdam, for example) which may well be cheaper. **Alitalia** is the major carrier, but from the USA, **TWA, United Airlines** and **Delta** also fly from a number of cities. From Canada, **Air Canada** and **Canadian Airlines** operate from Toronto and Montreal. Summer round-trip fares from New York cost around US$1,000; rather more from Canada, so you may prefer to fly from the States. As elsewhere, fares are very seasonal and much cheaper in winter, especially mid-week.

Many inexpensive charter flights are available to popular Italian destinations in summer, though you are unlikely to find the sort of rock-bottom bargains as, say, to Spain. One of the biggest UK operators is **Italy Sky Shuttle**, which uses a variety of carriers. You may find cheaper fares by combing the small ads in the travel pages, or from a specialist agent. Use a reputable ABTA-registered one, such as **STA Travel**, **Trailfinders** or **Campus Travel**. All these companies offer particularly good student and youth rates too. The main problems with cheaper flights tend to be inconvenient or unreliable flight schedules, and booking restrictions, i.e. you may have to make reservations far ahead, accept given dates and, if you miss your flight, there's no redress. Take good travel insurance, however cheap your ticket is.

From North America, standard scheduled flights on well-known airlines are expensive, but reassuringly reliable and convenient: older travellers or families may prefer to pay extra for such a long journey (9–15 hours' flying time). Resilient, flexible and/or youthful travellers may be willing to shop around for budget deals on consolidated charters, stand-bys or perhaps even courier flights (remember you can usually only take hand luggage with you on the last). In the USA, **Airhitch** and **Council Charter** are leading reputable cheap-flight specialists. Check the *Yellow Pages* for courier companies (**Now Voyager** is one of the largest USA ones, ✆ (212) 431 1616; **Board Courier Services** operates in several Canadian cities, ✆ (514) 633 0740). For discounted flights, try the small ads in newspaper travel pages (e.g. *New York Times, Chicago Tribune, Toronto Globe & Mail*). Firms like **STA** or Canada-based **Travel Cuts** are worth contacting for student fares. Numerous travel clubs and agencies also specialize in discount fares, but may require an annual membership fee.

### *discount agencies*

#### UK

**Campus Travel**, 52 Grosvenor Gardens, SW1, or 174 Kensington High Street, London W8, ✆ (0171) 730 3402.

**Italy Sky Shuttle**, 227 Shepherd's Bush Rd, London W6 7AS, ✆ (0171) 748 1333.

**STA**, 74 and 86 Old Brompton Rd, London SW7, or 117 Euston Rd, London NW1, ✆ (0171) 937 9921.

**Trailfinders**, 194 Kensington High Street, London W8 (0171) 937 5400.

#### USA/Canada

**Airhitch**, 2790 Broadway Suite 100, New York, NY 10025, ✆ (212) 864 2000.

**Council Travel**, 205 E 42nd Street, New York, NY 10017, ✆ (800) 800 8222.

**Last Minute Travel Club**, 1249 Boylston St, Boston, MA 02215, ✆ (800) 527 8646.

**Now Voyager**, 74 Varick St, Suite 307, New York, NY 10013, ✆ (212) 431 1616.

**Courier Travel Service**, 530 Central Avenue, Cedarhurst, NY 11516, ✆ (516) 374 2299.

**STA**, 48 East 11th Street, New York, NY 10003, ✆ (212) 477 7166.

**Travel CUTS**, 187 College Street, Toronto, Ontario M5T 1P7, ✆ (416) 979 2406.

Italy is easily accessible by rail from the UK, and about to become more so as the Channel Tunnel becomes fully operational and new fast rail networks spread throughout Europe. From London the journey to Milan currently takes about 22 hours, to Rome about 24, via Lille and Basel; services run daily in summer. Return fares range from about £160 to £240. From Paris, fast journeys via Lyon get you to Milan in under 10 hours. Once you've added the cost of a couchette (£12 or so), rail travel is scarcely cheaper than flying unless you are able to take advantage of student or youth fares. Discounts are available for families, and young children, though the long journey can be irksome unless you book sleepers. For more information, contact the **International Rail Centre** at Victoria, ✆ (0171) 834 7066.

One supremely luxurious way of reaching Italy by rail deserves a special mention: the **Orient Express** whirls you from London through Paris, Zurich, Innsbruck and Verona to Venice in a cocoon of traditional 20s and 30s glamour, with beautifully restored Pullman/wagon-lits. It's fiendishly expensive—and quite unforgettable for a once-in-a-lifetime treat. Current prices are about £895 for a double cabin (London–Venice one-way); prices include all meals. Several operators offer packages including smart Venice hotel accommodation and return flights home. Ring Venice-Simplon Orient Express on (0171) 928 6000 for more information.

**Interail** (UK) or **Eurail** passes (USA/Canada) give unlimited travel for under-26s throughout Europe for one or two months. Various other cheap youth fares (BIJ tickets etc.) are also available; organise these before you leave home. Useful addresses for rail travel include **Eurotrain**, 52 Grosvenor Gardens, London SW1, ✆ (0171) 730 8518); **Wasteels Travel**, 121 Wilton Rd, London SW1, ✆ (0171) 834 7066; any branch of **Thomas Cook**, or **CIT** (*see* addresses below).

If you are just planning to see Italy, inclusive rail passes may not be worthwhile. Fares on FS (*Ferrovie dello Stato*), the Italian State Railway, are among the lowest (kilometre for kilometre) in Europe. A month's full Interail pass costs £249, though you can now buy cheaper zonal passes covering three or four countries only. If you intend travelling extensively by train, one of the special Italian tourist passes may be a better bet (*see* 'Getting Around').

### CIT Offices in Italy

**UK:** Marco Polo House, 3–5 Lansdowne Rd, Croydon, Surrey, ✆ (81) 686 0677.

**USA:** 342 Madison Ave, Suite 3207, New York NY 10173, ✆ (212) 697 2100. There's also an 800 number you can call from anywhere:, ✆ (800) 223 0230.

**Canada:** 1450 City Councillors St. Suite 750, Montreal H3A 2E6, ✆ (514) 845 910.

A convenient pocket-sized **timetable** detailing all the main and secondary Italian railway lines is now available in the UK, costing £6 (plus 50p postage). Contact **Accommodation Line Ltd**, 11–12 Hanover Square, London W1; **Y Knot Travel**, Morley House, 1st Floor, 314/320 Regent Street, London W1; or **Italwings**, Travel & Accommodation, 87 Brewer Street, London W1. If you wait until you arrive in Italy, however, you can pick up the Italian timetable (in two volumes) at any station for about L4,500 each.

From USA and Canada, contact **Rail Europe**, central office at 226–230 Westchester Ave, White Plains, NY 10604, ✆ 914 682 2999 or 800 438 7245. **Wasteels** also have a USA office at 5728 Major Boulevard, Suite 308, Orlando, 32819 Florida.

## By Road

### by bus and coach

**Eurolines** is the main international bus operator in Europe, with representatives in Italy and many other countries. In the UK, they can be found at 52 Grosvenor Gardens, Victoria, London SW1, ✆ (0171) 730 0202, and are booked through National Express. Regular services run to many northern Italian cities, but terminate in Rome. Needless to say, the journey is long and the relatively small savings on price (a return ticket from London to Rome costs about £140) make it a masochistic choice in comparison with a discounted air fare, or even rail travel. Italian companies linked with Eurolines include **Lazzi** in Florence and Rome, and **Sadem** in Milan and Turin. Regular buses leave many Italian destinations for capitals throughout Europe, including Paris, Prague, Barcelona and Istanbul. **Magic Bus** is one of the major European operators (head office is at 20 Filellinon, Syntagma, Athens, ✆ (01) 32 37 4714), but it is represented in many other countries. Within Italy, you can obtain more information on long-distance bus services from any CIT office.

### by car

Driving to Italy from London is a rather lengthy and expensive proposition. If you're only staying for a short period, check costs against airline fly-drive schemes. It's the best part of 24 hours' driving time from the UK, even if you stick to fast toll roads. Calais–Florence via Nancy, Lucerne and Lugano is about 1042km. The most scenic and hassle-free route is via the Alps, avoiding crowded Riviera roads in summer, but, if you take a route through Switzerland, expect to pay for the privilege (£14 or 30SFr for motorway use). In winter the passes may be closed and you will have to stick to those expensive tunnels (one-way tolls range from about L22,000 for a small car). You can avoid some of the driving by putting your car on the train, though this is scarcely a cheap option. **Express Sleeper Cars** run to Milan from Paris or Boulogne (infrequently in winter). Foreign-plated cars may be entitled to free breakdown assistance from the ACI (Italian Touring Club), but it's wise to take out copper-bottomed insurance cover beforehand.

To bring a GB-registered car into Italy, you need a **vehicle registration document**, **full driving licence**, and **insurance papers**. Non-EU citizens should preferably have an **international driving licence** which has an Italian translation incorporated. Your vehicle should display a nationality plate indicating its country of registration. Before travelling, check everything is in perfect order. Minor infringements like worn tyres or burnt-out sidelights can cost you dear in any country. A **red triangular hazard sign** is obligatory; also recommended are a spare set of bulbs, a first-aid kit and a fire extinguisher. Spare parts for non-Italian cars can be difficult to find, especially Japanese models. Before crossing the Italian border, remember to fill up with petrol; *benzina* is still very expensive in Italy.

For more information on driving in Italy, *see* 'Getting Around By Car' (p.12) or contact the motoring organisations (**AA**, ✆ 0256 20123, or **RAC**, ✆ (0181) 686 0088 in the UK, and **AAA**, ✆ (407) 444 4000 in the USA.

### Passports and Visas

EU nationals with a valid passport can enter and stay in Italy as long as they like, or they may stay a year with a British Visitor's Passport, available from the post office. Citizens of the USA, Canada, Australia and New Zealand need only a valid passport to stay up to three months in Italy, unless they get a visa in advance from an Italian embassy or consulate:

**UK:** 38 Eaton Place, London SW1X, ✆ (0171) 235 9371.
32 Melville Street, Edinburgh 3, ✆ (0131) 226 3631.
2111 Piccadilly, Manchester, ✆ (0161) 236 3024.

**Ireland:** 63–65 Northumberland Road, Dublin, ✆ (0116) 2601 744.
7 Richmond Park, Belfast, ✆ (01232) 668 854.

**USA:** 690 Park Avenue, New York, NY, ✆ (212) 737 9100.
12400 Wilshire Blvd, Suite 300, Los Angeles CA, ✆ (213) 8200622.

**Canada:** 136 Beverley Street. Toronto, ✆ (416) 977 1566.

**Australia:** 61–69 Macquarie St, Sydney 2000, NSW, ✆ (02) 2478 442.

**New Zealand:** 34 Grant Rd, Thorndon, Wellington, ✆ (04) 7473 5339.

**France:** 47 rue de Varennes, 73343 Paris, ✆ (1) 45 44 38 90.

**Germany:** Karl Finkelnburgstrasse 49–51, 5300 Bonn 2, ✆ (0228) 82 00 60.

**Netherlands:** Herengracht 609, 1017 CE Amsterdam, ✆ (3120) 624 0043.

By law you should register with the police within eight days of your arrival in Italy. In practice this is done automatically for most visitors when they check in at their first hotel. Don't be alarmed if the owner of your self-catering property proposes to 'denounce' you to the police when you arrive—it's just a formality.

### Customs

EU nationals over the age of 17 can now import a limitless amount of goods for personal use, provided duty has already been paid. Non-EU nationals have to pass through the Italian Customs which are usually benign. How the frontier police manage to recruit such ugly, mean-looking characters to hold the submachine guns and dogs from such a good-looking population is a mystery, but they'll let you be if you don't look suspicious and haven't brought along more than 200 cigarettes or 100 cigars, or not more than a litre of hard drink or three bottles of wine, a couple of cameras, a movie camera, 10 rolls of film for each, a tape-recorder, radio, record-player, one canoe less than 5.5m, sports equipment for personal use, and one TV (though you'll have to pay for a licence for it at Customs). Pets must be accompanied by a bilingual Certificate of Health from your local Veterinary Inspector. You can take the same items listed above home with you without hassle—except of course your British pet. USA citizens may return with $400 worth of merchandise—keep your receipts.

### Currency

There are no limits to how much money you bring into Italy: legally you may not export more than L20,000 000 in Italian banknotes, a sum unlikely to trouble many of us, though officials rarely check.

Dozens of general and specialist companies offer holidays in Italy. Some of the major ones are listed below. Not all of them are necesssarily ABTA-bonded; we recommend you check before booking.

### UK general

**Bladon Lines**, 56–58 Putney High Street, London SW15 1SF.    (0181) 785 3131 ©

**Citalia**, Marco Polo House, 3–5 Lansdowne Road, Croydon CR9 1LL.    (0181) 686 5533 ©

**Cosmos**, Tourama House, 17 Holmesdale Rd, Bromley, Kent BR2 9LX. (0181) 464 3444 ©

**Cresta Italy**, Holiday House, Victoria Street, Altrincham, Cheshire WA14 1ET.
(01345) 125333 ©

**Crystal Premier**, Crystal House, The Courtyard, Arlington Rd, Surbiton, Surrey KT6 6BW.
(0181) 399 5144 ©

**First Choice** (formerly Enterprise), Groundstar House, London Road, Crawley, West Sussex RH10 2TB.    (01293) 560777 ©

**Inghams**, 10–18 Putney Hill, London SW15 6AX.    (0181) 785 7777 ©

**Italian Escapades**, 227 Shepherds Bush Road, London W6 7AS.    (0181) 748 2661 ©

**Italiatour**, 205 Holland Park Avenue, London W11 4XB.    (0171) 371 1114 ©

**Magic of Italy**, 227 Shepherds Bush Road, London W6 7AS.    (0181) 748 7575 ©

**Owners Abroad Travel**, 2nd Floor, Astral Towers, Betts Way, Crawley, West Sussex.
(01293) 554455 ©

**Page & Moy**, 136–140 London Road, Leicester LE2 1EN.    (01533) 524433 ©

**Sovereign**, Astral Towers, Betts Way, Crawley, West Sussex RH10 2GX. (01293) 599900 ©

**Sunvil**, Sunvil House, 7–8 Upper Sq, Old Isleworth, Middx TW7 7BJ.    (0181) 568 4499 ©

**Thomson**, Greater London House, Hampstead Rd, London NW1 7SD. (0181) 200 8733 ©

### UK special-interest

**Abercrombie & Kent** (art and architecture, botany and gardens), Sloane Square House, Holbein Place, London SW1W 8NS.    (0171) 730 9600 ©

**Alternative Travel** (walking and cycling tours), 69–71 Banbury Road, Oxford OX2 6PE.
(01865) 310399 ©

**Arblaster & Clarke** (wine tours, truffle hunts), 104 Church Road, Steep, Petersfield, Hants GU32 2BR.    (01730) 266883 ©

**Aria** (opera), 69 Cranbrook Road, London W14 2LT.    (0181) 994 0977 ©

**British Museum Tours** (guest lecturers, art and architecture), 464 Bloomsbury Street, London WC1B 3QQ.    (0171) 323 8895 ©

**Brompton Travel** (gardens and opera), Brompton House, 64 Richmond Road, Kingston-upon-Thames, Surrey KT2 5EH.    (0181) 549 3334 ©

**Cox & Kings** (gardens and villas, botany tours), St James Court, 45 Buckingham Gate, London SW1E 6AF.    (0171) 873 5002 ©

**Gordon Overland** (painting holidays), 76 Croft Road, Carlisle, Cumbria CA3 9AG.
(01228) 26795 ℭ

**JMB** (opera and gardens), Rushwick, Worcester WR2 5SN.
(01905) 425628 ℭ

**Kirker** (city breaks), 3 New Concordia Wharf, Mill Street, London SE1 2BB.
(0171) 231 3333 ℭ

**Leahys Travel** (pilgrimages), 116 Harpenden Road, St Albans, Herts AL3 6BZ.
(01727) 852394 ℭ

**Martin Randall Travel** (art and architecture, wines, gardens—guest lecturers), 10 Barley Mow Passage, Chiswick, London W4 4PH.
(0181) 742 3355 ℭ

**Prospect Music & Art** (opera; villas and gardens), 454/458 Chiswick High Road, London W4 5TT.
(0181) 995 2151 ℭ

**Ramblers** (walking tours), Box 43, Welwyn Garden City, Hertfordshire AL8 6PQ.
(01707) 331133 ℭ

**Saga** (art and architecture—senior citizens), The Saga Building, Middelburg Square, Folkestone, Kent CT20 1AZ.
(01303) 857000 ℭ

**Solo's** (singles holidays), 41 Watford Way, London NW4 3JH.
(0181) 202 0855 ℭ

**Special Tours** (escorted tours), 81a Elizabeth St, London SW1W 9PG. (0171) 730 2297 ℭ

**Tasting Italy** (cookery courses), 97 Bravington Road, London W9 3AA. (0181) 964 5839 ℭ

**Time Off**, Chester Mews, Chester Street, London SW1X 7BQ.
(0171) 235 8070 ℭ

**The Travel Club of Upminster** (painting holidays, garden tours), Station Road, Upminster, Essex RM14 2TT.
(01708) 225000 ℭ

**Travel for the Arts** (opera), 117 Regent's Park Rd, London NW1 8UR. (0171) 483 4466 ℭ

**Travelsphere** (coach tours), Compass House, Rockingham Road, Market Harborough, Leicestershire LE16 7QD.
(01858) 464818 ℭ

**Venice Simplon-Orient Express** (luxury rail tours) Sea Containers House, 20 Upper Ground, London SE1 9PF.
(0171) 928 6000 ℭ

**Voyages Jules Verne** (garden and villa tours), 21 Dorset Square, London NW1 6QG.
(0171) 723 5066 ℭ

**Wallace Arnold** (coach tours), Gelderd Road, Leeds, LS12 6DH.
(0532) 310739 ℭ

### in the USA/Canada

**Amelia Tours** (Sicily), 280 Old Country Road, Hicksville NY 11801.    (516) 433 0696 ℭ

**American Express Vacations** (prepacked or tailor-made tours), 300 Pinnacle Way, Norcross, GA 30093.
(800) 241 1700 ℭ

**Buddy Bombard Balloon Adventures** (ballooning in Tuscany), 6727 Curran Street, McLean, VA 22101 3804.
(703) 448 9407 ℭ

**CIT Tours** (general and skiing) 342 Madison Ave, Suite 3207, New York, NY 10173.
(212) 697 2100 ℭ

**Connaissance & Cie** (wine tours), 790 Madison Avenue, New York, NY 10021.
(212) 472 5772 ℭ

**Dailey-Thorp Travel** (music/opera), 330 West 58th Street, New York, NY 10019.
(212) 307 1555 ℂ

**Esplanade Tours** (art and architecture), 581 Boyston Street, Boston, MA 02116.
(617) 266 7465 ℂ

**Italiatour**, 666 5th Avenue, New York, NY 10103.    (212) 765 2183 ℂ

**Maupintour**, 1515 St Andrew's Drive, Lawrence, Kansas 66047.    (913) 843 1211 ℂ

**Olson Travelworld**, 970 West 190th Street, Suite 425, Torrance, California 90502.
(310) 354 2600 ℂ

**Trafalgar Tours**, 11 East 26th Street, New York, NY 10010.    (212) 689 8977 ℂ

**Travel Concepts** (wine/food), 62 Commonwealth Ave, Suite 3, Boston, MA 02116.
(617) 266 8450 ℂ

For self-catering and camping specialists *see* **Practical A–Z**, 'Where to Stay', pp.42–44.

## Getting Around

Italy has an excellent network of airports, railways, highways and byways and you'll find getting around fairly easy—until one union or another takes it into its head to go on strike (to be fair they rarely do it during the high holiday season). There's plenty of talk about passing a law to regulate strikes, but it won't happen soon if ever. Instead, learn to recognize the word in Italian: *sciopero* (SHO-per-o), and do as the Romans do—quiver with resignation. There's always a day or two's notice, and strikes usually last only a day, just long enough to throw a spanner in the works if you have to catch a plane. Keep your ears open and watch for notices posted in the stations. For more detailed information, *see* the relevant 'Getting Around' sections within each chapter.

### By Air

Air traffic within Italy is intense, with up to ten flights a day on popular routes. Domestic flights are handled by Alitalia, ATI (its internal arm) or Avianova. Air travel makes most sense when hopping between north and south, or to the islands of Sicily and Sardinia. Shorter journeys are often just as quick (and much less expensive) by train or even bus if you take check-in and airport travelling times into account. Mainland cities with airports include Ancona, Bari, Bergamo, Bologna, Brindisi, Florence, Genoa, Lamezia Terme (near Catanzaro), Milan, Naples, Parma, Pisa, Reggio Calabria, Turin, Trieste, Venice and Verona, all of which have direct flights to and from Rome.

Domestic flight costs are comparable to those in other European countries: a full-price return fare from Rome to Milan (an hour's journey) costs about L430,000 (one-way tickets are half-price). A complex system of discounts is available (some only at certain times of year) for night flights, weekend travel, senior (60 plus) and youth fares (12–26-year-olds; half-price or less for younger children). Family reductions are also available (up to 50%). Each airport has a bus terminal in the city; ask about schedules as you purchase your ticket to avoid hefty taxi fares. Baggage allowances vary between airlines. Tickets can be bought at CIT offices and other large travel agencies.

Italy's national railway, the **FS** (*Ferrovie dello Stato*) is well run, inexpensive (despite recent price rises) and often a pleasure to ride. There are also several private rail lines around cities and in country districts. Some, you may find, won't accept Interail or Eurail passes. On the FS, some of the trains are sleek and high-tech, but much of the rolling stock hasn't been changed for fifty years. Possible FS unpleasantnesses you may encounter, besides a strike, are delays, crowding (especially at weekends and in the summer), and crime on overnight trains, where someone rifles your bags while you sleep. The crowding, at least, becomes much less of a problem if you reserve a seat in advance at the Prenotazione counter. The fee is small and can save you hours standing in some train corridor. On the more expensive trains, **reservations** are mandatory. Do check when you purchase your ticket in advance that the date is correct; tickets are only valid the day they're purchased unless you specify otherwise. A number on your reservation slip will indicate in which car your seat is—find it before you board rather than after. The same goes for sleepers and couchettes on overnight trains, which must also be reserved in advance.

**Tickets** may be purchased not only in the stations, but at many travel agents in the city centres. Fares are strictly determined by the kilometres travelled. The system is computerized and runs smoothly, at least until you try to get a reimbursement for an unused ticket (usually not worth the trouble). Be sure you ask which platform (*binario*) your train arrives at; the big permanent boards in the stations are not always correct. If you get on a train without a ticket you can buy one from the conductor, with an added 20% penalty. You can also pay a conductor to move up to first class or get a couchette, if there are places available.

There is a fairly straightforward **hierarchy of trains**. At the bottom of the pyramid is the humble *Locale* (euphemistically known sometimes as an *Accelerato*) which often stops even where there's no station in sight; it can be excruciatingly slow. When you're checking the schedules, beware of what may look like the first train to your destination—if it's a *Locale*, it will be the last to arrive. A *Diretto* stops far less, an *Expresso* just at the main towns. *Intercity* trains whoosh between the big cities and rarely deign to stop. *Eurocity* trains link Italian cities with major European centres. Both of these services require a supplement— some 30% more than a regular fare. New supertrains similar to the French TGV services are just being introduced in Italy; the *ETR 500* series can travel at up to 186mph. Reservations are free, but must be made at least five hours before the trip, and on some trains there are only first-class coaches. Trains serving the most important routes have names such as the *Vesuvio* (Milan, Bologna, Florence, Rome, Naples), the *Adriatico* (Milan, Rimini, Pesaro, Ancona, Pescara, Foggia, Bari), or the *Colosseo/Ambrosiano* (Milan, Bologna, Florence, Rome). The real lords of the rails are the *ETR 450 Pendolino* trains, kilometre-eaters that will speed you to your destination as fast as trains can go (in Italy!). For these there is a more costly supplement and on some only first-class luxury cars.

The FS offers several **passes**. One which you should ideally arrange at a CIT or Italian rail agent office (e.g. Wasteels) before arriving in Italy, is the 'Travel-at-Will' ticket (*Biglietto Turistico Libera Circolazione*), available only to foreigners. This is a good deal only if you mean to do some very serious train riding on consecutive days; it does, however, allow you to ride the *Intercity/Eurocity* without paying a supplement. Tickets are sold for 8-, 15-, 21-, or 30-day periods, first or second class, with 50% reductions for children under 12. At the time of writing an 8-day second-class ticket is around £88 and the 30-day ticket is £152. A more flexible option is the 'Flexi Card' (marketed as a 'Freedom Pass' in the UK). It allows unlimited travel for either four days within a nine-day period (second class £66, first class £98), 8 days within 12 (second class £94, first class around £140), 12 days within 30 (second class £120, first class £190), and you don't have to pay any supplements. Another ticket, the *Kilometrico*, gives you 3000 kilometres of travel, made on a maximum of 20 journeys and is valid for two months; one advantage is that it can be used by up to five people at the same time. However, supplements are payable on *Intercity* trains. Second-class tickets are currently £90, first-class £152. Other discounts, available only once you're in Italy, are 15% on same-day return tickets and three-day returns (depending on the distance involved), and discounts for families of at least four travelling together. Senior citizens (men 65 and over, women 60) can also get a *Carta d'Argento* ('silver card') for L40,000 entitling them to a 20% reduction in fares. A *Carta Verde* bestows a 20% discount on people under 26 and also costs L40,000.

**Refreshments** on routes of any great distance are provided by bar cars or trolleys; you can usually get sandwiches and coffee from vendors along the tracks at intermediary stops. Station bars often have a good variety of take-away travellers' fare; consider at least investing in a plastic bottle of mineral water, since there's no drinking water on the trains.

Besides trains and bars, Italy's stations offer other **facilities**. All have a *Deposito*, where you can leave your bags for hours or days for a small fee. The larger ones have porters (who charge L1000–L1500 per piece) and some even have luggage trolleys; major stations have an *Albergo Diurno* ('Day Hotel', where you take a shower, get a shave and have a haircut, etc.), information offices, currency exchanges open at weekends (not at the most advantageous rates, however), hotel-finding and reservation services, kiosks with foreign papers, restaurants, etc. You can also arrange to have a rental car awaiting you at your destination—Avis, Hertz, Aurotrans and Maggiore are the firms most widespread in Italy.

Beyond that, some words need to be said about riding the rails on the most serendipitous national line in Europe. The FS may have its strikes and delays, its petty crime and bureaucratic inconveniences, but when you catch it on its better side it will treat you to a dose of the real Italy before you even reach your destination. If there's a choice, try for one of the older cars, depressingly grey outside but fitted with comfortably upholstered seats, Art Deco lamps and old pictures of the towns and villages of the country. The washrooms are invariably clean and pleasant. Best of all, the FS is relatively reliable, and even if there has been some delay you'll have an amenable station full of clocks to wait in; some of the station bars have astonishingly good food (some do not), but at any of them you may accept a well-brewed cappuccino and look blasé until the train comes in. Try to avoid travel on Friday evenings, when the major lines out of the big cities are packed. The FS is a lottery; you may find a train uncomfortably full of Italians (in which case stand by the doors, or impose on the salesmen in first class, where the conductor will be happy to change your ticket). Now and then, you may just have a beautiful 1920s compartment all to yourself for the night even better if you're travelling with your beloved—and be serenaded on the platform.

Inter-city coach travel is sometimes quicker than train travel, but also a bit more expensive. The Italians aren't dumb; you will find regular coach connections only where there is no train to offer competition. Coaches almost always depart from the vicinity of the train station, and tickets usually need to be purchased before you get on. In many regions they are the only means of public transport and well used, with frequent schedules. If you can't get a ticket before the coach leaves, get on anyway and pretend you can't speak a word of Italian; the worst that can happen is that someone will make you pay for a ticket. The base for all **country bus** lines is the provincial capitals. Some of the larger bus companies are **Autostradale** (Lombardy and the Lakes), **Lazzi** (Tuscany and central Italy), and **SITA** (all over Italy).

**City buses** are the traveller's friend. Most cities (at least in the north) label routes well; all charge flat fees for rides within the city limits and immediate suburbs, at the time of writing around L1200. Bus tickets must always be purchased before you get on, either at a tobacconist's, a newspaper kiosk, in bars, or from ticket machines near the main stops. Once you get on, you must 'obliterate' your ticket in the machines in the front or back of the bus; controllers stage random checks to make sure you've punched your ticket. Fines for cheaters are about L50,000, and the odds are about 12 to 1 against a check, so many passengers take a chance. If you're good-hearted, you'll buy a ticket and help some overburdened municipal transit line meet its annual deficit.

## By Car

The advantages of driving in Italy generally outweigh the disadvantages, but, before you bring your own car or hire one, consider the kind of holiday you're planning. For a tour of Italy's great art cities, you'd be better off not driving at all: parking is impossible, traffic impossible, deciphering one-way streets, signals and signs impossible. In Naples, don't even think about it. But for touring the countryside a car gives immeasurable freedom.

Third-party **insurance** is a minimum requirement in Italy (and you should be a lot more than minimally insured, as many of the locals have none whatever!). Obtain a Green Card from your insurer, which gives automatic proof that you are fully covered. Also get hold of a **European Accident Statement** form, which may simplify things if you are unlucky enough to have an accident. Always insist on a full translation of any statement you are asked to sign.

Breakdown assistance insurance is obviously a sensible investment (eg AA's Five Star or RAC's Eurocover Motoring Assistance).

**Petrol** (*benzina*, unleaded is *benzina senza piombo*, and diesel *gasolio*) is still very expensive in Italy (around L1500 per litre; fill up before you cross the border). Many petrol stations close for lunch in the afternoon, and few stay open late at night, though you may find a 'self-service' where you feed a machine nice smooth L10,000 notes. Motorway (*autostrada*) tolls are quite high (the journey from Milan to Rome on the A1 will cost you around L60,000 at the time of writing). Rest stops and petrol stations along the motorways stay open 24 hours. Other roads—*superstrade* on down through the Italian grading system—are free of charge.

Italians are famously anarchic behind a wheel. The only way to beat the locals is to join them by adopting an assertive and constantly alert driving style. Bear in mind the ancient maxim that he/she who hesitates is lost (especially at traffic lights, where the danger is less great of crashing into someone at the front than being rammed from behind). All drivers from boy racers to elderly nuns seem to tempt providence by overtaking at the most dangerous bend, and no matter how fast you are hammering along the *autostrada* (toll motorway), plenty will whizz past at apparently supersonic rates. North Americans used to leisurely speed limits and gentler road manners will find the Italian interpretation of the highway code especially stressful. Speed limits (generally ignored) are officially 130kph on motorways (110kph for cars under 1100cc or motorcycles), 110kph on main highways, 90kph on secondary roads, and 50kph in built-up areas. Speeding fines may be as much as L500,000, or L100,000 for jumping a red light (a popular Italian sport).

If you are undeterred by these caveats, you may actually enjoy driving in Italy, at least away from the congested tourist centres. Signposting is generally good, and roads are usually excellently maintained. Some of the roads are feats of engineering that the Romans themselves would have admired—bravura projects suspended on cliffs, crossing valleys on vast stilts and winding up hairpins.

Buy a good road map (the Italian Touring Club series is excellent). The **Automobile Club of Italy** (ACI) is a good friend to the foreign motorist. Besides having bushels of useful information and tips, they offer a free **breakdown service**, and can be reached from anywhere by dialling **116**—also use this number if you have to find the nearest service station. If you need major repairs, the ACI can make sure the prices charged are according to their guidelines.

### ACI Offices in Italy

**Florence:** Viale Amendola 36, ✆ (055) 24 861.

**Milan:** Corso Venezia 43, ✆ (02) 7745.

**Naples:** Piazzale Tecchino 49d, ✆ (0181) 614 511.

**Pisa:** Via S Martino 1, ✆ (050) 47 333.

**Rome:** Viale C. Colombo 261, ✆ (06) 514 971.

 Via Marsala 18, ✆ (06) 4959352.

**Siena:** Viale Vittorio Veneto 47, ✆ 0577) 49 001.

## Hiring a Car

Hiring a car or camper van is simple but not particularly cheap. In Italian it's called *autono-leggio*. There are both large international firms through which you can reserve a car in advance, and local agencies, which often have lower prices. Air or train travellers should check out possible discount packages. Most companies will require a deposit amounting to the estimated cost of the hire. VAT of 19% is applied to car hire, so make sure you take this into account when checking prices. Most companies have a minimum age limit of 21 (23 in some cases). A credit card makes life easier. You will need to produce your licence and a passport when you hire. Current 1994 rates are around L90,000 per day for a small car (Fiat Panda, for instance) with unlimited mileage and collision damage waiver, including tax (hire for three days or longer is somewhat less pro rata). Most major rental companies have offices in airports or main stations, though it may be worthwhile checking prices of local firms. If you need a car for longer than three weeks, leasing may be a more economic alternative. The National Tourist Office has a list of firms in Italy that hire caravans (trailers) or camper vans. Non-residents are not allowed to buy cars in Italy.

## Hitchhiking

It is illegal to hitch on the *autostrade*, though you may pick up a lift near one of the toll booths. Don't hitch from the city centres, head for suburban exit routes. For the best chances of getting a lift, travel light, look respectable and take your shades off. Hold a sign indicating your destination if you can. Never hitch at points which may cause an accident or obstruction; Italian traffic conditions are bad enough already! Risks for women are lower in northern Italy than in the more macho south, but it is not advisable to hitch alone. Two or more men may encounter some reluctance.

## By Motorcycle or Bicycle

The means of transport of choice for many Italians; motorbikes, mopeds and Vespas can be a delightful way to see the country. You should only consider it, however, if you've ridden them before—Italy's hills and alarming traffic make it no place to learn. You must be at least 14 for a *motorino* (scooter) and 16 for anything more powerful. Helmets are compulsory. Costs for a *motorino* range from about L20,000–L35,000 per day, scooters somewhat more (up to L50,000). Some travel insurance policies exclude claims resulting from scooter or motorbike accidents. Italians are keen cyclists; racing drivers up the steepest hills; if you're not training for the Tour de France, consider the region's topography well before planning a bicycling tour - especially in the hot summer months. You can hire a bike in most Italian towns. Prices range from about L10,000–L20,000 per day, which may make buying one interesting if you plan to spend much time in the saddle (L190,000–L300,000), either in a bike shop or through the classified ad papers put out in nearly every city and region. Alternatively, if you bring your own bike, do check the airlines to see what their policies are on transporting them. Bikes can be transported by train in Italy, either with you or within a couple of days—apply at the baggage office (*ufficio bagagli*).

## Practical A–Z

## Children

Even though a declining birthrate and the legalization of abortion may hint otherwise, children are still the royalty of Italy, and are pampered, often obscenely spoiled, probably more fashionably dressed than you are, and never allowed to get dirty. Surprisingly, most of them somehow manage to be well-mannered little charmers. If you're bringing your own *bambini* to Italy, they'll receive a warm welcome everywhere. Many hotels offer advantageous rates for children and have play areas and most of the larger cities have permanent **Luna Parks**, or funfairs. Rome's version in the EUR (a residential suburb south of the city) is huge and charmingly old-fashioned (a great trade-off for a day in the Vatican Museums). Italians don't like zoos and there are only a few small ones, but several so-so drive-through **Safari Parks** (near Rome, Verona, Novara, Brindisi and Cuneo) may amuse for a while. Apart from endless quantities of pizza, spaghetti and ice cream, other major attractions specifically designed for children include the **Bomarzo Monster Park** (Parco dei Mostri) in northern Lazio (a collection of huge, weird sculptures in the grounds of a 16th-century palace); the Disneyesque amusement parks of **Edenlandia** near Naples and **Gardaland** on Lake Garda; **Mini Italia** between Bergamo and Milan (a relief model of Italy studded with replica monuments); **Pinocchio Park** in Collodi, near Pisa; the fairy-tale playground of **Città della Domenica** in Perugia; and the whole city of **Venice**. If your kids know some Italian, there are **puppet theatres** in Rome and Milan, while the marionettes of Sicily (*pupi Sicilani*) are world-famous. If a **circus** visits town, you're in for a treat: it will either be a sparkling showcase of daredevil skill or a poignant, family-run, modern version of Fellini's *La Strada*. Try to catch one or two of Italy's more vivacious **festivals** or **carnivals** (Venice and Sicily have especially colourful processions).

## Climate and When to Go

*O Sole Mio* notwithstanding, all of Italy isn't always sunny; it rains just as much in Rome every year as in London, and Turin's climate in the winter is said to be about the same as that of Copenhagen. **Summer** comes on dry and hot in the south and humid and hot in much of the northern lowlands and inland hills; the Alps and high Apennines stay fairly cool, while the coasts are often refreshed by breezes, except for Venice, which tends to swelter. You can probably get by without an umbrella, but take a light jacket for cool evenings. For average touring, August is probably the worst month to stump through Italy. Transport facilities are jammed to capacity, prices are at their highest, and Rome, Milan, Florence, Venice and the other large cities are abandoned to hordes of tourists while the locals take to the beach. In Milan especially so many restaurants close down that you could starve, and the few staff left behind to man the galleys are sullen captives.

**Spring** and **autumn** are perhaps the loveliest times to go; spring for the infinity of wildflowers in Italy's countryside, autumn for the colour of the trees in the hills and the vineyards. The weather is mild, places aren't crowded, and you won't need your umbrella too much, at least until November. From December to March the happiest visitors are probably those on skis in the Alps or Apennines or opera buffs in La Scala, San Carlo or La Fenice, but it's the best time to go if you want the art and museums to yourself. Beware though, it can rain and rain, and mountain valleys can lie for days under banks of fog and mist. The Italian Riviera enjoys the mildest **winter** climate on the peninsula.

## Average Temperatures in °C (°F)

|  | January | April | July | October |
|---|---|---|---|---|
| Bari | 8.4 (46) | 13.9 (57) | 24.5 (76) | 18.2 (64) |
| Florence | 5.6 (42) | 13.3 (55) | 25.0 (77) | 15.8 (60) |
| Genoa | 8.4 (47) | 14.5 (58) | 24.6 (76) | 18.1 (64) |
| Milan | 1.9 (35) | 13.2 (55) | 24.8 (77) | 13.7 (56) |
| Cortina | 2.3 (28) | 5.2 (41) | 15.8 (61) | 7.6 (44) |
| Naples | 8.7 (47) | 14.3 (58) | 24.8 (77) | 14.5 (58) |
| Rome | 7.4 (44) | 14.4 (58) | 25.7 (79) | 17.7 (63) |
| Venice | 3.8 (38) | 12.6 (54) | 23.6 (74) | 15.1 (59) |
| Lake Garda | 4.0 (39) | 13.2 (55) | 24.5 (76) | 14.7 (58) |

## Average Monthly Rainfall in Millimetres (inches)

|  | January | April | July | October |
|---|---|---|---|---|
| Bari | 39 (2) | 35 (1) | 19 (1) | 111 (4) |
| Florence | 61 (3) | 74 (3) | 23 (1) | 96 (4) |
| Genoa | 109 (4) | 82 (3) | 35 (2) | 135 (5) |
| Milan | 62 (3) | 82 (3) | 47 (2) | 75 (3) |
| Cortina | 51 (2) | 138 (5) | 148 (6) | 119 (4) |
| Naples | 87 (3) | 55 (2) | 14 (1) | 102 (4) |
| Rome | 74 (3) | 62 (3) | 06 (3) | 123 (5) |
| Venice | 58 (2) | 77 (3) | 37 (1) | 66 (3) |
| Lake Garda | 31 (1) | 62 (3) | 72 (3) | 89 (3) |

The Rome rainfall in July in the official average. *That* you can believe if you like.

## Crime

There is a fair amount of petty crime in Italy—purse-snatchings, pickpocketing, minor thievery of the white collar kind (always check your change) and car break-ins and theft—but violent crime is rare. Nearly all mishaps can be avoided with adequate precautions. Scooter-borne purse-snatchers can be foiled if you stay on the inside of the pavement and keep a firm hold on your property (sling your bag-strap across your body, not dangling from one shoulder); pickpockets strike in crowded buses or trams and gatherings; don't carry too much cash, and split it so you won't lose the lot at once. In cities and popular tourist sites, beware groups of scruffy-looking women or children with placards, apparently begging for money. They use distraction techniques to perfection. The smallest and most innocent-looking child is generally the most skilful pickpocket. If you are targeted, the best technique is to grab sharply hold of any vulnerable possessions or pockets and shout furiously. (Italian passers-by or plain-clothes police will often come to your assistance if they realize what is happening.) Be extra careful in train stations, don't leave valuables in hotel rooms, and always park your car in garages, guarded lots or on well-lit streets, with portable temptations well out of sight. Purchasing small quantities of soft drugs for personal consumption is technically legal in Italy, though what constitutes a small quantity is unspecified, and if the police don't like you to begin with, it will probably be enough to get you into big trouble.

Political terrorism, once the scourge of Italy, has declined greatly in recent years, mainly thanks to special quasi-military squads of black-uniformed national police, the *Carabinieri*. Local matters are usually in the hands of the *Polizia Urbana*; the nattily dressed *Vigili Urbani* concern themselves with directing traffic, and handing out parking fines. If you need to summon any of them, dial 113.

## Disabled Travellers

Italy has been relatively slow off the mark in its provision for disabled visitors. Cobblestones, uneven or non-existent pavements, the appalling traffic conditions, crowded public transport and endless flights of steps in many public places are all disincentives. Progress is gradually being made, however. A national support organization in your own country may well have specific information on facilities in Italy, or will at least be able to provide general advice. The Italian tourist office, or CIT (travel agency) can also advise on hotels, museums with ramps and so on. If you book rail travel through CIT, you can request assistance if you are wheelchair-bound.

In the UK, contact the **Royal Association for Disability & Rehabilitation** (RADAR), and ask for their guide *Holidays & Travel Abroad: A Guide for Disabled People* (£3.50). They are based at 25 Mortimer St, London W1N 8AB (✆ (0171) 637 5400). Americans should contact SATH (**Society for the Advancement of Travel for the Handicapped**), 347 Fifth Avenue, Suite 610, New York 10016, ✆ (2112) 447 7284. Another useful organisation is **Mobility International**, at 228 Borough High Street, London SE1, ✆ (0171) 403 5688 or PO Box 3551, Eugene, Oregon 97403, USA, ✆ (503) 343 1284. If you need help while you are in Italy, contact the local tourist offices.

## Embassies and Consulates

**UK**

Bari: Via Dalmazia 127, ✆ (080) 554 3668.

Florence: Lungarno Corsini 2, ✆ (055) 284 133.

Milan: Via San Paulo 7, ✆ (02) 723 001.

Naples: Via Crispi 122, ✆ (081) 663 511.

Rome: Via XX Settembre 80/a, ✆ (06) 482 5441.

Venice: Palazzo Querino, Accademia 1051, Dorsoduro, ✆ (06) 522 7202.

## Ireland

Rome: Largo Nazareno 3, ✆ (06) 678 2541.

## USA

Florence: Lungarno Vespucci 38, ✆ (055) 239 8276.
Milan: Via Priv Amedeo 2–10, ✆ (02) 290 351.
Naples: Piazza Repubblica 2, ✆ (081) 583 8111.
Palermo: Via Vaccarini 1, ✆ (091) 307 813.
Rome: Via V. Veneto 119/a, ✆ (06) 46741.

## Canada

Milan: Via Vittorio Pisani 19, ✆ (02) 669 7451.
Rome: Via G. B De Rossi 27, ✆ (06) 445 981.

## Australia

Milan: Via Turati 40, ✆ (02) 659 8727.
Rome: Via Alessandria 215, ✆ (06) 852 721.

## New Zealand

Rome: Via Zara 28, ✆ (06) 440 2928.

## France

Milan: Corso Venezia 42, ✆ (02) 794 341.
Rome: Palazzo Farnese, ✆ (06) 686 011.

## Germany

Milan: Via Solferino 40, ✆ (02) 655 4325/655 4888.
Rome: Via Po 25c, ✆ (06) 884 741.

## Netherlands

Milan: Via San Vittore 45, ✆ (02) 480 11723.
Naples: Via Depretis 114, ✆ (081) 551 3003.
Rome: Via Michele Mercati 8, ✆ (06) 322 1141.

## Festivals

There are literally thousands of festivals answering to every description in Italy. Every *comune* has at least one or two honouring patron saints, at which the presiding Madonna is paraded through the streets decked in fairy lights and gaudy flowers. Shrovetide and Holy Week are great focuses of activity. *Carnival*, after being suppressed and ignored for decades, has been revived in many places, displaying the gorgeous music and pageantry of the *Commedia dell'Arte* with Harlequin and his motley crew. In Venice, the handmade carnival masks now constitute a new art form and make delightful, if expensive, souvenirs. Holy Week celebrations take on a dirgelike Spanish flavour in the south, when robed and hooded penitents haul melodramatic floats through the streets. Meanwhile in Rome the Supreme Pontiff himself officiates at the Easter ceremonies. Other festivals are more earthily pagan, celebrating the land and the harvest in giant phallic towers. Some are purely secular affairs sponsored by political parties (especially the Communists and Socialists), where everyone goes to meet friends. There are great costume pageants dating back to the Middle Ages or Renaissance like the Sienese *Palio* (a bareback horserace), an endless round of carnivals, music festivals, opera seasons and antique fairs. Relaxed village *festas* can be just as enjoyable as (or more so than) the big national crowd-pullers. Outsiders are nearly always welcome. Whatever the occasion, eating is a primary pastime at all Italian jamborees, and all kinds of regional specialities are prepared. Check at the local tourist office for precise dates, which alter from year to year, and often slide into the nearest weekend.

| | |
|---|---|
| Jan–July | Opera and ballet at La Scala, **Milan.** |
| Jan 5–6 | Epiphany celebrations throughout Italy: Epiphany Fair in Piazza Navona, **Rome**; Three Kings Procession, **Milan**; Piana degli Albanesi (Byzantine). |
| Late Jan | Festival of Italian Popular Song, **San Remo.** |
| 30–31 Jan | Sant'Orso handicrafts fair, **Aosta.** |
| Feb/March | Shrovetide Carnivals all over Italy, especially in **Venice**; **Viareggio**; Sa Sartiglia (medieval tournament masquerade). |
| March | Fashion collections, **Milan.** |
| | Sant'Ambroggio carnival, **Milan.** |
| March/April | Holy Week and Easter celebrations: processions **Taranto**, **Bari**, **Brindisi**; Scoppio del Carro (Explosion of the Cart), **Florence**; Good Friday Procession led by the Pope, **Rome**; concerts at San Maurizio church in Monastero Maggiore, **Milan.** |
| April | Reanactment of the Oath of the Lombard League (historical costume pageant), **Bergamo.** |
| End April | Ortafiori flower festival, **Orta San Giulio.** |
| April–May | Jazz festival, **Milan.** |
| May | Feast of San Nicola, **Bari** |
| | Festival of Snakes, **Cocullo** (Abruzzo). |
| | *Palio del Carroccio*, **Legnano** (Milan), celebrating defeat of Barbarossa by the Lombard League in 1176 (medieval parade and horse-race). |
| | Feast of San Gennaro (first of three such occasions when the faithful assemble in **Naples** cathedral to await the miraculous liquefaction of a phial of the saint's blood). |

Corsa dei Ceri (Race of the Candles), **Gubbio** (Umbria)—(huge wooden shrines are raced uphill to the basilica).

Palio della Balestra (Crossbow Palio), **Gubbio**—medieval contest with antique weapons.

Vogolonga, **Venice** (the 'long row' from San Marco to Burano).

**May/June**    Maggio Musicale Fiorentino, **Florence**.

**June**    Festival Cusiano di Musica Antica, **Orta San Giulio**.

Historical Regatta of the Four Ancient Maritime Republics (boat race between the rival sea-towns of **Pisa**, **Venice**, **Amalfi** and **Genoa**—location alternates).

Gioco del Ponte (Game of the Bridge), **Pisa** (mock battle).

Festival of Two Worlds, **Spoleto** (Umbria) (major arts festival).

**June 21**    Infiorata, **Genzano** (Rome) and **Spello** (Umbria) (Corpus Domini celebrations with flower decorations).

Feast of St Antonio, **Padua**.

Gioco del Calcio, **Florence** (football in medieval costume).

Festa dei Gigli, **Nola** (Naples) ('lily' procession).

**July**    Joust of the Bear, **Pistoia**.

Feast of the Redeemer, **Venice** (fireworks and gondola procession).

Umbria Jazz Festival.

Archery contest, **Fivizzano** (Massa).

**July and August**    Palio, **Siena**—bareback horserace (held twice).

Summer Operetta Festival, **Trieste**.

Verona Outdoor Opera Season.

Baths of Caracalla, **Rome**: outdoor opera.

**August**    Joust of the Quintana, **Ascoli Piceno** (Marches).

Palio dei Normanni, **Piazza Armerina** (historic pageant).

Bravo delle Botti, **Montepulciano** (barrel race).

Festa del Redentore, **Nuoro** (Sardinia) (folk festival).

International Film Festival, **Venice**.

Regatta, **Ventimiglia**.

Festival of the Straw Cart, **Avellino** (thanksgiving ritual).

Wheat Festival, **Foglianise** (Benevento) (decorated tractors).

**Aug–Sept**    Settimane Musicali, **Stresa** (musical weeks).

**September**    Joust of the Saracen, **Arezzo** (knights in armour).

Historic Regatta, **Venice**.

Living Chess Game, **Marostica** (Veneto) (even years).

Feast of San Gennaro, **Naples**.
Luminaria di Santa Croce, **Lucca** (torchlit procession).
Italian Grand Prix, **Monza**.
Neapolitan song contest, **Piedigrotta**.

| | |
|---|---|
| October | Truffle Fair, **Alba**. |
| | Feast of St Francis, **Assisi**. |
| November | Festa della Salute, **Venice**. |
| | San Martino, **Sigillo** (Perugia) (wine and chestnut festival). |
| December | La Scala opera season opens, **Milan**. |
| | Opera and ballet at La Fenice and Teatro Goldoni, **Venice**. |
| | Advent and Christmas celebrations. |
| | Christmas Fair of the presepi, **Naples**. |
| | Sausage and polenta festival, **Benevento**. |

## Food and Drink

There are those who eat to live and those who live to eat, and then there are the Italians, for whom food has an almost religious significance, unfathomably linked with love, La Mamma, and tradition. In this singular country, where millions of otherwise sane people spend much of their waking hours worrying about their digestion, standards both at home and in the restaurants are understandably high. Few Italians are gluttons, but all are experts on what is what in the kitchen; to serve a meal that is not properly prepared and more than a little complex is tantamount to an insult.

For the visitor this national culinary obsession comes as an extra bonus to the senses—along with Italy's remarkable sights, music, and the warm sun on your back, you can enjoy some of the best tastes and smells the world can offer, prepared daily in Italy's kitchens and fermented in its countless wine cellars. Eating *all'Italiana* is not only delicious and wholesome, but now undeniably trendy. Foreigners flock here to learn the secrets of Italian cuisine and the even more elusive secret of how the Italians can live surrounded by such delights and still fit into their sleek Armani trousers.

**Breakfast** (*colazione*) in Italy is no lingering affair, but an early morning wake-up shot to the brain: a *cappuccino* (espresso with hot foamy milk, often sprinkled with chocolate—incidentally first thing in the morning is the only time of day at which any self-respecting Italian will touch the stuff), a *caffè latte* (white coffee) or a *caffè lungo* (a generous portion of espresso), accompanied by a croissant-type roll, called a *cornetto* or *briosce*, or a fancy pastry. This repast can be consumed in any bar and repeated during the morning as often as necessary. Breakfast in most Italian hotels seldom represents great value.

**Lunch** (*pranzo*), generally served around 1pm, is the most important meal of the day for the Italians, with a minimum of a first course (*primo piatto*—any kind of pasta dish, broth or soup, or rice dish or pizza), a second course (*secondo piatto*—a meat dish, accompanied by a *contorno* or side dish—a vegetable, salad, or potatoes usually), followed by fruit or dessert and coffee. You can, however, begin with a platter of *antipasti*—the appetizers Italians do so brilliantly, ranging from warm seafood delicacies, to raw ham (*prosciutto crudo*), salami in a hundred varieties, lovely vegetables, savoury toasts, olives, pâté and many many more. There are restaurants that specialise in *antipasti*, and they usually don't take it amiss if you decide to forget the pasta and meat and just nibble on these scrumptious hors-d'œuvres (though in the end it will probably cost more than a full meal). Most Italians accompany their meal with wine and mineral water—*acqua minerale*, with or without bubbles (*con* or *senza gas*), which supposedly aids digestion—concluding their meals with a *digestivo* liqueur.

*Cena*, the **evening meal**, is usually eaten around 8pm. This is much the same as *pranzo* although lighter, without the pasta; a pizza and beer, eggs or a fish dish. In restaurants, however, they offer all the courses, so if you have only a sandwich for lunch you have a full meal in the evening.

In Italy the various terms for types of **restaurants**—*ristorante*, *trattoria*, or *osteria*—have been confused. A *trattoria* or *osteria* can be just as elaborate as a restaurant, though rarely is a *ristorante* as informal as a traditional *trattoria*. Unfortunately the old habit of posting menus and prices in the windows has fallen from fashion, so it's often difficult to judge variety or prices. Invariably the least expensive eating place is the *vino e cucina*, a simple establishment serving simple cuisine for simple everyday prices. It is essential to remember that the fancier the fittings, the fancier the **bill**, though neither of these points has anything at all to do with the quality of the food. If you're uncertain, do as you would at home—look for lots of locals. When you eat out, mentally add to the bill (*conto*) the bread and cover charge (*pane e coperto*, between L2000 and L3500), and a 15% service charge. This is often included in the bill (*servizio compreso*); if not, it will say *servizio non compreso*, and you'll have to do your own arithmetic. Additional tipping is at your own discretion, but never do it in family-owned and -run places.

People who haven't visited Italy for years and have fond memories of eating full meals for under a pound will be amazed at how much **prices** have risen; though in some respects eating out in Italy is still a bargain, especially when you figure out how much all that wine would have cost you at home. In many places you'll often find restaurants offering a *menu turistico*—full, set meals of usually meagre inspiration for L20,000–30,000. More imaginative chefs often offer a *menu degustazione*—a set-price gourmet meal that allows you to taste their daily specialities and seasonal dishes. Both of these are cheaper than if you had ordered the same food à la carte.

We have divided restaurants into the following price categories:

| | |
|---|---|
| *very expensive* | over L80,000 |
| *expensive* | L50,000–80,000 |
| *moderate* | L30,000 50,000 |
| *inexpensive* | below L30,000 |

When you leave a restaurant you will be given a receipt (*scontrino* or *ricevuto fiscale*) which according to Italian law you must take with you out of the door and carry for at least 60 metres. If you aren't given one, it means the restaurant is probably fudging on its taxes and thus offering you lower prices. There is a slim chance the tax police (*Guardia di Fianza*) may have their eye on you and the restaurant, and if you don't have a receipt they could slap you with a heavy fine.

There are several alternatives to sit-down meals. The 'hot table' (*tavola calda*) is a stand-up buffet, where you can choose a simple prepared dish or a whole meal, depending on your appetite. The food in these can be truly impressive; many offer only a few hot dishes, pizza and sandwiches, though in every fair-sized town there will be at least one *tavola calda* with seats where you can contrive a complete dinner outside the usual hours. Little shops that sell pizza by the slice are common in city centres. At any grocer's (*alimentari*) or market (*mercato*) you can buy the materials for countryside or hotel-room picnics; some places in the smaller towns will make the sandwiches for you. For really elegant picnics, have a *tavola calda* pack up something nice for you. And if everywhere else is closed, there's always the railway station—bars will at least have sandwiches and drinks, and perhaps some surprisingly good snacks you've never heard of before. Some of the station bars also prepare *cestini di viaggio*, full-course meals in a basket to help you through long train trips. Common snacks you'll encounter include *panini* of prosciutto, cheese and tomatoes, or other meats; *tramezzini*, little sandwiches on plain, square white bread that are always much better than they look; and pizza, of course.

The pace of modern urban life militates against traditional lengthy homecooked repasts with the family, followed by a siesta. Many office workers in northern cities behave much as their counterparts elsewhere in Europe and consume a rapid slimline snack at lunchtime, returning home after a busy day to throw together some pasta and salad in the evenings. But those with more leisure can still eat extremely well, and (if you avoid obvious expense-account places) inexpensively. Many Italian dishes need no introduction—pizza, spaghetti, lasagne and minestrone are now familiar well beyond national boundaries. What is perhaps less well known is the tremendous regional diversity at the table. Each corner of Italy prides itself on its own specialities, the shape of its pasta, its soups and sauces, its wines and desserts. You'll find many of these described and listed in the 'Eating Out' sections in the text, and in the menu vocabulary at the back of this book, but even so, expect to be overwhelmed, especially since many Italian chefs have wholeheartedly embraced the concept of *nouvelle cuisine*, or rather *nuova cucina*, and are constantly inventing dishes with even more names.

In northern Italy, look for dishes prepared with butter and cream. Egg pasta and *risotto* (Italian rice, often cooked with saffron) are favourite first courses, while game dishes, liver, *bollito misto* (mixed boiled meats), *ossobuco* (veal shin cooked in tomato sauce), seafood and sausages appear as main courses. Towards the Trentino-Adige the cooking displays hearty Austrian influences, with goulash and smoked meats with rye bread. Sometimes you may find dishes served with *polenta* (a pudding or cake of yellow maize flour), a brick-heavy substance to be approached with caution. But here, too, is Emilia-Romagna, Italy's gourmet region par excellence, the land of delicious tortellini and lasagne, Parmesan cheese, Parma ham, balsamic vinegar and a hundred other delicacies. Central Italy is the land of beans and chick peas, game, tripe, salt cod (*baccala*), *porchetta* (whole roast pork with rosemary), Florentine steaks, *saltimbocca alla romana* (veal scallops with ham and sage), and freshwater fish in interesting guises. Tuscan and Umbrian cooking uses fresh, simple, high-quality ingredients flavoured with herbs and olive oil, and the local *porcini* mushrooms or truffles. The further south you go, the spicier and oilier things get, and the richer the puddings and cakes. Modern Romans are as adventurous at the table as their classical ancestors, and include some stomach-churning offal in their diets. But the capital is an excellent place to delve into any style of regional cooking, with dozens of restaurants from all over Italy. Southern Italy is the land of homemade pasta, wonderful vegetables and superb seafood, often fried or laced with olive oil. Naples, of course, is the birthplace of pizza, and home of rich tomato sauces. Regional specialities are often seasoned with condiments like capers, anchovies, lemon juice, oregano, olives and fennel. If you are ever bored poring over a menu in Italy, you've been nipped in the tastebuds.

## Wine and Spirits

Italy is a country where everyday wine is cheaper than Coca-Cola or milk, and where nearly every family owns some vineyards or has some relatives who supply most of their daily needs—which are not great. Even though they live in one of the world's largest wine-growing countries, Italians imbibe relatively little, and only at meals.

If Italy has an infinite variety of regional dishes, there is an equally bewildering array of **regional wines**, many of which are rarely exported because they are best drunk young. Even wines that are well known and often derided clichés abroad, like Chianti or Lambrusco, can be wonderful new experiences when tasted on their home turf. Unless you're dining at a restaurant with an exceptional cellar, do as the Italians do and order a carafe of the local wine (*vino locale* or *vino della casa*). You won't often be wrong. Most Italian wines are named after the grape and the district they come from. If the label says DOC (*Denominazione di Origine Controllata*) it means that the wine comes from a specially defined area and was produced according to a certain traditional method. DOCG (*Denominazione d'Origine Controllata e Garantia*) is allegedly a more rigorous classification, indicating that the wines not only conform to DOC standards, but are tested by government-appointed inspectors (who are now more in evidence since a hideous methanol scandal claimed 20 lives in 1986). At present few wines have been granted this status, but the number is planned to increase steadily. *Classico* means that a wine comes from the oldest part of the zone of production, though is not necessarily better than a non-Classico. *Riserva*, *superiore* or *speciale* denotes a wine that has been aged longer and is more alcoholic; *Recioto* is a wine made from the outer clusters of grapes, with a higher sugar and therefore alcohol content. Other Italian wine words are *spumante* (sparkling); *frizzante* (pétillant), *amabile* (semi-sweet), *abbocato* (medium dry), *passito* (strong sweet wine made from raisins). *Rosso* is red, *bianco* white; between the two extremes lie *rubiato* (ruby), *rosato*, *chiaretto* or *cerasuolo* (rose). *Secco* is dry, *dolce* sweet, *liquoroso* fortified and sweet. *Vendemmia* means vintage, a *cantina* is a cellar, and an *enoteca* is a wine-shop or museum when you can taste and buy wines.

The regions of Piedmont, Tuscany and Veneto produce Italy's most prestigious red wines, while Friuli-Venezia Giulia and Trentino-Alto Adige are the greatest regions for white wines. King of the Tuscans is the mighty Brunello di Montalcino (DOCG), an expensive blockbuster. Pinot Grigio and the unusual Tocai make some of the best whites. But almost every other corner of Italy has its vinous virtues, be it the Lambrusco of Emilia-Romagna, the Orvieto of Umbria, the Taurasi of Campania or the Frascati of Lazio. The well-known Valpolicella, Bardolino and Soave are produced on the shores of Lake Garda. Even in the south, with much of its stronger, rougher wine shipped north for blending, you will find some wonderful varieties, such as the Sicilian Corvo (red and white).

Italy turns its grape harvest to other uses too, producing Sicilian **Marsala**, a famous fortified wine fermented in wooden casks, ranging from very dry to flavoured and sweet and **vin santo**, a sweet Tuscan speciality often served with almond biscuits. **Vermouth** is an idea from Turin made of wine flavoured with Alpine herbs and spices. Italians are fond of post-prandial brandies (to aid digestion)—**Stock** or **Vecchia Romagna** appear on the best-known Italian brandy bottles. **Grappa** is a rough, Schnapps-like spirit drunk in black coffee after a meal (a *caffè corretto*). Other drinks you'll see in any Italian bar include **Campari**, a red bitter drunk on its own or in cocktails; **Fernet Branca**, **Cynar** and **Averno** (popular aperitif/digestifs); and a host of liqueurs like **Strega**, the witch potion from **Benevento**, apricot-flavoured **Amaretto**, cherry **Maraschino**, aniseed **Sambuca** or the herby **Millefiori**.

Spirits like whisky or gin are reasonably priced in Italy; locals rarely drink them, despite intensive advertising.

## Health and Emergencies

You can insure yourself for almost any possible mishap—cancelled flights, stolen or lost baggage and health. While national health coverage in the UK and Canada takes care of their citizens while travelling, the USA doesn't. Check any current policies you hold to see if they cover you while abroad, and under what circumstances, and judge whether you need a special **traveller's insurance** policy for the journey. Travel agencies sell them, as well as insurance companies.

Citizens of EU countries are entitled to **reciprocal health care** in Italy's National Health Service and a 90% discount on prescriptions (bring **Form E111** with you). The E111 does not cover all medical expenses (no repatriation costs, for example, and no private treatment), and it is advisable to take out separate travel insurance for full cover. Citizens of non-EU countries should check carefully that they have adequate insurance for any medical expenses, and the cost of returning home. Australia has a reciprocal health care scheme with Italy, but New Zealand, Canada and the USA do not. If you already have health insurance, a student card, or a credit card, you may be entitled to some medical cover abroad.

In an **emergency**, dial **115** for fire and **113** for an ambulance in Italy (*ambulanza*) or to find the nearest hospital (*ospedale*). Less serious problems can be treated at a *Pronto Soccorso* (casualty/first aid department) at any hospital clinic (*ambulatorio*), or at a local health unit (*Unita Sanitarial Locale*—USL. Airports and main railway stations also have **first-aid posts**. If you have to pay for any health treatment, make sure you get a receipt, so that you can make any claims for reimbursement later.

Dispensing **chemists** (*farmacia*) are generally open from 8.30am to 1pm and from 4 to 8pm. Pharmacists are trained to give advice for minor ills. Any large town will have a *farmacia* that stays open 24 hours; others take turns to stay open (the address rota is posted in the window).

No specific **vaccinations** are required or advised for citizens of most countries before visiting Italy; the main health risks are the usual travellers' woes of upset stomachs or the effects of too much sun. Take a supply of **medicaments** with you (insect repellent, anti-diarrhœal medicine, sun lotion and antiseptic cream), and any drugs you need regularly.

Most Italian doctors speak at least rudimentary English, but if you can't find one, contact your embassy or consulate for a list of English-speaking doctors. Standards of health care in the north are generally higher than in the deep south.

### Public Hospitals and Medical Services

**Rome:**  Policlinico Umberto I, Viale del Policlinico 255 (near Stazione Termini), ✆ (06) 499 71.

**Milan:**  Ospedale Maggiore Policlinico, Via Francesco Sforza 35, ✆ (02) 551 3518.

**Florence:**  Tourist Medical Service, Via Lorenzo il Magnifico 59, ✆ (055) 475 411 (English-speaking doctors, 24-hr service).

**Venice:**  Ospedale Civilis Riuniti di Venezia, Campo SS Giovanni e Paolo, ✆ (041) 520 5622 or Ospedale del Mare, 1 Lungomare d'Annunzio, Lido, ✆ 526 5900.

**Naples:**  Ospedale Monaldi, Vico L Bianchi, ✆ (081) 545 1417 or contact the Guardia Medica Permanente, ✆ 751 31 77 (24-hr holiday emergency service).

## Living and Working in Italy

### Registration and Residency

If you are planning to stay in Italy long-term without working, you should register with the police within eight days of arrival and apply for a *permesso di soggiorno* from the local **Questura** (police station)—get there early in the morning as most state offices close in the afternoon. You need a *permesso* in order to open a bank account in Italy, or buy a car. It lasts for three months, after which you will need to renew it. If you can prove you have enough money to live on, permission is usually granted, though non-whites may have a hard time with some officials. However frustrating the process of obtaining documentation in Italy, try to appear calm and remain polite, or things will only get worse. Take your passport, a supply of photographs and as much convincing ID as you can muster.

If you wish to be registered as a resident you should apply to the local **Ufficio Anagrafe** (registry office). If you are in Italy for work, your employer should help you with the red-tape, though many small businessmen prefer to take unregistered foreigners (so that they don't have to declare them and pay tax). Students attending courses at Italian universities must obtain a declaration from the Italian Consulate in their home countries before their departure, certifying their 'acceptability' for further study, and that they have adequate health insurance. A surprising number of scholarships are offered to foreign students (especially post-graduates) by the Italian Ministry of Foreign Affairs; ask your Italian embassy for details, or write to the Ministry directly (Direzione Generale per la Cooperazione Culturale Scientifica e Tecnica, Piazzale della Farnesina 1, Roma).

## Renting a House or Flat

Many landlords in Italy will accept only non-residents as tenants (these are not covered by the same legislation and have fewer rights). Leases (usually for one year) may well specify that you are not to take out resident status in Italy, so if you do, keep quiet about it or you may find yourself homeless. Rents in the major cities can be astronomical. To find a place, scan appropriate local noticeboards and newspapers or place an ad yourself (e.g. in Rome's *Porta Portese* or Milan's *Secondomano*). Most landlords insist on a deposit of two or three months' rent in advance which may be very difficult to recover at the end of your stay, so bear this in mind when giving notice. Estate agents usually charge a 10% fee (of a year's rent). Rental leases are signed through a *commercialista* (lawyer-accountant) who represents both you and the landlord and is paid to know all the complicated legal niceties (landlords often bring their own lawyers and you may want your own as well).

## Buying a House

Ritzy villas and downtown apartments command awesome prices, but rural real estate is still one of Italy's great bargains. Even in today's saturated marketplace, you can achieve a life-time's dream by buying a run-down property and restoring it lovingly to your own tastes and needs. But beware the pitfalls.

One estate agent is constantly amazed that his English clients invariably express two major concerns about a property: drainage and the presence of a bidet in the bathroom (as if it were an instrument of the devil). What they should be asking are questions about water supply, electricity, and road access—often big problems for that isolated, romantic farmhouse. Another thing to remember before purchasing a home or land is that you need permission from the local *comune* to make any changes or improvements, and it's no good buying anything unless you're pretty sure the *comune* will consent (for a sizeable fee, of couse) to let you convert the old cellar or stable into a spare bedroom. Another thing to remember is that though there are no annual rates (property tax) to pay, there's a 10% IVA (VAT) to be paid on the purchase price for a house and 17% on land, as well as a hefty Capital Gains Tax on selling price and profit to be paid by the seller. Italians tend to get round this by selling at one price and writing down another on the contract. But remember if you sell you'll be in the same bind.

Once you've agreed to buy, you pay a deposit (usually 25–30%) and sign a *compromesso*, a document that states that if you back out, you lose your deposit, and if the seller changes his mind, he forfeits double the deposit to you (be sure your *compromesso* includes this feature, called *caparra confirmatoria*). Always transfer payment from home through a bank, taking care to get and save a certificate of the transaction so you can take the sum back out of Italy when you sell. After the *compromesso*, your affairs will be handled by a *notaio*, the public servant in charge of registering documents and taxes who works for both buyer and seller. If you want to make sure your interests are not overlooked, you can hire a *commercialista* who will handle your affairs with the *notaio*, including the final transfer deed (*rogito*), which completes the purchase at the local Land Registry. Upon signing, the balance of the purchase price generally becomes payable within a year. The next stage for most buyers, restoration, can be a nightmare if you aren't careful. Make sure the crew you hire is experienced and that you're pleased with their work elsewhere—don't hesitate to ask as many other people in your area as possible for advice. One book that offers some clues on the ins and outs of taxes, inheritance law, residency, gardening, etc. is *Living in Italy*, published by Robert Hale, London 1991.

## Finding a Job

Theoretically, all EU residents are entitled to work in Italy if they can find a job and have the correct permits. They may register at the local *Ufficio di Collocamento* (Manpower Office) to look for employment. In practice, permanent work is hard to come by (even harder for North American or Australasian citizens) outside the well-trodden paths of English language teaching, au pair work and casual labour in bars or restaurants. To find this kind of work, keep your eyes peeled for ads in local papers, shop windows and so forth, or ask around. In Italy, a grey area exists between black and white economies and it is possible to have a *codice fiscale*, which registers you as a taxpayer, even if you have no official work permit. This may enable you to find a better job. For any sort of office job, a sound knowledge of Italian is essential. Some cities, like Venice, have long been saturated with wannabee English teachers, but you can always try your luck. Private teaching is nearly always more lucrative than working for a language school, but obviously previous qualifications and experience affect your chances of obtaining a steady flow of clients. A TEFL (Teaching English as a Foreign Language) certificate is usually a prerequisite for any reputable language school post. Busking and selling goods on the street are illegal without a municipal permit.

## Keeping a Car

You have to be a resident to buy a second-hand car in Italy; non-residents are allowed to purchase a new car only on condition that it leaves the country within five days. Residents must switch their driving licences and number plates to Italian versions within one year. Non-residents may keep a foreign car in Italy for up to six months.

## Maps and Publications

The maps in this guide are for orientation only and, to explore in any detail, invest in a good, up-to-date regional map before you arrive.

For an excellent range of maps in the UK, try **Stanford's**, 12–14 Long Acre, London WC2 9LP, ✆ (0171) 836 1321, or **The Travel Bookshop**, 13 Blenheim Crescent, London W11 2EE, ✆ (0171) 229 5360. In the USA, try **The Complete Traveller**, 199 Madison Ave, New York, NY 10016, ✆ (0212) 685 9007. Excellent maps are produced by **Touring Club Italiano**, Michelin, and **Istituto Geografico de Agostini**. They are available at all major bookshops in Italy (e.g. Feltrinelli) or sometimes on news stands. Italian tourist offices are helpful and can often supply good area maps and town plans.

Books are more expensive in Italy than in the UK, but some excellent shops stock English-language books. A few useful ones are listed below.

### English Language Bookshops

**Florence:** The Paperback Exchange, Via Fiesolana 31r; Seeber, Via Tornabuoni 70r; Feltrinelli, Via Cavour 12–20r.

**Milan:** The American Bookstore, Via Camperio 16 (at Largo Cairoli); The English Bookshop, Via Mascheroni 12.

**Naples:** Universal, Rione Sirignano 1.

**Rome:** Anglo-American Book Co, Via della Vite 57; Lion Bookshop, Via del Babuino 181; Corner Bookshop, Via del Moro 48; Open Door Bookshop, Via della Lungaretta 25.

**Venice:** Sangiorgio, Calle Larga XXII Marzo 2087, San Marco;Serenissima, Merceria dell'Orologio 739, San Marco.

## Money

It's a good idea to order a wad of lire from your home bank to have on hand when you arrive in Italy, the land of strikes, unforeseen delays and quirky banking hours (*see* below). Take great care how you carry it, however (don't keep it all in one place). Obtaining money is often a frustrating business involving much queueing and form-filling. The major banks and exchange bureaux licensed by the Bank of Italy give the best exchange rates for currency or traveller's cheques. Hotels, private exchanges in resorts and FS-run exchanges at railway stations usually have less advantageous rates, but are open outside normal banking hours. Weekend exchange offices can be found in most large cities, e.g. **Milan:** Banca Ponti, Piazza del Duomo 19; Banca delle Comunicazioni, Stazione Centrale; American Express, Via Brera 3; **Florence:** Thomas Cook, Lungarno Acciaioli 6r; American Express, Via de'Guicciardini 49r; **Rome:** Banco Nazionale delle Comunicazione, Stazione Termini; Thomas Cook Piazza Barberini 21D; **Naples:** CIT, Piazza Municipio 70, Ashiba, Piazza Municipio 1; **Venice:** American Express, S. Moise 1471; CIT Piazza S. Marco. In addition there are exchange offices at most airports. Remember that Italians indicate decimals with commas and thousands with full points.

Besides traveller's cheques, most banks will give you cash on a recognised credit card or Eurocheque with a Eurocheque card (taking little or no commission), and in big cities such as Naples you can find automatic tellers (ATMs) to spout cash on a Visa, American Express or Eurocheque card. You need a PIN number to use these. Make sure you read the instructions carefully, or your card may be retained by the machine. MasterCard (Access) is much less widely acceptable in Italy. Large hotels, resort area restaurants, shops and car hire firms will accept plastic as well; many smaller places will not. From sad experience, Italians are wary of plastic—you can't even use it at motorway petrol stops.

You can have money transferred to you through an Italian bank but this process may take over a week, even if it's sent urgent *espressissimo*. You will need your passport as identification when you collect it. Sending cheques by post is inadvisable.

Although it varies from region to region, with the north bearing more resemblance to the rest of Europe than the Mediterranean south, most of Italy closes down at 1pm until 3 or 4pm to eat and properly digest the main meal of the day. Afternoon hours are from 4 to 7, often from 5 to 8 in the hot summer months. Bars are often the only places open during the early afternoon. Some cities (notably Milan) close down completely during August when locals flee from the polluted frying pan to the hills, lakes or coast. In any case, don't be surprised if you find anywhere in Italy unexpectedly closed (or open for that matter), whatever its official stated hours.

### banks

Banking hours vary, but core times in large towns are usually Monday to Friday 8.30am–1.00pm and 3–4pm, closed weekends and on local and national holidays (*see* below). Outside normal hours though, you will usually be able to find somewhere to change money (albeit at disadvantageous rates).

### shops

Shops usually open Monday–Saturday from 8am to 1pm and 3.30pm to 7.30pm, though hours vary according to season and are shorter in smaller centres. In some large cities hours are longer. Some supermarkets and department stores stay open throughout the day.

### offices

Government-run dispensers of red-tape (e.g. visa departments) often stay open for quite limited periods, usually during the mornings, Monday to Friday. It pays to get there as soon as they open (or before) to spare your nerves in an interminable queue. Anyway, take something to read, or write your memoirs.

### museums and galleries

Many of Italy's museums are magnificent, many are run with shameful neglect, and many have been closed for years for 'restoration' with slim prospects of reopening in the foreseeable future. With two works of art per inhabitant, Italy has a hard time financing the preservation of its national heritage; it's would be as well to inquire at the tourist office to find out exactly what is open and what is 'temporarily' closed before setting off on a wild-goose chase.

### churches

Italy's churches have always been a prime target for art thieves and as a consequence are usually locked when there isn't a sacristan or caretaker to keep an eye on things. All churches, except for the really important cathedrals and basilicas, close in the afternoon at the same hours as the shops, and the little ones tend to stay closed. Always have a pocketful of coins for the light machines in churches, or whatever work of art you came to inspect will remain clouded in ecclesiastical gloom. Don't do your visiting during services, and don't come to see paintings and statutes in churches the week preceding Easter—you will probably find them covered with mourning shrouds.

In general, Sunday afternoons and Mondays are dead periods for the sightseer—you may want to make them your travelling days. Places without specified opening hours can usually be visited on request—but it is best to go before 1pm. We have listed the hours of important sights and museums, and specified which ones charge admission. Entrance charges vary widely; major sights are fairly steep (L10,000 plus), but others may be completely free. EU citizens under 18 and over 65 get free admission to state museums, at least in theory.

## National Holidays

Most museums, as well as banks and shops, are closed on the following national holidays.

**1 January** (New Year's Day)

**6 January** (Epiphany)

**Easter Monday**

**25 April** (Liberation Day)

**1 May** (Labour Day)

**15 August** (Assumption, also known as *Ferragosto*, the official start of the Italian holiday season)

**1 November** (All Saints' Day)

**8 December** (Immaculate Conception)

**25 December** (Christmas Day)

**26 December** (*Santo Stefano*, St Stephen's Day)

In addition to these general holidays, many towns also take their patron saint's day off.

## Packing

You simply cannot overdress in Italy; whatever grand strides Italian designers have made on the international fashion merry-go-round, most of their clothes are purchased domestically, prices be damned. Now whether or not you want to try to keep up with the natives is your own affair and your own heavy suitcase—you may do well to compromise and just bring a couple of smart outfits for big nights out. It's not that the Italians are very formal; they simply like to dress up with a gorgeousness that adorns their cities just as much as those old Renaissance churches and palaces. The few places with dress codes are the major churches and basilicas (no shorts, sleeveless shirts or strappy sundresses—women should tuck a light silk scarf in a bag to throw over the shoulders), casinos, and a few posh restaurants.

After agonizing over fashion, remember to pack small and light: trans-Atlantic airlines limit baggage by size (two pieces are free up to 1.5m in height and width; in second-claass you're allowed one of 1.5m and another up to 110cm). Within Europe limits are by weight; 20 kg (44lbs) in second-class, 30 kg (66lbs) in first. You may well be penalized for anything larger. If you're travelling mainly by train, you'll want to keep bags to a minimum: jamming big suitcases in overhead racks in a crowded compartment isn't much fun for anyone. Never take more than you can carry; but do bring the following: any prescription medicine you need, an extra pair of glasses or contact lenses if you wear them; a pocket knife and corkscrew (for picnics), a flashlight (for dark frescoed churches, caves and crypts), a travel alarm (for those early trains) and a pocket Italian-English dictionary (for flirting and other emergencies; outside the main tourist centres you may well have trouble finding someone who speaks English). If you're a light sleeper, you may want to invest in ear-plugs. Your electric appliances will work in Italy if you adapt and convert them to run on 220 AC with two round prongs on the plug. Beyond that, what you bring depends on when and where you go (*see* 'Climate' above).

## Photography

Film and developing are much more expensive than they are in either the UK or the USA, though there are plenty of outlets where you can obtain them. For example, a roll of film or *pellicola* (36 exposures, 100 ASA) costs around L8500, and L23,000 for developing. The equivalent slide film costs about L6000 (L10,000 to develop). You are not allowed to take pictures in most museums and in some churches. Most cities now offer one-hour processing if you need your pics in a hurry. Light conditions vary widely in Italy: a Venetian sea fog is a vastly different photographic problem from the harsh glare of Sicily, so you may need a range of filters and films if you are touring extensively.

## Post Offices

Dealing with *la posta italiana* has always been a risky, frustrating, time-consuming affair. It is one of the most expensive and slowest postal services in Europe. Even buying the right stamps requires dedicated research and saintly patience. One of the scandals that mesmerized Italy in recent years involved the minister of the post office, who disposed of literally tons of backlog mail by tossing it in the Tiber. When the news broke, he was replaced—the new minister, having learned his lesson, burned all the mail the post office was incapable of delivering. Not surprisingly, fed-up Italians view the invention of the fax machine as a gift from the Madonna. From these harsh judgements, however, we must exempt the Vatican City, whose special postal service (on angelic wings?) knocks spots off the rest of the country for speed and efficiency. If you're anywhere in Rome, be sure to post your mail in the Holy See. You need to buy special Vatican stamps, which provide a tidy profit for the papal coffers.

Post offices in Italy are usually open from 8am until 1pm (Monday to Saturday), or until 6 or 7pm in a large city. To have your mail sent poste restante (general delivery), have it addressed to the central post office (*Fermo Posta*) and expect three to four weeks for it to arrive. Make sure your surname is very clearly written in block capitals. To pick up your mail you must present your passport and pay a nominal charge. Stamps (*francoboli*) may be purchased in post offices or at tobacconists (*tabacchi*, identified by their blue signs with a white T). Prices fluctuate. The rates for letters and postcards (depending how many words you write!) vary according to the whim of the tobacconist or postal clerk.

You can also have money telegraphed to you through the post office; if all goes well, this can happen in a mere three days, but expect a fair proportion of it to go into commission.

## Shopping

'Made in Italy' has become a byword for style and quality, especially in fashion and leather, but also in home design, certamics, kitchenware, jewellery, lace and linens, glassware and crystal, chocolates, bells, Christmas decorations, hats, straw work, art books, engravings, handmade stationery, gold and silverware, bicycles, sports cars, woodworking, a hundred kinds of liqueurs, aperitifs, coffee machines, gastronomic specialities, and antiques (both reproductions, and the real thing). You'll find the best variety of goods in Milan, Rome, Florence and Venice—in other words, where the money is. Design-conscious Milan is Italy's major shopping centre and a cynosure of innovative style and fashion throughout the world.

If you are looking for antiques, be sure to demand a certificate of authenticity—reproductions can be very, very good. To get your antique or modern art purchases home, you will have to apply to the Export Department of the Italian Ministry of Education—a possible hassle. You will have to pay an export tax as well; your seller should know the details. Be sure to save receipts for Customs on the way home. Italians don't much like department stores, but there are a few chains—the classiest is the oldest, Rinascente, while COIN stores often have good buys in almost the latest fashions. Standa and UPIM are more like Woolworth's; they have good clothes selections, housewares, etc., and often contain basement supermarkets. The main attraction of Italian shopping, however, is to buy classy luxury items; for less expensive clothes and household items you can nearly always do better at home on price and quality. Prices for clothes are generally very high.

## Sports and Activities

### casinos

Italy has four casinos, all in the north, at Venice, Campione (on Lake Lugarno), San Remo, and St Vincent (Aosta). To enter, you must be over 18 and produce your passport.

### cycling

About three-quarters of Italy is hilly or mountainous, so a cycling holiday is no soft option. It is best to bring your own bike (a mountain bike if possible) and spare parts; cycling is growing fast in popularity, but nowhere near as fanatically practised in Italy as, say, in France or Denmark. Facilities for hiring or repairing bikes are less widespread. You can buy a good bike in Italy, however (L200,000–300,000). Good biking regions include Tuscany and Umbria, Puglia and the Alpine areas, where there are some good trails. Most airlines and rail companies will transport bikes quite cheaply; ferries to Sicily and Sardinia will take them free. The spring *Tour d'Italia* is Italy's great annual cycling event.

### fishing

You don't need a permit for sea-fishing (without an aqualung), but Italy's coastal waters, polluted and over-exploited, may disappoint. Many freshwater lakes and streams are stocked, however, and if you're more interested in fresh fish than the sport of it, there are innumerable trout farms where you can practically pick the fish up out of the water with your hands. To fish in fresh water you need to purchase a year's membership card (currently L189,000) from the **Federazione Italiana della Pesca Sportiva**, which has an office in every province; they will inform you about local conditions and restrictions. Bait and equipment are readily available.

### football

Soccer (*il calcio*) is a national obsession. For many Italians its importance far outweighs tedious issues like the state of the nation, the government of the day, or any momentous international event—not least because of the weekly chance (slim but real) of becoming an instant lira billionaire in the Lotteria Sportiva. All major cities, and most minor ones, have at least one team of some sort. The sport was actually introduced by the English, but a Renaissance game, something like a cross between football and rugby, has existed in Italy for centuries. Modern Italian teams are known for their grace, precision, and coordination; rivalries are intense, scandals, especially involving bribery and cheating, are rife. The tempting rewards offered by such big-time entertainment attract all manner of corrupt practices, yet crowd violence is minimal compared with the havoc wreaked by Britain's lamentable fans. Big-league matches are played on Sunday afternoons from September to May. For information, contact the Federazione Italiana Giuoco Calcio, Via G Allegri 14, 00198 Rome, ℗ (06) 84911. Rugby and baseball are also played increasingly in most cities; even American football and basketball have their devotees.

### golf

Italians have been slower than some nationalities to appreciate the delights of biffing a small white ball into a hole in the ground, but they're catching on fast. New courses are now spawning all over the country. The northwest is a good place to practise inexpert swings on a wide variety of beautifully set courses, particularly around Lake Como. Write or ring beforehand to check details before turning up. Most take guests and hire equipment.

Contact the Federazione Italiana Golf, Via Flaminia 388, 00196 Rome, ℗ (06) 323 1825 for more information.

### hiking and mountaineering

These sports are becoming steadily more popular among native Italians every year. The Alps (particularly the Dolomites) and Lombardy now have a good system of waymarked trails and mountain refuges run by the Italian Alpine Club (CAI), represented in all the hilly provinces. If you are planning to use the more popular routes in summer, write beforehand to reserve beds in refuges. Local tourist offices can put you in touch with the right people and organizations. Walking in the Alps is generally practicable between May and October, after most of the snow has melted; all the necessary gear—boots, packs, tents, etc—are readily available in Italy but for more money than you'd pay at home.

The CAI can put you in touch with Alpine guides or climbing groups if you're up to some real adventure, or write to the Italian national tourist board for a list of operators offering mountaineering holidays. Some Alpine resorts have taken to offering *Settimane Verdi* (Green Weeks)—good-value accommodation and activity packages for summer visitors similar to skiers' White Weeks. Tuscany and the Apennines (Abruzzo National Park) offer less strenuous but equally enjoyable walking country.

### hunting

Italy's most controversial sport pits avid enthusiasts against a growing number of environ-mentalists. The debate is fierce and the start of the season is marked by huge protests. Indiscriminate trapping, netting and shooting is responsible for the decimation of many migrant Mediterranean songbirds. Less controversial, at least from the conservation point of view, is duck- and pigeon-shooting.

### motor racing

The homeland of Ferrari, Maserati and Alfa Romeo naturally fosters a keen interest in motor sports, proof of which can be witnessed along any Italian road, which Italians regard as prac-tice tracks. Monza, near Milan, hosts the Italian Grand Prix every September. The Formula I track, built in 1922, is 15km out of town.

### riding holidays

They are now available in many parts of Italy, particularly in areas where AGRITURIST (see 'Where to Stay—Rural Self-Catering') is well represented, such as Tuscany, Umbria and Lazio, where tours staying at country estates are organized. There are riding stables in most cities and resorts. For more information, contact the local Agriturist office, or the Associazione Nazionale per il Turismo Equestre, Via A Borelli 5, 00161 Rome, © (06) 444 1179. Rome's International Riding Show in the Villa Borghese draws a big crowd each May. Horse-racing is staged in many large cities, notably Rome, Milan and Palermo. The most exciting event by far, however, is Siena's bareback **Palio**, a medieval pageant arousing huge local rivalries.

### rowing and canoeing

The annual regatta between the four ancient maritime republics of Venice, Amalfi, Genoa and Pisa (held in turn at each city) is a splendidly colourful event. Lake Piediluco in Umbria hosts an international rowing championship. If you prefer the DIY version, try the Arno or any of Lombardy's lakes. The fast rivers of the mountain areas provide exciting white-water sport. Kayak races are held in the Dolomites. For more information contact the Federazione Italiana Canoa e Kayak, Viale Tiziano 70, 00196 Rome, © (06) 368 58215.

### skiing and winter sports

Italy still lacks the cachet of neighbouring Switzerland or Austria among the skiing fraternity, but has caught up significantly and now has a better reputation for safety and efficiency than it once did, though erratic snow cover is always a problem. Its main resorts are obviously in the Alps, particularly the scenic Dolomites. Downhill and cross-country (sci di fondo) skiing are available, along with more exotic variants (for experts only) like helicopter skiing. Equipment hire is generally not too expensive, but lift passes and accommodation can push up the cost of a winter holiday. Some of the most fashionable (and expensive) resorts include **Cortina** and **Courmeyeur**. The Sella Ronda links several resorts in an exhilarating day's circuit. The Marmolada glacier in Trentino-Adige and Cervinia at the foot of the Matterhorn provide year-round sources of snowy runs. Lombardy's most famous ski resort is **Bormio**, at the entrance to Italy's largest national park, which has hosted world events in recent years (glacier skiing is practised above the Stelvio pass). Prices are highest during Christmas and New Year holidays, in February and at Easter. Most resorts offer *Settimane Bianche* (White Weeks)—off-season packages at economical rates. Other winter sports such as ice-skating and bob-sleighing are available at larger resorts.

### tennis

If soccer is Italy's most popular spectator sport, tennis is probably the game most people actually play. Every *comune* has public courts for hourly hire, especially resorts. Private clubs may offer temporary membership to passing visitors, and hotel courts can often be used by non-residents for a reasonable fee. Contact local tourist offices for information. Italy's big tennis event is the Grand Prix tournament held in Rome in May.

### watersports

Despite Italy's notorious coastal pollution, watersports are immensely popular, especially sailing and windsurfing. Best areas for sailing include the Ligurian Riviera, northern Sardinia, and the Tuscan or Lazio coasts. Lakes Como and Garda also have well-equipped sailing and windsurfing schools. Waterskiing is possible on all the major lakes, as well as at many coastal resorts. A few areas are good for diving, e.g. Alassio (Liguria), Capri, and Sicily. Boat and equipment hire is often quite expensive.

Mainland Italy is not remarkable for its **beaches**. Much of the coast is disappointingly flat and dull and many seaside resorts are plagued by that peculiarly Italian phenomenon, the concessionaire, who parks ugly lines of sunbeds and brollies all the way along the best stretches of coast, and charges all comers handsomely for the privilege. During the winter you can see what happens when the beaches miss out on their manicures; many get depressingly rubbish-strewn. The beaches in the south (Calabria, Basilicata and Apulia) are generally cleaner and less developed than those further north; those around the Bay of Naples, Rome's Lido di Ostia and the Venetian Lido are best avoided for swimming. Head for the islands for cleaner water and prettier scenery. In Lombardy, the smaller, less crowded lakes like Viverone, Varese and Mergozzo are preferable to the larger lakes for swimming. No one bats an eye at topless bathing, though nudism requires more discretion.

For further information, contact the **Italian State Tourist Office** or write to the following organizations:

**Federazione Italiana Vela** (Italian Sailing Federation), Via Brigata Bisagno 2/17, Genoa, ✆ (010) 56 57 23.

**Federazione Italiana Motonautica** (Italian Motorboat Federation), and **Federazione Italiana Sci Nautico** can both be found at Via Piranesi 44b, Milan, ✆ (02) 76 10 50.

## Telephones

Public, telephones for international calls may be found in the offices of **SIP** (Societa Italiana Telefoni, Italy's telephone company). They are the only places where you can make reverse charge calls (*a erre*, collect calls) but be prepared for a wait, as all these calls go through the operator in Rome. Rates for long-distance calls are among the highest in Europe. Calls within

Italy are cheapest after 10pm; international calls after 11pm. Most phone booths now take either coins, *gettoni* (L200 tokens often given to you in place of change) or phone cards (*schede, telefoniche*) available in L5000 or L10,000 amounts at tobacconists and news-stands. In smaller villages and islands, you can usually find *telefoni a scatti*, with a meter on it, in at least one bar (a small commission is generally charged). Try to avoid telephoning from hotels, which often add 25% to the bill. Telephone numbers in Italy currently change with alarming regularity as the antiquated system is updated.

Direct calls may be made by dialling the international prefix (for the UK 0044, Ireland 00353, USA and Canada 001, Australia 0061, New Zealand 0064). If you're calling Italy from abroad, dial 39 and then drop the first 0 from the telephone prefix. Many places have public fax machines, but the speed of transmission may make costs very high.

## Time

Italy is on Central European Time, one hour ahead of Greenwich Mean Time and six hours ahead of Eastern Standard Time. From the last weekend of March to the end of September, Italian Summer Time (daylight saving time) is in effect.

## Toilets

Frequent travellers have noted a steady improvement over the years in the cleanliness of Italy's public conveniences, although as ever you will only find them in places like train and bus stations and bars. Ask for the *bagno, toilette,* or *gabinetto*; in stations and the smarter bars and cafes, there are washroom attendants who expect a few hundred lire for keeping the place decent. You'll probably have to ask them for paper (*carta*). Don't confuse the Italian plurals; s*ignori* (gents), *signore* (ladies).

## Tourist Offices

Known under various initials as EPT, APT or AAST, Italian tourist offices usually stay open from 8am to 12.30 or 1pm, and from 3 to 7pm, possibly longer in summer. Few open on Saturday afternoons or Sundays. Information booths can also be found at major railway stations and can provide hotel lists, town plans and terse information on local sights and transport. Queues can be maddeningly long. English is spoken in the main centres. If you're stuck, you may get more sense out of a friendly travel agency than an official tourist office.

**UK:**       1 Princes Street, London W1R 8AY, ✆ (0171) 408 1254.

**USA:**      630 Fifth Ave, Suite 1565, New York NY 10111, ✆ (212) 245 4822

             12400 Wilshire Blvd, Suite 550, Los Angeles, CA 90025, ✆ (310) 820 0098

             500 N. Michigan Ave, Suite 1046, Chicago IL 60611, ✆ (312) 644 0990.

**Canada**:  1 Place Ville Marie, Suite 1914, Montréal, Quebec H3B 3M9,
             ✆ (514) 866 7667 .

**Japan:**   2–7–14 Minimi, Aoyama, Minato-Ku, Tokyo 107, ✆ (813) 347 82 051—
             also responsible for Australia and New Zealand.

France: 23 Rue de la Paix, 75002 Paris, ☎ (01) 42 66 66 68

14 Avenue de Verdun, 06048 Nice, ☎ 93 87 75 81

**Germany**: Berliner Allee 26, 4 Düsseldorf, ☎ (211) 13 22 32

Kaiserstrasse 65, 6000 Frankfurt/Main 1, ☎ (069) 2374

Goethestrasse 20, 80336 München, ☎ (089) 53 03 69.

**Netherlands**: Stadhouderskade 6, 1054 ES Amsterdam, ☎ (020) 616 8244.

Tourist and travel information may also be available from **Alitalia** (Italy's national airline) or **CIT** (Italy's state-run travel agency) offices in some countries. In the UK, contact the **Italian Travel Centre**, at Thomas Cook, 45 Berkeley Street, London W1A 1EB, ☎ (0171) 499 4000.

## Weights and Measures

1 kilogramme (1000g)—2.2 lb

1 etto (100g)—0.25 lb (approx)

1 litre—1.76 pints

1 metre—39.37 inches

1 kilometre—0.621 miles

1 lb—0.45 kg

1 pint—0.568 litres

1 quart—1.136 litres

1 Imperial gallon—4.546 litres

1 US gallon—3.785 litres

1 foot—0.3048 metres

1 mile—1.161 kilometres

Clothes sizes are tailored for slim Italian builds. Shoes, in particular, tend to be narrower than in most western countries.

*clothing sizes*

**Women's Shirts/Dresses**

| UK | 10 | 12 | 14 | 16 | 18 |
|---|---|---|---|---|---|
| USA | 8 | 10 | 12 | 14 | 16 |
| Italy | 40 | 42 | 44 | 46 | 48 |

**Sweaters**

| | | | |
|---|---|---|---|
| 10 | 12 | 14 | 16 |
| 8 | 10 | 12 | 14 |
| 46 | 48 | 50 | 52 |

**Women's Shoes**

| | | | | | |
|---|---|---|---|---|---|
| 3 | 4 | 5 | 6 | 7 | 8 |
| 4 | 5 | 6 | 7 | 8 | 9 |
| 36 | 37 | 38 | 39 | 40 | 41 |

**Men's Shirts**

| UK/USA | 14 | 14.5 | 15 | 15.5 | 16 | 16.5 | 17 | 17.5 |
|---|---|---|---|---|---|---|---|---|
| Italy | 36 | 37 | 38 | 39 | 40 | 41 | 42 | 43 |

**Men's Suits**

| UK/USA | 36 | 38 | 40 | 42 | 44 | 46 |
|---|---|---|---|---|---|---|
| Italy | 46 | 48 | 50 | 52 | 54 | 56 |

**Men's Shoes**

| UK | 2 | 3 | 4 | 5 | 6 | 7 | 8 | 9 | 10 | 11 | 12 |
|---|---|---|---|---|---|---|---|---|---|---|---|
| USA | 5 | 6 | 7 | 7.5 | 8 | 9 | 10 | 10.5 | 11 | 12 | 13 |
| Italy | 34 | 36 | 37 | 38 | 39 | 40 | 41 | 42 | 43 | 44 | 45 |

All accommodation in Italy is classified by the Provincial Tourist Boards. Price control, however, has been deregulated since 1992. Hotels now set their own tariffs, which means that in some places prices have rocketed. After a period of rapid and erratic price fluctuation, tariffs are at last settling down again to more predictable levels under the influence of market forces. Good-value, interesting accommodation in cities can be very difficult to find. Milan has the most expensive and heavily booked hotels in Italy; check the calendar of events with the tourist office—a major trade fair or conference could put all your travel plans in jeopardy.

The quality of furnishings and facilities has generally improved in all categories in recent years. Many hotels have installed smart bathrooms and electronic gadgetry. At the top end of the market, Italy has a number of exceptionally sybaritic hotels, furnished and decorated with real panache. But you can still find plenty of older-style hotels and *pensioni* , whose eccentricities of character and architecture (in some cases undeniably charming) may frequently be at odds with modern standards of comfort or even safety.

### prices

| Category | Double with bath |
|---|---|
| *luxury* (\*\*\*\*\*) | L450–800,000 |
| *very expensive* (\*\*\*\*) | L250–450,000 |
| *expensive* (\*\*\*) | L160–250,000 |
| *moderate* (\*\*) | L85–160,000 |
| *inexpensive* (\*) | up to L85,000 |

### Hotels and Guesthouses

Italian *alberghi* come in all shapes and sizes. They are rated from one to five stars, depending what facilities they offer (not their character, style or charm). The star ratings are some indication of price levels, but for tax reasons not all hotels choose to advertise themselves at the rating to which they are entitled, so you may find a modestly rated hotel just as comfortable (or more so) than a higher rated one. Conversely, you may find a hotel offers few stars in hopes of attracting budget-conscious travellers, but charges just as much as a higher-rated neighbour. *Pensioni* are generally more modest establishments, though nowadays the distinction between these and ordinary hotels is becoming blurred. *Locande* are traditionally an even more basic form of hostelry, but these days the term may denote somewhere fairly chic. Other inexpensive accommodation is sometimes known as *alloggi* or *affittacamere*. There are usually plenty of cheap dives around railway stations; for somewhere more salubrious, head for the historic quarters. Whatever the shortcomings of the decor, furnishings and fittings, you can usually rely at least on having clean sheets.

Price lists, by law, must be posted on the door of every room, along with meal prices and any extra charges (such as air-conditioning, or even a shower in cheap places). Many hotels display two or three different rates, depending on the season. Low-season rates may be about a third lower than peak-season tariffs. Some resort hotels close down altogether for several months a year. During high season you should always book ahead to be sure of a room (a fax reservation may be less frustrating to organise than one by post). If you have paid a deposit, your booking is valid under Italian law, but don't expect it to be refunded if you have to cancel. Tourist offices publish annual regional lists of hotels and pensions with current rates, but do not generally make reservations for visitors. Major city business hotels may offer significant discounts at weekends.

Main railway stations generally have accommodation booking desks; inevitably, a fee is charged. Chain hotels or motels are generally the easiest hotels to book, though not always the most interesting to stay in. Top of the list is CIGA (*Compagnia Grandi Alberghi*) with some of the most luxurious establishments in Italy, many of them grand, turn-of-the-century places that have been exquisitely restored. Venice's legendary Cipriani is one of its flagships. The French consortium *Relais et Châteaux* specializes in tastefully indulgent accommodation, often in historic buildings. At a more affordable level, one of the biggest chains in Italy is *Jolly Hotels*, always reliable if not all up to the same standard; these can generally be found near the centres of larger towns. Many motels are operated by the ACI (Italian Automobile Club) or by AGIP (the oil company) and usually located along major exit routes.

If you arrive without a reservation, begin looking or phoning round for accommodation early in the day. If possible, inspect the room (and bathroom facilities) before you book, and check the tariff carefully. Italian hoteliers may legally alter their rates twice during the year, so printed tariffs or tourist board lists (and prices quoted in this book!) may be out of date. Hoteliers who wilfully overcharge should be reported to the local tourist office. You will be asked for your passport for registration purposes.

Prices listed in this guide are for double rooms; you can expect to pay about two-thirds the rate for single occupancy, though in high season you may be charged the full double rate in a popular beach resort. Extra beds are usually charged at about a third more of the room rate. Rooms without private bathrooms generally charge 20–30% less, and most offer discounts for children sharing parent's rooms, or children's meals. A *camera singola* (single room) may cost anything from about L25,000 upwards. Double rooms (*camera doppia*) go from about L40,000 to L250,000 or more. If you want a double bed, specify a *camera matrimoniale*.

Breakfast is usually optional in hotels, though obligatory in *pensioni*. You can usually get better value by eating breakfast in a bar or café if you have any choice. In high season you may be expected to take half-board in resorts if the hotel has a restaurant, and one-night stays may be refused.

## Hostels and Budget Accommodation

There aren't many youth hostels in Italy (where they are known as *alberghi* or *ostelli per la gioventù*), but they are generally pleasant and sometimes located in historic buildings. The **Associazione Italiana Alberghi per la Gioventù** (Italian Youth Hostel Association, or AIG) is affiliated to the International Youth Hostel Federation. For a full list of hostels, contact AIG at Via Cavour 44, 00184 Roma (© (06) 487 1152; ℻ (06) 488 0492). An international membership card will enable you to stay in any of them. You can obtain these in advance from the following organizations.

| UK: | Youth Hostels Association of England and Wales, Trevelyan House, 8 St Stephen's Hill, St Albans, Herts AL1 2DY, ✆ (0727) 55215. |
|---|---|
| USA: | American Youth Hostels Inc., Box 37613, Washington DC 20013-7613, ✆ (202) 783 6161. |
| Canada: | Canadian Hostelling Association, 1600 James Naismith Drive, Suite 608, Gloucester, Ontario K1B 5N4, ✆ (613) 748 5638. |

(Cards can usually be purchased on the spot in many hostels if you don't already have one.)

Religious institutions also run hostels; some are single sex, others will accept Catholics only. Rates are usually somewhere between L12,000 and L18,000, including breakfast. Discounts are available for senior citizens, and some family rooms are available. You generally have to check in after 5pm, and pay for your room before 9am. Hostels usually close for most of the daytime, and many operate a curfew. During the spring, noisy school parties cram hostels for field trips. In the summer, it's advisable to book ahead. Contact the hostels directly.

---

### Villas, Flats and Chalets

If you're travelling in a group or with a family, self-catering can be the ideal way to experience Italy. The National Tourist Office has lists of agencies in the UK and USA which rent places on a weekly or fortnightly basis. CIT offices also rent flats and villas. The small ads in the weekend papers are crammed with property suggestions, especially for Tuscany. If you have set your heart on a particular region, write ahead to its tourist office for a list of local agencies and owners, who will send brochures or particulars of their accommodation. Maid service is included in the more glamorous villas; ask whether bed linen and towels are provided. A few of the larger operators are listed below:

#### in the UK

**Citalia**, Marco Polo House, 3–5 Lansdowne Road, Croydon CR9 1LL, ✆ (0181) 686 5533.

**Eurovillas**, 36 East Street, Coggeshall, Essex CO6 1SH, ✆ (01376) 561156.

**Inghams**, 10–18 Putney Hill, London SW15 6AX, ✆ (0181) 785 7777.

**Interhome**, 383 Richmond Road, Twickenham, Middx TW1 2EF, ✆ (0181) 891 1294.

**International Chapters**, 102 St John's Wood Terrace, London NW8 6PL, ✆ (0171) 722 9560.

**Magic of Italy**, 227 Shepherds Bush Road, London W6 7AS, ✆ (0181) 748 7575.

**Sovereign**, Astral Towers, Second Floor, Betts Way, Crawley, West Sussex RH10 2GX, ✆ (01293) 599999.

**Vacanze in Italia**, Bignor, Pulborough, West Sussex RH20 1QD, ✆ (017987) 426.

#### in the USA

**At Home Abroad**, 405 East 56th Street, New York, NY 10022, ✆ (212) 421 9165.

**CUENDET: Posarelli Vacations**, Suzanne T. Pidduck, 1742 Colle Corva, Camarillo, CA 93010, ✆ (805) 987 5278.

**Hideaways International**, PO Box 4433, Portsmouth, New Hampshire 03801, ✆ (603) 430 4433.

**Homeowners International**, 1133 Broadway, New York, NY 10010, ✆ (212) 691 2361.

**RAVE**, (Rent-a-Vacation Everywhere), 383 Park Avenue, Rochester, NY 146007, ✆ (716) 256 0760 .

---

### Rural Self-catering

For a breath of rural seclusion, the normally gregarious Italians head for a spell on a **working farm**, in accommodation (usually self-catering) that often approximates to the French *gîte*. Often, however, the real pull of the place is a restaurant in which you can sample some home-grown produce (olives, wine, etc.). Outdoor activities may also be on tap (riding, fishing, and so forth).

This branch of the Italian tourist industry is run by a special agency, **Agriturist**. It has burgeoned in recent years, and every region now has several Agriturist offices. Prices of farm-house accommodation, compared with the over-hyped 'Tuscan villa', are still reasonable (expect to pay around L40,000–60,000 for a cottage or double room). To make the most of your rural hosts, it's as well to have a little Italian under your belt. Local tourist offices will have information on this type of accommodation in their areas; otherwise you can obtain complete listings compiled by the national organisation **Agriturist**, Corso Vittorio Emanuele 101, 00186 Rome (✆ (06) 6512342), or **Turismo Verde**, Via Mariano Fortuny 20, 00196 Rome (✆ (06) 3669931). Both publications are available in Italian bookshops.

---

### Alpine Refuges

The Italian Alpine Club operates refuges (*rifugi*) on the main mountain trails (some accessible only by *funivie*). These may be predictably spartan, or surprisingly comfortable. Many have restaurants. For an up-to-date list, write to the Club Alpino Italiano, Via Fonseca Pimental 7, Milan, ✆ (02) 2614 1378. Charges average L18,000–L25,000 per person per night, including breakfast. Most are open only from July to September, but those used by skiers are about 20% more expensive from December to April. Book ahead in August.

---

### Camping

Life under canvas is not the fanatical craze it is in France, nor necessarily any great bargain, but there are over 2000 sites in Italy, particularly popular with holidaymaking families in August, when you can expect to find many sites at bursting point. Unofficial camping is generally frowned on and may attract a stern rebuke from the local police. Camper vans (and facilities for them) are increasingly popular. You can obtain a list of local sites from any regional tourist office. Campsite charges generally range from about L7000 per adult; tents and vehicles additionally cost about L7000 each. Small extra charges may also be levied for hot showers and electricity. A car-borne couple could therefore spend practically as much for a night at a well equipped campsite as in a cheap hotel. To obtain a camping carnet and to book ahead, write to the **Centro Internazionale Prenotazioni Campeggio**, Casella

Postale 23, 50041, Calenzano, Firenze, ℂ (055) 882 381; ✎ (055) 882 3918 (ask for their list of campsites as well as the booking form). The **Touring Club Italiano** (TCI) publishes a comprehensive annual guide to campsites and tourist villages throughout Italy. Write to: TCI, Corso Italia 10, Milan, ℂ (02) 85261/852 6245.

## Women Travellers

Italian men, with the heritage of Casanova, Don Giovanni, and Rudolph Valentino as their birthright, are very confident in their role as Great Latin Lovers, but the old horror stories of gangs following the innocent tourist maiden and pinching her bottom are way behind the times. Italian men these days are often exquisitely polite and flirt on a much more sophisticated level, especially in the more 'Europeanised' north. Milan is a much easier city for single women than Rome or Naples.

Still, women travelling alone may frequently receive hisses, wolf-whistles and unsolicited (complimentary or lewd, depending on your attitude) or 'assistance' from local swains— usually of the balding, middle-age-crisis variety. A confident, indifferent poise is usually the best policy. Failing that, a polite 'I am waiting for my *marito*' (avoiding damaged male egos which can turn nasty), followed by a firm '*no!*' or '*Vai via!*' (Scram!) will generally solve the problem. Flashers and wandering hands on crowded buses may be an unpleasant surprise, but rarely present a serious threat (unless they're after your purse!).

Risks can be greatly reduced if you use common sense and avoid lonely streets or parks and train stations after dark. Choose hotels and restaurants within easy and safe walking distance of public transport. Travelling with a companion of either sex will buffer you considerably from such nuisances (a guardian male, of course, instantly converts you into an inviolable chattel in Italian eyes). Avoid hitchhiking alone in Italy.

# History

# The First Italians

Some 50,000 years ago, when the Alps were covered by an ice cap and the low level of the Mediterranean made Italy a much wider peninsula than it is now, Neanderthal man graced the Ligurian Riviera with his low-browed presence. Even that, however, is not the beginning of the story. Recently, scientists have become excited over the discovery of a new type, *Homo Aeserniensis*, the first known inhabitant of Europe, living in caves around Isernia a million years ago. Italy makes a convenient bridge from Africa to Europe, and it seems that there was a lot of traffic throughout prehistory. Nevertheless, none of the earliest inhabitants of Italy left much in terms of art or culture, and the peninsula remained a backwater until about the 8th century BC. At that time, most of the population were lumped together as 'Italics', a number of powerful, distinct tribes with related languages. Among them were the **Samnites**, who dominated much of Campania and the south, the dolmen-building **Messapians** in Apulia, the **Picentes** and **Umbrii** along the northern Adriatic coast, and a boiling kettle of contentious peoples in the centre: **Sabines, Aequi, Volscii** and **Latins**. The mighty walls of their cities, called *cyclopean walls*, can still be seen today around southern Lazio. Two of Italy's most culturally sophisticated peoples lived on the islands: the **Siculi** of Sicily and the castle-building, bronze-working **Sards** of the Nuraghe culture. Both kept to themselves and interfered little with affairs on the mainland. Much of the north, the classical Cisalpine Gaul, was the stomping ground of Celtic Ligurians; at the time this area north of the Po was not really thought of as part of Italy.

## 750–509 BC: Greeks and Etruscans

The most interesting nations of the time, however, were two relative newcomers who contributed much towards bringing Italy out of its primitive state, the **Etruscans** and **Greeks**. With their shadowy past and as yet undeciphered language, the Etruscans are one of the puzzles of ancient history. According to their own traditions, they arrived from somewhere in western Anatolia about 900 BC—Etruscan inscriptions have been found on the Greek island of Lemnos—probably as a sort of warrior aristocracy that imposed itself on the existing populations of Tuscany and north Lazio. By the 8th century BC they were the strongest people in Italy, grouped in a loose confederation of 12 city states called the *Dodecapolis*. At the same time, the Greeks, whose trading routes had long covered Italy's southern coasts, began to look upon that 'underdeveloped' country as a New World for exploration and colonization. Cumae, on the Campanian coast, became the first Greek foundation in 750 BC, a convenient base for trading with the Etruscans and their newly discovered iron mines. A score of others soon followed, in Sicily and along the Ionian Sea, and soon they were rivalling the cities of Greece itself in wealth and culture. A third new factor in the Italian equation also appeared at this time, without much fanfare. The year 753 BC, according to the legends, saw the foundation of **Rome**.

Italy was ripe for civilization. In the centuries that followed, the Etruscans spread their rule and their culture over most of the north while the Italic tribes learned from Etruscans and Greeks alike. Some of them, especially the Latins and the Samnites, developed into urbanized, cultured nations in their own right. For the Greek cities, it was a golden age, as Taras (Táranto), Metapontum, Sybaris, Croton, and especially the Sicilian cities like Syracuse and Akragas grew into marble metropolises that dominated central Mediterranean trade and turned much of inland Italy into tribute-paying allies. In the 6th century BC, they had more wealth than was probably good for them; stories are told of the merchants of Sybaris sending across the Mediterranean, offering fortunes for a cook who could produce the perfect sauce for seafood, and of the sentries of Akragas' army going on strike for softer pillows. From the first, also, these cities dissipated their energies by engaging in constant wars with each other. Some, like Sybaris, were completely destroyed, and by c.400 BC, the failure of the rest to work together sent them into a slow but irreversible economic decline.

The Etruscan story is much the same. By about 600 BC the 12 cities and their allies ruled almost all northern Italy (excluding Cisalpine Gaul), and wealth from their Tuscan mines made them a political force on a Mediterranean scale. Their decline was to be as rapid as that of Magna Graecia. Repeated defeats at the hands of the wild Gauls weakened their confederation, but the economic decline that led to Etruria's virtual evaporation in the 4th century BC is harder to account for. Rome, a border city between the Etruscans and Latins, threw out its Etruscan king and established a **Republic** in 509 BC (see 'Rome': History p.839). Somehow, probably by the absorption of conquered populations, this relatively new city managed to grow to perhaps 100,000 people, ranking it with Taras and Capua, an Etruscan colony in the growing region of Campania, as the largest on the peninsula. With an economy insufficient to support so many Romans, the city could only live by a career of permanent conquest.

## 509–268 BC: The Rise of Rome

After the expulsion of the Etruscans, Rome spent a hundred years at war with the various cities of Etruria, while gradually subjugating the rest of the Latins and neighbouring tribes. The little republic with the military-camp ethic was successful on all fronts, and a sacking by marauding Gauls in 390 BC proved only a brief interruption in Rome's march to conquest. Southern Etruria and Latium were swallowed up by 358 BC, and Rome next turned its attention to the only power in Italy capable of competing with her on an equal basis: the Samnites. These rugged highlanders of the southern Apennines, with their capital at Benevento, had begun to seize parts of coastal Campania. The Romans drove them out in 343–41BC, but in the **Second Samnite War** the Samnites dealt them a severe defeat (Battle of Caudine Forks, 321 BC). In the third war, feeling themselves surrounded by Roman allies, the Samnites formed an alliance with the Northern Etruscans and Celts, leading to a general Italian commotion in which the Romans beat everybody, annexing almost all of Italy by 283 BC.

A strange interlude, delaying Rome's complete domination of Italy, came with the arrival of **Pyrrhus of Epirus**, a Greek adventurer with a large army who was invited in by the cities of Magna Graecia as a protector. From him we get the term 'Pyrrhic victories', for he outmatched the Romans in one battle after another, but never was able to follow up his advantage. After finally losing one in 275 BC, at Benevento, he quit and returned to Epirus, while the Romans leisurely took the deserted Greek cities one by one. Now the conquest was complete. All along the Romans had been diabolically clever in managing their new demesne, maintaining most of the tribes and cities as nominally independent states, while planting Latin colonies everywhere (re-founded cities like Paestum, Ascoli Piceno, and Benevento were such colonies, together with new ones in the north like Florence). The great network of roads centred on Rome was extended with great speed, and a truly united Italy seemed close to becoming a reality.

## 268–91 BC: Empire Abroad, Disarray at Home

After all this, Rome deserved a shot at the Mediterranean heavyweight title. The current champ, the powerful merchant thalassocracy of Carthage, was alarmed enough at the successes of its precocious neighbour, and proved happy to oblige. Rome won the first bout, beating Carthage and her ally Syracuse in the **First Punic War** (264–41 BC), and gained Sicily, Sardinia, and Corsica. For the rematch, the **Second Punic War** (219–202 BC), Carthage sent **Hannibal** and his elephants from Spain into Italy over the Alps to bring the war into the Romans' backyard. Undeterred by the brilliant African general's victory at Cannae in 216 BC, where 4 legions were destroyed, the Romans hung on tenaciously even when Hannibal appeared at the gates of Rome. In Hannibal's absence, they took Spain and much of Africa, and after Scipio Africanus' victory at Zama in 202 BC, Carthage surrendered. The **Third Punic War** was a sorry affair. Rome only waited long enough for Carthage to miss a step in its treaty obligations before razing the city to the ground. The west conquered, Rome looked east. Already by 200 BC she had been interfering in Greek affairs. The disunited Greeks and successor states of Alexander's empire proved easy targets, and by 64 BC the legions were camped on the Cataracts of the Nile, in Jerusalem, and half across Asia Minor.

Nothing corrupts a state like easy conquests, and all this time things in Italy were going very wrong. Taxation ceased for Roman citizens, as booty provided the state with all the revenues it needed, and tens of thousands of slaves were imported. Thus Italy became a parasite nation. Vast amounts of cheap grain brought from Africa and Egypt ruined the Italian farmer, who had the choice of selling his freehold and becoming a sharecropper, joining the army, or moving to Rome as part of the burgeoning lumpenproletariat. The men who profited the most from the wars bought up tremendous amounts of land, turning Italy into a country of huge estates (*latifundia*), and becoming a new aristocracy powerful enough to stifle any attempts at reform. Only Rome, of course, and a few other cities prospered. In this period many of the Greek and Etruscan towns withered. Many country districts became abandoned, and rural Italy knew constant famine and plagues, while in Rome the new rich were learning the delights of orgies, gladiatorial combats, and being carried about the streets by slaves.

Not that degeneracy and social disintegration had proceeded far enough for Italy to fail to resist. Rome, and indeed all Italy divided into extremist factions, the reactionary 'Senatorial Party' and the radical 'Popular Party'. (The Senate, and the senatorial class, were not yet a nobility per se. A hefty fortune was all that was needed for entry. Their populist opponents included not only the poor, but most of the businessmen and the hard-pressed middle class.) In 133 BC, a remarkable reformer named **Tiberius Gracchus** was elected Tribune, but his plans for land reforms earned him assassination the following year. His brother **Gaius Gracchus** went even further, attempting to expand citizenship to most of the Italians when he gained the Tribunate in 123 BC, but he, too, was murdered after the Senate declared martial law that same year. By this time Rome's Constitution was reduced to a travesty, and both sides realized that the only real power lay with the legions. The populists staked their hopes on **Gaius Marius**, an illiterate but good-hearted general who saved Italy from the last surprise Celtic raid in 113 BC. Marius' ascent to power proved a disappointment, and a whole new generation of populist statesmen was assassinated one by one.

## 91–31 BC: Sixty Years of Civil War

Italy had had enough; the year 91 saw a coordinated revolt among the southern peoples called the **Social War**, which was defeated by the campaigns of Marius and **Sulla** (the Senate's darling in the army), and by an offer to extend Roman citizenship to all Italians. A military coup by Sulla followed, with the backing of the Senate; it was the first time armed Roman soliders ever actually entered Rome, a religious and constitutional taboo. However, when Sulla's army left for conquest and booty on the Black Sea, a populist counter-movement succeeded in taking power, and ruled Rome for the next three years. Sulla's triumphal return threw them out, and the haughty general unleashed a bloody reign of terror, unlike anything Italy had ever seen. An effective dictatorship was created, and all opponents either murdered or exiled (a redoubtable populist general named Quintus Sertorius still held Spain, and defeated five separate legions sent against him). Italy careened into anarchy, with many rural districts reverting to bandit-ridden wastelands, a setting for the remarkable revolt in 73 BC of **Spartacus**, an escaped gladiator who led a motley army of dispossessed farmers and runaway slaves—some 70,000 of them— back and forth across the south until the legions finally defeated him in 71 BC.

All this had exhausted both sides, and finally discredited senatorial rule. After Sulla's death, no one minded when the consulship and real power passed to **Pompey**, another successful general but one who cared little for politics. Like Sulla before him, Pompey soon set out for the east, where the most glory and booty were to be gained, and his departure left the stage in Rome open to 33-year-old **Julius Caesar**, a tremendously clever soldier-politician, but a good man anyhow. With his two surpassing talents, one for rhetoric and the other for attracting money, he took up the popular cause in better style than anyone had done it before. A taint of connection to the **Catiline conspiracy** of 68 BC, a revolt of adventurers, disaffected nobles, and other loose ends, proved a temporary setback, just as it advanced the fortunes of **Marcus Tullius Cicero**, the great orator, writer, and statesman who still dreamed of founding a real republic with a real constitution, opposing both extreme parties and pinning his hopes on the still-surviving Italian middle class. Few people in Rome cared for such principles, however, and after Pompey returned from bashing the Pontic Kingdom and the Cilician pirates, he, Caesar, and a wealthy building contractor named Licinius Crassus sliced up the republic between them, forming the **First Triumvirate** in 59 BC.

What Caesar really wanted, of course, was a military command. Following the accepted practice, he managed to buy himself one in the north, and undertook the conquest of most of Gaul, with well-known results. When Pompey grew jealous and turned against him, Caesar led his army back into Italy, defying the Senate by 'crossing the Rubicon', the river boundary between Italy and Gaul that Roman armies were not allowed to cross without senatorial authorization. Resistance collapsed before him, and he became unchallenged master of Rome while not even holding public office. Pompey and most of the Senate fled to Greece, where Caesar caught up with them three years later. In his four years as ruler of Rome, Caesar surprised everyone, even his enemies; everything received a good dose of reform, even the calendar, and a beginning was made towards sorting out the economic mess and getting Italy back on its feet. His assassination by a clique of republican bitter-enders in 44 BC plunged Italy into civil war again, and left historians to ponder the grand question of whether Caesar had really intended to make himself a king and finally put the now senile republic to sleep. A **Second Triumvirate** was formed, of Caesar's adopted son Octavian, a senatorial figurehead named Lepidus, and Caesar's old friend and right-hand man, a talented, dissipated fellow named Marcus Antonius (Mark Antony), who according to one historian spent the equivalent of $3 billion (of other people's money) in his brief lifetime. While he dallied in the east with Cleopatra, Octavian was consolidating his power in Italy. The inevitable battle came in 31 BC, at Actium in Greece, and it was a complete victory for Octavian.

## 31 BC–AD 251: The Empire

With unchallenged authority through all the Roman lands, Octavian (soon to rename himself **Augustus**) was free to complete the reforms initiated by Caesar. He maintained the forms of the republic while accumulating enough titles and offices for himself to have constitutional justification for his absolute rule. The title he chose for public use was 'first citizen', while behind the scenes the machinery was being perfected for the deification of the Caesars (a practical policy in the eastern half of the empire, where such things were common practice), and for a stable monarchy after his death. It all worked brilliantly; peace was restored, an effective administration created, and Italy in particular was able to recover from its time of troubles with the help of Augustus' reforms and huge programmes of public works.

For his career, and those of his successors, you may read the gossipy, shocking, and wonderfully unreliable *Lives of the Caesars* of Suetonius. All Rome tittered at the scandals of the later Julian Emperors, but reality was usually much more prosaic. **Tiberius** (AD 14–37) may have been a monster to his girlfriends and boyfriends, but he proved an intelligent and just ruler otherwise; his criminally insane successor **Caligula**, or 'Bootkin', lasted only four years (37–41) while the bureaucracy kept things going. **Claudius** (41–54) governed well and conquered southern Britain, while his stepson **Nero** (54–68) generally made a nuisance of himself in Rome but did little to disturb the system. Nevertheless, a commmander in Spain (Galba) declared him unfit to be emperor and marched on Rome to take his place; Nero just managed to commit suicide before they caught him. Now the genie was out of the bottle again, as the soldiers once more realized that the real power lay with them. Another general, Otho, commander of the emperors' Praetorian Guard, toppled Galba, and soon lost out in turn to Vitellius, commander on the Rhine. The fourth emperor of the fateful years AD 68–69 was **Vespasian**, leader of the eastern armies. He had the strongest legions and so got to keep the job; his reign (69–79) and those of his sons **Titus** (79–81) and **Domitian** (81–96), the three Flavian Emperors, were remembered as a period of prosperity. Vespasian began the Colosseum; whether intentionally or not, this incomparable new charnel house made a perfect symbol for the renewed decadence and militarization of the state.

For the moment, however, things looked rosy. After the assassination of Domitian, another bad boy but not an especially calamitous ruler, Rome had the good fortune to be ruled by a series of high-minded and intelligent military men, who carefully chose their successors in advance to avoid civil war. The so-called Antonine Emperors presided over the greatest age of prosperity the Mediterranean world ever knew; in Italy they ran a surprisingly modern state (though one still based on slave labour) that would seem familiar to us today: public libraries, water boards to maintain the aqueducts, rent control, agricultural price supports, low-cost loans for starting new businesses and many other such innovations. The first of the Antonines was **Nerva** (96–98), followed by **Trajan** (98–117) and **Hadrian** (117–138), both great soldiers and builders on a monumental scale, especially in Rome; after them came **Antoninus Pius** (138–61), little known only because his reign was so peaceful, and **Marcus Aurelius** (161–80), soldier, statesman, and Stoic philosopher. His choice for successor was his useless son **Commodus** (180–93) and the string of good emperors was broken.

The 2nd-century prosperity was not without its darker side. The arts were in serious decline, as if the imagination of the Greco-Roman Mediterranean was somehow failing. Education was in poor shape, and every sort of fatuous mysticism imported from the East permeated the minds of the people. Economically, this period saw the emergence of the well-known north-south split in Italy. The rural south, impoverished by the Roman Republic, now sank deeper into decline, while even the commerce of wealthy Campania began to fail, ruined by foreign competition. In the north, especially Cisalpine Gaul, a sounder, more stable economy led to the growth of new centres, Milan, Padua, Verona, and Ravenna the most prominent, beginning the economic divide that continues even today. In the balance, though, both politically and economically Italy was becoming an increasingly less significant part of the empire. Of the 2nd-century emperors, fewer came from Italy than from Spain, Illyria, or Africa.

## 251–475: Decline and Fall

For all it cost to maintain them, the legions were no longer the formidable military machine of Augustus' day. They were bureaucratic and a little tired, and their tactics and equipment were also falling behind those of the Persians and even some of the more clever German barbarians. The Goths were the first to demonstrate this, in 251, when they overran the Balkans, Greece, and Asia Minor. Five years later Franks and Alemanni invaded Gaul, and in 268 much of the east detached itself from the empire under the leadership of Odenathus of Palmyra. Somehow the empire recovered and prevailed, under dour soldier-emperors like **Aurelian** (270–75), who built Rome's walls, and **Diocletian** (284–305) who completely revamped the structure of the state and economy. His fiscal reforms, such as the fixing of prices and a decree that every son had to follow the trade of his father, ossified the economy and made the creeping decline of Italy and all western Europe harder to arrest. A gigantic bureaucracy was created, taxes reached new heights as people's ability to pay them declined, and society became increasingly militarized in every respect. The biggest change was the division of the empire into halves, each ruled by a co-emperor equally called 'Augustus'; Diocletian, significantly, chose the wealthier east for himself. The new western emperors usually kept their court at army headquarters in Mediolanum (Milan), and later at impregnable Ravenna on the Adriatic, and Rome itself became a marble-veneered backwater.

More than ever, the empire had become an outright military dictatorship, in a society whose waning energies were entirely devoted to supporting a bloated, all-devouring army and bureaucracy. Medieval feudalism actually had its origins in this period, as the remaining freehold farmers sold their lands and liberty to the local gentry—for protection's sake, but also to get off the tax rolls. In the cities, the high taxes and uncertain times ruined business and trade; throughout Italy and the West towns both large and small began their fatal declines. Diocletian reduced Italy to the status of a mere province, and the peninsula had little to do with imperial events thereafter. The confused politics of the 4th century are dominated by

**Constantine** (306–337), who ruled both halves of the empire, defeated various other contenders (Battle of the Milvian Bridge, outside Rome, in 312), and founded the new eastern capital of Constantinople. He adroitly moved to increase his and the empire's political support by favouring Christianity. Though still a small minority in most of the Empire, the Christians' strong organization and determination made them a good bet for the future. The religious revolution that followed was unexpected and remarkable. Diocletian had been the most ferocious of the persecutors of Christianity; by 400, it was the turn of the pagans and Jews to be persecuted. In the next decades, as the Empire's cities became Christianized, the Church itself became the most powerful and coherent instrument of the Roman élite.

The military disasters began in 406, with Visigoths, Franks, Vandals, Alans, and Suevi overrunning Gaul and Spain. Italy's turn came in 408, when Western Emperor Honorius, ruling from the new capital of Ravenna, had his brilliant general Stilicho (who himself happened to be a Vandal) murdered. A Visigothic invasion followed, leading to Alaric's sack of Rome in 410. St Augustine, probably echoing the thoughts of most Romans, wrote that it seemed the end of the world must be near. Rome should have been so lucky; judgement was postponed long enough for **Attila the Hun** to pass through Italy in 451. Then Gaiseric the Vandal, who had set up a pirate kingdom in Africa, raided Italy and sacked Rome again in 455. So completely had things changed, it was scarcely possible to tell the Romans from the barbarians. By the 470s, the real ruler in Italy was a Gothic general named **Odoacer**, who led a half-Romanized Germanic army and probably thought of himself as the genuine heir of the Caesars. In 476, he decided to dispense with the lingering charade of the Western Empire. The last emperor, young, silly Romulus Augustulus, was packed off to premature retirement in Naples, and Odoacer had himself crowned King of Italy at Pavia.

## 475–1000: The Dark Ages

At the beginning, the new Gothic-Latin state showed some promise. Certainly the average man was no worse off than he had been under the last emperors; trade and cities even revived a bit. In 493, Odoacer was replaced (and murdered) by a rival Ostrogoth, **Theodoric**, nominally working on behalf of the Eastern Emperor at Byzantium. Theodoric proved a strong and able, though somewhat paranoid ruler; his court at Ravenna witnessed a minor rebirth of Latin letters with Cassiodorus, Symmachus, and the great Christian philosopher Boethius. Nevertheless, stability was compromised by religious quarrels between the Arian Christian Goths and the orthodox Catholic populations in the cities.

A disaster as serious as those of the 5th century began in 536, with the invasion of Italy by the Eastern Empire, part of the relentlessly expansionist policy of the great **Justinian**. The historical irony was profound; in the ancient homeland of the Roman Empire, Roman troops now came not as liberators, but foreign, largely Greek-speaking conquerors. Justinian's brilliant generals, Belisarius and Narses, ultimately prevailed over the Goths in a series of terrible wars that lasted until 563, but the damage to an already stricken society and economy was incalculable. Italy's total exhaustion was exposed only five years later, when the **Lombards**, a Germanic tribe who worked hard to earn the title of barbarian, overran northern Italy and parts of the south, establishing a kingdom at Pavia and separate duchies in Benevento and Spoleto. A new pattern of power appeared, with semi-independent Byzantine dukes defending many coastal areas, the Byzantine Exarchs of Ravenna controlling considerable territory on the Adriatic and in Calabria, and Lombard chiefs ruling most of the interior. The popes in Rome, occasionally allied with the Lombards against Byzantium, became a force during this period, especially after the papacy of the clever, determined **Gregory the Great** (590–604). Scion of the richest family in Italy, Gregory took political control in Rome during desperate times, and laid the foundations for the papacy's claims to temporal power.

With trade and culture at their lowest ebb, the 7th century marks the rock bottom of Italian history. The 8th showed some improvement; while most of the peninsula lay in feudal darkness, **Venice** was beginning its remarkable career as a trading city, and independent Amalfi and Naples emulated its success on the Tyrrhenian coast. The popes, along with other bishops who had taken advantage of the confused times to become temporal powers, intrigued everywhere to increase their influence; they finally cashed in with a Frankish alliance in the 750s. At the time the Lombard kings were doing well, finally conquering Ravenna (751) and considerable territories formerly under the dominion of the popes, who invited in **Charlemagne** to protect them. He eliminated the last Lombard king, Desiderius (his father-in-law, incidentally), and tucked all Italy as far south as Rome (with the exception of Venice) into his short-lived patchwork empire, sanctified by a papal coronation as the heir of the Roman Empire. A Lombard Duchy of Benevento survived for centuries up in the mountains, and the Byzantines kept a tenuous hold on the heel and toe; the Greek villages and relics of troglodyte Greek monasticism in Calabria and Apulia date from this period. Arabs from Tunisia were beginning a gradual conquest of Sicily, and their raiders menaced all the peninsula's coasts; they sacked Rome itself in 746.

When Charlemagne's empire disintegrated following his death in 814, Italy reverted to a finely balanced anarchy. Altogether the 9th century was a bad time, with Italy caught between the Arab raiders and the endless wars of petty nobles and battling bishops in the north. The 10th century proved somewhat better—perhaps much better than the scanty chronicles of the time attest. Even in the worst times, Italy's cities never entirely disappeared. Sailing and trading over the sea always lead to better technologies, new ideas and economic growth, and in these respects the maritime cities of Italy had become the most advanced in Europe; even inland cities like Florence and Milan were developing a new economic importance and self-consciousness. Cities do not grow by magic in such unpromising times; even though few of them had managed to attain complete freedom of action, it is clear that even in the 900s many were looking to their own resources, defending their interests against the Church and nobles alike.

A big break for the cities, and for Italy, came in 961 with the invasion of the German **Otto the Great**, heir to the imperial pretensions of the Carolingians. He deposed the last feeble King of Italy, Berengar II of Ivrea, and was crowned Holy Roman Emperor in Rome the following year. Not that any of the Italians were happy to see him, but the strong government of Otto and his successors beat down the great nobles and allowed the growing cities to expand their power and influence. A new pattern was established; Germanic Emperors would be meddling in Italian affairs for centuries, not powerful enough to establish total control, but at least usually able to keep out important rivals.

## 1000–1154: The Rise of the *Comuni*

On the eve of the new millennium, most Christians were convinced that the turn of the calendar would bring with it the end of the world. On the other hand, if there had been economists and social scientists around, they would have had ample evidence to reassure everyone that things were looking up. Especially in the towns, business was very good, and the political prospects even brighter. The first mention of a truly independent *comune* (plural: *comuni*; a term used throughout this book, meaning a free city state; the best translation might be 'commonwealth') was in Milan, where in 1024 a popular assembly is recorded, deciding which side the city would take in the Imperial Wars.

Throughout this period the papacy had declined greatly in power and prestige, a political football kicked between the Emperors and the piratical Roman nobles. Beginning in the 1050s, a remarkable Tuscan monk named Hildebrand controlled papal policy, working behind the scenes to reassert the influence of the Church. When he became pope himself, in 1073, **Gregory VII** immediately set himself in conflict with the emperors over the issue of investiture—whether the church or secular powers could name church officials. The various Italian (and European) powers took sides on the issue, and 50 years of intermittent war followed, including the famous penance in the snow of Emperor Henry IV in Canossa (1077). The result was a big revival for the papacy, but more importantly the cities of Lombardy and the rest of the north used the opportunity to increase their influence, and in some cases achieve outright independence, defeating the local barons in war, razing their castles and forcing them to move inside the towns.

Southern Italy knew a different fate. The first **Normans** arrived about 1020, on pilgrimages to Monte Sant'Angelo in the Gargano. The liked the opportunities they saw for conquest, and soon younger sons of Norman feudal families were moving into the south, first as mercenaries but gradually gaining large tracts of land for themselves in exchange for their services. Usually allied to the popes, they soon controlled most of Apulia and Calabria. One of their greatest chiefs, **Roger de Hautville**, began the conquest of Sicily from the Arabs in 1060, six years before William the Conqueror sailed for England. Roger eventually united all the south into the 'Kingdom of Sicily', and by the 1140s, under Roger II, this strange Norman-Arab-Italian state, with its glittering, half-oriental capital of Palermo, had become the cultural centre of the Mediterranean, as well as one of the strongest, best-organized states in Europe.

## 1154–1300: Guelphs and Ghibellines

While all this was happening, of course, the First Crusade (1097–1130) occupied the headlines. It was, in part, a result of the new militancy of the papacy begun by Gregory VII. For Italy, especially Pisa and Venice, the two states with plenty of boats to help ship Crusaders, the affair meant nothing but pure profit. Trade was booming everywhere, and the accumulation of money helped the Italians to create modern Europe's first banking system. It also financed the continued independence of the *comuni*, which flourished everywhere, with a big enough surplus for building-projects like Pisa's cathedral complex, perhaps the biggest undertaking since the time of Trajan and Hadrian. Culture and science were flourishing, too, with a big boost from contact with the Byzantines and the Moslems of Spain and Africa. By the 12th century, far in advance of most of Europe, Italy had attained a prosperity unknown since Roman times. The classical past had never been forgotten—witness the attempt of Arnold of Brescia (1154) to recreate the Roman Republic. Similarly, free *comuni* in the north called their elected leaders 'consuls', and artists and architects turned ancient Roman styles into the Romanesque. Even Italian names were changing, an interesting sign of the beginnings of national consciousness; quite suddenly the public records (such as they were) show a marked shift from Germanic to classical and Biblical surnames: fewer Ugos, Othos, and Astolfos, more Giuseppes, Giovannis, Giulios, and Flavios.

Emperors and popes were still embroiled in the north. **Frederick I Barbarossa** of the Hohenstaufen—or Swabian—dynasty, was strong enough in Germany, and he made it the cornerstone of his policy to reassert imperial power in Italy. Beginning in 1154, he crossed the Alps five times, molesting free cities that asked nothing more than the right to continually fight one another. He spread terror, utterly destroying Milan in 1161, but a united front of cities called the Lombard League defeated him in 1176. Frederick's greatest triumph in Italy came by arranging a marriage with the Normans, leaving his grandson **Frederick II** not only emperor but king of Sicily, giving him a strong power base in Italy itself.

The second Frederick's career dominated Italian politics for 30 years (1220–50). With his brilliant court, in which Italian was used for the first time (alongside Arabic and Latin), his half-Moslem army, his incredible processions of dancing girls, eunuchs, and elephants, he provided Europe with a spectacle the like of which it had never seen. Frederick founded universities (as at Naples), gave Sicily a written constitution (perhaps the world's first), and built geometrically arcane castles and towers all over the south. The popes excommunicated him at least twice. The battle of pope and emperor had become serious. All Italy divided into factions: the **Guelphs**, under the leadership of the popes, supported religious orthodoxy, the liberty of the *comuni*, and the interests of their emerging merchant class. The **Ghibellines** stood for the emperor, statist economic control, the interests of the rural nobles, and religious and intellectual tolerance. Frederick's campaigns and diplomacy in the north met with very limited success, and his death in 1250 left the outcome very much in doubt.

His son **Manfred**, not emperor but merely King of Sicily, took up the battle with better luck; Siena's defeat of Florence in 1260 gained that city and most of Tuscany for the Ghibellines. The next year, however, Pope Urban IV began an ultimately disastrous precedent by inviting in **Charles of Anjou**, a powerful, ambitious leader and brother of the King of France. As protector of the Guelphs, Charles defeated Manfred (1266) and murdered the last of the Hohenstaufens, Conradin (1268). He held unchallenged sway over Italy until 1282, when the famous revolt of the Sicilian Vespers started the party wars up again. By now, however, the terms Guelph and Ghibelline had ceased to have much meaning; men and cities changed sides as they found expedient, and the old parties began to seem like the black and white squares on a chessboard. If your neighbour and enemy were Guelph, you became for the moment Ghibelline, and if he changed so would you. (Strangely enough, black and white were respectively the Ghibelline and Guelph colours. They also had distinctive styles of architecture. When you see a castle in Italy with simple rectangular crenellations along the walls, you'll know that Guelphs built it; ornate 'swallow-tail' crenellations are Ghibelline.)

Some real changes did occur out of all this sound and fury. In 1204 Venice hit its all-time biggest jackpot when it diverted the Fourth Crusade to the sack of Constantinople, winning for itself a small empire of islands in the Adriatic and Levant. Genoa emerged as its greatest rival in 1284, when its fleet put an end to Pisa's prominence at the Battle of Meloria. And elsewhere around the peninsula, some cities were falling under the rule of military *signori* whose descendents would be styling themselves counts and dukes—the Visconti of Milan, the della Scala of Verona, the Malatesta of Rimini. Everywhere the freedom of the *comuni* was in jeopardy; after so much useless strife the temptation to submit to a strong leader often proved overwhelming. During Charles of Anjou's reign the popes extracted the price for their invitation. The Papal State, including much of central Italy, was established in 1278. But most importantly, the Italian economy never seemed to mind the trouble. Trade and money flowed as never before; cities built new cathedrals and created themselves incredible skyscraper skylines, with the tall tower-fortresses of the now urbanized nobles. And it was, in spite of everything, a great age for culture—the era of Guelphs and Ghibellines was also the time of Dante (b. 1265) and Giotto (b. 1266).

## 1300–1494: Renaissance Italy

This paradoxical Italy continued into the 14th century, with a golden age of culture and an opulent economy side by side with almost continuous war and turmoil. With no serious threats from the emperors or any other foreign power, the myriad Italian states were able to menace each other joyfully without outside interference. One of the secrets to this state of affairs was that war had become a sort of game, conducted on behalf of cities by bands of paid mercenaries led by a condottiere, who were never allowed to enter the cities themelves. The arrangement suited everyone well. The soldiers had lovely horses and armour, and no real desire to do each other serious harm. The cities were usually free from grand ambitions; everyone was making too much money to want to go and wreck the system. Without heavy artillery, walled towns and castles were nearly impossible to take, making the incentives to try hard even less. Best of all, the worst schemers and troublemakers on the Italian stage were fortuitously removed from the scene. Shortly after the election of the French Pope Clement V in 1305, the papacy moved to Avignon, becoming a puppet of the French king that temporarily had little influence in Italian affairs.

By far the biggest event of the 14th century was the **Black Death** of 1347–48, in which it is estimated Italy lost one-third of its population. The shock brought a rude halt to what had been 400 years of almost continuous growth and prosperity, though its effects did not prove a permanent setback for the economy. In fact, the plague's grim joke was that it actually made life better for most of the Italians who survived; working people in the cities, no longer overcrowded, found their rents lower and their labour worth more, while in the country farmers were able to increase their profits by only tilling the best land.

It is impossible to speak of 'Italian history' in this period, with the peninsula split up into long-established, cohesive states pursuing different ends and warring against one another. Italian statesmen understood the idea of a balance of power long before political theorists invented the term, and, despite all the clatter and noise, most probably believed Italy was enjoying the best of all possible worlds. Four major states, each a European power in its own right, dominated the region's politics: first **Venice**, the oldest and most glorious, with its oligarchic but singularly effective Constitution, and its exotic career of trade with the East.

The Venetians waged a series of wars against arch-rival Genoa, finally exhausting her after the War of Chioggia in 1379. After that, they felt strong enough to make a major change in policy. Once serenely aloof from Italian politics, Venice now carved out a small land empire for itself, by 1428 including Verona, Padua, Vicenza, Brescia and Bergamo.

**Florence**, the richest city-state thanks to its banking and wool trade, also enjoyed good fortune, extending its control over most of Tuscany, and gaining a seaport with its conquest of now decadent Pisa in 1406. In 1434, **Cosimo de' Medici**, head of the largest banking house, succeeded in establishing a de facto dictatorship. Even though the forms of the old Republic were maintained, Florence was well on its

*Medici - coat of arms*

way to becoming a signorial state like its greatest rival, **Milan**. Under the Visconti, Milan had become rich and powerful, basing its success on the manufactures of the city (arms and textiles) and the bountiful, progressively managed agriculture of southern Lombardy. Its greatest glory came during the reign of **Gian Galeazzo Visconti** (1385–1402), who bought himself a ducal title from the Emperor and nearly conquered all north Italy, before his untimely death caused his plans to unravel.

In the south, the huge **Kingdom of Naples** suffered from the heritage of the Normans, who had made it the only part of Italy where north-European-style feudalism had ever taken root. When times changed, the backward rural barons who dominated the south retarded its commerce and its culture. Despite such promising periods as the reign of the King of Aragon, **Alfonso the Magnanimous** (1442–58), a prototypical Renaissance prince and patron of the arts who seized Naples and added it to his domains, the south was falling far behind the rest of Italy. The other Italian states included Genoa, a nasty little oligarchy that made money but contributed nothing to the cultural life of the times; the Duchy of Savoy-Piedmont, a quiet backwater still more closely tied to France than Italy; the tiny, stalwart Republics of Lucca and Siena; refined independent courts in Ferrara, Mantua, Modena and Rimini, surviving the rough seas of Italian politics; and finally the Papal States, anarchic while the popes were in France (until 1378), and woefully misgoverned when they came back.

And what of the Renaissance? No word has ever caused more mischief for the understanding of history and culture—as if Italy had been Sleeping Beauty, waiting for some Prince Charming of classical culture to come and awaken it from a 1000-year nap. On the contrary, Italy even in the 1200s was richer, more technologically advanced, and far more artistically creative than it had ever been in the days of the Caesars. The new art and scholarship that began in Florence in the 1400s and spread across the nation grew from a solid foundation of medieval accomplishment. The gilded, opulent Italy of the 15th century felt complacently secure in its long-established cultural and economic pre-eminence. A long spell of freedom from outside interference lulled the nation into believing that its political disunity could continue safely forever; except perhaps for the sanguinely realistic Florentine Niccolò Machiavelli, no one realized that Italy in fact was a plum waiting to be picked.

## 1494–1529: The Wars of Italy

The Italians brought the trouble down on themselves, when Duke Ludovico of Milan invited the French King Charles VIII to cross the Alps and assert his claim to the throne of Milan's enemy, Naples. Charles did just that, and the failure of the combined Italian states to stop him (at the inconclusive Battle of Fornovo, 1494) showed just how helpless Italy was at the hands of emerging monarchies like France or Spain. When the Spaniards saw how easy it was, they, too, marched in, and restored Naples to its Spanish king the following year (an Aragonese dynasty, cousins to Ferdinand and Isabella, had ruled Naples since 1442). Before long the German emperor and even the Swiss entered this new market for Italian real estate. The popes did as much as anyone to keep the pot boiling. Alexander VI and his son Cesare Borgia carried the war across central Italy in an attempt to found a new state for the Borgia family, and Julius II's madcap policy led him to egg on the Swiss, French and Spaniards in turn, before finally crying 'Out with the barbarians!' when it was already too late.

By 1516, with the French ruling Milan and the Spanish in control of the south, it seemed as if a settlement would be possible. The worst possible luck for Italy, however, came with the accession of the insatiable megalomaniac **Charles V** to the throne of Spain in that year; in 1519 he bought himself the crown of the Holy Roman Empire, making him the most powerful ruler in Europe since Charlemagne. Charles felt he needed Milan as a base for communications between his Spanish, German and Flemish possessions, and as soon as he had emptied Spain's treasury, driven her to revolt, and plunged Germany into civil war, he turned his attentions to Italy. The wars began anew, bloodier than anything Italy had seen for centuries, climaxing with the defeat of the French at Pavia in 1525, and the sack of Rome by an out-of-control imperial army in 1527. The French invaded once more, in 1529, and were defeated this time at Naples by the treachery of their Genoese allies. All Italy, save only Venice, was now at the mercy of Charles and the Spaniards.

## 1529–1600: Italy in Chains

The final treaties left Spanish viceroys in Milan and Naples, and pliant dukes and counts toeing the Spanish line almost everywhere else. Besides Venice and the very careful Republic of Lucca, the last bastions of Italian liberty were Siena and Florence, where the Medici had been thrown out and the Republic re-established. Charles' army besieged and took the city in 1530, giving it back to the Medici, who gained the title of Grand Dukes of Tuscany. They collaborated with Spain in extinguishing Siena's independence, despite a desperate resistance of seven years (1552–59), and the new Medici state assumed roughly the borders of Tuscany today.

The broader context of these events, of course, was the bitter struggles of the Reformation and Counter-Reformation. In Italy, the new religious angle made the Spaniards and the popes natural allies. One had the difficult job of breaking the spirit of a nation that, though conquered, was still wealthy, culturally sophisticated and ready to resist; the other saw an opportunity to recapture by force the hearts and minds it had lost long before. With the majority of the peninsula still nominally controlled by local rulers, and an economy that continued to be sound, both the Spanish and the popes realized that the only real threat would come not from men, but from ideas. Under the banner of combating Protestantism, they commenced a reign of terror across Italy. In the 1550s, the revived Inquisition began its manhunt for free-thinkers of every variety; the Index of Prohibited Books followed in 1559 (some works of Dante included), accompanied by public book-burnings in Rome and elsewhere. A long line of Italian intellectuals trudged to the stake, while many more buried their convictions or left for exile in Germany or England. The job of re-educating Italy was put in the hands of the new Jesuit order; their schools and propaganda campaigns bore the popes' message deeply into the Italian mind, while their sumptuous new churches, spectacles and dramatic sermons helped redefine Catholicism.

Despite the oppression, the average Italian at first had little to complain about. Spanish domination brought peace and order to a country that had long been a madhouse of conflicting ambitions. Renaissance artists attained a virtuosity never seen before, just in time to embellish the scores of new churches, palaces, and villas of the mid 16th-century building boom. The combined Christian forces had turned back the Turkish threat at Malta (1566) and Lepanto (1571), and some Italians were benefiting greatly from Spanish imperialism in the New World—especially the Genoese, who rented ships, floated loans, and snatched up a surprising amount of the gold and silver arriving from America.

## 1600–1796: The Age of Baroque

Nevertheless, the first signs of decay were already apparent. Palladio's country villas for the Venetian magnates, and Michelozzo's outside Florence, are landmarks in architecture but also one of the earliest symptoms. In both cities, the old mercantile economies were failing, and the wealthy began to invest their money unproductively in land instead of risking it in business or finance. Venice, between its wars with the Turks and its loss of the spice trade when the Portuguese discovered the route to the Indies, suffered the most. By 1650 she no longer had an important role to play in European affairs, though the Venetians kept their heads and made their inevitable descent into decadence a serene and enjoyable one.

The troubles were not limited to these two cities. After 1600 nearly everything started to go wrong for the Italians. The textiles and banking of the north, long the engines of the economy, both withered in the face of foreign competition, and the old port towns (with the exceptions of Genoa and the new city of Livorno) began to look half empty as the English and Dutch muscled them out of the declining Mediterranean trade. Worst off of all was the south, under direct Spanish or papal rule. Combining incompetence and brutality with outrageously high taxes (the Spaniards' to finance foreign wars, the popes' to build up Rome), they rapidly turned the already poor south into a nightmare of anarchic depravity, haunted by legions of bandits and beggars, and controlled more tightly than ever by its violent feudal barons. To everyone's surprise, the south rose up and staged an epic rebellion. Beginning in Naples (Masaniello's Revolt, 1647), the disturbances soon spread all over the south and Sicily. For over a year peasant militias ruled some areas, and makeshift revolutionary councils defended the cities. When the Spanish finally defeated them, however, they massacred some 18,000, and tightened the screws more then ever.

Bullied, humiliated and increasingly impoverished, 17th-century Italy at least tried hard to keep up its ancient prominence in the arts and sciences. Galileo looked

Galileo Galilei

through telescopes, Monteverdi wrote the first operas, and hundreds of talented though uninspired artists cranked out pretty pictures to meet the continuing high demand. Bernini and Borromini turned Rome into the capital of Baroque—the florid, expensive coloratura style that serves as a perfect symbol for the age itself, an age of political repression and thought control where art itself became a political tool. Baroque's heavenly grandeur and symmetry helped to impress everyone with the majesty of Church and State. At the same time, Baroque scholars wrote books that went on for hundreds of pages without saying anything, but avoided offending the government and the Inquisition. Baroque impresarios managed the wonderful pageantry of Church holidays, state occasions and carnivals that kept the ragged crowds amused. Manners and clothing became decorously berserk, and a race for easily bought noble titles occurred that would have made a medieval Italian laugh out loud. Italy was being rocked to sleep in a Baroque cradle.

By the 18th century, there were very few painters, or scholars, or scientists. There were no more heroic revolts either. Italy in this period hardly has any history at all; with Spain's increasing decadence, the great powers decided the futures of Italy's major states, and used the minor ones as a kind of overflow tank to hold surplus princes and those dispossessed by wars elsewhere (Napoleon on Elba was the last and most famous of these). In 1713, after the War of the Spanish Succession, the Habsburgs of **Austria** came into control of Milan and Lombardy, Mantua and the Kingdom of Naples. The House of Lorraine, related to the Austrians, won Tuscany upon the extinction of the Medici in 1737.

These new rulers improved conditions somewhat. Especially during the reigns of the Empress Maria Theresa (1740–80) and her son Joseph II (1780–92), two of the most like-able Enlightenment despots, Lombardy and the other Austrian possessions underwent serious, intelligent economic reforms—giving them the head-start over the rest of Italy that helped Milan to its industrial prominence today. Naples' hard luck continued when the Austrians transferred it to a branch of the House of Bourbon (1731); under them the southern kingdom was independent, but just as poorly governed as before. A new player in Italian affairs, and from the start an important one, was **Piedmont**, which during the War of the Austrian Succession shook loose from the tutelage of France and joined the winning side, earning a royal title in 1720 for **Vittorio Amedeo II**. The infant kingdom, with its brand-new capital of Turin, was poor and a little backward in many ways, but as the only strong and free state in Italy it would be able to play the leading role in the events of the next century, and in Italian unification.

## 1796–1830: Napoleon, Restoration, and Reaction

**Napoleon**, that greatest of Italian generals, arrived in the country in 1796 on behalf of the French revolutionary Directorate, sweeping away the Piedmontese and Austrians and setting up republics in Lombardy (the 'Cisalpine Republic'), Liguria, and Naples (the 'Parthenopean Republic'). Italy woke with a start from its Baroque slumbers, and local patriots gaily joined the French cause. In 1799, however, while Napoleon was off in Egypt, the advance through Italy by an Austro-Russian army, aided by Nelson's fleet, restored the status quo. This was often accompanied by bloody reprisals, as peasant mobs led by clerics like the 'Army of the Holy Faith' marched across the south massacring liberals and French sympathizers.

In 1800 Napoleon returned in a campaign that saw the great victory at Marengo, giving him the opportunity once more to reorganize Italian affairs. Napoleon crowned himself King of Italy; Joseph Bonaparte and later Joachim Murat ruled at Naples. Elisa Bonaparte and her husband got Tuscany. Rome was annexed to France, and the pope was carted off to Fontainebleau. Napoleonic rule lasted only until 1814, but in that time important public works were begun and laws, education and everything else reformed after the French model; immense Church properties were expropriated, and medieval relics everywhere put to rest—including the Venetian Republic, which Napoleon for some reason took a special delight in liquidating. The French, however, soon wore out their welcome. Besides hauling much of Italy's artistic heritage off to the Louvre, implementing high war taxes and conscription (some 25,000 Italians died in the invasion of Russia), and brutally repressing a number of local revolts, they systematically exploited Italy for the benefit of the Napoleonic élite and the crowds of speculators who came flocking over the Alps. When the Austrians and English came to chase all the little Napoleons out, no one was sad to see them go.

The experience, though, had given Italians a taste of the opportunities offered by the modern world, as well as a sense of national feeling that had been suppressed for centuries. The 1815 Congress of Vienna put the clock back to 1796; indeed the Habsburgs and Bourbons seemed to think they could pretend the Napoleonic upheavals never happened, and the political reaction in their territories was fierce. The only major change from the *ancien régime* was that Venice and its inland empire now belonged to Austria. (Two name changes help to confuse students of this period; Piedmont is often referred to as the 'Kingdom of Sardinia', and Naples acquired the name 'Kingdom of the Two Sicilies'.)

Almost immediately, revolutionary agitators and secret societies like the famous *Carbonari* emerged that would keep Italy convulsed in plots and intrigues. A large-scale revolt in Naples forced the reactionary King Ferdinand to grant a constitution (1821), but when Austrian troops came down to crush the rebels he revoked it. The French July Revolution of 1830 also spread to Italy, encouraged by the liberal King **Carlo Alberto** in Piedmont-Savoy, but once more the by now universally hated Austrians intervened.

## 1848–1915: The Risorgimento and United Italy

Conspirators of every colour and shape, including the legendary **Giuseppe Mazzini**, had to wait another 18 years for their next chance. Mazzini, a sincere patriot and democrat, agitated frenetically all through the years 1830–70, beginning by founding the *Young Italy* movement. Generally followed by a small cloud of cops and spies, Mazzini started parties, issued manifestos, plotted dozens of doomed revolts, defined great theories and strategies, checked in and out of exile, and chaired meetings of eternal committees, all with little practical effect. In retrospect, his career as a revolutionary can bear a slight comparison to Marx's—though less Karl than Groucho. It was typical of the times, and the disarray and futility among republicans, radicals, and those who simply wanted a united Italy set the stage for the stumbling, divisive process of the Risorgimento.

The big change came in the revolutionary year of 1848, when risings in Palermo and Naples (in January) anticipated even those in Paris itself. Soon all Italy was in the streets. Piedmont and Tuscany won constitutions from their rulers, and the people of Milan chased out the Austrians after a month of extremely bloody fighting; at the same time the Venetian Republic was restored. Carlo Alberto, the hope of most Italians for a war of liberation, marched against the Austrians, but his two badly bungled campaigns allowed the enemy to re-establish control over the peninsula. By June 1849, only Venice, under Austrian blockade, and the recently declared Roman Republic were left. Rome, led by Mazzini, and with a small army under **Giuseppe Garibaldi**, a former sailor who had fought in the wars of independence in Latin America, beat off several attacks from foreign troops invited in by the Pope. The republic finally succumbed to a large force sent by, of all people, the republic of President Louis Napoleon (soon to declare himself Napoleon III) in France. Garibaldi's dramatic escape to safety in San Marino (he was trying to reach Venice, itself soon to surrender) gave the Risorgimento one of its great heroic myths.

Despite failure on a grand scale, at least the Italians knew they would get another chance. Unification was inevitable, but there were two irreconcilable contenders for the honour of accomplishing it. On one side, the democrats and radicals dreamed of a truly reborn, revolutionary Italy, and looked to the popular hero Garibaldi to deliver it; on the other, moderates wanted the Piedmontese to do the job, ensuring a stable future by making **Vittorio Emanuele II** King of Italy. Vittorio Emanuele's minister, the polished, clever **Count Camillo Cavour**, spent the 1850s getting Piedmont in shape for the struggle, building its economy and army, participating in the Crimean War to earn diplomatic support, and plotting with the French for an alliance against Austria.

War came in 1859, and French armies did most of the work in conquering Lombardy. Tuscany and Emilia revolted, and Piedmont was able to annex all three. In May 1860, Garibaldi and his red-shirted 'Thousand' sailed from Genoa—Cavour almost stopped them at the last minute—and landed in Sicily, electrifying Europe by repeatedly beating the Bourbon forces in a quick march across the island. The Thousand had become 20,000, and when they crossed the straits bound for Naples it was clear that the affair was reaching its climax. On 7 September, Garibaldi entered Naples, and though he proclaimed himself temporary dictator on Vittorio Emanuele's behalf, the Piedmontese were alarmed enough to occupy Umbria and the Marches. The King met Garibaldi on 27 October, near Teano, and after finding out what little regard the Piedmontese had for him, the greatest and least self-interested leader modern Italy has known went off to retirement on the island of Caprara.

Just as the French made all this possible, some more unexpected help from outside allowed the new Italy to add two missing pieces and complete its unification. When the Prussians defeated Austria in the war of 1866, Italy was able to seize the Veneto. Only Rome was left, defended by a French garrison, and when the Prussians beat France at Sedan in 1870, the Italian army marched into Rome almost without opposition.

The first decades of the Italian Kingdom were just as unimpressive as its wars of independence. A liberal constitutional monarchy was established, but the parliament almost immediately decomposed into cliques and political cartels representing various interests. Finances started in disorder and stayed that way, and corruption became widespread. Peasant revolts occurred in the south, as people felt cheated by inaction after the promises of the Risorgimento, and organized brigandage became a problem, partially instigated by the Vatican as part of an all-out attempt to discredit the new regime. The outlines of foreign policy often seemed to change monthly, though like the other European powers Italy felt it necessary to snatch up some colonies. The attempt revealed the new state's limited capabilities, with embarrassing military disasters at the hands of the Ethiopians at Dogali in 1887, and again at Adowa in 1896.

After 1900, with the rise of a strong socialist movement, strikes, riots, and police repression often occupied centre stage in Italian politics. Even so, important signs of progress, such as the big new industries in Turin and Milan, showed that at least the northern half of Italy was becoming a fully integral part of the European economy. The 15 years before the war, prosperous and contented ones for many, came to be known by the slightly derogatory term *Italietta*, the 'little Italy' of modest bourgeois happiness, an age of sweet Puccini operas, the first motorcars, blooming 'Liberty'-style architecture, and Sunday afternoons at the beach.

## 1915–1945: War, Fascism, and War

Italy could have stayed out of the First World War, but let the chance to do so go by for the usual reasons—a hope of gaining some new territory, especially Trieste. Also, a certain segment of the intelligentsia found the *Italietta* boring and disgraceful: irredentists of all stripes, some of the artistic futurists, and the perverse, idolized poet **Gabriele D'Annunzio**. The groups helped Italy leap blindly into the conflict in 1915, with a big promise of boundary adjustments dangled by the beleaguered Allies. Italian armies fought with their accustomed flair, masterminding an utter catastrophe at Caporetto (October 1917) that any other nation but Austria would have parleyed into a total victory. No thanks to their incompetent generals, the poorly armed and equipped Italians somehow held firm for another year, until the total exhaustion of Austria allowed them to prevail (at the battle of *Vittorio Veneto* you see so many streets named after), capturing some 600,000 prisoners in November 1918.

In return for 650,000 dead, a million casualties, severe privation on the home front, and a war debt highter than anyone could count, Italy received Trieste, Gorizia, the South Tyrol, and a few other scraps. Italians felt they had been cheated, and nationalist sentiment increased, especially when D'Annunzio led a band of freebooters to seize the half-Italian city of Fiume in September 1919, after the peace conferences had promised it to Yugoslavia. The Italian economy was in shambles, and, at least in the north, revolution was in the air; workers in Turin raised the Red Flag over the Fiat plants and organized themselves into soviets. The troubles had encouraged extremists of both right and left, and many Italians became convinced that the liberal state was finished.

Enter **Benito Mussolini**, a professional intriguer in the Mazzini tradition with bad manners and no fixed principles. Before the War he had found his real talent as editor of the Socialist Party paper *Avanti*—the best it ever had, tripling the circulation in a year. When he decided that what Italy really needed was war, he left to found a new paper, and contributed mightily to the jingoist agitation of 1915. In the post-War confusion, he found his opportunity. A little bit at a time, he developed the idea of **fascism**, at first less a philosophy than an astute use of mass propaganda and a sense for design. (The *fasci*, from which the name comes, were bundles of rods carried before ancient Roman officials, a symbol of authority. *Fascii* also referred to organized bands of rebellious peasants in 19th-century Sicily.) With a little discreet money supplied by frightened industrialists, Mussolini had no trouble in finding recruits for his black-shirted gangs, who found their first success beating up Slavs in Trieste and working as a sort of private police for landowners in stoutly socialist Emilia-Romagna.

The basic principle, combining left- and right-wing extremism into something the ruling classes could live with, proved attractive to many, and a series of weak governments stood by while the fascist *squadre* cast their shadow over more and more of Italy. Mussolini's accession to power came on an improbable gamble. In the particularly anarchic month of October 1922, he announced that his followers would march on Rome. King Vittorio Emanuele III refused to sign a decree of martial law to disperse them, and there was nothing to do but offer Mussolini the post of prime minister. At first, he governed Italy with undeniable competence. Order was restored, and the economy and foreign policy handled intelligently by non-fascist professionals. In the 1924 elections, despite the flagrant rigging and intimidation, the Fascists only won a slight majority. One politician who was not intimidated was Giacomo Matteotti, and when some of Mussolini's close associates took him for a ride and murdered him, a major scandal erupted. Mussolini survived it, and during 1925 and 1926 the Fascists used parliamentary methods to convert Italy into a permanent fascist dictatorship.

Compared to the governments that preceded him, Mussolini looked quite impressive. Industry advanced, great public works were undertaken, with special care towards the backward south, and the Mafia took some heavy blows at the hands of a determined Sicilian prefect named Mori. The most lasting achievement was the Concordat of 1929 with the pope, founding the Vatican State and ending the Church's isolation from Italian affairs. The regime evolved a new economic philosophy, the 'corporate state', where labour and capital were supposed to live in harmony under syndicalist government control. But the longer fascism lasted, the more unreal it seemed, a patchwork government of Mussolini and his ageing cronies, magnified and rendered heroic by cinematic technique—stirring rhetoric before oceanic crowds, colourful pageantry, magnificent, larger-than-life post offices and railway stations built of travertine and marble, dashing aviators and winsome gymnasts from the fascist youth groups on parade. In a way it was the Baroque all over again, and Italians tried not to think about the consequences. In the words of one of Mussolini's favourite slogans, painted on walls all over Italy, 'Whoever stops is lost'.

Mussolini couldn't stop, and the only possibility for new diversions lay with the chance of conquest and empire. His invasion of Ethiopia and his meddling in the Spanish Civil War, both in 1936, compromised Italy into a close alliance with Nazi Germany. Mussolini's confidence and rhetoric never faltered as he led an entirely unprepared nation into the biggest war ever. Once more, Italian ineptitude at warfare produced embarrassing defeats on all fronts, and only German intervention in Greece and North Africa saved Italy from being knocked out of the War as early as 1941. The Allies invaded Sicily in July 1943, and the Italians began to look for a clever way out. They seized Mussolini during a meeting of the Grand Council, packed him into an ambulance and sent him off first to Ponza, then to a little ski hotel up in the Apennines. The new government under Marshal Badoglio didn't know what to do, and confusion reigned supreme.

While British and American forces slogged northwards, in this ghetto of the European theatre, with the help of the Free French, Brazilians, Costa Ricans, Poles, Czechs, New Zealanders and Norwegians, the Germans poured in divisions to defend the peninsula. They rescued Mussolini, and set him up in a puppet state called the Italian Social Republic in the north. In September 1943, the Badoglio government signed an armistice with the Allies, too late to keep the War from dragging on another year and a half, as the Germans made good use of Italy's difficult terrain to slow the Allied advance. Meanwhile Italy finally gave itself something to be proud of, a determined, resourceful Resistance that established free zones in many areas, and harassed the Germans with sabotage and strikes. The *partigiani* caught Mussolini in April 1945, while he was trying to escape to Switzerland; after shooting him and his mistress, they hung him by his feet from the roof of a petrol station in Milan.

## 1945–the Present

Post-war Italian *cinema verità*—Rossellini's *Rome, Open City*, or de Sica's *Bicycle Thieves*—captures the atmosphere better than words ever could. In a period of serious hardships that older Italians still remember, the nation slowly picked itself up and returned things to normal. A referendum in June 1946 made Italy a Republic, but only by a narrow margin. The first governments fell to the new Christian Democrat Party under Alcide de Gasperi, which has run the show ever since in coalitions with a preposterous band of smaller parties. The main opposition has been provided by the Communists, surely one of the most remarkable parties of modern European history. With the heritage of the only important socialist philosopher since Marx, Antonio Gramsci, and the democratic and broadminded leader Enrico Berlinguer, Italian communism is something unique in the world, with its stronghold and showcase in the well-run, prosperous cities of the Emilia-Romagna.

The 50's was Rome's decade, when Italian style and Italian cinema caught the imagination of the world. Gradually, slowly, a little economic miracle was happening; *Signor Rossi*, the average Italian, started buzzing around in his first classic Fiat *cinquecento*, northern industries boomed, and life cruised slowly back to normal. The south continued to lag behind, despite the sincere efforts of the government and its special planning fund, the *Cassa per il Mezzogiorno*. Though the extreme poverty and despair of the postwar years gradually disappeared, even today there is little evidence that the region is catching up with the rest of the country. Nationally, the *Democristiani*-controlled government soon evolved a Byzantine style of politics that only an Italian could understand. Through the constant parade of collapsing and reforming cabinets, nothing changed; all deals were made in the back rooms and everyone, from the Pope to the Communists, had a share in the decision-making. One wouldn't call it democracy with a straight face, but for four decades it worked well enough to keep Italy on its wheels. The dark side of the arrangement was the all-pervasive corruption that the system fostered. It is fascinating to read the work of journalists only five years ago, seeing how almost without exception they would politely sidestep the facts; Italy was run by an unprincipled political machine, whose members were raking in as much for themselves as they could grab, and everyone knew it, only it couldn't be said openly, for lack of proof. Even more sinister was the extent to which the machine would go to keep on top. The 70s Italy's 'years of lead' witnessed the worst of the political sleaze, along with a grim reign of terrorism, culminating in the kidnapping and murder in 1978 of an honorable Christian Democrat prime minister, Aldo Moro. All along, the attacks were attributed to 'leftist groups', though even at the time many suspected that some of the highest circles in the government and army were controlling or manipulating them, with the possible collusion of the CIA. They were indeed, and only recently has some of the truth begun to seep out. On another front, Italians woke up one morning in 1992 to find that the government had magically vacuumed 7% of the money out of all their savings accounts, an 'emergency measure' to meet the nation's colossal budget deficit—a deficit caused largely by the thievery of the political class and its allies in organized crime.

Italians are a patient lot but, as everyone knows, the lid has blown off, and at the time of writing Italy is well into a very Italian sort of revolution. The business started in the judiciary, the one independent and relatively uncorrupt part of the government. In the early 90's, heroic prosecutors Giovanni Falcone and Paolo Borsellino went after the Sicilian Mafia with some success, and were spectacularly assassinated for it, causing national outrage. Meanwhile, in Milan, a small group of prosecutors and judges found a minor political kickback scandal that has led them, through years of quiet and painstaking work, to the golden string that is currently unravelling the whole rotten tangle of Italian political depravity— what Italians call the *tangentopoli*, or 'bribe city'. For over a year, the televised hearings of Judge Antonio di Pietro and his Operation *Mani Pulite* ('clean hands') team from Milan were the nation's favourite and most fascinating serial.

All the kingpins have fallen, notably Socialist leader Bettino Craxi, currently hiding from extradition in Uruguay. Others, especially long-time prime minister Giulio Andreotti, have lost their parliamentary immunity, and everyone is looking forward to their rendezvous in Milan. The two ruling parties, the Christian Democrats and the Socialists, are dead; the 1993 municipal elections, held at the height of the *tangentopoli* hearings, were nearly a sweep for the PDS, the old Communists, beating the neo-fascist MSI and the Lega, the new regional party that has grown up in the north based on a resentment of corruption—and of southern Italian migrants. The Lega's demagogic leader, Umberto Bossi, has himself ironically come under Judge di Pietro's scrutiny over alleged kickbacks.

Other forces on the scene include the enigmatic Mario Segni, who led a successful drive for constitutional reform of the electoral system, and most surprising of all, Silvio Berlusconi, the television and publishing magnate (and former protégé of Craxi) whose near-monopolies were seriously threatened by a possible PDS government. Berlusconi thinks big—the only way out was to buy the government for himself. He used his big bankroll and control of television to create a new, totally synthetic party, called Forza Italia, and his pitchmen sold it to Italians the same way they sell them soap and sex every day. Meanwhile, Berlusconi managed an improbable three-way alliance with the MSI and the Lega. It all worked brilliantly. In the parliamentary elections of 1994, the first of what Italians are already calling their 'Second Republic', Berlusconi's rightist alliance won an impressive victory, and 'Mr Television' himself became prime minister.

So far it has been a rocky road for the new government. Berlusconi's refusal to distance himself from his communications empire while in office, and his heavy-handed attempt to cripple the *Mani Pulite* investigators, have made many Italians start to feel the egg on their faces—that they struggled so hard to topple a malodorous old order, only to merrily vote it back into office at the first chance. At the time of writing, Judge di Pietro is still in business, the coalition partners are quarrelling daily, the economy remains totally out of control, and the future of the Italian 'revolution' looks more uncertain than ever. Expect bigger and stranger surprises in the years to come.

# Art and Architecture: A Bare Outline

You'd have to spend your holiday in a baggage compartment to miss Italy's vast piles of architecture and art. The Italians estimate there is one work of art per capita in their country, which is more than anyone could see in a life-time—especially since so much of it is locked away in museums that are in semi-permanent 'restoration'. Although you may occasionally chafe at not being able to see certain frescoes, or at finding a famous palace completely wrapped up in the ubiquitous green netting of the restorers, the Italians on the whole bear the burden of keeping their awesome patrimony dusted off and open for visitors very well. Some Italians find it insupportable living with the stuff all around them; the futurists, for instance, were worried that St Mark's might be blown up by foreign enemies in the First World War— but only because they wanted to do it themselves, as was their right as Italian citizens.

## Pre-Etruscan

To give a chronological account of the first Italian artists is an uncomfortable task. The penin-sula's mountainous terrain saw many isolated developments, and many survivals of ancient cultures even during the days of the sophisticated Etruscans and Romans. Most ancient of all, however, is the palaeolithic troglodyte culture on the Riviera, credited with creating some of the first artworks in Europe—chubby images of fertility goddesses. These and other curious trappings may be seen in the Ligurian museums at **Balzi Rossi**, **Pegli**, and **Finalborgo**. The most remarkable works from the Neolithic period up until the Iron Age are the thousands of graffiti rock incisions in several isolated Alpine valleys north of Lake Iseo, especially the **Val Camonica**, where these ancient outdoor masterpieces are protected in a national park.

After 1000 BC Italic peoples all over the peninsula were making geometrically painted pots, weapons, tools, and bronze statuettes. The most impressive culture, however, was the tower-building, bronze-working Nuraghe civilization on the island of **Sardinia**, of which echoes are seen in many cultures on the mainland. Among the most intriguing and beautiful artefacts to have survived are those of the Villanova culture in the archaeological museum in **Bologna**; the statues and inscriptions of the little-known Middle Adriatic culture in the museum at **Chieti** in Abruzzo, and the statue-steles of an unknown people at **Pontrèmoli**, north of Viareggio; others, of the Luini culture, are in the civic museum in **La Spezia**. Dolmens and strange little temples survive in many corners of central and southern **Apulia**. If you wish to see what was going on across the Mediterranean at the same time, there's also one of the best Egyptian museums in the world in **Turin**.

## Etruscans and Greeks (8th–2nd centuries BC)

With the refined, art-loving Etruscans (see **Topics**) we begin to have architecture as well as art. Not much has survived, thanks to the Etruscans' habit of building in wood and deco-rating with terracotta, but we do have plenty of distinctive rock-cut tombs, the best of which are at **Cerveteri** and **Tarquinia**; many of them contain exceptional frescoes that reflect

Aegean Greek styles. The best of their lovely sculptures, jewellery, vases, and much more are in the museums in **Rome** (Villa Giulia—where you can also see a reconstructed temple facade), **Chiusi**, **Volterra**, and **Tarquinia**. There are also fine Etruscan holdings in **Perugia**, and in the archaeology museums in **Florence** and **Bologna**.

The Etruscans imported and copied many of their vases from their ancient Greek contemporaries, from Greece proper and the colonies of Magna Graecia in Southern Italy. The Doric temple at **Paestum** is the best surviving Greek structure on the peninsula (though there are many others in Sicily); **Cumae** west of Naples and **Metapontum** near Táranto are also worth a visit; there are many other excavated Greek cities, but usually only foundations remain. The archaeological museums in **Reggio Calabria, Táranto, Naples, Bari**, and the **Vatican** contain the most impressive collections of ancient Greek vases, statues, and other types of art.

## Roman (3rd century BC–5th century AD)

Italian art during the Roman hegemony is mostly derivative of the Etruscan and Greek, with a special talent for mosaics, wall paintings, glasswork and portraiture; architecturally, the Romans were brilliant engineers, the inventors of concrete and grand exponents of the arch. Even today their constructions such as aqueducts, amphitheatres, bridges, baths, and the Pantheon are most impressive.

Of course, **Rome** itself has no end of ancient monuments; also in the vicinity there is **Ostia Antica**, Rome's ancient port, and **Tivoli**, site of Hadrian's great villa. Rome also has a stellar set of museums filled with Roman antiquities—the National Museum in Diocletian's Baths, the Vatican Museum, the Capitoline Museums, and the Museum of Roman Civilization at EUR. **Naples** is the other outstanding destination for Roman art, with the ruins of ancient **Pompeii** and **Herculaneum** on its outskirts, and a spectacular museum, not only of artefacts found in the Pompeii excavations, but of statues from Rome dug up by Renaissance collectors like the Farnese.

Other impressive Roman monuments may be seen in **Benevento** (with the best triumphal arch, and another good museum, full of unusual Roman-Egyptian art); **Capua** (huge amphitheatre and Mithraeum); **Verona** (the arena, gates and theatre complex); **Aosta** (theatre and gates); the museum and excavations of **Aquileia** in Friuli and **Sepina** in Molise; the temples in **Brescia** and **Assisi**; 'the villa of Catullus' in **Sirmione** on Lake Garda; villas, tunnels, canals, markets and other surprises in **Pozzuoli** and **Baia** and elsewhere along the western Bay of Naples, and odds and ends in **Fiesole, Bologna, Trieste, Perugia, Cori** (in Lazio), **Spoleto, Rimini, Ancona, Susa, Lecce**, and **Alba Fucens** in Abruzzo.

## Early Middle Ages (5th–10th century)

After the fall of the Roman Empire, civilization's lamp flickered most brightly in **Ravenna**, where Byzantine mosaicists adorned the glittering churches of the Eastern Exarchate. Theirs was to be the prominent style in pictorial art and architecture until the 13th century.

Apart from Ravenna, there are fine mosaics and paintings of the period in **Rome**, in a score of churches such as Sant'Agnese, San Clemente, and Santa Prassede; in Rome the Italian preference for basilican churches and octagonal baptistries began in Constantine's day, and the development of Christian art and architecture through the Dark Ages can be traced there better than anywhere else. There are also many paintings in the catacombs of Rome and **Naples**. Other good Ravenna-style mosaics may be seen in the cathedrals of **Aquileia** and Torcello in **Venice**, where the fashion lingered long enough to create St Mark's. In the vicinity of **Táranto** there are the remains of Greek monasteries and cave paintings, and interesting early Christian churches at **Nocera** in Campania, and in Benevento. In **Albenga** on the Riviera and **Novara**, you'll find unusual 5th-century baptistries with artworks.

'Lombard' art, really the work of the native population under Lombard rule, revealed an original talent in the 7th–9th centuries, especially evident in the churches of **Cividale di Friuli**, in the works in the cathedral of **Monza**, in and around **Spoleto** and in the Abbey of San Salvatore in **Brescia**. A new style, presaging the Romanesque, may be seen in Sant'Ambrogio in **Milan**.

## Romanesque (11th–12th centuries)

At this point, when an expansive society made new advances in art possible, north and south Italy went their separate ways, each contributing distinctive styles in sculpture and architecture. We also begin to learn the identities of some of their makers. The great Lombard cathedrals, masterworks of brick art and adorned with blind arcading, bas-reliefs, and lofty campaniles are best exemplified at **Modena** (by the master builder-sculptor Wiligelmo), San Michele in **Pavia**, **Cremona** cathedral, and the Santo Stefano complex in **Bologna**. In **Verona**, the cathedral and San Zeno were embellished by Wiligelmo's talented student Nicolò; in **Parma**, the great baptistry by Benedetto Antelami is a milestone in the synthesis of sculpture and architecture.

In Tuscany, the rapidly accumulating wealth of **Pisa** permitted the undertaking of the cathedral complex, which was the largest building programme in Italy in a thousand years; its exotic style owed something to contacts with the Moslem world, but the inspiration for the design was completely original—and in part a very conscious attempt to recapture the grandeur of the ancient world. Inland, **Florence** developed its own particularist black and white style, exemplified in truly amazing buildings like the baptistry and San Miniato. Interesting variations appeared in all the other Tuscan cities, each showing some Pisan stripes or Florentine rectangles.

In the south, Byzantine and Moslem influences helped create an entirely different tendency. **Amalfi** and **Caserta** built a very Saracenic cathedral and cloister dating from this period; Amalfi's was adorned with incised bronze doors from Constantinople in a style that was later copied in towns all over the south, notably at **Trani** and **Monte Sant'Angelo** in Apulia. The tradition of Byzantine painting and mosaics continued, mostly in Sicily, though there is a fine example at Sant'Angelo in Formis at **Capua**. From Moslem geometrical patterns, southern artists acquired a taste for intricate designs using enamel or marble chips in church furnishings and architectural trim—as seen in pulpits and candlesticks in the churches of **Salerno, Ravello**, and many others.

The outstanding architectural advance of this period is the Apulian Romanesque, as shown in excellent cathedrals in almost every Apulian city (**Troia, Sipontum, Monte Sant'Angelo, Ruvo di Apulia, Trani, Bari** and **Altamura** have perhaps the best) a style closely related to contemporary Norman and Pisan work—to say who gets the credit for being first would not be easy. Another impressive cathedral of the southern Romanesque is that of **Anagni** in Lazio; in the same region are the two extremely unusual church facades in **Tuscania**. The Norman influence also appears in churches like the Abbazia della Trinità in **Venosa** (Basilicata) and in the wonderful mosaic pavement of **Otranto** cathedral.

This period also saw the erection of urban skyscrapers by the nobility, family fortress-towers built when the *comuni* forced local barons to move into the towns. Larger cities once had literally hundreds of them, before the townspeople succeeded in getting them demolished. **San Gimignano** and **Ascoli Piceno** have the most surviving examples. In many cases extremely tall towers were built simply for decoration and prestige. **Bologna's** Garisendi and Asinelli Towers, along with Pisa's Campanile, are the best examples of medieval Italy's occasional disdain for the horizontal.

## Late Medieval–Early Renaissance (13th–14th centuries)

In many ways this was the most exciting and vigorous phase in Italian art history, an age of discovery when the power of the artist was almost like that of a magician. Great imaginative leaps occurred in architecture, painting, and sculpture, especially in Tuscany. From Milan to Assisi, a group of masons and sculptors known as the *Campionese Masters* built magnificent brick cathedrals and basilicas. Some of their buildings reflect the Gothic style of the north (most spectacularly **Milan**) while in **Como** cathedral you can see the transition from that same Gothic to Renaissance. In **Venice**, an ornate, half-oriental style called Venetian-Gothic still sets the city's palaces and public buildings apart, and influenced the exotic Basilica di Sant'Antonio in **Padua**.

This was also an era of transition in sculpture, from stiff Romanesque stylization to the more realistic, classically inspired works of the great Nicola Pisano and his son Giovanni (in the churches of **Pisa, Pistoia** and **Siena**) and his pupil Arnolfo di Cambio (**Florence**). Other outstanding works of the 14th century are Lorenzo Maitani's cathedral in **Orvieto** and the Scaliger tombs of **Verona**, by the Campione masters.

Painters, especially in Rome and Siena, learned from the new spatial and expressive sculpture. Most celebrated of the masters in the dawn of the Italian Renaissance is, of course, the solemn Giotto, whose greatest works are the fresco cycles in **Padua** and **Assisi**. In the town of St Francis you can also see some excellent works by Giotto's merrier contemporaries from **Siena**. That city's artists, Duccio di Buoninsegna, Simone Martini and Pietro and Ambrogio Lorenzetti, gave Italy its most brilliant exponents of the International Gothic style—though they were also important precursors of the Renaissance. Their brightly coloured scenes, embellished with a thousand details, helped make Siena into the medieval dream-city it is today; the style carried on into the quattrocento with the courtly frescoes of the northern painter Pisanello. In Florence, the works of Orcagna, Gentile da Fabriano and Lorenzo Monaco continued that city's unique approach, laying a foundation for Florence's launching of the Renaissance. Cathedral complexes and public buildings in the northern cities, especially at **Siena** and **Pistoia**, show a sophisticated understanding of urban design and an original treatment of the established forms. Northern European Gothic never made much headway in Italy, though French Cistercians did build fine abbey churches like those at **San Galgano** in Tuscany and **Fossanova** in Lazio, and the English-financed Sant'Andrea in **Vercelli**. The south had relatively little to contribute during this period, but **Naples** developed its own neo-Gothic architecture, and unique geometrically patterned church façades appear at **L'Aquila** and **Brindisi**.

**Rome,** for one of the few times in its history, achieved artistic prominence with home-grown talent. The city's architecture from this period (as seen in the campaniles of Santa Maria in Cosmedin and Santa Maria Maggiore) has largely been lost under Baroque remodellings, but the paintings and mosaics of Pietro Cavallini and his school, and the intricate, inlaid stone pavements and architectural trim of the Cosmati family and their followers, derived from the Amalfi coast style, can be seen all over the city; both had an influence that extended far beyond Rome itself.

## The Renaissance (15th–16th centuries)

The origins of this high-noon of art are very much the accomplishment of quattrocento **Florence**, where sculpture and painting embarked on a totally new way of educating the eye (see art section under 'Florence', p. 652). The idea of a supposed 'rediscovery of antiquity' has confused the understanding of the time. In general, artists broke new ground when they expanded from the traditions of medieval art; when they sought merely to copy the forms of ancient Greece and Rome, the imagination often faltered.

Florentine art soon became recognized as the standard of the age, and examples can be seen everywhere in Tuscany. By 1450, Florentine artists were spreading the new style to the north, especially **Milan**, where Leonardo da Vinci and Bramante spent several years; the collections in the Brera and other galleries, the *Last Supper*, and the nearby **Certosa di Pavia** are essential works of the Renaissance. Other good museum collections are in **Rome, Parma, Turin** and **Bergamo**; the core of the latter city is a Renaissance masterpiece. **Mantua** has important works by Alberti and Mantegna, and nearby lies the 'ideal' Renaissance town of **Sabbioneta**. Michelangelo and Bramante, among others, carried the Renaissance to **Rome**, where it thrived under the patronage of enlightened popes. Other Renaissance diversions can be seen as far afield as **Rimini**, with its remarkable Malatesta Temple, and **Urbino**, with the lovely palace and art collection of the archetypal Renaissance prince, Duke Federico di Montefeltro.

The most significant art in the north came out of **Venice**, which had its own distinct school led by Mantegna and Giovanni Bellini (see 'Venetian Art', p. 345); one of the best painters of the school, the fastidious Carlo Crivelli, did much of his work in the Marches (**Ascoli Piceno** and **Ancona**). Under the patronage of the Este family, Renaissance **Ferrara** produced its own fascinating school of quattrocento painters (Cosmè Tura, Ercole Roberti).

In **Perugia**, Perugino was laying the foundations of the Umbrian school, in which Raphael and Pinturicchio earned their stripes. In **Orvieto** cathedral, the Tuscan painter Signorelli left a *Last Judgement* that inspired Michelangelo. Piero della Francesca is a special case, the most important non-Florentine painter before Raphael; his revolutionary works can be seen at **Urbino**, **Sansepulcro** and **Arezzo**. Southern Italy, trapped in a decline that was even more artistic than economic, hardly participated at all in the Renaissance, though many examples of the northerners' art can be seen at **Naples**, such as the Triumphal Arch in the Castel Nuovo.

Despite the brilliant triumphs in painting and sculpture, the story of Renaissance architecture is partially one of confusion and retreat. **Florence**, with Brunelleschi, Alberti and Michelozzo, achieved its own special mode of expression, a dignified austerity that proved difficult to transplant elsewhere. In most of Italy the rediscovery of the works of Vitruvius, representing the authority of antiquity, killed off Italians' appreciation of their own architectural heritage; with surprising speed the dazzling imaginative freedom of medieval architecture was lost forever. Some work still appeared, however, notably Codussi's palaces and churches in **Venice**.

## High Renaissance and Mannerism (16th century)

At the beginning of the cinquecento, an Olympian triumvirate of Michelangelo, Raphael, and Leonardo da Vinci held court at the summit of European art. But in this time when Italy was losing her self-confidence, and was soon to lose her essential liberty, artistic currents tended toward the dark and subversive. More than anyone, it was Michelangelo who tipped the balance from the cool, classical Renaissance into the turgid, stormy, emotionally fraught movement the critics have labelled **Mannerism**. Among the few painters left in exhausted Florence, he had the brilliant, deranged Jacopo Pontormo and Rosso Fiorentino to help. Other painters lumped in with the Mannerists, such as Giuliano Romano in Mantua and Il Sodoma around Siena broke new ground while maintaining the discipline and intellectual rigour of the early Renaissance. Elsewhere, and especially among the fashionable Florentine painters and sculptors, art was decaying into mere interior decoration.

For **Venice**, however, it was a golden age, with the careers of Titian, Veronese, Tintoretto, Sansovino, and Palladio, whose works may seen throughout Venetia. Another art centre of the age, **Parma**, is embellished with the Mannerist brushes of Correggio and Parmigianino. In **Cremona**, Milan, and other lucky galleries you can see works by Arcimboldo, the cinquecento surrealist.

In architecture, attempts to recreate ancient styles and the classical orders won the day. In **Milan**, and later in **Rome**, Bramante was one of the few architects able to do anything interesting with it, while Michelangelo's great dome of St Peter's put a cap on the accomplishments of the Renaissance. Other talented architects found most of their patronage in Rome, which after the 1520s became Italy's centre of artistic activity: Ligorio, Peruzzi, Vignola and the Sangallo family among them.

## Baroque (17th–18th centuries)

First and foremost, **Rome** continued its artistic dominance to become the capital of Baroque, where the socially irresponsible genius of artists like Bernini and Borromini was approved by the Jesuits and indulged by the tainted ducats of the popes. As an art designed to induce temporal obedience and psychical oblivion, its effects are difficult to describe, but you can see for yourself in the three great churches along Corso Vittorio Emanuele in Rome and a host of other works (Bernini's Piazza Navona fountains and St Peter's colonnades).

More honest cities, such as Florence and Venice, chose to sit out the Baroque era, though **Florence** at first enthusiastically approved the works of 16th century proto-Baroque sculptors like Ammannati, Giambologna and Cellini. Not all artists fit the Baroque mould; genius could survive in a dangerous, picaresque age, most notably in the person of Michelangelo Merisi da Caravaggio (works in **Milan, Rome** and **Naples**) not to mention other painters such as Mattia Preti, with works in Naples and **Taverna**, in his native Calabria.

Southern Italy, with a long tradition of religious emotionalism, found the Baroque entirely to its tastes, though few towns could afford to build much in this expensive style. **Naples** could, and Cosimo Fanzago's Monastery of San Martino marks the apotheosis of the Neapolitan Baroque. Painting and sculpture flourished in Naples while they were dying in the Renaissance towns of the north; southern art's ever-increasing eccentricity reached a climax in Naples' 18th–century Sansevero Chapel. A very different sort of Baroque appeared in the deep south, where the studied excess seemed to strike a deep chord in the popular psyche. Much of it is in Sicily, though the sedate Spanish-looking city of **Lecce** developed a Baroque style all its own that lasted from the 16th century to the late 18th, consistent and beautiful enough to make Lecce as impressive an architectural ensemble as any of the medieval or Renaissance cities of the north.

The town plan, churches, palaces, and royal hunting lodges of **Turin**, designed by the priest Guarini and the early 18th-century Sicilian Juvara are the most elegant representations of the Baroque spirit in northern Italy. This was a great age of palaces and ornately arranged Italian gardens, most famously those in **Tivoli**, Isola Bella in **Lake Maggiore**, and Villa Borghese and innumerable other locations in and around **Rome**, though there are also many around **Padua** and **Vicenza**.

## Neoclassicism and Romanticism (late 18th–19th centuries)

Baroque proved to be a hard act to follow, and in these centuries Italian art and architecture almost cease to exist. Two centuries of stifling oppression had taken their toll on the national imagination, and for the first time Italy not only ceased to be a leader in art, but failed even to make significant contributions.

The one bright spot in 18th-century Italian painting was **Venice**, where Giambattista Tiepolo and son adorned the churches and palaces of the last days of the Serenissima; their works can be seen in many places in the Veneto and **Udine** in Friuli. Other Venetians, such as Antonio Canaletto and Francesco Guardi, painted their famous canal scenes for Grand Tourists. In the 19th century, the Italian Impressionist movement, the *Macchiaioli*, led by Giovanni Fattori, was centred in the city of **Florence**. In sculpture, the neoclassical master Antonio Canova stands almost alone, a favourite in the days of Napoleon. His best works may be seen in the Villa Carlotta, on **Lake Como**, in Rome's Villa Borghese and at **Possagno**. In architecture, it was the age of grand opera houses, many designed by the Bibiena family of Bologna. The late 19th-century Gallerias in **Milan** and **Naples**, and the extravagances of the Piedmontese Alessandro Antonelli (**Turin** and **Novara**) are among the most impressive public buildings, and the neoclassical royal palaces at **Caserta** and **Stra** near Venice the grandest private addresses.

## 20th Century

The turn-of-the-century Liberty Style (Italian Art Nouveau) failed to spread as widely as its counterparts in France and central Europe. There are a few good buildings in **Milan**, but the best works are linked with the then burgeoning tourist industry. The age saw the construction of new Grand Hotels, casinos, and villas in nearly every resort, especially in **Venice**, the **Lakes**, the **Riviera, Pesaro, Viareggio**, and the great spas at **Merano, Montecatini**, and **Sanpellegrino**.

In the 20th century, two Italian art movements attracted international attention: futurism, a response to Cubism, concerned with the relevancy to the present ('the art that achieves speed, achieves success'), a movement led by Boccioni, Gino Severini, and Giacomo Balla (best seen in the Museum of Modern Art, **Rome**, and in several museums in **Milan**); and the mysterious, introspective metaphysical world of Giorgio De Chirico, whose brethren—Modigliani, Giorgio Morandi and Carlo Carrà—were masters of silences. Their works, and others by modern Italian and foreign artists are displayed in the museums of **Rome, Venice** and **Milan**.

Architecture in this century reached its (admittedly low) summit in the Fascist period (the **EUR** suburb in Rome, and public buildings everywhere in the south). Mussolinian architecture often makes us smile, but, as the only Italian school in the last 200 years to have achieved a consistent sense of design, it presents a challenge to all modern Italian architects—one they have so far been unable to meet.

In **Turin** and **Rome** you can see the works of the most acclaimed Italian architect of this century, Pier Luigi Nervi; good post-War buildings are very difficult to find, and the other arts have never yet risen above the level of dreary, saleable postmodernism. Much of the Italians' artistic urges have been sublimated into the shibboleth of Italian design—clothes, sports cars, suitcases, kitchen utensils, etc. At present, though business is good, Italy is generating little excitement in these fields. Europe expects more from its most artistically talented nation; after the bad centuries of shame and slumber a free and prosperous Italy may well find its own voice and its own style to help interpret the events of the day. If Italy ever does begin to speak with a single voice, whatever it has to say will be worth hearing.

# Topics

The only people in the world who read travel brochures, of course, are travel writers, and from long experience we are convinced that Italy produces some of the most astounding examples anywhere of this difficult art. In fact, stuck in your hotel room on some rainy evenings you may often find them the best entertainment Italy has to offer.

Brochures from the deep south often whisper startling propositions: '…nothing better before going into lanes which will remind you the Arabian rule, or before coming, if you like it, into some typical local inns to discover the boiled octopus or the moray on fire.' Those of the north often try to ensure that we are properly impressed with the grandeur of the locality: 'Turin stick in the mud? Its cars race by; its planes fly over it, it penetrates interstellar space…' Others increase our knowledge of Italian art and literature: 'From Malgrate, Foscolo hymned the sledge-hammers of Lecco, subjugators of iron; at Pescarenico young Manzoni wrote to Monti about the Adda.'

Almost every region has some wonderful thoughts to express; translated literally into English with painstaking care, they take us on a strange voyage through the darker corners of the Italian mind: 'Holidays and rest are fine, but are they absolute or relative?' Take this sober evaluation from the south: 'By now it has become a commonplace. In order to re-evaluate Irpinia, it is necessary to re-launch the long suffering and much-debated internal zones… Here, then, are the maxi-projects of the Parthenio, which has the honour of carrying Montevergine, with its enchanting colours, inside its ample womb.' In earnest, communist-run Emilia-Romagna, they'll give you a 100-page booklet with a complete socio-economic history, to make sure you understand the region's heritage of class struggle and bourgeois-capitalist contradictions before you begin your sightseeing.

Nevertheless, real connoisseurs of tourism prose know that the old-fashioned way is still the best, and Italy is happy to oblige with rousing eulogies that would have impressed the great Barnum himself: 'Immersed in the perfume of quaint essences, in the strange light between magic and reality, discover this handful of earth and granite: Calabria! Its strong and harsh aspect, of unexpected and incredible loveliness at times, induces those who speak of it to do so in a hushed voice… fragrance of bergamots and jasmine—stunning and evocative of past amours— sharp rocks, dense woods that open into small lakes as a maiden would open her shy eyes…Calabria!'

## Bella Figura

The longer you stay in Italy, the more inscrutable it becomes. Nothing is ever quite as it seems, and you'll find yourself changing your ideas about things with disconcerting frequency. Part of the reason why is the obsession to *fare una bella figura*, 'to make a good impression or appearance', one of the most singular traits of the Italian people. You notice it almost immediately upon arrival. Not only is every Italian an immaculately smart fashion victim (they are by far the biggest consumers of their own fashion industry), but they always seem to be modelling their spiffy threads—posing, gesturing, playing to an audience when they have one, which is nearly always because Italians rarely move about except in small herds. Their cities are their stage, with perfectly arranged piazze and streets designed like movie sets, with lights suspended over the middle. Long-time observers of the phenonemon have even noted that each city's women tend to dress themselves in colours that complement the local brick or stone.

The Italians' natural grace and elegance may be partly instinctive; even back in the 14th century, foreigners invariably noted their charming manners and taste for exquisite clothes. Many a painting of the Madonnna served not only piety's sake, but also advertised the latest Milanese silks cuts or Venetian brocades. Appearance supplanted reality in a thousand ways in the Renaissance, especially after the discovery of artificial perspective, which made artistic representations seem much more clever and interesting than the real thing. Fake, painted marble supplanted real marble, even if the fake cost more; Palladio built marble palaces out of stucco; *trompe l'œil* frescoes embellished a hundred churches; glorious façades on cathedrals and palaces disguise the fact that the rest is shabby, unfinished brick. Even castles were built more to impress rather than keep out the enemy, in a day when battles had become brilliant bloodless games, and gorgeous Italian armour deflected few blows.

The gentleman's bible of the day, Castiglione's *The Courtier*, advises that it is no use doing a brave and noble deed unless someone is watching; honour, like almost every other virtue, is something bestowed from without. After the French and Spanish burst the Italians' lovely soap-bubble of superiority in the 16th century, the country's history becomes a saga of trying to do everything to keep up appearances, of nobles desperately mending their socks in the dim light to save up the money for hiring a servant when they expected visitors.

Bella figura pleases the eye but irritates just about everything else. Fashionable conformity has a way of spreading from mere clothing and gestures to opinions, especially in the provinces; the Italians remain the masters of empty flattery and compliments (don't think for a moment that a Roman bartender is mistaking you for someone else when he addresses you as 'duke' or 'cavalier'), and will say anything to please: 'Yes, straight ahead!' they'll often reply when you need directions, hoping it will make you happy even if they've never heard of your destination.

Nor does fashion slavery show any sign of abating; now that more Italians have more money than ever before, they are using it for fur coats, rarely necessary in most of the country's winters, and for designer clothes for the whole family. Even little children go to bed with visions of fashion dancing in their heads; Italy is the last stand of Barbie and Ken dolls, where each little girl owns at least a dozen.

## Brick Italy, Marble Italy

'Italy', begins the 1948 Constitution, 'is a Republic based on labour' an unusual turn of phrase, perhaps, but one entirely in keeping with a time when a thoroughly humbled Italy was beginning to get back on its feet after the War. The sorrows of the common man occupied the plots of post-War *cinema verità*, and artists and writers began to celebrate themes of Faith, Bread, and Work as if they were in the employ of the Church's *Famiglia Cristiana* magazine. To outsiders it must have seemed that Italy was undergoing a serious change, but careful observers would have noted only another oscillation in the grandest, oldest dichotomy in Italian history. Brick Italy was once more in the driver's seat.

Brick Italy is a nation of hard work, humility and piety that knows it must be diligent and clever to wrest a comfortable living from the thin soil of this rocky, resource-poor peninsula. Marble Italy knows its citizens are perfectly capable of doing just that, just as they always have, and seeks to celebrate that diligence and cleverness by turning it into opulence, excess and foreign conquest. The two have been contending for Italy's soul ever since Roman quarrymen discovered the great veins of Carrara marble during the republican era. Brick Italy's capital in former times was brilliant, republican Siena; right now it is virtuous, hard-working socialist Bologna, a city with more bricks that Woolworth's has nickels. Its triumphs came with the Age of the Comunes, with the modest genius of the Early Renaissance, and with the hard-won successes of the last 40 years. Marble Italy reached its height in the days of Imperial Rome; its capital is (can you guess?) Rome, always and forever. After the medieval interlude, marble made its great comeback with the High Renaissance, Spaniardism, and Michelangelo, the high priest of marble. The Age of Baroque belonged to it completely, as did the brief era of Mussolini. Some confirmed Marble Cities are Naples, Genoa, Turin, Pisa, Parma, Trieste, Perugia and Verona. Brick partisans include Pavia, Livorno, Lucca, Arezzo, Cremona, and Mantua. Florence and Venice, the two medieval city-republics that eventually became important states on their own, are the two cities that most successfully straddle the fence. Look carefully at their old churches and palaces, and you will often find marble veneer outside, and solid brick underneath.

Keep all this in mind when you ponder the infinite subtleties of Italian history. It isn't always a perfect fit; medieval Guelphs and Ghibellines each had a little brick and a little marble in them, and the contemporary papacy changes from one to the other with every shift of the wind. Mussolini would have paved Italy over in marble if he had been able--but look at the monuments he could afford, and you'll see more inexpensive travertine and brick than anything else. For a while in the 80's, with Italy's economic successes and the glitz of Milanese fashion and design, it looked as if Marble Italy was about to make another comeback. But today, with Italy in the midst of its long and torturous revolution, the situation is unclear. If and when a new regime emerges, will its monument to itself be a beautiful symbol of republican aspirations like Siena's brick Palazzo del Pubblico, or a florid marble pile like Rome's Altar of the Nation, the monument to Italian unification (and one of the biggest hunks of kitsch on this planet).

## Commedia dell'Arte

The first recorded mention of Arlecchino, or Harlequin, came when the part was played by a celebrated actor named Tristano Martinelli in 1601—the year that also saw the debut of *Hamlet*. Theatre as we know it was blooming all over Europe in those times: Shakespeare and Marlowe, Caldéron and Lope de Vega in Spain, the predecessors of Molière in France. All of these had learned their craft from late-Renaissance Italy, where the *commedia dell'arte* had created a fashion that spread across the continent. The great companies, such as the Gelosi, the Confidenti and the Accesi, toured the capitals, while others shared out the provinces. Groups of ten or twelve actors, run as co-operatives, they could do comedies, tagedies or pastorals, to their own texts, and provide music, dance, magic and juggling between acts.

The audiences liked the comedies best of all, woth a set of masked stock characters, playing off scenes between the *magnificos*. the great lords, and the *zanni*, or servants, who provide the slapstick, half-improvised comic relief. These represented every corner of Italy: Arlecchino is a Bergamese; Balanzone, the wise doctor who 'cures with Latin' is from Bologna; white-clad, warbling Pulcinello a true Neapolitan; Meneghino, the piratical warrior, a Milanese; the drunkard Rugantino is a Roman; and the nervous rich merchant Pantalone is a Venetian; while the maid Colombina apparently belongs to all. To spring the plot there would be a pair of lovers, or *inamorati*—unmasked, to remind uis that only those who are in love are really alive.

It had nothing to do with 'art'. *Arte* means a guild, to emphasize that these companies were made up of professional players. The term was invented in 1745 by Goldoni (who wrote one of the last plays of the genre, *Arlecchino, servitore di due padrone*); in the 1500s the companies were often referred to as the *commedia mercenaria*—they would hit town, set up a stage on trestles, and start their show within the hour.

Cultured Italians of the day often deplored the way the 'mercenary' shows were driving out serious drama, traditionally written by scholarly amateurs in the princely courts. In the repressive climate of the day, caught between the Inquisition and the Spanish bosses, a culture of ideas survived only in free Venice. Theatre retreated into humorous popular enter-tainment, but even then the Italians found a way to say what was on their minds. A new stock character appeared, the menacing but slow-witted 'Capitano', who always spoke with a Spanish accent, and Italians learned from the French how to use Arlecchino to satirize the hated emperor Charles V himself—playing on the French pronunciation of the names *harle-quin* and *Charles Quint*.

Arlecchino may have been born in Oneta, a village north of Bergamo, but he carries a proud lineage that goes back to the ancient Greeks and Romans. From his character and appear-ance, historians of the theatre trace him back to the antique [planipedes, comic mimes with shaved heads (everyone knew Arlecchino wore his silly nightcap to cover his baldness). Other scholars note his relationship to the 'tricksters' of German and Scandinavian mythology, and it has even been claimed that his costume of patches is that of a Sufi dervish. No doubt he had a brilliant career all through the Middle Ages, though it was probably only in the 1500s that he took the form of the Arlecchino we know. At that time, young rustics from the Bergamasque valleys would go to Venice, Milan and other cities to get work as *facchini*, porters. They all seemed to be named Johnny—*Zanni* in dialect, which became the common term for any of the clownish roles in the plays; it's the origin of our word 'zany'.

The name 'Arlecchino' seems actually to have been a French contribution. At the court of Henri III, a certain Italian actor who played the role became a protégé of a Monsieur de Harlay, and people started calling him 'little Harlay', or Harlequin. The character developed into a stock role, the most beloved of all the *commedia dell'arte* clown masks: simple-minded and easily frightened, yet an incorrigible prankster, a fellow as unstable as his motley dress. His foil was usually another servant, the Neapoloitan Puricinella, or Punchinella—Punch—more serious and sometimes boastful, but still just as much of a buffoon. Try to imagine them together on stage, and you'll get something looks very much like Stan Laurel and Oliver Hardy. No doubt these two have always gone through the world together, and we can hope they always will.

## That Etruscan Smile

Everything about them is mysterious, and that's the way they seemed to like it. Their everyday lives were wrapped up in magic and superstition, and we know only the most superficial details about their religion, headquartered in the sacred wood called the *Fanum Voltumnae*, around modern Viterbo, where no outsider was ever allowed. No one knows anything for sure about their origins, though they seem to have come from western Anatolia, and their sudden decline and eventual complete disappearance after the 4th centuryBC was just as shadowy and unaccountable. Their language has resisted all attempts at deciphering, but they never wrote that much anyhow.

What the Etruscans did leave behind are portraits of themselves, some of the most remarkable achievements of ancient art. They weren't the most original of artists, but every style and fashion that came their way from Greece was adapted and given an Etruscan twist. Even more than the Greeks, they had a talent for capturing expression and character on every level, from the astute, gentlemanly *Orator* in the Florence museum, to the happy, worldly couples lounging on their stone sarcophagi, the beautiful terracotta heads of children in Rome's Villa Giulia, and the grinning, rosy-cheeked grotesques that peer out from every sort of Etruscan decoration. Usually they are smiling, a faraway smile as mysterious as anything else they have left us. Battered by dour Romans on one side and crazed Celts on the other, the Etruscans simply faded away. Or else they may have gone right into the ground, like the lost ancient people that became the fairies of Ireland. Certainly their presence is still felt in central Italy, especially in art. The Romans and the other Italic nations learned much about art from the Greeks, but when you look at their painting—at Pompeii, in the Naples Museum, or in Nero's Golden House, it will be clear that something essential, something in the soul, was their heritage from Etruria.

The thread of it has never been lost in all the centuries since. When you get to know Etruscan art, you'll see subtle reflections of it in everything that came after, from Botticelli's paintings to Mussolini's post offices. From the grotesques, revived by Raphael and now gazing out at us from the cornices of old buildings everywhere—even sometimes from the faces of the Italians themselves—one gets the feeling that somehow those mysterious Etruscans are still with us.

## Fungus Fever

If you've brought the children, ignore their unkind scoffing. That's not spaghetti with dirt on your plate, but spaghetti *al tartufo*, with truffles, the most prized gourmet delicacy in Italy, earthy, aromatic, aphrodisiac, the totem food of the Italian tribe. Admittedly truffles aren't much to look at, lumpy, subterranean fungi, bulbous tubers that consent to sprout only in certain corners of France and Italy with the proper calcareous soils, oak trees, and exposure. Per ounce these ugly lumps are the most expensive comestibles in the world. Fortunately, a little truffle goes a long way, and Italians will travel a long way to look, dreamy-eyed, at little glass jars of them displayed at truffle fairs. Two types of truffles are regarded as outstanding by connoisseurs—the black, found in south-west France and, in Italy, in the Apennines; and the white truffle, found in the Alba and Asti area of Piedmont. The white is usually the most prized, being rarer, and so more expensive. It's a creamy colour, smooth and irregularly shaped, and can vary in size from that of a walnut to something more like a football. Curiously, truffles actually have very little intrinsic taste—it's their power to impart flavour to other foods that has made them so highly valued. They are usually eaten raw, sliced very finely over virtually any dish—though most popularly with meat, fish or pasta—or used in stuffing for meat, poultry or game.

Truffles are so expensive because they are so hard to track down. An aura of mystery hangs over their birth; according to legend they are spawned by lightning bolts flicking through the oak groves. Although prices of late have led to serious experiments in truffle cultivation, most truffles are still brought to market by truffle-hunters with keen-nosed truffle-hounds; unlike the French, who have long used pigs to seek out the delicacy, the Italians swear by their dogs, suckled as young pups on teats rubbed with truffle juice.

Moreover, the truffle season is short—from October until the snows fall about Christmas— and during this time daily truffle auctions take place in Asti and Alba in the wee hours of the morning, when the secretive truffle hunters arrive with their dogs to sell the night's harvest (it's traditional to hunt at night, when truffles smell the strongest, or perhaps because the best ones are always on someone else's property). A walnut-sized *tartufo* can easily sell for I.100,000. However, if you are offered Tartufo ice cream, don't despair for the sanity of the Italian kitchen—it's made of cream and chocolate, and like French chocolate truffes only resembles the shape of its namesake.

## Leaning Towers

It isn't always a subject the Italians like to discuss. They will be happy to sell you all the little plastic souvenirs you want of the most celebrated of the species—the leaning tower of Pisa but a mention of the other dozens of listing landmarks scattered around Italy makes them uneasy. Italians, of course, rightfully think of themselves as the most skilled engineers on this planet. They built the Roman roads and aqueducts, the Pantheon, and the dome of St Peter's, the biggest in the world. They invented concrete. Today, their endless *autostrade* zoom through mile-long tunnels and skim over deep valleys on stilts, remarkable *tours de force* of engineering that would make the Romans proud. They have built more railway tunnels, perhaps, than the rest of Europe put together. Why can't they keep their towers from drooping?

The answer may well be that they built them that way. For centuries there has been a dark undercurrent of thought on the subject that claims Pisa's tower was meant to lean. Goethe thought so, and architects who carefully measured the foundation stones came to the same conclusion. A certain Professor Goodyear, who wrote over a hundred years ago, exposed the whole business as what he called 'symmetrophobia'—not really a fear of the symmetrical, but more a disdain for it. Italy's medieval master builders, not yet squeezed into the Renaissance straitjacket of monumental symmetry, could still be playful now and then—witness for instance the parfait stripes on so many cathedrals, or the floral wallpaper print that covers Florence's.

The Italians of today do not like this explanation any better; they brusquely reject any suggestion that their ancestors could have been tempted away from the perpendicular on a whim. You can judge for yourself at Pisa—that campanile simply would not look right without the tilt—or at the Garisenda and Asinelli towers of Bologna, a pair of elephantine monstrosities that seem ready to topple any minute. None of Venice's, except for the new St Mark's, are close to being straight; Ravenna has two that are even more precarious, and other examples can be seen at Rovigo and Rome. In Naples they have tilting domes—nothing intentional, but perhaps Providence's gentle reminder that nothing around the Bay of Naples is allowed to stand forever.

## Non-leaning Towers

In most of Italy, where there are no billboards and power lines to block the view, you will see landscapes that have not essentially changed since 1500. Long ago, Italian farmers began the job of making the country into one great formal garden, planting their olives and vines in neat rows, and creating long avenues of Lombardy poplars or parasol pines. Medieval designers added cities, towns, and castles in a constantly changing variety of styles, each one complementary to and respectful to those that came before. The basic feature in many parts of the rugged peninsula is the *hill town*, orderly and compact, its buildings draped carefully on a peak or slope as if arranged there by the hand of a sculptor. By 1500, after a half-millennium of prosperity, the builders' work was done, and the Italian garden was perfect, cohesive, and complete.

Visitors from over the Alps never ceased to be amazed; even those without an eye for beauty could be impressed by the richness and size of Italian towns, and especially by their monumental urge to the vertical. By 1150, Italians were building towers on a scale unmatched until the American cities of the 1900s. Indeed, larger Italian cities had a decidedly Manhattanish aspect with, in some cases, hundreds of tall, square defence towers creating incredible skylines—as with skyscrapers, it soon became a matter of prestige among the baronial families to try to have the tallest, and many reached over 60m (200ft). In those rough times, the towers weren't just for show; city officials had to take constant complaints from neighbours about siege engines parked on the street, stray showers of boiling oil, and noisy, pitched battles keeping the children up at night. The *comuni* managed to get most of these towers pulled down by about 1350. The great bell-towers of the cathedrals and city halls survive, and even today they are usually still the tallest buildings in the city. To give some idea of how ambitiously Italy could build, here are the 10 tallest structures completed before the year 1500:

| | | |
|---|---|---|
| Florence (Cathedral) | 110 m | (364ft) |
| Milan (Cathedral) | 107 m | (351 ft) |
| Cremona (Campanile) | 105 m | (345 ft) |
| Siena (Palazzo Pubblico) | 101 m | (332 ft) |
| Venice (Campanile) | 97 m | (319 ft) |
| Bologna (Asinelli tower) | 96 m | (316 ft) |
| Florence (Palazzo Vecchio) | 94 m | (309 ft) |
| Modena (Ghirlandina) | 84 m | (276 ft) |
| Florence (Giotto's Campanile) | 83 m | (273 ft) |
| Verona (Torre dei Lamberti) | 82 m | (270 ft) |

## Pasta

Croton and Sybaris, among other Greek cities of the Ionian Sea, take the credit for introducing the Italians to their future hearts' delight. A small, cylindrical form of pasta called *makarta*—perhaps the original *macaroni*—was a ritual food eaten at funeral banquets; by 600BC, the Sybarites, always on the hunt for new culinary experiences, had invented the rolling pin and were turning out *tagliatelle* and maybe even *lasagne*. Not yet having tomatoes, they were unable to perfect the concept, but in a nation that often has trouble baking a decent loaf of bread this delicious, aesthetically stimulating and eminently practical new staple found a warm welcome everywhere. Pasta's triumphal march northwards finally slowed to a halt in the rice paddies and treacherous *polenta* morasses of Lombardy, but everywhere else it remains in firm control.

Pasta does have its cultural ramifications. The artists of the Futurist movement wanted to declare war on spaghetti, and many of today's Italian *nouveaux riches* wouldn't be caught dead ordering any form of pasta in a restaurant (this, ironically, at a time when their counterparts in northern Europe and America wax ever more enthusiastic about it). Do you think that pasta is all the same? Well, so do millions of Italians, though an equal number revel in the incredible variety of pasta forms and fashions; in your travels you'll find the same flour and water turned into broad *pappardelle* and narrow *linguini* ('tiny tongues'), stuffed delights like *ravioli* and *tortellini*, regional specialities like Apulian *orecchietti* ('little ears') and Sardinia's *malorreddus*, that resemble miniature trilobites. Other inviting forms, among the 400 or so known shapes, include *vermicelli* ('little worms'), *lumacconi* ('slugs'), *bavette* ('dribbles'), and *strangolopreti* ('priest chokers'). But even these fail to satisfy the nation's culinary whims, and every so often one of the big pasta companies commissions a big name fashion designer to come up with a new form.

## The Pinocchio Complex

The Italians, as much as they adore their *bambini*, have produced but one recognized classic of children's literature, the story of a naughty wooden puppet who must pass through trials and tribulations before he can become a real boy—a stable, responsible child, a blessing to his father in his old age.

Since the Risorgimento, the Italian government has been a bit of a Pinocchio to the old country that painfully carved it out of wood, admittedly half petrified and half rotted from the start. Each ring of the thick trunk told a dire tale of defeat and tyranny, corruption, papal misgovernment, foreign rule and betrayal. From this piece of flotsam the Italians created a new creature, a national state that sits in the class of real governments like a mischievous, exasperating puppet. This Pinocchio is the bad boy of the EC, with more violations of its trade rules than any other nation. Every day its parliament is in session, its nose grows a little bit longer. With its creaky, wooden bureaucracy, unpredictable and not blessed with the soundest of judgements, it is constantly led astray by scheming foxes and cats—like the Mafia, power-hungry cabals of 'freemasons', southern landowners, Mussolinis, popes, Jesuits, and whale-sized special interests that threaten to gobble it down whole. The parties that make up its Commedia dell'Arte coalitions, like flimsy wooden limbs and joints, are liable to trip up or fly off at any moment, making the poor marionette collapse (something that since 1946 has occurred on the average of once every 11 months).

Just as Pinocchio, by some unexplained power, is able to walk without strings, so Italy, without a real government, functions with remarkable smoothness, and even prospers. Understandably, as Europe grows ever closer together, having a wooden-headed political system becomes more and more embarrassing. Constitutional reform, with the 1993 referendum that changed the electoral system, may prove a bigger threat to this puppet's career than any whale. And, with the revelations of the last few years, Italians are beginning to interest themselves in the all-important question of who, all this time, has been pulling the strings.

# Italian Culture

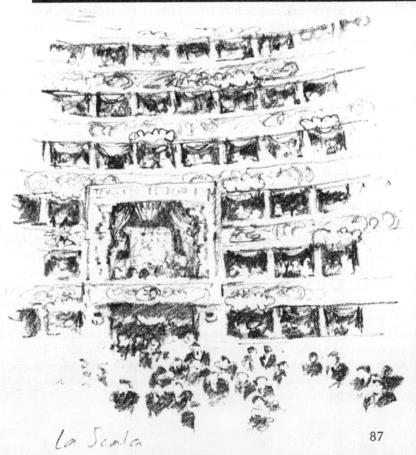

*La Scala*

After the Second World War, when Italy was at its lowest ebb, when it was financially and culturally bankrupt, when its traditional creativity in painting, architecture, and music seemed to have dried up, along came a handful of Italian directors who invented a whole new language of cinema. Neorealism was a response to the fictions propagated by years of Fascism; it was also a response to the lack of movie-making equipment after the Romans, their eyes suddenly opened after a decade of deception and mindless 'White Telephone' comedies, pillaged and sacked Cinecittà in 1943. Stark, unsentimental, often shot in bleak locations with unprofessional actors, the genre took shape with directors like Roberto Rossellini (*Roma, Open City*, 1945), Vittorio de Sica (*Bicycle Thieves*, 1948), and Luchino Visconti (*The Earth Trembles*, 1948).

Although neorealism continued to influence Italian cinema (Rossellini's films with Ingrid Bergman, like *Europa 51* and *Stromboli*, Fellini's classic *La Strada* with Giulietta Masina and Anthony Quinn, Antonioni's *The Scream*), Italian directors began to go off in their own directions. The post-War period was the golden age of Italian cinema, when Italy's Hollywood, Cinecittà, produced scores of films every year. Like the artists of the Age of Mannerism, a new generation of individualistic (or egoistic) directors created works that needed no signature, ranging from Sergio Leone's ultra-popular kitsch westerns to the often jarring films of the Marxist poet Pasolini (*Accattone, The Decameron*). This was the period of Visconti's *The Damned*, Antonioni's *Blow Up*, Lina Wertmuller's *Seven Beauties*, De Sica's *Neapolitan Gold*, Bertolucci's *The Conformist*, and the classics of the indefatigable maestro Federico Fellini—*I Vitelloni, La Dolce Vita, Juliet of the Spirits, The Clowns, Satyricon*.

In the 70s, the cost of making films soared and the industry went into recession. Increasingly, directors went abroad or sought out actors with international appeal in order to reach a larger audience, to help finance their films (Bertolucci's *Last Tango in Paris* with Marlon Brando and *1900* with Donald Sutherland, the overripe Franco Zeffirelli's *Taming of the Shrew* with Taylor and Burton, Visconti's *Death in Venice*). Fellini was one of the few who managed to stay home (*Roma, Amarcord*, and later *Casanova* (although admittedly with Donald Sutherland in the lead role), *City of Women, The Ship Sails On, Orchestra Rehearsal*, and *Intervista*, a film about Cinecittà itself).

Although funds for films became even scarcer in the '80s, new directors appeared to recharge Italian cinema, often with a fresh lyrical realism and sensitivity. Bright stars of the decade included Ermanno Olmi (the singularly beautiful *Tree of the Wooden Clogs* and *Cammina, Cammina*), Giuseppe Tornatore's sentimental and nostalgic *Cinema Paradiso* (1988), Paolo and Vittorio Taviani (*Padre Padrone, Night of the Shooting Stars, Kaos* and *Good Morning Babilonia*), Francesco Rosi (*Christ Stopped at Eboli, Three Brothers, Carmen* and *Cronaca d'una morte annunciata*), and Nanni Moretti (*La Messa é finita*), unfortunately rarely seen outside of festivals and film clubs abroad, while Zeffirelli (*La Traviata*) and Bertolucci (*1900, The Last Emperor*) continued to represent Italy in the world's moviehouses. Comedy found new life in Mario Monticelli's hilarious *Speriamo che sia femina* and in Bruno Bozzetto, whose animation features (especially *Allegro Non Troppo*, a satire of Disney's *Fantasia*) are a scream.

So far the 1990s have served up fairly thin gruel, a recession of inspiration to go with the economy. Worthy exceptions have been *Il Ladro dei bambini* (1992) by Gianni Amelio, *Mediterraneo* (1991) by Gabriele Salvatores, about Italian soldiers marooned on a Greek island, and Nanni Moretti's travelogue to the Ionian islands, *Caro Diario* (1994). This was also the decade that Fellini spun his final reel. Although critics at home and abroad sometimes complained that he repeated himself in his last films (*Ginger and Fred* and *La Voce della Luna*, 1990), his loyal fans eagerly awaited each new instalment of his personal fantasy, his alternative hyper-Italy that exists on the other side of the looking glass in the gossamer warp of the silver screen. The last director regularly to use Cinecittà ('Cinecittà is not my home; I just live there' he once said), his demise may well bring about the end of Rome's pretensions as Hollywood on the Mediterranean altogether.

Italian films are windows of the nation's soul, but if you don't understand Italian you may want to see them at home, where you have the advantage of subtitles. English language films in Italy rarely receive the same courtesy, however—Italians like their movies dubbed. Check listings for films labelled '*versione originale*'—you're bound to find a few in Rome (*see* p.906) and Milan (p.248), and often in other big cities as well. There are also Italy's film festivals (where films tend to be subtitled); the most important one is in Venice (last week of August to first week of September); also, Messina (July); Verona (June); Florence (documentaries, in December); Salerno (16 and 18mm films, in September); and Trieste (science fiction, in July).

## Literature

Few countries have as grand a literary tradition—even Shakespeare made extensive use of Italian stories for his plots. Besides all the great Latin authors and poets of ancient Rome, the peninsula has produced a small shelf of world classics in the Italian language; try to read a few before you come to Italy, or bring them along to read on the train. (All the books listed below are available in English translations, and may often be found in the English sections of Italian bookstores). Once you've visited some of the settings of Dante's *Divine Comedy*, and come to know at least historically some of the inhabitants of the Inferno, Purgatorio, and Paradiso, the old classic becomes even more fascinating. Dante was one of the first poets in Europe to write in the vernacular, and in doing so incorporated a good deal of topographical material from his 13th-century world. His literary successor, Petrarch (1304–74), has been called by many 'the first modern man'; in his poetry the first buds of humanism were born, deeply thought and felt, complex, subtle, and fascinating today as ever (his *Canzionere* is widely available in English). The third literary deity in Italy's late medieval/early Renaissance trinity is Boccaccio (1313–75), whose imagination, humour and realism is most apparent in his 'Human Comadey' the

*Dante*

*Decameron*, a hundred stories 'told' by a group of young aristocrats who fled into the countryside from Florence to escape the plague of 1348. Boccaccio's detached point of view had the effect of disenchanting Dante's ordered medieval cosmos, clearing the way for the renaissance of the secular novel.

Dante, Petrarch, and Boccaccio exerted a tremendous influence over literary Europe, and in the 15th and 16th centuries a new crop of Italian writers continued in the vanguard—Machiavelli in political thought (*The Prince*), though he also wrote two of the finest plays of the Renaissance (*Mandragola* and *Clizia*); Ariosto in the genre of knightly romance (*Orlando Furioso*, the antecedent of Spenser's *Faerie Queene*, among many others); Benevenuto Cellini in autobiography; Vasari in art criticism and history (*The Lives of the Artists*); Baldassare Castiglione in etiquette, gentlemanly arts and behaviour (*The Courtier*); Alberti in architecture and art theory (*Della Pintura*); Leonardo da Vinci in a hundred different subjects (the *Notebook*, etc.); even Michelangelo had time to write a book's worth of sonnets, now translated into English. Other works from the period include the writings and intriguing play (*The Candlemaker*) of the great philosopher and heretic Giordano Bruno (perhaps the only person to be excommunicated from three different churches); the risqué, scathing writings of Aretino, the 'Scourge of Princes'; the poetry and songs of Lorenzo di Medici; and the *Commentaries* by Pope Pius II (Eneo Silvio), a rare view into the life, opinions, and times of one of the most accomplished Renaissance men, not to mention the only autobiography ever written by a pope.

Baroque Italy was a quieter place, dampened by the censorship of the Inquisition. The Venetians kept the flame alight: Casanova's picaresque *Life*, the tales of Carlo Gozzi, and the plays of Goldoni. Modern Italian literature, unlike many, has an official birthdate—the publication in 1827 of Alessandro Manzoni's *I Promessi Sposi* ('The Betrothed'), which not only spoke with sweeping humanity to the concerns of pre-Risorgimento Italy, but spoke in its language—a new everyday Italian that nearly everyone could understand, no matter what their regional dialect; the novel went on to become a symbol of the aspiration of national unity. The next writer with the power to capture the turbulent emotions of his time was Gabriele D'Annunzio, whose life of daredevil, personally tailored patriotism and superman cult strongly contrast with the lyricism of his poetry and some of his novels—still widely read in Italy. Meanwhile, and much more influentially, Pirandello, the philosophical Sicilian playwright and novelist obsessed with absurdity, changed the international vocabulary of drama before the Second World War.

The post-War era saw the appearance of neorealism in fiction as well as cinema, and the classics, though available in English, are among the easiest books to read in Italian—Cesare Pavese's *La luna e i falì* (The Moon and the Bonfire), Carlo Levi's tragic *Cristo si è fermo a Eboli* (Christ Stopped at Eboli), or Vittorini's *Conversazione in Sicilia*. Other acclaimed works of the post-War era include *The Confessions of Zeno* by Italo Svevo of Trieste, *The Garden of the Finzi-Contini* (about a Jewish family in Fascist Italy), by Giorgio Bassani, and another book set during the Fascist era, *That Awful Mess on Via Merulana* by Carlo Emilio Gadda; then there's the Sicilian classic that became famous around the world—*The Leopard* by Giuseppe di Lampedusa.

The late Italo Calvino, perhaps more than any other Italian writer in the past two decades, enjoyed a large international following—his *Italian Folktales, Marcovaldo, Baron in the Trees*, and *If on a Winter's Night a Traveller* (which includes the first chapters of about 10 novels) were all immediately translated into English; perhaps the best of them is *Invisible Cities*, an imaginary dialogue between Marco Polo and Kublai Khan. Much maligned Sicily continued to produce some of Italy's best literature, from the pens of Leonard Sciasca and Gesualdo Bufalino. The current celebrity of Italian literature is of course Umberto Eco, professor of semiotics at Bologna university, whose *The Name of the Rose* kept readers all over the world at the edge of their seats over the murders of a handful of 14th-century monks in a remote Italian monastery, while magically evoking, better than many historians, all the political and ecclesiastical turmoil of the period.

Italy has also inspired countless of her visitors, appearing as a setting in more novels, poems, and plays than tongue can tell. There is also a long list of non-fiction classics, some of which make fascinating reading and are readily available in most bookshops: Goethe's *Italian Journey*, Ruskin's *The Stones of Venice*, D. H. Lawrence's *Etruscan Places* and *Twilight in Italy*, Hilaire Belloc's *The Path to Rome*, Norman Douglas's *Old Calabria*, James/Jan Morris's *Venice*, Mary McCarthy's *The Stones of Florence* and *Venice Observed*, and many others, including the famously over-the-top travellers' accounts of Edward Hutton and the ever-entertaining H. V. Morton. For the Italian point of view from the outside looking in, read the classic *The Italians* by the late Luigi Barzini, former correspondent for the *Corriera della Sera* in London.

## Music and Opera

Italy has contributed as much to Western music as any country—and perhaps a little more. It was an Italian monk, Guido d'Arezzo, who devised the musical scale; it was a Venetian printer, Ottavino Petrucci, who invented a method of printing music with movable type in 1501—an industry Italian printers monopolized for years (which is why we play *Allegro* but not *schnell*). Italy also gave us the piano, originally the *pianoforte* because unlike the harpsichord you could play both soft and loud, and the accordion, invented in the Marches, and the violins of the Guarneri and Stradivarius of Cremona, setting a standard for the instrument that has never been equalled. But Italy is most famous as the mother of opera, in many ways the most Italian of arts.

Italian composers first came into their own in the 14th century, led by the half-legendary, blind Florentine Landini, whose *Ecco la Primavera* is one of the first Italian compositions to come down to us. Although following international trends introduced by musicians from France and the Low Countries, musicologists note from the start a special love of melody, even in the earliest Italian works, as well as a preference for vocal music over the purely instrumental.

Landini was followed by the age of the *frottolas* (secular verses accompanied by lutes), especially prominent in the court of Mantua. The frottolas were forerunners of the *madrigal*, the greatest Italian musical invention during the Renaissance. Although sung in three or six parts, the text of the madrigals was given serious consideration, and was sung to be understood; at the same time church music had become so polyphonically rich and sumptuous (most notoriously at St Mark's in Venice) that it drowned out the words of the Mass. Many melodies used were from secular and often bawdy songs, and the bishops at the Council of Trent (1545–63) seriously considered banning music from the liturgy. The day was saved by the Roman composers, led by Palestrina, whose solemn, simple, but beautiful melodies set a standard for all subsequent composers.

Two contrasting strains near the end of the 16th century led to the birth of opera: the Baroque love of spectacle and the urge to make everything, at least on the surface, more beautiful, more elaborate, more showy. Musically there were the lavish Florentine *intermedii*, performed on special occasions between the acts of plays; the *intermedii* used elaborate sets and costumes, songs, choruses, and dances to set a mythological scene. At the same time, in Florence, a group of humanist intellectuals who called themselves the 'Camerata' came to the conclusion from their classical studies that ancient Greek drama was not spoken, but sung, and took it upon themselves to try to recreate this pure and classical form. One of their chief theorists was Galileo's father Vincenzo, who studied Greek, Turkish, and Moorish music and advocated the clear enunciation of the words, as opposed to the Venetian tendancy to merge words and music as a single rich unit of sound.

The first result of the Camerata's debates was court musician Jacopo Peri's *L'Euridice*, performed in Florence in 1600. Peri used a kind of singing speech (recitative) to tell the story, interspersed with a few melodic songs. No one, it seems, asked for an encore; opera had to wait a few years, until the Duchess of Mantua asked her court composer, Claudio Monteverdi (1567–1643), to compose something like the work she had heard in Florence. Monteverdi went far beyond Peri, bringing in a large orchestra, designing elegant sets, adding dances and many more melodic songs, or *arias*. His classic *L'Orfeo* (1607), still heard today, and *L'Arriana* (unfortunately lost but for fragments) were the first operatic 'hits'. Monteverdi moved on to bigger audiences in Venice, which soon had 11 opera houses. After he died, though, Naples took over top opera honours, gaining special renown for its clear-toned *castrati*.

Other advances were developing in the more pious atmosphere of Rome, where Corelli was busily perfecting the concerto form and composing his famous *Christmas Concerto*. In Venice, Vivaldi greatly expanded the genre by composing some four hundred concerti for whatever instruments happened to be played in the orchestra of orphaned girls where he was concert-master.

The 18th century saw the sonata form perfected by harpsichord master Domenico Scarlatti. Opera was rid of some of its Baroque excesses and a division was set between serious works and the comic *opera buffa*; Pergolesi (1710–36, his *Il Flaminio* was the basis for Stravinsky's *Pulcinella*) and Cimarosa (1749–1801) were the most sought-after composers, while the now infamous Salieri, antagonist of Mozart, charmed the court of Vienna. Italian composers held sway throughout Europe; with others, like Sammartini, who helped develop the modern symphony, they contributed more than is generally acknowledged today towards the founding of modern music.

Italy innovated less in the 19th century; at this time most of its musical energies were devoted to opera, becoming the reviving nation's clearest and most widely appreciated medium of self-expression. All of the most popular Italian operas were written in the 19th and early 20th century, most of them by the 'Big Five'— Bellini, Donizetti, Rossini, Verdi, and Puccini. For Italians, Verdi (1813–1901) is supreme, the national idol even in his lifetime, whose rousing operas were practically the battle hymns of the Risorgimento. Verdi, more than anyone else, re-established Italy on the musical map; his works provided Italy's melodic answer to the ponderous turbulence of Richard Wagner. After Verdi, Puccini held the operatic stage, though not entirely singlehandedly; the later 19th century gave us a number of composers best remembered for only one opera: Leoncavallo's *Pagliacci*, Mascagni's *Cavalleria Rusticana*, Cilea's *Adriana Lecouvreur*, and many others down to obscure composers like Giordano, whose *Fedora*, famous for being the only opera with bicycles on stage, is revived frequently in his hometown of Foggia.

Of more recent Italian, and Italian-American composers, there's *The Pines of Rome* of Respighi (whose works were the only 20th-century productions that the great Toscanini deigned to direct), Gian Carlo Menotti, surely the best loved, not only for his operas but for founding the Spoleto Festival. Lately there are the innovative post-War composers Luigi Nono and Luciano Berio, two respected names in contemporary academic music.

Next to all of this big-league culture, however, there survives remnants of Italy's traditional music—the pungent tunes of Italian bagpipes (*zampogna*), the ancient instrument of the Apennine shepherds, often heard in the big cities (especially in the South) at Christmas time; the lively *tarantellas* of Apulia, country accordion music, the fare of many a rural festa; and the great song tradition of the country's music capital, Naples, the cradle of everyone's favourite cornball classics, but also of many haunting, passionate melodies of tragedy and romance that are rarely heard abroad—or, to be honest, in Italy itself these days. Naples now prides itself on being the capital of Mediterranean rock 'n' roll, a spurious claim, and not too impressive even if it's true. Listen for yourself; on the *bancarelle* in the street markets of Naples you'll have ample opportunity to audition a wide range of locally produced cassettes and see if anything catches your fancy. Italian pop music climbs to the top of its modest plateau every February at the San Remo song festival, the national run-off for the Eurovision Song Contest and just as hilariously tacky; the likes of *Volare* are nowhere to be seen.

Opera season in Italy runs roughly from November to May. Don't limit your explorations to the prestigious La Scala in Milan. The San Carlo in Naples and La Fenice in Venice are equally old and impressive houses, in cities with a longer and more intense operatic tradition, and the Teatro dell'Opera in Rome and the Teatro Comunale in Florence can both put on excellent and innovative productions. On the next rung down (in size and finances, though not necessarily in quality) are the houses in Parma, Trieste, Genoa, Bergamo, Turin, Modena, Bari and Foggia. Summer festivals are an excellent place to hear music; check through the list of festivals on pp.19–22.

Non è questo 'l terren, ch' i' toccai pria?
Non è questo il mio nido,
Ove nudrito fui sí dolcemente?
Non è questa la patria in ch' io mi fido,
Madre benigna e pia,
Che copre l'un e l'altro mio parente?
Per Dio, questo la mente
Talor vi mova; e con pietà guardate
Le lagrime del popol doloroso,
Che sol da voi riposo,
Dopo Dio, spera: e, pur che voi mostriate
Segno, alcun di pietate,
Vertú contra furore
Prenderà l'arme; e fia 'l combatter corto;
Ché l'antiquo valore
Ne l' italici cor non è ancor morto.

Petrarch (1304–74)

*Is not this precious earth my native land?*
*And is not this the nest*
*From which my tender wings were taught to fly?*
*And is not this soil upon whose breast,*
*Loving and soft, faithful and true and fond,*
*My father and my gentle mother lie?*
*'For love of God,' I cry,*
*'Some time take thought of your humanity*
*And spare your people all their tears and grief!*
*From you they seek relief*
*Next after God. If in your eyes they see*
*Some marks of sympathy,*
*Against this mad disgrace*
*They will arise, the combat will be short*
*For the stern valour of our ancient race*
*Is not yet dead in the Italian heart.*

*trans. William Dudley Foulke LL D (1915)*

# Piedmont, Valle d'Aosta and Liguria

Piedmont (Piemonte), 'the foot of the mountains', is not only the birthplace of the modern Italian state, the source of its greatest river, the cradle of its industry, and the originator of such indispensable Italian staples as vermouth, Fiats and breadsticks, but also a beautiful region full of surprises. To the north and west tower some of the most important peaks of the Alps such as Gran Paradiso and Monviso, while the small autonomous region of Valle d'Aosta is dominated by world-class heavyweights like Mont Blanc, the Matterhorn, and Monte Rosa. The south is walled off from Liguria and the Mediterranean by the lush green Maritime Alps, which, like the rest of Piedmont, are unspoiled, ill-equipped with the amenities of international tourism, and utterly delightful. Between the Maritime Alps and the Po are miles of rolling hills clad in the noble pinstripe patterns of some of the world's most prestigious vineyards. North of the Po the scenery changes again, going as flat as a railway station pizza, criss-crossed by a complicated web of small canals that feed Europe's most important rice fields. And in the centre of the hills, plains and mountains lies the regional capital Turin, not an industrial by-product as one might suppose, but a charming Baroque city.

Historically, Piedmont is one of Italy's newer regions, its name not even in existence until the 13th century, when it gradually came to encompass the former Marquessates of Monferrato, Ivrea, Saluzzo, and the County of Turin. The French dynasty of Savoy first got a foothold in Piedmont by marriage in the 11th century, and from the very beginning kept a much tighter reign on their realm than other Italian princes. The rise of independent *comuni*, the republics and heady ideas of the Renaissance failed to penetrate their feudal fastness. For centuries the population didn't even consider itself Italian, and instead spoke Provençal, which still survives in many a remote valley. Yet, as unprogressive and as uninspired as Piedmont remained throughout Italy's Golden Age, it was the first region to re-surface when the peninsula went under in the tidal wave of invasions and looting of the 16th century; Piedmont's French occupation, begun in 1502, ended 60 years later when Duke Emanuele Filiberto won back his lands with a series of gritty battles. From that point on, the Savoys linked Piedmont's destiny with Italy, treading the troubled political waters of the day with an astute choice of alliances and cautious diplomatic manoeuvring that earned them the title of King of Sardinia in 1713, and then, in the Risorgimento, the crown of Italy herself.

There were violent riots in Turin when the first king of Italy, Vittorio Emanuele II, moved his capital to Florence, en route to Rome; the Piedmontese rightly sensed that they had been relegated to the knick-knack shelf of history. But rather than collect dust, they began Italy's industrial revolution, building the first wool and cotton mills in the torrent-sliced valleys of Biella, the first cars in Turin, the first typewriters in Ivrea, and creating a felt hat empire in Alessandria. Piedmont's economy has always been one of the strongest in Italy, with tourism playing only an insignificant supporting role.

But if the Italy you seek includes sensational Alpine scenery, snowy peaks and emerald valleys, and mountain resorts, either ultra-sophisticated or rustic, or somewhere in between; if it includes un-hyped medieval hill villages and castles standing like islands above rolling seas of vines; if it includes fantastic regional cuisine, with a French touch; or if you have a special interest in white truffles, caves, St Bernards, trout fishing, Egyptology, Romanesque architecture, rare flowers, wildlife or kayaking, you will love Piedmont and Aosta. On the other hand, if your Italy consists of Renaissance art, lemon groves and endless sunshine, you'd better do as Hannibal did and just pass right on through.

## Piedmont and Valle d'Aosta: Itineraries

Crossing the Alps: most people driving to Italy from Britain take the convenient Mont Blanc Tunnel between Chamonix and Courmayeur. Alternative routes include the Great St Bernard Tunnel, or in the summer the Little St Bernard Pass, all wonderfully scenic and not far from the A5 to Turin, Milan, or Genoa—though, unless you're in a rush, the parallel SS26 is prettier. The Valle d'Aosta, of course, is worth lingering in, with more facilities for tourism than Piedmont: **Courmayeur** and **Breuil-Cervinia** are world-class ski resorts, and there are a score of others in the region's dozen valleys. One of Europe's largest casinos is at **St-Vincent** in the main valley, as are the storybook castles of **Issogne** and **Fénis**. **Ayas** and **Cogne** are perhaps the most beautiful valleys in Aosta, the latter leading to the spectacular **Gran Paradiso National Park**, for many people the star attraction of the region with its population of ibex, chamois and golden eagles. From Courmayeur you can take what must be the most thrilling ride in all Europe, the cablecar over Mont Blanc to Chamonix. **Aosta**, the capital of the autonomous region, is adorned with Roman and medieval monuments lent a special enchantment by a magnificent backdrop of mountains.

There are several alternative passes further south. A fine approach is via Val d'Isère and the Col du Mt Cenis to **Susa**, or in winter through the Frejus Tunnel from St-Jean-de-Maurienne, or through the Col de Mongenèvre, between Briançon and Sestriere. All three routes leave you west of Turin, in the **Valle di Susa** or **Valle del Chisone**, among the most rewarding in Piedmont and easily visited in a circular tour, with stops at the medieval village of **Avigliana** and its provocative Romanesque abbey the **Sacra di San Michele**, then at the fine old town of **Susa**, and beyond at the well-equipped resorts of **Sauze d'Oulx**, **Bardonecchia**, **Claviere** or fashionable **Sestriere**. In the Valle del Chisone, there's the interesting Waldenses capital of **Pinerolo**, and the magnificent 'hunting lodge' of the Savoys at Stupinigi.

**Turin** is the cultural centre of Piedmont, having inherited the Savoys' art collections, now housed in the splendid Egyptian Museum, the Galleria Sabauda, and the Museum of Ancient Art, while Turin cathedral inherited the dynasty's most sacred relic, the Shroud of Turin.

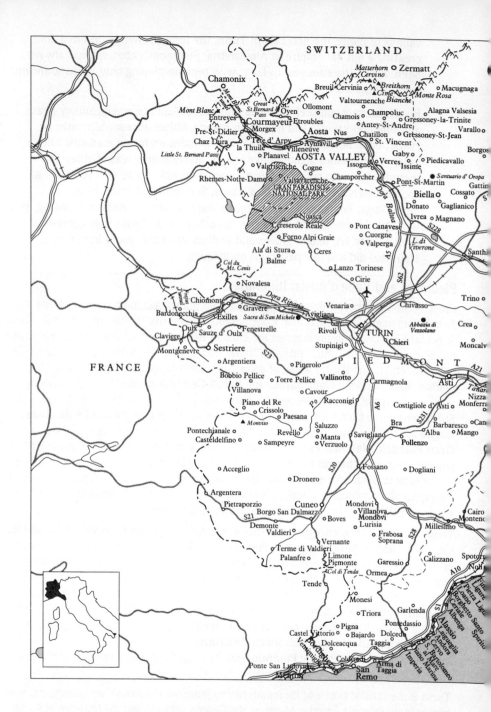

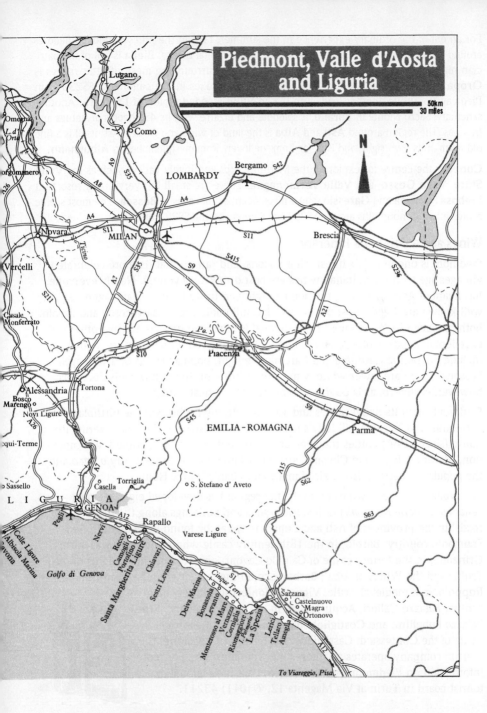

# Piedmont, Valle d'Aosta and Liguria

50km
30 miles

N

Lugano

Como

Omegna
L. d'
Orta

Borgomanero

LOMBARDY

Bergamo

S42

A26

A8

S35

A9

A4

Novara

S11

MILAN

Brescia

S11

Vercelli

A7

S35

S9

A1

S415

S236

Casale
Monferrato

S11

Po

Piacenza

A4

S10

Tortona

Alessandria

A21

Bosco
Marengo

Novi Ligure

A26

S45

EMILIA - ROMAGNA

Parma

A1

S9

Acqui-Terme

A7

Sassello

Casella

Torriglia

S. Stefano d' Aveto

A15

S62

LIGURIA

GENOA

Pegli

A12

S63

Celle Ligure

Nervi

Recco

Rapallo

Camogli

Portofino

Varese Ligure

Albisola Marina

Santa Margherita Ligure

Savona

Chiavari

Sestri Levante

Golfo di Genova

Deiva Marina

Bonassola

Levanto

Monterosso al Mare

Vernazza

Corniglia

Riomaggiore

I. Palmaria

La Spezia

Cinque Terre

S1

Sarzana

Castelnuovo

Magra

Ortonovo

Lerici

Tellaro

Ameglia

A12

To Viareggio, Pisa

99

For an out-of-the-ordinary experience in the summer, take in the miles of flooded paddies around **Vercelli**, the interesting but scarcely visited capital of rice. **Biella** is full of the patrician mansions of Italy's early textile tycoons; in the surrounding mesh of little valleys is **Oropa**, the holy shrine of Piedmont. Another route takes in the panoramic SS232 from Piedicavallo, while another leads into the beautiful wooded region of **La Serra**. Another sanctuary, Sacro Monte in **Varallo**, is splendid and bizarre with its 45 chapels of statues and frescoes. The region around **Asti** and **Alba** is the land of wine and castles; Asti itself is a fine old town in its own right, and isn't far from the lovely Romanesque abbey in **Albugnano**.

**Cuneo** is the centre for exploring the Maritime Alps and lovely valleys such as the **Valle Stura**, **Valle Gesso**, and **Valle Vermenagna**. There are small but very pretty resorts at **Frabosa Soprana** and **Garessio**, and a magnificent set of caves at **Bossea**. The most scenic routes into the mountains are the SS20 from Cuneo and the SS29 from Alba.

## Wines and a Drinker's Itinerary

Piedmont is one of Italy's finest wine regions, and rare in that its more celebrated vintages age well (most Italian wines are best drunk very young). Nearly everyone has heard of Asti Spumante, the popular light and fruity Italian 'champagne'; equally well known are Italy's most prestigious dry, full bodied reds, Barbaresco and Barolo, both produced from Piedmont's exceptional Nebbiolo grapes, as are two other excellent dry reds, Dolcetto and Barbera. Other fine red wines from the region include the tannic Gattinara and Carema, the light, popular Freisa or a well-aged Lessona. There are fewer white wines from Piedmont; the light Arneis dei Roeri, however, is superb, as is *Gavi*, both among Italy's finest whites.

Piedmont, with its native wines and access to Alpine herbs, was the birthplace of vermouth, and Turin is still Italy's major producer. Carpano, the oldest vermouth house (since 1786) bottles the popular bittersweet Punt e Mes, while the competition, Martini & Rossi and Cinzano, are better known for the classic dry *bianco* and the popular sweet reddish elixir of many an Italian's Happy Hour.

To savour Piedmont's wines properly, the region has developed eight regional cellars (*enoteche regionali*) in historic castles and buildings along the main 'wine roads' in the provinces of Asti and Cuneo: they can be found in **Mango**, in Asti Spumante country; **Barolo**, in the 18th-century castle where the wine was born; **Grinzane**, in the former castle of Camillo Cavour, operated by the 'Knights of the Truffle and the Wines of Alba'; **Barbaresco**, in the former church of San Donato; **Roppolo**, in a medieval castle; **Vignale Monferrato**, in the 17th-century Palazzo Callori; Acqui Terme, in the ancient cellars of the Palazzo Robellini; and **Costigliole d'Asti**, in the 18th-century castle of the Contessa di Castiglione. Near Turin in **Pessione**, the Martini company operates an interesting wine museum. For more information on Piedmont's wine roads, contact the regional tourist board in Turin at Via Magenta 12, © (011) 43211.

Detroit without the degradation, the aristocratic capital of the Savoys, an elegantly planned Baroque city of arcades and harmonious squares, frequent venue of international bridge tournaments, the home of the famous shroud, of Juventus, the Red Brigades and vermouth, and reputedly *the* centre of black magic in the Mediterranean, Turin (Torino) is the traditional and yet rather unexpected 'Gateway to Italy'. It stands on the Po, so close to its Alpine sources that this longest and most benighted of Italy's rivers is almost clean. Its cuisine is influenced by France; its winters are colder than Copenhagen's; its most renowned museum is Egyptian.

As important Italian cities go, Turin is a relative newcomer. In 1574, a time when the king of Spain held the rest of the peninsula by the bootstrap, fiesty 'iron-headed' Emanuele Filiberto of Savoy, descendant of Europe's most ancient ruling house, drove the French and Spanish troops from his territory and moved his capital from Chambéry to Turin, previously little more than a fortified Roman outpost (*Augusta Taurinorum*) and medieval university town. It was a move symbolizing the dynasty's new identity with the Italian portion of Savoy, or Piedmont, a move that was to have the greatest impact on the future. No one at the time suspected that the highly centralized duchy in this hitherto neglected corner of the peninsula would one day unite the land, and that Turin would be the first capital of the Kingdom of Italy.

It's a common cliché that the Agnelli family's Fiat Corporation is Turin's new dynasty; founded in 1899, it is not only Europe's largest car manufacturer, but the sixth-largest corporation in the entire world. While the historic centre of Turin retains its refined air of a courtly drawing room (no city in Italy looks anything like it), the glitter and sleekness of the shops are thanks mostly to Fiat money, which is also responsible for the vast suburb of Mirafiori south of Turin, built by the company to house the thousands of workers who have come up from Calabria and other points south. Paradoxically, while Turin takes credit for Italy's unification, it has suffered the consequences of that union most acutely, plagued by perhaps the worst relations and bigotry between northern and southern Italians. The latter became Italy's first and most organized proletariat: during the First World War, Gramsci, the great philosopher of the Italian Communist party, led the workers' factory councils in occupying the Fiat works in what he hoped would become an Italian Petrograd. The failure taught him that Italians required a different solution, and made him rightly fear that extremism in one form or another would be the end result.

Gramsci died in a fascist prison; fifty years after his factory councils experiment, the Red Brigades were born in the urban anonymity of Mirafiori. Their militant sympathizers and radical unionism crippled Fiat in the seventies. Since then, prosperity perhaps more than anything has exorcised most of Turin's extremist bogeys. Despite increasing European competition—and partly due to a far-sighted 'understanding' with Japanese car-makers not to intrude into each other's home markets—Fiat still supplies well over three-quarters of all the cars in Italy, through Fiat itself, through Fiat-owned Lancia, or through Alfa Romeo, also bought up by Fiat in the eighties.

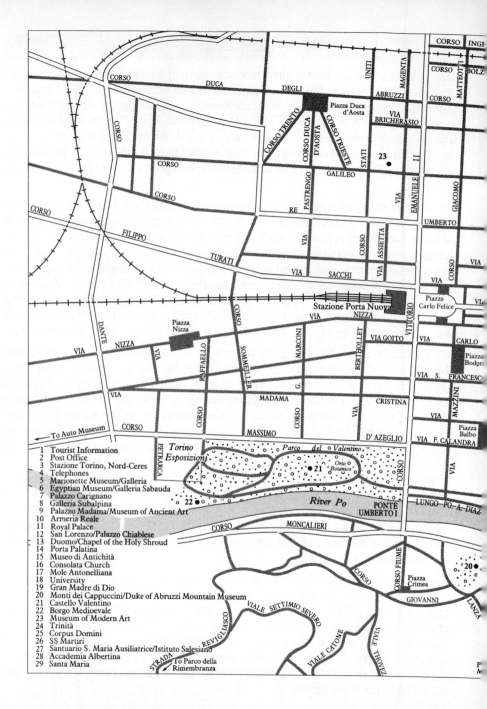

1 Tourist Information
2 Post Office
3 Stazione Torino, Nord-Ceres
4 Telephones
5 Marionette Museum/Galleria
6 Egyptian Museum/Galleria Sabauda
7 Palazzo Carignano
8 Galleria Subalpina
9 Palazzo Madama/Museum of Ancient Art
10 Armeria Reale
11 Royal Palace
12 San Lorenzo/Palazzo Chiablese
13 Duomo/Chapel of the Holy Shroud
14 Porta Palatina
15 Museo di Antichità
16 Consolata Church
17 Mole Antonelliana
18 University
19 Gran Madre di Dio
20 Monti dei Cappuccini/Duke of Abruzzi Mountain Museum
21 Castello Valentino
22 Borgo Medioevale
23 Museum of Modern Art
24 Trinità
25 Corpus Domini
26 SS Martiri
27 Santuario S. Maria Ausiliatrice/Istituto Salesiano
28 Accademia Albertina
29 Santa Maria

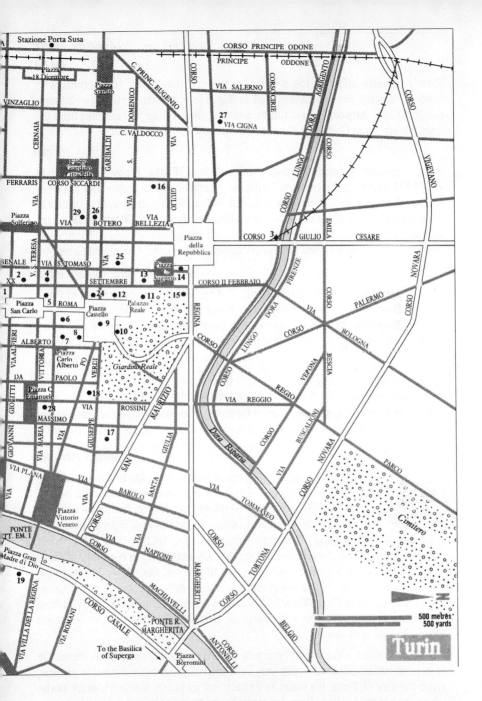

### by air

Turin's **Caselle airport**, 15km north of the city, has direct connections with London, Paris call and Frankfurt as well as flights to major Italian cities. For information ✆ 57781. **Airport buses,** run by SADEM, depart every 30 minutes from the main bus station at Corso Inghilterra 1. Tickets cost L5000 each way.

### by rail

Turin's massive neoclassical main train station, **Porta Nuova** (information ✆ 5613333), is near the centre of Turin, with connections to France and to Genoa (2 hrs), Milan (1½ hrs), Aosta (2½ hrs), and Venice (5 hrs); arrive in time or take in Porta Nuova's nightmarish bar at your own risk. Another station, **Porta Susa**, on the west side of town, can be a convenient getting-off point when arriving in Turin, while a third station, **Torino Ceres**, serves the regional line to Cirié, Lanzo, and Ceres.

### by long-distance bus

The **bus terminal** is on Corso Inghilterra, ✆ 4332525, at the western end of Corso Vittorio Emanuele II, though many buses also stop near Porta Susa station. Buses head out from here for Aosta's ski resorts as far as Chamonix. There are year-round connections to Cuneo, Saluzzo, Claviere, Sestriere, and other towns in the province.

### by road

The five *autostrade* serving Turin—the A32 from France via the Frejus tunnel, the A5 from Aosta and the Mont Blanc tunnel, the A4 to Milan in the east, the A21 from Parma and Alessandria, and the A6 from Genoa and Savona—all connect up in an arc that skirts the city to the west, making it possible to avoid it completely if necessary.

### Getting Around

Getting around Turin itself is easier than in most Italian cities, thanks to a regular grid of streets, served by old-fashioned **trams** and **buses**. Tickets (L1000 each) must be bought in advance, from tobacco shops or from the city transport office at Porta Nuova train station. This office also provides a good free city transport map. Bus route 1 links Porta Nuova with Porta Susa; No.4, Porta Nuova station (Via XX Settembre) to the Duomo; no.15 departs from Via XX Settembre, goes through the centre, then down Via Po to the Superga cog tramway. No.16 goes from the Piazza della Repubblica down Corso Regina Margherita to Piazza Vittorio Veneto and the Parco di Valentino. Bus 34 from Porta Nuova heads out to the Auto Museum; suburban bus 41 from Corso Vittorio Emanuele goes to Stupinigi.

If you intend to use a **car** in Turin you will find that parking is not quite as impossible as in most Italian cities, but is still very restricted in the old city centre. In general, given the size of Turin, it's easier to get around by public transport, or by **taxis,** which are not hard to find. There are ranks by the train and bus stations and in many of the main piazzas; alternatively, call for a taxi on ✆ 5730 or 5748.

The main tourist office is at Via Roma 226, ℂ 535181 (*open 9am–7.30pm Mon–Sat*), and there is also a branch office at Porta Nuova station (ℂ 531327). Both offices have a free room-finding service. For information on concerts, film times, and so on, check out the listings in Turin's local/national daily, *La Stampa*.

**Fire**, Corso Regina Margherita 330, ℂ 115.

**Police**, Corso XI Febbraio 22, ℂ 26091.

**Ambulance (Red Cross)**, Via Bologna 171, ℂ 280333.

**Ambulance (Green Cross)**, Via T. Dorè 4, ℂ 549000.

**Hospital**: Ospedale Molinetto, Corso Bramante 88/90, ℂ 66251/66261.

**24-hour pharmacy: Boniscontro**, Corso Vittorio Emanuele II 66, ℂ 538271, open 24 hours daily.

There is a cash exchange machine open 24 hours every day at Via Roma 224, beside the main tourist office.

The central post office is at Via Alfieri 10, ℂ 546800, just off the Piazza San Carlo and very near the main tourist office. Attached to it there is a phone centre.

The phone prefix for Turin is **011**.

## Via Roma

Central Turin is laid out in a stately rhythm of porticoed streets and jewel-like squares. Few railway stations in Italy deposit the weary traveller in a piazza as inviting as Porta Nuova's manicured **Piazza Carlo Felice**, where even the traffic intersections are covered with porticoes and pots of flowers. The fashionable **Via Roma** leads from here into the heart of the city, passing through an impressive 'gateway' of twin churches, **Santa Cristina** and **San Carlo**, designed by the Sicilian Baroque genius Filippo Juvarra, court architect to the King of Sardinia in the early 18th century.

Behind the churches lies Turin's finest square, **Piazza San Carlo**, a 17th-century confection with a flamboyant centrepiece in its bronze **equestrian statue of Duke Emanuele Filiberto** 'the Iron Head', sheathing his sword after battle, by local sculptor Carlo Marochetti (1838). Turin is a city of ornate elegant cafés, and in Piazza San Carlo you can sip your cappuccino in the most celebrated of them all, the 19th-century **Caffè Torino**, a veritable palace of coffee with chandeliers and frescoed ceilings. Just west of the piazza, the **Museo della Marionetta** has a collection of Italian puppets from various periods (Via S. Teresa 5; closed indefinitely for restoration at time of writing). The glass-roofed shopping arcade, or **Galleria**, between Santa Teresa and Via Bertola contains an outstanding Art Deco movie palace, well named the Lux.

### The Egyptian Museum and Galleria Sabauda

These, Turin's most outstanding treasure troves, are just off Piazza San Carlo, sharing the former **Palazzo dell'Accademia delle Scienze**. This palace, designed as a Jesuit college, is the most ponderous of Turin's landmarks designed by the remarkable Guarino Guarini, a Theatine priest and architect who came to work for Carlo Emanuele in 1668 and changed the face of the city.

The **Egyptian Museum** (*open 9am–2pm Tues–Sun; adm exp*) is rated the second most important in the world, after the museum in Cairo. It was begun as a collection of curios in 1628 by Carlo Emanuele I, but later Savoys took their pharaohs and mummies rather more seriously, especially Carlo Felice, who acquired the collection of the French Consul General of Egypt and confidant of Mohammed Ali, Bernardo Drovetti (who happened to be from Piedmont), and founded the museum itself in 1824—the first Egyptian museum in the world. Two major Italian expeditions in this century added considerably to the collections, and the museum played a major role in the Aswan Dam rescue digs. It was rewarded with one of the temples it had preserved—the 15th-century BC rock-cut Temple of Ellessiya, with a relief of Thothmes III, now reconstructed in the museum.

Other rooms display portions of an immense papyrus library, including several copies of the *Book of the Dead* and the *Royal Papyrus*, listing all the kings of Egypt, from the Sun itself down to the 17th dynasty; Turin's papyrus collection is so extensive that after Jean François Champollion cracked the Rosetta Stone, he came to complete his study of hieroglyphics here. The ground floor houses an excellent collection of monumental public sculpture, notably the black granite Rameses II (13th century BC), the 15th-century BC Thothmes III, and the sarcophagus of a vizier of the 26th Dynasty, Ghemenef-Har-Bak.

Upstairs you can spend hours wandering through the essentials and the trivialities of ancient Egypt: here are artefacts from the Egyptians' daily lives, notably a reconstruction of the 14th-century BC **Tomb of the architect Khaiè and his wife Meriè** (18th Dynasty) that somehow managed to escape the grave robbers—even the bread and beans prepared for their afterlife remains intact; other rooms contain mummies in various stages of deshabille, wooden models of boats and funerary processions, paintings, statuettes, canopic vases, jewellery, clothing and textiles.

*Museo Egisio*

On the top floor, the **Galleria Sabauda** (*open 9am–2pm Tues–Sun; adm*) houses the principal collections of the House of Savoy. The Savoys liked Flemish and Dutch art just as much as Italian, which gives the Sabauda a variety most Italian galleries lack. Among the Italians are two fine Florentine works, *Tobias and the Archangel Raphael* by Antonio and Piero del Pollaiuolo, and a fine study of Botticelli's newborn *Venus*, thought to be by one of his students; other works are by Mantegna, Taddeo Gaddi, Sodoma, Tintoretto, Titian, Veronese, and Bergognone. Among the Northerners are Jan Van Eyck's *St Francis*, Memling's drama-filled *Scenes from the Passion*, Van Dyck's beautiful *Children of Charles I*, popular scenes and landscapes by Jan Brueghel, *Portrait of a Doctor* by Jacobs Dirk, and Rembrandt's *Old Man Sleeping.* The French have a room to themselves, with works by Poussin, Claude, and Clouet.

Across from the museum, the **Palazzo Carignano**, much more representative of Guarini's work, was begun in 1679 for the Savoy-Carignano branch of the royal family—the branch that was to produce Vittorio Emanuele II, who, as the inscription on top states, was born here. The palace itself is one of Italy's finest Baroque concoctions, with an undulating brick façade and ornate rotunda. The palace served as the Piedmontese Subalpine Parliament, and later as the first Italian Parliament, which met here on 14 March 1861 to proclaim Vittorio Emanuele King of Italy. The Chamber now forms part of the **Museo Nazionale del Risorgimento** (*open 9am–6.30pm Tues–Sat; 9am–12.30pm Sun; adm Tues–Sat; free Sun*), the most interesting of Italy's scores of Risorgimento museums.

## Palazzo Madama

Parallel to the Via Accademia, the **Galleria Subalpina** (just right, off Via Battisti) is Turin's other shopping arcade, inspired by the Galleria Vittorio Emanuele in Milan. The Galleria Subalpina leads to an elegant coffeehouse, the Caffè Baratti & Milano, and the huge expanse of the **Piazza Castello**, the main square of Turin, with the **Palazzo Madama** in the middle. Named for the two royal widows ('Madama Reale') who lived here, the palace dates back to the 15th century, though it incorporates in its structure fragments from the eastern Roman gate, the Porta Decumana, as well as the original 13th-century castle. In 1718 one of the Madamas had Juvarra give the old place a facelift—a task Juvarra responded to with a beautiful, serene façade that has little to do with the typical Baroque of his period. The palace houses the **Museo Civico di Arte Antica** (also closed for restoration), with a notable collection of medieval and Renaissance sculpture and painting, stained glass, and books and manuscripts. Among the highlights of the museum's holdings, if anyone is ever allowed in again to see them, are the illuminated 14th-century law codes of the city of Turin, several unique pieces of 15th-century glassware, copies of the famous *Book of Hours* of the Duc de Berry, illustrations by Jan Van Eyck, and the superb *Portrait of an Unknown Man* (1476) by Antonello da Messina, one of his last works.

Under the arcade flanking the north side of Piazza Castello, the **Armeria Reale** (*open 2.30–7.30pm Tues, Thurs; 9am–2pm Wed, Fri, Sat; adm*) contains one of the finest collections of medieval and Renaissance arms, armour, and guns in the world; the library upstairs contains a famous self-portrait in red ink by Leonardo da Vinci.

## The Royal Palace and the Cathedral

The dark apricot **Palazzo Reale** (*open 9am–2pm Tues–Sun; guided tours only; adm*) lies just off the Piazza Castello, behind a gate of mounted 'Dioscuri' and Turin's largest parking lot, which doesn't do much for its already bureaucratic façade. This, however, was the main residence of the princes of Savoy from 1646 until 1865, and you can take the tour to learn that they lavished a considerable amount of their subjects' taxes on a tired architectural lullaby with chandeliers and fluffy frescoes. The cases of Chinese porcelain try hard to relieve the anomie. The Palace's **Gardino Reale** is a far more pleasant place to while away an afternoon, with the Mole Antonelliana (*see* below) rising above the trees like the headquarters of Ming the Merciless.

The former royal chapel, **San Lorenzo**, stands on the corner of Piazza Castello. Although the outside is bland, an unusual octagonal dome its only distinguishing feature, the interior by Guarini (1668–80) is an idiosyncratic Baroque fantasia. Between the Palazzo Reale and San Lorenzo, the **Museo Nazionale del Cinema** is housed in the Palazzo Chiablese, commemorating Turin's role in the early days of Italian cinema, with early projectors, posters, and much more, and in normal circumstances screenings in the winter and spring in a replica of an early theatre (but currently also closed indefinitely for 'works').

Around the corner is Turin's plain **Cathedral of San Giovanni** built by three dry 15th-century Tuscan architects. What it lacks in presence it compensates for with one of the most provocative artefacts of Christendom: the **Shroud of Turin**, brought to the city from the old Savoy capital of Chambéry in the 16th century by Emanuele Filiberto. To house the relic properly, Guarini designed the striking, black marble **Cappella della Sacra Sindone** or Chapel of the Holy Shroud, crowned by a bold oliaphonous dome-cone zig-zagging to a climax of basketweave arches full of restless energy. The chapel is at time of writing closed indefinitely for restoration, but much of it can well be appreciated from outside.

The shroud, shown only on special occasions, is kept in a silver casket in an iron box in a marble coffer in the urn on the chapel altar; an exact replica, however, is displayed in the cathedral along with a multilingual explanation of the results of several scientific investigations, which tried to determine whether it was possible that the shroud was used at Christ's burial. Although forensic scientists and their computers have concluded that it would have been impossible to forge the unique front and back impressions of a crucified man with a wound in his side and bruises from a crown of thorns, the shroud failed a carbon-dating test in 1989, and is now believed to date from the 12th century.

Besides the shroud, the cathedral contains in its second chapel a fine polyptych of SS. Crispin and Crispinian by Defendante Ferrari, and a copy of Leonardo da Vinci's *Last Supper*, painted when the original began to crumble. Near the cathedral's campanile are the remains of a Roman theatre, while across the piazza stands the impressive Roman gate, the **Porta Palatina**, with its two unusual 16-sided towers. On Saturdays the circular **Piazza della Reppublica** is the site of the 'Balôn' antique and flea market.

More of ancient Augusta Taurinorum lies to the north along Corso Regina Margherita: a fine museum of artefacts, the **Museo delle Antichità** (*open 9–1, 3–7, Tues–Sat; 9am–1pm Sun; adm*) at No.105, and at the **Consolata Church**, just off the Corso on Via Consolata. The Consolata is a regular ecclesiastical hodgepodge, with a Roman tower adjacent to its apse, an 11th–century campanile inherited from the demolished church of San Andrea, and two churches, a hexagon and an oval, knitted together by Guarini.

## The Mole Antonelliana

Turin's towering, idiosyncratic landmark, the **Mole Antonelliana** on Via Montebello (*open 9am–7pm Tues–Sun; adm*), which translates as 'Antonelli's massive bulk', can be seen from many corners of the city. Begun in 1863 by the quirky Piedmontese architect-engineer

Alessandro Antonelli, the Mole was intended originally as a synagogue. The project ran out of steam until 1897, when the city completed it, and declared it a monument to Italian Unity. Nowadays it serves mainly as an exhibition hall.

Standing some 167m high, the Mole is a considerable engineering feat. It manages to be harmonious and bizarre at the same time—a vaguely Greek temple façade, stacked with a colonnade, a row of windows, a majestic, sloping glass pyramid, a double-decker Greek temple, and a pinnacle crowned with a star, which the city illuminates at night. The Mole has been a lightning rod of madness   Nietzsche thought it was marvellous then permanently went over the edge. There is a lift up to the observation terrace (86m up) for a fine view of Turin and the Alps beyond.

The lively, arcaded **Via Po**, two blocks from the Mole, is the main funnel from the centre down to the river; it is also the main artery of the city's student life. Although founded in the 14th century, Turin University never gained the prestige of the schools in Padua, Bologna, Naples, Salerno, or Pavia. Its headquarters since 1720, the **Palazzo Università**, lies a block down from Piazza Castello on Via Po; in its courtyard there's a plaque to Erasmus, the most renowned of its alumni. Via Po widens out to form the long and bewildering **Piazza Vittorio Veneto**, half street and half parking lot, giving onto a bridge over the Po. Across the river, in a commanding setting, stands an imitation Pantheon, the **Gran Madre di Dio** church, while on the wooded hill to the right, on the **Monte dei Cappuccini**, stands the Capuchin church and the **Museo Nazionale della Montagna Duca degli Abruzzi** (*open 8.30am–7:15pm Tues–Fri; 9–12.30, 2.45–7.15, Sat–Mon; adm*), dedicated to Italy's mountains and their geography and folk traditions.

## Parco del Valentino

Back along the west bank of the Po stretches Turin's largest park, the **Parco del Valentino**, named after the 1660 **Castello del Valentino**, built by Madama Reale Maria Cristina, who felt her royal dignity required a French château. This lost château now does time as the university's School of Architecture, with the city's **Botanical Garden** laid out beneath it, but it isn't the only castle on the block; Turin built another one, along with a mock medieval hamlet, the **Castello e Borgo Medioevale**, as part of its 1884 Exposition. The houses are modelled on various traditional styles found in Piedmont, while the castle is furnished with baronial fittings (*castle open 9.30am–6pm Tues–Sat; 10.30am–6pm Sun; adm, free Fri; Borgo Medioevale open 8am–8pm daily; adm free*). A place near the castle loans out bicycles by the day, while along the riverbank you can rent a rowing boat for a fish-eye view of Turin. At the end of Parco del Valentino are the massive buildings of the Turin Exhibition, where it holds its famous springtime Auto Show in even-numbered years.

## The Motor Museum

Three kilometres south of the Parco Valentino, at Corso Unità d'Italia 40, is the modern **Museo dell'Automobile Carlo Biscaretti di Ruffia** (*open 10am–6.30pm Tues–Sun; adm exp*). Founded in 1933, its present quarters are an elephantine vintage-1960s exposition hall; highlights of the collection include the classics of the great age of Italian car design—Lancias, Maseratis, Alfa Romeos, Italicas, and of course Fiats—as well as some oddities like the asymmetrical 1948 Tarf 1. Further along the Corso d'Italia is another huge exposition hall, the **Palazzo del Lavoro**, built in 1961 by Pier Luigi Nervi.

One last museum, the **Galleria d'Arte Moderna** (*open 9am–7pm Tues, Wed, Fri, Sat; 9–1, 3–9, Thurs; 9–1, 2–7, Sun; adm*), is in another corner of the city, off Corso Vittorio Emanuele west of the Porta Nuova Station, on Via Magenta. It has one of Italy's best collections of modern art, with works by Klee, Chagall, Modigliani, Renoir, Picasso and others.

## Basilica di Superga

Northeast along the Po, on the metropolitan fringe, a rack railway will take you up to the stately Baroque **Basilica di Superga** (*trains run April–Sept 9.30–12, 3–6, daily; Oct–Mar 10–12, 3–5, daily*). The delightful trip through the greenwood culminates

*Museo dell' automobile*

with Juvarra's acknowledged masterpiece, built on top of a commanding 672m hill to fulfil a vow made by Vittorio Amedeo II during the French siege of Superga. Two fine towers flank a magnificent drum dome, set above a deep neoclassical porch; the crypt contains the tombs of Vittorio Amedeo II and subsequent Kings of Sardinia. The views from the top stretch from the city to the snowy Alps. Another fine viewpoint, east of Turin, the **Colle della Maddalena** (770m) is also the site of the mile-and-a-half-long **Parco della Rimembranza**, a memorial to Turin's First World War dead, planted with some 10,000 trees and crowned by a **Victory** with her torch (1928), the largest cast bronze statue in the world, nearly 18m tall.

**Pessione**, 19km east of Turin, has Italy's best wine museum, the **Museo Martini di Storia dell'Enologia**, (*open 9–12.30, 2.30–5.30, daily*) where the history of wine-making is vividly recounted, and some of the end products are available for sale.

## Stupinigi

Nine kilometres southeast of Turin, past the dreary suburbs of Mirafiori and the Fiat works, Stupinigi is the site of Vittorio Amedeo II's grand hunting lodge, the **Palazzina Mauriziana di Caccia**, (*open April–Sept 10–12.30, 2–6, daily; Oct–Mar 9.30–12, 2–5.30, closed Mon and Fri; adm exp*) built by Juvarra in 1730 on land belonging to the royal Mauritian Order, which now again owns the surrounding park and 'hunting lodge'. The lodge is actually a magnificent, asymmetrically complex Rococo palace, although the statue of a stag perched on the top, statues and frescoes of hunting scenes by Carle Van Loo, and *trompe-l'œil* scenes of hanging game remind the visitor of the palace's original purpose. The main oval salon is especially lovely, and was used for royal wedding receptions. The Mauritians run Stupinigi as a furniture museum.

Turin is a good shopping city, with the smartest shops around Via Roma and Piazza Castello, including such names as Chanel, Max Mara and Fendi. Two of the best places for strolling and window shopping, if not necessarily for buying, are the city's great *gallerie* off the Via Roma. There are a number of local designers of note who have resisted the move to Milan, perhaps most prominently Borbonese, which does stylish costume jewellery and 'partridge eye' leatherwork. Another good buy in Turin are fine chocolates, *gianduiotti*, named after Gianduia, a comic figure associated with St John's Day. Art books and very expensive books in English are available at the **Libreria Luxemburg**, Via Cesare Battista 7, near Piazza Carignano, and a cheaper range can be found at **Susan's Book Shop**, Via S. Quintinos, 8. For bargains, don't miss the Saturday morning 'Balon' flea market in Piazza della Repubblica.

## Sports and Activities

During the season, from September to May, you can take in a match played by two of Italy's premier first-division **football** clubs, Juventus or Torino, both of whom play in the **Stadio Comunale**, Strada Altessana 131, ✆ 7380081 (tram 9). In the summer the city's finest outdoor swimming hole is the **Lido di Torino**, in pools overlooking the Po at Via Villa Gloria 21 (on the west bank, between Parco del Valentino and the Auto Museum).

*Turin ✆ (011–)*                                                    **Where to Stay**

Turin's hotels tend to be either modern, expensive, and designed for business clients, or cheap and fairly seedy, with little in between. Nearly all are within easy walking distance of Porta Nuova Station.

### very expensive

★★★★ **Turin Palace**, Via Sacchi 8, ✆ 5625511, 🖷 5612187. For comfort and convenience, this is Turin's top choice. It is a traditional old grand hotel across from the Porta Nuova station which has spacious, soundproof rooms that land guests gently in the lap of luxury, as well as opulent public rooms and an excellent restaurant.

★★★★ **Jolly Hotel Principi di Piemonte**, Via P. Gobetti 15, ✆ 5625693, 🖷 5620270, is one of the most elegant hotels in the Jolly chain, with beautiful antique public rooms and luxurious bedrooms fitted out with every convenience an auto magnate could wish for, including a well-stocked minibar and cable TV.

★★★★ **Jolly Hotel Ligure**, Piazza Carlo Felice 85, ✆ 55641, 🖷 535438 which is directly opposite the Porta Nuova station is another in the Jolly chain, not quite as opulent as its brother, but a fine choice nevertheless. A freshly scrubbed 19th-century exterior hides a slick modern interior with extensive conference facilties, good restaurant and well-insulated, air-conditioned rooms. It also has facilities for disabled visitors.

★★★★ **Villa Sassi**, Via Traforo del Pino 47, ✆ 890556, 🖷 890095, is located in the hills east of the Po, in a lovely park; it is the most evocative hotel in the city, with 12 rooms in a building converted from a 17th-century patrician villa. In its conversion it has maintained most of its original features—marble floors, Baroque fireplaces, and portraits—and each room has been individually designed. The Villa also has one of Turin's finest restaurants, El Toulà (*see* below). You do need a car. (*Minimum stay three days; closed Aug.*)

*moderate*

★★★ **Victoria**, Via Nino Costa 4, ✆ 5611909, ✉ 5611806, is tucked away in a very pleasant part of town, near the centre, but in a quiet area. It has to be one of Turin's most attractive hotels in this category, recently refurbished and with lots of character—each room has been separately designed with many individual touches, and hydro-massage baths in some rooms. There's no restaurant, but a breakfast room, a garden and lovely reception rooms.

★★★ **Genova & Stazione**, Via Sacchi 14, ✆ 5629400, ✉ 5629896, is another good choice near Porta Nuova station; it has excellent, recently renovated rooms, all with TV and private bathrooms.

★★★ **Hotel Piemontese**, Via Berthollet 21, ✆ 6698101, ✉ 6690571, newly refurbished, also comfortable, and not far from the station. No restaurant, but there is a garage.

★★★ **Roma & Rocca Cavour**, Piazza Carlo Felice 60, ✆ 5612772, ✉ 5628137, is a very pleasant, more personal option, which has retained all its character as one of the oldest hotels in town. Each room is different, some modern and small, others old-fashioned and huge. There are satellite TV and sound-proofing in all rooms, and disabled facilities. Prices, moderate during peak seasons, drop into the inexpensive range at other times, and there's a 30% discount at weekends.

★★★ **Hotel Gran Mogol**, Via Guarini 2, ✆ 5612120, ✉ 5623160, is slick and modern and part of the Best Western chain. The wonderfully named hotel has been recently renovated, and its rooms now feature satellite TV and all other mod-cons, and it has parking and conference facilities.

★★★ **Nazionale**, Piazza CLN 254, ✆ 5611280, ✉ 538989, is also good and just off the main square it has large, comfortable modern rooms and bathrooms, a good restaurant and a garage.

*inexpensive*

★ **Alfieri**, Via G. Pomba 7, ✆ 8395911, is among the cheaper (and cheap places—mostly seedy dives—are plentiful in Turin, in the streets flanking Porta Nuova). It is one of the best, offering 11 rooms in a quiet, central area, at a very reasonable price, with some singles for under L30,000.

★ **Canelli**, Via San Dalmazzo 7, ✆ 546078, is shabbier, but very popular with young travellers. Its rooms are adequate, and all have bathrooms.

**Ostello Torino**, Via Alby 1, ✆ 6602939, the town's youth hostel, is on the other side of the river, near the Piazza Crimea (bus 52 from the station). It has very pleasant, renovated rooms at L16,000 a head, bed and breakfast. (*Closed 9am–6pm.*)

The kitchens of Piedmont are famous for their flavoursome and sophisticated specialities, combining the best of Northern Italian cuisine with the traditions of Provence. *Grissini* (breadsticks) were invented in Turin and so charmed Napoleon that he introduced them over the border. White truffles are a local obsession, and are often served grated in a *fonduta* (with melted *fontina* cheese from the Valle d'Aosta). The wintertime speciality, *bagna cauda*, a rich hot dip made with butter, olive oil, garlic, anchovies, and cream, is often served with *cardi*, raw artichoke-like thistle, or roasted meats. *Bolliti misti* (mixed boiled meats) and *fricandò* (Piedmontese stew) are other popular *secondi*, while the classic first course is *agnolotti*, pasta squares similar to ravioli, stuffed with meat or cheese. The pastries are among the best in Italy—the *Bocca di Leone* is a sinfully rich calorific heavyweight, *torta di nocciole* a divine hazelnut torte.

### very expensive

Turin's temple of fine cuisine, the **Vecchia Lanterna**, Corso Re Umberto 21, ✆ 537047, is a subdued and classy turn-of-the-century restaurant. The food is an artistic achievement—specialities include gourmet delights like quail pate, ravioli filled with duck and covered with truffle sauce, shellfish salad, a wide variety of stuffed trout, sea bass in the old Venetian style, and much more, accompanied by a perfect wine list. Be sure to reserve. (*Closed Sat evenings, Sun, Aug.*)

Turin's oldest restaurant, **Cambio**, at Piazza Carignano 2, ✆ 543760, opened in 1757, offers a nostalgic trip back to the old royal capital, where the menu invites you every Friday 'to eat like a king', with dishes that were served by the Savoys to their guests. The décor, the chandeliers, gilt mirrors, frescoes and cream coloured walls, red upholstery, and even the costume of the waiters, have all been carefully preserved—Prime Minister Cavour's favourite corner, where he could keep an eye on the Palazzo Carignano (if he were urgently needed a handkerchief would be waved from the window) is immortalized with a medallion. The old recipes have, though, been lightened to appeal to modern tastes. Antipasto choices include *cardi in bagna cauda*; other specialities are *agnolotti*, trout with almonds, boar, beef braised in Barolo, and *finanziera*, Cavour's favourite dish (made of veal, sweetbreads, cock's combs, and porcini mushrooms, cooked in butter and wine). Top it off with a slice of homemade tarte tatin, all for a kingly bill. (*Closed Sun, Aug.*)

Another of Turin's best, **El Toulà**, is a little way outside the city, in the **Villa Sassi** hotel. Its menus feature garden-fresh ingredients from the estate, and there is a renowned wine cellar containing over 90,000 bottles.

### expensive

Less regal than the most renowned establishments, but still charming, the **Due Lampioni**, Via Carlo Alberto 45, ✆ 546721, serves a delightful array of antipasti, many featuring salmon, scampi, and lobster. In the spring try the *gnocchi agli'asparagi*, followed by rack of lamb, or tournedos with foie gras. (*Closed Sun, mid-July–mid-Aug.*) **Montecarlo**, Via San Francesco da Paola 37, ✆ 830815, is one of Turin's most romantic restaurants, located in the atrium of the palazzo of the notoriously well-loved Contessa di Castiglione. Under the stone arches a delectable variety of antipasti (marinated swordfish, a flan of peas and scampi) may be followed by carrot soup with barley and well-prepared *secondi* like baked liver, lamb, or duck. The desserts are excellent, as is the wine list. (*Closed Sat evenings, Sun, Aug.*)

### moderate

There are many less expensive choices. **Alberoni**, Corso Mancalieri, 288, ✆ 6615433, is on the periphery of Turin, but compensates by having a pretty terrace over the Po, where you can dine out in the summer on Turin's most die-hard traditional dishes, from *bagna cauda* for starters to *panna cotta* for dessert, accompanied by garden-fresh vegetables. (*Closed Tues.*) **Arcadia**, Galleria Subalpina 16, ✆ 5613898, on the other hand, is a popular lunchtime spot right in the centre, with excellent antipasti, pasta and country-style meat dishes. (*Closed Mon.*).

**Da Giuseppe**, Via San Massimo 34, ✆ 8122090, offers a wide array of Piedmontese antipasti and specialities very popular with local diners; you'd do well to reserve. (*Closed Mon, Aug.*) **La Campannina**, Via Donati 1, ✆ 545405, is a pleasant, very reasonably priced old-style Piedmontese trattoria, with some slightly more elaborate specialities, many with truffles or mushrooms, a delicious risotto al Barolo, and game dishes (chamoix is one of the more exotic choices). (*Closed Sun, Aug.*) **Il Blu**, Corso Siccardi 15bis (a few blocks from La Consolata church) ✆ 545550, with prices near the bottom of this range, stars enormous, delicious salads and excellent pasta dishes, followed by good grilled meats if you still have room. (*Closed Sun, Aug.*) **Trattoria Toscana**, Via Rattazzi 5, ✆ 595513, also offers good food and plenty of it at accessible prices. (*Closed Sat, Aug.*)

### inexpensive

For a light meal under the arcades of Piazza Carlo Felice, across from the Porta Nuova Station, join the crowd at the **Ristorante Brek**, a trendy self-service place with islands of salads, soups, fresh breads and so on, where you can get a full meal for around L16,000. Another popular choice with those not wanting to spend too much cash is **Lullaby**, Via XX Settembre 6, ✆ 531024, which serves delicious, filling local fare in a still-smart but unpretentious atmosphere. It's hard to spend over L20,000, and it's one of the few restaurants in Italy with no *coperto*!

---

### Entertainment and Nightlife

There's always something to do in Turin. Anyone interested in taking a look at the industrial heart of the city might like to know that tours of the **Fiat works** are possible by inquiring at the company's office on Corso G. Marconi 10. On another plane entirely, **St John's Day** (24 June) is Turin's big folklore festival. If you'd like to know the future, Turin's sedate fortune-tellers and sorcerers run their operations around Porta Pila.

### opera, classical music and theatre

Turin's opera house, the **Teatro Regio**, in Piazza Castello, was rebuilt after a fire in the seventies, and is one of the few modern ones in Italy. From late autumn to late spring it stages ballet and symphony concerts as well as opera; call ✆ 8815241 to see what's coming up, or enquire at tourist offices. The grand old **Teatro Carignano**, Piazza Carignano, is used for theatre performances.

In July and August the city sponsors the **Punti Verdi**, a festival of plays, ballets, and concerts, performed in Turin's parks by international companies. **Settembre Musica**, logically enough in September, is another festival that's entirely devoted to classical music, featuring two concerts a day in the city's theatres and churches. Look for posters or check the listings in *La Stampa*.

### cafés

 No visitor to Turin, hot-chocolate fan or not, should pass over the city's most distinctive and seductive catering establishments—its grand 19th-century **cafés**, lavishly decorated with gilt, mirrors, chandeliers and art nouveau swirls, where sober, white-coated waiters have been serving tea, coffee and cakes to local ladies (and other clients) for over a hundred years. They're rarely cheap, but their chocolate, cakes, sandwiches and ice cream are usually superb, and they're very much part of the atmosphere of the city. Classic cafés include **Baratti & Milano**, in the Piazza Castello near the Galleria Subalpina, largely unchanged since 1873; the **Caffè Torino**, Piazza San Carlo 204, famed for its cocktails; and the beautifully decorated **Mulussano**, Piazza San Carlo 15.

### bars, clubs and discos

Turin's **nightlife** may not be quite as kicking as that to be found in Bologna or Milan, but there are still a fair amount of bars and clubs to choose from. Best areas to look around are the student area of Via Po leading down to Piazza Vittorio Veneto, and across the river on Corso Moncalieri. An excellent little book to pick up at the tourist office is *Torino Giovani*, which, although in Italian, gives full listings of what's going on in the city relevant to young people.

The **Brittania Pub**, Via Carlo Alberto 34, is where the odd homesick English-speaker might be found. It can look pretty authentic, but doesn't really capture the atmosphere. For cringeworthy fun, the **Blob Karaoke Club**, Via dei Mille 24, ✆ 837547, is as bad as it sounds. Best to go with a group so you feel no shame in singing along to Golden Italian Greats. In contrast, **Doctor Sax**, Lungo Po Cadorna 4, ✆ 878416, is hip and happening, with a selection of jazz and African rhythms. More jazz can be found at **Leri Jazz Club** Corso Vittorio Emanuele II 64, ✆ 546042, which has a more traditional feel to it. Rock fans might want to investigate **Manhattan**, Via Giachino 46, ✆ 218054, which hosts live rock and blues during the week.

For later-hours nightlife, be prepared to dig deep in your pockets, as most clubs are out of town and cost at least L15,000–25,000 admission. The ticket usually entitles you to a free drink, and official closing time is at 3am, though some will stay open way beyond this. **Hennesy**, Via Traforo del Pino 23, ✆ 890079, is *the* place to be seen, with all the latest top tunes and beautiful people. **El Patio e Invidia**, Corso Moncalieri 346/14, ✆ 674089, is much nearer to town but not quite as trendy, as is **Studio 2** on Via Nizza 32, ✆ 6502355, also popular at the moment.

Gay clubs are few and far between in Turin, but a good source of information is the **InfoGay** phoneline, ✆ 4365000.

## West of Turin: the Susa Valleys

Some of the most spectacular and accessible scenery in Piedmont lies in the Upper Valleys of Susa. Skiing is the main attraction in the winter, and the resorts are especially popular among the French, who find the prices considerably more congenial than those on the other side of the Alps. Old villages and churches are a constant reminder that this corner of Italy sat out the Renaissance; whereas Baroque dominates in Turin, Romanesque monuments grace the Valle di Susa.

### Getting There

**Trains** from Turin go through the Valle di Susa to the French border at the Mont Cenis Tunnel (note that only local trains make more than a few stops en route) and there are frequent SADEM **bus** services from Turin bus station to Susa, Pinerolo, Sestriere, and Claviere, which also call at most of the valley villages.

**By road** drivers can now take the A32 *autostrada* along the Valle di Susa into France and reach Sestriere and the high valleys in little more than an hour, but anyone wanting to see the area itself will prefer the SS25 road which runs more or less alongside it. To get to the Valle del Chisone an alternative route to take is the SS23 or SS589 out of Turin past Stupinigi and Pinerolo, and then the SS23 up into the valley.

### Tourist Information

There are tourist offices in the **Valle di Susa** at Avigliana, Piazza del Popolo, ✆ (011) 938650, and much further up in the ski resorts of **Sauze d'Oulx**, Piazza Assietta, ✆ (0122) 858009 ✆ 850479, and **Bardonecchia**, at Via della Vittoria 44, ✆ (0122) 99032, ✆ 980612. In the Valle del Chisone there are offices at **Claviere**, Via Nazionale 30, ✆ (0122) 878857; and in **Sestriere**, at Piazza G. Agnelli 11, ✆ (0122) 755444, ✆ 755171.

## Turin to Susa

**Rivoli**, the first large town west of Turin, once the residence of the Savoys, preserves one of their 18th-century castles, now a museum of contemporary art. The 12th-century **Abbey of Sant'Antonio di Ranverso** is five kilometres further west in Buttigliera Alta. The unique façade of the church, dominated by three high-pitched gables over the three doors, dates from the quattrocento; inside (*open 9–12, 3–6, Tues–Thurs, Sat, Sun*) fine frescoes from the same period by Giacomo Jaquerio adorn the walls, and the altar has a polyptych by Defendante Ferrari (1531). Outside are the remains of a medieval pilgrims' hostel.

**Avigliana**, the next town, is a Romanesque gem, with many fine buildings clustered about the medieval Piazza di Conde Rosso, including two churches and a 12th-century castle of the Savoys. From Avigliana it's 14km up to the most provocative church in Piedmont, the **Sacra di San Michele** (*open April–Sept 9–12.30, 3–7, daily; Oct–Mar 9–12.30, 3–5, daily*), an abbey founded around the year 1000 on the 615m ridge of Monte Pichiriano, overlooking the Dora Riparia valley and the Alps beyond. (An alternative route up to the abbey is a stout 2-hour trek up the mule path from Sant' Ambrogio di Torino, on the main valley road.)

Like all mountaintop shrines dedicated to the Archangel Michael, the Sacra is a strange place, full of mysterious, half-pagan nuances, a temple dedicated to God's celestial aide-de-camp, built like a seal over an ancient dragon's lair. Similar churches are thought to have had roles in medieval initiation rites, and it's significant that the Sacra di San Michele is located just off one of the main pilgrimage routes to Rome—the pilgrimage itself being an important rite of passage of the faith. The Sacra di San Michele, piled on a complicated mass of 90-foot substructures, is reached by the covered *Scalone dei Morti*, the 154-step 'Stair of the Dead' hewn out of the rock, and under the *Porta dello Zodiaco*, the Romanesque carvings of the zodiac. The ceiling of the mostly 12th-century church is supported by a massive, 18m stone pillar; in the crypt are buried the early dukes and princes of the House of Savoy-Carignano. The abbey was suppressed in 1622.

## Susa

The fine old town of Susa (Roman *Segusio*) may sound Persian, but actually was the seat of the Gaulish chieftain Cottius. Cottius was the kind of fraternizing Gaul that Asterix and Obelix would have liked to slap around with a menhir, one who so admired the Romans and Augustus that he erected the fine **Arco d'Augusto** in the emperor's honour, carved with reliefs of a triumphant procession. Augustus returned the compliment by making Cottius a prefect, and naming the Cottian Alps after him. Other remains of ancient Segusio lie above the Arco d'Augusto, including another arch, baths, and part of an aqueduct. The 11th-century **castle of Countess Adelaide** (the one who gave her hand to Otho of Savoy in 1045) dominates the pretty medieval **Piazza della Torre**; inside there is a **Museo Civico** with a small archaeological collection. (*Open April–Sept 3.30–5.30pm Tues–Sun; Oct–Mar 2.30–4.30pm Thurs, Sun only*.)

The centre of Susa is overlooked by the massive tower of the **Cathedral of San Giusto**. Dating from the 11th century, it contains the the prized *Triptych of Rocciamelone*, a Flemish brass portraying the Virgin, saints, and donor, made in 1358; another chapel houses a polyptych by Bergognone. Note the rare 10th-century baptismal font, made of serpentine.

From Susa the Monte Cenis road leads to **Giaglione**, a tranquil hamlet spread out under the mountains; its **Chapel of Santo Stefano** has unusual 15th-century exterior frescoes of the Virtues and seven Deadly Sins. On 22 January the village celebrates its patron's feast day with a 'Dance of the Swordmaker', Another ancient village visited from Susa, **Novalesa**, has the ruins of a Romanesque Benedictine abbey and chapels, one of which, **Sant'Eldrado** is still in use and contains good 13th-century frescoes.

# The Upper Valley

From Susa the road ascends steeply, past the ancient villages of **Gravere** and **Chiomonte**, the latter also the first of the valley's important ski resorts; the nearby hamlet **Ramats** produces a good local wine. **Exilles**, further on, lies under a mighty fortress that long dominated the valley; illuminated at night it seems to spill over the hill like molten gold. Exilles also has a fine 11th-century parish church.

**Oulx, Sauze d'Oulx**, and **Bardonecchia**, at the crossroads of several valleys, near the Mont Cenis Tunnel, are fashionable winter sport centres in what the Italians like to call the Via Lattea, or 'Milky Way'. Sauze d'Oulx, the 'Balcony of the Alps', and its plateau **Sportinia**, surrounded by a fine natural amphitheatre, are especially popular with Italian and foreign ski-package tours. They are also adored by motorcyclists, some of whom attempt to scale the **Chamberton**, apparently the highest point in Europe accessible by bike. There are also tennis and riding schools, and the town has, in season, the most in the way of nightlife in the area. Bardonecchia, a pretty village of old stone houses known as *grangia*, is an even more developed resort, with summer skiing on the Sommeiller glaciers (3000m), skating, an indoor tennis, swimming and sports centre, riding, hiking and boating in addition to downhill and cross country skiing. Bardonecchia has four separate ski areas with their own lifts; one, Fregiusia-Jaffereau, is for experts only. Inside the village, there is a small **Museo Civico** (*open April–Oct 10.30–12.30, 5.30–7.30, daily; in winter by request, © (0122) 999350*) in Piazza Vittorio Veneto which houses various local artefacts, old costumes and tools from the area. The best views in the neighbourhood are from **Monte Colomion** (2026m), reached by a chair lift.

The **Mont Cenis Pass** was a favoured French route into Italy, used by conquerors from Hannibal and his elephants (one of several possible routes proposed by scholars) to Charlemagne and Napoleon, who began the carriage road in 1808. The **Mont Cenis tunnel**, or Traforo del Frejus, at 12.8 kilometres, is the second-longest road tunnel in Europe, opened in 1980, though the rail tunnel was finished back in 1871. It was a bad business for Marseilles, which lost much of its importance as an eastern port, but a boon to the port of Brindisi and the rest of Europe in the increased speed in communications with that part of the world.

---

# The Valle del Chisone

The 'Milky Way' of winter resorts sweeps around the Upper Susa Valley to **Cesana** and its ultramodern satellite **Sansicario**, lying at the junction of the road to Oulx. Besides being a ski resort, Cesana is also a good base for summer walks, as is **Claviere**, lying just below the **Monginevro Pass** (the Roman *Mons Janus*). This was the favoured pass of the Roman emperors and Napoleon (again) in his frequent comings and goings. The Roman god Janus had two faces, and his mountain does, too; Italian Claviere on one face and French Montgenèvre on the other, which nevertheless share lifts and ski passes.

**Sestriere**, Piedmont's most fashionable playground, was never a real village, but planned as a summer and winter resort, with tall cylindrical hotels and modern flats and hotels, as charming as university dormitories. But the mountains are the main attraction, and Sestriere boasts exceptional slopes and lifts, cross country trails, ice tracks for winter races, a skating rink, and more; in summer you can try to shoot par at Europe's highest golf course, or play tennis or ride.

Above Sestriere are the old villages of **Sauze di Cesana** and **Grangesises**, with traditional wooden Alpine houses, and the tiny village and lovely wooded valley of **Argentiera**, a popular destination for cross-country skiers and hikers. A smaller resort, the old town of **Fenestrelle**, lies further down the valley.

At the foot of the Valle del Chisone stands **Pinerolo**, once the capital of the Princes of Acaia, predecessors of the Savoys. Splendidly situated at the junction of two valleys, it preserves several memories of its day as a capital, including the 14th-century **Palazzo dei Principi d'Acaia**, the Romanesque church of **San Maurizio**, with the princes' tombs, the Gothic **cathedral**, and several streets of medieval houses. In the 17th century the **Fortress of Pinerolo** belonged to the French (who called it *Pignerol*), and here, between 1668–78, they imprisoned the mysterious Man in the Iron Mask. Further south, between Pinerolo and Saluzzo lies **Cavour**, birthplace of the great Prime Minister and 'architect of Italian unity'.

## Pinerolo and the Waldenses

The Valle del Chisone and the Val Péllice, south of Pinerolo, are commonly known as the **Valli Valdesi,** or Waldensean valleys. The Waldenses were followers of Peter Waldo of Lyon, who, like St Francis of Assisi, was the son of a wealthy merchant who renounced all his possessions to preach the gospel; unlike Francis, however, Peter Waldo deeply criticized the corruption of the Church, and was branded a heretic instead of a saint.

Condemned by a Lateran Council in 1184, his followers, many from the south of France, took refuge in Piedmont's secluded valleys. The Waldenseans joined up with Protestantism during the Swiss Reformation, but were frequently persecuted, especially under Carlo Emanuele and Louis XIV of France, in 1685. They briefly took refuge in Switzerland, but returned in 1698 to reconquer their mountain valleys. Vittorio Amedeo of Savoy agreed to tolerate them as his subjects, although they had to wait until 1848 to gain complete freedom of religion. Today nearly every town in Northern Italy has a small Waldensean community; **Torre Péllice** is their centre, with a Waldensean college and small museum. It is also a base for scenic excursions up the valley to **Bobbio Péllice** and **Villanova**, which still has a flood embankment built with money sent by the Waldenses' great supporter, Oliver Cromwell.

---

*✆ (0122–)*                                                                                         **Where to Stay**

### Susa

The ★★★**Napoleon**, Via Mazzini 44, ✆ 622855, ✉ 31900 (moderate), is the top place to stay, with a garage and fairly good restaurant in addition to its comfortable rooms, all with bath. Between Chiomonte and Frais, near Susa, there is a youth hostel, the **Ostello lo Yoti**, ✆ 54492 (inexpensive) with beds for L12,000 per night.

## Sauze d'Oulx

The ★★★★**Capricorno**, in Le Clotes, ✆ 850273 (expensive) is a very pleasant eight-room lodge reached by chairlift. Very intimate and quiet, it's open all year, and has doubles only. You'll have to reserve well in advance to get a room here. The ★★★**Savoia Debili**, Via Clotes 20, ✆ 850185, @ 850613 (moderate) is just above the town centre, enjoys good views and has big rooms with modern bathrooms, and a restaurant. ★★**Villa Daniela**, Via Monfol, ✆ 850196 (moderate) is smaller and more personal, with a very pleasant little restaurant. ★★**Stella Alpina**, Via Miramonti, ✆ 850120 (moderate), is English-run, has recently been refurbished, and is worth the slightly higher cost. (*Open Dec–April, July–Sept.*) The ★★**Florida Prata**, Via Villaggio Alpino, ✆ 850195 (inexpensive), is one of the best-value places in town, with good size rooms and bathrooms.

## Sestriere

The ★★★★**Grand Hotel Sestriere**, Via Assietta 1, ✆ 76476, @ 76700 (very expensive) is the most luxurious and elegant on the slopes, with an indoor pool, spacious rooms, and a fairly good restaurant. (*Open 3 Dec–5 April.*) The twin towers that dominate Sestriere belong to two establishments of the Club Méditerranée: the ritzy one, the ★★**Duchi d'Aosta**, ✆ 77123, @ 77125 (expensive) has comfortable if functional rooms. Reservations for both this hotel and **La Torre**, (*see* below; expensive) can be made at the Club's offices at Largo Corsica dei Servi 11, Milan, ✆ (02) 704445. (*Open mid-Dec–30 April; full board only.*)

The ★★★**Miramonti**, Via Cesana 3, ✆ 755333, @ 755375 (moderate) is a good little hotel with single rooms only, new like everything else in Sestriere (*Open all year except 11 Oct–19 Nov.*) ★**La Torre** is the cheaper of the two Club Med towers, ✆ 77123, @ 77125 (moderate) with more simply furnished rooms. (*Open mid-Dec–30 April; full board only.*)

## Bardonecchia

The best hotels are the ★★★★**Des Geneys-Splendid**, Viale Einaudi 21, ✆ 99001, @ 999295 (moderate), which enjoys a tranquil setting in the trees and has more character than many resort hotels. (*Open mid-Dec–mid-Apr, July–mid-Sept, all rooms with bath.*) Also the very pleasant ★★★★**Park Hotel Rosa**, Viale della Vittoria 37, ✆/@ (0122) 999848 (moderate) has recently been refurbished, and also has a small and attractive garden. Other good choices include ★★★**Ca' Fiore**, Via Melebet 2, ✆/@ 96591 (moderate), a cosy and modern hotel on the road out of town. All rooms have bathroom and balcony, with wonderful views.

The ★★★**Riky Grand Hotel**, in the middle of Bardonecchia, ✆ (0122) 999353, @ 999355 (inexpensive), is ultra-modern and very comfortable, yet offers full board for under L80,000. (*Open Dec–first week of April, July–Aug; full board only.*) ★★**La Quiete**, Via San Francesco 26, ✆ (0122) 999859 (inexpensive), lives up to its name, as inside it's warm and cosy, log-cabin style, with good-size rooms all with TV, phone and bathroom, and some with balcony.

## Susa

For an excellent meal, **Del Pesce**, Via Monte Grappa 25, ✆ 622217 offers good solid Piedmontese cooking with a French touch, as in gnocchi Paris-style. The wine list is just as good, but prices remain in the moderate category.

## Bardonecchia

The restaurants in Bardonecchia are mostly fairly simple; **Tabor**, Via della Stazione 6, ✆ 999857, is one place that doesn't just slap out plates of mediocre pasta for the crowds, yet keeps to moderate-level prices.

## Sestriere

Among the restaurants in Sestriere, **La Baita**, Via Louset 4/a, ✆ 77496 (moderate) is famous for its polenta, served with hare, boar, or tamer dishes. (*Closed Tues.*) And for something completely different, try **La Tana della Volpe**, Monte Banchetta Sestiere, ✆ (0122) 70169, (moderate) set in the mountains above the town. After a delicious meal, guests ski back to town carrying flaming torches! Do reserve beforehand.

### Entertainment and Nightlife

Sauze d'Oulx has the most in the way of nightlife, especially around the bars. The best in town are **Moncrons**, Via Monfol, a very friendly English-run place with good music and reasonable prices, **Gossips**, Via Chaberton, with live music until 3am, and **Lampioni**, Via Assietta, which also serves food until 3am. The most popular, though not necessarily the best, disco in town is **New Life**, Piazza Miramonti, playing mainly Europop and chart sounds; whereas those in the know head to **Subway**, Via Clotes, which has a funkier atmosphere and more varied music. Both are open until 3am and charge around L15,000 for admission. In Bardonecchia, **Clacson**, Via Medail 38/a, plays a mix of house/techno/chart, depending on the dj's mood. (*Open until 3am; adm.*)

## North of Turin: the Valli di Lanzo and Ivrea

### Getting There

**Trains** on a regional rail line head north from the Torino Ceres station in Turin into the Valli di Lanzo, as far as Ceres, and to Cuorgné. For the valleys further north, trains run from Turin to Aosta about every two hours, stopping at Ivrea. Any destinations not on the rail line can easily be reached by SADEM **bus** services.

To reach the Valli di Lanzo **by road**, take the provincial road P2 from Turin to Caselle airport, and then continue on towards Ciriè. For destinations further north, both the A5 *autostrada* and the SS26 run from Turin to Aosta via Ivrea. For the Orco valley and the south side of the Gran Paradiso, take the SS460 directly from Turin through Rivarolo.

## The Valli di Lanzo

The northern valleys are much less visited than the Valle di Susa and Valle del Chisone. The long arm of Turin's industry extends as far as Cirè, but just beyond the outskirts of the metropolis lies the beautiful park of **La Mandria**, formerly used by royal hunting parties, with a toy palace of a hunting lodge; grander digs were built in 1660 at nearby **Venaria**, with Baroque flourishes added later by Juvarra. Although now it is used as a barracks, part of it may be visited. **Lanzo Torinese** is a pretty town, and a base for excursions into the branching valleys; its most famous monument is the 1378 **Ponte del Diavolo** spanning the River Stura. Impressive even today with its soaring single arch like most medieval bridges, the architect was none other than the devil himself. **Usseglio**, in the Val di Viù (bus from Lanzo) is a fine little ski resort.

The railway from Turin peters out at **Ceres**, a summer excursion centre at the fork of two pretty valleys. Buses from Ceres continue up the Val Grande to **Forno Alpi Graie**, the base for several good walks; another bus winds up the Valle d'Ala to the small ski resort of **Balme**, passing by way of **Ala di Stura** with a chair lift, and **Mondrone** with a lovely waterfall.

## Turin to the Valle d'Aosta

A pretty glacier-carved amphitheatre, the Canavese is a peaceful woody region. Its capital is Ivrea (Roman Eporedia), famous for its carnivals and typewriters. It reached its peak of influence in 1002, when its Marquess Arduin was crowned King of Italy. Up in the narrow lanes of the old town stands the 11th-century **cathedral**, which, despite an unfortunate neoclassical façade, preserves the original towers by the apse and dome. Here and there you can pick out pieces from older buildings, including Roman columns and a sarcophagus. Artworks include 12th-century frescoes, and paintings in the sacristy by Defendante Ferrari. The mighty **Castle of Ivrea**, built in 1358, guards the River Dora with four lofty towers. In 1908 the Olivetti-office machine company was founded in Ivrea, and continues to dominate the town's economy. South of Ivrea is pretty lake Candia, guarded by a 14th century castle and surounded by vineyards producing Doc Erbaluce and sweet Plassito di Canluso. West of Ivrea, the N565 leads into **Gran Paradiso National Park**. It passes through the ancient town of **Cuorgné** (also linked separately by rail from Turin), with a cluster of fine medieval buildings, especially on Via Arduino, where King Arduin once resided. **Valperga**, just south, has an attractive castle and church from the 15th century; both towns are known for cottage industries producing beaten copper. From Cuorgné the road follows the River Orco, the scenery becoming increasingly splendid as it nears the waterfalls around **Noasca**. The peaks of Gran Paradiso rise up majestically around the meadows of **Ceresole Reale** at the park entrance; the 'Reale' in its name is derived from a battle in 1544, when French troops of Francis I defeated the army of Emperor Charles V. It stands on the banks of a deep blue lake among the rough and tumble snowy giants that frown down from above.

## Valle d'Aosta

At French-speaking **Pont-St-Martin**, the road from Turin enters the autonomous Valle d'Aosta—one of the most spectacularly beautiful regions in Italy. Rimmed by the highest mountains in Europe—Mont Blanc (4807m/15780ft), the Matterhorn (Cervino in Italian,

4478m/14,690ft), Mount Rosa (4554m/15200ft) and Gran Paradiso (4061m/13,402ft), the Aosta valleys are one of Europe's most popular summer and winter playgrounds, dotted with lakes and serenaded by rushing streams. Emerald meadows lie beneath great swathes of woodlands; hills and gorges are defended by fairytale castles. With Piedmont, Aosta shares one of Italy's most beautiful and largest national parks, **Gran Paradiso**. The opening of the Mont Blanc tunnel (1968) and Great St Bernard tunnel (1964) have created an international boom in winter sports in the region, while *autostrade* link the resorts with Turin and Milan. The Valle d'Aosta has been compared to a leaf, traversed by a main vein (the Dora Baltea valley) with a dozen smaller veins, or valleys, branching off on either side. Each valley has its own character; in most of them French or Provençal is the dominant language, although Italian is understood everywhere. English comes in a poor third, outside of the major resorts. Although the Valle d'Aosta has traditionally owed allegiance to the House of Savoy, from the 11th to the 18th century it governed itself by an Assembly of the three estates, a Council, and its own body of law, the *Coutumier*. Union with Italy aggravated linguistic differences, a wound which Mussolini proceeded to rub salt in with his policy of cultural imperialism that insisted on the use of Italian. In defiance, the Aostans played a leading role in the Resistance, and in 1945 the region was granted cultural and a certain amount of administrative autonomy. Most towns are officially bilingual.

## Skiing

The major resorts in the Valle d'Aosta are Courmayeur, Breuil-Cervinia, St-Vincent, Brusson, Pila, and Cogne, but there are many smaller, quieter, and less expensive bases; write ahead for the region's ski handbook with maps of the slopes, lifts, and facilities in each of Aosta's valleys. Prices on the sunny side of the Alps are, like the weather, milder than in France or Switzerland, but can be very high by Italian standards. High season at the resorts, when prices go up about 15 per cent, are in force during Christmas–first week of Jan; second week of Feb–mid-March; Easter holidays; and July–Aug. If you come during the peak periods, reserve at least three months in advance. Although picking up a week's ski package (*settimana bianca*), including hotel and ski pass, from a travel agent is the easiest and least expensive way to go, families and groups of more than two may save money by writing in advance to the Aosta tourist office for their list of privately owned self-catering flats in the region (*elenco di apparta-menti da affittare*); but again, be sure to do so several months in advance.

**Trains** from Turin or Milan (a 5-hour trip, changing at Chivasso) go through the main valley as far as Pré-St-Didier. The valleys are all served by **buses**, run by the SAVDA company, though services to some of the smaller valleys are infrequent. Regular **coach** connections include Turin (also by SAVDA) or Milan to Courmayeur/Chamonix; Turin–Chamonix–Geneva (2 a day); Aosta–Val d'Isère–Col Iseran (1 a day); Aosta–Martigny (2 a day). In summer additional services include Genoa–Alessandria–Courmayeur; Courmayeur–San Remo–Rimini; and Aosta–Florence–Rome. There are regularly scheduled excursion buses in summer from Aosta to Mont Blanc, Lake Geneva, and the Two Savoys/Annecy.

The main **roads** that run up the middle of the Valle d'Aosta are the A5 *autostrada* and the SS26, from which the SS27 breaks off at Aosta to go up to the Great St Bernard pass. Both main roads can be heavily congested at times with commercial traffic.

The most breathtaking way to enter Aosta is by **cable car** from Chamonix over the glaciers of Mont Blanc to Courmayeur. It's expensive (L90,000 round trip) but unforgettable, especially if you're lucky enough to catch the mountain without its frequent veil of mist. The cable car runs during the ski season and in July and August, leaving roughly every hour.

The central office of the regional tourist organization is in **Aosta**, at Place Chanoux 8, © (0165) 236627, ✆ 34657. They have an office in Rome, at Via Sistina 9, © (06) 4741044, ✆ 4823837. As well as the usual services they provide very complete information on hiking routes in all the Aosta valleys, and publish a useful monthly listings booklet, *Dove, Come, Quando*, with information on restaurants and entertainments of all kinds, plus a little history, in four languages including English. Branch offices in the valley are at **Courmayeur**, at Piazza Monte Bianco, © (0165) 842060, ✆ 842070; **St-Vincent**, at Via Roma 50, © (0166) 512239, ✆ 513149; **Breuil-Cervinia**, at Via J. A. Carrel 29, © (0166) 949136, ✆ 949731; **Ayas-Champoluc**, Via Varasc, © (0125) 307113, ✆ 307785; **Gressoney**, Villa Margherita, St-Jean, © (0125) 355185, ✆ 355895; and in **Cogne**, at Place Chanoux 36, © (0165) 74040, ✆ 749125.

## The Eastern Valleys

### Pont-St-Martin and the Val Gressoney

Besides its stunning Alpine splendour, the Valle d'Aosta is known for its picturesque castles and Roman remains that seem to mark every narrow defile and bend in the valleys. One of Italy's most remarkable Roman bridges, dating from the 1st century BC, lies just within the region, at **Pont-St-Martin**; a span later attributed to the devil. According to legend he made a deal with the village: the bridge for the first soul that wandered across, only to be cheated when St Martin sent a dog over at dawn. Pont-St-Martin itself is a fine old town, encompassed by vineyards that produce one of Aosta's finest wines.

At Pont-St-Martin two valleys meet: the main Valle d'Aosta along the River Dora, and the wide and pleasant **Val du Gressoney** (or Val de Lys), gracefully meandering up to the crystal glaciers spilling off mighty Monte Rosa. The natives of the Val du Gressoney are Walser, who speak neither French nor Italian but an obscure dialect of German, having migrated here from the Swiss Valais in the 12th century. Their valley is utterly wholesome, with a solid family feel to it; their traditional Alpine chalets, with wooden balconies bursting with pots of geraniums, are a vision as fresh as childhood and Heidi. The main resorts of the valley are **Gressoney-St-Jean**, with its **Castello Savoia**, and the loftier, trendier **Gressoney-la-Trinité**, both good bases for laid-back skiing and walking holidays, the latter with chairlifts up Monte Rosa and ski facilities shared with the Val d'Ayas, the next valley to the west. **Issime**, on the way up from Pont-St-Martin, merits a stop for its gabled parish church, with a façade frescoed with a large 16th century scene of sinners taking their licks in the Last Judgement as a warning to all passers-by. Issime is a small climbing centre and, like most of the valley, prefers to speak German; oddly the next village, **Gaby**, only 4km away, is an island of French Provençal.

## Pont-St-Martin to Issogne

From Pont-St-Martin, the main valley road continues past the **Donnaz** station, with the impressive remains of the Roman highway hewn 200 yards into the living rock, and then through the narrow **Gorge de Bard**. At the other end, the gloomy **Fortress of Bard** looms up on its promontory, over the village of the same name; in 1800 Napoleon slipped his cannons past in the dead of night, spreading the road with sacking and straw to muffle their wheels. Picturesque old **Arnaz**, the next village up the valley, has a number of medieval houses and an intriguing Romanesque church built around the year 1000, adorned with 15th-century frescoes. Another ancient town, **Verrès**, lies at the junction of the Val d'Ayas, a crossroads defended by the massive, almost cubic **Fortress of Verrès** (*open for tours April–Sept 9–6, Oct–Mar 10–4; closed Wed; adm*), looming up on its promontory. Built in the 14th century by the Lord of Verrès, Ibelto di Challant, it's a stiff climb up from the town (or a quick drive). Although a treat for true castle fiends, most people will find the nearby residence of the Challant lords, the **Castle of Issogne** (*open April–Sept 9–7 Tues–Sun; Oct–Mar 9–12.30, 2–5.30, Tues–Sun; adm exp*), far more enchanting, with a frescoed courtyard that lacks only knights and fair ladies dallying by the fountain, in the shade of the mysterious iron pomegranate tree; the upper apartments, with their period furnishings and tapestries, are equally evocative.

## Val d'Ayas

Thickly forested with pines and chestnut groves, the Val d'Ayas winds northwards, with Monte Rosa on the right and the Matterhorn on the left, a walker's paradise and a good place to see traditional, massive Alpine chalets. The first *comune* of hamlets from Verrès, **Challant-St-Victor**, was the cradle of the noble Challant family who ran Aosta before the Savoys and their duke; their ruined castle still hangs over Villa, the main settlement. An even more impressive derelict castle stands further up the Val d'Ayas in **Graines**—an intriguing, 13th-century ruin with a Romanesque chapel. You can reach it from the little resort of **Arcesaz**.

**Brusson** lies at the crossroads of the Val d'Ayas and the scenic road through the pine forests of the **Colle di Joux** from St-Vincent (*see* below). Brusson has good holiday facilities amidst its scattered hamlets; one of the best excursions is to walk up to the miniature mountain lakes under Punta Valfredda. From Brusson the road climbs steeply to the picturesque villages of **Lignod** and **Antagnod**, both enjoying fine views of Monte Rosa, then to the most important resort in the Val d'Ayas, **Champoluc**. Here, you can take the cableway and chair-lift to the slopes just below **Testa Grigia** (3315m), one of the grandest belvederes of the Western Alps. A guide is recommended if you want to continue up all the way to the summit, an ascent rewarded with a breathtaking panorama of Mont Blanc, the Matterhorn, Gran Paradiso, and Monte Rosa, with a sea of peaks paying court around these mighty kings. Lift installations link the ski slopes of Champoluc with those of Gressoney-La-Trinité in the next valley. Beyond Champoluc the road ends at quiet Saint-Jacques, an excellent base for walks in the lovely, uninhabited valleys on either side of the village.

## St-Vincent and Châtillon

The valley widens at St-Vincent, the 'Riviera of the Alps', an élite spa for the rich and dissipated since the 18th century, boasting more than a mild climate and waters these days, with one of Europe's largest casinos. Besides blackjack, other St-Vincent activities include excursions through the shady chestnut groves and mountains to **St Germain Castle** in **Montjovet**, or up the funicular to the source of the mineral spring, the **Fons Salutis**, or a cultural call at St-Vincent's frescoed Romanesque church, built over the baths of a Roman villa. (*Open 6.30am–12, 2–7.30, daily.*)

The main road continues to the Valle d'Aosta's second city, **Châtillon**, given over to industry and with little to detain the visitor apart from another **Challant castle**, completely renovated in the 18th century (closed to the public), and a **Roman Bridge**. This, however, is where many travellers leave the train to catch a bus up Valtournenche.

## Valtournenche and Breuil-Cervinia

Valtournenche is Italy's picture window on the fabled Matterhorn (in Italian, Cervino), its unique profile rising up majestically at the top of the valley, and visible from nearly every point. The first small resort in the Valtournenche, **Antey-St-André**, is known for its healthy, mild climate. Roads from here branch off to the west for **Torgnon**, a very quiet base for walks in the woods, and to the east for **La Magdeleine**, a small settlement with ski facilities. For complete tranquillity, take the cable car from **Buisson** to the otherwise inaccessible hamlet of **Chamois**; from Chamois a chair lift continues up to the lovely green banks of Lake Lod and the ski slopes in the winter.

**Valtournenche**, the valley capital, is a popular ski resort, and hometown of the renowned Matterhorn guides—memorial plaques posted around the church are a grim reminder of the dangers they face. From Valtournenche you can get a cable car up the **Cime Bianche**, or take a dramatic walk along the specially constructed galleries through the **Gouffre des Buserailles**, a narrow gorge carved out by the river Marmore above Crépin.

The valley road ends at sparkling new and smart **Breuil-Cervinia**, one of Italy's most renowned ski resorts. It enjoys a uniquely grand setting—the Matterhorn to the north, the sweep of the Grandes Murailles to the west, and the Fruggen massif to the east. The resort dates from the construction of the road up in the late 1930s, and although Breuil-Cervinia may look more like a frontier boom town rather than anything vaguely quaint or even Italian, the mountains are everything, with 190km of ski run, and summer skiing on the glacier at **Plateau Rosà** (3500m); a cablecar and lift from here can take you to the top of Piccolo Cervino, from where fantastic ski trails continue down to Zermatt in Switzerland, or along the valley to Valtournenche. The descents are so lengthy that the KL time trials for the world speed record are held here. Other winter sports at Breuil-Cervinia include ice skating, bob sledding, hockey, and an indoor swimming pool and bowling alley. In the summer months, it is the base for ascents of the Matterhorn for experienced climbers, a feat first achieved from this side in 1867; the route's most precipitous passages are now fitted out with ropes. Other, far less demanding excursions include the easy hike from Plateau Rosà over the **Colle Superiore delle Cime Bianche**, either to emerald Lake Goillet and its view encompassing the Val d'Ayas, or to the summit of the **Breithorn** (4171m); the tourist office has maps and information on the trails and ascents.

## The Mian Valley: Chambave and Nus

West of Châtillon, **Chambave** is a village swathed in vineyards, under a promontory draped with the ruins of the **Castle of Cly**. Chambave produces a rare and prized golden dessert wine called Passito di Chambave. Wine and a modest amount of tourism are the main industries of **Nus**, the next town, a base for visiting two of the region's most remote valleys, the **Val Clavalité**, with the striking **Tersive Pyramid** at its head, or the **Val St-Barthélemy**, with its scattered villages lost in the trees.

The main attraction of Nus, however, is the **Castle of Fénis**, another built by the Challants, the Viscounts of Aosta throughout the Middle Ages. At Fénis, they outdid themselves in creating a genuine fairy-tale castle, all turrets and swallowtail crenellations. Within, the castle's court, chapels, and loggias are covered with fine 14th-century frescoes (*open April–Sept 9am–7pm Wed–Mon; Oct–Mar 9–12.30, 2–5.30, Wed–Mon; adm*). From here it's 13km to Aosta, in the way you can tour the distilleries at St-Marcela and Quart.

---

### Where to Stay

#### Gressoney-La-Trinité

The ★★★**Residence**, Via Elboden 30, ✆ (0125) 366148, ✉ 366076 (moderate), is a modern hotel in a garden with good views. All rooms have baths, and there's a garage on the premises. (*Open Dec–April, July–mid-Sept.*)

#### Val d'Ayas

The ★★★**Hotel Castor**, Via Rameï 2, ✆ (0125) 307117 (phone in the evenings), ✉ 308040 (moderate) is in an enchanting setting in its own grounds in Champoluc, with breathtaking views of Monte Rosa. It has wood-panelled rooms with all facilities, modern bathrooms, plenty of space and a very nice restaurant. (*Open Dec–May, June–mid–Sept.*) The ★★★**Anna Maria**, Via Croues 5, ✆ (0125) 307128 (inexpensive) is a lovely old mountain chalet, brimful of charm and simple, rustic bonhomie in a magnificent setting, with a garden; the food is also delicious. There are both singles and doubles, and some rooms without baths. (*Open Oct–April, June–Sept.*) Lower down the valley in Brusson is the ★**Beau Site**, Rue Trois Prois Village 2, ✆ (0125) 300144, (inexpensive) modern, cosy and warm and very reasonably priced, with singles and doubles.

## St Vincent

The ★★★★**Grand Hotel Billia**, Viale Piemonte 18, ✆ (0166) 5231, ✉ 201799 (very expensive) is one of those elegant, terribly grand turn-of-the-century hotels, originally built to take advantage of St-Vincent's curative mineral springs—which it still does, although it is also a magnet for those who come to get soaked at its roulette tables as well. The rooms are superb, many enjoying excellent views. Amenities include an indoor pool, sauna, tennis, and a large, lovely park.

Near the centre of St-Vincent is the ★★★**Posta**, Piazza 28 Aprile 1, ✆ (0166) 512250, ✉ 537093 (inexpensive) which has comfortable if not very glamorous rooms and a nice little garden. The ★★★**Haiti**, Via E. Chanoux 15/17, ✆ (0166) 512144, ✉ 512937 (moderate) is the top choice in this category, with modern rooms, with lots of space and light, all with TV and phone. A good second choice in the same town is ★★★**Elena**, Via Biavaz, ✆ 512140, ✉ 537459 (moderate) which offers big rooms with balconies and great views, all with marble-fitted bathrooms, and a restaurant next door.

## Breuil-Cervinia

The top hotel is ★★★★**Cristallo**, Strade Piolet 6, ✆ (0166) 943411, ✉ 948377 (very expensive), standing above the town in all its smart, modern glory. It has bold colours and styling, and very comfortable rooms, all equipped with TV; also an indoor swimming pool, tennis, and sauna. (*Closed Sept–Nov.*) Near Breuil-Cervinia, but a bit out of the way, in Avouil, ★**Leonardo Carrel**, ✆ (0166) 949077 (inexpensive) is a fine, basic Alpine chalet operated by a ski instructor. There are 10 pine-panelled rooms, all with bath, and good food in the restaurant. (*Open all year; one week minimum stay.*) The ★★★★**Hermitage**, ✆ (0166) 948998, ✉ 949032 (expensive) is another excellent hotel near the ski lifts, with a pool and garden and well-furnished rooms.

The ★★★**President**, Via S. Jamenet, ✆ (0166) 949476, ✉ 948335 (moderate), in Breuil-Cervinia, offers some of the finest views of the Matterhorn from its windows. Rooms are large and very comfortable, and all have private bath. (*Open end-Oct–May, July–Sept.*) ★★**Les Neiges d'Antan**, ✆ (0166) 948775, ✉ 948852 (moderate) 4km from the centre of Breuil at Perrères, is a pretty Alpine chalet in tranquil surroundings, where the resort's skyscrapers are hidden from view. The rooms are small but pleasant, all with bath, and the restaurant is the best in the area, so even if you don't stay you may want to drop by for a traditional mountain meal of salt beef, polenta, cheeses, Valdostana wines, and homemade desserts. (*Open Dec–April, July–Sept.*)

### Periasc

Near Antagnod, the ★★★**Monte Rosa**, ✆ (0125) 305735 (moderate) is a very pleasant, get-away-from-it-all mountain hotel, with tennis courts and a garden, though not all the rooms have baths.

### Beilciuken

The ★★**Stadel**, on Franzione, 3km from St-Jean, ✆ (0125) 355264, @ 356407 (inexpensive) is one of the more atmospheric places, with 12 very cosy rooms, all with private bath. It is very small and homely. (*Open Dec–April, June–mid-Sept.*)

---

*Eating Out*

### St Vincent

The place to celebrate after a lucky streak is the elegant **Batezar da Renato**, Via Marconi 1, ✆ (0166) 53164, (very expensive) in easy walking distance of the casino, with such delicacies as salmon mousse flavoured with wild fennel, or duck with peaches, or pigeon stuffed with mushrooms, accompanied by a classy wine list. (*Closed Wed, May, end-June–mid-July.*)

### Verrès

There's elegant dining at **Chez Pierre**, Via Martorey 43, ✆ (0125) 92376 (expensive). The menu varies according to season, as does the favoured spot to dine—in winter by the blazing hearth, in summer in the pleasant little garden. Try the *agnolotti alla savoiarda* and venison in bayberry sauce, topped off with a warm slice of apple pie smothered in cream.

If you're looking for slightly more economical dining, some of the best local food can be found in the restaurants in some of the hotels mentioned previously, notably **Les Neiges d'Antan** (moderate) and **Leonardo Carrel** (inexpensive), both are near Breuil-Cervinia.

## Aosta

The 'Rome of the Alps', Aosta enjoys one of the most splendid positions of any Italian city, encircled by regal mountains, divine emanations that appear to support the very sky overhead, and that on clear mornings envelop the city in a total, shimmering blueness, while their brilliant snowy peaks merge with the clouds to form a magic circle around the city. Aosta owes its historical importance to its position at the crossing of roads from the Mont Blanc and St Bernard passes—a piece of sunny Italy at the crossroads of France and Switzerland. Although looped in by industry, army installations and dull, modern suburbs, the city's ancient core, with its grand Roman and medieval monuments, retains its unique charm. The street plan has changed little since the days when Aosta was *Augusta Praetoria*, built in 23 BC, after the conquest of the Salassian Gauls, the terror of the Alps. In the Middle Ages Aosta (a corruption of 'Augusta') was ruled by the Challant Viscounts, and then by the Dukes of Aosta, who owed allegiance to the Savoys. But here the French influence remained stronger than in Piedmont, and you are more likely to hear French or a French dialect in the streets than Italian. Aosta is touristy, but in a relaxed way it is part resort and part an everyday workplace.

As the centre of transport to all sections of the Valle d'Aosta, the city makes a good base; it also has its 'own' ski resort at nearby Pila, and hosts a full calendar of cultural activities. On 31 January it holds the famous **Sant'Oro Fair**, a market dating back to the year 1000, where Aosta's talented woodworkers display and sell everything from ladders and chairs to toys and fine sculpture. In July there's a series of organ concerts, and in October the finals of a peculiar Valdostana sport, the *Bataille des Reines*, the 'Battle of Cows', in which two heifers butt heads.

## Place Emile Chanoux

Aosta is a hard town to get lost in, with its straight Roman streets branching out from the central **Place Emile Chanoux**. Here are Aosta's French-style town hall, the tourist office, and the IVAT (the local handicrafts association), where local arts and crafts are displayed year-round. A short distance from the square tower are the mighty double arches of the **Porta Pretoria**, the original Roman gate, its impressive strength a compliment to the ferocity of the local Gauls. The central arch was used for cart traffic, while the other two were for pedestrians. To the left of the gate stands the lofty façade of the **Roman Theatre**, one of the best-preserved in Italy, with its cavea and scena. (*Open April–Sept 9am–7pm Tues–Sun; Oct–Mar 9.30–12, 2–4.30, Tues–Sun.*) Through the Porta Praetoria, Via Sant'Anselmo is Aosta's main drag, named after St Anselm (1033–1109), Archbishop of Canterbury, the founder of Scholasticism, and a Doctor of the Church, who was born in the street now awash in stuffed St Bernards and garishly labelled bottles of mysterious Alpine elixirs.

Via Sant'Orso to the left leads shortly to the curious Romanesque-Gothic hybrid **Collegiata dei Santi Pietro ed Orso** (*open April–Sept 9am–7pm, Tues–Sun; Oct–Mar 9.30–12, 2.30–5.30, Tues–Sun*), founded in the late 10th century. The church is famous for the rare Ottonian frescoes dating from its construction and for its charming little cloister, begun in 1133, its short columns topped by wonderfully carved capitals of white marble, darkened with an artificial patina. The scenes vary in inspiration, from Biblical stories to mythology; traditionally cloister capitals were one of the few places where monkish sculptors could let their imaginations run wild. The 11th-century crypt contains the remains of Aosta's patron Sant'Orso. Across the lane from the collegiata are the excavations of the palaeo-Christian **Basilica di San Lorenzo** which was built in the 6th century and destroyed in the 9th. (*Closed for restoration.*)

Via Sant'Anselmo ends at the triumphal **Arch of Augustus**, built at the founding of the city, to celebrate the victory over the Salassi; the rather incongruous roof was added in the 18th century. On the other side of the arch and above the river Buthier, a fine, single-span **Roman bridge** has outlasted the channel it once crossed, but is still used by Aostans to pass over the dried-up bed.

## The Cathedral and Forum

From Place Emile Chanoux, Via Xavier de Maistre leads, on the right, to the scanty remains of the **Roman Amphitheatre** and the 12th-century **Torre del Balivi**. To the left is the **cathedral**, off Via Monseigneur de Sales, an ancient church rebuilt several times, with a neoclassical façade hiding a Gothic interior. The stained-glass windows are 15th–16th-century Swiss workmanship, while the choir contains finely inlaid 15th-century stalls, and two excellent mosaics, one a 12th-century *Labours of the Months*, the other a 14th-century scene of Mesopotamia. Next to the choir, behind the glass doors, is the newly arranged **Cathedral Museum** (*open 10–12, 3–6, Tues–Sat; 3–5.45pm Sun; adm*). Although small, the museum contains such outstanding treasures as an ivory diptych from the year 406, portraying the Emperor Honorius, tombs (especially the 13th-century effigy of Tommaso II of Savoy, visible in the choir), and Romanesque reliquaries and statues, all well-described in a free audio guide in English.

In front of the cathedral, in Piazza Giovanni XXIII, are the remains of the **Roman Forum** (*open April–Sept 9am–7pm Tues Sun; Oct–Mar 10–12, 2.30–4.30, Tues–Sun*). Most intriguing here is the huge 92m by 87m **Cryptoporticus** or underground corridor that extended under most of the Forum, though whatever purpose it might have served is a mystery. You can also make out the foundations of a Roman temple under the **Casa Arcidianale**.

Beyond the forum stands a nearly intact portion of the **Roman Wall**, with **La Torreneuve**, formerly belonging to the House of Challant. Other intact sections of the walls remain in the south, near the station, where three towers survive: **Il Pailleron**, in a garden nearest the station, most maintains its Roman character; the impressive, round **Torre Bramafam** was a Challant defensive work; and the third, the **Torre del Lebbroso**, earned its sad name from a family of lepers who were incarcerated here from 1733 until the last survivor died in 1803. It is used today to house temporary exhibitions. (*Open during exhibitions April–Sept 9am 7pm, Oct–Mar 9.30–12.30, 3.30–6.30.*)

*Tomba di Tommaso II*

---

*Aosta ☉ (0165–)*         **Where to Stay**

Aosta is not only the central transport hub for the region, but it's more likely than most of the resorts to have rooms available if you haven't booked in advance.

### very expensive

The best hotel in the region is the very new ★★★★**Hostellerie du Cheval Blanc**, Via Clavalitè 1, ☉ 239140, ✆ 239150, set in its own grounds, slightly out of town. It was designed by the Florentine architect Bartolini, and it's clear that no expense has been spared: the big, ultra-modern rooms are arranged around a central courtyard with emphasis on lots of space and light. There are luxurious suites, all bathrooms have marble and granite fittings and there is also an indoor pool, sauna, gym and extensive conference facilities. It is also home to the finest restaurant in the region (*see* below).

### *expensive*

In the centre, the **★★★★Europe**, Via Ribitel 8, © 236363, ✆ 40566, is an excellent second choice, a cosy, older hotel, with a private garage, and TVs in each room. The **★★★★Valle d'Aosta**, Corso Ivrea 146, © 41845, ✆ 236660, is a kilometre from the centre and used mainly as a stopover by travellers on the *autostrada*. Behind its rippled, modern façade, the furnishings are very comfortable, and all rooms have private baths and minibar.

### *moderate*

If you're driving, the **★★★Rayon de Soleil**, above Aosta in Saraillon, © 262247, ✆ 236085, is a pleasant, medium-sized hotel, with fine views, a garden, and indoor pool. Back in town, best choice is the oddly named **★★★Bus**, Via Malherbes 18, © 43645, ✆ 236962, located in a quiet street off Via Aubert, with rooms that are comfortable and tastefully decorated, ample parking and a good restaurant. **★★★Cecchin**, Via Ponte Romano 27, © 45262, enjoys an enviable position near the Arco Augusto and virtually on the Roman bridge. There are just 10 rooms, all with TV and phone, and a quiet, homely atmosphere. Two other adequate choices in town are **★★★Turin**, Via Torino 14, © 44593, ✆ 361377, with good sized rooms and all mod-cons, albeit fairly characterless, and **★★★Roma**, opposite, © 40821, ✆ 32404, with slightly bigger rooms and cosy public rooms.

### *inexpensive*

The best choice near the station, the **★Monte Emilius**, Via G. Carrel 9, ©/✆ 35692, offers clean, bathless rooms at low prices.

**Rural Tourism** is popular in the region. Full details can be obtained from the tourist office, but possibilities include: **La Ferme**, Azienda Agrituristica, Reg Chabloz 11, © 551647, or **Plan d'Avia**, Turismo Rurale, Loc Avie-Arupilles, © 51126.

---

*Aosta © (0165–)*

### *Eating Out*

### *very expensive*

Gourmets agree that the best restaurant in the entire region is **Le Petit Restaurant** (formerly **Cavallo Bianco**), located in the **Hostellerie du Cheval Blanc** (*see* above). Although it has lost something of the character of its 16th-century setting, it has lost nothing in the way of quality. Two fixed-price menus are offered: one for L95,000, and a gourmet menu at L130,000, with three antipasti, and sorbets between the courses. The menu changes daily, according to market availability, and wines are extra. (*Closed Wed.*)

A traditional favourite in the heart of town, **Piemonte**, Via Porta Pretoria 13, © 40111, features excellent, home-style Piedmontese and French cuisine—*bagna cauda* in the winter, boar steaks in the autumn, crêpes, and apple pie, all at reasonable prices. (*Closed Sun.*) **Vecchia Aosta**, Via Porta Pretoria 4, © 361186, built right into the Roman walls, has the most striking dining room in town. The food is good, too, featuring homemade pasta, cured venison and trout with almonds, and lots of wines to help it down. The **Vecchio Ristoro**, Via Tourneuve 4, © 33238, is housed in a windmill that functioned until only a few years ago. The food is excellent—hot antipasti, smoked trout and salmon, and an especially good selection of local cheeses. (*Closed Sun, mid-July–Aug.*) For lighter, less expensive food, there are also several places along Via Porta Pretoria and Via Aubert that offer pizza by the slice or *tavola calda* service. **Carillon**, Via Aubert 74, © 40106, provides both crêpes and Italian dishes at inexpensive prices. (*Closed Wed.*)

---

## Entertainment and Nightlife

Aosta's night-time life begins about 10pm in any of the bars and cafés that line Via Aubert, Via Porta Pretoria and Via Sant'Anselmo, particularly **Café Aubert,** which attracts a young, hip crowd, and **Café Duc**. Just off the main drag, on Via Croix de Ville, is the only place in town with any character, **Papa Marcel's**, with graffiti scribbled all over the walls, and hundreds of bottles containing weird liquids on the shelves. A must. The best disco in town is **Help**, on Via Aosta (*adm*).

# Around Aosta

Pila, 20km south of Aosta, is the nearest winter/summer resort to the city, with chair lifts up Mt Chamolé (2300m) that operate all year round, though much less frequently in summer. There are trails up the slopes of **Mont Emilius** (3559m), Via Chamolé, that offer stupendous views over the ranges to the north.

More castles loom over the valley west of Aosta, on the Courmayeur road, beginning with the solemn 13th-century **Castle of Sarre** (*closed for restoration*), rebuilt in the 18th century. After the Risorgimento the kings of Italy, who spent 99.5 per cent of their time hunting, used it as one of their lodges, and the interior is still full of trophies bagged in the surrounding valleys. Two other restored medieval castles guard the pretty village of St-Pierre, a bit further on; one, the 14th-century **Sarriod de la Tour**, is used for art exhibitions.

# The Western Valleys

## Aosta to the Great St Bernard Pass

From Aosta at least two buses a day make the 34km trip to the Swiss frontier at perhaps the most famous of Alpine passes, the **Colle del Gram Bernardo** (*closed Nov–May*), its importance now somewhat diminished by the new tunnel, open all year round. The road up (SS27) is uncommonly pretty, affording splendid Alpine vistas through the various valleys and back towards Aosta itself. **Etroubles** is the main resort in the valley, and **Sant Oyen**, in the midst of emerald meadows, is a quieter holiday centre, with skiing at Flassin.

The legendary **Hospice of St Bernard** lies just on the other side of the Swiss border (passports required). According to legend, the great stone monastery was founded in the 11th century by St Bernard, archdeacon of Aosta, and operated by canons from Marigny, who made it their business to minister to weary and snowbound travellers, many of them pilgrims or churchmen en route to Rome. The hospice is located at the exposed summit of the pass (2469m), and to aid them in finding people lost in the heavy snows the canons developed a uniquely hardy breed of dog. Magnificent specimens abound near the hospice, and when not engaged in saving the lives of intrepid skiiers, they happily mug for the cameras of the intrepid tourist.

Before St Bernard, the pass was known as *Mont Jovis*, after an ancient temple of Jupiter Poeninus, and was frequently crossed by Celts and Romans, and later by the Emperors; Napoleon moved 40,000 troops through in 1800 to defeat the Austrians at Marengo.

The Valpelline, branching off from the SS27 at **Variney**, is a handful of unfrequented valleys of unspoiled scenery. Head for **Ollomont**, the base for visiting the lovely Alpine basin known as the Conca di By. There is more fine scenery around the scattered hamlets of **Oyace**, above the river Buthier.

## Val di Cogne and Gran Paradiso National Park

From Aosta and St-Pierre, the Val di Cogne stretches south towards the blunt peak of the Gran Paradiso massif (4061m). The valley's rich magnetite and iron mines were exploited long before its tourism potential; the latter began in earnest with the opening of the national park in the 1920s.

The mouth of the valley is defended by the Challant **Castle of Amayavilles**, its four round-turreted towers dating from the 18th century. Further up, at **Pondel**, the stunning, torrential gorge of the Grand'Eyvia is spanned by a steep **Roman bridge**, still in use today. Beyond lies the *comune* of **Cogne**, a pleasant, busy town that commemorates the traditional source of its livelihood with a fine cast-iron fountain, erected in 1819.

Now a popular resort, Cogne is the main gateway to the **Gran Paradiso National Park**, which encompasses the entire massif in its protected boundaries. Set aside as a Savoy hunting reserve in the 19th century, the park was donated to the state by Vittorio Emanuele III in 1919. It played

*Gran Paradiso*

the lead role in preserving the ibex (or stambecco, or steinbock), a pretty deer-like creature with long, ridged horns, which numbered only 420 in 1945, all of them in the confines of the park. Since then their numbers have increased tenfold, and animals from the park have been reintroduced into many of their old Alpine haunts. Although ibex prefer high altitude, rugged crags, they may be seen around the valleys in the winter and early spring. They share their paradise with the more numerous, shorter-horned chamois, who have a wider range and are more easily spotted—if not here, on a number of local dinner menus. In November and December the males of both species may be seen furiously butting heads for the ladies.

Among the birds you may be lucky enough to see a Wall Creeper, Chough, Golden Eagle, Ptarmigan, Nutcracker, or Black Grouse. The flowers are at their most spectacular in early June; even if you're not up to a long trek over hill and dale to see them, visit the **Paradisia Alpine Botanical Garden**, laid out in 1955 in the lovely **Valnontey** near Cogne. (*Open Jun–Sept 9.30–12.30, 2.30–6.30, daily; adm.*)

Cogne has seven campsites as well as its hotels; within the park there are eight Alpine refuges, many used as hostels during ski season. If you only have a limited amount of time, the best one to aim for is **Vittorio Sella** (2584m), a gorgeous walk away through Cogne's vast meadow of Sant'Orso, up into the deep, flower-spangled vale of **Loson**, a favourite rendezvous of ibex and chamois now that the refuge is no longer a royal hunting lodge. You can return the next day to Cogne through Valnontey.

The western reaches of the park, the lush, unspoiled **Valsavarenche** and the **Val de Rhêmes** may be reached from Villeneuve on the Courmayeur road. In the Valsavarenche, the ideal base is **Dégioz**; from here a track leads up to the Vittorio Sella Refuge, while another, a former royal hunting road, goes to the **Nivolè Pass**, site of yet another former hunting lodge, now the **Rifugio Albergo Savoia**; an alternative route diverges from this at Lake Djuan for the Entrelor pass and the prettily situated village of **Rhêmes-Notre-Dame** in the Val de Rhêmes. The Valsavarenche summer bus terminus, **Pont**, is the base for ascents of Gran Paradiso.

## The Main Valley: Villeneuve to Pré-St-Didier

Medieval castles abound in this region. **Villeneuve** is sprawled under the massive, ruined, 12th-century **Châtel-Argent**, while the next town, **Arvier**, is dominated by the slightly later **Château de la Mothe**. Arvier is even more renowned for its wine, *Vin de l'Enfer*. Here, a road forks for the wild and rocky **Valgrisenche**, dominated by the melancholy **Castle of Montmayeur** high on its rock. The Valgrisenche's main villages, **Planaval** and **Valgrisenche**, have the shimmering Rutor glacier for a backdrop; just beyond the latter towers the massive Beauregard dam and its artificial lake.

Back in the main valley, **Avise** is a charming village with two medieval castles on the hill side. It lies at the foot of a romantic gorge, where the **Pierre Taillée** has remains of the Roman road cut into the rock. On the far side you get your first memorable glimpse of Mont Blanc; above the road to the left, **Derby** has a fine collection of fortified medieval houses, a little Gothic church, and a waterfall, the **Cascata di Linteney**. To the right of the road the landmark is the 13th-century **Châtelard tower** in La Salle.

The medieval tower of **Morgex**, headquarters of the upper main valley, or Valdigne, was the administrative seat of the Savoys in the region. The little resort of **Pré-St-Didier**, just beyond, lies at the confluence of the Dora de la Thuile and Dora Baltea rivers. Its warm chalybeate springs are used for skin complaints; its station is the last rail link in the Valle d'Aosta. From here you can pick up buses to La Thuile or Courmayeur.

## Little St Bernard Valley

At Pré-St-Didier begins the scenic road up to the Little St Bernard Pass, threading forests and dizzily skirting the ravine of the Dora de la Thuile. The town of **La Thuile** is a growing winter resort, with excellent skiing on the slopes of Chaz Dura. In summer the most striking excursion is up to the **Colle San Carlo** and the **Tête d'Arpy**, with an azure lake and remarkable view of Mont Blanc.

Above La Thuile, Mont Blanc also forms a stunning backdrop to pretty **Lac Verney**, a mirror in a setting of emerald meadows. A bit beyond, the **Little St Bernard Pass** (2188m; *open June–Oct*) is marked by a statue of St Bernard on a column and a neolithic **Cromlech**, or burial circle marked by stones, with the ruins of two structures on the side. Just on the other side of the French frontier the ancient **Hospice du Petit-St-Bernard** was founded even before St Bernard, with the purpose of sheltering destitute travellers. Formerly run by the same order as the Great St Bernard monastery, this hospice was bombed during the Second World War, then ceded to France, and has been left abandoned. A former abbot, Pierre Canous, planted an **Alpine botanical garden** here in 1897, which, after years of neglect, has been re-established and reopened. From the pass it's 31km to the first French town, Bourg-St-Maurice.

## Courmayeur

In more ways than one Valle d'Aosta reaches its climax in Courmayeur, which is one of the most stunning, best equipped and most congenial resorts in the Alps. Lying at the foot of Mont Blanc, it is perhaps Italy's most fashionable winter and summer resort, rivalling Chamonix in chic but warmer both in its climate and atmosphere. The skiing is matchless, the scenery mythic in its grandeur, and the accommodation and facilities among the best in the western Alps.

Besides the 100km of downhill ski runs at **Chécrouit-Val Veny**, served by nine cableways, seven chair lifts, 13 ski lifts and helicopters for jet-set thrills, Courmayeur offers magnificent cross-country skiing, ice skating, and an indoor swimming pool: in summer there is skiing on the glacier of Colle del Gigante, a rock-climbing school, golf, tennis, riding, hang gliding, fishing, and spectacular walks, with some 20 alpine refuges in the area.

One thing Courmayeur isn't is a bargain. A one-way trip through the Mont Blanc tunnel will set you back L36,000, and a trip on the thrilling, unforgettable cableway to Chamonix over Mont Blanc and back is L90,000 (passports required), though for L37,000 you can go only part of the way to **Punta Helbronner**, with fantastic views of the mountain. The tunnel itself is entered above Courmayeur, beyond the medieval fortress-village of **Entrèves** and **La Palud**, the loftiest of the scattered hamlets of the Courmayeur *comune*; La Palud is also the base for the cableway to France. Another scenic summer excursion is to take the Funivia Courmayeur, departing from the centre of town, to the **Plan Chécrouit**, and from there up to Col de Chécruit. This pass is the base for climbing **Mont Chétif** (1½ hours), the peak just before Mont Blanc, offering tremendous views into the mighty abyss of the **Aiguille Noire**. An alternative is to take another cable car from the Col de Chécruit to **Cresta d'Arp** (2755m), with more fantastic views and a ski run descending all the way to **Dolonne**. For a less adventurous outing, there is a little

*Monte Bianco* Alpine Museum at the top of town, housing a small collection of various Alpine artefacts. (*Open 9–12.30, 3–6, daily; May–Jun, Oct–Nov, closed Mon; adm*).

Two gorgeous valleys run in opposite directions from Entrèves. The **Val Veny** may be ascended by bus as far as Lac Combal, the base for a fairly easy hike to the Rifugio Elisabetta and from there, a three-hour walk up to the **Colle de la Seigne** which is on the French border, with fabulous views in either direction. The most common ascent of Mont Blanc starts at Lac Combal.

The **Val Ferret** beginning at La Palud is enchanting and serene, the site of a golf course, trout streams, and the finest cross-country walks; there is accommodation in **Plampincieux**, a quiet resort in the pine trees.

---

*Where to Stay*

*© (0165–)*

### Cogne

★★★★**Bellevue** Cogne's poshest hotel, Rue Grand Paradis 20, *©* 74825,  *@* 749192 (expensive), is a very comfortable family-run inn, cosy and well-furnished, in one of the village's prettiest areas. All rooms have private bath and telephones, and most have balconies; there is a garden, a friendly pub, and sauna. (*Open Christmas holidays–Oct.*) ★★★**Petit Hotel**, Viale Cavagnet 19, *©* 74010, *@* 749131 (expensive) is good value for money, with a garden and tennis court and a friendly atmosphere. All rooms have private baths. (*Open all year.*) ★★★**Vallée de Cogne**, Via Cavagnet 7, *©* 74079, *@* 749279, (expensive) is another pleasant little hotel.

### Courmayeur

In Courmayeur Christmas, Easter, July, August, and from the second week of February through to the end of March are high season, when reservations are a must. At other times, if the hotel stays open, you'll find lower prices and more room.

The ★★★★**Pavillon**, (very expensive) Strada Regionale 60, *©* 846120, *@* 846122, is a Relais & Château member which has 40 very cosy, commodious rooms with balconies enjoying priceless views, all furnished with colour TVs as well as anything else you might need. A welcoming large stone fireplace, a mellow bar, a heated indoor pool and sauna, and a good restaurant are the Pavillon's other attractions; perhaps best of all, however, it's a mere 100m from the funivia to Plan Chécrouit. (*Open 3 Dec–2 May, 19 June–3 Oct.*)

Try ★★★**Hotel del Viale**, Viale Monte Bianco, ✆ 846712, ✉ 844513 (expensive) for old-fashioned Alpine charm in Courmayeur. It will win your heart with its woodsy, cosy atmosphere in an attractive old chalet. Private baths, phones and radios are bows to modernity. ★★★**Bouton d'Or** (moderate) Strada Statale 26, No.10, ✆ 846729, ✉ 842152, (moderate) is a pleasant choice in easy walking distance of the centre of town. It offers modern bedrooms with sparkling bathrooms, and often balconies looking up to Mont Blanc, as well as a garden, solarium and sauna. It's owned by the same family that runs the restaurant, **Le Vieux Pommier**.

★★★**Hotel Croux**, Via Circonvalazione 94, ✆ 846735, ✉ 845180 (moderate) in the centre of town enjoys outstanding views and modern bedrooms all with bathrooms and equipped with TV and other amenities. ★★**Petit Meublé** Via Margherita 25, ✆ 842426 (inexpensive) is a pleasant option, with tranquil rooms near the river, a short walk from the centre. All rooms have bathrooms. ★**Bel Soggiorno**, Viale Monte Bianco 63, ✆/✉ 846774, (inexpensive) is a delightful bargain and has ten simple but lovely rooms, showers down the hall except for a few rooms, and an attractive garden.

## Entrèves

★★★**La Brenva** ✆ 89285, ✉ 89301 (moderate) was once a simple royal hunting lodge but has been a hotel since 1897. The décor has changed little since then, though TVs, air-conditioning and private baths have all been added.

## La Palud

In La Palud, up the road, hotels are much more reasonable. ★★**Astoria**, Sr. La Palud 23, ✆ 869740, ✉ 869750, (inexpensvive) is an excellent choice with big, modern rooms in a cosy old style, all with TV and bathroom. ★**Funivia**, Via San Bernardo, ✆ 89924 (inexpensive) also has big rooms, modern bathrooms, old wood furniture and priceless views, at bargain prices.

## Plan Gorret

★★★★**Palace Bron**, ✆ 842742, ✉ 844015 (very expensive), is a luxury white chalet at Plan Gorret which is little more than a kilometre above Courmayeur on a pine forested hill, with beautiful views over the Mont Blanc massif from nearly every room. It's close enough to Courmayeur to be convenient for the slopes, but far enough away to enjoy a rarefied tranquillity. Next to the hotel is an outdoor, lake-like pool; the restaurant and piano bar are elegant. (*Open Dec–April, July–Sept.*)

✆ (0165–)

### *Eating Out*

Courmayeur, as international and trendy as it might be, doesn't usually measure up in the kitchen. Hotel meals are usually watered-down Italo-

French cuisine, while decent non-affiliated restaurants are few and far between. In Entrèves, however, the **Maison de Philippe**, © 896 797, 🖃 896 719 (moderate/expensive) has a fame that extends not just into Italy but also into France and Switzerland as well, and there are those who don't mind paying the tunnel fares just to come over to feast at this jovial temple of Alpine cuisine. And feast is no exaggeration, for if Philippe's all-you-can-eat doesn't bust your buttons, no place will. The décor is charming, rustic without fussiness, and the tables are laid out on three different levels; in the summer you can dine out in the garden. The food, from the antipasti of salami and ham, to the delicious ravioli filled with porcini mushrooms, the tasty fondue, trout, or game, and the grand dessert finale, is all delicious. (*Closed Tues.*) **Le Vieux Pommier**, Piazzale Monte Bianco 25, Courmayeur, © 842281 (moderate), is a tourist favourite with a rustic hyper-Alpine interior and a good solid, Valdostana cuisine. (*Closed Mon, Oct.*)

The best restaurant in Cogne, **Lou Ressignon**, Via Mines de Cogne, © 74034 (moderate) is an attractive chalet serving good, honest Valdostan specialities—chamois (*camoscio*) with polenta for something out of the ordinary, topped off with a good homemade dessert. (*Closed Tues.*)

### Entertainment and Nightlife

In Courmayeur, this is to be found on Via Roma, in a cluster of pubs and bars about halfway down the street. For those missing home, **The Red Lion** attempts to recreate an authentic-English atmosphere with its draught lager and pub memorabilia. Opposite, **Steve's** has a warm atmosphere and cold beers. (*Both open until about 3am.*)

## East from Turin: Vercelli and Novara

East of Turin and north of the Po is a landscape that runs the gauntlet from flood plain to Alpine splendour. This section includes the province of Vercelli and part of Novara; for convenience, the northern part of Novara, from Lake Orta and Lake Maggiore to Domodossola and the Simplon Pass, is dealt with in the chapter on Lombardy and the Italian Lakes (*see* p.269).

### Getting Around

This area is especially well served by **rail**. Frequent trains travel to Vercelli and Novara from Turin and Milan; both cities are also linked with Biella (1 hour). The main rail and road approach to the Valsesia is also from Novara; if coming directly from Turin, you can change trains at Romagnano. Trains run into the valley as far as Varallo (from Novara, 1½ hours), where you can catch a **bus** up to Alagna (another 1½ hours). Other rail links from Vercelli continue south to Casale Monferrato, Asti, and Alessandria, while Novara has trains to Lakes Orta and Maggiore and beyond. An extensive network of **buses** into the alpine valleys operates from Biella.

**By road** the A4 *autostrada* goes directly to Novara from Turin, while the slower SS11 also runs to Novara passing through Vercelli on the way. For Biella from Turin take the SS11 and then turn onto the SS593 in Cigliano. This road joins the SS143 to Biella. The quickest way to drive to the Valsesia from Turin is by the A4 and then the A26 to Romagnano, where you will meet up with the SS299 road which leads from Novara up and along the length of the valley.

---

### Tourist Information

 The main tourist offices in the region are in **Vercelli**, at Viale Garibaldi 90, ✆ (0161) 64631, 🖂 64632; **Novara**, Via Dominioni 4, ✆ (0321) 623398, 🖂 393291; **Biella**: Piazza V Veneto 3, ✆ (015) 351128, 🖂 34612; and **Varallo**, Corso Roma 38, ✆ (0163) 51280, 🖂 53091.

---

## Vercelli

Several million plates of risotto are born every year on the plain between Turin and Milan, a region that is no less than Europe's greatest producer of rice. Its capital, **Vercelli**, is surrounded by a seemingly endless patchwork of paddies divided by hundreds of irrigation canals that criss-cross the plain, dating back to the 15th century. In summer, when they're newly flooded, they become magical, reflecting the clouds and sunset in an irregular checkerboard of mirrors, a landscape bordering on the abstract, uncanny and desolate, melancholy and beautiful.

Of all the cities in Piedmont, only Vercelli stirred from its feudal hibernation in the Renaissance, producing in the 16th century a school of painters, even though the most brilliant of them, Il Sodoma (born in 1477), soon escaped to more promising territory in Tuscany. Even so, as a minor 'city of art' Vercelli is an old, atmospheric place. If you have only an hour between trains, you can take in its chief marvel, the **Basilica di Sant'Andrea**, which looms up just across from the station. The basilica was begun in 1219, funded by Cardinal Guala Bicchieri, papal legate and guardian and 'saviour' of England's Henry III. To thank Cardinal Bicchieri for his aid in obtaining the throne, Henry gave him the the revenues from the Abbey of St Andrew in Chesterton, near Cambridge, and the cardinal used the money to finance the basilica and monastery in Vercelli. Completed nine years later—a lightning clip in those days, thanks to the cardinal's unstinting resources—the basilica, though basically Romanesque, is famous in Italian architectural history as one of the first to display signs of the great new Gothic style from the Ile de France, first adopted by the Cistercian Order; the Gothic whispers in Sant'Andrea's twin bell towers, the flying buttresses, the vaulting in the nave and the plan of the church and cloister.

The change of materials halfway up the façade at first gives the same incongruous impression as a 1960s demi-wood station wagon. The three arched portals are Romanesque, with lunettes over the door attributed to the great 12th-century sculptor Antelami. The lofty interior is majestic and striking in its simple red and white decoration. The cloister, with its cluster columns and sculptural details, is quite lovely, and offers the best view of the unusual cupola and the basilica's Romanesque and Gothic features. The massive detached campanile, in the style of the towers, was added in 1407.

Vercelli's grand 16th-century **cathedral** is a short way to the left, in Piazza Sant'Eusebio; of the original Romanesque construction only the bell tower remains. It has an especially valuable library of codices, including some 11th-century Anglo-Saxon poems perhaps brought to Vercelli by Cardinal Bicchieri. The one saintly member of the House of Savoy, the Blessed Amedeo IX, who died in Vercelli castle in 1472, is buried in an octagonal chapel. From the cathedral, the Via Duomo leads past the **Castello d'Amedeo** (to the left, behind Santa Maria Maggiore), then to Via Gioberti and Via Borgogna, site of the **Pinacoteca Borgogna** (*open 3–5.30pm Tues, Fri; 9.30am–12 midday Sat, Sun*), with paintings by Vercelli natives—most famously Sodoma, Gaudenzio and Defendante Ferrari, as well as works from the rest of Italy.

Via Borgogna gives into old Vercelli's main street, **Corso Libertà**. At No.204 be sure to look in at the lovely courtyard of the 15th-century **Palazzo Centori**. The Corso continues to the main square, Piazza Cavour, where markets are held under the Palazzo Municipio. Down Via Lucca is the Church **of San Cristoforo**, its interior adorned with a famous series of frescoes (1529–33) by Gaudenzio Ferrari, including his masterpiece, the *Madonna of the Oranges*. Vercelli has an interesting archaeological and historical museum, the **Museo Leone** (*open Mar–Nov 3–5.30pm Tues, Thurs; 10am–12 midday Sun*) on Via Verdi, off Piazza Cavour, located in a 15th-century house and Baroque Palace. From Piazza Cavour, Corso Libertà continues into the newer part of town; in Piazza Zumaglini rice prices are decided in the Rice Exchange, or **Borsa Risi**; here, too, is the national rice board's headquarters.

## Novara

Novara is an ancient city, but one that has preserved only a few traces of its past. In the central Piazza della Repubblica there's the restored 15th-century **Broletto**, housing Novara's **Museo Civico**, with paintings by Gaudenzio Ferrari and others from Piedmont, as well as one attributed to Antonello da Messina. Unfortunately, it has been closed for an indefinite period. Across the piazza stands the **Duomo**, built over an earlier Romanesque temple in the 1860s by the flamboyant Antonelli (who designed the Mole in Turin). This time instead of bulding tall, he designed one of the largest doorways in Europe in Europe (38 by 19ft). Parts of the original cathedral survive, including the campanile, the 12th-century chapel of **San Siro**, with contemporary frescoes, the red brick cloister frescoes, and some mosaics in the chancel; there are fine frescoes and paintings by Gaudenzio Ferrari and others of the Vercelli school, and a collection of 16th-century Flemish tapestries. The ancient **Baptistry** dates back to the 5th century, and contains very unusual frescoes of the Apocalypse which were painted in the 10th century.

From the piazza, Via San Gaudenzio leads to Novara's landmark the church of **San Gaudenzio**, designed in the 16th century by Pellegrino Tibaldi and topped in the 19th by Italy's most phallic dome, by the inimitable Antonelli, who crowned this tall, narrow creature with a slender spire and a shining figure of the saint who seems to poke the very sky. San Gaudenzio's equally unusual 8th-century campanile makes an interesting companion piece. Inside, look for Il Tanzio's nightmarish *Battle of Sennacherib* (1627).

# Biella

Easily reached from Vercelli, Novara or Turin, the wool and textile town of Biella is divided into two—the lower half, **Biella Piano** and the upper, **Biella Piazzo**, linked since 1885 by an incline railway. Biella Piano's chief monuments are clustered in the Piazza Duomo: the lovely little **Baptistry**, dating back to the late 10th century, the mighty nine-storey Romanesque **Campanile** of a now-demolished church, and the town's white elephant, the Gothic **cathedral**, unfortunately prettified in the last century.

Biella Piano also has a fine Renaissance church—one of the few in Piedmont—**San Sebastiano**, begun in 1504 and housing a number of works by the Vercelli school, especially Bernardino Lanino's *Assumption*, and some beautifully carved choir stalls. The city's **Museo Civico** (*open 3–5.30pm; closed Wed*) is on Via P. Micca 36, with archaeological finds, ceramics, and paintings.

During the Renaissance, wealthy textile merchants built their showy mansions up in Biella Piazzo, which retains much of its patrician air and offers fine views over the city and surrounding mountains. A three-storey **cotton mill** from 1859 stands near the centre, a reminder of what is still the region's lifeblood. Across the river Cervo, in San Gerolamo Park, the former villa of the great Alpine explorer and photographer Vittorio Sella is now the **International Museum of Alpine Photography**, founded in 1948, with his old equipment and photographs of the world's greatest peaks. To visit, call or write ahead © (015) 23778.

On the map the environs of Biella look like a plate of spaghetti, a confusing network of squiggly yellow valley roads winding between the mountains. The main attractions, all connected by bus with Biella, include the stately, 16th-century castle in **Gagliànico**, 5km from Biella; and 12km to the north, the **Santuario d'Oropa**, the most venerated shrine in Piedmont, founded by St Eusebius in the 4th century when he returned from the Holy Land with the image of the *Black Madonna and Child*, reputedly carved by St Luke.

The sanctuary consists of three vast quadrangles, a new Baroque basilica, and a remnant of the original frescoed church, sheltering the icon, perhaps the most exotic and pagan image in Christian Italy, jet-black and embellished with a towering golden crown, a starry halo, and costly jewels. A cable-way near the sanctuary ascends **Monte Mucrone** (2335m), with its lake, good hiking in summer and skiing in the winter.

In the next valley to the east, **Piedicavallo**, the highest town, is a base for hikes into the

*Battistero di Biella*

Val Gressoney in Valle d'Aosta, or into the Valsesia (*see* below). A few kilometres south of Piedicavallo begins the **Strada Panoramica Zegna**, (SS232), which winds across to the Valsesia, and is noted for its spectacular views of Monte Rosa.

West of Biella, in late spring thick clusters of rhododendrons and azaleas burst into a dazzling pageant of colour on Burcina Hill, in the village of **Pollane**. From here the road twists around to another popular hill sanctuary, **Graglia**, dedicated to Our Lady of Loreto; the Piedmontese mania for hill shrines derives straight from the pagan past. To the southwest of Graglia, at Donato, begins a district known as **'La Serra'** because of its steep green moranic ridge. Oaks, chestnuts, birches, and vineyards grow here in arcadian harmony, dotted with unspoiled villages. At the end of the ridge lies the clear, spring-fed **Lago di Viverone**, an unglamorous but soothing place to camp, swim, fish, or mess about on a boat. There's an 18-hole golf course nearby at **Magnano**.

## Varallo and the Valsesia

The industrial, lower part of this lovely Alpine valley is dotted with textile and cotton mills, but at **Varallo** the scene begins to change. Varallo is a fine, friendly town embraced by wooded slopes; the river Sesia froths and tumbles here, making for exciting white-water kayaking or rafting. Varallo has a good Pinacoteca, with works by the Vercelli school, sharing space with the Natural History Museum in the **Palace of Museums** (*hours change by season — inquire at the tourist office*), as well as a fine church, **San Gaudenzio**, artistically piled on top of a stair, best known for its polyptych by Gaudenzio Ferrari. An entire wall of his work, depicting the Life of Christ, is in the church of **Madonna delle Grazie**, located at the bottom of the steps up to Sacro Monte.

Located high above the town (608m; a cable car also makes the trip up), **Sacro Monte** is the five-star attraction of Varallo. It was founded as the Sanctuary of New Jerusalem in 1491 by the Blessed Bernardo Caimi, who wanted to recreate in Piedmont the Holy Shrines of Palestine. The idea caught the fancy of St Charles Borromeo, the Archbishop of Milan, and when the two holy men were done, the result is nothing tub-thumping less than the Disneyland of the Counter-Reformation. The high altar is gilded, exploding Baroque, but what makes the 'Bible really come alive' are the 45 chapels containing what must be the world's first dioramas—16th-century 3D scenes of statuary with fresco backgrounds—some 1000 statues and 4000 painted figures, depicting scenes from the scriptures. When you can pull yourself away from this sincere but slightly nutty extravaganza, step outside to appreciate the fine **Piazzale della Basilica**, a little gem of porticoes, palm trees and a fountain under a pavilion.

North of Varallo extends the **Val Mastallone**, a scenic valley of deep ravines and Alpine scenery; **Fobello**, famous for its Walser lace-making and embroidery traditions, with a lace museum and school, and **Rimella** are two small resorts. The upper extension of the Valsesia, the **Val Grande**, is more touristy with main resorts at **Riva Valdobbia**, with Monte Rosa as a background and a parish church with curious exterior frescoes. There are a number of walks beginning here, with the hike over the Colle Valdobbia to the Val Gressoney in Aosta the most popular. **Alagna**, the last town in the valley, is a popular summer and winter resort under Monte Rosa, with funiculars up into the massif. The Walser population (who immigrated from the Swiss Valais in the 12th century), have converted one of their wooden 17th-century homes in the charming hamlet of Pedemonte (3km up the road from Alagna) into the **Walser Museum** (*hours change by season*), furnished in the traditional manner.

## Where to Stay

Vercelli isn't exactly a popular stopover, and its hotels are indifferent, whereas Novara and Biella do rather better in the hospitality field.

### Vercelli

★★★**Giardinetto**, Via Luigi Sereno 3, ✆ (0161) 61558, ✉ 62570 (moderate) is one of the best places to stay. It is in its own grounds with an attractive little restaurant and bar. There are only eight rooms, but all are modern doubles with TV, bar, safe and phone. ★★**Da Cinzia**, Corso Magenta 71, not far from the river, ✆ (0161) 253585 (inexpensive) is a convenient establishment in the centre of Vercelli where all the rooms have private baths.

### Novara

★★★★**Italia** is centrally located on Via Solaroli 10, ✆ (0321) 399316, (expensive). The most elegant hotel in Novara, it's very modern, well furnished and comfortable, with a garage and one of the best restaurants in the city, with good rice dishes and some surprises, like chicken curry. The ★★★**Europa**, Corso Cavallotti 38, ✆ (0321) 35801, ✉ 629993 (moderate), is large and comfortable, convenient for both the centre and the station. It has a garage, and all rooms have baths. For a place with a bit of character, try the ★★★**Parmigiano**, Via dei Cattaneo 4, ✆ 623231 (moderate), a family-run hotel. An old façade conceals a sparkling modern interior with clean, simple rooms, and a very pleasant restaurant.

### Biella

★★★★**Augustus**, Via Italia 54 (in the centre), ✆ (015) 27554, ✉ 29257 (expensive); this medium-sized hotel offers very comfortable accommodation, with bath, TV, and minibar in every room. ★★★**Principe** is centrally located at Via Gramsci 4, ✆ (015) 2522003, ✉ 351669 (moderate), and has a friendly bar, and TV in every room.

### Varallo

★**Monte Rosa**, Via Regaldi 4, ✆ (0163) 51100 (inexpensive), Varallo has a few modest inns, one of which is this one with 18 rooms in a tranquil garden, as well as one of Varallo's few restaurants. ★★**Indren**, a few kilometres from the centre of Alagna at Reale Inferiore, ✆ (0163) 91151 (inexpensive), small and simple, serene and in a pretty setting. All rooms have baths, but prices are very reasonable.

### Valesesia

★★★★**Cristallo**, ✆ (0163) 91285, ✉ 91114 (moderate). Although small it has the best accommodation in the resort, with luxurious rooms and lots of mountain atmosphere, but still at moderate-range prices. (*Open Christmas–April, July–Aug.*)

## Roppolo

***Castello di Roppolo**, near Lake Viverone, ✆ (0161) 987313, ✉ 987165 (moderate), has 11 elegant rooms in a former medieval castle, in a lovely setting. Each room is well-furnished, with private bath. The same building also houses the **Enoteca della Serra** wine cellar and restaurant (*see* below).

---

*Eating Out*

## Vercelli

The province of Vercelli is not known for its cuisine, in spite of its rice, though at **Il Paiolo**, Via Garibaldi 72, ✆ (0161) 250577, you can dine well on good hearty risotto at moderate-range prices. (*Closed Thurs.*)

## Novara

The shrine of Novarese cuisine is the **Trattoria del Amicizia ai Tre Scalini**, Via Sottile 23, Novara (expensive). The food—antipasti of the local salame *della duja*, risotto al Barolo or *pasta e fagioli*, and a wide variety of *secondi* is excellent, and accompanied by a good list of Piedmontese wines. (*Closed Sun, Aug.*) Another of Novara's best restaurants, and slightly cheaper, is the one in the **Italia** hotel, and there is also an excellent, moderately priced restaurant in the hotel **Parmigiano**, which is a good place to try out local specialities (for both *see* above).

## Biella

On the road to the Sanctuary of Oropa from Biella, **Il Baracca**, Via Santuario d'Oropa 6, ✆ (015) 21941, (expensive) is the oldest and best place to eat in the area, with Piedmontese treats like *bagna cauda, salame della duja*, rice dishes, and mixed roast or boiled meats. (*Closed Wed.*) To the south of Biella, and in the moderate price range, the **Enoteca della Serra**, ✆ (0161) 98501, shares the **Castello di Roppolo** with a hotel (*see* above). It offers a wide selection of Piedmont's finest wines, local specialities in the adjacent restaurant. (*The Enoteca is open Wed–Sun from March to October, and weekends only for the rest of the year.*)

## The Valsesia

It is not well-supplied with restaurants, and most of the best ones are in hotels. The Monte Rosa in Varallo (*see* above), offers good local fare at inexpensive prices.

## Southeast Piedmont: Alessandria and Asti

When the Turinese or Milanese come to this region on weekends, their thoughts are more on victuals and drink than on sights. Alba and Asti are the main wine-growing centres of Piedmont, producing its most famous wines in a supremely civilized landscape, characterized by lovely, rolling hills and winding roads, and dotted with small villages and fortifications. The region's other speciality, white truffles, *tartufi*, the pungent ambrosia of the Italians, are harvested in the autumn with a barrage of ecstatic festivals devoted to gluttony, and sold at daily auctions in the main towns.

## Getting Around

Alessandria, Casale Monferrato, Acqui Terme, Asti, and Alba are all linked to one another by **rail**, and Alessandria and Asti also have good connections to Turin, Genoa and Milan. To really explore the district's scenic 'wine roads' (*strade dei vini*), though, you need a **car**. The *autostrade* A21 (Brescia–Turin) and A26 (Genoa–Simplon Pass) intersect just outside Alessandria, but you can also get to Asti and Alessandria from Turin on the less stressful SS10, and from Savona on the coast on the slow but sometimes spectacular SS30. Some of the most interesting routes to follow in the region are the SS457, from Asti to Casale Monferrato, and any of the roads leading into the wine region south of Alba.

**Bus** schedules are rarely convenient to many of the outlying villages.

## Tourist Information

Tourist offices can be found in **Alessandria**, at Via Savona 26, ✆ (0131) 51021, ✉ 253656; **Casale Monferrato**, Via L Marchino 2, ✆ (0142) 70243, ✉ 781811. **Acqui Terme**, at Corso Bagni 8, ✆ (0144) 322142, ✉ 322143; Asti, Piazza Alfieri 34, ✆ (0141) 530357, ✉ 538200; and in **Alba**, at Piazza Medford, ✆ (0173) 35833, ✉ 363878.

## Casale Monferrato and Alessandria

Between Vercelli and Alessandria, **Casale Monferrato**, Italy's biggest producer of cement, once held the more glamorous position as capital of the medieval and Renaissance duchy of Monferrato, though it retains few traces of the Paleologhi dukes who held court here—principally, a fairly good Romanesque **cathedral**, and some walls of the old **castle** across the piazza. Monferrato was one of the most important safe havens for Jews in Italy during the Renaissance and Counter-Reformation, and Casale's most unusual monument is its Baroquely ornate **Synagogue**, Via S. Olper 44, (*open 10–12, 3–5, Sun, public holidays only*) built in 1595, which now doubles as a Jewish museum.

**Alessandria**, the provincial capital, was founded in the 12th century by disgruntled nobility from Monferrato who opposed Emperor Frederick Barbarossa and named their new town after his arch-enemy, Pope Alexander III. The city these days is best known as the city of Borsalino hats, famed as the world's finest. The company has its own hat museum, the **Museo del Cappello Borsalino**, which is now normally closed, though if you're interested in visiting you could try inquiring at the tourist office or calling ✆ (0131) 202111. There's little else to see; most impressive is the 12-pointed **Cittadella**, built in 1728 by the Savoys and one of the best-preserved fortresses from the period, with most of its outer works still intact. North of Alessandria, **Valenza** is a major producer of gold and silver jewellery; the goldsmiths' association, the Associazione Orafa Valenzana, has a permanent exhibition of their craft in the centre of town.

Just 8 kilometres south of Alessandria on the Genoa road, Napoleon defeated the Austrians on 14 June 1800 in what he considered the greatest battle of his career, **Marengo**. The battlefield is marked by a column, and in the village there are monuments to Napoleon and General Desaix, who perished on the field, as well as a museum of the battle in the **Villa di Marengo** (*closed for 'works'; inquire at Alessandria tourist office on possible opening times*). Another 6 kilometres further south lies **Bosco Marengo**, birthplace of Pope Pius V (1504–72), whose reign was particularly notable for the victory over the Turks at Lepanto. Pius built the magnificent church of **Santa Croce** in the village to serve as his tomb, a masterpiece of green marble and porphyry. The Romans, however, interred him in Santa Maria Maggiore.

## Tortona and Acqui Terme

**Tortona**, east of Alessandria, was the Roman *Dertona*, and still has a sprinkling of Roman remains, most importantly two monumental tombs at the corner of Viale De Gasperi and Via Emilia. The **Museo Civico** (*temporarily closed for restoration*), in the Piazza Marconi, is housed in a 15th-century palace and contains interesting Roman artefacts and medieval art. From Tortona the railway continues to Voghera, Pavia, and Milan.

More Roman remains may be seen at the spa south of Alessandria on the SS30 road, **Acqui Terme** (Roman *Acquae Statiellae*), most notably the four arches of the **Aqueduct** in the park near the hotel and bathhouse of Antiche Terme. An **Archaeological Museum** (*open 4–7pm Tues–Sat; 10–12 Sun, public holidays*), in the half-ruined Castello dei Paleologhi, contains mosaics and remains from the ancient baths. Next to the castle stands the fine Romanesque **cathedral**, with a good doorway and campanile. The most intriguing site in Acqui, however, is the octagonal pavilion and fountain in the centre of town, called the **Bollente** after the hot sulphuric spring that bubbles up here, leaving the earth amid a diabolical cloud of steam.

---

## Asti

Former rival of Milan, **Asti** is an old and noble city that well repays a visit. Although nowadays synonymous with fizzy wine, Asti is proudest of its poet, Vittorio Alfieri (1749–1803),who ran off with the young wife of the not-so-bonny Prince Charlie. Corso Alfieri is the main street, and all of the city's monuments are within a block of its length. On the Corso's end stands the church and cloister of **San Pietro in Consavia**, built in the 15th century and housing a small archaeological collection (*open April–Sept 9–12, 3–7, Tues–Sat; 3–7pm Sun; Oct–Mar 9–12, 3–6, Tues–Sat; 3–6pm Sun*). Most intriguing, however, is its round baptistry, perhaps dating as far back as the 10th century, supported by eight thick columns with cubic capitals.

Six streets further west, the Corso passes by the large **Piazza Alfieri**, which houses the tourist office and the Public Gardens; behind the piazza is the **Campo del Palio**, the site of Asti's bare-back horse race, a tradition of neighbourhood rivalry dating back to 1275 and revived in 1967. As in Siena, the Palio combines medieval pageantry, daredevil riding, and much feasting and celebration afterwards: it takes place on the third Sunday of September, coinciding with Asti's great wine fair. A week before the Palio, in the *Festival della Sagra*, people from the surrounding villages parade in traditional 19th-century costumes, and present displays recreating cooking and working practices from that era. Their produce is on sale in the Campo del Palio afterwards.

South of the Campo is Asti's train station. Just a short distance from the Piazza Alfieri is the attractive Romanesque-Gothic **Collegiata di San Secondo** (*open 7–12, 3.30–7, daily*), which houses the relics of Asti's patron saint, the Palio Astigiano (the banner awarded at the horse race) and a polyptych by Asti's greatest Renaissance artist, Gandolfino d'Asti. There are several old palaces in the neighbourhood, and medieval towers loom over the rooftops—the tall, elegant **Torre Troyana**, across the Corso, and further down the Corso, the **Torre Comentina**, with the swallowtail merlins of the Ghibelline party, and then the octagonal **Torre dei De Regibus**. Here, detour to the right (north), for the tall **cathedral**, a 14th-century Gothic monument, with Baroque frescoes, paintings by Gandolfino d'Asti, and Holy Water stoups constructed from Roman and Romanesque capitals and columns.

Back on the Corso, there's a museum and wild-eyed bust devoted to Vittorio Alfieri, in his old house, at Corso Alfieri 375 (*open 10–12, 3.30–5.30, Tues–Fri; 10–12 Sat, Sun*). In the basement of the neighbouring Liceo, at Via Gualtieri 1, you can visit the 8th-century **Crypt of Sant'Anastasio**, with notable carved capitals, and the **Museo Lapidario** (*open 9–12, 3–6, Tues–Sat; 9–12 Sun*). On Via Mazzini, across from the Alfieri museum, is the **Palazzo Malabayla**, the finest Renaissance palace in Asti. At the end of the Corso is another of Asti's medieval towers, the **Torre Rossa**, an unusual cylindrical tower on a Roman foundation, with a checkerboard crown. Four kilometres to the north, the **Chiesetta di Viatosto** is a pretty little Romanesque-Gothic chapel on a hill, with quattrocento frescoes inside, and enchanting views over the hilly and fertile countryside to the Alps.

## North of Asti: Monferrato

The province of Asti divides itself into two sections, Monferrato in the north and the Langhe in the south. The gastronomic capital of Monferrato is **Moncalvo** (bus from Asti), with famous wine and truffle festivals. The towers and moats remain of its castle, there's a good Gothic church, **San Francesco**, and many old houses, and most spectacularly, a view of the countryside from the large Piazza Carlo Alberto. Just northeast of Moncalvo, another ancient *Black Madonna*, similar to the icon at Oropa, is venerated at the **Santuario di Crea**. Its 23 chapels contain late 15th–17th century frescoes and statues; the highest chapel, del Paradiso, has more fine views over the vineyards. Another town just northeast of Asti, **Castagnole Monferrato**, holds a special festival on the second Sunday in October, called *La Vendemmia del Nonno* (Grandpa's Grape Harvest), with old-fashioned grape picking, barefoot wine crushing, dancing and music. More sophisticated features include a truffle auction, and stalls

Tartufi d'Alba

serving glasses of Barbera and Grignolina, as well as Ruch 130, a new red dessert wine from the region—accompanied by a huge buffet.

In the northwest, in the middle of the countryside near **Albugnano** (22km from Asti, off the road to Chivasso) the **Abbazia di Vezzolano** (*open April–Sept 9.30–12.30, 3–6, Tues–Sun; Oct–Mar 9.30–12.30, 2–4, Tues–Sun*), is the finest Romanesque building in Piedmont, founded according to legend in 773 by Charlemagne, who had a vision on the site while out hunting. It has a remarkable façade from the early 12th century, adorned with blind arcades and sculpture, and an even more remarkable rood screen that divides the nave in two and is carved with two strips, the upper one depicting the *Four Evangelists* and the *Deposition*, *Assumption*, and *Incarnation of the Virgin*, while the lower one has a cast of solid medieval characters sitting in a row, with their names draped over their chests like beauty contestants. On the high altar are 15th-century terracotta figures of the *Virgin and Child*, worshipped by kneeling figures of *St Augustine* and *Charlemagne*, all under a florid Gothic baldacchino. Part of the **cloister** is even older than the church, with sculpted capitals, while the newer section is adorned with frescoes of biblical scenes and Charlemagne. Between the abbey and Turin, **Chieri** is a fine old town with an especially interesting **Gothic cathedral**, finished in 1436, built over Roman and early medieval foundations; its frescoed baptistry dates back to the 13th century.

---

## Le Langhe and Alba

South of Asti lie the beautiful, fertile hills of Le Langhe, swathed with the intricate woven patterns of the vines that produce Italy's finest red wines—Barolo, Barbera, Barbaresco, Dolcetto, and Nebbiolo. Little villages are clustered on the tallest hills, crowned by their castles, like **Montegrosso**, the main producer of Barbera wine; gastronomic **Costigliole d'Asti**, and **Canelli**, surrounded by vineyards producing muscat grapes, the centre of Asti Spumante production. Most of these castles are now *enoteche*, open for the tasting and sale of the local product—one of the most interesting is in Grinzane, but local tourist offices provide a leaflet with details of all of them (*see* also 'Wines and a Drinker's Itinerary', p.100). **Nizza Monferrato** is the site of the **Bersano Museum**, Piazza Dante 24, ℂ (0144) 721273 (*open Mar–Oct 10–12, 2–6, Mon–Fri*), with a collection of artefacts related to the history of wine.

Further south, the hills become higher, and vineyards give way to hazelnuts and maize. **Alba** is the capital of Le Langhe, on the banks of the Tanaro, an austere medieval city of narrow winding alleys and brick towers, famous for its cuisine and truffles as well as its noble wines. At the beginning of the 16th century it produced its greatest painter, Macrino, whose *Vergine Incoronata* (1501) hangs in the council chamber of the **Palazzo Comunale**, along with the *Piccolo Concerto* by Mattia Preti, a follower of Caravaggio. The highlight of the 14th-century **Duomo** is the choir stalls, inlaid in 1500 by Cidonio. Traditionally a bitter enemy of Asti, Alba is now content to send up its old rival in a donkey Palio complete with clown jockeys the first Sunday in October. But Alba can be serious when it has to deny the Second World War. Its resistance fighters were the bravest in Italy and defended the "Free Republic of Alba" from the Germans for 23 days in 1944.

# Around Alba

Around Alba, hilltop villages, ruined castles and vineyards are set in lovely rolling country. A few kilometres south of the town the oldest Piedmontese enoteca, in the castle of **Grinzane di Cavour**, © (0173) 262159 (*open 9–12, 2.30–6.30; closed Tues, Jan*) is also the meeting point of the 'Order of the Knights of the Truffle and Wines of Alba', and contains a restaurant and a small museum dedicated to wine-making, folk traditions, and the castle's most famous former resident, Count Camillo Cavour. **Barbaresco**, to the east of Alba, and **Barolo**, to the south, have respectively given their names to renowned red wines; in Barolo the 16th-century **Castello Falletti** is used as a vintage cellar, wine museum, and well-stocked enoteca. The village of **La Morra**, the belvedere of Le Langhe, is a good base for walks through the vineyards, and for visiting the former Abbey of the Annunciation, now the **Ratti Wine Museum** (*open 8.30–12, 2:30–6, Mon–Fri*). Nearby, **Verduno** is dominated by a 17th-century castle in Juvarra's elegant Baroque style that was used as a summer residence by King Carlo Alberto. Another good castle, this one from 1340, dominates the concentric village of **Serralunga d'Alba** to the east.

**Brà** has some odds and ends from Roman *Pollentia* (modern Pollenza), in the Gothic Palazzo Traversa on Via Serra and Barnardo Vittone's *S. Chiara* (1742) with a delightful Rococo inteior. **Pollenza** itself retains a circular funerary monument, the foundations of the forum, theatre and amphitheatre with seating for 17,000 reflecting the fortune; Roman *Pollentia* made in textiles, **Cherasco**, south of Brà, is smaller and more atmospheric—the **Torre Civica** in the centre of town has a rare clock of the phases of the moon. The local museum houses an interesting collection of historical and archaeological items. The local castle is a comfortable residence built by the Visconti in the 14th century.

---

### Activities

Organized nature rambles through the vineyards, villages and woods, on horseback or foot (known as 'trekking' in Italy), are popular here, ranging from a one-day stroll to a more strenuous three days, spending the night in castles along the way. For details © (0172) 490018/495300, @ 495110.

---

### Where to Stay

**Farm holidays**, at varying levels of comfort and price, are available throughout this area, for those looking for a return to nature, or perhaps just Piedmontese home cooking. Details are available from local tourist offices, particularly in Asti and Alba, and should be obtainable through Italian tourist offices abroad.

## Alessandria

Alessandria's most comfortable hotel, ★★★★**Alli Due Buoi Rossi**, Via Cavour 32, © (0131) 254444, @ 445255 (very expensive) also has the city's best restaurant. Located in the heart of town, the rooms are luxurious, and the meals feature the full range of Piedmontese specialities. There are several other four-star hotels in Alessandria, but none are particularly impressive for the price. ★★★★**Domus**, Via T. Castellani 12, © (0131) 43305, @ 232019 (expensive) is the best of the bunch, centrally located with small, modern rooms. The ***Londra**, next to the station at Corso Cavalotti 51, ✆ (0131) 251721 (moderate) has adequate, if rather nondescript rooms. **Rex**, Via San Francesco d'Assisi 48, ✆ (0131) 252297 (inexpensive) is bright, modern and centrally located.

## Acqui Terme

In Acqui Terme, you can take the water or mud cure in the pampered environment of the ****Antiche Terme**, Viale Donati, ✆ (0144) 322101, ✍ 324909 (moderate), set in a pretty park, but nevertheless still in the moderate price bracket. (*Open June–end-Sept.*) ***Nuove Terme**, another thermal establishment, at Piazza Italia 1, ✆ (0144) 322106, ✍ 324909 (moderate), also has comfortable rooms, again in a quiet garden setting. (*Open mid-Mar–Dec.*)

## Asti

Just outside Asti (convenient for drivers) is the ****Hasta Hotel**, at Valle Benedetta 25, ✆ (0141) 213312, ✍ 219580 (expensive) which is tranquil and very cosy, with tennis courts, garden, and TV and air-conditioning in every room. It also has a good restaurant, featuring local dishes. ****Alermo**, Via E. Filiberto 13, ✆/✍ (0141) 595661 (moderate) is one of the city's finest hotels, with every room furnished with private bath, TV, and air-conditioning; advance reservations are advisable for the Palio. Enjoying the best position in town is the ****Reale**, Piazza Alfieri 6, ✆ (0141) 530240, ✍ 34357 (moderate) which has large, sumptuously decorated modern rooms all with balconies looking out onto the square, and is extremely good value. A good alternative is the ****Palio**, Via Cavour 106, ✆ (0141) 34371, ✍ 34373 (moderate) though without so much character. ***Rainero**, Via Cavour 85, ✆ (0141) 353866, is an oldish, medium-sized, central hotel with air-conditioning. Asti can offer the **Cavour**, Piazza Marconi 18, ✆ (0141) 530222 (inexpensive) a clean, modern hotel with well-equipped rooms, and also **Genova**, Corso Alessandria 26, ✆ (0141) 593197, slightly outside the town, but which has a restaurant, too.

## Alba

The best place to stay is the ***Savona**, Via Roma 1, ✆ (0173) 440440, ✍ 364312 (moderate) which has recently been refurbished with very stylish, comfortable and modern rooms, as well as a restaurant, bar and garage. ***Ave**, Via Einaudi 5, ✆ (0173) 361256, ✍ 441878 (inexpensive) is not as well situated or as original, but slightly cheaper. The **Piemonte**, Piazza Rosetti 6, ✆ (0173) 441354, is nicely situated, though the rooms are small.

## Monta

About 20 minutes north of the town in Monta, the *Belvedere**, Via San Giovanni 3, ✆ (0173) 976156 (inexpensive) is a very reasonably priced hotel that enjoys wonderful views across the valley, and has fine food in the restaurant below.

## Alessandria

The restaurant generally recognized as Alessandria's best is in the hotel **Alli Due Buoi Rossi** (*see* above). An alternative, **Il Grappolo**, Via Casale 28, ✆ (0144) 253217 (expensive) at the top end of town, is a smart, modern restaurant installed in a 19th-century palazzo, with a fine selection of local wines.

## Acqui Terme

The best place to dine in is **Carlo Parisio**, at Via Mazzini 14, ✆ (0144) 56650 (expensive), in the centre of town, with a menu of Piedmontese specialities—*bagna cauda*, stuffed vegetables, *agnolotti*, and good roast meats. (*Closed Mon, mid–July.*)

## Costigliole d'Asti

Here is one of the top restaurants in all Piedmont: **Da Guido**, Piazza Re Umberto 1, ✆ (0141) 966012 (very expensive), where reservations are essential to partake of the beautiful masterworks of the kitchen, all made of the freshest local ingredients, with a predilection for porcini mushrooms and truffles. The wine cellar is one of the best endowed in the entire country. (*Closed Sun, public holidays.*)

## Asti

You can also dine extremely well at **Gener Neuv**, Largo Tanaro 4, ✆ (0141) 557270 (very expensive), overlooking the river. In this elegant gourmet haven you can enjoy a superb *menu degustazione* based on Piedmontese traditions, but prepared in an imaginative and exquisite manner. The desserts are light and beautiful to behold, and the list of Piedmontese wines is matchless. Reservations advisable. (*Closed Mon, Aug.*) A less expensive choice in than the Gener Neuv, but nearly as well known, is **Falcon Vecchio**, Via San Secondo 8, ✆ (0141) 593106 (expensive), in a wonderfully atmospheric old building. All its dishes are *tipici Astiani*—making it *the* place to try truffles or local meats. (*Closed Sun evenings, Mon.*). **La Greppia**, Corso Alba 140, ✆ (0141) 59 262, is another gastronomic rendezvous, with delicious truffled dishes in season. (*Closed Mon.*)

**Il Cenacolo**, Viale Pilone 59, ✆ (0141) 511110 (moderate), is an attractive, atmospheric old place with delicious savoury dishes based on local ingredients. (*Closed Tues.*) There is a good choice of cheapish restaurants in Asti. Right at the heart of town, **Pizzeria Palio**, Piazza Alfieri 28, ✆ (0141) 592474 (inexpensive) offers good and very ample pizzas at a very nice price. Another good and inexpensive restaurant is in the **Genova** hotel (*see* above).

## The Langhe Villages

La Morra's **Belvedere**, Piazza Castello 5, ✆ (0173) 50190 (moderate) is where, according to many, Piedmont's finest *agnolotti* are served; it is also a lovely place to try *finanziera*, good mushroom and truffle dishes in the autumn, and naturally, fine wines. In the villages of the Langhe, many of the *enoteche* offer meals of local specialities at reasonable prices. One of the best value places to sample the local fare is the **Belvedere** hotel in Monta (inexpensive) north of Alba (*see* above).

## Alba

Ther is a large selection of restaurants here. One of the best, **Osteria dell'Arco** Vicolo dell'Arco 2, ✆ (0173) 363974 (moderate), is in the very centre of town, in a historic building. The small menu includes a tasty tarragon risotto, stuffed guinea fowl, and a good selection of wine, all for a price between the moderate and the inexpensive categories. (*Closed Sun, Aug.*)

## Casale Monferrato

**La Torre**, Via Gargoglio 3, ✆ (0142) 70295 (expensive), is a restaurant that the Turinese and Milanese drive out of their way to patronize. The offerings are based almost entirely on ingredients procured in the immediate environs, such as risotto with crayfish, spinach-filled tortelli, or breast of duck. (*Closed Aug.*)

## Verduno

You can eat in Carlo Alberto's castle, the **Real Castello**, Via Umberto I 9, ✆ (0172) 459125 (expensive), and dine like a king on the region's favourite pasta, *tajarin* (tiny tagliatelle), roast guinea fowl, and hazelnut torte. (*Open mid-April–Nov.*)

## Barolo

The classic place to dine from among a substantial selection of restaurants is **Del Buon Padre**, Via delle Viole 30, in the outskirts at Vergne, ✆ (0173) 56192 (moderate), where the Piedmontese cuisine is solid and simply very good, and the wines are divine. (*Closed Wed.*)

## Southwest Piedmont: Cuneo and the Maritime Alps

Despite the long frontier this district shares with France, the difficult mountainous terrain has made this one of the least known corners of Italy. The French influence is strong, both in the dialect and kitchen. Traditions in handicrafts, costumes, and festivals have lingered longer than almost anywhere else on the peninsula.

### Getting Around

Cuneo is linked by **rail** with Turin via Saluzzo, and with Genoa via Ceva and Mondovì. It is also linked by one of Italy's most spectacular railways to southwest Piedmont's main mountain resort, Limone Piemonte, and then via French territory to Ventimiglia, a 98km stretch that only reopened in 1979 after suffering grave damage in the Second World War. The journey takes roughly three hours, with all its windings and hairpin bends over the mountains. **Bus** services also run from Cuneo to all the towns in the province and to Turin and Genoa.

Cuneo is also a major **road** junction. The A6 Turin–Genoa *autostrada* runs past Mondoví, but more interesting routes from Turin to Cuneo are the SS20 through Savigliano, or the SS663 and its continuation through Saluzzo. The SS20 continues past Cuneo alongside the rail line to Limone Piemonte, a dramatic road that also tunnels into France before returning to Italy at Ventimiglia. West of Cuneo, the SS21 also leads to France, via the Colle della Maddalena (*closed in winter*). The SS564 leads from Cuneo to Mondoví and the SS28 or the A6 to Savona and Genoa.

*Tourist Information*

The main provincial tourist office is in **Cuneo**, at Corso Nizza 17, ✆ (0171) 66615, ✉ 695440. There are also offices in **Saluzzo**, at Via Griselda 6, ✆ (0175) 46710, ✉ 46718; Limone Piemonte, Piazza Municipio, ✆ (0171) 92101; **Mondoví**, Via Vittorio Veneto 17, ✆ (0174) 40389, ✉ 481266; in **Roccaforte Mondoví**, near Lurisia Terme, at Via Radium, ✆ (0174) 683119, ✉ 683 440; **Frabosa Soprana**, Piazza del Municipio, ✆ (0174) 34010; and in Garessio, on Via del Santuario, ✆ (0174) 81122, ✉ 82 092.

For serious hikers, the provincial tourist office provides a full list of **Alpine refuges** in the Maritime Alps, most of which are inaccessible by road, and which are particularly concentrated in the Natural Parks south of Cuneo.

## South from Turin to Saluzzo

Students of the French Revolution will recognize the name of one of the first towns south of Turin, **Carmagnola**, as the origin of the popular Parisian song of that period, the 'Carmagnole'. The song was originally sung by Piedmontese minstrels about an early 15th-century condottiere nicknamed Il Carmagnola; how it made Danton's hit parade is anyone's guess. **Racconigi**, a silk-making town further south, is the site of the **Castello Reale** of the Savoys, begun in 1676 and finished in 1842; behind the castle extends a beautiful park with ancient trees and a lake.

Mellow, old **Saluzzo** was the capital of a marquisate founded in 1142, that knew its golden age period in the 15th century. The upper town retains much of its character from that period, especially in the lanes below the castle. The church of **San Giovanni** has a good 14th-century Romanesque-Gothic campanile; the church itself was built in 1280, and contains among its treasures the tomb of Saluzzo's great Marquess Ludovico II, who died in 1503. The choir stalls and cloister are also worth a look. On Via San Giovanni, the charming 15th–16th-century **Casa Cavassa** is now used as the **Museo Civico** (*open 10–12.30, 2–6, Tues–Sun; adm*). Four kilometres south of Saluzzo, in **Manta**, the marquesses had one of their favourite castles. It's not much to look at, but contains in its baronial hall excellent frescoes by Giacomo Jaquerio of Turin, of nine heroes and nine heroines, believed by some to be portraits of the marquesses and their wives, all posing by the Fountain of Youth (1420s).

## Western Valleys: the Po, Varaita and Maira

Buses calling at Saluzzo ascend the rugged Upper Valley of the Po just to the west. **Revello**, near the entrance of the valley, was fortified by the first Marquess of Saluzzo. Part of their palace has been incorporated in the Municipio, including their chapel, containing intriguing portraits of the marquesses and a Leonardoesque fresco of the *Last Supper*. The fine 15th-century **Collegiata** has a Renaissance marble portal by Matteo Sanmicheli, and some good artworks inside. According to ancient tradition, when Charlemagne exiled the last old Lombard king, Desiderius, in 774, he took refuge in **Ghisola**, a tiny, ancient hamlet near Paesana, at the valley crossroads.

Further up the valley, **Crissolo** is a small resort under the attractive pointed peak of **Monviso** (3841m), the highest peak in the Maritime Alps. From Crissolo, with a guide and a sense of adventure, you can visit the stalactite-full **Grotta del Rio Martino**. The valley road ends at the **Piano del Re**, the source of the Po, Italy's longest river (652km). If you've always wanted to drink a glass of pure Po, this is the place to do it; by the time it flows out into the Adriatic it becomes one of the most toxic substances in Europe. Above Piano del Re, you can walk through the curious **Pertuis de la Traversette** (2882m), a tunnel, 75 metres long, dug in 1480 by the Marquess Ludovico II, a remarkable feat of Renaissance engineering undertaken to facilitate the passage of mule caravans between Saluzzo and the Dauphiny. The pass above Piano del Re is believed by some to have been used by even bigger freight— Hannibal's elephants.

Starting once again from Saluzzo, from **Verzuolo** (south of Manta) you can take a lovely detour or an entire holiday in the pretty and luxuriant **Valle Varaita**, a Provençal-speaking valley retaining many of its ancient handicrafts and folklore. The most interesting villages include **Sampeyre**, manufacturer of ironwork and eiderdowns, where early frescoes have recently been discovered in its parish church of **SS. Pietro e Paolo**. During Carnival Sampeyre celebrates the *Baio*, a thousand-year-old lay custom that features a variety of historical characters and dramatic scenes with Napoleonic-era costumes, topped with hats made of bright ribbons. Another village, **Casteldelfino**, recalls in its name the days in the 14th century when it was the headquarters of the Dauphin's Cisalpine lands; and then there's the small summer and winter resort of **Pontechianale**. Above it, in good weather, an asphalted road leads into France by way of the **Colle dell'Agnello**.

The **Valle Maira**, the next valley to the south, is known for its lush fruit orchards. It begins at **Dronero**, with an attractive 15th-century bridge, yet another one named the Ponte del Diavolo. Some three kilometres from Dronero, **Villar San Costanzo** has a beautiful 12th-century crypt, a survivor of an ancient Benedictine Abbey, entered from the parish church of **San Pietro in Vincoli**. This village is also the base for visiting some of the strangest sights in the area: the weird chimney rocks known as *ciciu* (puppets, in local dialect), on the slopes of the Pragamonti ridge. Formed by glacial erosion millions of years ago, and standing anything from 2–8m high, they resemble giant mutant mushrooms, and look especially haunting in winder or at night. The upper part of the Valle Maira, around **Acceglio**, is completely unspoiled.

# Cuneo

The provincial capital, Cuneo is an important market town at the confluence of the rivers Gesso and Stura, which here form a wedge, in Italian a *cuneo*, which lends the city its unusual triangular shape. If you're coming by rail, you'll pass over the impressive **Viadotto**

**Soleri**, built in the early 1930s. Although mostly rebuilt in the 18th and 19th centuries, Cuneo is a pleasant city, built around its vast porticoed main square, the **Piazza Galimberti**, site of an enormous market every Tuesday. Via Roma, leading off from the piazza, and Via Mondovì are the town's most characteristic streets, with their old porticoes built to shelter merchants from the snow. Of the churches, the most interesting is **San Francesco**, built in 1227, with a good Gothic portal from 1481. Recently restored, it now houses the small collection of the local museum, containing some Piedmontese paintings from the 18th and 19th centuries and prehistoric, Roman and medieval artefacts (*open 8.30–1, 2.30–5.30, Tues–Sat; on request Sun*). In the first part of November, Cuneo hosts the Piedmontese Cheese Exposition, starring the celebrated 'art cheeses'—Castelmagno, Brà, Murazzano, Rashera, and more, which you can nibble on while sipping the vintages of Le Langhe.

Buses from Cuneo will take you up any of the surrounding valleys, the closest of which, the little **Valle Grana**, is reached by way of Caraglio. Here the tiny village of **Monterosso Grana**, spread under its ruined watchtower, has a chapel with good 15th-century frescoes and a small ethnographic museum, with a school aimed at reviving the old crafts of furniture-making and weaving. **Pradleves** is a small summer resort, while **Castelmagno** is the producer of a famous cheese named after the village. A serpentine road leads up and up to the austere and lonely **Santuario di San Magno**, dedicated to a Roman legionary martyred on this site. Its oldest section, the choir, dates back to the 15th century.

**Borgo San Dalmazzo**, named after another martyr, Dalmatius (3rd century), is more famous these days for its snails, the main attraction of the *Fiera Fredda* (the Cold Fair), an early December market founded by Emanuele Filiberto. Borgo's most notable monument, the **Santuario della Madonna del Monserrato**, a miniature version of the famous Catalan shrine, can be reached by foot in 20 minutes along the chapel-dotted Via Crucis. Alternatively, as another reflection of the Piedmontese fascination with all kinds of fungi, there is a **Mushroom Museum** in the nearby village of Boves, at Piazza Borelli 6, ✆ (0171) 38005. (*Open on request.*)

## Three Valleys

Borgo San Dalmazzo lies at the junction of three valleys. The longest, the wooded **Valle Stura**, is a botanical paradise for its rare flowers, and throughout history was a major route of salt merchants and armies. **Demonte** is the chief town of the valley, retaining a number of medieval buildings; on the mountain of Podio stand the ruins of the once mighty **Fortress of Consolata**, destroyed by the French in 1796. Further up the valley, **Terme di Vinadio** is a small, hot sulphur-spring spa, open summers only; at Pietraporzio begins the **Stretta delle Barricate**, a narrow ravine closed in by tall walls on both sides. **Argentera**, the last and highest *comune*, is a cool summer resort; between May and mid-October the pass into France above Argentera, the **Colle della Maddalena**, is open, lined with pastures and meadows brimful of flowers in the late spring.

The second valley, the **Valle Gesso**, leads from Borgo San Dalmazzo into the heart of the Maritime Alps, the southernmost to have snow all year round, with three peaks—Argentera, Gelas, and Matto—at over 3000m. Much of the region lies within the boundaries of the **Parco Naturale dell'Argentera**, with many Alpine refuges and huts for hikes and ascents.

The main resort is the **Terme di Valdieri**, in the middle of the park—a spa that was favoured by the Savoys, but rebuilt in the 1950s. It is famed for its hot sulphur springs; near the pool the waters flow down a series of steps covered with a rare, multi-coloured algae called 'muffa' (*ulva labyrinthiformis*), which has special healing properties when applied to wounds or inflammations. From here you can walk up to the pretty **Pian del Valasco**. **Entracque** is a small resort in a branch of the valley.

To the east of Borgo, the **Valle Vermenagna**, the route taken by the railway and the SS20 road, is steep and wooded. From Vernante, an 8km side road leads up to **Palanfre**, a small Alpine village on the fringe of an enchanting beech forest, itself a natural reserve. The unusual circumstance of mountains over 3000m so close to the sea, and the high level of rainfall, combine to create a lush climatic environment of extraordinary richness; within the not-large confines of the **Parco Naturale di Palanfre** alone, there are over 650 different trees and flowers. Back in the main valley, and not far from the French frontier, **Limone Piemonte**, where the natives speak Provençal, is a popular winter sports centre with excellent skiing and full facilities, and the area's best nightlife during the season. Its name derives not from 'lemon' but from the Greek for meadow, *leimon*, one of the village's most charming features. Amidst the new development stands the Gothic parish church, **San Pietro in Vincoli**, with good examples of local 17th-century woodcarving.

There's another natural park at the head of the **Valle del Pesio**, the next valley, with interesting karstic formations and pine forests, spread under the loftiest peak, Marguareis. In the spring be sure to look for what the Italians call the 'Piss del Pesio' a spectacular 30-metre jet of subterranean water into a void, which resembles just what it sounds like. In the centre of the valley is the **Certosa di Pesio**, founded in 1173 and dominated by its large cloister. Although abandoned after Napoleon, the Certosa is now once again used as a religious house, and the monks take in guests.

## Mondovì

Like several other towns in Piedmont, **Mondovì** is divided into two sections, an older, upper half called Piazza, and a lower part known as Breo. Piazza's heart beats in the attractive, asymmetrical **Piazza Maggiore**, where in contrast to the older, Renaissance buildings, the elegant **Chiesa della Missione** (or San Francesco Saverio, 1675–1733) adds an elegant Baroque touch. The florid interior is topped by a vault frescoed with *trompe-l'œil* figures by the 17th-century Tridentine painter Andrea Pozzo. The **cathedral** (1763), also up in Piazza, has a chapel dedicated to Universal Suffrage, which was introduced in Italy by five-times-Prime-Minister Giovanni Giolitti, born in Mondovì. At Piazza's highest point, the **Giardino del Belvedere** is planted about the old civic tower, affording excellent views over the countryside. Down in mostly 18th-century Breo, the city's symbol, the 'Moor', sounds the hours atop the church of **SS. Piero e Paolo**.

Mondovì is the base for visiting a number of interesting sites in its mountainous environs. Near Bastia Mondovì, the 11th–15th-century church of **San Fiorenzo** is covered inside with a series of 51 late-Gothic frescoes in the Provençal style. Just east of the town of Mondovì in **Vicoforte**, the huge 16th–18th-century **Sanctuary** has an unusual, enormous dome and an impressive interior.

To the south lies yet another hot-spring spa, **Lurisia** (*open between June and September*). **Frabosa Soprana** is a popular winter and summer resort with ski slopes; from here the road continues south over the hills to Bossea (bus from Mondovì), site of the **Grotte di Bossea** among the most interesting and important in Italy, with a wide variety of beautiful stalactite formations, narrow passages and huge caverns, an underground river and lakes, and a skeleton of a prehistoric bear, *Ursus Spelaeus*. The caves maintain a year-round temperature of 9°C, and can be visited daily with a guide.

From the rail junction at **Ceva**, you can take a train south along the Tanaro river as far as Ormea. **Garessio**, a collection of four little hamlets, is a picturesque hill resort, with ski slopes, mineral water cures, and a summer palace of the Savoys, the **Castello di Casotto**. Pretty **Ormea** is a woodsy summer resort, its ruined castle once a nest of Saracen corsairs in the 10th and 11th centuries, when they controlled the Ligurian coast. Ormea is a good base for lovely walks into the mountains.

---

*Where to Stay*

## Cuneo

Cuneo is a good base if you intend to explore several of the region's valleys. One of the town's best hotels is the ★★★★**Principe**, Piazza Duccio Galimberti 5, ✆ (0171) 693355, ✉ 67562 (moderate) right in the centre, which has 42 modern rooms, and good parking facilities. The ★★★**Royal Superga**, Via Pascale 3, ✆ (0171) 693223 (moderate) is also a comfortable, medium-sized hotel, with a garage, and slightly cheaper. In the oldest quarter, the ★★**Ligure**, Via Savigliano 11, ✆ (0171) 68942 (inexpensive) is a good place both to sleep and to eat, a bit old and worn at the edges, but brightened with old-fashioned courtesy. Rooms vary in price, depending on the plumbing, and tasty meals of homemade pasta and roast meat or trout are equally inexpensive. In the Cunean valleys there are many often simple and rustic places to stay and eat. Good suggestions are the ★★**Tre Verghe d'Oro**, ✆ (0171) 986116 (inexpensive) in Pradleves in the Valle Grana, a long-established, old-fashioned mountain inn.

## Limone Piemonte

One of Limone Piemonte's best hotels, the ★★★**Principe**, ✆ (0171) 92389, ✉ 927070 (expensive), a scenic position, with a pool, restaurant and disco, is currently closed; call ✆ (0171) 92101 for information. ★**Mignon**, in Limone Piemonte, Via San Giovanni 3, ✆ (0171) 92363 (inexpensive) has seven simple rooms without baths and a good restaurant, where Piedmontese specialities are complemented by a cosy atmosphere.

## Limone

The ★★★**San Secondo**, Via Genova 4, ✆ (0171) 92373 (moderate), enjoys a lovely position by the river. The rooms are big, if slightly old-fashioned, and it also has a good restaurant. (*Open 1 Dec–30 April, July–mid-Sept.*) ★★★**Touring**, Via Roma 4,

℗ (0171) 92393, is warm and cosy, with log fires and period furniture, and rooms all with TV and private baths, as well as a restaurant and garage. (*Open 1 Dec–30 April, July–mid-Sept.*) Slightly out of town in Colle di Tenda is the ★★★**Tres Amis**, Panice Soprana, ℗ (0171) 928175, ✆ 928177 (moderate) which has 70 modern rooms, all with bathroom and lovely views, as well as a restaurant and indoor swimming pool.

## Valle del Pesio

**Certosa di Pesio** (*see* above), ℗ (0171) 738123. The monks have in recent years provided accommodation for travellers, though this facility may not be continued in future, so it's best to check before arriving. Rooms have cost L40,000 per night.

## Mondovì

The ★★★**Park Hotel**, Via Delvecchio 2, ℗ (0174) 46666, ✆ 47771 (inexpensive) in the old town, is smart and modern, with well-equipped rooms.

## Corsaglia

In a pretty setting south of Mondovì in Corsaglia, a tiny hamlet on the way to Bossea, ★**Corsaglia**, ℗ (0174) 349109, is a lovely little place by the river that makes a delightful rural retreat, with fine home cooking, and single and double rooms with balconies at very reasonable rates.

---

*Eating Out*

## Carmagnola

Like the rest of Piedmont, the southwest corner is a happy hunting ground for the galloping, or even the bus-riding gourmet. In Carmagnola, for instance, there's **La Carmagnola**, Via Chiffi 31, ℗ (011) 9712673 (very expensive) a lovely restaurant in a 17th-century Piedmontese mansion, featuring dishes based on the freshest of fresh ingredients, offering a delicious *menu degustazione* including exotic dishes like pheasant galantine in Sauternes and raspberry vinegar, and local specialities like *ossobuco* and *porcini* mushrooms in cream. The desserts and wines, from Le Langhe and Friuli, are also exceptional. (*Closed Mon, Aug.*)

## Cuneo

An old favourite in old Cuneo is **Tre Citroni**, near Piazza Galimberti on Via Bonelli 2, ℗ (0171) 602048 (expensive), a family-run citadel of fine dining, with delightful *agnolotti* and roast lamb, among other dishes. Back in Cuneo town, the **Ligure** hotel (inexpensive) is also a favourite place for sampling local food at inexpensive prices (for details of all three, *see* above).

## Centallo

A little way north of Cuneo in Centallo is the excellent **Due Palme**, Via Busca 2, ℗ (0171) 211567 (expensive) which serves mouthwatering *agnolotti*, lamb chops with porcini mushrooms, duck à l'orange and other delicacies.

## Pradleves

To the west of Cuneo, the restaurant in the pretty **Tre Verghe d'Oro** (moderate/inexpensive) features *gnocchi al Castelmagno* and other mountain specialities.

## Boves

9km south of Cuneo, **Rododendro** (very expensive) at Frazione San Giacomo, © (0171) 380372, is the wood-surrounded atelier of one of Italy's finest woman chefs. Her leek soup, truffles with eggs and exquisitely tender Chateaubriand have put the restaurant on Italy's gourmet map, with an extensive wine list of French and Italian bottles.

In the birthplace of Saluzzo's great republican patriot, Silvio Pellico, **La Gargotta del Pellico** (expensive), Piazzetta dei Mondagli 5, © (0175) 46833, is another exceptionally good restaurant—try the quail in pastry, or the raviolini with marjoram and mushroom butter, followed by superb desserts like pear mousse, and several varieties of Piedmontese cheese.

## Limone Piemonte

There are many more restaurants than is the norm for the area—**Mac Miche**, Via Roma 64, © (0171) 92449 (moderate) , offers a fairly standard Italian menu at moderate prices. For excellent but less expensive food in a friendly atmosphere, also in Limone, try the family-run **La Crubarsela**, Via Comm. Beltrandi 7, © (0171) 92391 (moderate/inexpensive) just down from the tourist office, which serves fine local dishes in a homely setting, at a very nice price, and has an unusually good wine selection. (*Closed Mon.*)

## Corsaglia

Many of the medium-priced restaurants in the country towns and villages are found in hotels, particularly in the mountain valleys, where the village hotels often have the only restaurants around. This is so, for example, in the excellent **Corsaglia** (inexpensive; *see* above) south of Mondovì.

---

### *Entertainment and Nightlife*

Limone has the most going on in the area, and most of the action takes place on or just off Via Roma. **The English Pub** bears little resemblance to its name, but is quite friendly, and a good place to start the evening off. As a contrast, the big, brash **Ayo American Bar**, is also popular. There are a few discos in Limone—all cost L15–20,000 admission, which gets you a free drink, and stay open until 3am. The most popular are **La Lanterna**, the ultra-modern **Boccaccio**, and, on the way out of town, **Maco**.

Limone also has its own lively **beer festival** every year, in mid-September.

# Liguria (the Italian Riviera)

'Riviera' in Italian simply means shore, but in Liguria the shore is THE Riviera, a rugged, rock-bound rainbow of coast linking France to Tuscany, endowed with what is surprisingly one of the rarer Italian commodities—beautiful beaches. Usually not large, buxom, sandy beaches, but rather refined, slender strands in magical settings, beneath swaying palms and bright gardens, backed by old fishing towns tumbling down the hillsides, or resorts that fit as comfortably as an old pair of shoes. After Liguria, you'd have to continue all the way down to the Bay of Naples to find a shore comparable in interest and beauty. And if you're approaching from the haughty French Riviera, the Italian Riviera comes as a pleasant surprise, wonderfully relaxed and ever so gently faded—no one cares if your socks don't quite match, or you've brought the children along. There are splendid grand hotels, but they are outnumbered by small and unpretentious pensioni.

Although August is peak season on the Riviera these days, people first came to this fabled shore for its sunny and mild winter climate. Sheltered by the Maritime Alps from inclement weather from the north, Liguria enjoys a sensuously lush growth of lemons, oranges, and flowers—one of the region's principal exports. The oil from its ancient groves is legendary. Bathed in a luminous, warm light, the Riviera's colours are dazzling, the reds, blues, yellows and greens like glistening newborns to the beleaguered mist-shrouded vision of the northerner.

The delights of sun and sea are only part of what the region has to offer. Liguria has a distinct regional identity and a distinct language. Poor in resources but full of intrepid, tenacious seamen and merchants, it has always looked to the sea for its survival, its commerce; early on, the native Ligurians traded with the Phoenicians and the Greeks, before Genoa became an important Roman seaport. In the Middle Ages, after ejecting the Saracen pirates who had long harassed the coast, Genoa grew to become a seapower rivalled only by Venice, the bitterest of its many enemies. And although its importance declined in the 15th century, the Ligurian character had been formed by then—frugal, feisty, shrewd, adventurous, but not without a sense of humour. Columbus, of course, came from Liguria, as did the great admiral Andrea Doria, and the Risorgimento heroes Garibaldi and Mazzini.

In Liguria look for ancient popular festivals and folk traditions, for great regional cuisine, especially fish dishes prepared in a hearty style similar to neighbouring Provence—try cacciucco, Ligurian bouillabaisse, or cappon magro, pickled fish with vegetables or Brasato di manzo alla genovese, braised beef with vegetables and mushrooms in red wine. Even the snacks are different, like focaccia, Ligurian pizza, made with a softer dough than the Neapolitan version and the ingredients baked inside, and farinata, a mixture of baked, ground chickpeas best eaten hot from the oven. Pasta (especially trenette, similar to linguini) is often served with Genoa's famous pesto sauce of basil, garlic, pine nuts, olive oil and parmesan, ground with a mortar and the pestle which gave it its name. And, although Liguria isn't one of Italy's great wine-growing regions, you may want to try its best, Pigato, a fine, dry white, or Rossese, a fine dry red.

# Ligurian Itineraries

The **Via Aurelia** (SS1), successor to the ancient Roman road, runs along the coast offering the finest scenery, although the *autostrade* A10, between Ventimiglia and Genoa, and the A12, from Genoa to Pisa, also both have lovely stretches overlooking the coast. Transport, especially buses along the coast, is especially good. The best thing to do on the Riviera is to base yourself in one place and explore from there, at least once venturing into the green mountains behind the beaches. The most scenic mountain routes include the SS28 from Imperia to Ormea and Garessio in Piedmont, from where you can circle back down on the SS582 to Albenga on the coast. Between Savona and Millesimo runs the A6 *autostrada* to Turin, more or less following the prettier old route. The A26 or SS456 from Pegli towards Milan via Alessandria are attractive at least as far as Vignole Barbera, though the A7 is much faster. East of Genoa, the ideal way to see the most stunning scenery—the Monti di Portofino and the Cinque Terre, is by boat and foot.

The highlights of the Riviera, from west to east, include the fascinating prehistoric caves of **Balzi Rossi**, the medieval hill villages of **Dolceacqua** and **Taggia**, and the ghost town of **Bussana Vecchia**, all near the Riviera's old capital of fun, **San Remo**. Further along the coast is the almost undiscovered village of **Cervo** and ancient **Albenga**, near the beautiful caves of **Toirano**. And in the great embrace of the Genoan metropolitan area, **Pegli**, with its museums, villas, and gardens.

**Genoa** has several palaces full of art, including a great oriental museum, and a wonderfully evocative old quarter, worth a couple of days in itself. East of Genoa there are more villas and gardens at **Nervi**, then the magnificent promontory, the **Monte di Portofino**. Here are a number of beautiful places—the charming fishing village of **Camogli**, the ancient abbey of **San Fruttuoso**, and the ultra chic international resort and yacht port of **Portofino**, a base for beautiful walks. **Chiavari** is an interesting old seamen's town, and beyond it are the **Cinque Terre** villages, hanging on cliffs or below them, immersed in vineyards and laced together by a stunning seaside footpath. **La Spezia** has a good naval museum, and nearby, beautiful old **Portovenere** is almost as chic as Portofino these days. The whole Gulf of La Spezia, known as the 'Gulf of Poets', is enchanting, and can be combined in a boat excursion with the Cinque Terre.

## Riviera di Ponente: Ventimiglia to San Remo

This part of the Riviera, especially the coast west of Imperia, enjoys one of the mildest winter climates in the country. Flowers thrive here even in February, and are cultivated in fields that dress the landscape in a brilliant patchwork (albeit increasingly shrouded in plastic!), lending this stretch the well-deserved name of the 'Riviera of Flowers'.

### Getting Around

Trains run frequently up and down the coast from Ventimiglia to Genoa; from Ventimiglia a line branches off for Cuneo, in Piedmont, one of the country's most scenic rail routes (*see* under Cuneo, p.153). Inland the hill towns are easily reached by bus, from their nearest coastal towns.

Road connections are equally convenient, as virtually all roads link up with the SS1 coast road, the Via Aurelia, or, if you're in a hurry, the A10 autostrada.

### Tourist Information

There are tourist offices in **Ventimiglia**, at Via Cavour 61, ✆ 351183; **Dolceacqua**, Via Patrioti Martiri 56, ✆ 206666; **Bordighera**, Palazzo del Parco, Via Roberto, ✆ 262322, ✉ 264455; **San Remo**, Via Nuvoloni 1, ✆ 571571, ✉ 507649; **Ospedaletti**, at Corso Regina Margherita 1, ✆ 59085; and in **Arma di Taggia**, in the Villa Boselli, ✆ 43733. The phone prefix for the whole of this area is **0184**.

## Ventimiglia

Ventimiglia is tricky: if you arrive by train it can seem seedy and dull. On the other hand, if you come by the coastal road from the west it is pure enchantment, a garden-town by the sea where roses and carnations are the main crops, and in June the main festival is the 'Battle of the Flowers'. Ventimiglia is also a garden of history, with some of the most ancient roots in Liguria, as evinced by the relics left by Neanderthal man in the **Balzi Rossi** ('Red Cliffs') caves, near the French frontier, on the beach below the village of Grimaldi. Here, between 40 and 100 thousand years ago, thrived one of the most sophisticated prehistoric societies discovered in Europe. In the caves themselves are the traces of several elaborate burials, the dead adorned with seashell finery; and in one cave, the *Grotto del Caviglione*, is an etching of a horse, of a breed now common only on the Russian steppes. The **Museo Preistorico**, (*museum and caves open April–Sept 9.30–12.30, 5–7, Tues–Fri; 10–12 Sat, Sun; Oct–Mar 10–12, 3–5, Tues–Fri; 10–12 Sat, Sun; adm*) at the caves' entrance, displays the most important finds from within—ornaments, tools, weapons and some of the earliest works of art ever discovered, lumpy fertility figures called "Venuses".

In the same area, at Mortola Inferiore (and reached by the same municipal bus from Ventimiglia) you can take in the world-famous **Hanbury Gardens** (*open April–Sept 9–6; Oct–Mar 10–4; closed Wed; adm exp*), an enchanted botanical paradise founded in 1867 by Sir Thomas Hanbury and acquired by the Italian state in 1960. Spread out on the slopes around a castle-like villa, planted with some 5000 rare and exotic plants that Sir Thomas acclimatized from Africa and Asia to co-exist with native Mediterranean flora, the gardens are among the most important in Italy. Near the gardens part of the ancient Via Aurelia can be seen, with a plaque alongside listing the famous who have passed this way, from St Catherine of

Siena to Napoleon. The main road, passing underneath the gardens, leads to the customs post at Ponte San Ludovico with its landmark, the **Castle** where Serge Voronoff performed his experiments, seeking the Fountain of Youth in monkey glands.

In ancient times Ventimiglia was an important Ligurian station on the Via Aurelia, which the Romans called *Albintimilium*. The ruins of **Albintimilium** stand one kilometre east of the modern town; best preserved here is the small 2nd-century AD **amphitheatre** (*open 3–7pm Wed, Fri; 9–1 Thurs, Sat*). Most of the finds from the excavations of the Roman town are on view in the nearby **Museo Archeologico**, Via Verdi 15. (*Open April–Sept 9.30–12.30, 5–7, Tues–Fri; 10am–12 midday Sat, Sun; Oct–Mar 10–12, 3–5, Tues–Fri; 10am–12 midday Sat, Sun; adm.*)

Ventimiglia itself is divided into old and new by the river Roja, the modern town built around the great winter flower market and lined with typical Riviera seaside promenades, while the old town, with its medieval plan of twisting lanes, has the attractive ensemble of an 11th–12th-century **cathedral** and **Baptistry** for its focal point; the latter still shows vestiges of the Byzantine and Lombard original. Another fine Romanesque church of the same period, **San Michele**, was built with Roman columns and milestones. Overlooking the coast west of Ventimiglia are the ruins of the 12th-century **Castel D'Appio**, former head-quarters of the piratical Counts of Ventimiglia.

## Dolceacqua

Inland from Ventimiglia there are several pretty valleys, the Val Nervia perhaps the most appealing (buses hourly from Ventimiglia). The gem here is the picturesque old stone village of **Dolceacqua** occupying both banks of the river, spanned here by the single arch of a medieval bridge, and crowned by a 16th-century and reputedly haunted **Doria Castle**, where the lords are said to have taken full advantage of their *droit de seigneur* to spend the first night with local brides. On St Sebastian's Day (20 January) Dolceacqua celebrates a unique religious procession, led by the 'tree man' who bears a huge tree branch hung with large, coloured communion hosts, a curious mixture of Christianity with ancient fertility rites.

The hillsides around Dolceacqua are terraced with vineyards producing the good red wine, *Rossese*, available in the local cafes. Further up, **Pigna**, cradled in the foothills of the Maritime Alps, is another pretty village with an adjacent thermal spa; some three kilometres away you can visit **Castelvittorio**, a fortified hamlet that has changed little since the 13th century, when its thick walls defended it from predatorial Saracen raids. From here drivers can circle back, by way of Baiardo (*see* below), to the coast at San Remo.

## Bordighera

Once a favourite winter residence of Europe's pampered set, and of literati like Katherine Mansfield, blessed with a good beach and regal promenades, Bordighera is now one of the most jovial resorts on the Riviera: from the end of July until the end of August its International Humour Festival does everything possible to make you laugh, with films, comedy acts and routines. As at Ventimiglia the environs contain vast fields of cultivated flowers, but here the speciality is palms; since Sant'Ampelio legendarily brought the first seeds from Egypt, Bordighera has had a monopoly in supplying the Vatican with fronds during Easter week.

You can learn all about the ancient Ligurians at Bordighera's **Museo dell'Instituto Internazionale di Studi Liguri** (*open 8.30–1, 2.30–6, Mon–Sat; closed first two weeks of Aug.*) There are plaster casts of the curious Neolithic rock engravings from the Valle delle Meraviglie (part of France since the Second World War) and finds from Roman *Albintimilium*. The tiny medieval nucleus of Bordighera, above the Spianata del Capo, is shoe-horned behind its gates; further up the flower bedecked **Via dei Colli** there are excellent views of the shimmering coast. Below, the Romanesque Chapel of **Saint'Ampelio** stands on its little cape, above the grotto where the saint lived; from here you can walk along the pleasant Lungomare Argentina west to the spa, or east along the seaside Via Arziglia to Bordighera's palm and mimosa plantations at the **Winter Garden** and the **Giardino Madonna della Ruota**, a 45-minute walk.

## San Remo

San Remo is the opulent, ageing queen of the Italian Riviera, her grand hotels and aristocratic villas as beautiful and out of date as antimacassars on an armchair. Yet even if the old girl isn't young, she's still a game corker with a Mae West twinkle in her eye. Other resorts may be more glamorous, but few have more character. San Remo also has considerable bargains, both in hotels and in the shops—the French pour over from the Côte d'Azur to purchase designer clothes and furnishings that cost 20–30 per cent more in Paris.

San Remo stands on a huge, sheltered bay and was long a favourite watering hole for a variety of drifting aristocrats, most famously Empress Maria Alexandrovna, wife of Czar Alexander II; she was followed by a sizeable Russian colony, including Tchaikovsky, who composed *Eugene Onegin* and the Fourth Symphony during his stay here in 1878. The duke of nonsense, Edward Lear, ended his lifelong travels through the Mediterranean here in 1888, as did the father of dynamite and founder of the famous prizes, Alfred Nobel, who died in 1896 in the **Villa Nobel**, on the eastern edge of town, near the Parco Ormond, and closed to the public at time of writing.

A legacy from these golden days of fashion, the white, brightly lit, Liberty-style **Municipal Casino** is still the lively heart of San Remo's social life, with its gaming rooms (the French room, with a jacket-and-tie dress code and cover charge, or the free, un-dress-coded American room), roof garden cabaret, and celebrated restaurant with a live orchestra. It is also, in February, the setting for the biggest event in the world of Italian pop, the unabashedly tacky *Festival della Canzone*, an extravagant, five-day-long lip-synch ritual built of glitter and hype, where this once gloriously musical nation parades its contemporary talents with all the self-confidence of the Emperor in his new clothes.

From the Casino you can take the famous *passegiata* down the lovely, palm-lined **Corso dell'Imperatrice**, named in honour of Maria Alexandrovna; here, springing out of luxuriant, almost tropical foliage are the utterly incongruous onion domes of the dainty **Russian Orthodox Church** (*open April–Sept 9.30–12.30, 4–7, Tues, Thurs, Sat; Oct–Mar 9.30–12.30, 3–6.30, Tues, Thurs, Sat*), built in the 1920s by the exiled nobility, who lavished a considerable sum on this bright little jewel box. It contains the tombs of some other deposed blue-bloods, the royal house of Montenegro. On the other side of the Casino the Corso becomes Via Matteotti, San Remo's main shopping street. Early risers can take in the almost intoxicating colour and scent of the **San Remo Flower Market** on Corso Garibaldi, just off Piazza Colombo—very much a working, wholesale market, but fascinating for visitors nonetheless.

The old town, **La Pigna**, has been called San Remo's 'casbah', a tangled, mystery-laden mesh of steep lanes and stairs weaving under archways and narrow tunnels. In the Piazza San Siro is the 12th-century, but much altered, **Cathedral of San Siro**, with an unusual black crucifix by an unknown sculptor. Above the vegetable market looms **Monte Bignone**, the highest peak in the amphitheatre of hills wrapped around San Remo (1305m). A bus goes part of the way to the top, from where there are great views of the Riviera. Below lies the 18-hole **Ulivi golf course**, and the most panoramic road in San Remo, the **Corso degli Inglesi**. This leads on to the **Via Crucis Monumentale**, lined with statues of the Stations of the Cross.

Standing majestically above San Remo is the **Shrine of Our Lady of the Coast** (*open April–Sept 9–12, 3–6.30, daily; Oct–Mar 9–12, 3–5.30, daily; buses run regularly from San Remo*). The madonna inside is believed to have saved a local sailor from shipwreck, who subsequently donated the first gold coin to establish the shrine. On *Ferragosto*, 15 August, this event is celebrated with fireworks and a feast, in one of the Riviera's most attractive traditional festivals.

## Around San Remo

San Remo has several interesting neighbours, all easily reached by buses departing from the train station. Just to the west, the quieter seaside resort of **Ospedaletti** is shaded by a luxuriant ensemble of pines, palms, and eucalyptus; its name is said to derive from the Knight Hospitallers of Rhodes, who had a pilgrims' hospice here in the 14th century. They also bestowed their name on the nearby hill town of **Coldirodi**, known for its **Rambaldi Art Gallery**, ✆ 670131 (*open 3–6pm Tues, Thurs, Sat; 9–12 Wed, Fri, Sun; adm*), with paintings by Veronese and Guido Reni, and a library.

Most unusual is **Bussana Vecchia**, Italy's trendiest ghost town. On 23 February 1887, a mighty earthquake shook Bussana, killing thousands and turning the town into the picturesque ruin you see today, while the inhabitants rebuilt a new Bussana 2km closer to the sea. It is a rather typical Italian contradiction that although Bussana Vecchia officially no longer exists, it has a number of artistically minded inhabitants who are equally officially non-existent, but who have restored the interiors (though not the exteriors) of the ruined houses and been hooked up with water, lights, telephones and, somehow, two mild-mannered llamas from Peru, and make a living selling paintings and all sorts of artsy fartsy duet magnets. The earthquake knocked in the roof of the Baroque church (packed at the time for the Ash Wednesday service), but nearly all the parishioners managed to escape death in the side chapels; one survivor, Giovanni Torre detto Merlo, went on to invent the ice cream cone in 1902. The church is open to the sky behind its façade, the stucco decorations now sprout weeds, trees grow in the nave and apse, and cherubs smile down like broken dolls on a shelf.

Further inland, **Bajardo**, spread out over its conical hill with a grand backdrop of mountains and forests, was also devastated by the earthquake. An intriguing relic is the ruined church at the top of the town, with 13th-century capitals carved roughly with the heads of Mongols, some of whom are believed to have accompanied the Saracens to Liguria. Bajardo, unlike Bussana, was rebuilt on the same site as the old town, and its reputation for healthy air has made it a modest summer resort. Bajardo celebrates an ancient rite, the *Festival della Barca* (of the boat) on Pentecost Sunday, when a large tree trunk topped by a smaller pine tree is erected in the middle of the piazza, around which the people dance and sing—a rare survival of a pagan fertility rite left almost untouched by the Church.

To the east, **Arma di Taggia** has one of the finest sandy beaches in the area, lying at the mouth of the Valle Argentina; three kilometres inland, picturesquely medieval **Taggia** is the site of a popular antiques fair held on the fourth Saturday and Sunday of every month. The **Dominican Convent** (*open 9.30–12, 3–5; closed Thurs*), founded in 1400 and now a national monument, contains a number of fine paintings of the local Ligurian school. A pretty drive or walk from Taggia is the road up to the **Sanctuary of the Madonna di Lampedusa**, a fine viewpoint, reached via the remarkable, dog-leg 16-arched **medieval bridge** at Castellaro. Come on the third Sunday of July for the ancient Festival of Mary Magdalen, who according to tradition once paid Taggia a call, and is remembered by members of her red-capped confraternity with an eerie Dance of Death, performed by two men, one playing the role of 'the man', and the other of Mary Magdalen, who dies and is brought back to life with a sprig of lavender—Taggia's principal cash crop for centuries.

There are a number of attractive old villages dotting the Valle Argentina, most intriguing of which is **Triora**, a fortified 15th-century village high in the mountains. This is a small summer resort, also visited in the winter for skiing at **Monesi**, just under the lofty Cima di Piano Cavallo.

---

© (0184–)   ## Where to Stay

In San Remo, if you arrive without a booking, there's a hotel-finding service in the station, © 80172 (*closed Sun*). On the whole, though, you shouldn't have too much trouble finding a room outside of July and August.

Note that many hotels in this area still prefer to follow traditional practice and require that their guests take full- or half-pension, particularly in high season. At other times, they are more open to negotiation.

## Ventimiglia

Although Ventimiglia is midway between Monte Carlo and San Remo, prices here are reasonable. The top hotel choice is **★★★La Riserva**, © 229533 (moderate), up in the olive groves at Castel d'Appio 5km west of the town, a fine family-run inn with magnificent views, a pool, and very comfortable rooms, all with bath. (*Open April–Sept and Christmas holidays only.*) In Ventimiglia itself the **★★★Sea Gull**, Via Marconi 13, © 351726 (inexpensive) is a comfortable establishment on the water-front, with a bit of garden, parking, and a private beach. All its rooms have baths. **★Lido**, Via Marconi 11, © 351473 (inexpensive), is another pleasant beachfront choice, and very reasonably priced. (*Open April–Sept.*)

## Bordighera

Bordighera is excellently equipped with hotels in all price ranges, but real elegance can be found at the modern ★★★★**Del Mare**, Via Portico della Punta 34, ✆ 262201 (very expensive), in a beautiful panoramic position over the sea, with such amenities as private beach, sea-water pool, gardens and tennis courts. (*Closed Nov–Christmas.*) Another luxurious hotel is the ★★★★**Cap Ampelio**, Via Virgili 5, ✆ 264333 (expensive) which overlooks both the town and the sea, and can offer designer furnishings and heated pool, garden, and Italian or French TV.

Some way up the hill in Bordighera, the ★**Virginia**, Via Romana 55, ✆ 260477 (inexpensive) has pleasant rooms, some without baths, and a pretty garden. Lower down in the town, in front of the station, ★**Palme**, Via Roma 5, ✆ 261273 (inexpensive) offers basic rooms at a reasonable price.In Bordighera the ★★★**Britannique & Jolie**, Via Regina Margherita 35, ✆ 261464, is a traditional favourite, with a garden near the sea. All rooms have private bath. (*Closed Oct–Nov.*) ★★★**Villa Elisa**, Via Romana 70, ✆ 261313, is an inviting villa above the town, standing in pretty gardens, with very attractive rooms, some without bathrooms.

## San Remo

The top hotel in San Remo is more of a palace than accommodation for rent: the ★★★★★**Royal**, near the Casino on Corso Imperatrice 80, ✆ 5391, ✉ 61445 (very expensive). Surrounded by lush gardens, with palms, flowers, tennis court, and an enormous heated sea-water pool, this turn-of-the-century *grande dame* has rooms that vary from imperial suites to more modest, refurbished bedrooms, all, however, fully equipped with modern conveniences. And, true to tradition, the hotel orchestra serenades guests in the afternoon and gets them dancing in the evening.

One of the region's oldest hotels, the ★★★★**Astoria West End**, Corso Matuzia 8, ✆ 667701, ✉ 65616 (very expensive) sounds as if it belongs in New York, but instead sits in all its confectionery elegance opposite the sea in San Remo. Although recently renovated, its grand chandeliers, elaborate stucco ceilings and carved lifts have been left unchanged. It also has luxuriant gardens with a pool, and a pretty outdoor terrace. If you prefer something with a Liberty-style touch, ★★★★**Grand Hotel Londra**, Corso Matuzia 2, ✆ 666000, ✉ 668073 (expensive) can oblige. Built around the turn of the century, it has a lovely garden, pool, and fine original interior details. (*Closed Oct–Nov.*)

If you seek peace and quiet, there are two good choices, ★★★**Paradisio**, Via Roccasterone 12, ✆ 571211, ✉ 578176 (moderate), located above most of the hurly burly, and enveloped with flowers on the terrace and balconies, with a distinguished salon, glass-enclosed dining room, and well-furnished rooms, all with bath and many with TVs (*closed Nov–first half of Dec*) or, behind the casino, the ★★★**Riviera**, Corso degli Inglesi 86, ✆ 502215, ✉ 502216 (moderate) which is less plush, but quiet and substantially cheaper than the seafront hotels. If you don't mind being in the middle of the resort's bustle, then the ★★★**Lolli Palace**, Corso dell'Imperatrice 70, ✆ 531496, ✉ 541574, (moderate) right on the seafront and recently refurbished, is a good choice. Rooms are big and bright with all modern fittings, some facing the sea. It also has a garage and restaurant. Further along the front, at Corso dell'Imperatrice 27, the ★★★**Europa**, ✆ 578170, ✉ 508661 (moderate) is one of the few hotels not to have been fully refurbished, and so retains its rather *fin de siècle* character in its main rooms. Another alternative is the recently refurbished ★★★★**Nazionale**, Via Matteotti 3, ✆ 577577, ✉ 541535 (moderate) which enjoys a privileged position beside the casino. It has 87 modern, air-conditioned rooms, all with bathrooms, and most with fine views.

In the centre of San Remo, the ★★★**Eletto**, Via Matteotti 44, ✆ 531548 (inexpensive) is a very pretty 19th-century hotel, furnished with antiques, and also blessed with a welcoming little garden. Prices range from the moderate to the inexpensive categories, depending on season and the room. Tiny, eight-room ★★**Sole Mare**, Via Carli 23, ✆ 577105, ✉ 532778 (inexpensive) is a comfortable choice, especially popular with Italians. All rooms have baths, and it also has parking space.

Cheaper hotels like the old-fashioned ★**Terminus**, Via Roma 8, ✆ 577110, and ★★**Zabora** at Via Roma 54, ✆ 503170, ✉ 503171 (both inexpensive) abound in San Remo on Via Matteotti, Via Roma, Corso Mombello, and Corso Massini, where rooms can be found for around L20,000 a head. Most of these hotels have rooms with and without baths.

---

✆ *(0184–)*

# Eating Out

## Ventimiglia

**Balzi Rossi**, Piazzale De Gasperi, ✆ 38132 (very expensive) is the premier restaurant in the Ventimiglia area and is right on the frontier at San Lodovico—which has an almost seaworthy dining room overlooking the Mediterranean. The cuisine magnificently blends the best of France and Liguria, and includes a legendary *terrina di coniglio*, pasta dishes with fresh tomatoes and basil, scallops of sea bass, divine desserts and excellent wines. Definitely reserve. Other than this one, Ventimiglia's restaurants are fairly undistinguished.

## Dolceacqua

**Gianni**, Via della Liberazione 35, ✆ 206136, (expensive) has good Ligurian and mountain specialities, which go down easily with a bottle of Rossese.

## Bordighera

The most spectacular place to eat in Bordighera, inserted in the cliffs, is **La Reserve Tastevin**, at Capo Sant'Ampelio, Via Aurelia 20, ✆ 261322 (expensive). The views are fantastic, and so is the food, a delightful combination of ingredients from the sea and the Valle Argentina.

The very elegant and tiny **La Chaudron**, Piazza Bengasi 2, ✆ 263592 (expensive), will win your heart with delicious dishes like spaghetti with artichokes, and the

Ligurian speciality, *pesce al sale* (fish baked in a bed of salt, skinned, then dressed with olive oil). Be sure to reserve. There are many more restaurants, including several cheaper ones in the old part of town: still in the expensive range, **Degli Amici**, Via Lunga 2, ℰ 260591 (expensive), has some well-prepared seafood and rabbit dishes.

### San Remo

**Giannino**, Lungomare Trento e Trieste 23, ℰ 50514 (very expensive) offers exquisitely prepared dishes based of fresh, natural ingredients, including a speciality of the region, *tagliolini al sugo di triglia*—wholewheat pasta with red mullet sauce—polenta with cheese and vegetable sauce, pigeon with ginger, and much more. An excellent wine list accompanies it all. San Remo's **Pesce d'Oro**, Corso Cavallotti 300, ℰ 576332, (expensive) is one of the town's most famous restaurants, although one would never guess from the rather funky location. Inside, however, the *lasagnette al pesto, zuppa di frutti di mare*, and sea bass in lobster sauce will make you a convert to the Pesce d'Oro's numerous fan club. Just outside San Remo, at Verezzo Cava, is **Silvestro**, ℰ 559066 (inexpensive) which offers an alternative to the constant barrage of seafood in the shape of delicious homecooked meat, chicken, and rabbit dishes, at prices close to the inexpensive range.

There is a wide selection of medium/lower-price pizzerias and restaurants in San Remo—the largest concentration of them around the Piazza Eroi Sanremesi and the Via Palazzo, between the seafront and the old town. In Bordighera, similarly, most cheaper restaurants are found in the old town.

### Arma di Taggia

Along the coast at Arma di Taggia, **La Conchiglia**, Via Lungomare 33, ℰ 43169 (expensive) serves Ligurian delights based on seafood, local cheese, and delicate olive oil—the prawn and white bean salad is delicious. Reservations recommended; as well as the main menu they also offer a very good set lunch.

---

### *Entertainment and Nightlife*

In all the Riviera resorts, most of the clubs, night bars and discos are very expensive. Probably the most popular places in San Remo are **Boccaccio**, a disco beside the Casino, and, next to it, **Pascia Club**, which is more of a cabaret-revue venue. Most of the rest are on the outskirts of the town, but one perennially popular venue in the centre is the **Odeon Music Hall**, Via Matteotti 178 (*adm*).

## Riviera di Ponente: Imperia to Savona

Imperia divides the 'Riviera of Flowers' from the more rugged, silvery 'Riviera of Olives'. Connoisseurs of olive oil rate Liguria's the tops in Italy, although of course there are plenty of other regions ready to dispute this most slippery of crowns.

Road and rail connections are as easy as in the sections of the Riviera further west. Among the more spectacular drives in the area are the SS582, from Albenga to Garessio, and the SS490, inland from Finale Ligure.

There are official tourist offices in **Imperia**, at Viale G. Matteotti 54/a, © (0183) 24947, @ 24950; **Diano Marina**, Piazza Martiri della Libertà 1, © (0183) 496956, @ 494365; **San Bartolomeo al Mare**, Piazza XXV Aprile 1, © (0183) 400200, @ 403550; **Cervo**, at Piazza Castello 1, © (0183) 408197, @ 403133; **Alassio**, Via Gibb 26, © (0182) 640346, © 644690; **Albenga**, Viale Martiri della Libertà 17, © (0182) 50475; **Finale Ligure**, Via San Pietro 14, © (019) 692581, @ 680052; and Savona, at Via Paleocapa 59, © (019) 25305. In Finale Ligure there is also a very friendly and helpful general information office run by the local bus company, near the rail station at Via Mazzini 28, ©/@ (019) 692275, and also a Hotel Information service, © (019) 694252, that operates from June to September only.

# Imperia

In 1923 two towns, Porto Maurizio and Oneglia, were married by Mussolini to form a provincial capital, Imperia. The bustling oil port (olive oil, that is) of Oneglia was the birthplace of the great Genoese Admiral Andrea Doria, while the old quarter of Porto Maurizio (connected by city bus) has most of Imperia's charm, with steep lanes and steps, though even here the town lacks the typical Riviera resort ambience, for better or worse. Imperia does have a small **Naval Museum**, Piazza Duomo 11, © (0183) 651541 (*open Sept–June 4–7.30pm Wed–Sat; July–Aug 9am–11pm Wed–Sat*), containing amongst other artefacts a variety of memorabilia of the Doria family.

Imperia is also the base for exploring old villages in the hinterland, like **Dolcedo**, the site of the most renowned olive groves in the region, with several medieval bridges, one of which is carved with the cross of the Knights of Malta. In another valley, further east, the main SS28 road leads to pretty **Pontedassio**.

East of Imperia are a string of popular resorts: **Diano Marina**, famous for its olives, and site of a small **Museo Civico** (*open April–Sept only*), that contains a reconstruction of some rooms from Roman houses unearthed in the area; modern **San Bartolomeo al Mare**; and, prettiest of the three, **Cervo**, a curl of white, cream, and pale yellow houses sweeping up from the sea. At the top of the curl stands the pretty, cream pastry Baroque **Church of the Corallini** (of the coral fishermen), with a distinctive concave façade emblazoned with a stag, or *cervo* in Italian. The old town has a delightful, sunny, Moorish atmosphere. Although it hosts a chamber-music festival in July and August, with only five small hotels near its shingle beach it is hardly spoiled.

**Andora**, next along the coast, consists of a Marine Quarter with a beach and, up in the Merula valley, a fortified medieval hamlet, reached by way of an ancient bridge. The old town is dominated by its picturesque ruined castle and the lovely 13th-century Romanesque-Gothic Church of **SS. Giacomo e Pietro**. On the other side of Capo Mele ('Cape Apples') lies the attractive old fishing town of **Laigueglia**, with a majestic Baroque church from 1754.

## Alassio and Albenga

With one of the best beaches on the Riviera, and one of the mildest climates, **Alassio** has long been a popular winter resort. Of pre-resort Alassio little more remains to be seen than some old palazzi on its main street, the pretty 1597 church of **Sant'Ambrogio** with a Romanesque campanile, and a defence tower. Visiting celebrities have autographed the 'Muretto', or little wall, Alassio's version of Hollywood Boulevard; in August there's even a 'Miss Muretto' beauty contest. Excursion boats make the short trip to the tiny islet, **Isola Gallinaria**, especially popular with skin-divers; another pleasant outing is up the **Roman Road** to the 13th-century Benedictine church of **Santa Croce**, one of the best view-points in the area.

Ancient **Albenga** is the most historic and interesting town on the Riviera del Ponente. Once the Roman port of *Album Ingaunum*, Albenga was prosperous throughout the Middle Ages, until its harbour shifted away with the course of the Cento river; nowadays Albenga stands a kilometre from the sea, and grows asparagus in the old river bed. Albenga's impressive collection of 13th-century brick towers, built during its day as a *comune*, stand like bridesmaids around the elegant 1391 campanile of the Romanesque **cathedral**. One of the towers (*c.* 1300) belongs to the Palazzo Vecchio del Comune, and now houses the **Museo Civico Ingauno** (*open 10–12, 3–6, Tues–Sun*), which contains archaeological odds and ends, and provides a good view from the top floor.

Steps lead down from the piazza to Albenga's most celebrated monument, the 5th-century **baptistry** (*same hours as museum*). In the 5th and 6th centuries there was a great fondness for geometrical forms, and Albenga's baptistry is a minor tour de force of the genre, its architects combining an unusual 10-sided exterior with an octagonal interior. Some of the original mosaics remain in blue and white stone, depicting 12 doves, symbols of the Apostles.

To the north of the cathedral, the **Piazzetta dei Leoni** is named after the three mysterious lions who stand guard here. Nearby on Via Episcopio, the Bishop's Palace, with exterior frescoes, houses the **Diocesan Museum** (*same times as Museo Civico*), with 17th-

*Cattedrale*

century tapestries, paintings, reliquaries and illuminated manuscripts. The 13th-century **Loggia dei Quattro Canti**, nearby, marks the centre of the Roman town.

Another tower, on Piazza San Michele, belongs to the **Palazzo Peloso Cipolla** ('Hairy Onion Palace'), built in the 14th century, with a Renaissance-era façade; it now contains the **Roman Naval Museum** (*same times as Museo Civico*). The collection features rows of amphorae and other items salvaged from a 1st-century BC Roman shipwreck discovered near the Isola Gallinaria, as well as 16th–18th-century blue and white pharmacy jars from Albisola.

From Albenga you can walk to the west and along the Cento, through the scattered remains of Roman *Album Ingaunum*—the old Roman road and tombs on the hill, the amphitheatre below, and the foundations of the city on the river banks. Towards the east stands the 13th-century bridge, the Ponte Lungo, spanning the former course of the Cento. **Garlenda**, some 12 kilometres further inland, is a pretty hill resort, with a fine 18-hole golf course.

## Inland: the Grottoes of Toirano

Heading east of Albenga, **Ceriale** is a small seaside resort with a famous Good Friday procession. **Borghetto Santo Spirito**, the next coastal town, is mainly of interest as the junction (and bus pick-up point) for **Toirano**, a medieval hill village that seems spanking new compared to the relics of its Middle Palaeolithic inhabitants (80,000 BC), discovered in the two large caves nearby—the **Grotta della Basura** and the **Grotta di Santa Lucia**. The Grotta della Basura has a section called the Bear Cemetery because of all of the bones found there, and a 'Room of Mystery', with animal and human footprints as if left from a ritual dance. Near the entrance to the grottoes the **Prehistoric Museum of the Val Varatella** (*open 9–12, 2–5*) contains remains found in these and other caverns in the valley, and a reassembled bear skeleton. Like modern Italians, Toirano's ancient cave dwellers had excellent taste, and chose as their abode one of the loveliest caves in the region, where Mother Nature, their interior decorator, added draperies and designs of pastel-coloured stalactites. (*Half-hour guided tours of the caves operate 9–12, 2–5, daily; adm.*).

Another medieval village nearby, **Balestrino**, is still defended by a picturesque **Del Carretto** castle; other castles constructed by the same clan of local lordlings may be seen further up the Val Varatella at cheese-making **Bardineto** and at a popular summer resort—the mountain village of **Calizzano**, which, besides the castle, has a small zoo with a contemporary descendant of the carnivorous cave bear and a flock of Tibetan goats.

## The Coast: Loano to Noli

Loano is an attractive, palm-shaded town and resort best known for its 16th-century **Palazzo Doria** (now the Municipio), containing a rare 3rd-century AD mosaic pavement, and for the fine views to be had from its 1608 Carmelite convent. Another old seaside town, **Pietra Ligure**, has the ruins of a Genoese fortress; from Borgio, the next tiny resort, you can turn off for Valdemino and the **Grotta di Borgio**, with more good stalactites (*open 9–11.30, 2:30–5, Tues–Sun; adm*).

**Finale Ligure** is yet another pleasant garden resort, spread between Finale Marina and the medieval village of Finalborgo, two kilometres inland. This area is especially rich in caves, many of which contain fascinating traces of Palaeolithic man and woman—most famously the **Grotta delle Arene Candide**. Although none of the caves is open to visitors, pottery, tools, tombs, Venuses and another huge bear skeleton found inside them are on display in the **Finale Civic Museum**, housed in the cloister of the convent of Santa Chiara in Finalborgo (*open April–Sept 10–12, 3–6, Tues–Sun; Oct–Mar 9–12, 2.30–4.30, Tues–Sun; adm*). Finalborgo itself is dominated by an impressive if derelict **castle**, another property of the Del Carretti, and the splendid 13th-century octagonal campanile of the **Basilica di San Biagio**. One of the prettiest excursions from Finalborgo is to make your way along the old Roman Via Aurelia, which here weaves through the Valle di Ponci (near Finale Pia) and the Val Quazzola, traversing a dozen Roman bridges.

**Noli** thrived as a small maritime republic before its bigger neighbours elbowed it out of business, though its independence is still commemorated in a festival of traditional regattas every August. Lying under the **Castello di Monte Ursino** and still protected by its medieval walls, gates, and towers, its most important monument is the 11th-century church of San Paragorio, founded in 820; its treasures include a 13th-century bishop's throne and a 12th-century crucifix called a *Volto Santo* because of the picture on it, said to be a true portrayal of Christ—similar to the more famous one in Lucca. But sure, too, to note Noli's antique street lamps. There's a good beach here, and an even better one nearby at **Spotorno**.

## Savona

The provincial capital, Savona is a working city rather than a resort, as well as one of Italy's busiest ports; one of the most interesting things to do is hang around the docks and watch the aerial cable cars unload coal for the ironworks at San Giuseppe di Cairo. The harbour tower, the **Torre di Leon Pancaldo** dates from the 13th century, but was renamed to honour Magellan's Savonese pilot, Leon 'Hot Bread'. Other natives of Savona include the della Rovere family, which gave the world two popes, Sixtus IV (who built the Sistine Chapel in the Vatican) and his nephew, Julius II, who hired Michelangelo to paint the thing.

Sixtus and Julius left their mark on the old quarter of Savona (take pretty Via Pia from the harbour); their **Della Rovere Palace** (now the law courts) faces the 16th-century **cathedral**, flanked by another **Sistine Chapel**. This contains a marble tomb with two fine statues of the popes. The cathedral contains a few relics of its medieval predecessor, which the Genoese demolished in 1528 to build a fortress—not to protect Savona, but to put a damper on its considerable ambition. The best art is tucked away in the **cathedral Museum** (*open on request*), with a fine *Adoration of the Magi* by the Hoogstaeten master, 14th-century English alabaster statues, and items donated by the popes. Near the quay, at Via Quadra Superiore 7, the medieval Palazzo Pozzobonello houses the **Museo Civico** (*open 8.30am–12.30pm Mon–Sat; adm*), with a good collection of Ligurian Renaissance works by Donato De Bardi, Lodovico Brea, and Taddeo di Bartolo, as well as a polyptych by Vincenzio Foppa.

From Savona rail lines branch off for Turin (also linked by the A6 *autostrada*) and Milan. Along the first route you'll pass through the traditional boundary between the Alps and the Apennines at **Bocchetta di Cadibona**, and stop off at **Millesimo** (connected by bus from Savona), a charming, fortified hill town, where even the bridge, the **Gaietta**, has a watch tower. It is a popular excursion destination, with a clutch of artisans' workshops and pastry shops selling scrumptious rum chocolates called *millesimini.*

## Savona to Genoa

Although the bathing quality declines the closer you get to the big city, there are some tempting stopovers: **Albisola**, Liguria's most important ceramics centre, or **Celle Ligure** and **Varazze**, popular resorts, the latter still partly surrounded by its walls which incorporate the façade (but nothing else) of the 10th-century church of **Sant'Ambrogio**. The rebuilt 1535 Sant'Ambrogio, with a lovely medieval campanile, contains some fine Renaissance and Baroque art. Further east, **Cogoleto**, according to one tradition, was the birthplace of Columbus. At least everyone in the village thinks so, and they've erected a statue and plaque to him in the main piazza.

**Pegli**, a longtime weekend retreat of the Genoese, has been sucked into metropolitan Genoa, but like Nervi to the east maintains its beauty and most of its tranquillity. The grounds of two seigneurial villas are now used as parks. One park, the **Villa Doria**, was formerly the gardens of the interesting, frescoed 16th-century Villa Centurione Doria, now used as the **Naval History Museum** (*open 9–1, 2–5, Tues–Sat*), with a fine collection of artefacts relating to Genoa's proud maritime traditions, including ships' models, paintings (among them a portrait of Columbus), compasses, astrolabes, weapons, armour, and maps. Another park, the magnificent **Villa Durazzo-Pallavicini** is an elegantly arranged garden with statuary, rotundas, temples, and ponds, designed in the 19th century. The house itself contains **Museum of Ligurian Archaeology** (*open 9am–5pm Tues–Sat; 9am–12.30pm Sun; adm*), with an interesting collection of pre-Roman and Roman finds from Genoa, and especially from the prehistoric caves of the Riviera di Ponente. The star exhibit is the so-called 'Young Prince', a buried figure discovered in the Grotta delle Arene Candide, with a seashell headdress and a dagger in his hand.

### Where to Stay

Note that many hotels in this area still prefer whenever possible to follow traditional practice and require that their guests take full- or half-pension, particularly in high season. At other times they will be more open to negotiation.

### Imperia

The **★★★Robinia**, Via Pirinoli 14, ✆ (0183) 62720, 🖂 60635 (moderate) is a pleasant, albeit unexceptional choice, with its own beach, a lovely terrace, parking, restaurant, and 55 rooms, most with a sea view. There are any number of one and two-star hotels in Imperia, mainly around the Corso Matteotti.

### Diano Marina

The **★★★★Bellevue & Méditerranée**, Via Gen. Ardoino 2, ✆ (0183) 402693 (moderate) is one of the most pleasant hotels on the beach, with a pool and garden in addition to its beach facilities. Diano Marina also has the **★★★Caprice**, Corso Roma

19, ☎ (0183) 495061 (inexpensive; quite a classy place for this price range, with private baths in all rooms as well as a garden and beach, and a fine restaurant.

## Cervo

The accommodation available in Cervo is measly compared to the rest of the Riviera, but the ★★★**Columbia**, Via Aurelia 71, ☎ (0183) 400079 (inexpensive), does its best to please, with 20 comfortable rooms, a garden, and private beach. (*Closed Oct–Nov*). In the old town, ★★**Bellavista**, Piazza Castello 2, ☎ (0183) 408094 (inexpensive) has pleasant enough rooms, without bath.

## Alassio

Alassio is the biggest resort in the area, and the top hotel there is now the recently refurbished and newly promoted ★★★★★**Spiaggia**, Via Roma 78, ☎ (0182) 643403, ✆ 640279 (very expensive) which, despite its name, is not actually on the beach, although it does have a private one. The rooms are modern, air-conditioned, and well-equipped, but rather small. There is a pool and a restaurant, but it's not really five-star material. Another the finest hotels is the ★★★★**Grand Hotel Diana**, Via Garibaldi 110, ☎ (0182) 642701, ✆ 640304 (expensvie) directly on the sea. Rooms without a sea view are considerably cheaper than those on the front, but all have private bath, and there's an indoor pool as well as a private beach.

Out of a very extensive choice, the ★★★★**Ambassador**, Corso Europa 64, ☎ (0182) 472034 (moderate) is one of the more popular hotels, with comfortable rooms, all with private bath. Directly on the beach, ★★★**Beau Sejour**, Via Garibaldi 102, ☎ (0182) 640303, ✆ 646391 (moderate) has well-furnished rooms, and is good for a longer stay, with a fine terrace and garden for dawdling.. (*Open April–Sept.*) The ★★★**Majestic**, Corso Leonardo da Vinci 300, ☎ (0182) 642721 (moderate) is a good-value resort hotel, with beach facilities. (*Open mid-April–mid-Oct.*) The excellent ★★★**Milano**, Piazza Airaldi e Durante 11, ☎ (0182) 640597, ✆ 640598 (moderate) has been recently remodelled and is literally right on the beach, and all rooms are well-equipped, have balconies and enjoy fine sea views. There is also a very nice restaurant serving various Ligurian specialities. The ★★★**Ligure**, Passeggiata Italia 25, ☎ (0182) 640653, ✆ 660641 (moderate) is another good medium-price hotel, in the heart of the old town but still with sea views, with modern, airy rooms and a very good restaurant. There are several budget options. The pleasant, seafront ★★★**Eden**, Passeggiata Cadorna 20, ☎ (0182) 640281, ✆ 643037, also has beach facilities. The ★★**Bel Air**, Via Roma 40, ☎ (0182) 642579, ✆ 640238, is wonderful value, as its rooms have all modern fittings and the hotel has its own beach. The similar ★★**Kon Tiki**, Via delle Palme 11, is a short walk from the beach, with its own bar and restaurant, and modern facilities in all rooms.

## Albenga

There is not a great choice of accommodation in Albenga, but prices are convivial. ★★★**La Gallinara**, Via Piave 66, ☎ (0182) 53086, ✆ 541280 (expensive) is the top choice, and there's also ★★★**Tre Torri**, Via Piave 2, ☎ (0182) 50692, ✆ 540442 (expensive) set in its own grounds and with parking facilities. For beach views, there's the **Sole e Mare**, Lungomare Colombo, ✆ (0182) 51817, @ 52752 (expensive) with simple but pleasant rooms with baths at reasonable prices. Albenga's *Il Bucaniere, Lungomare Colombo 8, ✆ (0182) 50220 (inexpensive) has rather basic rooms without baths, but a nice garden.

## Garlenda

The ****La Meridiana**, Via ai Castelli, ✆ (0182) 580271, @ 580150 (very expensive) is a golfers' paradise, amid pretty olive groves, ancient oaks, and vineyards. A member of the Relais et Châteaux chain, it is a contemporary building constructed with traditional stone walls and wooden ceilings, and with simple but very attractive furnishings. As well as the golf course, there is a large pool in the grounds, tennis courts, and a riding school, and the sea is only 10km away. The really adventurous can even take parachuting lessons at the little airport nearby, and the food is excellent. (*Open all year.*) Golf duffers with smaller budgets than the residents of La Meridiana (*see* above) can still be near the links at the ***Foresteria Golf Club**, at Bra, ✆ (0182) 580013 (expensive) which offers all of seven simple but nice rooms, all with bath.

## Finale Ligure

Hotels in Finale Ligure mainly cater to families. Among the best are the ***Park Hotel Castello**, Via Caviglia 26, ✆ (019) 691320 (expensive) a pleasant hotel near the top of the town, with more character than most and a pretty garden; it's also one of the few that remains open all year. Also good is the rather unfortunately named ****Moroni**, Via San Pietro 38, ✆ (019) 692222, @ 680330 (expensive), which has big, air-conditioned rooms without sea views, or smaller ones with. Rooms are well-equipped throughout, and very reasonably priced.

For a change from the fairly anonymous modern establishments try the ***Conte**, Via Genova 16, ✆ (019) 600670 (expensive) in its own secluded garden in a lovely setting. Inside, it's like stepping back in time fifty years—old prints line the walls, and period furniture sits in reception. All the rooms are different, and large, and some have modern fittings.

In the old town, ***Colibri**, Via Colombo 57, ✆ (019) 692681, @ 694206 (expensive) is a very efficiently run, modern place, whose rooms have views of the hills—making a change from the sea. There is also a sun-roof, parking, and a good restaurant.

*San Marco, Via Concezione 22, ✆ (019) 692533 (inexpensive) is a fairly basic cheap hotel that has the advantage of being right on the sea front, and a good restaurant. Enjoying the best views in town, and in the castle itself, is a fine **youth hostel** ✆ (019) 690515 (inexpensive) with a pretty garden. To get there, turn left at the station, and then it's a stiff 15-minute climb up a seemingly endless flight of steps. It is, though, worth it. (*Open Mar–Oct; L14,000 per person, including breakfast.*)

## Imperia

Imperia has some fine restaurants, particularly the **Lanterna Blù**, Via Scarincio 32 in Porto Maurizio, ✆ (0183) 63859 (very expensive). The ingredients for its fine dishes come directly from two local farms; be sure to try the hot seafood antipasti, a splendid accompaniment to the views from the seaside veranda. (*Closed Wed.*) Excellent seafood is the main attraction at **Nannina**, Viale Matteotti 56, ✆ (0183) 20 208, (very expensive) in Imperia, a haven for lovers of scampi and prawns. (*Closed Mon.*) The Imperia-ites are proud of their prize-winning pizzeria, **Hobo's**, at Via Rambaldo in Porto Maurizio, (inexpensive) where an exquisite *Quattro Stagioni* with a beer is L8500, and full meals are also available at inexpensive prices.

## Cervo

Those who reserve in advance can enjoy a meal at **San Giorgio**, in the old town on Via Volta 19, ✆ (0183) 400175, (expensive) where in an intimate, art-filled setting you can dine on well-prepared Ligurian specialities like *trenette al pesto* or *verdure ripiene* (stuffed vegetables).

## Alassio

What Alassio may lack in grand hotels it makes up for with a gourmet palace, **La Palma**, Via Cavour 5, ✆ (0182) 40314 (expensive), where you can choose each day between two *menus degustazione*, one highlighting basil, the sacred herb of Liguria, and the second, Provençal-Ligurian specialities with an emphasis on seafood. La Palma is not large, so be sure to reserve. For a seafood orgy, head out to the local yacht club's **Al Mare**, Porticciolo Ferrari, ✆ (0182) 44186, (expensive) where each course (except the delicious ice cream for dessert), is delightfully fishy. In the heart of the old town, **La Cave**, Passeggiata Italia 7, ✆ (0182) 640693, (expensive) is an atmospheric old restaurant, serving typical Ligurian cuisine like *troffie al pesto* and fish soups. (*Closed Wed.*) For pizza in a traditional atmosphere, try **Della Quintana**, Via Gastaldi 5, ✆ (0182) 643301 (inexpensive), housed in a medieval building.

## Finale Ligure

The first-choice restaurant in Finale is **Raffa**, Via Concezione 64, ✆ (019) 692495 (expensive), run by Raffaele Ciuffo, who prides himself on choosing only the freshest of local fish, which is served in an intimate atmosphere. Don't leave without trying the speciality, *pescespada alla Raffa*. (*Closed Wed.*) One of the best reasonably priced places to eat in Finale is **Al Cantuccio**, Via Torino 54, ✆ (019) 691394, (inexpensive) which offers two fixed-price menus of local delicacies, one around L12,000 and the other at L30,000. There is also an extremely good wine list. Further along the coast in Noli, a friendly restaurant serving good Ligurian food is **Da Ines**, Via Vignolo 1, ✆ (019) 748086 (moderate) in the middle of the old town.

During the summer season, this area is one of the liveliest on the Italian coast, with several festivals and events as well as lots of clubs, bars and discos. Throughout summer, the **Musica nei Castelli di Liguria** music festival takes place, in which a series of classical concerts by Italian and international ensembles are presented in the many castles of the region. Full details are available from local tourist offices.

Anyone with children should also keep in mind that in Ceriale, just to the east of Albenga, is the only **aquapark** in the region, at **Le Caravelle**, Via Sant'Eugenio, © (0182) 931755 (*open April–Sept 10am–7pm daily*). It has loads of slides, chutes, and waterfalls, and is serious fun.

As regards **nightlife**, Alassio attracts a fairly young, hip crowd who meet up from about 10pm in the bars lining the sea-front such as **Zanzibar**, Via Vittorio Veneto 143, with lots of loud music and 50s memorabilia, and **Breakfast**, Via Dante 213, *the* place to meet both before and after clubbing. Clubs and discos generally get going about midnight and close at 4 or 5am.

The trendiest places in Alassio are **Rapsodia**, Vico Berna 6, which plays an excellent selection of 70s disco to latest chart, and **U Brecche**, Via Dante 204. A slightly older clientele patronises the more mainstream **Boccaccio Club**, in Via Privata Londra. In summer, roofs and inhibitions come down in Alassio at **La Vela**, Via Giancardi 46, and in nearby Laigueglia at **La Suerte**, just by the sea, which gets very crowded very early. In Albenga there's **Blackout**, Via Martiri della Libertà 21, small and trendy, with an interesting mixture of rock and funk.

**Live music** can also be found in Alassio, at **Fred Music Bar**, on Via XX Settembre, and **Tropicana**, Passeggiata Italia 3, where you can sit outside and listen to the bands. In Ceriale, there's live **jazz** every night till 3am at the **Blue Monk Pub**, Via Ponetto 2, from local and international performers.

Finale is the other hot-spot for nightlife: plenty of bars line the seafront, including **Clipper**, with an old-style atmosphere. Of the discos, **Caligola**, on Via Colombo, plays mainly dance, and **El Patio**, Lungomare Italia, provides less frantic music for a slightly older crowd.

## Genoa

There's always a tingling air of danger, excitement, unexpected fortune or sudden disaster in real port cities. The streets are enlivened with sailors, travellers and vagrants of all nationalities, and there's always the volatility of the sea itself, ready to make or break a fortune. Of the country's four ancient maritime republics (Venice, Amalfi, and Pisa are the others), only Genoa (Genova) has retained its salty tang and thrill. It is Italy's largest port, and any possible scenographic effect it could have, enhanced by its beautiful location of steep hills piling into the sea, has been utterly snuffed out by the more important affairs of the port: an elevated highway, huge docks, warehouses, stacks of containers and unloading facilites hog the shoreline for miles, so that from many points you can't even see the sea. And behind the docks wind the dishevelled alleys lined with typical piquant portside establishments that cater to weasely men of indeterminate nationality, old pirates, and discreetly tattooed ladies.

Counterbalancing this fragrant zone of stevedores is the Genoa that Petrarch called *La Superba*, the Superb City (or 'Proud', as in one of the Seven Deadly Sins) of palaces, gardens, and art; the city whose merchant fleet once reigned supreme from Spain to the southern Russian ports on the Black Sea, the city that gave the Spaniards Columbus but which in return controlled the contents of Spain's American silver fleets, becoming the New York City of the 16th century, flowing with money, ruled by factions of bankers and oligarchs, populated by rugged individualists and entrepreneurs, and leaving a mark in the fashion industry with its silks and a sturdy blue cotton cloth the French called *de Gênes*, which came to be made into jeans.

Modern Genoa is a teeming, neon-flashing, kinetic antidote to the Riviera's resortarama. Even its impossible topography is exciting: squeezed between mountains and sea, greater Genoa stretches for 30 kilometres—there are people who commute to work by lift or funicular, tunnels bore under green parks in the very centre of the city, and apartment houses hang over the hills so that the penthouse is at street level. The old quarter is a bustling warren of alleys, or *carugi*, miniature canyons under eight-storey palaces and tenements, streaming with banners of laundry. There are fine streets of Renaissance palaces and Art Nouveau mansions, fine art (though the Genoese produced no painters or sculptors of note themselves, they amassed some fine collections), and one of the most amazing cemeteries on earth.

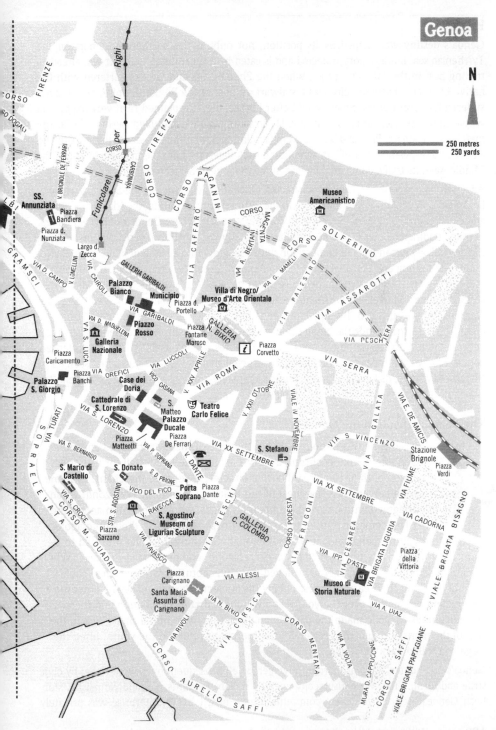

Genoa

N

250 metres
250 yards

FIRENZE

Righi

Il per Funicolare

CORSO DOGALI

CORSO FIRENZE

CORBINARA

CORSO

V. BRIGNOLE DE FERRARI

SS. Annunziata

Piazza Bandiera

Piazza d. Nunziata

Largo d. Zecca

GALLERIA GARIBALDI

GRAMSCI

VIA D. CAMPO

V. LOMELLINI

VIA CAIROLI

Palazzo Bianco

Municipio

VIA GARIBALDI

Piazza d. Portello

VIA D. MADDALENA

Piazza Rosso

Galleria Nazionale

VIA S. LUCA

Piazza Caricamento

Piazza Banchi

VIA OREFICI

Case dei Doria

VICO CASANA

Palazzo S. Giorgio

VIA TURATI

Cattedrale di S. Lorenzo

VIA S. LORENZO

S. Matteo

Palazzo Ducale

Piazza Matteotti

Piazza De Ferrari

VIA P. SOPRANA

S. Mario di Castello

VIA S. BERNARDO

S. Donato

S. D. PRIONE

SOPRAELEVATA

VIA S. CROCE

STR. S. AGOSTINO

VICO DEL FICO

CORSO M. QUADRIO

Piazza Sarzano

S. Agostino/ Museum of Ligurian Sculpture

V. RAVECCA

VIA RAVASCO

VIA RIVOLI

Piazza Carignano

Santa Maria Assunta di Carignano

VIA N. BIXIO

VIA ALESSI

CORSO AURELIO SAFFI

VIA CAFFARO

PAGANINI

CORSO

CORSO MAGENTA

VIA A. BERTANI

VIA G. MAMELI

Museo Americanistico

CORSO SOLFERINO

VIA PALESTRO

Villa di Negro/ Museo d'Arte Orientale

GALLERIA N. BIXIO

Piazza Fontane Marose

VIA LUCCOLI

V. XXV APRILE

VIA ROMA

Piazza Corvetto

VIA ASSAROTTI

VIA PESCHIERA

VIA SERRA

V. XXII OTTOBRE

Teatro Carlo Felice

V. DANTE

Porta Soprano

Piazza Dante

VIA FIESCHI

GALLERIA C. COLOMBO

VIALE IV NOVEMBRE

S. Stefano

VIA XX SETTEMBRE

CORSO PODESTÀ

VIA FRUGONI

VIA GALATA

VIA S. VINCENZO

VIA XX SETTEMBRE

VIA DE AMICIS

Stazione Brignole

Piazza Verdi

VIA FIUME

VIA CADORNA

Piazza della Vittoria

VIA IPP. D'ASTE

VIA CESAREA

VIA BRIGATA LIGURIA

VIALE BRIGATA BISAGNO

Museo di Storia Naturale

VIA A. DIAZ

VIA CORSICA

CORSO MENTANA

VIA A. VOLTA

CORSO A. SAFFI

MURA D. CAPPUCCINE

VIALE BRIGATA PARTIGIANE

181

# History

Genoa's destiny was shaped by its position, not only as the northernmost port on the Tyrrhenian sea, but as a port protected and isolated by a ring of mountains. It was already a trading post in the 6th century BC, when the Phoenicians and Greeks bartered with the native Ligurians. Later the city was a stalwart outpost of the Roman Empire, and as such suffered the wrath of Hannibal; rebuilt after his sacking, it remained relatively happy and whole until the Lombards took it in 641, initiating a dark, troubled period. While the merchants of Amalfi, Pisa, and Venice were creating their maritime republics in the 10th and 11th centuries, Genoa was still an agricultural backwater, far from the main highways of the Middle Ages, its traffic dominated by Pisa, its coasts prey to Saracen corsairs.

Adversity helped form the Genoese character. Once it rallied to defeat the Saracens, the city began a dizzily rapid rise to prominence in the 12th century, capturing the islands of Sardinia and Corsica, and joining the Normans to conquer Antioch, where Genoa established its first of many trading colonies in the Middle East. The city walls had to be enlarged in 1155, as the city quickly expanded and competition with Pisa grew into a battle of blows as well as of trade. The turning point for their duel for supremacy in the Western Mediterranean came in 1284, when Genoa soundly pummelled Pisa into naval obscurity at the battle of Meloria—a victory Genoa followed up with another over a more troublesome rival, Venice, at the Curzonali islands in 1298. By this time Genoa had merchant colonies stretching from the coast of North Africa, to Syria, along the Black Sea, and in Spain, where Genoese captains became the first to sail to the Canaries and the Azores. Genoa itself was the most densely populated city in Europe, as its patricians constructed their towering houses that seemed so 'superb' to visitors; its fame was so widespread that Genoa served as a setting for a tale in the Arabian Nights, the only Western city to be so honoured.

## The Famous Insult to the Genoese

 It was during this period, in 1316, that one of the most beloved anecdotes of Genoese history occurred, a story the Genoese like to tell for its perfect evocation of their proud, stubborn character: a Genoese merchant, by name Megollo Lercari, was the guest of the Eastern Emperor at Trebizond, when he disagreed with one of the emperor's pages, who slapped him across the face. The emperor refused to let the Genoese strike back, though he apologized for the youth's behaviour. It was not enough. Seething, Megollo returned to Genoa, got up a private fleet, sailed back to Trebizond, and demanded the page. When the emperor refused, the Genoese besieged the city, capturing whoever they could and chopping off their ears or noses. Finally his subjects' despair made the emperor give in, and he handed over the youth, and watched, first in trepidation and then amazement, as Megollo made the page stoop over, then gave him a smart kick in the seat of the pants. Honour thus regained, the merchant returned the youth, lifted the siege and sailed back to Genoa.

Genoa's first golden age was marred, however, as all subsequent ones were to be, by civic strife and turmoil that were disgraceful even by Italian standards. The individualistic, stubborn Genoese refused to accept communal unity; nearly every enterprise was privately funded, including even most of the city's military expeditions. The city itself was divided into factions, nobles against each other, nobles against the mercantile classes, the merchants against the artisans—while the ruling families each dominated their own quarter of the city, forming *alberghi*, or brotherhoods, of their partisans, running their own prisons and armies, and fighting for political control of their city.

In 1339 the popular classes won a victory by electing Genoa's first doge, Simone Boccanegra, the hero of Verdi's opera. Genoa's doges, though, were figureheads from the beginning, and Boccanegra's victory was Pyrrhic: the nobles responded to his election by inviting in the Visconti of Milan; Boccanegra was exiled to Pisa; the Visconti were thrown out; Boccanegra returned—for nearly two centuries Genoese civic history is an ignoble chronicle of one faction momentarily gaining the upper hand, and all the others doing everything to undermine it, even inviting in a foreign lord.

## The Bank of St George

The real power in Genoa turned out to be a bank. When the city sank deep into debt during its prolonged war with Venice for the eastern Mediterranean (ending in Genoa's traumatic defeat at Chioggia in 1380), its creditors—Genoa's oligarchs—formed a syndicate, the Banco di San Giorgio, to guarantee their increasingly precarious loans. This the bank did by gradually assuming control of the city's overseas territories, castles, towns, and even its treasury. Genoa from then on, for all practical purposes, was run as a business proposition—once, in 1421, when the bank was short of cash, it sold Livorno to Florence for a tidy sum. The Genoese never had any reason to identify with their municipal government like the Venetians did, but, as Machiavelli noted, they were very loyal to their bank.

Genoa recovered quickly from the defeat at Chioggia by transforming its economy from the mercantile sphere to the financial. The cinquecento found the city Europe's leading economic power, a position Genoa maintained for a long time thanks to the foresight of Andrea Doria (1468–1560), the 'Saviour of Genoa' and the greatest admiral of his day. During the Wars of Italy between Charles V of Spain and Francis I of France, Doria drove Genoa's traditional French allies from the city and welcomed Spanish protection, then wrote a new Republican constitution for the strife-torn city, institutionalizing the shared rule of the 28 *alberghi*. Charles V rewarded Doria with the title of Prince of Melfi, and he and other Genoese took prominent posts throughout the Empire. Meanwhile the Bank of St George became fat and sleek financing the wars in the Low Countries for Charles V and Philip II, processing Spain's silver, and taking over the international money market from Besançon and Antwerp: millions of *scudi* passed through Genoa every year. Andrea Doria was also Genoa's first great patron of the arts, introducing the High Renaissance to the city that had formerly managed without it.

Nevertheless, after the crusty old admiral, Genoa began to decline. Spain's bankruptcies came too frequently; Atlantic commerce overtook in importance the old Mediterranean trade; the Ottoman Empire gobbled up Genoa's last trading colonies in the east. The French (1668), and then the Austrians (1734), took the city itself; Corsica, Genoa's last colony, revolted in 1768, and the Bank of St George could do nothing but sell it to France.

By the 1815 Treaty of Vienna, Genoa and Liguria joined Piedmont, and almost at once the city became a hotbed of unification sentiment, led by the conspiring philosopher of the

Risorgimento, Giuseppe Mazzini, and such patriot luminaries as Nino Bixio, Goffredo Mameli, the Ruffini brothers, and of course Garibaldi himself.

## Getting There

### by air

Genoa's international airport, **Cristoforo Colombo**, 6km from the city in Sestri Ponente, has direct flights to Britain and many European destinations as well as to Italian cities. For information, © 2415410, @ 2415437. **Buses** to the airport depart an hour before each flight from Brignole Station and Piazza de Ferrari.

### by sea

From Genoa you can sail away to exotic lands on a ferry from the **Stazione Marittima**, © 2412439, just below the Stazione Principe. Nearly any travel agency in Genoa can sell you a ticket, or you can make reservations by phone. **Grandi Traghetti**, Via Fieschi 17, © 589331, sails several times a week to Palermo, and Porto Torres in Sardinia; **Tirrenia**, Ponte Colombo, © 258606, has ferries to the Sardinian ports of Porto Torres, Cagliari, and Olbia, as well as to Palermo and Tunis; **Sardinia Ferries**, Piazza Dante 5, © 593301, has services to several points on that island from Genoa; and **Corsica Ferries**, Piazza Dante 5, © 543751, sails to Bastia.

### by rail

Genoa has two main train stations: **Principe**, in Piazza Acquaverde, just west of the centre, and **Brignole**, to the northeast. Principe in general handles trains from the north and France, while Brignole takes trains from the south, though most long-distance trains actually call at both. Also, city bus no.37 links the two.

### by long-distance bus

Intercity services and buses to the rest of the province and the Riviera depart from the Piazza della Vittoria, south of Brignole station, or from Piazza Acquaverde, in front of Stazione Principe.

### by road

Three major *autostrade* actually meet just north of the centre of the city—the A10 from France and the Riviera di Ponente, the A12 along the Riviera di Levante, and the A7 to Milan, which also connects with the A21 for Turin. The elevated branch of the A10, the *Sopraelevata*, runs right along the old port before ending near the Fiera di Genova; use it to get in or out of the city, and to connect up with all three main highways.

## Getting Around

 Chances are you won't need to make much use of city **buses**, as most of Genoa's points of interest are in the centre, between the two train stations—the main thoroughfares are Via XX Settembre, running from near Brignole to the central Piazza de Ferrari; and Via Balbi, from Stazione Principe towards Piazza di Nunziata and the Piazza Corvetto, from where Via Roma leads to the Piazza de Ferrari. If you do take the buses, a single **ticket**—which must be purchased before getting on the bus, from tobacco shops or the transport authority (ATM) information kiosks at the rail stations—costs L1200; a one-day unlimited-travel **tourist ticket** is also available from the ATM, for L4000.

There are also **funiculars** from Piazza Portello and Largo della Zecca, which ascend to the city's upper residential quarters; the one served by the former, **Righi**, has a splendid outlook over the city and harbour. A **lift** from Piazza Portello will also take you up to the nearer belvedere at Castelletto. Tickets for funiculars and lifts are the same as for the city buses.

Genoa also now has a **Metro**, but at time of writing most of it is of theoretical usefulness, as there is only one functioning line, with three stops open. Another seven are under construction.

**Driving** in Genoa is not much fun, and probably best avoided. The old quarter is closed to traffic, and the street plan is chaotic, though one consolation is that the *Soprelevata*, the ugly elevated motorway that runs along the harbour, is never hard to find for a quick getaway. **Taxis**, on the other hand, are plentiful. For a radio taxi, call ℭ 2696.

---

### Tourist Information

The main local EPT office is at Via Roma 11, ℭ 541541, ℮ 581408, though visitors are usually better served at the multilingual branch offices at Stazione Principe, ℭ 262633, Stazione Brignole, ℭ 562056, and at the airport, ℭ 2415247. The offices are open Monday to Friday during office hours and on Saturday mornings (airport office Saturday pm also). Genoa has a very easy-to-grasp **museum/monument admission policy**— each one costs L4000 admission, and all are free on Sundays. Except where stated this applies to all the monuments etc. listed below.

For information about entertainments, special events and what's on in general in Genoa at any one time a good source is the city's daily paper, *Il Secolo XIX*. The tourist offices are only just getting used to an increase in visitors, but are also very helpful.

**Fire,** ℭ 115
**Police**, Via Diaz, ℭ 53661
**Ambulance,** ℭ 363159

**Hospital: Ospedale Evangelico Internazionale**, Via Benedetto XV 10, ℭ 35351.
**24-hour Pharmacy: Pescetto**, Via Balbi 31, ℭ 252786.

There is a 24-hour automatic change machine at **Bancomat**, Piazza de Ferrari 10.

The **main post office** is at Via Boccardo 2, off Via Dante and near the Piazza de Ferrari, and is open 8.15am–7.40pm Mon–Sat. There are also offices at the two main train stations. There is a **telephone centre** open 24 hours at the SIP office at Via XX Settembre 139.

The telephone prefix for Genoa is **010**. Note, too, that Genoa is one of several Italian cities with an unnecessarily complicated street-numbering system: any commercial establishment receives a red (r) number, but any residence a black or blue numberplate.

## Stazione Principe to Via Garibaldi

Both of Genoa's two main stations are lovely—the Stazione Principe could serve as a setting for a fancy-dress ball. In its Piazza Acquaverde visitors are greeted by a **Statue of Columbus**, a view of the port, and the stately Via Balbi. If you're catching a ferry, Via Andrea Doria will take you down to the Stazione Marittima, but even if you're not you may want to wander down to take in Genoa's most celebrated landmark, the **Lanterna**, a medieval lighthouse standing 117m high, and last restored in 1543. In the old days a huge fire would be ignited on top to guide vessels into the port. Near the Stazione Marittima there are two other ancient monuments: the **Commandery**, a loggia belonging to the Knights of St John, who used Genoa as a Crusader port, and the 12th-century church of San Giovanni di Pré, with an attractive spire-clustered campanile.

**Via Balbi** has some fine late Renaissance palaces, among them the yellow and red **Palazzo Reale** (*open 9am–1.30pm daily*), with its hyper-decorated 18th-century ballroom and Hall of Mirrors, and a *Crucifixion* by Van Dyck, who spent several years working in Genoa. Via Balbi gives on to Piazza Nunziata, so named because of its 16th-century **Annunziata Church**, with a façade almost Puritan in its austerity, hiding a voluptuous Rococo interior. From the next square, the **Largo della Zecca**, you have several options: the thrilling funicular ride up to Righi, where you can dine at the top of the town, the lift up to the Castelletto, the tunnel through to Piazza Portello, some browsing through the district's antique shops, or, by continuing round on Via Cairoli, Genoa's most famous street, **Via Garibaldi**.

Via Garibaldi, the former *Strada Nuova*, was laid out in 1558, and for centuries was Genoa's 'Millionaires' Row,'with uninterrupted lines of 16th- and 17th-century palazzi. Many have since been converted into banks and municipal offices, but the street's unique and elegant character has been carefully maintained. Two of the palaces hold important art collections: the **Palazzo Bianco** (*open 9am–7pm Tues–Sat; 9–12 Sun*), at No.11, former residence of the Grimaldis, is no longer very white, but has the most noteworthy collection in the city, with a good assortment of Italian paintings, including Filippino Lippi's *Madonna with Saints*, Pontormo's *Florentine Gentleman*, Veronese's *Crucifixion*, and an even more impressive collection of Flemish art. Among the latter are Gerhard David's sweetly domestic *Madonna della Pappa*, paintings by Cranach, Van der Goes, Van Dyck and Rubens (who also worked for a while in Genoa), and there is also a fine *San Bonaventura* by the Spaniard Zurbarán. The portrait of Andrea Doria by Jan Matsys has remarkable hands. Across the street at No.18, the **Palazzo Rosso** (*open 9am–7pm Tues–Sat; 9–12 Sun*), still retains some of its palatial fittings, as well as a picture gallery with an especially good collection of portraits by Van Dyck, Pisanello, Dürer, and works by Caravaggio and his pupil Mattia Preti; here, too, is *La Cuoca*, a favourite work by Genoa's own Bernardo Strozzi.

Next to the Palazzo Rosso, the former **Palazzo Tursi** is now Genoa's Municipio, with the city's most beautiful courtyard and such municipal treasures as native son Paganini's violin, in the Sala della Giunta, and three letters from Columbus in the Sala del Sindaco. You can

*Piazza de' Ferrari*

enter the courtyard of No.7, the **Palazzo Podestà**, with an elaborate fountain in the shape of a grotto. The façade of No.3, the 16th-century **Palazzo Parodi-Lercari**, was built by the descendants of Megollo Lercari, who recalled the 'Insult to the Genoese' at Trebizond with earless and noseless caryatids.

## The Villa di Negro

Via Garibaldi ends at Piazza Marose, with more palaces, especially the 15th-century **Palazzo Spinola dei Marmi**, embellished with black and white bands and statues of the Spinola family. From here Salita Santa Caterina leads into the circular **Piazza Corvetto**, a major junction of the city bus lines and the entrance to the park of **Villa di Negro**, an urban oasis that takes full advantage of Genoa's crazy topography, with streams, cascades, grottoes and walkways, culminating at the top with the **Museo d'Arte Orientale** (*open 9am–5pm Tues–Sat; 9–12.30 Sun*), Italy's finest museum of Oriental art, a lovely collection of statues, paintings, theatre masks, and an extraordinary set of Samurai helmets and armour, all well displayed in a sun-filled modern building.

At the corner of Piazza Corvetto and Via Roma you can stop off for a history-imbued break at the early 19th-century **Caffè Mangani**. Via Roma continues down to tumultuous **Piazza de Ferrari**, on one side marked by the neoclassical **Teatro Carlo Felice**, built in 1829, bombed in 1944, and then left crumbling until 1992, when it was restored and reopened as part of the Columbus celebrations. Across the piazza, and separating it from the Piazza Matteotti below, is the giant, black-and-white mass of the 16th-century **Palazzo Ducale**, since 1992 a shopping and exhibition centre (see below). The way down from the Piazza de Ferrari to the Piazza Matteotti is by a huge monumental staircase, formerly used for the city's processions.

From Piazza de Ferrari you can descend into Old Genoa; the most picturesque way is to head down Via Dante to Piazza Dante and the **Porta Soprana**, the tall twin-towered 1155 gateway where, according to documents, Columbus' father was gatekeeper; his 'boyhood home' is nearby, as are the 12th-century ruins of the **Cloister of Sant'Andrea**, set out on the lawn.

## The Old City

Within the Porta Soprana are the tall houses, sliced by corridor-like alleys, of the old city, some so narrow that they live in perpetual shade. Partly bombed and mostly unrepaired after the War, leaning ever so gently towards the harbour below, many houses have white marble and black slate portals, permitted only to those families who performed a deed of benefit to the city, while corners and wall niches are decorated with hundreds of little shrines known as *madonnette*, the little madonnas.

The old town is for exploring, although single women should exercise caution, especially after dark. To see the highlights of the quarter, take the Via Ravecca down from Porta Soprana to the 13th-century Gothic church of Sant'Agostino, its ruined cloisters converted into the well-designed **Museum of Ligurian Sculpture and Architecture** (*open 9am–7pm Tues–Sat; 9am–12 midday Sun*) containing artworks and architectural fragments salvaged from Genoa's demolished churches. One of the finest works is the 1312 fragment of the tomb of Margherita of Brabant, wife of Emperor Henry VII, sculpted by Giovanni Pisano. Margherita died suddenly in Genoa while accompanying her husband to Rome for his coronation, and Henry, whom Dante and many others had hoped would be able to end the feud between Italy's Guelphs and Ghibellines, died in Siena two years later, many believe of sorrow; his last request was that his heart be taken to Genoa to be interred with his wife. There are also Roman works, Romanesque sculpture, frescoes, the 14th-century wooden *Christ of the Caravana*, and much more.

From Sant'Agostino the Stradone di Sant'Agostino leads to another good church, the 12th-century Romanesque **San Donato**, with an exceptionally lovely octagonal campanile, portal and interior, combining a pleasant mix of Roman and medieval columns. The nearby Via San Bernardo, one of the few straight streets in the old city, was laid out by the Romans. Their *castrum* (fort) up the hill (take the Salita della Torre degli Embriaci) provided the foundations for Genoa's most venerable church, the evocative **Santa Maria di Castello**, founded in the palaeo-Christian era and incorporating numerous Roman columns and stones in its Romanesque structure. The crusaders used Santa Maria's complex as a hostel. Fairest of its artworks is the 15th-century fresco of the *Annunciation* in the cloister, while the strangest is the *Crocifisso Miracoloso* in a chapel near the high altar—miraculous in that the Christ's beard is said to grow whenever Genoa is threatened with calamity.

## Around Piazza Matteotti

Another entrance into the historic centre from Piazza de Ferrari is by way of Piazza Matteotti, dominated by the main façade of the vast and grandiose **Palazzo Ducale**, once the residence of Genoa's doges. First built in the 16th century, it was greatly altered in the following century to serve as the city law courts. It stood neglected for years, but, like the

Carlo Felice theatre, it was also restored and renovated for 1992, and now you can walk through its attractive courtyards, one adorned with a fountain, or sample the restaurants, bars, and shops, and also an exhibition centre (*guided tours also available, adm, Ⓒ 562440*). Sharing the square is the Baroque church of the Gesù, designed in the late 16th century by Pellegrino Tibaldi. The interior is a colourful Baroque fantasia, all *trompe-l'œil* stage effects that highlight its frothy Baroque treasures: a *Circumcision* and *St Ignatius Exorcising the Devil* by Rubens, and an *Assumption* by the 'Divino' Guido Reni.

Just off the square stands the jauntily black-and-white-striped **Cathedral of San Lorenzo**, begun in the 12th century, and modified several times; the façade was last restored in 1934. Odds and ends from the ages embellish the exterior—two kindly 19th-century lions by the steps on the main façade, and a carving of St Lawrence toasting on his grill above the central of three French-Gothic-style portals. On the north side there's a pretty 12th-century **Portal of San Giovanni**; on the south, Hellenistic sarcophagi, another Romanesque portal, and a 15th-century tomb. The rather morose interior also wears jailbird stripes. The first chapel on the right contains a good marble *Crucifixion* of 1443, and a British shell fired from the sea 500 years later that hit the chapel but miraculously failed to explode. On the left, note the sumptuous Renaissance **Chapel of St John the Baptist**, with fine sculptures and marble decorations, and a 13th-century sarcophagus that once held the Baptist's relics.

The well-arranged **Cathedral Treasury** (*open 9.30–11.45, 3–5.45, Tues–Sat*), in the vaults off the nave to the left, contains a number of genuine treasures, acquired during the heyday of Genoa's mercantile empire: a crystal dish said to have been part of the dinner service of the Last Supper, the blue chalcedony dish on which John the Baptist's head was supposedly served to Salome, an 11th-century arm reliquary of St Anne, the golden, jewel-studded Byzantine *Zaccaria Cross*, and an elaborate 15th-century silver casket built to hold St John the Baptist's ashes.

The Salita del Fonaco follows the back of the Palazzo Ducale, then veers right for the **Piazza San Matteo**, a beautiful little square completely clothed in the honourable black and white bands of illustrious civic benefactors—and it's no wonder, for Piazza San Matteo was the public foyer of the Doria family, encompassed by their proud palazzi and their 12th-century church of **San Matteo**, inscribed with their great deeds. Inside the church, the highlight is the early 14th-century cloister, with charming capitals on twinned columns. Andrea Doria's palace was No.17 on the square, while No.14, belonging to Branca Doria, has a beautiful portal with Genoa's patron St George.

## Between Via San Lorenzo and Via Garibaldi

This northern section of the historic centre, built up mostly in the Renaissance, has survived somewhat better than the area around Porta Soprana, and has, amid its monuments, fine shops, pubs, restaurants, and cafés. From Piazza San Matteo it's a short walk to the **Campetto**, a lovely square adorned with the ornate 16th-century Palazzo Imperiale; in the nearby Piazza Soziglia you can take a break at one of the oldest coffee houses in Genoa, **Kainguti**, at No.98r, or **Romanegro**, at No.74r, both founded by a Swiss at the beginning of the 19th century. From the Piazza Soziglia and the Campetto, the pretty Via degli Orefici meanders down to the major intersection of medieval Genoa, the **Piazza Banchi**, with its

Renaissance Loggia dei Mercanti. From here Via Ponti Reale descends to the harbourside **Piazza Caricamento**, lined with the ancient arcades of Via Sottoripa and dominated by the gaudily decorated **Palazzo di San Giorgio**. This was built originally in 1260 for the Capitani del Popolo, but was taken over in 1408 by the famous Bank of St George, the shrewd Genoese bankers requiring a headquarters from where they could scrutinize the comings and goings of the port. It's now occupied by the Harbour Board, but you can ask the guard to show you some of the rooms that have been refurbished in their original 13th-century style.

Seawards, on the other side of the *Sopraelevata* from the Piazza Caricamento, the whole of the port area around the old quay or *Molo Vecchio* was extensively refurbished for 1992. Former cotton warehouses are now conference and exhibition centres, and a new attraction has been built, the **Gran Bigo** or 'Great Crane', designed by Renzo Piano, which now towers over the port from the end of one of the quays. A lift goes up the tower (*tickets L4000*), and there are superb views from the top. By 1994, the **Aquarium**, too the largest in Europe, should be fully functional. This area is pleasant for strolling after the at times somewhat claustrophobic *centro storico*.

Returning to the old city, **Via San Luca**, the main street passing through Piazza Banchi, was the principal thoroughfare of medieval Genoa, and in its day, home turf of another prominent Genoese family, the Spinola. One of their palaces, just off Via San Luca in little Piazza di Pelliccena, now houses the **National Gallery of Liguria** (*open 9–5 Tues–Sat, 9–1 Sun*). Most of its paintings were donated by the Spinola, along with the palace, which retains most of its 16th–18th-century decor. The paintings are arranged as in a private residence, and include Antonello da Messina's sad, beautiful *Ecce Homo*, Joos Van Cleve's magnificent *Adoration of the Magi*, works by Van Dyck (*Portrait of a Child* and the *Four Evangelists*), and another fragment of Giovanni Pisano's tomb of Margherita di Brabante, a statue of Justice. A little further to the north, back towards Largo della Zecca, stands one of the chief shrines of 19th-century Italian history, the **Casa Mazzini**, Via Lomellini 11, where the romantic prophet of Italian unification Giuseppe Mazzini was born in 1805. It now houses Genoa's **Museo del Risorgimento** (*open 9am–7pm Tues–Sat; 9–12 Sun*), centred on various relics of Mazzini himself.

---

## East Genoa

East of the Piazza de Ferrari runs the arcaded **Via XX Settembre**, the main thoroughfare of 19th-century Genoa, adorned here and there with Liberty-style touches. This is Genoa's main shopping street, and it and the area around Brignole station make up one of the city's most lively and genteel neighbourhoods, aglow with neon lights. Via XX Settembre is traversed by the Ponte Monumentale, which carries the Corso A. Podesta overhead. Next to the bridge a lane leads up to another of Genoa's striped medieval churches, **Santo Stefano**, which contains a *Martyrdom of St Stephen* by a less flamboyant than usual Giulio Romano. Beyond the bridge the avenue continues to the large Piazza della Vittoria, a Fascist-era square presided over by a 1931 War Memorial Arch. Nearby is the **Giacomo Doria Museum of Natural History**, Via Brigata Partigiane 9, © 566319, (*open 9–12, 3–5:30, Tues–Thurs, Sat, Sun*), an interesting collection garnered by 19th-century Genoese noblemen in their travels abroad.

## The Hills and Staglieno Cemetery

Some of the loveliest corners of Genoa are to be found up in the surrounding hills. The **Circonvallazione a Monte** is the scenic route, made up of several *corsi*, that skirts the slopes, a route followed by city bus 33, from Stazione Brignole or Piazza Manin, up to Corso Armelilini and Corso Solferino, where at No.39, in the 17th-century Villa Grüber, the **Museo Americanistico F. Lunardi** (*open 9.30–12, 3–5.30, Tues–Sat; 3–5.30pm Sun*) is installed. It holds a beautiful and important collection of pre-Columbian art, especially strong in Mayan work. The hillside route continues along Corsos Magenta, Paganini, Firenze, and U. Bassi, passing on the way the imposing **Castello d'Albertis**, which is medieval, though it was rebuilt in the 19th century. This, too, houses a **Museo Etnografico**, with a pre-Colombian collection, though it has been closed to visitors for some years.

Just over the mountains, along the Torrente Bisagno, lies Genoa's famous **Staglieno Cemetery** (*open 8am–5pm daily; bus 34 from Piazza Acquaverde or Piazza Corvetto*). Founded in 1844, the cemetery covers 160 hectares, and even has its own internal bus system. The Genoese have a reputation for being tight-fisted, but when it comes to post-mortem extravagance they have few peers. Staglieno is a veritable Babylon of the dead, with miniature cathedrals, Romanesque chapels, Egyptian temples, and Art Nouveau palaces and statuary—a fantastic, often surreal ensemble. In the centre of the hills, Genoa's great revolutionary idealist of the Risorgimento, Giuseppe Mazzini, is buried in a simple tomb behind two massive Doric columns, surrounded by laudatory inscriptions by Tolstoy, Lloyd George, D'Annunzio, and others. After a life of plots, conspiracies, and exile, Mazzini died in semi-exile in Pisa, hiding out under the assumed name of American abolitionist John Brown. Mrs Oscar Wilde is buried in the Protestant section.

## Around Genoa

**Nervi**, one of the oldest resorts on the Riviera, is just east of Genoa, and has been incorporated into the metropolis. To get there from the city, take bus 17 from Piazza de Ferrari, or bus 15 from the Piazza Caricamento. On the way, in Genova Quarto, is another monument to the Risorgimento, the **Garibaldi Museum**, in Villa Garibaldi (*open 9am–1pm, closed Thurs*), which houses some of the original red shirts of Garibaldi's Thousand (originally intended for slaughterhouse workers in South America), some of their guns, and a variety of documents. In Nervi itself, two of the town's oldest Genoese villas have been converted to museums: the **Galleria d'Arte Moderna** is in the former Villa Serra in the Parco Municipale (Via Capolungo 3) and contains a large collection of 19th and 20th-century Italian art, but has been closed indefinitely for restoration. The other, the **Villa Luxoro** (*open 9–1.15, 3–6, Tues–Sat; 9am–1.15pm Sun*), is further east in one of the Riviera's loveliest parks, at Via Mafalda di Savoia, 29. It, too, has a small modern art collection, but is especially noteworthy for its decorative arts holdings: clocks (some of the first luminous timepieces), furniture, fabrics and lace.

There are also two popular excursions into the hinterland from Genoa: **Casella**, a small mountain resort reached by a small electric train from Piazza Manin, and **Torriglia** (reached by bus, or by car on the SS45 road towards Piacenza), with an impressive if utterly derelict medieval castle, a small resort offering skiing in winter and pretty walks in summer.

Sea-bathing around Genoa being a dubious proposition, you may want to take advantage of municipal **swimming pools**—there are two pools at the Lido d'Albara, by the sea on the east side of town, with a restaurant attached, and another in Nervi. Anyone wanting to get closer to the sea can also take the **tour of Genoa's port**. Excursions are run by the Cooperativa Battellieri, © 265712 for reservations, and by Alimar, © 256775; both companies depart from the Calata Zingari, near the Stazione Marittima, and the trip costs L19,000 return.

Genoa's two first-division **football** teams, the star-name-laden Sampdoria and the lately less successful, though older, club Genoa, both play at the Stadio Luigi Ferraris, on the north side of the city. Buses KV and KM run to there from Brignole station.

*Genoa © (010–)*

### Where to Stay

Genoa's hotels range from the fabulous to the scabrous. Most are near one or other of the main train stations—around Brignole is the better area if you're looking for something cheap. Only crusty sailors and bodyguards would feel comfortable in the very cheapest establishments near the port.

### *very expensive*

★★★★★ **Colombia** is temporarily closed.

★★★★ **Starhotel President**, Corte dei Lambruschini 4, © 5727, ✉ 5531820, is the top hotel in the city while Colombia is closed. It is a two-year-old part of a complex in front of Brignole station built specifically for the 1992 celebrations, and something like the ultimate in nineties luxury and design. Ultra-modern and super-sleek, it has 192 double rooms, including some vast suites, all air-conditioned, sound-proofed, and fully equipped with all modern facilities. There are also extensive conference and business facilities, a palatial reception area, a gourmet restaurant, and an underground garage, and prices, as one might expect, are close to the luxury range.

★★★★ **Savoy Majestic**, Via Arsenale di Terra 5, © 261641, ✉ 261883, in contrast to Starhotel President, is not quite so expensive and retains an old-world charm with high ceilings and period-piece furniture. Its rooms, however, are big and modern, many with fine views, and there is a restaurant and garage too.

★★★★ **Bristol Palace**, Via XX Settembre 35, © 592541, ✉ 561756, is not far from Brignole station, is another elegant choice with sumptuous, antique furnishings and beautiful air-conditioned rooms, and a pleasant English bar downstairs.

★★★★ **Brittania**, Via Balbi 38, © 26991, ✉ 269242, There are also some good upper-range hotels near Principe station, of which the best is perhaps this one. It is very smart and slick, if maybe rather garishly designed in black and red, and modern and comfortable. The top floor rooms enjoy fantastic views, and though there's no restaurant, it does have a café, gym and billiard room.

★★★ **Milano Terminus**, Via Balbi 34, ✆ 262264, ✇ 267176, is a good, recently refurbished hotel near Principe station that's reasonably priced and has bright modern rooms, all with bathrooms.

★★★★ **Europa**, Via Monachette 8, ✆ 256955, ✇ 261047 is also totally refurbished, fully air-conditioned and with modern rooms.

★★★★ **Jolly Hotel Plaza**, Via Martin Piaggio 11, ✆ 8393641, fax, 8391850. There is a good choice in the centre, near Piazza Corvetto and the pretty Villa di Negro park—this is a very pleasant modern hotel with large, cosy rooms, all with mini-bars and air conditioning.

★★★★ **Moderno Verdi**, Piazza G Verdi 5, ✆ 5532104, ✇ 581562, is opposite Brignole station and near the Starhotel President (*see* above), but much less flamboyant, with all the standard facilities for this category, and fully equipped, smallish rooms with bathrooms.

★★★★ **Astor**, Viale delle Palme 16, ✆ 3728325, ✇ 3728486. Nervi means 'nerves' in Italian, but you can escape the hurly burly of Genoa there at the fashionable and elegant Astor hotel in an enchanting garden near the sea.

★★★ **Agnello d'Oro**. Via Monachette 6, ✆ 262084, ✇ 262327, is housed in a 17th-century property of the Doria family, near Via Balbi. Although most of the old-fashioned charm is concentrated in the lobby, the rooms are very comfortable, and most have private bath.

★★★ **Vittoria e Orlandini**, Via Balbi 45, ✆ 261923, ✇ 262656, is also not far from the Principe station, had good rooms, and optional air-conditioning.

★★★ **Bellevue**, Salita Provvidenza 1, ✆ 262400, ✇ 265932, is slightly more expensive but enjoying a wonderful view of the port. It has been recently refurbished, is fully air-conditioned and has smart, modern rooms throughout, though no restaurant.

★★ **Bel Soggiorno**, Via XX Settembre, 19/2, ✆ 542880, ✇ 581418, is near the centre, is the friendliest hotel in this category, also recently refurbished, and in an excellent position, though it can be slightly noisy. English is spoken, and all rooms have bathrooms.

★★ **Cairoli**, Via Cairoli 14, ✆ 206531, ✇ 280041. Among the more respectable and hygienic of the city's inexpensive choices, the very best is the one of the excellent 'family hotel' chain. Very centrally located, it's more like a 3 star place, with sparkling, modern rooms with TV, phone and bathroom, and a relaxed, friendly and personal atmosphere. Although prices approach the moderate range, it's still excellent value.

★ **Major**, Vico Spada 4, ✆ 293449, is a cheaper alternative and is the in a great position just inside the centro storico, and close by Piazza Ferrari and Via Garibaldi. The rooms are clean and modern, some with bath, and a real bargain.

★ **Carletto**, Via Colombo 16 (signposted off Via XX Settembre), ✆ 561229, ⊕ 588412. In the station areas, not far from Brignole, with good rooms in a pleasant area, with lots of focaccia stands nearby.

★★ **Della Posta e Nuova Genova**, Via Balbi 24, ✆ 262005, also in the same area near Brignole, has the best, inexpensive-to-moderate accommodation in a building that's entirely full of pensioni.

★★ **Villa Bonera**, Via Sarfatti 8, Nervi, ✆ 3726164, ⊕ 3728565. Outside the city in Nervi this is also a very attractive but inexpensive option which has 26 charming rooms, some without baths, in a 17th-century villa surrounded by a pretty garden.

---

*Genoa ✆ (010–)*                                                          **Eating Out**

Besides various forms of pasta with pesto, the Genoese are fond of putting basil in numerous other dishes. Also a popular pasta dish, *pansotti* are little ravioli filled with spinach and served in a walnut sauce. *Torta pasqualina* consists of vegetables and hard-boiled eggs rolled in a pastry; *cima alla Genovese* is breast of veal filled with similar ingredients.

### *expensive*

One of Genoa's most famous restaurants, **Toe Drue**, is in the working-class district of Sestri Ponente, west of the centre, at Via Corsi 44, ✆ 671100. Toe Drue means 'hard table', and this very fashionable restaurant has kept the furnishings of the rustic inn that preceded it. On these hard tables are served an array of delightful and unusual Ligurian specialities, many featuring seafood. Reservations are definitely necessary. **Gran Gotto**, Via Fiume 11 (near Piazza della Vittoria), ✆ 564344, is another of the city's classic eateries, featuring imaginative and delicately prepared seafood like turbot in radicchio sauce, warm seafood antipasti, famous kidney (*rognone*) dishes, and delectable desserts, at prices only just above the moderate range. More expensive, but enjoying a romantic sea view over the cliffs, is **Vittorio al Mare**, east of the port and past the Lido at Boccadasse (Belvedere Firpo 1, ✆ 3760147), which has good pasta and seafood. In the old centre, near the Piazza Banchi, is **Trattoria del Mario**, Via Conservatori del Mare 35/r, ✆ 297788, an old Genoese favourite that offers the freshest of fish prepared in the authentic Genoese style, and pasta with pesto as well as *cima*; the delicious seafood salad is a popular starter. (*Closed Sat, Aug.*) One of the best traditional choice in the old city, **Pancetti Antica Osteria**, Borgo Incrociati 22/r, ✆ 8392848, offers *pansotti*, chick pea soup, and some other Ligurian classics that are rarely prepared elsewhere, accompanied by the region's best vintages.

### *moderate and inexpensive*

In the maze of the southern old city, **Archivolto Mongiardino**, at number 2 in the street of the same name, ✆ 203614, is the place to go for lobster (*aragosta*) and other excellent seafood dishes. Interior decoration is not their forte, but the prices, though on the border of the moderate and expensive ranges, are still among the most reasonable anywhere for the type and quality of the seafood. **Genio**,

Salita San Leonardo 61, © 546463, off Via Fieschi near Piazza Dante, is another popular moderate-range restaurant serving great traditional Ligurian food, and offering a wider choice for non-seafood fans.

Good inexpensive restaurants abound in Genoa, especially in the *centro storico*. Try the fresh fish in the **Trattoria da Pino** in Piazza Caricamento, © 362395, one of Genoa's top greasy spoon districts. **Orlando Vegia Zena**, on Vico del Serriglio, © 299891, features Sard as well as Ligurian specialities. **Trattoria del Castello**, Salita Santa Margherita del Castello, has some of the best cheap food in town, with good Genoese specialities. And, just off Via XXV Aprile, near the Piazza de Ferrari, the wonderfully authentic **Trattoria da Maria**, Vico Testadora 14/r, © 581080, serves up filling three-course meals for under L15,000. (*Closed Sat.*)

### Entertainment and Nightlife

In Paganini's home town there is bound to be plenty of music. The **Genoa Opera**, now back in the Teatro Carlo Felice in Piazza de Ferrari after years of being without a proper home, presents its main season from January to April, and in the summer sponsors the prestigious **Ballet Festival** in the park in Nervi. In the summer there's also a full schedule of music and theatre in the city itself, and year-round there's **jazz** every Thursday at the **Louisiana Jazz Club**, Piazza Matteotti 20. **The Patio**, Via Oberdan 22, in Nervi, has live bluegrass on Mondays and jazz on Wednesdays. Every year Genoa competes with Venice, Pisa, and Amalfi in the **Regatta of the Ancient Maritime Republics**, hosted by winner of the previous year. There are frequent flower shows in the Fiera district, and a lively flea market in Piazzetta Lavagna. English books are available at **Bozzi**, on Via Cairoli 6.

The main centre of **café and bar life** is around the Via XX Settembre, though a noisier and seamier choice of places can be found around the port. Anyone feeling a need for a more English drinking ambience can find it at the **Brittania Pub** on Vico della Casana just off Piazza Ferrari, which is very popular with both foreigners and Italians.

## Riviera di Levante: Recco to Sestri Levante

East of Genoa, the coast, fairly tame up to this point, becomes a creature of high drama and romance. The beaches aren't as prominent, nor the climate quite as mild, but from the Monte di Portofino to the once nearly inaccessible fishing villages of the Cinque Terre, the mountains and sea tussle and tumble in a voluptuous chaos of azure, turquoise and piney green. Against these deep-coloured coves, cliffs and inlets rise the villages of weathered pastels and ochres, originally painted even brighter, with silvery groves of olives, gazing out over bobbing fleets of fishing craft, sailing boats, and sleek white yachts.

### Getting Around

The Genoa–Pisa **railway** hugs the coast, but in many places you can only get glimpses of the scenery between the tunnels. The same holds true of the A12

*autostrada* between Genoa and La Spezia; most scenic of all is the old coastal road, the Via Aurelia (SS1), which is also the route used by most of the **buses**. A number of villages are linked by **boat** services (*see* below).

***Tourist Information***

There are tourist offices all along the coast, in **Camogli**, Via XX Settembre 33, ✆ 771066, an office which is particularly helpful; **Portofino**, at Via Roma 35, ✆ 269024; **Santa Margherita Ligure**, Via XXV Aprile 2/b, ✆ 287485, 🖃 290222; **Rapallo**, at Via A. Diaz 9, ✆ 51282, 🖃 63051; **Uscio**, Via IV Novembre 96, ✆ 91101; **Zoagli**, Piazza San Martino 8, ✆ 299127; **Chiavari**, at Piazza G. Mazzini 1, ✆ 324848, and at Corso Assarotti 1, ✆ 29862; **Lavagna**, Piazza Libertà 40, ✆ 392766; and in **Sestri Levante**, at Via XX Settembre 33, ✆ 41422. The phone prefix for the whole of this area is **0185**.

## Recco and Camogli

Of all the nubs and notches in the Italian coastline, one of the best beloved is the squarish promontory of Monte di Portofino, which comes into view as you leave Nervi, and forms, on its western side, the Gulf of Paradiso. **Recco**, at the crossroads to Camogli, was bombed into dust during the War, and has since been completely rebuilt, but **Camogli**, only a kilometre or so away on the promontory, was spared. Built on a pine-wooded slope, it is an old sea town, once home port of a renowned fleet that fought with Napoleon; its fishing and merchant vessels were equally prominent along the Riviera. Its name derives from *Casa Mogli* (home of wives), since the menfolk were almost always at sea. The old harbour, piled high with tall, faded houses with dark green shutters, is the site of Camogli's famous *Sagra del Pesce*, an ancient festival that takes place on the second Sunday in May, where Italy's largest frying pan (4m across) is used to cook up thousands of sardines, which are distributed free to all comers—a display of generosity and abundance that carries with it the hope that the sea itself will be equally generous and abundant in the coming year. Another popular festival, the *Stella Maris* (first Sunday of August), honours those lost at sea and features a nautical procession to Punta Chiappa.

A small promontory separates Camogli's little pebble beach from its fishing port. Near here, **Dragonara Castle**, originally built in the Middle Ages to defend the port from Saracens, now contains the **Tyrrhenian Aquarium** (*open April–Sept 10–11.45, 3–6.45; Oct–Mar 10–11.45, 3–5.45*), with 22 tanks of Mediterranean creatures. Camogli recalls its own history in the **Maritime Museum** (*open April–Sept 9–12, 4–7, Wed–Mon; Oct–Mar 9–11.45, 3–5:40, Wed, Sat, and Sun; 9–12 Mon, Thurs, and Fri*) at Via Gio Bono Ferrari 41. The archaeological section (*open 9am–12 midday Wed–Mon*), contains artefacts from, and a reconstruction of, an Iron Age settlement discovered nearby; the maritime section contains an interesting array of ship's models, nautical instruments, maps, paintings, and documents that recall Camogli's thrilling days as a rough and tumble sea power.

From Camogli there's a regular boat service, run by the **Golfo Paradiso** company, Via Scalo 2, ✆ 772091, 🖃 771263, to the tiny fishing hamlet of **San Fruttuoso** on the seaward side of the promontory, and inaccessible save by sea or on foot (from Camogli it's a three-hour hike; there are also boats from Portofino, Santa Margherita, and Rapallo, so in summer it can be elbow-room only). The same company also runs services to Recco, Nervi and Genoa. On the way from Camogli the boats pass the **Punta Chiappa**, a point famous for the changing colours of the sea, though thanks to the quantity of rubbish floating around nowadays the water is no longer as clear as it once was.

San Fruttuoso is named after its famous **Abbey**, founded in 711 by the bishop of Tarragona, who fled Spain from the Moors, bringing with him the relics of San Fruttuoso. The Benedictines subsequently took over the abbey, with the protection of Genoa's powerful Doria family. In the 13th century six of the Dorias were buried in the abbey (while their home church of San Matteo was being done up), and in the 16th century Andrea Doria added the **Torre dei Doria** to defend the abbey from Turkish corsairs, who plagued the coast in the name of the king of France. The Dorias have recently donated the abbey and surrounding land to an environmental conservation group; you can stroll through the complex of palace, pretty white 11th-century church, and cloister (*open May–Oct 10–1, 2–6, Tues–Sun; Mar, April 10–1, 2–4, Tues–Sun; Nov–Feb public holidays only*). San Fruttuoso is surrounded by a lush growth of palms and olives, and from here it's a two-hour walk through these groves to Portofino. Another sight, best appreciated by skin-divers, is the 1954 bronze **Cristo degli Abissi** (Christ of the Depths), off shore, and eight fathoms under the sea, a memorial to those lost at sea and protector of all who work underwater.

## Portofino and Santa Margherita

The stunning **Monte di Portofino** (610m) is easiest reached from **Ruta** and **Portofino Vetta** (buses from Camogli). Protected as a natural park, it offers several lovely walks, especially up to

Baia di Portofino

the summit (one hour from Ruta), with its priceless views of the Riviera and out to sea as far as Elba, or in another hour to the lighthouse on the cliffs (the Semaforo Nuovo), or in two hours to Portofino.

One of Italy's most romantic little nooks, **Portofino** was discovered long ago by artists, then by the yachting set, who fell in love with its delightful little port framed by mellowed, narrow houses, and then by the rich and trendy, who fell in love with its spectacular beauty and seclusion and made it a favourite setting for illicit trysts and such, far, they hoped, from the clicking cameras of the paparazzi. The exclusiveness still exists to a certain extent—if you don't sleep on your yacht, there are only a handful of small hotels—but the seclusion vanishes every weekend and every day in summer, when thousands of trippers pour in for an afternoon's window-shopping in the smart boutiques (some selling the district's famous lace), and a drink in the portside bars. In the evening, though, the yachtsmen and the residents of the hillside villas descend once again to their old haunts and reclaim Portofino as their own.

Portofino's name is derived from the Roman *Portus Delphini*, which had a *mithraeum* (an initiatory sanctuary dedicated to the popular Persian god Mithras, a favourite of Roman soldiers). This is now the site of the delightful **church of St George**, housing the relics of the defrocked saints. Note the new sculpted bronze doors: as often as not there's a cat sleeping under the altar. Further up, **the castle** which was built as a defence against the Turks affords enchanting views of the little port (*open 10am–6pm Tues–Sun; adm*). Another lovely walk, beyond the castle, is to the Faro, the old lighthouse, taking in magnificent views of the Gulf of Tigullio through the pine forest. Boats travel from Portofino to San Fruttuoso and Santa Margherita.

If you're driving to Portofino, you'll have to take the narrow road from **Santa Margherita Ligure**, passing by way of the **Abbey of La Cervara**, where King Francis I was imprisoned for a while after the Battle of Pavia. Santa Margherita is a pleasant resort, with a beautiful harbour—not as spectacular as Portofino, but friendly and lively, a popular winter hideaway for the British, and a summer resort with accommodation priced for all budgets. The main sight in town is the **Basilica di Santa Margherita**, a rococo extravaganza with Italian and Flemish art. There are boat excursions to Portofino, San Fruttuoso, and the Cinque Terre.

## Rapallo and Inland

**Rapallo**, at the innermost corner of the Gulf of Tigullio, is perhaps the most famous resort on the Riviera di Levante, enjoying a mild year-round climate, and endowed with a fairly good beach, an 18-hole golf course, busy tourist harbour, indoor swimming pool, tennis, riding school and stables, and marvellous natural surroundings. Rapallo was the longtime home of Max Beerbohm, who lived in the Villino Chiaro and attracted a notable literary circle to the resort; it is also a favourite venue for conferences—at the **Villa Spinola** Italy and Yugoslavia signed the Treaty of Rapallo in 1920. This villa lies along the Santa Margherita road, as does **San Michele di Pagana** containing a *Crucifixion* by Van Dyck, and the site of large fire-work-popping festivals in July and September. In Rapallo itself, the **Castle**, surrounded by the harbour's waters, is used for changing exhibitions; and there's a **Museo Civico** on Piazza delle Nazioni (*open 3–6pm Tues, Wed, Fri, Sat; 10–11.30am Thurs*) with religious art, *presepi* figures, and antique lace. There's a funicular (which probably won't be working, so you'll have to walk, drive or take the bus) up to the 16th-century **Santuario di Montallegro**, with a Byzantine icon which miraculously flew here from Dalmatia. Above the church it's a short walk up to Monte Rosa for a spectacular view.

Inland from this stretch of coast there are two attractive hill resorts: one is **Uscio**, reached by the SS333 road from Recco, a health spa and manufacturer of large campanile clocks. From Rapallo and the Montallegro, a long, winding road arrives after about an hour at **Santo Stefano d'Aveto**, up in the Ligurian Apennines, where Rapallo's wintertime visitors can head for a taste of snow and a bit of skiing at just over 1000m, as well as a scenic 8km cable car excursion. Santo Stefano's landmark is the imposing **Castello Malaspina**.

## Chiavari and Lavagna

East of Rapallo, **Zoagli** is a small seaside village that has produced patterned velvets ever since they were fashion's rage in the Middle Ages, although nowadays people prefer it for dressing their furniture instead of themselves; most of the velvet factories are open for visits on request. Dominating the shoreline is a curious, eclectic castle-villa with a red tiled roof. **Chiavari**, the next town, is another specialized craft centre, in ship-building, fine wooden and straw chairs, and macramé, an art brought back by the town's sailors from the Middle East, and still used to adorn towels and tablecloths with intricate fringes and tassels. Orchids are another local speciality, their blooms best seen at the annual show at the end of February.

Chiavari has a quaint main street, called in dialect the 'Carruggio Drittu', lined with a couple of kilometres of medieval arcades. One of the most interesting buildings in the historic centre, the 17th-century **Palazzo Torriglia** in Piazza Mazzini, houses both the tourist office and a picture gallery (*open 10–12, 4–7.30, Mon–Fri*), with art by the Genoese school and a *Pietà* by Quentin Matsys. There are two museums open to visitors in the **Palazzo Rocca**, one of them an art gallery, at Via Costaguta 2, with mostly local work from the last four centuries (*open 10–12, 4–7.30, Sat, Sun*). Next to it the **Civico Museo Archeologico**, Via Costaguta 4 (*open 9am–1.30pm Mon; 9am–7.15pm Tues–Sat*), has items discovered in the nearby 8th–7th-century BC necropolis, demonstrating trade links with the Phoenicians, Greeks, and Egyptians. The Palazzo Rocca also has a beautiful garden. In Chiavari's newer quarters, there's a small pleasure port, near the long sandy beach. A road leads from here to Santo Stefano d'Aveto.

**Lavagna**, separated from Chiavari by a bridge over the Entella, has an equally long beach. It was ruled in the Middle Ages by the Fieschi, who produced a 13th-century pope, Innocent IV, and Count Opizzo Fieschi, whose marriage to Bianca dei Bianchi in 1230 made such an impression on Lavagna that the anniversary (14 August) is annually re-enacted, a ceremony that climaxes in the communal eating of the gargantuan *Torta dei Fieschi*. Innocent IV, on the other hand, is remembered in the beautiful early Gothic church he built, the **Basilica di San Salvatore dei Fieschi**, a half-hour's walk inland near Cogorno. There is also a market here on Thursdays where you can hunt out local handicrafts in wood, slate and iron.

## Sestri Levante and Varese Ligure

**Sestri Levante** is endowed with a lovely, curving peninsula called the Isola, dividing the 'Bay of Silence' from what Hans Christian Andersen himself christened the 'Bay of Fables'. It has a picturesque sandy beach, and perhaps more than its share of touristic development. The magnificent garden on the peninsula belongs to Albergo dei Castello, where Marconi performed his first experiments with radio waves; below it stands the fine Romanesque church of **San Nicolò** and the Piazza Matteotti, with fine views of the two bays. The **Galleria Rizzi**, Via Cappuccini 10, on the Bay of Silence (*open April–Sept 4–6pm Thurs, Sat, Sun; adm*), contains works by the Florentine, Emilian, and Ligurian schools, ceramics, and a small furniture collection.

From Sestri a bus heads inland along the SS523 to Borgo Val di Taro in Emilia, passing by way of **Varese Ligure**, the chief town of the mountainous Val di Vara. Like many villages in the region, its medieval architecture and town design are interesting for their adaptation to the hilly terrain, as seen most typically in Varese in the ancient **Borgo Rotundo**. Its great 15th-century **Castle** belonged to the Fieschi clan of Lavagna.

---

✆ *(0185–)*  **Where to Stay**

Note that many hotels in this area still insist, or at least prefer, that guests take full board, particularly in high season.

### Camogli

The top hotel is the ★★★★**Cenobio dei Dogi**, Via Cuneo 34, ✆ 770041, ✆ 772796 (very expensive), a former palace of Genoa's doges, in a tranquil, secluded location in a splendid flower-filled park overlooking the gulf. The rooms are well appointed and comfortable, many with balconies enjoying the charming view, and there's a salt-water pool, tennis courts, and pebble beach. (*Closed Jan, Feb.*) The ★★★**Casmona**, Salita Pineto 13, ✆ 770015, ✆ 770016 (moderate) is a quiet, tidy place with a restaurant, and a shady little patio. ★★**Pensione La Camogliese**, Via Garibaldi 55, ✆ 771402, ✆ 774024 (inexpensive) is very pleasant, not far from the sea, and also has an attractive restaurant (*see below*). ★★**Il Faro**, Via P. Schiaffino 116–118, ✆ 771400 (inexpensive) is also a good budget choice, at the top of town with excellent views, and a restaurant too.

### Portofino

Nothing stays inexpensive when the jet set comes to town, but ★★★★★**Splendido**, Viale Baratta 13, ✆ (0185) 269551, ✆ 269614 (luxury) is nevertheless worth every lira; the view alone, from every balcony of every room, of the town, its tiny harbour and the deep blue sea beyond, is priceless. Rose and white, the Splendido is adorned with a huge terrace, large heated pool, tennis courts, and splendid garden. Inside, each of the 88 spacious, very comfortable rooms has a hydromassage bath, air-conditioning and everything else you might desire. (*Open April–Oct.*)

The ★★★★**Nazionale**, Via Roma 8, ✆ 269575, ✆ 269578 (very expensive), smack on the port in the centre of the action, has a slightly faded charm to it, furnished with antiques or reproductions, with modern baths. The best rooms, rather more expensive, have Venetian furniture and overlook the harbour. It has no parking though, which can be a big problem in Portofino. The ★★**Eden**, Vico Dritto 18, ✆ 269091, ✆ 269047 (expensive), is far from cheap and still within this category, but is actually the town's least expensive hotel, a charming 12-room establishment in the centre of town, but endowed with a fine garden and good Ligurian restaurant. Some, cheaper, rooms do not have bathrooms.

## Santa Margherita

Two hotels have long rivalled one another in the luxury category, although the ★★★★★**Imperial Palace**, Via Pagana 19, on the edge of town, ✆ 288991, @ 284223 (luxury), has been rated one more star. Formerly a private villa, it was converted into a hotel at the turn of the century; the original villa contains the palatial marble and gilt-encrusted public rooms, in one of which, in 1922, the Weimar Republic signed an agreement with Russia to reopen diplomatic relations. Concerts are frequently held in the afternoons in the music room. The bedrooms too are furnished with Genoese antiques, some more elaborately than others, and each has a full range of facilities. There's a heated pool and tennis amid the hotel's semi-tropical garden, and a private beach. (*Open Mar–Oct.*) The shining white ★★★★**Grand Hotel Miramare**, Via Pagana 8, ✆ 287013, @ 284651 (luxury) is almost as palatial, though purpose-built as a posh winter hotel in the early 1900s. Surrounded by a lovely garden, with a heated salt-water pool (as well as a pebbly beach across the road), it has lovely air conditioned rooms, many with fine views of the gulf from their balconies. The Miramare's water skiing school is one of the best in Italy. The ★**San Giorgio**, Via Cuneo 59, ✆ 286770 (inexpensive), a bit outside of the centre, has nine pleasant rooms, all with bath, and a garden.

Santa Margherita has several less extravagant choices than those mentioned above, such as ★★★**La Vela**, Corso Cuneo 21, ✆ 286039, @ 286463 (moderate), a former villa located a bit above town and enjoying good sea views. With only 16 rooms, all with bathrooms, it has a friendly, intimate atmosphere. (*Closed Nov–Christmas.*) The ★★**Conte Verde**, Via Zara 1, ✆ 287139, @ 284211 (moderate), also a villa, is in the centre, a short walk from the sea, and is a cheerful place with a small terrace, garden, and bar. Santa Margherita's best option in this category, though, and bordering on the inexpensive range, is the very friendly and welcoming. (*Closed Nov–Christmas.*) ★★**Albergo Fasce**, Via L. Bozzo 3, ✆ 286435, @ 283580 (moderate) is part of the 'family hotel' chain. Its rooms are large, modern and immaculately maintained (as is the whole hotel), with satellite TV, phone and safe in each, and it also offers a laundry service, free bike hire, parking, sun roof and a small garden, making it exceptional value. There's also an excellent restaurant (*see* below). Also very good value and at the lower end of this range is the ★★★**Albergo Terminus**, Piazza Nobili 4, ✆ 286121, @ 282546 (moderate) run by the former owner of two London restaurants, at the top of town just beside the station. All rooms have TV and phone, and some offer wonderful views of the bay and town.

## Rapallo

Rapallo has more hotels than any resort on the Riviera di Levante. The ★★★★**Eurotel**, Via Aurelia Ponente 22, ✆ 60981, @ 50635 (expensive) overlooks Rapallo and the sea. A modern building, with pretty gardens and pool, all of its rooms have balconies, minibar, and full facilities. In the centre of Rapallo, the ★★★**Riviera**, Piazza IV Novembre 2, ✆ 50248, ✉ 65668 (moderate) is a converted villa near the sea. Remodelled inside, it has a popular glass terrace in the front and a garden at the rear, and comfortable rooms, all with bath. ★★★**Minerva**, Corso Colombo 57, ✆ 50356, ✉ 230388 (moderate) is good value: an up-to-date hotel, near the seashore, with tasteful décor, garden and bar. All rooms have baths. Close to the sea front in Rapallo and right in the middle of town, the **Pensione Bandoni**, Via Marsala 24, ✆ 50423 (inexpensive) is a comfortable, simple hotel that's good value. There are a good many more inexpensive hotels to choose from around the same area.

## Sestri Levante

Sestri Levante competes with Rapallo for being the most touristy resort of the Eastern Riviera, but you'll never notice it if you stay at the ★★★★★**Hotel dei Castelli**, Via Penisola 26, ✆ 485780, ✉ 44767, occupying the tip of the Isola peninsula. Built in the twenties on the site of a Genoese castle, it was constructed from the castle's stone. The views of both bays and the sea crashing against the cliffs all around the hotel's park are magnificent, especially from the dining terrace. There's also a natural sea pool cut into the rock for safe swimming. (*Open 10 May–10 Oct.*) The seaside ★★★★**Villa Balbi**, Viale Rimembranza 1, ✆ 42941, ✉ 482459 (expensive) is a pink palace, its core an 18th-century Genoese villa. Rooms are large, many with views of the sea, and the public rooms are palatial. In the garden there's a heated sea-water pool. (*Open April–Oct.*) Alternatively, right on the 'Bay of Silence', there's the ★★★★**Miramare**, Via Cappellini 9, ✆ 480855, ✉ 41055 (expensive) with 45 large, airy and fully equipped modern rooms, including 11 'family rooms', plus a private beach, terrace restaurant and garage.

Sestri Levante's ★★★**Helvetia**, Via Cappuccini 43, ✆ 41175, ✉ 47216 (moderate) is a fine welcoming little hotel in the prettiest part of town, right on the 'Bay of Silence'. It has a large terraced garden. At the lower end of this price bracket, ★★★**Eden**, Via XXV Aprile 170, ✆ 45771 (moderate) is a very reasonably priced, family-run place, just off the main square, and with some rooms with views of the 'Bay of Fables'. (*Open April–Sept.*) A good choice on the seafront is ★★★**Mira**, Via Rimembranza 15, ✆ 41576, ✉ 41577 (moderate) a family-run hotel with rooms with a view and an excellent restaurant, too (*see* below).

A good budget hotel in Sestri Levante is the **Pensione Jolanda**, Via Pozzetto 15, ✆ 41354 (inexpensive) which has a sea view from some rooms.

---

✆ *(0185–)*                                                                    *Eating Out*

## Recco

Though lacking much in the way of scenic attractions, Recco is something of a gourmet mecca, famous for its *focaccia* with cheese and *trofie*, a helix-shaped pasta made of chestnut flour and wheat. The mayor of Recco runs two of the best places to eat: the celebrated **Manuelina**, Via Roma 278, ✆ 74128 (expensive), just outside the centre, where you can try *trofie* with pesto and seafood prepared in a variety of styles for the *secondo*; alongside it is his **Focacceria** (expensive) with full meals in the moderate range (*see* below). Another much-renowned restaurant in Recco is the hundred-year-old **Da-o Vittorió**, Via Roma 160, ℗ 74029 (expensive), whose specialities include utterly superb *minestrone di verdura alla Genovese* and *trofie al pesto*. Recco has many medium- and low-price restaurants of unusually high quality, and at the **Focacceria**, (moderate) the cheaper half of the Manuelina (*see* above) at Via Roma 278, ℗ 74128, you can dine on one of the town's most famous specialities, *focaccia*, as well as full meals of such Ligurian dishes as *cima*, for exceptionally reasonable prices, from moderate down to the inexpensive range. Recco, again, has some of the best budget-price restaurants in the area, particularly along the seafront and around the Via Roma. In Camogli a good place to eat is the restaurant of the Pensione La Camogliese (inexpensive; *see* above), which has an attractive veranda overlooking the port, and good, reasonably priced fish dishes.

## San Fruttuoso

There are a couple of good seafood restaurants: **Da Giovanni**, ℗ 770047 (expensive), a small, charming place, which also doubles as an inexpensive hotel, and **La Cantina**, ℗ 772626 (expensive), on the beach, offering fish cooked to order at very reasonable prices.

## Camogli

A tiny, charming place on the harbour in Camogli that bases its existence entirely on the luck of the town's fishing fleet is **Vento Ariel**, Calata Prospero Castelleto, ℗ 771080 (expensive). Fish and seafood only are served, and reservations are essential in summer. Daily set menus are offered, as well as à la carte choices. (*Closed Wed.*) There are several restaurants near Camogli at Portofino Vetta, of which the **Rosa**, Via J. Ruffini 11, ℗ 771088, enjoys some of the finest views, and prepares some of the best seafood, bought in the morning's catch.

## Portofino

Dining out in Portofino can be a rarefied experience at **Il Pitosforo**, Molo Umberto I 9, ℗ 269218 (very expensive), overlooking Portofino's little piazza and port A tree goes out of the middle of the dining room, and one whole wall is lined with a collection of spirits from around the world that will make any serious drinker eyes glaze over in delight. Every night at 10pm, all the lights are switched off to highlight the magical view of the golden lights in the port. The Ligurian cuisine is among the finest anywhere, whether you order bouillabaisse, spaghetti with prawns and mushrooms, the red mullet or sea bream with olives. (*Closed Tues.*) An excellent restaurant in Portofino is **Da Puny**, Piazza Martire Olivetta 7, ℗ 269037 (expensive), which serves delicious pasta and seafood dishes for starters, and well-prepared fish, like sea bass baked in salt.

## Santa Margherita

If you can escape the board requirements of your hotel, try the finest restaurant in Santa Margherita, **Cesarina**, Via Mameli 2/c, ℰ 286059 (very expensive), located under an arcade in the old part of town. The décor is fresh and modern, and goes well with such specialities as *zuppa di datteri* (razor clam soup) or Liguria's famous spaghetti with red mullet (*triglie*) sauce. Reservations are advisable. (*Closed Wed.*). More seafood and tasty fresh fish dominates the menu at **Dei Pescatori**, Via Bottaro 44, ℰ 86747 (expensive). **Ancora**, Via Maragliano 7, ℰ 280599, (moderate) offers seafood specialities (especially the *insalata di pesce*), and a good-value set tourist menu. (*Closed Tues.*) Also excellent is another small hotel restaurant, the one in the **Albergo Fasce** (inexpensive; *see* above) in Santa Margherita, where you can find a full meal of delicious Ligurian specialities for not much more than L20,000 a head.

## Rapallo

One of many restaurants in Rapallo, **Cuoco d'Oro**, Via della Vittoria 5, ℰ 50745 (moderate) is an intimate, authentic place, where each order is freshly prepared, but is still very reasonable. Reservations are advisable. Rapallo and Sestri Levante both have any number of cheap and cheap-ish restaurants. In Rapallo, though, the best are not found among those crowding the seafront, but more around the Piazza Garibaldi and Via Venezia. Similarly, in Sestri the best budget eateries are around the Via XXV Aprile, which runs along the middle of the Isola.

## Chiavari

**Copetin**, Piazza Gagliardo 16, ℰ 309064 (expensive), serves delicious fish and scampi dishes, risotto *mare-monti*, and fresh desserts.

## Sestri Levante

For excellent seaside dining, **Angiolina**, Viale della Rimembranza 49, ℰ 41198 (expensive) is the place to go for an exquisite *zuppa di pesce* and other delicious denizens of the deep. Seafood and traditional Ligurian cuisine comprise the menu at **Fiammenghilla Fieschi**, Via Pestella 6, ℰ 481041 (expensive). It's a great place to try marinated swordfish, lobster, *focaccia*, or *pansotti*. There's also a very good Ligurian wine list. (*Open evenings only, housed in an old patrician villa.*) The restaurant of the **Mira** hotel (*see* above), Via Rimembranza 15, ℰ 41576, (moderate) serves excellent fish specialities, including *riso marinara* and *nasello alla mira*, and offers a pleasant outlook over the sea.

## Levi

In Levi, six kilometres from Chiavari, is **Ca' Peo**, Strada Panoramica, ℰ 319696 (very expensive), one of the best restaurants on the Riviera. The atmosphere is elegant and charming, and the food imaginatively and delicately prepared, featuring ingredients like radicchio from Treviso, truffles from Alba, porcini mushrooms, and very fresh fish, followed by excellent desserts and accompanied by noble wines. Reservations are a must.

In super-chic and élite Portofino two port-side drinking holes have long competed for the biggest celebrities: **La Gritta American Bar** and **Scafandro American Bar**, both of them elegant and glamorous in the resort's studied, laid-back and very expensive style.

Not many places along the coast can compete with Portofino in the glitz stakes, but less chic places like Rapallo and Sestri also have their fair share of nightlife. In Sestri, for early drinking, there's an excellent bar, **Il Bistro di Sestri Levante**, Piazza Matteotti 13, ✆ 41613, notable for its vast collection of beer cans and good music. It also serves good, inexpensive food. For later on, **Piscina Disco**, at the far end of the Bay of Fables, is what it says: a pool/disco, playing a varied selection of house/chart music until the early hours (*adm* ).

## Riviera di Levante: the Cinque Terre and La Spezia

Before sliding down to the comparatively dull and flat coast of Tuscany, the Riviera bows out with a dramatic flourish, around the rugged, almost inaccessible cliffs of the Cinque Terre, the rocky peninsula of Portovenere, and La Spezia's lovely 'Gulf of Poets'. One particular plus point of this area is that prices, especially for accommodation, are noticeably lower for a given level of quality than elsewhere along the Riviera.

### Getting Around

The easiest way to reach the Cinque Terre is by **train** from Genoa or La Spezia. Each of the five towns has a station, only a few minutes apart and separated by long tunnels; afterwards the train drills through the mountains straight to La Spezia and Sarzana, from where you can continue on towards Parma or Pisa.

The A12, beyond Sestri Levante, heads inland to avoid the wild coast, until arriving at La Spezia. The SS1 follows a similar route, though it runs more directly into La Spezia and up to Portovenere. The controversial coastal road to the Cinque Terre (*Litoranea delle Cinque Terre*; Italian engineers' bulldozers begin to twitch at the mention of the word 'inaccessible') has succeeded so far in reaching Monterosso (approaching from Genoa) and Riomaggiore and Manarola (approaching from La Spezia). Drivers should be aware, also, that the villages at the end of the winding cliff roads are tiny, and parking is a perennial problem. There are **buses** from Piazza Chiodo in La Spezia to Riomaggiore and Manarola, Portovenere (every 15 minutes), Lerici, Sarzana, and Florence.

There are also seven **boat** lines serving the area. From La Spezia, In-Tur, Viale Italia, (✆ 24324), and Battellieri del Golfo, Via Banchina Revel, (✆ 28066), and from Lerici Navigazione Golfo dei Poeti (✆ 967676), Verde Azzurro (✆ 967860) and Cap Baracco, Via San Bernardino 1, (✆ 964412), all have regular sailings between La Spezia, Lerici, Portovenere, and the Cinque Terre; NGP goes as far as Portofino to the north, and Marina di Massa and Marina di Carrara in Tuscany. Another company, Fratelli Rossignoli (✆ 817456) sail between Monterosso and Viareggio during summer. Also, Corsica Ferries (✆ 21282) and NAVARMA (✆ 35484) make the five-hour run between La Spezia and Bastia in Corsica daily in summer, and less frequently at other times.

Local tourist offices are in **Levanto**, at Piazza C. Colombo 2, ✆ 808125; **Monterosso al Mare**, Via Fegina 38, ✆ 817506; in La Spezia, at both Viale Mazzini 45, ✆ 770900, and in the railway station, ✆ 743717; **Portovenere**, Piazza Bastreri 1, ✆ 900691, ✉ 770908; and in **Lerici**, at Via Gerini 40, ✆ 967346.

## Sestri Levante to the Cinque Terre

After Sestri Levante, the Apennines move in and crowd the coast, admitting here and there little glens and sandy strands—at **Moneglia** with its two castles, **Deiva Marina** (near the pretty village of Framura), **Bonassola**, and, most importantly, **Levanto**, which has a good sandy beach, flower gardens, and several monuments from the 13th century—the **Loggia** (town hall), the church of **Sant'Andrea**, and chunks of its walls.

Next on the coast, **Monterosso al Mare** is the first of the five towns of the **Cinque Terre** ('The Five Lands'), as they've been known since the Middle Ages. Perched wherever the cliffs and hills permitted enough space to build, surrounded by steep slopes corrugated by hundreds of terraces laboriously carved out of the earth and rock, the Cinque Terre towns are visually stunning. They also enjoy a fine, mild climate, and the vineyards that occupy the near-vertical terraces produce the region's finest (and most potent) wines—the ones labelled Sciacchetrà are made from raisins, and can be either dry or sweet. Formerly accessible only by sea or by a spectacular series of cliff-skirting footpaths, the towns have maintained much of their charm, even though nowadays they are far from being undiscovered.

Monterosso, reachable by car, is the most touristy of the five, with beaches (free and 'organized'), hotels, rooms in private houses, and so on, and boats to hire for personal tours of the coast. Most of the facilities are in the new half of town called Fegina, separated from the old by a hill crowned with the 1622 **Convento dei Cappuccini** and a medieval tower; the 18th-century **Sanctuary of Soviore**, built over an older church, hosts a music festival in the summer. From Monterosso it's a momentary train ride or a lovely hour and a half walk to the next town, **Vernazza**, founded by the Romans on a rocky spit, a striking vision from the footpath above. Its parish church, **Santa Margherita of Antioch**, was built in 1318.

The hour and a half walk from Vernazza to **Corniglia** is one of the most strenuous, for Corniglia, unlike the other towns, is high up on the cliffs and not on the sea, though it does have the longest (though pebbly) beach. From Corniglia another hour's walk through splendid scenery leads to **Manarola**, at the terminus of the coastal road from La Spezia. Manarola is a colourful fishing village built along steep lanes. It is linked in 20 minutes or so to **Riomaggiore** by the most popular section of the footpath, the 'Via dell'Amore', carved

Riomaggiore

into the cliff face over the sea. Riomaggiore, one of the prettiest towns, also sees plenty of visitors, who crowd its lively cafés and rocky beaches.

## La Spezia

The largest city in the region, the provincial capital, and one of Italy's most important naval bases, La Spezia was bombed heavily in the Second World War and presents a modern but cheerful face to the world, standing at the head of one of Italy's prettiest gulfs. Mostly used by visitors as a base for visiting the Cinque Terre, Portovenere, and other locations around the 'Gulf of Poets', it has a number of attractions in its own right—among them a promenade of swaying palms and lush public gardens. At Via Curtatone 9, the **Museo Civico** (*open 8.30–1.15, 2.30–7.15, Tues–Sat; 9–1 Sun*) contains an important archaeological section, with prehistoric finds from Palmaria's Grotta dei Colombi, pre-Roman and Roman material from Luni, and most notably Ligurian stelae from the Bronze and Iron Ages. It also has an ethnographic collection, with traditional costumes and tools from villages in the province. The excellent **Naval Museum** (*open 2–6pm Mon, Fri; 9–12, 2–6, Tues–Thurs, Sat; adm*) in Piazza Chiodo, next to the Naval Arsenal, contains a fine collection begun in 1560 by Emanuele Filiberto, with relics of the ships sent by the Savoys to the Battle of Lepanto; there are models, a gallery of figureheads, and momentoes from Italy's naval battles. A very new museum, still being completed at time of writing, is Italy's first **Transport Museum**, Via de Canaletto 100, which contains all forms of transport, including the only double-decker buses ever built in the country. In the church of **Santa Maria Assunta** there's a terracotta *Incoronation of the Virgin* by Andrea della Robbia.

## Portovenere and Palmaria

The road between La Spezia and Portovenere is lovely and winding (if you're prone to motion sickness you may prefer to take the equally scenic boat), and passes by way of the pretty cove of **Le Grazie**. At the end of the road stands ancient, fortified **Portovenere**, with its long promontory, castle, and tall pastel houses, one of the loveliest towns on the Riviera. It's named after the goddess of love herself, protectress of fishermen, and her temple stood at the tip of the promontory, on the site of the church of **San Pietro**, another patron of fishermen. This is a strange little church, of black and white striped marble, dating from 1277, and built over a few colourful marble remains of a 6th-century predecessor. There are splendid views from here, of Palmaria and the coast of the Cinque Terre; the pretty cove below once held the Grotta Arpaia, where Byron wrote *The Corsair*, and from where he swam across the gulf to Lerici and Shelley's villa. It collapsed in the 1930s.

The best thing to do in Portovenere is wander through its narrow, cat-crowded lanes (Portovenere is Italy's champion kitty city), past tall ancient houses on the waterfront, built under the Genoese, who fortified the town in the early 12th century (as the Pisans had fortified Lerici across the gulf), with interesting details on the doorways. From the port a narrow lane leads up to the lovely church of **San Lorenzo**, with a bas-relief over the door of St Lawrence being toasted on his gridiron, built in 1130; inside is Portovenere's most precious relic, the *Madonna Bianca*, said to have floated to the town encased in a cedar log in the 13th century (the log, too, is on display). Further up, a steep but worthwhile walk leads to the 16th-century Genoese **Castello**, with marvellous views. (*Open April–Oct 10–12, 2–6, daily; Nov–Mar 3–5pm daily.*)

From Portovenere you can cross the 400m channel to **Isola Palmaria** and visit its famed **Grotta Azzura**—though a much cheaper proposition is to book a passage from La Spezia. Palmaria produces the black, gold-veined marble you may have noticed in Portovenere, and was the site of a neolithic settlement. A much smaller islet, **Isola del Tino**, with a lighthouse and the ruins of an 8th-century monastery, and the tinier **Tinetto**, lie further out.

## Lerici

Lerici, on its own little bay, is the most important town and resort on the east shore of the 'Golfo dei Poeti'. Lerici is dominated by its imposing **Castello** (*open 9am–midnight daily; adm*), towering up on its promontory. Built by the Pisans, it was enlarged by the Genoese in the 15th century; inside you can visit the Chapel of Sant'Anastasia (1250). Lerici has a nice beach and mild winter climate, and its environs were beloved by Shelley, whose last home was the Casa Magni in **San Terenzo**, the charming fishing village across the bay from Lerici: it was from here that he sailed, in 1822, to meet Leigh Hunt at Leghorn (Livorno), only to shipwreck and drown by Viareggio. To the south is the enchanting, tranquil, tiny cove and beach of **Fiascherino**, where D. H. Lawrence lived in 1913–14; beyond is the unspoiled medieval hamlet of **Tellaro**. Another road continues around the gulf and begins to climb up the Val di Magra to **Ameglia**, with its remains of the Roman port of Luni, its 10th-century castle, and the slate portals of the older houses.

## Sarzana and Ancient Luni

From La Spezia, trains and the *autostrada* cross the Val di Magra for **Sarzana**, once on the easternmost edge of the Republic of Genoa: an ancient, fortified town dominated by the **Fortezza di Sarzello**, a castle built in the early 14th century by the tyrant of Lucca, Castruccio Castracani. The 14th-century **cathedral** contains one of the best works of Master

Guglielmo, a *Crucifixion* of 1138; other churches of note include **Sant'Andrea** and **San Francesco**, with good sculptures. To the north in **Fosdinovo**, the Malaspina castle hosted Dante in 1306; he is also said to have visited the ruined 13th-century castle in **Castelnuovo Magra**. The church contains a *Calvary* by Brueghel the Younger.

**Ortonovo** lies near the site of the ancient Roman town of **Luni**, built as a bulwark against the fierce Ligurians. The city survived until the Middle Ages; the power-hungry Bishop of Luni survived until 1929, when the bishopric was combined with that of La Spezia. Excavations have revealed a sizeable amphitheatre, forum, houses, temples, and so on, on the site there is a **Museo Nazionale di Luni** (*open April–Sept 9–12, 3–7, Tues–Sun; Oct–Mar 2–7pm Tues–Sun; adm*), with an interesting collection of marble statuary, coins, jewellery, portraits, etc., as well as a display of archaeological techniques used in excavating the site, which can be toured with a guide.

If you're continuing down the coast from here, see p.718.

---

*✆ (0187–)* **Where to Stay**

### Monterosso

Of the five towns of the Cinque Terre Monterosso has the best accommodation, with the ★★★★**Porto Roca**, Via Coroni 1, ✆ 817502, @ 817692 (expensive) as the top choice, located on the headland, with lovely views of the sea from all the rooms. ★★★★**Palme**, Via IV Novembre 18, ✆ 817541, @ 818265 (moderate) is a modern hotel  with 49 rooms, all with bathroom, set in a large garden and just 5 minutes from the sea. It also has some parking space. The largish, modern ★★★**Cinque Terre**, Via IV Novembre 22, ✆ 817543 (moderate) has a private beach and plain but comfortable rooms, some without bathrooms. Large and friendly ★★**Villa Adriana**, Via IV Novembre 23, ✆/@ 818109 (moderate) is also on the waterfront in Monterosso, with a beach. Rooms are simple, but all have baths. Probably the best budget option is ★★★**Amici**, Via Burranco 36, ✆ 817544, @ 817424 (inexpensive) in the old part of town, and 150m from the beach. The rooms are light and airy, some with balcony, and there's an excellent restaurant. ★★★**Jolie**, Via Gioberti 1, ✆ 817539, @ 817273 (inexpensive) is much the same, but more expensive.

### Vernazza

There's the ★★**Sorriso**, Via Gavino 4, ✆ 812224 (inexpensive) an honest little inn with very inexpensive rooms, the doubles with baths, and a well-known restaurant (*see* below). The cheapest option in Vernazza is ★**Barbara**, ✆ 812201 (inexpensive) where the rooms are all pretty basic, but have lovely views overlooking the square. Enquire for a room in the **Capitano** restaurant, also in the main square (*see* below).

### Manarola

There are two hotels, the ★★★**Marina Piccola**, ✆ 920103, @ 920966 (inexpensive) with all of 10 simple rooms, is a good place to get away from it all, even if you may not feel especially pampered. Rooms are better in the main hotel, rather than in the annexe, and there is also a very nice restaurant. The new ★★★**Ca'd'Andrean**, Via Discovolo 25, ✆ 920040 (inexpensive) is a spotlessly clean little family-run place with ten large rooms (some with terrace), a garden and bar.

## La Spezia

The finest accommodation is at the ★★★★**Jolly del Golfo**, Via XX Settembre 2, ✆ 27200, ✉ 22129 (very expensive), a modern and rather stylish member of the strangely named Italian hotel chain, with views stretching to the gulf. Each room has air-conditioning, and TV. Among the bargains the best are ★**Flavia**, Vicolo dello Stagno, off Via del Prione, not far from the station, ✆ 27465 (inexpensive) with rooms with baths for under L50,000, and ★**Terminus**, Via Paleocapa 21, ✆ 714935 (inexpensive) slightly more expensive, with large, clean rooms, albeit a bit noisy. Near the station is the ★★★**Firenze & Continental**, Via Paleocapa 7, ✆ 713200 (moderate) is a comfortable hotel that's convenient for making rail hops into the Cinque Terre. All the rooms in the main hotel have bathrooms, but it has a cheaper annex (*dipendenza*) nearby on Via Fiume 60.

## Portovenere

In Portovenere the large and modern ★★★★**Hotel Royal Sporting**, Via dell' Olivo 345, ✆ 900326, ✉ 529060 (expensive) is the finest hotel, with a fantastic location overlooking sea and town, a salt-water pool, beach, garden, tennis courts, and air-conditioning in every room. There is also a place to park, an important consideration in this little town. (*Open April–Oct.*) ★★★**San Pietro**, ✆ 900616 (expensive) has hardly any of the facilities of the Royal, but a lot more character. Located up at the old castle, it has charming 1920s Liberty-style décor, and superb views. ★★**Genio**, Piazza Bastrieri 8, ✆ 900611 (inexpensive) has the cheapest rooms in Portovenere, all with baths, and a nice little garden, too. ★**Lorena**, on the Isola Palmaria, ✆ 900678, is also an attractive option, though the rooms are without baths and prices are getting into the moderate category. (*Open 1 May–30 Sept.*)

## Lerici

There is the ★★★★**Shelley & Delle Palme**, Lungomare Biaggini 5, ✆ 967127(moderate), one of the largest and most comfortable hotels on the 'Gulf of Poets', with fine views of the sea and baths in all rooms, though prices are still very reasonable. Still with the Romantics, on the left as you approach the town is the ★★★**Byron**, ✆ 967104, ✉ 967409 (moderate) also a good choice, where the slightly small rooms—though all with bath—are compensated for by fine views across the bay and, on the third floor, huge balconies. ★★★**Doria**, just over the headland, Via Privata Doria, ✆ 967124, ✉ 966459 (moderate) is slightly cheaper and also enjoys great views. Outside the town on the cove of Fiascherino ★★★★**Il Nido**, Via Fiascherino 75, ✆ 967286 (moderate) enjoys a lovely location, with enchanting views over the sea and beach. It has good rooms (though not quite so good in the annexe) that are perfect for rest and relaxation. The only inexpensive-range hotel in Lerici is ★★**Hotel del Golfo**, Via Gerini 37, ✆ 967400 (inexpensive) just up from the tourist office. It's new and clean, and all rooms have bathrooms, and some balconies. Near Lerici, in the more laid-back San Terenzo, ★★★**Elisabetta**, Via Mantegazza 21, ✆ 970636 (inexpensive) is tiny but comfortable, with a garden, and rooms with baths. ★★★**Mulino** (inexpensive), Via Garibaldi 30, ✆/✉ 970801, on the road into the village, is not as well positioned but has similar prices. There are even cheaper options along the seafront, including ★**Il Nettuno**, Via Mantegazza 1, ✆ 971093 (inexpensive) which has clean, big rooms, all with bathroom, and some with balconies for under L70,000, or, slightly more expensive, ★★**Giglio**, Via Garibaldi 16, ✆ 970805, on the left coming into the village, with well-equipped rooms, most with bathrooms, and a restaurant and garage.

## Ameglia

Ameglia, south of Lerici in the Val di Magra, is the site of the most famous hotel and restaurant in the region, the ★★★★**Paracucchi Locanda dell'Angelo**, at Ca' di Scabello, Viale XXV Aprile 60, ✆ 64391, ✉ 64393 (moderate) owned and run by a master chef. The hotel, though still moderately priced, is modern, stylish, and slick, with each room equipped with private bath, air-conditioning and TV, and the sea is only a couple of minutes away. The restaurant is one of the finest in the country (*see* below).

---

### Eating Out

## Monterosso

The best food in Monterosso is served at **Il Gigante**, Via IV Novembre, ✆ 817401, (moderate) with especially good Ligurian specialities—*pansotti, trenette al pesto* and fresh fish.

## Vernazza

The **Gambero Rosso** in Piazza Marconi 7, ✆ 812265 (moderate) is a well-known restaurant that's partly carved out of the rock; try the *tegame di acciughe*, a tasty dish made with anchovies, a Cinque Terre speciality. There's also plenty of less piquant seafood, too. On the square in Vernazza, the **Capitano**, ✆ 812201, (moderate) serves fine fish fare—try the *linguine ai granchi*, washed down with a glass of the genial Captain's own wine.

## Manarola

The choice trattoria is **Aristide**, Via Roma, ✆ 920 000 (moderate), serving a delicious minestra and exquisite fish dishes, also rabbit, game, and other meat in season.

## La Spezia

**La Posta**, in the centre of town on Via Don Minzoni 24, ✆ 34419 (expensive) has some of the city's most diverse and expert cuisine, with game, truffles and mushrooms in season, and good pasta dishes. (*Closed weekends.*) **Il Rossetto**, Via dei Colli 105, ✆ 29393 (expensive) has good views, from up on a hillside over the gulf; its menu features beef, chicken, rabbit and boar, but there's not a minnow in sight. Its hearty roast and grilled meats are accompanied with good red Tuscan wines. La

Spezia has a good number of low-price restaurants, much-patronized by the naval personnel who are everywhere in the town, and mainly concentrated around the Via del Prione, near the port. One of the best is **Dino**, Via de Passano 17, ✆ 736157 (inexpensive), near the main street, a charming, unpretentious place with good food and service, and an excellent-value fixed price menu. (*Closed Sun evenings, Mon.*)

## Portovenere

You can dine in a former fisherman's house in the picturesque Calata Doria, at **Al Gavitello da Mario**, ✆ 900215 (expensive). The menu—surprise!—is devoted to seafood, but prepared in unusual ways—for *primo*, try fish ravioli with prawn sauce, and for *secondo*, scampi with pear brandy. At the beginning of the promontory, **La Taverna del Corsaro**, Lungomare Doria 182, ✆ 900622 (expensive) has one of the most delightful locations in Portovénere, where you can savour delicacies like prawn in bell-pepper sauce and *zuppa di datteri* (razor clams). As well as well-prepared seafood, there's a good selection of wines and desserts.

## Lerici

The best restaurant in Lerici is **Due Corona**, Via G Mazzini, ✆ 967417 (very expensive), beside the port, the deserving winner of two culinary awards. Seafood is, of course, a speciality, try their *cocktail di antipasti mare* and *grigliata mista*. (*Closed Thurs.*) Lerici's **Paolino**, Via S. Francesco 14, ✆ 967801 (expensive) offers three dining choices—light, medium, and full, depending on your appetite—with particularly good salads and pasta dishes. Another place in the area to find good budget meals is Lerici, where there are a great many open-air pizzerias and restaurants along the waterfront. family-run **La Spiaggia**, on the quay at Piazza Basteri 2, ✆ 0187 901670 (inexpensive) in Portovenere, serves some of the best fried squid rings in Italy and other fishy delights, along with a refreshing house wine.

## San Terenzo

**Palmira**, Via Trogo 13, ✆ 971094 (expensive) is a very popular trattoria that serves delightful *zuppa di vongole* and other seafood, though meat dishes are available as well. (*Closed Wed, Sept, Oct.*)

## Fiascherino

**Miranda**, Via Fiascherino 92, ✆ 968130 (expensive) serves mouthwatering seafood dishes like prawn flan in white truffle sauce and fish *gnocchi* with pesto.

## Ameglia

Hotel-restaurant **Dell'Angelo** (very expensive; *see* above for details) is the region's most prestigious place to eat, a haven for gourmets. The menu changes often, but each and every dish is a superb, and often amazingly simple, example of pure wizardry. The desserts are exquisite, and the wine list contains many a rare and prestigious vintage.

## Lombardy and the Lakes

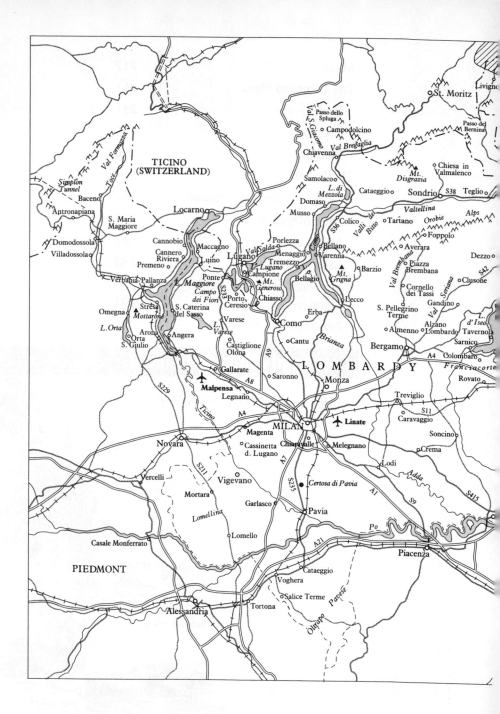

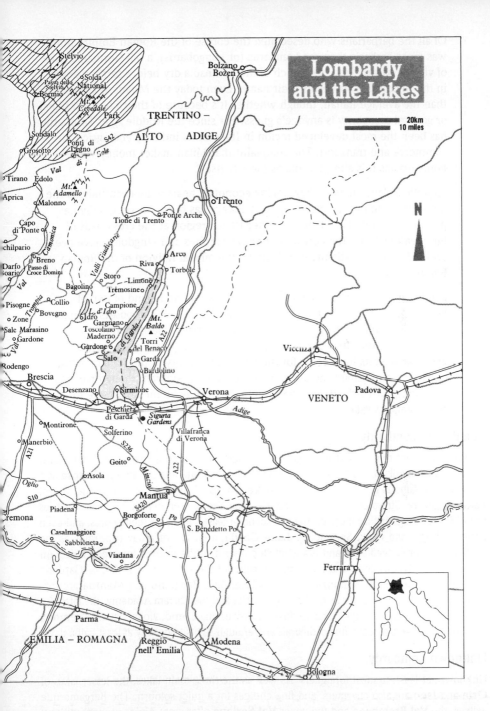

Of all the barbarians who desecrated the corpse of the Roman Empire none was more barbaric than the Lombards (or Longobards), a tall Germanic tribe of violent pagans who bled much of the peninsula dry before settling down in the region that still bears their name. Even today the Milanese are taller than the average Italian, though whether it's because of their Lombard blood or general prosperity is anyone's guess. For since the Middle Ages Lombardy has been the most developed region in Italy, in its industry and agriculture, commerce and transport. The complaint that Milan makes money while Rome wastes it is almost as old as the city itself.

Frenetic Milan, the pounding, racing economic heart of modern Italy, is the transport node for the entire north. It always has been, for geography has placed Lombardy more than any other Italian region at the crossroads of European history—the destinies of entire empires and kingdoms have been decided here; Christianity was declared the official religion of the Roman Empire in Milan.

Lombardy has its gentle side as well. This was the homeland of two of Rome's greatest poets, epic Virgil and lyric Catullus, of composers Donizetti and Monteverdi, of the great violin masters, Amati, Guarneri and Stradivarius. And since the 18th century countless poets, composers and weary aristocrats have come for the peace and beauty of the Italian Lakes, one of the most charming districts in the country—which, though partially in Piedmont, Switzerland, and the Veneto, have all been included here for convenience's sake.

## The Best of Lombardy

**Milan** is far more than a centre of finances and fashion, but an art city in its own right, where you can easily spend three days, taking in nearby **Pavia** and its famous **Certosa** as a day trip. The famous gardens and villas of **Lake Como** (Villa Carlotta and Bellagio) or of **Lake Maggiore** (Stresa and the Borromean isles) can also be seen in rather hurried day trips from Milan, though it's far more pleasant to spend at least a night on their shores, and even better to linger and relax. Spectacular **Lake Garda**, a bit far for a day trip, rates as the liveliest for a prolonged stay, and is a good stop-over if you're headed towards Venice; on Garda don't miss Sirmione and its Romantic ruins of the Grotte di Catullo, or Gardone Riviera, with Gabriele D'Annunzio's kitsch palace. Both **Bergamo** and **Mantua** are top-notch art cities, the former for its medieval Città Alta and the Carrara Academy, the latter for the Renaissance palaces of the Gonzaga dukes. Silk-weaving **Como**, violin-making **Cremona** and Roman **Brescia** all have fine cathedrals and enough sights to occupy at least half a day.

## Unknown Lombardy

Unknown, at least, to most foreigners. As well as the three main lakes, the lesser lakes of **Orta** and **Iseo** are also charmers, and fine choices for a quiet sojourn. The Bergamasque valleys, the **Val Brembana** and the upper **Val Seriana** offer great Alpine scenery without the hype, while the beautiful **Val Camonica** above Lake Iseo is the home of the remarkable **National Park of Prehistoric Engravings**. The rugged Alpine valleys of Sondrio province, the **Valchiavenna** and the **Valtellina**, are dotted with castles and quiet villages; **Bormio**, at the top of the Valtellina, is one of Italy's top winter sports centres and the gateway to glacier-encrusted **Stelvio National Park**. More splendid scenery lies to the north of Lake Maggiore, especially around **Domodossola** and the Romantic **Val Formazza**.

Artistic treasures pale before Lombardy's natural wonders, but certainly worth a mention are **Sabbioneta**, an ideal Renaissance town near Mantua; the lovely frescoes of Masolino da Panicale in **Castiglione Olona**, east of Lake Maggiore; and the ancient Cathedral of **Monza**, with the treasure of the 6th-century Lombard Queen Theodolinda.

# Milan

Most tourists don't come to Italy looking for slick and feverishly busy Milan, and most of those who somehow find themselves here take in only the obligatory sights—Leonardo's Last Supper, La Scala, the Duomo, and the Brera Gallery—before rushing off in search of designer fashions. Most Italians (apart from the almost 2,000,000 Milanese, that is) have little good to say about their second city, either: all the Milanese do is work, all they care about is money, and they defiantly refuse to indulge the myth of *la dolce vita*.

The Italians who deride Milan (most of whom work just as many hours themselves) are mostly envious, and the tourists who whip through it in a day are mostly ignorant of what this great city has to offer. Milan is indeed atypical, devoid of the usual Italian daydreams and living-museum mustiness. Like Naples it lives for the present, but not in Naples' endearing total anarchy; as one of Europe's major financial centres and a capital of fashion, Milan dresses in a well-tailored, thoroughly cosmopolitan three-piece suit. The skills of its workers, above all in the luxury clothing trades, have been known for centuries—as evoked in the English word 'millinery'.

And yet, as the Milanese are the first to admit, Milan has made its way in the world not so much by native talent as through the ability to attract and make use of those from other places, from St Ambrose and Leonardo da Vinci to its most celebrated designer of the moment. It has produced no great music of its own, but La Scala opera house is one of the world's most prestigious places to sing; it has produced but one great artist of its own (the extraordinary Arcimboldo) but managed to amass enough treasures to fill four first-class galleries. Milan is Italy's New York, its greatest melting pot, the Italians' picture window on the modern world, where the young and ambitious gravitate to see their talents properly appreciated and rewarded. Here history seems to weigh less; here willowy Japanese models slink down the pavement with natty young gents whose parents immigrated from Calabria. Luigi Barzini complained that foreigners are interested only in dead Italians, but Milan is one city where the live ones are equally captivating and overflowing with ideas.

## History

Milan was born cosmopolitan. Located far from any sea or river, in the middle of the fertile but vulnerable Lombard plain, it nevertheless lies at the natural junction of trade routes

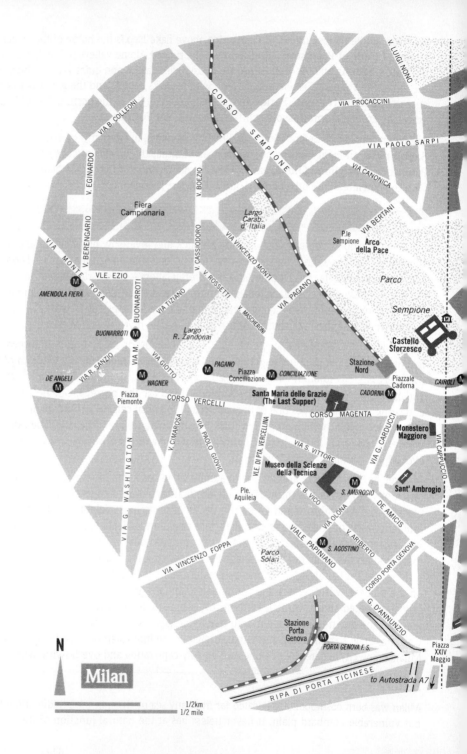

Milan

1/2km
1/2 mile

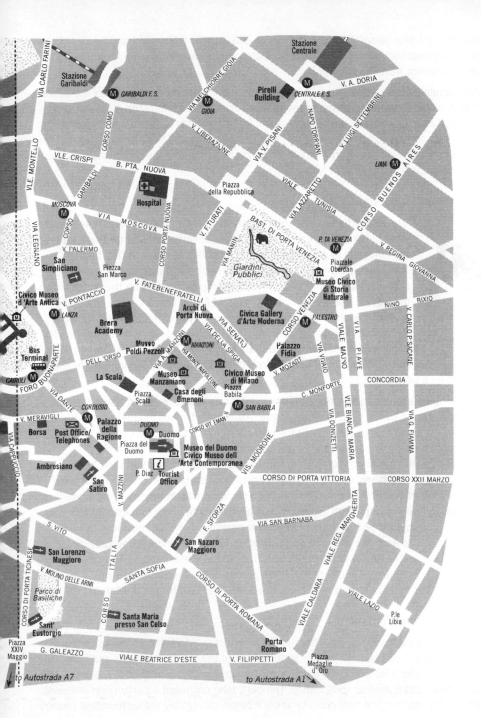

through the Alpine passes, from the Tyrrhenian and Adriatic ports, and from the river Po. A great advantage commercially, this strategic position has also put Milan right in the path of every conqueror tramping through Italy.

Mediolanum, as it was originally called, first became prominent in the twilight of the Roman Empire, when, as the headquarters of the Mobile Army and the seat of the court and government of the West, it became the de facto capital for long periods of time; Diocletian preferred it to Rome, and his successors spent much of their time here. The Christianization of the Empire was given official support here in 313, when Constantine the Great established religious toleration with his Edict of Milan.

## St Ambrose (Sant'Ambrogio)

 No sooner had Christianity received the stamp of approval than it was split between two camps: the orthodox, early-Catholic tradition and the followers of Arianism. Arians, followers of the Egyptian bishop Arius, denied that Christ was of the same substance as God, and the sect was particularly widespread among the peoples on the fringes of the Roman Empire. An early bishop of Milan was an Arian and persecutor of the orthodox, and a schism seemed inevitable when he died. When the young consular governor Ambrose spoke to calm the crowd during the election of the new bishop, a child's voice suddenly piped up: 'Ambrose Bishop!' The cry was taken up, and Ambrose, who hadn't even been baptized, suddenly found himself thrust into a new job.

According to legend, when Ambrose was an infant in Rome, bees had flown into his mouth, attracted by the honey of his tongue. Ambrose's famous eloquence as bishop (374–97) is given much of the credit for preserving the unity of the Church; when the widow of Emperor Valentine desired to raise her son as an Arian, demanding a Milanese basilica for Arian worship, Ambrose and his supporters held the church through a nine-day siege, converting the Empress's soldiers in the process. His most famous convert was St Augustine, and he also set what was to become the standard in relations between Church and Empire when he refused to allow Emperor Theodosius to enter church until he had done penance for ordering a civilian massacre in Thessalonika. St Ambrose left such an imprint on Milan that even today genuine Milanese are called Ambrosiani; their church, practically independent from Rome until the 11th century, still celebrates Mass according to the Ambrosian rite. The Milanese even celebrate their own civic carnival of Sant'Ambrogio in March.

## The Rise of the Comune

During the barbarian invasions of the next few centuries 'Mediolanum' was shortened to Mailand, the prized Land of May, for so it seemed to the frostbitten Goths and Lombards who came to take it for their own. In the early 11th century Milan evolved into one of Italy's first *comuni* under another great bishop, Heribert, who organized a *parlamento* of citizens and a citizen militia. The new *comune* at once began subjugating the surrounding country and especially its Ghibelline rivals Pavia, Lodi, and Como. To inspire the militia Heribert also invented that unique Italian war totem, the *carroccio*, a huge ox-drawn cart that bore the city's banner, altar and bells into battle, to remind the soldiers of the city and church they fought for.

It was Lodi's complaint about Milan's bullying to Holy Roman Emperor Frederick Barbarossa that first brought old Red Beard to Italy in 1154. It was to prove a momentous battle of wills and arms between the Emperor and Milan, one that would define the relationship of Italy's independent-minded *comuni* towards their nominal overlord. Barbarossa besieged and sacked Milan in 1158; the Ambrosiani promised to behave but attacked his German garrison as soon as the Emperor was back safely over the Alps. Undaunted, Barbarossa returned again, and for two years laid waste to the countryside around Milan, then grimly besieged the defiant city. When it surrendered he was merciless, demanding the surrender of the *carroccio*, forcing the citizens to kiss his feet with ropes around their necks, and inviting Milan's bitterest enemies, Lodi and Como, to raze the city to the ground, sparing only the churches of Sant'Ambrogio and San Lorenzo.

But this total humiliation of Milan, meant as an Imperial example to Italy's other *comuni*, had the opposite effect to that intended; it galvanized them to form the Lombard League against the foreign oppressor (only Pavia hated Milan too much to join). Barbarossa, on his next trip over the Alps, found the *comuni* united against him, and in 1176 was soundly defeated by the Lombard League at Legnano. Now the tables had turned and the empire itself was in danger of total revolt. To preserve it, Barbarossa had to do a little foot-kissing himself in Venice, the privileged toe in this case belonging to Pope Alexander III, whom Barbarossa had exiled from Rome in his attempt to set up a pope more malleable to his schemes. To placate the Lombard *comuni*, the Treaty of Constance was signed after a six-year truce in 1183, in which the signatories of the Lombard League received all that they desired: their municipal autonomy and the privilege of making war—on each other! The more magnanimous idea of a united Italy was still centuries away.

## The Big Bosses

If Milan was precocious in developing government by the *comune*, it was also one of the first cities to give it up. Unlike their counterparts in Florence, Milan's manufacturers were very varied in their trades (though mainly involved in textiles and armour) and limited themselves to small workshops, failing to form the companies of politically powerful merchants and trade associations that were the power base of a medieval Italian republic. The first family to fill Milan's vacuum at the top were the Torriani (della Torre), feudal lords who became the city's *signori* in 1247, only to lose their position to the Visconti in 1277.

The Visconti, created dukes in 1395, made Milan the strongest state in all Italy, and marriages into the French and English royal houses made the family prominent in European affairs as well. Most ambitious of them all was Gian Galeazzo (1351–1402), married first to the daughter of the king of France, and then to the daughter of his powerful and malevolent uncle Bernabò, whom Gian Galeazzo neatly packed off to prison, before conquering most of northern Italy, the Veneto, Romagna, and Umbria. His army was ready to march on Florence, the gateway to the rest of the peninsula, when he suddenly died of plague. In his cruelty, ruthlessness and superstitious dependence on astrology, and in his love of art and letters (he founded the Certosa of Pavia, began the Duomo, held a court second to none in its lavishness, and supported the University of Pavia) Gian Galeazzo was one of the first 'archetypal' Renaissance princes. The Florentines and the Venetians took advantage of his demise to carry off pieces of his empire, and while his sons, the obscene Gian Maria (who delighted in feeding his enemies to the dogs) and the gruesome, paranoid Filippo Maria, did what they could to regain their father's conquests, Milan's influence was eventually reduced to Lombardy, which its leaders ran as a centralized state.

Filippo Maria left no male heirs, but a wise and lovely daughter named Bianca, whom he betrothed to his best condottiere, Francesco Sforza (1401–66). After Filippo Maria's death, the Milanese declared the Golden Ambrosian Republic, which crumbled without much support after three years, when Francesco Sforza returned peacefully to accept the dukedom. One of Milan's best rulers, he continued the scientific development of Lombard agriculture and navigable canals and hydraulic schemes, and kept the peace through a friendly alliance with the Medici. His son, Galeazzo Maria, was assassinated, but not before fathering Caterina Sforza, the great Renaissance virago, and an infant son, Gian Galeazzo II.

## Lodovico il Moro

It was, however, Francesco Sforza's second son, Lodovico il Moro (1451–1508) who took power and became Milan's most cultured and intriguing leader. He was helped by his wife, the delightful Beatrice d'Este, who ran one of Italy's most sparkling courts until her early death in childbirth. Lodovico was a great patron of the arts, commissioning the *Last Supper* and many of Leonardo da Vinci's engineering schemes, as well as his theatrical pageants. Nevertheless Lodovico bears the blame for one of the first great Italian political blunders, when his quarrel with Naples grew so touchy that he invited King Charles VIII of France to march through the peninsula to claim the Kingdom of Naples. Charles took him up on it and marched unhindered through the country. Lodovico soon realized it was a terrible mistake, and joined the last-minute league of Italian states that united to trap and destroy the French at Fornovo. They succeeded, partially, but the damage was done: the French invasion had shown the Italian states, beautiful, rich and full of treasures, to be disunited and vulnerable. Charles VIII's son, Louis XII, took advantage of a claim on Milan through his Visconti grandmother and captured the city, and Lodovico with it. He died a prisoner in France. After more fights between French and Spanish, Milan ended up a strategic province of Charles V's empire, ruled by a Spanish Viceroy.

In 1712 the city came under the Habsburgs of Austria, and with the rest of Lombardy profited from the enlightened reforms of Maria Theresa, who did much to improve agriculture (especially the production of rice and silk), rationalize taxes, and increase education; under her rule La Scala opera house was built, the city's greatest art gallery, the Brera Academy, was founded, and most of central, neoclassical Milan was built. After centuries of hibernation the Ambrosiani were stirring again, and by the time Napoleon arrived the city welcomed him fervently. With a huge festival Milan became the capital of Napoleon's 'Cisalpine Republic' and was linked with Paris via the new Simplon Highway.

# The Powerhouse of United Italy

Austrian rule was restored once more after Napoleon's collapse in 1814, but Milan was to be an important centre of Italian nationalist sentiment during the Risorgimento, and rebelled against the repressive Habsburg regime in 1848. The city's greatest contribution during this period, however, was the novelist Manzoni, born in Lecco on Lake Como, whose master-piece, *I Promessi Sposi*, caused a sensation through his use of language—a new, popular, national Italian that everyone could understand, no small achievement in a country of a hundred dialects, where the literary language had remained practically unchanged since Dante. It was also a work that observed history from the point of view of the common man, and was a landmark in sparking feelings of Italian unity.

After joining the kingdom of Italy, Milan rapidly took its place as Italy's economic and indus-trial leader, attracting thousands of workers from the poorer sections of the country. Many of these workers joined the new Italian Socialist Party, which was strongest in Lombardy and Emilia-Romagna. In Milan, too, Mussolini founded the Fascist Party and launched its first campaign in 1919. The city was bombed heavily in air raids during the Second World War. In May 1945 its well-organized partisans liberated it from the Germans before the Allies arrived, and when Mussolini's corpse was hung up on a meat hook in the Piazzale Loreto the Milanese turned out to make sure that the duke of delusion was truly dead before beginning to rebuild their battered city on more solid ground.

Milan was, again, perhaps *the* centre of Italy's postwar economic miracle when it began to take off in the late fifties, drawing in still more thousands of migrants from the south. Despite economic ups and downs and a few hiccups, the city's wealth has continued to grow by near-mathematical progression ever since, while its political affairs were dominated from the seventies onwards by the Socialist Party and their ineffable boss Bettino Craxi. Since the beginning of the nineties, however, as anyone exposed to any of the Italian media has not been allowed to forget for even one minute, the whole structure has of course come crashing down, for it was in Milan, too, that the first allegations of the large-scale taking of *tangenti* (bribes) came to light, initially involving the Socialists, though the mud later spread to touch all the established parties. Craxi and his cronies have virtually disappeared from the political map, and power in Milan's affairs is now disputed between a left/green alliance and the regionalist Northern League. The effects of this new broom are awaited with a mixture of hope, curiosity and apprehension.

---

### Getting There

The transport hub of northern Italy, Milan is naturally well served by a full range of international services—with two international airports, several train stations and many long-distance coach services. It is also the centre of the Italian motorway (*autostrada*) network, and the main point of arrival for many roads from the north through or across the Alps, though anyone driving to the city would be well advised to leave their car wherever they are staying as soon as possible, and do any sight-seeing by public transport. Milan's expanding Metro network is, as well as one of the best means of getting from A to B, a very useful aid to orientating oneself within the city, and stops (indicated **Ⓜ**) are listed in the text below.

Both of Milan's airports, **Linate** (8km from the centre) and the larger **Malpensa** (50km to the west) receive national and international flights. As a rule, intercontinental flights use Malpensa, while Linate handles most of the European and domestic traffic—but be sure to check. For all flight enquiries for both airports ✆ 74852200. Buses run every 20 minutes between Linate and Porta Garibaldi station or Piazza Luigi di Savoia, next to the Stazione Centrale, in Milan. City bus 73 also runs to Linate from Piazza San Babila (Ⓜ line 1) in the city centre. Ticket prices are the same as for other city buses (L1200). For Linate bus information ✆ 66984509.

Buses to and from Malpensa also run from Porta Garibaldi and Piazza Luigi di Savoia, 2½ hours before each flight. Check the full schedule in the nearby **Agenzia Dorea**, or call for information on ✆ 40099260/80. Tickets cost L12,000 each way.

Milan's splendiferous main **Stazione Centrale** (Ⓜ lines 2, 3), designed in the thirties with the travelling Fascist satrap in mind, dominates the Piazza Duca d'Aosta northeast of the centre. Centrale (information ✆ 675001) handles nearly all international trains, as well as most of the domestic routes. From Centrale you can take tram 1 to Piazza Scala and Nord Station, and 33 to Stazione Garibaldi and the Cimitero Monumentale; bus 60 goes to Piazza Duomo and Castello Sforzesco and bus 65 runs down Corso Buenos Aires, Corso Venezia and through the centre to Corso Italia.

**Stazione Garibaldi** (Ⓜ2) is the terminus for car-train services, as well as trains for Pavia, Monza, Varese, Como, and Bergamo. **Stazione Lambrate** (Ⓜ2), on the east side of the city, has connections to Genoa, Bergamo, and towards the Simplon Pass. **Milano-Nord** (Ⓜ Cadorna) is the main station of Lombardy's regional railway network, with connections to Lake Como, Varese, Novara, Lake Maggiore and several other local destinations.

Most intercity buses arrive in the Piazza Castello (Ⓜ Cairoli), where several bus companies have their offices. **Autostradale** (✆ 801161) is the largest, and it's worth giving them a call if you're aiming for one of the less frequented lake shores or Alpine valleys with no train link.

The various *autostrade*, from France and Turin in the west and across to Venice in the east (A4), to Genoa (A7) and to Bologna, Florence and the south (A1), all link up around Milan with the *tangenziale* ring road, which like the *autostrade* is a toll road. From there several streets connect with the three inner ring roads and the centre; one of the most direct is the Viale Certosa, from the northwest. To the north the A8 runs from the *tangenziale* towards Domodossola and the Simplon Pass, and the A9 towards Lake Como and into Switzerland via Lugano.

Milan is not a difficult place to find your way around in—unless you've brought a car.

## by bus and tram

The buses and rather dashing Art Deco trams run by the Milan transport authority (ATM) are convenient and their routes well marked. As usual in Italy you must purchase **tickets** (L1200) in advance at tobacco shops, news-stands, or in the coin-gobbling machines at the main stops, and stamp them in the machines on board; one ticket is valid for 75 minutes' travel anywhere on the network, regardless of how many transfers you make. Most bus routes run from about 6am to midnight, after which time special night bus routes operate with reasonable frequency.

If you plan to be riding around a fair bit, buy a one-day pass (L4100), which is valid for buses, trams and the Metro, and is available from the tourist office, tobacconists, or the ATM information office in the Piazza del Duomo, ✆ 89010797. The ATM also publishes a very useful, but cheap, large map showing all the bus routes and metro stops, the *Guida Rete dei trasporti pubblici*, available from the same outlets.

## by metro

The **Metropolitana Milanese** (Ⓜ), begun in the sixties, is sleek and well run, and a boon for the bewildered tourist. There are three lines, the Red (Ⓜ1), Green (Ⓜ2), and Yellow (Ⓜ3), the last of which was only completed in 1990. The Red and Green Lines intersect at Cadorna and Loreto; the Yellow and Green lines cross only at Stazione Centrale, while the Yellow and Red meet at Duomo. The Metro is open 6am to midnight daily, and tickets are the same as those used for the buses or trams.

## by taxi

Milanese taxis are yellow, and their drivers generally honest and reliable. If it's not possible to flag a free cab down in the street they can be found waiting at ranks in the Piazza del Duomo, by the Stazione Centrale, and in several other central piazzas. Alternatively, call for a taxi on ✆ 8585.

## by car

Driving in Milan requires chutzpah, luck, and good navigation skills. One-way streets are the rule, signs confusing, parking impossible (outside a handful of usually full underground garages), and bringing a vehicle into the city centre between 7 and 10am or trying to park during rush hours is not only foolhardy but illegal. Also, remember that even though Milan looks like a bloated amoeba on the map, since it has grown outward in concentric circles, most of its sights are in the highly walkable inner ring, the *Cerchia dei Navigli*, which follows the former medieval walls and now-buried canals. Within this area, getting anywhere by car is usually the least convenient means of doing so. Traffic moves only slightly more freely within the second ring, the *Viali*, which follows the line of the 16th-century Spanish walls.

The main tourist office is in the Piazza del Duomo on Via Marconi 1, © 809662, @ 72022999. Other branch offices are at the Stazione Centrale, © 6990432, and Linate Airport, © 744065. All three will make free hotel reservations on the spot, and provide good city maps and other practical information; they also organize daily coach tours of the city, departing from the Piazza del Duomo, and canalboat trips in summer. The municipal information office in the Galleria Vittorio Emanuele, © 870545, is especially good for information on exhibitions, concerts, and other special events. Other good places to find out what's on are Milan's excellent daily *Corriere della Sera*, and the weekly tabloid *Viva Milano*.

**Fire, © 115**

**Police**, Via Fatebenefratelli 11, © **62261**

**Ambulance, © 7733**

**Hospital: Ospedale Maggiore di Milano**, Via F Sforza 35, © 55031 (Ⓜ Crocetta).

**24-hour Pharmacy: Carlo Erba**, Piazza Duomo 21, © 72023120. By the entrance of each pharmacy you will find a list of other out-of-hours possibilities.

There are two 24-hour change offices in the Piazza del Duomo, one at No.19 and the other next to the Virgin megastore. There are also two more outside the **Stazione Centrale**.

The **main post office** is situated at Piazza Cordusio (Ⓜ Cordusio), and is open 8.15am–7.40pm Mon–Fri, and 8am–5.30pm Sat. Alongside it there is also a phone centre.

## Piazza del Duomo

In the exact centre of Milan towers its famous **Duomo**, a monument of such imposing proportions (third largest in the world after St Peter's and Seville Cathedral) that on clear days it is as visible from the distant Alps as the Alps are visible from its dome. Bristling with 135 spires, defended by 2244 marble saints and one sinner (Napoleon, who crowned himself King of Italy here in 1805), guarded by some 95 leering gargoyles, energized by sunlight pouring through the largest stained-glass windows in Christendom, Milan Cathedral is a remarkable bulwark of the faith. And yet for all its monstrous size, for all the hubbub of its Times-Squarish piazza of throbbing neon signs, traversed daily by tens of thousands of Milanese and tourists, the Duomo is utterly ethereal, a rose-white vision of pinnacles and tracery woven by angels.

Gian Galeazzo Visconti founded it in 1386 as a votive offering to the Mother of God, hoping in return that she would favour him with a male heir. His prayers for a son were answered in the form of Giovanni Maria, a loathsome degenerate assassinated soon after he attained power; as the Ambrosiani have wryly noted, the Mother of God got the better of the deal. For, along with the money to build the church, Gian Galeazzo threw in the Candoglia quarries (source of the fine marble still used by the Cathedral Building company) and hired the finest architects and masons of the day, including the masters of Campione of Lake Lugano, who are accredited with the design, assisted by Gothic artisans from the North. However, before the cathedral could be completed, the Gothic style—which the Italians never liked much to begin with—had become unfashionable, and the bewildered façade went through several overhauls of Renaissance and Baroque, then back to Gothic, with the end result, completed in 1809 under Napoleon's orders, resembling a shotgun wedding of Isabelline Gothic with Christopher Wren. In the 1880s there were plans to tear it down and start again, but no one had the heart, and the Milanese have become used to it. Walk around, though, to the glorious Gothic **apse**, to see what its original builders were about. The subjects of the bas-reliefs on the bronze doors, all cast in this century, are a Milanese history lesson: the Edict of Constantine, the Life of St Ambrose, the city's quarrels with Barbarossa, and the history of the cathedral itself.

The remarkable dimensions of the interior challenge the eyes to take in what at first seems like infinity captured under a canopy. Its tremendous volume is defined into five aisles by 52 pillars of titanic dimensions, crowned by rings of niches and statues, and is dazzlingly lit by acres of stained glass; the windows of the apse, embellished with flamboyant Gothic tracery, are among the most beautiful anywhere. In them you can see the mysterious alchemical symbol adopted as the Visconti crest, and now the symbol of the city: a twisting serpent in the act of swallowing a man. All other decorations seem rather small afterthoughts, but you may want to seek out in the right transept Leoni's fine Mannerist tomb of Gian Giacomo de' Medici, better known as *Il Medeghino*, the pirate of Lake Como—erected by his brother Pope Pius IV. Near Il Medeghino's tomb is the most disconcerting of the cathedral's thousands of statues: that of San Bartolomeo being flayed alive, with an inscription assuring us that it was made by Marco Agrate and not by Praxiteles, just in case anyone couldn't tell the difference. Other treasures include the 12th-century Trivulzio Candelabrum, by Nicola da Verdun, as well as medieval ivory, gold, and silverwork in the Treasury, located below the main altar by the crypt, where St Charles Borromeo (nephew of Il Medeghino; *see* below, 'Arona' on Lake Maggiore) lies in state. Near the entrance of the cathedral is a door leading down to the **Baptistry of St Ambrose** (*open 10–12, 3–5, daily; adm*), excavated in the 1960s, containing the octagonal baptismal font where the good bishop baptized St Augustine.

For a splendid view of Milan, take a walk through the enchanted forest of spires and statues on the **cathedral roof** (*open 9–5.30 daily; steps, or lift from outside the cathedral; adm*).

The 15th-century dome by Amadeo, topped by the main spire with the gilt statue of *La Madonnina* (who at 4m tall, really isn't as diminutive as she seems 100m from the ground) offers the best view of all—on a clear morning all the way to the Matterhorn.

## Museo del Duomo and Palazzo Reale

On the south side of the cathedral, the **Museo del Duomo** (*open 9.30–12.30, 3–6, Tues–Sun; adm ; disabled access*) is housed in a wing of the Palazzo Reale, for centuries home of Milan's rulers, from the Visconti to the Austrian governors. The latter were responsible for its current neoclassical make-up. The museum contains artefacts related to the Duomo, including some of the original stained glass and fine 14th-century French and German statues and gargoyles, tapestries, and a Tintoretto among many other artworks. Other rooms document the history of the cathedral's construction, including a magnificent wooden model built in 1519, designs from the 1886 competition for the new façade, and castings from the bronze doors.

In the main core of the Palazzo Reale is the recently installed **Civíco Museo dell'Arte Contemporanea (CIMAC)** (*open 9.30–5.30 Tues–Sun; disabled access*), with temporary exhibits on the second and the main collection on the third floor. It's devoted to mainly Italian art of this century, and has early works by the futurists (especially Boccioni), as well as others by Modigliani, De Chirico, Morandi, De Pises, Melotti, the mystical Carrà, and current artists like Tancredi and Novelli.

Behind the palace, on Via Palazzo Reale, be sure to note the beautiful 14th-century **campanile di San Gottardo**, formerly belonging to the palace chapel. The main flanks of the Piazza del Duomo are occupied by porticoes sheltering some of the city's oldest bars; in the centre stands a florid equestrian statue of Vittorio Emanuele II.

## The Galleria and La Scala

Opening up from the north side of the Piazza del Duomo is Milan's majestic drawing room, the elegant **Galleria Vittorio Emanuele**, a great glass-roofed arcade designed by Giuseppe Mengoni, who tragically fell from the roof the day before its inauguration in 1878. Here are more elegant bars (especially the venerable **Il Salotto**, serving perhaps Milan's best cup of coffee) and some of the city's finest shops. In the centre, under a marvellous 48m glass dome, is a ring of mosaic figures of the zodiac; the Milanese believe it's good luck to step on Taurus's testicles.

At the other end of the Galleria lies the **Piazza della Scala**, address of one of the world's great opera houses, the modest looking neoclassical **La Scala Theatre**, its name derived from the church of Santa Maria alla Scala which formerly stood on the site. Inaugurated in 1778 with Salieri's *Europa Riconosciuta*, La Scala saw the premieres of most of the 19th-century classics of Italian opera, and when bombs smashed it in 1943 it was rebuilt as it was in three years, reopening under the baton of its great conductor Arturo Toscanini. The **Museo Teatrale alla Scala** (*open June–Oct 9–12, 2–6, daily; Nov–May Mon–Sat only; adm*), entered through a door on the left, has recently been rearranged to house better its excellent collection of opera memorabilia, scores, letters, portraits and photos of legendary stars, and set designs; there's even an archaeological section with artefacts related to ancient

Greek and Roman theatre. From the museum you can look into the beautiful 2800-seat theatre, with its great chandelier; try to imagine the scene in 1859, when the crowded house at a performance of Bellini's *Norma* took advantage of the presence of the Austrian governor to join in the rousing war chorus.

An unloved 19th-century statue of Leonardo stands in the middle of the Piazza della Scala, while opposite the theatre the imposing **Palazzo Marino** is a fine 16th-century building hiding behind a 19th-century façade; now the Palazzo Municipale, it has one of the city's loveliest courtyards. A few steps away, on Via Catena, the unusual 1565 **Casa degli Omenoni** is held up by eight uncomfortable giants; around the corner on the lovely cobble-stoned Piazza Belgioioso, the **Museo Manzoniano** (*open 9.30–12, 2–4, Tues–Fri*) is located in the fine old house where Manzoni lived, and contains items relating to the novelist's life and work, including illustrations from *I Promessi Sposi* and an autographed portrait of his friend Goethe.

## The Museo Poldi-Pezzoli

In front of La Scala runs one of Milan's busiest and most fashionable boulevards, the **Via Manzoni**. Verdi lived for years and died in a room in the Grand Hotel (No.29); at No.10 is the lovely 17th-century palace of Gian Giacomo Poldi-Pezzoli, who decorated his home to fit his fabulous art collection, then willed it to the public in 1879. Repaired after bomb damage in the War, the **Museo Poldi Pezzoli** (*open 9.30–12.30, 2.30–6, Tues–Fri; 2.30–7.30pm Sat; closed Sun pm April–Sept, and Sat in Aug; adm*) houses one of Italy's best-known portraits, the 15th-century *Portrait of a Young Woman* by the Tuscan Antonio Pollaiuolo, depicting an ideal Renaissance beauty. She shares the most elegant room of the palace, the Salone Dorato, with the other jewels of the museum: Mantegna's Byzantine *Madonna*, Giovanni Bellini's *Pietà*, Piero della Francesca's *San Nicolò* and from a couple of centuries later, Guardi's *Grey Lagoon*. Other outstanding paintings include Vitale da Bologna's *Madonna*, a polyptych by Moretti, and works by Luini, Foppa, Turà, Crivelli, Lotto, Cranach (portraits of Luther and wife) and a crucifix by Raphael. The museum also has a fine Islamic collection of metalwork and rugs, including a magnificent 1532 Persian carpet depicting a hunting scene (in the Salone Dorato), medieval and Renaissance armour, Renaissance bronzes, Flemish tapestries, Murano glass, and much more.

## Via Montenapoleone

A couple of blocks up Via Manzoni from the museum is Milan's high fashion vortex, the palace-lined **Via Montenapoleone** and a bit beyond, the elegant, pedestrian-only **Via della Spiga**. Even if you're not in the market for astronomically priced clothes by Italy's top designers, these exclusive lanes make for good window shopping and perhaps even better people-watching. It's hard to remember that up until the 1970s Florence was the centre of the Italian garment industry. When Milan took over this status, thanks mainly to its superior transportation network, it added the essential ingredient of public relations to the Italians' innate sense of style to create a high-fashion empire rivalling Paris, London and New York.

There are two recently established museums in the sumptuous 18th-century Palazzo Morando Bolognini, on Via S. Andrea 6, between 'Montenapo' and Via della Spiga: the

**Civico Museo di Milano** and the **Civico Museo di Storia Contemporanea** (*both open 9.30–5.30 Tues–Sun; disabled access*), the first documenting the story of the city, the second devoted to Italian history between the years 1914 and 1945.

Near the intersection of Via della Spiga and Via Manzoni, the **Archi di Porta Nuova**, the huge stone arches of a gate, are one of the few survivals of the 12th-century walls. The original moat that surrounded the walls was enlarged into a canal to bring in the marble for the construction of the cathedral; it was covered in the 1880s when its stench became greater than its economic benefits. (A useful bus, no.96/97, from the Piazza Cavour makes the circuit of the former canal, and is convenient for reaching the Castello Sforzesco, Santa Maria delle Grazie, or Sant'Ambrogio.)

## Giardini Pubblici

From Piazza Cavour, Via Palestro curves between the two sections of Milan's Public Gardens. The Romantic **Giardini di Villa Reale** (Ⓜ Palestro) were laid out in 1790 for the Belgiojoso family by Leopoldo Pollak, who also built the Villa Reale, Napoleon's residence while in town. This is now the **Civica Galleria d'Arte Moderna** (*open 9.30–5.30 Tues–Sun; disabled access*); it specializes in Lombard art of the 19th century, in which local artists reflected international movements and invented one of their own, the self-consciously Romantic *Scapigliati* (the 'Wild-haired Ones'). Besides the Italians, there are works by Millet, Corot, Cézanne, Gauguin, Manet, and Van Gogh. A third section contains early 20th-century works by the futurists and others, while a recent donation has added paintings by Picasso, Renoir, and Matisse.

The **Giardini Pubblici** proper, with its fine old trees, lies between Via Palestro and the Corso Veneziaand was laid out in 1782; artificial rocks were added to this shady corner of arcadia to compensate for Milan's flat terrain. A good place to take the children, with its zoo, swans, peddle cars, and playgrounds, it is also the site of Italy's premier **Natural History**

**Museum** (*open 9.30–12.30, 2.30–5.30, Tues–Fri; 9.30am–7.30pm Sat, Sun*), near the Corso Venezia; another victim of the War, it has been rebuilt in its original neo-medieval style. Look out for the Canadian cryptosaurus, the stuffed white rhino, the Colossal European lobster, the Madagascar aye-aye and the 40-kilo topaz.

**Corso Venezia** itself is one of Milan's most interesting thoroughfares, with its neoclassical and Liberty style palaces—most remarkably, the 1903 **Palazzo Castiglione** at No.47 and the neoclassical **Palazzo Serbelloni**, Milan's press club, on the corner of Via Senato. The quarter just west of the Corso Venezia was the most fashionable in the city in the 1920s. It has a smattering of unusual buildings: on Via Malpighi 3, off the Piazza Oberdan, the **Casa Galimberti** with a colourful ceramic façade; the good Art Deco foyer at Via Cappuccini 8; the eccentric houses on Via Mozart (especially No.11); and the romantic 1920s **Palazzo Fidia** at Via Melegari 2.

## Lo stile Liberty

'Liberty style' is the name given in Italy to Art Nouveau, the short-lived artistic and architectural movement that flourished in many European countries around the turn of the century. It refers, curiously, to Liberty's, the London shop, whose William Morris-influenced, flower-patterned fabrics and ceramics were some of the first articles in the style imported into Italy, and became enormously popular at the time (the style is also, less commonly, known as the *stile floreale*). The ethos behind the movement was an avoidance of architectural precedents, an embracing of 'naturalistic' ornament and smooth, flowing lines, and a desire to 'integrate' all the arts—hence the importance given not just to painting and fine art, but also to architecture and interior and practical design. Decoration, an integral part of every design, was the key. Liberty style was never as important in Italy as were its equivalents in France, Austria or Catalonia—nor was it usually as extravagant as they often were—but it did for a time become the vogue among the newly wealthy middle classes of Italy's industrializing north. As the prosperity of this class grew in the 1900s, so too did demand for Liberty-style buildings and products—seen most notably in the villas around the lakes, or along the Riviera. Perhaps the most important figure working in the style in Italy was Giuseppe Sommaruga (1867–1917), whose achievements include the Palazzo Castiglione in Milan and the Hotel Tre Coli, near Varese. Both are characterized by their richly ornamental lines and an uninhibited use of space. In a similar style, but more refined, is the architecture of Raimondo D'Aronco (1857–1932), who worked mainly on public buildings, particularly for conferences and exhibitions. His most famous work is the Palazzo Comunale in Udine. There are few examples of Liberty style in the less affluent, less industrialized South. Most are in Sicily, thanks to the exceptional talent of architect-designer Ernesto Basile (1857–1932) whose chief works, the Villa Igiea and Villino Florio (both in Palermo), are marked by an almost vertiginous degree of sinuous decoration.

Northwest of the Giardini Pubblici, the **Piazza della Repubblica** has many of the city's hotels; the Mesopotamian-scale Stazione Centrale, blocking the end of Via Vittor Pisani, is the largest train station in Italy. The nearby skyscraper, the **Pirelli Building**, is one that the Milanese are especially proud of, built in 1960 by Gio Ponti. Pier Luigi Nervi designed its concrete structure. It's now the seat of Lombardy's regional government, and you can see most of the city from its terrace (call ahead, ✆ 67651).

## Brera and its Accademia

Another street alongside La Scala, Via G. Verdi, leads into the **Brera**, one of the few old quarters to survive in central Milan. Although some of the old cobblestone streets of Brera have maintained their original flavour (especially the Corso Garibaldi), local trendies are busily turning the remainder into Milan's version of Greenwich Village, full of antique and curiosity shops, late night spots, and art galleries. At the corner of Via Brera and the pungently named Via Fiori Oscuri ('Street of the Dark Flowers') is the elegant courtyard of the **Brera Academy** (*open 9–5.30 Tues–Sat; 9–12.30 Sun; adm , free on 1st, 3rd Sun, and 2nd, 4th Sat of each month*), one of Italy's most important hoards of art. Credit for the collection goes mainly to Napoleon, whose bronze statue, draped in a toga, greets visitors as they enter; a firm believer in centralized art as well as central government, he stripped northern Italy's churches and monasteries of their treasures to form a Louvre-like collection for Milan, the capital of his Cisalpine Republic. The museum first opened in 1809.

Perhaps the best known of the Brera's scores of masterpieces is Raphael's *Marriage of the Virgin*, a Renaissance landmark for its evocation of an ideal, rarefied world, where even the disappointed suitor snapping his rod on his knee performs the bitter ritual in a graceful dance step, all acted out before a perfect but eerily vacant temple in the background. In the same room hangs Piero della Francesca's last painting, the *Pala di Urbino*, featuring among its holy personages Federico da Monfeltro, Duke of Urbino, with his famous nose. The Venetian masters are well represented: Carpaccio, Veronese, Tintoretto, Jacopo Bellini and the Vivarini, but especially Giovanni Bellini, with several of his loveliest madonnas and the great *Pietà*, as well as a joint effort with his brother Gentile, of *St Mark preaching in Alexandria*; there are luminous works by Carlo Civelli and Cima da Conegliano; and several paintings by Mantegna, including his remarkable study in foreshortening, the *Cristo Morto*. Other Italian works include a unique panel painting by Bramante, Caravaggio's striking *Supper at Emmaus*, the *Pala Sforzesca* by an unknown 15th-century Lombard artist, depicting Lodovico il Moro and his family; a polyptych by Gentile da Fabriano; and fine works by the Ferrarese masters, da Cossa and Ercole de' Roberti.

Outstanding among the foreign artists' works are Rembrandt's *Portrait of his Sister*, El Greco's *St Francis*, and Van Dyck's *Portrait of the Princess of Orange*. When the Great Masters become indigestible, take a breather in the new 20th-century wing of the gallery, populated mainly by futurists like Severini, Balla, and Boccioni, who believed that to achieve speed was to achieve success, and the metaphysical followers of De Chirico, who seem to believe just the opposite.

Brera's other principal monument is **San Simpliciano**, just off the Corso Garibaldi to the north. Founded perhaps by St Ambrose, it retains its essential palaeo-Christian form in a 12th-century wrapping, with an excellent fresco in the apse by Bergognone, one of the leading 15th-century Lombard painters.

# Castello Sforzesco

*Open 9.30–5.30 Tues–Sun; disabled access.*

Marking the western limits of the Brera quarter, the **Castello Sforzesco** is one of Milan's best-known monuments. Originally a fortress in the walls, the Visconti made it their castle, and as a symbol of their power it was razed to the ground by the Ambrosian Republic in 1447. Three years later, with the advent of Francesco Sforza, it was rebuilt, though since then its appearance has suffered many vicissitudes. Air raids damaged it and its treasures, and when it was rebuilt, its stout towers were made to double as cisterns. Today it houses the city's main art collection, the **Civico Museo d'Arte Antica del Castello**. The entrance is located across the vast Piazza d'Armi, in the lovely Renaissance Corte Ducale. Housed in what was the principal residence of the Sforza, the museum contains intriguing odds and ends from Milan's history—the equestrian tomb of Bernabò Visconti and a beautiful 14th-century monument of the Rusca family; reliefs of Milan's triumph over Barbarossa, and the city's gonfalon. Leonardo designed the ilex decorations of the **Sala delle Asse**.

The next room, the **Sala dei Ducali**, contains a relief by Duccio from Rimini's Tempio Malatestiano; the Sala degli Scarlioni contains the two finest sculptures in the museum, the *Effigy of Gaston de Foix* (1525) and Michelangelo's unfinished *Rondanini Pietà*, a haunting work that the artist laboured on for nine years, off and on, until his death.

Upstairs, most notable among the fine collection of Renaissance furnishings and decorative arts, is the 15th-century Castello Roccabianca frescoes illustrating the popular medieval tale of Patient Griselda. The **Pinacoteca** contains a tender *Madonna with Child* by Giovanni Bellini, his brother-in-law Mantegna's more austere, classical madonna in the *Pala Trivulzio*, and the lovely *Madonna dell'Umiltà* by Filippo Lippi. From Lombardy there are several fine works by Bernardino Bergagnone (especially the serene *Virgin with SS. Sebastian and Gerolamo*) and Il Bramantino, one of the strangest of mannerists, with an eerie *Noli me tangere*. There's a roomful of Leonardo's followers, then a painting by Milan's Giuseppe Arcimboldi (1527–1593), who was no one's follower at all, but the first surrealist. Before going on to become court painter for the Habsburgs in Prague, he left this *Primavera*, a portrait of a woman made up entirely of flowers.

The castle's third court, the beautiful **Cortile della Rocchetta**, was designed by the Florentines Bramante and Filarete, both of whom worked for several years for Francesco Sforza. Filarete also built Milan's great Ospedale Maggiore (1450s, the centrepiece of the Università degli Studi) with ornate brickwork and terracotta and the first cross-shaped wards, and wrote an architectural treatise on the ideal city he called *Sforzinda* in honour of his patron. The basement of the cortile is filled with the *comune*'s extensive **Egyptian collection** of funerary artefacts and the **Prehistoric Collection** of items found in Lombardy's Iron Age settlements. The first floor houses the **Museum of Musical Instruments** with a beautiful collection of string and wind instruments, and a spinet that was played by Mozart. The **Sala della Balla**, where the Sforza played ball, now contains the *Tapestries of the Months* designed by Bartolomeo Suardi, better known by his nickname 'Bramantino' for having been Bramante's pupil.

## Parco Sempione and Cimitero Monumentale

Behind the Castello lies the **Parco Sempione**, Milan's largest city park, the site of De Chirico's **Metaphysical Fountain**; the 1930s **Palazzo dell'Arte**, used for exhibitions; the **Arena**, designed in 1806 after Roman models, where 19th-century dilettantes staged mock naval battles; and the triumphal arch, **Arco della Pace**, marking the terminus of Napoleon's great highway (Corso Sempione) that extended from Milan to the Simplon Pass. The arch, originally intended to glorify Napoleon, was instead dedicated to peace by the Austrians. The **Casa Rustici** at Corso Sempione 36, designed in 1931 by Terragni, has proportions that follow Euclid's Golden Rule; many consider it Milan's finest modern building.

Further out (tram 4 from Piazza Scala) lies the **Cimitero Monumentale** (*open 8.30am–5pm daily*), the last rendezvous of Milan's well-to-do burghers. Their lavish monuments—Liberty-style temples and pseudo-ancient columns and obelisks—are just slightly less flamboyant than those of the Genoese. The cemetery keeper has guides to the tombs—Manzoni, Toscanini, and Albert Einstein's father are among the best-known names; the memorial to the 800 Milanese who perished in German concentration camps is the most moving.

---

## West of the Duomo

Milan's greatest painting, Leonardo da Vinci's *Last Supper* (or the *Cenacolo*), is in the refectory of the convent of **Santa Maria delle Grazie** (Ⓜ *Cadorna, then Via Boccaccio and left on Via Caradosso; open 8.15–1.45 daily; adm; disabled access*). But before entering, get into the proper Renaissance mood by first walking around the 15th-century church and cloister. Built by Guiniforte Solari, with later revisions by Bramante under Lodovico Il Moro, it is perhaps the most beautiful Renaissance church in Lombardy, its exterior adorned with fine brickwork and terracotta. Bramante's greatest contribution is the majestic Brunelleschi-inspired tribune, added in 1492; he also designed the choir, the unusual crossing under the dome, the sacristy, and the elegant little cloister, the **Chiostrino** (*open 7–12, 3–7, daily*).

### The Last Supper

Leonardo painted two of his masterpieces in Milan, the mystery-laden *Virgin of the Rocks* and *The Last Supper*. The former is in the Louvre, and the latter would have been, too, had the French been able to figure out a way to remove the wall. Unfortunately, the ever-experimental artist was not content to use proper, established fresco technique (where the paint is applied quickly to wet plaster) but painted with tempera as if on a wood panel (*fresco secco*), enabling him to return over and over again to achieve the subtlety of tone and depth he desired. The result was exceedingly beautiful, but almost immediately the moisture in the walls began its deadly work of flaking off particles of paint. As the painting deteriorated, various restorers through the centuries have come to try their hand at the most challenging task in their profession, with mixed success. In the Second World War the refectory was decimated by a bomb, and the *Last Supper* only preserved thanks to precautionary measures. Since

1977 restorers have been at work once again, this time cleansing the work of its previous restorations, and stabilizing the wall to prevent further damage; scaffolding will hide portions of the work for several years.

Deterioration or no, the *Last Supper* still thrills, especially in the mellow afternoon light. Painted at the moment when Christ announces that one of his disciples will betray him, it is a masterful psychological study, a single instant caught in time, the apostles' gestures of disbelief and dismay captured almost photographically by one of the greatest students of human nature. According to Vasari, the artist left the portrait of Christ purposely unfinished, believing himself unworthy to paint divinity; Judas was another problem, but Leonardo eventually found the proper expression of the betrayer caught guiltily unawares but still nefariously determined and unrepentant.

## Monastero Maggiore

From Santa Maria delle Grazie the Corso Magenta leads back towards the centre; at the corner of Via Luini stands the Monastero Maggiore. The monastery's pretty 16th-century church of **San Maurizio** (*open 9.30–12, 3.30–6.30, Wed, Sat, Sun only; closed June–Sept*) contains exceptional frescoes by Bernardino Luini, one of Leonardo's most accomplished followers. The former Benedictine convent (entrance at Corso Magenta 15) houses the city's Etruscan, Greek, and Roman collections in the **Civico Museo Archeologico** (*open 9.30–5.30 Tues–Sun*), with good Greek vases, Roman glass, a 1st-century AD head of Jove discovered under the Castello Sforzesco, finds from Caesarea in the Holy Land, and Etruscan funerary objects. As important as Milan was in the late Empire, next to nothing has survived the city's frequent razing and rebuilding.

## Sant'Ambrogio

The last resting place of Milan's patron saint, the ancient church of Sant'Ambrogio lies just off San Vittore and Via Carducci (Ⓜ Sant'Ambrogio) behind the restored medieval gate, the **Pusterla di Sant'Ambrogio**. Founded by St Ambrose in 379, it was enlarged and rebuilt several times, the last time in the 1080s; the result became the prototype of Lombardy's Romanesque basilicas.

The church (*open 7–12, 2–7, Mon–Sat; 7–1, 3–8, Sun*) is entered through a porticoed **Atrium**, lined with fragments of tomb which sets off the simple, triangular façade with its rounded arches and ancient towers; the one to the right, the Monks' Campanile, was built in the 9th century, while the more artistic Canons' Campanile on the left was finished in 1144. The bronze doors, in their decorated portals, date from the 10th century. In its day the finely proportioned interior was revolutionary, for its new-fangled rib vaulting; rows of arches divide the aisles, supporting the women's

*S. Ambrogio - Milano*

gallery, or Matroneum. On the left, look for the 10th-century bronze serpent (said to symbolize Moses' staff) and the **pulpit**, one of the masterpieces of Italian Romanesque. The apse is adorned with 10th–11th century mosaics of the Redeemer and saints, while the sanctuary contains two ancient treasures: the 9th-century *Ciborium* (a casket on columns containing the Host) and a magnificent gold, silver, enamel and gem-studded **altar** (835), portraying scenes from the lives of Christ and St Ambrose. In the crypt below moulder the bones of Saints Ambrosio, Gervasio, and Protasio. At the end of the south aisle the 4th-century **Sacello di San Vittore in Ciel d'Oro** ('in the sky of gold') contains brilliant 5th-century mosaics in its cupola and a presumed authentic portrait of St Ambrose.

After working on Santa Maria delle Grazie, Bramante spent two years on Sant'Ambrogio, contributing the unusual **Portico della Canonica** (entered from the door on the left aisle) and the two cloisters, now incorporated into the adjacent Università Cattolica; these display Bramante's new interest in the ancient orders of architecture, an interest he was to develop fully when he moved on to Rome. The upper section of the Portico houses the **Museo della Basilica di Sant'Ambrogio** (*open 10–12, 3–5, Mon, Wed–Fri; 3–5 Sat, Sun; adm*), which contains illuminated manuscripts, medieval capitals and other architectural fragments, as well as ancient fabrics and vestments, some dating back to the 4th century, known as the 'Dalmatiche di Sant'Ambrogio,' tapestries, and paintings by Luini and Bergognone. The 1928 **War Memorial** in the Piazza Sant'Ambrogio was designed by Giovanni Muzio and inspired by Athens' Tower of the Winds.

## Museum of Science and Technology

From Sant'Ambrogio Via San Vittore leads to the former Olivetan convent of San Vittore, repaired after the War to house the **Leonardo da Vinci Museum of Science and Technology** (*open 9.30–4.30 Tues–Sun; adm; disabled access*). Most of this vast and diverse collection, still arranged in its original 1950s format, is rather mysterious for the uninitiated, and if you're not keen about smelting and the evolution of batteries you may want to head straight for the **Leonardo da Vinci Gallery**, lined with wooden models and explanations of his machines and inventions; his knowledge of hydraulic engineering was put to good use in canal-building Milan. Other rooms include musical instruments and displays on optics, radios, computers, clocks and astronomy; downstairs you can push buttons and make waterwheels turn. Another building is devoted to trains, and another to ships and naval history.

## Milan's Financial District

Between Sant'Ambrogio and the Duomo lies what has been the centre of Milan's merchant guilds, bankers, and financiers for centuries, the bank-filled **Piazza Cardusio** (Ⓜ Cardusio), and the area around the Via degli Affari and the Via Mercanti, which gives into the Piazza del Duomo. Milan's imposing **Borsa** (stock exchange) was founded by Napoleon and is now the most important in the nation. On Via Mercanti, the 13th-century **Palazzo della Ragione**, the old Hall of Justice, was given an extra floor with oval windows by Maria Theresa. It has recently been restored and is adorned on the Via Mercanti side with a curious statue of a sow partly clad in wool that recalls the city's Roman name, Mediolanum, which could be translated as 'half-woolly'; on the Piazza Mercanti side the building is adorned with a beautiful early 13th-century equestrian relief.

## The Ambrosiana

In the Piazza Pio XI (off Via Spadari and Via Cantù) is the most enduring legacy of the noble Borromeo family, the **Ambrosiana**, founded by Cardinal Federico Borromeo (cousin of Charles), who amassed one of Italy's greatest libraries here in 1609, containing 30,000 rare manuscripts, including ancient Middle Eastern texts collected to further the Cardinal's efforts to produce a translation of the Bible, a 5th-century illustrated *Iliad*, Leonardo da Vinci's famous *Codice Atlantico*, with thousands of his drawings, early editions of *The Divine Comedy*, and many more unique items. Unfortunately, the library is currently indefinitely closed for restoration.

The restoration hasn't affected the Cardinal's art collection, the **Pinacoteca** (*open 9.30–5 Mon–Fri, Sun; adm*), housed in the same building. Although a number of paintings have been added over the centuries, the gallery is a monument to one man's taste—which showed a marked preference for the Dutch, and for the peculiar; the art here ranges from the truly sublime to some of the funniest paintings ever to grace a gallery: here are Botticelli's lovely *Tondo*, and his *Madonna del Baldacchino* nonchalantly watering lilies with her milk; a respectable *Madonna* by Pinturicchio and the strange, dramatic *Transito della Vergine* by Baldassarre Estense. Further along an *Adoration of the Magi* by the Master of Santo Sangue is perhaps the only one where Baby Jesus seems thrilled at receiving the wise men's gifts. A small room is illuminated by a huge pre-Raphaelitish stained-glass window of Dante by Giuseppe Bertini (1865), and contains the glove Napoleon wore at Waterloo, a 17th-century bronze of Diana the Huntress, so ornate that even the stag wears earrings, and a number of entertaining paintings by Cardinal Borromeo's friend Jan Brueghel the Younger, who delighted in a thousand and one details and wasn't above putting a little pussycat in Daniel's den of lions.

These are followed by more masterpieces: Giorgione's *Page*, Luini's *Holy Family with St Anne* (from a cartoon by Leonardo), Leonardo's *Portrait of a Musician*, a lovely portrait of Beatrice d'Este attributed to Ambrogio De Predis, and then Bramantino's *Madonna in Trono fra Santi*, a scene balanced by a dead man on the left and an enormous dead frog on the right. Challenging this for absurdity is the nearby *Female Allegory* by 17th-century Giovanni Serodini, in which the lady, apparently disgruntled with her lute, astrolabe and books, is squirting herself in the nose.

The magnificent cartoon for Raphael's *School of Athens* in the Vatican is as interesting as the fresco itself; the copy of Leonardo's *Last Supper* was done by order of the Cardinal, who sought to preserve what he considered a lost work (the copy itself has recently been restored). A 16th-century *Washing of Feet* from Ferrara has one Apostle blithely clipping his toenails. Another room contains pages of drawings from Leonardo's *Codice Atlantico*. The first Italian still-life, Caravaggio's *Fruit Basket*, is also the most dramatic; it shares the space with more fond items like Magnasco's *The Crow's Singing Lesson*. Further on is Titian's *Adoration of the Magi*, painted for Henri II of France, and still in its original frame.

## San Satiro

On the corner of Via Spadari and busy Via Torino is the remarkable Renaissance church of **San Satiro** (officially Santa Maria presso San Satiro), rebuilt by Bramante in 1476, his first

Milanese project, but with a mostly 19th-century façade. Faced with a lack of space in the abbreviated, T-shaped interior, Bramante came up with the ingenious solution of creating the illusion of an apse with *trompe l'œil* stucco decorations. Bramante also designed the beautiful octagonal **Baptistry** off the right aisle, decorated with terracottas by Agosto de Fondutis; to the left the **Cappella della Pietà** dating from the 9th century is one of the finest examples of Carolingian architecture in North Italy, even though it was touched up in the Renaissance, with decorations and a Pietà by De Fondutis. San Satiro's 11th-century **Campanile** is visible on Via Falcone.

## South of the Duomo: Porta Romana

This corner of Milan is the main traffic outlet of Milan towards the *autostrada* to the south. Tram 13 will take you past its two monuments—firstly, **San Nazaro Maggiore** on Corso Porta Romana, a church that has undergone several rebuildings since its 4th-century dedication by St Ambrose, and last restored in the Romanesque style. The most original feature of San Nazaro is the hexagonal **Cappella Trivulzio** by Bramantino, with the tomb of the condottiere Giangiacomo Trivulzio, who had inscribed on his tomb, in Latin: 'He who never knew rest now rests: Silence.' Trivulzio did have a busy career; a native Milanese who disliked Lodovico Sforza enough to lead Louis XII's attack on Milan in 1499, he became the city's French governor, then went on to lead the League of Cambrai armies in thumping the Venetians at Agnadello (1509), when they threatened to create a land empire as great as the one they already possessed at sea. Further down Corso Porta Romana, in the Piazza Medaglie d'Oro, is one of the original Renaissance gates, the **Porta Romana** (1598).

**Corso Italia**, another main artery to the south, leads to **Santa Maria presso San Celso**, finished in 1563; its façade is a fine example of the Lombard love of ornament, which reaches almost orgiastic proportions in the Certosa di Pavia (*see* below, p.253). Within, beyond an attractive atrium, the interior is paved with an exceptional marble floor and decorated with High Renaissance paintings by Paris Bordone, Bergognone, and Moretto. The adjacent 10th-century church of **San Celso** has a charming interior restored in the 19th century, and a good original portal.

## Ticinese Quarter

Southwest of the city centre, Via Torino leads into the artsy quarter named for the Ticino river, and traversed by the main thoroughfare, Corso di Porta Ticinese (tram 15 from Via Torino). In the Ticinese you can find pieces of Roman Mediolanum, which had its centre in modern **Piazza Carrobbio**: there's a bit of the Roman circus on Via Circo, off Via Lanzone, and the **Colonne di San Lorenzo**, on the Corso: these 16 Corinthian columns, now a rendezvous of Milanese teenagers but originally part of a temple or bath, were transported here in the 4th century to construct a portico in front of the **Basilica di San Lorenzo Maggiore**. This is considered the oldest church in Milan, perhaps dating back to the palaeo-Christian era. It acquired its octagonal form, encircled by an ambulatory, in the 4th century. Along with Sant'Ambrogio it was preserved when Barbarossa sacked the city in 1164, but since then it has suffered severe fires, and in the 16th century came near total collapse. The dome and interior were then rebuilt, conserving as much of the old structure as possible. The most interesting section of the church is the **chapel of S. Aquilino** (*adm*) with beautiful 5th-century mosaics of Christ and his disciples and an early Christian sarcophagus.

Near the neo-classical **Porta Ticinese** built in the Spanish walls, stands another 4th-century church, **Sant'Eustorgio**, rebuilt in 1278 and modelled along the lines of Sant'Ambrogio, with its low vaults and aisles. The pillars have good capitals, and the chapels are finely decorated with early Renaissance art. One chapel is dedicated to the Magi, and held their relics until Frederick Barbarossa took them to Cologne. The highlight of the church, however, is the pure Tuscan Renaissance **Cappella Portinari**, built for Pigello Portinari, an agent of the Medici bank in Milan. Attributed to Michelozzo and often compared with Brunelleschi's Pazzi Chapel in Florence in its elegant simplicity and proportions, the chapel is crowned by a lovely dome, adorned with stucco reliefs of angels. This jewel is dedicated to one of the more dreadful saints, the Inquisitor St Peter Martyr (who was axed in the head in 1252), whose life was frescoed on the walls by Vincente Foppa and whose remains are buried in the magnificent *Arca di San Pietro Martire* (1339) by the Pisan Giovanni di Balduccio.

## The Navigli District

Beyond Porta Ticinese is Milan's Navigli district (Ⓜ Porta Genova, or tram 8 or 19) named for the navigable canals, the **Naviglio Grande** and **Naviglio Pavese**, that break up the endless monotony of streets, and meet to form the *Darsena* near the Porta Ticinese. Up until the 1950s Milan, through these canals, handled more tonnage than seaports like Brindisi, and like any good port the Navigli was a funky working class district of warehouses, workshops, sailors' bars, and public housing blocks. Although some of this lingers, Navigli is Milan's up and coming trendy area, where many of the city's artists work, and much of the city's new night spots are opening up.

### Shopping

Milan is the cloud cuckoo land of conspicuous consumption, where buying and selling is a veritable art form, a city that can wilt the strongest-backed credit card in the solar system. Few places on earth offer such a variety of designs and goods, especially in clothes and home furnishings. There are few bargains to be had, but a couple of interesting weekly markets offer high fashion for terrestrial prices. In Milan most shops are closed all day Sunday and Monday morning; food stores close on Monday afternoons.

Many of the big names in designer apparel and jewellery have their boutique 'headquarters' in what is known as the **Quadrilatero**, defined by Via Montenapoleone, Via della Spiga, Via S. Andrea and Via Borgospesso. Nearly all the shops here have branch offices elsewhere in Milan and in other cities; some of the better established, like Gucci, Armani, and Krizia, are glorified international chain stores. You may just find the latest of the latest pret-à-porter designs on Montenapoleone, but be assured they'll soon show up elsewhere, expensive enough, but without the high snob surcharges. The aura and status created around the Italian garment industry is as much due to quality as to a certain wizardry with words and images; a language of gloss and glamour that could provide the subject for a doctoral thesis for an anthropologist from New Guinea. But then again, Italians have always liked to put on the dog, *la bella figura*; it's in their blood. The hype machine has turned this traditional trait into a national obsession—there are countless Italian fashion magazines (most of them emanating from Milan, naturally), and a weekly television programme devoted to *La Moda*. The bright lights and glitter of modern Milan, with its celebrity designers, resembles that of Hollywood in its glory days; this is an Italian fantasyland that dreams are made of, diverting the attentions of thousands whose attentions might otherwise be unoccupied. After an hour of window-shopping, however, only a die-hard fashion slave would disagree with Walter Benjamin's 'Monotony is nourished by the new.'

### *in the Quadrilateral*

The **jewellers** were here first, in the 1930s; since then, to have an address on Via Montenapoleone has meant status and quality. Among the most interesting on the street are **Buccellati** (No.4), considered by many the best jewellery designer in Italy, featuring exquisitely delicate gold work and jewels, each piece individually crafted. **Calderoni** (No.8) is fun for lavishly kitsch creations, while for something more traditional, try **Maboussin**, at No.29.

The artsy displays of clothing and, increasingly, shoes (in 1987 the Milanese staged a demonstration in protest at the takeover of their sacrosanct Montenapo by such 'Millipedes') are a window shopper's paradise. **Missoni's** ravishing knits for women and men are at Montenapoleone 1; **Valentino** and his classics are at Via Santo Spirito 3; **Krizia** sells her famous knits, evening dresses, and children's wear at Via della Spiga 23, and there's more designer children's wear at **Gio Moretti**, Via della Spiga 29. **Armani's** chief Milanese outlet is at Via Sant'Andrea 9, featuring his famous 'unstructured' jackets for men and women, while **Mila Schön** sells both her women's and her men's styles at Montenapoleone 2, and her men's at No.6. For quiet sophistication from a designer who has an 'architectural' approach, visit **Gianfranco Ferré**, who was the first Italian in years to branch out from pret-à-porter into individualist haute couture (women's clothes, Via della Spiga 11; men's next door). **Gianni Versace** displays his innovations on Via della Spiga 4 and at Montenapoleone 11, **Adriana** at Via della Spiga 22, and **Yves Saint Laurent** at Via Sant'Andrea 10. Three classics of couture are on Via Sant'Andrea, **Hermès** at 21, **Fendi** at 16 and **Chanel** at 12. The two bad boys of fashion are also represented, **Gaultier** at Via della Spiga 20 and **Moschino** at Via Sant'Andrea 14, and Via Durini 14 (near, also, to **Emporio Armani**).

Lace and leather are also well represented. Italian leather goods are known in most parts of the world simply through the name **Gucci**, which has a shop at Montenapoleone 5. **Ferragamo** sells his famous designs and shoes for men and women at Montenapoleone 3. **Beltrami**, at Montenapoleone 16 and in the Galleria San Babila, has the most outrageous and colourful women's shoes in Italy. Interesting shoes can also be found on Montenapoleone at **Sergio Rossi**, and **Della Vane**, at numbers 15 and 20 respectively.

Amongst the profusion of jewels, clothes, leathers and shoes there are also some antique dealers and furriers. **Lorenzi**, Montenapoleone 9, is the city's most refined pipe and male accessories shop. The **Salumaio di Montenapoleone**, at No.12, has an infinite array of hams, salamis, pasta, and cheeses, and nearly every gourmet item imaginable. If you need a break from shopping, **Café Cova** at Via Montenapoleone 8, or **Baretto**, Via Sant'Andrea 3, will keep you caffeinated while floating in the ozone of chic.

### the city centre

Besides the great Galleria Vittorio Emanuele, several minor gallerias branch off the Corso Vittorio Emanuele, each a shopping arcade lined with good quality and reasonably priced shops. In Piazza del Duomo a monument almost as well known as the cathedral itself is Milan's biggest and oldest department store, **La Rinascente**; it's also the only one to have been christened by Gabriele D'Annunzio. La Rinascente has six floors of merchandise, with especially good clothing and domestic sections, offering a wide array of kitchen appliances dear to the heart of an Italian cook. There's a cafeteria on the top floor with great views over the cathedral. Other central shops include those of **Fiorucci**, who has his main headquarters in the Galleria Passerella; **Mandarina Duck**, in Galleria San Carlo, with a vast variety of bags and travelling cases; **Fratelli Prada**, Galleria Vittorio Emanuele, with classic, beautifully crafted leather goods; and **Guenzati**, Via Mercanti 1, which will make a velvet lover's heart flutter; they also do made-to-order clothes. Cheeses, from the most exotic to the most everyday, have been sold since 1894 at the **Casa del Formaggio**, Via Speronari 3, near the Duomo. **Rizzoli**, in the Galleria Vittorio Emanuele, is one of the city's finest, best-stocked bookshops (with many English titles), owned by the family that founded the Corriere della Sera. Also in the Galleria, **Messaggerie Musicali** is one of the best in town for musical scores. On Sunday morning, a **Stamp and Coin Market** is held in Via Armorari, behind the Central Post Office.

The shops on busy Via Torino have some of Milan's more affordable prices, especially in clothes and footwear. **Frette** at No.43 has an excellent section of moderately priced household linens, while **La Bottega del Tutù**, No.48, has everything for your favourite ballerina; at **Vergelio**, No.23, you can find reasonably priced shoes, and a bit further down **Foot Locker** is handy for sports shoes and accessories.

### Brera district

As well as a Monday market in the Piazza Mirabello and the **Antiques Fair** (every last Sunday of the month, along Naviglio Grande), Brera offers some of Milan's most original shops. Unusual and bizarre antiques are the mainstay of **L'Oro dei Farlocchi**, Via Madonnina 5; **Naj Oleari**, Via Brera 5, has unusual children's clothes and household items; **Piero Fornasetti**, Via Brera 16, has rather eccentric home decorations; exotic handmade papers can be found at the **Legatoria Artistica**, Via Palermo 5; and **Surplus**, Corso Garibaldi 7, has a marvellous array of second-hand garments. The latest Italian fashions are also reasonably priced at the big **COIN** department store, Corso Garibaldi 72.

On **Corso Buenos Aires** (Ⓜ Lima), one of Milan's longest and densest shopping thoroughfares, you can find something of every variety and hue; one unusual shop is **Le Mani d'Oro**, Via Gaffurio 5 (near Piazzale Loreto), which specializes in *trompe l'œil* objects and decorations, while **Guerciotti**, Via Tamagno 55 (parallel to Corso Buenos Aires), makes bicycles to order. Another shopping street with excellent merchandise and reasonable prices is **Via Paolo Sarpi** (Ⓜ Moscova), formerly the city's Chinatown. Other interesting shops: **Sardinia Shop**, Largo Cairoli 2, with carpets and baskets from the island of the *nuraghi*; **Faenze di Faenza**, Via Stoppani 10, with faience ware; **Franco Leoni**, Via Urbano III 1 (just off Corso Porto Ticinese), has antique Italian dolls; and **Il Discanto**, Via Turati 7, with exotic instruments and jewellery from Asia and Africa. For an excellent selection of books in English, try either **The English Bookshop**, Via Mascheroni 12 (Ⓜ Conciliazione) or **The American Bookstore**, Largo Cairoli, near the castle. If you're interested in the latest designs in all kinds of furniture, Milan has a major concentration of showrooms and stores near the centre: well worth a look are **Artemide**, Corso Monforte 19; **De Padova**, Corso Venezia 14; **Dilmos**, Piazza San Marco 1; and **Alias**, Via Fiori Chiari 3.

Perhaps the best place to hunt for designer bargains in Milan is the Saturday market in **Viale Papiniano**, in the Navigli. On December 7 (St Ambrose's Day) there's a fine antiques market, the **O Bei, o Bei**, in the Piazza Sant'Ambrogio.

---

### Sports and Activities

A dip in one of Milan's public **swimming pools** can make a hot day of summer's sightseeing far more tolerable: two of the nicest and most convenient are situated in the **Parco Solari**, Via Solari and Via Montevideo (Ⓜ San Agostino), and the outdoor **Lido di Milano**, Piazzale Lotto 15 (Ⓜ Lotto). East of town, the **Parco dell'Idroscalo**, built around an artificial lake designed as a 'runway' for seaplanes in the 20s, has a lovely complex of three pools known as Milan's Riviera (Viale dell'Idroscalo 1), reached by a special bus departing from Piazza Cinque Giornate.

The best **golf** course in the Milan area is the **Golf Club Milano**, in the delightful Parco di Monza in Monza, a short distance north of the city (*see* below). A popular **bicycle excursion** from Milan is to pedal along the Naviglio Grande canal from the Darsena to the Ticino river (around 40km), passing by way of **Cassinetta di Lugagnano**, which has one of Italy's finest restaurants (*see* below, p.246). Like the Venetians with their villas along the Brenta canal, the 18th-century Milanese built sumptuous summer houses along the Naviglio. Only one, the 15th-century frescoed **Villa Gaia** in Robecco, is open to visitors, and only if you call ahead (✆ 9470512). Bicycles can be **rented** for any period of time from Vittorio Comizzoli's shop in Via Washington 60, ✆ 4984694 (Ⓜ Wagner).

Milan's two prestigious first division football clubs, AC Milan and Inter, play on alternate Sundays during the September–May season at **San Siro** stadium, Via

Piccolomini 5 (Ⓜ Lotto, then walk). Arrive early to be sure to get a ticket; alternatively, tickets for AC games can be bought in branches of the Cariplo bank, and for Inter games in branches of the Banca Popolare Milano. American football (the 'Rhinos') and rugby are semi-professional and can often be seen at the Giurati sports centre. Milan has a good basketball team, which plays in the Super Palatenda sports facility, on Via Sant'Elia. There are two race tracks, the Ippodromo and the Trottatoio for trotters, both near San Siro. For a real escape, travel agencies throughout Milan can book you a week's package holiday in the mountains, for skiing or hiking.

## Milan Ⓒ (02–) — *Where to Stay*

Milan has basically two types of accommodation: smart hotels for expense-accounted business people, and seedy dives for new arrivals from the provinces, still seeking their first job in the city. This bodes ill for the pleasure traveller, who has the choice of paying a lot of money for an up-to-date modern room with little in the way of atmosphere, or paying less for a place where you may not feel very comfortable (or worse, very safe). Reserve in advance if possible, because the exceptions to the rule are snapped up fast. Tourist offices (*see* above) provide a free hotel reservation service. Bear in mind also that in August in Milan only a handful of shops, restaurants and so on remain open, so that at this time it can be surprisingly easy to find a hotel. On the other hand, during the city's great trade fairs (especially the big fashion show in March and autumn, and the April Fair) you may find no room at the inn.

### *luxury*

Milan's deluxe hotels are clustered between the centre and the Stazione Centrale; four are owned by the reliable and imaginative CIGA chain.

★★★★★ **Excelsior Gallia**, Piazza Duca d'Aosta 9, Ⓒ 6785, ✆ 66713239, is a deluxe hotel near the Stazione Centrale that has hosted most of Milan's visiting potentates since it first opened in 1932. Lately spruced up with briarwood furnishings and oriental rugs, its spacious, elegant, and air-conditioned rooms are equipped with satellite television that receives English channels; the Health Centre offers Turkish baths, massages, solarium and beauty treatments, and the Baboon Bar (ask how it got the name during the War) is a mellow place to while away the evening.

★★★★★ **Hotel Palace**, Piazza della Repubblica 20, Ⓒ 6336, ✆ 654485, is a CIGA hotel that caters primarily for executives who demand heated towel racks in addition to very tasteful bedrooms and public rooms; many have balconies, and there's a nice roof garden as well.

★★★★★ **Hotel Principe di Savoia**, Piazza della Repubblica 17, Ⓒ 6230, ✆ 6595838, is the most elegant and prestigious of the CIGA hotels, originally built in 1927 and since lavishly redecorated. Rooms and service are designed to pamper and please even the most demanding clients—when Margaret Thatcher and Jerry Lewis are in Milan, they stay here. The hotel has its own buses to the airports, a good bar, and also a private garage.

★★★★ **Cavour**, Via Fatebenefratelli 21, ✆ 6570251, ✉ 6592263, an elegantly furnished hotel in the Brera, a few blocks from the Giardini Pubblici and Via Montenapoleone, and a good choice in the 4-star category.

★★★★ **De La Ville**, Via Hoepli 6, ✆ 867651, ✉ 866609, is a modern hotel that's very centrally located, between the Duomo and La Scala, and has antique furnishings and courteous service.

★★★★ **Diana Majestic**, Viale Piave 42, ✆ 29513404, ✉ 201072, (Ⓜ Porta Venezia) is a stylish CIGA hotel built at the turn of the century, with charming rooms and views over a garden.

★★★★ **Manin**, Via Manin 7, ✆ 6596511, ✉ 6552160, is a comfortable hotel facing the shady Giardini Pubblici, in one of central Milan's quieter corners; reception is friendly and the rooms modern.

★★★ **Ariosto**, Via Ariosto 22, ✆ 4817844, has more character than most Milanese hotels of its class, and is conveniently close to Ⓜ Conciliazione stop. An early 20th-century mansion converted to a hotel in 1969, it has a lovely little courtyard, overlooked by the nicer rooms.

★★★ **Hotel Manzoni**, Via Spirito Santo 20, ✆ 76005700, ✉ 784212. This pleasant and tranquil hotel enjoys one of the most privileged locations in Milan—on a quiet street in easy walking distance of Montenapoleone and La Scala, with the plus of a private garage. Its cheap prices for its location, however, make it extremely popular, so book well in advance.

★★★ **Soperga**, Via Soperga 24, ✆ 6690541, ✉ 66980352, two blocks east of the Stazione Centrale, is rather expensive, but has good, safe rooms, all with baths.

★★ **Antica Locanda Solferino**, Via Castelfidardo 2, ✆ 6570129, ✉ 26571361. Among the less expensive offerings, the most enjoyable is this 19th-century inn in Brera that has been brought back to life, complete with its former furnishings. All 11 rooms are different in shape and decoration, though the baths are modern. This is another place that requires advance reservations.

★★ **London**, Via Rovello 3, ✆ 72020166, ✉ 8057037. Between the castle and the cathedral, this hotel lacks the charm of the Solferino, but offers good rooms with baths, and breakfast included.

★★★ **Giulio Cesare**, Via Rovello 10, ✆/✉ 72003915, among the more pleasant and wholesome of Milan's cheaper accommodation, with air-conditioning.

★ **Pensione Valley**, Via Soperga 19, ✆ 6692777. Good budget hotels in Milan are thin on the ground, but this one, a short distance from the Stazione Centrale, has comfortable rooms at accessible prices, some with baths.

**Sabrello**, Via Sammartini 15, © 6697786. Also very conveniently situated near the station, very clean, and exceptional value for the city.

*cheap*

**Ostello Piero Rotta**, Via Salmoiraghi 2, © 367095, Milan's modern youth hostel, near San Siro stadium and **Ⓜ** QT8 on line 1. An IYHF card is required, and it is *open all year, 7–9am, 5–11pm*. L20,000 per person per night, including breakfast.

---

*Milan* © *(02–)*                                             **Eating Out**

In moneyed Milan you'll find some of Italy's finest restaurants, and some of its most expensive; an average meal will cost you considerably more than it would almost anywhere else in Italy. Butter is preferred in local cooking to oil, and polenta appears more often on the menu than pasta. Perhaps the best-known Milanese speciality, found even in the most obscure corners of Calabria, is the breaded cutlet (*cotoletta alla milanese*), with *risotto alla milanese* (prepared with broth and saffron) a close second. The Lombards also favour hearty dishes like *ossobuco alla milanese* (veal knuckle braised with white wine and tomatoes, properly served with risotto) and *cassoeula* (a stew of pork, cabbage, carrots and celery). Milan also lays claim to minestrone and *busecca*, tripe soup with eggs and cheese. The Milanese cake *panettone,* filled with raisins and fruit, has become a Christmas tradition all over the country.

Good Lombard wines include the reds from the Valtellina (Grumello, Sassella, or the diabolical-sounding Inferno); the various wines from Oltrepó Pavese, or Franciacorta's crisp dry whites and mellow reds. Visconti's Lugana is a very pleasant and dry white; Barbacarlo, a dry, fruity red; Buttafuoco, a dry, heartier red.

In August (and on Sundays, for that matter) so few restaurants remain open that their names are printed in the paper; in the past few years the *comune*, taking pity on the famished hordes, has operated an open-air mess hall in August in the Parco Sempione providing inexpensive meals. At other times, the best places to find a sizeable selection of cheaper restaurants are in the Brera, Ticinese and Navigli districts.

*very expensive*

**Savini**, © 8058343 , in the Galleria Vittorio Emanuele (since 1867), is considered the most traditional Milanese restaurant of all, a cultural institution where you can try Lombard classics at the pinnacle of perfection—here the often-abused *cotoletta* and risotto retain their primordial freshness, as do the more earthy *cassoeula* and *ossobuco*. Oenophiles will appreciate the vast cellar of Italian and French wines. (*Closed Sun.*) Another culinary bastion is **La Scaletta**, Piazzale Stazione Porta Genova 3, © 8350290. Don't let the location, in one of the city's more banal corners, fool you; this little restaurant is the workshop of Italy's *nuova cucina* sorceress, Pina Bellini, who does exquisite things to pasta and risotto, to fish and rabbit, all beautifully presented. Excellent desserts and wines finish off a truly memorable meal. (*Closed Sun, Mon; reservations strongly advised.*) If you prefer the ultimate in traditional Italian cuisine, **Aimo e Nadia**, Via Montecuccoli 6,

© 416886, in another dull, out-of-the-way corner north of the Stazione San Cristoforo, will serve you such mouth-watering delights as hot ricotta with radicchio (that slightly bitter red chicory from the Veneto), an exquisite liver pâté, risotto with zucchini (courgettes) and white truffles, sole tarragon, and pigeon with artichokes. Fantastic light desserts top off the meal. (*Closed Sat midday, Sun.*) Alternatively, if you're looking for delectable gourmet treats, **Peck**, Via Victor Hugo 4, © 876774, is a name that has meant the best in Milan for over a hundred years, either in its epicurean delicatessen and shop at Via Spadari 9, or here, at its restaurant, which offers different tantalizing fixed-price menus every week. If you need a break from Italian cuisine, **Suntory**, Via G. Verdi 6, © 8693022, serves some of the best Japanese food in all Italy, and is much patronized by Milan's large Japanese business community. (*Closed Sun.*)

Although it's 20km from Milan, along the Naviglio Grande in Cassinetta di Lugagnano, the **Antica Osteria del Ponte**, © 9420034, is known as a holy temple of Italian cuisine that shouldn't be missed by any serious gourmet, featuring heavenly dishes like ravioli filled with lobster and zucchini, fresh foie gras, marvellously prepared fish, cassata with pistachio sauce and perfect little pastries—nearly every dish based in Italian traditions. The décor is beautiful, intimate and elegant. The fixed-price menu in the evening will set you back L150,000. (*Closed Sun, Mon.*)

### *expensive*

For a glimpse of Milanese intellectuals like Umberto Eco and fashion's trend-setters, dine at their favourite restaurant, **Decio Carugati** in the Navigli at Vias Vigevano and Corsico, © 860036, where *la cucina nuova* is as interesting as its elegant patrons. **La Zelata**, Via Anfossi 10 (off Corso Porta Vittoria) © 5484115, is a quiet and refined place run by the former head chef of the Palace hotel. Specialities here include the unusual *raviolone* (one big raviolo, with a delightful sauce) and turbot in a delicate sauce of zucchini flowers; there are also great desserts, and a fine French and Italian wine list. (*Closed Sun.*) **Trattoria del Ruzante**, Corso Sempione 17, © 316102, has gained a reputation for its exquisite and utterly simple approach to Lombard dishes, especially their famous *tagliatelle alle verdure*. **Aurora**, Via Savona 23 (in the Navigli), © 89404978, has lovely belle epoque dining rooms and an equally lovely cuisine, with an emphasis on mushrooms and truffles; another speciality is the cart of boiled meats, from which you can chose a vast array of sauces, or the salad cart, which offers a quick lesson in Italian olive oil and vinegar dilettantism—the former especially is treated as circumspectfully as vintage wine. Yet another cart will overwhelm you with its bewildering array of cheeses. Exceptional value for this quality of cuisine, the Aurora has been greatly praised by readers. (*Closed Mon.*)

Another good, but again out-of-the-way place, **Osteria del Binari**, Via Tortona 1 (by the Porta Genova station), © 89409428, has delightful Lombard and Piedmontese specialities, served outdoors in a shady garden in the summer, complemented by homemade bread and pasta, and fine wines.

Championship pizzas, with a vast selection to choose from, are the speciality at **Vecchia Napoli Da Rino**, Via Chavez 4 (between Stazione Centrale and Parco Lambro); ✆ 2919056; besides pizzas, they also do good antipasti, gnocchi, and fish dishes. (*Closed Mon.*) The **Osteria del Pallone**, Via Gorizia, is a popular, noisy traditional *osteria* with an old-style Milanese atmosphere on the banks of the Naviglio Grande canal, serving hearty Lombard cuisine at good-value prices. It's also a popular bar, and they have exquisite ice-cream.

Inexpensive by Milanese standards, anyway. Besides the places listed below, Milan is well endowed with American and Italian fast-food joints, for those without the money or time for a genuine Italian sit-down feast.

**Pizzeria Carmignani Angelo e Gianfranco**, Corso S. Gottardo 38 (Navigli district), ✆ 8391959 , offers excellent value and tasty pizza from a wood oven as well as good fish, pasta, and other dishes. (*Closed Tues, Wed.*) In Brera, spaghetti-lovers will want to try one of the over 100 varieties offered at **Emilio**, Viale Piave 38, ✆ 29401982. (*Closed Mon, Tues midday.*) Late-night eaters, except on Sundays, can find delicious victuals at **Topkapi**, Via Ponte Vetero in Brera, ✆ 808282 —good pizza, risotto, *involtini* and more, topped off with homemade pies. (*Closed Wed.*) One of the best bargains in town is the **Grand'Italia**, Via Palermo 5, Brera, ✆ 877759, which serves up good pizza and *focacce* (Ligurian pizza), as well as a daily if limited choice of first and second courses. Exceptionally cheap but nevertheless full sized meals are also available at one of Brera's best-known bars, the **Bar Giamaica** (*see* below).

---

## Entertainment and Nightlife

### opera, classical music and theatre

For many people, an evening at **La Scala** is one of the major reasons for visiting Milan. The opera season traditionally opens on 7 December, St Ambrose's Day, and continues until July, while a symphony concert season runs from September through November. The programme is posted outside the theatre, and the box office is located on the left side of the façade. For information, ✆ 807041; reservations ✆ 809126, but be warned that finding a good seat at a moment's notice is all but impossible. You can try through your hotel's concierge, or show up at the box office an hour before the performance to see what's available. Chances are it'll be a vertiginous gallery seat, just squeezed in under the ceiling, but what you can't see you can at least hear. More **classical music** is performed in the Giuseppe Verdi Conservatorio, Via del Conservatorio 12, ✆ 701755, and at the Angelicum, Piazza Sant'Angelo 2, ✆ 6592748. The city of Milan sponsors a series of **Renaissance and Baroque music concerts** in the lovely church of San Maurizio on Corso Magenta, while the province puts on, between October and June, a series of contemporary concerts called *Musica nel nostro tempo*. Keep an eye out for posters and bannners, and tourist offices will have full details.

Milan is also the home of Italy's best **theatre** company, the **Piccolo Teatro**, Via Rovello 2, near Via Dante, ✆ 872352. Founded after the Second World War and run for years by brilliant director Giorgio Strehler, the Piccolo is ideologically sound, with a repertory ranging from Commedia dell'Arte to the avant-garde. Tickets are priced low so anyone can go—but reserve in advance as far as possible. Sometimes the Piccolo performs at the much larger **Teatro Lirico**, near the Duomo at Via Larga 14, ✆ 876889. Even if your Italian is only so-so you may enjoy a performance at the puppet theatre, the **Teatro delle Marionette**, Via Olivetani 3/b, ✆ 4694440, near Piazza Sant'Ambrogio. **Films** in English are shown regularly at the Angelicum, Piazza Sant'Angelo 2. The *Corriere della Sera* has complete listings of theatre and films, but if the films aren't listed under *Versione Originale* you can be sure that they're dubbed.

### jazz

The *Corriere* also lists under 'Ritrovi' the cabarets and nightclubs with live music; for **jazz** Milan's best club is **Scimmie**, Via Ascanio Sforza 45, in Brera, with diverse but high-quality offerings from Dixieland to fusion. The more informal **Capolinea**, Via Lodovico il Moro, at the end of the no.19 tramline (in the Navigli), has attractive low prices and often excellent sessions. Two spots in Brera offer jazz on a more intimate scale: **Il Ponte**, Via Brera 32, and **Club Due**, Via Formentini 2, with live music in the basement.

### cafés and bars

Milan has some good, lively **bars**, concentrated in the Brera, Navigli and Ticinese quarters. The old rendezvous of artists and intellectuals in the twenties and thirties, the **Bar Giamaica**, is still open for business at Via Brera 26, as is another old bar, **Moscatelli**, Corso Garibaldi 93, a beloved Milanese oasis for the fashion-weary. **El Tumbun de San Marc**, Via San Marco 20, serves some of Milan's best beer, but for a hearty atmosphere, and a balm to the heart of a homesick Brit, try the **Matricola** pub, tram no.23 to corner of Vias Giovanni Pascoli and Romagna (*open 11pm–1am Mon–Sat; L8000/pint*), a Guinness-owned place with the black stuff on tap plus full pub lunches and 'English' breakfasts served.

As in the rest of Italy, a favourite evening activity is a promenade topped off with an ice cream stop at the *gelateria*. Traditional favourites include **Pozzi**, Piazza Gen. Cantore 4, in the Navigli, and **Passerini**, Via Hugo 4, near the Duomo. **Viel** in Piazza Castello (Via Beltrami) has the most surprising flavours, while totally natural ingredients go into the treats at the **Ecologica**, Corso di Porta Ticinese 40.

After a hard day's shopping Milanese also like nothing more than to pop in for a drink at **Taveggia**, near the Duomo, a traditional bar that has a tapas-style selection of free food. The **Pois**, by the Colonne di San Lorenzo in the Ticinese, is a place for the young and stylish. If you have James Bondish tastes and the wallet to match, the exclusive **Champagneria**, Via Clerici 1 (near La Scala), will soothe your palate with 850 labels of champagne, to wash down the equally vast selection of caviars.

For a sophisticated drink try too **Bar Magenta**, Via Carducci 13, near ⓜ Cadorna, renowned for the models to be found among its young and trendy crowd. A place popular for both lunchtime and evening drinking is **Bar Cavour**, Via Meravigli (ⓜ Cordusio), a large, well-lit bar open till 2am, which attracts a fairly smart crowd and gets very busy at weekends. For a less formal night out try **Tropical Latino**, Via Ozanam (ⓜ Lima), a Mexican bar with food, lots of imported Mexican beer, salsa music, and a loud atmosphere. Arrive early to avoid queueing.

### clubs and discos

The **club scene** in Milan, as in the rest of Italy, is concerned more with appearance than dancing. However, it is possible to discover some places where the emphasis is reversed—though you have to look hard. Generally, places open every day until 3am (though this is often extended at weekends), and the admission fee entitles you to one free drink.

One of the biggest clubs in town, the warehouse-style **City Square**, Via Castelbarco 11–13 (*adm*), near the university, plays techno and house to a young crowd. There's an incredible light show, and live bands during the week, when admission is substantially cheaper. Milan's very fashion-conscious rock'n'rollers get down at the **Rolling Stone**, Corso XXII Marzo 32, (bus 90/91), perhaps the most famous club in town. The atmosphere is relaxed, the music—anything from rock to rap to reggae—and clientele are varied, and despite a capacity of 1000, it's still advisable to arrive early (before midnight). The recently trendy **Zimba**, Via Gratosoglio 108 (*open Tues–Sun*), plays a mixture of African/tribal/reggae sounds and occasionally presents a top-name band in that genre, while the wonderful, bizarre and very chic **Plastico**, Viale Umbria 120 (*open Mon–Sat; adm*) is Milan's version of Studio 54— small and shiny with a very eclectic clientele and fussy doormen. It also has a sizeable gay following. Milan's foremost gay club, though, the biggest in the country, is **Nuova Idea**, Via Castiesa 30.

The super-exclusive, membership-only **Soul 2 Soul** (*adm*) plays a mixture of jazz, hip-hop and R&B in an ultra-modern setting. The other big disco **Time**, Corso Lodi, has three dance floors playing three different types of music and a capacity of 1500. The emphasis is on techno, and sometimes it gets so hot that the whole place steams up. By way of contrast, **Stella Alpina**, Via Bocconi (*adm; tram 29/30*), is small and trendy and plays an interesting mixture of jazz/disco and salsa. Brazilian music and drinks are on tap at Brera's **Leoncino**, Corso Garibaldi 50.

## Short Excursions from Milan

## Monza

Only 15 minutes by train from the Porta Garibaldi Station, or 20 minutes by bus from Piazza IV Novembre, Monza is synonymous with the Italian Grand Prix, which is held in early

September on the famous Monza race course. The course, built in 1922, lies in the heart of one of greater Milan's 'lungs', the beautiful Parco di Monza, formerly part of the Villa Reale of the kings of Italy. It includes the 27-hole **Golf Club Milano** as well as other recreational facilities in its acres and acres of greenery; the single sombre note is struck behind the 18th-century residence—an expiatory chapel built by Vittorio Emanuele III that marks the spot where his father Umberto was assassinated by an anarchist in 1900.

Monza itself is a pleasant if industrial town, once highly favoured by the Lombard Queen Theodolinda, who founded its first cathedral in the late 6th century after being converted from Arianism by Pope Gregory the Great. The present **Duomo** on Via Napoleone dates from the 13th century, and bears a lovely if crumbling multi-coloured marble façade by the great Campionese master, Matteo (1390s), who also did some of the fine carvings inside. Theodolinda's life is depicted in a series of 15th-century frescoes near her tomb, honouring the good queen who left Monza its most famous relic, preserved in the high altar: the **Iron Crown of Italy**, a crown believed to have belonged to the Emperor Constantine, named after the iron strip in the centre said to be one of the nails from the True Cross. In the old days, new Holy Roman Emperors would stop in Monza or Pavia to be crowned King of Italy, before heading on to Rome to receive the Crown of Empire from the Pope. The cathedral's precious treasury is displayed in thee **Museo Serpero** (*open 9–11.30, 3–5, Tues–Sun*) and includes many objects that once belonged to Theodolinda: a processional cross given her by Gregory the Great, her crown and her famous silver hen and seven chicks symbolizing Lombardy and its provinces.

## Lodi

The southeast corner of the province of Milan, watered by the river Adda, is called La Bassa. La Bassa's main city, **Lodi**, was a fierce rival of Milan until the year 1111, when the Milanese ended the feud by decimating Lodi, leaving only the ancient church of San Bassiano intact; they then forbade the citizens of Lodi from returning. Even in the cruel and bitter period of inter-city rivalries Milan's treatment was unduly harsh, and in 1153 Lodi brought a formal complaint to the newly elected Emperor Frederick Barbarossa, hoping he would act as a referee. The emperor warned Milan to leave Lodi alone, and when the proud Ambrosiani mocked his threats he levied a terrible penalty, the brutal sacking of Milan. He also founded a new city of Lodi, but it showed its gratitude by joining Milan in the Lombard league as soon as the Emperor was safely back across the Alps—the first Italian city to learn that calling in foreign intervention was a Pandora's box best left closed. History, though, was to repeat itself over and over again before 1796, when another emperor, Napoleon, won an important battle over the Austrians here.

Besides the ancient church of **San Bassiano** in Lodi Vecchio (Old Lodi, 5km to the east), Lodi's greatest monument is its elegant Renaissance church of the 1490s, **La Incoronata**, containing paintings by Bergognone. It is located near the city's central arcaded Piazza della Vittoria, site of its Broletto and 12th-century Duomo.

# The Lombard Plain

The three small capitals of the Lombard plain are among Italy's most rewarding art cities, each maintaining its individual character: Pavia, the capital of the ancient Lombards and the region's oldest centre of learning, embellished with fine Romanesque churches and its famous Renaissance Certosa; Cremona, the graceful city where the raw medieval fiddle was reincarnated as the lyrical violin; and Mantua, the dream shadow capital of the wealthy Gonzaga dukes and Isabella d'Este.

## Pavia

Pavia is one of those rare cities that had its golden age in the three digit years before the millennium, that misty half-legendary time historians have shrugged off as the Dark Ages. But these were bright days for Pavia, when it served as capital of the Goths, and saw Odoacer proclaimed King of Italy after defeating Romulus Augustulus, the last Roman Emperor in the West. In the 6th century the heretical Lombards led by King Alboin captured Pavia from the Goths and formed a state the equal of Byzantine Ravenna and Rome, making Pavia the capital of their *Regnum Italicum*, a position the city maintained into the 11th century; Charlemagne came here to be crowned (774), as did the first King of Italy, Berenguer (888), and Emperor Frederick Barbarossa (1155). At the turn of the millennium, the precursor of Pavia's modern university, the *Studio*, was founded, and among its first students of law was the first Norman Archbishop of Canterbury, Lanfranc, born here in 1005.

Pavia was a Ghibelline *comune*, the 'city of a hundred towers' and a rival of Milan, to whom it lost its independence in 1359. It was favoured by the Visconti, especially by Gian Galeazzo, who built the castle housing his art collection and founded the Certosa di Pavia, one of the most striking landmarks in Italy. It, and many other churches in the city, bear the mark of Pavia's great, half-demented sculptor-architect of the High Renaissance, Giovanni Antonio Amadeo.

### Getting There

There are **buses** roughly every 45 minutes between Milan and Pavia, and this is also the best way to travel if you wish to stop off and visit the Certosa, some 8km north of Pavia. Buses arrive in and depart from Via Trieste, in the brand-new station-cum-shopping centre. Frequent **trains** link Pavia to Milan (30min) and Genoa (1½ hours), and there are less frequent services to Cremona and Mantua, Alessandria and Vercelli, and Piacenza. The train station is an easy walk from the centre, at the end of Corso Cavour and Via Vittorio Emanuele II. If you're travelling by **car**, Pavia can be reached very quickly from Milan by the A7 *autostrada*, or in a more leisurely fashion by the SS35, which has the advantage of passing by the Certosa.

### Tourist Information

Via Fabio Filzi 2, © (0382) 22156, @ 32221, very near the new shopping centre.

## The Duomo and San Michele

Pavia retains its street plan from the days when it was the Roman city of *Ticinum*, the cardus (Corso Cavour) and the decumanus (Strada Nuova) intersecting by the town hall, or **Broletto**, begun in the 12th century, and the **Duomo**. Begun in 1488, the cathedral owes its imposing design to Amadeo, Leonardo da Vinci, Bramante, and a dozen other architects, and its strange, unfinished appearance—from a distance it looks as if it's covered with corrugated cardboard—to an unusual lack of interest and funds. The last two apses in the transept were added only in 1930, while the vast cupola that dominates the city skyline was added in the 1880s. Next to the cathedral is the rubble of what was once the singularly unattractive 12th-century **Torre Civica**; its collapse in 1989 prompted serious attention to its rather more famous Pisan relation.

From the Duomo, the Strada Nuova continues south down to the river and the pretty **Covered Bridge**, which has replaced the original Renaissance model damaged during the last War. From Strada Nuova Via Maffi leads to the small, brick, 12th-century **San Teodoro**, notable for its early 16th-century fresco of Pavia when it still had a forest of a hundred towers and the original covered bridge.

East of the Strada, Via Capsoni leads in a couple of blocks to Pavia's most important church, the Romanesque **Basilica di San Michele**, founded in 661 but rebuilt in the 12th century after its destruction by lightning. Unlike the other churches of Pavia, San Michele is made of sandstone, mellowed into a fine golden hue, though the weather has been less kind to the intricate friezes that cross its front like comic strips, depicting a complete 'apocalyptic vision' with its medieval bestiary, mermaids, monsters, and human figures involved in the never-ending fight between Good and Evil. The solemn interior, where Frederick Barbarossa was crowned Emperor, contains more fine carvings on the capitals of the columns; the most curious, the fourth on the left, portrays the 'Death of the Righteous'. Along the top runs a Byzantine-style women's gallery, while the chapel to the right of the main altar contains the church's most valuable treasure, a 7th-century silver crucifix.

## The University and Castello Visconteo

The great yellow neoclassical quadrangles of the **University of Pavia**, famous for law and medicine, occupy much of the northeast quadrant of the ancient street plan. The ancient Studio was officially made a university in 1361. St Charles Borromeo, a former student, founded a college here (still supported by the Borromeo family in Milan), while Pope Pius V founded another, the Collegio Ghislieri, in 1569. In the 18th century Maria Theresa worked hard to bring the university back to life after scholarship had hit the skids, and financed the construction of the main buildings. Three of Pavia's medieval skyscrapers, or **Torri**, survive in the middle of the university, in the Piazza Leonardo; the roof in the Piazza shelters what is believed to be the crypt of the demolished, 12th-century **Sant'Eusebio church**; nearby you can meet some of the university's 17,000 students (many of whom commute from Milan), at the Bar Bordoni, on Via Mentana. In the Piazza Cairoli, northeast of the main university, the 1228 **San Francesco d'Assisi** was one of the first churches in Italy dedicated to the saint; it has an unusual façade, adorned with lozenge patterns and a triple-mullioned window.

At the top of Strada Nuova looms the mighty **Castello Visconteo**, built in 1360 by the Campionese masters for Gian Galeazzo II, but partially destroyed in the Battle of Pavia (24 February 1525) when Emperor Charles V captured Francis I of France, who succinctly described the outcome in a letter to his mother: 'Madame, all is lost save honour'. Three sides of the castle and its beautifully arcaded courtyard with terracotta decorations managed to survive as well, and now house Pavia's **Museo Civico** (*open 10–12, 2.30–4, Tues–Sun; Dec, Jan, July, Aug 9am–1pm only, Tues–Sun*). The archaeological and medieval sections contain finds from Roman and Gaulish Pavia, as well as robust Lombard and medieval carvings salvaged from now-vanished churches, and colourful 12th-century mosaics. One room contains an impressive wooden model of the cathedral, built by the architect Fugazza in the early 16th century. The picture gallery on the first floor contains works by Giovanni Bellini, Correggio, Foppa, Van der Goes and others.

## San Pietro in Ciel d'Oro

Behind the castle, Via Griziotti (off Viale Matteotti) leads to Pavia's second great Romanesque temple, **San Pietro in Ciel d'Oro** ('St Peter in the Golden sky'), built in 1132 and named for its once-glorious gilded ceiling, mentioned by Dante in Canto X of the *Paradiso*. The single door in the façade is strangely off-centre; within, the main altar is one of the greatest works of the Campionese masters, the **Arca di Sant'Agostino**, a magnificent 14th-century monument built to shelter the bones of St Augustine, which, according to legend, were retrieved in the 8th century from Carthage by the Lombard king Luitprand, staunch ally of Pope Gregory II against the Iconoclasts of Byzantium. Luitprand himself is buried in a humble tomb to the right, and in the crypt lies another Dark Age celebrity, the philosopher Boethius, slain by Emperor Theodoric of Ravenna in 524.

There are two other notable churches in Pavia. In the centre of town (walk down the Piazza Petrarca from Corso Matteotti), **Santa Maria del Carmine** (1390s) is an excellent example of Lombard Gothic, with a fine façade and rose window and, inside, a beautifully sculptured lavabo by Amadeo. Outside the centre, to the west (Corso Cavour to Corso Mazzoni and Via Riviera) it's a 15-minute walk to the rather plain, vertical, 13th-century **San Lanfranco**, especially notable for its lovely memorial, the *Arca di San Lanfranco*, sculpted by Amadeo in 1498, his last work (though Archbishop Lanfranc was actually buried in Canterbury); the same artist helped design the church's pretty cloister.

## The Certosa di Pavia

The pinnacle of Renaissance architecture in Lombardy, and according to Jacob Burckhardt 'the greatest decorative masterpiece in all of Italy', the Certosa, or Charterhouse, of Pavia, was built over a period of 200 years. Gian Galeazzo Visconti laid the cornerstone in 1396, with visions of the crown of Italy dancing in his head, and the desire to build a splendid pantheon for his hoped-for royal self and his heirs. Although many architects and artists worked on the project (beginning with the Campionesi masters of Milan cathedral), it bears the greatest imprint of Giovanni Antonio Amadeo, who with his successor Bergognone worked on its sculptural programme for 30 years, and who contributed the design of the lavish façade.

Napoleon disbanded the monastery, but in 1968 a small group of Cistercians reoccupied the Certosa. The monks of today live the same style of contemplative life as the old Carthusians, maintaining vows of silence. A couple, however, are released to take visitors around the complex (*open 9–11.30, 2.30–6pm, Tues–Sun in summer; it closes at 5pm in the spring and autumn, and 4pm in winter; weekends are often very crowded*). If you arrive by the Milan-Pavia bus, the Certosa's a 1½km walk from the nearest stop, a beckoning vision at the end of the straight, shaded land, surrounded by well-tended fields and rows of poplars once part of the vast game park of the Castello Visconteo in Pavia.

Once through the main gate and **vestibule** adorned with frescoes by Luini, a large grassy court opens up, lined with buildings that served as lodgings for visitors and stores for the monks. At the far side rises the sumptuous, detailed façade of the **church**, a marvel of poly-chromatic marbles, medallions, bas reliefs, statues, and windows covered with marble embroidery from the chisel of Amadeo, who died before the upper, less elaborate level was begun. The interior plan is Gothic but the decoration is Renaissance, with later Baroque addi-tions. Outstanding works of art include Bergognone's five statues of saints in the chapel of Sant'Ambrogio (sixth on the left); the tombs of Lodovico il Moro and his young bride Beatrice d'Este, a masterpiece by Cristoforo Solari; the beautiful inlaid stalls of the choir, and the tomb of Gian Galeazzo Visconti, all works of the 1490s and surrounded by fine frescoes. The old sacristry contains a magnificent, early cinquecento ivory altarpiece by the Florentine Baldassarre degli Embriachi, with 94 figures and 66 bas reliefs.

From the church, the tour continues into the **Little Cloister**, with delicate terracotta deco-rations and a dream-like view of the church and its cupola, a rising crescendo of arcades. A lovely doorway by Amadeo leads back into the church. The **Great Cloister** with its long arcades is surrounded by the 24 house-like cells of the monks—each contains a chapel and study/dining room, a bedroom upstairs and a walled garden in the rear. The frescoed **Refectory** contains a pulpit for the monks who read aloud during otherwise silent suppers.

---

*Pavia © (0382–)*                                              **Where to Stay**

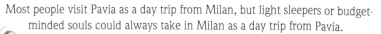

Most people visit Pavia as a day trip from Milan, but light sleepers or budget-minded souls could always take in Milan as a day trip from Pavia.

### expensive and moderate

The most comfortable, if expensive hotel in town is the recently refur-bished ★★★★**Moderno**, Viale Vittorio Emanuele II 45, © 303401, next to the railway station. For convenience and a slightly more old-fashioned touch try the centrally located ★★★★**Ariston**, Via A. Scopoli 10/d, © 34334, @ 25667, with air-conditioning, private bath, and television in each room, for much less than you'd pay in Milan. ***Excelsior**, Piazza Stazione 25, ✆ 28596, @ 23060, is also conveniently located, and slightly cheaper.

*inexpensive*

There are not many options in this category: **Aurora**, Via Vittorio Emanuele II 25, ✆ 23664, is another hotel near the station and has showers in each room, while the elderly but friendly *Splendid, Via XX Settembre 11, ✆ 24703 has plenty of rooms, though none of them has baths.

---

### Pavia ✆ (0382–)                                          Eating Out

Pavia is well endowed with good restaurants. Specialities include frogs, salami from Varzi and *zuppa pavese* (a raw egg on toast drowned in hot broth ); good local wines to try are from the Oltrepó Pavese region, one of Lombardy's best. Cortese is a delicious dry white, Bonarda a meaty, dry red, Pinot a fruity white.

*expensive*

For excellent, innovative cuisine, eat at the small but chic **Locanda Vecchia Pavia**, right under the cathedral on Via Cardinal Ribodi 2, ✆ 304132; its young chefs base the day's menu on what looks good in the market, with some surprising but delicious results like salmon and caviar tartare, truffle filled ravioli, and equally fine desserts.( *Closed Wed, Aug.*) Pavia's other temple of fine cuisine is **Al Cassinino**, Via Cassinino 1, ✆ 422097, just outside the city on the Giovi highway. Sitting on the Naviglio, the restaurant is done out in the style of a medieval inn, complete with rare antiques. Dishes are whatever the market provides—from truffles to frogs' legs, oysters to caviar. ( *Closed Wed, Christmas* .)

*moderate and inexpensive*

**Osteria della Madonna**, Via de Liguri, ✆ 302833  is a jumping place featuring good, solid lunches for around L20,000 and more elaborate dinners, often with live entertainment, for L50,000. ( *Closed Sun, Mon, Aug.*) In the old 16th-century mill of the Certosa, the **Vecchio Mulino**, Via al Monumento 5, ✆ 925894 , serves up delicious food with ingredients garnered from the fertile countryside—foie gras, risotto with crayfish or asparagus, frog's legs, *coniglio al Riesling* (rabbit in wine), crepes filled with artichokes, and much more. The wine list has nearly every label produced in Lombardy. ( *Closed evenings Sun, Mon.*) Cheapest of all, **Il Senatore**, on the street of the same name, serves good, solid local fare at a very reasonable price in a cosy atmosphere.

## Around Pavia: Lomello and Vigévano

West of Pavia and the Certosa lies the little-known Lomellina, a major rice-growing and frog-farming district, irrigated by canals dug by order of the Visconti in the 14th century. The feudal seat, **Lomello**, has some fine early medieval buildings, most notably a lovely little 5th-century polygonal **Baptistry** near the main church, the 11th-century **Basilica di Santa Maria**.

Also in the Lomellina is the old silk town of **Vigévano** (better known these days for its high-fashion footwear manufacturers), the site of another vast **castle** of the Visconti and Sforza clans; it was the birthplace of Lodovico il Moro, and for the past few years has been undergoing a lengthy restoration process. Below it lies the majestic rectangular **Piazza Ducale**, designed in 1492 by Bramante (with help from Leonardo) as Lombardy's answer to Venice's Piazza San Marco. Originally a grand stairway connected the piazza to one of the castle towers, though now the three sides are adorned with slender arcades, while on the fourth stands the magnificent concave Baroque façade of the **cathedral**, designed by a Spanish bishop, Juan Caramuel de Labkowitz. Inside there's a good collection of 16th-century paintings and a 15th-century Lombard polyptych on the life of St Thomas of Canterbury, and an especially rich **treasury** (*open 3–5pm public holidays only, or upon request*), containing illuminated codices, Flemish tapestries, and golden reliquaries.

## Cremona

*violin making*

Charming Cremona is Italy's graceful capital of violin masters, and has been since 1566, when Andrea Amati developed the modern violin in his Cremona workshop. The next two centuries were a musical golden age for the city, the era when Andrea's son Nicolò Amati, and his famous pupils Antonio Stradivarius and Giuseppe Guarneri built the workshops (*Botteghe Liutarie*) that today still house some 50 violin masters, many of whom have learnt their trade in Cremona's International School of Violin-making. To celebrate the tradition the city hosts a festival of stringed instruments every third October (the next in 1994). Violins even seem to be reflected in the curving spiral cornices and pediments that adorn Cremona's elegant brick and ornate terracotta palaces, while the sweetness of their tone is recalled in the city's culinary specialities—*torrone*, a nougat made of almonds and honey and sold in bars throughout the city, and *mostarda di Cremona*—candied cherries, apricots, melons, and so on in a sweet mustard sauce, served with boiled meats.

In the 14th century the *comune* of Cremona was captured by Milan, and the city's history is closely linked with the Lombard capital. In 1441, it was given to Bianca Maria Visconti as her dowry when she married Francesco Sforza, marking the change of the great Milanese dynasties. The city enjoyed a happy, fruitful Renaissance as the apple of Bianca's eye, and the fertile countryside is littered with lovely villas and castles.

### Getting There

Even Cremona's railway station is delightful: there are frequent **train** services there from Milan (about 2 hours' journey), Pavia, Mantua, Brescia, and Piacenza, as well as three times a day from Bergamo. If you are coming from Parma or Bologna, change in Fidenza. The station lies north of the centre, at the end of Via Palestro. **Buses** arrive in and depart from Piazza Marconi, southeast of the Piazza del Comune, for Genoa, Trieste, Mantua, Bergamo, Padua, Milan, Iseo and all destinations in Cremona province; for information, ℂ (0372) 29212.

Travelling **by car**, the most convenient road to take from Milan is the SS415 via Crema, leaving Milan by the Corso Lodi. If you are approaching from the west or the east, Cremona is also near the A21 Brescia-Turin *autostrada*.

### Tourist Information

Piazza del Comune 5, © (0372) 23233. If you're in the market for a violin or just want to visit a workshop, ask for their free list of *Botteghe Liutarie*. The tourist office also operates a useful **museum entry scheme**—a single L5000 ticket, valid for a three-day period, gives admission to all the town's main museums.

## Via Palestro to the Piazza del Comune

Cremona can be easily visited by foot in a day, starting from the station and the Via Palestro. Here, behind a remodelled Baroque façade at No.36, the 15th–16th century **Palazzo Stanga**'s courtyard is an excellent introduction to the Cremonese fondness for elaborate terracotta ornament. The **Museo Stradivariano** nearby at No.17 (*open 9am–6pm Tues–Sat, 9–12.30, 3–6, Sun; closed Aug; adm*) is an equally good introduction to the cream of Cremona's best known industry. Around the corner, on Via Dati, the Palazzo Affaitati (begun in 1561) houses a grand theatrical staircase added in 1769 and the **Museo Civico** (*open 9am–6pm Tues–Sat; 9–12.30, 3–6, Sun; closed Aug; adm*), which has sections devoted to art, with paintings by the Cremonese school (Boccaccino and the Campi family), and one of the 16th-century Surrealist Arcimboldo's most striking portraits, *Scherzo con Ortaggi*, a vegetable face with onion cheeks and walnut eyes. The interesting archaeology section includes a fine labyrinth mosaic from the Roman colonia at Cremona; another section houses the Cathedral Treasury, with some fine Renaissance illuminations.

Via Palestro becomes Via C. Campi, and at an angle runs into the boxy, Mussolini-era Galleria Venticinque Aprile, leading to the **Piazza Roma**, a little park; along Corso Mazzini is Stradivarius' tombstone, transferred from a demolished church. Corso Mazzini forks after a block; near the split, at Corso Matteotti 17, is Cremona's prettiest palace, the 1499 **Palazzo Fodri** (now owned by the Banca d'Italia; ask the guard to unlock the gate), with a courtyard adorned with frescoed battle scenes and terracottas.

## The Duomo and its Torrazzo

By now you've probably caught at least a glimpse of the curious pointed crown of the tallest bell tower in Italy, the 112m **Torrazzo**, looming high over Cremona's equally remarkable Duomo in Piazza del Comune, itself a square seductive enough to compete in any urban beauty contest. The Torrazzo, only slightly shorter than Milan Cathedral, was built in the 13th century, and has battlements as well as bells, though any warlike purpose it may have had is belied by a fine astronomical clock, added in 1583 by Giovanni Battista Divizioli, and the twin 'wreaths' and spire on top. The stout-hearted can ascend to the top for an eye-popping view of Cremona. An added attraction on the lower levels is a violin workshop, a reproduction of one of Stradivarius' time, where a violin maker often works and explains his art (*open Mar–Oct 10–12, 3–6.30, Tues–Sat; 10–12.30, 3–7, Sun; Nov–Feb 3–6pm Sat only; adm*).

The **Duomo**, linked to the Torrazzo in the early 15th century by a double loggia, the *Bertazzola*, is the highest and most exuberant expression of Lombard Romanesque, with a trademark Cremonese flourish in the façade's graceful curls and immense rose window. Built by the Comacini masters after an earthquake in 1117 destroyed its predecessor, the cathedral is just as captivating, especially the main door **Porta Regia**, flanked by two nearly toothless lion telamones and four flat prophets, and crowned by a small portico, known as the Rostrum, where 13th- and 14th-century statues of the Virgin and two saints silently but eloquently hold forth above a frieze of the months by the school of Antelami.

The cathedral was begun as a basilica, but as Gothic came into fashion it was decided to add arms to make a Latin cross; the new transepts, especially the north one, are almost as splendid in their exteriors as the marble-coated main façade. Inside, the nave and apse have opulent frescoes (early 15th century) by Romanino, Boccaccino, Pordenone and others, and fine Flemish tapestries. The twin pulpits have reliefs attributed to Amadeo or Pietro da Rho.

Before leaving the cathedral, look at the medieval capital in the presbytery supported by tired telamones, while behind them an impassive mermaid holds up her forked tail—a Romanesque conceit nearly as popular as the two lions by the main door. Such mermaids, displaying the entrance to the womb, with birds or dragons whispering in their ears, come straight from medieval mysticism, perhaps as a symbol of the cosmic process: the sirens, representing desire, become the intermediaries by which nature's energy and inspiration (here represented by the birds) are conducted into the conscious world.

Across from the Duomo, the Gothic **Loggia dei Militi** was used as a rendezvous by the captains of the *comune*'s citizen militia; behind it lies the 13th-century **Palazzo del Comune**(*open 9am–6pm Tues–Sat, 9–12.30, 3–6, Sun; closed Aug; adm*), a lavish town hall that retains some of its original frescoes, doorways, and windows. One room, the **Saletta dei Violini**, contains four violins by Cremona's greatest masters—Andrea Amati, Nicolò Amati, Stradivarius, and Guarneri del Gesù, the latter formerly owned by Pinchas Zukerman.

## Back Towards the Station

From the Galleria Venticinque Aprile, Via Cavallotti leads to the Via Plasio and the 14th-century church of **Sant'Agostino**. Its Gothic façade is adorned with fine terracotta decorations, and within are good Renaissance frescoes by Bembo; the fifth chapel on the left contains a lovely *Madonna with Saints* (1494) by Perugino. Further up Via Plasio joins the Corso Garibaldi, site of the 11th-century church of **Sant'Agata**, hiding behind a neoclassical façade; inside are more frescoes and a medieval masterpiece, the 13th-century wooden panel painted with the life of St Agatha. Across the street stands (just barely) the dilapidated 1256 **Cittanova**, former headquarters of the Guelph party in Cremona, now attached to the flamboyant but phoney Gothic façade of the **Palazzo Trecchi**. Further up Corso Garibaldi, the pink and white **Palazzo Raimondi** (1496) is the home of the **International School of Violin-making**; while across the street stands the city's most peculiar palace, crowned with strange iron dragons. Further up, near the station, **San Luca** has a beautiful terracotta façade and a little detached octagonal baptistry.

One other church, **San Sigismondo**, is 1km east of the centre, beyond the Piazzale Libertà, on Via A. Ghisleri. Built in 1463 by Bianca Maria Visconti to commemmorate her marriage in an earlier church on the same site, it is adorned with colourful Renaissance frescoes by the Cremona school, in a harmonious marriage of art and architecture.

## Activities

**Boating** on the River Po is possible at **SNI**, Via Robolotti 7, © (0372) 25546. Or, for dinosaur-obsessed children (and adults!), there is a **Prehistoric Zoo Park** in nearby **Rivolta d'Adda**, © (0373) 78184, with over 20 life-size reproductions of various prehistoric animals in their natural habitat.

*Cremona © (0372–)*

## Where to Stay
### moderate

Cremona has a small selection of fairly good hotels, with the ★★★★**Continental**, Piazza della Libertà 27, © 434141, near the top of the moderate price range. It's modern, comfortable and near the centre, and has a display of its own collection of Cremona-made fiddles. All rooms have bath and television, and there's parking in the garage. Another very nice option is the ★★★★**Impero**, Piazza Pace 21, © 460337, just behind the main square. Rooms are stylish and modern, and good value. The ★★★**Duomo**, Via Gonfalonieri 13, © 35242, on a street leading from the main square, has a very nice restaurant as well as comfortable rooms, while the ★★★**Astoria**, Via Bordigallo 9, © 461616, ✆ 461810, is a cheaper option, a very pleasant hotel in a quiet street near the Duomo and the Piazza Roma.

### inexpensive

It's worth remembering that hotels at the lower end of the price scale are virtually all closed from late July to early September. Those that aren't, however, include ★**Albergo Touring**, Via Palestro 3, © 36976, a good, simple choice midway between the centre and the station; ★**Bologna**, Piazzale Risorgimento 7, © 24258, right by the station and perhaps the most reasonably priced; and ★**Ideale**, just down from the station on the corner of Via Trieste, with clean, if rather noisy, doubles. Also available in the area are **Farming Holidays**—information can be obtained either from the tourist office, or c/o Piere d'Olmi, Azienda Borlenga, © 63670.

## Eating Out

Cremona is not one of Italy's gastronomic capitals, but you can dine very well at the elegant **Ceresole**, at Via Ceresole 4, © (0372) 23322 (expensive; reservation advisable), near the Piazza del Comune. Recently remodelled, it serves a balance of traditional and innovative dishes—eel with leeks, *gnocchetti* with ricotta and herbs, and duck are among the specialities. An older, more traditional restaurant, the **Trattoria Bissone**, Via F. Pecorari 3 (moderate), features boiled meats with *mostarda di Cremona* and other hearty fare. On Via Bordigallo, a Chinese restaurant, **Fou-Lu**, offers full meals adapted for Italian tastes, in the same price category. In the inexpensive range, **Marechiaro**, Corso Campi 49, serves fairly basic, but very tasty, fare at reasonable prices. **Bar Voglia Pizza**, Corso Garibaldi 38, is the place to go for *pizza al taglio* (by the slice).

On the northwest outskirts of **Crema**, in Via Crocicchio, is the **Trattoria Guada il Canal**, © (0373) 200133 (expensive), considered the finest restaurant in the area, with a warm, country atmosphere. The cuisine is based entirely on seasonal availability, and though the menu is usually brief, everything is sublime, from the pâtés to the various pasta dishes (try the *tagliolini* with scallops and broccoli), the well-prepared seafood, succulent rack of lamb with thyme, and many more specialities.

## Around Cremona: Soncino and Crema

Lying between the rivers Po and Oglio, the mainly agricultural province of Cremona is fortified with a number of castles and towers that recall the days when the Italians had nothing better to do than beat each other up. The best surviving one, the **Castello Sforza**, is in **Soncino** on the river Oglio, originally built in the 12th century, was expanded in 1473 by Galeazzo Maria Sforza as an advance base against the Venetians, who possessed the Brescian-built fortified town of Orzinuovi directly across the river. The castle's now-dry moat and dungeons survive, as well as its imposing quadrangle of towers (open for visits, but check at Cremona's tourist office before setting out).

**Crema**, also west of Cremona, is an attractive town that belonged to Venice for three centuries, and still bears a Lion of St Mark on its town hall. In the same piazza stands the 14th-century Lombard Romanesque **Duomo**, especially notable for its finely worked windows and tower. The **Museo Civico di Crema**, housed in the former convent of Sant'Agostino on Via Dante (*open 2.30–6.30pm Tues–Fri; 9am–12 midday Sat; 10am–1pm Sun and holidays*), has an interesting collection of Lombard armour discovered in local tombs; the Refectory contains 15th-century frescoes by Da Cemmo. A kilometre or so north of Crema, the rotund **Santa Maria Croce** is a lovely Renaissance church inspired by Bramante, with three orders of loggias encircling the façade, and four polygonal chapels with spherical cupolas. Crema also has a number of fine palaces and villas dating from its Venetian period, of which the 18th-century **Villa Ghisetti-Giavarina** in nearby Ricengo is the most interesting and stately, with fine arches and statues.

## Mantua

By its setting Mantua (Mantova) hardly answers to many people's expectations of Italy, sitting as it does in a fertile, table-flat plain, on a wide thumb of land protruding into three swampy, swollen lakes formed by the River Mincio. Its climate is moody, soggy with heat and humidity in the summer and frosty under blankets of fog in the winter. The local dialect is harsh, and the Mantuans, when they feel chipper, dine on braised donkey with macaroni. Verdi made it the sombre setting of his opera *Rigoletto*. And yet this former capital of the art-loving, fast-living Gonzaga dukes is one of the most atmospheric old cities in the country, masculine and stern, dark and handsome, with none of neighbouring Cremona's gay architectural arpeggios—melancholy with memories of past glories, poker-faced but holding in its hand a royal flush of dazzling Renaissance art.

# History

Mantua gained its fame in Roman times as the beloved home town of the poet Virgil, who recounts the legend of the city's founding by the Theban soothsayer Manto, daughter of Tiresias, and her son, the hero Ocnus. Virgil was born around 70 BC, and not much else was heard from Mantua until the 11th century, when the city formed part of the vast domains of Countess Matilda of Canossa. Matilda was a great champion of the pope against the Emperor; her adviser, Anselmo, Bishop of Lucca, became Mantua's patron saint. Even so, as soon as Mantua saw its chance it allied itself with the opposition, beginning an unusually important and lengthy career as an independent Ghibelline *comune*, dominated first by the Bonacolsi family, and then the Gonzaga.

Naturally defended on three sides by the Mincio, enriched by river tolls, and enjoying the protection and favour of the emperor, Mantua became prominent as a neutral buffer state between the expansionist powers of Milan and Venice. The three centuries of Gonzaga rule, beginning in 1328, brought the city unusual peace and stability, while the refined tastes of the marquesses brought out artists of the highest calibre: Pisanello, Alberti, and especially Andrea Mantegna, who was court painter from 1460 until his death in 1506. Gianfrancesco I Gonzaga invited the great Renaissance teacher, Vittorino da Feltre, to open a school in the city in 1423, where his sons and courtiers, side by side with the children of Mantua's poorer families, were taught according to Vittorino's humanist educational theories, which gave equal emphasis to the intellectual, the physical, and the moral. His star pupil was Ludovico (1412–78), who was considered one of the most just princes of his day, and did much to embellish Mantua according to Florentine principles. Ludovico's grandson, Gianfrancesco II, was a military commander, who lead the Italians against the French at Fornovo, but is perhaps best known in history as the husband of the brilliant and cultivated Isabella d'Este, the foremost culture vulture of her day as well as an astute diplomat, handling most of Mantua's affairs of state for her not very clever husband.

The family fortunes reached their apogee under Isabella's two sons. The eldest, Federico II (1500–40), godson of Cesare Borgia, married Margherita Palaeologo, the heiress of Monferrato, acquiring that duchy for the family, as well as a ducal title for the Gonzaga; he brought Raphael's pupil, the great Giulio Romano (called 'that rare Italian master' by Shakespeare in *The Winter's Tale*), from Rome to design and adorn his pleasure dome, the Palazzo del Te. When he died his worthy brother, Cardinal Ercole, served as regent for his son Guglielmo, and both of these men, too, proved to be busy builders and civic improvers. The last great Gonzaga, Vicenzo I, was a patron of Rubens and Monteverdi, who composed the first modern opera, *L'Orfeo*, for the Mantuan court in 1607.

The Gonzaga and Mantua suffered a mortal blow in 1630 when their claims for Monferrato came into conflict with the Habsburgs, who sent Imperial troops to take and sack the city. The Gonzaga's great art treasures were stolen or sold, including Mantegna's great series, the *Triumphs of Caesar*, now at Hampton Court. The duchy, under a cadet branch of the family, limped along until the Austrians snatched Mantua in 1707, eventually making it the south-west corner of their Quadrilateral.

Mantova is linked directly by **train** with Verona, Milan, Modena, and Cremona, and indirectly with Brescia and Parma (change at Piadena). There are also **buses** to Lake Garda and frequent services to towns in the province, such as Sabbioneta (*see* below). Both the bus and train stations are near Piazza Porta Belfiore, at the end of Corso Vittorio Emanuele, about 10 minutes walk from the centre.

**By car** the quickest way to get to Mantua from Milan is to take the A4 *autostrada* towards Venice, and then take the exit onto the SS236 just beyond Brescia. A more interesting route is to take the SS415 to Cremona, and then continue on the SS10 to Mantua. Mantua is also close to the A22 *autostrada*, between Modena and the Brenner Pass.

## Tourist Information

On the corner of Piazza dell'Erbe/Piazza Mantegna 6, ✆ (0376) 350681.

## Piazza Mantegna

From the station, Corso Vittorio Emanuele and Corso Umberto I lead straight into the Renaissance heart of Mantua, where the narrow cobbled streets are lined with heavy porticoes. Rising up above the rest of the city, in Piazza Mantegna, is the lofty dome of Mantua's great basilica, **Sant'Andrea**, built by Leon Battista Alberti in 1472 to house the Gonzaga's most precious holy relic, a chalice of Christ's blood, said to have been given to St Andrew by St Longinus, the Roman centurion who pierced Christ's side with his lance. Ludovico Gonzaga had asked Alberti to create a truly monumental edifice to hold the relic and form a fitting centrepiece for the city, and Alberti complied. In Florence Alberti had found himself constrained as an architect by his patrons' tastes, but in Mantua he was able to experiment and play with the ancient forms he loved. Sant'Andrea is based on Vitruvius's idea of an Etruscan temple, with a single barrel-vaulted nave supported by side chapels, fronted with a unique façade that combines a triumphal arch and a temple. Inside, Andrea Mantegna is buried in the first chapel on the left, next to a rather stern self-portrait in bronze. He designed much of decoration in the spacious interior, later executed by his pupils.

On the east side, the unfinished flank of the basilica is lined with the porticos and market stalls of the **Piazza dell'Erbe**. Across the square is the attractive 1082 **Rotonda di San Lorenzo,** built by the Countess Matilda over an earlier Lombard structure, and restored in 1908 after many centuries of neglect; fragments of medieval frescoes in the beautiful apse were discovered by the restorers. Also on the Piazza dell'Erbe, the lovely **Casa di Boniforte** has delicate stucco decoration, almost unchanged since it was built in 1455, while the 13th-century **Palazzo della Ragione** has a stout clock tower topped by an odd little temple and astronomical clock, added during Ludovico's restoration of the palace. The adjacent **Broletto,** built in 1227, faces the Piazza del Broletto, with a medieval figure of Virgil seated near the door.

An archway leads right into the grand, cobbled **Piazza Sordello**, traditional seat of Mantua's ruling lords. On one side rise the sombre palaces of the Bonacolsi, the Gonzaga's predecessors, with their **Torre della Gabbia**, named for the iron torture cage (*gabbione*) they kept to suspend prisoners over the city (though the Mantuans claim it was only used once). At the head of the piazza stands Mantua's **Duomo**, with a silly 1756 façade topped with wedding-cake figures that hides a lovely Renaissance interior by Giulio Romano. The 15th-century house at No.23 has been restored as the official **Casa di Rigoletto**, and contains a little exhibition on the opera.

## Palazzo Ducale

*Open 9–1, 2.30–6, Mon–Sat; 9–1 Sun; guided tours every half-hour; adm.*

Opposite the Bonacolsi palaces stands that of the Gonzaga, its unimpressive façade hiding one of Italy's most remarkable Renaissance residences, both in its artwork and in sheer size. The never-satisfied Gonzaga kept on adding on until they had some 500 rooms in three main structures—the original **Corte Vecchia**, first built by the Bonacolsi in 1290, the 14th-century **Castello**, with its large towers overlooking the lake, and the **Corte Nuova**, designed by Giulio Romano. Throw in the Gonzaga's **Basilica di Santa Barbara** and you have a complex that occupies the entire northeast corner of Mantua. If you go in the winter, dress warmly—it's as cold as a dead duke.

Although stripped of its furnishings and many of its artworks, the palace is still imposing, majestic, and seemingly endless. One of the first rooms on the tour, the former **chapel**, has a dramatic if half-ruined 14th-century fresco of the Crucifixion, attributed by some to Tommaso da Modena, while another contains a painting of a battle between the Gonzaga and the Bonacolsi in the Piazza Sordello, in which the Gonzaga crushed their rivals once and for all, in 1328—although the artist, Domenico Monore, painted the piazza as it appeared later in 1494. More fascinating than this real battle is the vivid **fresco of Arthurian knights** by Pisanello, Italy's Gothic master. For centuries the work was believed lost, until layers and layers of plaster were stripped away in 1969, revealing a remarkable, if unfinished, work that was commissioned by Gianfrancesco Gonzaga in the mid 15th century to commemorate his receiving from Henry VI the concession to use the heraldic SS collar of the House of Lancaster, an insignia that forms the border of Pisanello's mural, mingled with the marigold motif of the Gonzaga.

Beyond this are the remodelled **neoclassical rooms**, holding a set of Flemish tapestries based on Raphael's Acts of the Apostles cartoons (now in the Victoria and Albert Museum). Woven in the early 1500s, these copies of the Vatican originals are in a much better state of preservation; note the curiously pagan borders. Beyond these lies the **Sala dello Zodiaco**, with vivacious 1580 frescoes by Lorenzo Costa il Giovane, and the **Sala del Fiume**, named for its fine views over the river, and the **Galleria degli Specchi**, with its mirrors and mythological frescoes, and, by the door, a note from Monteverdi on the days and hours of the musical evenings he directed there in the 1600s.

The Gonzaga were mad about horses and dogs, and had one room, the **Salone degli Arcieri**, painted with *trompe l'œil* frescoes of their favourite steeds standing on upper ledges; they were used in a family guessing game, when curtains would be drawn over the figures. Sharing the room are works by Tintoretto and a painting by Rubens of the Gonzaga family, so large that Napoleon's troop had to cut it into pieces to carry it off. Further on lie the duke's apartments, with the family's fine collection of classical statuary, including busts of the emperors, a Hellenistic torso of Aphrodite, and the 'Apollo of Mantova', a Roman copy of a Greek original. The **Sala di Troia** has vivid 1536 frescoes by Giulio Romano and his pupil, Rinaldo Mantovano, while another ducal chamber has a beautiful seicento labyrinth on the ceiling, each path inscribed in gold with 'Maybe yes, maybe no'. From some of the rooms you can look out over the grassy **Cortile della Cavallerizza**, with rustic façades by Giulio Romano.

The **castle** is reached by a low spiral ramp, built especially for the horses the Gonzaga apparently could never bear to be long without. Here, in the famous **Camera degli Sposi**, are the remarkable frescoes by Mantegna, who like a genie captured the essence of the Gonzaga in this small bottle of a room. Recently restored to their brilliant, original colours, the frescoes depict the life of Ludovico Gonzaga, with his wife Barbara of Brandenburg, his children, dwarves, servants, dogs, and horses, and important events—greeting his son Francesco, recently made a cardinal, and playing host to Emperor Frederick III and King Christian I of Denmark. The portraits are unflattering and solid, those of real people not for public display, almost like a family photo album. The effect is like stumbling on the court of the Sleeping Beauty; only the younger brother, holding the new cardinal's hand, seems to suspect that he has been enchanted. Wife Barbara and her stern dwarf stare out, determined to draw the spectator into the eerie scene. And in truth there is a lingering sorcery here, for these frescoes are the fruit of Mantegna's fascination with the mysterious new science of perspective that gave artists the power to recreate three-dimensional space. The beautiful backgrounds of imaginary cities and ruins reflect Mantegna's other love, classical architecture, and add another element of unreality, as do his *trompe l'œil* ceiling decorations.

From here the tour continues to the **Casetta dei Nani**, residence of the dwarfs, tiny rooms with low ceilings and shallow stairs, although there are party-poopers who say the rooms had a pious purpose, and were meant to bring the sinning dukes to their proud knees. The last stop is the **suite of Isabella d'Este**, designed by her as a retreat after the death of her husband. Her fabulous art collection has long gone to the Louvre, but the inexplicable symbols she devised with her astrologers remain like faint ghosts from a lost world on the walls and ceiling.

## Other sights

There are several sights within easy walking distance of the Palazzo Ducale. On Via Accademia, just east of the Broletto, Piazza Dante has a monument to the poet and the **Teatro Scientifico** (*open 9.30–12.30, 3–6, Mon–Sat; adm*). Also known as the Teatro Bibiena, it was built by Antonio Galli Bibiena, a member of the famous Bolognese family of theatre builders. Mozart, aged 13, performed at the inaugural concert in 1770; father Leopold thought it was the most beautiful theatre he had ever seen.

West of the Piazza Sordello, Via Cairoli leads to the city's main park, the **Piazza Virgiliana**, with a Mussolini-era statue of Virgil. The **Museo Gonzaga**, Via Cairoli 55 (*open April–June, Sept, Oct 9.30–12, 2.30–5, Tues–Sun; July–Aug Thurs, Sat, Sun only; Nov–Mar Sun only; adm*), contains a variety of artefacts and treasures that once belonged to the family. Further west, in the Piazza d'Arco, the 18th-century **Palazzo d'Arco** has been opened to the public (*open Mar–Oct 9–12, 3–5, Thu, Sat, Sun, 9–12 only Tues, Wed, Fri; Nov–Feb 9–12, 2.30–4, Sun and holidays only; adm*); former residence of the Counts d'Arco, it contains period furnishings, instruments, and a section of the original 15th-century palace, with beautiful zodiac frescoes. The nearby 1304 church of **San Francesco** was rediscovered in 1944, when a bomb hit the arsenal that had disguised it for a century and a half. It was restored to its original state in 1954, and contains frescoes attributed to Tommaso da Modena.

South of the medieval nucleus lies Mantua's second great sight, the Palazzo del Te; on the way there, just off the main Via Principe Amedeo, you can take a look at **Giulio Romano's House**, designed by the artist, as was the quaint palace decorated with monsters opposite. Mantegna also designed his dream house, the **Casa di Mantegna**, in the same neighbourhood, at Via Acerbi 47 (*open 9–12.30, 3–6, daily*). Designed as a cube built around a circular courtyard, it was intended partially as his personal museum. Embellished with classical 'Mantegnesque' decorations, the house is used for frequent art exhibitions. Nearby stands the rather neglected **San Sebastiano**, the second church in Mantua designed by Alberti, this one in the form of a Greek cross.

## Palazzo del Te

*Open 10am–6pm Tues–Sun; adm.*

At the end of Via Acerbi is Giulio Romano's masterpiece, the marvellous **Palazzo del Te**, its name derived not from tea, but from *tejeto*, a local word for a drainage canal. The palace grounds were formerly swampland, drained for a horsey Gonzaga pleasure ground. In 1527 Federico II had Giulio expand the stables to create a little palace for his mistress, of whom his mother, Isabella d'Este, disapproved. The project expanded over the decades to become a guest house suitable for Emperor Charles V. In the Palazzo del Te Giulio Romano created one of the great Renaissance syntheses of architecture and art, combining *trompe l'œil* with a bold play between the structure of the room and the frescoes; in the **Sala dei Giganti** the Titans, wrestling with pillars, seem to be bringing the ceiling down upon the spectator's head. Another room has more life size Gonzaga horses up on ledges, and another, the **Camera di Psiche**, is painted with lusty scenes from *The Golden Ass* of Apuleius, all in contrast with the serene Pompeii-style decorations in between. In the garden Giulio Romano added the little **Casino della Grotta**, adorned with pretty stuccoes.

---

### Activities

Several **boat** companies operate on the lakes and the river Mincio around Mantua, among them **Andes**, Piazza Sordello 8, ✆ (0376) 322875, @ 322869. A pleasant 1½hr trip costs L10,000 (less for children).

---

*Mantua ✆ (0376–)*

### Where to Stay

*expensive and moderate*

Mantua has a small selection of typical hotels, the best of which is the ★★★★**Rechigi**, Via Calvi 30, ✆ 320781 (moderate), conveniently located in the historic centre. All rooms have private bath, air conditioning, and comfortable furnishings, and the hotel has ample parking.

Also a fine choice is ★★★★**San Lorenzo**, Piazza Concordia 14, ℰ 220500 (expensive). Housed in a restored late Renaissance building, with all modern comforts, in the centre's pedestrian zone, this hotel has many rooms with views over the Piazza dell'Erbe. Another pleasant hotel housed in an older building is ★★★**Due Guerrieri**, ℰ 325596 (moderate), overlooking the Piazza Sordello and the Palazzo Ducale. There are baths in every room, and parking nearby. ★★**Albergo Bianchi**, Piazza Don Leoni, ℰ 321504 (moderate), is near the station, and handy for train travellers.

### *inexpensive and cheap*

Two good-value options are ★**ABC Moderno**, ℰ 322329 (inexpensive), next door to the Bianchi, which has small cell-like rooms arranged around an inner courtyard with space for parking, and ★**Rinascita**, Via Concezione 4, ℰ 320607 (inexpensive), a spotlessly clean budget hotel off Piazza Virgiliana, with a delightful inside garden and marble floors throughout. Mantua also has an exceptional **youth hostel**, the **Ostello Sparafucile**, Lunetta di San Giorgio, ℰ 372465 (cheap) is Mantua's exceptional **youth hostel**, located just outside the city. The hostel is in a cinquecento castle, popularly believed to be the headquarters of the baddie in Rigoletto. The interior has been remodelled, but without losing any of its character. The charge is L14,000 a person a night, with breakfast; cheap meals are also available. (*Closed 15 Oct–1 April; to get there, take bus nos.2 or 9 from Piazza Cavallotti.*)

A programme initiated in the last few years has developed five old country **villa-farmhouses** as inexpensive accommodation, averaging around L20,000 per person per night. One, the **Villa Schiarino-Lena**, ℰ 398104 (inexpensive), is only a few kilometres from Mantua, on the other side of Lago Superiore; the rooms surrounding a 16th-century agricultural courtyard have been converted into apartments. Another, a fully functioning farm, the **Feniletto**, ℰ 650262 (inexpensive), is 13km from Mantua at Rodigo, in the midst of the Regional Park of the Mincio; boating excursions are possible on the river. Reserve well in advance, as there are only five beds. A few kimometres southeast of Mantua in Serravale Po, **Due Madonne**, ℰ/✉ (0386) 40056 (inexpensive), offers horse riding, walking and cycling as well as hearty local cooking. For more information on stays in traditional buildings in the Mantuan countryside, contact the tourist office.

---

*Mantua ℰ (0376–)*                                                    ***Eating Out***

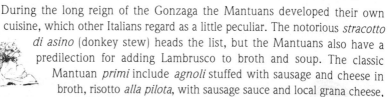

During the long reign of the Gonzaga the Mantuans developed their own cuisine, which other Italians regard as a little peculiar. The notorious *stracotto di asino* (donkey stew) heads the list, but the Mantuans also have a predilection for adding Lambrusco to broth and soup. The classic Mantuan *primi* include *agnoli* stuffed with sausage and cheese in broth, risotto *alla pilota*, with sausage sauce and local grana cheese, or *tortelli di zucca* (little pasta caps stuffed with pumpkin, served with melted butter). The local lake and river fish—deep-fried frog's legs, catfish, eel, crayfish, pike and bass—are traditional second courses.

Long considered Mantua's finest restaurant, **Il Cigno**, Piazza d'Arco, ✆ 327101, does many local specialities in a very elegant setting. The menu changes according to season—when it's cold, the *agnoli* in broth with Lambrusco will take off the chill; the eel in balsamic vinegar is a delicious second course. (*Closed Mon, first part of Aug.*) The lovely **Aquila Nigra**, Vicolo Bonaclosi 4, ✆ 350651, offers both local dishes and some from other regions, including seafood and risotto with scampi. There's a large selection of Italian and French wines, and delicious desserts like chestnut torte. (*Closed Sun, Mon, most of Aug.*) **Al Garibaldini**, Via S. Longino 7, ✆ 328263, is right in the historic centre of Mantua, in a fine old structure with a shady garden for al fresco dining in the summer. The menu features many Mantuan dishes, with especially good risotto and *tortelli di zucca*, fish, and meat dishes. (*Closed Wed, most of Jan.*)

*inexpensive*

For no atmosphere but delicious Mantuan cooking at a very accessible price try the **Trattoria al Lago**, Piazza Arche 5, ✆ 323300. The **Due Cavallini**, Via Salnitro 5 (near Lago Inferiore, off Corso Garibaldi), ✆ 322084, is the place if you want to bite into some donkey meat—though it has other, more typical dishes as well. (*Closed first part of July.*)

## Around Mantua

Although the Po plain isn't generally known for its natural beauty, Mantua's western lake, Lago Superiore, is noted for its delicate lotus blossoms, planted in the 1930s as an experiment. They have since thrived, and bloom in July and August around the city's park, the Valletta Belfiore. Another of Mantua's parks, the Bosco della Fontana, lies 5km to the north off the road to Brescia. The Bosco's ancient broad-leafed trees are believed to be a relic of the ancient forest that once covered the Po plain, and its shady paths and streamlets are a tempting retreat from the afternoon heat. Within its confines stand the ruins of a 12th-century Gonzaga castle. If you're in Mantua in the middle of August, be sure to visit the Sanctuary of the Madonna delle Grazie, on the banks of Lago Superiore at Curtatone, where there's an unusual art competition, for the madonnari—artists who draw pavement chalk portraits of the Madonna—among other diversions. Inside, the church is chock-full of votive offerings, some curious and some inexplicable, left in thanks by people who invoked the name of the Madonna in an hour of need. There is also a stuffed crocodile hanging from the roof, apparently the last in the area when the remaining land around the church was drained.

### San Benedetto Po

Some 22km southeast of Mantua (connected in the summer by small tourist boats, sailing down the Mincio to the Po), San Benedetto Po grew up around the Benedictine abbey of **Polirone** (*open 8am–7pm daily*), the 'Monte Cassino of the North', established in the year 1007 and especially favoured by the feisty Countess Matilda of Canossa (d.1115), whose alabaster sarcophagus survives in the apse of the **Basilica**, rebuilt in the 1540s by Giulio Romano. The basilica is connected to the 12th-century Church of Santa Maria, which has a fine contemporary mosaic. There are several cloisters from various periods, and a refectory with recently discovered frescoes attributed to Correggio. Another part of the monastery contains the **Museo della Cultura Popolare Padana**, © 615977 (*open June–Oct 9–12, 3–6.30, Tues–Sun; Mar–May 9–12.30, 2–5.30 daily; Nov–Mar, call in advance; adm.*), devoted to the traditions and culture of the surrounding countryside.

## Sabbioneta

An hour's bus ride southwest of Mantua on the Parma road, Sabbioneta was built as a capital and ideal dream city by the prince of Bozzolo, Vespasiano Gonzaga, member of a cadet branch of the Gonzaga family. Vespasiano was a firm believer that the city should be a rational expression in the measure of man, and had the streets of his 'Little Athens' laid out straight and square within its irregular hexagonal walls; his humanistic philosophy attracted many Jewish settlers, who founded a famous printing press. To see the interiors of the historic centre, contact the Pro Loco on Via V. Gonzaga 31, © (0375) 52039 (*open April–Sept 9–12, 2.30–6, Tues–Sun; Oct–Mar 9–12, 2.30–5, Tues–Sun; adm*).

The classical utopian vision of Vespasiano was out of fashion before Sabbioneta was even built, and its spark died with its creator, leaving a silent little museum city with a declining population. Around the central Piazza Castello, Vespasiano constructed a long frescoed corridor, the **Galleria degli Antichi,** to display his collection of classical statues (now in Mantua's Palazzo Ducale). At one end lies the **Palazzo del Giardino**, the prince's pleasure palace, richly adorned with frescoes and stuccoes by the school of Giulio Romano.

The next piazza contains the symmetrical **Palazzo Ducale** with its five arches, housing wooden equestrian statues of Vespasiano and his kin; other rooms, with fine frescoes and ceilings, include the **Sala d'Oro** with its golden ceiling, the **Sala degli Elefanti** with elephants, or the **Sala delle Città Marinare** with paintings of port towns and a small **Museum of Sacred Art**. Behind the palace, the 1586 church of the **Incoronata** houses Vespasiano's mausoleum, with a bronze statue of the prince in classical Roman garb. The last stop on the tour is the small 1588 **Teatro Olimpico**, designed by the Vicenzan Scamozzi after Palladio's theatre in Vicenza. Twelve plaster statues of the ancient Olympians grace the balcony, and some of the original Venetian frescoes have recently been rediscovered. Also in the centre of town is the 16th-century **synagogue**, derelict for the past 50 years.

---

### Eating Out

In Sabbioneta, the **Ca' d'Amici**, Via d'Aragona 2, © (0375) 52318, is the best restaurant, featuring local and national specialities (expensive). For a real treat, however, just getting into the very expensive price range, drive 20km north to Canneto sull'Oglio (just beyond Piadena), where you can feast at one of Lombardy's finest and most tranquil restaurants, **Dal Pescatore**, Via Runate 13, © (0376) 70304, located in an old and elegant country house. The menu and its preparation are authentic and delightful; offerings include *tortelli* with pumpkin, grilled eel, delectable fish dishes and magnificent desserts and wines. (*Closed Mon, Tues, mid-Aug, two weeks Jan.*)

# The Italian Lakes

Just to mention the Italian Lakes is to evoke a soft, dreamy image of romance and beauty, a Latin Brigadoon of consumptive gentlemen and gentle ladies strolling through gardens, sketching landscapes, and perhaps indulging in a round of whist on the villa veranda in the evening. The backgrounds to their fond pleasures are scenes woven of poetry, of snow-capped peaks tumbling steeply into ribbons of blue, trimmed with the silver tinsel of olives and the daggers of dark cypress; of mellowed villas gracing vine-clad hillsides and gold-flecked citrus groves; of spring's excess, when the lakes become drunken with colour, as a thousand varieties of azaleas, rhododendrons and camellias spill over the banks. For even though the Swiss border is just around the corner, the three largest lakes—**Maggiore, Como** and **Garda**—cover enough area to create their own climatic oases of Mediterranean flora, blooming even at the foot of the starlit Alps.

Lake holidays faded from fashion in the post-War era, when a suntan became a symbol of leisure instead of manual labour and summer's mass trek to the seashore became as fixed a ritual as the drowning of lemmings. But the lakes are simply too lovely to stay out of fashion for long, and today a new generation is busily rediscovering what their grandparents took for granted, polishing up the old Belle Epoque fixtures of the villas and grand hotels. For better or worse, the Italians have ringed the lakes with finely engineered roads, making them perhaps too accessible, whereas before visitors had to make do with small boats, or leisurely steamers. Prices have risen with demand, and between July and September rest and relaxation, or even peace and quiet, may seem a Victorian relic, unless you book into one of the grander villa hotels. Quiet havens, however, still exist on the smaller, less developed lakes of Iseo and Orta, the east shores of lakes Maggiore and Como, and in the mountain valleys to the north of the lakes, around Domodossola and in the beautiful Valtellina.

Lake resorts are generally open between April and October. The best times to visit are in spring and autumn, not only because there are fewer crowds, but because the lakes themselves are less subjected to winter mists and summer haze. In the restaurants, look for lake fish and trout, served either fresh or sun-dried. The finest wines from the lake district come from Bardolino on the east shore of Lake Garda; try too the reds from the Valtellina, or the vintages from Franciacorte near Lake Iseo or La Brianza near Lake Como.

Below, the lakes are described geographically from west to east, from Piedmont's Lake Orta and the valleys around Domodossola, through Lombardy's lakes and the Valtellina, the art cities, Bergamo and Brescia, and then to Lake Garda on the border of the Veneto.

# Lake Orta and Domodossola

The green waters of Lake Orta run still and quiet, and in the centre they hold a magical isle, illuminated on summer nights, to hang like a golden fairy-tale castle. A mere 13km long, Orta is a lake 'made to the measurements of man', and blessed with an exceptional dose of charm. Nietzsche, who never fell in love, did so on its soft green shores. He didn't get the girl, but the world got *Thus Spake Zarathustra*.

## Getting Around

The main resorts on Lake Orta, Orta San Giulio and Omegna, are easily reached from Turin or Milan on **trains** heading north to Domodossola. There are frequent **buses** from Orta to Arona on Lake Maggiore, and from Omegna to Verbania. A small railway makes the trip between Domodossola and Locarno (Switzerland) while the other mountain valleys are served by bus from Domodossola.

**By road** Orta is easily accessible from Milan by the *autostrada* A8, which also connects with the A26 from Turin, Alessandria and Genoa, and from Switzerland via the Simplon Pass road, which meets the A8.

## Tourist Information

There are three tourist offices in the area: in **Orta San Giulio**, at Via Orlina, ✆ (0322) 90355; in **Macugnaga**, Piazza Municipio, ✆ (0324) 65858; and in **Santa Maria Maggiore**, at Piazza Risorgimento 5, ✆ (0324) 95091.

# Lake Orta

The east bank of Lake Orta is dominated by the district's highest peak, the 1491m **Mottarone**; below it, located on its own little peninsula, is the lake's charming main village, **Orta San Giulio**, with many attractive 17th- and 18th-century houses and shops built around a fine little palazzo, where art exhibitions are held frequently. Orta San Giulio has its own acropolis, **Sacro Monte**, dedicated to St Francis; its 21 chapels, mostly built in the Renaissance style between the 1590s and the 1660s, contain frescoes and terracotta statues by different artists related to the life of St Francis. A path from the village follows the lake for about a kilometre.

From Orta, steamboats run to the ports of Pella, Oira and Omegna, and **Isola San Giulio**, a pretty islet directly in front of the village, but, according to legend, once inhabited by loathsome serpents and monsters. They were banished by Orta's version of St Patrick, St Julius, who arrived in 390 and founded the precursor to the island's **Basilica**. Most of what you see today dates from around the 12th century, including the intriguing carving of griffons and serpents on the black marble pulpit. There are some good 15th-century frescoes by Ferrari and his school, and a marble sarcophagus with ancient carvings, believed to have belonged to the Lombard Duke Meinulphus, who had betrayed the island to the Franks and was beheaded by Agilulf; and indeed a decapitated skeleton was found inside in 1697. Pride of place, however, goes to the big vertebrae displayed in the

sacristy, belonging to one of the dragons Julius dismissed from the island. The other sizeable town on the lake, **Omegna**, has a small beach and less expensive lodgings.

## From Lake Orta to Domodossola: Valle Anzasca

From Omegna, the railway and *autostrada* continue into the northernmost reaches of Piedmont. Between Omegna and Domodossola, two lovely valleys diverge to the west—first and foremost, the enchanting **Valle Anzasca** (buses there can be caught from Domodossola or from the station at Piedimulera at the foot of the valley). A number of little villages lie scattered among the woods and vineyards—tiny **Colombetti**, its slate roofs huddled under a lofty cliff; **Bannio-Anzino**, the 'capital' of the valley, across and above the river Anzo, with modest ski facilities and a 7-foot-tall, 16th-century bronze Christ in its parish church, brought here from Flanders; **Ceppo Morelli** has a famous, vertiginous bridge over the Anza; beyond Ceppo the road plunges through a gorge to the old mining town of **Pestarena**.

The various hamlets that comprise **Macugnaga**, the Valle Anzasca's popular resort, lie under the majestic frowning face of **Monte Rosa** (4638m). As in the Valle d'Aosta's Val Gressoney on the southern side of Monte Rosa, Macugnaga was settled by German-speaking Swiss from the Valais (the Walser) in the 13th century. A small museum in **Staffa**, the chief village of Macugnaga, is devoted to Walser folklore, while other old Swiss traces remain in the parish church, built in the 13th century. Macugnaga has a number of ski lifts, and a chair lift that operates in the summer as well, to the magnificent **Belvedere** with views over the Macugnaga glacier; a cableway from Staffa to the **Passo Monte Moro** (2868m) is used by skiers in both the winter and summer seasons.

From Macugnaga, fearless alpinists can attempt the steep east flank of Monte Rosa, one of the most dangerous ascents in the Alps; walkers can make a three day trek over the mountains to Gressoney-St-Jean and other points in the Valle d'Aosta (trail map essential).

North of the Valle Anzasca, the much less visited **Val d'Antrona** is a pretty wooded valley famed for its trout fishing. The valley begins at **Villadossola**, from where you can catch a bus to the chief village **Antronapiana**, a pleasant place lost in the trees, near the lovely lakelet of Antrona.

## Domodossola

The largest town in the Valley of the River Toce, or Valle d'Ossola, Domodossola is best known for its location at the foot of the **Simplon Pass** (*Passo del Sempione*), through which, after the Battle of Marengo, Napoleon constructed his highway from Geneva to Lombardy, completed in 1805. Exactly 100 years later the even more remarkable Simplon Tunnel was completed. At 19.8 kilometres it is the longest in the world.

Domodossola is a pleasant old town with an arcaded main square and an interesting **Museo Civico**, with exhibits relating to the construction of the Simplon tunnel and the flight of the Peruvian Georges Chavez, the first man to fly over the Alps (29 September 1910), only to die in a crash near Domodossola.

The road and railway line between Domodossola and Locarno (the largest Swiss town on Lake Maggiore) pass through the extraordinary **Val Vigezzo**, a romantic beauty that has attracted so many artists through the years that it's been nicknamed the Valley of Painters. The place to stay if you're tempted to linger is the main town, **Santa Maria Maggiore**; from nearby Maleco a road descends the Val Cannobina to Cannobio on Lake Maggiore.

Buses from Domodossola also plunge north into the spectacular scenery that leads up into the picturesque **Val Formazza**, colonized by German-speaking families from the Valais. Their charming, scattered, villages are small summer and winter resorts, offering excursions to the Alpine lakes, especially from **Ponte** (with a chair lift), where the bus terminates. One of the most breathtaking waterfalls in all the Alps is six kilometres up the road from Ponte, known as the **Cascata della Frua**, but like all of Italy's best waterfalls it is almost always dry, its water diverted for hydroelectric power. However, between 10 and 20 August, or on a Sunday from June until September between 9 am and 5 pm, the power company releases the thundering 300m veil of mist.

---

## *Where to Stay*

### Orta San Giulio

****San Rocco**, Via Gippini 11, © (0322) 905632, ✆ 905635 (very expensive) is the lake's most luxurious hotel, located in a former 17th-century monastery with a pretty garden right on the water. All rooms have private baths and balconies, and air-conditioning. There are two moderate category hotels on the main square, opposite the island, the

***Orta**, © (0322) 90253, ✆ 905646 (moderate), modern and stylish with big rooms and bathrooms, and the ***Leon d'Oro**, © (0322) 905666, ✆ 90303 (moderate), which has rather smaller rooms and is not quite as stylish as its neighbour, but is slightly cheaper. A pleasant choice is ***La Bussola**, Via Panoramica 24, ©/✆ (0322) 90198 (moderate). Set back on a quiet hill, this 16-room hotel (all rooms with bath) enjoys a magnificent panorama of the lake; there's a pretty garden with a swimming pool and a good restaurant. In the centre of the village, *Antico **Agnello**, Via Olina 18, © (0322) 90259 (inexpensive) is a simple, inexpensive little inn with warm, cosy rooms and an excellent restaurant (*see* 'Eating Out').

### Pettenasco

***Hotel Giardinetto**, Via Provinciale 1, © (0323) 89118, ✆ 89219 (moderate). A friendly, family-run hotel, also right on Lake Orta, with beautiful views of the Isoletta di San Giulio, which offers reduced rates for children; there's a swimming pool, private beach, and water sports facilities, and an excellent restaurant. All rooms have private bath or shower. (*Open April–Oct only.*)

### Omegna

**Vittoria**, Via Zanoia 37, © (0323) 62237 (inexpensive). This is the pick of the inexpensive-range *locande*.

### Valle Anzasca

Most of the Valle Anzasca's accommodation is clustered in Macugnaga. The ***Nuova Pecetto**, in the hamlet of Pecetto, © (0324) 65025 (moderate) is one of the most charming, a tiny, traditional hotel with a garden and fine views of Monte Rosa All rooms have baths.(*Closed mid-Sept–Nov.*) In Staffa, the largest and most luxurious choice, **★★★Zumstein**, Via Monte Rosa 63, ✆ (0324) 65118 (moderate), has attractive rooms in a pretty location (*Open mid-Dec–April, mid-June–mid-Sept.*) Also in Staffa, **★★Chez Felice**, Via Ville 14, ✆ (0324) 65229 (inexpensive), is a little mountain villa which has both simple but charming rooms with bath and the best restaurant in the valley (*see* below).

## Domodossola

**★★★Europa**, ✆ (0324) 481032, ✉ 481011 (moderate). Above the town in the suburb of Calice, 4km away, this has fine views and a garden, and the rooms all have private bath and toilet.

## Santa Maria Maggiore

**★★La Jazza**, Via Domodossola, ✆ (0324) 94471 (inexpensive) is a pleasant hotel with a garden. (*Open all year.*)

---

### *Eating Out*

The nicest restaurant in Orta is the **Antico Agnello** inn (*see* above). The menu changes with the season and varies between traditional dishes like fish from the lake, and more unusual fare such as pumpkin soup and *torta di verdura* (vegetable pie). Add to this a charming atmosphere, an extensive wine list and excellent service and you have a perfect recipe. It's still in the moderate price category, but reservations are necessary. Also in Orta San Giulio, **Sacro Monte**, Via Sacro Monte 5, ✆ (0322) 90220 , has delicious food and wine with the Piedmontese touch, in the same price range. (*Closed Tues.*)

In Staffa **Chez Felice** (*see* above, moderate) is a lively haven of mountain *nuova cucina*, where you can find salmon mousse with herbs, warm artichokes with a sauce of anchovies and capers, delicious soups, risotto with almonds, cheese and herb soufflé and many other delights; for afters, there's a magnificent array of local cheeses and exquisite desserts. (*Closed Thurs, and reservations advisable if you're not staying at the hotel.*)

## Lake Maggiore

> *Have you not read in books how men when they*
> *see even divine visions are terrified?*
> *So as I looked at Lake Major in its halo*
> *I also was afraid ...*

Hilaire Belloc, *The Path to Rome*

Italy's second-largest lake after Garda, Lago Maggiore winds majestically between Piedmont and Lombardy, its northern corner lost in the towering, snow-capped Swiss Alps. In Roman times Maggiore was called *Lacus Verbanus*, for the verbena that still grows luxuriantly on its shores. What really sets the lake apart, though, are its three jewel-like islands, which for many people make it the best lake to visit if there's only time for one. These, the fabled Borromean isles, still belong to the Borromeo family of Milan, who also possess the fishing rights over the entire lake—as they have since the 1500s.

The western shore of the lake, especially in the triad of resorts Stresa, Baveno, and Verbania, are the most scenic places to aim for, with the best and most varied accommodation. Unless you reserve well in advance, however, avoid July and August.

---

### Getting Around

**Trains** from Milan's Stazione Centrale to Domodossola stop at Arona and Stresa; from Porta Garibaldi station in Milan trains go to Luino on the east shore. A third option is the regional railway from Milano-Nord, which goes by way of Varese to Laveno. Trains from Turin and Novara go to Arona and Stresa. **By road** Lake Maggiore is directly connected with Milan by both the A8 *autostrada* and the SS33, and with Turin, Alessandria and Genoa by the A26.

From Lake Orta, there are **buses** from Omegna to Verbania, every 20 minutes. Buses that connect the two lakes also run from Stresa and Arona stations.

*Navigazione Lago Maggiore* runs **steamers** to all corners of the lake, with the most frequent services in the central lake area, between Stresa, Baveno, Verbania, Pallanza, and Laveno; **hydrofoils** buzz between Arona and Locarno (in Switzerland). Frequent services by steamer or hydrofoil from Stresa sail to the Borromean Isles—a ticket for the furthest, Isola Madre, entitles you to visit all. **Car ferries** run between Intra and Laveno. Pick up a boat schedule at one of the tourist offices, or from the company's headquarters at Viale F. Baracca 1, in Arona.

---

### Tourist Information

There are several tourist offices around the lake, at **Luino**, Viale Dante Alighieri 6, © (0332) 530019; in **Stresa**, Principe Tommaso 70, © (0323) 30150, @ 32 561; in **Verbania**, Corso Zanitello 6, © (0323) 503249; in **Baveno**, Corso Garibaldi 4, ©/@ (0323) 924632; and in **Arona**, at Piazza Duca d'Aosta, ©/@ (0322) 243601.

---

## Arona

Arona is the southernmost steamer landing, and the most interesting town in the southern reaches of Lake Maggiore. Even if you're just passing through it is hard to avoid **San Carlone**, a copper colossus towering 35m high above the old town. San Carlone (St Big Chuck) is perhaps better known as Charles Borromeo (1538–84), born in the now-ruined **Castle of Arona**, and the statue was erected by a family member in 1697.

## The World's Biggest Saint

 Charles Borromeo was the most influential churchman of his day, appointed 'Cardinal Nephew and Archbishop of Milan' at the age of 22 by his maternal uncle, Pope Pius IV. In Rome he was a powerful voice calling for disciplinary reforms within the Church, and was an instigator of the Council of Trent, in which he played a major role. There was one legendary point in the Council when the cardinals were ready to ban all church music, which by the 16th century had degenerated to the point of singing lewd love ballads to accompany the Te Deum. Charles and his committee, however, decided to let the musicians have one more go, and gave Palestrina the chance to compose three suitable masses that reflected the dignity of the words of the service (and Charles reputedly told the composer that the cardinals expected him to fail). To their surprise, and to the everlasting benefit of Western culture, Palestrina succeeded, and sacred music was saved.

After the death of his uncle-pope, Charles went to live in his diocese of Milan, the first archbishop to do so in 80 years. Following the mandate of the Council of Trent to the letter, he at once began reforming the cosy clergy to set the example for other bishops. In Milan he was so hated that he narrowly escaped an assassination attempt (the bullet bounced off his heavy brocade vestments). He was a bitter enemy of original thought and not someone you would want to have over for dinner, but for a queer sensation walk up the steps in his statue's hollow heart for the view.

The Borromeo family's chapel in **Santa Maria**, also in the upper part of town, contains a lovely 1511 altarpiece by Ferrari.

More Borromeana awaits at **Angera**, across the lake in Lombardy and the first steamer call. Angera has an interesting, well-preserved castle, the **Rocca di Angera** (*open April–June, Sept–Oct 9.30–12, 2–5 daily; July–Aug 9.30–12.30, 3–7, daily; adm*). The original owners, the Visconti, had it frescoed in the 14th century with battle scenes from their victory over the Della Torre family. The Borromei picked it up in 1439, and have lately added some detached frescoes from their palace in Milan.

## Stresa

The best-positioned and most charming town on the lake, **Stresa** has been a holiday resort since the last century, soaring in popularity after the construction of the Simplon Tunnel in 1906; Hemingway used its **Grand Hotel des Iles Borromées** as Frederick Henry's refuge from war in *A Farewell to Arms*. The town is also a favourite of international congresses, and has an annual music festival in late summer (*see* below).

While Stresa itself is lovely, bursting with flowers and sprinkled with fine old villas, it serves primarily as a base for visiting the isles and **Monte Mottarone** (1491m), via the cableway beginning at Stresa Lido. The views are famous, taking in a vision of glacier-crested Alpine peaks, stretching all the way from Monte Viso (far west) and Monte Rosa over to the eastern ranges of Ortles and Adamello by Lake Garda, as well as the Lombard plain and the miniature islands below. Stresa's golf course is on the slopes of Monte Mottarone, at **Vezzo**

(9 holes); both it and **Gignese**, site of a curious little **Umbrella Museum** (*open April–Sept, mornings only*), can be reached from Stresa by bus.

---

*Stresa ✆ (0323–)* **Where to Stay**

Opened in 1863, ★★★★★**Des Isles Borromées**, Corso Umberto I 67, ✆ (0323) 30431, ✉ 32405, (luxury) is opulent in both its aristocratic Belle Epoque furnishings and its modern conveniences. Overlooking the lake, the islands, and a lovely flower-decked, palm-shaded garden, the hotel has a pool, beach, tennis courts, and the *Centro Benessere* ('well-being') where doctors are on hand to give you a check-up, exercises and improve your diet. There's even a heli-pad, should you need one. The magnificent rooms all have sumptuous private bathrooms and minibars. (*Open all year.*) Some 40 years younger than the former, the ★★★★**Regina Palace**, Corso Umberto I, ✆ (0323) 933777, ✉ 933776, (very expensive) is a lovely, bow-shaped palace with Liberty-style touches, tranquil in its large park. It has a heated swimming pool, tennis courts, beach, and splendid views.(*Open April–Oct.*) ★★★★**Milan au Lac**, Piazza Marconi, ✆ (0323) 31190, ✉ 32729, (expensive) is another lake-front hotel, with good-size rooms, many with balconies and, of course, wonderful views. A hotel that enjoys the most ravishing view of the islands is the ★★★★**Villaminta**, at Stresa Lido, on the Sempione road, ✆ (0323) 933818, ✉ 933955 (expensive). In addition to its comfortable rooms, there's a beach, pool, and tennis courts, and its good restaurant serves excellent lake fish and dishes from nearly every region in Italy. (*Open mid-Mar–Oct.*)

In the moderate category, the ★★★**Primavera**, Via Cavour 39, ✆ (0323) 31286, ✉ 33458, (moderate) is a friendly hotel with a touch of style, and pretty balconies, but no restaurant. ★★★**Moderno**, at Via Cavour 3, ✆ (0323) 933773, ✉ 93375, (moderate) is a charming place, with rooms set round an inner patio. All have TV and minibar, and there are also two very good restaurants. ★★★**Italia e Suisse**, Piazza Marconi, ✆ (0323) 30540, ✉ 32621, (moderate) is near the lake and the steamer landing. (*Open all year.*) A good budget option in Stresa, with big, modern rooms, many with balcony and TV, is ★★**Elena**, Piazza Cadorna 15, ✆ (0323) 31043, ✉ 33339, (inexpensive). It also has a garage.

---

*Stresa ✆ (0323–)* **Eating Out**

Stresa's gourmet haven, **Emiliano**, is on the lakefront at Corso Italia 52, ✆ (0323) 31396, (very expensive), and offers *nuova cucina* with a Bolognese touch, with specialities such as their delicious seafood dishes, a beef and lobster 'mosaic' and calves' liver in balsamic vinegar. They also have excellent desserts, and a superb wine list. The grand *menu degustazione* is L90,000, but others are less. **La Chandelle**, Via Sempione 23, ✆ (0323) 30097, (expensive), offers a mixed Italian-French menu in an elegant atmosphere; fondues, escargot, French onion soup, and curried shrimp are some of the choices on the menu.

From the last week of August through September the town of Stresa sponsors a highly acclaimed series of music weeks, the *Settimane Musicali di
Stresa*, featuring orchestras from around the world. As to nightlife, Maggiore
has a more sedate feel than the other lakes, and the place is awash with softly
tinkling piano bars. In Stresa, for a quiet drink in atmospheric surroundings,
the **Casa del Caffè**, Via A. M Bolognaro 26, is ideal.

## The Borromean Islands

Rare and probably myopic is the visitor to Lake Maggiore who can resist a trip to at least one
of these lush beauties, dotting the mouth of the wide bay of Pallanza. Actually, the three
Borromean Islands include the **Isola dei Pescatori** in the middle, with its almost too quaint
and picturesque fishing village, and another private islet called **San Giovanni**, just off the
shore at Pallanza, with a villa once owned by Toscanini. Stresa has the most boats to the
islands (you can even rent a rowing boat in town to avoid the crowds), but there are also
frequent excursions from Baveno and Pallanza.

The closest island to Stresa, **Isola Bella**, is also the most celebrated. It was a barren rock
until the 17th century, when Count Carlo III Borromeo decided to make it a garden for his
wife, Isabella (hence the name of the islet), hiring the architect Angelo Crivelli to plan its
impressive series of 10 terraces and formal arrangements. Later 17th-century Borromei
added the palace and 'artificial grottoes' and finished the gardens, endowing them with statuary, fountains, and perhaps the first of its famous white peacocks. The only problem is that
the 17th century was not an auspicious time for doing much of anything, especially art, and
on Isola Bella sighs of rapture over the splendour of the views and gardens intermingle with
groans of disbelief at the 'art'. The conducted palace tour goes down best after a few drinks
(*open Mar–Oct 9–12, 1.30–5.30, daily; adm*).

The delightful, larger **Isola Madre** stands as an interesting contrast to Isola Bella, planted
with a colourful, luxuriant garden in a more informal English style. It also has a smaller, more
refined palace, with an interesting collection of Borromeo family portraits, and the family's
18th-century marionette theatre and puppets (*opening times and adm as Isola Bella*).

## Beyond Stresa

**Baveno** is Stresa's quieter sister, connected by a beautiful, villa-lined road. It has been fashionable among the international set ever since 1879, when Queen Victoria spent a summer
at the Villa Clara, now Castello Branca. A pretty road leads up **Monte Camoscio,** behind
Baveno, while another leads back to the little Lake Mergozzo, a corner of Lake Maggiore that
has been cut off in the last 100 years by silt from the river Toce. The main shore road carries
on to **Pallanza**, which has a famously mild winter climate. Pallanza was united with Suna
and Intra in 1939 to form Verbania (from the old Roman name of the lake), and is mostly
visited for the **Villa Taranto,** some 50 acres planted with 20,000 kinds of plants by a Scot,
Captain Neil McEacharn. The aquatic plants, including giant Amazonian water lilies and
lotus blossoms, the spring tulips and autumn colour are exceptional, as are some of the rarer

species—the handkerchief tree, bottle bush, and copper-coloured Japanese maple. The house is used by the Italian prime minister for special conferences (*otherwise open April–Oct 8.30am–sunset; adm*). Intra, Verbania's industrial quarter, is the departure point for a ferry-boat across to Laveno, and buses up to the mountain resort of **Premeno**, with skiing in the winter and a beautiful 9-hole golf course.

North of Intra, **Ghiffa** is a pretty, rural village with an attractive castle and 13th-century Lombard Gothic church. **Cannero Riviera**, further up the shore, is a quiet resort amid the citrus groves, facing two islets, formerly haunted by medieval banditti. **Cannobio**, the last stop before Switzerland, is an ancient town, one that, though in Piedmont, is famous for adhering to the Milanese Ambrosian Rite, itself revived by Cardinal Charles Borromeo in an effort to promote local pride. It has a fine Bramante-inspired Santuario della Pietà, with an altarpiece by Ferrari. The village lies at the foot of the Val Cannobina, where you can hire a boat to visit the pretty **Orrido di Sant'Anna** with its waterfall.

## The Eastern Shore and Santa Caterina del Sasso

The main place of interest on the Lombard shore is the romantic, deserted Carmelite convent of **Santa Caterina del Sasso**, hanging on a sheer cliff over the water, with grand views over the Borromean islands and mountains. The convent is visible only from the lake (if you're driving, follow the signs from the shore road after Leggiuno; boats call here between April and September). According to legend, in the 12th century a wealthy merchant and usurer named Alberto Besozzi was sailing on the lake when his boat sank. In deadly peril he prayed to St Catherine of Alexandria, who saved him from the waves and cast him upon this rock-bound shore. Alberto henceforth repented of his usury and lived as a hermit in a cave. When his prayers brought an end to a local plague, he asked that as an *ex voto* the people construct a church to St Catherine. Over the centuries, other buildings were added as the cave of 'Beato Alberto' became a popular pilgrimage destination, especially after a huge boulder fell on the roof, only to be miraculously wedged just above the altar, sparing the priest who was saying mass. The boulder finally crashed through in 1910, without harming anyone, because nobody was there; the monastery had been suppressed in 1770 by Joseph II of Austria. In 1986 a 15-year long restoration of Santa Caterina was completed, revealing medieval fresco fragments (especially notable is one in the Sala Capitolare, of 13th-century armed men). There's also a 16th-century fresco of the *Danse Macabre* in the Loggia of the Gothic convent.

**Laveno**, the most important town in the district, is well known for its ceramics. If you're taking the train from Milan or Varese, the Milano-Nord line will leave you right next to the lake. The best thing to do in Laveno is to take the cable car up to the **Sasso del Ferro** (1062m), from where you can walk up for a marvellous view over the lake. Or come at Christmas-time, when Laveno can claim Italy's only underwater *presepio* (Christmas crib), floodlit and visible from terra firma—and no, the figures don't wear snorkles!

The northern reaches of the lake on the eastern side are not very exciting. **Luino** is the largest and most important town, believed to have been the birthplace of Bernardino Luini. To the north the two Maccagnos, **Maccagno Inferiore** and **Maccagno Superiore**, are on the whole more pleasant places to take refuge from the crowds.

### Sports and Activities

There are any number of beaches around the lake, though many are privately owned, often by hotels. There are 9-hole **golf courses** near Stresa, at Vezzo, and in the mountain resort of Premeno, reached by bus from Verbania. Premeno also offers good **skiing** in winter.

### Where to Stay

Easter and July to mid-September are the high season on Lake Maggiore, when you should definitely reserve.

### Isola dei Pescatori

★★★**Verbano**, ✆ (0323) 30408, 🖷 33129, (moderate) is a lovely, quiet little hotel on the lake, which offers the chance to see the picturesque island after the hordes return to the mainland. It also has a good restaurant. The ★**Belvedere**, ✆/🖷 (0323) 30047, (inexpensive) is a less expensive choice, with doubles at very reasonable prices.

### Verbania-Pallanza

Right on the lake is the grand old ★★★★**Majestic**, Via Vittorio Veneto 32, ✆ (0323) 504305, 🖷 556379, (expensive), a very comfortable hotel endowed with a good restaurant and plenty of amenities—an indoor pool, tennis, park and private beach.(*Open April–Oct.*) ★★★**Belvedere**, Viale Magnolia 6, ✆ (0323) 503202, 🖷 504466, (moderate) is a good hotel for thie price-range, located on the lake near the steamer landing. In the same town the recently refurbished ★★★**Pace**, Via Cietti 1, ✆ (0323) 557207, 🖷 557341, (moderate) offers excellent value, with modern rooms and bathrooms and old-style writing desks and other furniture. (*Open Mar–Oct.*) A hotel which enjoys a lovely position in a park near the lake is the ★**Villa Serena**, Via Crocetta 26, ✆ (0323) 556015 (inexpensive).

### Cannero Riviera

★★★**Hotel Cannero**, Lungolago 2, ✆ (0323) 788046, 🖷 788048, (moderate). A fine hotel with terraces overlooking the lake. There's a swimming pool, better than average food in the restaurant, and a garage. Guests must stay for a minimum of three days. (*Open end Mar–Oct.*)

## Luino

In Luino, the top choice is the ★★★★**Camin**, Via Danta 35, ✆ (0332) 530118, ✉ 537226, (expensive), a hotel in the old style, with big rooms, plush fittings and heavy wooden furniture, combined with the modern: TV (and in some rooms, video), hydro-massage baths and twin basins in marble. There are two good, reasonably inexpensive hotels: just down from the station, the ★**Elvezia**, Via XXV Aprile 107, ✆ (0332) 531219 (inexpensive) is neat, clean, convenient; it's towards the top of this price range, but still good value. ★★**Internazionale**, ✆ (0332) 530193, ✉ 537882, (inexpensive), opposite the station, has a smart modern interior, fully equipped and good-size rooms, and parking facilities. You could also try the ★★★**Ancora**, on the main square, ✆/✉ (0332) 530451, (inexpensive). A bit basic for this price range, it nevertheless enjoys fine views.

---

*Eating Out*

## Pallanza

The best place to eat in Pallanza, the **Milano**, Corso Zanitello, ✆ (0323) 556816 (expensive), is located in a fine old villa on the lake, with dining out on the terrace for a very romantic evening. The food is some of the finest on Maggiore: wonderful antipasti and lake fish prepared in a number of delicious styles. (*Closed Tues.*)

## Ranco

Just north of Angera on the Lombard side of the lake, is **Del Sole**, Piazza Venezia 5, ✆ (0331) 976620, (very expensive), the finest restaurant on the lake, in a lovely old inn with a charming terrace for outdoor dining in summer. The exquisitely and imaginatively prepared lake fish and crayfish are worth the journey; they're complemented by magnificent wine lists and delicate desserts. (*Closed Mon evenings, Tues, and all Jan.*)

---

*Entertainment and Nightlife*

Lake Maggiore is one of the quieter lakes; however, if you do feel the need to dance, **Kursaal**, in Pallanza, at Via Veneto 16 (*adm*) is a big, plush place in its own grounds, and with occasional live acts too.

## Lake Varese and Castiglione Olona

Between Lake Maggiore and Milan lies the quiet **Lago di Varese**, 8½km long and the big, sleepy head of the 'minor lakes'. The main settlement, **Gavirate**, makes hand-carved pipes. Just south, in Voltorre, in the cloister of the 11th-century monastery of **San Michele** (now a cultural centre) there are splendid, older carvings on the capitals, attributed to Lanfranco. From Biandronno boats depart for little Isolino Virginia, site of the **Museo Preistorico di Villa Ponti**, which chronicles a prehistoric lake settlement (3000 BC–Roman times).

More lovely, though, is the little Renaissance town of **Castiglione Olona**, southeast of the lake (there's a local station about 3km away, on the Nord-Milano line to Varese). Castiglione

Olona owes its quattrocento Florentine charm to Cardinal Branda Castiglioni (1350–1443), a native who went on to serve as a bishop in Hungary and briefly in Florence, where he was so enchanted by the blossoming Renaissance that he brought Masolino and other Florentine artists home with him to do up the town. Among their works are the frescoes in the cardinal's birthplace, the **Casa dei Castiglioni**, with Masolino's fresco of Veszprem, Hungary, as decribed to him by the cardinal; and the Brunelleschi-style **Chiesa di Villa** on Piazza Garibaldi, a cube surmounted by a hemispherical dome. Walk up Via Cardinal Branda to the Gothic-Lombard **Collegiata**, built over the Castiglioni castle. It contains beautiful frescoes, with Masolino contributing several on the life of the Virgin; his greatest work is in the separate **Baptistry**, the old tower of the castle. On the first Sunday of each month, Castiglione holds the *Fiera del Cardinale*, an antiques fair and flea market.

In **Castelséprio**, there are even more surprising wall paintings in the ancient Longobard **Santa Maria Foris Portas**, once the parish church of a town that was destroyed in the 13th century. Its unique, 8th-century frescoes were discovered during the Second World War by a partisan hiding here; no one knows who painted them, but the style shows an exotic, Eastern influence.

## Lake Lugano

Zigzagged Lake Lugano with its steep, wooded fjord-like shores is more than half Swiss; the Italians, when they want to make a point about it, call it Lake Ceresio. Its most important town, Lugano, is the capital of the Canton of Ticino. The Swiss snatched it from Milan way back in 1512, and when the canton had a chance to return to Italy a couple of centuries later it stalwartly refused. Nevertheless, Italy maintains a wee island of territory in the middle of the lake, Campione d'Italia, which is just big enough to support a prosperous casino that more than welcomes Swiss francs. If you can't beat them, soak them.

### Getting Around

The main approach to the lake is from Varese, which has a **train** to Porto Ceresio and a bus to Ponte Tresa. Both of these are **steamer** calls on the *Società Navigazione Lago di Lugano* line, with several links daily to Lugano, from where you can continue east back to Italian territory (Porlezza or Osteno). You can also approach from Lake Como; **buses** from Como or Menaggio go to Porlezza. Varese is served by both the FS and Milano-Nord from Milan—the stations in Varese are next to each other.

**By road** you can approach the lake from Milan via Varese, to reach the Italian side, on the A8, or via Como on the A8 and then the A9, which runs directly to Lugano.

### Tourist Information

The **Varese** tourist office is at Via Carrobbio 2, ℰ (0332) 283604. There is also an office in **Campione d'Italia**, at Via Volta 16, ℰ (091) 685051.

## Varese

A garden city of shoe-manufacturers, Varese serves as a departure point for visiting lakes
Maggiore or Lugano, Castiglione Olona or **Sacro Monte**, reached by bus from the station.
Supposedly founded by St Ambrose in gratitude for Lombardy's safe deliverance from the
Arian heresy, Sacro Monte's church of Santa Maria has since been lavishly rebuilt in the
Rococo style; pilgrims ascend from the Prima Cappella along the Sacred Way, marked by 14
11th-century chapels dedicated to the Mysteries of the Rosary. There are fine views from
Sacro Monte, and even finer ones if you continue up to the karst massif of the **Parco
Naturale di Campo dei Fiori**. If you just have an hour or two to kill in Varese, head for the
**Giardino Pubblico**, formerly the 18th-century park of the Este dukes of Modena; there's a
hodgepodge of archaeology and art in the park's **Museo Civico** (*open 9–12, 3–5,
Tues–Sun*), housed in the Villa Mirabello.

## Lake Lugano

Lugano slowly drains its rather polluted waters into Lake Maggiore through the Tresa, a river
that forms the border between the Italian and Swiss halves of the village of **Ponte Tresa**.
There's not much to see in either half beyond the steamer landing, but if from Varese you
head instead to Lugano's other Italian landing at **Porto Ceresio**, you can take in along the
way the pretty 16th-century **Villa Cicogna Mozzoni** (*open May–Oct 9–12, 2–6, daily*) at
Bisuschio, near the little resort of **Viggiú**; the villa is especially interesting for its frescoes by
the Campi brothers and their school, and also has a fine garden. From Porto Ceresio the
steamer enters Swiss territory (bring your passport), passing the pretty village of **Morcote** on
route to **Campione d'Italia**.

In the Middle Ages, before state-sanctioned gambling was invented, the once-independent
fief of Campione was celebrated for its master builders, who like other medieval artists
worked anonymously, and are known to history only as the Campionesi Masters. They had a
hand in most of Italy's great Romanesque cathedrals—in Cremona, Monza, Verona,
Modena, and Sant'Ambrogio in Milan—and such was their reputation that when the Hagia
Sophia in Constantinople began to sag, the Byzantine Emperor hired the Campionesi Masters
to prop it up. In their hometown they left only a small sample of their handiwork, **San
Pietro** (1326). A later, Baroque-coated church of the **Madonna dei Ghirli** (Our Lady of the
Swallows) has a fine exterior fresco from 1400 of the Last Judgement, and several others
from the same period in the interior. Campione uses Swiss money and postal services and
has no border formalities.

## Lugano

The scenery improves as you near Lugano, set between Monte Brè and Monte San Salvatore.
A popular resort, it has two main sights, the 16th-century Franciscan church of **Santa Maria
degli Angioli**, containing striking frescoes by Bernardino Luini, considered his greatest
masterpiece; Ruskin, who wrote that Luini was 'ten times greater than Leonardo', saw these
frescoes and gushed, 'Every touch he lays is ethereal; every thought he conceives is beauty
and purity...' The second sight, the **Villa Favorita**, has a collection of paintings amassed by

Baron Heinrich von Thyssen-Bornemisza: most of the Old Masters are at present showing in Madrid and Barcelona, but the villa retains a permanent exhibition of European and American modern art. A popular excursion is to continue down the south arm of the lake to **Capolago** and take the rack railway up to the summit of Monte Generoso for the view.

East of Lugano, the lake returns to Italy, in the province of Como. **Santa Margherita** on the south shore has a cableway up to the panoramic Belvedere; 2km above the Belvedere, from the resort of **Lanzo d'Intelvi**, there are even more wide ranging views. **San Mamete**, a steamer landing on the north shore, is the prettiest village in the area, with its castle and the quiet Valsolda behind. **Osteno** has fine views of the lake, and boat excursions up the watery ravine of the River Orrido. From **Porlezza** you can catch a bus for Menaggio on Lake Como, passing on the way the tiny, enchanting Lago di Piano.

---

℗ *(0344–)*                                              *Where to Stay and Eat*

In San Mamete, the ★★★**Stella d'Italia**, ℗ 68139, @ 68729, is a lovely, moderate-range lakeside hotel, with a lido, garden, and waterside terraces. Each room has a balcony looking over a tranquil vision of mountain and lake, and you can borrow the hotel's boat for outings. All rooms have private bath. (*Open April–Oct.*)

In Porlezza there are more choices; try the inexpensive ★★**Rosen-Garden**, ℗ 62228, which has ten comfortable rooms, all with bath near the lake, and is open all year, or, in the moderate price category, ★★**Regina**, Piazza Matteoti 11, ℗/@ 61228 (moderate) with quiet and simple rooms on the lake, all with bath. The Regina also has a fine restaurant, featuring good homemade pasta and specialities like breast of duck with grapes.

## Lake Como

Sapphire Lake Como has been Italy's prestige romantic lake ever since the earliest days of the Roman empire, when the Plinys wrote of the luxuriant beauty surrounding their several villas on its shores. It was just the sort of luxuriant beauty that enraptured the children of the Romantic era, inspiring some of the best works of Verdi, Rossini, Bellini, and Liszt, as well as enough good and bad English verse to fill an anthology. And it is still there, the Lake Como of the Shelleys and Wordsworths, the grand villas and lush gardens, the mountains and beloved irregular shore of wooded promontories. The English still haunt their traditional English shore, but most of the visitors to Como these days are Italian, and there are times when the lake seems schizophrenic, its nostalgic romance and mellowed dignity battered by modern demands that it be the Milanese Riviera. Even so, Como is large and varied enough to offer retreats where, to paraphrase Longfellow's ode to the lake, no sound of Vespa or high heel breaks the silence of the summer day.

Third-largest of the lakes, 50km long but only 4.4km at its widest point, Como (or Lario) is one of the deepest lakes in Europe, plunging down 410m near Argegno. It forks in the middle like a pair of legs, the east branch known as the Lago di Lecco for its biggest town, while the prettiest region is the centre, where Como appears to be three separate lakes, and where towns like Tremezzo and Bellagio have been English enclaves for 200 years. One legacy of the English are the seven excellent golf courses in the province, while the waters around Domaso are excellent for windsurfing. As a rule, the further you go from the city of Como, the cleaner the lake.

## Getting Around

There are frequent FS **trains** from Milan's Centrale or Porta Garibaldi stations, taking you in some 40 minutes to Como's main San Giovanni Station (information ℂ (031) 261494). Slower trains run on the regional Milan-Nord line to the lakeside station of Como-Lago. From Como, trains to Lugano and Lecco all depart from San Giovanni. Lecco is connected by rail with Milan, Como, and Bergamo; from Lecco the line up to the Valtellina follows the eastern shore as far north as Cólico (Lecco rail information ℂ (0341) 364130). **Buses** from Como run to nearly every town on the lake.

To get to the west shore of the lake **by road** from Milan the most direct route is to take the A8 *autostrada* out of the city, and then the A9, which leads directly past Como town. For Lecco and the eastern lake the main roads are the SP42 from Milan and the SS342 from Bergamo.

**Steamers** and **hydrofoils** are operated by *Navigazione Lago di Como*, based on the lake in Como at Piazza Cavour, ℂ 304060, and in Lecco at Lungolario C. Battisti, ℂ 364036, where you can pick up schedules and tourist passes. There are frequent connections between Como, Tremezzo, Menaggio, Bellagio, Varenna, and Cólico, with additional services in the central lake, and generally at least one boat a day to Lecco. **Car ferries** run between Bellagio, Varenna, and Cadenabbia. Some services cease altogether in the winter.

## Tourist Information

In **Como** there are tourist offices at Piazza Cavour 17, ℂ (031) 262091, @ 261152, and in the San Giovanni railway station, ℂ (031) 267214. They distribute a free monthly booklet, *Turismo Proposte*, with a complete list of events and concerts around the lake. There are also offices in **Bellagio**, Lungolago A. Manzoni 1, ℂ (031) 950204; **Cernobbio**, at Via Regina 33b, ℂ (031) 510198; **Lecco**, Via Nazario Sauro 6, ℂ (0341) 362360, @ 286231; **Menaggio**: Via Lusardi 8, ℂ (0344) 32924; and **Tremezzo**, at Piazza Fabio Filzi 2, ℂ (0344) 40493

## The City of Como

Magnificently located at the southern tip of the lake, Como was captured from the Gauls by the Romans in the 2nd century BC. In AD 23 it was the birthplace of Pliny the Elder, compiler of antiquity's greatest work of hearsay, the *Natural History*, and later of his nephew and heir, Pliny the Younger, whose letters are one of our main sources for the cultured Roman life of the period. In the 11th century Como enjoyed a brief period as an independent *comune*, but it was too close to Milan and the Visconti to remain so for long, and from 1335 on it has been ruled by Milan. For centuries it has been the leading Italian silk city, and, while silk worms are no longer raised on the lake, Chinese thread is woven and dyed here to the specifications of the Milanese fashion industry (as displayed in Como's biggest silk shop, Centro della Seta, at Via Volta 64 and Via Bellinzona 3). Even if you're just passing through to the more serene resorts, Como merits a brief visit; part of its charm is that the historic centre, still bearing the imprint of its Roman plan, is closed to traffic.

Life in Como revolves around the busy lakeside **Piazza Cavour**, with its cafés, hotels, steamer landing, and pretty views. West of Piazza Cavour, the *Giardini Pubblici* have two landmarks: the circular neoclassical **Tempio Voltiano**, dedicated to Como's electrifying native son, physicist Alessandro Volta, which contains a display of his instruments (*open April–Sept 10–12, 3–6, Tues–Sun; Oct–Mar 10–12, 2–4, Tues–Sun; adm*); and the War Memorial by futurist architect Antonio Sant'Elia.

From Piazza Cavour Via Plinio leads back to the elegant Piazza Duomo, adorned with the colourful striped town hall, or **Broletto**, the **Torre del Comune** (both early 13th century), and the magnificent **Duomo**, considered Italy's best example of the transition from Gothic to Renaissance. The Gothic is revealed in the lovely rose window and in the pinnacles on the main façade; over the side doors note the fine carving by the Rodari brothers, while on either side of the central portal under delicate stone canopies are Renaissance statues of Pliny the Elder on the left and Pliny the Younger on the right. What, you might ask, are ancient Romans doing on a cathedral? Although Pliny the Younger did once write a famous letter to Emperor Trajan on the subject of Christians, praising their hard work and suggesting that they be left alone, in fact the Renaissance tended to look at all noble figures of antiquity as honorary saints. Inside, the three Gothic aisles combine happily with a Renaissance choir and transept; the rows of 16th-century tapestries lend a palatial feel, and there are paintings by two of Leonardo's followers, Luini (*Madonna and Child*) and Ferrari (*Marriage of the Virgin*).

Down the main street, Via Vittorio Emanuele, the 12th-century **San Fedele** has a unique pentagonal apse and a doorway carved with portly medieval figures. Further up the street, in the Piazza Medaglie d'Oro Comasche, the **Museo Civico** (*open 9.30–12.30, 2–5, Tues–Sat; 9.30–12.30 Sun*) is the city's attic of artefacts, dating from the Neolithic era up until the Second World War. Como also has a small **Pinacoteca**, Via Diaz 84 (*open 9.30–12.30, 2–5, Tues–Sat; 9.30–12.30 Sun; adm*), which contains carved capitals and wonderful medieval paintings from the old monastery of Santa Margherita del Broletto. Particularly striking are a placid *St Sebastian* shot through with arrows, and the poignant *Youth and Death*, both anonymous.

From the Piazza Medaglie d'Oro Comasche, continue down Via Giovio to the **Porta Vittoria**, a striking gate from 1192 topped with five tiers of arches. Como's Romanesque gem, the 11th-century **Sant'Abbondio**, is a short walk away in an industrial suburb; from the Porta Vittoria, follow Viale Cattaneo to Viale Roosevelt, cross and turn left to Via S. Abbondio. Well restored in the 19th century, the church has five aisles, and 14th-century frescoes of knights in medieval armour coming to arrest Christ in Gethsemane.

For great views over the lake take the funicular up **Brunate**, the hill overlooking Como. The station is on the Lungolario Trieste, near the main beach.

A short hop away on the train towards Lecco is lace-making **Cantù**, where you'll find the 10th-century **Basilica di San Vicenzo** (a 20-minute walk to the east of the station, in the neighbouring village of Galliano; follow the signs); inside it is decorated with a remarkable fresco cycle painted just after the millennium (check opening hours in the Como tourist office before setting out). The chief landmark of Cantù is the tall, minaret-like Romanesque campanile of its parish church.

---

*Como ℰ (031–)*  ***Where to Stay***

One of the newest and most luxurious hotels in town is the ★★★★**Palace Hotel**, Lungolago Trieste 16, ℰ (031) 303303, ℯ 303170 (very expensive). Partly built in the former palace of the Archbishop, its rooms are big and modern, and some have fax machines. There are extensive conference facilities, and a huge banqueting hall. On Como's main Piazza Cavour, overlooking the lake, the ★★★★**Barchetta Excelsior**, ℰ (031) 3221, ℯ 302622, (expensive) is a grand old hotel, with many rooms boasting balconies over the piazza and lake. (*Open all year.*) In a garden just outside Como on the west shore is ★★★★**Villa Flori**, Via Cernobbio 12, ℰ (031) 573105, ℯ 570379, (expensive). All rooms with bath. (*Open all year.*) For character, charm and a large amount of history, *the* place to stay in Como is ★★★★**Le Due Corti**, Piazza Vittoria 15, ℰ (031) 328111, ℯ 328800, (expensive). Originally an ancient monastery, and then a post house, it reopened in 1992 as a hotel. Rooms are arranged around the original monastic courtyard and all are individual, preserving much of their original architecture. Design is meticulous, with only local fabrics used, antique furniture and old prints on the walls. Concessions to modernity include air-conditioning, satellite TV, minibar and jacuzzis in some bathrooms. The suites are particularly lovely.

★★★**Park Hotel**, Viale Rosselli 20, ℰ (031) 572615, ℯ 574302, (moderate) is a medium–sized establishment near the lake, without a restaurant; also a ghood choice is ★★★**Marco's**, Via Coloniola 43, ℰ (031) 303628, ℯ 302342, (moderate), with 11 small rooms, all with TV, phone, bathroom and balcony. A clean, cosy and friendly little hotel, with a small restaurant, is the ★**Sole**, Via Borgovico 89/91, ℰ/ℯ (031) 573382 (inexpensive).

---

*Como ℰ (031–)*  ***Eating Out***

Como is one of those towns where the restaurants tend to process clients with slipshod food and service, especially in summer. **Perlasca**, Piazza de'Gasperi 8, ℰ/ℯ (031) 303936 (expensive) run by four brothers, two in the kitchen and two out front, is one place that does not. The menu changes almost every day and according to season, and features typical dishes like *filetto di laverello*, a fish only found in this part of the lake, and *fettuccine e funghi*, a peerless pasta with local mushrooms. The restaurant also enjoys wonderful views over the lake.

**Sant'Ana**, Via Filippo Turati 3, ℰ (031) 505266, (expensive) is also a good, old, family establishment, more frequented by toilers in the silk trade than tourists, featuring well-prepared if unadventurous Lombard specialities; good risotto with radicchio, and trout with almonds. (*Closed Mon.*)

There are not many good cheap restaurants in the area, but in Como the **Sole** hotel (inexpensive) has a pleasant little restaurant with reasonable prices.

## From Como to Tremezzina

Zigzagging back and forth from shore to shore, the steamer is the ideal way to travel around the lake, allowing you to drink in the marvellous scenery. The first steamer landing, **Cernobbio**, is an old resort, the 1816-17 retreat of Queen Caroline of England, who held her wild parties in what is now the fabulous Hotel Villa d'Este. Across the lake, near the steamer landing of ancient **Torno**, stands the 16th-century **Villa Pliniana**, which so charmed Shelley that he tried to buy it; its name is derived from its peculiar intermittent spring described in a letter of Pliny the Younger (check at the Como tourist office to see if it's been reopened for visits.) The area has been fertile soil for operas; Rossini composed *Tancredi* in the Villa Pliniana, while Bellini composed *Norma* and *La Sonnambula* in other villas nearby.

Back on the west shore, **Argegno** enjoys one of the most privileged positions on the lake, with views of the snow-clad mountains to the north and access to the west into the pretty Val d'Intelvi, which culminates at the summer/winter resort of **Lanzo d'Intelvi**, overlooking Lake Lugano.

Beyond Argegno (still on the west shore), lies the pretty islet of **Comacina**, sprinkled with the ruins of ancient churches, and beyond that the district of **Tremezzina**, where the description of the lake as the 'mirror of Venus' hardly seems extravagant. Totally sheltered, the Tremezzina enjoys the most benign climate on Lake Como, lined in the spring with carpets of azaleas, agaves, camellias, rhododendrons and magnolias under the towering cypresses and palms. **Lenno**, the southernmost village, is believed to have been the site of Pliny the Younger's villa 'Comedia'; in one of his letters he describes how he could fish from his bedroom window. No remains of the villa have ever been found, but you can visit the fine 11th-century octagonal **baptistry** of the parish church. It was in this lovely setting, in front of a posh villa in nearby Mezzegra, that Mussolini and his mistress Claretta Petacci were executed by local partisans. They had been captured along the north shore of the lake, attempting to flee in a German truck to Switzerland. Claretta was killed trying to shield *Il Duce* from the bullets.

## Villa Carlotta

The main towns of the Tremezzina are the popular English resorts of **Tremezzo** and **Cadenabbia**, served by an old Anglican church. Between the two lies the most popular attraction on Lake Como, the **Villa Carlotta** (*open Mar, Oct 9–12, 2–4.30, daily; April–Sept 9am–6pm daily; adm*). Originally built in 1747 as the Villa Clerici, the villa took its name from its subsequent owner, Princess Carlotta of Prussia, who laid out the magnificent formal gardens and park in the 1850s. In April and May the thousands of azaleas and rhododendrons put on a dazzling display of colour, but no matter when you come you can also take in the neoclassical interior with its cool, virtuoso, irritatingly insufferable neoclassical statuary, among which Canova's passionate *Cupid and Psyche* holds pride of place. Ponder, if you can, the Icelander Bertel Thorvaldsen's frieze of Alexander entering Babylon, commissioned by Napoleon but completed after Waterloo for another client who picked up the considerable tab. In another villa in Cadenabbia, Verdi composed *La Traviata*.

## Bellagio

High on the headland where the lake forks, enjoying one of the most scenic positions in all Italy, Bellagio (from the Latin *bi-lacus*) is a fine old town that has managed to maintain an air of quiet dignity through the centuries, perhaps because even now, with its silk industry, it doesn't depend totally on tourism. A bus from the pier will take you to the **Villa Serbelloni**, now the Study and Conference Centre of the Rockefeller Foundation. Most scholars believe this stands on the site of Pliny's villa 'Tragedia', higher over the lake than his villa 'Comedia', and so named not only because tragedy was considered a 'loftier' art, but because in his day tragic actors wore high heels. The villa itself is closed to visitors, but you can walk through the park on a two-hour guided tour between April and October (*open 10.30am–4pm Tues–Sun; adm*). Another villa in Bellagio open for visits, the **Villa Melzi** (*open April–Oct 9am–6.30pm daily*), also has a fine garden and greenhouse, while the villa itself contains a collection of Egyptian sculpture. In the centre of Bellagio, the 12th-century church of **San Giacomo** has interesting carvings.

Back on the west shore, **Menaggio** is another pleasant resort, with a lovely golf course and beach. It lies at the head of two valleys: the Val Menaggio, an easy route to Lake Lugano, and the **Valle Sanagra**, from where you can make one of the finest ascents on the lake, the day-long walk up to panoramic **Monte Bregagno**, departing from the Villa Calabi.

**Varenna**, the main village on the east shore of the lake, is near Lake Como's most curious natural wonder, the **Fiumelatte** ('river of milk'), Italy's second shortest river, running only 250m before hurtling down in creamy foam into Lake Como. For the Fiumelatte, as its name implies, is as white as milk. Not even Leonardo da Vinci, who delved deep into the cavern from which it flows, could discover its source, or why it abruptly begins to flow in the last days of March and abruptly ceases at the end of October. The best route up is to follow the signposted path from Varenna, passing a tiny cemetery on the way. The walk takes only 15min, and the views along the way are wonderful. Varenna also has a couple of villas and gardens open for tours, including the **Villa Monastero** (*open April–Sept 10–12.30, 2.30–6.30, daily; adm*), built on the site of a 13th-century monastery; the garden, adorned with statues and bas-reliefs, is especially known for its citrus trees. The nearby **Villa Cipressi** (*same times and price*) has a very fine garden. The most interesting church is the Romanesque **San Giorgio**, adorned with a giant exterior fresco of St Christopher, while the nearby **Oratorio di San Giovanni Battista**, built around the millennium, is one of the oldest surviving churches on the lake. The castle high above Varenna, the ruined **Castello Vezio**, was, according to legend, founded by Queen Theodolinda; you can drive up for the fantastic view. Another east shore village, **Bellano**, lies at the bottom of the steep gorge of the River Pioverna. It has a fine Lombard church, **Santi Nazaro e Celso** (1348), by the

Campionesi masters (*open Easter–Sept 9.30am–5.30pm, closed Wed*) and a remarkable walkway through the gorge over the river.

Across on the west shore, visitors to Venice will recognize the name of the hamlet of **Rezzonico**, cradle of the family that built one of the grandest palaces on the Grand Canal and produced Pope Clement XIII. Further up, looming over Musso, the lofty, almost inaccessible **Rocca di Musso** was the castle stronghold of Lake Como's notorious pirate, Gian Giacomo de' Medici, nicknamed 'Il Medeghino', born during the Medici exile from Florence in 1498. He gained the castle from Francesco II, Duke of Milan, for helping to remove the French from Milan and assassinating the duke's best friend; he made it the base for his fleet of armed ships that patrolled the lake and extorted levies from towns and traders. He ended his career as the Marquis of Marignano, helping Charles V oppress the burghers of Ghent. His brother became the intriguing Pope Pius IV, while his nephew was St Charles Borromeo, the holy scourge of Milan.

Next on the lake, **Dongo, Gravedona**, and **Sorico** once formed the independent republic of the Three Parishes that endured until the arrival of the Spaniards. In the Middle Ages the little republic was plagued by the attentions of the inquisitor Peter of Verona, who sent scores of citizens to the stake for daring to doubt that the pope was Christ's representative on earth. Peter got a hatchet in his head for his trouble—and a quick canonization from the pope as St Peter Martyr. Gravedona was and still is the most important town of the three; it has a 12th-century church, the small **Santa Maria del Tiglio**, believed to have been originally a baptistry, with frescoes of St John the Baptist; it has some fine carvings (the centaur pursuing a deer is Early Christian symbolism, representing the persecution of the Church), and an unusual tower. Nearby is another ancient church, **San Vicenzo**, with a 5th-century crypt. Back on the east shore, **Cólico**, near the mouth of the Adda, is the gateway to the Valtellina (*see* below).

---

## Lecco and its Lake

The Lago di Lecco, the less touristy leg of Lake Como, resembles a brooding fjord, with granite mountains plunging down steeply into the water, a misty landscape beloved by Leonardo. **Lecco** itself is an industrial but pleasant city, lying at the foot of jagged Mount Resegone, where the River Adda continues its journey south (a typical entry in Pliny's *Natural History* records how the River Adda passes through the entire lake without mingling its waters). Lecco was the birthplace of Alessandro Manzoni (1785–1873) and the setting of his novel, *I Promessi Sposi* ('The Betrothed'), a 19th-century classic that embodies Manzoni's liberal, pro-unification attitudes. There is a small museum in his boyhood home, the **Villa Manzoni** on Via Guanella (*open Mar–May 9.30am–6pm, Tues–Sun; June–April 9.30am–2pm, Tues–Sun; adm*). Also to see in Lecco are the 14th-century fortified bridge over the Adda built by the Visconti, which survives without its towers, and Lecco's **basilica**, adorned with 14th-century Giottoesque frescoes. The prettiest square in town is the Piazza XX Settembre, just under the Visconti tower.

The villages on the lake shore seem rather melancholy after the gardens and villas on the west branch of the lake. The mighty **Grigna mountains** dominating the east shore offer a number of ascents and excursions departing from **Mandello del Lario**.

# La Brianza

Between Lecco and Como are five baby-sized lakes in the pretty, wine-growing, furniture-making region called **La Brianza**. The first town, **Civate**, was the site of a famous Benedictine abbey, **San Calocero**, founded in 705, with 11th-century frescoes and nothing less than the keys of St Peter given him by Christ. Ask the sacristan at Civate's parish church for the key before setting out on the 1hr walk to 10th-century **San Pietro al Monte**, with its remarkable frescoes of the Apocalypse, rare baldacchino from 1050 and ornate crypt. The adjacent **Oratorio di San Benedetto** has an unusual 12th-century painted altar.

### Sports and Activities

There are superb walks and hikes of varying degrees of difficulty from virtually every one of the towns around the lake; local tourist offices can suggest possible itineraries. Boats too can be hired in most of the lakeside towns, and there are good public beaches in Como, at Villa Geno, and at the Lido in Menaggio, where there is also a large swimming pool. There are also plenty of golf courses around the lake—Como town has a full 18-hole course 4km from the town in Montorfano, and there is a particularly beautiful course at Menaggio.

### Where to Stay

#### Erba

★★★★★**Castello di Pomerio**, Via Como 5, ℰ (031) 627516, ℰ 628245 (very expensive). Away from the lake itself and halfway between Como and Lecco, a 12th-century castle has been converted into a lovely hotel. The interior has been meticulously restored, right down to the frescoes. Many rooms have fireplaces, and massive wooden beds (but modern bathrooms); the public rooms are furnished with antiques, and it has indoor and outdoor pools and tennis courts.

#### Cernobbio

★★★★★**Villa d'Este**, Cernobbio, Lago di Como, ℰ (031) 511471, ℰ 512027, (luxury). This famous hotel, the most palatial on Lake Como, was originally built in 1557 by Cardinal Tolomeo Gallio, the son of a local fisherman who went on to become one of the most powerful men in the Vatican—besides this villa, he had seven along the road to Rome so he never had to spend a night not under his own roof. Queen Caroline was not the only crowned head to make use of the Cardinal's old digs, and since 1873 it has been a hotel. Each room is individual, furnished with antiques or fine reproductions, the public rooms are regal, the food is superb, and the glorious gardens in themselves a reason to stay. There is a swimming pool literally on the lake, another indoor pool, a fine golf course, squash, tennis, sailing, nightclub, dancing and more. Be warned that the rooms cost a king's ransom too, at L600,000 or more for a double. (*Open April–Oct.*) On the other hand there is the ★★**Terzo Crotto**, Via Volta 21, ℰ (031) 512304 (inexpensive), with nine rooms, all with bath, and also an excellent good-value restaurant.

## Tremezzo

A large, comfortable 19th-century hotel next door to Villa Carlotta is the ★★★★**Grand Hotel**, Via Regina 8, Tremezzo, ✆ (0344) 40446, ✉ 40201 (expensive). Besides its garden and pool, it has large rooms with good views on all sides. (*Open mid-Feb–mid-Dec.*) ★★**Villa Marie**, Via Regina 30, ✆ (0344) 40427 (inexpensive) is an intimately Victorian hotel with 15 pleasant rooms overlooking the lake and a shady garden. (*Open April–Oct.*)

## Cadenabbia

On the western shore in Cadenabbia, right on the lake and charmingly old-fashioned, the ★★★★**Bellevue**, Via Regina 1, ✆ (0344) 40418, ✉ 41466, (moderate) is a large but very pleasant place to stay, with plenty of sun terraces, garden, and pool. (*Open 20 Mar–10 Oct*) ★★★**Britannia Excelsior**, Via Regina 42, ✆ (0344) 40413, (inexpensive) is a cosy old hotel in Cadenabbia set in a piazza overlooking the lake; lots of rooms with balconies, some without bathrooms. (*Open April–Oct.*)

## Bellagio

★★★★★**Grand Hotel Villa Serbelloni**, Via Roma 1, ✆ (031) 950216, ✉ 951529 , (very expensive). Bellagio is one of the most romantic places to stay on the lake, and it has several fine hotels. This is a magnificent ornate villa, set in a flower-filled garden, and enjoying some of Como's finest views. The frescoed public rooms are glittering and palatial, and there's a heated pool and private beach, tennis, boating and water-skiing, and dancing in the evening to the hotel orchestra. The rooms range from palatial suites to some that are a bit faded. (*Open April–Oct.*)

A genial 16th-century hotel near the centre of Bellagio is the ★★★**Hotel Du Lac**, Piazza Mazzini, ✆ (031) 950320, ✉ 951 624, (moderate), located on a terrace next to the lake. The rooftop garden has a fine view over the lake, and the comfortable rooms all have bath. Located in a 19th-century villa, the ★★★**Firenze**, Piazza Mazzini 46, ✆ (031) 950342, ✉ 951722 (moderate) is right next to Bellagio's harbour. The terraces and many of the rooms have lake views, and there's a cosy lobby with heavy beams and a Florentine fireplace. The rooms (some without baths) are good and unpretentious. (*Open mid-April–mid-Oct.*) Also on the lake-front, the ★★★**Excelsior Splendide**, Via Lungo Lario Manzoni 28, ✆ (031) 950225, ✉ 951224, has a touching, fading charm, big, old rooms (most with a view, though be sure to ask), a pool and its own garden. With slightly smaller rooms, and less character, but lake views, there's the ★★★**Metropole**, Piazza Mazzini 1, ✆ (031) 950409, ✉ 951534, (moderate), and for simple accommodation available all year round, near the lake, try ★**La Spiaggia**, Via Paolo Carcano 21, ✆ (031) 950313 (inexpensive); most of its rooms are without baths.

## Menaggio

A hotel that was built in 1806 next to the lake is the ★★★★**Grand Hotel Victoria**, Via Castelli 7, ✆ (0344) 32003, ✉ 32992 (expensive), and during recent renovation its original décor was carefully preserved while it was complemented with creature comforts like designer bathrooms, TVs, and minibars. The public rooms are quite elegant, and there's a pool in the garden. (*Open all year.*) A more modern establishment which also stands in its own grounds on the lake is the ★★★★**Grand Hotel Menaggio**, Via IV Novembre 69, ✆ (0344) 32640, ✉ 32350, (expensive). Rooms are modern and fully equipped, most of them with a stunning view, and there's a pool and conference facilities. ★★★**Bellavista**, Via IV Novembre 21, ✆ (0344) 32136, ✉ 31793 (moderate) is right on the lake, and also has nice rooms. (*Open Mar–Dec.*) Menaggio's very fine **youth hostel**, the **Ostello La Primula**, Via IV Novembre 38, ✆ (0344) 32356, (inexpensive) has beds at L12,000 per night and a restaurant serving some of the best cheap meals in the area. (*Open Mar–Oct.*)

## Varenna

★★★★**Hotel Royal Victoria**, Piazza S. Giorgio 5, ✆ (0341) 830102, ✉ 830722 (expensive) is a fine old hotel on the eastern shore of the lake which was completely renovated in 1981. Right on the lakeside, in the midst of a 19th-century Italian garden, it has 45 very comfortable rooms, all with en suite bath and minibar. (*Open all year.*) There is also the ★★★★**Hotel du Lac**, Via del Prestino 4, ✆ (0341) 830238, ✉ 831081 (expensive), which, as its name suggests, is right on the lake, with rooms and bathrooms that are very small though fully equipped, and marvellous views. There's also a good lakeside restaurant at lake level. One of the best places to stay in Varenna is the ★★★**Albergo Milano**, Via XX Settembre 29, ✆ (031) 830298 (moderate), a lovely, family-run place in an exquisite setting, with eight rooms all of which have bathrooms, balconies and wonderful views. The ones to request, though (months in advance), are numbers 1 or 2, with their large terraces, ideal for couples and incurable romantics.

## Lecco

Just over a kilometre outside Lecco, at Malgrate, ★★★★**Il Griso** Via Statale 29, (0341) 202040, ✉ 202248 (expensive) is a moderate-sized but elegant hotel with fine views of the lake from its wide terrace. There's a pool in the garden, and one of the region's best gourmet restaurants (*see* below). The ★★★**Moderno**, Piazza Diaz 5, ✆ (0341) 288519, ✉ 362177 (moderate) is not very characterful, but it has adequate rooms with all modern facilities. A tiny hotel which has the advantage of being right on the lake, and has very cheaply priced rooms without bathrooms, is the ★**Alberi**, Lungolago Isonzo 4, ✆ (0341) 363440, (inexpensive, *open all year.*)

---

### *Eating Out*

## Cernobbio

The restaurant in the **Terzo Crotto** in Cernobbio (inexpensive; *see* above) provides delicious dinners for around L35,000.

## Comacina

The islet of Comacina, dotted with the interesting ruins of its numerous churches, is deserted except for a restaurant, the 50-year-old **Locanda dell'Isola Comacina**, ℂ (0344) 55083. For one fixed price (L50,000) you are picked up in a boat at Cala Comacina or Ossuccio (near Lenno), and given a fine meal including an antipasto of vegetables, ham, and sausage, followed by grilled trout, fried chicken, wine, and dessert, and a return trip to the mainland. (*Open April–Nov.*)

## Tremezzo

The best place to dine in the area of Tremezzo is by common consent **Velu**, ℂ (0344) 40510 , 1½km up in the hills at Rogara di Tremezzo. From the terrace you can see the lake shimmering below, once the home of the fish on the menu. Good basic Italian meat courses are served as well, and excellent fresh vegetables. (*Open April Oct; closed Tues.*) Another of the best restaurants in the area is in the **Il Griso** hotel in Malgrate, near Lecco (*see* above). Reservations are essential.

## Menaggio

Some of the best cheap meals in the region, at around L12,000, are available in the youth hostel, the **Ostello La Primula**, in Menaggio (*see* above).

## Viganò Brianza

If you're touring in the Brianza south of Lake Como, the little village of Viganò Brianza, halfway between Como and Milan, is worth a special trip for its restaurant **Piero**, Via XXIV Maggio 26, ℂ (039) 956020 (expensive). Delicious regional specialities complement the chef's own innovations, and there's an excellent wine list. (*Closed Sun evenings, Mon, Aug.*)

## Beyond Como: the Valleys of Sondrio

North and east of Lake Como lies the mountainous and little-known province of Sondrio, sandwiched between the Orobie Alps and Switzerland. Its glacier-fed rivers not only flow into Como and the Mediterranean, but through the Danube to the Black Sea and through the Rhine into the North Sea. Only four roads link Sondrio's two main valleys, the Valchiavenna and the Valtellina, with the rest of Italy. The province is among the least-exploited Alpine regions, offering plenty of opportunities to see more of the mountains and fewer of your fellow creatures, especially in the western reaches.

When the Spanish Habsburgs took Milan, the Valtellina, with its many Protestants, joined the Swiss Confederation. Yet even though they didn't possess it, it was of prime importance to the Spaniards during the Counter-Reformation, assuring their trouble-making troops the link between Milan, Austria, and the Netherlands. In 1620, the Spanish in Milan instigated the 'Holy Butchery' of 400 Protestants in the valley by their Catholic neighbours. The valley rejoined Italy only in the Napoleonic partition of 1797.

## Getting Around

At Cólico the **railway** from Milan and Lecco forks, one line heading north as far as Chiavenna, the other heading east as far as Tirano before veering north towards St Moritz. Sondrio is served by an efficient network of **buses**. Several lines run into Switzerland from Sondrio, Tirano, and Chiavenna; and there are direct coach connections to Sondrio from Milan. If you're driving, the road up to the Valchiavenna is the SS36, which runs from Milan via Lecco, and from Bergamo via the SS342. Just north of Cólico the SS38 branches off the SS36 eastwards into the Valtellina.

## Tourist Information

The main tourist office in the region is in **Sondrio**, at Via C. Battisti 12, ℘ (0342) 512500, ✆ 212590. It can provide a full range of maps and information on walks and tracks in the surrounding mountains (*see* below, 'Sports and Activities'). There are also offices in **Aprica**, ℘ (0342) 746113, ✆ 747732; **Bormio**, Via Stelvio 10, ℘ (0342) 903300, ✆ 904696; **Chiesa in Valmalenco**, Piazza SS. Giacomo e Filippo 1, ℘ (0342) 451150, ✆ 452505; **Madesimo**, ℘ (0343) 53015, ✆ 53782; and **Livigno**, Via Gesa 55, ℘ (0342) 996379, ✆ 996881.

## Valchiavenna

In Roman times Lake Como extended as far north as **Samolaco**; between here and Cólico lies the marshy Piano di Spagna and the shallow Lake Mezzola, an important breeding ground for swans. On the west shore of the lake stands the 10th-century Romanesque chapel of **San Fedelino**; on the east **Novate Mezzola** is the base for walks in the enchanting and unspoiled **Val Codera**.

**Chiavenna**, the chief town in the district, is delightfully situated among the boulders of an ancient landslide in a lush valley. Amidst the rocks are natural cellars, the **Crotti**, which maintain a steady, year-round temperature and have long been used for ripening local cheeses and hams; some have been converted into popular wine cellars, celebrated in mid-September at the annual *Sagra dei Crotti*. The most important church in town, **San Lorenzo**, was begun in the 11th century and contains a treasure with a 12th-century golden 'Pax' cover for the Gospels; also note the carved octagonal font (1156) in the Romanesque Baptistry. Above the Palazzo Baliani you can walk up to **Paradiso** (*open 2–6pm Tues–Sat; 10.30–12.30, 2–6, Sun; adm*), the town's botanical park, with a small archaeological museum; another park, the **Marmitte dei Giganti**, 'the giants' kettles', actually contains glacial potholes and prehistoric etchings (*incisioni rupestri*).

East of Chiavenna, in the Val Bregaglia, the road towards Switzerland passes the **Acqua Fraggia**, a waterfall near Borgonuovo; a seemingly endless stair leads to the ancient hamlet of Savogno atop the cascade. In 1618, a huge landslide buried the town of **Piuro**, further up the valley; the excavations of this humble, 17th-century Pompeii, which you can visit, have revealed a number of finds now in the museum of the church of Sant'Abbondio in Borgonuovo. In another nearby village, **Aurogo**, the 12th-century church of **San Martino** contains contemporary frescoes.

North of Chiavenna, the **San Giacomo valley** becomes increasingly rugged and steep, with dramatic landslides, glaciers, and waterfalls. There are two summer/winter resorts on the road—**Campodolcino** and the more developed **Madesimo**—before you reach the **Splügen Pass** (2118m), generally closed six months of the year.

## The Valtellina

East of Cólico the SS38 enters the Valtellina, the valley of the River Adda. The old, vine-wrapped villages and numerous churches along the lower valley are part of the **Costiera del Cèch**, referring to its inhabitants, the Cèch, whose origin is as mysterious as the name. Their main town is **Morbegno**; from here buses make excursions towards the south, into the two scenic valleys, the **Valli del Bitto**, with iron ore deposits that made them a prize of the Venetians for two centuries, and the rural **Val Tartano**, a 'lost paradise', dotted with alpine cottages, woods, and pastures, its declining population still farming as their ancestors did centuries ago. The road through the valley was finished only in 1971, though many hamlets in the valley even today are accessible only by foot or mule. A third valley running to the north, the wild granite **Val Másino**, is traversed by the magnificent 'Sentiero Roma', and also serves as the base for the ascent of Monte Disgrazia (3680m) one of the highest peaks in the region. Near the village of Cataéggio, the landmark is an awesome granite boulder, the **Sasso Remenno**.

The provincial capital **Sondrio** is a modern town, dotted with a few old palaces and dominated by its oft-remodelled **Castello Masegra**, dating from 1041. The town's Palazzo Quadrio houses the ethnographic **Museo Valtellinese**, with archaeological and art collections. It is temporarily closed for restoration work, but in the same Palazzo you can also taste the upper Valtellina's famous red wines—Sassella, Grumello and the unusual Inferno. Rock hunters should not miss the valley north of Sondrio, the **Val Malenco**, mineralogically the richest valley in the Alps with 150 different kinds of minerals, including the commercially mined serpentine, or green marble. **Chiesa in Valmalenco** and **Caspoggio** are the main resorts, with skiing in the winter. The former has a small **Museo Storico Etnografico** (*open April–Oct 5–7pm daily; Nov–Mar 4.30–6.30pm Sun, holidays only; adm*), containing various stone objects found in the valley, from Roman times to the present day, such as ancient gourds and jars.

## The Upper Valtellina

The highway rises relentlessly through the valley; but if you're driving, take the scenic 'Castel road' running north of the highway and river from Sondrio, via Tresivio and the melancholy ruins of Grumello castle, then on to the old patrician town of **Ponte in Valtellina**. Ponte was the birthplace of astronomer Giuseppe Piazzi (1746–1826), discoverer of the first asteroid, but is mostly visited for its parish church of **San Maurizio**, and its unusual bronze *cimborio* (1578), or lantern, and frescoes by Bernardino Luini.

Further east along the castle road or highway, charming **Teglio** was the most important town of the Valtellina in the Middle Ages. It takes special pride in a dish called *pizzoccheri*, described as 'narcotic grey noodles with butter and vegetables', served up to bewildered visitors at the annual autumn *Sagra dei Pizzoccheri*. Teglio has the finest palace in the whole region, the **Palazzo Besta** (*open 9–12.30, 2.30–5.30, Tues–Sat; 9–12.30 Sun; adm*) from

1539, embellished with fine chiaroscuro frescoes in its Renaissance courtyard, and the **Antiquarium Tellinum** (*open April–Sept 9–1, 2.30–5.30 Tues–Sun; Oct–Mar 9–2 Tues–Sun; adm*), housing a fine example of local prehistoric rock carving, the 'Stele di Caven', among other examples of the valley's prehistoric art. **San Pietro** has a fine 12th-century campanile, while above Teglio the mighty stump of its old tower offers fine views of the valley. Among the old lanes, look for the house with blackened arcades, once residence of a particularly adept and sought-after executioner.

**Tirano**, the rail terminus, has a number of 16th- and 17th-century palaces and the Valtellina's Renaissance masterpiece, the **Sanctuary of the Madonna**, built in 1505 a kilo-metre from the centre; inside is an ornate, inlaid wood organ. Between Tirano and Teglio a road pushes southeast to the winter and summer resort of **Aprica**, with its school of competitive skiing, and beyond to Edolo in the Val Camonica (*see* p.307). Another road from Tirano follows the railway north into Switzerland to St Moritz.

The Stelvio road continues up to **Grosotto**; the organ in its church of the Virgin is a master-piece of the woodcarver's art. The large old village of **Grosio** has been important since prehistoric times, as witnessed by the engravings in its **Parco delle Incisioni Rupestri**, similar to those in the National Park in the Val Camonica. It's the last village in Lombardy where you can still see women wearing their traditional costumes; in the 16th century it was the birthplace of Cipriano Valorsa, nicknamed the 'Raphael of the Valtellina', who was responsible for most of the frescoes in the region's churches, including those in Grosotto's **San Giorgio** and the **Casa di Cipriano Valorsa**. The imposing if ruined castle and the finest palazzo in town belonged to the local lords, the Visconti-Venosta. **Sóndalo**, the next town, has a modern sanatorium and some courtly 16th-century frescoes in the church of Santa Marta.

# Bormio and Stelvio National Park

The seat of an ancient county, not unjustifiably called the 'Magnifica Terra', Bormio is a fine old town with many frescoed palaces, recalling the days of prosperity when Venice's Swiss trade passed through its streets. Splendidly situated in a mountain basin, it is a major ski centre (the 1985 World Alpine Ski Championships were held here), with numerous lifts and an indoor pool. The **Chiesa del Crocifisso** has fine 15th-century frescoes, and there's a spa in nearby **Bagni di Bormio**.

Bormio is the main entrance into the **Parco Nazionale Delle Stelvio**, Italy's largest national park, founded in 1935 and encompassing the grand alpine massif of Ortles-Cevedale. A tenth of the park's area is covered with glaciers, including one of Europe's largest, the *Ghiacciaio dei Forni*. The peaks offer many exciting climbs, on **Grand Zebrù** (3850m), **Ortles** (3905m) and **Cevedale** (3778m) among other peaks. It also includes Europe's second-highest pass, the **Passo di Stelvio**, through which you can continue into the Alto Adige and Bolzano between the months of June and October (*see* p.466); the pass is also an important winter and summer ski centre.

From Bormio the **Val di Dentro** heads east up towards the **Valle di Livigno**, another ski area, noted for its traditional wooden houses and trout fishing. Before reaching the valley, however, you must pass through Italian customs—it's a bustling duty-free zone, though its Forcola di Livigno, another pass into Switzerland, is open in summer only.

## Sports and Activities

Those interested in a trekking holiday through the region's most spectacular scenery should request the Sondrio tourist office's booklet *L'Avventura in Lombardia* which, though in Italian, details a fine 20-day trail from Novate Mezzola through Stelvio National Park down to Capo di Ponte; another booklet from the tourist office has a complete listing of the area's alpine refuges. Tourist offices also have information on **skiing** facilities in winter, but note that at popular resorts such as Bormio it's nearly always necessary to reserve in advance. Travel agents in Milan and other cities will have full information on individual resorts.

The Stelvio National Park is administered by the provinces of Sondrio, Trentino, and Bolzano, all of which have **park visitors' centres**. Bormio's is at Via Monte Braulio 56, ✆ (0342) 901582; they can tell you where the trails and alpine refuges are, where to find an alpine guide, or where to watch for the chamois, marmots, eagles, and other wildlife, or some of the park's 1800 species of flora.

## Where to Stay

Prices in Sondrio's resorts are a relief compared to those in the more fashionable mountain regions of the Val d'Aosta and the Dolomites.

### Valchiavenna

★★★★**Cascata e Cristallo**, Via Carducci 2, ✆ (0343) 53108, ✉ 54470, (expensive). This large hotel, with a pool and health centre, is at the top of the list of the many hotels in Madesimo.

### Valtellina

A real charmer in Morbegn, in the Valtellina, is the ★★★**Margna**, Via Margna 24, ✆/✉ (0342) 610377 (inexpensive), a fine old hotel which also has an excellent restaurant featuring local cuisine. All its rooms have baths. Another fine old hotel and restaurant, in Grosio in the Upper Valtellina (*see* below), is the ★★★**Sassella**, ✆ 847272, ✉ 845880, (inexpensive); the rooms are all fitted with private bath and TVs. On the north side of the Valtellina, in Chiesa in Valmalenco, ★★★**Chalet Rezia**, ✆/✉ (0342) 451271, (inexpensive) is a lovely little chalet in a peaceful setting, with a covered pool, that has been well recommended by readers. All the rooms have baths.

### Sondrio

★★★★**Bella Posta**, Piazza Garibaldi 19, ✆ 510404, ✉ 510210, (moderate). Formerly the old stage post, this grand old hotel is the best place to stay in Sondrio. Its rooms are big with lots of old-fashioned charm, as well as amenities like TV, phone and minibar. Public rooms include a cosy reading room, and a very good restaurant.

## Valtartano

**★★La Gran Baita**, Via Castino 7, ℭ (0342) 645043, (inexpensive). In Tartano, the main village of the serene Valtartano, is this comfortable hotel offering rooms with bath for around L50,000.

## Bormio

You can go upmarket at the **★★★★Palace**, Via Milano 54, ℭ (0342) 903131, ℮ 903366 (very expensive), a modern establishment with tennis, swimming pool, and very comfortable rooms all with bath and TV. (*Open 20 Dec–25 April, 28 June–6 Sept.*) **★★★Baita dei Pini**, Via Peccedi 15, ℭ (0342) 904346, ℮ 904700 (expensive) is a pleasant place, with very good rooms, all with bath. (*Open Dec–April, 15 June–Sept.*)

---

### Eating Out

Sondrio's cuisine is less influenced by international tastes than that in other alpine resort areas. Buckwheat is the stuff of life, in the Valtellina's grey *polenta taragna* and the narcotic noodles, *pizzoccheri*; there are delicious cheeses like *bitto* and the low-fat *matûsh*, chestnut-fed pork and salami, and fresh whipped cream on raspberries for dessert.

## Valchiavenna

Madesimo's **Osteria Vegia**, Via Cascata 7, ℭ (0343) 53335, (moderate) has been the place to go for *pizzoccheri* and other local treats for 280 years .

## Valtellina

A restaurant that readers have particularly recommended in Chiesa in Valmalenco in the Valtellina is the **Taverna Valtellinese**, Via Rusca, ℭ (0342) 451200, (moderate) which features excellent local cuisine including delicious pizzocheri, and an extensive wine list . Ponte in Valtellina, though, has the restaurant considered to be the region's best, **Cerere**, Via Guiccardi 7, ℭ (0342) 482284 (expensive), housed in a 17th-century palace. Cerere has long set the standard of classic Valtellina cuisine and its wine list includes the valley's finest. (*Closed Wed, July.*)

The **Sassella** hotel in Grosio (moderate; *see* above) serves a refined version of local specialities like *bresaola condita* (local cured beef served with olive oil, lemon and herbs), crêpes with mushrooms and local cheese, smoked trout, and Valtellina wines. Another good place to go wine tasting is Grosio's **Enoteca Valtellinese**, 'Al bun vin', near the centre of the village.

## Bormio

**Kuerc**, in the heart of old Bormio on Piazza Cavour 8, ℭ (0342) 904738, (moderate) is named after the ancient town council of Bormio, and is a good place to try local dishes in an attractive setting.

# Bergamo

At the end of *A Midsummer's Night Dream* everyone dances a 'Bergomask' to celebrate the happy ending. Bergamo itself is happy and charming in the same spirit as its great peasant dance, a city that has given the world not only a dance but also the maestro of *bel canto* in the composer Gaetano Donizetti, the Venetian painters Palma Vecchio and Lorenzo Lotto, and the great master of the portrait, Gian Battista Moroni.

Built on a hill on the edge of the Alps, the city owes much of its grace to the long rule of Venice (1428–1797), but this wasn't a one-way deal. Not only did Bergamo contribute two of Venice's most important late Renaissance artists, but the city's most brilliant and honourable condottiere, the 15th-century Bartolomeo Colleoni. Colleoni was so trusted by the Great Council that he was given complete control of Venice's armed forces; he also received the unique honour of an equestrian statue in Venice, a city that as a rule never erected personal monuments to anybody—though it helped that Colleoni left the Republic a fortune in his will in exchange for the statue. Somehow there was enough cash left over to build Colleoni a dashing tomb in his hometown as well, one of the jewels of the old Città Alta. Bergamo also contributed so many men to Garibaldi in its enthusiasm for the Risorgimento that it received the proud title 'City of the Thousand'.

## Getting There

Bergamo is an hour's **train** ride from Milan, and also has frequent connections to Brescia, but only a few trains a day to Cremona and Lecco; for information, ✆ (035) 247624. It is also very easily accessible **by road**, as it is just beside the A4 Milan-Venice *autostrada*.

There are regular **bus** services to Lake Iseo, as well as to Como, Lake Garda, the Bergamasque valleys, and Edolo and the Val Camonica. Both train and bus stations are located near each other at the end of Viale Papa Giovanni XXIII. Local bus 1 from the station will take you to the base of the funicular (L1100 one way) up to the historic upper city, or otherwise will take you there itself. Bergamo also has an **airport**, with flights to Rome and Ancona.

## Tourist Information

Bergamo has two tourist offices, one in the Lower Town, very near the train and bus stations, at Viale Papa Giovanni XXIII 106, ✆ (035) 242226, ✉ 242994; and one in the Upper Town, at Vicolo Aquila Nera 3, ✆ (035) 232730.

## Up to the Piazza Vecchia

There are two Bergamos: the **Città Alta**, the medieval and Renaissance centre up on the hill, and the **Città Bassa**, pleasant, newer and spacious on the plain below, most of its streets laid out at the beginning of this century. The centre of the Lower Town is the large, oblong **Piazza Matteotti** (from the station, walk up Viale Giovanni XXIII) with the grand 18th-century **Teatro Donizetti** and, on the right, the church of **San Bartolomeo**, containing a fine 1516 altarpiece of the *Madonna col Bambino* by Lotto. Further up Viale Vittorio

Bergamo

Emanuele II is the funicular up to the Città Alta; once you're at the top, Via Gombito leads from the upper station in a short distance to the beautiful **Piazza Vecchia**.

Architects as diverse as Frank Lloyd Wright and Le Corbusier have praised this square as one of Italy's finest, for its magnificent ensemble of medieval and Renaissance buildings, all overlooking a low, dignified lion fountain. At the lower end stands the **Biblioteca Civica** (1594), designed after Sansovino's famous library in Venice. Directly opposite, an ancient covered stair leads up to the 12th-century **Torre Civica**, with a 15th-century clock and curfew bell that still warns the Bergamasques to bed at 10pm; there is a lift to take visitors up for the fine views over Bergamo (temporarily closed at time of writing). Next to the stair, set up on its large rounded arches, is the 12th-century **Palazzo della Ragione**, with a Lion of St Mark added recently to commemorate the city's golden days under Venice, which seemed blessedly benign compared to some of the alternatives.

One of the best features of the Piazza Vecchia is that, through the dark, tunnel-like arches of the Palazzo della Ragione, are glimpses of a second square hinting more of a jewel box than an edifice. This is the Piazza del Duomo, and the jewel box reveals itself as the sumptuous, colourful façade of the 1476 **Colleoni Chapel**, designed for the old condottieri by Giovanni Antonio Amadeo while working on the Charterhouse at Pavia. The Colleoni Chapel is even more ornate and out of temper with the times, an almost-medieval tapestry that disregards the fine proportions and serenity of the Tuscans for the Venetian love of flourish. Amadeo also sculpted the fine tombs within, of Colleoni and his daughter Medea (Colleoni's, however, is empty—his remains were misplaced after a couple of temporary burials in the chapel before the tomb was finished). For some unknown reason, his empty tomb is double decked, one beautifully carved sarcophagus under another, all under a fine equestrian statue. Young Medea's tomb is much calmer, and was brought here in the 19th century from another church. The ornate ceiling is by Tiepolo, and there's a painting of the Holy Family by Goethe's constant companion in Rome, the Swiss artist Angelica Kauffmann.

Flanking and complementing the chapel are two works by Giovanni, a 14th-century master of Campione: the octagonal **Baptistry** and the colourful porch of the **Basilica of Santa Maria Maggiore**, crowned by an equestrian statue of St Alexander. The church itself was begun around 1137 and is austerely Romanesque, behind Giovanni da Campione's window dressing. He also designed the attractive door with a scene of the Nativity of Mary. The Baroque interior, however, hits you like a gust of lilac perfume. Poor lyrical Donizetti deserved better than his tomb near the back of the church; the best art is up along the balustrade of the altar, with four wonderful wood-inlaid scenes designed by Lorenzo Lotto and executed by Capodiferro ('Ironhead') di Lovere, who managed to find an amazing selection of colours and shades of natural wood to work into the vivid scenes. The third building on the square is an insipid neoclassical **Cathedral**.

Although lacking in famous monuments, the rest of the Città Alta deserves a stroll; walk along the main artery, the Via Colleoni (the condottiere lived at Nos 9–11) to the old fortress of the **Cittadella**, which houses the city's **Natural History Museum** (*open 8.30–12.30, 2.30–5.30, Tues–Sun*) and the **Archaeological Museum** (*open 9–12.30, 2.30–6, Tues–Sun*). Near the Cittadella is the bottom station of another funicular, up to **San Virgilio**—also a very pleasant, if steep, walk—where there is another fortress, the **Castello**, with superb panoramic views. Back at the Cittadella, the quiet, medieval Via Arena leads around to the back of the cathedral, passing by way of the **Museo Donizettiano** (*open 8–12, 2–5, Mon–Fri*), with an interesting collection of memorabilia and artefacts associated with the town's most famous son, including some of his musical instruments. Another good place to aim for is the ruined 14th-century **Rocca**, the castle of the Visconti, whose unpleasant rule preceded that of the Venetians.

## The Carrara Academy

Bergamo's great art museum lies half-way between the upper and lower cities. To get there from on the Città Alta's funicular station, walk along the mighty Venetian walls (the Via Della Mura) and exit through the Porta Sant'Agostino. The first left is the pedestrian-only Via della Noca, which descends to the **Pinacoteca Carrara**, Piazza dell'Accademia (*open 9.30–12.30, 2.30–5.30, Wed–Mon; adm Mon, Wed–Sat, free Sun*), founded in 1780 and housing one of Italy's great provincial collections. It has especially fine portraits—Botticelli's haughty *Giuliano de' Medici*, Pisanello's *Lionello d'Este*, Gentile Bellini's *Portrait of a Man*, Lotto's *Portrait of Lucina Brembati* with a vicious weasel under her arm and a sickly moon overhead, and another strange painting of uncertain origin, believed to be of Cesare Borgia, with an uncannily desolate background. There are fine portraits by Bergamo's master of the genre, Moroni, to whom Titian sent the *Rectors of Venice*, with the advice that only Moroni could 'make them natural'. There are some excellent *Madonna con Bambino* by the Venetian masters, Giovanni Bellini, Mantegna (who couldn't do children), and Crivelli (with his cucumber signature), as well as by the Sienese Landi. The plague saint San Sebastiano is portrayed by three contemporaries from remarkably different aspects—typically naked and pierced with arrows before a silent city, by Giovanni Bellini; well-dressed and rather sweetly contemplating an arrow, by Raphael; and sitting at a table, clad in a fur-trimmed coat, by Dürer. An eerie, black and silver *Calvary* is an unusual work by the same artist, and there is much, much more, by both Italian and foreign artists.

From the Carrara, Via San Tommaso, Via Pignolo, and Via Torquato Tasso lead back down to the central Piazza Matteotti. There are fine altarpieces by Lorenzo Lotto along the way, in **San Bernardino** and **Santo Spirito**.

---

*Bergamo ✆ (035–)*               ***Where to Stay***

 The city's finest hotel is the ★★★★**Excelsior San Marco**, Piazzale Repubblica 6, ✆ 366111, 🖷 223201 (very expensive), well located between the upper and lower towns, which offers air-conditioned, modern rooms, all with TV and bath, as well as one of Bergamo's best restaurants (*see* below). The recently refurbished and upgraded ★★★★**Capello d'Oro e del Moro**, Viale Giovanni XXIII 12, ☏ 232503, ✉ 242946 (expensive) is also now one of the top choices in town, with well-equipped modern rooms with satellite TV, lovely bathrooms, and a very good restaurant.

Most of Bergamo's hotels are in the Città Bassa, but one of the most atmospheric, the ★★**Agnello d'Oro**, Via Gombito 22, ☏ 249883, ✉ 235612 (moderate) is up in the medieval centre. It's a fine old 17th-century inn with cosy rooms, all with bath; the restaurant is also quite good. Another hotel in the Upper Town, on the corner of the Piazza Vecchia, is the ★★**Sole**, Via Rivola 2, ☏ 218238, ✉ 240011 (moderate), which isn't quite as nice, and a shade noisier, but homely, with baths in every room. Good cheaper options in the Lower Town are ★**Caironi**, Via Toretta 6, ☏ 243083 (inexpensive), which involves a 20min walk or bus nos.5, 7 or 8, or, nearer the station, ★**Sant'Antonio**, Via Paleocapa 1, ☏ 210284, ✉ 212316 (inexpensive); most rooms are without baths.

---

*Bergamo ☏ (035–)*  

***Eating Out***

*expensive*

Bergamo prides itself on its cooking, and the city is well endowed with excellent restaurants. Many, surprisingly, feature seafood—Bergamo is a major inland fish market. The classic for fish, **Da Vittorio**, Viale Papa Giovanni XXIII 21, ☏ 218060 (expensive) specializes in seafood prepared in a number of exquisite ways, as well as a wide variety of meat dishes, polenta, risotto, and pasta, and a superb bouillabaisse. (*Closed Wed, three weeks Aug.*) The other great fish restaurant is **Dell'Angelo**, Via S. Caterina 55, ☏ 237103 (expensive), a 17th-century inn with tables outdoors in a courtyard in summer, and delicacies like smoked *balik* salmon fillets and aubergine with ricotta. The great speciality of the house is baked sea bass with seashell crust. Also in the Lower Town, the Excelsior San Marco hotel (*see* above) houses another of the town's best eating places, the very modern and imaginative **Colona**, featuring both local and international specialities (expensive).

**Taverna dei Colleoni**, on the Piazza Vecchia, ☏ 232596 (expensive) features more classical Italian cuisine, and specialities including swordfish with mushrooms and *concerto di porcini*. An excellent choice in the Città Alta, just below the Piazza Vecchia, is the **Trattoria Tre Torri**, Piazza Mercato del Fieno 7, ☏ 244366 (moderate), a tiny, atmospheric place, featuring hearty cuisine and lots of delicious local specialities cooked in individual ways. As an antipasto, try the *guanciale* (pig cheek), followed by *casoncelli* (a kind of ravioli), and, as a main course, *polenta di Bergamo* with rabbit. There's an extensive wine list, including many labels from the restaurant's own vineyards, excellent service and friendly prices.

For good pizza by the slice and bread shaped like Commedia dell'Arte figures, try **Il Fornaio**, Via V. Colleoni near Piazza Vecchia.

# Around Bergamo

The year after Bartolomeo Colleoni was appointed Captain General of Venice he purchased a ruined castle at **Malpaga** (on the Cremona road), which he had restored; his heirs in the cinquecento added a fine series of frescoes commemorating a visit to the castle by King Christian I of Denmark in 1474, portraying Colleoni hosting the de rigueur splendid banquets, jousts, hunts and pageants of Renaissance hospitality. It's open for visits if you call ahead, ✆ (035) 840003.

Southwest of Bergamo, **Caravaggio** was the birthplace of Michelangelo Merisi da Caravaggio and is the site of a popular pilgrimage sanctuary designed in a cool Renaissance style by Pellegrino Tibaldi. **Treviglio**, a large, rather dull town nearby, has an exquisite 15th-century polyptych in the Gothic church of San Martino; to the south **Rivolta d'Adda** boasts the **Zoo di Preistoria** (*open Wed–Mon; adm*), with lifesize replicas of the denizens of the region in the Mesozoic era. An even more mind-boggling roadside attraction beckons in **Capriate San Gervasio**, off the autostrada towards Milan, where the **Parco Minitalia** (*open daily*) cuts Italy down to size—400 metres from tip to toe, with mountains, seas, cities, and monuments all arranged in their proper place. Even a miniature train is on hand to take visitors up and down the boot. Due east of Bergamo, **Sotto del Monte** was the birthplace of the beloved Pope John XXIII, and is an increasingly popular pilgrimage destination.

# The Bergamasque Valleys

North of Bergamo the scenery improves along the Bergamasque valleys, as they plunge into the stony heart of the **Orobie Alps**, the mighty wall of mountains that isolates the Valtellina further north. At the Bergamo tourist office pick up their booklets *Orobie Inverno* (winter) or *Orobie Estate* (summer), which, though in Italian, have lists of all hotels, refuges, winter sports, and trails.

## Val Brembana

There are two main Bergamasque valleys: the western one, the Val Brembana, follows the Bremba river, and was extremely important in the Middle Ages as the main route for caravans transporting minerals from the Orobie and Valtellina to Bergamo and Venice.

Just off the main road, in **Almenno San Bartolomeo**, the tiny, round 12th-century church of **San Tomè** is a jewel of Lombard Romanesque, composed of three cylinders, one atop the other, and prettily illuminated at night; its isolation makes it especially impressive. **Zogno**, further up the valley, is the site of the **Museo della Valle Brembana** (*open 9am–12 midday Tues–Sun*), with artefacts relating to the district's life and history. Zogno is also the base for visiting **La Grotta delle Meraviglie**, with a long gallery of stalactites and stalagmites. **San Pellegrino Terme**, next up the valley, means mineral water to millions of Italians and is Lombardy's most fashionable spa, developed at the turn of the century around two Baroque/Liberty-style confections, the Grand Hotel and the Casino. Excursions include a ride up the funicular for the view, and a visit to the 'Dream Cave', the **Grotta del Sogno**. According to legend, the humorously frescoed **Casa dell'Arlecchino** at Onerta in **San**

**Giovanni Bianco** was the birthplace of Harlequin; the role was invented by a *Commedia dell'Arte* actor who lived there, named Ganassa.

The next town, medieval **Cornello dei Tasso** (pop.30) preserves its appearance as a relay station on the merchant's road, with an arcaded lane to protect the caravans of mules. In the 13th century much of the business of expediting merchandise here was in the hands of the Tasso family, whose destiny, however, was far bigger than Cornello. One branch went on to run the post between Venice and Rome, while another moved to Germany in the 1500s to organize for Emperors Maximilian I and Charles V the first European postal service. Their extensive network of postal relay stations were in use into the 19th century, while the German spelling of their name, Taxis, went on to signify their privately licensed vehicles and from that, our modern taxis. One member of the family operating out of Sorrento was the father of the loony Renaissance poet Torquato Tasso. As well as the muleteer's arcades, you can see the ruins of the Tasso ancestral home, frescoes in the 15th-century church, and a number of fine medieval buildings.

Beyond **Piazza Brembana** the road branches out into several mountain valleys. The most important and developed resort is **Foppolo**; besides winter sports it offers an easy ascent up the **Corno Stella**, with marvellous views to the north and east. Other good ski resorts include **Piazzatorre** and **San Simone** near Branzi; **Carona** is a good base for summer excursions into the mountains and alpine lakes. Another important village on the merchants' road, the prettily situated **Averara**, was the first station after the Passo San Marco, through which the road entered from the Valtellina. Besides the covered arcade for the caravans, there are a number of 16th-century exterior frescoes.

## Valle Seriana

Bergamo's eastern valley, the **Valle Seriana**, is industrial in its lower half and ruggedly Alpine in the north. At the bottom of the valley, some 8km from Bergamo, **Alzano Lombardo** is worth a brief stop for one of Italy's most striking Rococo pulpits completely covered with reliefs and soaring cherubs (by Antonio Fantoni) in the **Basilica di San Martino**, along with some fine 17th-century inlaid and *intarsia* (wooden mosaic) work.

Fine old **Gandino** is another town to aim for, just off the main valley road. In the Middle Ages it was the chief producer of a heavy, inexpensive cloth called bergamasque. The finest structure in town is the **Basilica**, a 17th-century garlic-domed church, with more fine works by Fantoni and a museum housing religious art and relics of the city's medieval textile industry. **Clusone**, further up, is the capital and prettiest town of the Valle Seriana, with many frescoes, a beautiful 16th-century astronomical clock in the Piazza dell'Orologio, and a market every Monday with many fascinating varieties of cheeses, sausages and other local produce. Near the clock, the **Oratorio del Disciplini** is adorned with an eerie 1485 fresco of the *Danse Macabre* and the *Triumph of Death*, where one skeleton mows the nobility and clergy down with arrows, while another fires a blunderbuss. There are more frescoes inside, and a *Deposition* by Fantoni. Winter and summer resorts further north include the **Passo della Presolana** and **Schilpàrio**, both located near dramatic Dolomite-like mountain walls.

The least visited of the larger lakes, Iseo (the Roman *Lacus Sebinus*) is the fifth in size, and a charming alternative for anyone wishing to avoid the glittering hordes that blacken the more celebrated shores. Even back in the 1750s it was the preferred resort of such eccentric Italophiles as Lady Mary Wortley Montagu, who disdained the English who 'herd together' by the larger lakes. Besides its wooded shores and backdrop of mighty mountains, Iseo bears triplet islands in its bosom, among them Monte Isola, the largest island in any European lake. Along the river Oglio, the main source of Iseo, runs the Val Camonica, a magnificent Alpine valley with nothing less than one of the world's greatest collections of prehistoric art.

### Getting Around

**Buses** run frequently from Bergamo to the lake towns of Tavèrnola and Lovere, and there's also a direct bus from Milan to Lovere. Iseo town and the south side of the lake are best approached from the southeast—there are frequent buses from Brescia, and a **regional railway** (not an FS train) runs to Iseo and along the entire east shore of the lake from Brescia or the rail junction at Rovato, between Bergamo and Brescia. From Pisogne at the north end of the lake several trains a day continue up the Val Camonica as far as Edolo. The main **road** to Iseo is the SS510, which leaves the A4 *autostrada* not far west of Brescia. The SS42 also runs to Lovere at the north end of the lake, from Bergamo.

**Steamers** ply the lake between Lovere and Sarnico, calling at 15 ports; there's also a service from Sale Marasino to Monte Isola. All boats on the lake are run by **Navigazione Lago d'Iseo**, Via Nazionale 16, Bergamo, ✆ (035) 971 482, and timetables are available at all local tourist offices.

### Tourist Information

The main tourist office on Lake Iseo is in **Iseo** town, Lungolago Marconi 2, ✆ (030) 980209, ✉ 981361. A useful tourist organization based in Iseo is **Co-optur**, Via Duomo 17, ✆ (030) 981154, ✉ 9821742, a local co-operative which has a booking service for hotels, day trips and restaurants. In the Val Camonica there are tourist offices in **Darfo-Boario Terme**, at Piazza Einaudi 2, ✆ (0364) 531609, ✉ 532280; **Capo di Ponte**, Via Briscioli, ✆ (0364) 42080; **Edolo**, Piazza Martiri della Libertà 2, ✆ (0364) 71065; and in **Ponte di Legno**, at Corso Milano 41, ✆ (0364) 91122.

## Franciacorta and Lake Iseo

Between Brescia and Iseo lies the charming wine-growing region known as **Franciacorta**, the 'free court', which, owing to its poverty, paid no taxes, a fact that endeared it to the villa-building patricians of Lombardy. Today, the name of the region is also synonymous with one of Italy's best-known varieties of champagne-method sparkling wine, as well as with mellowing old estates surrounded by vineyards producing a fine DOC red and Pinot Bianco. While the countryside as a whole is a prime attraction, the village of **Erbusco** is now also home to perhaps the best and certainly the most talked-about restaurant in Italy, that of Gualtiero Marchesi, **L'Albereta**.

The **Villa Lana** (now Ragnoli) in Colombaro is also worth a stop for Italy's oldest cedar of Lebanon in its garden. Two other villages closer to Brescia have ancient churches—the Romanesque Olivetan abbey church at **Rodengo**, with three cloisters and frescoes by Romanino and Moretto, and **San Pietro in Lamosa**, founded by monks from Cluny in 1083, located in **Provaglio**. San Pietro overlooks an emerald peat moss called **Le Torbiere**, which blossoms into an aquatic garden of pink and white waterlilies in late spring; the tourist office in Iseo rents out rowing boats to enable you to paddle through.

**Iseo**, between the lake and Le Torbiere, is one of the main shore resorts, with its beaches and a venerable 12th-century church, **Pieve di Sant'Andrea**, on one of its shady streets. Steamers link it with **Sarnico**, a smaller resort to the south, sprinkled with Liberty-style villas, and with the arcadian, car-less island of **Monte Isola**, a resort of poets with genteelly decaying fishing villages and inviting walks through olive and chestnut groves. Another steamer port, **Sale Marasino**, is one of the prettier spots on the lake, ringed by mountain terraces. From the nearby village of **Marone** you can hike up to the panoramic view point of **Monte Guglielmo** (1949m, with an alpine refuge), passing along the way **Zone** and its spiky 'erosion pyramids', similar to the pyramids of the Dolomites. Next along the shore, the old village of **Pisogne** has the last train station on the lake shore, and bus connections to Lovere; its church of **Santa Maria della Neve** is covered with excellent frescoes by Romanino, who spent two years on the project.

**Lovere**, the oldest resort on Lake Iseo, has a fine church in its 15th-century frescoed **Santa Maria in Valvendra**, and a handful of good paintings in its **Galleria dell'Accademia Tadini** (*open May–Sept 2–6pm Tues–Sat*), especially a *Madonna* by Jacopo Bellini. The highlight of Iseo's west shore is **Riva di Solto** (a steamer port), with odd little bays and views across the water of the formidable Adamello mountains. **Tavèrnola Bergamasca** has a local steamer to Sarnico.

## A Temple of Nuova Cucina

For years, moneyed Milan flocked to the eponymous gourmet enclave of **Gualtiero Marchesi**, the innovative master chef and Pied Piper/founder of *la nuova cucina*. Marchesi is very much a celebrity in Italy—he has his own TV show and is author of several cookbooks, and his restaurant became more of an institution, frequented by the top politicos and industrialists of the day, than simply a place to eat. So it came as quite as surprise when in 1993 he shut up shop in Milan and moved to the country, to Erbusco, a tiny village in the heart of the Franciacorta wine region. He has opened a hotel, L'Albereta (*see* below, 'Where to Stay'), thus returning to his roots—his father, too, was a hotelier—and with it a new restaurant. Devotees need not have been too concerned, as the new establishment has quickly taken up its predecessor's status as one of the principal places of pilgrimage of the Italian cult of foodism. The setting, on a hill overlooking the rolling countryside, is exquisite, as is the decor, incorporating frescoes from the original villa. There are three set menus: a lunch menu at L50,000, a four-course evening meal at L80,000, and a seven-course gourmet menu at L110,000, wine not included. Marchesi usually bases his dishes on what is available at the market each day; specialities include, to begin, lightly scrambled egg with caviar, *crema di luccio*, a delicate mousse made from a lake fish, and *risotto con gamberi e seppie*, a risotto with prawns and cuttlefish. A trademark is his unusual marriages of flavours—such as pigeon and lobster ravioli, or ratatouille of sweet and sour aubergines with salted prawns. The hotel also has its own vineyard, as well as a superb selection of other wines. The seven-course meal can easily take three hours to get through, but it is meant to be savoured, rather than rushed!

## Val Camonica

From Pisogne the road and railway continue northeast into the Val Camonica, one of the loveliest and most fertile of Alpine valleys. Its name is derived from a Rhaetian tribe, the Camuni, whose artistic ancestors used the smooth, glacier-seared permian sandstone of their valley as tablets to engrave solar discs and labyrinths, mysterious figures and geometric designs, animals, weapons, and people. What is especially remarkable is the unbroken length of time during which the engravings were made: the oldest are from the Neolithic era (before 2200 BC) and the latest date from the arrival of the Romans—a period spanning some 25 centuries, enabling scholars to trace intriguing prehistoric stylistic evolutions, from the random scratched symbols of the late Stone Age to the finely drawn, realistic and narrative figures of the Bronze and Iron Ages. Although it's impossible to understand the significance these etchings had for their makers, their magic must have been extraordinary: in the valley 180,000 have been discovered so far. Some are beautiful, some ungainly, some utterly mystifying, while a few are fuel for crackpot theories. Recently UNESCO has put the Val Camonica on its select list of sites to be protected as part of the artistic patrimony of humanity.

Some 12km from Pisogne some early rock incisions from the 3rd millennium BC may be seen in a lovely park at Luine, near the busy spa of **Boario Terme**. Unfortunately the rock here has weathered more than further north at Capo di Ponte, and the graffiti are often hard to decipher. Boario also offers the opportunity for a scenic detour up the **Valle d'Angolo** and its wild and narrow **Dezzo Ravine**.

When the Romans conquered the valley their capital was **Cividate Camuno**, and it remembers their passing with mosaics, tomb stones and other local finds in its small **Archaeological Museum** (*open 8am–2pm Tues–Sun*). It also has a fine 12th-century tower, and churches with frescoes by the excellent quattrocento painter Da Cemmo in the environs, at **Esine** and **Bienno** (Santa Maria Annunziata). **Breno**, the modern capital of the valley, lies under an imposing medieval castle; its 14th-century church of **Sant'Antonio** contains frescoes by Romanino, and its **Museo Camuno** in the town hall has an interesting ethnographic collection from the valley. From here a mountain road winds eastwards up to the Passo di Croce Domini and Lake Idro, and then down towards Brescia (*see below*).

## Capo di Ponte

**Capo di Ponte** is the centre for visiting the best of the prehistoric engravings, located in the **Parco Nazionale delle Incisioni Rupestri Preistoriche** (*open 9am–one hour before* *sunset daily; adm; guided visits can be arranged through Capo di Ponte tourist office or the park itself, © 42140*). The main attraction is the **Naquane rock**, etched with some 900 figures during the Iron Age. Across the Oglio, in **Cemmo**, there are two other magnificent rocks, the first ones to be discovered, and a few kilometres south of Capo di Ponte, in the tiny medieval hamlet of **Foppe** (near **Nardo**) a second section of the park was opened after the discovery in 1975 of another great concentration of engravings, reached via a path from the village. In Nardo, Capo di Ponte's *Centro Camuno di Studi Preistorici* has its museum, with plans of the Camuni culture's sites among other explanatory items. Besides prehistoric art, Capo di Ponte also has two 11th-century churches: **San Siro**, with its three tall apses built on a hill directly over the river, and the Cluniac monastery church of **San Salvatore**.

Further up the valley the scenery becomes grander as the Adamello group of the Brenta Dolomites looms up to the right. Beautiful excursions into the range are possible from **Cedegolo**, into the lovely **Val di Saviore** with its mountain lakes Arno and Salarno or up Mount Adamello (3555m). From **Malonno** you can drive or walk along a scenic road through the chestnut woods of the **Valle Malga**, with more pretty lakes and easy ascents (Corno delle Granate, 3111m).

Surrounded by majestic mountains, **Edolo** stands at the crossroads of the valley and the road from Sondrio and the Valtellina to the Passo di Tonale. It is a base for a whole range of mountain excursions, and for the ski resorts of the **Valle di Corteno**, **Ponte di Legno** (the most developed) and **Passo di Tonale**. From the Passo di Tonale you can continue east into Trentino's lovely Val di Sole (*see* p.464), while a road from Ponte di Legno cuts north through Stelvio National Park to Bormio.

---

### *Where to Stay*

### Erbusco

Italy's master chef Gualtiero Marchesi has recently decamped from Milan to open **L'Albereta**, © (030) 7267003, (very expensive), a hotel and gourmet restaurant in the tiny village of Erbusco in the Franciacorta. It's an old, entirely renovated villa, and the accommodation consists of 39 rooms and suites, all individual and all  beautifully designed. There's every possible attention to detail, with wall paintings by Jacques Margerin, open log fires, jacuzzis in the bathrooms and a swimming pool, sauna, tennis and garage. Even so, it's still in the very expensive rather than luxury category, with rooms at around L200,000.

### Iseo

The top choice in Iseo and one of the best places to stay in the region is ★★★★**I Due Roccoli**, © (030) 9821853, ✆ 9821877 (expensive), set amid its own large gardens in the hills above the town. A member of the prestigious *Relais du Silence* hotels, the hotel occupies part of an old hunting lodge. The modern suites, rooms and bathrooms are beautifully designed and equipped, some with garden views, and others with breathtaking views of the lake. There's a banqueting hall, sun terrace, pool and one of the finest restaurants in the area (*see* below). In Iseo town, ★★★**Ambra**,

Piazza G. Rosa, ℭ (030) 980130, ✉ 9821361(moderate) is on the lake and near Iseo town centre. All its rooms have modern fittings, and most have nice bathrooms and balconies, though there's no restaurant. A short distance away along the lake shore, the **Milano, ℭ (030) 980449, ✉ 9821361 (inexpensive) has smaller rooms in an old-fashioned style, many with views, and a small restaurant and bar. ***Moselli, in Pilzone, just outside Iseo, ℭ (030) 980001, ✉ 981868, (inexpensive) is a good choice as it's near the beach, in a garden; all the rooms have baths. One of the newer and more interesting places to stay and dine on Lake Iseo is the ****Cantiere in Sarnico, Via Monte Grappa 2, ℭ (035) 910091, ✉ 912722 (moderate), in an old building remodelled by its new owners, with very comfortable rooms.

## Monte Isola

A pleasant, tranquil hotel on Monte Isola is the ***Montisola Palace, in the village of Menzino, ℭ (030) 9825138 (moderate), with a pool in addition to its beach, tennis courts, and fine rooms, all with private bath; it also has self-catering flats available (*Open April–Oct.*) **Bellavista, Via Roma 14, in Siviano, also on Monte Isola, ℭ (030) 9886106 (inexpensive) is a wonderful place to get away from it all—its rooms are comfortable, small and simple with, of course, outstanding views, and there's a nice little restaurant, too. Another choice in Siviano is **Canogola, Porto di Siviano, ℭ (030) 9825310 (inexpensive), a small hotel which offers quiet lakeside rooms, all with bath.

## Sale Marasino

On the east side of the lake, in the small village of Sale Marasino, ***Rotelli, ℭ (030) 986115, ✉ 986241 (inexpensive) is an excellent bargain, with magnificent views, a pool, tennis, sauna and gym and well-sized, modern rooms at, incredibly, inexpensive-category prices of around L60,000 per night.

## Val Camonica

Most of the hotels in the Val Camonica are concentrated in Boario Terme or in the mountain resorts at the northern end. In Boario the plush ****Grand Hotel Boario e Delle Terme, Via Manzoni 2, ℭ (0364) 531 061, is the duchess of valley accommodation, but at time of writing is unfortunately closed for restoration. Second choice is the ****Rizzi, Via Caroucci 5/11, ℭ (0364) 531617 (moderate), which is old and slightly frayed at the edges, but has comfortable rooms all with TV, phone, safe etc. It has its own garden, with a lovely outside verandah and a very nice restaurant featuring local dishes. The stylish ***Diana, Via Manifattura 12, ℭ/✉ (0364) 531403 (moderate) is a modern hotel in Boario, opposite the Terme, with good-size rooms with all mod cons, large bathrooms and wonderful views of the mountains, as well as a restaurant and garden, too. The ***Brescia, Via Zanardelli 6, ℭ (0364) 531409, ✉ 532969 (moderate) is a slightly old-fashioned hotel in Boario, but its rooms are fully equipped, and there are conference facilities, a very stylish dining room and a pub/disco downstairs. A good budget option in Boario Terme, in the station forecourt,**Ariston, ℭ/✉ (0364) 531532 (inexpensive), which offers small, clean rooms with modern fittings, great views, and old-fashioned hospitality.

At the head of the valley in Ponte di Legno the sleek and modern ★★★★**Mirella**, Via Roma 21, ℗ (0364) 900500, ℗ 900530 (expensive) is the top choice, with a pool and tennis courts among its facilities. A less glamorous but adequate choice up at the Passo del Tonale is the ★★★**Dolomiti**, ℗ (0364) 900260, ℗ 900251 (moderate). All rooms are with bath. (*Open all year.*)

---

## Eating Out

### Clusane

Fish from the lake are, of course, a speciality, and nowhere more so than the village of Clusane, near Iseo, where the foremost speciality is *tinca al forno* (tench from the lake). The village could also lay claim to having the most restaurants per capita in the area—20, seating 4000, in a place with a population of 1500!

### Erbusco

The region can now boast one of Italy's most prestigious restaurants, Gualtiero Marchesi's **L'Albereta** in Erbusco, ℗ (030) 7267003 (very expensive).

### Iseo

The best place to eat in Iseo is **I Due Roccoli** hotel, ℗ (030) 9821853, ℗ 9821877 (expensive, *see* above), though it's outside the town, and you'll need a car to get there. The dining room is tasteful and intimate, with an open log fire, service is impeccable, and much of the food is home grown, from the small farm in the hotel grounds. Favourite dishes include an antipasto of salad and truffles, *insalata di lambetto tartufato*, a delicious green pasta with mushrooms known as *pappardelle verdi con funghi porcini*, various fish from the lake, and, for dessert, a *mousse di cioccolato bianco* that's one of the best in the country. (*Open to non-residents Thurs–Mon only.*)

In Iseo town, for a fine glass of wine (from Franciacorta and beyond) and a good plate of lake trout, among other local specialities, try **Il Volto**, Via Mirolte 33, ℗ (030) 981462 (moderate).

### Rovato

In Rovato, on the edge of the Franciacorta, there's another excellent place to feast on the freshest of fish: **Tortuga**, Via A. Angelini 10, ℗ (030) 722980, (expensive). Specialities include wonderful seafood antipasti, and delicate scampi as a recommended choice for seconds. There's a garden for outdoor dining as well.

### Sarnico

The restaurant of the **Cantiere** hotel (*see* above) features a wonderful *menu degustazione* for moderate prices, featuring dishes like risotto with oysters and prosciutto, veal cutlets with asparagus, wild mushroom soup, exquisite fish dishes, and desserts that hit the spot.

#### Val Camonica

In the Val Camonica most of the best restaurants are in the valley's hotels (*see* above). A good place to eat in Ponte di Legno, **Al Maniero**, ℰ (0364) 91093 (moderate). features hearty local cuisine in a cosy, happy atmosphere.

## Brescia

The second city of Lombardy, Brescia may be busy and prosperous, but it's no one's favourite art town, even though it has a full day's supply of art, architecture, and delightful corners to visit. Perhaps it's the vaguely sinister aura of having been Italy's chief manufacturer of arms for the last 400 years. Perhaps it's because the local Fascists saw fit to punch out the heart of the old city and replace it with a soulless, chilling piazza designed on the principles that might makes right. The Brescians seem to detest it, but it's hard to avoid; they would do well to raze it and the subliminal memories it evokes.

## History

Brescia was originally a Gaulish settlement, an origin remembered only in its name Brixia, from the Celtic *brik* ('hill'). Brixia was an ally of Rome early on, and in 26 BC achieved the favoured status of a *Colonia Civica Augusta*, when it was embellished with splendid monuments. By the 8th century Brescia had recovered enough from the barbarian invasions to become the seat of a Lombard duchy under King Desiderius, whose daughter Ermengarda was sought in marriage by Charlemagne as the condition for the Emperor's crown. He later repudiated her, and the forlorn Ermengarda returned to Brescia to die in the Abbey of San Salvatore, founded by her mother.

In the 11th century Brescia joined the Lombard League against the tyranny of Frederick Barbarossa and produced the great Benedictine monk, Arnold of Brescia, who went to Rome to preach against the tyranny of possessions and the worldly materialism of the Church, only to be burned at the stake for his troubles by the Pope. Brescia itself was too tempting a prize to be left in peace by the region's thugs. Power struggles began with the unspeakable Veronese Ezzelino da Romana in 1258 and ended with the detested Visconti in 1421, when the notables, weary of the game of musical chairs in their government, invited the Venetians to adopt the city. The Venetians were grateful to get it, for strategic reasons, and for the access it gave to the area's unusually pure iron deposits. By the 16th century Brescia had become Italy's major producer of firearms, and so indispensable to Venice that the Republic imposed emigration restrictions on Brescia almost as severe as those placed on the glassmakers of Murano.

Venetian rule not only brought a great measure of peace and prosperity to the town, but initiated an artistic flowering as well. The Brescian Vincenzo Foppa (1485–1566) was a key figure in the Lombard Renaissance, whose monumental paintings were among the first to depict a single, coherent atmosphere. Towards the end of the century, Girolamo Romanino (1485–1566) synthesized Lombard and Venetian schools, while his contemporary Moretto da Brescia (1498–1554) was an ardent student of Titian and contributed the first Italian full-length portrait. His star pupil was Moroni of Bergamo. Recently, a forgotten painter,

Giacomo Antonio Ceruti (1698–1767), has been the centre of interest for his realist genre paintings of Brescia's poor and humble artisans—a rare subject for the place and time.

Brescia is the main transport hub for western Lombardy and Lake Garda, a major **road** junction as the meeting-point of the A4 Turin-Venice *autostrada* and the A21 from the south. It is also on the main Milan-Venice **rail** line, 55 minutes from Milan, an hour from Verona, and less to Desenzano del Garda, the main station on Lake Garda. There are also frequent services to Bergamo (1 hour) and Lecco (2 hours); to Cremona (just over an hour); and to Parma via Piadena (2 hours). For FS rail information, ✆ (030) 37961. Another, regional, railway line wends its way north along the east shore of Lake Iseo and then through the mountains to Edolo in the Val Camonica (2½ hours).

There is an even more extensive **bus** network, with frequent links to the towns of Lakes Garda and Iseo and less frequently to Idro; also to Turin and Milan, Padua and the Euganean Hills, Marostica, Bassano del Grappa, and Belluno; to Trento via Riva and to the resorts of Pinzolo and Madonna di Campiglio in Trentino, as well as to all points within the province. For information, ✆ (030) 44061.

The **bus and railway stations** are located next to each other just south of the city centre on Viale Stazione. Bus C connects them to the centre, or you can walk there in 10 minutes up the Corso Martiri della Libertà.

Corso Zanardelli 38, ✆ (030) 293284, near the central Piazza del Duomo.

## The Central Squares

Hurry, as the Brescians do, through the deathly pale and grim 1930s **Piazza Vittoriale**, duck behind its varicoloured post office, and enter into a far more benign display of power in Brescia's Venetian-style **Piazza della Loggia**, the city's most elegant square. It has two fine loggias—one belonging to the Venetian Renaissance **Monte di Pietà Vecchia** (1489), and the other to the three-arched building known simply as the **Loggia**, an almost frilly confection designed in part by Sansovino and Palladio, the greatest Renaissance architects of the Veneto. Another remainder of the Serenissima is the **Torre dell'Orologio**, a copy of the one in St Mark's Square, complete with two bell-ringing figures on top.

Looming up behind the clock tower is the third-highest dome in Italy, the pearl-white, green-lead-roofed crown of the **Duomo**, built in 1602 by Giambattista Lantana. From the **Piazza del Duomo** itself, however, the dome is hidden by a high, marble false front, its upper section as insubstantial as the wooden façades of a frontier town. Over the door a bust of Brescia's great Cardinal Querini 'winks mischievously, as if inviting the faithful to enter'. You should take him up on it, not so much for the few paintings by Romanino (by the bishop's throne) and Moretto that try to warm the cold interior, as to visit the adjacent **Duomo Vecchio** (*open April–Sept 9–12, 3–7.30, Wed–Mon*). Built in the 11th century over the ruins of the ancient Basilica of San Filastrio and the ancient Roman baths, the singular cathedral may well be the only one in Italy designed in the shape of a top hat, low and rotund, with a massive cylindrical tower rising from its centre, supported by eight pillars. Inside its simple form is broken only by a 15th-century raised choir. The altarpiece, an *Assumption* by Moretto, is one his greatest works. The crypt of San Falastrio, the only part of the ancient church to survive, contains a mixed bag of Roman and early medieval columns, and mosaics from the Roman baths. Several medieval bishops are entombed around the walls, most impressively Bishop Mernardo Maggi in his sarcophagus of 1308; the cathedral treasure contains two precious 11th century relics—the *Stauroteca*, a reliquary box containing a titbit of the True Cross, and the banner once borne on the *Carroccio* (sacred ox cart) of the Brescian armies.

Just behind the new cathedral, on Via Mazzini 1, you can visit the **Biblioteca Queriniana**, containing the 18th-century collection of rare books and manuscripts compiled by Cardinal Querini *(open 8.30–12, 2–6, Tues–Fri, Sun; 8.30–12 Sun)*, including the 6th-century 'Purple Evangeliary' and Eusebius' 11th-century Concordances of the Gospels; the cardinal is said to have snubbed the Vatican library in order to favour his own collection. On the other side of the Duomo, the 12th-century **Broletto** was the civic centre prior to the construction of the Loggia; its formidable tower, the **Pegol**, predates it by a century.

## Roman Brixia

From behind the Broletto, take a right on to the ancient *Decumanus Maximus*, now the Via dei Musei, which soon leads to the heart of the old Roman city and the ruins of its forum in the **Piazza del Foro**. Looming above are the mighty columns of the **Capitoline Temple** *(open 9–12.30, 2–5, Tues–Sun; adm)*, erected by the Emperor Vespasian in AD 73 and preserved for posterity by a medieval mud-slide that covered it until its discovery in 1823. In 1955 an earlier, Republican-era Capitoline temple was discovered beneath Vespasian's, with unusual mosaics of natural stone.

The Capitoline Temple is divided into three *cellae*, which were probably dedicated to the three principle Roman deities—Jupiter, Juno, and Minerva. They are filled with the inscriptions, tombstones, and mosaics of the **Civico Museo Romano**—a considerable collection thanks to the foresight of the 1485 municipal council, which forbade the sale or transport of antiquities outside Brescia. The museum's best treasures, however, are upstairs, and include a 6-foot bronze Winged Victory, who, without the object she once held, seems to be snapping her fingers in a dance step. She, and six gilded bronze busts of emperors, were found during the excavations of the temple. There's a gilt bronze figurine of a prisoner, believed to be the great Gaulish chief Vercingetorix, a beautiful Greek amphora from the 6th century BC, and a facsimile of the fascinating, 25-foot-long Peutringer Map of Vienna, itself a 12th-century copy of a Roman road map.

Next to the temple is the unexcavated *cavea* of the **Roman Theatre**, while further down the Via dei Musei stands the most important complex of Lombard Brescia, the **Abbey of San Salvatore**, founded in the 8th century and disbanded at the end of the 18th. Its church of Santa Giulia, added in the 16th century, and the 8th-century Basilica of San Salvatore, have been restored to house Brescia's **Museo Civico**. San Salvatore is especially interesting for the fragments of its lovely stucco decoration, in the same style as Cividale del Friuli's 8th-century Tempietto Lombardo. The old nunnery contains a **Museum of Modern Art**, Via Monti 9 (*open 4–7pm Thurs–Sun; adm*) while Santa Giulia houses the **Museum of Christian Art** (*under restoration; for visiting times call © 44327*), a magnificent collection with two exceptional masterworks. One is the 8th-century Lombard *Cross of Desiderius*, studded with 212 gems and cameos, including one from the 4th century of a Roman woman with her two children, all peering warily into the approaching Dark Ages; the Brescians like to believe it is the great Galla Placidia of Ravenna. The other treasure is a 4th-century ivory coffer called the *Lipsanoteca*, adorned with beautiful bas-reliefs of scriptural scenes. One of the lovely 5th-century ivory diptychs originally belonged to the father of the philosopher Boethius. Lombard jewellery, medieval art, and Renaissance medals round out the collection.

## The Cydnean Hill

The lyric poet Catullus, who considered Brixia the mother of his native Verona, was the first to mention the Cydnean hill that rises up behind the Via dei Musei. This was the core of Gaulish and early Roman Brixia—if you take Via Piamarta from Santa Giulia you'll pass by the ruins of the city's one surviving **Roman gate**, as well as the attractive 1510 **San Pietro in Oliveto**, named after the ancient silvery olive grove that surrounds the church. Up on top are the imposing walls of the medieval **Castello**, with its round 14th-century **Mirabella Tower**, built on a Roman foundation. There's a small children's zoo in the castle garden, a dull Risorgimento museum (*open 9–12.30, 2–5, Tues–Sun; adm*), and the remodelled **Luigi Marzoli Museum of Arms** (*open June–Sept 10–12.45, 2–5, Tues–Sun; Oct–Mar 9–12.45, 2–6, Tues–Sun; adm*), one of Italy's most extensive collections of Brescia's bread-and-butter industry.

## The Pinacoteca

From the Capitoline Temple Via F. Crispi descends to the Via Carlo Cattaneo; at No.3, in the Piazza Labus near the intersection, you can make out the columns and lintels of the ancient Roman **Curia**, imprinted like a fossil in the wall of a house. Further down, Via Crispi opens up into the Piazza Moretto, site of the **Galleria Tosio-Martinengo** (*open 9–12.30, 2–5, Tues–Sun; adm*), Brescia's main art repository. This houses a fine collection of the local school, including paintings by Foppa, Moretto (his *Salome* is a portrait of the great Roman courtesan-poetess Tullia d'Aragona), Romanino, Moroni, and the later Ceruti, as well as a painting by Lorenzo Lotto and two early works by Raphael—a not altogether wholesome, beardless *Redeemer* and a lovely *Angel*.

From the gallery Via Moretto takes you back to the centre and the shops under the porticoes of Via Mazzini and Corso Zanardelli.

## The West Side

In the neighbourhoods west of the Piazza della Loggia and the Corso Martiri della Libertà there are a handful of monuments worth a look if you have an hour to spare. Just west of the Via S. Faustino (which leads north from the Piazza della Loggia) there are two unusual churches—**San Faustino in Riposo**, a cylindrical, steep-roofed drum of a church from the 12th century (near the intersection with Via dei Musei), and further up, the 14th-century **Santa Maria del Carmine**, crowned with a set of Mongol-like pinnacles; it contains frescoes by Foppa and a 15th-century terracotta Deposition group.

Just off the Corso G. Mameli (the western extension of Via dei Musei) **San Giovanni** is a Renaissance church with good works by Moretto and the Bolognese painter Francia. Further along the corso stands the giant **Torre Palata**, a survivor from the rough and tumble 13th century, with a travesty of a 16th-century fountain like a bunion on its foot. From here Via della Pace heads south to the venerable 13th-century **San Francesco** with frescoes, and the nearby (at the intersection of Corso Martiri) **Santa Maria dei Miracoli** with a fine, ornate Renaissance façade. Further south, off the Corso Martiri on Via Bronzetti, the 18th-century **Santi Nazaro e Celso** houses a 1522 polyptych by Titian, portraying a *Risen Christ* in the central panel; as is often the case, Titian's care to produce the last word in emotional realism in his religious art goes overboard into a numbing vision of spiritual banality.

---

*Brescia ℭ (030–)* **Where to Stay**

Brescia's hotels cater mainly to business clients, and its best hotels are comfortable if not inspiring. The city's premier hotel, the **★★★★★Vittoria**, Via X Giornate 20, ℭ 280061, @ 280065, (very expensive) has everything one would expect—large, sumptuous rooms, palatial bathrooms of French *Rosa* marble, banqueting suites, conference facilities and liberal use of marble and chandeliers throughout. It is, though, chilly and a bit soulless, due no doubt to its severe Fascist-era architecture. Near the centre by the castle, the **★★★★Master**, Via L. Apollonio 72, ℭ 399037, @ 3701331 (expensive) also has some of the best rooms in town, all with TV and other facilities A bit further out of the centre, the very modern **★★★★Ambasciatori**, Via Crocifissa di Rosa 92, ℭ 308461, @ 381883, (moderate) with a garage is a good bet for drivers; it also has very good, air-conditioned rooms, all with private bath and TV. A slightly less expensive choice is **★★★Cristallo**, Via Stazione 12, ℭ 3772468, @ 3772615, (moderate), an adequate albeit nondescript place near the station. **★★Astron**, Via Togni 14, ℭ 48220, (inexpensive) is another very pleasant option, with clean, simple rooms at a nice price.

---

*Brescia ℭ (030–)* **Eating Out**

Brescians are not known for their cooking, and in fact are looked upon as rather stolid conservatives at the table. Kid is a popular item on the local menu, and the stews, meat on a skewer and polenta dishes the Brescians favour have been in vogue since the Renaissance. The city's most celebrated restaurant, **La Sosta**, Via San Martino della Battaglia 20, ℭ 295603 (expensive) is charmingly set in a 17th-century stable that has been stripped and made elegant, though a few horsey reminders may be seen in the pictures on the wall and the hitching rings on the pillars. The food, though good, is 'international' and a bit dull. ( *Closed Mon, Aug.*) In the same price range, you can have more imaginative dining but rather less atmosphere at **Alla Stretta**, Via Stretta 63, © 2002367 (expensive), with good fish and traditional Brescian meat dishes. If you're looking to fill up at the other end of the price scale, **Bersagliera**, Corso Magenta 38, near the tourist office (inexpensive) is a good, cheap and popular pizzeria.

One of the best restaurants in the Brescia area is actually 10km away to the north, in Concesio, where the excellent **Miramonti L'Altro**, Via Crosette 34, © 2751063, (expensive) features a menu that delights both the gourmet and traditionalist, with specialities that include raw and smoked salmon, seasonal wild mushrooms, breast of duck in ginger, and kid Brescian-style. For afters, there's a fine array of mountain cheeses, or one of Miramonti's great desserts ( *Closed Mon, Aug.*)

## Around Brescia

Besides Lakes Garda and Iseo, there are a number of worthwhile excursions into the region's mountain valleys—as well as one to the south in the plain, to **Montirone** and the fine **Villa Lechi**, built in 1740 by Antonio Turbino, and little changed since the day when Mozart slept there. It has frescoes by Carlo Carloni and period furnishings, and the stables and park are equally well preserved.

To the north stretches the **Valtrompia**, a scenic agricultural valley. Its largest town, **Gardone Val Trompia**, was one of the main producers of firearms for Venice, and enjoyed the special protection of the Republic; it still makes hand-crafted sports rifles. North of Gardone the valley narrows as the road climbs to two summer resorts, **Bovegno** and **Collio**. The high mountains around the latter permit skiing in the winter. Beyond Collio a new road continues up to the scenic **Passo del Maniva** and over to the Passo di Croce Domini.

Long, narrow **Lake Idro** lies over the mountains from Collio, at the head of the Val Sabbia. Surrounded by rugged mountains and rural villages, it is the highest of the Lombard lakes, and one of the best for trout fishing. Named after the small resort town of **Idro**, its small sandy beaches are all low-key, family-oriented places. **Anfo** is another resort, while the most interesting lake settlement is **Bagolino**, on the trout-filled River Caffaro, with its peaceful medieval streets and the 15th-century church of **San Rocco**, frescoed in the 1400s by Da Cemmo. From Lake Idro you can continue up the Chiese river into Trentino's Val Giudicarie, towards Tione (*see* p.463).

## Lake Garda

The Italian lakes culminate in Garda, the largest (48km long, and 16km across at its widest point) and most dramatic, the Riviera of the Dolomites. With the profile of a tall-hatted witch, its romantic shores have enchanted poets from the days of Catullus and Virgil, who both knew it by its Roman name, *Lacus Benacus*. For travellers from the north, its olive and lemon groves, its slender cypress and exotic palm trees have long signalled the beginning of their dream Italy. No tourist office could concoct a more scintillating Mediterranean oasis to stimulate what the Icelanders call 'a longing for figs', that urge to go south.

Perhaps it's because Lake Garda is more 'Italian' that it seems less infected by the maiden auntiness of its more northerly, Swissified sisters. Less stuffy and status-conscious, it is the most popular lake, attracting a wide range of visitors, from beach bums to package tourists, and sailors and windsurfers come to test their mettle on Garda's unusual winds, first mentioned by Virgil: the *sover* which blows from the north from midnight and through the morning, and the *ora*, which blows from the south in the afternoon and evening. Storms are not uncommon, but on the other hand the breezes are delightfully cool in the summer. In the winter Garda enjoys a mild climate, less oppressed by clammy fogs and mists than the other lakes. Although services are at a minimum, winter is an ideal time to visit, when the jagged peaks of its shore shimmer with snow and you can better take in the voluptuous charms that brought visitors to its shores in the first place.

## Getting Around

 There are two **train stations** at the southern end of Lake Garda, at Desenzano and Peschiera, both of which are also landings for the lake's **hydrofoils** (*aliscafi*) and **steamers**. **Buses** from Brescia, Trento, and Verona go to their respective shores; Desenzano, the principal starting point for Lake Garda, is served by buses from Brescia, Verona and Mantua, and two exits from the *autostrada* A4. **Drivers** going to the north-west side of the lake (above Salò) and coming from the west should leave the A4 earlier, shortly after Brescia, and take the SS45.

Other local bus lines run up and down the road that winds around the lake shores— a marvel of Italian engineering, called *La Gardesana*, Occidentale (SS45) on the west and Orientale (SS249) on the east. In summer, however, their scenic splendour sometimes pales before the sheer volume of holiday traffic.

All **boat services** on the lake are operated by *Navigazione sul Lago di Garda*, Piazza Matteotti 2, Desenzano, © (030) 9141321, where you can pick up a timetable; the tourist offices have them as well. The one **car ferry** crosses from Maderno to Torri; between Desenzano and Riva there are several hydrofoils a day, calling at various ports (2 hours the full trip), as well as the more frequent and leisurely steamers (4½ hours). Services are considerably reduced in the off season, from October to March. Full fare from Desenzano to Riva on steamer is L14,200, and on the hydrofoil L19,200. There are also regular afternoon cruises from July to mid-September, calling at various different points.

## Tourist Information

While Lake Garda's west shore belongs to the province of Brescia in Lombardy, its northern tip is in Trentino and its eastern shore is in Venetia, in the province of Verona. This is a product of history, not of any plan to divvy up tourist cash among regions, and each region parochially often fails to acknowledge that Lake Garda exists beyond its own boundaries; their maps often leave the opposite shores blank, if they draw them in at all. Be sure to check area codes when telephoning.

However, an excellent joint publication that does cover the whole lake, and is available from any of the tourist offices around the shore, is *Garda Pocket*, which has extensive listings of museum opening times, sports facilities (riding, windsurfing, golf, tennis, and so on), discos, cinemas, boat times, and a bit of history about the area—all in English.

There are tourist offices in all the main lake resorts. Some of the more important are those in **Desenzano del Garda**, at Porto Vecchio 27, ✆ (030) 9141510, ✆ 9144209; **Sirmione**, at Viale Marconi 2, ✆ (030) 916114, ✆ 916222; **Gardone Riviera**, Corso Repubblica, ✆ (0365) 20347; **Gargnano**, at Piazza Feltrinelli 2, ✆ (0365) 71222; **Limone sul Garda**, Piazzale A. De Gaspari, ✆ (0365) 954781, ✆ 954355; **Riva del Garda**, Giardini di Porta Orientale 8, ✆ (0464) 554444, ✆ 520308; and in **Arco**, at Via delle Palme 1, ✆ (0464) 516161, ✆ 532353.

# The South and West Shores

## Desenzano and Solferino

**Desenzano del Garda** is the lake's largest town and its main gateway (if you arrive by train, a bus will take you to the centre). Life in Desenzano is centred around its port cafés, and a dramatic statue of Sant'Angela, foundress of the Ursuline Order. Originally a settlement of pile dwellings, Desenzano was a popular holiday resort of the Romans, and one of their **villas** has been excavated on Via Crocifisso, revealing colourful mosaics from the 4th century and a range of artefacts now kept in the small museum on the site (*villa and museum open April–Sept 9am–6.30pm Tues–Sun; Oct–Mar 9am–5pm Tues–Sun; adm*). Nearby in the parish church there's an unusual *Last Supper* by Gian Domenico Tiepolo.

As well as Lake Garda, Desenzano is also the base for visiting the low, war-scarred hills to the south. The two most important battles occurred on the same day, 24 June 1859, when Napoleon III defeated Emperor Franz Joseph at **Solferino** and King Vittorio Emanuele defeated the Austrian right wing at **San Martino della Battaglia**, 8km away. It was the beginning of the end for the proud Habsburgs in Italy, but the Battle of Solferino had another consequence as well—the terrible suffering of the wounded so appalled the Swiss Henry Dunant that he formed the idea of founding the Red Cross. At San Martino you can climb the lofty **Torre Monumentale** (*open 8.30–1, 2–5, Wed–Mon*), erected in 1893, which contains paintings and mementoes from the battle. Solferino is marked by an old tower of the Scaligeri of Verona, the **Spia d'Italia**, with a collection of uniforms; there's a battle museum by the church of **San Piero**, containing 7000 graves, and a memorial to Dunant and the Red Cross, erected in 1959 (all hours same as for the San Martino tower).

## Sirmione

> *Sweet Sirmio! thou, the very eye*
> *Of all peninsulas and isles,*
> *That in our lakes of silver lie,*
> *Or sleep enwreathed by Neptune's smiles*

*Sirmione*

So gushed Catullus, Rome's greatest lyric poet, born in Verona in 84 BC. Like many well-to-do Romans he had a villa out on the narrow 4km-long peninsula of **Sirmione** that pierces Lake Garda like a pin, just over 90m across at its narrowest point. Sirmione is the most visually striking resort on the lake, especially at the lovely **Grotte di Catullo**, entwined with ancient olive trees on the tip of the rocky promontory—romantic ruins with a capital R, not of Catullus' villa, but of a Roman bath complex (Sirmione is famous even today for its thermal spa). The views across the lake to the mountains are magnificent; there's also a small **antiquarium** on the site, with mosaics and frescoes (*open 9am–sunset Tues–Sun; adm*).

The medieval centre of Sirmione is dominated by one of the most memorable of Italian castles, the fairytale **Castello Scaligero** (*open April–Oct 9–1, 9–6; adm*), built by Mastino I della Scala of Verona in the 13th century, and surrounded almost entirely by water. There's not much to see inside, but fine views from its swallowtail battlements. Also worth a look is the ancient Romanesque church of **San Pietro in Mavino**, with 13th-century frescoes. Cars are not permitted over the bridge into the town of Sirmione, and the best swimming is off the rocks on the west side of the peninsula.

## Salò

From Sirmione the steamer passes the lovely headlands of Manerba and Punta San Fermo and the **Island of Garda**, the lake's largest, where there was a monastery once visited by St Francis. Long in ruins, it provided the base for a monumental 19th-century Venetian-Gothic-style palace, now owned by the Borghese family, one of whom, Scipione, made the famous drive from Peking to Paris in the early days of the automobile.

**Salò** (the Roman *Salodium*) enjoys one of the most privileged locations on the lake, but is best known internationally for having given its name to *Il Duce*'s last dismal stand, the puppet 'Republic of Salò' of 1943–45, formed after the Nazis rescued him from his prison in an Abruzzo ski lodge. It also has, though, a number of fine buildings, including a late Gothic **Cathedral** with a Renaissance portal of 1509, and paintings within by Romanino and Moretto da Brescia, and a golden polyptych by Paolo Veneziano. There's also a small museum, the **Museo del Nastro Azzuro**, containing information on the history of the region. **L'Ateneo**, in the Renaissance Palazzo Fantoni, contains a collection of 13th-century manuscripts and early printed books. North of Salò begins the **Brescia Riviera**, famous for its exceptional climate and exotic trees and flowers.

## Gardone Riviera and D'Annunzio's Folly

**Gardone Riviera** has long been the most fashionable resort on the Brescia Riviera, if not in the whole of Lake Garda, ever since 1880 when a German scientist noted the almost uncanny consistency of its climate. One place that profits most from this mildness is the loveliest sight in Gardone, the **Giardino Botanico Hruska** (*open April–Sept 9am–6pm; adm*), with an enormous range of exotic blooms growing between imported tufa cliffs and artificial streams. Above the garden it's a short walk to

*Il Vittoriale*

Gardone's most confounding sight, **Il Vittoriale**, the last home of Gabriele D'Annunzio (1863–1938). The house, a luxurious Liberty-style villa designed by Gian Carlo Maroni, was presented to the extravagant writer by Mussolini in 1925, ostensibly as a reward to the poet from a grateful nation for his patriotism and heroic efforts during the First World War, but also as a sop with which the *Duce* hoped to get this unpredictable figure out of the way and keep him quiet. D'Annunzio dubbed the villa, formerly owned by a German family, 'Il Vittoriale' after Italy's victory over Austria in 1918, and began to redecorate it and pull up its lovely garden, creating perhaps the world's most remarkable pile of kitsch.

## More Italian than any other Italian

D'Annunzio was a poor boy from the Abruzzo who became one of the most famous writers and poets of his generation, but not one who was convinced that the pen was mightier than the sword; a fervent right-wing nationalist, he was one of the chief warmongers urging Italy to intervene in the First World War. Later he led his 'legionaries' in the famous unauthorized invasion of Fiume, which, though promised to Italy before its entrance into the war, was to be ceded by the Allies to Yugoslavia. D'Annunzio instantly became a national hero, stirring up a diplomatic furore before coming home. For Mussolini, however, the still-popular old nationalist was a loose cannon who eventually became an acute embarrassment, and he decided to pension him off into gilded retirement on Lake Garda, correctly calculating that the gift of the villa would appeal to the great man's delusions of grandeur.

Luigi Barzini has described D'Annunzio as 'perhaps more Italian than any other Italian' for his love of gesture, spectacle, and theatrical effect—what can you say about a man who would announce that he had once dined on roast baby? Yet for the Italians of his generation, no matter what their politics, he exerted a powerful influence in thought and fashion; he seemed a breath of fresh air, a new kind of 'superman', hard and passionate yet capable of writing exquisite, intoxicating verse; the spiritual father of the futurists, ready to destroy the old bourgeois *Italia vile* of museum curators and parish priests and create in its stead a great modern power, the 'New Italy'. He lived his life of total exhibitionism, according to the old slogan of an American brewery, 'with all the gusto he could get'—extravagantly, decadently and beyond his means, at every moment the trend-setting, aristocratic aesthete, with his borzois and passionate, melodramatic affairs with the actress 'the Divine' Eleanora Duse and innumerable other loves (preferably duchesses). Apparently he thought the New Italians should all be equally eccentric and clever, and disdained the corporate state of the Fascists.

D'Annunzio made Il Vittoriale his personal egomaniacal monument, probably suspecting that one day the gaping hordes would come tramping through to marvel at his cleverness and taste. Instead, he managed to leave posterity one of the most hilarious clutter bins of all time. Unfortunately the guides only speak Italian, so the following is a summary to fill in some of the gaps if you don't. The tour begins with what must be called a 'cool reception' room for guests D'Annunzio disliked—it's austere and formal, compared to the comfy one for favourites. When Mussolini came to call he was entertained in the former; D'Annunzio, it is said, escorted *Il Duce* over to the mirror and made him read the inscription he had placed above: 'Remember that you are of glass and I of steel.' Perhaps you can make it out if your eyes have had time to adjust to the gloom. Like Aubrey Beardsley and many of the horror-movie characters played by Vincent Price, D'Annunzio hated the daylight and had the windows painted over, preferring low electric lamps.

The ornate organs in the music room and library were played by his young American wife, who gave up a promising musical career to play for his ears alone. His bathroom, with 2000 pieces of bric-à-brac, somehow manages to have space for the tub; the whole house is packed solid with a feather-duster's nightmare of art and junk. In his spare bedroom, adorned with leopard skins, you can see the cradle-coffin he liked to lie in to think cosmic thoughts. He made the entrance to his study low so all would have to bow as they entered; here he kept a bust of Duse, but covered, to keep her memory from distracting him. The dining room, with its bright movie-palace sheen, is one of the more delightful rooms. D'Annunzio didn't care much for it, and left his guests here to dine on their own with his pet tortoise, which he had had embalmed in bronze after the creature expired of indigestion, to remind the company of the dangers of overeating.

In the adjacent auditorium hangs the biplane D'Annunzio used to fly over Vienna in the War, while out in the garden the prow of the battleship *Apulia* from the Fiume adventure juts out mast and all through a copse of cypresses. Walk above this to the **Mausoleum** on its hill, a disturbing, bizarre and alien monument to delusions of grandeur, the white travertine stone glaring on bright sunny days. Within three concentric stone circles the sarcophagi of legionary captains respectfully pay court to the plain tomb of D'A himself, raised up on columns high above the others like a pagan sun-king, closer to his dark star than anyone else, the whole in hellish contrast to the Mausoleum's enchanting setting over the lake.

The Vittoriale is *open 9–12.30, 2.30–6.30, Tues–Sun; adm exp.* There's an option of buying a ticket only for the uninteresting museum and grounds; try to arrive at 9am to avoid the crowds and tour buses. In the summer there are performances of D'Annunzio's plays in the outdoor theatre.

## Toscolano-Maderno and Gargnano

The single *comune* of Toscolano-Maderno has one of the finest beaches on Lake Garda, a fine 9-hole golf course, the car ferry to Torri, and the distinction of having been the site of *Benacum*, the main Roman town on the lake. Toscolano had a famous printing press in the 15th century, and was the chief manufacturer of nails for Venice's galleys. Most of the Roman remains, however, have been incorporated into the fine 12th-century church of **Sant'Andrea** in Maderno, restored in the 16th century by St Charles Borromeo. **Gargnano** seems more of a regular town than a resort, though it was from here, in a villa owned by the publisher Feltrinelli (whose chain of bookstores are today a blessing to the English-speaking traveller in Italy), that Mussolini ruled the Republic of Salò. The main sight in town is the 13th-century Franciscan church and cloister; in the latter the columns are adorned with carvings of lemons and oranges, a reminder of the ancient tradition that the Franciscans were the first to cultivate citrus fruits in Europe.

North of Gargnano the lake narrows and the cliffs come close to the shore; here the Gardesana road pierces tunnel after tunnel like a needle as it hems through some of the most striking scenery along the lake. An equally splendid detour is to turn off at **Campione**, a tiny hamlet huddled under the cliffs, along the old military road for **Tremósine**, atop a 300m precipice that dives down sheer into the blue waters below; from the top there are views that take in the entire lake. The road from Tremósine rejoins the lake and La Gardesana at the next town along the lake, **Limone sul Garda**.

Although it seems obvious that Limone was so named because of its lemon groves, prominent in their neat rows of terraced white posts and trellises, scholars sullenly insist it was derived instead from the Latin *limen*. Nor is it true that Limone was the first place to grow lemons in Europe (the Arabs introduced them into Sicily and Spain), but none of that detracts from one of the liveliest resorts on the lake, with a beach over 3km long.

# Riva del Garda

After Limone the lake enters into the Trentino region and reaches the charming town of Riva, snug beneath an amphitheatre of mountains. Riva first blossomed as a resort during the days of Austrian rule (1813–1918), when it was labelled the 'Southern Pearl on the Austro-Hungarian Riviera'. It is one of the best bases for exploring both the lake and the Trentino mountains to the north.

The centre of town is the Piazza III Novembre with its plain, 13th-century **Torre Apponale**; just behind it, surrounded by a natural moat, stands the sombre grey bulk of the 12th-century castle, the **Rocca**, housing a civic museum with local archaeological finds from the prehistoric settlement at Lake Ledro and from Roman Riva (*open 9–12, 2.30–6, Tues–Sun*). The early 17th-century **Church of the Inviolata** was built by an unknown but imaginative Portuguese architect with a fine gilt and stucco Baroque interior. A funicular (or a steep path) makes the ascent to the Venetian watchtower, the 1508 **Bastione**.

A number of pleasant excursions are possible from Riva, but one of the best is the closest, the **Cascata del Varone**, a lovely 87m waterfall in a tight gorge only 3km away, by the village of Varone (*opening times variable according to season; adm*). Another fine excursion is up over the exciting Ponale Road (N240) to **Lake Ledro**, noted not only for its scenery but also the remains of a Bronze Age settlement of lake dwellings. One has been reconstructed on the site at **Molina**, where there's also a museum (*open Mar–June, Sept–Nov 9–12, 3–6, daily; July, Aug 9–12, 3–7 daily*). From here you can continue to Lake Idro, through the shadowy narrow gorge of the **Valle d'Ampola**.

There are also several attractive small and unspoilt villages around Riva, including **Arco**, a small resort town under its castle-crowned rock, the former property of the cultured Counts of Arco. Their 16th-century palace, and the botanical garden once owned by the Archduke, are Arco's other sights. **Dro** a little to the north in the Sarca valley is near the small lakes of Cavedine and Toblino, and on the edge of the site of an ancient glacier that left behind a vast field of boulders when it thawed. Further on lies **Drena**, and the site of another of the Counts of Arco's castles. All of these villages make good bases for walks into the surrounding countryside. Maps are, as usual, available from local tourist offices.

---

## Where to Stay

If you come to Garda in July or August without a reservation, it can mean big disappointment. For lower prices and more chance of a vacancy, try the small towns on the east shore; also check at the tourist offices for rooms in private homes. At least half-pension will be required in season at most hotels, and despite the mild climate most close up after October or November until March.

### Sirmione

For a total immersion in the peninsula's romance, the ★★★★★**Villa Cortine**, Via Grotte 12, © (030) 9905890, ✆ 916390 (very expensive) cannot be surpassed, offering its guests perhaps the rarest amenity to be found in the town—tranquillity.

Its enchanting, century-old Italian garden occupies almost a third of the entire peninsula, with exotic flora, venerable trees, statues and fountains running down to the water's edge. The neoclassical villa itself was built by an Austrian general, and was converted into a hotel in 1954, conserving its frescoed ceilings and elegant furnishings. The rooms are plush, the atmosphere perhaps a bit too exclusive, but it's ideal for a break from the real world, with private beach and dock, pool and tennis courts. (*Open April–Oct*).

Alternatively, another top choice in Sirmione, without quite the same atmosphere, is the ★★★★★**Grand Hotel Terme**, Via Marconi 7, ✆ (030) 916261, ✆ 916568 (very expensive), right beside the castle, with a private beach, pool, gym and a full health and beauty treatment programme, as well as a lovely lakeside restaurant.

A less expensive but still very comfortable place to stay is the ★★★★**Hotel Eden**, Piazza Carducci 18, ✆ (030) 916481, ✆ 916483 (moderate), housed in a medieval building in the centre that has been beautifully remodelled with fine marbles, and co-ordinated bedrooms with princely bathrooms, TV, and air-conditioning. Unusually, it does not have a restaurant. (*Open Mar–Oct.*)

Another good place to stay is ★★★**Catullo**, Piazzi Flaminia, ✆ (030) 916181 (moderate), in the heart of the old town and refurbished in 1991, with good-sized rooms and bathrooms with beautiful views and all modern amenities. Although it's more attractive on the outside than in the rooms, the ★★**Hotel Grifone**, near the Scaliger castle on Via delle Bisse 5, ✆ (030) 916014, (inexpensive) has a great location, and some of its rooms, all of which have baths, have lovely lake views. (*Open April–Oct.*) Alternatively, Sirmione has the ★★**Speranza**, Via Casello 4, ✆ (030) 916116, ✆ 916403 (inexpensive), which has all the fittings of a three-star hotel, including air-conditioning and marble bathrooms, but at significantly lower prices.

## Salò

Although less glamorous than some of its neighbours, Salò has one of Lake Garda's loveliest hotels, the ★★★★**Laurin**, Viale Landi 9, ✆ (0365) 22022, ✆ 22382, (expensive), an enchanting Liberty-style villa converted into a hotel in the 1960s, but retaining its elegant décor. The charming grounds include a swimming pool and beach access; all rooms have bath and TV.

The first-floor rooms are the ones to request in the ★★★★**Duomo**, Via Luno Lago Zanardelli 91, ✆ (0365) 21026, ✆ 21028, (expensive)—all lead out to a huge balcony, where lake-gazing can be appreciated to its fullest. The rooms are also big and modern, and there's a fine restaurant. ★★★**Benaco**, Via Lungo Lago Zanardelli 44, ✆ (0365) 20308, ✆ 20724, (moderate) is a pleasant choice on the lake front which has modern rooms, all with bathroom, TV, phone and lovely lakeside views, and a good restaurant.

The ★★★**Vigna**, Via Lungo Lago Zanarcelli 62, ✆ (0365) 520510, ✆ 520144, (moderate) has rooms that are none too individual, but comfortable and modern, and views that really steal the show.

## Gardone Riviera

Further north, Gardone Riviera and its suburb Fasano Riviera have competing Grand Hotels, both old pleasure domes. When Gardone's contender, the ★★★★**Grand Hotel**, Via Zanardelli 72, ✆ (0365) 20261, ✉ 2269, (expensive) was built in 1881, its 180 rooms made it one of the largest resort hotels in Europe. It is still one of Garda's landmarks, and its countless chandeliers glitter as brightly as when Churchill stayed there in the late forties. Almost all of the palatial air-conditioned rooms look on to the lake, where guests can luxuriate on the garden terraces, or swim in the heated outdoor pool or off the private sandy beach. The dining room and delicious food match the quality of the rooms. (*Open mid-April–mid-Oct.*)

Fasano's ★★★★**Grand Hotel Fasano**, Corso Zanardelli 160, ✆ (0365) 21051 (expensive) was built in the early 19th century as a Habsburg hunting palace and converted into a hotel around 1900. Surrounded by a large park, it's furnished almost entirely in Belle Epoque style; there are tennis courts, a heated pool, and private beach, and the restaurant is one of Lake Garda's best. (*Open May–Sept.*)

In Gardone, the lovely ★★★**Villa Fiordaliso**, Via Zanardelli 132, ✆ (0365) 20158, ✉ 290011, (expensive) is a fine turn-of-the-century hotel, where the historically minded can request (for a considerable price) the suite where Mussolini and his mistress Claretta Petacci spent the last few weeks of their lives. Located in a serene park, with a private beach, it has only seven rooms, all finely equipped; it also boasts an elegant restaurant, featuring classic Lombard and Garda dishes. (*Open all year.*)

One of the best places to stay in Fasano, just outside Gardone, is the ★★★★**Villa del Sogno**, Viale Zanardelli 106, ✆ (0365) 290181, ✉ 290230 (very expensive), its creator's 'Dream Villa' of the 1920s—done in grand Renaissance style. Although not on the lake, it has a private beach five minutes' walk away and a pool in its flower-filled garden. (*Open April–10 Oct.*) A well-aged outward appearance hides a fully refurbished and very modern interior of the ★★★**Monte Baldo**, ✆ (0365) 20951, (moderate). It now has stylish rooms, most of them with bathroom, as well as a swimming pool and restaurant. (*Open April–Oct.*) Above the main road overlooking the lake, the ★★★**Bellevue**, ✆ (0365) 20235, ✉ 290080 ((inexpensive) has a pretty garden sheltering it from the traffic. The rooms are modern, and all have private bath. (*Open Apr–10 Oct.*) Half-way up the road to Il Vittoriale is another former villa in a pleasant garden, the ★**Pensione Hohl**, ✆ (0365) 20160 (inexpensive). None of the rooms has a bath, but they're quiet, and a steal in Gardone at under L60,000.

## Gargnano

In Villa di Gargnano, just outside the main village of Gargnano, the ★★★**Baia d'Oro**, Via Gamberera 13, ✆ (0365) 71171, ✉ 72568 (moderate) is a small but charming old hotel on the lake front with an artistic inn-like atmosphere. It has a private beach, and picturesque terrace; all rooms have baths. (*Open 20 Mar–Oct.*) For a pure Victorian ambience, even if the furnishings are replicas, reserve at the ★★★**Giulia**, Viale Rimembranza 20, in Gargnano, ✆ (0365) 71022, ✉ 72774 (moderate); added attractions are its fine lake views, beach, and good food. All rooms have baths. (*Open April–15 Oct.*)

## Limone

Prices in Limone are not as high as in other resorts, and the town's best hotel, ★★★★**Le Palme**, Via Porto 36, ✆ (0365) 954681, ✉ 954120 (moderate) is housed in a pretty Venetian villa, preserving much of its original charm alongside modern amenities. In the old centre of Limone, and named after its two ancient palm trees, it has a fine terrace and tennis courts, though no beach. All 28 rooms have private baths. (*Open end Mar–Oct.*) Many of the lakeside hotels in Limone are large and ungainly, if inexpensive by Garda standards, but the ★★★**Sogno del Benaco**, Lungo Lago Marconi 3, ✆ (0365) 954026, ✉ 954327 (inexpensive) is of a more reasonable size, and has fairly standard rooms at very reasonable prices.

## Riva del Garda

When German intellectuals from Nietzsche to Günter Grass have needed a little rest and relaxation in Italy they have for many decades flocked to Riva del Garda to check in at the ★★★★**Hotel du Lac et du Parc**, Viale Rovereto 44, ✆ (0464) 520202, ✉ 555200 (very expensive). Set in a large lakeside garden, the hotel is spacious, airy and tranquil, and there are indoor and outdoor pools, a beach, sailing school, gym, sauna, and tennis courts. (*Open April–Oct.*). The turn-of-the-century ★★★★**Grand Hotel Riva**, Piazza Garibaldi 10, ✆ (0464) 521800, ✉ 552293 (expensive), majestically positioned on the main square, has 87 modern rooms looking out over the lake, and a rooftop restaurant combining fine food with incomparable views. There is also a private beach. (*Open Mar–Oct.*) Right on the port in Riva's main square, the ★★★**Hotel Sole**, Piazza III Novembre, ✆ (0464) 552686, ✉ 552811 (expensive) has plenty of atmosphere and a beautiful terrace; most rooms have private baths and look out over the lake, though they vary widely in size and quality. (*Open all year.*)

One of the best of the many hotels in the moderate category in Riva is the ★★★**Centrale**, Piazza III Novembre 27, ✆ (0464) 552344, ✉ 552138, beside the harbour, with fully equipped, spacious rooms and bathrooms. Almost as good as the Centrale, and slightly cheaper is the ★★★**Portici**, Piazza III Novembre 19, ✆ (0464) 555400, ✉ 555453 (moderate), in a nice position on the square, competely refurbished and with modern rooms all with bathrooms. The ★**Villa Minerva**, Viale Roma 40, ✆ (0464) 553031 (inexpensive) is a good economy choice which is not far from the centre, very pleasant, and very popular. (*Open all year.*) Riva also has a **youth hostel**, at Piazza Cavour 10, ✆ (0464) 554911, with beds for around L12,000 per night. (*Open Mar–Oct.*)

---

*Eating Out*

## Sirmione

One of Italy's finest restaurants is near the Sirmione peninsula, at Lugana di Sirmione: the classy **Vecchia Lugana**, Via Lugana

Vecchia, © (030) 919012 (expensive). The menu changes four times a year to adapt with the changing seasons, and the food is exquisite, prepared with a light and wise touch—try the divine mousse of lake trout. The elegant **Ristorante Grifone di Luciano**, © (030) 916097 (moderate), which shares its ancient location with the Hotel Grifone (*see* above) serves simple but delicious fish and more at moderate prices. Another fine place to dine nearby with views that rival the food is the **Piccolo Castello**, Via Dante 7, © (030) 916138 (moderate) facing the Scaliger *castello*, with fish and meat specialities from the grill.

## Gargnano

In Gargnano is the celebrated **La Tortuga**, Via XXIV Maggio 5 (near the harbour), © (0365) 71251 (expensive), a gourmet haven on Lake Garda whose specialities are delicate dishes based on seasonal ingredients and fish from the lake, perfectly prepared; there are also delicious vegetable soufflés, innovative meat courses, mouth-watering desserts and fresh fruit sherbets, and an excellent wine and spirits cellar. (*Closed Wed, three weeks in July.*)

## Salò

For a good, reasonably priced and traditional meal try the **Trattoria alla Campagnola**, Via Brunati 11, © (0365) 22153 (moderate). Garden-fresh vegetables are served with every dish, the pasta is homemade, and they make great use of wild mushrooms in season.

---

### Entertainment and Nightlife

Riva enjoys quite a hectic nightlife in season, much of it geared towards the hordes of Brits and Germans that invade the town. Many can be found in the **Lord Nelson Pub**, Viale Dante 91, © (0464) 55412, with its fairly authentic pub interior that becomes a disco in summer. For a more sedate evening's entertainment there are a couple of pleasant piano bars: **Bellavista**, Via Lungolago Verona, with a fairly calm atmosphere, except on Sunday evenings when karaoke takes over, and **Cantina Marchetti**, Piazza Marchetti, which stays open till 4am. The main place in town to get on down is **Tiffany** (*open all year 8pm–3am daily; adm*), in a lovely position in the gardens leading down to the lake. There's also live music on most Fridays.

## The East Shore: Riva to Peschiera

### Tourist Information

There are tourist offices along the eastern side of the lake in **Malcésine**, at Via Capitanato 6/8, © (045) 7400044, 🖂 7401633; **Torri del Benaco**, Via Gardesana 5, © (045) 7225120; in **Garda**, Lungolago Regina Adelaide 3, © (045) 7255194, 🖂 7256720; **Bardolino**, at Piazza Matteotti 53, © (045) 7210078, 🖂 7210872; and in **Peschiera del Garda**, at Piazza Bettelloni, © (045) 7550381.

# Torbole

The northern part of the east shore is dominated by the chain of **Monte Baldo**, rising up over **Torbole** at the mouth of the Sacra, the main river flowing into Lake Garda. Torbole is a pleasant resort, but it's also famous in the annals of naval history. In 1437, during a war with the Visconti, the Venetians were faced with the difficulty of getting supplies to Brescia because the Milanese controlled Peschiera and the southern reaches of Lake Garda. A Greek sailor came up with the following suggestion: that the Venetians sail a fleet of provision-packed warships up the Adige to its furthest navigable point, then transport the vessels over Monte Baldo into Lake Garda. Anyone who has seen Herzog's film *Fitzcarraldo* will appreciate the difficulties involved, and the amazing fact that, with the aid of 2000 oxen, the 26 ships were launched at Torbole only 15 days after leaving the Adige. Unfortunately, after all that trouble, the supplies never reached Brescia. The same trick, however, perhaps even suggested by the same Greek, enabled Mohammed II to bring his fleet into the upper harbour of Constantinople the following year, leading to the capture of the city.

# Malcésine

South of Torbole and the forbidding sheer cliffs of the Monte di Nago hanging perilously over the lake (which nevertheless attract their share of human flies), the Gardesana Orientale passes into the Veneto at **Malcésine**, the loveliest town on the east shore. The Veronese lords have always taken care to protect this part of the coast, or the 'Riviera degli Olivi' as they dubbed it, and the town is graced by a magnificent 13th-century Scaliger castle rising up on a sheer rock over the water. The castle offers a small museum and beautiful views from its tower (*open 9am–7pm daily*). It was while sketching this castle that Goethe was suspected of spying; Malcésine has since made up by erecting a bronze bust of the poet.

As well as the Scaliger castle, there's also the 16th-century **Palace of the Captains of the Lake** of Verona, now the Municipio, in the centre of Malcésine's web of medieval streets. A cableway runs up to **Bocca Tratto Spino**, just below the highest peak of Monte Baldo, the Punta del Telegrafo (2201m); its ski slopes are very popular with the Veronese, and its views are ravishing. Malcésine is also a popular walking base—for anything from a short stroll through the woods to a full-day hike—and there are numerous *rifugi* in the hills above the town (for details ask at the tourist office).

# Torri del Benaco and Garda

Further south, past a stretch of shore silvery with olives, there are two pretty resort towns on either side of the promontory of San Vigilio. The first, **Torri del Benaco**, is defended by a 1383 **Scaliger castle**, (*open 9.30–1, 4.30–7.30; adm*); in the church of **Santa Trinità** there are 14th-century Giottoesque frescoes. The ferry boat crosses over from here for Maderno; the steamer continues around the pretty **Punta di San Vigilio** with its Renaissance **Guarienti villa** by the great Venetian architect Sammicheli and old church of San Vigilio.

**Garda**, which gave the lake its modern name, predates the Romans but is known by the name the Lombards gave it, *Warthe*, 'the watch'. After Charlemagne defeated the Lombards Garda became a county, and in the now-disappeared castle, the wicked Count Berenguer secretly held Queen Adelaide of Italy prisoner in 960, after he murdered her husband Lotario and she refused to marry his son. After a year she was discovered by a monk, who spent another year plotting her escape. She then received the protection of King Otto I of Germany, who defeated Berenguer, married the widowed queen, and thus became Holy Roman Emperor. Garda has many fine old palaces, villas, and narrow medieval lanes, and is the last really scenic spot on the lake.

## Bardolino and Peschiera

Bardolino's most important crop is familiar to any modern Bacchus, and between the vine-yards rises a fine collection of 19th-century villas. It has two important churches: the 8th-century **San Zeno** and the 12th-century **San Severo**, with frescoes. The next town, **Lazise**, was the main Venetian port, and near the harbour retains a fine ensemble of Venetian buildings, as well as another Scaliger castle. Between here and Verona at Pescantina, there's a **Dinosaur Park** for addicts of concrete brontosauri, with a zoo and reptiliarium all rolled up in one, and an autosafari if you've brought the car.

**Peschiera del Garda** is an old military town on the railway from Verona, near the mouth of the River Michio that drains Lake Garda. Its strategic position has caused it to be fortified since Roman times, though the imposing walls that you see today are 16th-century Venetian, reinforced by the Austrians when Peschiera was one of the corners of the Empire's 'Quadrilateral'. Today, like Desenzano, Peschiera is mainly a transit point to the lake, but its purifying plant still helps it to fulfil its ancient role as a defender, this time of the lake's ecology and fish population. Here, too, you can treat the children—at **Gardaland**, © (045) 6410355, Italy's largest, and most massively popular, theme park (*open Mar–June, Sept–Oct 9am–6pm daily; July–mid-Sept 12 midday–12 midnight daily; adm exp*).

---

© (045–) **Where to Stay**

The east shore of Garda is more family-orientated, slower paced, and less expensive than the western side.

### Malcésine

The excellent ★★★★**Val di Sogno**, © 7400108, @ 7401694 (expensive) is situated about three minutes out of town in a beautiful setting in its own grounds right on the lake shore. There is a pool, private beach, lakeside restaurant, and modern rooms with bathroom and balcony, and all at very reasonable prices, not far above the moderate price category. ★★★**Vega**, Via Roma, © 6570355, @ 7401604 (moderate) is an inviting hotel, with big, modern rooms, all with satellite TV, minibar, safe and air-conditioning, and a private beach. Next to the lake and not far from the centre of Malcésine, the ★★★**Excelsior Bay**, © 7400380, @ 7401675 (moderate), a fine resort hotel with a pool and garden, has splendid views from the balconies of its rooms. (*Open end Mar–end Oct.*) The ★★★**Malcésine**, © 7400033, @ 7400173 (moderate, with some rooms at inexpensive-level rates) is a hotel pleasantly situated in its garden with swimming terrace, and with pleasant rooms, all with baths. A good budget option which has a good position, with lake views, and a restaurant, is ★★**Miralago**, Via Roma, © 7400111 (inexpensive). Another good cheaper place is ★★**Sirena**, Via

Roma, © 740019 (inexpensive), with some rooms with a view, and TV in most rooms, but no restaurant.

## Torri del Benaco

The most comfortable hotel in the town is the **★★★Gardesana**, Piazza Calderini 20, © 7225411, @ 7225771 (moderate), right on the harbour with splendid views of lake and castle. All rooms have baths, and breakfast and meals are served on the harbour patio when the weather is good. (*Open all year.*)

## Garda

Garda's best hotel is the **★★★★Hotel du Parc**, © 7255343, @ 7256970 (expensive), a lakeside villa that has recently been entirely refurbished and upgraded. (*Open all year.*) The **★★★★Eurotel**, © 62703333, @ 7256640, (moderate) is a large, modern, quite luxurious hotel which, again, is good value compared to the west shore hotels. It has a fine garden and pool. (*Open 9 April–Oct.*) **★★★Flora**, Via Madrina 4, ©/@ 7255348 (moderate) is an exceptionally well-priced hotel situated slightly above the town in its own grounds, and slick and modern with pine fittings, spacious rooms, all with bathroom and balcony, and fantastic amenities—tennis, mini-golf and *two* pools. Next door to the Flora, also in its own grounds and well-priced, but not quite as modern or comfortable, is **★★★Continental**, Via Giorgione 6, © 7255398, @ 7255927 (moderate)—which only has one swimming pool. The best inexpensive hotel in Garda is the **★Vittoria**, Lungolago Regina Adelaide, © 7255065 (inexpensive), at the end of the main lakefront walk. The rooms are big, with simple fittings, and service is very friendly.

---

© (045–)                                                               *Eating Out*

On the landward side of Garda, almost outside the town, the **Ristorante Stafolet**, Via Poiano 12, © 7255427, is worth asking directions to, for its wild duck and plump, spinach-filled *strangolopreti*, all at moderate prices. Less distinguished, but a good and very cheap place in which to find a full meal of stout local cooking is **Al Ponte Sel**, Via Monte Baldo 75.

A short way further south in Bardolino, you can dine well at **Aurora**, Via San Severo 18, © 7210038, near the town's pretty Romanesque landmark, the church of San Zeno. Specialities include the produce of the lake, especially trout prepared in a variety of styles, again at moderate prices.

## Venetia

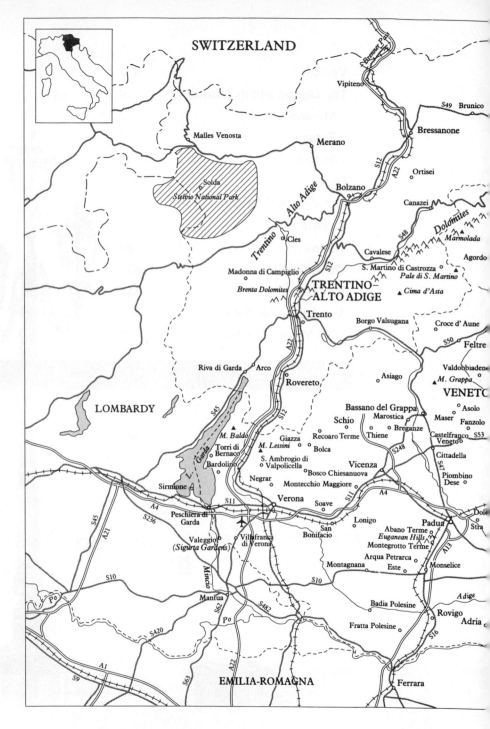

Venetia:
Veneto, Trentino-Alto Adige
and Friuli Venezia-Giulia

Venetia, sometimes known as the Three Venetias, is one of Italy's ripest showpieces and most chic holiday playgrounds, bursting at the seams with brilliant art, palaces, villas, and beautiful cities. To these add some of Europe's most ravishing mountains, Alpine lakes, and sophisticated winter sports facilities; add too a few of Italy's most famous wines, delicious seafood, and a very noticeable cultural diversity and richness. If you want to limit your holiday to a certain region of Italy, Venetia would make an exciting choice, though its very popularity can make it a trying and much more expensive one in the peak season of July and August. Late May–June and late September–October are the ideal periods to hike in the mountains or dispute with a gondolier.

Venetia encompasses roughly the region controlled by Venice from the 14th and 15th centuries until the conquest of Napoleon. It includes three modern Italian regions: the Veneto itself, and the autonomous regions of Trentino-Alto Adige (Trento and Bolzano provinces), and Friuli-Venezia Giulia (Trieste, Udine, Pordenone, and Gorizia)— stretching from the Po to the Dolomites, from Lake Garda to the border of Slovenia. In this book they have been divided into four sections: Venice, the Veneto, the Dolomites (northern Veneto and Trentino-Alto Adige) and Friuli-Venezia Giulia.

## Itineraries

For art and architecture, the best cities are the best known—Venice, Padua, Vicenza, and Verona. Veneto beauty spots include the Euganean hills near Padua, the pre-Alps (Bassano, Asolo, Conegliano, Alpago), the Monti Lessini north of Verona, and the Delta of the Po. See 'The Dolomites' section for entirely mountain itineraries, and 'Friuli-Venezia Giulia' for a special week-long itinerary in that obscure region. The best beaches by the rather grey and turgid Adriatic are at Sottomarina, Cavallino, Caorle, Lignano-Sabbiadoro and Grado; in between you will still find places which are not yet too built up, but these are becoming increasingly rare.

### The Best of Venetia: a Circular Route in a Fortnight

**Days 1–4**: Highlights of Venice and the Lagoon. **Day 5**: Padua in the morning, evening and overnight in Bassano del Grappa. **Day 6**: Maser and Asolo, in the afternoon to Vicenza, via Maròstica. **Day 7**: Vicenza, on to Verona in the afternoon. **Days 8–9**: Verona. **Day 10**: Scenic drive along Lake Garda to Trento. **Day 11**: To Bolzano and Cortina d'Ampezzo, down the Great Dolomite Road. **Days 12–13**: Around Cortina (Lake Misurina, Dobbiaco). **Day 14**: Return to Venice, via Pieve di Cadore and Conegliano.

### The Palladian Villas: Five Days to and from Padua

**Day 1**: Burchiello excursion down Brenta canal to Venice (Villa Nazionale, Villa Widmann Foscari, and La Malcontenta). Return to Padua by bus. **Day 2**: To the Euganean Hills (Villa Barbariga and Arquà Petrarca) and Fratta Polèsine, near Rovigo (Villa Badoer). **Day 3**: To

Vicenza (Villa Rotonda, Villa dei Nani, Villa Cordellina-Lombardi). **Day 4**: North to Lonedo di Lugo (Villa Godi-Valmarana and Villa Piovene) and Thiene (Castello Colleoni), on to Bassano. **Day 5**: Maser (Villa Barbaro), and if you're flush, an overnight stay in Browning's villa in Asolo, now the Hotel Villa Cipriani.

## Outstanding Roman and Medieval Art and Architecture: Ten Days

For when you begin to be satiated with Renaissance beauty—**Days 1–2**: Venice (St Mark's, Murano, Torcello). **Day 3**: Padua (Scrovegni chapel, St Anthony's) to Monselice. **Day 4**: Este and Montagnana. **Day 5**: Verona (Roman Arena, San Zeno). **Day 6**: to Maròstica, Bassano, and Cittadella. **Day 7**: to Castelfranco Veneto (morning) and to Cividale del Friuli in the afternoon. **Day 8**: Cividale. **Days 9–10**: Aquileia and Grado, and back to Venice.

## Wines in Venetia

Such a varied region as Venetia obviously produces a huge range of wines, which are enthusiastically made available for your palette and pocket at hundreds of *enoteche*, *cantine* and other outlets. There are several specific wine routes. The area around Verona, for instance, is criss-crossed with trails, passing between vineyards that produce some of Italy's best-known and most exported DOC wines, such as Soave whites and the massively marketed Valpolicella and Bardolino reds (see p.432). Further east, the best place to try Prosecco, the champagne of Italy, other than in a restaurant in Treviso, is on the *Strada del Vino Bianco* which runs from Conegliano to Valdobbiadene. As well as the very familiar labels, however, Venetia also produces many others that can be more of a discovery for wine buffs. Trentino produces some 23 DOC wines, and is especially notable for its whites and, increasingly, its sparkling wines. Try the superb whites like Riesling Renano, fruity Chardonnay, Pinot Bianco or Pinot Grigio; for a red, try Marzemino. Some of Italy's best white wines are also produced in the Alto Adige/Süd Tirol, with a marked Germanic flavour—Rieslings, Gewürtztraminer, and Sylvaner (*see* p.467). Lastly, there are seven more excellent DOC areas in the Friuli, on the far eastern borders of Italy, and a region whose products are as yet not so well known internationally (*see* p.479).

## Venice

Venice seduces, Venice irritates, but Venice rarely disappoints. She is a golden fairy-tale city floating on the sea, a lovely mermaid with agate eyes and the gift of eternal youth. On the surface she is little changed from the days when Goethe called her the 'market-place of the Morning and the Evening lands', when her amphibious citizens dazzled the world with their wealth and pageantry, their magnificent fleet, their half-Oriental doges, their crafty merchant princes, their splendidly luminous art, their lack of scruples, their silken debauchery, and their long decline and fall into a seemingly endless carnival. One can easily imagine Julius Caesar bewildered by modern Rome, or Romeo and Juliet missing their rendezvous in the traffic of modern Verona, but Marco Polo, were he to return from Cathay today, could take a

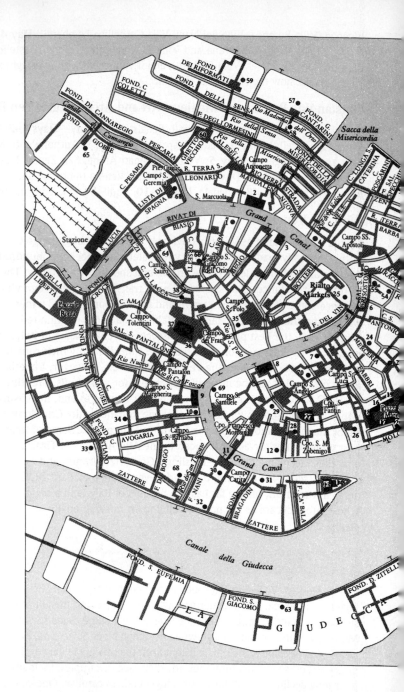

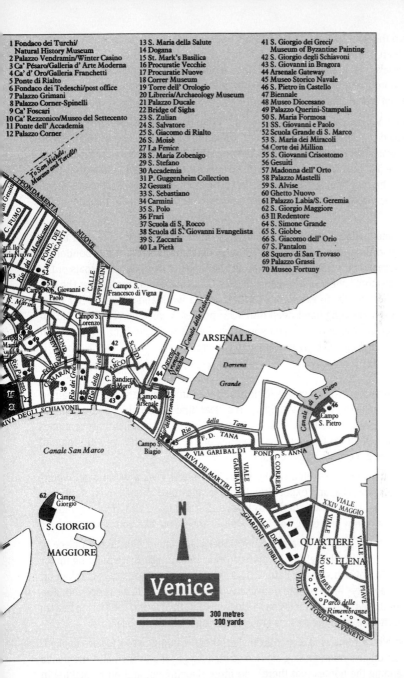

familiar gondola up the familiar Grand Canal to his house in the Rialto, astonished more by the motor-boats than anything else. Credit for this unique preservation must go to the Lagoon and the canals, the amniotic fluid of Venice's birth and the formaldehyde that has pickled her more thoroughly than many more venerable cities on the mainland, where Fiats and industry have not feared to tread.

For a thousand years Venice called herself the 'Most Serene Republic' (*la Serenissima*), and at one point she ruled 'a quarter and a half' of the Roman Empire. The descent to an Italian provincial capital was steep, if gracefully bittersweet; and sensitive souls find gallons of melancholy, or, like Thomas Mann, even death, brewed into the city's canals that have nothing to do with the more flagrant microbes. In the winter, when the streets are silent, Venice can be so evocative that you have to kick the ghosts out of the way to pass down the narrower alleys.

But most people (some million of them a year) show up in the summer, and like their ancestors, have a jolly good time. For Venice is a most experienced old siren in her boudoir of watery mirrors. International organizations pump in the funds to keep her petticoats out of the water as well as smooth the worst of her wrinkles. Notices posted throughout the city acknowledge that she 'belongs to everybody', while with a wink and swivel of her fascinating hips she slides a knowing hand deep into your pocket. Venice has always lived for gold, and you can bet she wants yours—and you might just as well give it to her, in return for the most enchanting, dream-like favours any city can grant.

## When to Go

Venice (Venezia) is as much a character as a setting, and the same may be said of its weather. In no other city will you be so aware of the light; on a clear, fine day no place could be more limpid and clear, no water as crystal bright as the Lagoon. The rosy dawn igniting the domes of St Mark's, the splash of an oar fading in the cool mist of a canal, the pearly twilit union of water and sky are among the city's oldest clichés.

If you seek solitude and romance with a capital R, go in January. Pack a warm coat, water-resistant shoes and an umbrella, and expect frequent fogs and mists. It may even snow—in 1987 you could even ski jump down the Rialto bridge. But there are also plenty of radiant diamond days, brilliant, sunny and chill; any time after October you take your chances.

As spring approaches there is Carnival, a game but rather bland attempt to revive a piece of old Venice; Lent is fairly quiet, though in the undercurrent the Venetians are building up for their first major invasion of sightseers at Easter. By April the tourism industry is cranked up to full operational capacity; all the hotels, museums, and galleries have reopened, the gondolas are un-mothballed, the café tables have blossomed in the Piazza, the Casino has relocated to the Lido. In June even the Italians are considering a trip to the beach.

In July and August elbow room is at a premium. Peripheral camping grounds are packed, queues at the tourist office's room-finding service stretch longer and longer, and the police are kept busy reminding the hordes that there's no more sleeping out and no picnicking in St Mark's Square. The heat can be sweltering, the canals nastily pungent, the ancient city gasping under a flood of cameras, shorts, sunglasses and rucksacks. Scores head off to the Lido for relief; a sudden thunderstorm over the Lagoon livens things up, as do the many festivals. In the autumn the city and the Venetians begin to unwind, the rains begin to fall, and you can watch them pack up the parasols and *cabanas* on the Lido with a wistful sigh.

## History

Venice has always been so different, so improbable, that one can easily believe the legend that once upon a time the original inhabitants sprang up from the dew and mists on the muddy banks of their Lagoon. Historians who don't believe in fairies prefer to think that Venice was born of adversity: the islands and treacherous shallows of the Lagoon provided the citizens of the Veneto a refuge from Attila the Hun and the damning heresies sweeping the mainland. Twelve Lagoon townships grew up between modern Chioggia and Grado; when Theodoric the Great's secretary visited them in 523 he wrote that they were 'scattered like sea-birds' nests over the face of the waters'.

In 697 the 12 townships united to elect their first duke, or Doge. Fishing, trading—in slaves, among other things—and their unique knowledge of the Lagoon brought the Venetians their first prosperity, but their key position in between the Byzantine Empire of the East and the 'barbarian' kings on the mainland also made them a bone of contention. Early Venice grew up helped by Byzantine patronage, but towards the end of the 8th century the Franks, who had defeated the Lombards in the name of the Pope and claimed dominion over the whole of northern Italy, turned their attention to the obstinate Venetians, hoping to add their islands to their possessions. In 810 they expected to achieve their goal when the Doge, Obelario de'Antenori, who was engaged in a bitter internal feud with other Venetian factions, invited Charlemagne's son Pepin to send his army into the city.

The Venetians, until then undecided amongst themselves whether to support Rome or Constantinople, united in response to the approach of Pepin's fleet, deposing the reviled Doge, defiantly declaring for Byzantium, and entrenching themselves on the islands of the Rialto. The shallows and queer humours of the Lagoon confounded Pepin, and after a gruelling six-month siege he gave up. It was there on the Rialto that the city republic of Venice was born, and a subsequent treaty between the Franks and the Eastern Emperor Nicephorus (814) recognized the city as a subject of Byzantium, with all-important trading concessions. Byzantine authority over the city was, though, a matter of pure theory, so from then on Venice was effectively independent.

The Venetians lacked only a dynamic spiritual protector; their frumpy, obscure St Theodore with his crocodile was too low in the celestial hierarchy to fulfil the destiny they had in mind. In 829 some Venetian merchants, supposedly on secret orders from the Doge, carried off one of the Republic's greatest coups when they purloined the body of St Mark from Alexandria; they smuggled him past the Egyptian authorities by claiming that the Saint was a shipment of pickled pork, so that the Moslem guards turned away in disgust. To acquire an Evangelist for themselves was, in itself, a demonstration of the Venetians' ambition.

## Marriage to the Sea

As the East–West trade grew in importance, the Venetians designed their domestic and external policies to accommodate it. At home they required peace and stability, and by the beginning of the 11th century had squelched aristocratic notions of an hereditary dogeship by exiling the most over-ambitious families; Venice would never have the despotic *signori* who plagued the rest of Italy.

The raids of Dalmatian pirates spurred the Venetians to fight their first major war in 997, when the great Doge Pietro Orseolo captured the pirates' coastal strongholds. The Venetians were so pleased with this first victory that they celebrated the event with a splendidly arrogant ritual every Ascension Day, the *Sensa* or 'Marriage of the Sea', in which the Doge would sail out to the Lido in his sumptuous barge, the *Bucintoro*, and cast a diamond ring into the sea, proclaiming 'We wed thee, O sea, in sign of our true and perpetual dominion'.

Venice, because of her location and her mighty fleet, supplied a great deal of the transport for the first three Crusades, and in return received her first important trading concessions in the Middle East. Arch-rival Genoa became increasingly envious, and in 1171 convinced the Byzantine Emperor to all but wipe out Constantinople's Venetian quarter. Rashly the Doge Vitale Michiel II set off with a fleet himself to launch a revenge attack upon the Empire, which was an utter failure; on his return he was killed by an angry mob (Venetians were always sore losers), and the Great Council, the *Maggior Consiglio*, was brought into being to check the power of the Doge and avert future calamities.

Vengeance stayed on the back-burner until the next Doge, the spry and cunning old Enrico Dandolo, was contracted to provide transport for the Fourth Crusade. When the Crusaders turned up without the Venetians' fee, Dandolo offered to forgo it in return for certain services: first, to reduce Venice's rebellious satellites in Dalmatia, and then, in 1204, to take Constantinople itself. Aged 90 and almost blind, Dandolo personally led the attack; Christendom was scandalized, but Venice had gained, not only a glittering hoard of loot, but three-eighths of Constantinople and 'a quarter and a half' of the Roman Empire—enough islands and ports to control the trade routes in the Adriatic, Aegean, Asia Minor and the Black Sea.

To ensure their dominance at home, in 1297 the merchant princes limited membership in the *Maggior Consiglio* to themselves and their heirs (an event known in Venetian history as the *Serrata*), inscribing their names in the famous *Golden Book*. The Doges were slowly reduced to honorary chairmen of the board, bound up by a complex web of laws and customs to prevent any dictatorial ambitions.

## A Rocky 14th Century

First the people (1300) and then the snubbed patricians (the 1310 Tiepolo Conspiracy) unsuccessfully rose up against their disenfranchisement under the Republic's government. The latter threat was serious enough that a committee of public safety was formed to hunt down the conspirators, and in 1335 this committee became a permanent institution, the infamous Council of Ten. Because of its secrecy and speedy decisions, the Council of Ten took over much of Venice's government; in later years it was streamlined into a Council of Three. Membership was for one year, and over the centuries the council (and especially its offshoot, the State Inquisition, set up in 1539) developed a reputation that fairly dripped with terror. Its techniques—inviting private denunciations, torture, secret trials and executions, all supported by a network of spies and informers—have often been compared to those of a modern police state.

Away from home the 14th century was marked by a fight to the death with Genoa over eastern trade routes. Each city annihilated the other's fleet on more than one occasion before things came to a head in 1379, when the Genoese, fresh from a victory over the Venetian commander Vittor Pisani, captured Chioggia and waited for Venice to starve, boasting that they had come to 'bridle the horses of St Mark'.

As was their custom, the Venetians had imprisoned Pisani for his defeat, but the republic was now in such a jam, with half of its fleet far away, that he was released to lead what remained of their navy. A brilliant commander, Pisani exploited his familiarity with the Lagoon and in turn blockaded the Genoese in Chioggia. When the other half of Venice's fleet came dramatically racing home, the Genoese surrendered (June 1380) and never recovered in the East.

## Fresh Prey on the Mainland

After Genoa's defeat, Venice was determined never to feel hungry again, and set her sights on the mainland—not only for the sake of farmland, but to control her trade routes into the west that were being increasingly harried and taxed by the *signori* of the Veneto. Opportunity came in 1402 with the death of the Milanese duke Gian Galeazzo Visconti, whose conquests became the subject of a great land grab. Venice snatched Padua, Bassano, Verona, and Belluno in the first round, and in 1454 added Treviso, Ravenna, Friuli, and Bergamo. In 1489 the republic reached its furthest extent when it was presented with Cyprus, a gift from the king's widow, a Venetian noblewoman named Caterina Cornaro.

But just as Venice expanded, Fortune's wheel gave a creak and conspired to squeeze her back into her Lagoon. The Ottoman Turks captured Constantinople in 1453, and although the Venetians tried to negotiate trading terms with the sultans (as they had previously done with the infidel Saracens, to the opprobrium of the West), they soon found themselves fighting and losing three centuries' worth of battles for their eastern territories. Far graver to the merchants of Venice was Vasco da Gama's voyage around the Cape of Good Hope to India, blazing a cheaper and easier route for Venice's prime markets that broke her monopoly of oriental luxuries.

On the mainland, Venice's rapid expansion had excited the fear and envy of Italy's potentates, who responded by forming the League of Cambrai (1508) with the sole aim of humbling the proud Venetians. They snatched her possessions after her defeat at Agnadello in 1509, but quarrelled amongst themselves afterwards, and before long all the territories they conquered voluntarily returned to Venice. The Republic, however, never really recovered, and although her renowned arsenal produced a warship a day, and her captains won a glorious victory over the Turks at Lepanto (1571), she was increasingly forced to retreat.

## A Most Leisurely Collapse

The odds were stacked against her, but in her golden days Venice had accumulated enough wealth and verve to cushion her fall. Her noble families retired into the country, consoling themselves in the classical calm of Palladio's villas, while the city was adorned with the solace of great masterpieces of Venice's golden age of art. Carnival, ever longer, ever more licentious, was sanctioned by the state to bring in moneyed visitors, like Lord Byron, who dubbed it 'the revel of the earth, the masque of Italy'. In the 1600s the city had 12,000 courtesans, many of them dressed as men to whet the Venetians' passion.

By the time of the French Revolution the Lion of St Mark had lost his remaining teeth, and Napoleon, declaring he would be 'an Attila for the Venetian state', took it with scarcely a whimper in 1797, neatly ending the story of the world's most enduring republic, in the reign of its 120th doge. Napoleon took the horses of St Mark to Paris as his trophy, and replaced the old *Pax tibi, Marce, Evangelista Meus* inscribed in the book the lion holds up on Venice's coat-of-arms with 'The Rights of Men and Citizens'. Reading it, a gondolier made the famous remark, 'At last he's turned the page'.

Napoleon gave Venice to Austria, whose rule was confirmed by the Congress of Vienna after the Emperor's defeat in 1815. The Austrians' main contribution was the railway causeway linking Venice irrevocably to the mainland (1846). Two years later, in the revolutionary year of 1848, Venice gave its last gasp of independence, when a patriotic revolt led by Daniele Manin seized the city and re-established the republic, only to fall to the Austrian army once again after a heroic one-year siege.

## Modern Venice

The former republic did, however, finally join the new kingdom of Italy—the last of the great Italian cities to do so—in 1866, after Prussia had conveniently defeated the Austrians. Already better known as a magnet to foreign visitors than for any activity of its own, Venice played a quiet role in the new state, though the economy did begin to change, particularly under Mussolini, when the industrial zones of Mestre and Marghera were begun on the mainland, and a road was added to the railway causeway. Luckily the city escaped damage in the two World Wars, despite heavy fighting in the environs; according to one legend, when the Allies finally occupied Venice in 1945 they arrived in a fleet of gondolas.

But Venice was soon to engage in its own private battle with the sea. From the beginning the city had manipulated nature's waterways for her own survival and defence, diverting a major outlet of the Po, the Brent, the Piave, the Adige, and the Sile rivers to keep her Lagoon from silting up. All but three outlets to the sea were blocked; and most famously, in 1782, Venice completed the famous *murazzi*, the 4-kilometre-long, 6-metre-high sea walls to protect the Lagoon. But on 4 November 1966 a combination of wind, torrential storms, high tides and giant waves breached the *murazzi*, wrecked the Lido and left Venice under record *acque alte* (high water) for 20 hours, with disastrous results to the city's architecture and art. The catastrophe galvanized the international community's efforts to save Venice. Even the Italian state, notorious for its indifference to Venice (historical grudges die slowly in Italy) passed a law in 1973 to preserve the city, and contributed to the construction of a new flood barricade similar to the one on the Thames.

This giant sea gate, known as 'Moses', has now been completed, but arguments continue over whether it will ever be effective if needed, and what its ecological consequences might be. Venice today is perennially in crisis, permanently under restoration, and seemingly threatened by a myriad potential disasters—the growth of algae in the Lagoon, the effects of the outpourings of Mestre on its foundations, the ageing of its native population, or perhaps most of all the sheer number of its tourists. Fears of an environmental catastrophe have, though, receded of late; somehow, the city contrives to survive, as unique as ever, and recent proposals to give it more of a function in the modern world, as, for example, a base for international organizations, may serve to give it new life as well.

## The Face of Venice

The historic centre of Venice stands on 117 islets, divided by over 100 canals that are spanned by some 400 bridges, each with steps that after a day's walking put enough kinks in your legs to make you want to pay the king's ransom asked for a café chair. The longest bridges are the 4.2km rail and road causeways that link Venice to the mainland. The open sea is half that distance across the Lagoon, beyond the protective reefs or *lidi* formed by centuries of river silt and the Adriatic current.

The Grand Canal, Venice's incomparable main street, was originally the bed of a river that fed the Lagoon. It snakes majestically through the heart of Venice; the other canals, its tributaries (called *rio*, singular, or *rii*, plural), were shallow channels meandering through the mud banks, and are nowhere as grand—some are merely glorified sewers. But they add up to 45km of watery thoroughfares.

A warren of 2300 alleys, or *calli*, handle Venice's pedestrian-only traffic, and they come with a colourful bouquet of names—a *rio terrà* is a filled-in canal; a *piscina* a filled-in pool; a *fondamenta* or *riva* a quay; a *salizzada* is a street that was paved in the 17th century; a *ruga* is one lined with shops; a *sottoportico* passes under a building. A Venetian square is a *campo*, recalling the days when they were open fields; the only square dignified with the title of 'piazza' is that of St Mark's, though the two smaller squares flanking the basilica are called *piazzette*, and there's one fume-filled *piazzale*, the dead end for buses and cars.

All the *rii* and *calli* have been divided into six quarters, or *sestieri*, since Venice's earliest days: **San Marco** (by the piazza), **Castello** (by the Arsenal) and **Cannaregio** (by the Ghetto), all on the northeast bank of the Grand Canal; and **San Polo** (by the church), **Santa Croce** (near the Piazzale Roma), and **Dorsoduro**, the 'hard-back' by the Accademia, all on the southwest bank. Besides these, the modern *comune* of Venice includes the towns on the Lagoon islands, the Lido, and the mainland townships of Mestre and Marghera, Italy's version of the New Jersey Flats, where most Venetians live today. There is some concern that historic Venice (population around 79,000, down from 200,000 in its heyday) may soon become a city of second homes belonging to wealthy northern Italians and foreigners.

## Dialect and Directions

Venetian dialect is still commonly heard—to the uninitiated it sounds like an Italian trying to speak Spanish with a numb mouth—and it turns up on the city's street signs. Your map may read 'San Giovanni e Paolo' but you should inquire for 'San Zanipolo'; 'San Giovanni Decollato' (decapitated John) is better known as 'San Zan Degola'. Still, despite the impossibility of giving comprehensible directions through the tangle of alleys (Venetians will invariably point you in the right direction, however, with a blithe *'sempre diritto!'*— 'straight ahead!'), it's hard to get hopelessly lost in Venice. It only measures about 1.5 by 3 kilometres, and there are helpful yellow signs at major crossings, pointing the way to San Marco, Rialto, and the Accademia, or the Piazzale Roma and the Ferrovia if you despair and want to go home. When hunting for an address in Venice, make sure you're in the correct *sestiere*, as quite a few *calli* share names. Also, beware that houses in each *sestiere* are numbered consecutively in a system logical only to a postman from Mars; numbers up to 5000 are not unusual.

## Architecture

At once isolated on her islands but deeply linked to the traditions of East and West, Venice developed her own charmingly bastard architecture, adopting only the most delightfully visual elements from each tradition. Ruskin's *The Stones of Venice* is the classic work on the city's buildings, which harsher critics—and Ruskin was one—disparage for being all artifice and show, void of any proper theories and conceptional ideals. The Venetians inherited the Byzantines' fondness for colour, mosaics, rare marbles and exotic effects, epitomized in the magnificently garish **St Mark's**. Venetian Gothic is only slightly less elaborate, and achieved its most notable products in the great palaces, most notably the **Palazzo Ducale** and the **Ca' d'Oro**, with their ogival windows and finely wrought façades.

The Renaissance arrived in Venice relatively late, and its early phase is called Lombardesque, after the **Lombardo** family (Pietro and sons Tullio and Antonio) who designed the best of it, including the small but flawless **Santa Maria dei Miracoli** and the rich **Scuola di San**

**Marco**. Later Renaissance architects brought Venice into the mainstream of the classical revival, and graced Venice with the arcaded **Piazza San Marco**, the **Libreria** of Sansovino, the **San Michele** of Mauro Codussi (also named Coducci), and two of **Palladio**'s finest churches, which stand out in clear contrast to the exuberant jumble that surrounds them. Venice's best Baroque works are by **Longhena**, the spiritual heir of Palladio.

To support all this on the soft mud banks, the Venetians drove piles of Istrian pine 5 metres into the solid clay—over a million posts hold up the church of Santa Maria della Salute alone. If Venice tends to lean and sink (2–3mm a year, according to the tourist office), it's due to erosion of these piles by the salty Adriatic, pollution, and the currents and wash caused by the deep channels dredged into the Lagoon for the large tankers sailing to Marghera. Or, as the Venetians explain, the city is a giant sponge.

Most Venetian houses are between four and six storeys high. On the tops of some you can see the wooden rooftop loggias, or *altane*, where the Renaissance ladies of Venice were wont to idle,

*Ca' d'Oro*

bleaching their hair in the sun; they wore broad-brimmed hats to protect their complexions, and spread their tresses through a hole cut in the crown.

## Venetian Art

Though a late-bloomer in painting, Venice is rivalled only by Florence when it comes to the artistic treasures she has to offer. Before the 14th century the Venetians excelled primarily in mosaic, an art they learned from the Byzantines and produced most memorably in the cathedrals of Torcello and St Mark's. But change was in the air: in 1306 Giotto was working on his great series of paintings in the Scrovegni Chapel in Padua, and his influence can be seen in the works of **Paolo Veneziano**, the first Venetian painter of note (14th century). Byzantine and Gothic tendencies, however, remained strong for a long period, especially in the works of later Venetians, the **Vivarini** dynasty of Murano and **Jacobello del Fiore**.

All of these gave way in the 15th century before the advanced styles of two great Veneto masters. **Andrea Mantegna** (1431–1506), trained in Padua, influenced generations of artists and sculptors with his strong interest in antiquity and powerful sculptural figures, while the long career of his brother-in-law, **Giovanni Bellini** (1440?–1516) marked the transition in Venice from the Early to the High Renaissance. Giovanni's father, **Jacopo Bellini**, instilled a love of nature and the senses in his son, who was later influenced by the luminous oil painting techniques of **Antonello da Messina** (who visited Venice in 1475). The light and colour that are the hallmarks of Venetian painting were first explored by Giovanni Bellini, and his sweet Madonnas are one of the delights of the Italian Renaissance. Other noteworthy artists of the Venetian quattrocento include **Vittore Carpaccio** (1470–1523), the charming master of narrative painting, and **Carlo Crivelli** (1432–1493), a lover of clear detail—and cucumbers—who spent his later career in the Marches.

## The Cinquecento

The 16th century is often called the Golden Age of Venetian Art. While the rest of Italy followed the artists in Rome in learning drawing and anatomy, the Venetians went their own way, obsessed with the dramatic qualities of atmosphere. **Giorgione of Castelfranco** (1475–1510), a pupil of Bellini, was the seminal figure in this new manner; his *Tempest* in the Accademia is a remarkable study in brooding tension. Giorgione is also credited with inventing 'easel painting'—art that served neither Church nor State nor the vanity of a patron, but stood on its own for the pleasure of the viewer.

Giorgione's pupil, Tiziano Vecellio, or **Titian** (1477–1576), was another major transitional figure in Venetian art; while his early works are often confused with his master's, his later career is marked by dramatic, often spiralling compositions and striking tonal effects produced by large brushstrokes. His contemporary, **Tintoretto** (1518–94), took these Mannerist tendencies to unforgettable extremes, while *trompe l'œil* master **Paolo Veronese** (1528–88), originally of Verona, painted visually lavish canvases that are the culmination and epitome of all that Venice had to teach.

Other outstanding Venetians of the period include **Cima da Conegliano**, creator of some of Venice's loveliest landscapes, and **Palma il Vecchio**, Titian's rival, fond of depicting luscious blonde Venetian goddesses.

Venetian painting, from Titian on, was the international style of its day, and it enjoyed a healthy revival in the 18th century when demand was high in Venice and abroad. **Giambattista Tiepolo** (1696–1770) and his son **Giandomenico** were the masters of a huge school of theatrical, buoyant ceiling art and narrative frescoes, while **Antonio Canaletto** (1697–1768) and **Francesco Guardi** (1712–93) produced countless views of Venice that were the rage among travellers on the Grand Tour; even today the majority of their works are in Britain and France. **Pietro Longhi**, their contemporary, devoted himself to genre scenes that offer a delightful insight into the Venice of 200 years ago.

## Getting There

### by air

Venice's **Marco Polo Airport** is 13km north of the city near the Lagoon, and has regularly scheduled connections from London, New York (via Milan), Paris, Vienna, Nice, Zürich, Frankfurt, Düsseldorf, Rome, Milan, Palermo, and Naples. For flight information in Venice, © 661262.

The airport is linked with Venice by water-taxi (© 964084), the most expensive option (L100,000); or by *motoscafi* with San Marco (Zecca) roughly every hour and a half (L15,000 per person), although there are connections with most flights from Mar–Oct, and if you're catching an early flight, you can reserve a departure (© 5222303). There is also an ATVO bus to the Piazzale Roma (L7000) or, cheapest of all, the ACTV city bus no.5 (L1000), which runs once an hour.

Some **charter flights** arrive at Treviso, 30km to the north. If a transfer is not included with your ticket the way to get into Venice is to catch bus no.6 into Treviso, from where there are frequent trains and buses to the city.

### by sea

Adriatica lines (Zattere 1412, © 5204322), has connections every 10 days in June–September with Split (15 hours) and Dubrovnik (24 hours). There are also 34 car-ferry journeys a year—roughly every 10 days between Venice and Piraeus (2 days), Heraklion, Crete (2½ days), and Alexandria (3½ days). An easier way to approach Venice on water is by taking the *Burchiello* from Padua along the Brenta Canal (see p.395).

### by rail

Venice's **Stazione Santa Lucia** is the terminus of the *Venice Simplon-Orient Express* and numerous other less glamorous trains from the rest of Europe and Italy. There are frequent connections to Padua (every half-hour, and a ½-hr journey), where the budget-conscious visitor may prefer to stay; and also frequent trains from Milan (3½-hr journey time), Bologna (2hrs), Florence (4hrs), Rome (8hrs), and Trieste (2½hrs). All trains from Santa Lucia stop in Mestre, where you may have to change for some destinations. For rail information, © 715555.

Water-taxis, *vaporetti*, and gondolas (see below) wait in front of the station to sweep you off into the city. If you've brought more luggage than you can carry, one of

Venice's famous/infamous porters (distinguished by their badges) will lug it to your choice of transport, and if you pay his fare on the water-taxi, will take it and you to your hotel (official price for one or two pieces of luggage is L8350 between any two points in the historic centre, an extra bag is L2350)—or you can track down a porter once you disembark at one of the main landings or the Lido.

### by bus

Piazzale Roma is Venice's bus terminus; there are frequent city buses from here to Mestre, Chioggia, Marghera, and Malcontenta; regional buses every half-hour to Padua, and less frequently to other Veneto cities and Trieste. It has its own helpful tourist information office, © 5227404.

### by car

All roads to Venice end at the monstrous municipal parking towers in **Piazzale Roma** or its cheaper annex, **Tronchetto**, nothing less than the largest car park in Europe. You can leave your car there for L24,000 a day, if they're not bursting at the seams, as they often are in summer. The Italian Auto Club (ACI) runs three alternative car parks (open to non-members): **Fusina**, © 969460, with a shady, year-round campsite, located at the mouth of the Brenta Canal south of Marghera (car park open summer only; *vaporetto* no.16 to Venice); **S. Giuliano**, © 970434, in Mestre near the causeway (bus service to Venice), and **Punta Sabbioni**, © (0421) 92002, in between the Lido and Jesolo, (reached by ferry boat no.17 from Tronchetto).

---

## Getting Around

 Apart from the obvious fact of there being no road traffic, one other peculiarity in finding one's way around Venice is the street numbering system—the addresses given you will be for individual streets, but houses are numbered not by those streets but by each one of the six *sestieri* or districts, so that numbers along tiny alleys can frequently reach into the thousands.

### vaporetti and motoscafi

Public transport in Venice means by water, by the grunting, canal-cutting **vaporetti** (the all-purpose water-buses), or the sleeker, faster *motoscafi*, both run by the ACTV (© 5287886). Each line has a number, and timetables and prices are posted at each stop. There is a flat ticket price for any one journey on each route (*see* below). A *vaporetto* that only calls at some of the stops on a route, and so is slightly speedier, is called a *diretto*; the deviously-named *accelerato* pulls in at every one. A third type, a *traghetto*, simply makes a direct crossing of a body of water, be it the Grand Canal, the Giudecca Canal, or whatever, and so is quite a bit cheaper. Note that the only canals served by public transport are the Grand Canal, the Rio Nuovo, the Canale di Cannaregio and the Rio dell'Arsenale; between them, you'll have to rely on your feet, which is not as gruelling as it sounds, as Venice is so small you can walk across it in an hour.

If you intend to hop on a boat at least six times in a given day, consider purchasing a **24-hour tourist pass**, valid for unlimited travel on all lines, for L9000, or the **3-day pass**, for L17,000. Single tickets need to be purchased and validated in the machines at the landing stages, and as many of these don't always have staff on duty to sell tickets it's best to stock up. Most *Tabacchi* and other shops displaying an ACTV sticker sell them in blocks of ten. If you plan to spend more than a few days in Venice, the **Carta Venezia** is a good investment; it costs L8000, but is valid for three years and entitles you to sizeable discounts on all ACTV services. To get one take your passport and a photo to ACTV central office in Corte dell'Albero, on the Grand Canal by the S. Angelo stop.

Lines of most interest to visitors are listed below; most run until midnight. Summer-only services usually run from April to September. Precise schedules are listed in the tourist office's free monthly guide, *Un Ospite di Venezia*.

**Line 1** (*accelerato*, L2500) runs from the Piazzale Roma and the Ferrovia (station), down the Grand Canal, to San Marco and the Lido, stopping everywhere; around the clock, every 10min, although much less frequently after 9pm. The entire journey takes one hour.

**Line 2** (*diretto*, L2500) takes the short cut from Piazzale Roma, Tronchetto and the Ferrovia through the Rio Nuovo to Rialto, Accademia, San Marco and Lido. Every 10min during the day, approximately once an hour at night.

**Line 5** (*servizio circolare*, L2500) the circular route, makes a circuit of the whole city and two of the nearest islands, running either to the left (*sinistra*) or right (*destra*) and departing every 15min. Main points of interest are the Fondamente Nuove, the islands of Murano and San Michele, Campo della Tana (where you can take a peek inside the Arsenale), San Zaccaria, Isola di San Giorgio Maggiore, Redentore, Zattere, Piazzale Roma, Ferrovia, Ponte delle Guglie (Canale di Cannaregio) and Madonna dell'Orto.

**Line 5bar** (*direttissimo*, L2500), a summer-only line from Tronchetto, Piazzale Roma, the Ferrovia, Murano and S. Elena to S. Zaccaria and vice versa (every 30min).

**Line 6** (*diretto motonave*, L1750) is the large steamer from the Riva degli Schiavoni to the Lido (every 20min).

**Line 8** (L2500), the motorists' friend, from S. Zaccaria via Giudecca, Zattere and Sacca Fisola to Tronchetto, and vice versa.

**Line 9** (*traghetto*, L1200), from Zattere to Giudecca every 15min.

**Line 12** (L3300), Fondamente Nuove to Murano, Burano, Torcello and Treporti (one an hour).

**Line 13** (L3300), Fondamente Nuove to Murano, Vignole and S. Erasmo (one an hour).

**Line 14** (L3300), Riva degli Schiavoni to the Lido and Punta Sabbioni (every half-hour).

**Line 16** (L3,300), Zattere to the Fusina car park, on the mainland (summer only).

**Line 17** Car ferry from Tronchetto (Piazzale Roma) to the Lido (every 50min).

**Line 28** (L2,500), from Piazzale Roma and Tronchetto to S. Zaccaria and the Lido (summer only).

**Line 34** (*diretto*, L2500), from S. Marco via Giudecca, Tronchetto, Piazzale Roma, Ferrovia, Rialto, Accademia, San Marco and Giardini della Biennale to the Lido, and vice versa (summer only).

At San Marco you can also find a number of **excursion boats** to various points in the Lagoon; they are more expensive than water buses, but may be useful if you're pressed for time.

### water-taxis

These are really more tourist excursion boats—they work like taxis, but their fares are de luxe. Stands are at the station, Piazzale Roma, Rialto, San Marco, Lido, and the airport. These stylish motor boats can hold up to 20 passengers, and fares are set for destinations beyond the historic centre, or you can pay L125,000 per hour. Within the centre the basic fare for up to four people is L27,000 for the first four minutes, after which the meter starts spinning; additional passengers are L2500 each, and there are surcharges for baggage, holiday or nocturnal service (after 10pm), and for using a radio taxi (© 5232326).

### gondolas

Gondolas, first mentioned in the city's annals in 1094, have a stately mystique that commands all other boats to give way. Shelley and many others have compared them to a funeral barque or the soul ferry to Hades, and not a few gondoliers share the infernal Charon's expectation of a solid gold tip for their services. Like Model Ts, gondolas come in any colour as long as it's black, still obeying the Sumptuary Law of 1562, though nowadays hardly any gondolas have their traditional cabins, once notorious for clandestine trysts.

Once used by all and sundry like carriages or taxis, gondolas now operate quite frankly for tourists who can pay the official L70,000 for a 50-minute ride (L90,000 after 8pm). Most gondolas can take six people, and before setting out agree with the gondolier on where you want to go and how long you expect it to take to avoid any unpleasantness later on. The above prices are the official tariff, but many gondoliers, especially in high season, will wish to negotiate a premium.

In addition, gondolas retired from the tourist trade are used for **gondola traghetti** services across the Grand Canal at various points between its three bridges— your only chance to enjoy an economical, if brief, gondola ride for L500. *Traghetto* crossings are signposted in the streets nearby. For appearance's sake you'll have to stand up for the short but precarious experience: only sissies ever sit down on *traghetti*.

### hiring a boat

Perhaps the best way to spend a day in Venice is by bringing or hiring your own boat—a small motor boat or a rowing boat—though beware of the Venetian type of oar, which requires practice to use. It can be difficult to find a boat for hire, but ask Bruno Bianchini in the Piazza San Marco tourist office for suggestions. *Motoscafi* for hire are easier to find, especially with chauffeurs: try Cooperativa Motoscafi, S. Marco 978, © 5235775; Narduzzi & Solemar, S. Marco 2828, © 5287701; or La Lagunare Motoscafi, Viale S. Marco 119/10, Mestre, © 5315039.

### car hire

If you want to explore the mainland by car, several hire firms have offices at Piazzale Roma, Marco Polo airport, or Mestre station: Autorent, © 5289494; Avis, © 5225825; Budget, © 5414299; Europcar, © 5238616; International, © 5206565; Maggiore, © 5415040.

---

## Tourist Information

The main information office of the local tourist board (APT) is under the arcades in one corner of Piazza San Marco, to the far left as you face the square (Ascensione 71/c, © 5226356, ✆ 5298730). Branch offices at the station (© 715016) and the bus station in Piazzale Roma (© 5227402) offer accommodation services. There are also offices on the Marghera *autostrada* (© 921638), and on the Lido at Gran Viale 6 (© 765721).

Tourist offices provide a free, if not too detailed, street map, and also have a separate free booklet and map, *Veneziapertutti*, with information on **disabled access** and facilities in the city. The main source for information in English on any current events is the magazine *Un Ospite di Venezia*, distributed free at tourist offices. Otherwise, the two local papers *Il Gazzettino* and *Nuova Venezia* both have listings of films, concerts and so on in Venice and the *terraferma*. The phone code for Venice from elsewhere in Italy is **041**.

Venice offers a free youth pass (**Carta Giovani**) to people aged between 14 and 29, which gives discounts to the city's attractions, from films in the Film Festival to shops and restaurants. Apply at the APT offices, with a photo and your passport. Also, anyone of whatever age interested in visiting more than two out of five specified museums—the Museo Correr, the Palazzo Ducale, Ca' Pésaro, Ca' Rezzonico and the Glass Museum in Murano—might wish to buy a **Biglietto Cumulativo**, sold at the museums themselves, which gives you admission to each of them for L16,000.

**Fire,** © 115
**Police emergencies,** © 113
**Police**, Fondamenta S. Lorenzo, Castello, © 5200754.
**Ambulance,** © 523

**Hospital: Ospedale Civili di Venezia**, Campo SS. Giovanni e Paolo, ✆ 5294516.

**24-hour pharmacies:** Call ✆ 192 for a list of those open each day.

Places that exchange money outside normal banking hours include **American Express**, S. Moisè 1471, S. Marco, ✆ 5200844, open April–Oct 8am–8pm Mon–Sat; **CIT**, Piazza S. Marco 4850, ✆ 5285480, open 8am–6pm Mon–Sat; **INTRAS**, Piazza S. Marco, open 8.30am–6pm Mon–Sat.

The main post office is in the Fondaco dei Tedeschi, near the Ponte Rialto, and is open 8.15am–7pm Mon–Sat. There are also smaller offices off Piazza San Marco (Calle dell'Ascensione; open 8.15am–1.25pm Mon–Fri, 8.15am–12 midday Sat) and on the Zattere. There are phone centres alongside the Fóndaco dei Tedeschi post office and in Piazzale Roma.

---

# The Grand Canal

A ride down Venice's bustling and splendid main artery is most visitors' introduction to the city, and there's no better one. The Grand Canal has always been Venice's status address, and along its looping banks the aristocrats, or *Nobili Homini*, as they called themselves, built a hundred marble palaces with their front doors giving on to the water, framed by the peppermint-stick posts where they moored their watery carriages. The oldest palaces, dating back to the 12th century, reveal Byzantine influences, but most are either Venetian Gothic or Lombardesque, or a combination of several periods and styles remodelled over the years.

Connoisseurs of palaces can purchase guides of the Grand Canal that give details of each structure, but in brief the most acclaimed, heading from Piazzale Roma to the Piazza San Marco, are: the **Fóndaco dei Turchi** (on the right after the Station Bridge), formerly the Turkish warehouse, and now the Natural History Museum; almost opposite, Mauro Codussi's Renaissance **Palazzo Vendramin-Calergi**, where Richard Wagner died in 1883, now the winter home of the casino. Back on the right bank, just after the San Stae landing, the Baroque **Palazzo Pésaro** is adorned with masks by Longhena. And then comes the loveliest of them all, the **Ca' d'Oro**, by its own landing stage, with an elaborate florid Gothic facade, formerly etched in gold, now housing the Galleria Franchetti (see p.371).

After the Ca' d'Oro Europe's most famous bridge, the **Ponte di Rialto**, swings into view. 'Rialto' recalls the days when the canal was the Rio Alto; originally it was spanned here by a bridge of boats, then by a 13th-century wooden bridge. When that was on the verge of collapse, the republic held a competition for the design of a new stone structure. The winner, Antonio da Ponte, was the most audacious, proposing a single arch spanning 48m; built in 1592, it has since defied the dire predictions of the day and still stands, even taking the additional weight of two rows of shops. The reliefs over the arch are of St Mark and St Theodore.

To the right stretch the extensive **Rialto Wholesale Markets**, and on the left the **Fóndaco dei Tedeschi** (German Warehouse), once the busiest trading centre in Venice, where merchants from all over the north lived and traded. The building (now the post office) was remodelled in 1505 and adorned with exterior frescoes by Giorgione and Titian, of which only some fragments survive (now in the Ca' d'Oro).

Beyond the Ponte di Rialto are two Renaissance masterpieces: across from the S. Silvestro landing, Sanmicheli's 1556 **Palazzo Grimani**, now the Appeals Court, and Mauro Codussi's **Palazzo Corner-Spinelli** (1510) just before Sant'Angelo landing stage. A short distance further along the left bank are the **Palazzi Mocenigo**, actually three palaces in one, where Byron lived for two years. A little way further on on the same side a space opens up in the wall of buildings, the Campo San Samuele, dominated by the **Palazzo Grassi**, an 18th-century neoclassical residence that has been completely renovated by the Fiat Corporation as a modern exhibition and cultural centre.

On the right bank, just after the bend in the canal, the lovely Gothic **Ca' Foscari** was built in 1437 for Doge Francesco Foscari: two doors down, by its own landing-stage, is Longhena's 1667 **Ca' Rezzonico**, where Browning died. Further on the canal is spanned by the wooden **Ponte dell'Accademia**, built in 1932 to replace the ungainly iron 'English bridge'.

On the left bank, before S. Maria del Giglio landing, the grand Renaissance **Palazzo Corner** (Ca' Grande) was built by Sansovino in 1550. On the right bank, Longhena's famous Baroque **Santa Maria della Salute** and the Customs House, or **Dogana di Mare**, crowned by a golden globe and weathervane of Fortune, guard the entrance to the Grand Canal. The next landing-stage is San Marco.

## Byron Goes Swimming

Byron arrived in Venice in 1816, his heart full of romance as he rented a villa on the Brenta to compose the last canto of his *Childe Harolde's Pilgrimage*. The city's canals at least afforded him the personal advantage of being able to swim anywhere (his limp made him shy of walking); on one occasion he swam a race from the Lido to the Rialto bridge and was the only man to finish.

It wasn't long before the emotional polish of *Childe Harolde* began to crack. To Byron's surprise, Venice didn't aggravate his romantic temperament, but instead cured him of it. He went to live in the Palazzo Mocenigo on the Grand Canal, in the company of 14 servants, a dog, a wolf, a fox, monkeys and a passionate, garlicky baker's wife, *La Fornarina*, who stabbed him in the hand with a fork—which so angered Byron that he ordered her out, whereupon she threw herself into the Grand Canal. Under such circumstances, all that had been breathless passion reeked of the ridiculous, as he himself admitted:

> *And the sad truth which hovers o'er my desk*
> *Turns what was once romantic to burlesque*

Venice, its women, its ironic detachment and its love of liberty set Byron's mind free to write first *Beppo: A Venetian Story*, spoofing Venice's *cavalieri serventi* (escorts/lovers—even nuns had them) while celebrating the freedom of its people. He wrote two bookish plays on Venetian themes, *Marino Faliero* and *The Two Foscari*, and most importantly began his satirical masterpiece, *Don Juan*.

Meanwhile too much debauchery took its toll: an English acquaintance wrote in 1818 that 'His face had become pale, bloated and sallow, and the knuckles on his hands were lost in fat'. Byron became infatuated with a young Countess, Teresa Guiccioli, and left Venice to move in with her and her elderly husband in Ravenna. But, having tasted every freedom in Venice, Byron once more began to chafe; the Contessa was 'taming' him. He bundled up the manuscript of *Don Juan* and left, only to die of fever at the age of 36 in the Greek War of Independence.

## Piazza San Marco

Napoleon described this grand asymmetrical showpiece as 'Europe's finest drawing-room', and no matter how often you've seen it in pictures or in the flesh, its charm never fades. There are Venetians (and not all of them purveyors of souvenirs) who prefer it in the height of summer at its liveliest, when Babylonians from the four corners of the earth outnumber even the pigeons, who swoop back and forth at eye level, while the rival café bands provide a schmaltzy accompaniment. Others prefer it in the misty moonlight, when the familiar seems unreal under hazy, rosy streetlamps.

The piazza and its two flanking *piazzette* have looked essentially the same since 1810, when the 'Ala Napoleonica' was added to the west end, to close in Mauro Codussi's long, arcaded **Procuratie Vecchie** (1499) on the north side and Sansovino's **Procuratie Nuove** (1540) on the south. Both, originally used as the offices of the 'procurators' or caretakers of St Mark's, are now lined with jewellery, embroidery and lace shops. Two centuries ago they contained an equal number of coffee-houses, the centres of the 18th-century promenade. Only two survive—the **Caffè Quadri** in the Procuratie Vecchie, the old favourite of the Austrians, and **Florian's**, in the Procuratie Nuove, its hand-painted décor unchanged since it opened its doors in 1720, although with coffees at L7000 a head the proprietors could easily afford to remodel it in solid gold.

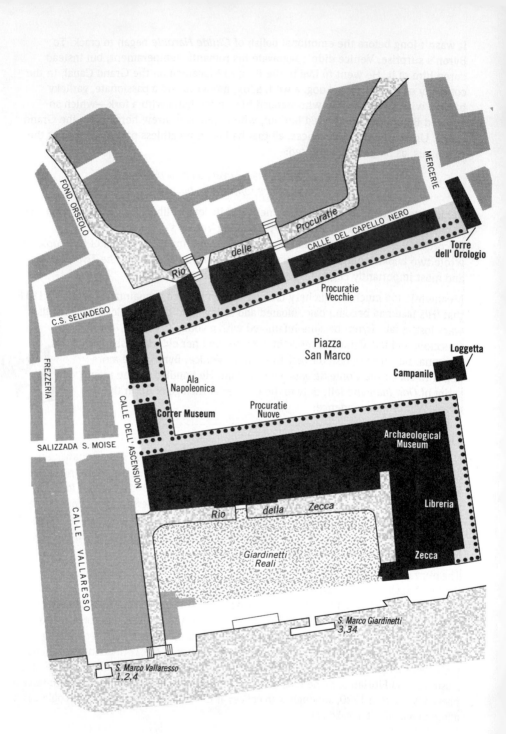

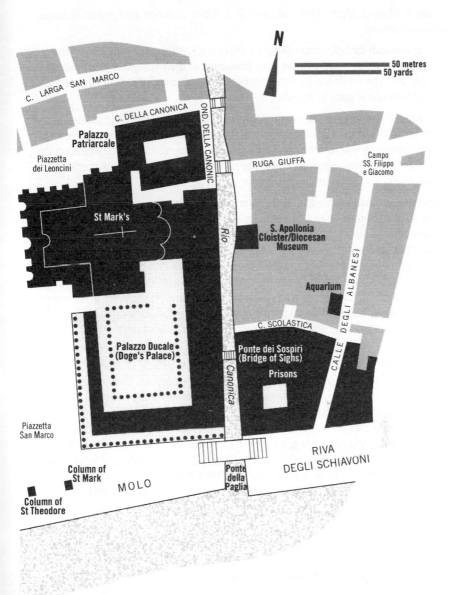

C. LARGA SAN MARCO

C. DELLA CANONICA

OND. DELLA CANONIC

**Palazzo Patriarcale**

Piazzetta dei Leoncini

RUGA GIUFFA

Campo SS. Filippo e Giacomo

**St Mark's**

Rio

**S. Apollonia Cloister/Diocesan Museum**

**Aquarium**

CALLE DEGLI ALBANESI

C. SCOLASTICA

**Palazzo Ducale (Doge's Palace)**

Canonica

**Ponte dei Sospiri (Bridge of Sighs)**

**Prisons**

Piazzetta San Marco

RIVA DEGLI SCHIAVONI

**Column of St Mark**

MOLO

**Ponte della Paglia**

**Column of St Theodore**

N

50 metres
50 yards

**Piazza San Marco**

# St Mark's Basilica

*Open 9.30am–5.30pm, Mon–Sat, and 2–5.30pm, Sundays and public holidays; adm (see below).*

This is nothing less than the holy shrine of the Venetian state. An ancient law decreed that all merchants trading in the East had to bring back from each of their voyages a new embellishment for St Mark's. The result is a glittering robbers' den, the only church in Christendom that would not look out of place in Xanadu.

Until 1807, when it became Venice's cathedral, the basilica was the private chapel of the doge, built to house the relics of St Mark after their 'pious theft' in 828, a deed sanctioned by a tidy piece of apocrypha that had the good Evangelist mooring his ship in the Rialto on the way from Aquileia to Rome, when an angel hailed him with the famous *'Pax tibi...'*, or 'Peace to you, Mark, my Evangelist. Here your body shall lie.'

The present structure, consecrated in 1094, was begun after a fire destroyed a previous St Mark's in 976. Modelled after Constantinople's former Church of the Apostles, five rounded doorways, five upper arches and five round Byzantine domes are the essentials of the exterior, all frosted with a sheen of coloured marbles, ancient columns and sculpture ('As if in ecstasy,' wrote Ruskin, 'the crests of the arches break into marbly foam...'). The spandrils of the arches glitter with gaudy, Technicolor mosaics—the High Renaissance, dissatisfied with the 13th-century originals, saw fit to commission cartoons from several painters for the scenes, leaving intact only the *Translation of the Body of St Mark* on the extreme left, which includes the first historical depiction of the basilica itself.

Front and centre, seemingly ready to prance off the façade, the controversial 1979 copies of the bronze **horses of St Mark** masquerade well enough—from a distance. The ancient originals (cast some time between the 3rd century BC and 2nd century AD, and now inside the basilica's Museo Marciano) were one of the most powerful symbols of the Venetian Republic, part of a 'triumphal quadriga' taken by Constantine the Great from Chios to grace the Hippodrome of his new city, only to be carried off in turn by the artful Doge Dandolo in the 1204 Sack of Constantinople. Another prize from Byzantium are the four porphyry 'Moors' huddled in the corner of the south façade near the Doge's Palace; according to legend, they were changed into stone for daring to break into St Mark's treasury, though scholars prefer to believe that they are four chummy 3rd-century Roman Emperors, the Tetrarchs.

There are separate admission charges for many of the smaller chapels and individual attractions, and different sections of the basilica are also frequently closed for restoration. Beadles enforce a dress code fairly strictly; shoulders must be covered, and shorts above the knee and anything that looks like beachwear are not allowed for men or women. There is a ramp for wheelchair access at the Piazzetta dei Leoncini entrance.

## The Interior

The best mosaics, most of them 13th-century originals, cover the six domes of the **atrium**, or narthex, their old gold glimmering in the permanent twilight. The oldest mosaic in St Mark's is that of the *Madonna and Saints* above the central door, part of the original 11th-century decoration of the basilica. A slab of red marble in the pavement marks the spot where the Emperor Barbarossa knelt and apologized to 'St Peter and his pope'—Alexander III, in 1177. This, a favourite subject of Venetian state art, is one of the few gold stars the republic ever earned with the papacy; mistrust and acrimony were far more common.

The interior, in the form of a Greek cross, dazzles the eye with the intricate splendour of a thousand details. The domes and upper vaults are adorned with golden mosaics on the New Testament, the oldest dating back to the 11th century, though there have been several restorations since. Ancient columns of rare marbles, alabaster, porphyry and verdantique, sawn into slices of rich colour, line the lower walls; the 12th-century pavement is a magnificent geometric mosaic of marble, glass, and porphyry. Like a mosque, the central nave is covered with Eastern carpets.

The first door on the right leads to the 14th-century **baptistry**, much beloved by John Ruskin and famous for its mosaics on the life of John the Baptist, with a lovely Salome in red who could probably have had just as many heads as she pleased. It has been closed for restoration for several years, but with luck may have reopened by the time you visit. A door from the baptistry leads into the **Cappella Zen**, designed by Tullio Lombardo in 1504 to house the tomb of one Cardinal Zen, who had left a fortune to the Republic on condition he be buried in St Mark's. Further along the right transept you can visit the **treasury** (*adm*), containing the loot from Constantinople that Napoleon overlooked—fairy-tale-like golden bowls and crystal goblets studded with huge coloured gems.

Near the Altar of the Sacrament, at the end of the right transept, a lamp burns 'eternally' next to one pillar: after the 976 fire, it appeared that the body of St Mark had been lost, but in 1094 (after Bari had beaten Venice to the relics of St Nicolaus) the good Evangelist was made to stage a miraculous reappearance, popping his hand out of the pillar during Mass. St Mark is now said to be be buried in a crypt under the high altar, in the **sanctuary** (*adm*). The highlight of the sanctuary is the retable of the altar, the fabulous, glowing **Pala d'Oro**, a masterpiece of medieval gold and jewel work. The upper section may originally have been in the Church of the Pantocrator in Constantinople, and the lower section was commissioned in that same city by Doge Pietro Orseolo I in 976. Over the years the Venetians added their own scenes, and the Pala took its present form in 1345.

In the left transept the **Chapel of the Madonna of Nicopeia** shelters a much-venerated 10th-century icon, the *Protectress of Venice*, formerly carried into battle by the Byzantine Emperor. More fine mosaics are further to the left in the Chapels of St Isidore (whose body the Venetians kidnapped from Chios—and in the mosaic he seems happy to go, grinning like a chimp). In the **Chapel of the Madonna dei Máscoli**, there are fine mosaics on the *Life of the Virgin* by Andrea Castagno and Michele Giambono (1453), that were among the first harbingers of the Renaissance in Venice.

Before leaving the narthex, climb the steep stair near the west door to the **Museo Marciano, Galleria and Loggia dei Cavalli** (*adm*), where you can walk through part of the former women's gallery in the basilica, for a closer look at the dome mosaics; outside on the loggia, as well as the superb views of the piazza, you can inspect the replica horses and compare them with the excellently restored, gilded, almost alive originals in the museum.

## The Campanile

*Open April–Sept 9.30–7.30 daily; Oct–Mar 9.30–3.30 daily, or till later in the day according to light; adm.*

St Mark's bell tower, to those uninitiated in the cult of Venice, is an alien presence, a Presbyterian brick sentinel in the otherwise delicately wrought piazza. But it has always been there, having been begun in 912 and last altered in 1515, and when it gently collapsed into a pile of rubble on 14 July 1902 the Venetians felt its lack so acutely they began to construct an exact replica, only a few hundred tons lighter and stronger, completed in 1912. It is just shy of 100m tall, and you can take the lift up for a bird's-eye vision of Venice and its Lagoon; from up here the city seems amazingly compact. Though you have to pay for the view, the republic's misbehaving priests had it for free; the Council of Ten would suspend them in cages from the windows. Under the campanile, Sansovino's elegant **loggetta** adds a graceful note to the brick belfry. Its marbles and sculptures glorifying Venice took it on the nose when the campanile fell on top of them, but they have been carefully restored.

## The Correr Museum and Clock Tower

At the far end of the piazza from the basilica, in the Procuratie Nuove, the **Museo Civico Correr** (*open 10–4 Mon, Wed–Sat; 9–12.30 Sun; closed Tues; adm*) contains an interesting collection of Venetian memorabilia—the robes, ducal bonnets and old-maidish nightcaps of the doges, the 20-inch heeled *zoccoli*, once the rage among Venetian noblewomen, and a copy of the statue of Marco Polo from the temple of 500 Genies in Canton. Upstairs is a fine collection of Venetian paintings, including two great works by Carpaccio, *Two Venetian Ladies (The Courtesans)* and the *Young Man in a Red Beret*, with his archetypal Venetian face; works by Jacopo Bellini and his sons, Gentile and Giovanni; Antonello da Messina's *Pietà*, one of his best works; and the Bosch-esque *Temptation of St Anthony* by Il Civetta (the little owl).

At the head of the Procuratie Vecchie two bronze wild men, called the 'Moors', sound the hours atop the clock tower, the **Torre dell'Orologio**, built to a design by Mauro Codussi in 1499 above the entrance to Venice's main shopping street, the Merceria. The old Italians were fond of elaborate astronomical clocks, but none is as beautiful as this, with its richly coloured enamel and gilt face, its Madonna and obligatory lion: the Council of Ten (which encouraged false rumours) supposedly blinded its builders to prevent them creating such a marvel for any other city. If restoration work has been completed, you can climb to the top to examine its workings close to, and be deafened by its bell (*if open 9–12, 3–5, Tues–Sat; 9–12 Sun; adm*). Two porphyry lions and a fountain stand in the nearby **Piazzetta Giovanni XXIII** (named after the beloved Venetian patriarch who became pope), flanking the basilica's north façade.

## Piazzetta San Marco

To the south of the basilica, the Piazzetta San Marco was the republic's foyer, where ships would dock under the watchful eye of the doge. The view towards the Lagoon is framed by two tall Egyptian granite columns, trophies brought to Venice in the 1170s. The Venetians had a knack for converting their booty into self-serving symbols: atop one of the columns several Roman statues were pieced together to form their first patron saint, St Theodore with his crocodile (or dragon, or fish), while on the other stands an ancient Assyrian or Persian winged lion, under whose paw the Venetians slid a book, creating their symbol of St Mark.

Opposite the Doges' Palace stands the **Libreria**, built in 1536 by Sansovino (finished by Scamozzi) and considered by Palladio to be the most beautiful building in the world, one especially notable for the play of light and shadow in its sculpted arcades. Sansovino, trained as a sculptor, was notorious for paying scant attention to architectural details, and the library was scarcely completed when its ceiling collapsed, a miscalculation that cost him a trip to the Council of Ten's slammer. He was only released on the pleading of Titian. In the library scholars with prior permission, obtainable from the director's office, can examine such treasures as the 1501 *Grimani breviary*, a masterwork of Flemish illuminators; Homeric *codices*, the 1459 world map of Fra Mauro, and Marco Polo's will.

Next to the library, at No 17, Venice's **Archaeology Museum** (*open 9–2 Tues–Sat; 9–1 Sun; adm*) has just been remodelled, and is one of the few museums in the city heated in the winter. It has an excellent collection of Greek sculpture, including a violent *Leda and the Swan* and ancient copies of the famous *Gallic Warriors of Pergamon*, all given to the city by Cardinal Grimani in 1523. On the other side of the Libreria, by the waterfront, is another fine building by Sansovino, the 1547 **Zecca**, or Old Mint, which once stamped out thousands of gold *zecchini*, which gave English a new word: 'sequin'.

## The Palace of the Doges (Palazzo Ducale)

*Open 15 April–Oct 8.30am–7pm daily; Nov–14 April 8.30am–1pm, or later in the day some months, daily; adm.*

What St Mark's is to sacred architecture, the **Doges' Palace** is to the secular—unique and audacious, dreamlike in a half-light, an illuminated storybook of Venetian history and legend. Like the basilica, it was founded shortly after the city's consolidation on the Rialto, though it didn't begin to take its present form until 1309—with its delicate lower colonnade, its loggia of lacy Gothic tracery, and the massive top-heavy upper floor, like a cake held up by its own frosting. Its weight is partly relieved by the diamond pattern of white Istrian stone and red Verona marble on the façade, which from a distance gives the palace its wholesome peaches-and-cream complexion. Less benign are the two reddish pillars in the loggia (on the

*Palazzo Ducale*

359

Piazzetta façade) said to have been dyed by the blood of Venice's enemies, whose tortured corpses were strung out between them.

Some of Italy's finest medieval sculpture crowns the 36 columns of the lower colonnade, depicting a few sacred and many profane subjects—animals, guildsmen, Turks, and Venetians. Beautiful sculptural groups adorn the corners, most notably the 13th-century *Judgement of Solomon*, on the corner nearest the palace's grand entrance, the 1443 **Porta della Carta** (Paper Door), a Gothic symphony in stone by Giovanni and Bartolomeo Bon.

Fires in 1574 and 1577 destroyed much of the palace, and at the time there were serious plans afoot to knock it down and let Palladio start again *à la* Renaissance. Fortunately, however, you can't teach an old doge new tricks, and the palace was rebuilt as it was, with Renaissance touches in the interior. Just within the Porta della Carta, don't miss Antonio Rizzo's delightful arcaded courtyard and his finely sculpted grand stairway, the **Scala dei Giganti**, named for its two Gargantuan statues of *Neptune* and *Mars* by Sansovino.

Visitors enter the palace via another grand stairway, Sansovino's **Scala d'Oro**. The first floor, once the private apartments of the doge, is now used for frequent special exhibitions (*separate adm*), while the golden stairway continues up to the *Secondo Piano Nobile*, from where the Venetian state was governed. After the fire that destroyed its great 15th-century frescoes, Veronese and Tintoretto were employed to decorate the newly remodelled chambers with mythological themes and scores of allegories and apotheoses of Venice—a smug, fleshy blonde in the eyes of these two. These paintings are the palace's chief glory, and signboards in each room identify them. Some of the best works are in the first room, the **Anticollegio** (with Tintoretto's *Bacchus and Ariadne* and Veronese's *Rape of Europa*), and the **Sala del Collegio**, with several masterpieces by both artists. Visiting ambassadors and other foreign official guests would be required to wait in the first of these two rooms before being ushered into the second to be presented to the hierarchy of the Venetian state, and so their decoration had to be suitably impressive.

Tintoretto dominates in the **Sala del Senato**—less lavish, since only Venetians were admitted here—while the main work in the **Sala del Consiglio dei Dieci** is Veronese's ceiling, *Old Man in Eastern Costume with a Young Woman*. Under this the dread Council of Ten deliberated and pored over the anonymous accusations deposited in the *Bocche dei Leoni*—the lions' mouths, the insidious suggestion boxes spread over the city. Next to the Ten's chamber, the old **Armoury** (Sala d'Armi) houses a fine collection of medieval and Renaissance arms and armour.

From here the visit continues downstairs, to the vast and magnificent **Sala del Maggior Consiglio**, built in 1340 and capable of holding the 2500 patricians of the Great Council. At the entrance hangs Tintoretto's crowded, and recently restored, *Paradiso*—the biggest oil painting in the world (7m by 22m), looking up at Veronese's magnificent *Apotheosis of Venice*, on the ceiling. The frieze along the upper wall portrays the first 76 doges, except for the space that would have held the portrait of Marin Falier (1355) had he not led a conspiracy to take sole power; the dry inscription on the black veil that is there in his stead notes that he was decapitated for treason. The portraits of the last 44 doges, each painted by a contemporary painter, continue around the **Sala dello Scrutinio**, where the votes for office were counted. Elections for doge were Byzantine and elaborate—and frequent; the Maggior Consiglio preferred to choose doges who were old, and wouldn't last long enough to gain a following.

## A Doge's Life

Senator in Senate, Citizen in City were his titles, as well as Prince of Clothes, with a wardrobe of gold and silver damask robes, and scarlet silks. Once the Doge was dressed, the rest of his procession would fall in line, including all the paraphernalia of Byzantine royalty: a naked sword, six silver trumpets, a damask umbrella, a chair, cushion, candle and eight standards bearing the Lion of St Mark in four colours symbolizing peace, war, truth and loyalty. Yet for all the pomp this was the only man in Venice not permitted to send a private note to his wife, or receive one from her, or from anyone else; nor could he accept any gift beyond flowers or rose-water, or go to a café or theatre, or engage in any money-making activity, while nevertheless having to meet the expenses of his office out of his own pocket. Nor could he abdicate, unless requested to do so.

The office was respected, but often not the man. When a Doge died he was privately buried in his family tomb before the state funeral—which used a dummy corpse with a wax mask, after a 16th-century Doge had died during a plague. An 'Inquisition of the Defunct Doge' was held over the dummy, to discover if the Doge had kept to his *Promissione* (his oath of coronation), if his family owed the state any money, and if it were necessary to amend the *Promissione* to limit the powers of his successor still further. Then the dead Doge's dummy was taken to St Mark's to be hoisted in the air nine times by sailors, to the cry of 'Misericordia' (Mercy), and then given a funeral service at Santi Giovanni e Paolo.

At the end of the tour the **Bridge of Sighs** (*Ponte dei Sospiri*) takes you to the 17th-century **Palazzo delle Prigioni**, mostly used for petty offenders. Those to whom the Republic took real exception were dumped into uncomfortable *pozzi*, or 'wells' in the lower part of the Palazzo Ducale, while celebrities like Casanova got to stay up in the *piombi* or 'leads' just under the roof (*see* below).

In 1984 the section of the palace where the real nitty-gritty business of state took place, a maze of narrow corridors and tiny rooms, was restored and opened to the public. Because the rooms are so small the 1½-hour guided tour, the **Itinerari Segreti** ('Secret Itinerary') is limited to 20 people, and the reason why it's not better known is that it's only available in Italian. If you're still game, reserve a place (well in advance in summer) by calling © 5204287. There are normally two tours a day and tickets cost L5000.

The tour begins at the top of the Scala d'Oro, with the snug wood-panelled offices of the **Chancellery** and the 18th-century **Hall of the Chancellors**, lined with cupboards for holding treaties, each bearing the arms of a Chancellor. In the justice department is the **Torture Chamber**, where the three Signori della Notte dei Criminali (judges of the night criminals) would 'put to the question' their suspects, hanging them by the wrists on a rope at is still in place. These practices ended in the early 1700s, when Venice became one of the first states in Europe to abolish torture.

Next is the ornate **Sala dei Tre Capi**, the chamber of the three magistrates of the Council of Ten, who had to be present at all state meetings. As this chamber might be visited by foreign dignitaries, it was lavishly decorated with works by Veronese, Antonello da Messina and Hieronymus Bosch. From here it's up to the notorious **Piombi**, which despite their evil reputation appear downright cosy, as prisons go. Casanova's cell is pointed out, and there's an elaborate exploration of his escape through a hole in the roof.

Near the end of the tour comes one of Venice's marvels: the **attic of the Sala del Maggior Consiglio**, where you can see how the Arsenale's shipwrights made a vast ceiling float unsupported over the room below; built in 1577, it has yet to need any repairs.

## San Marco to Rialto

The streets between the piazza and the market district of the Rialto are the busiest in Venice, especially the **Mercerie**, which begin under the clock tower and are lined with some of the city's smartest shops. It was down the Mercerie that Baiamonte Tiepolo led his rebels in 1310, when an old lady cried 'Death to tyrants!' from her window and hurled a brick at his standard-bearer, killing him on the spot, and causing such disarray that Tiepolo was forced to give up his attempted coup. It was a close call that the republic chose never to forget: the site, above the Sottoportego del Capello Nero, is marked by a stone relief of the heroine with her brick.

The Merceria continues to the church of **San Zulian**, redesigned in 1553 by Sansovino, with a façade most notable for Sansovino's statue of its overly proud benefactor, Tommaso Rangone. Sansovino also had a hand in **San Salvatore** in the next campo, adding the finishing touches to its noble Renaissance interior and designing the monument to Doge Francesco Venier. An 89-year-old Titian painted one of his more unusual works for this church, the *Annunciation*, which he signed with double emphasis *Titianus Fecit—'Fecit'* because his patrons refused to believe that he had painted it. In a chapel north of the altar is the *Supper at the House of Emmaus*, by the school of Giovanni Bellini.

Humming, bustling **Campo San Bartolomeo**, next on the Mercerie, has for centuries been one of the social hubs of Venice, and still gets packed with after-work crowds every evening. Its centre is graced by the **statue of Goldoni**, whose comedies in Venetian dialect still make the Venetians laugh; and by the look on his jolly face, he still finds their antics amusing. Follow the crowds up to the **Ponte di Rialto** (see 'The Grand Canal' p.351), the geographical heart of Venice, the principal node of its pedestrian and water traffic.

The city's central markets have been just across the bridge for a millennium, divided into sections for vegetables and for fish. Near the former you may pay your respects to what has traditionally been considered Venice's oldest church, the little **San Giacomo di Rialto**, founded perhaps as long ago as the 5th century and substantially reworked in 1071 and 1601. In the same campo stands a famous Venetian character, the 16th-century granite figure of the hunchback, **Gobbo di Rialto**, who supports a little stairway and marble podium from which the decrees of the Republic were proclaimed to the populace.

## San Marco to the Accademia

Following the yellow signs 'To the Accademia' from the Piazza San Marco (starting by the tourist office), the first campo belongs to Baroque **San Moisè**, with a grimy opera-buffa façade, rockpile and altarpiece. For more opera and less buffa, take a detour up Calle Veste (the second right after Campo San Moisè) to monumental Campo San Fantin and **La Fenice** (1792), one of Italy's most renowned opera houses, and site of the premieres of Verdi's *Rigoletto* and *La Traviata*. Venice has a venerable musical tradition, albeit one that had become more tradition than music by the time of the era of grand opera—even though Lorenzo da Ponte, Mozart's great librettist, was himself a Venetian.

Back on route to the Accademia, in the next campo stands **Santa Maria Zobenigo** (or del Giglio), on which the Barbaro family stuck a fancy Baroque façade, not for God but for the glory of the Barbaros; the façade is famous for its total lack of religious significance. The signs lead next to the Campo Francesco Morosini, named after the doge who recaptured the Morea from the Turks, but who is remembered everywhere else as the man who blew the top off the Parthenon. It's better known as **Campo Santo Stefano**, and is one of the most elegant squares in Venice, a pleasant place to sit outside at a café table—particularly at **Paolin**, Venice's best *gelateria*. At one end, built directly over a canal, the Gothic church of **Santo Stefano** has the most gravity-defying campanile of all the leaning towers in Venice (most alarmingly viewed from the adjacent Campo Sant'Angelo). The interior is worth a look for its striking wood ceiling, soaring like a ship's keel, as well as its wooden choir stalls (1488).

## The Accademia

*Open 9am–2pm Tues–Sat; 9am–1pm Sun; adm.*

Just over the Accademia bridge lies the **Galleria dell'Accademia** itself, the grand cathedral of Venetian art, ablaze with light and colour; this is the best place in the world to study both the development of the school and some of its greatest masterpieces. The gallery has a policy of admitting a maximum of 180 visitors at a time, so to be sure of getting a place it's advisable to get there early, above all in high season.

The pictures are well labelled but in no particular order, though the earliest works are in the first room: among them, 14th-century altarpieces by Paolo and Lorenzo Veneziano, whose half-Byzantine Madonnas look like models for Venetian silks. Later altarpieces fill **Room II**, most importantly Giovanni Bellini's masterpiece the *Pala di San Giobbe*, which in its architecture repeats its original setting in the church of San Giobbe; on the left St Francis invites the viewer into a scene made timeless by the music of the angels at the Madonna's feet. Other altarpieces in the room are by Carpaccio, Basaiti, and Cima da Conegliano (the subtle *Madonna of the Orange Tree*).

The next rooms are small but, like gifts, contain the best things: Mantegna's confidently aloof *St George*, a trio of Madonnas by Giovanni Bellini, and Piero della Francesca's *St Jerome and Devotee*, a youthful study in perspective. In **Room V** you will find Giorgione's *La Vecchia*, with the warning '*Col Tempo*' ('With Time') in her hand, and the mysterious *The Tempest*, two of the few paintings scholars accept as being indisputably by this artist, but how strange they are! It is said Giorgione invented easel painting for the pleasure of bored, purposeless patricians in Venice's decline, but the paintings seem to reflect rather than lighten their ennui and discontent.

Highlights of the next few rooms include Lorenzo Lotto's *Portrait of a Gentleman*, which catches its sitter off-guard before he could clear the nervously-scattered scraps of paper from his table, and Paris Bordenone's 1354 *Fisherman Presenting St Mark's Ring to the Doge*, celebrating a miracle of St Mark.

The climax of the Venetian High Renaissance comes in **Room X**, with Veronese's *Christ in the House of Levi* (1573), set in a Palladian loggia with a ghostly white imaginary background, in violent contrast to the rollicking feast of Turks, hounds, midgets, Germans and the artist himself (in the front, next to the pillar on the left). The painting was originally titled *The Last Supper*, and fell foul of the Inquisition, which took umbrage (especially at the Germans). Veronese was cross-examined, and ordered to make pious changes at his own expense; the artist, in true Venetian style, saved himself both the trouble and the money by simply giving it the title by which it has been known ever since.

Room X also contains Veronese's fine *Annunciation*, and some early masterworks by Tintoretto—*Translation of the Body of St Mark*, and *St Mark Freeing a Slave*, in which the Evangelist, in true Tintoretto-esque fashion, nosedives from the top of the canvas. The last great painting in the room was also the last ever by Titian, the sombre *La Pietà*, which he was working on when he died, aged about 90, from the plague; he intended it for his tomb, and smeared the paint on with his fingers.

Alongside several more Tintorettos, the following few rooms mainly contain later work from the 17th and 18th centuries, but mixed in among them are a series of fascinating scenes of 15th-century Venice, by Carpaccio, Gentile Bellini, and others. Compare them to Canaletto and Guardi, whose 18th-century scenes of Venice were the picture postcards of the British aristocracy on their Grand Tour, and are well represented in **Room XVII**.

The final rooms of the Accademia were formerly part of the elegantly Gothic church of Santa Maria della Carità, and house more luminous 15th-century painting by Alvise Vivarini, Giovanni and Gentile Bellini, and Crivelli, above all the fascinating series depicting the *Miracles of the True Cross* against Venetian backgrounds, originally painted for the Scuola di S. Giovanni Evangelista, in **Room XX. Room XXI** contains the dreamily compelling *Cycle of S. Ursula* by Carpaccio, from the former Scuola di Sant'Orsola, and only recently restored. Finally, the last room, **Room XXIV**, the former *scuola* of the church, contains two fine paintings that were originally made for it: Titian's 1538 *Presentation of the Virgin* and a 1446 triptych by Antonio Vivarini and Giovanni d'Alemagna.

## Dorsoduro

The Accademia lies in the *sestiere* of Dorsoduro, which can also boast the second-most-visited art gallery in Venice, the **Peggy Guggenheim Collection** (*open April–Oct 11am–6pm Wed–Fri, Sun, Mon; 11am–9pm Sat; closed Tues; adm, free 6–9pm Sat*), just down the Grand Canal from the Accademia in her 18th-century Venetian palazzo. In her 30 years as a collector, until her death in 1979, Ms Guggenheim amassed an impressive quantity (if not always quality) of brand-name 20th-century art—Bacon, Brancusi, Braque, Calder,

Chagall, Dali, De Chirico, Duchamp, Dubuffet, Max Ernst (her second husband), Giacometti, Gris, Kandinsky, Klee, Magritte, Miró, Moore, Mondrian, Picasso, Pollock, Rothko, and Smith. Administered by the Solomon R. Guggenheim Foundation in New York, the collection can come as a welcome breath of fresh air after so much high Italian art, and also sponsors a number of temporary exhibitions, even in winter; look out for posters.

From here it's a five-minute stroll down to the serene, octagonal basilica of **Santa Maria della Salute** (*open 8–12, 3–5 daily*), on the pointed tip of Dorsoduro. One of five churches built in thanksgiving after the passing of plagues (Venice, a busy international port isolated in its Lagoon, was particularly susceptible), La Salute (1631–81) is the masterpiece of Baldassare Longhena, its snow-white dome and marble jelly rolls dramatically set at the entrance of the Grand Canal. The interior is a relatively restrained white and grey Baroque, and the **sacristy** (*adm*) contains the *Marriage at Cana* by Tintoretto and several works by Titian, including his *St Mark Enthroned Between Saints*. Almost next to the basilica, on the point, stands the distinctive profile of the **Dogana di Mare**, the Customs House (see 'The Grand Canal', p.352).

The **Fondamenta delle Zattere**, facing away from the city towards the freighter-filled canal and the island of Giudecca, leads from La Salute to the **Gesuati**, the only church in Venice decorated by Umbria artists. For a more elaborate feast, take the long stroll along the Fondamenta (or take *vaporetto* Line 5 to San Basegio) to Veronese's parish church of **San Sebastiano** on Rio di San Basilio. Veronese, it is said, murdered a man in Verona and took refuge in this neighbourhood, and over the next 10 years he and his brother Benedetto Caliari embellished San Sebastiano—beginning in 1555 with the ceiling frescoes of the sacristy and ending with the magnificent ceiling, *The Story of Esther*, and illusionistic paintings in the choir. The church is often closed, but the custodian can usually be found there on weekday mornings or Sunday afternoons, and he will open it up for you if he has not done so already; tip him for turning on the lights.

From San Sebastiano you can head back towards the Grand Canal (Calle Avogaria and Calle Lunga S. Barnaba); turn left up Calle Pazienza to visit the 14th-century church of the **Carmini** with a landmark red campanile and lovely altars by Cima da Conegliano and Lorenzo Lotto. The **Scuola Grande dei Carmini** (*open 9–12, 3–6, Mon–Sat; adm*), next door, was designed by Longhena in the 1660s, and contains one of G. B. Tiepolo's best and brightest ceilings, *The Virgin in Glory*.

The Carmini is on the corner of the delightful **Campo Santa Margherita**. Traditionally the main marketplace of Dorsoduro, it's also a good spot to find relatively inexpensive pizzerias, restaurants and cafés that are not aimed primarily at tourists. It is also close to **Ca' Rezzonico** (Rio Terrà Canal down to the Fondamenta Rezzonico), now home to the **Museo del Settecento Veneziano** (*open 10–5 Mon–Thurs, Sat; 9–12.30 Sun; closed Fri; adm*), Venice's attic of 18th-century art, with bittersweet paintings by Giandomenico Tiepolo, some wild Rococo furniture, a pharmacy, genre scenes by Longhi (*The Lady and Hairdresser*), and a breathtaking view of the Grand Canal. The house was owned in the last century by Robert Browning's son Pen, and the poet died there in 1889. One of the palaces you see opposite belonged to Doge Cristoforo Moro, whom the Venetians claim Shakespeare used as his model for Othello, confusing the doge's name with his race.

## San Polo and Santa Croce

From the Ponte di Rialto, the yellow signs towards the Piazzale Roma lead past the pretty **Campo** and church of **San Polo** (*open 7.30am–12 midday, 4–7pm, Mon–Sat; 7.30–12 Sun*), known for Giandomenico Tiepolo's dramatic *Stations of the Cross* in the Oratory of the Crucifix. The signs next take you before a venerable Venetian institution: the huge brick Gothic church of the **Frari** (*open 9.30–12, 2.30–6, Mon–Sat; 2.30–6 Sun; adm*), one of the most severe medieval buildings in the city, built between 1330 and 1469. Monteverdi, one of the founding fathers of opera and once choir director at St Mark's, is buried here, as is Titian, beneath a massive, and most inartistic, 19th-century monument. There is also a strange pyramid with a half-open door, which the neoclassical sculptor Antonio Canova intended to be Titian's tomb, but which eventually became a monument to the sculptor himself. The Frari is celebrated for its great art, and especially for the most overrated painting in Italy, Titian's *Assumption of the Virgin* (1516–18), in the centre of the Monk's Choir. Art historians marvel at Titian's revolutionary Mannerist use of space and movement, but its gaudy colours and big-eyed, heaven-gazing Virgin are as perceptive as a Sunday school holy card.

That, however, is not true of Giovanni Bellini's lovely *Triptych of Madonna with Child and Saints* in the sacristy, or Donatello's rustic *Statue of St John the Baptist* in the choir chapel. In the north aisle Titian's less theatrical and later *Madonna di Ca' Pésaro* was modelled on his wife Celia; the painting had a greater influence on Venetian composition than the *Assumption*. Also note the beautiful Renaissance **Tomb of Doge Nicolò Tron** by Antonio Rizzo in the sanctuary, from 1476.

## The Scuola di San Rocco

Next to the Frari, the **Scuola di San Rocco** (*open April–Sept 9–1, 3.30–6.30 daily; Oct–Mar 10am–1pm Mon–Fri; 3–6pm Sat, Sun; adm*) is one of Venice's numerous 'schools' or charitable confraternities. San Rocco, renowned for his juju against the Black Death, was so popular among the Venetians that they stole his body from Montpelier and canonized him before the pope did, and his confraternity was one of the city's wealthiest. The school has a beautiful, lively façade by Scarpagnino, and inside it contains one of the wonders of Venice— or rather, 54 wonders—all painted by Tintoretto, who worked on the project from 1562 to 1585 without any assistance.

Tintoretto always managed to look at old, conventional subjects from a fresh point of view; while other artists of the High Renaissance often composed their subjects with the epic vision of a Cecil B. de Mille, Tintoretto had the revolutionary eye of a 16th-century Orson Welles, creating audacious, dynamic 'sets', often working out his compositions in his little box-stages, with wax figures and unusual lighting effects. In the *scuola*, especially in the upper floor, he was at the peak of his career, and painted what is considered by some to be the finest painting cycle in existence. Vertigo is not an uncommon response—for an antidote, look at the funny carvings along the walls by Francesco Pianta. The greatest work in the cycle is the *Crucifixion*, where the event is the central drama of a busy human world. In the same room there are also several paintings on easels by Titian, and one of Christ that some attribute to Titian, some to Giorgione.

Just to the north, beyond the Campo San Stin, the **Scuola di San Giovanni Evangelista** (*open in theory 9.30–12.30 Mon–Fri, but advisable to ring ahead, © 5224134*) deserves a look inside for its beautiful Renaissance courtyard and double-ramp stairway by Mauro Codussi (1498), noted for the rhythms of its domes and barrel vaults.

From Campo San Stin, if you start along Calle Donà and keep as straight as possible, you should end up at **Ca' Pésaro** on the Grand Canal, a huge 17th-century pile by Longhena that is occupied by the **Galleria d'Arte Moderna** (*open 10–5 Tues–Sat; 9.30–12.30 Sun; adm*), with a collection principally of works exhibited in the Biennale exhibitions. Italian contemporary art, much of it unfamiliar to a foreign audience, is the mainstay, but some international figures are also represented, such as Gustav Klimt. Ca' Pésaro also houses a **Museum of Oriental Art** (*open 9–2 Tues–Sat; 9–1 Sun; adm*), with a higgledy-piggledy collection of Asian artefacts collected in the last century. If you really want to escape the crowds, however, head further up the canal to the stuffed Lagoon fowl in the **Natural History Museum** (*open 9–1.30 Tues–Sat; adm*) in the Venetian-Byzantine **Fóndaco dei Turchi**, last spruced up in 1858.

## San Marco to Castello

Starting at the Piazzetta San Marco, the gracefully curving and ever-bustling **Riva degli Schiavoni** took its name from the Slavs of Dalmatia. A few steps beyond the Palazzo Ducale is one of the city's finest Gothic palazzi, which since 1822 has been the famous **Hotel Danieli**, its name a corruption of the 'Dandolo' family who built it. Here on the quay stands a robust 1887 **Memorial to Vittorio Emanuele II**, where two of Venice's over 10,000 lions shelter—as often as not, with members of Venice's equally numerous if smaller feline population between their paws.

From the Riva, the Sottoportico San Zaccaria leads back to the lovely Gothic-Renaissance **San Zaccaria** (*open 10–12, 4–6, daily*), begun by Antonio Gambello in 1444 and completed by Mauro Codussi in 1515. Inside, look for Bellini's *Madonna and Saints* in the second chapel to the right, and the refined Florentine frescoes by Andrea del Castagno in the chapel of San Tarasio. Another church on the Riva itself, **La Pietà**, served the girls' orphanage which the red-headed priest Vivaldi made famous during his years as its concert master and composer (1704–38). The church was rebuilt shortly afterwards with a remarkable oval interior, in luscious cream and gold with G. B. Tiepolo's extravagant *Triumph of Faith* on top. It has particularly fine acoustics—due to Vivaldi's involvement in the design—and is still frequently used for concerts.

Due north of La Pietà stands the city's Greek Orthodox Church, the 16th-century **San Giorgio dei Greci**, with its tilting tower, and nearby the later *scuola*, now the **Museum of Byzantine Religious Painting** (*open 9–1, 2–5, Mon, Wed–Sat; 9–1 Sun; closed Tues; adm*). Run by the Hellenic Centre for Byzantine Studies, it contains icons from the 16th and 17th centuries, many painted by Greek artists who fled the Turkish occupation. In Venice the Greeks came into contact with the High Renaissance and shifted away from the rigid traditionalism of Orthodox painting, creating a Venetian-Cretan school of art, which nourished, most famously, El Greco.

Nearby, the Dalmatian minority—present in Venice almost throughout the history of the Republic—began the tiny **Scuola di San Giorgio degli Schiavoni** in 1951 (*open 9.30–12.30, 3.30–6.30, Tues–Sat; 9.30–12.30 Sun, holidays; adm*). Its interior, though minute by comparison with the city's grander monuments, is decorated with the most beloved art in all Venice: Vittore Carpaccio's charming paintings on the lives of the Dalmatian patron saints: Jerome with his patient little white dog; George charging a petticoat-munching dragon in a landscape strewn with maidenly leftovers from lunch, and more. Some of the greatest works by Carpaccio's more serious contemporaries, the Vivarini and Cima da Conegliano, hold pride of place in **San Giovanni in Brágora** (between San Giorgio degli Schiavoni and the Riva); the best work, Cima's *Baptism of Christ*, is in the sanctuary.

## The Arsenale

From the Riva, the Fondamenta dell'Arsenale leads to the twin towers guarding the **Arsenale**. Founded in 1104, this, first of all arsenals, derived its name from the Venetian pronunciation of the Arabic *darsina'a*, or artisans' shop, and up until the 17th century these were the greatest dockyards in the world, the very foundation of the Republic's wealth and power. In its heyday the Arsenale had a payroll of 16,000, and produced a ship a day to fight the Turks. Dante visited this great industrial complex twice, and as Blake would later do with his Dark Satanic Mills, confined it to the *Inferno*.

Today the Arsenale is occupied by the Italian military and is off-limits, but you can look at the **Great Gateway** next to the towers, built in 1460 and often regarded as the earliest Venetian Renaissance building, and constructed almost entirely from marble trophies brought over from Greece. Alongside them were later placed a line of stone lions, also picked up in Greece, including one ancient beast that Doge Francesco Morosini found in Piraeus, with 11th-century runes carved in its back in the name of Harold Hardrada, a member of the Byzantine Emperor's Varangian Guard who was later crowned king of Norway. Other very innocent-looking lions, eroded into lambs, were brought from the island of Delos in 1718. The only way to get a look at the inside of the Arsenale at present is by taking the Line 5 *vaporetto*, which goes through the middle of it.

Venice's glorious maritime history is the subject of the fascinating artefacts and models in the **Museo Storico Navale** (*open 9am–1pm Tues–Sat; adm*)—most dazzling of all is the model of the doge's barge, the *Bucintoro*. The museum is located a short way past the gateway to the Arsenale, near the beginning of Via Garibaldi; in a neighbouring house lived two originally Genoese seafarers who contributed more to the naval history of Britain than that of Venice, Giovanni and Sebastiano Caboto.

Via Garibaldi and the Fondamenta S. Anna continue to the Isola di San Pietro, site of the unmemorable **San Pietro di Castello** (*open April–Sept 8–12, 4–7, daily; Oct–Mar 8–12, 3–6, daily*), until 1807 Venice's cathedral, its lonely, distant site no small comment on the Republic's attitude towards the papacy. The attractive, detached campanile is by Codussi, and, inside, there is a marble throne incorporating a medieval Moslem tombstone inscribed with verses from the Koran, which for centuries was said to have been the Throne of St Peter in Antioch. To the south are the refreshing pines and planes of the **Public Gardens**, where the International Exhibition of Modern Art, on Biennale, takes place in even-numbered years in the artsy pavilions. This, and the **Parco delle Rimembranze** further on, were given to this sometimes claustrophobic city of stone and water by Napoleon, who knocked down four extraneous churches to plant the trees. From here you can take Line 1 or 2 back to San Marco, or to the Lido.

## San Marco to Santi Giovanni e Paolo

The calle that leads from the Piazzetta dei Leoncini around the back of San Marco and over the Rio di Palazzo will take you to one of Venice's newest museums, the **Museo Diocesano** (*open 10.30–12.30 daily*), in the Romanesque cloister of Sant'Apollonia. It features an exceptional collection of trappings and art salvaged from the city's churches. Through a web of alleys to the north there's more art in the 16th-century Palazzo Querini-Stampalia, home of the **Fondazione Querini-Stampalia** (*open 10–12.30, 3.30–6, Tues–Sun; adm*), which has an endearing assortment of genre paintings—the closest we have to photographs of 18th-century Venice by Pietro Longhi and the naïve Gabriel Bella, as well as works by Bellini, Palma il Vecchio, and G. B. Tiepolo. Other attractions of the palazzo are its décor and furnishings, which give an idea of the look of an 18th-century Venetian patrician's residence.

**Santa Maria Formosa**, in its charming campo just to the north, was rebuilt in 1492 by Codussi, who made creative use of its original Greek-cross plan. The head near the bottom of its campanile is notorious as being the most hideous thing in Venice, while inside, Palma il Vecchio's *Santa Barbara* is famed as the loveliest woman, modelled on the artist's own daughter. Another celebrated work, Bartolomeo Vivarini's *Madonna della Misericordia* (1473), is in the first chapel on the right; the parishioners shown under the protection of the Virgin's mantle earned their exalted position by paying for the painting.

The next campo to the north is dominated by **Santi Giovanni e Paolo** (*San Zanipolo*, in Venetian dialect), after St Mark's the most important church on the right bank (*open 7–12.30, 3.30–7.30, daily*). A vast Gothic brick temple begun by the Dominicans in 1246, then almost entirely rebuilt after 1333, and finally completed in 1430, no one could accuse it of being beautiful, despite its fine front doorway. San Zanipolo contains many superb pieces of Venetian art, but is, most of all, a pantheon of the doges; all their funerals were held here after the 1300s, and some 25 of them went no further, but lie in splendid Gothic and Renaissance tombs. Among them there are also monuments to other honoured servants of the Venetian state, such as Marcantonio Bragadin, the commander who in 1571 was flayed alive by the Turks after he had surrendered Famagusta, in Cyprus, after a long siege; his bust sits on an urn holding his neatly folded skin. The adjacent chapel contains Giovanni Bellini's excellent polyptych of *St Vincent Ferrer*, a fire-eating subject portrayed by the gentlest of painters; nearby is a small shrine containing the foot of St Catherine of Siena. The finest of the tombs is in the chancel, that of Doge Andrea Vendramin, by Tullio and Antonio Lombardo (1478), while the **Chapel of the Rosary** in the north transept, which was severely damaged by fire in the last century, has a fine ceiling by Veronese that was originally in the church of the Umiltà, long demolished.

Adjacent to San Zanipolo, the **Scuola Grande di San Marco** has one of the loveliest Renaissance façades in Italy, the fascinating *trompe-l'œil* lower half by Pietro and Tullio Lombardo, the upper floor by Mauro Codussi, and finished in 1495. The *scuola* is now used

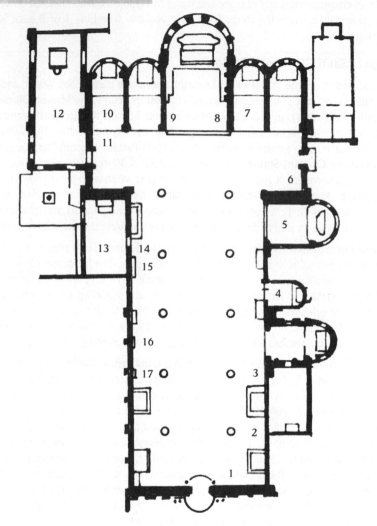

1   Tombs of the Mochenigo family
2   Bragadin monument
3   Tomb of Ludovico Diedo
4   Chapel of the Madonna della Pace
5   Chapel of St Dominic
6   Tomb of Nicola Orsini
7   Chapel of the Maddalena
8   Tombs of Doges Michele Morosini
    and Leonardo Loredan

9   Tombs of Doges Andrea Vendramin and
    Marco Corner
10  Tomb of Doge Giovanni Dolfin
11  Tomb of Doge Antonio Venier
12  Chapel of the Rosary
13  Sacristy
14  Tomb of Palma Giovane
15  Tomb of Doge Pasquale Malipiero
16  Tomb of Doge Tommaso Mocenigo
17  Tomb of Doge Nicolò Marcello

as Venice's municipal hospital, but it is possible to enter to see the lavish coffered ceiling in the library with the permission of the *Direttore di Sanità*.

Opposite stands the famous, superbly dynamic **Equestrian Statue of Bartolomeo Colleoni**, the condottiere from Bergamo (1400–76) who had done so much for the Republic's claims on the mainland. In his lifetime proud of his emblem of *coglioni* (testicles—a play on his name), Colleoni envied Donatello's statue of his predecessor Gattamelata erected by the Venetians in Padua, and in his will he left the Republic 100,000 ducats if it would erect a similar statue of him in front of St Mark's. Greedy for the money but unable to countenance a monument to an individual in their sacred Piazza, the wily Venetians put the statue up before the *scuola* of St Mark. Verrocchio, the master of Leonardo and Botticelli, had only finished the plaster moulds when he died in 1488, leaving Alessandro Leopardi to do the casting.

## Santa Maria dei Miracoli and the Ca' d'Oro

From the Campo San Zanipolo, Largo G. Gallini leads to the perfect little Renaissance church of **Santa Maria dei Miracoli** (*open 10–12, 3–6, daily*), built by Pietro Lombardo in the 1480s and often compared to an exquisite jewel box, elegant, graceful, and glowing with a soft marble sheen, inside and out. Just to the south are two enclosed courtyards, known as the **Corte Prima del Milion** and the **Corte Seconda del Milion**, which were once part of the home of Marco Polo. The latter in particular looks much as it did when the great traveller lived there; 'Million', his nickname in Venice, referred to the million tales he brought back with him from China.

Nearby, Codussi's **San Giovanni Crisostomo** (1504) is the master's last work, a seminal piece of Renaissance architecture that contains Giovanni Bellini's last altar painting (*SS. Jerome, Christopher, and Augustine*), as well as a beautiful high altarpiece by Sebastiano del Piombo.

Further towards the railway station up the Grand Canal, signposted off the Strada Nuova (Via 28 Aprile), stands the enchanting Gothic **Ca' d'Oro**, finished in 1440 and currently housing the **Galleria Franchetti** (*open 9am–7.15pm Tues–Fri; 9–2 Mon, Sat, Sun; adm*). In its collection are Mantegna's stern *St Sebastian*, Guardi's series of Venetian views, an excellent collection of Renaissance bronzes and medallions (some by Pisanello), a portrait of Sultan Mehmet II by Gentile Bellini, who did a stint in Istanbul, and now sadly faded fragments of the famous frescoes by Giorgione and Titian from the Fóndaco dei Tedeschi. Also present are some more minor works by Titian, including a voluptuous *Venus*, and a fine *Crucifixion* by a follower of Van Eyck. The building itself is most famous for the intricate traceries of its façade, best appreciated from the Grand Canal, and the courtyard, with a finely carved wellhead by Bartolomeo Bon.

Due north, near the Fondamente Nuove, stands the unloved, unrestored church of the **Gesuiti** (*open 10–12, 5–7, daily*), built in 1714–29: a Baroque extravaganza, full of *trompe l'œil* of white and green-grey marble draperies that would make a fitting memorial for Liberace. A previous church on this same site was the parish church of Titian, to which he contributed the *Martyrdom of St Lawrence*—the saint on a grill revered by Titian's patron, Philip II of Spain.

# Cannaregio

Crumbling, piquant Cannaregio is the least visited *sestiere* in Venice, and here, perhaps, more than anywhere else in the city, you can begin to feel what everyday life is like in Venice behind the tourist glitz—children playing tag on the bridges, old men in shorts messing around in unglamorous, unpainted boats on murky canals, neighbourhood greasy spoons and bars, banners of laundry waving gaily overhead.

Northern Cannaregio was Tintoretto's home base, and he is buried in the beautiful Venetian Gothic **Madonna dell'Orto** (*open April–Sept 9.30–12, 4.30–7, daily; Oct–Mar 9.30–12, 3.30–5, daily*). It also contains several of his jumbo masterpieces, such as the *Sacrifice of the Golden Calf*, in which Tintoretto painted himself bearing the idol—though he refrained from predicting his place in the *Last Judgement*, which hangs opposite it. He also painted the highly original *Presentation of the Virgin in the Temple* in the south aisle, near one of Cima da Conegliano's greatest works, *St John the Baptist*. The first chapel near the door contains a *Madonna* by Giovanni Bellini.

From the Campo Madonna dell'Orto, take a short walk down the Fondamenta Contarini, where, across the canal, in the wall of the eccentric **Palazzo Mastelli** you can see one of Venice's curiosities: an old, stone relief of a Moor confronting a camel. There are three more 'Moors' in the **Campo dei Mori**, just in front of the Madonna dell'Orto. The original identities of these mysterious old figures has long been forgotten, though a fourth one, embedded in one corner of the square and with a metal nose like Tycho Brahe, is formally known as Signor Antonio Rioba. He featured in many Venetian pranks of yore: anonymous satires or denunciations would be signed in his name (a tradition similar to that of Pasquino in Rome, see p.870), and new arrivals in the city would be sent off to meet him.

Also in the area is another church, **Sant'Alvise** (currently under restoration), which must be the loneliest church in Venice. Its main features are a forceful *Calvary* by Giambattista Tiepolo and a set of charming tempera paintings that Ruskin called the 'Baby Carpaccios', but are now actually attributed to Carpaccio's master, Lazzaro Bastiani, as Carpaccio himself would only have been about eight years old when they were painted.

Three *rii* to the south of Sant'Alvise is the **Ghetto**—THE Ghetto, that is, for, like '*Arsenal*', it is a Venetian word: '*ghetto*' derives from the word '*getto*' meaning 'casting in metals', and there was an iron foundry here which preceded the establishment of a special quarter to which all Jews were ordered to move in 1516. The name is poignantly, coincidentally apt, for in Hebrew 'ghetto' comes from the root for 'cut off'. And cut off its residents were in Venice, for the Ghetto is an island, surrounded by a moat-like canal, and at night all Jews had to be within its windowless walls. Cramped for space, the houses were built tall, but with very low ceilings, which, as many people have noted, eerily presages ghetto tenements of centuries to come. But the Venetians did not invent the mentality behind the Ghetto, even if they invented the name; Spanish Jews in the Middle Ages were segregated, as were the Jews of ancient Rome. Indeed, Venetian law specifically protected Jewish citizens and forbade preachers from inciting mobs against them—a common enough practice in the 16th century. Jewish refugees came to Venice from all over Europe; here they were safe, even if they had to pay for it with high taxes and rents. When Napoleon threw open the gates of the Ghetto in 1797, it is said that the impoverished residents who remained were too weak to leave.

The island of the **Ghetto Nuovo**, the oldest section, is a melancholy place, its small campo often empty and forlorn. The **Scuola Grande Tedesca** is the oldest of Venice's five synagogues, built by German Jews in 1528, and is in the same building as the small **Jewish Community Museum** (*open 10–7 Sun–Fri; closed Sat, Jewish holidays; adm, guided tours extra*). The informative tours (in English) organised by the museum visit this synagogue and two others, the **Scuola Spagnola**—an opulent building by Longhena—and the **Scuola Levantina**.

Light years from the Ghetto in temperament, but only three minutes away on foot, the **Palazzo Labia**, next to the 1580 **Ponte delle Guglie**, has a ballroom with Giambattista Tiepolo's lavish, sensuous frescoes on the *Life of Cleopatra*. The palazzo is now owned by RAI, the Italian state broadcaster, but the ballroom is open for concerts or by appointment; ℰ 781111. Away from the palazzo towards the railway station runs the garish, lively **Lista di Spagna**, Venice's tourist highway, lined with restaurants, bars, hotels and souvenir stands that are not always as cheap as they should be.

---

## San Giorgio Maggiore and the Giudecca

The little islet of San Giorgio Maggiore, crowned by the church of **San Giorgio Maggiore** by Palladio (*open 9–12.30, 2–6.30, daily*), dominates the view of the Lagoon from the Piazzetta San Marco (*vaporetto* Line 5). It is a church which strongly suggests that Renaissance architecture may well be a case of the Emperor's New Clothes; its white marble temple façade has nothing to do with the red-brick body of the church, and the whole building lacks any kind of vision. But hanging where it does, between the water and the sky, it is redeemed by the light that bathes it daily with as many variations as Monet's series on the Cathedral of Rouen. The stern white interior is relieved by Tintoretto's *Fall of Manna* and his celebrated *Last Supper* on the main altar, which is also notable for the fine carving on the Baroque choir stalls. A lift (*open 9–12, 2.30–5, daily; adm*) can whisk you to the top of the **Campanile** for a remarkable view over Venice and the Lagoon. The old monastery, partly designed by Palladio, is now the headquarters of the Giorgio Cini Foundation, dedicated to the arts and the sciences of the sea, and venue for frequent exhibitions and conferences. To make sure the monastery is open, call ahead (ℰ 5289900).

**La Giudecca** (Lines 5, 8 or 9) actually consists of eight islands that curve gracefully like a Spanish *tilde* just south of Venice; prominent among its buildings are a string of empty mills and factories—the product of a brief 19th century flirtation with industry—and for the most part the atmosphere is relatively quiet and homely. Like Cannaregio, it's seldom visited by the throngs, though a few people wander over to see Palladio's best church, **Il Redentore** (*open 7.30–12, 3.30–7, daily*). In 1576, during yet another plague that killed 46,000 Venetians, the doge and the senate vowed that if the catastrophe ended, they would build a church and visit it in state once a year. Palladio was duly commissioned to build the church, completed in 1592, and on the third Sunday of each July a bridge of boats was constructed to take the authorities across from the Zattere. This event, the *Festa del Redentore*, is still one of the most exciting events on the Venetian calendar. The Redentore itself provides a fitting backdrop; this time Palladio's classical façade, with its interlocking pediments, suits the rest of the church.

---

## Shopping

Venice is a fertile field for shoppers, whether you're looking for tacky bric-à-brac to brighten up the mantelpiece (just walk down the Lista di Spagna) or the latest in hand-crafted Italian design—but be warned that bargains are hard to find. Everything from fresh fish to lovely inlaid wooden boxes and huge quantities of tourist junk can be found at the **Rialto markets**. You will also come across food stalls in any number of squares and on barges along the smaller canals, but there is another large food and produce market in Castello, on **Via Garibaldi**. The main public auction house is **Franco Semezato**, Palazzo Giovanelli, Cannaregio 2292, ✆ 721811.

### antiques

A flea market appears periodically in Campo San Maurizio, near Campo Santo Stefano, which is also the area with the largest concentration of antique shops. **Antonietta Santomanco della Toffola**, Frezzeria 1504, S. Marco, has Russian and English silver, prints, and antique jewellery and glass, while the establishments of the print dealer **Pietro Scarpa** at Campo S. Moisè 1464 and Calle XXII Marzo 2089, S. Marco, are as much museums as shops. Away from the San Marco area, **Salizzada**, S. Lio 5672, in Castello, has old prints of Venice, clocks, and many other curious odds and ends, and **Xanthippe**, Dorsoduro 2773, near Ca' Rezzonico, is a new, highly eclectic little shop specializing in the 19th century.

### books

Venice has a good selection of bookshops. **Fantoni**, Salizzada di S. Luca 4121, S. Marco, has a monumental display of monumental art books, while **Sansovino**, Bacino Orseolo 84, S. Marco (just outside the Procuratie Vecchie), also has a large collection of art and coffee-table books combined with a huge stock of postcards. The best stock of books in Italian about every aspect of Venice, including some rare editions, is in **Filippi**, Calle del Paradiso 5763, Castello. If you're looking for books in English, then **Il Libraio a San Barnaba**, Fondamenta Gerardini 2835/a, Dorsoduro, has the best overall selection. **Sangiorgio**, Calle Larga XXII Marzo 2087, S. Marco, and **Serenissima**, Merceria dell'Orologio 739, S. Marco, both have good collections of books in English about Venice.

### fashion, fabrics and accessories

Most of Venice's high-fashion designer boutiques are located in the streets to the west of Piazza San Marco; fashion names like **Missoni**, with some of Italy's most beautiful knitwear, at Calle Vallaresso 1312, S. Marco, near Harry's Bar; the very exclusive **Elisabetta alla Fenice**, Campo S. Fantin, S. Marco; **Krizia**, Calle delle Ostreghe and Via XXII Marzo, S. Marco, for more youth-oriented, colourful knits; **Laura Biagiotti**, Via XXII Marzo 2400/a, S. Marco; **Roberta di Camerino**, Lungomare Marconi 32, on the Lido, one of Venice's home-grown designers; and Giorgio Armani, at both **Giorgio Armani da Elysée**, Frezzeria 1693, S. Marco, and

**Emporio Armani**, Calle dei Fabbri 989, S. Marco, with more accessible prices. For fashions by maverick Italian and French designers, try **La Coupole**, Via XXII Marzo of Frezzeria 1674, S. Marco. Then there's **M. Antichità**, S. Marco 1691, offering velour dresses of Renaissance richness, and jewels to match.

Most Venetians, however, buy at least some of their clothes at the **COIN** department store, Rio Terrà S. Leonardo 5788, Cannaregio, part of a national chain, and a variety of cheap clothes stalls can also be found on most days in the same street. Fashionable second-hand clothes are the mainstay at **Aldo Strausse**, Campo S. Giustina, in Castello, but **Emilio Ceccato**, Sottoportego di Rialto, S. Polo, is the place to find something very typically Venetian—gondoliers' shirts, jackets and tight trousers. Meanwhile, at the **Camiceria San Marco**, at Calle Vallaresso 1340, S. Marco, they will make up men's shirts and women's dresses to order for you within 24 hours.

For sensuous and expensive lingerie, visit **Jade Martine**, Frezzeria 1762, S. Marco. The great place to find Venetian lace, whether for lingerie or tablecloths, is on Burano (see p.394), though be aware that the bargains there are probably neither handmade nor even Buranese. Back in Venice itself, **Jesurum**, Ponte Canonica 4310, S. Marco, has a vast quantity of Venetian lace and linen of all kinds on display in a 12th-century former church behind St Mark's Basilica, as well as a good selection of swimwear and summer clothes.

Not just lace, but also other high-quality fabrics have figured equally among Venice's traditional specialities, using skills that in many cases have been reinvigorated in recent years. **Trois**, S. Marco 2666, is an institution selling colourful pleated Fortuny silks, invented in Venice and made to traditional specifications on the Giudecca; scarves, dresses and bags made from Fortuny silks are available from **Delphos**, S. Marco 2403. **Rubelli**, in the Palazzo Corner Spinelli, S. Angelo 3877, S. Marco, offers heavier damasks, velours and brocades, produced in the rich colours of the cinquecento. More modern designs in silks and fabrics can be found at **Valli**, Merceria S. Zulian 783, S. Marco.

For posh shoes, **La Fenice**, Via XXII Marzo 2255, S. Marco, has a good selection by French and Italian designers. The greatest name in Venetian leather is **Vogni**, Via XXII Marzo 1300, S. Marco, which has a comprehensive selection of bags and luggage, and a complete range by Venetian designer Roberta di Camerino.

Jewellery in Venice tends to be expensive and conservative—particularly in the many shops in and around San Marco—and so may be of more interest for looking than buying. **Codognato**, S. Marco 1295, is one of the oldest jewellers in Venice, with some rare Tiffany, Cartier and art deco items, and **Missiaglia**, Piazza S. Marco 125, where you can see some of the most elegant pieces produced by Venetian gold and silversmiths working today.

### food and drink

As well as in the markets (*see* above), other good places to pick up local specialities include **Pastificio Artigiano**, Strada Nuova 4292, Cannaregio, where Paolo Pavon has for nearly fifty years created Venice's tastiest and most exotic pastas, among them *pasta al cacao* (chocolate pasta) and lemon, beetroot and curry varieties. Similarly, **Il Pastaio**, Calle del Varoteri 219, in the Rialto market, offers pastas in over a score of different colours. **Colussi**, Rugheta S. Apollonia 4325, S. Marco, near Campo Santi Filippo e Giacomo, is a *pasticceria* with an enormous range of unusual pastries.

If you do want to picnic as you make your way round Venice then **Rizzo**, Calle delle Botteghe, S. Marco, just off Campo F. Morosini, is an *alimentari* where you'll find everything you need. For wines and other varieties of alcohol, **Cantinone già Schiavi**, Fondamenta S. Trovaso 992, Dorsoduro, is a fine old shop with plenty to choose from.

### gifts

Anyone seeking unusual gifts will find plenty to look at in Venice, though, again, prices sometimes need to be handled with care. At **La Scialuppa**, Calle Seconda dei Saoneri 2695, S. Polo, you can buy the wares of woodworker Gilberto Penzo, who makes beautiful *forcole* (gondola oar locks, made of walnut), replicas of Venetian guild signs and many other things. **Calle Lunga 2137**, in Dorsoduro, is a workshop specializing in decorative wrought iron, and **Fondamenta Minotto 154**, S. Croce, near S. Nicolò Tolentino and the railway station, has all sorts of gold and brass items, such as Venetian doorknockers. For children, **Signor Blum**, Calle Lunga S. Barnaba 2864, Dorsoduro, has beautiful jigsaw puzzles and brightly-painted wooden toys. For an overview, the **Consorzio Artigianato Artistico Veneziano**, Calle Larga S. Marco 412, S. Marco, has a fair selection of all kinds of handmade Venetian crafts.

The most renowned of Venice's ancient crafts are, of course, an obvious choice. As Burano is the centre for lace, so too Murano (*see* below) is still the place to go for glassware, but in the city one of the grand names in Venetian glass is **Pauly**, Ascensione 72, S. Marco, near Ponte Consorzi, which has 30 rooms of both traditional and contemporary designs in glass housed in a former doge's palazzo. At a less exalted level, **Paolo Rossi**, Campo S. Zaccaria 4685, S. Marco, has attractive reproductions of ancient glassware at still-reasonable prices, and **Arte Veneto**, Campo S. Zanipolo 6335, Castello, offers glass and ceramic trinkets that escape looking tacky or ridiculous. For interesting contemporary glassware, take a look at **Isola**, Campo S. Moisè, S. Marco. If you can contemplate carrying them home then mosaics, one of the oldest Venetian crafts, are also available, as individual *tessere* or larger items. Try **Arte del Mosaico**, Calle Erizzo 4002, Castello, or **Angelo Orsoni**, Campiello del Battello 1045, Cannaregio. All kinds of beautiful hand-crafted paper can be bought from one of Stravinsky's favourite shops, **Legatoria Piazzesi**, S. Maria del Giglio 2511, S. Marco, along with many other fine but useful things for the desk or study, nearly all of them locally made. Alternatively, **Cartoleria Accademia**, Accademia 1052, Dorsoduro, is jam-packed with paints, paper, easels and so on for those who want to make their own souvenir of Venice.

---

### Sports and Activities

Most of Venice's sporting facilities are found on the Lido or the other outer islands (*see* p.391).

The rule of thumb in Venice is that in whatever class of hotel you stay, expect it to cost around a third more than it would on the mainland, even before the often outrageous charge for breakfast is added to the bill. Reservations are near-essential from about April to October and for Carnival; many hotels close in the winter, though many of those that do stay open offer substantial discounts at this time. Single rooms are always very hard to find. If you arrive at any time without reservations, the tourist offices at the railway station and Piazzale Roma have a free room-finding service (a deposit is required, which is then deducted from your hotel bill), though they get very busy in season. Many hotels also have touts around the station looking for clients, who are not necessarily to be disregarded, as the prices they offer can be quite reasonable. Also, the central tourist office in Piazza San Marco will supply by post a list of agencies that rent self-catering flats in Venice and neighbouring resorts that can be reserved in advance.

### *luxury*

★★★★★ **Cipriani**, Giudecca 10, ℂ 5207744, ℮ 5203930. Since 1963 this has been one of Italy's most luxurious hotels, a villa isolated in a lush garden at one end of the Giudecca that's so quiet and comfortable you could forget Venice exists, even though it's only a few minutes away by the hotel's 24-hour private launch service. An Olympic-size pool, sauna, jacuzzis in each room, tennis courts, and a superb restaurant are just some of its facilities, and no hotel anywhere could pamper you more. Room prices vary according to the view and the facilities.

★★★★★ **Danieli**, Riva degli Schiavoni 4196, Castello, ℂ 5226480, ℮ 5200208. The largest and most famous hotel in Venice, in what must be the most glorious location, overlooking the Lagoon and rubbing shoulders with the Palazzo Ducale. Formerly the Gothic palazzo of the Dandolo family, it has been a hotel since 1822; Dickens, Proust, George Sand and Wagner checked in here. Nearly every room has some story to tell, in a beautiful setting of silken walls, Gothic staircases, gilt mirrors and oriental rugs. The new wing, much vilified ever since it was built in the 1940s, is comfortable but lacks the charm and the stories.

★★★★★ **Gritti Palace**, S. Maria del Giglio 2467, S. Marco, ℂ 794611, ℮ 5200942. The 15th-century Grand Canal palace that once belonged to the dashing glutton and womanizer Doge Andrea Gritti has been preserved as a true Venetian fantasy and elegant retreat, now part of the CIGA chain. All the rooms are furnished with Venetian antiques, but for a real splurge do as Somerset Maugham did and stay in the Ducal Suite. Another of its delights is the restaurant, the **Club del Doge**, on a terrace overlooking the canal.

### *very expensive*

★★★★ **Cavalletto & Doge Orseolo**, Calle Cavalletto 1107, S. Marco, ℂ 5200955, ℮ 5238184. Overlooking the basin where most of the gondoliers moor their vessels, in a building that in the Middle Ages was already a hostel for pilgrims waiting to embark for the Holy Land, it now offers far more luxury than the pilgrims ever enjoyed—air-conditioning, window boxes, minibar and TV. Off-season discounts.

**** **Londra Palace** Riva degli Schiavoni 4171, Castello, ℮ 5200533, ℮ 5225032. Tchaikovsky wrote his *Fourth Symphony* in room 108 of this hotel, and it was also a favourite of Stravinsky. The hotel was created by linking two palaces together, and it has an elegant interior, one of the cosiest lobbies in Venice, and exceptionally good service. There is also an excellent restaurant, **Les Deux Lions**.

**** **Metropole**, Riva degli Schiavoni 4149, Castello, ℮ 5205044, ℮ 5223679. A near-neighbour of the Londra Palace, it was built at the beginning of the 19th century and used by the military before becoming a hotel. Completely renovated, it has been finely and romantically furnished in traditional Venetian style, and many rooms have wonderful views over the Lagoon. There is also a picturesque gondola landing, on a side canal.

**** **Saturnia & International**, Via XXII Marzo 2398, S. Marco, ℮ 5208377, ℮ 5207131. A lovely hotel in a romantic quattrocento palazzo that has preserved centuries of accumulated decoration. Very near S. Marco, it has a garden court, faced by the nicest and quietest rooms. Off-season discounts.

### expensive

*** **Accademia-Villa Maravegie**, Fondamenta Bollani 1058, Dorsoduro, ℮ 5210188, ℮ 5239152. A hotel that offers a generous dollop of slightly faded charm in a 17th-century villa with a garden, just off the Grand Canal. Its 26 rooms are furnished with a menagerie of antiques, some of which look as if they were left behind by the villa's previous occupant—the Russian Embassy. The Accademia is a favourite of many, so book well in advance. Off-season discounts.

*** **La Fenice et Des Artistes**, Campiello de la Fenice 1936, S. Marco, ℮ 5232333, ℮ 5203721. A favourite of opera buffs in Venice, where you can sit out on a terrace at breakfast and hear the evening's soprano doing her scales. Inside there are lots of mirrors, antiques and chandeliers to make artistes feel at home. Air-conditioning is available.

*** **Flora**, Calle Bergamaschi 2283/a, S. Marco, ℮ 5205844, ℮ 5238217. A small hotel on a little street that's remarkably quiet so near to the Piazza, with a charming garden and patio, spilling flowers. It's comfortably furnished, but when booking ask for a large room. Air-conditioning and off-season discounts are available.

*** **Do Pozzi**, Corte do Pozzi 2373, S. Marco, ℮ 5207855, ℮ 5229413. With a bit of the look of an Italian country inn, this hotel has 29 quiet rooms on a charming little square, only a few minutes from Piazza San Marco. It's friendly and well run. Optional air-conditioning in all rooms.

*** **Malibran**, S. Giovanni Crisostomo 5864, Cannaregio, ℮ 5224626. In the Corte del Milion, next to, or perhaps even incorporating, the house of Marco Polo.

★★★ **Sturion**, Calle del Sturion 679, San Polo, ✆ 5236243, ✉ 5228378. A popular choice, as it's one of the least expensive hotels actually on the Grand Canal. It's advisable to book well ahead for one of its eight large, finely furnished rooms.

*moderate*

★★ **Agli Alboretti**, Rio Terrà S. Agnese 882/4, Dorsoduro, ✆ 5230058. A charming little hotel on a rare tree-lined lane near the Accademia; 19 rooms, all with baths.

★★ **La Calcina**, Zattere ai Gesuati 780, Dorsoduro, ✆ 5206466. Near the Gesuati church and overlooking the Giudecca canal, this was Ruskin's *pensione* in 1877. It is simply furnished, but comfortable. Off-season discounts.

★★ **Falier**, Salizzada S. Pantalon 130, S. Croce, ✆ 5228882. A small hotel near Campo San Rocco. Elegantly furnished, it has two flower-filled terraces to lounge around on when your feet rebel, and all rooms have baths.

★★ **Messner**, Salute 216, Dorsoduro, ✆ 5227443. A recently modernized hotel only a couple of minutes from the Salute, and very suitable for families. There are great showers, but awful coffee.

★★ **Mignon**, SS. Apostoli 4535, Cannaregio, ✆ 5237388. In a fairly quiet area, not far from the Ca' d'Oro, the Mignon boasts a little garden for leisurely breakfasts, though the rooms (some without baths) are rather plain.

★★ **Pensione Seguso**, Zattere ai Gesuati 779, Dorsoduro, ✆ 5222340. In a 15th-century house on the Zattere, next door to La Calcina, it has rooms in the front that overlook the Giudecca canal, while the side rooms have views over one of its finest 'tributaries'. The Seguso has plenty of character, antiques, and tables outdoors for a sunny breakfast.

★★ **La Residenza**, Campo Bandiera e Moro 3608, Castello, ✆ 5285315. Located in a lovely 14th-century palace in a quiet square between San Marco and the Arsenale. The public rooms are flamboyantly decorated with 18th-century frescoes, paintings and antique furniture, though the bedrooms are more simple.

*inexpensive*

The largest concentration of relatively cheap hotels in Venice is around the Lista di Spagna, running eastwards into Cannaregio from the train station, though they can be pretty tacky and noisy. A more relaxed, pleasant and attractive area in which to find less expensive accommodation is in Dorsoduro, particularly around the Campo Santa Margherita.

★ **Antico Capon**, Campo S. Margherita 3004/b, Dorsoduro, ✆ 5285292. With seven simple rooms, and, thankfully, no breakfast, this hotel owes most of its charm to its sociable and restaurant-filled *Campo*.

★ **Casa Carettoni**, Lista di Spagna 130, Cannaregio, ✆ 716231. The most pleasant and comfortable cheap hotel near the station; no breakfast is a plus, as you can do as Venetians do and take it in a nearby bar.

- ★ **Casa Petrarca**, Calle delle Colonne 4386, S. Marco, ✆ 5200430. Petrarch didn't really sleep in one of these six friendly rooms near the Piazza San Marco, but few people care when they bag one.

- ★ **Casa Verardo**, Ruga Giuffa 4765, Castello, ✆ 5286127. A classy, 9-room *locanda* with friendly owners, though none of the rooms has a bath.

- ★ **Da Pino,** Crosera S. Pantalon, Dorsoduro 3942, ✆ 5223646. A cheap and cheerful hotel in a busy shopping street that can be noisy at night.

- ★ **Montin**, Fondamenta di Borgo 1147, Dorsoduro, ✆ 5227151. One of the last old-fashioned Venetian hostelries, with seven character-filled rooms, and an excellent (but expensive) restaurant as well. Book *very* early.

- ★ **Sant'Anna**, S. Anna 269, Castello, ✆ 5286466. A fine little hotel popular with those who want to escape tourist Venice, located just north of the Giardini Pubblici. Only eight rooms, including some triples.

- ★ **Silva**, Fondamenta Rimedio 4423, Castello, ✆ 5227643. A bit hard to find—on one of the most photographed little canals in Venice, between the S. Zaccaria *vaporetto* stop and S. Maria Formosa. The rooms are fairly basic, but quiet, and there's a friendly owner, and Venice's most arrogant black cat.

### hostels and campsites

The tourist office has a list of all inexpensive hostel accommodation in Venice; as sleeping in the streets is now discouraged, schools are often pressed into use to take in the summer overflow, charging minimal rates for a place to spread out a sleeping bag.

**Camping** is big business in the north-east corner of the Lagoon, around Jesolo and Punta Sabbioni, where there are any number of plushly appointed sites. There are also several sites around the Brenta Canal. The tourist office provides a complete list. The nearest campsite to Venice is **San Nicolò**, Riviera S. Nicolò 65, on the Lido, ✆ 767415 (International Camping Card required); another good site, open all year, is **Fusina**, Via Moranzani, Malcontenta, near Fusina, ✆ 969064. The *vaporetto* Line 16 from there to Venice runs only in summer, but the regular Venice–Padua bus runs nearby.

**Ostello Venezia**, Fondamenta delle Zitelle 86, Giudecca, ✆ 5238211. Venice's official youth hostel enjoys one of the most striking locations of any in Italy, with views across the Giudecca canal to San Marco. From June to September you can only book in person—the office opens as 6pm, but doors open at noon for waiting. IYHF cards required (though they're available at the hostel) and there's an 11.30pm curfew. Beds are L17,000 a head, breakfast included; meals are L8000.

**Foresteria Valdese**, Calle della Madonnetta 5170, Castello, ✆ 5286797. An old palazzo converted into a dormitory/*pensione* by the Waldensians. Check-in 11am–1pm, 6–8.30pm; beds in dorm L20,000, breakfast included, and in rooms L24,000 per person.

**Domus Cavanis**, Rio Terrà Foscarini 912, Dorsoduro, ✆ 5287374. A Catholic-run hostel open June–Sept only. Single-sex single, double and triple rooms are available, at L35,000 per person; meals are L8000.

Venetian cuisine is based on fish, shellfish, and rice, often mixed together in a succulent seafood risotto. *Risi e bisi* (rice and peas) is famous, often served with anchovy sauce, while the favourite local pasta dish is *bigoli in salsa*, thick hollow spaghetti topped with butter, onions, and anchovies or sardines. There are various types of *risotti*: *di mare*, with seafood, *in nero*, with cuttlefish cooked in its own ink, or *alla sbirraglia*, with vegetables, chicken and ham. For *secondo*, liver and onions (*fegato alla veneziana*) with polenta (*tecia*) shares top billing with seafood dishes like scampi, Sile eel, cuttlefish in its own ink (*seppie alla veneziana*), *fritto* (Adriatic mixed fry) and lobster (*aragosta*). Bitter red *radicchio* is a favourite side-dish, and you can top it all off with a *tiramisù*, the traditional Veneto mascarpone, coffee and chocolate dessert. Wines are of a reliably high standard in most restaurants, mainly excellent Veneto reds and whites from Friuli and Trentino-Alto Adige.

Venice, however, is famous for its bad restaurants. Not only is cooking in general well below the norm in Italy, but prices tend to be about 15% higher, and even the moderate ones can give you a nasty surprise at *conto* time with excessive service and cover charges. The cheap ones, serving up 500 tourist menus a day to the international throng, are mere providers of calories to keep you on your feet; pizza is a good standby if you're on a budget. The restaurants listed here, though, all have a history of being decent or better, so chances are they still will be when you visit.

### *very expensive*

**Antico Martini**, Campo S. Fantin 1983, S. Marco, ✆ 5224121. Near La Fenice, this is a Venetian classic, all Romance and elegance. It started out as a Turkish coffeehouse in the early 18th century, but nowadays is better known for seafood, a superb wine list and the best *pennette al pomodoro* in Venice. The intimate piano bar-restaurant stays open until 2am. (*Closed Tues, Wed midday, Dec, Feb.*)

**La Caravella**, Calle Larga XXII Marzo 2397, S. Marco, ✆ 5208901, in an annexe to the Saturnia hotel (*see* above). For sheer variety of local and exotic dishes, prepared by a master chef, few restaurants in Italy can top this merrily corny repro of a dining hall in a 16th-century Venetian galley. Try *bouillabaisse*, French onion soup, gazpacho, or the house's famous *bigoli*, followed by scampi in champagne or the delicious chicken in a a paper bag (*en papillote*). Despite the décor, the atmosphere is fairly formal. (*Open Oct–April, closed Wed.*)

**Danieli Terrace**, in the Danieli Hotel, Riva degli Schiavoni 4196, Castello, ✆ 5226480. The Danieli's rooftop restaurant is renowned for classic cuisine (try the *spaghetti alla Danieli*, prepared at your table) and perfect service in an incomparable setting overlooking Bacino San Marco. (*Closed Tues.*)

**Do Forni**, Calle dei Specchieri 468, S. Marco, ✆ 5232148. For many Italians as well as foreigners, this is *the* place to eat in Venice. There are two dining rooms, one 'Orient Express'-style and the other rustic, and both are always filled with diners partaking of its excellent seafood antipasti, polenta, and well-prepared fish. (*Open Oct–April; closed Thurs.*)

**Harry's Bar**, Calle Vallaresso 1323, S. Marco, ✆ 5236797. In a class by itself, a favourite of Hemingway and assorted other luminaries, this is as much a Venetian institution as the Doges' Palace, though food has become secondary to its celebrity atmosphere. The sandwiches and house cocktails (a Bellini, Tiziano, or Tiepolo—delectable fruit juices mixed with Prosecco), served in the bar, are justly famous. The menu, served in the restaurant upstairs, is short, but features a wonderful assortment of antipasti (the *carpaccio* (raw beef) is especially good), risotto, baked lamb, liver, or scampi; the desserts are all exceptional. (*Closed Mon.*)

### *expensive*

**Dall'Amelia**, Via Miranese 113, Mestre, ✆ 913951. A restaurant that, despite its inconvenient mainland location, is of necessary inclusion, as all Italian gourmets cross the big bridge to dine here at least once. The oysters are delicious and there's a divine *tortelli di bronzino* (bass), plus a choice of wine from one of Italy's most renowned cellars.

**Antica Besseta**, Calle Savio 1395, S. Croce, ✆ 721687 . A family-run citadel of Venetian homecooking, where you can experience an authentic *risi e bisi*, or *bigoli in salsa*, scampi, and the family's own wine. (*Closed Tues, Wed, part of July, Aug.*)

**Corte Sconta**, Calle del Pestrin 3886, Castello, ✆ 5227024. It may be off the beaten track, but the reputation of this trattoria rests solidly on its exquisite molluscs and crustaceans, served in a setting that's a breath of fresh air after the exposed beams and copper pots that dominate the typical Venetian restaurant. The Venetians claim the Corte Sconta is even better in the off-season; be sure to order the house wine. Reservations are essential. (*Closed Sun, Mon, most of July–Aug.*)

**Hostaria da Franz**, Fondamenta San Isepo (or Giuseppe) 754, Castello, ✆ 5227505. A restaurant well out of the way just north of the Giardini Pubblici, but it's well worth the trouble of getting lost en route. This is one of Venice's best: great oysters, *gnocchi*, and seafood cooked the way it should be if all Venetians tried harder. The house wine, a delicate Tocai, is lovely. (*Closed Tues.*)

**Montin**, Fondamenta di Borgo 1147, Dorsoduro, ✆ 5227151. Part of the much cheaper Montin hotel (see above), this has long been Venice's most celebrated artists' eatery. The food, however, can range erratically in quality from first to third division, though the garden setting is guaranteed to enchant. (*Closed Tues evening, Wed, mid-Aug.*)

**Trattoria Vini da Arturo**, Calle degli Assassini 3656, S. Marco, ✆ 5286974. In an infamous little street near La Fenice, this is a tiny trattoria that marches to a different drum from most Venetian restaurants, with not a speck of seafood on the menu. Instead, try the *tagliatelle al radicchio* and *stinco* (shin) *all'Amarone*, or Venice's best steaks; its *tiramisù* is famous. (*Closed Sun, mid-Aug.*)

**A La Vecia Cavana**, Rio Terrà dei SS. Apostoli 4624, Cannaregio, ☎ 5238644. Cannaregio's smartest restaurant, where you can dine on Adriatic specialities. They sometimes offer a good reasonably priced lunch set menu. (*Closed Tues.*)

*moderate*

**Altanella**, Rio del Ponte Lungo 268, Giudecca, ☎ 5227780. A delightful old seafood restaurant with canal-side tables near the Redentore, where the *risotto di pesce* and *fritto* are worth the trip in themselves. (*Closed Mon evening, Tues, half of Aug.*)

**Antica Mola**, Fondamenta degli Ormesini, Cannaregio, no telephone, near the Ghetto. Superbly run by the same family since time immemorial, Mola has recently become newly fashionable, and serves some of Cannaregio's best food at good-value prices. (*Closed Wed.*)

**Antico Giardinetto da Erasmo**, S. Croce 2315, ☎ 721301, behind the church of S. Cassiano. The star feature is delicious seafood, in the form of antipasti or as a main course, cooked in a variety of styles. In good weather you can eat out in the little garden. (*Closed Sat, Sun, Aug.*)

**La Furatola**, Calle Lunga S. Barnaba 2870, Dorsoduro, ☎ 5208594. A small but dedicated trattoria where the fish are jumping (or almost) as you select one that strikes your fancy—definitely *the* place for an affordable seafood feast. (*Closed Wed evening, Thur, July–Aug.*)

**Alla Madonna**, Calle della Madonna 594, S. Polo, ☎ 5233824. A large, popular, and very Venetian fish restaurant. (*Closed Wed, Jan.*)

**Ai Promessi Sposi**, Calle dell'Oca 4367, Cannaregio, no telephone. Cheerful bar/trattoria with good basic fairly traditional food. (*Closed Tues.*)

**Da Remigio**, Salizzada dei Greci 3416, Castello, ☎ 5230089. A neighbourhood favourite, with solid Venetian cooking, that's frequently full of locals. (*Closed Mon, Tues.*)

**Tre Spiedi**, Salizzada S. Canciano 5906, Cannaregio, ☎ 5280035, near the Campiello F. Corner and the central post office. A cosy atmosphere to go with local specialities like *braciola Bruno* (pork chops). (*Closed Sun evening, Mon.*)

*inexpensive*

**Acciugheta da Fabiano**, Campo SS. Filippo e Giacomo, Castello, ☎ 5224292. One of the best cheap restaurants and bars near the Piazza San Marco, with good pizzas and atmosphere to boot. (*Closed Tues.*)

**Alle Oche**, Calle Tintor 1459, S. Croce, ☎ 5241496, south of S. Giacomo dell'Orio. Set in a quiet little square by the canal, with tables outdoors, this great pizzeria has over 50 varieties of pizza, including one topped with cream and prawns. There are also good pasta dishes, such as *tagliatelle al gorgonzola*. Get there early, as it fills up very quickly. (*Closed Mon.*)

**Casa Mia**, Calle dell'Oca 4430, Cannaregio, ☎ 5285590, near Campo SS. Apostoli. A lively pizzeria full of locals. (*Closed Tues.*)

**Latteria Veneziana**, Calle dei Fuseri, S. Marco, no telephone. Venice's only declaredly vegetarian restaurant, not famous for the lightness of its cooking, but good value.

**Paradiso Perduto**, Fondamenta della Misericordia 2540, Cannaregio, ℂ 720581. A great favourite with a young, studentish and arty clientele, with a bar at the front. The food varies in quality, but it stays open from midday till late, and often has jazz concerts at weekends. (*Closed Wed.*)

**Trattoria della Donna Onesta**, Calle della Madonna 3922, Dorsoduro, ℂ 5229586. A down-to-earth place where you'll find Venetian specialities served with an extra friendly touch. (*Closed Sun.*)

**Vino Vino**, Campo S. Fantin 1983, S. Marco, ℂ 5224121. A trendy offspring of the élite Antico Martini, where you can eat a well-cooked, filling dish with a glass of good wine at prices even students can afford. (*Closed Tues, Wed midday, Dec, Feb.*)

## Entertainment and Nightlife

Sadly, in a city that's clearly made-to-order for pleasure, revelry and romance, life after dark is notoriously moribund. The locals take an evening stroll to their local *campo* for a chat with friends and an *aperitivo*, before heading home to dinner and the TV—the hotblooded may go on to bars and discos in Mestre, Marghera or the Lido. Visitors are left to become even poorer at the **Municipal Casino**, out on the Lido from April to October, and at other times in the Palazzo Vendramin on the Grand Canal (hours are 3pm–2am, dress up and take your passport). You might prefer to spend less more memorably on a moonlit gondola ride, or you can do as most people do—wander about. Venice is a different city at night, when the *bricole* lights in the Lagoon are a fitting backdrop for a mer-king's birthday pageant.

Even so, there are places to go among all this peace and quiet, and against the absence of everyday nightlife should be put Venice's packed calendar of special events. For an up-to-date calendar of current events, exhibitions, shows, films, and concerts in the city, consult *Un Ospite di Venezia*, free from tourist offices.

### opera, classical music and theatre

Venice's music programme is heavily oriented to the classical. Opera (from December to May only), ballet, recitals and symphonic concerts may not always be top notch, but are presented at Venice's stunning opera house, **Teatro La Fenice**, Campo S. Fantin, S. Marco, ℂ 5210161, and its smaller chamber, Sala Apollinée. Two other concert venues that are worth visiting as much for the décor as the music are the **Palazzo Labia**, Campo S. Geremia, Cannaregio, ℂ 716666, with its Tiepolo frescoes, used for recordings by Italian state radio, and Vivaldi's lovely church of **La Pietà** (information and tickets, ℂ 5208722 or 5208711).

Venice's principal theatre is the **Teatro Goldoni**, Calle Goldoni 4650/b, S. Marco, ℂ 5205422, which is where the Goldoni repertory holds pride of place, but there are other plays, as well as concerts.

The classic cafés of Venice face each other across Piazza San Marco: **Florian's** and its great rival **Quadri**—avoided, it is said, by all true Venetians because of its popularity with the Austrian occupiers in the last century. Prices are correspondingly exorbitant. More fashionable with smart Venetians today, particularly on Sundays, is **Harry's Dolci**, Fondamenta S. Biagio 773 on the Giudecca, noted for its elegant teas, ice creams and cakes. Stand-up-only **Caffè Costarica**, Rio Terrà di S. Leonardo, Cannaregio, brews Venice's most powerful *espresso* and great iced coffee (*frappé*), and also sells ground coffees and beans over the counter. The **Campo Santa Margherita** in Dorsoduro, with plenty of bars and cafés and a good *gelateria*, is the square most favoured by young Venetians and the student community.

Throughout the day Venetians frequently drop into bars and wine bars for a 'shadow' (an *ombra*, a tiny glass of wine generally downed in one go) and *cichetti*, the Venetian equivalent of tapas. For the greatest variety of wines, try Venice's oldest wine bar, **Al Volta**, Calle Cavalli di S. Marco 4081, S. Marco , with over 2000 Italian and foreign labels to choose from and a sumptuous array of *cichetti*. (*Closed Sun.*) **Do Mori**, a resolutely traditional Rialto market bar, just off Ruga Vecchia San Giovanni, has delicious snacks to go with your *ombra*. (*Closed Wed afternoon, Sun.*) **Al Milion**, behind S. Giovanni Crisostomo at Cannaregio 5841, near Marco Polo's house, is a comfortable old wine bar full of venetians in the afternoon. (*Closed Wed.*) Between 5pm and dinner is the time to indulge in a beer and *tramezzini*, finger sandwiches that come in a hundred varieties, and some of the best are to be found at **Osteria alla Botteghe**, Calle delle Botteghe, by Campo Santo Stefano in San Marco.

The title of best *gelateria* in the city has by convention been accorded to **Paolin**, on the Campo Santo Stefano, S. Marco, above all for their divine pistachio. (*Closed Fri.*) However, **Nico**, on the Zattere ai Gesuati, Dorsoduro, is also a must on anyone's ice cream tour, specializing in luscious combinations. (*Closed Thurs.*)

## jazz, clubs and nightspots

Venice's few late-night bars and music venues can be fun, or just posy and dull, and what you find is pretty much a matter of pot luck. **Paradiso Perduto** (*see* above, 'Eating Out', for details) is the city's best-known and most popular late-night bar/ restaurant, often presenting live jazz at weekends, and also attracts some of Venice's low-profile gay community. The relaxed and informal wine bar **Osteria da Codroma**, Fondamenta Briati 2540, Dorsoduro, hosts a backgammon club, art shows and occasional live jazz, and serves excellent toasted sandwiches. (*Open 7pm–2am; closed Thurs.*) A funkier restaurant/bar with music, dancing and sometimes live rock or jazz is **Ai Canottieri**, Ponte Tre Archi 690, Cannaregio. (*Open 7pm–2am; closed Sun.*)

There are also quite a few fairly glitzy piano bars, such as **Linea d'Ombra**, Zattere ai Saloni, near the Salute. **El Souk**, Calle Corfu 1056/a, Dorsoduro, near the Accademia, is Venice's only actual disco (*open 10pm–4am; closed Sun*), though from July–Sept there's a more convivial place to dance open on the Lido, **Club 22**, Lungomare Marconi 22. The Lido's late-night bars—particularly along the Gran Viale and Lungomare Marconi—can be quite lively in summer. A favourite place for Venetians to make off to in Marghera is **Al Vapore**, Via Fratelli Bandiera 8, which hosts live rock and jazz.

Back in Venice, the main late-night drinking holes are **Harry's Bar** (*see* above, 'Eating Out'), especially if someone else is paying; **Osteria agli Assassini**, Calle degli Assassini, S. Marco, which has wines, beers, and good *cichetti* (*open till midnight; closed Sun*), and **Haig's**, Campo S. Maria del Giglio, S. Marco, a fashionable bar that attracts a mixed gay/straight clientele and what there is of Venice's *beau monde.* (*Open till 2am; closed Wed.*) For more filling victuals, try **Vino Vino** (*see* above, 'Eating Out'; *open till 2am*), or the **Creperia Poggi**, Cannaregio 2103, which has music and also stays open till 2am, flipping crêpes until midnight. (*Closed Sun.*) The last chance for an ice cream is at 3am at the Lido's **Gelateria Bar Maleti**, Gran Viale 47. (*Closed Wed.*)

### exhibitions and art festivals

Venice is one of Europe's top cities for exhibitions: major international shows fill the **Palazzo Ducale** and the **Palazzo Grassi**, Campo S. Samuele, S. Marco, which Fiat has transformed into a lavishly equipped exhibition and cultural centre. High calibre art and photographic exhibitions also appear frequently at the **Palazzo Querini-Stampalia**, the **Peggy Guggenheim Collection**, and **Ca' Pésaro**.

Then there's the **Biennale**, the most famous contemporary art show in the world, founded in 1895 and now held, in principle, in even-numbered years. The main exhibits of the forty or so countries officially represented are set up in the permanent pavilions in the Giardini Pubblici, but there is also an open section for younger and less-established artists, in venues across the city. Controversy has hummed around the Biennale for years, and the recent appointment as director of Achille Bonito Oliva, with the stated aim of turning it into a 'laboratory of ideas', has only reinvigorated the argument, drawing particular condemnation from Anglo-American critics.

The city's other great cultural junket is the **Venice Film Festival**, held in the Palazzo del Cinema and the Astra

Cinema on the Lido every year in late August and September. As well as spotting the stars, you can sometimes get in to see films if you arrive at the cinemas really early—tickets are only sold on the same day as each showing.

Venice also has two substantial music festivals, the **Vivaldi Festival**, held in La Fenice, and the **Contemporary Music Festival**, both in September.

### traditional festivals

Venice's renowned **Carnival**, first held in the ten days preceding Lent in 1094, was revived in 1979 after several decades of dormancy. It attracts huge crowds, but faces an uphill battle against the inveterate Italian urge to maintain their *bella figura*—getting dressed up in elaborate costumes, wandering down to San Marco and taking each other's picture is as much as most of the revellers seem to get up to. Concerts and shows are put on all over Venice, with city and corporate sponsorship, but there's very little spontaneity or serious carousing, and certainly no trace of what Byron called the 'revel of the earth'.

Even so, a **Carnival mask** can still make a good souvenir, either in inexpensive papier mâché (*cartapesta*) or in leather. There are mask shops all over Venice, but for the real, traditionally-crafted item, try **Giorgio Clanetti (Laboratorio Artigiano Maschere)**, Barbaria de la Tole 6657, Castello, near SS. Giovanni e Paolo, or the master of them all, **Emilio Massaro**, Calle Vetturi, by Campo Morosini, S. Marco, where you can watch them being made.

In 1988 Venice revived the medieval ceremony of **La Sensa**, held on the first Sunday after Ascension Day, in which the doge married the sea. Now the mayor plays the groom, in a replica of the state barge or *Bucintoro*. It's as corny and pretentious as it sounds, but on the same day you can watch the gondoliers race in the **Vogalonga** from San Marco to Burano and back again.

Venice's most spectacular festival, **Il Redentore**, held on the third Sunday of July, celebrates the end of the plague of 1576, when the Senate vowed that in thanksgiving they would build a church (Palladio's Il Redentore, on the Giudecca) and cross over to attend mass there once a year on a bridge of boats—which the Venetians continue to do today. The greatest excitement happens the Saturday night before, when Venetians traditionally row out for a picnic on the water, manoeuvring for the best view of the fabulous fireworks display over the Lagoon.

More adrenalin is expended in the **Regata Storica** (first Sunday in September), a splendid pageant of historic vessels and crews in Renaissance costumes and hotly contested races by gondoliers and a variety of other rowers down the Grand Canal. Another bridge of boats is built on 21 November, this time across the Grand Canal to the Salute, for the feast of **Santa Maria della Salute**, which also commemorates the ending of a plague, in 1631. This event provides the only opportunity to see Longhena's unique basilica as it would have been when it was built, with its doors thrown open on to the Grand Canal.

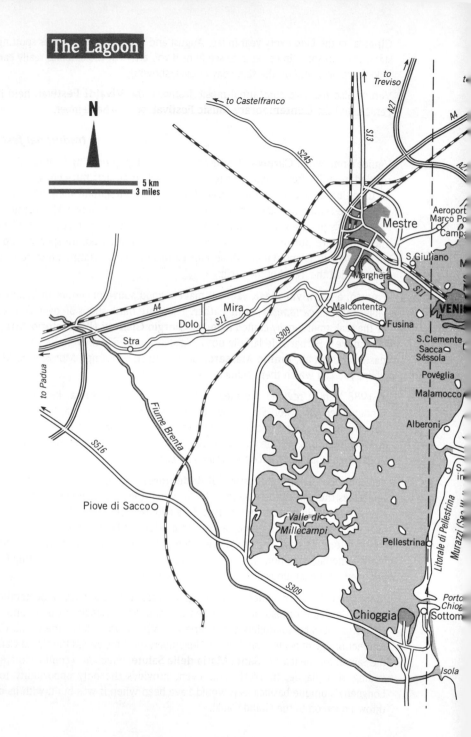

The Lagoon

N

5 km
3 miles

to Treviso

to Castelfranco

S245

S13

A27

A4

A2.

Mestre

Aeroport
Marco Po
Camp

S. Giuliano

Marghera

S11

VENI

A4

Mira

Malcontenta

S. Clemente
Sacca
Séssola

Dolo

S11

Fusina

Stra

Povéglia

Malamocco

to Padua

S309

Alberoni

S516

Fiume Brenta

S.
in

Piove di Sacco

Litorale di Pellestrina

Murazzi (Se

Valle di
Millecampi

Pellestrina

S309

Porto
Chio
Sottom

Chioggia

Isola

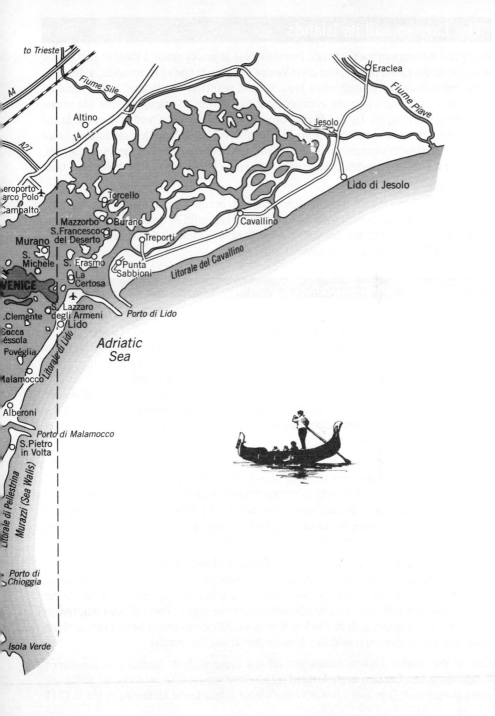

to Trieste

A4

Fiume Sile

A27

14

Altino

Aeroporto
Marco Polo

Campalto

Torcello

Mazzorbo    Burano
S.Francesco
del Deserto

Murano

S.
Michele    S. Erasmo    Punta
                          Sabbioni
.Clemente    S.Lazzaro
            degli Armeni
Vignole
La
Certosa

VENICE

Treporti

Litorale del Cavallino

Porto di Lido

Lido

Sacca
Sessola

Poveglia

Litorale di Lido

Adriatic
Sea

Malamocco

Alberoni

Porto di Malamocco

S.Pietro
in Volta

Litorale di Pellestrina

Murazzi (Sea Walls)

Porto di
Chioggia

Isola Verde

Eraclea

Fiume Piave

Jesolo

Lido di Jesolo

Cavallino

# The Lagoon and its Islands

Pearly and melting into the bright sky, iridescent blue or murky green, a sheet of glass yellow and pink in the dawn, or just plain grey: Venice's Lagoon is one of its wonders, a desolate, often melancholy and strange, often beautiful and seductive 'landscape' with a hundred personalities. It is 56km long and averages about 8km across, adding up to some 448 square kilometres; half of it, the *Laguna Morta* ('Dead Lagoon') consists of mud flats except in the spring, while the shallows of the *Laguna Viva* are always present, and cleansed by tides twice a day. To navigate this treacherous sea, the Venetians have developed highways of channels, marked by *bricole*—wooden posts topped by orange lamps—that keep their craft from running aground.

Once the numerous islands were densely inhabited, occupied by a town or a monastery. Now all but a few have been abandoned; many a tiny one, with its forlorn shell of a building, has been overgrown with weeds, while the whole of the Lagoon is threatened by the accumulation of algae, the curse of the post-industrial Adriatic.

# The Lido and South Lagoon

The Lido, one of the long spits of land that forms the protective outer edge of the Lagoon, is by far the most glamorous of the islands, one that has given its name to countless bathing establishments, bars, amusement arcades and cinemas all over the world. On its 12 kilometres of beach the poets, potentates and plutocrats of the turn of the century spent their holidays in palatial hotels and villas, making the Lido the pinnacle of *Belle Epoque* fashion, so brilliantly evoked in Thomas Mann's novel *Death in Venice*, and Visconti's subsequent film. The story was set and filmed in the **Grand Hotel des Bains**, just north of the renowned, Mussolini-style **Municipal Casino** and the **Palazzo del Cinema**, where Venice hosts its International Film Festival.

The Lido is still the playground of the Venetians and their visitors, with its riding clubs, tennis courts, golf courses and shooting ranges; it is also expensive, overcrowded and annoying, with its tedious hierarchy of private bathing establishments. The free beach, the **Spiaggia Comunale**, is on the north part of the island, a 15-minute walk from the *vaporetto* stop at San Nicolò (go down the Gran Viale, and turn left on the Lungomare d'Annunzio), where you can hire a changing hut and frolic in the fine sand and not-so-fine sea.

Further north, beyond the private airfield, the **Porto di Lido** is maritime Venice's front door, the most important of the three entrances to the Lagoon, where you can watch the ships of the world sail by. This is where the Doge would sail to toss his ring into the waves, in the annual 'Marriage of the Sea'. It is stoutly defended by the mighty **Forte di Sant'Andrea** on the island of Le Vignole, built in 1543 by Venice's fortifications genius Sanmicheli. In times of danger, a great chain was extended from the fort across the channel.

One of the smaller Lagoon islands just off the Lido, with its landmark onion-domed campanile, is **San Lazzaro degli Armeni** (*vaporetto lines 10, 20 from Riva degli Schiavoni, open to visitors 3–5pm daily*). It was Venice's leper colony in the Middle Ages, but in 1715 the then-deserted island was given to the Mechitarist Fathers of the Armenian Catholic Church after they were expelled from Greece by the Turks. Today their monastery is still one of the world's major centres of Armenian culture and its monks, always noted as linguists, run a famous polyglot press able to print in 32 languages, one of the last survivors in a city once renowned for its publishing. Tours of San Lazzaro include a museum filled with relics of the ancient Christian history of Armenia, as well as memorabilia of Lord Byron, who spent a winter visiting the fathers and bruising his brain with Armenian. Donations from visitors are appreciated.

Buses from the Lido's *vaporetto* landing run via ferries all the way south to Chioggia, passing through **Malamocco**, a tranquil fishing village named after one of the first Lagoon townships—the original sank into the sea in the 11th century. Next to it is the small resort of **Alberoni**, which boasts the Lido Golf Course.

A ferry takes the bus across the Porto di Malamocco to an even thinner island reef, **Pellestrina**, with two sleepy villages, **S. Pietro in Volta** and **Pellestrina**, where you can see the impressive sea walls, the **Murazzi**. The last great public works of the Republic, they were constructed with huge, white Istrian blocks and built, as their plaque proudly states: 'Ausu Romano—Aere Veneto' ('With Roman audacity and Venetian money').

## Chioggia

Another ferry crosses the third porto for **Chioggia**, the southernmost town on the Lagoon. Chioggia is one of the most important fishing ports on the Adriatic, a kind of working-class Venice where the canals and streets are arrow-straight, and the boats of the fishing fleet are painted with brightly coloured pictures and symbols. The morning **fish market**, brimming with exotic and tasty sea creatures, is one of the wonders of Italy.

The Chioggians have a not entirely undeserved reputation for grumpiness, a temperament that is hardly improved when the uppity Venetians call their little lion up on its column in the Piazzetta Vigo (where the ferry leaves you) the 'Cat of St Mark'. Goldoni was amused enough by it all to make the town the setting of one of his comedies, the *Baruffe Chiozzotte*. When you've had your fill of fish and the locals, you can stroll along the long bridge to Chioggia's resort island **Sottomarina**, or its more rural cousin **Isola Verde**, for a swim.

### *Sports and Activities*

Despite dire reports about the state of the waters of the Adriatic, people still swim off the Lido without becoming mutants, but there is an alternative in the **swimming pool** on Sacca Fisola, at the west end of the Giudecca, ✆ 5285430. If you're interested in **sailing**, inquire at the sailing club, the **Compagnia della Vela**, for information on boat hire.

The Lido has the attractive 18-hole **Alberoni Golf Course**, ✆ 831015, and two tennis clubs, the **Tennis Club Venezia**, Lungomare Marconi 41/d, ✆ 5260335, and the cheaper **Campi Comunali di Tennis**, ✆ 5265689. You can also ride along the Lido, like Byron and Shelley, though it's no longer such a romantic hooves-in-the-surf affair—inquire at **Circolo Ippico Veneziano**, Ca' Bianco, Lido, ✆ 5261820.

If you prefer to **cycle** along the Lido, bikes can be hired at **Giorgio Barbieri**, Via Zara 5. Another favourite bike ride in the area is along the Brenta Canal; bikes for hire are available from a stand at the first bus stop after Marghera, at Oriago.

## Venice © (041–)

### *Where to Stay*
### *luxury*

★★★★★ **Excelsior**, Lungomare Marconi 41, Lido di Venezia, © 5260201, ✆ 5267276. An immense confection, built in 1907 as the biggest and most luxurious resort hotel in the world. The outrageous exterior is part-Hollywood and part-Moorish neo-gothic, and the interior is paradise for the upwardly mobile. Private beach, swimming pool, tennis courts, golf, nightclub and private launch service to Venice are some of its amenities. Ogling the stars at the film festival is another. (*Closed Nov–Mar.*)

### *very expensive*

★★★★ **Des Bains**, Lungomare Marconi 17, Lido di Venezia, © 5265921, ✆ 5260113. A grand old luxury hotel that preserves much of its *Belle Epoque* revelries in its magnificent Liberty-style salon, private *cabanas*, and large garden designed for dalliance. Thomas Mann stayed here on several occasions, and has Aschenbach sigh his life away on the private beach. There's also a salt-water swimming pool, tennis courts, perfect service, and a launch service into Venice. (*Closed Nov–Mar.*)

★★★★ **Quattro Fontane**, Via delle Quattro Fontane 16, Lido di Venezia, © 5260227, ✆ 5260726. The best of the smaller Lido hotels, it was formerly the seaside villa of a Venetian family. Its cool walled-in courtyard is inviting and tranquil, and the public and private rooms are furnished with antiques. Tennis courts. Book well in advance. (*Closed Nov–Mar.*)

### *expensive*

★★★ **Villa Parco**, Via Rodi 1, Lido di Venezia, © 5260015. A recently renovated villa a short way from the beach with a fine little garden for a bit of privacy. Children are welcome.

---

## Venice © (041–)

### *Eating Out*

You can still find the classic turn-of-the-century Lido experience at the restaurant **Dall'Hotel Excelsior**, Lungomare Marconi 40, © 5260201 (very expensive), which will offer you nearly everything you could desire—including a traditional Venetian meal.

Chioggia bursts at the seams with fish restaurants, including the old-fashioned **Trattoria Buon Pesce**, Stradale Ponte Caneva 625, Chioggia, © 400861 (moderate/inexpensive). Start with *gnocchetti alla marinara* and follow it with oysters, crab or whatever the waiter suggests. Best of all, prices are half what you'd pay in Venice.

Most Venetian itineraries take in the islands of Murano, Burano, and Torcello, all easily reached by inexpensive *vaporetti*, as is the cypress-studded cemetery island of **San Michele** (*vaporetto Line 5*), with its simple but elegant church of **San Michele in Isola** by Mauro Codussi (1469), his first-known work and Venice's first taste of the Florentine Renaissance, albeit with a Venetian twist in the tri-lobed front. It contains the tomb of Fra Paolo Sarpi, the famous Venetian monk and philosopher who led the ideological battle against the pope when the republic was placed under the Great Interdict of 1607, in a major duel of secular and church authority. Venice, considering St Mark the equal of St Peter, had her priests say Mass despite the interdict and eventually won the battle of will, thanks mainly to Sarpi, who also authored a famous Protestant-sympathizing *History of the Council of Trent*. He also made significant discoveries in anatomy, particularly on the contraction of the iris, and shared notes on astronomy with Galileo.

The **cemetery** itself is entered through the cloister next to the church (*open 8.15am–4pm daily*). The Protestant and Orthodox sections contain the tombs of some of the many foreigners who preferred to face eternity from Venice, among them Ezra Pound, Sergei Diaghilev, Frederick Rolfe (Baron Corvo) and Igor Stravinsky. The gate-keeper provides a basic map.

## Murano

The island of Murano (*vaporetti Lines 5, 5bar, 12, 13*) is synonymous with glass, the most celebrated of Venice's industries. The Venetians were the first in the Middle Ages to rediscover the secret of making crystal glass, and especially mirrors, and it was a secret they kept a monopoly on for centuries by using the most drastic measures: if ever a glassmaker let himself be coaxed abroad, the Council of ten sent their assassins after him in hot pursuit.

However, those who remained in Venice were treted with kid gloves. Because of the danger of fire, all the forges in Venice were relocated to Murano in 1291, and the little island became a kind of republic within a republic—minting its own coins, policing itself, even developing its own list of NHs (*nobili homini*—noblemen) in its own *Golden Book*—aristocrats of glass, who built solid palaces along Murano's own Grand Canal.

But glass making declined like everything else in Venice, and only towards the end of the 19th century were the forges once more stoked up on Murano. Can you visit them? You betcha! In fact a trip to the glassblowers' is the single most touristy thing to do in Venice. After watching the glass being made, there's the inevitable tour of the 'Museum Show Rooms'; these have the same atmosphere as a funeral parlour, all respect and solicitude, carpets and hush-hush—not unfitting, as some of the blooming chandeliers, befruited mirrors and poison-coloured chalices begin to make Death look good. There is no admission charge, as it is hoped you might buy, though there's not too much pressure to do so. More of Murano's often grotesquely kitsch products are on sale in shops all over the island.

It wasn't always so. The **Museo Vetrario** or Glass Museum (*open 9–7; closed Wed; adm*), in the 17th-century Palazzo Giustinian on Fondamenta Cavour has some simple pieces from

Roman times, and a choice collection of 15th-century Murano glass, especially the delightful 1480 *Barovier Nuptial Cup*; later glass tends to prove that Murano's glassblowers have long had a wayward streak. A multilingual exhibit explains the history of glassmaking. Save your ticket (if you dare!) for the new **Modern and Contemporary Glass** annexe, on Fondamenta Manin, opposite Fondamenta dei Vetrai.

Nearby stands the primary reason to visit this rather dowdy island, the Veneto-Byzantine **Santi Maria e Donato** (*open 8–12, 4–7, daily*), a contemporary of St Mark's basilica, with a beautiful arcaded apse. Inside the floor is paved with a marvellous 12th-century mosaic, incorporating coloured pieces of ancient Murano glass, and on the wall there's a fine Byzantine mosaic of the Virgin. The relics of Bishop Donato of Euboea were nabbed by Venetian body-snatchers, but in this case they outdid themselves, bringing home not only San Donato's bones but those of the dragon the good bishop slew with a gob of spit; you can see them hanging behind the altar.

Back on the Fondamenta dei Vetrai, the 15th-century **San Pietro Martire** has a lovely Giovanni Bellini (*Madonna and Child with St Mark, St Augustine and Doge Barbarigo*) from 1488.

## Burano

Burano (*vaporetto Line 12*) is the Lego-land of the Lagoon, where everything is in brightly coloured miniature—the canals, the bridges, the leaning tower, and the houses, painted with a Fauvist sensibility in the deepest of colours. Traditionally on Burano the men fish and the women make Venetian point, 'the most Italian of all lace work', beautiful, intricate and murder on the eyesight. All over Burano you can find samples on sale (of which a great deal are machine-made or imported), or you can watch it being made at the **Scuola dei Merletti** in Piazza Galuppi (*open 9–6 Tues–Sat; 10–4 Sun; adm*), though '*scuola*' is misleading, as no young woman in Burano wants to learn such an excruciating art. The school itself was founded in 1872, when traditional lacemaking was already in decline. In the sacristy of the church of **San Martino** (with its tipsily leaning campanile) look for Giambattista Tiepolo's *Crucifixion*, which Mary McCarthy aptly described as 'a ghastly masquerade ball'.

From Burano you can hire a *sandola* (small gondola) to **San Francesco del Deserto**, some 20 minutes to the south. St Francis is said to have founded a chapel here in 1220, and the whole islet was subsequently given to his order as a site for a **monastery** (*visitors welcome 9–11, 3–5.30 daily*). In true Franciscan fashion, it's not the buildings you'll remember (though there's a fine 14th-century cloister), but the love of nature evident in the beautiful gardens. Admission is free, but donations are appreciated.

## Torcello

Though fewer than 100 people remain on Torcello (*vaporetto Line 12*), this small island was once a serious rival to Venice herself. According to legend, its history began when God ordered the bishop of *Altinum*, the old Roman town near Mestre, to take his flock away from the heretical Lombards into the Lagoon. From a tower the bishop saw some stars rise over

Torcello, and so led the people of Altinum to this lonely island to set up their new home. The town developed quickly, and for the first few centuries seems to have been the real metropolis of the Lagoon, with 20,000 inhabitants, palaces, a mercantile fleet and five townships; but malaria decimated the population, the *Sile* silted up Torcello's corner of the Lagoon, and the rising star of Venice drew its citizens to the Rialto.

Torcello is now a ghost island overgrown with weeds, its palaces either sunk into the marsh or quarried for their stone, its narrow paths all that remain of once bustling thoroughfares. One of these follows a canal from the landing stage past the picturesque Ponte del Diavolo to the grass-grown piazza in front of the magnificent Veneto-Byzantine **Cathedral of Santa Maria Assunta** with its lofty campanile, founded in 639 and rebuilt in the same Ravenna basilica-style in 1008. It is the oldest building in the Lagoon, and still one of the most impressive. The interior (*open 10–12.30, 2–5, daily; adm*) has the finest mosaics in Venice, all done by 11th- and 12th-century Greek artists, from the wonderful floor, to the spectacular, potent *Last Judgement* on the west wall and the unsettling, heart-rending *Teotoco*, the stark, gold-ground mosaic of the thin, weeping Virgin portrayed as the 'bearer of God'.

Next to the cathedral is the restored 11th-century octagonal church of **Santa Fosca**, surrounded by an attractive portico, one of the best works of late Byzantine architecture still in existence. Near here stands an ancient stone throne called the **Chair of Attila**, though the details of its connection with the Hunnish supremo are suspiciously nebulous. In the spring the basin in front of the cathedral is filled with frogs. Across the square from the cathedral the two main surviving secular buildings of Torcello, the Palazzo del Consiglio and Palazzo dell'Archivio, contain the small **Museo dell'Estuario** (*open 10–12.30. 2–5.30 Tues–Sun; adm*), with an interesting collection of archaeological finds and artefacts from Torcello's former churches.

## Cavallino and Jesolo

The Litorale del Cavallino, the 10km peninsula that protects the northern part of the Lagoon, was long known as a semi-wild place of beach, sand dunes and pine forests. There's still some of that left, among its 28 camping grounds and umpteen hotels and restaurants. There are two ports on the *litorale*: **Punta Sabbioni** (*vaporetto Line 14*) and **Treporti** (*vaporetto Line 12*). **Lido di Jesolo**, further north from Punta Sabbioni, is a far more developed and densely packed resort, attracting some six million tourists a year, though numbers have fallen off lately because of the Adriatic's pollution problems—driving hoteliers to install their own pools. Buses connect the Jesolo with Punta Sabbioni, timed to coincide with the ferries.

## Villas along the Brenta

In *The Merchant of Venice*, Portia, disguised as a young lawyer, left her villa of Belmont on the Brenta Canal and proceeded down to Fusina to preserve Antonio's pound of flesh. For about the same price you can trace her route on the stately, villa lined Brenta in a modern version of the patricians' canal boat, the *Burchiello*, which makes the day-long excursion from the end of March to the end of October, on Tuesday, Thursday, and Saturday from Venice, and Wednesday, Friday and Sunday from Padua. The journey may be booked through any travel agent or CIT office abroad; the very considerable L110,000 price includes admission into the three villas open to the public, lunch, guide, and coach back to the city of origin. You can also follow the Brenta on your own, less romantically and far less expensively, along the S11 road that follows the canal, by car or the half-hourly bus to Padua from Piazzale Roma. However, to get to the closest villa to Venice, at Malcontenta, you must take a different bus from Piazzale Roma that leaves only once an hour.

Often called an extension of the Grand Canal, the Brenta Canal was one of the choicest locations for Venetian patricians to go a-squiring in the country, and still be within easy communication with the city; over seventy villas and palaces lie on or just off the waterway. The classical proportions and stately symmetry that are the hallmarks of Palladio were especially suited to the landscape and the Venetians' conceit, and his celebrated, temple-fronted 1560 **Villa Foscari**, better known as **La Malcontenta**, was a major influence on all subsequent 17th- and 18th-century villa architecture (*the villa is between Fusina and Oriago; open April–Oct 9–12 Tues, Sat, and the first Sun of each month; adm L10,000; guided tours*). Viewed from the canal, the villa is a vision begging for a Scarlett O'Hara to sweep down the steps—not all that surprising, for Palladio's *Quattro Libri dell'Architettura* were Bibles for the 18th-century builders of America's old plantation homes, as well as for the important Palladian movement in Britain led by Inigo Jones. Inside, the villa houses some suitably delicate frescoes.

Further up the canal, Mira Ponte is the site of the 18th-century **Villa Widmann-Foscari** (*open 9am–6pm Tues–Sun; adm exp; guided tours*). If you only have time for one villa, don't make it this one—redone soon after its construction in the French Baroque style, the villa contains some of its original furniture and bright, gaudy murals by two of Tiepolo's pupils, but not much of real interest. Mira's post office occupies the **Palazzo Foscarini**, Byron's address while working on sections of *Childe Harold* in 1817–19.

One of the grandest villas in the entire Veneto region is further up at Stra: the 18th-century **Villa Nazionale** (or **Pisani**), built for Doge Alvise Pisani (*open June–Sept 9–6 Tues–Sun; Oct–May 9–1.30 Tues–Sun; adm; guided tours*). More of a royal palace than a country manor, it was completed in 1760, in time to be purchased by Napoleon for his viceroy in Italy Eugène Beauharnais, and in 1934 was chosen by Mussolini as a suitable stage for his first meeting with Hitler. Inside the villa has lost most of its decoration, but the ballroom makes up for the boredom with one of Giambattista Tiepolo's most shimmering frescoes, the *Apotheosis of the Pisani Family*. The vast park contains the monumental stables and one of Italy's finest mazes.

---

*Venice © (041–)*                                                    **Where to Stay**

### Burano

\*Raspo de Ua, Via Galuppi 560, Isola di Burano, © 730095 (moderate/ inexpensive) is a simple, 6-room *locanda* that offers visitors a chance to get to know the real Burano.

## Torcello

The most prestigious place to stay in the northern Lagoon is, however, the
★★★**Locanda Cipriani**, Piazza S. Fosca 29, Isola di Torcello, ✆ 730150 (expensive).
An offshoot of the Cipriani hotel in Venice, it has only five very comfortable rooms in
what is, once the day-trippers have melted back into the Lagoon, the most haunted
spot in the *comune* of Venice. Hemingway stayed here, writing his awful Venice
novel *Across the River and into the Trees*. It also houses a slightly over-rated restau
rant (*see* below).

## Brenta Canal

★★★**Villa Margherita**, Via Nazionale 312, Mira, ✆ 420879 (expensive) provides an
opportunity to live the life of a Venetian patrician, who in the old days would not
have been caught dead in the city in summer. The hotel restaurant, specializing in
seafood, is also one of the best in the area. (*Closed Jan.*)

---

## Burano

Burano is full of fish trattorias, of which the most popular is **Ai
Pescatori**, Via Galuppi 371, ✆ 730650 (expensive). The huge
seafood menu varies according to the catch; try their *risotto di
fagioli* (beans) and *anguilla in brodo di bronzino* (eel in sea bass
sauce)—the latter must be ordered in advance. (*Closed Mon.*)

## Torcello

In season, a private boat picks up lunchtime diners every day at 12.20pm by the
Danieli Hotel in Venice to transport them to the **Locanda Cipriani**, ✆ 730757 (very
expensive), returning them two hours later. A rather self-consciously rustic descendant of Harry's Bar, it offers grand feasts of a variety of the chef's specialities, such as
seafood risotto or gnocchi. The food is good, but not quite as much as it should be at
the price.

Torcello also has a few relaxing bars with outside tables, and another, less pretentious restaurant, **Villa 600**, ✆ 730999 (moderate), which has the charms of a late
Renaissance villa, and a pretty outdoor terrace in summer. (*Closed Wed, Jan.*)

## Brenta Canal

One of the traditional ways to round off an excursion along the Brenta Canal is to
dine on the lovely poplar-shaded veranda of the **Ristorante Nalin**, Via Nuovissimo
29, Mira, ✆ 420083 (moderate). The emphasis is on Venetian seafood, finely grilled,
and there are good Veneto wines as well. (*Closed Mon, Aug.*)

Although only half an hour from Venice by motorway, Padua (Padova) refuses to be over-shadowed by the old dowager by the sea, and can rightly claim its own place among Italy's most interesting and historic cities. Nicknamed *La Dotta* (The Learned), Padua is the brain of the Veneto, the home of the great Roman historian Livy as well as of one of Europe's most celebrated universities, founded in 1221 and a magnet to such luminaries as Petrarch, Dante, and Galileo.

Padua's churches, under the brushes of Giotto and Mantegna, were virtual laboratories in the evolution of the fresco, while two Padovan sculptors, Bellano and Il Riccio (Andrea Briosco), dominated the art of small bronze statues in the Renaissance. Padua attracts religious as well as art pilgrims; it is the last resting place of St Anthony of Padua, known locally simply as *Il Santo*, and his exotic, seven-domed mosque of a basilica is the city's greatest landmark. Although the northern half of Padua had to be rebuilt after bomb damage in the War, some of the arcaded southern streets could still serve as a stage for *The Taming of the Shrew*, which Shakespeare set in this lively, student-filled city.

---

### Getting There

Padua is easily reached by **train** from Venice (40min), Bologna (2hrs), Vicenza (45min) and other cities on the Milan–Venice line. Outside the train station, a booth dispenses tickets and directions for the city buses. The **bus station** is a 10-minute walk away in the Piazzale Boschetti, Via Trieste 40, © 8206811, and has buses every half-hour to Venice, and good connections to Vicenza, Treviso, Este, Monselice, Bassano, and Rovigo. Padua is also a major **road** junction, the meeting-point of the *autostrade* A4 (Milan–Venice) and A13 (to Bologna, Florence and the south) and the coast road via Chioggia to Ravenna (SS516/SS309).

The **Burchiello motor-launch** down the Brenta Canal to Venice departs from Padua on Wed, Thur, Sun; bus transport is provided to the Villa Pisani at Stra (see above, 'Villas along the Brenta'). The central reservation office for the Burchiello in Padua is Siamic Express, Via Trieste 42 (by the bus station), © 660944.

---

### Tourist Information

The main office of the local APT is at Riviera Mugnai 8, © 8750655, @ 650794; there are branch offices in the railway station, © 27767 (*open 9–6 Mon–Sat; 9–12 Sun*), and at the Eremitani (*open 9.30–4.30 Tues–Sun*). Admission to several of Padua's major attractions—the Cappella degli Scrovegni, the Museo Civico, the Orto Botanico, Palazzo della Ragione, Baptistry, and Oratorio di S.Giorgio—is available at a reduced rate with a **Biglietto Unico** or single ticket which lets you all of them. You can buy it from any one of the participating sites.

The phone code for Padua is **049**.

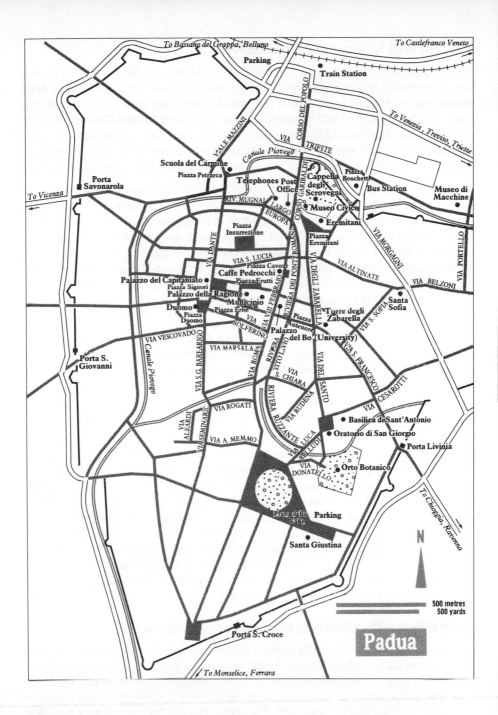

To Bassano del Grappa, Belluno

To Castlefranco Veneto

Parking

Train Station

To Venezia, Treviso, Trieste

CORSO DEL POPOLO

VIA TRIESTE

VIALE MAZZINI

VIA

Canale Piovego

Scuola del Carmine
Piazza Petrarca

Piazza
Boschetti

Cappella
degli
Scrovegni

Porta
Savonarola

Telephones Post
Office

CORSO GARIBALDI

Bus Station

Museo di
Macchine

To Vicenza

RIV. MUGNAI

LARGO
EUROPA

Museo Civico

Eremitani

VIA MORGAGNI

VIA PORTELLO

Piazza
Insurrezione

Piazza
Eremitani

VIA D'ANTE

VIA S. LUCIA

VIA DEGLI ZABARELLA

VIA ALTINATE

VIA BELZONI

Piazza Cavour

Caffè Pedrocchi

Palazzo del Capitaniato

Piazza Frutti

VIA VIII FEBBRAIO

RIVIERA DEI PONTI ROMANI

Torre degli
Zabarella

Santa
Sofia

Piazza Signori

Palazzo della Ragione

Municipio

Duomo

Piazza Erbe

VIA
SOLFERINO

VIA S. SOFIA

Piazza
Duomo

Piazza
Antenore

VIA VESCOVADO

Palazzo
del Bo (University)

Porta S.
Giovanni

Canale Piovego

VIA S.G. BAREARIO

VIA MARSALA

RIVIERA TITO LIVIO

VIA ROMA

VIA
S. CHIARA

VIA DEL SANTO

VIA S. FRANCESCO

VIA CESAROTTI

VIA ALEARDI

VIA SEMINARIO

VIA ROGATI

VIA A. MEMMO

RIVIERA RUZZANTE

VIA RUDENA

Basilica di Sant'Antonio

VIA LUCA

Oratorio di San Giorgio

Porta Livinia

VIA
BELLUDI

VIA
DONATELLO

Orto Botanico

Prato della
Valle

Parking

To Chioggia, Ravenna

Santa Giustina

N

500 metres
500 yards

Porta S. Croce

Padua

To Monselice, Ferrara

399

# Cappella degli Scrovegni and the Eremitani

Padua's attractions merit at least a day, but if you only have a couple of hours it's an easy walk from the bus or railway station to the city's most celebrated sight, the **Cappella degli Scrovegni** (or *Madonna dell'Arena*), sheltered by the crusty shell of Padua's ancient amphitheatre, and entered with the same ticket as the adjacent **Museo Civico** (*both open 9–6 daily; Oct–Mar closed Mon; adm exp; note that the chapel may be closed for long periods for restoration work in 1994–95*). Enrico Scrovegni erected it in 1303, in expiation for the sins of his father, whom Dante consigned to the *Inferno* for his usury (Canto XVII).

Giotto, Dante's favourite artist, was commissioned by Scrovegni to fresco the interior with a series of New Testament scenes (1304–13). The artist was then at the height of his powers, and this magical blue temple has been acclaimed as his greatest masterpiece. It is the best place to observe the characteristics that made Giotto so revolutionary at that time—his response to the problems of three-dimensional space and volume, and his skill at narrative composition, best represented here in the *Kiss of Judas* and the *Deposition*. Giotto's followers painted the frescoes in the apse, while the master is generally credited with the *Last Judgement* by the entrance and the strange allegories of the *Vices and Virtues* that run below the biblical cycle.

A path leads back to the **Nuovo Museo Civico e Museo Bottacin**, installed in the old Augustine convent of the Eremitani. Its historical collection features ancient Greek and Roman coins and other finds from ancient Veneto, of which the most important are 14 funerary *stelae* from the 6th to 1st centuries BC, a rare find this far north. The main attraction, though, are its paintings, particularly Giotto's *Crucifixion*, designed for the Cappella Scrovegni, and the small *Leda and the Swan* by Giorgione. Other paintings include little-known works by Giovanni Bellini, Tintoretto, Titian, Costa, Vivarini, Veronese, and Longhi.

Until an air raid in 1944, another wonder of Early Renaissance art stood by the Museo Civico: the 1306 Augustan church of the **Eremitani** (*open 8.30am–12 midday Mon–Sat; 8.30–12, 3.30–6.30 Sun, holidays*), with its magnificent Ovetari chapel, frescoed in 1454–7 by Andrea Mantegna when he was in his early twenties. Although the church was shattered, what could be salvaged of the frescoes has been painstakingly pieced together; *The Martyrdom of St Christopher and St James* is especially remarkable for the use of scientific perspective in its masterful foreshortening from below. Also note the church's beautifully restored wooden ceiling. Padua's oldest church, the 9th-century **Santa Sofia** (*open 9–12, 4–6.30, daily*), lies to the east at the corner of Via S. Sofia and Via Altinate; much rebuilt in the 11th century, it still has a lovely Byzantine apse.

## Central Padua: The University and Palazzo della Ragione

From the Eremitani it's a short walk down to Piazza Cavour, the historic heart of Padua, and the renowned **Caffè Pedrocchi**, built in 1831 by Giuseppe Jappelli in a kind of mausoleum-neoclassical-Egyptian-revival style, with columned stone porches at either end. Originally open 24 hours a day, it was famous for having no doors—and for its intellectual customers who came here to debate the revolutionary politics of Mazzini. You can still have a coffee at the Pedrocchi and then take in Jappelli's adjacent neo-Gothic, bullet-scarred **Pedrocchino**, where the students turned words into deeds in 1848, clashing with the Austrian police.

Diagonally opposite the café on Via VIII Febbraio is the central seat of the University, Andrea Moroni's 16th-century **Palazzo del Bo'** ('of the ox'), a nickname derived from the sign of a tavern that stood on this site before the University's foundation in 1221. It shelters the old wooden pulpit from which Galileo lectured, the golden Great Hall with walls covered with the armorial devices of its alumni, and the steep, uncomfortable **Anatomical Theatre** (1594), believed to be the first permanent one anywhere, designed by Fabricius, tutor of William Harvey, who discovered of the circulation of blood—only one of scores of Englishmen who earned degrees at Padua's renowned School of Medicine. Other famous professors there included Vesalius, author of the first original work on anatomy since Galen (1555), and Gabriello Fallopio, discoverer of the Fallopian tubes (*closed at the time of writing, but check at the tourist office*).

Two sarcophagi are the centrepiece of the nearby **Piazza Antenore**. The one on columns supposedly belongs to Antenor, the hero of the Trojan War who founded ancient *Patavium*, according to the town's most celebrated son Livy, while the other one was set up to commemorate the 2000th anniversary of the birth of Livy himself.

Across the street, behind the 16th-century **Municipio** with its uncomfortable-looking fascist-era façade, are the Piazza delle Erbe and Piazza delle Frutta, the liveliest squares in the city, where bustling markets are held every morning. They are separated by the massive, arcaded **Palazzo della Ragione**, also known as *Il Salone* (*open April–Sept 10–6 Tues–Sat; Oct–Mar 10–4 Tues–Sat; adm*). First constructed as Padua's law courts in 1218 and then rebuilt in 1306, this is one of the largest medieval halls in existence, measuring 79m by 27m, with a ceiling 26m high—like 'vaulting over a market square', as Goethe described it. Its great hull-shaped roof was rebuilt after a fire in 1756—an earlier blaze, in 1420, destroyed most of the original frescoes by Giotto and his assistants, though some *Virtues* by Menabuoi survived. The rest were replaced with a set of over 300 biblical and astrological scenes by Niccolò Miretto. Exhibitions are frequently staged in the Salone, but two exhibits never change: the *pietra del vituperio*, a stone block where debtors were made to sit bare-bottomed, and a giant **wooden horse**, built for a joust in 1466, its rather fierce glance complemented by testicles as big as bowling balls.

Just to the west, the stately **Piazza dei Signori** saw many a joust in its day, and can still boast of Italy's oldest astronomical clock, built by Giovanni Dondi (1344), incorporated into the Renaissance tower of the **Palazzo del Capitaniato**. On the left is the fine Lombard Renaissance-style **Loggia della Gran Guardia**, completed in 1523. Behind Dondi's clock, Padua University's Arts Faculty, the **Liviano**, was built in 1939 by Gio Ponti, incorporating the upper floor of the old Carrara palace, the **Sala dei Giganti**—a name derived from its huge 14th-century frescoes of ancient Romans, repainted by Domenico Campagnola in the 1530s. It also has a more intimate 14th-century portrait of Petrarch sitting at his desk, attributed to Altichiero. Around the corner from the square stands the **Duomo**, first begun in the 12th century, but tampered with considerably in the Renaissance—Michelangelo was only one of several cooks who spoiled the broth here before everyone lost interest, as the tell-tale blank façade reveals. Next to it, the Romanesque **Baptistry** (*open 9.30–12.30, 2.30–5.30, Tues–Sun; adm*), is far more rewarding to visit, its interior frescoed by the Florentine Giusto de' Menabuoi in the 1370s. The dome, with its multitude of saints seated in a circular paradise, is awesome, but chilling.

## Piazza del Santo and the Basilica di Sant'Antonio

Below the commercial heart of Padua rise the exotic domes of its most famous monument, the **Basilica di Sant'Antonio** (*open 6.30am–7pm daily*). St Anthony of Padua was a Portuguese missionary who was shipwrecked in Italy, fell under the influence of St Francis, worked a number of miracles, and was canonized the year after his death, in 1232. The basilica was begun in the same year over his tomb and finished the following century. For pure fantasy it is comparable only to St Mark's, and though it lacks the Venetian basilica's colourful decoration, its cluster of seven domes around a lofty, conical cupola, two octagonal *campanili* and two smaller minarets make it a delightful experiment in medieval fantasy.

Sharing the large piazza in front of the basilica, with the pigeons and exuberantly garish souvenir stands, is one of the most important works of the Renaissance, Donatello's great equestrian **Statue of Gattamelata** ('The Honeyed Cat'), the cool *condottiere* who served Venice so well and honestly that it paid for this monument. *Gattamelata* owes its importance not only to its excellence and serene Renaissance spirit, but for technical reasons as well: it was the first large equestrian bronze cast since antiquity.

More by Donatello awaits in the basilica's Byzantine-inspired **interior**—probably not what a monk vowed to poverty would have ordered, but certainly a sign of the esteem in which his devotees held and continue to hold him—today they throng his sumptuous chapel on the left, patiently waiting to touch or kiss his sarcophagus. A motley array of homemade votive offerings credit the Saint with the usual miraculous cures and interventions, while others thank him for finding things—Anthony apparently runs Heaven's Lost Property Office. The series

S. Antonio

of 16th-century marble reliefs lining the chapel are among the high points of the Venetian Renaissance: the fourth and fifth are by Sansovino, the sixth and seventh by Tullio Lombardo, and the last by Antonio Lombardo. Just outside the chapel is a fine work by their father, Pietro: the **tomb of Antonio Roselli** (1467).

The **high altar**, much rearranged over the centuries, is the work of Donatello and his helpers (1445–50), crowned by the famous *Crucifixion*, with bronze statues of the *Madonna* and *six patron saints of Padua* and reliefs of the *miracles of St Anthony* below. The great Paschal Candelabrum is the masterpiece of Il Riccio, who also, with his master Belluno, cast the 12 bronze reliefs of Old Testament scenes on the choir walls. Behind the high altar, in the ambulatory, don't miss the **Treasury** where a hundred glittering gold reliquaries include the tongue and larynx of Il Santo, whose humble Franciscan cassock is spread out in a glass case below. In the right transept, the **Cappella di San Felice** contains beautiful frescoes, and a remarkable *Crucifixion*, painted in the 1380s by Altichiero, the leading Giottoesque artist of the day. And if you've been wondering about the quaint blue stylized decoration of the apse and dome, it dates from 1903 to the 1940s.

Flanking the piazza opposite Gattamelata, the **Oratorio di San Giorgio** (*open April–Sept 8.30–12.30, 2.30–6, daily; Feb–Mar, Oct–Nov 9–12, 2.30–4.30, daily; Dec–Jan 9am–12 midday daily; adm*) was built in 1377, and beautifully frescoed by two heirs of Giotto, Altichiero and Jacopo Avanzi; it makes an interesting comparison with the Cappella Scrovegni. As part of the visit the same jovial custodian will also let you into the adjacent **Scuola del Santo**, an old confraternity with paintings on the *Life of St Anthony* by a variety of artists in the panelled upstairs room, including some, not the best, that are attributed to a teenage Titian.

A few streets to the south of the Piazza del Santo lies Padua's **Orto Botanico** (*open April–Sept 9–1, 3-6, Mon–Sat; 9.30–1 Sun; Oct–Mar 9–1 Mon–Sat; adm*), one of Europe's oldest botanical gardens, first established in 1545; it retains the original layout, and a few of the specimens. At 'Goethe's palm', planted in 1585 and still flourishing, the poet speculated on his Theory of the Ur-plant, that all plants evolved from one universal specimen.

Beyond, 'Italy's largest piazza', the **Prato della Valle** (1775), does service as municipal parking lot, flea market, amusement park and pantheon for 78 illustrious men associated with Padua, whose statues surround the moat. On one side stands the **Basilica of Santa Giustina** (*open 7.30–12, 3.30–7.30, daily*), designed by Il Riccio, its domes similar to St Anthony's, but its interior blandly Baroque. Further from the centre, Padua still retains large sections of its massive **walls**, built by the Venetians in the 16th century, with several impressive gates.

---

### Activities

For information on what's on read *La Mattina*, or the tourist office's bi-monthly *Padova Today*; every summer a series of concerts, exhibitions, open-air films and other events is organized under the umbrella of the *Padovacolore* programme. Padua has two good shops selling English books: **Libreria Internazionale Cortina**, on the corner of Via Mazolo and Via Jappelli, and **Feltrinelli**, Via S. Francesco 14. Every

Saturday a large general market is held in the Prato della Valle, and there are daily food markets in the Piazza delle Frutta and Piazza delle Erbe.

---

## Where to Stay

### expensive

Padua, accustomed to housing mainly students and pilgrims, has little to offer in the way of atmosphere in its better hotels. The ★★★★**Hotel Donatello**, Via del Santo 102, ℗ 8750634, ✉ 86750829, has a prime location, with Donatello's *Gattamelata* pointing right to it, and many rooms look out over the basilica itself. Its air-conditioned rooms have been recently renovated.

### moderate

Small and cosy, the ★★★**Leon Bianco**, Piazza Pedrocchi 7, ℗ 657225, ✉ 8756184, is right in the heart of Padua; from its roof terrace, where breakfast is served in summer, you can look down on the Caffè Pedrocchi. The ★★★**Grande Italia**, Corso del Popolo 81, ℗ 650877, ✉ 8750850, is in a beautiful building, conveniently placed opposite the railway station. The ★★**Hotel Sant'Antonio**, Via S. Fermo 118, ℗ 8751393, ✉ 8752508, is between the station and centre, beside the Porta Molino, and has a friendly, family atmosphere, and some cheaper rooms without baths.

### inexpensive

The ★**Pavia**, Via del Papafava 11, ℗ 661558, is deservedly popular, and is clean, central and friendly. There's also a large, pleasant, city-run youth hostel, **Ostello Città di Padova**, at Via Aleardi 30, ℗ 28369, which is open all year. IYHF cards are required. To get there, take bus 3, 8 or 11 from the station to the Prato della Valle.

---

Padua ℗ (049–)

## Eating Out

### very expensive

Bocking is essential for **San Clemente**, Corso Vittorio Emanuele II 142, ℗ 8754020, a new but prestigious restaurant which has as its specialities such delicacies as noodles with asparagus and quails, gnocchi with caviar and spring onions, or risotto with saffron and local herbs. (*Closed Sun, Mon midday, Aug.*)

### expensive

Right in the heart of Padua, **Dotto**, Via Squarcione 23, ℗ 8751490, offers elegant surroundings and inventive cookery based on the freshest of ingredients; for a first course, try their famous *pasta fagioli*. There's also a cheaper lunch menu, which changes daily. (*Closed Sun evenings, Mon, Aug.*)

### moderate

For classic Paduan homecooking, featuring succulent boiled and roast meats, the crowds venture outside the city walls to **Da Giovanni**, Via Maroncelli 22,

© 772620 (bus 9 from the railway station; if you're driving, there's parking opposite). The homemade pasta is good, as are the locally raised capons. (*Closed Sun, Aug.*) Back inside the city, behind the cathedral, is the **Enoteca Angelo Rasi**, Riviera Paleocapa 7, © 8719797, one of the most amiable and popular spots to drink the local vintages, especially those from the Colli Euganei; light meals accompany the wine. (*Closed Sun.*)

*inexpensive*

**Al Pero**, Via S. Lucia 72, not far from the Palazzo del Capitaniato, is popular and friendly, with sturdy home cooking. (*Closed Sun.*) The larger **Vecchia Padova**, Via Battista 37, offers more variety and excellent food, including very good pizza.

# The Veneto Heartland

Although the scenery is better to the north in the Dolomites and west around Lake Garda, you may like to spend a day or two exploring the heartland of the Veneto. The Padua tourist office has a booklet of the best villas; many of them admit visitors to the grounds, and a few allow you inside—but the only practical way to see more than one or two of them is by car.

## South of Padua to the Po Delta

### *Getting Around*

The spas and towns in the **Euganean Hills** are easily reached from Padua by **car** on the A13, the SS16 or local roads through Abano Terme, or by **bus** from the main station. There are also regular **trains** from Padua to Monsélice (23km), Este (32km), Montagnana (52km) and Rovigo (45km), which take about the same time as the buses, though with the train you may have to change at Monselice; trains via Montagnana continue to Mantua.

Arquà Petrarca is most easily reached by bus from Monsélice (10km); the Palladian villa at Fratta Polesine by bus from Rovigo (direction: Trecenta). From **Rovigo** there are frequent buses to Adria and the Delta towns; trains also run from Rovigo to Adria and Chioggia (1hr 20min), or south to Ferrara (30min) and Bologna (1hr). Rovigo's **bus station** is on the Piazzale G. Di Vittorio, © (0425) 361225; the **railway station** is on the Piazza Riconoscenza, © (0425) 33396. If you are driving, the SS443 leads from Rovigo towards Adria and the Delta, while the SS499, which turns off the main SS16 a few km south of Rovigo, runs westwards towards Fratta Polesine and Verona.

### *Tourist Information*

There are tourist offices in the Euganean Hills at **Abano Terme**, Piazza Pietro d'Abano 18, © (0439) 8669455, @ 8669053; **Teolo**, Palazzetto dei Vicar, © (0439) 86407; and **Montegrotto Terme**, Viale della Stazione 37, © (0439) 793384. The **Rovigo** tourist office is at Via J. H. Dunant 10, © (0425) 361481, @ 30416, and there is an office in the Delta at **Rosolina Mare**, Piazzale Albertin, © (0426) 664541, @ 664543.

# The Euganean Hills

Within sight of Padua, the conical Euganean Hills, or *Colli Euganei*, are a pleasant geological oddity plopped in the middle of the Veneto plain. They were volcanic islands when the surrounding land was still covered by the sea, and very early on attracted the region's first prehistoric settlers, whose main settlement was *Ateste* (Este). Later, the Romans discovered the two secrets of the Euganean Hills: hot mud and good wine. Livy, Suetonius and Martial all recommended the virtues of their hot mineral springs, which emerge from the ground at 87°C, and they have been appreciated ever since. Today there are some 130 hotels/thermal establishments in the area catering to those seeking health or beauty cures.

Because of their unique conditions, the hills are also home to some interesting flora; from **Teolo**, on the jagged, western flank of the hills, you can get on to a 42km circular nature trail around the district, from which there is a detour to visit natural springs. Near Galzignano, the tiny village of **Valsanzibio** has an 18-hole golf course and a wonderful garden, the park of the **Villa Barbarigo** (*open 15 Mar-31 Oct 9–12, 3–7, Tues–Sat; 3–7 Sun, Mon; adm exp*). Laid out in 1699, it also contains a fine maze. There are more villas dotted about the hills, but most are not open to the public.

To the south on the SS16 lies the prettiest village in the Euganean Hills, **Arquà Petrarca**. The world-weary Petrarch, accompanied by his daughter Francesca and his stuffed cat, the Laura II, chose Arquà as his last home; his villa, the charming **Casa del Petrarca** (*open April–Sept 9.30–12.30, 3.30–5.30, Tues–Sun; Oct–Mar 9.30–12.30, 2.30–4.30, Tues–Sat; 10–4 Sun; adm*), still preserves much of its 14th-century structure, and some of its furnishings. Even the view has changed little since the days of the great poet. Petrarch died here in 1374, and is entombed in a simple marble sarcophagus near the church.

## Monsélice, Este and Montagnana

On the southern slopes of the Euganean Hills, the natural citadel of **Monsélice** was first fortified by the Romans and later by Ezzelino da Romano, tyrant of Padua and henchman of Frederick II. Ezzelino's fortified palace, now the beautiful restored **Ca' Marcello**, houses a rich collection of medieval and Renaissance arms and antiques (*guided tours only, at 9, 10.30, 3.30, 5 Tues, Fri and Sat, and on the second and third Sun of the month at 3.30 and 5; adm*). Further up, via the Romanesque **Duomo** and Scamozzi's unusual **Via Sacra delle Sette Chiese** lined with seven little chapels, stands the elegant late 16th-century **Villa Duodo** (*grounds only open dawn–dusk daily*), also by Scamozzi, with fine views over the Veneto prairie.

Monsélice's old rival, **Este**, is only 9km to the west; its name, from the ancient *Ateste*, was adapted by a noble 11th-century Lombard family who conquered and ruled it before moving on to greater glory in Ferrara. Like Monsélice it was a hotly contested piece of real estate, as evidenced by the ruined walls and towers of the 1339 **Castello dei Carraresi**, now a public garden. Inside the garden, and partly made of material cannibalized from the castle walls, is the 16th-century Palazzo Mocenigo, home of the **Museo Nazionale Atestino** (*open April–Sept 9–1, 3–6, Tues–Sun; Oct–Mar 9–1, 3–6, Tues–Sun; adm*). This has one of northern Italy's finest pre-Roman collections, with some outstanding 6th–5th century BC bronze statuettes, and an 8th-century BC vase in the shape of a pig. Among the paintings, the most important is a *Madonna and Child* by Cima da Conegliano. Behind the castle, the **Villa De Kunkler** was Byron's residence in 1817–18; here Shelley, his guest, penned 'Lines written among the Euganean Hills', after the death of his daughter, Clara.

Some 15km west of Este lies **Montagnana**, famous for some of the best-preserved medieval fortifications in Italy, built by Ezzelino da Romano. The walls extend for two kilometres, and are defended by numerous towers—impressive but not very effective, as Venice lost and regained the town some 13 times during the War of the League of Cambrai. The **Duomo** has a portal by Sansovino, a huge, anonymous painting of *The Battle of Lepanto*, and an altarpiece by Veronese; the square it dominates was, by special permission of the Doge, modelled on the Piazza San Marco. Beside the Porto Padova is an interesting villa designed by Palladio, the **Palazzo Pisani**. The best day of the year to be in Montagnana is the first Sunday in September, when the town holds its **Palio**, or traditional horse race, a more bucolic version of the famous race in Siena (*see* 'The Palio in Emilia-Romagna', p.544).

## 'Little Mesopotamia'

About 20km south of Monsélice, **Rovigo** is the capital of the province wedged between the Adige and the Po rivers, known as the Polèsine or the 'Little Mesopotamia'. Like ancient Mesopotamia it has been blessed and cursed by its rivers, which make it fertile but often flood, while miles of silt have left its ancient capital and port Adria high and dry.

Rovigo, a prosperous little city, has a couple of tilted 10th-century towers, the **Torri Dona**, in a park near the cathedral, and in the central Piazza Vittorio Emanuele II, the **Pinacoteca dell'Accademia dei Concordi** (*open 10–12, 3.30–7, Mon–Fri; 10–12 Sat; July, Aug 10–12 Mon–Sat*), with a collection of minor Venetian paintings by major artists like Giovanni Bellini, Lorenzo Lotto, and Palma il Vecchio. Signs lead from there to the octagonal **La Rotonda**, a 16th-century church by Zamberlano, a pupil of Palladio, with a tower by Longhena. From Rovigo it's 18km southwest to **Fratta Polèsine**, where you can visit Andrea Palladio's **Villa Badoera**, (*open April–Sept 3.30–7pm Mon–Sat; 10–12, 3.30–7, Sun; Sept–Mar 2–5 daily; also Thurs mornings 9–12 from Sept–June; adm*), built in 1570 with a classical temple façade. No furniture survives inside, but the pseudo-Roman grotesques by Giallo Fiortino have been uncovered on the walls.

Buses and trains from Rovigo also head east for ancient **Adria**, founded by the Etruscans and colonized by the Greeks in the days when it stood on the shore of the sea that took its name. The Venice of its day, Adria has but one canal now, and a **Museo Archeologico Nazionale** at Via G. Badini 59 (*open April–Sept 9–1, 3–7, daily; Oct–Mar 9–1, 3–6, daily; adm*) to remind us of its glory; there's an interesting collection of material from old and modern excavations in the region, including a 4th century BC iron chariot of Gaulish workmanship, found entombed with its tiny horses.

## The Po Delta

The reed-filled delta of the Po is a marshy wonderland of a thousand islets, filled with waterfowl and migratory birds from the north. Plans to make this a natural park proceed slowly, while here and there resorts have mushroomed up along the sandy, pine-shaded shores—

namely **Rosolina Mare** and **Isola Albarella** (owned by Crédit Suisse), though it must be admitted that both resorts try hard to behave in an ecologically acceptable fashion. Unfortunately the same cannot be said of the industries that line the 652km length of the Po, at once Italy's greatest river and its greatest sewer. There are several **boat cruises** to chose from that explore the delta, most of them departing from **Porto Tolle** or **Taglio di Po**; arrangements can also be made for major fishing outings. Contact **Marino Cacciatori**, Via Nuovo Centro Trasferimento, Porto Tolle, ✆ (0426) 81508, or **Gorino Sullam**, Ca' Vendramin, Taglio di Po, ✆ (0426) 88019.

---

### *Where to Stay*

#### Euganean Hills

All of the thermal establishments in the Euganean Hills have mineral-water pools, therapists and gardens, but none can match the class of the ★★★★★**Gran Hotel Orologio**, Viale delle Terme 66, in Abano Terme, ✆ (0439) 8669111, ✆ 8669072 (very expensive), in business for over two hundred years. Its large park and verdant, landscaped pools attract many guests seeking pampered tranquillity instead of magic mud. (*Closed Dec–Feb.*)

#### Montagnana

★★★**Aldo Moro**, Via G. Marconi 27, ✆ (0429) 81351, ✆ 82842 (moderate), has fine rooms beside the Duomo, and a great restaurant where you can eat the famous local *prosciutto dolce*, alone, with melon, or in a risotto. Also in Montagnana, IYHF card-holders have the opportunity to stay in what is actually the best location in town, the magnificent **Rocca degli Alberi** ('Tree Castle') at the Legnano Gate, built in 1362 and now housing a comfortable, hospitable **Youth Hostel**, ✆ (0429) 81320 (inexpensive; *closed mid-Oct–Mar*).

#### Delta

A simple but cheap hotel is the ★**Renata**, Via del Mare 21, Porto Tolle, ✆ (0426) 89024 (inexpensive), which also has a restaurant.

---

### *Eating Out*

#### Arquà Petrarca

The rarefied, health-filled environment of the spas is not the place to look for a good meal; it's better to save your appetite for Arquà Petrarca and the lovely **La Montanella**, Via Costa 33, ✆ (0429) 718200 (expensive), where you can enjoy not only the garden and view over the village itself, but an exquisite risotto and well prepared game dishes. (*Closed Tues evenings, Wed, 2 weeks each in Aug, Jan.*)

#### Monsélice

**La Torre**, Piazza Marconi, ✆ (0429) 73729 (moderate), serves traditional food with extreme elegance; spaghetti with lobster is a speciality. (*Closed Sun evenings, Mon.*)

## Montagnana

An excellent trattoria that's always packed with locals is **I Stona**, Via Carrarese 51 (inexpensive). The menu is changed daily.

## Rovigo

If you're passing through Rovigo at mealtimes, you can eat well at the family-run **Tre Pini**, Viale Porto Po 68, ℗ (0425) 421111 (expensive). The nondescript décor grows rosier as you eat your way through such delights as homemade tortellini, and fresh salmon in champagne. (*Closed Sun, Aug.*)

## North of Padua

Some of the Veneto's best known sites are north of Padua, in the foothills of the Dolomites: Castelfranco, birthplace of Giorgione, Asolo, where the Queen of Cyprus held her fabled Renaissance court; several outstanding villas, including Masèr, where Palladio and Veronese collaborated to create a unique work of art; Bassano del Grappa, with its covered bridge, and Maròstica, the medieval village where they play chess with human players.

### Getting Around

From Padua there are both **buses** and **trains** to Bassano del Grappa (40mins), via Castelfranco; coming from Vicenza you would also change trains at Castelfranco, passing Cittadella on the way. If travelling by train from Venice, you must change in Treviso. From Castelfranco there are infrequent buses to Piombino Dese, on the local road to Venice.

From Bassano there are regular bus services to Possagno (roughly a half-hour journey), which is also served by a bus from Castelfranco. Buses from Bassano also head east to Asolo (14km) and Masèr (6km further). There are about 15 buses on this route daily, as it is part of the main Bassano–Treviso service. West from Bassano buses run to Maròstica (20 buses daily), Lonedo di Lugo, Thiene (25km) and Asiago (36km), all four of which may also be reached by bus from Vicenza. Bassano's **bus station** is in the Piazzale Trento, near the tourist office, ℗ 30850, while the **train station** is at the top of Via Chilesotti. Asolo and Maser are also linked by frequent buses from Montebelluna.

By **car** the main road to Bassano from Padua is the SS47, which runs through Cittadella. The SS307 leads to Castelfranco, and is a more direct route to get from Padua to Asolo and Maser than via Bassano. From Bassano a local road, to Crespano del Grappa, leads also to Possagno, and the SS248 to Asolo. A long but scenic route to Asiago from Bassano is by taking the SS47 north and then turning west onto the SS349, in Primolano.

### Tourist Information

The local tourist office in **Bassano** is Largo Corona d'Italia 35, ℗ (0424) 534351, @ 26703. In **Asiago** the office is at Piazza Carli 56, ℗ (0424) 62661, @ 462445.

## Castelfranco and Cittadella

**Piombino Dese**, just off the main SS307 road from Padua to Castelfranco, is a must-detour for Palladiophiles, for its 1554 **Villa Cornaro** (*open May–mid-Sept 3–6pm Sat only; adm*), one of the master's more monumental structures. The interior is frescoed with 18th-century biblical scenes. On the other hand, most people who come to **Castelfranco Veneto**, 9km to the north, do so to pay homage to an earlier and more important genius, Giorgione, who was born here in 1478. He left in the town one of the few masterpieces that are undisputedly from his brush, the *Castelfranco Madonna* (1504), now hanging in the **Duomo**. It's squirrelled away in a chapel behind a grille, but still casts the same ineffable, dreamlike spell as his paintings in Venice. There are also some fragments of allegorical frescoes by Veronese, in the sacristy. Near the cathedral, the **Casa del Giorgione** (*open 9–12, 3–6, Tues–Sun*) contains a chiaroscuro frieze of scientific instruments attributed to Giorgione, and a few exhibits related to this most elusive of painters.

Castelfranco itself is a fine old walled city built by the Trevisans in 1199 to counter the ambitions of the neighbouring Paduans. The Paduans, tit for tat, founded the egg-shaped **Cittadella** 15km to the west; one tower in its 13th-century walls was Ezzalino's infamous torture chamber (cf. *Paradiso* IX, 54). From Castelfranco you can also nip up to **Fanzolo**, 5km to the northeast, for another of Palladio's finest, the **Villa Emo** (*open April–Sept 3–5pm Sat, 3–6 Sun; Oct–Mar 2–5pm Sat, 2–6 Sun; adm*). The main rooms were frescoed in their entirety with mythological subjects by Giambattista Zelotti.

---

## Bassano del Grappa

Lying in the foothills of the Alps where the Brenta River begins its flow across the plain, picturesque, trendy Bassano del Grappa produced a well-known family of 16th-century painters, the Da Pontes, known by the adopted name Bassano. The 'Grappa' comes from lofty Monte Grappa to the north, scene of terrible fighting in the First World War.

The centre of town, the Piazza Garibaldi, is dominated by the square, medieval **Torre Civica** and the old Gothic church of **San Francesco**. The cloister behind the church leads to the **Museo Civico** (*open 9–12.30, 3.30–6.30, Tues–Sat; 3.30–6.30pm Sun; adm*), with works by the Bassano family, especially Jacopo (see his masterpiece, the twilit *Baptism of St Lucia*) and Alessandro Magnasco (the uncanny *Refectory*, full of racing, wraith-like friars). The museum also has drawings by another local boy who made good, the neo-classical sculptor Antonio Canova, and a good archaelogical collection. But it was Palladio who designed Bassano's most renowned landmark, the **Ponte degli Alpini**, the unique covered wooden bridge that spans the Brenta. First constructed in 1599, the bridge has subsequently been rebuilt several times to the same design. At one end is a 200-year old grappa distillery, Nardini, with a small museum where you can taste and buy (*open 8am–8pm Tues–Sun*).

## A Grappa Digression

 Although a lot of grappa does come from Bassano del Grappa, its name doesn't derive from the town or its mountains, but from *graspa*, the residues left at the bottom of the wine vat after the must is removed; it can be drunk unaged and white, or aged in oak barrels, where it takes on a rich, amber shade. First mentioned in a 12th-century chronicle, grappa, or *aqua vitae* ('the water of life'), was chugged down as a miracle-working concoction of earth and fire to dispel ill humours. In 1601 the Doge created a University Confraternity of Aqua Vitae to control quality; during the First World War, Italy's Alpine soldiers adopted Bassano's enduring bridge as their symbol and grappa as their drink. One of their captains described it perfectly:

> *'Grappa is like a mule; it has no ancestors and no hope of descendants; it zigzags through you like a mule zigzags through the mountains; if you're tired you can hang on to it; if they shoot you can use it as a shield, if it's too sunny you can sleep under it; you can speak to it and it'll answer, cry and be consoled. And if you really have decided to die, it will take you off happily.'*

These days the rough, trench quality of grappa does not appeal to many Italians; from 70 million litres guzzled in 1970, only 25 million were drunk in 1990. The Veneto with its 20 distilleries is a leading producer, and Bassano is a good place to seek out some of the better, more elusive labels; besides Nardini, look for Da Ponte, Folco Portinari, Jacopo de Poli, Maschio, Rino Dal Tosco, or Carpenè Malvolti.

From Bassano you can also visit **Possagno**, at the foot of Monte Grappa, birthplace of Antonio Canova (1757–1822), the ultimate neoclassical sculptor and favourite of Napoleon and several popes. As well as his house, where there is an collection of the clay and plaster models used for his work in the **Gypsoteca** (*open May–Sept 9–12, 3–6, Tues–Sat; 9–1, 3–7, Sun; Oct–April 9–12, 2–5, Tues–Sat; adm*), Possagno also contains the extraordinary tomb that the artist designed for himself, the **Tempio** (*open April–Oct 9–7; Nov–Mar 2–5pm, daily*), a mini-Pantheon that the town itself describes as 'one of the greatest monuments that man on earth has ever erected—in praise of God—to himself'.

## Maser and Asolo

Bassano is a good base for visiting the best of all villas, the **Villa Barbaro** at **Maser**, 20km to the east (*open June–Sept 3–6pm Tues, Sat, Sun; Oct–May 2–5pm Tues, Sat, Sun; adm*). Built in 1568 for Daniele Barbaro, Patriarch of Aquileia and one of Venice's most distinguished humanistic scholars, Maser is a unique synthesis of two great talents: Palladio and his friend Veronese, whose frescoes of its interiors are one of the masterworks of his career. Palladio, it is said, taught Veronese about space and volume, and nowhere is this so evident as in these ravishing, architectonic, *trompe-l'œil* paintings, where the figures literally seem to inhabit the villa. Legend has it that the famous huntsman in the bedroom is Veronese's self-portrait, gazing across the rooms at his mistress. Other rooms contain portraits of the original owners, gazing from painted balconies; a very convincing dog sits beneath a ceiling of allegorical figures; a little girl opens a door; painted windows offer views of totally convincing landscapes. In the grounds is a lovely and serene circular chapel, the **Tempietto**, a miniature pantheon designed by Palladio in 1580 and decorated with stuccoes by Alessandro Vittoria.

In the hills above Masèr, a few kilometres back towards Bassano, is the old walled town of **Asolo**, the consolation prize given by Venice to Queen Caterina Cornaro after demanding her abdication from the throne of Cyprus, in 1489. One of the most enchanting spots in Italy, Asolo is linked nostalgically to Caterina's court, famed in Renaissance times for its refinement and cultivation of art and literature. Pietro Bembo used it as a setting for his dialogues on love, *Gli Asolani*, and Giorgione is said to have strolled through its rose-gardens strumming the lute; the enforced idleness and boredom in Asolo might perhaps have inspired his invention of easel painting. In the last century, Asolo was also a beloved retreat of Robert Browning (his last volume of poems was entitled *Asolando*; 'Pippa Passes' was set here as well). Eleonora Duse is buried in the local cemetery; and Freya Stark lived in a house rebuilt by Browning's son, Pen. Today you can visit the **Castello** and remains of the garden where Queen Caterina lived in 'lace and poetry'; the **Loggia del Capitano** contains a museum of local works of art dedicated to Queen Caterina, Browning, Duse, but is closed for indefinite restoration. For Asolo's famous views of 'a hundred horizons' climb up to the **Rocca**, built over a Roman fort.

## West of Bassano

**Maròstica**, 7km west of Bassano, is a storybook medieval town, with 13th-century walls, an upper castle sprawled over the hill, and a lower castle in the piazza, once the abode of the Venetian lord and now the town hall. The piazza in front of the lower castle is the perfect setting for the storybook event that has put Maròstica on the map: the *Partita a Scacchi*, or the human chess match, which takes place on even-numbered years in early September. The game, announced in Venetian dialect and played with its human 'pieces' in medieval costume on a 22-square-metre board, commemorates the 1454 contest for the hand of Lionora Parisio; her father refused to let her two suitors fight the traditional duel for humanitarian reasons, and even offered the loser of the match the hand of his younger daughter. If you can't make the match, you can see the elaborate costumes and paraphernalia on display in the town hall.

Further west, in **Lonedo di Lugo**, near the town of Lugo (about 6km north of Breganze), there are two important villas by Palladio. The **Villa Godi Maliverni** (*open mid-Mar–Oct 2–6pm Tues, Sat; 3–5pm Sun; adm*), built in 1540, was his very first, with the central portion, usually the most prominent and decorated part of his villas, recessed behind two large wings. The interior was frescoed by Giambattista Zelotti and his assistants, and contains a fossil collection and museum of deservedly little-known Italian 19th-century painting. The later and more classically elegant **Villa Piovene** (*open April–Oct 2–6pm; Nov–Mar 3–5pm; adm*) is a couple of doors down, with its neat, neoclassical gardens.

In **Thiene**, 10km further to the west, the quattrocento **Castello Colleoni di Thiene** (*open 9–12, 3–6, Tues–Sat, but ring first: © (0445) 363556; Sun tours at 3, 4, and 5; adm*) is an attractive, pre-Palladian villa, with towers, battlements, and Venetian Gothic windows; inside there are frescoes, antique ceramics, and jumbo paintings of the former residents of the 18th-century stables behind the villa. From here you can catch a train to Vicenza.

When the Venetians feel claustrophobic, they head up into the foothills of the Dolomites and relax at **Asiago**, north of Thiene, a pleasant summer and winter resort known for its salubrious climate and pretty walks, rebuilt after the devastating Battle of Asiago in 1918; the British dead lie in five surrounding cemeteries.

*Where to Stay*

## Castelfranco

The ★★★**Roma** at Via Fabio Filzi 39, ✆ (0423) 721616, ✉ 721515 (moderate), is outside the fortifications, but offers a good view of them. All rooms have TV and air-conditioning.

## Bassano

In the centre of Bassano, the ★★★**Belvedere**, Piazzale Gen. Giardino 14, ✆ (0424) 529845, ✉ 529849 (expensive) has the best rooms in town, and is convenient, if not quiet; ask for one in the back if you're a light sleeper.

★★**Al Castello**, Piazza Terraglio 20, ✆/✉ (0424) 28665 (moderate) has cheerful rooms, with the castle rising behind them. ★★**Nuovo Mondo** Via Vittorelli 45, ✆ (0424) 522010 (inexpensive) is basic, clean and central; its rooms and hallways are packed with intriguing furniture.

## Asolo

Asolo can boast one of Italy's most charming and romantic hotels, the ★★★★★**Villa Cipriani**, Via Canova 298, ✆ (0423) 952166 (very expensive), in a house dating from the 16th century that belonged to Robert Browning, decorated with Persian carpets once owned by Eleonora Duse. Enveloped in a paradise of hills and cypresses, the hotel also has an enchanting garden filled with roses and song birds; some of its 32 rooms are located in its garden houses. The restaurant, in the tradition of Venice's Cipriani family, serves equally lovely meals.

Overlooking Asolo's central piazza, and with a little garden behind it, is ★★★**Duse**, Via Browning 190, ✆ (0423) 55241, ✉ 950404 (moderate).

*Eating Out*

## Castelfranco

One of the pleasures of visiting Castelfranco is dining at its celebrated restaurant, **Barbesin**, just above town on the Circonvallazione Est, ✆ (0423) 490446 (expensive). Its setting is as idyllic as the products of its kitchen, based entirely on fresh, seasonal ingredients; the veal with apples melts in your mouth. **Ai Due Mori**, Vicolo Montebelluno, ✆ (0423) 497174 (moderate) specializes in local dishes, served at reasonable prices.

## Bassano

Bassano is known for its restaurants, especially in the spring when asparagus is in season. Try it at the very elegant **Ristorante Belvedere**, Viale delle Fosse 1,

$\mathcal{O}$ (0424) 26602 (expensive), where you can enjoy other specialities such as risotto with shrimp and spinach, fish flavoured with fennel, and Venetian *tiramisù* for dessert. (*Closed Sun, last two weeks of Aug.*)

Just outside Bassano on the road up to Mt Grappa, **Ca' Sette**, Via Cunizza da Romano 4, $\mathcal{O}$ (0424) 25005, is installed in a lovely settecento villa, and offers asparagus specialities in season, and other dishes based on local mushrooms and red radicchio. In summer you may dine out in the garden.

Back in the centre of the town is **Al Sole**, $\mathcal{O}$ (0424) 523206 (moderate), which offers a perfect risotto, or delicious duck. (*Closed Mon, July.*) A short way back from the bridge, the **Trattoria El Piron** (inexpensive), is Bassano's best bargain, with an elegance that outstrips its price. (*Closed Sat.*) For good pizza, try **Bella Capri**, at Via J.Da Ponte 47 (inexpensive; *closed Tues*).

## Maser

Just up the road from Palladio's villa at Maser you can dine in enchanting surround-ings at **Da Bastian**, Via Cornuda, $\mathcal{O}$ (0423) 565400 (expensive); its pâté, risotto, tasty Venetian-style snails and desserts are renowned.

## Asolo

One of the oldest houses in Asolo is now the **Hosteria Ca' Derton**, Piazza D'Annunzio 11, $\mathcal{O}$ (0423) 52730 (moderate), featuring traditional specialities to match the setting.

## Maròstica

**Taverna de Morostega**, $\mathcal{O}$ (0424) 72866 (moderate), in the newly renovated upper castle, offers lovely views and some of the most popular cuisine in the region, starring great homemade pasta dishes; top it off with a *caffè corretto*, 'corrected' with one of a score of different grappas.

## Vicenza

'The city of Palladio', prettily situated below the Monti Bérici, is an architectural pilgrimage shrine and knows it; where other Italians grouse about being a nation of museum curators, the prim and often grim Vicentini glory in it. Perhaps classical, monumental High Renaissance cities are better to visit than live in; there's little room for chance or spontaneity in their planned, symmetrical perfection, the intellectual product of a gentry immersed in humanistic and classical thought (far better educated than those merchants and sailors in the lagoon, who ruled Vicenza in its heyday).

Although Vicenza was heavily damaged during the Second World War, restorers have tidied up most of the scars, for these days the rouble rolls in Vicenza. The city promotes itself as the *Città d'Oro*, the 'City of Gold', thanks to its gold-working industry; it is also the birthplace of the inventor of the silicon chip, Federico Faggin, and has electronics industries that allow it to call itself the 'Silicon Valley' of Italy. Add machine tools, textiles and shoes to the list, and you have one of Italy's wealthiest cities.

### *Getting There*

Vicenza is on the main **rail** line between Verona (45min) and Padua (35min) and Venice (1hr); there is also a branch line up to Thiene. The station is on the south side of the town, at the end of Viale Roma (✆ 325046). The FTV **bus station** (✆ 544333) is alongside it: buses depart from here for Bassano and Maròstica as well as to Asiago, Rovigo, Este, Lonigo, and other destinations in the region. Note that as in Venice, street names in Vicenza are in dialect—instead of *via* look for *contrà*.

If you are travelling by **car**, Vicenza is equally well-placed, being next to the A4 *autostrada* and on the SS11 Venice–Verona road. Parking is most convenient in the two large attended car parks, one at the west end of the town by the Mercato Ortofrutticolo, and the other to the east, by the stadium. Both are linked to the centre by special bus service every 5 minutes.

### *Tourist Information*

The information office at Piazza Matteotti 12, ✆ (0444) 320854 (open 9.30–12.30, 2–5.30 Mon–Sat, 9.30–12.30 Sun) is particularly helpful, and also lends bicycles free of charge to tourists on deposit of a passport or national identity card. The local APT tourist office is at Piazza Duomo 5, ✆ 544122, ✉ 325001. Ask about their free Palladio tour on Sunday mornings. The phone prefix for Vicenza is **0444**.

## Porta Castello to the Piazza Signori

The Viale Roma, the main road up from the station, enters the city proper through the **Porta Castello**, with its powerful 11th-century tower dominating one end of Vicenza's long main street, the pedestrians-only **Corso Palladio**, lined with palaces of various eras. One of the first, Piazza Castello's **Palazzo da Porto Breganze** of the enormous columns, designed by Palladio and partly built by his pupil Scamozzi, before the very monumentality of the design defeated him. Scamozzi also built the less exciting **Palazzo Bonin** at No.13, after his master's designs.

From the Piazza Castello, Contrà Vescovado leads to the **Duomo**, a Gothic temple with a diamond pattern façade that was carefully pieced together after the war; don't miss the polyptich by Lorenzo Veneziano (fifth chapel on the right). Nearby, down Contrà Proti, look in Via Pigafetta for the **Casa Pigafetta**, birthplace of Antonio Pigafetta, a local aristocrat who sailed with Magellan on his first journey around the world, and wrote the definitive account of the voyage. Just past it, to the left, lies the Piazza dei Signori.

## Piazza dei Signori

This large and kingly square is the heart and soul of Vicenza, its public forum in Roman times and today. In the 16th century, the Vicentines decided the piazza's crumbling old medieval

Palazzo della Ragione no longer matched their new, Renaissance-humanist aspirations. Having passed over such luminaries as Sansovino and Giulio Romano, they surprisingly hired a young unknown called Palladio to give it a facelift.

## Vicenza's Perfect Architect

 A Paduan by birth, Andrea di Pietro della Gondola (1508–80) received his classical nickname of Palladio in Vicenza, the city in which he began working at the age of 16. His first major commission, the Basilica, so captured the hearts of the Vicentine ruling class that they commissioned him to build their urban and suburban palaces, the theatre for their Academy, and other public buildings. He was, for them, the perfect architect, able to produce pomp and grandeur for very little money—mainly by using cheap brick coated with a marbly sheen of stucco. Palladio owes his continuing reputation not so much to his buildings, many of which were never completed, but to his books, of which Sir Reginald Blomfield, in his *Studies in Architecture*, wrote pointedly, 'With the touch of pedantry that suited the times and invested his writings with a fallacious air of scholarship, he was the very man to summarize and classify, and to save future generations of architects the labour of thinking for themselves'. To modern eyes, many of Palladio's buildings seem only too familiar, a tribute to the wide following he has had in Britain and America from the 17th century on. If not the best, always remember that Palladio was in many ways the first. The centre for Palladian studies, the **Centro Internazionale di Architettura 'A. Palladio'** ℂ 323014, housed upstairs in the Basilica, offers a popular architectural course each September.

Palladio began working on the building, ever since known as the **Basilica**, in 1549, and kept at it off and on until his death (*Basilica* was used here in its old Latin meaning of hall of justice, as the locals were keen to emulate the Romans; the building also housed the town council). The result perfectly fulfils its aims, with two tiers of rounded arches interspersed with Doric and Ionic columns that give an appearance of Roman regularity, although in truth Palladio had to vary the size of the arches to compensate for the irregularities in the Gothic structure. The roof is concealed behind a pediment lined with life-size statues in the Roman mould, a hallmark of Palladio's later work; stare at them long enough and the urge to shoot them off like ducks in a penny arcade becomes almost irresistible. (*The great Gothic hall of the basilica is open 9.30–12, 2.30–5, Tues–Sat; 9.30–12 Sun*). For a look at what Palladio was disguising with his monumental false front, go behind the basilica to **Piazza delle Erbe**, home to Vicenza's daily food and produce market, guarded by the **Torre del Tormento**, the medieval prison.

The basilica shares Piazza dei Signori with the needle-like **Torre di Piazza** (12th–15th-century), and Palladio's **Loggia del Capitaniato** (1571), built to celebrate the victory at Lepanto. If its grand columns and arches seem confined in too narrow a space, it's because the loggia was meant to extend over several more bays. The neighbouring 16th-century **Monte di Pietà**, built in two sections, was frescoed in the 1900s with amazing Liberty-style pin-up girls, some of whom still faintly survive moral outrage, war damage, and Father Time.

From the Piazza's Lion of St Mark column, obligatory souvenir of the Venetian Republic, a right turn down Via San Michele leads to the Retrone, one of Vicenza's two little rivers, spanned here by the pretty **Ponte S. Michele** (1620). On the opposite bank is the **Oratorio di S. Nicola** (*open July–Sept 9–12, 3–6*), remarkable for the creepiest altarpiece in Italy, *La Trinità* by the 16th-century artist Francesco Maffei, whose feverish brush infected some of the Oratorio's walls as well.

## Contrà Porti and Around

Returning to the Piazza dei Signori, a left turn at the columns will return you to the Corso Palladio and the city's prettiest Gothic palace, the 15th-century **Palazzo da Schio**, also known as the 'Ca' d'Oro'. It's enough to make the Palladian palaces, concentrated in the quarter just north of the Corso, seem as exciting as bank branches—the best are along the **Contrà Porti**, Vicenza's most dignified street, which leads off the Corso on the opposite side from the Piazza. Most noticeable is the huge **Palazzo Thiene**, another neoclassical addition grafted on to a medieval building, by Palladio himself.

Diagonally across the Contrà Zanella from the Palazzo Thiene is the church of **Santo Stefano**, which contains one of Palma Vecchio's most beautiful paintings, *Madonna with Saints George and Lucy*. More of Vicenza's finest art is to be found just at the other end of the Contrà S. Stefano in the chapels of the early Gothic church of **Santa Corona**(*open 9.30 12.30, 3.30 6.30, daily*). Veronese's *Adoration of the Magi* (1573) and Giovanni Bellini's *Baptism of Christ*, a late painting set in a rugged, very un-Venetian landscape. Alongside the church is the **Museo Naturalistico-Archeologico**, containing a mixture of Roman and Lombard relics discovered in and around the city (*open 9.30–12, 2.30–5, Mon–Sat; 9.30am–12 midday Sun; adm;* biglietto cumulativo *includes Pinacoteca and Teatro Olimpico*).

Nearby, at the north end of the Corso, more art is on display in Palladio's classic Palazzo Chiericati (1550–1650), now home of the **Pinacoteca** (*open 9.30–12, 2.30–5, Tues–Sat; 9.30–12 Sun; adm*). On the ground floor are some of the original frescoes, with a hilarious ceiling by a certain Busascorci, who took it upon himself to portray the sun god and his steeds in just the position earthlings would see them at noon—all bums and bellies. Upstairs are fine works by Paolo Veneziano, Memling, the Vicentine Bartolomeo Montagna (a follower of Mantegna), Cima da Conegliano, Sansovino (the lovely *Madonna col Bambino*), Tintoretto, Van Dyck (*Four Ages of Man*), Jan Brueghel the Elder, Bassano, Veronese and major works by the irrepressible Francesco Maffei (*Glorification of the Inquisitor Alvise Foscarini*).

## Teatro Olimpico

> *Open 16 Mar–15 Oct 9.30am–12.20pm, 3–5.30pm, Mon–Sat; Oct–Mar 9.30–12.20, 2–4.30, Mon–Sat; all year round 9.30–12.20 Sun; adm.*

Across Piazza Matteotti from the museum, the Teatro Olimpico was Palladio's swansong, and is one of his most original and fascinating works, a unique masterpiece of the Italian Renaissance, and said to be the oldest indoor theatre in Europe. Palladio himself was a member of the group of 25 literati and dilettantes who formed the high-minded 'Olympic

Academy' that built the theatre for their own plays and lectures. For the stage, Palladio as always went back to the ancient buildings he had seen during his sojourns in Rome, and designed an elegant and permanent set in wood and stucco, while his pupil Scamozzi added the amazing piazza and streets radiating out in the then popular Piazza del Popolo style in flawless, fake perspective—designed especially for the theatre's first production, Sophocles' *Oedipus Rex*, and meant to represent the city of Thebes. But here Thebes has become a pure ideal, a Renaissance dream city, so perfect that no one ever thought to change the set. If you come between April and October, you may be able to see a performance in this most historical of theatres.

## Monte Bérico and the Villa Rotonda

Vicenza's holy hill, Monte Bérico, rises just to the south of the city. Buses make the ascent approximately every half-hour from the bus station, or you can also walk up in half an hour (this area is not well signposted, so be sure to pick up the tourist office's map), through the 150-arch covered walkway, or **Portici**, built in the 18th century to shelter pilgrims climbing to the Baroque **Basilica di Monte Bérico** (*open 7–12, 2.30–7, Mon–Sat; 7am–7pm Sun, holidays*) that crowns the hill. The basilica commemorates two 15th-century apparitions of the Virgin, and contains two fine paintings: *La Pietà* by Montagna, hanging near the altar, and the *Supper of St Gregory the Great* by Veronese, appropriately hung in the refectory in the cloister (down the steps to the left), and carefully pieced together after Austrian soldiers sliced it to shreds in 1848. Outside, there are superb views of the city and the Villa Rotonda.

From here, walk back down the Portici as far as Via M. D'Azeglio; not far down this road on the right is an alleyway leading to the **Villa Valmarana**, nicknamed 'dei Nani' after the statues of dwarfs in the garden (*open 15 Mar–April 2.30–5.30; May–Sept 3–6, Oct–15 Nov 2–5, daily; also May–Sept only 10–12 Thurs, Sat, and Sun; adm exp*). Its main attraction is its sumptuous decoration by Giambattista and Giandomenico Tiepolo, who frescoed the *Palazzina* with charming scenes from the *Iliad*, *Orlando Furioso* and other Renaissance poems. Giandomenico's more intimate, ironical scenes of rural life in the *Foresteria* (guest house) seem to undermine his father's Grand Manner right under his nose.

From there a further five-minute walk along the Stradella Valmarana (alternatively, by bus no.8 from the railway station) brings you to the celebrated Villa Capra-Valmarana, better

*Villa Rotonda*

known as the **Villa Rotonda**, (*gardens open 10–12, 3–6, Tues–Thurs; adm; interior open 10–12, 3–6, Wed only; adm exp*) designed by Palladio for Cardinal Capra in 1551 and completed after his death, by the faithful Scamozzi. Unlike the master's other villas, which under their stuccoed, classical skins were functional farmhouses, the Villa Rotonda was built for sheer delight, the occasional garden party, and, though no one knew it at the time, as the perfect setting for Joseph Losey's film *Don Giovanni*. One of the main interests of the Accademia Olimpica was mathematics, and the Villa is, if anything, an exercise in geometrical form—a circle (expressed by the dome) in a cube, complemented by four symmetrical porches. It was the inspiration for a number of celebrated buildings in Britain and America, including Thomas Jefferson's Monticello and Chiswick House in London.

## Surrounding Villas

The tourist office publishes a helpful booklet in English describing the villas in Vicenza province, complete with maps and itineraries for drivers. Only a handful of them are open for visits at all, and the ones that are often have bizarre hours, so be sure to check before setting out. The northern part of the province is the most interesting (*see* above, 'North of Padua'); otherwise, it's easy to take a bus from Vicenza out to **Montecchio Maggiore**, 13km west along the road to Verona. This is one of the area's prettiest towns, defended by two castles that in Da Porto's 1529 tale of *Romeo and Juliet* belonged to the Montagues. Just before the village, the 18th-century **Villa Cordellina-Lombardi** (*open 9–12, 3–6, on Wed from 13–28 April; on Sat from 4 May–18 July; on Sun from 17 Aug–15 Oct; adm*) by Giorgio Massari is worth a visit for its colourful frescoes by a young Giambattista Tiepolo. The villa is now used as a provincial conference centre, but tours are provided at certain times.

---

*Vicenza ✆ (0444–)*     **Where to Stay**

*expensive*

Near the railway station, the ★★★★**Campo Marzo**, Via Roma 21, ✆ 545700, ✉ 320495, has modern, comfortable rooms, with air-conditioning, and a garage.

*moderate*

For comfort in a central location, complete with a parking area, try the ★★★**Cristina**, Corso B. Felice 32, ✆ 323751, ✉ 543656.

*inexpensive*

An older hotel in the midst of the historic district is the ★★**Due Mori**, Contrà da Rode 26 (near the Piazza dei Signori) ✆ 321888, ✉ 326127, which has reasonable rooms on a quiet street.

Up on the slopes of Monte Bérico, ★★**Casa Raffaele**, Viale X Giugno 10 (through an arch in the Portici), ✆ 323663, ✉ 545767, is a very good-value hotel that offers fine double rooms, all with bath, as well as tranquillity and great views.

Whatever airs Vicenza puts on in the culture department become somewhat draughty in the kitchen—this is polenta and *baccalà* (salt cod) country, and the local fare is not the most subtle on the stomach. Other, lighter specialities include *bigoli con l'anatra*, fat spaghetti with duck sauce, the unusual *paeta col melagrano* (guinea fowl with pomegranates) and spit-roast pigeon.

### expensive

For perfectly prepared fish, take a walk from the centre of town to Piazzetta Porta Padova, where **Cinzia & Valerio**, ☏ 505213, serves tagliatelle with salmon, cuttlefish risotto, or grilled sole, followed by homemade ice cream and crisp biscuits. (*Closed Sun midday, Mon, Aug.*)

### moderate

The author of the original version of *Romeo and Juliet*, Luigi Da Porto, was born in a 15th-century palace at the Contrà Porti 6 that was converted into an inn some 200 years ago. The **Tre Visi**, ☏ 324868, still serves food today, and with its fireplace and rustic fittings is a charming place to enjoy good, basic Veneto cooking and homemade pasta dishes. (*Closed Sun evenings, Mon, mid-July–mid-Aug.*) Another old inn in the centre of town, **Scudo di Francia**, Contrà Piancoli 4, ☏ 320898, has a more refined setting, antiques, and a more imaginative menu—try the ravioli stuffed with mushrooms and asparagus, or the *Menu Classico Alla Vicentina*, with a wine from the Colli Bérici. (*Closed Sun evenings, Mon, Aug.*)

### inexpensive

A good central trattoria is the **Vecchia Guardia**, Contrà Pescherie Vecchie 11, ☏ 321231, near the Piazza dell'Erbe, with pizza and straightforward meals. (*Closed Thurs.*) More basic but cheap, lively and very popular is the **Antica Casa della Malvasia**, Contrà delle Morette 5, near Piazza dei Signori, for real local home cooking. A popular stop for a cheap lunch is the **Righetti**, a bustling self-service canteen with seats spilling on to Piazza Duomo. (*Closed Sat, Sun.*)

## Verona

> *There is no world without Verona walls*
> *But purgatory, torture, hell itself*
> *Hence banished is banish'd from the world;*
> *And world's exile is death.*

*Romeo and Juliet*, Act III

Well, love leads one to extremes. When Cupid's pilgrims descend on Verona they sigh over 'Juliet's balcony' and other sights made up to be Shakespearean shrines. But the pale-pink city curling along the banks of the Adige, the Veneto's second metropolis both in size and in the importance of its cultural treasures, has far more to offer than postcards of the famous lovers. Some of Italy's finest Roman relics are now graced by popular summer productions of opera and ballet of Karnak proportions, and between them are scattered reminders of Verona's greatest days: the Middle Ages and early Renaissance, the era of the Scaligeri.

## History

Blessed with a navigable river at the bottom of a busy Alpine pass, Verona was favoured by the Romans from the time of its colonization in 89 BC, a period when it produced three of its greatest citizens—Vitruvius, the spiritual father of Renaissance architecture, the poet Catullus, and Pliny the Elder. The city maintained its status as a capital under the Ostrogoths and Franks, and in 1107 became a free *comune* in league with Padua, Vicenza, and Treviso. This inaugurated the most violent era of Verona's history, when the city's nobility spiced their eternal Guelph and Ghibelline disagreements with a sideshow of purely domestic feuds and vendettas. Their notoriety inspired the story of *Romeo and Juliet* (first written by Luigi Da Porto in 1529), and led to the *comune* inviting the tyrannical Ezzelino da Romano in to take power; he held on to it until 1259, when the reins of the city were taken over by the Della Scala family.

The Della Scalas (or the Scaligeri) were typical early Renaissance tyrant family, combining a bloodthirsty passion for power with an exquisite taste for the arts. Their names were, however, uniquely canine: 'Big Dog', Cangrande I (1311–29) both greatly expanded the family's claims in northern Italy and gave such generous hospitality to Dante that the poet dedicated his *Paradiso* to him (although one may well wonder if his famous 'Letter to Cangrande' on how to read poetry ever arrived; any modern postman who saw the name 'Big Dog of the Stair' written on the door would have walked straight past). Cangrande's heir, Mastino II (the Mastiff) consolidated his gains while his own successor, the fratricidal Cansignorio ('Lord Dog'; 1359–75) presided over the construction of some of the family's last great monuments. In 1387 the city was seized by the Milanese Gian Galeazzo Visconti.

By the time of Visconti's death in 1402, Verona had had enough of *signori* and annexed itself to the Venetian Republic. Yet relations with Venice were not always rosy. After Venice's defeat in the Wars of the League of Cambrai Verona opened its gates to the German army, not returning to St Mark's fold until 1517. The Venetians retaliated by making Verona foot the bill for its vast new fortifications system, designed by Sanmicheli. However, unlike Venice, Verona rose up against Napoleon in 1797—only to be partly destroyed for its presumption. There then followed a long period of Austrian rule, until most of the city joined the new Kingdom of Italy with Lombardy in 1859; the north bank of the Adige, the border between Lombardy and Venetia, remained Austrian along with Venice until 1866. Bombed in the Second World War, Verona quickly rebuilt and can still claim to be one of Italy's prettier cities graced with monuments spanning two millennia, dressed in rose-coloured stone. It has also been, for the last two decades, a major economic success story, one of the boom towns of modern industrial Italy.

### Getting Around

 Verona's **airport** is to the southwest near Villafranca and has scheduled flights to Rome and Munich, as well as occasional charter flights to

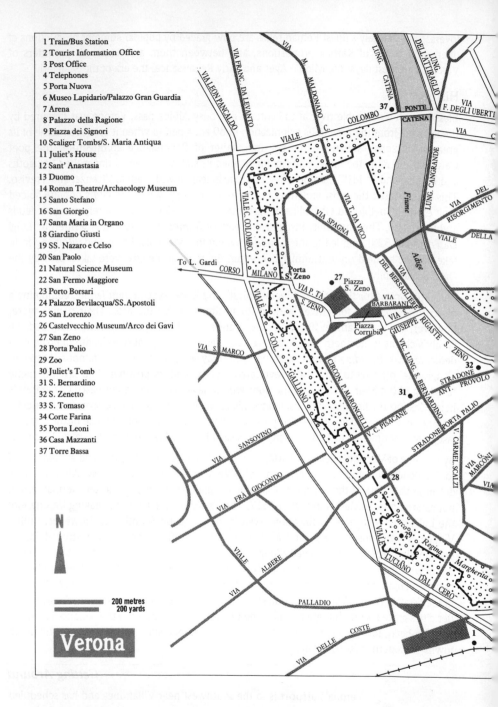

N

200 metres
200 yards

Verona

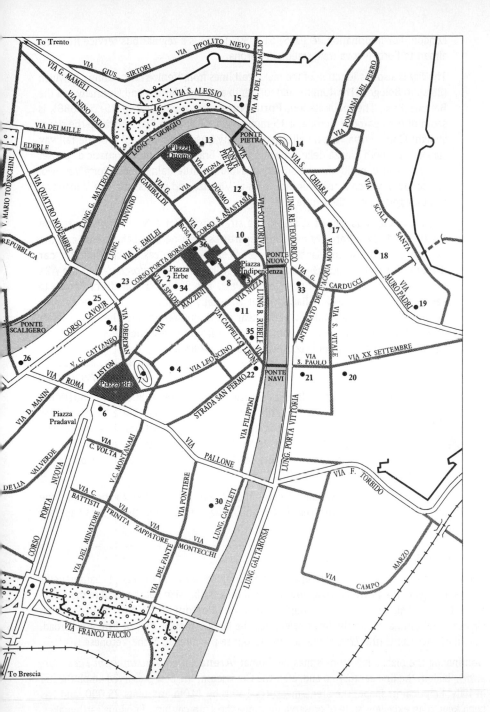

London. For information, ☏ (045) 513039. There is a regular bus service from the airport to Porta Nuova train station in Verona.

The city is also the junction of the major **rail** lines from Venice (1hr 45min), to Milan (2hrs), to Bologna (1hr 40min), and to Trento and then Austria and Germany, via the Brenner Pass. The main station, **Porta Nuova** (information ☏ (045) 590688), is south of the centre of Verona, a 15-minute walk from the Piazza Brà up the dead-straight Corso Porta Nuova; alternatively, city buses no.71 or 72 link the railway station with both Piazza delle Erbe and Piazza Brà. There's an automatic dispenser for bus tickets opposite the station. Try to avoid the little train station, Porta Vescovo, east of town, which is used for local runs to Vicenza and points east, but is inconvenient for getting into the centre.

The provincial **bus depot** is across the street from Porta Nuova railway station (☏ (045) 34129); there are frequent departures from here to Lake Garda and the mountains, and also to Mantua (1 hour). Verona is also easily accessible for **car drivers** as it is the crossing-point of the A4 Milan–Venice *autostrada* and the A22 from Modena to Trento and the Brenner Pass. The SS11 also runs from Verona to Lake Garda. As in most Italian cities it is usually pointless to drive once inside Verona—there are several car parks near the train station and the Corso Porta Nuova, the main entry point if you are coming from the A4. **Bicycles** can be hired on the south-east corner of Piazza Brà, ☏ (045) 596852.

## Tourist Information

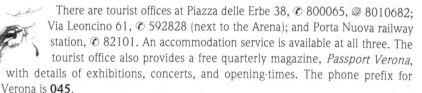

There are tourist offices at Piazza delle Erbe 38, ☏ 800065, 🖷 8010682; Via Leoncino 61, ☏ 592828 (next to the Arena); and Porta Nuova railway station, ☏ 82101. An accommodation service is available at all three. The tourist office also provides a free quarterly magazine, *Passport Verona*, with details of exhibitions, concerts, and opening-times. The phone prefix for Verona is **045**.

Note that on the first Sunday of every month admission is free to the Arena, the Museo Castelvecchio, the Teatro Romano, Juliet's tomb, and the Museo Lapidaro Maffeiano.

## Porta Nuova to the Arena

The first thing most people see of Verona, whether arriving by rail or road, is Sanmicheli's Renaissance gate, the **Porta Nuova**, now stranded on a traffic island at the head of the Corso Porta Nuova. This avenue leads straight under the **Portoni della Brà**, built by Gian Galeazzo Visconti, and into the heart of Verona: the large, irregular **Piazza Brà**, with broad, café-filled pavements (the *Liston*) that are the favourite promenade of the Veronese.

Dominating the piazza is Verona's massive Roman **Arena** (*open 7.30am–6pm Tues–Sun; adm*), built in the first century AD and, after the Colosseum, the best-preserved amphitheatre in Italy. Elliptical in shape, the arena measures 139m by 110m and seats 25,000, and has been kept in an excellent state of preservation since the 16th century. Previous earthquakes, however, have downed the outer arcade except for the four arches of the wing, or '*ala*'. As amphitheatres go, Verona's arena is exceptionally lovely in its pink and white stone, enough to make one almost forget the brutal sports it was designed to host; since 1913, the death and mayhem has been purely operatic.

Another side of Piazza Brà is dominated by the 17th-century **Palazzo della Gran Guardia**, with a Visconti tower peering over its shoulder; on the corner of Via Roma, the **Museo Lapidario Maffeiano** (*open 8am–1.30pm Tues–Sun; adm*), established in 1714, has an important collection of ancient inscriptions.

## Piazza delle Erbe and Piazza dei Signori

From Piazza Brà, Via Mazzini (the first pedestrian-only main street in Italy) is the most direct route to the core of medieval Verona. The former Roman forum, **Piazza delle Erbe**, is now filled with the parasols of stands selling fast food, souvenirs, and overpriced vegetables. Four old monuments on the piazza's spine poke their heads above the lake of parasols—a Lion of St Mark; a 1368 fountain built by Cansignorio topped by a Roman statue known as the 'Madonna Verona'; a 16th-century loggia called the 'Berlina' where malefactors used to be tied and pelted with rotten produce; and an elegant Gothic stone lantern.

A colourful variety of buildings encases the square, including the charming **Casa Mazzanti**, formerly part of a Scaligeri palace and brightened with 16th-century frescoes, and the 12th-century **Torre de Lamberti**, 84m high, with a lift to the top from the courtyard of the Palazzo della Ragione (*open 8–1.30 Tues–Sun; adm*). The smaller **Torre del Gardello** at the other end of the square was another work of Cansignorio. Six ancient gods pose atop the adjacent Baroque **Palazzo Maffei**, while the battlemented red-brick Chamber of Commerce near the centre of the piazza was built in 1301 for a medieval merchants' association.

From bustling Piazza delle Erbe the **Arco della Costa** ('of the rib'—named after the whale bone hung in the arch) leads into stately **Piazza dei Signori**, presided over by a rather severe 1865 statue of Dante. The civic centre of the Veronese city-state, the piazza contains the striped **Palazzo della Ragione** with its Romanesque-Gothic courtyard (*Cortile del Mercato Vecchio*) and unusual grand staircase. Behind Dante the **Loggia del Consiglio** (1493) with its yellow and red frescoes and statues of five ancient citizens of Verona is the city's finest

*Castelvecchio*

Renaissance building. The adjacent crenellated **Tribunale** (law courts), formerly a Scaliger palace, has a portal by Sanmicheli.

The arch adjoining it leads to the grandiose Gothic pantheon of the Della Scala family, the **Scaliger Tombs** or *Arche Scaligere* (still undergoing repairs from damage in the 1976 Friuli earthquake). The three major tombs portray their occupants in warlike, equestrian poses on top, and reposing in death below, although a copy has replaced the statue atop the Tomb of Cangrande (d. 1329), built into the wall of the 12th-century church of **Santa Maria Antica**. Don't miss the crowned dogs next to Cangrande's effigy, holding up ladders, the family emblem. More ladder motifs can be seen in the fantastical pinnacles of the tomb of Cansignorio (d. 1375), in the more sedate one of Mastino II (d. 1351), and in the web of their wrought-iron enclosure. The rather plain 14th-century house in the same Via delle Arche Scaligere traditionally belonged to the Montecchi family (Shakespeare's Montagues), and hence is known as the **Casa di Romeo**.

The tourist groups and postcard stands, however, are all over at the **Casa di Giulietta**, near the Piazza delle Erbe at Via Cappello 27 (*open 8–6.30 Tues–Sun; adm*). Although the association is slim (the 13th-century house was once an inn called 'Il Cappello', reminiscent of the Dal Cappello family, the original of the Capulets), the house has been well restored to fit the fancy of all but the most nit-picking romantics, with its lovely windows and balcony, though they may well complain that the bronze statue of Juliet in the courtyard is a bit busty for a 13-year-old. The house has an attractive interior, with a few period furnishings.

## Sant'Anastasia and the Duomo

Two of Verona's best Gothic churches are north of the Scaliger Tombs. The first, **Sant'Anastasia**, is Verona's largest church, begun in 1290 and never completed, as evidenced by its woebegone façade; only the fine portal, with its frescoes and reliefs of St Peter the Martyr, gives an idea of what its builders intended. In the dim light of the interior many people start at what at first sight appears to be two men loitering under the holy water stoops; these are the *Gobbi*, or 'hunchbacks'. The beautiful interior contains frescoes by Altichiero dated 1390, in the Cavalli Chapel (the horse-head helmets the worshippers wear on their backs are similar to the dragon head on Cangrande's statue); terracottas by Michele da Firenze and paintings by the school of Mantegna in the Pellegrini chapel; and best of all, Pisanello's 1438 fresco of *St George at Trebizond* in the sacristy. Pisanello, Italy's unrivalled interpreter of international Gothic, portrays a watchful, calculating princess who seems more formidable than any dragon.

A few streets down Via Duomo, almost at the tip of the river's meander, stands Verona's **Duomo**, consecrated in 1187, its exterior a charming Romanesque at the roots and Gothic in the crown. The portal, supported on the backs of two stylized lions, was carved by the same 12th-century master Nicolò as San Zeno (*see* below). Look for the knightly figures of Roland and Oliver guarding the west door, and on the south porch, the relief of Jonah and the Whale. Inside, highlights include the beautifully carved Tomb of St Agatha in the Cappella Mazzanti and an *Assumption* by Titian in the first chapel on the left. Painted in 1540, it shows us a very different Virgin from the heaven-gazing goddess in Venice's Church of the Frari—this one looks down sympathetically at her friends on earth. In the pretty cathedral cloister are a few remains of the Duomo's Pre-Romanesque predecessor, and in its ancient baptistry, **San Giovanni in Fonte**, there's an eight-sided font big enough to swim in, carved in 1200 from a single piece of marble and decorated with beautiful reliefs. The chapter library, the **Biblioteca Capitolare**, at Piazza del Duomo 13 (*open 9.30–12.30 Mon–Wed, Fri; also 4–6 Tues, Fri; closed Thurs, Jan*), claims to be the oldest library still operating in Europe, and contains a magnificent collection of medieval manuscripts.

## The Roman Theatre

Leading over the river beyond the Duomo is the **Ponte Pietra** (all of Verona's bridges were blown up in the War; this one was partly reconstructed from its original Roman stone, dredged up from the Adige), and just across it to the right rise the picturesque ruins of the **Teatro Romano** (*open 8–1.30 Tues–Sun; adm*), built into the hill of San Pietro. Begun under Augustus, the cavea, arches, and tiers of columns amid the cypresses are well preserved, though little is left of the stage. A lift goes up to the **Archaeology Museum** (*same hours and ticket as Teatro Romano*), located in the convent overlooking the theatre, containing an interesting collection of small bronzes and a few mosaics. Above it, the **Castel San Pietro** is a 19th-century fortification built over its Roman and Visconti-era predecessors, and one with famous views over Verona at sunset.

On the same northeast bank of the Adige, there are several ancient churches: just on this side of the Ponte Pietra stands the intriguing 12th-century **Santo Stefano**, pieced together from columns and capitals of older buildings and brightened with 14th-century frescoes, some by Altichiero. Five minutes further on the dull but large-domed Renaissance church of **San Giorgio in Braida** contains a number of first-rate paintings, especially Veronese's altarpiece of the *Martyrdom of St George*.

## South to the Ponte Navi

Also on the north bank, not far south of the theatre on the Interato dell'Acqua Morta, **Santa Maria in Organo** (*open 8–12, 4–6*) has a 1533 façade by Fra Giovanni da Verona and merits a visit inside for Fra Giovanni's charming wood-inlaid choir stalls, lectern, and cupboards (in the sacristy) depicting scenes of old Verona—as well as birds, animals, and flowers.

Across the street that runs at the back of the church, behind the facade of the Palazzo Giusti, are the cool **Giardini Giusti** (*open 9am–dusk; adm*) which the Englishman Thomas Coryat described as 'a second paradise, and a passing delectable place of solace'. That was in 1611; although they were unfortunately landscaped in the nineteenth century, the gardens retain their lush grass, fountains, and fine view of the city.

In the quarter south of the gardens there are a couple of other churches: the nearby **Santi Nazaro e Celso** (1484) on Via Muro Padri has frescoes and artwork by Montagna, while **San Paolo** (rebuilt 1763), south on Via San Paolo, contains Veronese's *Madonna and Saints*, which like his few other surviving works in his home town, was painted before he had to move on to Venice (supposedly after committing a murder). On the river bank, at Lungadige Porta Vittoria 9, there's the elegant Palazzo Pompei, built in 1530 by Sanmicheli and now housing the **Museo Civico di Scienze Naturale**, especially noted for its fossil collection (*open 8am–7pm; closed Fri; adm, but free on Sun*).

Just across the Ponte Navi on the south bank towers the splendid vertical apse of **San Fermo Maggiore**, unusual in that it is actually two churches, one built on top of the other. The lower Romanesque church was begun in the 11th century by the Benedictines, while the upper Gothic temple, with its attractive red and white patterns, was added by the Franciscans. The interior is covered with fine 14th-century frescoes, works by Caroto (*Madonna and Saints*), and a graceful *Annunciation* by Pisanello (1462). From San Fermo, the Via Leoni (which becomes Via Cappello) leads back to the centre of town, by way of the picturesque ruins of the Roman **Porta dei Leoni** (incorporated in a building) and an archaeological dig in the middle of the street.

## Piazza delle Erbe to Castelvecchio

From Piazza delle Erbe, Corso Porta Borsari leads to another, more impressive Roman gate, the **Porta dei Borsari**, built in the 1st century AD and named after the *borsarii*, who collected duties on goods entering the city. Beyond the gate the street becomes the Corso Cavour, embellished with palaces from various epochs, most notably Sanmicheli's *elegantissimo* 1588 **Palazzo Bevilacqua** (No.19), noted for its ornate, rhythmic alteration of large and small windows, columns, and pediments. Across the street the lovely Romanesque church of **San Lorenzo** (1117) preserves its upper, women's gallery, reached by way of its two cylindrical towers.

A little way further down the Corso Cavour opens up into a small square with a simple but refined commemorative arch, the **Arco dei Gavi**, designed by Vitruvius in honour of a local family. The French demolished it in 1805, but in 1932 it was put back together again.

## Castelvecchio

Next to the arch, Cangrande II's fortress of **Castelvecchio** (1355) has weathered centuries of use by other top dogs, from the Venetians to Napoleon and the Nazis, to become Verona's excellent and well-arranged civic **museum of art** (*open 7.30am–6.30pm Tues–Sun; adm*). Among the sculpture on the ground floor there's a sarcophagus (1179) carved with vivid reliefs of SS. Sergius and Bacchus, as well as some highly expressive 14th-century Veronese sculpture, especially a stark, painful *Crucifixion* and the uncanny equestrian statue of Cangrande I (displayed outside the window). The pyjama-clad charger, complete with an equine hood ornament and deathly eyes, and the moronically grinning 'Big Dog' himself, his ghastly dragon-helmet slung over his back, are an unforgettable odd couple.

Upstairs a bevy of lovely *Madonnas* (*of the Quail* by Pisanello, *of the Rose-garden* by Stefano da Verona, *della Passione* by Crivelli, two by Giovanni Bellini, and in Andrea Mantegna's *Holy Family*) hold court with paintings by Veronese, Tintoretto, and Caroto (including his well-known *Child with Sketch*, a happy insight into Renaissance childhood). Among the minor works, look for the strange, haunting *Orfeo* by 17th-century artist, Roelandt Savery. A room in the keep displays the garments and trappings found in Cangrande I's tomb in the 1920s. Behind the castle, Cangrande II's **Ponte Scaligero** spanning the Adige repeats the attractive 'swallowtail' battlements of the Castelvecchio; as with the Ponte Pietra, it was reconstructed from its original stones after the Second World War.

## San Zeno

A 15-minute walk west from the Castelvecchio, mostly along the riverbank (or bus 32 or 33 from Corso Porta Borsari) will take you to **San Zeno Maggiore** (*open 7–12.30, 3.30–6.30*), the belle of Verona's churches and one of the finest Romanesque buildings in Italy. Built originally in the 4th century, the church took its present form in the mid-14th century. Its magnificence demanded a legend: beneath its lofty campanile (finished in 1149) lies the tomb of a personage no less than the Frankish King Pepin the Short.

The rich façade of San Zeno is dominated by a magnificent 12th-century rose window of the *Wheel of Fortune* by Maestro Brioloto. Below, the finely carved porch by Masters Nicolò and Guglielmo depicts scenes from the months, the miracles of San Zeno, the Hunt of Theodoric and other allegories. The bronze doors, with their 48 panels nicknamed the 'poor man's Bible', are one of the wonders of 11th-century Italy, and still, after a millennium, have an unmatched freshness and vitality: in the Annunciation scene Mary covers her face in fear and anguish while the angel Gabriel does his best to comfort her; in the Descent into Hell, Christ and a large, leering Satan fight a tug-of-war for souls. Other scenes seem a bit strange to us, especially the one of two nursing mothers on the lower lefthand door, one suckling twin children, the other, what look to be twin crocodiles.

The interior boasts a beautiful Gothic ceiling, 13th-and 14th-century frescoes, and on the altar a magnificent triptych (1459) by Mantegna that brilliantly combines the master's love of classical architecture and luminous colouring. Although the French returned the painting after Napoleon carted it off, they kept the panels of the predella; the ones you see are copies of the originals in the Louvre. Below the altar, in the dim crypt, the body of St Zeno glows in the dark.

A short distance from the church is the Porta San Zeno, from where you can follow the Circonvallazione Maroncelli around the city walls to Sanmicheli's most beautiful gate, the **Porta Palio**. Next to it is the small city **zoo**, which is more worthy of anyone's time than the **Tomb of Juliet** (*open 8.30am–7pm Tues–Sat; adm*), back near the river on Via del Pontiere, south of Via Pallone and not far from the Piazza Brà. Even the Veronese admit no connection with any kind of tradition here, but the Romanesque cloister and the 14th-century sarcophagus would make fine props for the tragedy's last scene. A small museum of frescoes is an added attraction.

---

*Verona ℂ (045–)*  **Where to Stay**

Be sure to reserve or at least call ahead if you come in July or August, when opera fans fill the city. Rooms are also tight in March, when Verona hosts a huge agricultural fair.

### *luxury*

Verona has one exceptional luxury hotel, the ★★★★★**Due Torri**, Piazza Sant'Anastasia 4, ℂ 595044, @ 8004130. Goethe and Mozart slept here, and would feel just at home now in several of the hotel's 98 rooms—at least in the ones appointed in 18th-century antiques. Others come in different eras and styles, and if they're not too busy you can chose from photos the décor to suit your mood. The public rooms are equally resplendent, the ceilings adorned with 17th-century paintings, the banquet rooms with charming circus frescoes, and no matter where you turn, more antiques. Rooms are air-conditioned and service is first class.

### expensive

A more modest, but very comfortable choice on a quiet, trafficless street near the Arena, the ★★★★**Colomba d'Oro**, Via C. Cattaneo 10, ✆ 595300, offers very comfortable air-conditioned rooms behind its pleasant old stone façade, and secure parking in its garage.

### moderate

Centrally located near the Arena, ★★★**Giulietta e Romeo**, Vicolo Tre Marchetti 3, ✆ 23554, ✆ 8010862, is also on a quiet street and offers fine rooms (and parking facilities). The ★★**Cavour**, Via Chiodo 4, ✆ (045) 590508, just behind Piazza Brà, is stylish and eccentric; all rooms have baths.

### inexpensive

Two options offering cheaper rooms with or without bath are, near the station, the ★**Volto Cittadella**, Via Volto Cittadella 8, ✆ 8000077, or, right in the centre, the ★**Catullo**, Via Valerio Catullo 1, ✆ 8002786, some of whose pleasant rooms, appropriately, possess a balcony. If you have an IYHF card, however, you can't beat the **Ostello Verona**, Salita Fontana del Ferro 15, ✆ 590360, just beyond the Castel di San Pietro on the north side of the river (take bus no.72 to the first stop across the river). It's housed in a 16th-century villa, adorned with yet more frescoes, although the beds are up in the newer wing. The reception stays open all year round, 24 hours a day, but you won't be allowed in until 5pm; get there early in summer.

---

*Verona* ✆ *(045–)*            *Eating Out*

Although Verona is more famous for its wine than its food, the locals are especially fond of their gnocchi, the 'traditional symbol of abundance', and in the summer their tables are graced with Italy's finest peaches. The tall, light cake *pandoro* is a Veronese speciality that's sold all over the country, especially at Christmas time.

### very expensive

The grand master of the Veronese restaurant scene is **Il Desco**, Via dietro San Sebastiano 7, ✆ 595358, in a renovated palace in the heart of the city, not far from the Ponte Nuovo. Dishes are based on seasonal ingredients: gnocchi with ewe's milk cheese, red mullet with black olives and rosemary, goose liver in a sauce of sweet wine and grapes. (*Closed Sun.*) Another treat for the gourmet, **Arche**, Via delle Arche Scaligere 6, ✆ 8007415, is located near 'Romeo's house' and the Scaliger tombs. Long the classic place to go for a special meal in an aristocratic setting (it has been run by the same family for over a hundred years) the Arche specializes in the freshest of fish, brought in daily from Chioggia and imaginatively prepared by the maestro in the kitchen—the menu changes daily. The wine list is also excellent. (*Closed Sun, Mon, most of July.*) A glamorous as much as a gourmet experience is to sit outside in the Piazza dei Signori and have your every culinary care tended to by the elegant waiters of **Nuovo Marconi**, Via Fogge 4, ⓒ 591910. The food is as rooted in tradition as the surroundings: tagliolini with crab, gnocchi with pumpkin, and fine scampi and duck. (*Closed Sun.*)

*expensive*

An even older favourite, located a couple of streets away from the Piazza delle Erbe, **I Dodici Apostoli**, Corticella San Marco 3, ⓒ 596999, offers a traditional Renaissance setting—complete with frescoes of Romeo and Juliet. The name is derived from 12 18th-century 'apostles' of the kitchen who gathered here to dine. Some of the delicacies served today are adapted from Renaissance recipes, especially the *pastissada de caval* (a kind of horsemeat stew); the restaurant's *salmone in crosta* (marinated salmon in pastry) is famous. (*Closed Mon, two weeks June.*)

*moderate*

**Bottega del Vino**, Via Scudo di Francia 3 (off Via Mazzini), ⓒ 8004535 , has the interesting contrast of traditional recipes cooked using organically grown ingredients, with pasta made on the premises. (*Closed Tues.*) Real culinary adventurers should try **La Diga**, Lungadige Attiraglio 65, ⓒ 942942 (on the river bank near the hospital, on the north side of the city), which offers a menu based on fruit: risotto with kiwi fruit, veal with tuna sauce and cherries, and scrumptious, more socially acceptable desserts. **Verona Antica**, located on one of the city's oldest streets, Via Sottoriva 10, ⓒ 8004124, has a more traditional Italian menu, with seats outside or closeted in its cosy basement. (*Closed Sun, mid-July–mid-Aug.*)

*inexpensive*

You can also eat well for less at **Al Cacciatore**, Via Seminario 4, ⓒ 594291 (across the Ponte Nuovo). On Sunday or in August, when it is closed, try any of the other trattorias in this area; tourists rarely venture across the river, so culinary standards are high and prices low. Near San Zeno, at the junction of Via S. Giuseppe and Rigaste S. Zeno, with tables alongside the river, **Vesuvio** is *the* place for pizza.

---

### Entertainment and Nightlife

Verona bills itself as the 'city for all seasons' and offers a wide-ranging cultural programme throughout the year. It is best known for the **opera and ballet** in the Arena, a festival founded in 1913, with performances almost every day in July and August. Occasional classical concerts and big-name **rock shows** are also held there throughout the rest of the year. If you're travelling on a tight schedule, it's best to reserve your seat before coming to Italy: for programme details and tickets, write to the **Ente Lirico Arena di Verona**, Piazza Brà 28, ⓒ 590109 (but no reservations over the phone). Otherwise, tickets are on sale at the same address (it's in one of the arches of the Arena), 8.40–12.20, 3–5.30, Mon–Fri; 8.40–12.20 Sat. Seats cost from L30,000 to L220,000. At the same time Verona also hosts a **Shakespeare festival** (in Italian) in the Roman Theatre: same address as above for information and tickets.

From December to April there is **drama** in the Teatro Nuovo, and also more **opera and concerts** in the Teatro Filarmonico, sponsored by the Ente Lirico. For information on exhibitions and concerts coming up at any time, consult the tourist office's *Passport Verona*. For discos, films, and more casual artistic events, *Siri-Sera* is a broadsheet fly-posted weekly in cafés and around town.

From mid-December to mid-January Verona uses the arcades of the Arena for a massive show of Christmas cribs (*presepi*) from around the world. In the spring the city hosts one of Italy's oldest **carnivals,** first recorded in 1530; the last Friday of carnival is known as the 'Bacchanal of Gnocchi', presided over by the Papà dello Gnoco who walks about with a giant potato dumpling on a fork.

The Via Mazzini, the main shopping street, is filled in the evening as the Veronese stroll down to the Piazza Brà; it also has a fine bookshop with some English titles, the **Libreria Ghelfi e Barbato**. There are a number of **art galleries** in the historic centre around the Piazza delle Erbe, while the region between the Via Ponte Pietra, Via Duomo, Sottoriva, and Corso S. Anastasia is called the 'little city of antiques'. But buyer beware: the region is Italy's largest producer of reproductions.

Unlike the Venetians, the Veronese like to be out and about in the evening. The bars in Piazza Brà and Piazza delle Erbe are the busiest, but one of the most characterful and lively bars in the city is the **Osteria del Duomo**, Via Duomo 7/a. For live music, try **Corto Maltese**, Lungadige Porta Vittoria, near the Ponte Navi. For *gelato* fans, Verona's main magnet is the Piazza delle Erbe, where there are several outlets offering any number of flavours.

## Around Verona

### Wine Trails

Verona province, extending from the eastern shores of Lake Garda (see p.316) into the foothills of the Alps, produces some of Italy's best-known and most-exported DOC wines: Soave and Bianco di Custoza (both white) and Valpolicella and Bardolino (both red). The tourist office distributes glossy brochures on each region, which detail lists of growers, along with a map; drive along any of the official 'wine routes' (*strada del vino*), and you'll be assured of a hearty welcome.

The **Soave** region lies to the east of Verona along the Vicenza road (SS11), encompassing the old town of **Soave,** distinguished by the well-preserved 14th-century **Castle of the Scaligers,** a crenellated island in a sea of vineyards (*open 9–12, 3–6, Tues–Sun; adm*). On Via Roma, try a Soave Classico or the sweet Recioto di Soave, a dessert wine made from raisins at the **Enoteca del Castello.** The **Valpolicella** district is just north of Verona along the SS12, its nucleus in **Negrar** (with the pretty 15th-century Villa Bertoldi) and **Sant'Ambrogio,** where in addition to red wine they quarry Verona's famous red marble. From Sant'Ambrogio it's a half-hour walk northeast to the church of **San Giorgio,** built in the 7th century, and accompanied by a fine Romanesque cloister.

## The Monti Lessini

To the north of Valpolicella, Verona's 'Little Dolomites', the Monti Lessini, were settled in the 13th century by Bavarians. Over the centuries their language evolved into a now seldom heard dialect called Cimbro; their northern roots are also remembered in their folklore, costumes, and the huge *tromboni* that they blast at their festas. You can learn more about them at the small ethnographic museum in **Giazza**, one of the district's prettiest villages.

The Monti Lessini boast some growing winter sports centres, especially around **Bosco Chiesanuova**, the main town. To the west of here there's a pretty waterfall and botanical park at **Molina**; and northwards, just off the road to Corno d'Aquilio, is the bizarre **Spluga della Preta**, one of the world's deepest potholes (886m).

The **Ponte di Veja** is a spectacular natural arch (the Ponte di Malebolge of the *Divine Comedy*) that may be reached from Corrubio (on the road north of Negrar). Six kilometres along the same road by Camposilvano you can explore the **Valley of the Sphinxes** (*Valle delle Sfingi*), named for its mysterious rock formations. **Bolca**, southeast of Giazza, has an impressive fossil museum, while **Cogollo** and **Tregnago** nearby are important manufacturers of wrought iron.

## Into the Dolomites: Treviso to Belluno

The proximity of Venice to the Dolomites means that you can have a wonderfully varied holiday without having to spend too much time on the road: Belluno is only an hour and a half drive from Venice, and Cortina d'Ampezzo, the glamour-puss of winter sports in the Dolomites, another hour and a half further along.

### Getting Around

Treviso **airport** is southwest of the town; bus no.6 runs from there to the railway station.

There are **trains** from Venice or Mestre to Treviso (30min) and Belluno (2 hours), either directly or by changing at Padua or Conegliano; services are more frequent from Padua. One line goes via Conegliano and Vittorio Veneto; the other, longer but more scenic, via Montebelluna (also a getting-off point for Maser and Asolo; *see* above, 'North of Padua') and Feltre.

There are also **buses** to all main destinations from Venice's Piazzale Roma. If you want to go directly into the mountains, the **Dolomiti-Bus** company has daily routes to several destinations (including Agordo, Arabba, Falcade, Colle S. Lucia) from Venice; in the summer it's advisable to reserve a ticket in advance at a travel agent. Many bus services also run from Treviso.

For **cars** the A27 *autostrada* goes from Venice (just north of Mestre) as far as Vittorio Veneto; otherwise, take the SS13 through Treviso. From Conegliano and Vittorio Veneto the SS51 leads north to Belluno and on to Cortina d'Ampezzo. To get to Feltre directly take the SS348 from Treviso.

The **Treviso** tourist office is in the Palazzo Scotti, Via Toniolo 41, ✆ (0422) 547632, ✉ 541397, and is open 8.30–12.30, 3–6, Mon–Fri, and 8.30–12.30 only Sat. Other offices are in **Vittorio Veneto**, Piazza del Popolo 18, ✆ (0438) 57243; in **Tambre** in the Alpago valley, at Piazza 11 Gennaio 1945, ✆ (0437) 49277, ✉ 49246; and **Feltre**, at Piazza Trento-Trieste 9, ✆ (0439) 2540, ✉ 2839. **Belluno** has two offices, one that has detailed information on trails, alpine refuges, and skiing, at Via Sant'Andrea 5, ✆ (0437) 959111, ✉ 941222; and another for the town itself, at Via Pesaro 21, ✆ (0437) 940083.

## Treviso

Treviso is one of the pleasant surprises of the Veneto. Famous in Italy for its cherries and for the Benetton family, it is laced with little canals (or *canagi*) diverted from the river Sile, languorous with willow trees, and humming with more than a little discreet prosperity. Like Verona, it formed its character in the century preceding its domination by Venice (1389–1796), when it was ruled by the Da Camino family and when its churches were embellished by one of Giotto's greatest pupils, Tomaso da Modena, who did little outside Treviso.

Another unique and charming feature is the frescoed façades of its houses and palaces; attractive building stone was scarce, so it became the custom to cover the humble bricks with a layer of plaster and painted decoration—in the 1300s with simple colours and patterns, and, by the 1500s, with heroic mythologies and allegories. Although faded and fragmented since then—on Good Friday 1944 an air raid destroyed half of Treviso in five minutes—one of the delights of visiting the city is to pick out frescoes under the eaves, or hidden in the shadows of an arcade.

### Piazza dei Signori and Duomo

From the bus or train station, both located on Via Roma south of the centre, it's a 10-minute walk over the Sile along the Corso del Popolo and Via XX Settembre to the Piazza dei Signori, the heart of Treviso. Here stands the city's only surviving *comunale* palace, the large brick **Palazzo dei Trecento**, as well as the towered **Palazzo del Podestà** (rebuilt in the 19th century) and the **Monte di Pietà**. The latter contains the lovely Renaissance **Sala dei Reggitori** (*visits free, by appointment only:* ✆ *(0422) 654301*), with walls of gilt leather, a painted, beamed ceiling and works by Sebastiano Ricci and Luca Giordano.

The arcaded Calmaggiore leads from the square to the **Duomo** (*open 7.30–12, 3.30–7, daily*), a Venetian Romanesque building with a cluster of domes, founded in the 12th century; the adjacent baptistry gives an idea of what the cathedral looked like before its many alterations. Besides fine Renaissance tombs of local prelates there's a memorable 17th-century monument to Pope Alexander VIII. The Malchiostro chapel has frescoes by native son Pordenone and his enemy Titian (*The Annunciation*); Vasani wrote that Pordenone always painted with his sword at his hip in case Titian showed up.

## Museo Civico and San Francesco

From the Piazza Duomo, Via Ricca meets the Borgo Cavour near the **Museo Civico** (*open 9–12, 2–5, Tues–Sat; 9–12 Sun; adm*). Its archaeological collection on the first floor includes unusual 5th-century BC bronze discs from Montebelluna; upstairs, among several frescoes is the masterpiece of Tomaso da Modena, *The Life of St Ursula*, a series that's just as delightful as Carpaccio's St Ursulas in the Accademia. Borgo Cavour exits the city through the great Venetian gate, the **Porta dei Santi Quaranta** (1517), encompassed by an impressive stretch of the ramparts. Back towards the centre on the Via Canova, the **Casa Trevigiana** (*open only for special exhibitions*) is a reliquary of the city's architecture containing provocative bits and pieces salvaged from her ruins. Especially notable are the fire screens and other furnishings in wrought iron, a local craft since Renaissance times. Two streets behind Casa Trevigiana are the city walls, which, if you follow them to the right along Viale Fra Giocondo and across the bridge, will take you within sight of the tall, brick, Romanesque-Gothic **San Francesco**, with a fresco of the Madonna by Tomaso da Modena as well as the graves of Francesca Petrarch and Pietro Alighieri, the children of Italy's two greatest poets, whose final meeting-place here in Treviso was purely a coincidence. In the same area, on Via San Parisio is Treviso's lively and colourful **Fish Market**, open every morning except Sunday.

Back along the walls to the east, Viale Burchiellati leads shortly to the city's other great gate, Guglielmo Bergamasco's exotic **Porta San Tomaso**. From here Via Mazzini leads towards the deconsecrated church of **Santa Caterina**, with frescoes by Tomaso in the Cappella degli Innocenti (*open by appointment only; inquire at Museo Civico, © (0422) 51337*).

## San Nicolò

Treviso's best church, San Nicolò, is located in one of the city's most charming quarters, southwest of the Piazza dei Signori (take Via A. Diaz from the Corso del Popolo). San Nicolò is the finer twin of San Francesco, with an attractive triple apse. The interior is a treasure house of lovely frescoes—from a huge, luck-giving *St Christopher* on the south wall to the charming pages by Lorenzo Lotto by the d'Onigo tomb. Tomaso da Modena contributed the saints standing at attention on the columns, but even better are his perceptive portraits of 40 Dominicans, painted in 1352, in the chapter house of the adjacent **Seminario** (*open April–Sept 8–12.30, 3–7; Oct–Mar 8–12.30, 3–5.30*).

---

## Conegliano and Vittorio Veneto

Conegliano was the birthplace of Giambattista Cima (1460–1518)—'the sweet shepherd among Venetian painters' as Mary McCarthy called him—the son of a seller of hides, who often painted his native countryside in his backgrounds. If you haven't seen the originals, reproductions are displayed at his birthplace, the **Casa di Cima**, Via Cima 24 (*open 4–6pm Sat, Sun only; Dec–Feb 3–5pm Sat, Sun only*). An original and beautiful Cima forms the altarpiece of the 14th-century **Duomo**, its façade frescoed by Pozzoserrato, who with some help from his cinquecento fellows did the adjacent **Scuola di Santa Maria dei Battuti**, hall of a flagellants' confraternity (*open 9–12; closed Wed*). Be sure to stroll down **Via Venti Settembre**, lined with old palaces; the old **castle** on the hill has a small museum and even better view (*open 10–12.30, 2.30–6.30, Tues–Sun*). Conegliano has a wine-making school, and produces in its hills the much loved Prosecco of Treviso which you can go a-tasting along the 42-kilometre **Strada del vino bianco**—the white-wine road between Conegliano and **Valdobbiadene** to the west. On the way is the parish church of **San Pietro di Feletto**, frescoed in the 15th-century by an unknown painter, whose 'Poor Man's Bible' is a jewel of popular religious art.

The Venetian Pre-Alps saw a heavy share of battles in the First World War, and the hills around Asiago, Monte Grappa and the Piave are often crowned with Italian, British or French war cemeteries. **Vittorio Veneto**, north of Conegliano, was the site of Italy's final victorious battle (October 1918). The Vittorio's name, however, is for Vittorio Emanuele II; in 1866, to celebrate the birth of Italy, two rival towns were united: **Cèneda** down below, and upper, walled **Serravalle**, which conserves its old palaces and houses. In the **Loggia** in Cèneda, designed by Sansovino, there is a museum of the battle (*open 10–12, 4.30–6.30, Tues–Sun; adm*); in the **Duomo** there's an altarpiece by Titian of the *Madonna and saints*.

Vittorio is the base for visiting the lovely **Bosco del Cansiglio** to the northeast, a forest of beech and red pine on a lofty karstic plateau. Mt Cansiglio itself offers the closest downhill skiing to Venice; the slopes are reached from the beautiful **Alpago** valley on the northern side. The Alpago has a picturesque lake, **Lago di Santa Croce**, as a focal point for its small villages, which can offer ski and watersports facilities that have yet to become trendy and expensive.

## Belluno

A provincial capital, Belluno is notable not for any artistic or historic monuments but for its magnificent setting at the junction of the Piave and Ardo rivers, with the first peaks of the Dolomites as a backdrop. It is also a transportation hub for the mountains, and a good place to pick up information on hikes and ski resorts in the eastern Dolomites.

The most important building in Belluno, the **Duomo**, was designed by the great Tullio Lombardo, but never completed; from its campanile there are superb views of the town and its environs. It shares its Piazza with the 15th-century **Palazzo dei Rettori**, the ornate residence of Belluno's Venetian governors. In Via Duomo, the **Museo Civico** (*open 10–12, 3–6, Sun 10–12, closed Mon*) is a treat for fans of extrovert Baroque painter Sebastiano Ricci. Little **Piazza del Mercato**, lined with bars and with a fountain dating from 1410, is one of the prettiest corners of the old town. Nearby, Via Mezzaterra leads south to the 12th-century **Porta Ruga**, with a postcard view of the Piave valley and the mountains.

If you don't have time or the inclination for a major foray into the mountains, take the bus to the mountain of **Nevegal**, 11km south of Belluno. It has a little ski-resort and a chairlift to the Rifugio Brigata Alpina Cadore (1600 m), with its pretty alpine garden. From here it's an easy three-hour walk up to the **Col Visentin**, site of another refuge that commands a unique panorama: north across the sea of Dolomite peaks and south to the Venetian Lagoon.

## Feltre

West from Belluno the SS50 skirts the Piave and the southern flank of the Dolomites on its way to Feltre, one of the prettiest towns in the province. Sacked by the troops of Emperor Maximilian in 1510 during the War of the League of Cambrai, Feltre was rebuilt immediately afterwards and has changed little since, especially the houses along the main **Via**

**Mezzaterra**; along the way look for exterior frescoes by Feltre's own contribution to the Renaissance, Lorenzo Luzzo, better known by his punk nickname, *Il Morto da Feltre*, the 'Dead Man of Feltre', given to him because of his unusual pallor. The jewel on the Via Mezzaterra is the picturesque **Piazza Maggiore**, where a Lion of St Mark stands vigil over the castle, the

*Piazza Maggiore di Feltre*

church of San Rocco (with a fountain by Tullio Lombardo), and the 16th-century **Palazzo dei Rettori** (Municipio), decked out with a Palladian portico. Inside there's a small wooden theatre which saw the production of Goldoni's first plays.

The Palazzo Villabuono, by the town's east gate on Via L. Luzzo 23, now houses the **Museo Civico** (*closed for restoration at time of writing*) which has among its archaeological collection an altar to the *anna perrena* (the year), and among its paintings works by 'The Dead Man', Gentile Bellini, and Cima da Conegliano. The *Transfiguration*, Il Morto da Feltre's most acclaimed work, is nearby in the sacristy of the church of **Ognissanti**. Back towards the centre, on Via del Paradiso 8, the **Museo Rizzarda** (*open June–Sept 10–1, 4–7, Tues–Sun; adm*) features a collection of beautiful works in wrought iron, much of it from the forge of the local master Carlo Rizzarda, along with 19th and 20th-century paintings.

From Feltre it's an easy walk up to the Romanesque **Sanctuary of SS. Vittore e Corona** (1100) on Monte Miesna. Its frescoes go back to the 1200s and its views go as far as the southern plains. Roads from Feltre continue south to Asolo and Bassano del Grappa, or west and north to Asiago and Trento.

*Where to Stay*

## Treviso

North of Treviso in Paderno di Ponzano the lovely villa ★★★★★**El Toulà**, Via Postumia 63, ✆ (0422) 969191 (luxury) has only ten luxurious double rooms, guaranteeing lots of special touches and tranquillity. The extensive grounds contain a swimming pool and tennis courts, and there's a charming bar and excellent restaurant.

A convenient hotel is the modern ★★★★**Continental**, Via Roma 16, ✆ (0422) 411662, ✉ 411620 (expensive), near the station. All rooms have air-conditioning and TV, and there's a garage. Right in the centre of town is the **★★Campeol**, Piazza Ancillotto 8, ✆ (0422) 56601, ✆ 540871 (moderate). All its rooms have baths and good views of the historical centre, and there is a pleasant dining-room where breakfast is served. There are no cheaper hotels worth recommending in central Treviso, and not many in the region generally.

## Conegliano

A hotel with a very good restaurant is the **★★★Canon d'Oro**, Via XX Settembre 129, ✆ (0438) 34246 (moderate); its frescoed exterior conceals plush modern rooms, overlooking the town's main street. For an alternative, the **★★★Sporting**, Via Diaz 37, ✆ (0438) 412300, ✆ 412310 (moderate), set in parkland on Conegliano's outskirts, boasts tennis courts, a sizeable pool, sauna and satellite TV.

## Vittorio Veneto

**★★★Hotel Terme**, Via della Terme 4, ✆ (0438) 554345 (moderate) has good, comfortable rooms and an excellent kitchen, serving specialities with *radicchio* and garden-fresh vegetables. A basic but comfortable hotel is the **★Vecchia Locanda**, Via Tommaseo 80, ✆ (0438) 552121 (inexpensive).

## Belluno

Belluno caters mostly for ski bunnies, but the **★★★Hotel Astor**, Piazza dei Martiri 26-E, ✆ (0437) 942094, ✆ 942493 (moderate), offers good value and comfortable, central rooms. The **★★Centrale**, Via Loreto 2, ✆ (0437) 943349 (inexpensive), is between the station and centre; it has clean, cheap rooms, with or without bath.

## Feltre

For all modern facilities, from parking to a private park, the place to go in Feltre is the **★★★★Doriguzzi**, Viale del Piave 2, ✆ (0439) 2902, ✆ 83660 (expensive), set in a pleasant garden near the station.

In the Alpago there are some 6000 rooms available to rent in private homes, covering a wide range of prices and amenities. Contact the local tourist office for a list, or they can help you book.

---

### *Eating Out*

More people eat than stay in Treviso, and the city's fine restaurants are a tempting reason to follow the crowd. Besides cherries, Treviso produces the Veneto's finest red radicchio; a typical dish is *sopa coada*—a baked pigeon casserole. For an apéritif, a Prosecco, *naturalménte*.

## Treviso

Treviso's most acclaimed restaurant, **El Toulà da Alfredo**, Via Collalto 26, ✆ (0422) 40275 (expensive), disdains tradition for a lovely, elegant Belle Epoque décor and an imaginative menu that includes French and Viennese dishes alongside Veneto specialities such as *sopa coada*. (*Closed Sun evenings, Mon, Aug; reserve.*)

In a beautiful medieval building, **Al Bersagliere**, Via Barberia 21, ✆ (0422) 541988 (moderate), has a full selection of *sopa coada* and other Venetian specialities such as squid in its own ink, risotto, and liver Venetian-style, as well as delicious antipasti too. **Le Beccherie**, Piazza Anchillotto 11, ✆ (0422) 540871 (moderate), is one of Treviso's bastions of local atmosphere and cooking—a great place to try *pasta e fagioli* with red radicchio. A restaurant that's a fair bargain and a boon to homesick Americans is **Toni del Spin**, Via Inferiore 7, ✆ (0422) 543829 (inexpensive), which offers at the end of a Veneto meal (*biguli*, risotto, *risi e bisi* or, in the winter, roast suckling pig)—American apple pie! (*Closed Sun, Mon midday, Aug.*)

## Conegliano

Outside Conegliano there's the excellent **Tre Panoce**, Via Vecchia Trevigiana 50, ✆ (0438) 60071, located in an old farmhouse crowning a hill of vineyards, with outdoor tables in summer (if you're not driving, bus no.1 stops outside). And what really counts, the food, is exquisite, prepared with fresh ingredients from the surrounding countryside. The menu is always changing, but game specialities and mushroom dishes appear frequently. (*Closed Sun evenings, Mon, all of Aug.*) **Al Salisà**, Via XX Settembre 2, ✆ (0438) 24288 (moderate) is extremely elegant, featuring succulent snails (*lumache*) and game specialities in season, especially venison. There's also a good local wine list, and frequently special menus for lunch. (*Closed Tues evenings, Wed, Aug.*)

## Plois

One of the top restaurants in Venetia, **Dolada**, is located in the village of Plois, at Via Dolada 9, ✆ (0437) 479141 (expensive), overlooking Lago di Santa Croce and its surroundings. Wood panelling, candlelight and romance accompany homemade pasta, the celebrated *zuppa dolada*, superb fish, duck and lamb dishes and an exceptional wine list.

## Belluno

The best place to eat in Belluno is the hardest to find, located behind a plain door in the heart of town—**Al Sasso**, Via Consiglio 12, ✆ (0437) 22424 (moderate). The cooking is simple: homemade pasta and gnocchi, rabbit and kid, all served in a traditional setting. (*Closed Mon, last two weeks of Aug.*) A good, simple trattoria is **Da Mare**, Piazza Mazzini 24 (inexpensive).

# The Dolomites

There are mountains and there are the Dolomites. Born as massive corals in the primordial ocean, and heaved up from the seabed 60 million years ago, tempests and blizzards over the aeons have whittled away the malleable calcite that laces the Dolomites to form an extraordinary landscape. Otherworldly and majestic peaks claw and scratch at the sky between the valleys of the Adige and the Piave rivers, a petrified tempest of jagged needles, pinnacles and sheer cliffs.

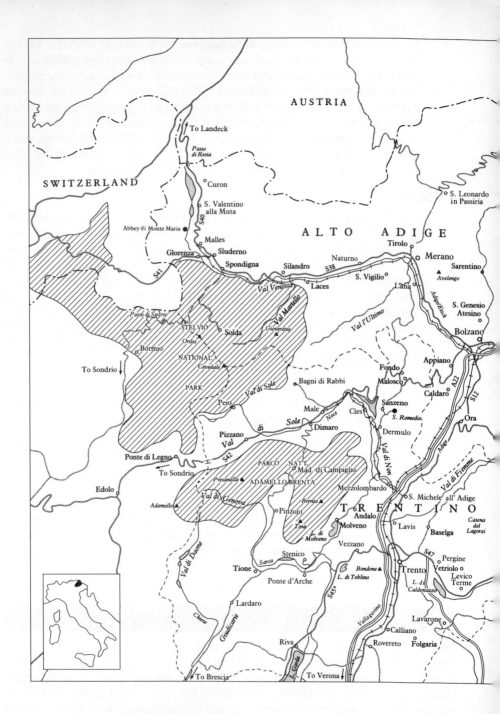

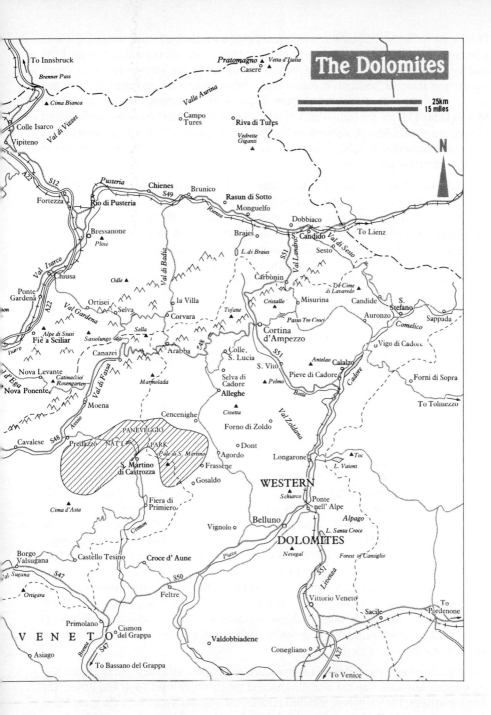

The Dolomites

25km
15 miles

N

To Innsbruck
Brenner Pass
Cima Bianca
Colle Isarco
Vipiteno
Val di Vizzes
Fortezza
S12
A22
Rio di Pusteria
Pusteria
Chienes
S49
Brunico
Rasun di Sotto
Monguelfo
Dobbiaco
To Lienz
Bressanone
Plose
Braies
S. Candido
Sesto
Val di Sesto
Val Landro
L. di Braies
S51
Carbonin
Tre Cime di Lavaredo
Candide
S. Stefano
Sappada
Chiusa
Val Isarco
Odle
la Villa
Tofane
Cristallo
Misurina
Auronzo
Comelico
Vigo di Cadore
Ponte Gardena
A22
Ortisei
Selva
Corvara
Val di Badia
Passo Tre Croci
Cortina d'Ampezzo
Val Gardena
Sella
Sassolungo
Arabba
Colle. S. Lucia
S. Vito
Antelao
Calalzo
Pieve di Cadore
Cadore
Forni di Sopra
Fiè a Sciliar
Alpe di Siusi
Canazei
Catinaccio Rosengarten
Marmolada
Selva di Cadore
Pelmo
Boite
To Tolmezzo
Nova Levante
Val d'Ega
Nova Ponente
Val di Fassa
Moena
Cencenighe
Alleghe
Civetta
Forno di Zoldo
Val Zoldana
Cavalese
S48
Predazzo
PANEVEGGIO NAT'L PARK
Passo di S. Martino
Dont
Agordo
Longarone
Toc
L. Vaiont
Cima d'Asta
S. Martino di Castrozza
Frassene
Gosaldo
WESTERN
Schiarco
Ponte nell' Alpe
Fiera di Primiero
Cismon
Vignolo
Belluno
Alpago
L. Santa Croce
Borgo Valsugana
Val Sugana
S47
Castello Tesino
Croce d' Aune
Piave
Nevegal
DOLOMITES
Forest of Cansiglio
Ortigara
S50
Feltre
S51
Livenza
Vittorio Veneto
Sacile
To Pordenone
Primolano
Cismon del Grappa
Brenta
S47
Valdobbiadene
Conegliano
A27
VENETO
Asiago
To Bassano del Grappa
To Venice

Pratomagno
Vetta d'Italia
Casere
Valle Aurina
Campo Tures
Riva di Tures
Vedrette Giganti
Rienza

These most romantic of mountains were named after a wandering French mineralogist with a fantastic name, Dieudonné Sylvain Guy Tancrède de Gratet de Dolomieu, who in 1789 was the first to describe their mineral content. They have since adorned countless jigsaw puzzles and attracted thousands of nature-lovers, hikers, sportsmen, mountain-climbers and skiers, who can slide down the slippery slopes even in summer on the glaciers of **Marmolada** (3341m), the highest peak in the range. In the summer the snow fields convert to bouquets of wild flowers, streaked with brilliant blue gentians, yellow alpine poppies and buttercups, edelweiss, and pink rhododendron. The air and light in autumn are so sharp and fine they can break your heart.

Culturally, especially in the bilingual Alto Adige/Süd Tirol, the Dolomites are more than half Austrian. In isolated mountain valleys people speak German and little Italian, while others still speak Ladin (Romansch), a language that owes its origins to the days when the Emperor Tiberius sent Roman soldiers to crush the Celts in the mountain valleys of Switzerland and the Tyrol. Some of the soldiers stayed behind in the valleys, and their descendents became known as the Ladini, or Latins. The cuisine in the Dolomites profits from both Italy and Austria, which make the region a great place to eat apple strudel and pasta *al dente*, if not a good place to make yourself understood if you only speak English.

## Highlights of the Dolomites

There are so many lovely walks and drives in the Dolomites it seems a bit presumptuous putting one above the other, though the stupendous **Great Dolomites Road** between Bolzano and Cortina (SS241 and SS48) justly deserves its fame. Other sensational **drives** are around the Pale di San Martino (SS50 and local roads); through the passes of the Sella Group (SS243 and SS244); along the western slopes of the Brenta Dolomites from Pinzolo to Folgarida (SS239); and around Cortina, to Misurina, Auronzo, the Val di Sesto and down the Val di Landro (SS48, SS51, SS52 and local roads).

It's also difficult to pinpoint the most memorable **walks**. It's never too far to a cable car or chairlift that can whisk you half-way up a mountain to begin your rambles. Among the best, requiring no special equipment, are two easy but ravishing paths in Paneveggio Natural Park; a beautiful walk above Misurina around Tre Cime di Lavaredo; above Santa Cristina to Sassolungo; around Madonna di Campiglio and Molveno in the Brenta Group; around Colle Santa Lucia; and above Merano, among countless others. If you've had some mountain experience, one of the most famous hikes begins in the Val di Fassa, and runs to the bizarre Torri del Vaiolet on Catinaccio (Rosengarten); another awesome experience is to walk the Via Bocchette above Madonna di Campiglio. The **High Trails of the Dolomites** (*see* below) were laid out to take in the best scenery and are accessible from many points. The Pale di San Martino, the Brenta, Cristallo, Tofane, Marmolada, and Sella Groups offer challenges to skilled climbers. Every tourist office has walking and climbing maps for their districts and can advise on the degree of difficulty.

The prettiest **lakes**—though again it seems unfair to mention only a few out of hundreds— are sapphire Misurina, Carezza, and Alleghe, and the strikingly hued Tovel and Braies. The prettiest **valleys**: the Val di Non with its orchards, the emerald Val di Sole, the grand Val di Fassa, the sunny Val Gardena, the rural Tyrolean Pusteria, and the picturesque Val di Sesto, the wild Val l'Ega, the enchanting Val di Genova, or the ravishing Val Zoldana.

Man-made sights pale before the handiwork of angels, but the **cities** of Trento, Bressanone, Vipiteno, Pieve di Cadore, Rovereto, Bolzano and Merano are all worth visits; as are the ancient **towns** of Cencenighe, Cavalese, Borgo Valsugana, Pergine, and Malles.

The mountains are also endowed with a fine collection of medieval **castles**— Castel Tirolo above Merano; Castello di Sabbionara at Avio; Castel di Pietra at Fiera di Primiero; Castello Toblino; Castel Telvana at Borgo Valsugana; Trostburg castle at Ponte Gardena; Sluderno castle; as well as several around Cles, Appiano, and Naturno. Quite a few now house hotels or restaurants. The **ecclesiastical highlights** include the ancient abbey of Novacella near Bressanone; the curious hermitage of San Romedio at Cles; the frescoes in San Rocco at Tesero, San Virgilio at Pinzolo, and Malles' parish church and Benedictine abbey.

*Polomiten, Tre cime di Loredo*

For **winter sports**, Cortina d'Ampezzo has the best facilities. However, San Martino di Castrozza, Madonna di Campiglio, Auronzo, Canazei, Selva di Cadore, Sappada, Solda, and San Candido could all come in close behind.

## When to Go

Prices skyrocket in the Dolomites during their high-season periods (Christmas holidays, end of January to Easter, mid-July to mid-Sept). To avoid high prices and colour-coordinated coachloads of Austro-Italian swingers and Gucci-equipped alpinists, try to go in June or October, when the alpine refuges are open but not packed to the gills, or immediately after the New Year holidays for skiing, when everyone else has to go back to work and the resorts offer big discounts.

## Hiking

One is almost tempted to lapse into Italian hyperbole about hiking in the Dolomites—but suffice to say it's as close as some of us will ever get to heaven. There are routes for everyone from semi-couch-potatoes to the rock-grappling Indiana Jones, and eight **High Trails of the Dolomites** (*Alte Vie delle Dolomiti*) specially designed for those 'vagabonds of the path' who fall in between the two extremes. The trails range from 120 to 180km in length, and are designed to take the average walker two weeks—though it doesn't hurt to plan a few days on top of that for rests and detours.

The High Trails have the virtue of keeping you on top of mountains and plateaux for nearly their entire length. While they do not require any special climbing skill (trails with a death-defying *via ferrata*, 'iron ladder', or other obstacles almost always have detours for the less intrepid), they do demand a stout pair of hiking boots with good rubber soles and protection against sudden storms, even in the middle of summer. Strategically placed alpine refuges provide shelter, but if you come in early June or October when the refuges closed you'll need to carry camping gear. The refuges are open from the end of June to the end of September; in July and August it's wise to book a bed or cot in advance to avoid disappointment.

## The High Trails

**No.1** From Lake Braies to Belluno, the most popular route.

**No.2** 'Trail of the Legends', from Bressanone to Feltre.

**No.3** 'Trail of the Chamois', from Villabassa to Longarone.

**No.4** The Grohmann route, from San Candido to Pieve di Cadore.

**No.5** The Titian route, from Sesto Pusteria to Pieve di Cadore.

**No.6** 'Trail of the Silences', from the sources of the Piave to Vittorio Veneto.

**No.7** Belluno Pre-Alps to the Alpago (a region covered in the preceding section).

**No.8** 'Trail of the Heroes', across the mountainous battlefields from Feltre to Bassano del Grappa (also covered in the preceding section).

There are two good sets of **maps** that include the above *Alte Vie* and other paths as well, and point out the location of the Alpine refuges: *Carta dei Sentieri e Rifugi*, Edizioni Tabacco Udine, and *Maps Kompass-Wanderkarten*, Edizioni Fleishmann-Starnberg. Both are scale 1:50,000, and are readily available at news-stands in the region. There is also an extensive literature and guides covering the paths if you can read Italian or German; alternatively, the tourist office in Belluno offers free booklets on each trail in English that contain all the basic information you need to know before you go, including the telephone numbers of the refuges. They also give you a good idea of the level of difficulty of each trail, so read them thoroughly before setting out.

**Alpine refuges** (*rifugi alpini*) vary. Many are owned by the Italian Alpine club, while others are privately owned, primarily by ski resorts. Some are along trails, while others may be reached via cable car. All offer bed and board. Prices vary mainly by altitude: the higher up and more difficult of access, the more expensive. Cots range from L10 to 15,000, beds from L12 to 25,000; complete meals from L15,000. Besides these refuges, there are the *baite* (wooden huts), *casere* (stone huts) and bivouacs (beds but no food) found along some trails: they generally have no custodians but offer shelter.

Write to the tourist offices in Belluno, Trento, and Bolzano (listed in the city sections) for more information, or the headquarters of the **Italian Alpine Club** (CAI, Via Fonseca Pimental 7, 20121 Milan, © (02) 26141378, @ 26141395. Alternatively, if you're coming up from Venice, inquire there at the CAI office at San Marco 1672, © (041) 5225407.

# Skiing

The Dolomites are like a candy shop for winter sports junkies. As the sunny side of the Alps they enjoy good clear weather and when it snows, it falls delightfully dry and powdery. There is a variety of slopes of all levels of difficulty, and country trails, toboggan and bobsled runs, ice rinks and speed-skating courses; if all of the ski runs were ironed out flat they would stretch from the Brenner Pass to Reggio Calabria. There are other bonuses as well: ski schools in July, and indoor, heated pools in the middle of winter. The only problem comes in trying to choose which out of scores of places to aim for.

To get some orientation, write ahead to the tourist offices: to Belluno for their *Dolomiti Neve* pamphlets, to Trento for *Snowy Planet*, or Bolzano for *Ski Panorama: South Tyrol*, all of which have suggestions that may narrow down the field. An easier option is to book a week's *Settimana Bianca* package (room and board at a hotel, ski-pass and instruction) from CIT (Citalia) or other travel offices all over Italy. This is especially good value outside the peak season. If you have your own transport and want to try as many resorts as possible, the *Superski Dolomiti* pass gives you unlimited access to most of the slopes for periods of one, two, or three weeks—the longer the period, the more economical the pass. Nearly all resorts hire out equipment and offer ski instruction; some have winter caravan camping.

---

## Getting Around

Even the heirs of the Romans can make the **trains** go only so far in the mountains. The line north from Venice, Treviso, and Belluno (*see* preceding section) passes through Pieve di Cadore before petering out in Calalzo di Cadore, 35km from Cortina d'Ampezzo (2½ hours from Venice). The western Dolomites in the Trentino-Alto Adige are linked by the main line between Verona and Munich/Innsbruck, which goes by way of Trento (1½ hours) and Bolzano/Bozen (2½ hours) to the Brenner Pass (4 hours). Branch lines run from Bolzano to Merano/Meran and Malles Venosta, to the west, and from near Bressanone/Brixen to Brunico/Bruneck and San Candido/Innichen to the east, on the line to Vienna.

The Dolomites are exceptionally well served by two major **bus** companies— *Dolomiti-Bus* in the east and *SAD Buses* in the west. Pick up their schedules at the main bus stations or tourist offices; many departures coincide with trains from the south. Besides their normal runs, the bus companies add special scenic tours in July and August from the major centres.

By **car** the major access routes into the Dolomites are, in the west, the A22 *autostrada* from Verona via Trento and Bolzano/Bozen to the Brenner Pass, and in the east the SS51 via Belluno to Cortina. At 38km north of Trento on the A22 (or parallel SS12) the SS48 branches off eastwards towards Cortina; alternatively, take the SS241 from Bolzano/Bozen, part of the 'Great Dolomites Road'. Bolzano/Bozen and Bressanone/Brixen are the main junctions for roads linking the western and eastern Dolomites.

# The Eastern Dolomites: the Cadore

Much of the district north of Belluno along the upper Piave, known as the Cadore, was incorporated into Italy only after the First World War. Its glitzy, gorgeous, somewhat over-ripe heart is Cortina d'Ampezzo, host of the 1956 Winter Olympics, which did much to introduce the Cadore to the world and make the district one of the most fashionable in Italy. The *Alte Vie* pass through this region as well, winding across some of the most renowned ridges and peaks in the range.

## From Belluno to Pieve di Cadore

### Tourist Information

As well as the main regional tourist offices in Belluno and Cortina there are local offices in **Pieve di Cadore**, at Via XX Settembre 18, ✆ (0435) 31644, @ 31645; **Santo Stefano di Cadore**, Via Venezia 40, ✆ (0435) 62230, @ 62077; **Sappada**, Borgata Bach 20, ✆ (0435) 469131, @ 66233; and in **San Vito di Cadore**, at Via Nazionale 9, ✆ (0436) 9405, @ 99345.

## The Piave Valley

The roads north along the river Piave from Belluno (SS50) and Treviso (SS51) meet at the junction of Ponte nelle Alpi before continuing up through scenery marked by the steep pyramids of **Monte Dolada** and **Piz Gallina**. A less benign mountain, **Toc** (1921m), looms ahead over the town of **Longarone**. In 1963 a landslide from the slopes of Toc crashed into the local reservoir, Lake Vaiont, creating a tidal wave in the Piave that killed some 2000 people. From Longarone the now-ruined dam, 6km to the east, is a main attraction, reached via the stupendous **Gola del Vaiont**.

From Longarone there's also the option of turning off to the west for the **Val Zoldana**, a lovely valley lining the River Maè. This road, the SS251, continues beneath the stunning peaks of Civetta and Pelmo up towards the resort of Selva di Cadore. The main road from Longarone continues north past the ruined **Tower of Gardona** into the foothills of the Antelao and Marmarole, and the pretty town and resort of **Pieve di Cadore**, 45km from Ponte nelle Alpi.

*Pieve* means parish, and from Roman days on this was the most important settlement in the Cadore. It is famed as the birthplace of that mighty wielder of the paintbrush, Tiziano Vecellio, or Titian, born some time between the late 1470s and 1490. You can visit his old house, the **Casa Natale di Tiziano** (*open June–Sept 9.30–12.30, 4–7, Tues–Sun; adm*), on Via Arsenale, and see the altarpiece *Madonna with Child and SS. Andrew and Titian* that he painted and donated to one of the chapels of the parish church. The most important building in Pieve doesn't leave room for any false modesty but calls itself the **Palazzo della Magnifica Comunità Cadorina** (*same hours as Titian's Birthplace*). Built in 1525, it now houses the local archaeological and historical museum, including an unusual collection of spectacles. But what Pieve is proudest of these days is that the Italian Santa Claus, Babbo Natale, has made it is his home, which you can visit in the town park.

The road and the Piave continue north past the end of the rail line at Calalzo to the winter resort of **Santo Stefano di Cadore**, located in the beautiful **Comelico valley**. From here you can continue northwest through the Passo Monte Croce to the Val di Sesto (*see* below, 'Excursions from Cortina'). Another highly scenic road from Santo Stefano heads east towards the trendy resort of **Sappada**, a town more Austrian in feel than Italian. All of the above may be reached by buses from the Calalzo station.

From Pieve di Cadore there is also a direct road to Cortina d'Ampezzo, the SS51, which winds through the **Valle del Boite** with its many rustic wooden chalets, between the Antelao massif, nicknamed the 'King of Cadore' and **Monte Pelmo**, the latter one of the most unusual and striking peaks in the Dolomites. The road passes through two summer/winter resorts, **Borca di Cadore** and the more important **San Vito di Cadore**, an excellent base for ascending Pelmo and nearby peaks.

### Where to Stay and Eating Out

As in the case of most Dolomite resorts, guests tend (or are usually obliged) to dine in their hotels on half- or full-pension terms.

### San Vito di Cadore

There are a number of comfortable hotels here: the best is the ★★★★**Marcora**, Via Roma 28, ✆ (0436) 9101, 🖂 99156 (very expensive), in a fine setting with a pool. (*Open 20 June–10 Sept, 20 Dec–20 Mar.*)

### Pieve di Cadore

Near Pieve di Cadore in the hamlet of Tai, the ★★★**Canada**, ✆ (0435) 31741, 🖂 500257 (moderate), is one of the most charming hotels in the Cadore, with a lovely garden in a beautiful setting.

### Sappada

One reason for Sappada's popularity is its relative abundance of reasonably priced accommodation. A couple of good choices are the ★★**Corona Ferrea**, Borgata Kratten 17, ✆ (0435) 469103 (moderate) , which has comfortable rooms, all with bath (*open 20 June–20 Sept, 20 Dec–15 April*), and the small ★★★**Sierra Hof**, Borgata Soravia 110, ✆ (0435) 469110 (moderate), which is near the centre of the village (*open all year*). All its rooms also have baths.

In the neighbouring village of Cima Sappada and slightly more pricy is the ★★★**Belvedere**, Piazza Cima 93, Cima Sappada, ✆ (0435) 469112 (moderate), which has only 14 rooms, but does have its own sauna. It also offers one of the area's best restaurants (*open to non-residents*): mountain specialities include several varia-tions on venison. (*Open Dec–15 April, July–Sept.*)

Among the many cheaper hotels in Sappada, try ★**Pachner**, at Borgata Bach 43, ✆ (0435) 469138, which is open all year, and has rooms with or without bath. In San Vito di Cadore, ★★**Il Cardo**, ✆ (0436) 9459, is pleasantly located outside the centre, and remains open all year.

### Getting Around

Cortina's **bus** station is just off Via Marconi, and is served by SAD and Dolomiti buses; for information ✆ (0436) 867130. Services are greatly augmented in June–Sept, when buses serve virtually every paved road in the region. The nearest **train** stations are Dobbiaco/Toblach, 32km north (on the Bolzano–Lienz line), or Calalzo di Cadore, 35km south; both have regular bus connections to Cortina. There are four **roads** into Cortina: the SS51 from north and south and the SS48, the *Grande Strada delle Dolomiti* or Great Dolomites Road, from east and west.

### Tourist Information

The main tourist office is at Piazzetta S. Francesco 8, ✆ (0436) 3231, ✐ 3235, near the central Piazza Venezia. They have an accommodation service, good maps of surrounding trails, and information about excursions. The local alpine guide organization is next door, and open in July, August, and September, ✆ (0436) 4740.

In the surrounding region there are offices at **Misurina**, ✆ (0436) 39016; **Auronzo**, Via Roma 10, ✆ (0435) 9359, ✐ 400161; and **Dobbiaco/Toblach**, Via Roma, ✆ (0474) 72132, ✐ 72730; and south of Cortina in **Alleghe**, Piazza Kennedy 17, ✆ (0437) 523333, ✐ 723881; **Agordo**, Via Sommariva 10, ✆ (0437) 65044, ✐ 65205; and **Frassene**, Viale della Vittoria, ✆ (0437) 67035.

## The Sporting Life

Cortina's the sort of place where David Niven and Audrey Hepburn would hang out in a café wearing sunglasses, but it also enjoys the best location in the Dolomites: a lofty (1224m), sunny, cross-shaped meadow at the junction of the Boite and Bigontina valleys, in the centre of a ring of extraordinary mountains—Tofane, the great mount 'owl'; Cristallo, the 'crystal' mountain; Sorapis, licked by stony flames; and the Cinque Torri, the 'five towers'. The 1956 Olympics endowed Cortina with superb winter sports facilities; here you can ski-jump, speed-skate, fly down bobsled and luge runs, and cut figures of eight in the ice stadium, not to mention the thousand and one downhill and cross-country ski runs in the vicinity. In the summer, Cortina, which has a number of 'Green Week' discount packages similar to the winter 'White Weeks', is an excellent base for hikers and alpinists and excursions of all kinds into the mountains, while in town there's a riding school, tennis, and summer/winter swimming pools, and activities like the Ice Disco Dance in the Olympic Ice Stadium.

Devoted heart and soul to fun times and the sporting life, Cortina is almost as well known for its night-time activities, especially in winter, when the *après ski* crowd fills its clubs and discotheques and trips the light fantastic until the wee hours of dawn. But whatever worldly pleasure and delight this snowy fleshpot offers, it comes at a price, rating right up there with Capri, Portofino, and Venice herself on the bottom line of the tab; those on a budget survive by camping and dining *à la* supermarket.

Cortina has more than its share of trendy shops, and a museum of contemporary art you can take in if it rains—the **Museo Ciasa de Ra Regoles**, Via del Parco, on the corner of Corso d'Italia, (*open Dec–Easter, July–mid-Sept 4–7.30pm; sometimes mornings also; adm*) with works by De Pisis, Morandi, De Chirico and others. Two cable cars from Cortina wait to whisk you up to the mountains, both at the end of the town bus lines: in the north, near the Olympic stadium, to **Tofana di Mezzo** (3243m; L36,000 round-trip) where there are privately run alpine refuges, and in the west, to **Tondi di Faloria** (2343m; L22,000). All-day ski passes for Faloria and Cristallo are available at the office on Ria de Zeto 8 in Cortina, © (0436) 2517.

*Cortina © (0436–)* **Where to Stay**

Expect to run up against the full-board requirement nearly everywhere in Cortina in its high season—which is mortifying to the pocketbook though not to the flesh; the local cuisine is as *haute* as the price.

### luxury

If you're putting on the dog in Cortina, the place to do it is the ★★★★★**Miramonti Majestic**, Via Miramonti 103, © 4201, @ 867019. Warm, traditional and rustic, it has pretty wooden balconies affording magnificent views. The well-designed rooms have most of the imaginable creature comforts, and there's an indoor pool, tennis courts, exercise facilities, and sauna. (*Open July–Aug, Dec–Mar.*)

### very expensive

If you'd rather be in the centre of action, ★★★★**De La Poste**, Piazza Roma 14, © 4271, @ 868435, is a large alpine chalet with classy rooms and balconies, and a terrace and bar that see much of Cortina's social round, especially in the evening.

### expensive

Ten minutes' walk from the centre, down at the bottom of the valley beside the river, is another alpine chalet, the ★★★★**Hotel Corona**, Via Val di Sotto 10, © 3251, @ 867339 . It's memorable for a modern art collection even more extensive than the one in the museum; it's also more convenient than most hotels for the ski lift. (*Open June–Sept, Dec Mar.*)

### moderate

The ★★★**Imperio**, Via C. Battisti 66, © 4246, @ 4248, is an unpretentious hotel with no restaurant but adequate rooms, all with bath, and open all year. The charmer in this price category is an 800-year-old farmhouse that's been run as an inn by the same family for the past century, the ★★★**Menardi**, Via Majon 110, © 2400, @ 862183, furnished with antiques and bedecked with fresh flowers. (*Open 20 June–20 Sept, 20 Dec–10 April.*) Small, friendly and, by Cortina standards, cheap, is the ★★**Cavallino**, Corso d'Italia 142, © 2614.

### inexpensive

The Tourist Office issues lists of rooms in private houses, and will book them for you; alternatively, watch out for *CAMERE/ZIMMER* signs beside the road.

Both of Cortina's best and most fashionable restaurants are outside the city and most easily reached by car. **Il Meloncino**, at Via Gillardon 17, © 861043 , is in the district of Gillardon, en route to Flazarego on the westbound SS48. With great views over Cortina, this small, intimate restaurant offers a delicious menu to complement its romantic setting; the risotto with myrtleberries is a real treat. Reservations are a must, and you may have to settle for lunch as dinner dates are sometimes booked up months in advance. (*Closed Tues, June, Nov.*) The more elegant **El Toulà**, Via Ronco 123, © 3339, is closer to Cortina, near Pocol. Located in a refurbished wooden farmhouse, the restaurant specializes in perfect grilled meats, roast lamb, and desserts with a Tyrolean touch. There's also a renowned wine list. (*Open Dec–Mar, 15 July–30 Aug only; closed Mon, except in very high season.*)

*moderate*

A brief, sturdy walk up the hill behind town brings you to **Al Camin**, Via Alverà 99, © 2010, a cosy restaurant with lots of wood and a big fireplace, serving the tasty local versions of polenta and goulash. (*Closed Mon.*)

## Excursions From Cortina

As a major crossroads, Cortina offers numerous forays into the surrounding mountains. The classic Dolomites excursion is to take the Great Dolomites Road between Cortina and Bolzano, but as most people approach it from the west, you'll find it described further on (*see* 'Bolzano' p.467).

A popular and beautiful short trip from Cortina is on the SS48 and SS48b eastwards over the lofty **Tre Croci pass** to **Lake Misurina**, one of the loveliest of Dolomite lakes, shimmering below the jagged peaks of Sorapis and the remarkable triple-spired **Tre Cime di Lavaredo**, 15km northeast of Cortina. The colours of Misurina are so brilliant they look touched-up on a postcard; as a resort it makes a fine alternative to Cortina, especially if ice skating is your sport. From Misurina it's a magnificent 7km drive up to the **Rifugio Auronzo**, located just beneath the Tre Cime di Lavaredo. From the refuge it's an easy walk to the fine 1916 **Bersaglieri Memorial**, honouring Italy's famous sharpshooters. More fine views await from **Monte Piana**, a lofty meadow 6km north of Misurina.

## Circular routes from Misurina to Cortina

There are two possible circular routes from Misurina back to Cortina that make rewarding, full-day excursions. Both begin to the east on the SS48 via **Auronzo**, past a peak known as the **Corno del Doge** for its resemblance to the Doge's bonnet. Auronzo, surrounded by fragrant spruce forests and on the shores of an artificial lake, is another resort town, with a cable car and chairlifts up **Monte Agudo**.

From Auronzo you can circle south around Pieve di Cadore and the Valle di Boite (161km altogether; see above 'From Belluno to Pieve di Cadore') or take the longer route around to the north (224km) through the **Comelico** and the beautiful **Val di Sesto,** noted for its traditional wooden houses. The route passes into the bilingual Alto Adige region through **San Candido/Innichen,** a pretty summer/winter resort on the river Drava; it has a Benedictine monastery and a lovely Romanesque collegiate church, the 13th-century **SS. Candidus e Corbinian.** The turn back to Cortina (SS51) is at **Dobbiaco/Toblach,** one of the original Dolomite resorts, in a magnificent setting, with good skiing, a nearby lake, and a railway station. The large **castle** in the old part of town was built for Venice's arch-enemy, the Emperor Maximilian, in 1500. Mahler spent some summers here, an association commemorated by a small museum.

## Dobbiaco to Cortina

The road passes the wooded Lago di Dobbiaco and enters into the dramatic **Val di Landro,** with the Cristallo group looming ahead over the town of **Carbonin/Schluderbach.** The road south of here is known as the 'Alemagna', for it was long the main route south from Germany. It passes by way of **Ospitale,** one of many towns in the region named after the hostels that once sheltered pilgrims on their way to Rome, and a pair of little lakes, the Black and the White, before reaching the lonely ruins of the **Castel Sant'Umberto.** The road then circles around castle-crowned Podestagno, before descending into the Ampezzo with the Le Tofane group storming up to the right.

## Cortina to Colle Santa Lucia and Agordo

There are two routes to this region south-west of Cortina: the main one follows the Great Dolomites Road through the Falzarego Pass before taking the SS203 southwards at Andraz, while an alternative, lesser-known but equally pretty route takes the smaller SS638 road through the Giau Pass to **Selva di Cadore,** at the head of the Valle di Zoldo and the road to Longarone. **Colle Santa Lucia,** near here, is a photographer's paradise, with its old agricultural hamlets and famous view of the Dolomites as a backdrop (31km from Cortina).

Continuing south from Colle the road passes **Caprile** and the lovely **Lago di Alleghe,** under the massive peaks of Civetta. At the fine old village of **Cencenighe** you have the option of turning off for Falcade and San Martino di Castrozza (see below 'East of Trento'). **Agordo** (45km) is an attractive town and resort in the Val Cordevole, along one of the principal branches of the Piave. The Passo Duran above Agordo leads back to Cortina via the Valle di Zoldo and the village of **Dont** (another 21km)—there are splendid views of Civetta and Pelmo, and you can buy samples of local woodcarving.

---

*Where to Stay*

### Lake Misurina

The ★★★**Lavaredo,** Via Monte Piana 11 ✆ (0436) 39227, 🖃 39127 (expensive) has tennis courts and a good restaurant, and is open all year, while the ★★**Dolomiti des Alpes,** Via Monte Piana, ✆ (0436) 39031, 🖃 39216 (moderate), just above the lake, has a sauna-solarium. (*Closed Oct–mid-Dec.*) Overlooking Lake Misurina is the ★**Sport,** Via Monte Piana 18, ✆/🖃 (0436) 39125 (inexpensive), with plain, simple rooms.

### Auronzo

In nearby Auronzo there are far more choices: one of the most comfortable, the **★★Juventus**, Via Padova 26, ✆ (0435) 9221 (moderate), is right on the beach of Lake Auronzo. The **★Vienna**, Via Verona 2, ✆ (0435) 9394 (inexpensive) has rooms with or without bath, and is near the beach with good views of the mountains.

### Dobbiaco/Toblach

The **★★★Cristallo-Walch**, Viale Roma 11, ✆ (0474) 72138, ✉ 72755 (expensive) is a fine resort hotel in a beautfiul setting, with an indoor pool and sauna. For real mountain splendour, stay in Monte Rota/Radsberg, just outside Dobbiaco/Toblach, at the **★★★Alpengasthof Ratsberg**, Monterota 10, Radsberg, ✆ (0474) 72213, ✉ 72916 (moderate), with a lovely park, indoor pool and views. It is on top of Monte Rota itself, and accessible by cable car.

### Selva di Cadore

A fine, economical place both to stay and to eat is the **★★★Giglio Rosso**, at Pescul, ✆ (0437) 720310. All rooms have baths, and the restaurant does a fine mulberry risotto and turkey in beer. (*Open Dec–Mar, June–Sept.*)

### Caprile

The 130-year-old **★★★★Alla Posta**, Piazza Dogliani 19, ✆ (0437) 721171, ✉ 721677 (expensive) is most prestigious hotel, with TVs in each of its comfortable rooms, and a fairly good restaurant. (*Open 20 Dec–15 April, 15 June–30 Sept.*)

---

*Eating Out*

On the road east of Auronzo at Cimagogna is **Dal Cavaliere**, ✆ (0435) 9834 (moderate), which serves delicious suckling pig and risotto with herbs or mushrooms, amid traditional, wood-panelled décor. Alternatively, 2km west at Reane is **La Stadiera** (moderate), with good gnocchi, or venison with polenta.

## The Western Dolomites: Trentino

The autonomous province of Trentino contains some of the finest scenery of the western Dolomites, especially in the Val di Fassa on the western slopes of Marmolada and in the isolated but hauntingly majestic Brenta Group, to the west of the Adige; it also includes the north shore of Lake Garda (see p.316, in 'Lombardy and the Lakes'). Unlike the Alto Adige/South Tyrol further north, Trentino is mostly Italian in language and heritage, sprinkled with a Ladin minority in the valleys. Many of the 200 alpine refuges in Trentino are operated by the *Società degli Alpinisti Tridentini* (SAT), which is a good source for mountain information. They can be contacted in Trento, at Via Manci 57, ✆ (0461) 21522. Trento itself is one of Northern Italy's finest little cities, worth a visit even if mountains aren't your cup of tea.

Trento is on the main FS **rail** line between Verona and the Brenner Pass; another line links the city with Bassano del Grappa and connections to Padua and Venice, passing through the Val Sugana. A private local rail line, the *Ferrovia Trento-Malè*, also runs from Trento up to Cles in the Val di Non. Otherwise **buses** are the main form of public transport, although service, especially out of season in the western reaches, is often skeletal. In addition to the main Dolomite bus lines, *Atesina Trento* provides links to the southern half of the region as well as connecting Trento to Riva del Garda, Feltre, Belluno, and Bassano. If you look wholesome enough **hitch-hiking** is also relatively easy around this area.

The main **roads** into Trentino are, again, the A22 *autostrada* and the SS12, which run in parallel straight through the middle of the province. The main junction points for roads off these main highways are Rovereto, Trento and Bolzano/Bozen. Also, about 15km north of Trento the SS43 turns off the SS12 to the west, for the Brenta, the Val di Non and the Val di Sole; another 20km north the SS48 turns off eastwards towards Cortina d'Ampezzo, later becoming part of the Great Dolomites Road.

## Tourist Information

No province in Italy has such an efficient and enthusiastic tourist board—it even has branches in **Rome** (Via Poli 47, ✆ (06) 6794216, @ 6970243) and **Milan** (Piazza Diaz 5, ✆ (02) 86461251, @ 72002188). The **Trento** head office is at Via Sighele 3, ✆ (0461) 980000, @ 238938. Between Verona and Trento the only tourist office is in **Rovereto**, at Via Dante 63, ✆ (0464) 430363, @ 435528.

# From Verona to Trento: Val Lagarina and Rovereto

Following the Adige up from Verona, passing through the Valpolicella region and the Monti Lessini, the A22 and SS12 enter Trentino near **Avio**, dominated by the proud 14th-century **Castello di Sabbionara** (*open Feb–Sept 10–12, 1–6, Tues–Sun; Oct–Dec 10–4, Tues–Sun; closed Jan; adm*). Its guardhouse preserves a wonderful fresco cycle of battling knights, the *Parata dei Combattenti*, while in the keep the frescoes portray scenes of courtly love. The castle was the first property of the Italian version of the National Trust, the *Fondo per l'Ambiente Italiano*.

Further up the road and the river Adige, past a sea of vineyards, **Rovereto** is the second city of Trentino, built around an imposing Venetian castle; from 1416–87 the city formed the northern extent of the Serenissima, before the Trentini, with the aid of the Tyroleans, pushed the Venetians back to Verona. This area was also hotly contested in the First World War, and the castle contains an evocative **War Museum** devoted primarily to that conflict (*open Mar–Nov 8.30–12.30, 2.30–6.30, Tues–Sun; adm*). After the War, cannons from each of the 19 belligerents were melted down to make the largest ringing bell in the world, the **Campana dei Caduti**, which is now located in the southern quarter of Rovereto; it rings in memory of the fallen every day at sundown.

Rovereto was the home town of the great archaeologist Paolo Orsi, who willed his private collection of statues, busts and vases from Magna Graecia to the city. They are displayed in the **Musei Civici** near the centre of town (*open 9–12, 3–6, Tues–Sat*). The Italian Futurist artist Fortunato Depero (1892–1960) also worked for many years in the town, and bequeathed it the **Museo Depero** (*open 9–12, 2.30–6, Tues–Sun; adm*), a perfect little museum in which the artist himself has designed the showcase for his art; his tapestries, puppets and paintings hang beside striking wooden furniture and interior decoration.

Just southeast of Rovereto, you can follow the 'Path of the Dinosaurs', marked by huge footprints planted 200 million years ago. The 'Path of Peace' (*Sentiero della Pace*), a long-distance path along the line of the First World War battlefields, also runs nearby and ends at Mount Zugna just to the south, after passing the Campana dei Caduti in Rovereto and some remaining traces of the 1915–17 front. The Rovereto Tourist Office provides detailed maps for both paths.

East of Rovereto are two small summer/winter resorts on a lofty plateau (1,000m) below Monte Cornetto, reached by the SS350 via Calliano: **Folgaria**, in a neighbourhood of mouldering Austrian fortifications left over from the First World War, and the larger **Lavarone**, near the lake of the same name, where Sigmund Freud spent three summers. In the tiny village of **Luserna**, near Lavarone, the inhabitants speak Cimbro, a dialect of High German.

Across the Adige from Rovereto, **Isera** is the centre for the production of Marzemino wine, one of Trentino's finest reds. To the north, visible from the road to Trento, the ruined but still imposing **Castle of Beseno** (*open April–Oct 9–12, 2–5.30, Tues–Sun; adm*) towers over the small town of Calliano.

---

© *(0464–)*

### Where to Stay and Eating Out

## Rovereto

The ★★★**Rovereto**, Corso Rosmini 82/d, © 435522, ✉ 439644 (expensive) is a fine central hotel for an overnight stay, with comfortable air-conditioned rooms, and a good restaurant that also serves a vegetarian menu. There's also an excellent, modern **Youth Hostel**, at Via della Scuola 16, © 433707 (inexpensive), which is very near the railway station.

The best place to eat in Rovereto is **Al Borgo**, Via Garibaldi 13, © 436300 (expensive), a surprisingly sophisticated little restaurant in the heart of town. The menu features delicious dishes like ham and spinach in puff pastry, risotto with lemon, or turbot with artichokes, all accompanied by piano music in the evening.

## Lavarone

Freud stayed at the ★★★**Hotel du Lac** in Frazione Chiesa, © 783112 (moderate). An indoor swimming pool and tennis courts in addition to its pretty setting on the lake make it a fine place to forget your favourite neurosis.

In the 16th century Emperor Charles V, haughty ruler of much of Europe, found his Germanic possessions in the throes of the Reformation, and his Catholic domains bracing for a hysterical reaction. A staunch Catholic himself, Charles sought to heal the rift in his realm by muscling the pope into calling a Council of the Church to look into some urgently needed counter-reforms.

When the pope finally agreed in 1536, another nine years passed while the two quibbled about venue—Charles wanted it on Imperial turf, while the pope insisted on an Italian city. Trento, an Italian city ruled by a powerful bishop-prince, but part of the Holy Roman Empire, was found to be the perfect compromise. The **Council of Trent** (1545-63), the initiation of the Counter-Reformation, was too late to bring the Protestant strays back into the fold, though it played an important role in defining the future shape and ritual of the Catholic Church and the role of the bishops, and in educating parish priests.

Influential in bringing the Council to Trento was the city's greatest ruler, Bernardo Clesio, Bishop of Trento, Count of Tyrol, president of the secret council of the Spanish King Ferdinand, and later Supreme Chancellor to Ferdinand's grandson, Charles V. A great patron of the arts, he personally brought at least the tail end of the Renaissance to the city.

The Council put Trento on the map, but the city has much more to offer than memories of the Counter-Reformation. Lying at the foot of Monte Bondone, between the banks of the Adige and the Fersina, it is refreshingly unpretentious and charming; many of its gently winding streets are embellished with colourful al fresco frescoes, and the former palace of its bishop is adorned with a cycle of medieval frescoes that alone is worth the trip.

### Getting Around

The **bus** and FS **railway** station are almost next to each other on the Piazza Dante. For FS rail information, ✆ (0461) 234545; for bus information, ✆ (0461) 983627. For the Trento-Malè station, with trains up the Val di Non to Cles, turn left out of the main station, and walk 500m to Via Seconda da Trento 7, ✆ (0461) 822725. From March to November the city lends bikes, for free: go to Piazza Mostra, in front of Castello del Buonconsiglio, and leave your passport as a deposit. (*Open 8am–7.30pm.*)

### Tourist Information

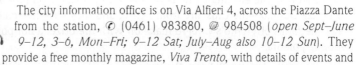

The city information office is on Via Alfieri 4, across the Piazza Dante from the station, ✆ (0461) 983880, @ 984508 (*open Sept–June 9–12, 3–6, Mon–Fri; 9–12 Sat; July–Aug also 10–12 Sun*). They provide a free monthly magazine, *Viva Trento*, with details of events and entertainments in the city. Regular exhibitions are held at the **Museo d'Arte Moderna**. Also, every year since 1952 Trento has staged the **International Alpine Film Festival**, in May or June; for information ✆ (0461) 238178, or @ 237832.

## To the Duomo

Trento's points of interest are easily seen on foot. The statues of the great poet and other celebrated Italians in the **Piazza Dante**, amid the public gardens in front of the station, were erected in 1896 by Trento's irredentist societies in defiance of their Austrian rulers. Next to the station itself, the attractive 12th-century collegiate church of **San Lorenzo** stands in a sunken lawn.

From San Lorenzo, Via Andrea Pozzo and Via D. Orfane lead to the gracious pink **Santa Maria Maggiore**, a simple and elegant Renaissance temple with ornate portals and a beautiful organ gallery from 1534. Beyond this, streets open into **Piazza Duomo**, Trento's loveliest square, lorded over by an 18th-century **fountain of Neptune** with his trident, recalling the city's Roman name, *Tridentum*. The 16th-century exterior-frescoed **Palazzo Cazuffi** stands on one side facing the **Duomo**, an austere marble temple designed in the 13th century and completed in 1515. Although it took 300 years to build, the style is all plain Romanesque, its extrovert galleries along its three apses its only flourish. But it sounds good—the campanile has one of the most melodious bells in Italy. The Council of Trent held its three major sessions in the stately interior of the Duomo, and its decrees were given divine blessing before the huge crucifix still to be seen in a right-hand chapel. The baldacchino over the altar is a replica of the one in St Peter's. Excavations in 1977 unearthed a 6th-century basilica under the cathedral, the original home of the relics of Trento's patron, San Virgilio.

## The Ciusi-Gobj Masquerade

 Virgilius (or Fergal) was an 8th-century Irish saint *en route* to Palestine when he met St Rupert, the Apostle of Austria, and decided to lend him a hand in the southern Alps. His intellect was held in awe by the Italian monks of the day, and he alarmed Rome with his 'outlandish' ideas, especially his belief that the world was a sphere. He is celebrated every 20–26 June with an enthusiastic *Palio dell'Oca*, in which teams from each of the city's districts don 17th-century costumes and race down the Adige on rafts, trying to slip a ring over the neck of a papier-mâché goose suspended over the river. On the last day, the Ciusi-Gobj Masquerade commemorates a day back in the Middle Ages when Trento hired a group of workers from Feltre to reinforce the walls. Food supplies being low, Trento's bishop realized that the city could not afford to feed the workers and sent them home—only the Feltrese returned in the night to raid the stores. The ensuing battle is re-enacted in costume on June 26 in the Piazza Duomo—the Ciusi are from Feltre, and they have five chances to break the ranks of Trento's Gobj to make off with the prize: a hot pot of bubbling polenta.

Next to the cathedral, the **Palazzo Pretorio**, crowned with swallowtail battlements, and its tall medieval **Torre Civica** house the excellent **Museo Diocesano Tridentino** (*open 9–12, 2–6, Thur–Tues; closed Wed; adm*), containing items from the Duomo Treasures and churches throughout Trentino. There are paintings of the Council of Trent; also a local 16th-century portrayal of a *Mass of St Gregory*, its nonchalant congregation including a large band of pious skeletons; three pretty 12th-century ivory caskets made by Moslem craftsmen; and an unusual 12th-century enamelled reliquary case and four charming 15th-century wooden altarpieces from the church of San Zeno in the Val di Non, portraying three local martyrs in scenes observed by a man in an incongruous beaver hat. The museum's greatest treasure, however, waits in the last room: a cycle of six early 15th-century Flemish tapestries by Peter Van Aelst, masterpieces of woven portraiture and detail, purchased and brought to Trento by Bernardo Clesio.

From the Piazza Duomo, be sure to stroll down Via Belenzani, with its fine Renaissance palaces. The best, the **Palazzo Geremia**, was one of the first built in Trento, and is embellished with 16th-century frescoes of the Wheel of Fortune and the local citizens receiving the Emperor Maximilian.

## Castello di Buonconsiglio

From Via Belenzani, Via Roma/Via Gian Antonio Manci leads to the residence of Trento's mighty bishop-princes, the **Castello di Buonconsiglio** (*open 9–12, 2–5, Tues–Sun; adm*). Because of its importance on the main highway between Germany and Italy, the German Emperors in the Middle Ages sought to keep the city under control by granting Trento's bishops a near-regal temporal status that they retained until the arrival of Napoleon. The castle actually consists of two buildings—the 13th-century Castelvecchio and the 1530 Magno Palazzo, built by bishop Clesio. The Palazzo houses the provincial museum of art.

The tour of the castle includes a number of richly frescoed rooms. One, with mythological figures on the ceiling, was touched up to conform to Counter-Reformation modesty levels— some of the gods wear turn-of-the-century bathing costumes, and the goddesses look like Tarzan's Jane. The great mirrors in the Sala degli Specchi were added in the 18th century to replace the Flemish tapestries now in the cathedral museum. The best art of the castle is reserved for last: the ravishing, colourful and detailed **Frescoes of the Months** in the Castelvecchio's Torre dell'Aquila, painted by an anonymous artist around the year 1400. While the nobles sport and flirt in the foreground, peasants perform their month-by-month labours, tending their flocks, making cheese, planting and harvesting their fields, and making wine. In one scene is the oldest-known depiction of Trento, dominated by the castle itself.

On a more solemn note, the Castel di Buonconsiglio was the sight of the imprisonment, trial, and execution in 1916 of the Italian patriot Cesare Battisti and his two companions, executed by the Austrians for high treason. Their cells, the courtroom where they were tried, and the ditch where they were shot may be seen; his prominent memorial, a marble circle of columns, stands on the hill of Doss Trento west of town.

## Around Trento: Monte Bondone

The slopes of Trento's mountain neighbour, Monte Bondone, can be easily reached by cable car (or mountain road), departing from the Ponte di San Lorenzo in Trento (behind the bus station) and climbing as far as **Sardagna**. The cable car runs 7am-9pm Mon–Sat; 9am-6pm Sun, and costs L1000. From Sardagna there are fine views over Trento. At least three buses a day continue from here up to **Vaneze** and **Vason**, Monte Bondone's ski resorts; from Vason a cable car ascends to one of Bondone's three summits (2098m).

Further along the road towards Riva del Garda, **Viotte** is the site of a nature reserve, an alpine refuge, and, near the latter, a **Botanical Garden** (*open May–Oct*), founded in 1938 on the banks of two artificial lakes, and planted with over two thousand species of high-altitude flora from around the world.

---

*Trento ℂ (0461–)*

### Where to Stay

### expensive

Trento isn't as well endowed with accommodation as the mountain resorts in its province, and one may wonder where all the bishops attending the Council of Trent put up for nine years. Some are said to have slept at the predecessor of the ★★★★**Albergo Accademia**, near Santa Maria Maggiore at Vicolo Collico 4/6, ℂ 233600, ℮ 230174. Two other buildings have since been added to form the modern hotel. The panelled rooms are comfortable and air-conditioned, and you can pick up German-language TV in every room.

### moderate

The ★★★**Aquila d'Oro**, Via Belenzani 76, ℂ/℮ 986282, is right in the centre and has extremely comfortable rooms, as well as café tables spilling out into the street. If you have a car, one of the nicest places to stay is the ★★★**Villa Madruzzo**, 3km east of Trento in Cognola, Via Ponte Alto 26, ℂ 986220, ℮ 986361. In a charming 19th-century villa located in a leafy park, it has modern, comfortable rooms.

### inexpensive

The ★**Venezia**, Piazza Duomo 45, ℂ/℮ 234144, has small, basic rooms, with and without baths. Ask for one overlooking the Duomo and fountain of Neptune.

---

*Trento ℂ (0461–)*

### Eating Out

Trentino cuisine is basically alpine: popular dishes include *canederli*, a kind of gnocchi made with salami and parsley; *patao*, a minestrone of yellow flour and sauerkraut, and *osei scampadi*, veal birds cooked with sage. Accompany them with some of the Trentino's excellent white wines.

### expensive

Trento's most celebrated restaurant, the **Chiesa**, Via Marchetti 9, ℂ 238766, is located in an elegant 17th-century palazzo near the Castello di Buonconsiglio. It's famous for its 'Apple Party Menu' in which Trentino's delicious apples appear in every dish; other choices include smoked trout and a tempting cheese strudel, or even a 1500s menu based on the preferred dishes of Bernardo Clesio, accompanied by an extensive wine list and scrumptious desserts. Reservations are always necessary. (*Closed Sun, Tues eves, mid-July–mid-Aug.*)

### moderate

In the centre of town is **Roma**, Via Simonino 6, ℂ 984150, which offers gnocchi with ricotta and truffles, or polenta with local cheeses and mushrooms. (*Closed Sun,*

*Aug.*) More expensive is **Orso Grigio**, Via degli Orti 19, ✆ 984400, with a meaty menu featuring goose liver, lamb chops, and venison. If you dare venture over the river, you can join the locals at the **Trattoria Piedicastello**, Piazza Piedicastello 11, ✆ 230730, for simple dishes such as *minestrone alla trentina*, broth, and tripe. (*Closed Sun, Aug.*)

### inexpensive

The popular **Ristorante-Pizzeria Forst**, located in the middle of Trento in the 16th-century palace on Oss Mazzurana 38, ✆ 235590, is the place to drink beer and Trentino's wines, eat a pizza *tirolese* (with mushrooms and *speck*) or a *piatta trentino* (a mixture of local specialities). The **Taverna-Enoteca Al Tino**, Via S. Trinità 10, ✆ 23987, on the east side of the Duomo near Piazza Vittoria, has good pizza amid a jolly atmosphere and traditional wine casks.

## East of Trento

### Tourist Information

The tourist office for the Levico and Vetriolo Terme area is in **Levico**, at Viale Dante Alighieri 6, ✆ (0461) 706101, @ 706004. Further north there are offices in **San Martino di Castrozza**, ✆ (0439) 768867, @ 768814; **Falcade**, Piazza Municipio 1, ✆ (0437) 599241, @ 599242; **Fiera di Primiero**, ✆ (0439) 62407, @ 62992; **Predazzo**, ✆ (0462) 501237, @ 502093; **Cavalese**, ✆ (0462) 41111, @ 20649; and **Canazei** in the Val di Fassa, ✆ (0462) 62466, @ 62278.

## The Val Sugana

The Val Sugana follows the course of the Brenta, and is mainly visited for its two lakes, Caldonazzo and Levico. **Pergine**, a few kilometres before the **Lago di Caldonazzo**, is the most interesting town in the valley, with its ruined castle and medieval streets. Below it, **San Cristoforo** is the main resort on the lake. From **Vetriolo Terme** you can hike up to the summit of Panarotta for splendid views of Caldonazzo, the adjacent **Lake Levico**, and its resort of **Levico Terme**. Both lakes are excellent for sailing and windsurfing.

Further downriver, the old town of **Borgo Valsugana** lies beneath the well-preserved 14th-century **Castel Telvana**. There are pretty views from the Val di Sella above Borgo; from nearby **Castello Tesino** a winding little road leads to San Martino (75km). Alternatively, continue on the SS47 for another 18km until Primolano, where the main SS50b turns off northwards for Feltre or San Martino.

## Pale di San Martino

The stunning, pinnacle-crowned Pale di San Martino (3191m) is the principal mountain group of the southern Dolomites, and **San Martino di Castrozza**, dramatically lying at its foot, is the biggest winter resort south of Cortina d'Ampezzo (complete with helicopters up to the more difficult slopes, skating, and a bobsled run). If the Beautiful People and international scene at Cortina make your flesh crawl, it's an excellent alternative. Like Cortina, the village is of recent construction—the Austrians demolished the medieval town in the First World War, leaving only the ancient church.

San Martino also makes a superb base for summer climbing and walking. Among the most popular excursions (be sure to pick up the map with its itineraries at the tourist office) is the ascent by cable car and chairlift to the summit of **Rosetta**. On the whole, however, the Pale is a mountain group reserved for experienced climbers. If you're not among them, the less demanding walks in the area include the path up Monte Cavallazza, facing the Pale (3hrs); or, closer at hand, to the Col Fosco or, more ambitiously, to Paneveggio.

## Paneveggio National Park

Much of the breathtaking scenery around San Martino lies within the **Parco Naturale Paneveggio–Pale di San Martino**, a wilderness of venerable woods, emerald meadows, rushing streams, wildflowers, and wildlife that is

*Cascate di Nardis*

altogether one of the most enchanting corners in Italy. Access to the park is from the visitors' centre (from San Martino, it's just a few kilometres north along the SS50 beyond the **Passo di Rolle**), in the village of **Paneveggio**, where there's a little natural history museum. There are two splendid paths that take in awesome vistas, including not only the Pale di San Martino, but also the distinctive peaks of Marmolada, Pelmo, and Civetta. In past centuries the forests here provided Venice with the timber for its fleet and Stradivarius and his colleagues from Cremona with the resonant wood for their fiddles; Venetians not only replanted trees a certain distance apart, to make sure the trunks were tall and straight for masts, but punished tree poachers with death. Rules are still strict: there are only a few campsites and no one may stay more than 24 hours.

The Pale di San Martino is encircled by a grandly scenic road. The northern part of the route (SS346 and SS203) on the way to Agordo (see p.446 above, 'The Eastern Dolomites: the Cadore') passes through the villages of **Canale d'Agordo** and **Falcade**, the latter a ski resort. The southern route, also via Agordo (SS347), passes first through **Frassene**, a summer resort, then climbs through the forests of Gosaldo to the **Passo di Cereda** and the resort of **Fiera di Primiero**, which like Cortina stands at the crossing of two valleys, the Cismon and the Canali. There's good skiing in the winter here, and in the summer a popular outing is the hour's walk from Fiera to the sinister ruined **Castel di Pietra**, precariously balancing on a jagged rock—according to legend, it was built by Attila the Hun. Two attractive traditional Alpine villages in this area are **Mezzano** and **Tonadico**.

## Val di Fiemme and Val di Fassa

The whole of the area to the north of Paneveggio, taking in the magnificent scenery dominated by the western slopes of the mighty Marmolada group, is known as the Val di Fassa. If you're approaching it from San Martino, you can join the main route north at Predazzo. If you're coming from Trento, an alternative road to the main A22/SS12 turns north a little to the east of the city at Civezzano and follows the river Avisio and the Val di Cembra, passing through a region of rocks eroded into spiky 'pyramids' near **Segonzano**. It then enters the **Val di Fiemme**, near its chief town, **Cavalese**.

For many years, thanks to the bishops of Trento, the Val di Fiemme was virtually independent, ruled by its own *Regolani* who held their parliament in the park of the Pieve (parish church); you can still see their circle of stone benches, the **Banco de la Reson**. The *Magnifica Comunità* of Cavalese still has considerable say in local affairs, running the Val di Fiemme from the grand **Palazzo della Comunità**, the former bishops' palace, its façade adorned with fine frescoes. Local rule had its disadvantages for some: in nearby **Doss delle Strie**, 11 witches were burnt alive in 1505. A cable car from Cavalese ascends to **Mt Cermis** (2229m).

The lake-spangled mountains between Cermis and the Val Sugana, the **Catena dei Lagorai**, are for the most part accessible only by foot, and are one of the least developed areas in the Dolomites. **Tesero**, just east of Cavalese, is a charming traditional village; its old church of San Rocco is frescoed with the 'Sunday Christ', surrounded by the tools forbidden on the Sabbath; at Panchià up the road there's a pretty covered bridge spanning the Avisio. Both have good downhill ski runs.

North of Predazzo the SS48 enters the **Val di Fassa**, where the seven *comuni* preserve their Ladin dialects. The main base for exploring the magnificent peaks in the area—Marmolada, Sassolungo, and Sella—is the town of **Canazei**, rebuilt after 1912, when another fire destroyed the town. Here you can pick up literature on the numerous trails, cable cars, and alpine refuges in the area; C. Artoni's *200 Itinerari in Val di Fassa* is a good bet for serious exploration. In nearby **Campitello** the parish church has a curious 15th-century fresco on the subject of Sabbath-breaking; were the mountaineers of old inveterate workaholics or merely avoiding the collection plate?

**Vigo di Fassa** is the centre of Ladin culture in the valley, where you can see *tabià*—the traditional log cabins of the Ladini, and learn more about them at the **Museo Ladino di Fassa**, spread out among several *tabià* at San Giovanni di Vigo di Fassa. From San Giovanni it's a 20-minute walk to the Gothic church of **Santa Giuliana a Vigo**, with fine quattrocento frescoes and a carved and gilded triptych by Giorgio Arzt of Bolzano (1517). From Vigo there's a cable car up to the Catinaccio group to the west, from where you can walk up to the peculiar sheer triple pinnacle, the **Torri del Vaiolet**. **Moena**, another modern community, is the largest town in the valley and an important winter sports centre.

In July and August, most rooms will have been booked months in advance. Out of season, however, prices drop considerably, and bargaining is also possible.

### expensive

San Martino's most luxurious hotel is the ★★★★**Hotel Savoia**, ✆ (0439) 68327, which has comfortable rooms equipped with all modern facilities.

### moderate

The ★★★**San Martino**, ✆ (0439) 68011, has an indoor pool, tennis courts, and sauna. Astride the Passo di Rolle north of San Martino, ★★★**Venezia**, Via Statale, ✆ (0439) 68315, has fantastic views stretching across the valley, which makes a good base for getting quickly into the National Park.

In Cavalese one of the nicest hotels has the funniest name, ★★★**Trunka Lunka**, Via Degasperi 4, ✆ (0462) 30233. It has only 21 rooms, and a sauna and solarium. Another hotel in Cavalese, the ★★★**San Valier**, ✆ (0462) 31285, is in a pretty setting and has an indoor pool and sauna. Up on the top of Mt Cermis above Cavalese ★★★**Sporting**, ✆ (0462) 31441, also has a pool and sauna to go with its magnificent views.

In Canazei the ★★★**Bellevue**, ✆ (0462) 61104, has great mountain views and pleasant rooms. Alternatively, try ★★★**Il Caminetto**, ✆ (0462) 61231, ✉ 61527. Both are open all year.

### inexpensive

Five minutes walk up the hill behind San Martino brings you to the ★★**Suisse**, Via Dolomiti 1, ✆ (0439) 68087, a simple but comfortable bed and breakfast, with rooms with or without bath. There are several cheaper hotels in Moena and Predazzo; in the latter, ★**Cimon**, ✆ (0462) 501691, is central, and has a garden.

---

## Eating Out

### expensive

In Moena, the **Malgo Panna**, Via Costalunga 29, ✆ (0462) 573489, offers a variety of menus, stretching from polenta with a selection of local cheeses and cold meats, to the *menu degustazione* of trout, rabbit, *tortelli ai porcini*, speck, venison, and strawberries. (*Closed Mon.*)

### moderate

In San Martino, the **Ristorante Malga Ces**, ✆ (0439) 68145, offers local specialities such as *canederli* or Tyrolean gnocchi, polenta with venison, local village cheeses and fruits of the forest.

*Tourist Information*

There are several tourist offices around the Brenta in **Fai della Paganella**, ℭ (0461) 583130, ℰ 583410; **Molveno**, ℭ (0461) 586924, ℰ 586221; **Pinzolo**, ℭ (0465) 51007; **Madonna di Campiglio**, ℭ (0465) 42000, ℰ 40404; **Folgarida**, ℭ (0464) 721133, ℰ 720250; and **Malé**, ℭ (0463) 901280, ℰ 901563.

## Around Monte Paganella

The Brenta Group, though a bit distant from the other Dolomites, is just as marvellous and strange, and a challenge for experienced alpinists, though there are a number of less demanding walks for non-alpinists as well. Even if you don't have time to plunge into the heart of the Brenta Dolomites, it's easy to visit the eastern flank of the mountains from Trento, first heading north via **San Michele all'Adige**, which has a museum of local handicrafts and costume, and **Mezzocorona**, the land of the 'prince of Trentino wines', Teròldego, as well as spumante.

From the crossroads at Mezzolombardo, the scenic local road climbs to three well equipped summer/winter resorts, served by four buses a day from Trento: **Fai della Paganella**, **Andalo** (both with cable cars to the summit of Monte Paganella—2125m) and **Molveno**, near the pretty Lago di Molveno, and a good base for hiking. From Molveno the road continues south to Ponte Arche, passing Fiavé, site of a 5000-year-old settlement of lake dwellers. East of Ponte Arche is pretty **Lake Toblino** with its castle (which now houses an excellent restaurant).

## The Giudicarie

The Valley of Giudicarie runs from Molveno down to the Lago d'Idro, near Brescia (*see* p.311). Along the way it passes San Lorenzo in Banale, where a track north up the **Val d'Ambiez** provides a quick route for hikers to approach the highest peaks of the Brenta group. Further on, the lovely castle at **Stenico** retains some faded but good Renaissance frescoes (*guided tours, daily except Mon 9–12 and 2–5.30; Jan–March 9 12 and 2–5; adm*). From Stenico, the road along the north bank of the river leads to the narrow Val d'Algone, with a waterfall near Airone, and another track into the mountains.

Trentino's most ruggedly stark scenery lies to the south, along the upper reaches of the River Chiese in the **Val di Daone** up to the artificial lakes of Maga Boazzo and Malga Bissina. These lie at the foot of lofty Mount Fumo (3418m), in the Adamello group. The other principal river runing through the Giudicarie is the Sarca, which feeds Lake Garda. North of **Tione**, the valley capital, the main road follows the sarca up to **Pinzolo**, an attractive town where the exterior of the parish church of San Virgilio (in the cemetery, at the northern end of town) was frescoed by the itinerant Lombard artist Simone Baschenis in 1539, portraying a vividly eerie medieval-style *Dance of Death*. Placid, business-like skeletons conduct princes, popes, soldiers and everyone else to their end, with a couplet of elegant poetry for each. More of Baschenis' precise, luminous work can be seen inside the church.

Pinzolo is a good base for exploring the glacier-clad Brenta and Adamello mountains, with their scores of lakes, as well as the lovely **Val di Genova**, part of the **Parco Naturale Adamello-Brenta**, one of the last Alpine refuges of the brown bear. The mouth of the Val di Genova is graced by the lofty **Cascate di Nardis**, a woodland waterfall flowing from the glacier on **Presanella** (3254m)—in Pinzolo you can find a guide to make the ascent. before the waterfall, the chapel of **Santo Stefano** at Carisolo has more frescoes by Simone Baschenis. To the east a chair-lift (the world's fastest, they claim) rises to the lower slopes of **Cima Tosa**, the highest peak of the Brenta Dolomites.

## Madonna di Campiglio

From Pinzolo the SS289 zigzags up to the most important resort in the Brenta Dolomites, Madonna di Campiglio, with extensive winter sports facilities that include a ski-jump, 31 lifts, speed-skating, a regular skating rink, and an indoor pool; in the summer it offers experienced climbers the chance to try their mettle on ice and a wild, rocky terrain; for inexperienced walkers it has the most scenic trails in the group. Even if you only have enough spunk to get into a chairlift and a funicular you can enjoy the marvellous views from the **Passo del Grostè**, some 2260m above Campiglio to the east, or from **Pradalago** (cable car) to the west. Get the tourist office's footpath map to take Campiglio's classic walk, through the beautiful Val di Brenta and Valsinella just to the south. A more difficult path, the fabulous **Via Bocchette**, takes in some of the region's most bizarre naked pinnacles and fantastic cliffs, but should only be attempted with proper equipment.

North of Campiglio the road passes through Passo Campo Carlo Magno, named after Charlemagne who supposedly stopped here on his way to Rome to receive the Emperor's crown. **Folgarida**, beyond the pass, is another well-endowed winter resort.

## Val di Sole

Occupying the upper reaches of the Noce river and the Trentino sector of the Stelvio National Park (*see* **Lombardy and the Lakes**, p.217), Italy's 'Sun Valley' is a cosy region of soft green meadows and villages, with the lofty peaks of Monte Cevedale as a backdrop; many valley churches have charming exterior frescoes, especially an Annunciation at Pellizzno and a St Christopher at Peio. The scenic roads up the **Val di Peio** and **Val di Rabbi** lead into the Stelvio; there is a park **visitors' centre** in Bagni di Rabbi, open all year.

**Malè**, the capital of the Val di Sole, is the site of an ethnographical museum, the **Museo della Civiltà Solandra**, with handicrafts and agricultural and domestic implements; these days, the town is an important woodworking centre, and has good skiing in the winter.

## Val di Non

The wooded Val di Non, the enchanting valley along the lower course of the River Noce, produces some of Italy's finest apples, especially Golden Delicious and 'Renetta del Canada', which look more like potatoes. The valley is especially lovely in the spring, when its apple blossoms, emerald meadows, and snow-clad mountains glow with colour.

**Cles**, the main town of the Val di Non (linked by local train to Trento), stands on the large artificial lake of Santa Giustina. It is the home town of Trento's great bishop Bernardo Clesio, who was born in the **Castello Cles**, the best of a score of castles in the valley. Cles has several Renaissance buildings, but the most attractive and unusual is across the lake at Sanzeno, the **Santuario di San Romedio**, a popular pilgrimage shrine on the cliff where the legendary hermit Romedio lived with his pet bear, as a kind of alpine St Jerome. Over the centuries, chapels in different styles were stacked down the rock—the end result lies somewhere between a dolls' house and a monastery. Don't miss the 11th-century barbaric reliefs on the portal or the disarming home-made ex-votos, or the ghastly souvenir shop.

South of Cles, a 15km road leads to one of the prettiest of alpine lakes, **Lago di Tovel**, lying deep in the folds of the Brenta Dolomites. Unlike other mountain lakes, famed for their sapphire hue, Tovel is famous for its ruby redness at certain periods, when a rare algae, *Glendodinium sanguineum* covers its surface. Nowadays you'll be lucky to see much red at all—this is perhaps the only case in the world where one regrets to say that pollution has made the water turn blue. From Lake Santa Giustina you can head east to Bolzano, through the **Passo Mendola**, or continue down the Val di Non past its orchards and old castles at **Taio** and **Vigo**. **Sfruz**, a small town above the valley, is a fine cross-country skiing centre and base for walks. The road continues south to Trento via San Michele all'Adige.

---

*Where to Stay*

## Molveno

In Molveno the most comfortable hotel is the ★★★**Belvedere**, Via Nazionale 9, ✆(0461) 586933, ✆ 586044 (expensive), which has fine rooms, overlooking the lake, with an indoor pool and solarium. An older hotel, the ★★★**Molveno**, Via Betega 16, ✆ (0461) 586934 (expensive), offers tennis and an outdoor pool among its amenities.

## Pinzolo

In Pinzolo, the ★★★**Centro Pineta**, Via Matteotti 43, ✆ (0465) 52758 (moderate) is a pleasant, medium-sized hotel, warm in the winter and cool in the summer, and pine-scented year-round.

## Madonna di Campiglio

Madonna di Campiglio is the one resort in the Brenta Dolomites with accommodation and facilities to please the most demanding customers, and prices tend to be correspondingly high. You can shoot long Alpine drives at the course of the ★★★★**Golf Hotel**, up at the Passo Carlo Magno, ✆ (0465) 41003, ✆ 40294 (very expensive). A former summer residence of the Habsburgs, the hotel is open in winter for skiers as well. In Madonna di Campiglio itself the ★★★★**Relais Club des Alpes**, Via Monte Spinale, ✆ (0465) 40000, ✆ 40186 (very expensive) is large and well furnished, with a large indoor pool; each of the airy rooms has air-conditioning and TV. Good value is the ★★★**Palù**, Via Valle Sinella 4, ✆ (0465) 41280, ✆ 43183, (moderate), a small, older hotel with comfortable air-conditioned rooms, all with TV. The resort has many self-catering flats; contact the local Associazione Albergatori, ✆ (0465) 42660.

### Lake Tovel

There are two little hotels by Lake Tovel, above the Val di Non, the **★Albergo Lago Rosso**, ✆ (0463) 31242 (inexpensive), and **★Miralago**, ✆ (0463) 40090 (inexpensive). Both have rooms without baths, and are open in summer only.

### Cles

Cles has a fine resort hotel in its **★★★Punta Verde**, Via S. Vito 20, ✆ (0463) 21275, ✉ 24358 (moderate), open all year, with tennis, indoor pool, and sauna. All rooms have private baths.

---

*Eating Out*

### San Michele all'Adige

You can dine well at **Da Silvio**, Via Brennero 2, ✆ (0461) 650324 (expensive). Ultra-modern in décor, serving imaginative dishes, Silvio's has a delicious speciality called the *Altamira*, a selection of mixed meats grilled at your table, with your choice of sauces.

### Pinzolo

Near Pinzolo, at Le Pozze 8, the little **Prima o Poi**, ✆ (0465) 57175 (moderate) is the most charming restaurant in the region, and serves such delicacies as a paté made with trout, homemade pasta and gnocchi, and mushroom dishes. (*Closed Wed, June.*)

### Val di Sole

In the Val di Sole, near the entrance of the Val di Peio at Comasine, you can dine well in a charming 15th-century mill, **Il Molino**, ✆ (0463) 74244 (moderate). The spacious interior has been attractively converted into a multi-level dining room, where such mountain specialities as goat with wild apples, trout, and venison are excellently prepared. (*Closed Tues, Oct.*)

## Alto Adige/Süd Tirol

Everything has two names on the sunny side of the Alps, in the bilingual province of Bolzano/Bozen, otherwise known as the Alto Adige/Süd Tirol. And yet ethnically the inhabitants are neither German nor Italian, but Ladin, who spent most of their history ruled by the bishop of Brixen/Bressanone and the counts of Tyrol, based near Merano/Meran. After the abdication of the 'Ugly Duchess', Margaret of Tyrol, in 1363, the whole region passed at least nominally to the Habsburgs. German influence was thus stronger here than in Trentino, and when Napoleon put the Süd Tirol under Austrian control it had no objection—unlike Trentino, which chafed and yearned to join Venetia.

After the First World War Italy gained Trentino, and in the 1920s absorbed the lands up to the Brenner Pass as the natural frontier. Mussolini, a dedicated cultural imperialist, immediately invented Italian names for all the towns and tried to stick the Italian language down the inhabitants' throats, until Hitler told him to lay off. It was hardly an auspicious beginning, and if the Trentini, led by Cesare Battisti, had defied the Austrians, the people of Süd Tirol, with their majority pro-Austrian party (the PPST) tend to be among the most disaffected Italians; if it weren't for the Italian vote from the southern half of the autonomous region of Trentino-Alto Adige, separatism would be a serious problem. As far as language goes, the figures are presently 69% German-speaking, 27% Italian, and 4% Ladin. Occasionally the more vicious malcontents show their resentment by sabotaging the train tracks. Yet the central Italian government, for its part, has done much to mollify the region, granting it a great deal of autonomy and enough economic perks to make it one of the country's wealthiest areas.

Its position at one of the great historical crossroads between north and south, its brilliant Alpine scenery, its winter sports (Bolzano traditionally produces Italy's finest skiiers), and renowned climatic spa at Merano made the Süd Tirol a tourist destination long before the other Dolomite provinces. The region also produces some of Italy's best wine, especially whites, and lots of it—there are some 40 vines for every inhabitant. The most reliable labels are Herrnhofer, Bellendorf, Kehlburg, von Elzenbaum and Hofstatter; good whites to try are the light and smooth Riesling Renano, dry and snappy Gewürtztraminer, Weissburgunder (Pinot Bianco), Welschriesling (known elsewhere as Riesling Italico), Sylvaner (with a dry, delicate perfume) and Muller-Thurgau (light and fruity).

## Bolzano/Bozen

The lively, cultured capital of Alto Adige, Bolzano is an excellent base for visiting the mountains that rise on either side. Located on the banks of the Isarco/Eisack and the Talvera/Talfer, which merge just downstream to form the Adige, Bolzano was an important market town in the Middle Ages, a tradition it remembers in its busy food market today. With its high, narrow gabled houses and arcaded streets it looks the part of a piece of Austria that got away. In the summer, however, you may want to base yourself somewhere higher in the mountains; the humidity in the valley turns Bolzano into a sauna.

### Getting Around

 **Trains** for Trento, Bressanone, Vipiteno, Brenner and Innsbruck, to the north; Merano and Malles/Venosta, to the north-west; and for Brunico, Dobbiaco, and Lienz to the east, all depart from the FS station, a short distance from the central Piazza Walther down the Via Stazione (information ✆ (0471) 974292). The **bus station** is across the street on Via Garibaldi, ✆ (0471) 971259. From here you can pick up a bus to Cortina and to nearly every town in the Alto Adige.

The main **road** from Bolzano apart from the A22/SS12 is the SS38, which runs northwest towards Merano and the Val Venosta. At the end of the valley it connects with the road to Bormio and the Valtellina, or you can continue into Austria.

The office for the city of **Bolzano** is at Piazza Walther 8, ℂ (0471) 970660, ✆ 980128 (*open 8.30–6 Mon–Fri; 9–12.30 Sat*). They provide a free monthly calendar of events in the town. For the Alto Adige/Süd Tirol region and the mountains the office is at **Piazza Parrochia** 11/12, ℂ (0471) 993808, ✆ 993899. The region also has a special Alpine information service, on ℂ (0471) 993809, and a winter traffic conditions information line on ℂ (0471) 993812, Another source of information on mountaineering, hiking and organised day-trips is the Club Alpino Italiano (CAI), Piazza dell'Erbe 46, ℂ (0471) 971694).

## Piazza Walther

Bolzano's cultural fusion manifests itself unexpectedly in the town's pretty parlour, **Piazza Walther-Platz**. In the centre there's a statue of Germany's greatest *minnesinger*, Walther von der Vogelweide, and at his feet slouch travellers from around the world munching on Big Macs from America's biggest chain, located just behind the great troubadour. In front of Walther stands Bolzano's Gothic **Duomo**, with a colourful roof and pretty tower. The art, however, is a block behind the cathedral, in the former **Dominican cloister** (*open 9am–6.30pm daily*), now the Music Conservatory, where the chapel of San Giovanni contains fine 14th-century frescoes by an admirer of Giotto.

From here Via Goethe/Goethestrasse leads up to the jovial **Piazza dell'Erbe**, Bolzano's commercial hub, where a fountain of Neptune watches over the daily fruit and vegetable market. To the right begins the city's main street, moody **Via Portici/Laubengastrasse**, lined with shops under its Tyrolean arcades, while behind Piazza dell'Erbe stands the **Church of the Francescani** with a pretty Gothic cloister, fresco fragments, and a beautiful 1500 altarpiece by woodcarver Hans Klocker. Near here too, on Via Museo/Museumstrasse, is Bolzano's **Museo Civico** (*open 9–12, 2.30–5.30, Tues–Sat; 10–1 Sun; adm*), with a small archaeological section, Gothic and Baroque art, and wood carvings and folk items. It stands near the bridge over the Talvera; to the right, in its own field, is the **Castel Mareccio**, with five stout towers and a 13th-century core, now used as a convention centre.

For a fine view of the castle and craggy mountains beyond Bolzano, cross the Talvera and stroll up its riverside park, the **Lungotalvera Bolzano**; bearing straight from the bridge, however, Corso Libertà/Freiheit Strasse leads to **Gries**, a suburb with two important churches—the imposing, Baroque **Abbey Church of the Benedettini** in the main piazza, and the old **parish church of Gries** (*open April–Oct 10–12, 2.30–4, Mon–Fri*), with a beautifully carved 15th-century wooden altar by Michael Pacher. Bus no.10 travels back from here to the centre.

## Walks around Bolzano

There are two fine walks you can take for views over Bolzano. Beyond the Gries parish church, at the end of Via Knoller/Knollerstrasse, begins the 1½km **Passeggiata del Guncina**, with an inn at the top for refreshments. A bit longer but more dramatic, the **Passeggiata Sant'Osvaldo** begins near the train station at Via Renico/Rentscherstrasse and descends by the head of the Lungotalvera promenade. Further up the river, the 1237 **Castel Roncolo/Schloss Runkelstein** (*open Mar–Nov 10–5* (*last entry 4pm*), *Tues–Sat*) guards the passage on its impregnable rock. Inside, there are fascinating 14th-century frescoes of chivalric knights.

There are three cable cars from Bolzano, but the most rewarding is that from Via Renon/Rittnerstrasse, near the station, which climbs 1221m up the slopes of Mt Renon/Rittner to **Soprabolzano/Oberbozen** (*cable car runs 7am–8pm daily*). The views of the Dolomites are splendid, but for a truly strange sight continue from here on the rack railway up to **Collabo/Klobenstein**, and from there follow the path to the **Longomoso Pyramids**—rocks eroded to form a dense forest of needles and bizarre stone drapery. More fine views of the Dolomites can be had from the San Genesio/Jenesien cable car, which departs from Via Sarentino (across the Talvera, and before the Castel Roncolo).

---

*Bolzano* ✆ *(0471–)*

### Where to Stay

#### very expensive

Bolzano is well equipped with hotels. The most lavish, the CIGA chain's ★★★★**Park Hotel Laurin**, Via 4 Laurino, ✆ 980500, ✉ 970953, is a lovely hotel built at the turn of the century in Viennese *Jugendstil*, and located in a fine old park and rose garden near the centre of Bolzano. It has a heated swimming pool, and the lounge and public areas are furnished with fine antiques clustered around black marble fireplaces. Rooms are large and very comfortable.

#### expensive

In Piazza Walther, the long-established ★★★★**Grifone-Greif**, ✆ 977056, ✉ 980613, may be in the very heart and soul of Bolzano, with a café giving on to the busy square, but in the back it has a fine swimming pool in a garden. The rooms are also very pleasant, and there's parking for your car. Downstairs is one of Bolzano's best restaurants, with outdoor tables in good weather.

#### moderate

For peace and quiet, the little 11-room ★★★**Eberle**, Passeggiata Sant'Osvaldo 1, ✆ 976125, offers guests a pool, tennis, sauna and gym, in addition to cosy rooms; there's also an excellent restaurant. Less luxurious, but on a lively shopping-street lined with frescoed buildings is ★★**Feichter**, Via Grappolo/Weintraubengrasse 15, ✆ 978768, which has pleasant rooms, some without bath.

#### inexpensive

The ★**Croce Bianca-Weisses Kreuz**, Piazza del Grano/Kornplatz 3, ✆ 977553, is cheerful and welcoming, with clean rooms; its lobby is a café that opens onto the pavement. If it's hot in Bolzano, take the Colle cable car (Italy's oldest) from the opposite bank of the Isarco (Bus no.11 or a short walk from the train station) up to the refreshing breezes of Colle/Kohlern, where there are two small but very pleasant hotels—★★**Kohlern**, Colle 11, ✆ (0471) 971428, with 14 rooms, or the ★**Klaus**, Colle 14, ✆ (0471) 971294, an old farmhouse with 10 rooms, some without bath.

## Eating Out

Like the language, the cuisine of Alto Adige/Süd Tirol is a bit more than half Germanic—instead of *prosciutto*, expect *speck* (smoked Tyrolean ham) on pizza. Other specialities are Wiener schnitzel, sauerkraut dishes, goulash, *knodel* (breadcrumb dumplings in a variety of styles), *Terlaner* (wine soup) with apple, cheese, and poppy-seed strudels, Sachertorte, and rich mousse for dessert.

### expensive

The restaurant in the Hotel Laurin (*see* above), the **Belle Epoque**, not only has elegant, turn-of-the-century décor, but also delicious, reasonably priced antipasti and fish dishes, and great desserts.

### moderate

Contemporary elegance and very good Italian food may be had at **Da Abramo** in Piazza Gries 16, ☎ (0471) 280141; the speciality is seafood, and among their offerings are a divine risotto, turbot with rosemary, and escalopes in a white pepper sauce. For a mixture of both Austrian and Italian cuisines, try **Heller Keller**, Erbsengasse 10, which may leave you confused or strangely satisfied: spaghetti, wurstel, and strudel. (*Closed Sun.*)

### inexpensive

The jovial Tyrolean **Cavallino Bianco/Weisses Rossel**, Via dei Bottai/Bindergasse 6, is extremely popular, with an eclectic menu stretching from ham and eggs to *Bolognerschnitzel*. **Zum Bogen Weinstrube**, Via Streiter/Streiterstrasse 31, is the place to eat cheap wurstel and goulash. (*Closed Sat evening, Sun, July.*)

## East of Bolzano: the Dolomites

Bolzano lies just to the west of the Süd Tirol's most spectacular Dolomite scenery. Scores of Alpine refuges, chairlifts and cable cars, and fast buses from Bolzano to towns and funicular stations in the valleys make access easy. Bolzano's tourist office has information on trails and refuges; for more detail, buy a copy of *I Rifugi Dell'Alto Adige*, by Willy Dondio.

### Tourist Information

There are tourist offices in the Val Gardena at **Ortisei/St Ulrich**, ☎(0471) 796328, ✆ 796749; **Santa Cristina**, ☎ (0471) 793046, ✆ 793198; **Selva di Val Gardena/Wölkenstein**, ☎ (0471) 795122, ✆ 794245; and **Corvara**, at Ciasa de Comun 198, ☎ (0471) 836176, ✆ 836540. On the Catinaccio road there is an office at **Nova Levante**, ☎ (0471) 613126, ✆ 613360.

## Val Gardena/Grödnertal

The most accessible and certainly one of the most beautiful excursions from Bolzano is to take the Brenner road north to the Ladin-speaking Val Gardena, lying between the Alpe di Siusi/Seiser Alm and the jagged Odle/Geislergruppe. The dominant feature of the **Alpe di**

**Siusi** is a magnificent plateau, noted for its skiing in winter and seemingly endless meadows of flowers in the late spring; there are numerous lifts up from the Val Gardena, or a road up from the resort town of **Siusi**. A classic, but not strenuous hike from Siusi is the 4-hour trek up **Monte Pez**, rewarded with remarkable views and an optional stay at one of the grand dames of 19th-century Alpine refuges, the **Rifugio Bolzano di Monte Pez**.

The SS242 turns off the main highway and enters the Val Gardena at **Ponte Gardena/Waidbruck**, in the shadow of the medieval **Trostburg Castle** (*guided tours Easter–Oct at 10, 11, 2, 3 and 4; closed Mon; adm*). The first and largest town in the valley, **Ortisei/St Ulrich**, and the next two villages in the valley, **Santa Cristina** and **Selva di Val Gardena/Wölkenstein** are all well-equipped resorts, with cable cars ascending the Alpe di Siusi. Santa Cristina has cable cars up into the Odle group on the north side of the valley and up to the foot of the most distinctive peak in the region, the spiralling, dream-like **Sassolungo/Langkofel** (3180m) to the south.

## The Woodcarvers of the Val Gardena

The most important town of the Val Gardena, **Ortisei/St Ulrich**, has specialized in wood carving for several centuries, and is now a good place to buy works ranging from the moving to the stomach-churning. It is said that farmers began carving to while away the long winter evenings, using a soft pine from the valley's slopes. By the 17th century, some farmers were neglecting their land to hike across the hillside, selling carved toys, ornaments, household furniture and implements. By 1820, 300 craftsmen were working in the valley, and a school was set up in 1872 to consolidate skills, and bring in foreign influence and trade.

Today there are more than 3000 wood-carvers up and down the Gardena. The tourist office issues a list of workshops that can be visited, and which sell to casual callers; the Chamber of Commerce of Bolzano issues a certificate with every piece of work, ensuring that it is entirely carved by hand. Ortisei's museum has a permanent exhibition of ancient and modern works, as does the local church, which has attracted a good number of donations over the years from artists grateful for their worldly success. In July and August the school of woodcarving holds weekly courses, each of nine lessons: contact the tourist office for details, and to book a place.

From the crossroads in Selva you have a choice of two spectacular routes, either over the fabulous **Passo di Sella** to Canazei in Trentino, where you can pick up the Great Dolomites Road (*see* below), or over the grand **Passo di Gardena** down into the **Val Badia** to the east, another beautiful valley that has retained its Ladin culture. **Corvara** and **La Villa/Stern** are its main resorts. To the north the SS244 through the valley leads to San Lorenzo, near Brunico, while to the south the road descends to Arabba.

## Catinaccio/Rosengarten

The other main group accessible from Bolzano, Catinaccio/Rosengarten, is among the most celebrated of all the Dolomites. Its name first appears in a 13th-century Tyrolean epic poem, describing how King Lauren of the Dwarves was made prisoner and dragged away from his mountain realm. Furiously Lauren put a curse on the roses that had betrayed him, that no one would ever see them again, neither by night nor by day. But he neglected to mention the dawn or the twilight, when the enchanted roses redden the stony face of Rosengarten.

From Bolzano, the road to Rosengarten (SS241) begins at Cardara/Kardaun, just east of town, and passes through the breathtaking narrow gorge of the **Val d'Ega/Eggental**. As the road nears the valley's main settlement and winter and summer resort, **Nova Levante/ Welschnofen**, the craggy peaks of the **Latemar** group loom up to the right, while the massive wall of Rosengarten rises to the left. You can reach the slopes of Rosengarten from Nova Levante or the Passo di Costalunga/Karer, near gorgeous Lake Carezza, up the road from Nova Levante. For an even more spectacular approach, continue along the SS241, which only becomes more magical the further you go, to **Pozza di Fassa** on the eastern slopes of Rosengarten.

## The Great Dolomites Road: Bolzano to Cortina d'Ampezzo

This stretch of road from Bolzano, the SS241 through the Val d'Ega to Rosengarten and Pozza, is the first leg of the fabled 110km *Strada delle Dolomiti*, or Great Dolomites Road. Buses from Bolzano or Cortina make the journey in summer three times a day, and you should take one—for who could bear to keep their eyes on these mountain roads and miss some of Europe's greatest scenery?

After Pozza the road, (now the SS48), continues up Trentino's Val di Fassa to the resort of Canazei, the best base for the ascent of the Dolomites's mightiest peak, the **Marmolada** (3342m). The road from Canazei climbs in zigzags, past the peculiar tower of **Sassolungo** and Sella glowering on the left, on its way to the **Passo Pordoi**, with fabulous views of Sella and Marmolada.

From the pass the road writhes down towards **Arabba**, a ski resort, and **Pieve di Livinallongo**, below the odd-shaped **Col di Lana**, its summit blown off by an Italian mine in the First World War. The road then climbs again, past the haunting, eroding **Castello d'Andraz**, (just after the settlement of Andraz) to the **Sasso di Stria** (Witch's Rock) and the tunnel at **Passo di Falzarego**.

From here the road begins the descent to Cortina, with views of the strange **Cinque Torri** (Five Towers) and nearly vertical slopes of Tofane, before reaching the top of the Boite valley, with beautiful views over Cortina (see p.448).

---

*©* (0471–)          *Where to Stay and Eating Out*

## Val Gardena

The Val Gardena is well equipped with excellent hostelries. In Ortisei, the ★★★★**Aquila-Adler**, Via Rezia 7, *©* 796203, *@* 796210 (very expensive) is the most glamorous hotel, located in a large garden, with an indoor pool and tennis courts, and cosy rooms. (*Open mid-Dec–mid-Mar, mid-May–Oct.*) Just outside Ortisei, ★★★**La Perla**, Via Digon 1, *©* 796421, *@* 798198 (expensive) is a year-round pleasure to visit, with its park and indoor pool. In the centre of Ortisei, **★★Ladinia**, Via Razia 174, ✆ 796281 (inexpensive) has pleasant, airy rooms. Rooms can also be hired in private houses along the valley: tourist offices have lists.

In the village of Ortisei, **Janon** (moderate) serves home-made tortelloni with local mushrooms, a selection of fried meats, and delicious desserts .

In Selva, the small but very comfortable **★★★★Alpenroyal**, Via Meisules 43, ✆ 75178, @ 794161 (expensive) is one of the few hotels in the area that are open all year, with plenty of facilities to keep its guests fit and happy—indoor pool, whirlpool baths, sauna, solarium, and fitness room.

In Santa Cristina, **★★★★Diamant**, at Sacun 17, ✆ 796780, @ 793580 (very expensive), has lovely mountain views, an indoor pool and sauna, and tennis courts, all in a quiet park. (*Open Easter–Oct.*) There are several hotels just outside Santa Cristina at Monte Pana, which open only for the summer and winter seasons: one that's pleasant is the **★★★Cendevaves**, Monte Pana 48, ✆ 796562, @ 793567 (moderate), which has an indoor pool and good views. Another choice that's convenient for the slopes, the **★★Freina**, Via Centro 403, ✆ 795110 (moderate) has 12 rooms with bath At least half-pension is required, but the food is excellent— stop here to eat if you're just passing through.

## Rosengarten

In Nova Levante the **★★★★Posta Cavallino Bianco/Weisses Roessel**, Strada Carezza 30, ✆ 613113, @ 613390 (expensive) is a fine resort hotel, with a name that recalls the former postal relay station, though its facilities—indoor and outdoor pools, tennis, and much more—are contemporary and very comfortable. (*Open mid-Dec–mid-Apr, mid-May–mid-Oct.*) Good value in Nova Levante, and open all year, is the **★★★Stella-Stern**, Strada Carezza 51, ✆ 613125 (moderate), with nice rooms, all with bath, an indoor pool and fitness room.

# North Towards the Brenner Pass

### Tourist Information

The largest office in this area is in **Bressanone/Brixen**, at Viale della Stazione 9, ✆ (0472) 36401, @ 36067. There are also offices at **Brunico/ Bruneck**, Via Europa 22, ✆ (0472) 555722, @ 555544; and **Vipiteno/ Sterzing**, Piazza Città 3, ✆ (0472) 765325, @ 765441.

## Val Isarco

North of Bolzano and Ponte Gardena lies the Val Isarco/Eisacktal, the main route to the Brenner Pass. On the way to Bressanone is the ancient town of **Chiusa/Klausen**, lying under its 17th-century monastery, and a base for visits to the quiet Val di Funès.

**Bressanone/Brixen** was the capital of the region for a millennium, ruled by a bishop continually at odds with the Counts of Tyrol. Now a popular resort under Monte Plose, the city is one of the most charming in the Alto Adige, with medieval buildings and arcaded streets. Its ancient **Duomo**, however, was metamorphosed into a dull Baroque church in the 18th century. Fortunately the remodellers neglected the Romanesque cloister, with its fine 14th-century frescoes. Even earlier frescoes decorate the cathedral's 11th century **Baptistry**. The cathedral treasure and a fine collection of *presepi* (carved Christmas cribs) may be seen in the Museo Diocesano in the **Hofburg** (*open Mar–Oct 10–5, Mon–Sat; Dec–Feb crib section open 2–5pm daily*). This former bishops' palace has an exquisite arcaded, three-storey courtyard.

Besides excursions on Mount Plose, Bressanone is a good base for visiting **Schloss Feldthurns** (*guided tours Mar–Nov at 10, 11, 2.30, 3.30, Tues–Sun; adm*), built for the local bishop in the 16th century in the hills to the southwest. Another short excursion from Bressanone is to the fortified **Convento di Novacella/Neustift** (*guided tours at 10, 11, 2, 3, 4, Mon–Fri; 10, 11 Sat; adm*), some 3km north of town, at the head of the Pusteria. Begun for the Augustine Order in 1142, the convent is a fascinating study in the evolution of architecture, with its 12th century tower, fine Baroque church, beautiful frescoed 14th-century cloister, and the strange, round 12th–16th century chapel of San Michele. Visitors can also see a small art gallery and the library with a collection of medieval manuscripts.

## The Pusteria

The Pusteria is the wide and pleasant valley running eastwards along the river Rienza towards Dobbiaco/Toblach. It is dotted with typical Tyrolean villages and castles, and many of its attractive little churches contain works by the valley's 15th-century master woodcarver Michael Pacher, most notably in the 13th-century parish church of **San Lorenzo di Sebato/St Lorenzen**. Prominent nearby is the convent of **Castel Badia/Sonnenburg**, now a hotel.

The capital of the Pusteria, **Brunico/Bruneck** is a pleasant town and transport hub of the region. From here you can head north into the heavily wooded **Val di Tures**, where **Campo Tures/Sand in Taufers** clustered under its medieval baronial castle is the main centre. Glacier alpinists come here for the **Vedrette Giganti**, reached from Riva di Tures (with a pretty waterfall), while extremists may carry on north of Campo up the Valle Aurina to **Casere** and 2km beyond to the hamlet of **Pratomagno**, the northernmost village in Italy.

East of Brunico, **Monguelfo/Welsberg** is a resort under a 12th-century castle; from here a road turns south into the Val di Braies/Prags. The **Lago di Braies**, fast in the Dolomites' embrace, is celebrated for its intense green colour. East of Monguelfo the road continues to Dobbiaco/Toblach (see p.450, 'Excursions from Cortina').

## The Upper Val Isarco to the Brenner

**Vipiteno/Sterzing**, the main town between Bressanone and the pass, formerly belonged to the great banking dynasty, the Fuggers. The attraction it held for them was its mines; although abandoned in the 18th century they were lucrative enough in renaissance times for their owners to build splendid battlemented houses. The end of the Corso is framed by the tall **Torre di Città**. The **Museo Multscher** (*open May–mid-Nov 10–12, 2–5, Mon–Sat*), in Piazza Città, is devoted to a handful of elegant works by the 15th-century painter Hans Multscher. To house pilgrims on their way to Rome, the Knights Templar built a **hospital** on the edge of Vipiteno in 1241, though most of what you see today dates from the 16th century. Excursions into the mountains around Vipiteno include the scenic **Val Ridanna** with skiing to the west, the tranquil **Val di Vizze** to the east, and through the **Val Passiria** and the **Passo di Giovo** towards Merano.

**Colle Isarco/Gossensass** is another summer/winter resort, with skiing and hiking on Cima Bianca and in the Val di Fleres. Beyond this lies the **Brenner Pass** (1375m), the lowest of Alpine passes, and the route of countless invaders from the north; during the Second World War it was heavily bombed. From here it is 125km to Innsbruck.

---

*Bressanone* ℭ *(0472–)*          **Where to Stay**

### very expensive

Bressanone is perhaps better known for a hotel than any of its sights, a venerable inn that recalls a day back in the year 1500 when the King of Portugal sent an Indian elephant to Emperor Maximilian as a gift for his zoological park. The elephant, on his way to his new home, spent a week in Bressanone's best hostelry. The locals were so impressed that they had his portrait done by the door of the inn for all to see, and there it remains to this day, on the front of the **★★★★Elefant**, Via Rio Bianco 4, ℭ 32750, ✆ 36579. Of the old Renaissance inn, only the fresco remains, but inside the ceilings and walls still have antique panelling, and there are beautiful tile stoves. Many of the lovely rooms are furnished with antiques, though no one remembers which one the elephant slept in. There's also a swimming pool and pleasure garden, as well as a dairy and vegetable garden that provides many of the fresh ingredients for the Tyrolean and international dishes served in the Elefant's fine restaurant. (*Closed Nov–Feb.*)

### moderate

A minute's walk from the centre of Bressanone, **★★★Chiavi d'Oro**, Via Torre Bianco 10, ℭ 22379, has full air-conditioning and central heating, depending on the season, along with TVs in every room and a small garden.

### inexpensive

Inside the old city walls of Bressanone are the **★★Goldene Traube**, Via Portici Minori/Kleine Lauben 9, ℭ 36552, and the **★Schwarzer Adler**, Via Portici Minori/Klein Lauben 2, ℭ 36127; predictably, because of their perfect positioning right in the town's heart, they both fill up fast.

---

*Bressanone* ℭ *(0472–)*          **Eating Out**

In Bressanone the old walls are ringed with cafés; one of them, **Fink**, Via Portici Minori/Kleine Lauben 4, ℭ 34883 (moderate) has a restaurant upstairs, serving traditional Südtirolese cooking: saddle of venison, *polenta nera* (made from buckwheat), and a wide variety of cold meats and cheeses. (*Closed Tues evenings, Wed, most of July.*)

In Vipiteno/Sterzing **Hotel Krone**, Via Città Vecchia 31, ✆ 765210 (moderate) is the place to eat (and sleep) for the total mitteleuropean experience: refined Tyrolean cuisine, an Italian olive oil menu, and lavish desserts.

# The Upper Adige

## Merano and the Val Venosta

Just 28km up the Adige from Bolzano, **Merano/Meran** has been a favourite spa for central Europeans since the 1830s. Owing to a quirk of the Alpine weather it has a particularly balmy microclimate, and has long been a retreat for convalescents suffering respiratory complaints. The soothing effects of the climate, clean air and graded walks into the mountains are complemented by specific cures, such as the notorious grape cure: the patient eats nothing but grapes, starting at two pounds daily and ending with eight or ten. Apart from inflicting digestive disorders, Merano is most notable for its exclusive hotels, for the elderly and sedate, for its quiet atmosphere and for the fantastic scenery.

However, Merano does have other attractions. It offers plenty of opportunities for skiing, in the Meran 2000 recreation area above the town. It's also an attractive town, full of flowers, grapes and wine, with a stern 15th-century Gothic **Cathedral** and a fine medieval centre, set around the arcaded Via dei Portici.

From Torre della Polvere/Pulvertürm, between the cathedral and the river, the favourite promenade of the Meraner, the **Passeggiata Tappeiner/Tappeinerweg**, leads up into the mountains, with memorable views. For centuries, the landowners of these valleys were generally left alone to govern their own territories, and as a result the area bristles with a large proportion of the Alto Adige's more than 350 castles. A list of those that are open, as museums, restaurants, or hotels, is available from any tourist office in the area. **Schloss Tirol**, north of Merano in Tiroler Dorf, is one of the best, headquarters of the independent Counts of Tyrol until 1363, when the Habsburgs muscled in. It contains a Romanesque chapel and the **Archaeological Museum of the Süd Tirol** (*open Mar–Nov 10am–5pm Tues–Sun; adm*). Nearby **Brunnenberg** was the last home of Ezra Pound. **Schloss Schenna**, north of Merano, (*guided visits Easter–Nov at 10.30, 11.30, 2, 3, 4, 5, Mon–Sat; adm*) has an impressive collection of arms and armour. It stands at the foot of the Passiertal valley, home of Andreas Hofer, the Austrian national hero who stood up to Napoleon.

East of Merano, the Val Venosta/Vinschgau follows the Adige west towards Austria. At **Naturno/Naturns**, the little church of San Prokulus has some fresco fragments that may go back to the 8th century. A little way west on the SS38 a narrow but very scenic road digresses north up another valley, the **Val di Senales/Schnalstal**, passing the little Lago di Vernago/Stausee. **Latsch**, on the main Adige road, has the only all-year skiing in this area.

Two genuine treats await anyone who makes it as far up the valley as **Sluderno/ Schluderns**: the castle of **Coira/Churburg** (*open Mar–Nov 10–12, 2–4, Tues–Sun; adm*), with gloriously painted loggias and a fine collection of armour, and **Monte Maria/Marienburg**, a 17th-century Benedictine house, gleaming white with a crown of towers and gables, in a woodland setting (*still a monastery, but guided tours June–Sept at 10, 11, 3, 4.30, Mon–Fri; 10, 11, Sat; Oct–May 10.45, 3, Mon–Sat*).

At Sluderno the SS41 branches off westwards into Switzerland; the main road continues to the ancient **Malles/Mals**, the largest town in the west of the Val Venosta, before plunging north to Austria. On the way it passes the romantically ruined castle of **Lichtenburg**, and an artificial lake, the **Lago di Resia/Reschensee**, with the church spire of a submerged village poking out above its calm surface.

## Stelvio National Park

If you leave the main valley road (the SS40) at Spondigna/Spondinig just before Sluderno and stay on the SS38, you'll enter the **Stelvio National Park**, the largest in Italy. As well as offering endless possibilities for climbers, the park also encompasses fifty lakes, a hundred glaciers (a tenth of the 134,620 hectares is ice), and Europe's second-highest pass, the **Passo dello Stelvio**, open only between June and October. Through it the road makes its way down towards Bormio and the Valtellina, in Lombardy (*see* pp.295–6).

Stelvio is administered by the provinces of Sondrio, Trento, and Bolzano, all of which have **park visitors' centres** that can tell you where to find the marked trails, alpine refuges, and the best flowers and wildlife: look out for chamois, marmots, eagles, and the ibex, reintroduced in 1968. Unfortunately, the last bear was shot in 1908. Hunting is now illegal in the Lombard section of the park, but contines in Trentino and Alto Adige, causing endless controversy each autumn.

*Merano ☎ (0473–)* **Where to Stay**

As one might expect of a rather old-world, faded-aristocratic spa like Merano, there are a good number of luxury hotels, but not much in the lower ranges. You can sleep like a lord in one of several renovated castles set in greenery: ★★★★**Schloss Rundegg**, Via Schenna/Schennastrasse 2, ☎ 34100 (very expensive) has every luxury, while ★★★**Schloss Labers**, Località Labers 25, ☎ 34484, ✉ 34146 (expensive), a castle-villa, is a little more modest.

Franz Kafka preferred the luxurious ★★★★**Hotel Palace**, Via Cavour 2, ☎ 34734 (very expensive), set in beautifully maintained grounds with a pool.

A less exalted but very comfortable moderate-range hotel is the ★★★**Minerva**, Via Cavour 95, ☎ 36712, a turn-of-the-century hotel with period furnishings, as well as a garden and pool. All rooms have baths, and most balconies with great views. (*Closed Nov–Mar.*)

Merano's restaurants are concentrated around the Via dei Portici. If it's a special occasion, book a table at **Andrea**, Via G. Galilei 44, © 37400 (very expensive), run by star chef Andreas Hellrigl. He specializes in local dishes—*zuppa al vino Terlano*, rack of lamb in rosemary, and so on—and offers two different gourmet menus at each meal. (*Closed Mon, mid-Jan–mid-Mar.*)

Alternatively, an excellent but less economically trying meal of typical Tyrolean soup, trout or venison, and a superb dessert can be had at the **Terlaner Weinstube**, Via dei Portici 231, © 35571 (moderate), amid traditional rustic décor. (*Closed Mon, mid-Jan–mid-Feb.*)

# Friuli-Venezia Giulia

For many British or American visitors, this region east of Venice is terra incognita, a jumbly name that sometimes turns up on the wine list in Italian restaurants. Trieste, at the far end of Italy, evokes cloudy images of pre- and post-War intrigue, a kind of *Third Man* on the Mediterranean. In between Trieste and Venice the imagination fails.

One problem is that the region is burdened with a history as messy as its name. In Roman days Aquileia was the most important city and seat of the patriarchate. Its ecclesiastical and temporal authority was gradually usurped by Cividale del Friuli, the Lombard capital in the Dark Ages, and then in the Middle Ages by Udine, before all was snatched away by the Venetians in the 14th century. Trieste was sometimes under the doges' thumb, sometimes Venice's bitter rival under the Counts of Gorizia or the Austrians.

Napoleon threw the region in with the 'Kingdom of Illyria', a piece of real estate subsequently picked up by the Austro-Hungarian Empire until 1918, when Italy inherited it, as well as all of Istria down to Fiume (modern Rijeka). A major dispute broke out over the territory following the Second World War. Tito's Yugoslav partisans took Trieste from the Germans; the western Allies then forced them to leave, occupying the city themselves as a neutral free port until 1954, when it was readmitted into Italy, leaving the rest of Istria to Yugoslavia. A disastrous earthquake in 1976 shook Friuli to the core, killing a thousand people, levelling entire towns, and causing widespread structural damage. Now rebuilt with modern apartments and bungalows, parts of the central Friulian plain bear an uncanny resemblance to the American Midwest.

Weary of being marginal, Friuli-Venezia Giulia is now grasping for an identity of its own, but it's like trying to put together pieces from several different jigsaw puzzles. The population in the east speaks Slovenian, while the north has a sizeable German minority. In Trieste there are large Jewish, Greek, and Serb minorities, and in the middle, around Udine, a majority Friulian ethnic group, like the Ladini in the South Tyrol, who speak a language similar to the Swiss Rhaeto-Romansch. In 1963 the central government threw up its hands in despair and gave the region autonomy.

## Friuli-Venezia Giulia Itineraries

The two greatest monuments in the region are the cathedral of **Aquileia**, with its fabulous 4th-century mosaics, and the Tempietto Longobardo in **Cividale del Friuli**, a unique relic of the Dark Ages. There are four good **beaches** between Venice and Trieste: Caorle and Bibione (both in the Veneto) and Lignano-Sabbiadoro and Grado. The **Carnic** (Carniche) and **West Julian Alps** offer less expensive and less crowded mountain resort alternatives to the Dolomites.

You could see the highlights of Friuli in four days by car, starting from Venice and ending up in the Cadore region of the Dolomites: the first day in ancient Aquileia and nearby **Grado**, a beach resort with a medieval core (114km from Venice). The next day, **Trieste** (52km), including the Archduke's palace at Miramare and the Grotta Gigante in Trieste's *Carso* hinterland. Third day: the 8th-century wonders of Cividale del Friuli and **Udine**, an art city (105km). Day four: **Codroipo**, site of the villa of the last doge, and from there into the mountains, either via the interesting small town of **Spilimbergo** to the resort area of **Piano di Cavallo**, ending up in the Eastern Dolomites at Longarone (85km from Udine); or north, following the scenic valley of the **Tagliamento** to Pieve di Cadore (200km).

You can follow the same itinerary by public transport, except on the last day's stretch from Udine. Possible options are a train west through Codroipo and Pordenone to Conegliano, one of the crossroads of the Veneto, from where you can return to Venice or head north to Pieve di Cadore; alternatively, take the train north to **Carnia** from Udine, and a bus from there to Sappada.

## Wine in Friuli

The Friuli region has seven of its own DOC regions. Italian-reading wine lovers should pick up a copy of *La Terra dell'Oro* from any tourist office for a complete description of the various vintages and a list of cellars open to visitors. The best-known region is **Collio** (around Cormons), famous for its whites, especially Pinot Bianco and Riesling. The **Collio Orientale**, a much larger region, also produces good whites and a brisk red, Refosco. Rochi di Cialla and Giovanni Dri are just two of the best-known labels. The other DOC regions—**Aquileia, Isonzo, Carso, Latisana**, and **Grave del Friuli**—produce good reds; names to look out for are Schiopettino, Carso Terreno, and Riva Rossa.

## From Venice to Trieste: the Coast

### *Getting Around*

**Trains** from Venice along the coast run roughly every two hours (journey time to Trieste 2 hours). **Buses** from Piazzale Roma are less frequent, though Caorle and Bibione can most easily be reached by direct bus from Venice. The alternative is to take the train to S. Donà di Piave and the local bus to Caorle from there. For Bibione or Lignano-Sabbiadoro, take the train to Latisana, from where a bus will take you to the coast in about 30 minutes. For

Aquileia and Grado, take the train to Cervignano del Friuli and then a bus, or a direct bus from Trieste.

The main **roads** that go along the coast are the A4 *autostrada* and the SS14, both of which run all the way to Trieste, though the SS14 runs closer to the sea and is more convenient for the coastal towns.

It is also possible to fly directly to this area, to Trieste's **airport** at Ronchi di Legionari, between Trieste and Grado (see below, 'Trieste').

## Tourist Information

There are tourist offices with accommodation services in **Caorle**, at Piazza Europa 3, ✆ (0421) 81085; **Lignano-Sabbiadoro**, Via Latisana 42, ✆ (0413) 71821, ✉ 70449; **Aquileia**, Piazza Capitolo, ✆ (0431) 919491 (*open April–Nov only*); and **Grado**, at Viale Dante Alighieri 72, ✆ (0431) 8991, ✉ 899278.

## Old Roman Towns and Beaches

The SS14 from Venice passes first Marco Polo airport and then **Altino**, the modern name of the Roman city of Altinum. Once renowned for its wealth and villas, it was put to the sack by Attila the Hun—only the first of many hardships that led its inhabitants to found a new city on the island of Torcello in the Venetian Lagoon. What Attila and the Lombards didn't wreck was removed to Torcello, so that all that remains in the **museum** (*open 9am–2pm Tues–Sun*) are mosaics and a few odds and ends.

The route continues over the Piave near **San Donà di Piave**; it was near here that Ernest Hemingway, then an ambulance driver for the Red Cross, was wounded in 1918, an experience that became the germ of *A Farewell to Arms*. From San Donà a detour to the attractive old fishermen's town of **Caorle** (the Roman port of Caprulae) is tempting, not only for its isthmus, its beaches, and its pretty lagoon beloved of wildfowl, but for the splendid gilded Venetian *pala* on the altar of the **cathedral**, built in 1075. The **Valle Grande** along the inner lagoon preserves a relic of the primordial pine woods that once scented the shore from Grado to Ravenna. **Bibione**, on the eastern side of the lagoon (best reached via Portogruaro and Latisana) is another pleasant resort.

Caorle was the port of ancient Concordia Sagittaria, now **Portogruaro**, a seductive old town laid out under the delicately worked but very tilted campanile of its **cathedral**, worth a visit for its frescoes. Portogruaro conserves its ancient gates and winding arcaded streets. Finds excavated in town and nearby Concordia are displayed in the **museum** (*open April–Oct 9–12, 3–6, Tues–Sun; Nov–Mar 9–1 Tues–Sun; adm*).

## Lignano-Sabbiadoro, the 'Austrian Riviera'

From a few kilometres east of **Latisana**, where a new road, the SS354, branches off to the coast, you can follow the crowds south to the Laguna di Marano and the fastest-growing resort area on the Adriatic, **Lignano-Sabbiadoro**. With a lovely 9km sandy beach and scores of new hotels, apartments, bungalows and campsites, Lignano-Sabbiadoro and its two adjacent resorts of **Lignano-Pineta** (the prettiest section, under the pinewoods) and smart **Lignano Riviera** offer fun in the sun and Viennese sausages just like Mutter makes.

## Palmanova

In the Renaissance, despite all Alberti's theories on town planning, only a handful of entirely new towns were ever constructed, and none of them has survived more intact than **Palmanova**, 10km north of Cervignano del Friuli. Built in 1593 by the Venetians as a bulwark against the Austrians and Turks, it is a fine example of 16th-century 'ideal' radial military planning and a geometrical *tour de force*: the star formed by its walls has nine points, while the large, somewhat eerie, piazza in the heart of town is a perfect hexagon that originally contained the arsenal servicing the nine bastions. Even though most of the walls and moat are now overgrown, their stone softly moulded into serpentine hills and gullies, they are still defended by young conscripts. At the **Museo Storico** (*open 10–1, 4–8, Tues–Sun; adm*), ask about the torchlight tour of the recently discovered walkways within the walls. From Palmanova there are frequent buses to Aquileia, Grado, and Udine.

## Aquileia

If Palmanova is unique in its plan, Aquileia, directly south of Cervignano, is unique in that it's the only major Roman city in Italy to die on the vine, so to speak. While most other Roman metropolises are still notable towns or cities, Aquileia has dwindled to 3,500 inhabitants, who no longer receive emperors but tend vineyards and the tourists who flock to see the most important archaeological site in Northern Italy.

Founded as a Roman colony in 181 BC, Aquileia ('Eagle') earned its name from the eagles that flew over the town while plans were being laid for Augustus' German campaign. It was a good augury. Augustus himself was in and out, and received Herod the Great here. The famous Patriarchate of Aquileia was founded in 313, but after the sack of the city by Attila (452) and the Lombards (568), the patriarch moved to a safer home in Grado, the ancient outer port of Aquileia. When Aquileia wanted the patriarchate back in the 7th century, Grado refused to surrender the title, and for 400 years rival patriarchs sat in Grado and in Cividale del Friuli, the Lombard capital. When they were reconciled in 1019, Aquileia's great basilica was rebuilt, but it was the old city's last hurrah. Aquileia's port on the Natissa silted up, malaria chased out the remaining citizens, and the patriarchate moved on to Udine and became a mere archbishopric.

### The Basilica

Aquileia's magnificent **Basilica** (*open April–Sept 8.30–7.30 daily; Oct–Mar 9–12, 3–6, daily*) with its lofty campanile is a landmark on the Friulian plain for miles around. It was founded in 313 by the first Patriarch Theodore, and when the basilica was rebuilt in 1023 Theodore's floor was merely covered up. Rediscovered and uncovered in this century, the pavement is a vast, ancient carpet of vivid and often whimsical mosaics, where portraits, animals and geometric patterns happily mingle with Christian and pagan scenes. Original

floor of
Aquilea
basilica

frescoes from 1031 survive in the apse, where you can see Patriarch Poppo dedicating the basilica he clutches in his hands, accompanied by Emperor Conrad II and Gisela of Swabia. Bas-reliefs in the north-east chapel portraying Christ with St Thomas of Canterbury, carved only a few years after his martyrdom, show just how fast news of church politics travelled in the 1170s. Another treasure is the 11th-century **San Sepolcro**, a reproduction of the Holy Sepulchre in Jerusalem.

Next to the San Sepolcro is the entrance to the **Cripta degli Scavi**, containing more great mosaics from 313, sandwiched in between pagan Roman mosaics and some others from the 8th century. Another crypt, the **Cripta degli Affreschi**, is adorned with colourful 12th-century Byzantine-style frescoes (*both crypts open April–Sept 9–6 daily; Oct–Mar 9–1 Tues–Sun; adm*).

## The Museo Archeologico

> *Open April–Sept 9.30am–7pm Tues–Sun; 9am–2pm Mon; Oct–Mar 9am–2pm Tues–Sun only; adm.*

This museum, housed in an old palace across the road from the basilica, contains an excellent collection of artefacts from Roman Aquileia, including a fine set of highly individualized Republican portrait busts; unlike the Greeks who idealized themselves in marble (or perhaps were just better looking), the Romans insisted that all their warts, cauliflower ears, and crumpled Roman noses be preserved for posterity. Among the bas-reliefs there's a smith with his tools, amber and gold ornaments, and a thousand and one household items that breathe life into ancient Aquileia. The ancient Aquileians could be lighthearted: there are flies made of gold, and a wee bronze figurine of a springing cat.

# The Excavations

A circular walk, beginning on the Via Sacra behind the basilica, takes in most of Aquileia's excavations; an unfortunate proximity to Venice, that quarrying magpie, has shorn them of most of their grandeur. The Via Sacra first passes by recently unearthed **Roman houses and palaeo-Christian oratories** (some with beautiful mosaics intact), then continues up through the considerable ruins of the ancient **harbour**. Continue straight and bear right after the crossroads with the modern Via Gemina to the **Palaeo-Christian Museum** (*same hours as Museo Archeologico, adm free*), with reliefs and sarcophagi, and a walkway over the undulating mossy mosaics. Return by way of Via Gemina to Via Giulia Augusta (the main Cervignano-Grado road). To the right of this road you can see the old Roman road, and on the left, the **Forum** with its re-erected columns. Just off a fork to the right, the **Grand Mausoleum** (1st century AD) was brought here from the distant suburbs. The meagre ruins of the amphitheatre, the baths (terme), and another tomb, the **Sepolcreto**, are on Via XXIV Maggio and Via Acidino, north of the village's central Piazza Garibaldi.

# Grado

Aquileia had an inner port and an outer port, or *grado*, on the island that still bears its ancient name. Modern Grado lies at the end of a causeway 11km to the south, the queen of its own little lagoon and archipelago. Even the narrow alleys of its picturesque old town, the **Castrum Gradense**, are called *calli* as in Venice. With a long beach and a thermal spa that specializes in baking its visitors in hot sand baths, Grado is a popular resort. The free beaches, however, are dirty: to find cleaner ones with sparser crowds, walk east to **Pineta**, or catch the boat to **Barbana**, an island in the lagoon with a resident religious community (*boats run frequently every day in summer; Nov–May, Sat, Sun only; tickets L6,000*). Grado owes its origin as a beach resort to medicine. Keen to bring children to the seaside, in order to effect cures for TB, Italian doctors set to work trying to discover a fresh-water spring on the peninsula of Grado. In 1892 the spring was discovered, and very quickly a town grew up to accommodate burgeoning numbers of visitors. Nowadays, alongside common-or-garden holidaymakers, its clients include athletes, models, and business people undergoing specific programmes of recuperation. The popular 'sand cure' involves being buried up to your neck in warm sand.

In the 6th century the Patriarch of Nova Aquileia, as he called himself, was installed in the **Duomo** (Basilica of Sant'Eufemia), a simple solid temple preserving a fine 6th-century mosaic floor, though the scriptural adages and geometrical patterns that cover it seem austere after the garden on the floor of Aquileia's basilica. A fine silver Venetian-style *pala* glows on the altar. An alley of early sarcophagi separates Sant'Eufemia from another, smaller basilica, **Santa Maria delle Grazie** and the octagonal, 6th-century **Baptistry**, both with mosaic floors.

From Grado there are daily excursions in summer into the lagoon, where several islets have traditional thatched fishermen's cottages, or *casoni*. If you're lucky you'll see herons in the mystery-laden fens of the lagoon. There are also daily sea connections from Grado to Trieste and the Istrian coast in summer (*see* below, 'Trieste'), and to the quaint fishing village of **Porto Buso**.

In the beach resorts, count on high season prices from mid-June to the end of August; book ahead, easpecially for the first three weeks of August. Out of season, many hotels are shut, but those that stay open often offer discounts.

## Lignano

In shady Lignano-Pineta you can stay first class at the ★★★★**Greif**, Arco del Grecale 18, ☎/@ 42226, (very expensive/expensive), a large resort hotel with a pool and garden, parking and private beach. (*Open 19 May–15 Sept.*) The ★★★**Medusa Splendid**, Raggio dello Scirocco 33, ☎ 422211 (moderate) is more intimate, and also has a pool, very good rooms, and a garden.

The fashionable place to stay in Lignano Riviera is the ★★★★**Eurotel**, Calle Mendelssohn 13, ☎ 428991 (very expensive/expensive), which enjoys perhaps the most beautiful setting in the area and offers lovely rooms, a heated pool and more. (*Open 14 April–20 Sept.*)

Built up in the last 25 years, Lignano-Sabbiadoro is a good place to look for self-catering bungalows as well as hotels, although none really stands out. For comfortable rooms try ★★★**Miramare**, Via Aquileia 49, ☎ 71260, @ 720051 (moderate), with parking and a garden as well as its own beach. (*Open May–Sept.*)

In the less expensive range there's the ★★**Pensione Astro**, Via Miramare 48, ☎ 71309 (inexpensive), or ★**La Perla**, Via Padana 10, ☎ 71445 (inexpensive, *open 15 May–22 Sept*). Both have rooms with or without baths.

## Aquileia

If you want to stop over in Aquileia, the ★★★**Patriarchi**, Via Julia Augusta 12, ☎ 919595, @ 919596 (moderate), overlooks the excavations; all rooms are air-conditioned. The old ★**Aquila Nera**, Piazza Garibaldi 5, ☎ 91045 (inexpensive), offers small rooms, with or without bath, in the quiet main square.

## Grado

There are lots of choices in Grado, but a couple that stand out, within sight of one another in the centre of the town, are the ★★★★**Antica Villa Bernt**, Via Colombo 5, ☎ 82516, @ 82517 (very expensive/expensive), a refurbished old villa with only 22 lovely rooms, all with bath, air-conditioning, and TV (*open May–Sept*); and the ★★★★**Savoy**, Via Carducci 33, ☎ 81171, @ 83305 (very expensive/expensive), which has a thermal pool, garden, parking, and very comfortable rooms.

To avoid the full-pension tyranny, try the ★★**Villa Lucilla**, Viale del Capricorno 3, ☎ 80814 (inexpensive), in the pinewoods opposite the island of Barbana in Pineta. All rooms have baths, and there's a garden. (*Open May–Sept.*)

## Caorle

Caorle's **Duilio**, Via Strada Nuova 19, ℗ 81087 (expensive) is celebrated for its succulent seafood, in the antipasti, with the pasta, and as the main course. A charming setting, a huge wine list, and reasonably priced menus are particular attractions. (*Closed Mon, Jan.*)

## Lignano

In Lignano-Sabbiadoro there's the small but convivial **Bidin**, Via Europa 1, ℗ 71988 (expensive), which has a separate *menu degustazione* for either fish or meat. (*Closed Tues.*) **Al Bancut**, Via Friuli 30, ℗ 71926 (moderate), in the centre of town, has fine grilled fish and meats. (*Closed Tues.*) You can sit outside to eat plain food on a quiet street at **Osteria Sache Burache**, Viale dei Plantini, ℗ 71498 (inexpensive; *closed Mon*).

In Lignano Riviera **Al Cason**, Corso Continenti 169, ℗ 428527 (moderate), is housed in an old thatched fishing cottage, with beautiful views over the lagoon. It offers fine seafood dishes, and an exquisite Adriatic mixed seafood grill, among other choices. (*Open Easter–Oct.*)

## Aquileia

The restaurant attached to the **Aquila Nera** hotel (*see* above, inexpensive) is small, traditional and homely, with good gnocchi and basic meat dishes. Near Aquileia **La Colombara**, Via S. Zilli 34, ℗ 91513 (moderate), 2km outside the village on the Trieste road, serves up the finest cuisine in the area, specializing in seafood prepared in a number of excellent and unusual ways, accompanied by good wines from the Collio. (*Closed Mon, June.*)

## Grado

The most celebrated restaurant in Grado, the **Antica Trattoria da Nico**, Via Marina 10, ℗ 80470 (expensive), in the old town, is run by the jolly Nico who meets Grado's sizeable fishing fleet at dawn to select the pick of the catch, which he expertly prepares and serves up surrounded by a properly nautical décor. The menu adapts to the catch. (*Closed Thurs.*) In the winding streets around the cathedral is the **Tavernetta All'Androna**, Calle Porta Piccola 4, ℗ 80950 (moderate), with a daily changing menu of fresh fish, and homemade bread and pasta. (*Closed Tues, Dec–Feb.*) There is also the **Trattoria de Toni**, Piazza Duca D'Aosta 37, ℗ 80104 (inexpensive), which offers fine fresh fish. (*Closed Tues.*)

## Trieste

Once the main seaport of the Austro-Hungarian Empire, Trieste became after two world wars the woebegone widow of the Adriatic, a grandiose neoclassical city shorn of its *raison d'être*. But, as Europe opens up to the east, it is regaining its former central position and slick cosmopolitan air, something that the inhabitants accept as simply another twist in a confused history. The shops bubble with different languages, and a bewildering variety of car license plates clog up the stern, straight, very central European 19th-century streets. Trade is picking up, too: not from tourists who once passed through on their way to Yugoslavia, but from Slovenes flashing new-found wealth, other East Europeans carting off cheap goods to sell back home, and tankers moored in the bay.

Don't come to Trieste for great art or beautiful buildings: its capitalist wealth has been firmly invested in banks, shipping-lines and the stock exchange. Instead, come to sense the energy and excitement of a city shaking off decades of nostalgic sloth, and picking up the threads of its most vibrant time, the beginning of this century. Or you could just come for the stone breasts: plastered with naked statues, Trieste must have more of them than any other city in the world.

## History

Founded as the busy Celtic port of Tergeste, Trieste first became an important city under Augustus. From the 9th to the 13th centuries it maintained a precarious independence under its arrogant, princely bishops; by the 14th and 15th centuries it was Venice's chief rival in the Adriatic.

Austria, always longing for a convenient port, is deeply woven into Trieste's history. It first offered the city its protection in 1382, and in 1719 gave it its special favour when Charles VI made it a free port. These were Trieste's happiest days. It returned to Austrian rule after the fall of Napoleon in 1815, though by now bereft of free-port status and without its medieval heart, as the Viennese rebuilt the centre of the city in a heavy-handed neoclassical style. They governed in a similar fashion, turning the majority Italian population into ardent 'Irredentists', turbulently desiring union with Italy.

Italian troops were welcomed in 1918, but Italian government all too soon proved to be another disappointment for Trieste, when Mussolini tried to force the heterogeneous population into an Italian cultural strait-jacket, larding the city with Fascist monuments. The real disaster came in the aftermath of the Second World War, when Trieste found itself permanently divorced from its Istrian hinterland in Slovenia and Croatia. Tito's Yugoslavia only gave up its last claims to Trieste itself in 1954, and the border was not finally settled until 1975.

At the turn of the century Trieste sparkled with intellectuals and literati. Sir Richard Burton, translator of the *Arabian Nights*, was consul here from 1870 until his death in 1890. James Joyce, after eloping with Nora Barnacle, lived in Trieste for long periods in 1904–15 and 1919–20; here his two children were born, and he began writing *Ulysses*. He also befriended, translated, and helped to publish Ettore Schmitz, better known as Italo Svevo—epitomising Trieste's troubled history, his nom-de-plume literally means 'the Italian Swabian'. Unknown to either of them, Rainer Maria Rilke was nearby at Duino. Of the Grand Cafés, once the symbol of Triestine society and filled with fervent cross-cultural conversation, ideas, and spies, most have vanished, or deal primarily in memories.

# Getting There

## by air

Trieste's **airport** is at Ronchi dei Legionari, ✆ (040) 773224, 30km to the north of the city near Monfalcone; the airport bus is run by F.lli Cosulich, ✆ (040) 422711, and departs from the main bus station.

## by sea

The mammoth offices of Lloyd Triestino in Piazza dell'Unità d'Italia dispense information on all ship departures from Trieste, and most anywhere else as well. Inquire at Via del'Orologio 1, ✆ (040) 7785428.

A ferry sails from the **Stazione Marittima** to Istria every day except Wednesday during June to Sept, calling at Grado and Lignano in Italy on the way, and then Piran (Slovenia) and Umag, Porec, Rovinj and Pula (Croatia). Remember to take a passport for Slovenia and Croatia. Sample return fares are Grado, L15,000, Rovino L50,000 and Pula L63,000. At other times of the year service is a less frequent.

There are also weekly ferries from Trieste in summer to Igoumenitsa, Patras and Corfu in Greece.

## by rail

There are frequent trains to Venice, Gorizia, Udine, as well as to Austria, Slovenia and several other destinations in Eastern Europe, from Trieste's **Stazione Centrale**, on Piazza della Libertà 8, ✆ (040) 418207.

## by long-distance bus

The main **bus station** is in front of the Stazione Centrale, in the Piazza della Libertà, ✆ (040) 62030. It has bus services to Venice, Treviso, Padua, Belluno, Trento, and Cortina and Sappada in the Dolomites; long-distance coaches to Milan, Mantua, and Genoa; and international services to Ljubljana, Rijeka, and Zagreb.

## by road

The A4 *autostrada* from Turin finally comes to an end in Trieste, as does the parallel SS14 from Venice. Just outside the city, however, they link up with roads that lead east, towards Ljubljana in Slovenia, and south-east into Croatia. The Ljubljana road is motorway for part of its length.

# Getting Around

Trieste's many long, straight Habsburger streets make finding one's way around relatively simple, and **buses** are quite frequent. As usual, tickets must be bought in advance. Most routes run from or by the central bus station; for information, ✆ (040) 370160. There is also a **tram** line (*tranvia*) from Piazza Oberdan up to Villa Opicina above the city.

The main information office is at Via San Nicoló 20, ✆ (040) 369881, 🖂 369981. There is also an office at the Stazione Centrale, ✆ (040) 420182 (*both open 9–1, 4–7, Mon–Fri; 9–1 Sat*). For information on the whole of Friuli-Venezia Giulia the office is at Via Rossini 6, ✆ (040) 363952, 🖂 365496.

There are British and American **consulates** in Trieste, the UK at Vicolo delle Ville 16, ✆ (040) 302884, and the United States at Via Roma 45, ✆ (040) 660177.

## Piazza dell'Unità d'Italia

From the train or bus station, the Corso Cavour leads directly into the **Borgo Teresiano**, the commercial centre laid out by Maria Theresa's tidy planners in an orderly grid, and planted with neoclassical architecture. The street passes over the **Canale Grande**, an inlet with moorings for small craft; the adjacent Piazza Ponterosso is the site of the daily market. At the head of the canal stands the classical temple church of **Sant'Antonio**, and near it, the blue-domed Serbian Orthodox **Santo Spiridone**, an exotic orchid in a regimented garden.

Trieste's whale of a heart, vast **Piazza dell'Unità d'Italia**, is one of Italy's largest squares. Facing the harbour, it is framed by the hefty **Palazzo del Comune**, topped by two Moors who ring the bell in the clock tower; on one side the **Palazzo del Governo** glows in its bright skin of neo-classical mosaics, on the other broods the huge palace of Lloyd Triestino. In the summer flowers brighten the piazza, while in winter, plants that look appropriately like cabbages hold pride of place, unless they are cowering beneath the mighty *bora*, a north-east wind that whips over the Carso. The centrepiece of all this, a mind-boggling pile of rocks and statuary purported to represent the *Four Continents* (1750), may send you staggering off for a drink at the piazza's **Caffè degli Specchi**, in business since 1839 and once a famous Irredentist meeting place.

## Up the Capitoline Hill

Catch bus no.24 from the station or Piazza dell'Unità to ascend the Capitoline Hill, the nucleus of Roman and medieval Trieste. In the 5th century the Triestini raised the first of two basilicas here to their patron San Giusto, a martyr drowned during the persecution of Diocletian. An adjacent basilica, built in the 11th century, was linked to the first in the 14th century, thus giving the **Cathedral of San Giusto** (*closed 12 midday–3pm*) its curious plan. The doorway, under a splendid Gothic rose window, is framed by the fragments of a Roman sarcophagus: six funerary busts gaze solemnly ahead like a corporate board of directors, while embedded in the adjacent, squat campanile there's a frieze that looks like a fashion plate for Roman armour. The interior has some fine mosaics, especially the 13th-century *Christ with SS. Giusto and Servulus*, as well as good 12th-century frescoes. Buried on the right is Don Carlos, the Great Pretender of Spain's 19th-century Carlist Wars, who died as an exile in Trieste in 1855.

Next to San Giusto are the fragments of the Roman forum and a 1st-century basilica, of which two columns have been re-erected. The excellent view over Trieste from here is marred by a 1933 **Monument to The Fallen**, which admirably extols the principal fascist virtues of strength and vulgarity. The 15th-century **Castello** was begun by the Venetians and finished by the Austrians, and offers more views from its ramparts and a small **Museo Civico** (*open 9am–1pm Tues–Sun; adm*), full of armour and weapons.

Just down the lane from the cathedral is the **Museo di Storia ed Arte**, and the **Orto Lapidario** (*both open 9am–1pm Tues–Sun; adm*). The first collection houses some intriguing finds from ancient Tergeste, and a famous 5th-century deers' head silver *rhyton*, or drinking vessel, from ancient Tarentum. The Orto Lapidario contains Roman altars, stelae, a red granite Egyptian sarcophagus and the tomb of the great archaeologist J. J. Winckelmann, who was murdered in Trieste in 1768 by a Tuscan cook. On the way down to the centre, stop at the well-preserved 1st-century **Roman theatre** on the Via Teatro Romano.

## Other Sites Around Trieste

The **Museo Revoltella**, in Piazza Venezia (from Piazza dell'Unità, continue along the harbour past the Stazione Marittima, and the museum entrance is at Via Diaz 27), was founded by Baron Pasquale Revoltella, one of the financiers of the Suez Canal, which was a big boon to Trieste's port. Full of original furnishings, it contains a gallery of 19th-century art that evokes the city's golden days, as well as modern works by a range of Italian artists, including Morandi and De Chirico (*tours only, with a guard but not a guide, at 9, 10.30, 12, 3, 4.30, 6, Mon, Wed–Sat; 9, 10.30, 12, Sun; closed Tues; adm exp*).

On the other side of town (off the Via Carducci, between Piazza Oberdan and the Capitoline Hill), at Via Cesare Battisti 18, is Trieste's best surviving Belle Epoque coffee house, the **Caffè San Marco**, physically unchanged since it opened in 1914. Its name and the Venetian scenes painted on the walls betrayed the owner's pro-Italian sentiments. According to the Triestini, the masked carnival figures in the oval over the bar portray Vittorio Emanuele and Mussolini. You won't find a classier joint to shoot a round of pool or sit at a marble table to chug down one of the local micro-cappuccinos. One street away, on Via S. Francesco, stands the most beautiful **Synagogue** in Italy, built in 1910 on ancient Syriac models.

*Castello Miramare*

In sombre counterpoint stands the only Second World War concentration camp in Italy to be used for mass exterminations, the **Risiera di San Sabba** at the southern extreme of the city, an old factory that was taken over by the Nazis in September 1943. The building now houses a small museum (*bus no.8; museum open 9–1 Tues–Sun*).

## Habsburgs and Karst: Excursions from Trieste

You can't go too far from Trieste without running into Slovenia. For a short jaunt, take the old Opicina **Tranvia** (tramway) from Piazza Oberdan up to Poggioreale for the fine panorama from the belvedere **Vedetta d'Opicina**. Another popular excursion is to **Miramare**, some 7km up the coast (bus 36 from Piazza Oberdan or Stazione Centrale; in summer, boat excursions from Riva del Mandracchio). On the way, watch for the **Faro della Vittoria**, a powerful lighthouse and 1927 war memorial to sailors, crowned by a heavy-sinewed, big-busted Valkyrie in a majorette's costume.

## Miramare

Towering up on its own little promontory overlooking the sea, the castle of Miramare hides a dark history behind its charming 19th-century facade. It was built by the Habsburg Archduke Maximilian and his Belgian wife Carlotta, and visitors are greeted by a stone sphinx with a cryptic smile that seems to ask the world: why did Maximilian leave this pleasure palace and like a *dummkopf* let Napoleon III's financiers con him into becoming Mexico's puppet emperor in 1864, and why did he linger around there to face a firing squad three years later? Was he an idealist like his apologists claim, or too much of a Habsburg to know any better?

Carlotta, after desperately trying to rally European support for her husband, went mad after his execution and survived him for another 50 years in Belgium, while Miramare rapidly acquired the ominous reputation of putting a curse on anyone who slept within its walls. Most unfortunately, another Habsburg—the Archduke Ferdinand—stayed here on his way to assassination in Sarajevo, the incident that sparked off the First World War. When the Americans occupied it in 1946, their commander insisted on sleeping out in the park in a tent. You can hear the whole sad story in the sound and light show 'Miramare's Imperial Dream' (*in English on Tues at 9 or 9.30 pm in July, Aug and Sept. Palace open April–Sept 9–1.30, 2.30–6, Mon–Sat; 9am–12.30pm Sun; adm*).

Inside, the palace retains its original overblown Victorian-era décor and furnishings. Miramare's charming park was designed by Maximilian, who made a better botanist than emperor; it's free, and open daily until sunset.

## The Carso

Most of Trieste's slender province is within the Carso, named from its karst topography. Karst is pliable limestone, easily eroded by the rain into remarkable shapes—and here, pale cliffs that form Italy's most dramatic Adriatic coastline north of the Gargano peninsula. Inland the karst has been buffeted into petrified waves of rock dotted with *dolinas* (swallow holes), while underground, aeons of dripping water have formed vast caverns, subterranean lakes and rivers inhabited by blind amphibians. Vineyards grow wherever there's room, and elsewhere the landscape is dominated by sumac, which autumn ignites into a hundred shades of scarlet.

Between Miramare and the industrial shipbuilding town of Monfalcone lies the fishing village of **Duino**, with its two castles; the ruined **Castello Vecchio** and the 15th-century **Castello Nuovo**, perched on a promontory over the sea. Castello Nuovo has long been owned by the Princes von Thurn und Taxis, one of whom played host to Rilke here in 1910–14, when the poet composed his famous *Duino Elegies*. The castle is now a Rilke study centre, and there's a scenic 'Rilke walk' along the promontory. Nearby **Sistiana** is a pretty resort with a yacht harbour in its own little bay.

Born in a karstic abyss in Slovenia, the **Timavo river** continues underground for 30km before reappearance near the winsome Romanesque church and inland village of **San Giovanni al Timavo**, above Duino. Also inland are the caves, the most famous of which, the **Grotta Gigante** near Opicina, is the largest and easiest to visit (bus 45, every half hour from the Piazza Oberdan). So vast it could swallow the entire basilica of St Peter, the Grotto is embellished with well-lit stalactites and stalagmites. A **Museum of Speleology** outside has displays on cave geology and exhibits of palaeolithic and neolithic remains discovered on the site (*open April–Sept 9–12, 2–7, Tues–Sun; Oct–Mar 10–12, 2–5, Tues–Sun; adm*).

The cave is not far from **Sgonico** (bus 46 from Piazza Oberdan), site of a Karstic botanical garden, while bus 40, also from Oberdan, offers an excursion through some fine scenery to the perilous Karstic cliffs in the **Val Rosandra**, south of Trieste and the site of an alpine school. Bus 20 (and in the summer, boats) heads south along the coast from Trieste to **Muggia**, an attractive old Venetian fishing port and Italy's last bit of Istria.

---

### Activities

The **opera** season at Trieste's **Teatro Comunale Verdi** runs from November to March. Performances of different kinds—music, drama, dance—are frequently presented at the castle on summer evenings, and classical Italian plays are occasionally put on at the **Teatro Romano**. Summer **boat tours** of the Triestine Riviera depart from Trieste's Riva del Mandracchio. Nearest beaches are at Riviera di Barcola, Grignano and Sistiana. **Carnival** is celebrated with a Venetian flair in Muggia, south of Trieste (*see* below, 'The Carso'), with a lavish parade that's well beyond what you would expect in a small town.

---

*Trieste ✆ (040–)*  **Where to Stay**
**very expensive**

On Trieste's finest square, Piazza dell'Unità d'Italia, is the city's finest hotel, the **★★★★Duchi d'Aosta**, ✆ 7351, @ 366092, in a neo-Renaissance palace erected in 1873. Now owned by the CIGA chain, it exudes a dignified Belle Epoque ambience; upstairs the luxurious rooms are fitted with all modern comforts. It has a fine restaurant, and there is parking outside or in the garage.

**moderate**

Another fine neoclassical building, the **★★Hotel Al Teatro**, Via Capo di Piazza G. Bartoli 1 (near Piazza dell'Unità), ✆ 366220, @ 366560, is, as its name suggests, near the opera. The hotel served as British headquarters after the Second World War and is a bit of a nostalgic trip back to the Trieste of yore. Near the station is the comfortable ★★★**Milano**, Via Ghega 17, ✆ 369472, ✉ 369727.

Alternatively, it might be more fun to take the tram up to Opicina and lodge at the ★★**Daneu**, Via Nazionale 11, ✆ 211241, a comfortable hotel with a good restaurant. Outside Trieste there are many more choices beside the sea, as for example in Duino (*see* below) at the ★★★**Duino Park**, ✆ 208184, ✉ 208526, which has its own pool and a private piece of beach. South of the city at Muggia the ★★★**Lido**, Via Battista 22, ✆ 273338, ✉ 271131, has a good restaurant serving local seafood.

### *inexpensive*

There are many less expensive choices in the centre of Trieste (look around Via Roma, Via della Geppa, or Via XXX Ottobre). The ★**Alabarda-Flora**, Via Valdirivo 22, ✆ 630269, is a clean, comfortable, good-value hotel.

At Muggia, the ★★**Arciduca**, Strada per Chiampore 46, ✆ 271131, is pleasantly situated near the sea, and has cosy rooms. The **Youth Hostel** for the area is idyllically but inconveniently placed overlooking the sea at Viale Miramare 331, ✆ 224102, 8km north of Trieste near Miramare. To get there, take bus 36 from Trieste.

---

*Trieste* ✆ *(040–)*                                         **Eating Out**

Trieste is a good place to eat dumplings instead of pasta—Slovenian and Hungarian influences are strong in the kitchen. A famous first course is *jota*, a kind of minestrone with beans, potatoes, and sauerkraut, or you could try *kaiserknödel* (bread dumplings with grated cheese, ham, and parsley). For *secondo*, there's a wide variety of fish like *sardoni* (big sardines), served fried or marinated, and both tasty and inexpensive. Goulash, roast pork, and *stinco* (veal knuckle) are also popular. The middle-European influence, however, is especially noticeable in the desserts: the lovely strudels, the *gnocchi di susine* (plums), or *zavate*, a warm cream pastry.

### *expensive*

The ideal place to partake of this *cucina Triestina* is **Suban**, Via Comici 2, ✆ 54368, in the suburb of San Giovanni (and quite hard to find, so call ahead and take a taxi). Founded out in the country in 1863, this wonderful old inn has since been absorbed by urban growth, though it maintains much of its old feel and its fine views over Trieste. Suban offers a famous *jota*, *sevapcici* (Slovenian grilled meat fritters), sinful desserts, and good wines. Readers have warned us, though, that the quality of the food is not entirely consistent, as the regular chef is sometimes absent; ask when booking if he's on duty, and if not, wait till he is. (*Closed Sun, most of Aug.*)

The smartest restaurant in Trieste is beside the sea, the **Elefante Bianco**, Riva III Novembre 3, ✆ 365784 , with Italian nouvelle cuisine served up in an atmosphere of greenery, wrought iron, and wood—though its prices can be outrageous considering the size of the portions. (*Closed Sun and Aug.*) Another of the best-known restaurants in Trieste is **Harry's Grill**, in the Duchi d'Aosta hotel (*see* above), which serves excellent international specialities.

The elegant seafront **Nastro Azzurro**, Riva N. Saura 12, ℭ 305789, is near the fish market, and specializes in its wares; the seafood antipasti and *fritto di mare* are mouth-watering. (*Closed Sun.*) A few doors down, the **Trattoria Alla Cantina Sociale**, Riva N. Sauro 18, ℭ 300689, is scruffier and more familial: the popular seafood menu changes according to the catch. For finer views, try **Allo Squero**, north of the city at Viale Miramare 42, ℭ 410884, which has fine fish soup, mussels and lobster. (*Closed Sun evenings, Mon, Feb.*)

*inexpensive*

**Bella Trieste**, Via Pane Bianco 96, ℭ 815262 (in the Servola quarter: take bus 29 from Piazza Goldoni, get off at the fourth stop in Via dei Soncini and take the first right-hand turning), is a little cathedral of good home cooking, and well worth the effort of getting there. Back in the centre of Trieste, on Via Cassa di Risparmio, **Pepi** overflows at lunchtime with crowds eager for sausage, pickles, and beer, and serves as a reminder of how long Austria ruled Trieste. For more Italian inexpensive fare, there are several pizzerias around Piazza Sant'Antonio.

## Eastern Friuli: Gorizia, Udine and Cividale

*Getting Around*

These three cities are linked by **rail** from Trieste, Pordenone and Venice. Gorizia, Cormons and Udine are all on the line from Trieste; a private local railway line links Udine station with Cividale (20min). Udine's railway **station** is on Viale Europa Unita, ℭ (0432) 503656; the **bus station** is not far away on the other side of the same street, ℭ (0432) 506941. If you're travelling by **car**, an *autostrada*, the A23, now runs north from the A4 near Palmanova to Udine and then on to the Carnia and Villach in Austria. Alternatively, the main road to Udine from Trieste is the SS305 from Monfalcone, with turnings for Gorizia and Cividale.

*Tourist Information*

The **Gorizia** tourist office is at Via Diaz 16, ℭ (0481) 533870; there is also another office nearby in **Gradisca d'Isonzo**, in the Palazzo Torriani, Via M Ciotti, ℭ (0481) 99180, ✉ 99880. In **Udine** the information office is at Piazza 1 Maggio 7, ℭ (0432) 295972, ✉ 504743, and in **Cividale del Friuli**, at Largo Boiani 4, ℭ (0432) 731398.

## Gorizia

The frontier town of Gorizia was for centuries ruled by a powerful dynasty of counts, who were always ready to stir up trouble against Venice, with the winking approval of the Kings of Hungary. When the last count died without an heir in 1500, the city was briefly controlled by Venice before being taken over by the Habsburgs. As in Trieste, the Austrians provided Gorizia with broad, straight boulevards, several parks and pronounced the result an 'Austrian Nice' (minus the seashore).

It saw fierce fighting in the First World War, but it was after the Second World War that Gorizia became Italy's Berlin, cut in two in such a thoughtless manner that the city almost choked. The eastern section of the town, called Nova Gorica in Slovenian, was left as Yugoslav (now Slovenian) territory. Things were improved in 1979, when residents on either side of the barbed-wire fence were granted a 16km zone around the city to transact their affairs freely. In 1991, Gorizia saw the first shots of the new Balkan War, when Slovenia declared independence and the Yugoslav army was sent in to wrest back the lucrative border posts. Today, as Slovenia prospers in its independence, the town is a peculiar mix of flashy boutiques catering for cross-border traffic, and grim reminders of recent strife.

Crowning Gorizia, the **Borgo Castello** is a little village within the city, built within the 1509 Venetian fortress that also encompasses the 12th-century **Castle** of the Counts of Gorizia (*open April–Sept 9.30–1, 3–7, Tues–Sun; Oct–Mar 9.30–1, 3–5.30, Tues–Sun; adm*). The castle has good views over Gorizia, and 17th-century furniture inside. The Borgo contains solemn medieval houses, the 1386 **Church of Santo Spirito**, and the **Formentini House**, now the museum of history, art, and handicrafts (*same hours as castle*). The **Duomo**, tinkered with repeatedly since the 14th century, contains a treasure bestowed by Maria Theresa.

The area around Gorizia, the **Collio**, is the most important wine region in Friuli. In the many-towered town of **Gradisca d'Isonzo**, you can taste any or all of the Friulian wines at the **Enoteca Regionale Serenissima** (*open 10am–1pm, 4–11pm; closed Wed*). **Cormons** is the only town in Italy to erect a statue to Emperor Maximilian. Visit its Cantina Produttori Vini del Collio, © (0481) 60579.

---

## Udine

Legend states that Udine's *castello* sits on a mound erected by Hunnish warriors, who carried the soil to the site in their helmets so that their commander Attila could watch the burning of Aquileia. The story is apocryphal, as Udine went on to take Aquileia's place as Friuli's capital after the 13th century, and become seat of Aquileia's patriarch from 1238 to 1751. Udine's chief rivals were Cividale and Venice, and after a nine-year resistance Udine surrendered to the latter in 1420. In the Second World War it was the last city to be liberated in Italy (May 1945).

Udine has a discreet charm and many old streets interwoven with little canals; it's also the centre of Friulian nationalism, where you're likely to hear people conversing in the Friulian tongue. Unless you've been smitten by the works of Giambattista Tiepolo, none of Udine's attractions is exceptional, but the whole is admirable, and away from the major tourist trails.

### Piazza della Libertà

The heart of Udine, Piazza della Libertà, has been called 'the most beautiful Venetian square on terra firma'. Its most striking building, the candy-striped **Loggia del Lionello**, was built by a goldsmith in 1448 and faithfully reconstructed after a fire in 1876; a second loggia, the **Loggia di San Giovanni** (1533), supports a clock tower and a bell rung by two Venetian-inspired 'Moors'. There is the usual Venetian column topped by a Lion of St Mark, accompanied by a statue of Justice, with Bette Davis eyes; below this is a rather unhappy monument to the unhappy Peace Treaty of Campo Formio, in which Napoleon gave this part of Italy to Austria.

Palladio's rugged **Arco Bollari** (1556) is the gateway to the hill of the **Castello**, former seat of the Patriarch and the Venetian governor. In 1487 the latter built the sweeping portico that still shields visitors from inclement weather, but could do nothing against the 1976 earthquake that severely damaged all the buildings on the hill. Its three museums—civic, ancient and modern art, and the Risorgimento—finally reopened in 1987. Among the paintings are works by Tiepolo, Pordenone, Pellegrino di San Daniele, and Carpaccio; in the modern gallery are works by the brothers Afro, Mirko, and Dino Basaldell, natives of Udine. There are fine views of the Alps from the walls (*museums open 9.30–12.30, 3–6, Tues–Sat; 9.30am–12.30pm Sun; adm*).

## Down in the City

The oft-altered **Duomo**, just to the south of the Piazza Libertà, has a charming 14th-century lunette over the door with figures so weathered they look like gingerbread. The interior is a dignified Baroque symphony of grey and gold, with a handful of works by Tiepolo. In the heavy-set campanile there's a small **Cathedral Museum**, adorned with excellent 1349 frescoes of the *Funeral of St Nicolas* by Vitale da Bologna, and a 14th-century sarcophagus. The **Oratorio della Purità**, added to the cathedral in 1757, is a Tiepolo shrine, with its partly frescoed, partly painted *Assumption* on the ceiling, the altarpiece of the *Immaculate Conception*, and the chiaroscuro frescoes on the walls by G. B. Tiepolo's son Giandomenico (*closed for restoration at time of writing, but worth checking at tourist office*).

Near the Duomo (down Via Calzolai) is the austere 14th-century church, **San Francesco**, on Piazza Venerio; from here take a left on Via Savorgnana for the more ornate **San Giacomo**, with its clock tower and lifesize figures gazing over the arcaded **Piazza Matteotti**, Udine's centuries-old market square. An unusual feature of San Giacomo is the outdoor altar on the balcony over the door, once used to celebrate mass on market days.

From here, Via Sarpi leads around to join the Riva Bartolini with Palladio's **Palazzo Antonini** (now the Banca d'Italia). The Tiepolo trail, however, continues in the other direction: from the Piazza Libertà, take Via Manin through a gate to the Piazza Patriarcato and the **Palazzo Arcivescovile**, frescoed by Tiepolo with fine Old Testament scenes (*closed for restoration at time of writing; check with tourist office*). More recent art (Severini, Carrà, De Chirico, De Kooning, Segal, Lichtenstein, Dufy, and so on) is on display in the new **Galleria d'Arte Moderna** (*open 9.30–12.30, 3–6, Tues–Sat; 9.30–12.30 Sun; adm*), located on the northern fringes of the old town. To get there, follow Riva Bartolini to Via Palladio, then go straight on Vias Mazzini, Mantica and A. L. Moro, or take bus 2 directly from the station or Piazza 1 Maggio.

## Cividale del Friuli

Only a hop and a skip from Udine in the valley of the Natisone, Cividale del Friuli is a grand old town, founded in 50 BC by Julius Caesar as *Forum Iulii*, a name that was condensed for centuries into 'Friuli'. The Lombards invaded in 568, and made Cividale the capital of their first duchy. The city grew so important that the Patriarch of Aquileia moved here in 737, initiating a magnificent 8th century, documented by Paulus Diaconus, the contemporary

Lombard historian. Born in Cividale, Diaconus is one of the chief sources scholars have for the early Middle Ages in northern Italy. Cividale's patriarchal state endured from 1077 to 1366, when Udine took control. Though many of the town's monuments were damaged in the 1976 earthquake, all have since been repaired.

## South Bank

From the Cividale Città station, the corso leads to the main piazza, with the 13th–15th-century **Palazzo Comunale**, a statue of Julius Caesar, and the **Duomo**, begun in 1453 and given its plain but attractive Renaissance façade by Pietro Lombardo. It contains unique treasures: the 12th-century silver altarpiece, the *Pala di Pellegrino II*, with its 25 saints and two archangels; a fine gilded equestrian monument (1617) and the Renaissance sarcophagus of Patriarch Nicolò Donato. Beside the Duomo is the **Museo Cristiano** (*open April–Sept 9–7 daily; Oct–Mar 9.30–12, 3–6.30; adm*), which contains two masterpieces from the 8th century: the octagonal Baptistry of Callisto and the Altar of Ratchis, dating back to 749, a period when there was still considerable confusion about the way hands and arms are attached to the human form. Yet, compare this charming primitive work with the six virgins in the Tempietto (*see below*).

*Tempietto Longobardo*

The **Museo Archeologico Nazionale** (*open April–Sept 9–7 daily; Oct–Mar 9–1; adm*) is in the Palazzo Pretorio, designed by Palladio, across the square from the Duomo. The collection is celebrated for the glories of its early medieval section; some of the most intriguing items came from the sarcophagus of the 6th-century Lombard Duke Gisulphus—a fibula, cross, and ring all wrought in gold. There are ancient weapons and ivory chess-men from a knight's tomb, the early 9th-century *Pax del Duca Orso*, adorned with an ivory crucifix in a golden frame and studded with jewels; a 1400 embroidered altar cover, a 10th-century ivory casket, the delightful *Psalter of Egbert of Tièves* (990), owned by St Elizabeth of Hungary, an 8th-century copy of Paulus Diaconus' *History of the Lombards*, and much more.

Corso Ponte d'Aquileia descends to the Natisone and the 1442 **Ponte del Diavolo**. In the Middle Ages, it was a common folk belief that bridges were magical, and many stories grew up on how they were erected overnight by the Devil himself. In Cividale's case,

Satan hung around in the morning to snatch the first soul that ventured across as his payment. But the wily Cividalesi outsmarted him by sending over a cat.

## The Tempietto Longobardo

The Tempietto Longobardo, also known as Santa Maria in Valle (*open 10–1, 3.30–6.30, daily; adm*), stands on the banks of the Natisone in Piazzetta San Biagio. It is the greatest work of the 8th century in Italy, despite the fact that it had to be restored in the 13th century after an earthquake shattered three-quarters of its ornamentation and all of its mosaics. The stucco reliefs that remain, however, are ravishing, uncanny, and perhaps even miraculous: there are six gently smiling white virgin saints, standing at either side of a beautiful and intricately carved window, all positioned over an even more intricately carved arch with a vine motif—a love letter from the Dark Ages to posterity.

Artistically, Europe wasn't to see the likes of the Tempietto again for 400 years. Besides the stuccoes there is a finely carved and inlaid wooden choir of 1371, and some excellent frescoes of the same period, replacing the lost mosaics; the *Adoration of the Magi* is lovely.

On the same north bank of the Natisone, another attraction is the mysterious **Ipogeo Celtico** under the house at Via Monastero 21. This peculiar man-made cave is believed to have served as a funeral chamber in the 3rd century BC, though no one's sure, because there's nothing to compare it with. Later the Romans and Lombards used it as a prison, where unfortunates would have had to look at the three monstrous, carved heads that peer out of the walls seemingly from the dawn of time itself (*for it to be opened, inquire at the Museo Archeologico*).

---

### *Where to Stay*

### Gorizia

The most attractive place to stay in Gorizia is the **★★Palace**, Corso d'Italia 63, ⑦ (0481) 82166, ⊕ 31658 (moderate), with large modern rooms on the main street. Opposite Gorizia railway station, the **★Albergo Silvano** (inexpensive) has basic rooms, none with bath.

### Udine

**★★★★Astoria Hotel Italia**, Piazza XX Settembre 24, ⑦ (0432) 207091 (expensive) is the *grande dame* of the city's hotels, conveniently located in the heart of town; it has a fine restaurant, specializing in meat and fish dishes in the Veneto style. Just outside the centre of Udine, but only five minutes' walk from the train station, is **★★★San Giorgio**, Piazzale Cella 2, ⑦ (0432) 505577, ⊕ 506110 (moderate), which has good, modern, air-conditioned rooms. Of the cheap hotels in Udine, the **★Piccolo Friuli**, Via Magrini 9, ⑦ (0432) 507817 (inexpensive) is streaks ahead, with baths in all its comfortable rooms. Not quite such good value but nearer the centre is **★Da Arturo**, Via Pracchiuso 75, ⑦ (0432) 299070 (inexpensive).

### Cividale del Friuli

Cividale del Friuli's hotel **★★★Al Castello**, Via del Castello 18, ⑦ (0432) 733242 (moderate), slightly outside the town in the suburb of Fortino, is not in a castle but a former fortified Jesuit Seminary, and now offers Cividale's most atmospheric rooms, as well as a fine restaurant with views from its balcony. The **Locanda Pomo d'Oro**, Piazza S. Giovanni 20, © (0432) 734189 (moderate) is the cheapest option in Cividale itself; the only real bargains to be found are in surrounding villages.

---

### Eating Out

## Gorizia

In Gorizia's Borgo Castello, with views over the town and the surrounding hills, you can sup in medieval splendour at the **Lanterna d'Oro al Castello**, © (0481) 85565 (moderate). The menu features Friuli specialities like *prosciutto di San Daniele*, and well-prepared dishes of venison, kid and boar. (*Closed Mon.*) For funksters, the **Bastione Fiorito** (inexpensive) has cheap food and a disco inside one turret of Gorizia's castle.

## Cormons

Cormons has several fine restaurants. The best is outside the centre on a hilltop in Subida, **Al Cacciatore della Subida**, © (0481) 60531 (moderate), enjoying a charming country setting that's complemented by perfect local cuisine. The cold breast of pheasant in mushroom cream is a popular summer dish, and there are excellent Collio wines. (*Closed Tues, Wed, Feb.*) **Al Giardinetto**, Via Matteotti 54, © (0481) 60257 (moderate) is in the centre of town, with a Hungarian-flavoured menu: gnocchi with plums, goulash, rack of pork, Sachertorte and poppy-seed cakes. (*Closed Mon evenings, Tues.*)

## Udine

Udine's **Alla Buona Vita**, Via Treppo 10, © (0432) 21053 (expensive) is Venetian in its ownership and menu. Good seafood antipasti and seafood risotto, liver *alla veneziana*, bigoli, and that good Lagoon cuisine in a refined setting. (*Closed Mon.*) **All'Antica Maddalena**, Via Pelliccerie 4, © (0432) 25111 (moderate) consists of two small but lovely Renaissance and Baroque dining rooms, where good Veneto cuisine is served, with an emphasis on seafood, truffles in season, and steaks with various sauces prepared at your table. The oldest restaurant in Udine, **Alla Vedova**, Via Feletto 43, © (0432) 470291 (moderate) is quite a way from the historic centre, off the SS13 to Tarvisio (bus no.2); but what better way to spend an evening than at a table near the great hearth (or outdoors in the summer), dining on wild duck risotto? The house's red Refosco is famous. **Da Arturo**, attached to the hotel (inexpensive, *see* above for details), is a good neighbourhood trattoria that will fill you in on local Friulian specialities.

For an exceptional meal, head 7km north of Udine to Tricesimo and its gourmet haven, **Da Boschetti**, Piazza Mazzini 9, © (0432) 851230 (very expensive), where the innovative chef bases his dishes entirely on the availability of fresh ingredients and old Friulian traditions—try pappardelle with porcini mushrooms, scallops with

French beans in almond oil, or steamed salmon with vegetables, followed by exquisite desserts.

### Cividale del Friuli

If you're making a day trip to Cividale, stop in at **Alla Frasca**, Via di Rebesi 10, ℂ (0432) 731270 (moderate), with a charming Renaissance atmosphere and tasty Friulian dishes, including a *menu di funghi* that offers truffles and mushrooms with everything. (*Closed Mon.*) Also pleasant is **Al Fortino**, Via Carlo Alberto 46, ℂ (0432) 731217 (moderate), with typical Friuli fare, and homemade pasta. (*Closed Mon evenings, Tues.*) Behind the Duomo in Cividale, **Trattoria Al Paradiso**, Via Cavour 21, ℂ (0432) 732438, is a place that's always full of locals. (*Closed Mon.*)

## The Carnia and Central Friuli

### *Tourist Information*

There are tourist offices in the mountains of the Carnia region in **Tarvisio**, Via Roma 10, ℂ (0428) 2135, @ 2972; in the Carnia Centrale in **Arta Terme**, near Tolmezzo, at Via Umberto 15, ℂ (0433) 929290, @ 92104; and in **Savorgnani/Forni di Sopra**, on the way west towards the Cadore, at Via Cadore 1, ℂ (0433) 886767, @ 886686. There is also an office in **Pordenone**, at Piazza della Motta 13, ℂ (0434) 21912.

### The Carnia

Sadly, the Carnia region north of Udine, with the lovely old towns of Gemona and Venzone, was the epicentre of the great '76 earthquake, and few of their monuments survive, though they are now linked by a bright new *autostrada*, one of Italy's most recent engineering marvels. The mountain valleys, especially in the eastern Julian Alps, are Slovene-speaking, and if the peaks lack the imposing grandeur of their Dolomite neighbours, they also lack their crowds and lofty prices in their summer and winter resorts. Trail maps, ski information, and a list of the forty *rifugi* in the region may be had from the regional tourist offices.

The mountains around the pass at **Tarvisio** (near the Austrian and Slovenian borders) are stern, but cradle an up-and-coming winter and summer resort, **Sella Nevea**, near two pretty lakes at the national park in **Fusine**. One of the prettiest excursions in the area is up to **Lago del Predil** under Monte Magante on the border with Slovenia.

**Tolmezzo** is the main town of the Carnia and the transportation hub of the mountains, with buses to most of the villages. To the west of Tolmezzo the scenery grows increasingly delightful. Resorts have sprung up at **Arta Terme**, with its mineral springs, **Ravascletto** and **Villa Santina**. The district around **Paularo** is especially rich in *casolari*, the unusual wooden multi-storied chalets resembling walk-up barns. **Forni di Sopra** has a fine 15th-century triptych in the Romanesque church of San Floriano, and good skiing, as does **Forni di Sotto**, a village rebuilt after the Nazis burnt it to the ground in reprisal for partisan activities. **Sauris** has a beautiful lake with ski slopes on the surrounding mountains. From **Comeglians** in the north of the valley there is a lovely scenic road up to **Sappada** in the Cadore (see p.446).

## Udine to Pordenone

West from Udine you can take a detour through the Friulian heartland to **San Daniele del Friuli**, famous for its sweet cured hams and the fine frescoes by Pellegrino di San Daniele in the church of **San Antonio**. Every August, a *festa del prosciutto* is held, when hundreds of varieties of ham are lined up in the central piazza for tasting. **Spilimbergo**, on the west bank of the Taglimento, is the site of the 'painted castle' with lovely exterior frescoes, a Gothic cathedral with paintings by Pordenone, and a Mosaic school, founded in 1922 and open for tours. Another town in the district, **Maniago**, produced swords and daggers for the Republic of Venice, and now manufactures cutlery, axes, nailclips and more, all on display in the *comunale* cutlery shop.

On the main Udine-Pordenone road, **Codroipo** is the site of the enormous **Villa Manin** (1738), residence of Venice's last doge (*interior open 9–12.30, 3–6, Tues–Sun*). When he was elected, his chief rival declared, 'A Friulian as Doge! The republic is dead.' The prediction was correct, but the villa, with its air-headed frescoes and elegant park, recalls better days. Napoleon was one of its guests, if not a welcome one.

## Pordenone

Pordenone is a working city and provincial capital that gave its name to the Renaissance artist G. A. Sacchiense, whose works may be seen in the **Museo Civico**, housed in the pretty 15th-century Palazzo Richiere (*open 9.30–12.30, 3–6.30, Tues–Sun; adm*) and in the **Duomo**, where his odd masterpiece the *Madonna della Misericordia* hangs. The cathedral has a beautiful campanile in Romanesque brickwork. The bizarre **Palazzo Comunale**, focal point of Pordenone's arcaded *corso*, has a Venetian clock tower topped by two bell-ringing Moors, superimposed on a graceful 13th-century building. The city has a number of shady green parks along the river Noncello.

South of Pordenone, the wee hamlet of **Sesto al Reghena** is the site of the fortified **Abbey of Santa Maria in Sylvis**, founded by the Lombards in the 8th century. It possesses some fine early bas-reliefs, a 13th-century *Annunciation*, and unique frescoes; look especially for the *Albero della Vita*, depicting Christ crucified on a voluptuous pomegranate tree.

**Sacile** to the west is a pleasant town on the willowy banks of the Livenza, which has, ever since 1351, held a bird festival (the *Dei Osei*) on the last Sunday in August. Thousands of songbirds are assembled in the main piazza, and prizes are awarded to the birds and the person who can do the best imitation of their songs. To the north, the mountain basin of **Piancavallo** (1300m) is the most important winter resort in Friuli, under the towering slopes of Monte Cavallo. From **Montereale** near Maniago a 50km road, the SS251, threads through a steep mountain gorge to Longarone in the Eastern Dolomites.

## Emilia-Romagna

S. Apollinare Nuovo – Mosaic

Between the sparkling wines of Lombardy, the elegant Soave of the Veneto and the full-bodied Chianti of Tuscany, Emilia-Romagna seems like a glass of warm beer. It is mostly flat, on the southern plain of the Po, hot and humid in the summer, and cold and fog-bound in the winter. Most tourists see it only from the train window when chugging between Venice and Florence.

But for anyone interested in cracking the surface of this glossiest and most complex of nations, Emilia-Romagna is an essential region to know. For this is Middle Italy, agricultural, wealthy, progressive, a barometer of Italian highs and lows—the birthplace of the country's socialist movement, but also of Mussolini and Fascism. In Emilia-Romagna hard-working cities like Modena, Parma, and Bologna share space with Rimini, Italy's vast, madcap international resort, with Ravenna, the artistic jewel of the region with its stupendous Byzantine mosaics, and with traditional Apennine villages. Emilia-Romagna is the cradle of Italy's greatest and most innovative film directors—Fellini, Bertolucci, and Antonioni; of musical giants like Verdi, Toscanini, Pavarotti, Tebaldi, and Bergonzi; and of such diverse talents as Marconi, Savonarola, Ariosto, and Ferrari.

As a united region, Emilia-Romagna is a child of the Risorgimento. Emilia, the land west of Bologna, was named after a Roman road, the Via Aemilia, the modern Via Emilia, built by M. Aemilius Lepidus in 187 BC between Piacenza and Rimini running almost dead straight for hundreds of kilometres along the course of the Apennines. Nearly all of Emilia's large cities grew up at intervals along the road, like beads on a string. Romagna, the land to the east of Bologna, recalls the period from the 5th century to 751 when this was 'Rome', when Ravenna was the last enclave of the Roman Empire in the west, ruled by the exarchs of the Eastern Roman Empire in Byzantium. By the Middle Ages most of these cities had gone their own way, controlled by dynasties of dukes and *signori*—the Farnese, Este, Malatesta, Bentivoglio, and Da Polenta—who claimed at least nominal allegiance to the pope, and held the front line between the Papal States and the not always friendly Venetians and Milanese.

In Emilia-Romagna you'll find, besides the unique art of the Byzantines and Ostrogoths in Ravenna, some of Italy's finest Romanesque churches (Parma and Modena), two of its crookedest towers (Bologna), some of its most beau-tiful Renaissance art (Parma, Bologna, and Ferrara) and the Renaissance's most unusual building, the Malatesta Temple in Rimini. The province of Parma has some of Italy's finest castles, and there's a veritable plethora of spas, most famously at Salsomaggiore. You can ski, hike, ride, or hang-glide in the Apennines, observe the wildfowl in the Po Delta, sunbathe in style on the Adriatic, go duty-free shopping in San Marino, visit Italy's ceramics capital at Faenza, or attend a grand opera in Parma, Reggio, Bologna, or Modena. You'll also find the best food in Italy in Emilia-Romagna—this is the

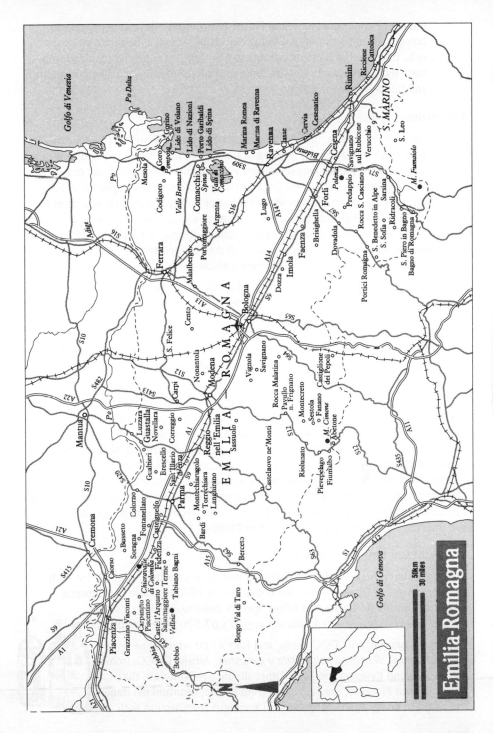

Emilia-Romagna

home of Parmesan cheese and Parma ham, tortellini, lasagne, spaghetti bolognese, and a hundred different kinds of sausages, balsamic vinegar and eels. It is also the home of Lambrusco, which if it's the right stuff should foam like a beer when it's first poured, only to reveal a sparkling, elegant, and full-bodied wine below.

## Itineraries

The region's art and architectural highlights can easily be seen in eight days or so—from west to east, begin with a half day in **Piacenza**, and from there take a bus to **Busseto**, with its Verdian memories. **Parma** requires an entire day to take in its magnificent cathedral and Baptistry, its museums in the Farnese palace, and its frescoes by Correggio. Leave half a day too for the cathedral and museum in **Modena**, and at least two and a half days for **Bologna**, perhaps Italy's most underestimated art city. **Faenza**'s great ceramics museum and shops deserve a half day, easily divided with the Malatesta temple in **Rimini**. Give **Ravenna**'s marvellous churches and monuments a very full day, or even two, and the cathedral, Este castle, and fine Renaissance palaces of **Ferrara** a whole day as well.

It would, though, be a shame to race through the monuments of the flatlands without taking a breather in the country. From Piacenza you can visit the attractive Roman ruins at **Velleia**, or ancient **Bobbio**, with its monastery founded by an Irish monk, or the fine medieval village of **Castell'Arquato**. In Parma it's worthwhile hiring a car to visit its fine castles, especially **Torrechiara** and **Soragna**, or the Farnese's 'little Versailles', in **Colorno**. There are several interesting old towns north of Reggio Emilia like **Novellara**, **Guastalla**, and **Luzzara**, home of Italy's museum of *naif* painting.

From Modena you can take a lovely detour into the northern Apennines for some fine mountain scenery; the resort of **Sestola** is an excellent base for excursions around Monte Cimone, the tallest peak in the range. In the spring **Vignola**, also south of Modena, is a wonderland of cherry blossoms. Southern Forlì province, especially around **Portico di Romagna**, **Santa Sofia**, and **Campigna** is also good for mountain excursions. The wetlands and forests of the **Po Delta** and the great medieval **abbey of Pomposa** are worth a visit from Ferrara, which also has a string of seven beach resorts, which are quieter and more Italian than **Rimini**, **Riccione**, and **Cattolica** further south. These southern resorts, though, are all an easy bus hop from the pigmy mountain republic of **San Marino**.

## The Wines of Emilia-Romagna

The most comprehensive place in Emilia-Romagna to try wines is inside the 13th-century fortress of **Dozza**, which was converted in 1970 to house the **Enoteca Regionale Emilia-Romagna** (see below 'East of Bologna/Imola'). It stocks around 450 vintages, selected from the region's 67,500 wine-producers.

The region has thirty-six DOC wines, and Italy's first white wine with *denominazione di origine controllata e garantita*, Albana DOCG, from the area around Ravenna and Forlì. Other distinctive wines are the Malvasia from Piacenza; the Sauvignon from Parma; Montuni del Reno, from around Bologna; and Sangiovese di Romagna from around Forlì.

Lambrusco comes in four DOC varieties: Lambrusco Salamino di Santa Croce, Lambrusco di Sorbrara, and Lambrusco Grasparossa di Castelvetro, all from the hills surrounding Modena, and Lambrusco Reggiano from Reggio Emilia. Drink it with the fatty foods typical of the region—parmesan, salami, ham.

## Piacenza

Competing with the more famous and obvious charms of nearby Parma and Cremona, Piacenza is the unassuming wallflower of Renaissance art cities. Nevertheless, it can boast of two of the most gallant horses in Italy, a Botticelli, and an amazing liver.

A Roman colony established in 218 BC at the conjunction of the Via Aemilia and the Po, Piacenza was an important *comune* in the 12th and 13th centuries, and a member of the Lombard League in 1314. It spent much of the subsequent centuries under the Farnese thumb, as part of the Duchy of Parma. In 1848, after a plebiscite, Piacenza became the first city to unite with Piedmont in the new nation of Italy, earning itself the nickname of *Primogenita* or 'first-born'.

### Getting Around

The **train station**, on Piazzale Marconi, is about a 10-minute walk from the centre. There are frequent connections to Milan (1½hrs), Parma (40min) and Cremona. The **bus station** is in the Piazza Cittadella, near the Palazzo Farnese, with buses to Cremona, Bobbio (10 a day, 1hr 20min), Grazzano Visconti, Castell'Arquato (1hr) and other destinations in the province. Buses to the excavations in Velleia (1hr 40min) are infrequent; if you go make sure you don't get stranded.

Piacenza is a major **road** junction. The historic Via Emilia, now also known as the SS9, heads south-east from the city towards Parma, Bologna and the coast, and northwards to Milan. Parallel to it there now runs the *autostrada* A1, which is, though, not quite as straight. Just north of Piacenza both are crossed by the A21 from Turin to Cremona and Brescia, which is accompanied for most of its route by the more peaceful SS10. South-west of the city the SS45 leads off towards Bobbio and Genoa.

### Tourist Information

The provincial tourist office is at Piazzetta dei Mercanti 10 (flanking Piazza Cavalli), © (0523) 29324. The city information office is at Via S. Siro 17, © (0523) 34347, @ 34348.

## Piazza Cavalli

Piacenza's excellent Piazza Cavalli (to get there from the station, cut across the park to Vias G. Alberoni and Roma, then turn left on Via Carducci) takes its name from its two bronze horses with flowing manes, the **Cavalli**, masterpieces of the early Baroque cast in the 1620s by Francesco Mochi. Riding them are two members of the Farnese clan: Alessandro, the 'Prince of Parma', who served as Philip II of Spain's governor in the Low Countries during the Dutch War of Independence (not a position that won him any popularity contests, despite the fine statue), and his son Ranuccio. The piazza also contains the Gothic **Palazzo del Comune** (1280), with swallowtail crenellations, mullioned windows and a rose window, and the 13th-century church of **San Francesco**, noted for its Gothic interior.

Rising up at the end of the main street, Via XX Settembre, the Lombard-Romanesque **Duomo** (1122–1233) is an imposing pile; viewed from the side and apse it's a picturesque confusion of columns, caryatids, and galleries in the shadow of the mighty campanile. The transitional interior (from Romanesque to Gothic) includes some good 15th-century frescoes. From here Via Chiapponi leads to **Sant'Antonino**, Piacenza's most ancient church, with an 11th-century octagonal lantern believed to be the first built in Italy, and a fine Gothic porch called the *Paradiso*. Just southwest on Vias San Siro and Santa Franca, across the street from a picturesque but derelict Art Nouveau theatre, is the **Ricci-Oddi Gallery** (*open April–Oct 10–12, 3–5, Tues–Sun; Nov–Mar 2–4pm Tues–Sun; adm*), a well-arranged collection that offers an excellent idea of what Italian artists were up to between the years 1800 and 1930.

## The Palazzo Farnese

From Piazza Cavalli, Corso Cavour leads to the pachydermic, uncompleted Palazzo Farnese, local headquarters of the ducal family (begun in 1558). Inside is the **Museo Civico** (*open 9am–12.30pm Tues–Thurs; 9–12.30, 3–6, Fri–Sun; adm*). Botticelli's lovely *Tondo* is the highlight of the paintings, and in the archaeological section you can see the most famous Etruscan bronze of them all: the *Fegato di Piacenza*, a model of a sheep (or some say human) liver, designed for apprentice augurs, diagrammed and inscribed with the names of the Etruscan deities. The Etruscans regarded the liver as a microcosm of the sky, ruled over by various gods, and looked in it for blemishes to see which deity had anything to communicate. Another section of the museum contains medieval arms, and another 18th- and 19th-century coaches.

About 2km southwest of the city is **San Lazzaro Alberoni** (*visits by appointment only, ✆ 63198*). This college contains a fine collection of Flemish tapestries, and among its 16th–18th century Flemish and Italian paintings, Antonello da Messina's *Christ at the Column*—an unusual composition and the Renaissance's most sorrowful Christ.

---

## Environs of Piacenza

The rarely visited hills and mountains south of Piacenza offer several possibilities for excursions or road stops. The main SS45 to Genoa follows the Trebbia valley to **Bobbio** (46km), where St Columbanus founded a monastery in 612, shortly before his death. Columbanus, one of several scholarly Irish monks who came to the illiterate continent as missionaries in the Dark Ages, was also the founder of the great abbey of Luxeuil (Vosges), which he had been forced to leave because of his outspoken views of the Frankish count and the Celtic observances in his church. The **Basilica**, rebuilt in the 15th century, has traces of Columbanus's church and his Renaissance sarcophagus. The **Museo di San Colombano** (*open 10–12, 3–6, Sat, Sun only; adm*) contains a famous 4th-century ivory bucket with reliefs, Romanesque statuary, and painting; in the town of Bobbio, clustered around the monastery and castle, there are many fine old stone houses.

Emilia's best-preserved Roman town, prettily situated on a hillside, is **Velleia**, 33km south of Piacenza between Bobbio and Salsomaggiore. It was never very large, but retains an interesting forum, temple, amphitheatre and mysterious large carved stones that resemble bathtub plugs. Most of the items excavated are now in Parma, though bits and pieces remain in Velleia's **antiquarium** on the site (*open 9am–sunset daily*). If you're driving you can cut over the hills from here to Lugagnano and **Castell'Arquato**, a lovely walled hill town built around an asymmetrical **Palazzo Pretorio** (1293) and a Romanesque church of the same period—a picturesque ensemble Placenza likes to put on its brochures. Just as picturesque, closer to Piacenza, but not as authentic, **Grazzano Visconti** was recently rebuilt in the medieval style. The result is charming, and the village is a good place to purchase ornamental wrought iron.

---

*Piacenza ℂ (0523–)*  **Where to Stay**

**expensive**

Piacenza's most prestigious hotel, the ★★★★**Grande Albergo Roma**, Via Cittadella 14, ℂ 23201, is just off Piazza Cavalli; it offers old-fashioned service, comfortable air-conditioned rooms, a garage, and a good restaurant.

**moderate**

For modern rooms, with TV and air-conditioning, try the ★★★**Nazionale**, Via Genova 35, ℂ 712000, @ 456013. It has an underground garage. ★★**Bivio**, Via Pennazzi 5, ℂ 62737, is good value, with rooms with or without baths.

**inexpensive**

Near the station there are a couple of plain, simple choices—★**Rangoni**, Piazzale Marconi 1, ℂ 21778, and ★**Moderno**, Via Tibini 31, ℂ 29296, @ 384438. Both offer basic rooms, with or without baths. (*Be warned that, along with most of Piacenza, they close for August.*)

---

*Piacenza ℂ (0523–)*  **Eating Out**

**expensive**

Piacenza can claim an exceptional gourmet restaurant, the delightful **Antica Osteria del Teatro**, Via Verdi 16, near Sant'Antonino, ℂ 384639, where local recipes merge delectably with French *nouvelle cuisine* under the chef's magic touch. (*Closed Sun evenings, Mon, Aug.*)

**moderate**

The nearby **Ginetto**, Piazza Sant'Antonino 8, ℂ 335785, is the Osteria's main rival for honours at the table, its tantalizing menu also featuring a French touch or two—vol-au-vent, quiche and crêpes filled with artichokes and cheese, or with spinach and ricotta, and a celebrated strawberry torte. For interesting risottos, and good seafood, try the **Antico Caffè**, Via Garibaldi 49, ℂ 24918. (*Closed Sun, Aug.*)

**Trattoria Brianza**, Vicolo Manzini 3, © 37638, specializes in both Piacentine and Spanish dishes such as gazpacho and paella for the pasta-weary.

## From Piacenza to Parma

North of the Via Emilia between Piacenza and Parma is the flat countryside of the Po valley known as the *Bassa*, often featured in Italian films. Down the Via Emilia itself, 30km east of Piacenza, the **Abbey of Chiaravalle della Colomba** (*open 9–12, 2–7, daily*), 4km north of Alseno, has a Romanesque church and beautiful brick cloister. More elaborate Romanesque awaits at **Fidenza**, the Roman *Fidentia Iulia*, known for centuries as the Borgo San Donnino until Mussolini resurrected its old, more imperial-sounding name. Fidenza's interest is concentrated in its 13th-century **Duomo**, with a porch adorned with statues by the followers of the great Antelami, the master of Parma's Baptistry.

South of Fidenza, **Salsomaggiore** ('Big Salt') with its 109 hotels is the largest and best-known of a cluster of saline water spas specializing in arthritic and rheumatic cures. It was popular with Italian royalty at the turn of the century, and is now soemtimes favoured by operatic celebrities. Its main baths, the **Terme Berzieri**, are concentrated in an intriguing half-baked Liberty-style palace. Better, stop in at the **Palazzo dei Congressi** on Viale Romagnosi. Once this was the town's grandest hotel, built in Salsomaggiore's pre-First World War golden era and owned by Cesar Ritz; past clients have included Caruso, Toscanini and Queen Margherita of Italy. The lobby is still one of the grandest in Italy, a Liberty-arabesque fantasy with fabulously colourful frescoes by Italy's Art Nouveau master Galileo Chini. Another important spa nearby is **Tabiano Bagni**, with stinky sulphur springs.

## Busseto

Lying some 15km north of Fidenza on the road to Cremona, Busseto is the attractive, neatly rectangular walled town that gave the world Joe Green—Giuseppe Verdi. To Italians Verdi is not just another great composer, but the genius who expressed the national spirit of the Risorgimento in music: Italy's answer to Richard Wagner.

Opera buffs can have a field day and take in the complete 'Swan of Busseto' tour, beginning in the house at **Roncole**, 9km southeast of Busseto (*open April–Nov 9.30–12.30, 3–7, Tues–Sun; adm*) where the composer was born in 1813, son of a grocer and tavern-keeper . While in Roncole, you may also visit the parish church where little Giuseppe was baptized and played the organ.

In Busseto proper a statue of Verdi relaxes in an armchair near the medieval castle, or **Rocca**, built by the Pallavicini lord Oberto, who became the subject of Verdi's first and seldom heard opera, *Oberto*. The Rocca contains the **Teatro Verdi**, modelled after La Scala, built in the composer's honour in 1845; Verdi frequently attended performances here. The Rocca's Palazzo Pallavicino is now the **Museo Civico** (*castle, theatre and museum open April–Nov 9.30–12.30, 3–7, Tues–Sun; Dec–Mar call © (0524) 92487; adm*) packed full of Verdian memorabilia. In Sant'Agata di Villanova, 3km north of Busseto, the composer built the **Villa**

Verdi (*open April–Oct; adm*) with the proceeds from *Rigoletto*. It is privately owned, but guided tours are offered of the house and a replica of the hotel room in Milan where Verdi died in 1901.

## The Castles of Parma

The province of Parma is known for its beautiful castles, some of which lie between Busseto and Parma. The **Palace of Soragna** (*open April–Oct 9–12, 3–7, Sun, Tues, Thurs; Nov–Mar 9–12, 2–5, Sun; adm*), was begun in the 8th century as a castle and converted into a palace ten centuries later by its current owners, the Princes of Meli Lupi. It contains some fine original furnishings and frescoes by Parmigianino, Gentile da Fabriano, and others. In **Fontanellato** the fairytale **Castello di Sanvitale** (*open 9.30–11.45, 3–6, Tues–Sun; Nov–Mar closes at 5pm; adm*) is much more castle-like, surrounded by a proper moat that's still in use and adorned inside with frescoes; the rich, sensuous *Diana and Actaeon* in the boudoir is by Parmigianino. Another imposing fortress nearby, **Castel Guelfo** (*visible from the outside only*) once belonged to the Ghibelline Pallavicini family of Busseto, but was renamed as an insult by its Guelph captors in 1407.

In **Colorno**, just north of Parma on the road to Mantua, one of the Farnese dukes, Ranuccio II, converted an old castle into a 'miniature Versailles' in 1660. It has beautiful gardens, an orangerie—and tunnels; the later Bourbon rulers must have been nervous, for they installed escape hatches leading all over the countryside, one supposedly running all the way to Parma (*open to visitors by appointment, © (0521) 816939*).

### *Where to Stay and Eating Out*

#### Salsomaggiore

The ★★★★★Grand Hotel & Milano, Via Dante 1, © (0524) 572241, @ 573884 (very expensive) is the plushest place in town to take the waters, with lovely air-conditioned rooms, and a heated pool in a pretty garden. (*Open April–Oct.*). The ★★★**Valentini**, Viale Porro 10, © (0524) 578251, @ 578266 (moderate) is another old hotel, with its own spa, swimming pool, and parking, all in a quiet park setting. (*Open 23 Mar–16 Nov.*)

Salsomaggiore has by far the largest choice of hotels in the less expensive price range. One plain but reasonable hotel in the centre of town is the ★**Albergo Livia**, Piazzale Berzieri 6, © (0524) 573166 (inexpensive).

The classic place to eat in Salsomaggiore is **Al Tartufo**, Viale Marconi 30, © (0524) 573696 (expensive); besides *tartufi* (truffles), which star in many of the dishes, you can try the chef's famous grilled mushrooms. **Alle Querce da Giorgio**, Via Parma 85, © (0524) 572484 (moderate) is a peaceful restaurant by the side of a little lake filled with trout and carp. The patron suggests a menu, which will probably feature *porcini* mushrooms, truffles and homemade pasta among other good things. (*Closed Mon.*)

## Busseto

The finest place to stay in Busseto is, naturally, named after one of Verdi's operas, and is owned by the family of a tenor who often performs in them, Carlo Bergonzi: **★★★I Due Foscari**, Piazza Carlo Rossi 15, ✆ (0524) 92337, ✉ 91625 (moderate). It's small, very comfortable and will probably have no vacancies unless you reserve in advance; modern air-conditioning is not the least of its charms. Here, too, you can find one of Busseto's best restaurants, featuring solid, traditional Parmigiano cooking.

## Roncole

Verdi-ites can lunch (or on Saturday, dine) at one of the region's best-known and yet simplest restaurants, **Guareschi**, Via Processione 113, ✆ (0524) 92495 (moderate), where many of the ingredients of its specialities are made, or grown, on the family farm, including the Lambrusco, the prosciutto, the pasta, and the vegetables. All are well prepared and delicious. It's often booked out by wedding parties, so reserve in advance. (*Closed Fri.*)

## Sacca di Colorno

**Stendhal-Da Bruno**, Via Sacca 80, ✆ (0521) 815493 (moderate) is the perfect complement to a visit to the Farnese palace, inhabited in Stendhal's time by Marie Louise. Fish is the speciality here—eels and small fry from the Po, and denizens of the deep brought in daily from Chioggia. There's also great homemade charcuterie, desserts, and wine, all served in a serene setting.

## Parma

The French daily *Le Monde* rated Parma as the best Italian city to live in, for its prosperity and quality of life. Even the air in Parma is lighter and less muggy in the summer than that in other cities along the Po. One of Italy's great art cities and the second city in Emilia-Romagna after Bologna, Parma's many admirers can cite her splendid churches and elegant lanes, her artworks and antiquities, the lyrical strains of grand opera that waft from her Teatro Regio— a house that honed the talents of the young Arturo Toscanini—and the glories of its famous cheese and ham at table as reasons not only to visit, but to return again and again.

Parma is the place to see the masterpieces of Benedetto Antelami (1177–1233), the great sculptor trained in Provence (in Arles and St Gilles especially) and whose Baptistry here introduced the Italians to the idea of a building as a unified work in its architecture and scuptural programme. Parma's distinctive school of art began relatively late, with the arrival of Antonio Allegri Correggio (1494–1534), whose highly personal and self-taught techniques of *sfumato* and sensuous subtlety deeply influenced his many followers, most notably Francesco Mazzola, better known as Parmigianino.

### History

Parma is a fine example of how Italians have learned to adapt and even prosper in the face of continual political uncertainty. After starting out as a small Roman-way station on the Via Emilia, the fledgling medieval town of Parma found itself insecurely poised on the edge of

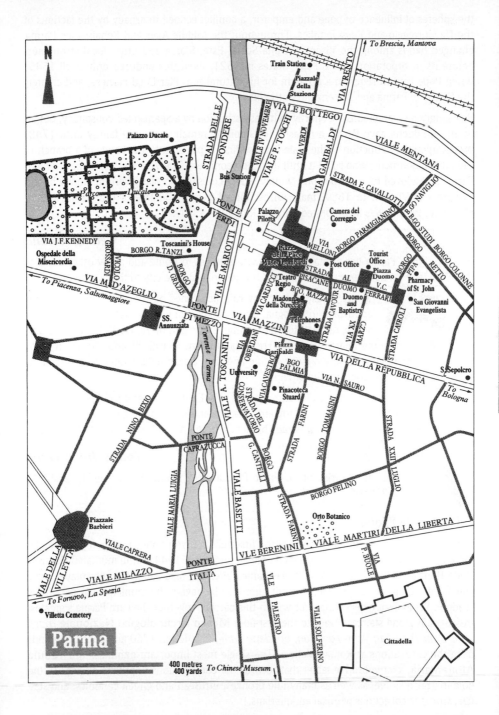

Parma

400 metres
400 yards

the spheres of influence of pope and emperor, a conflict echoed internally by the factions of the Da Correggio and Rossi families. Throughout the Middle Ages and Renaissance Parma changed hands among the Visconti, Della Scala, Este, Sforza and other local strongmen before its incorporation in the Papal States in 1521. Even this endured only until 1545, when Pope Paul III required a tax farm for his natural son, Pier Luigi Farnese, and created the Duchy of Parma and Piacenza to fit the bill.

Pier Luigi's own ambitions led shortly to his assassination by a Spanish-led conspiracy, but all in all, the duchy gave Parma a measure of stability, remaining in the family until 1748, when, upon the extinction of the male Farnese line, it passed into the hands of a branch of the French Bourbons, who ruled it until the Napoleonic era. The year 1815 saw the arrival of Parma's best-loved ruler, Napoleon's widow Marie-Louise, who was given the duchy by the Congress of Vienna. In 1859, mass unrest forced her to abdicate; a year later, after a plebiscite, the city was incorporated into the Kingdom of Italy.

## Getting Around

Parma has a small **airport**, with services to Rome and a few other destinations, mostly within Italy. It is just outside the city to the northwest.

The city is easy to reach by **rail**, positioned on the main line from Turin and Milan to Bologna, Florence and Rome. The station is north of the centre, on Via Monte Altissimo, at the end of Via Garibaldi; buses 1 and 8 link it to the heart of Parma. The **bus station**, ℰ (0521) 283178, is on Viale P. Toschi, between the railway station and the Palazzo della Pilotta. It has frequent services to all points in the province.

The main **roads** that cross in Parma are the Via Emilia (SS9) and parallel A1, and the north-south roads, the SS343 towards Mantua and the SS62 to La Spezia. Just to the west of Parma the A15 *autostrada* branches off the A1 and runs south to La Spezia.

## Tourist Information

The city tourist office is at Piazza del Duomo 5, ℰ (0521) 234735, ℰ 238605.

## Palazzo della Pilotta

Arriving by train or bus in Parma, one of the first buildings you notice is also, unfortunately, the most pathetic: the ungainly, never-completed and, since 1944, bomb-mutilated **Palazzo della Pilotta**, built for the Farnese. It was named after *pelote*, a ball game once played in its courtyard. The palace's appearance is not improved by having the municipal car park in its shadow. Yet looks are deceiving—for within this patched-together shell are Parma's greatest treasures. A grand staircase leads to the first-floor **Museo Archeologico Nazionale** (*open 9am–2pm Tues–Sat; 9am–1pm Sun, holidays; adm*), founded in 1760 and containing finds from the excavations at Roman Velleia. The single most important exhibit is the **Tabula Alimentaria**, a large bronze tablet that records the contributions of private citizens to the dole in Trajan's time, as well as many fine bronzes, Etruscan and Greek ceramics, and statuary from the collections of ducal antiquarians.

On the second floor, the **Galleria Nazionale** (*open 9am–2pm Tues–Sat; 9am–7.30pm Sun; separate adm exp*) was founded even earlier, in 1752. To reach the gallery you pass first through the wooden **Teatro Farnese**, built in 1618 by Palladio's pupil, Giambattista Aleotti; unlike his master's Teatro Olimpico in Vicenza, he created a living theatre, with rotating scenery and a stage that doesn't dwarf the actors. In 1944 a bomb tore most of the theatre into splinters and sawdust, but it has since been carefully reconstructed.

Most of the gallery's paintings are from Emilia-Romagna and Tuscany. The Early Renaissance collection features works by the Tuscans Gaddi, Spinello Aretino, Giovanni di Paolo and Fra Angelico and the Emilians Simone dei Crocifissi and Loschi (whose charming *St Jerome* holds a toddler of a lion paternally by the paw). Further along there's a lovely portrait sketch by Leonardo, *La Scapigliata*, four fine works by the Venetian Cima da Conegliano, and a portrait by Sebastiano del Piombo of the handsome Medici pope, Clement VII. Some of Correggio's most celebrated works are here, the tender *Madonna di San Gerolamo* and the *Madonna della Scodella* , as well as Parmiginiano's *Marriage of St Catherine* and the flirtatious *Turkish Slave*; among the non-Italian pictures are works by Peter Brueghel the Younger, Van Dyck, and Holbein's famous portrait of the sharp-featured Erasmus. In a room of their own are portraits of the Farnese clan, and Canova's statue of Marie Louise on her throne.

On the same floor as the gallery, the **Palatine Library** (*open 9–12 midday Tues–Sat; free*) has a vast collection of incunabula, codices, manuscripts and editions published by the city's famous printer Bodoni, who gave his name to the popular type he invented.

## Piazza della Pace

Behind the Palazzo and across the Verdi bridge is the restful, grassy Parco Ducale, with cafés, a lake, and exotic ducks; if, instead of crossing the river, you walk south from here along Viale Mariotti you will come to the excellent daily market in Piazza Ghiaia, a cornucopia of the region's gastronomic delicacies can be found on sale. Alternately, from the front of the Palazzo della Pilotta cross the **Piazza della Pace**, with its statue of a rugged partisan, to the **Glauco Lombardi Museum**, on Via Garibaldi 15 (*open April–Oct 9.30–12.30, 4–6, Tues–Sat; 9.30am–1pm Sun; Nov–Mar 3–5pm Tues–Sat; 9.30am–1pm Sun*), entirely devoted to the life and times of the former Empress of France and Duchess of Parma, Marie Louise. The south side of Piazza della Pace is occupied by the celebrated **Teatro Regio** (entrance in Via Garibaldi), built by Marie Louise in 1829. This is one of operatic Italy's holy-of-holies, and the best place to hear the region's favourite son, Verdi. Its audiences are legendarily contentious and demanding, and each year tenors and sopranos from all over the world submit either to avalanches of flowers or catcalls from the famous upper balconies, the *loggioni*. Toscanini began his career here playing in the orchestra, which has since been renamed in his honour.

Just off the Via Melloni, which leads away on one side of the Piazza, is the **Camere del Correggio** (*open 9am–7.30pm daily*), in the ex-convent of San Paolo. In 1519 its worldly abbess, Giovanna Piacenza, hired Correggio to fresco her refectory with sensuous mythological scenes; he portrayed the abbess herself as the goddess Diana over the fireplace. The decorative scheme in the vault is unique, with sixteen putti set over sixteen mythological emblems, of mysterious symbolic import; some claim to see a vast thematic allegory. The abbess wasn't the only woman in the High Renaissance to hide her meaning in secret images (*see* p.264, Isabella d'Este's rooms in Mantua). The second room contains fine 1514 frescoes and grotesques by Araldi.

## Piazza Duomo

Strada Pisacane connects the Piazza della Pace to the Piazza Duomo, the heart of medieval Parma and the site of its remarkable Romanesque cathedral and baptistery. The exterior of the **Duomo** (*open 9–12, 3–7, daily*) is ambitious, angular Romanesque, embellished with rows of shallow arches; three tiers of them cross the façade, creating an illusion of depth around the central arched window, and the pattern continues in the rich decoration of the sides, apses, and dome. The central portal of the façade, added in 1281, has reliefs of the Labours of the Months. The fine interior contains two masterpieces: a bas-relief of the *Deposition from the Cross* by Antelami, and, in the dome, Correggio's *Assumption* (1526-30), a work of art celebrated since the days of Vasari for its almost three-dimensional portrayal of clouds, angels and saints.

The octagonal **Baptistry** (*open 9–12, 3–6, daily; adm*) is one of the jewels of Italian Romanesque, constructed of pale rose-coloured marble from Verona. It was designed in 1196 by Antelami, who carved the remarkable ribbon frieze of animals and allegories that encircles the lower part of the exterior. The meaning behind all the winged cats, archers, griffons and sea serpents is as elusive as Correggio's ceiling; many are repeated in mirror images elsewhere in the frieze. Antelami is also responsible for the doorways dedicated to the Virgin Mary and the Last Judgement, and the statues in the niches. Inside are the master's famous reliefs of the Twelve Months, and spring and winter. The lovely 13th-century tempera paintings are by an unknown but masterly hand—be sure to bring enough lire coins to light them up.

Save some lire, however, for **San Giovanni Evangelista**, the church just behind the cathedral (*open 7–12, 3.30–7.30, daily*). Under its Baroque skin it shelters one of the masterpieces of the High Renaissance, Correggio's *Vision of St John* fresco in the dome. Unfortunately, when the church was remodelled in 1587 all of Correggio's other ceiling decorations were lost, though a fresco of St John writing down his vision survives over the door north of the altar. Other frescoes here are by Parmigianino. Near the church you can visit the historic

*Battistero di Parma*

**Pharmacy of St John** (*open 9am–1.45pm Tues–Sun; adm*) on Borgo Pipa, which has been dispensing drugs since 1298 and contains old jars, pots, 16th-century decoration and medieval pharmaceutical instruments.

## Piazza Garibaldi

In company with the rest of the old gents of Parma, Garibaldi and Correggio, or at least their statues, spend their day in the modern centre of the city, the **Piazza Garibaldi**. Here, too, stands the yellow 17th century **Palazzo del Governatore**, with its intricate sundial. Behind the palazzo, the church of **Madonna della Steccata** (*open 9–12, 3–6, daily*) was built in 1539 on Bramante's original design for St Peter's. Its sumptuous interior contains excellent 16th-century frescoes in its chapels by Parmigianino and his contemporaries.

## Paganini, Toscanini, and Stendhal

There are three musical and literary pilgrimages to make in Parma. The first is to the tomb of the embalmed wizard of catgut and bow, Paganini, who lies decked out in virtuoso splendour in **Villetta cemetery** (*a 15-minute walk from the centre of Parma on the west side of the river, open April–Oct 8–12, 2–7, daily; Nov–Mar closes at 5pm*). The **Birthplace of Arturo Toscanini** (1867–1957) is at Via Rudolfo Tanzi 13, between the Ponte di Mezzo and the Parco Ducale; it contains a variety of memorabilia and a copy of every record he ever made (*open 10am–1pm Tues–Sun*).

Stendhal aficionados will be glad to know that there really is a **Charterhouse of Parma**, the Certosa (*open April–Oct 9–12, 3–6, daily; Nov–Mar 2–5pm daily*), although it bears no resemblance to his imagination's invention in atmosphere, architecture, or history. Located 4km east of town (bus no.10), it was founded in 1281, but totally rebuilt in the 17th century, and now serves as a military school. The cloister is out of bounds, but you can visit the church's frescoed interior.

## Four Castles

Further afield there are Parma's famous castles (see above 'From Piacenza to Parma' for those to the west of the city). There are buses to each of them from Parma, but not between them, so to do a full tour you need a car. In the foothills south of Parma (on the road to Langhirano) towers **Torrechiara** (*open 9am–1pm Tues–Sat; 9–1, 3-7, Sun; adm*) a castle of brick and fantasy almost unchanged since the 15th century, and defended by four mighty towers. Inside there is an elegant courtyard and good frescoes by an artist named Bembo, who exceeded himself in the beautiful 'Golden Room' .

Another castle, the 15th-century **Bardi**, perches atop its own hill southwest of Parma (*to visit the interior, call ahead, ☎ (0525) 71321*). It retains its beautiful beamed ceilings and 16th-century frescoes. On the local road to Reggio Emilia via Montecchio lies **Montechiarugolo** (*Again, you must call ahead to visit (☎ (0521) 686600*). Built in 1406 and architecturally resembling Torrechiara, it contains fine 15th- and 16th-century paintings. At **Compiano**, further up in the mountains on the SS513 road, there is a half-ruined castle with something surprisingly rare in Italy—ghosts.

# The Gourmet in Emilia-Romagna

Emilia-Romagna is packed with things to buy and take home: ceramics in Faenza or Sassuolo, mosaics in Ravenna, wrought iron in Bologna, and lace or wicker baskets throughout the region. But nothing sums up this area so well as food, and, beside the countless wonderful experiences waiting in restaurants, it's easy to find tastes to take home. Cheese, meat, wine, liqueurs or sweets travel well.

Most Parmesan cheese, called *grana*, on account of its grainy quality, is actually *Parmigiano-Reggiano*, and is produced around Parma, Modena, and Reggio Emilia. Even more revered than the famous ham of Parma is *culatello*, a sausage made from a pig's buttocks, which can be prepared only in the humid lowlands of the Po valley. Much commoner is Parma ham itself, according to tradition left to dry in the sweet air of the hills in the Magra valley, where it loses its excessive saltiness while gaining the scent of pine and olives, then dried by the Cisa Pass, and flavoured with chestnut by the Apennines, before being brought down the valley of the River Parma.

Nocino is a liqueur which tradition states must come from Sassuolo, near Modena, and be made from unripe walnuts picked on St John's Day, the 24th of June. Pure alcohol is poured over the crushed nuts, then sugar, cinnamon, cloves and lemon rind are added; the mixture is left for forty days before being sieved through cotton. The other great specialities of Modena are balsamic vinegar—the finest of which is as prized and precisely regulated as any DOCG wine—and cherries, from Vignola.

In Bologna, delicatessens sell fresh tortellini, stuffed with any combination of ricotta cheese, minced beef or veal, bread, chicken, nutmeg, fresh herbs, or whatever else crosses the chef's mind. Bologna is also famous for its deserts and pâtisserie, the most specialised of which is *torta di riso*, a sweet, thick rice pudding.

---

### Shopping

The main market in Piazza Ghiaia, by the river, is the most convenient place to stock up for a picnic or pick up some local specialities to take home. Otherwise, try **Specialità di Parma**, Via Farina 9/c, a magnificently stocked emporium supplying all the regional delicacies. There are a number of antique shops in Parma, mainly along or around Via N. Sauro; fashion shops are clustered around Borgo Angelo Mazza. A world food fair, the **Cibus**, is held in May, and an antiques fair in late autumn. For tours of the plants that make Parma's prime products, prosciutto and Parmesan cheese, call each trade's cooperatives: the Consorzio Prosciutto, ✆ (0521) 243987, and the Consorzio Parmigiano, ✆ (0521) 292700.

---

*Parma ✆ (0521–)*

### Where to Stay

Parma's trade fair grounds are bustling in May and September, months when you may well find no room at the inn if you haven't reserved a couple of months in advance.

*very expensive*

Top of the range is the **★★★★Grand Hotel Baglione**, Via La Piacenza, ℭ 292929, ℘ 292828. Slightly outside the centre, it has modern rooms with every possible convenience.

*expensive*

The **★★★★Park Hotel Stendhal**, Via Bodoni 3, ℭ 208057, ℘ 285655, right in the heart of town alongside the Piazza Pilotta, is a rather old hotel, but still with good facilities.

*moderate*

The **★★★Torino**, Via A. Mazza 7, ℭ 281046, ℘ 230725, near the centre, offers plush rooms and garage parking in addition to the convenience of its location. In the knot of small streets behind the Duomo is **★★★Button**, Borgo Solina 7, ℭ 208039, ℘ 238783, with small but very comfortable rooms.

*inexpensive*

Two popular budget hotels are the **★★Croce di Malta**, Borgo Palmia 8, ℭ 235643, one street away from Piazza Garibaldi and pleasant, quiet and small, and the **★Brozzi**, Via Trento 11, ℭ 272717, ℘ 272724, near the station. Both have rooms with or without baths, and good cheap restaurants. Parma's youth hostel, **Ostello Cittadella**, Via Passo Buole, ℭ 581546, is housed in the Farnese's 17th-century pentagonal fortress, which now serves as a municipal park (bus no.9 from the station). IYHF card required.

---

*Parma ℭ (0521–)*                                                    **Eating Out**

*The pig is like the music of Verdi; nothing in it of waste*

supposed old Parma saying

It is just like the *Parmigiani* to link their two ruling passions, music and food; a perfect onion is greeted with the same rapt silence as a perfect dish of pasta, dusted with freshly grated parmesan cheese. Other dishes to look out for are *stracotto* (roast beef), *carpaccio* (raw beef), and its various methods of serving artichokes (*carciofi*)—in fritters, pasta dishes, and in crêpes.

*very expensive*

**La Greppia**, Via Garibaldi 39, ℭ 233686 , is housed in a former stable, with a delicious selection of *pasta di verdure* (made with spinach or tomatoes) and other original vegetable dishes, and good second courses, all prepared before your eyes in the glass kitchen. (*Closed Thurs, Fri, July.*)

*expensive*

An ideal place to dip into Parma's specialities is **Parizzi**, Strada della Repubblica 71, ℭ 285952, a large, cheerful restaurant with delicious antipasti of prosciutto di Parma and salami, followed by crêpes alla parmigiana, asparagus in pastry, or *cappelletti*,

Parma's favourite shape of pasta. Among the chef's very own specialities are, for a main course, *scaloppe Parizzi*, with fontina and ham, and great desserts. Reservations definitely necessary. (*Closed Sun evenings, Mon, most of Aug.*) Near the Duomo is **Angiol d'Or**, Vicolo Scutellari 1, © 282632 (closed Sun, Mon, Aug), with seating outside; expect risotto with quails, *tortelli d'erbetta* (filled with ricotta, eggs, and beet leaves), *tortellini di zucca* (with pumpkin, grated cheese and bread), and tripe with *parmigiano*.

### moderate

The **Vecchio Molinetto**, Via Milazzo 39, © 253941, near the Villetta cemetery, is an unpretentious place offering good honest local cuisine—great risotto baked with veal and *involtini alla Molinetto*. (*Closed Mon, Aug.*) A comfortable traditional restaurant in the centre of the city, **Sant'Ambrogio**, Vicolo Piaghe 1/a, © 34482, serves particularly good pasta and local meats. Another excellent place to get to grips with the local cuisine in the middle of Parma is the restaurant in the **Croce di Malta** hotel (*see* above).

### inexpensive

Traditional Parma cuisine at very reasonable prices is served at the **Trattoria dei Corrieri**, Strada del Conservatorio 1, © 234426, in an old postal relay station in the centre of town. The menu usually features salami and ham antipasti, pasta *alla parmigiana* and a filling and tasty *bollito misto* (boiled meats).

## Entertainment and Nightlife

**Opera** mobilizes a more enthusiastic local audience in Parma than just about anywhere else in Italy. The main season at the Teatro Regio runs from December to March, with some concerts during the rest of the year; there are also occasional performances at the Teatro Farnese. Parma also hosts two **music competitions**, one for conductors, at the end of August, and another for operatic singers, in October. In September there's also the **Verdi Festival**; for information, contact Fondazione Verdi Festival, Via Farini 34, © (0521) 289028, @ 282141. Throughout the summer concerts are also held in the surrounding castles—the tourist office provides a full list of forthcoming events.

## Reggio Emilia

A bright, prosperous agricultural city, Reggio nell'Emilia, now usually called just Reggio Emilia, was the Roman *Regium Lepidi*. It lines either side of the Via Emilia, which also divides the old part of the city from the new streets to the north. From 1409 to 1796 Reggio was ruled by the Este family of Ferrara, during which time its most famous son, Ludovico Ariosto (1474–1533), author of *Orlando Furioso*, was born. Nowadays it is noted for its numerous ballet schools, its balsamic vinegar and its version of Parmesan cheese, Parmigiano-Reggiano, which tastes exactly the same as Parma's to any sane person.

The tourist office is right in the centre of the town at Piazza Prampolini 5, © (0522) 451152, ✆ 436739.

## Piazza Prampolini

The **Piazza Prampolini**, just south of the Via Emilia, is the civic and ecclesiastical heart of Reggio, with its peculiar **Duomo** topped by a single octagonal tower. Most of its original Romanesque features were remodelled in the 16th century, though on the façade the fine statues of Adam and Eve remain, and in the tower niche, a copper Madonna flanked by the cathedral donors. On the same piazza, the **Palazzo Comunale**, begun in 1414 and often remodelled, was where the *Tricolore* was proclaimed the Italian national flag in 1797 during the second congress of Napoleon's Cispadane Republic, a very short-lived entity that covered the area between Reggio, Mantua, Ferrara and Bologna. Behind the cathedral, and beyond the main market in Piazza San Prospero—another wonderful place to see and stock up on local produce—the 16th-century church of **San Prospero** is noted for its fine choir, with frescoes and inlaid stalls.

## North of the Via Emilia

In the centre of Reggio's new broad streets is the vast Piazza Cavour and the renowned 19th-century **Teatro Municipale**, the town's opera house, crowned by a surplus of musing statuary; performances of opera, concerts and plays (from December to March) are of a high quality if not quite as prestigious as the Regio in Parma. The **Museo Spallanzani** (*open 9am–12 midday Tues–Sat; 3–5pm Sun*), near a powerful monument to the Martyrs of the Resistance, has various collections—Natural History, archaeology in the **Museo Chierici** (with the buxom Neolithic 'Chiozza Venus'), the Museum of the Risorgimento and Resistance, and the Museo Numismatico. In Reggio's public garden at the back of the theatre, there is an imposing funerary monument of a Roman family (50 BC) discovered in Boretto. Near here is the very eclectic **Galleria Parmeggiani** (*opening times still spitefully irregular; check with tourist office*), which until recently had been closed for restoration for years. If nothing else, note the 16th-century Moorish-style doorway brought over from Valencia. If you can get in to see them, many of the artworks inside are Spanish as well.

In San Maurizio, 3km east of Reggio, the 16th-century villa **Il Mauriziano** was the home of Ariosto's family, and some of the rooms have been restored to their appearance when the poet came to visit from his new home in Ferrara (*again, check for opening times*).

## Around Reggio

Some 15km northeast of Reggio, **Correggio** is a pretty town with old arcaded streets, the birthplace of the painter Antonio Allegri, better known as Correggio (d. 1534). His home on Borgo Vecchio was reconstructed in 1755. The **Palazzo dei Principi** (*open 9am–1pm Tues–Sun*), begun in 1506, contains the town's Museo Civico, with a *Christ* by Mantegna and some lovely cinquecento Flemish tapestries. The Renaissance church of **San Quirino** is attributed to the Farnese's favourite architect, Vignola. Northwest in **Novellara** the 14th-century Gonzaga dukes built a fine castle, the **Rocca**; this now serves both as the town hall and museum, housing medieval and Renaissance frescoes and a unique collection of chemists' jars.

Near the banks of the Po, **Gualtieri**, the Lombard *Castrum Walterii*, has a Spanish-style *plaza mayor*, the arcaded **Piazza Bentivoglio,** and the 16th-century brickwork **Palazzo Bentivoglio**. The latter has some fine frescoes, particularly those in the *Sala dei Giganti*. Another old Lombard town, **Guastalla** (*Wartstal*), was a capital of the Gonzaga, and conserves many 16th-century memories, including a statue of Ferrante Gonzaga the Condottiere, as well as the **Basilica della Pieve**, a fine Romanesque church begun in the 10th century, and the 1671 Teatro Ruggeri. Further down the Po on the outskirts of **Luzzara**, the former convent of Agostiano has been converted into the bright and charming **Museo Comunale dei Pittori Naif**, with a permanent collection of *naif* art. Many of the works are by Antonio Ligabue, who lived and died in Gualtieri. There are also frequent temporary exhibits, and a New Year's competition and show that lasts throughout January. The museum was founded by Cesare Zavattini, a great cinema verità director and collaborator of Vittorio De Sica.

Back towards the west along the river, **Brescello**, (Roman *Brixellum*), is adorned wih a statue by Sansovino of Ercole II d'Este in the guise of his namesake Hercules. The town is famous in Italian popular culture as the hometown of Giovanni Guareschi's *Don Camillo*, the priest of the post-war era (immortalized in films by Fernandel) eternally, fraternally at war with the Communist mayor Peppone. For obsessive fans, the Reggio tourist board produces a guide detailing places with which Guareschi was connected.

All of these villages are accessible by bus or train from Reggio; for **Canossa**, south of Reggio, you'll have to drive, or else walk 7km from the nearest bus stop. Its name will ring a bell with anyone who ever studied medieval history—it was the original family seat of the powerful feudal family of Da Canossa, whose most famous member was the mighty, charismatic and warlike Countess Matilda. In 1077, after Emperor Henry IV deposed Pope Gregory VII and the pope in turn excommunicated the emperor, Matilda, a partisan of the Guelfs, was instrumental in bringing Henry to Canossa on his knees in the snow to apologize to Gregory. It was a turning point; for the next two centuries, popes would hold the moral high ground (Henry IV and sons were soon avenged) over the kings and barons of Europe. Today Canossa is scenic and tranquil, with a ruined castle as a dim reminder of the days of Countess Matilda; every now and then historical pageants are staged inside.

---

© (0522–)                                                              *Where to Stay*

## Reggio

The ★★★★**Grand Hotel Astoria**, Viale L. Nobili 2, © 435245, @ 453365 (expensive) offers fine views over the municipal gardens. It has its own garage, comfortable, air-conditioned rooms, and great service.

The historic ★★★**Scudo d'Italia**, Via Vescovado 5, © 434345, @ 452602 (moderate) has traditionally accommodated most of Reggio's visiting actors and opera singers in its slightly old-fashioned but very pleasant rooms. On the ground floor is an excellent, but expensive, restaurant.

Slightly out of the centre, **★Stella**, Via Blasmatori 5, ℂ 432280 (inexpensive) offers basic rooms with or without bath. The youth hostel, **Ostello Tricolore**, Via dell'Abbadessa 8, ℂ (0522) 454795 (inexpensive) is modern, well-equipped, and near the station.

## Guastalla

North of Reggio, Guastalla has the most in the way of accommodation. **★★★Old River**, Viale Po 2, ℂ 838401, ✆ 824676 (moderate) offers excellent air-conditioned rooms (which can be crucial in August) in a pleasant green setting. It also has garage parking. **★Pacian**, Via Trieste 3, ℂ 824195 (inexpensive) has cheap rooms, with or without bath. There's also a youth hostel here, outside town at Viale Po 11, ℂ 824915. (*Open Mar–Oct.*)

---

ℂ (0522–)                                         *Eating Out*

## Reggio

Like Parma, Reggio is a major producer of Parmesan cheese (properly called here Parmigiano-Reggiano); like Modena, too, it distils *aceto balsamico*, or balsamic vinegar, as valuable as frankincense in the Middle Ages.

Reggio's smartest restaurant is **Italo**, Via Sessi 14, ℂ 454465 (expensive), a calm, comfortable environment in which to taste *pecorino* in *aceto balsamico*, risotto *alla parmagiana*, or veal with truffles. (*Closed Mon, Tues.*)

**Canossa**, Via Roma 37, ℂ 454196 (moderate) is a fine place to try the various hams of this area, served together as an *antipasto*; other specialities include *cappelletti* in broth, and tortelli made on the premises. (*Closed Wed.*) **Dulcamara**, Via Blasmatori 1, ℂ 48223 (moderate) is that rare fruit, a vegetarian restaurant: expect spaghetti with tofu or pesto, and organic wines. (*Closed Mon evenings, Tues.*)

For pizza, paella, and tagliatelle with peppers, at tables out on the street, try **La Casseruola**, Via S. Carlo 5, ℂ 49550 (inexpensive; *closed Wed*). In an arcade leading off Piazza Prampolini is a thriving pizzeria, **Sotto Broletto**, Via Broletto 1, ℂ 439676 (inexpensive; *closed Thurs*).

## Modena

Modena puts on a class act—'Mink City' they call it, the city with Italy's highest per capita income, a city with 'a psychological need for racing cars' according to the late Enzo Ferrari, whose famous flame red chariots compete with the shiny beasts churned out by cross-town rival Maserati. Sleek and speedy, Modena also has a lyrical side of larger-than-life proportions: Luciano Pavarotti was born here, and its scenographic streets take on an air of mystery and romance when enveloped in the winter mists rising from the Po.

Known in Roman days as *Mutina*, Modena first came to note in the 11th–12th centuries under Countess Matilda, powerful ally of the pope, (*see* above, 'Around Reggio'). When it became an independent *comune*, however, Modena's Ghibelline party was to dominate in response to the Guelph politics of the city's chief rival, Bologna. In 1288 the city came under control of the Este dukes of Ferrara, and the Este Duchy of Modena endured until 1796. A feebly independent duchy was recreated by the Vienna Congress in 1815, only for Modena, like Parma, to be swept into the Kingdom of Italy by the wave of nationalistic feeling in 1859–60.

### Getting Around

There are frequent **rail** connections with Bologna (30min), Parma (35min) and Milan (2 hours), and also to Mantua (50min), via Carpi. The station is on Piazza Dante, a 10-minute walk from the centre (or take bus 7); for train information, ✆ (059) 308811. You can hire bikes cheaply inside the left-luggage office (*Deposito Bagagli*).

The **bus station** at Via Bacchini, ✆ (059) 308800 has frequent connections to Bologna, Ferrara, and destinations in Modena province and the Apennines (to Vignola every hour; to Fanano and Sestola six a day; to Fiumalbo, via Pievepelago, eight a day).

The city of Ferrari is naturally a major **road** junction. Just to the west of Modena the A22 *autostrada* leaves the main A1 from Verona, Trento and the Brenner Pass. The Via Emilia runs through the city but there is also a bypass that skirts round it to the north, linking up with the SS12 (north, to Verona) and the P3/SS12 southwards to the Apennines and Tuscany.

### Tourist Information

The city tourist office is at Via Scudari 30, ✆ (059) 222482, @ 214591, very near the Duomo and the Piazza Grande.

## Duomo di San Geminiano

The Via Emilia is Modena's main thoroughfare, and it is in the centre of this city where the old Roman highway picks up one of its loveliest gems, the **Piazza Grande**, site of Modena's celebrated Romanesque **Duomo di San Geminiano**. Begun with funds and support from Countess Matilda in 1099, the cathedral was designed by a master-builder named Lanfranco, and completed in the 13th century; a thorough cleaning in 1985 has restored it to its original ivory appearance.

Curiously, the main features of the cathedral are Ghibelline-Lombard, and scholars believe Lanfranco designed it thus at the bidding of Modena's burghers as a show of independence, both from Matilda and the powerful Abbey of Nonantola (*see* below). Complementing the Duomo's fine proportions are the magnificent carvings by the 12th-century sculptor Wiligelmo above the three main entrances. His friezes on either side of the main Lion Portal are believed to illustrate scenes from the medieval mystery play on the Book of Genesis, the *Jeu d'Adam*. Wiligelmo's South Portal depicts the life of Modena's 4th-century patron,

St Geminiano, and he was also responsible for the delicate floral decorations on the door facing the piazza. The weights and measures carved into the façade recall the days when the daily market was held in the square.

Wiligelmo's contemporary, the 'Master of the Metopes', executed the eight fascinating reliefs of mythological creatures and allegorical subjects on top of the buttresses—monsters relegated to the ends of the cathedral just as they are relegated to the ends of the earth. Those on the cathedral are copies; the originals, which deserve a much closer look, are in the adjacent **Museo Lapidario** on Via Lanfranco (*for admission, call ahead, © (059) 216078, or plead with the sacristan*). Yet another sculptor was responsible for the 12th-century carving of King Arthur in the lunette over the Porta della Pescheria.

Later 12th-century work, including the rose window, was done by the Campionesi masters from Lake Lugano in Lombardy, who added the final touches to Lanfranco's charming interior, with its rhythm of arches supported by slender columns and ponderous piers. The altar is split in the Lombard style, the choir raised above the crypt. This is supported by lion pillars and adorned with remarkable tinted bas-reliefs of the Passion by the Campionese masters. The mighty, if slightly askew, campanile, called the **Ghirlandina**, was also completed by the Campionese masters. It houses a famous trophy, an ancient wooden bucket stolen during a raid on Bologna in 1325, when the two cities were at war. It is the subject of a 17th-century mock-heroic epic, *La Secchia Rapita*. The Bolognese make periodic attempts to steal it back; according to rumour, they have it now, and the one you see is only a replica. At the base of the campanile is a photo memorial to Modena's martyred partisans.

## Palazzo dei Musei

The other main sight in Modena is the Palazzo dei Musei (with your back to the cathedral, turn left along Via Emilia), housing the **Biblioteca Estense** (*open 9am–5pm Mon–Thurs; 9am–1pm Fri, Sat*). Among its famous collection of illuminated manuscripts is one of the most fabulous anywhere, the *Bible of Borso d'Este*, made for the Duke of Modena, a gorgeously coloured 1200-page marvel illustrated in the 15th century by the Emilians Taddeo Crivelli and Franco Rossi.

Upstairs, the **Galleria Estense** (*open 9am–2pm Mon–Sat; 9am–1pm Sun; adm*) is a well-arranged collection founded by Francesco I d'Este, whose excellent bust by Gian Lorenzo Bernini greets visitors at the entrance. His taste wasn't quite as fine as that of some other dukes, but here's your chance to see a Tomaso da Modena outside of Treviso, as well as some good early Emilian works, bronzes by Il Riccio of Padua, a good Flemish collection, several works by Venetian Renaissance artists (Palma Vecchio, Tintoretto, Cima da Conegliano, and Veronese), and Velásquez' *Portrait of Francesco I d'Este*.

On the way back to the Piazza Grande, stop by to see the *Deposition* by Guido Mazzoni (1476) in **San Giovanni Battista**. From Piazza Grande Via C. Battisti leads to the huge Baroque **Palazzo Ducale**, now the National Military Academy and off limits unless you happen to stumble into Modena on the Sunday nearest 4 November. Between this behemoth and the station the main landmark is the interesting neo-Romanesque **Tempio Monumentale**, erected in 1923.

Eleven kilometres east of Modena lies the **Abbey of Nonantola**, founded in 652 by the Lombard abbot Anselmo, rebuilt in the 12th century and suffering various Baroque vicissitudes since. The portal, however, retains its beautiful carving by the workshop of Wiligelmo. The church is dedicated to and contains relics of the 4th-century St Sylvester, pope under Constantine, while the crypt contains 64 columns with carved capitals and the tomb of another pope, St Adrian III, who died here in 885 *en route* to the diet of worms.

## The Modenese Apennines and Carpi

From Modena you can break away from the flatlands of the Po by heading south into the Apennines, which near the border with Tuscany achieve majestic proportions. The region has perfect updrafts for hang-gliding and sailplanes, especially around **Pavullo** and **Montecreto**. In April the emerald-green foothill region around **Vignola** and **Savignano** is covered with the lacy blossoms of Vignola's famous cherry trees; from here continue further south to **Guiglia** and the peculiar pinnacles of Rocca Malatina in the **Parco Naturale di Sassi**. Just south of Guiglia, don't miss the 11th-century country church at **Pieve Trebbio** with primitive capitals inside. Motorheads can make the pilgrimage to **Maranello**, where the **Galleria Ferrari** is dedicated to the legendary marque, with scale models, trophies, vintage cars, and a reconstruction of Enzo Ferrari's office (*open 9.30–12.30, 3–6, Tues–Sun; adm exp*). **Sassuolo**, southwest of Modena, is the centre of Italy's flourishing ceramic tile industry, which has been booming since Italian designers have discovered that people spend money on decorating their bathrooms and kitchens as well as their persons. It also produces Nocino, a liqueur flavoured by green walnuts that must be picked on St John's Day.

The most striking scenery is up at **Sestola**, a winter and summer resort near the highest peak of the Northern Apennines, **Monte Cimone** (2165m). From Sestola you can visit the pretty glacial **Lago della Ninfa** and the **Giardino Esperia**, planted by the local Alpine club in 1950 at the Passo del Lupo, a botanical frontier, where Alpine and Apennine flowers, trees, and herbs grow side by side. Another excursion from Sestola is to **Pian Cavallaro** and from there to the summit of Monte Cimone for a unique view—on a clear day you can see both the Tyrrhenian and Adriatic seas, and all the way north to the Julian Alps and Mont Blanc. You can also make the ascent from the old village of **Fiumalbo**, just below the Passo Abetone that separates Emilia from Tuscany. Two other mountain lakes are just south of Fiumalbo: **Lago Santo** and **Lago Bacio**, connected by an easy footpath. Not as pretty, but more unusual, is the small **Lago Pratignano**, in the meadows south of Fanano, a little to the east of Sestola. In the spring its banks are strewn with unusual wild flowers and carnivorous plants—bring your waders.

North of Modena both buses and trains run to **Carpi**, a wealthy, workaholic town dominated by the vast and impressive **Piazza dei Martiri**. Beside it stands the 16th-century **Castello del Pio**, which holds a museum, the **Museo al Deportato**, remembering the prisoners and civilians deported to Germany from a Nazi camp that stood outside the town during the Second World War (*open 9–12, 3–6, Thurs, Sat, Sun*).

### Activities

Modena sponsors an Antiques Fair on the 4th Saturday and Sunday of every month in the Parco Novisad (except in July and December). Vignola celebrates its cherry blossom festival in April, with horse races, bicycle tours, exhibitions and other events. On 15 August there's a traditional festival at Pievepelago, and in nearby Riolunato there are two ancient popular festas, the *Maggio delle Ragazze* and *Maggio delle Anime*, both celebrated in May. For exact dates, contact the tourist office in Sestola, at Via Passerini 18, ✆ (0536) 62324, ✉ 62398. For a ski report, call ✆ (0536) 223222.

## Where to Stay

### Modena

The palatial ★★★★**Canalgrande**, Corso Canalgrande 6, ✆ (059) 217160, ✉ 221674 (expensive) has richly decorated public rooms, with crystal chandeliers and frescoes on the ceiling, and plush, air-conditioned bedrooms with all modern comforts. Ancient trees grace the hotel's pretty garden.

The ★★★**Hotel Estense**, Via Berengario 11, ✆ (059) 219057, ✉ 211755 (moderate) is near the Palazzo dei Musei, offering unpretentious but comfortable rooms with the option of air conditioning and guarded parking for your car. More central, ★★★**Roma**, Via Farini 44, ✆ (059) 222218, ✉ 223618 (moderate) has rooms in a 17th-century Este property, fitted out with a garage.

The ★★**Albergo Centrale**, Via Rismondo 57, ✆ (059) 218808, ✉ 238201 (inexpensive) near the cathedral, has smart rooms, with or without baths. ★**Sole**, Via Malatesta 45, ✆ (059) 214245 (inexpensive) is in a small, ancient street, and offers seven basic but spacious rooms, without baths.

### Sestola

In Sestola in the Apennines, ★★★**Tirolo**, Via delle Rose 19, ✆ (0536) 62523 (moderate), is endowed with tennis courts and very comfortable rooms (*open June–Sept, mid-Dec–mid-May only*). The nearby ★★★**San Marco**, Via delle Rose 2, ✆ (0536) 62330 (moderate) also has comfortable rooms with air-conditioning, and tennis courts in a lovely garden.

A pleasant small hotel that's open all year in Sestola is the ★★**Sport Hotel**, Via delle Ville 116, ✆ (0536) 62502 (inexpensive). It has double rooms only, with or without baths.

There are also numerous small hotels in **Fiumalbo**, especially at Dogana Nuova near the ski resort.

## Eating Out

Modena's kitchen has a long and notable tradition. In the heart of Emilia's pig country, it prides itself on its variety of *salumeria* and prosciutto; minced pork fills its tortellini and its famous main course, *zampone* (pig's trotter) which is boiled and sliced. Modena's famous balsamic vinegar is distilled from Trebbiana grapes, which after a few years of diligently pouring it from one barrel to another achieves a delicate taste between sweet and sour. The plump cherries of Vignola are among the best in Italy. Modena is also the best place to taste true, natural Lambrusco, which must be drunk young (a year or so old) to be perfectly lively and sparkling; the test is to see if the foam vanishes instantly when poured into a glass.

## Modena

The cathedral of Modenese cuisine is a restaurant almost as famous as the real cathedral, **Fini**, Largo San Francesco, ✆ (059) 223314 (very expensive). Founded in 1912, Fini has an almost endless menu of hearty regional pasta (lasagne and tortellini prepared in a variety of ways—the *pasticcio di tortellini* is exceptional), meat dishes, the famous *zampone* or *bollito misto* and appetizers (hams and sausages and salami), all deliciously prepared. (*Closed Mon, Tues, most of Aug.*) The very elegant **Borso d'Este**, Piazza Roma 5, ✆ (059) 214114 (expensive) is opposite the Palazzo Ducale, and offers a light, experimental menu, with such dishes as shrimp and artichoke salad, risotto with Venetian radicchio and marrow flowers, and duck in balsamic vinegar. There are also equally imaginative desserts, and French and Italian wines. (*Closed Sun, Aug.*)

A brief drive out of the centre is **Vinicio**, Via Emilia Est 1526, ✆ (059) 280313 (expensive) which does an excellent job of adapting the rather heavy local cooking to modern tastes—try tortelli with ricotta and spinach. In addition there are very fine salads and vegetables, meat courses prepared with balsamic vinegar, and an excellent wine list. (*Closed Mon, Aug.*) The most Modenese restaurant in Modena is **Bianca**, Via Spaccini 24, ✆ (059) 311524 (moderate) which serves all the famous local specialities, from an antipasto of several varieties of sausage, to beef in balsamic vinegar. (*Closed Sat midday, Sun, Aug.*)

An excellent trattoria in Modena, serving local specialities without fuss or expense, is **Alla Redocca**, Piazzetta Redocca 8, ✆ (059) 242750 (inexpensive). At weekends, the Modenese embark on gastronomic voyages into the Apennines: stop at any roadside restaurant (choose the one with the most cars parked outside), and you will find simple meals served of various smoked meats, cheeses, freshly baked breads, and raw vegetables. The meal is named *tigelle* or *crescente* after its distinctive breads—one like a flat, baked muffin, the other thin dough fried in fat. During the week you won't have to wait for a table.

## Sestola

**Il Faggio**, Via Libertà 68, ✆ (0536) 62211 (moderate) serves dishes all based on fresh, locally available ingredients—including venison and wild boar. (*Closed Mon.*)

## Soliera

North of Modena towards Carpi is **Da Lancellotti**, at Via Grandi 120 in Soliera, ✆ (059) 567406 (moderate), whose chef grows his own vegetables, and edible, aromatic flowers that flavour all the food.

*Entertainment and Nightlife*

The **concert, ballet, and opera season** at the Teatro Comunale runs from September to May, while from late October to May **plays** are performed at the Teatro Storico. In addition, for the past few years, in mid-September, Pavarotti has been giving a concert in his home town's Piazza Grande. It's expensive and booked up well in advance, but crowds still come to sit in the neighbouring bars, and listen to the music while watching the show on TV.

## Bologna

'You must write all the beautiful things of Italy,' said the Venetian on the train, but the man from Bologna vehemently shook his finger. 'No, no,' he insisted. 'You must write the truth!' And it is precisely that, a fervent insistence on the plain truth as opposed to the typical Italian delight in appearance and *bella figura*, that sets Bologna apart. A homespun realism and attention to the detail of the visible, material world are the main characteristics of the Bolognese school of art (recall Petrarch's comment that while only an educated man is amazed by a Giotto, anyone can understand a Bolognese picture). The city's handsome, harmonic, and well preserved centre disdains imported marble or ornate stucco, preferring honest red brick. Bologna's municipal government, long in the hands of the Italian Communist Party (now the PDS), is considered the least corrupt and most efficient of any large city in the whole country. In the 11th century it was the desire for truth and law that led to the founding of the University of Bologna, whose first scholars occupied themselves with the task of interpreting the law codes of Justinian in settling disputes over investitures between pope and emperor. And it is Bolognese sincerity and honest ingredients in the kitchen that has made *la cucina bolognese* by common consent the best in all Italy.

*La Dotta*, *La Grassa*, and *La Rossa* (the Learned, the Fat, and the Red) are Bologna's sobriquets. It may be full of socialist virtue, but the city is also very wealthy and cosy, with a quality of life often compared to Sweden. The casual observer could well come away with the impression that the reddest things about Bologna are its telephone booths and its suburban street names like Via Stalingrado, Via Yuri Gagarin, and Viale Lenin. But Bologna is hardly a stolid place—its bars, cafés and squares are brimming with youth and life, and there's a full calendar of concerts from rap to jazz to Renaissance madrigals, as well as avant-garde ballet, theatre, and art exhibitions. Visitors, though, should be aware that in July and August Bologna can be as exciting as cheap supermarket salami, *bologni*, that bears its name.

## History

Born as the prosperous Etruscan outpost of Felsina, and renamed Bononia by the Gauls, Bologna grew up at the junction of the Via Emilia and the main road over the Apennines from Florence. Dominated by Ravenna for centuries, Bologna broke away in the 11th century and became an independent *comune* in the 12th and 13th centuries, a golden age when it was one of the principal Guelph cities of the Lombard League. As such it warred with Ghibelline Modena, and defeated that city in the Battle of Fossalta in 1249, capturing

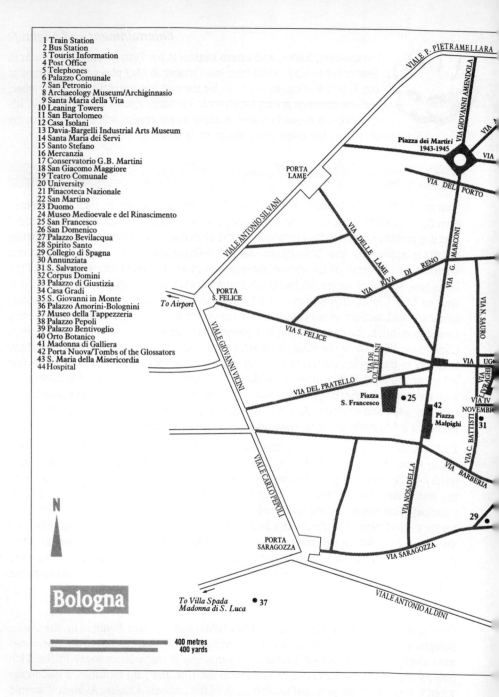

1 Train Station
2 Bus Station
3 Tourist Information
4 Post Office
5 Telephones
6 Palazzo Comunale
7 San Petronio
8 Archaeology Museum/Archiginnasio
9 Santa Maria della Vita
10 Leaning Towers
11 San Bartolomeo
12 Casa Isolani
13 Davia-Bargelli Industrial Arts Museum
14 Santa Maria dei Servi
15 Santo Stefano
16 Mercanzia
17 Conservatorio G.B. Martini
18 San Giacomo Maggiore
19 Teatro Comunale
20 University
21 Pinacoteca Nazionale
22 San Martino
23 Duomo
24 Museo Medioevale e del Rinascimento
25 San Francesco
26 San Domenico
27 Palazzo Bevilacqua
28 Spirito Santo
29 Collegio di Spagna
30 Annunziata
31 S. Salvatore
32 Corpus Domini
33 Palazzo di Giustizia
34 Casa Gradi
35 S. Giovanni in Monte
36 Palazzo Amorini-Bolognini
37 Museo della Tappezzeria
38 Palazzo Pepoli
39 Palazzo Bentivoglio
40 Orto Botanico
41 Madonna di Galliera
42 Porta Nuova/Tombs of the Glossators
43 S. Maria della Misericordia
44 Hospital

Bologna

400 metres
400 yards

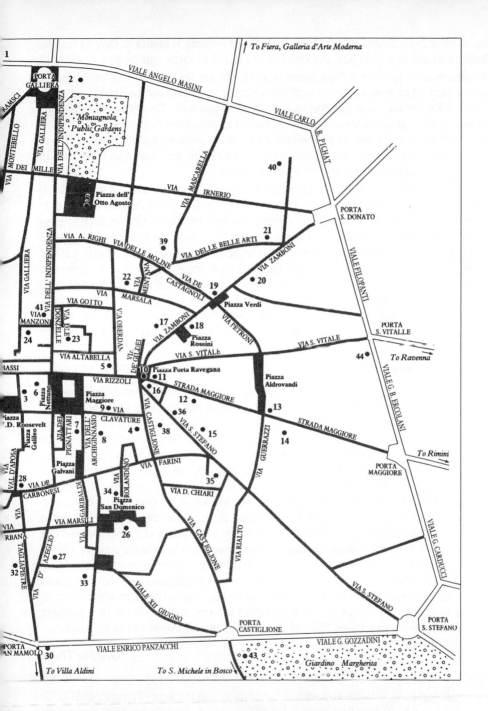

the talented Enzo, King of Sardinia and natural son of Emperor Frederick II. Defying custom, Bologna refused to ransom him, and kept him in a nice little castle until he died in 1272.

Bologna became part of the Papal States in 1278, though for the next few centuries real power was held by several different local 'first citizens', most famously the Bentivoglio family (1401–1506), whose name translates quaintly as 'Wish-you-well'. They heralded a flowering of local culture, despite a sensational family saga of assassination, high-living and questionable legitimacy—the paternity of Annibale, father of the great art patron Giovanni II, was decided by a throw of the dice. Giovanni II ruled for 43 years, until ousted by Pope Julius II, after which Bologna was ruled directly by a papal legate.

Bologna witnessed one of the turning points in Italian history in 1530, when Charles V insisted on being crowned Holy Roman Emperor in its basilica of San Petronio instead of in Rome, which his troops had mercilessly sacked three years previously. Charles felt that going to Rome would seem like an act of contrition, and such was the low standing of papal authority that when he told Pope Clement VII that he did not need to seek crowns, but that crowns sought him, the pope could only agree. Charles' coronation, both as Emperor and King of Italy, was celebrated with tremendous pomp, but marked the beginning of three centuries of foreign domination in Italy, and the first symptoms of death for the Renaissance. Luigi Barzini notes that from then on the Italians put away their bright clothes and began to wear black in the Spanish style, as if they were in mourning—just as the Fascisti donned black shirts under Mussolini.

## Modern Bologna

In the 19th century Bologna was the birthplace of Guglielmo Marconi, who carried out his first experiments with radio at the Villa Grifone, and of the composer Ottorino Respighi (1879–1936), whose music was popularized abroad by his fellow-Emilian Toscanini. It was also at this time that Bologna took the lead in the Italian socialist movement—as well as in enduring the brunt of the Fascist reaction in the 20th. And although it was on the 'Gothic Line', where the Germans held the Allies at bay in 1944–45, and the scene of fervid partisan activity, Bologna emerged from the War relatively unscathed. The city's historic centre is considered one of the best preserved and maintained in Italy, to the credit of the city administration's policy of 'active preservation'—old houses in the centre are gutted and renovated for municipal public housing, maintaining the character and diversity of the old quarters. Nor is this the first time that Bologna has found a creative solution to its housing needs. One of the first things you notice is how every street is lined with arcades, or *portici*. The original ones date from the 12th century, when the *comune*, faced with a housing shortage caused by 10,000 university students, ordered rooms to be built onto existing buildings over the streets. Over time the Bolognese became attached to them and the shelter they provided from the weather; now it claims 35km of *portici*, more than any other city in the world.

---

### Getting There

#### by air

Bologna's G. Marconi **airport** is to the northwest in the Borgo Panigale, ✆ 311578; city bus no.91 runs from there to the railway station. Bologna has flight connections with major Italian and European cities, and Sicily and Sardinia.

### by rail

Bologna is one of the prime nodes of the FS rail network, with frequent and fast connections to Venice, Florence, Milan, Ravenna, Rimini and just about anywhere else in Italy from the **Stazione Centrale** in Piazza delle Medaglie d'Oro, information © 246490. It is on the north side of the city centre, about a 10–15 minute walk from Piazza Maggiore; alternatively, bus no.25 goes straight there. Because of the tragic ultra-Right bombing here in August 1980 that killed 85 people, Bologna is the one station in Italy certain to inspect your bags minutely if you leave them at the *Consegna*.

### by long-distance bus

The **bus station** is near the FS at Piazza XX Settembre, © 248374, and has services every hour for Ferrara, Imola, Modena, and Ravenna, and less frequent services to many other destinations in the region.

### by road

The *autostrade* approaching Bologna skirt around the city to the north in a ring road, the *tangenziale*, which connects up with most major routes. At Bologna the A1 from Milan leaves the Via Emilia and turns south towards Florence, but the A14 continues on to Ravenna and Rimini. The A13 runs north from Bologna to Ferrara and Padua.

Within the *tangenziale* the state roads leading into Bologna connect up with an inner ring road around the city centre, though the SS9-Via Emilia still runs through its middle. The SS64 (Via Stalingrado, inside the *tangenziale*) branches off north for Ferrara, and the SS253 for Ravenna. South of Bologna the SS64 runs to Pistoia and the SS65 to Florence.

### Getting Around

Most of Bologna's sights are within easy walking distance of one another, but the city also has an efficient local **bus** system. Tickets must be bought before boarding the bus, and are available from *tabacchi* shops. There are also offices that dispense both tickets and city bus maps and information at the main bus station in Piazza XX Settembre, at a booth outside the railway station, and at 1/1 Piazza Re Enzo, near Piazza Maggiore, © 247005.

For drivers, similarly, walk or use public transport rather than try to use a car within Bologna's Tangenziale ring road, which encircles a typically Italian imbroglio of pedestrian and one-way streets with no place to park. You may find a parking space in Piazza XX Settembre, where it is also possible to hire **bicycles** inside the Porta Galliera, at Piazza XX Settembre 7, © 6302015 (*open 7am-8pm daily*). For a **taxi**, © 372727 or © 534141.

### Tourist Information

The main tourist information office is right in the centre of the city at Piazza Maggiore 6, © 239660 (*open 9am–7pm daily*). There's also an office at the railway station, ☏ 246541 (*open 9–12.30, 2.30–6.30, Mon–Sat*), and a desk at the airport. The local APT head office is at Via Marconi 45, ☏ 237413, @ 261878. Telephone area code for Bologna is **051**.

**Fire, ☏ 115.**
**Police**, Piazza Galileo 7, ☏ **113**.
**Ambulance, ☏ 333333.**

**Hospital: Ospedale Sant'Orsola**, Via Massarenti 8, ☏ 6363111.

**24-hour pharmacy: Piazza Maggiore**, next to the tourist office; if it is not open check the list outside to see which pharmacies are on duty that night, or call ☏ 192 for information.

In the wall of **Credito Romagnolo**, Via Rizzoli 34, there is a cash exchange machine open 24 hours every day.

The main post office is at Piazza Minghetti, not far from the Archiginnasio, and is open 8.15am–6.30pm Mon–Fri, 8.15am–1pm Sat. There are SIP **telephone** offices in Piazza VIII Agosto, and Via Fossalta (off Via Rizzoli). Area code for Bologna from elsewhere in Italy is **051**.

---

## Piazza Maggiore

The centre stage of Bolognese public life is Piazza Maggiore and its antechamber, **Piazza Nettuno**, graced with the virile and vaguely outrageous **Fountain of Neptune**, 'who has abandoned the fishes to make friends with the pigeons', designed in the 16th century by Tomaso Laureti of Palermo and executed by Giambologna. Adjacent, and occupying part of both squares are the 13th-century **Palazzo di Re Enzo** and the **Palazzo del Podestà**, begun about the same time and remodelled in 1484 by Aristotele Fioravanti, who went on to design part of the Kremlin. The corners of the **Voltone** (the big portico in front) contain 16th-century statues of Bologna's four patron saints.

Filling the western side of the Piazza Maggiore, the crenellated **Palazzo Comunale** incorporates the 1287 Casa Accursio (the arcaded section), and the 1425 annexe by Fioravante Fioravanti, father of Aristotele. Over the main door presides a bronze statue of Pope Gregory XIII, the reformer of the calendar and a native of Bologna. Under a canopy to the left is a beautiful terracotta Madonna by Nicolò dell'Arca, a Renaissance sculptor from Apulia who left his best work in Bologna. Inside there are two museums—the **municipal art collection**, reached via Bramante's grand staircase (1505), which contains important works by the Bolognese school, and the new **Museo Morandi**, devoted to Bologna's greatest contemporary painter, Giorgio Morandi (1890–1964). He hardly ever left the city, and, although friends with futurists and metapysicists in Ferrano, kept to himself, quietly producing some of this century's best paintings. The subject matter—boxes, a vase of flowers—is mundane, but under Morandi's fierce gaze is transformed with startling intensity. There are also landscapes of Grizzana, the nearby village where Morandi spent his summers, portraits, drawings, sculptures, his library and personal art collection, and a reconstruction of his studio (*both museums open 10am–6pm Tues–Sun; adm*).

The **Basilica di San Petronio**, by Antonio da Vicenza (1390), opposite the Palazzo del Podestà, is the largest structure on the square, yet had the Bolognese had their way, this temple to their patron saint would have been far grander, and even larger than St Peter's in Rome. However, the Cardinal Legate ordered them to spend their money on the university's Archiginnasio, instead of on municipal prestige.

San Petronio's façade was never finished. The white and red marble stripes, recalling the city's heraldic emblem, only made it up to the door. The central portal has a remarkable doorway, with bas-reliefs of biblical scenes by Jacopo della Quercia of Siena, begun in 1425. Like Ghiberti's doors to the Baptistry in Florence (for which job della Quercia had been one of the unsuccessful candidates), they are landmarks in the visual evolution of the early Renaissance, and seem strangely modern—almost Art Deco in sensibility.

The lofty, spacious interior saw the crowning of Charles V as Holy Roman Emperor and, according to tradition, the conversion of a visiting monk named Martin Luther who became so nauseated by papal pomp and pageantry that he decided to go ahead and start the Reformation. In 1655 the astronomer Cassini traced the meridian on the floor and designed the huge astronomical clock, which tells the time with the shaft of light admitted through an oculus in the roof. Two of the chapels are noteworthy—one with 15th-century frescoes of Heaven and a rather alarming Hell, and another containing Lorenzo Costa's *Madonna and Saints*, both to the left as you enter. In the museum at the end of the aisle are models of some of the grand schemes that the Bolognese have had in mind for the church and its façade since building began (*museum open 10am–12 midday; closed Tues, Thurs*).

Missing from the front of San Petronio, however, is Michelangelo's colossal bronze statue of Pope Julius II, commissioned by that pope in 1506, after he regained the city for the Papal States. Julius also commissioned a large castle in the centre of Bologna. Both were torn to bits by the population as soon as the pope's luck changed; and to rub salt into his wounded pride the bronze was sold as scrap to his arch-enemy, Alfonso I of Ferrara, who melted it down to cast an enormous cannon—which he fondly called 'Julius'.

## Via dell'Archiginnasio

Bologna's excellent **Museo Civico Archeologico** is just to the left of San Petronio, on Via dell'Archiginnasio 3 (*open 9am–2pm Tues–Sat; 9–1, 3.30–7, Sun; adm*). Into its dim and dusty wooden cases is crammed one of Italy's best collections of antiquities—beautifully wrought items from the Iron Age Villanova culture, native Italics who were eventually conquered by the Etruscans, and artefacts from Bologna's beginnings as Etruscan *Felsina*. Felsina may have been a frontier town, but it is richly represented here with tomb art, proto-chesspieces shaped like gravestones and the embossed bronze urn, the *Situla di Certosa*, similar to others found in Tuscany. The Etruscans traded through their port of Spina (near Comacchio) with the Greeks, whose Attic vases are one of the highlights of the museum. There are a few items from Gallic Bononia, Roman artefacts (a lovely copy of Phidias' bust of Athena Lemnia), and an excellent Egyptian collection.

Further down the street is the old university, the **Archiginnasio** (*open 9am–1.45pm Mon–Sat*), its walls covered with the escutcheons and memorials of famous university scholars. Bologna's university is the oldest in Europe, but was not provided with a central building until 1565. After 1803 this became the municipal library, but if you ask the porter, he'll admit you to the ornate old **anatomical theatre**, shattered by a bomb in the Second World War and painstakingly rebuilt in 1950. The monument in the piazza in front of the Archiginnasio commemorates Luigi Galvani, the 18th-century Bolognese discoverer of electrical currents in animals who gave his life and name ('galvanize') to physics.

Just off the Piazza Maggiore on Via Clavature, the church of **Santa Maria della Vita** is worth a visit for the terracotta *Lament Over the Dead Christ* by Nicolò dell'Arca, a work harrowing in its grief and terror, a 15th-century version of Edvard Munch's *Scream.*

## Two Leaning Towers

In the passage under Via Rizzoli (the main street flanking the Piazza Maggiore) you can see the remains of the old Roman Via Aemilia, which followed the same route. To the east the end of Via Rizzoli is framed by the beautiful **Piazza Porta Ravegnana** and a pair of towers that might have wandered off the set of *The Cabinet of Dr Caligari.* After the initial shock wears off, however, fondness invariably sets in for this odd couple, the Laurel and Hardy of architecture. The taller one only looks respectable because the other is so hilarious.

According to legend, the **Due Torri** were built in 1119 in a competition between two powerful families. The winner, the svelte 97m **Torre degli Asinelli** (*open 9am–6pm daily; adm*), is the highest in Bologna, which once had 180 such skyscrapers. It tilts about 1 metre out of true, though the 500 steps that lead to the top are more likely to make your head spin than the tilt. The view over Bologna is worth the trouble, however. Its side-kick, the **Torre Garisenda**, sways tipsily to the south, 3.2m out of true; the Garisenda contingent failed to prepare a solid foundation, and when they saw their tower pitching precariously, gave up. In 1360 it became such a threat to public safety that its top was lopped off, leaving only a squat, 48m stump; inscribed in its base you can read what Dante wrote about it in the *Inferno.*

From the towers, five streets fan out to gates in the eastern walls of the old city. One of these, the palace-lined **Strada Maggiore**, follows the route of the Via Aemilia, passing first in front of **San Bartolomeo**, notable for its two works by Bolognese masters: Albani's *Annunciation*, in a chapel on the south aisle, and Guido Reni's *Madonna.* In the 19th century Italians considered the 'Divine Guido' as their greatest artist; since then he has taken a precipitous and admittedly deserved fall from fashion. At Strada Maggiore 13, the **Casa Isolani** is one of the best-preserved 13th-century houses left in Bologna; at No.44 the 18th-century **Palazzo dei Giganti** (or Davia) (*open 9am–2pm Tues–Sat; 9am–1pm Sun*) contains the Museum of Industrial Art and the Galleria Davia-Bargelli, housing Vitale da Bologna's famous *Madonna with Teeth,* perhaps the most characteristic work of the Bolognese school . At this point the *portici* of the street intermingle with those of the arcades of the city's Gothic jewel, **Santa Maria dei Servi**, which contains among its works of art a rare *Madonna* by Cimabue (in the apse) which you'll need to illuminate to see.

## Santo Stefano

Via Santo Stefano, another of the streets radiating from the two towers, may be reached from Santa Maria dei Servi on Via Guerrazzi (where, at No.13, the 14-year-old Mozart was elected to the Academia Filarmonica). A street back towards the centre along Via Santo

Stefano is a quartet of churches, with a cloister and two chapels thrown in, all once part of the monastery of **Santo Stefano** founded by St Petronius, who reproduced here the general layout of the holy sites of Jerusalem. Three of the churches of this unique and harmonious Romanesque ensemble face Piazza Santo Stefano—the largest is the **Crocifisso**, with an altar in its façade, begun in the 11th century and containing an ancient crypt below its raised choir. To the left is the entrance to **San Sepolcro**, a polygonal temple containing the curious tomb of San Petronio, modelled after the Holy Sepulchre and adorned with bas-reliefs. **SS. Vitale e Agricola**, further to the left, is Bologna's oldest church, built in the 5th century, with bits and pieces of old Roman buildings and alabaster windows. Beyond it is the **Cortile di Pilato**, containing an 8th-century Lombard bathtub that has somehow gained the sinister reputation of being the basin in which Pontius Pilate washed his hands. From here you can enter the fourth church, the 13th-century **Trinità**, the lovely 11th-century **cloister**, and the **museum**, with works by Simone de' Crocifissi and others (*all open 9–12, 3.30–6, daily*).

Still further up Via Santo Stefano towards the Due Torri is the lovely Gothic **Palazzo della Mercanzia** (1384); it has an ornate loggia by the architect of San Petronio, Antonio da Vincenzo.

## Via Zamboni

Again from the towers, the Via Zamboni leads shortly to the Piazza Rossini. Rossini, composer of the *Barber of Seville* and *William Tell*, studied from 1806 to 1810 at the **Conservatorio G.B. Martini** on the piazza (*open 9am–1pm Mon–Sat*), and spent much of his life in a nearby palazzo. The Conservatory houses original scores by Mozart, Monteverdi and Rossini, and oddly, a portrait by Thomas Gainsborough. Also on the square is **San Giacomo Maggiore**, begun in 1267 and later enlarged. It was the parish church of the Bentivoglio, who adorned it with art. Giovanni II hired the Ferrarese Lorenzo Costa to paint the frescoes in the **Cappella Bentivoglio** of the *Triumph of Death*, the *Apocalypse*, and *Madonna Enthroned*, in the midst of Giovanni II and his family. In these pictures, the Bentivoglio seem benign enough, though the Bolognese hardly found them so; when the clan were deposed their palace was torn apart brick by brick. The fresco itself was commissioned in thanksgiving for Giovanni's escape from hired assassins. The fine altarpiece in the chapel is by Francesco Francia, a native of Bologna, while the high-mounted tomb opposite, of Anton Galeazzo Bentivoglio (1435) is by Quercia. Be sure to ask the sacristan to let you into the **Oratory of Santa Cecilia**, frescoed by Costa and Francia.

The **Teatro Comunale**, further up Via Zamboni in Piazza Verdi, was built in 1763 over the ruins of the Bentivoglio Palace by Antonio Bibiena. The Bibiena clan of theatre and stage designers were in demand all over Europe in the 17th and 18th centuries, and did much to popularize the typical Baroque tiers of boxes, which the Teatro Comunale preserves behind its 1933 façade.

## The University

Beyond the theatre is the **University**, which was moved in 1803 from the too-central Archiginnasio (where the students could cause trouble) into Pellegrino Tibaldi's Mannerist **Palazzo Poggi**, topped by the eclectic observation tower, or *speculum*, and adorned with

Tibaldi's frescoes of Ulysses. Famed for medicine, astronomical studies (Copernicus studied here), and the sciences, Bologna was, however,.known best of all for its studies in jurisprudence, ever since its founding by the Glossatori (who 'glossed' or annotated Justinian's codes). One student, Vacarius, founded the law school at Oxford in 1144.

There are a number of small museums connected to the university, including one dedicated to the university itself, in the main building at Via Zamboni 33, which also houses the **Museum of Astronomy** (*both open 9am–1pm Mon–Sat*). The **Botanical Garden**, is at Via Irnerio 42; the **Museum of Human Anatomy**, Via Irnerio 48, houses a somewhat bizarre collection of 18th-century medical models (*both same hours as university museums*); or, for a sobering idea of what Fido looks like under the skin, there's the **Anatomy Museum of Domestic Animals**, Via Belmeloro 12 (*call ahead, © 243414*).

## Pinacoteca Nazionale

*Open 9am–2pm Tues–Sat; 9am–1pm Sun; adm.*

Across from the university, at Via Belle Arti 56, Bologna's most important art is stored in the Pinacoteca Nazionale . Represented here are 14th-century Bolognese artists, of which Vitale da Bologna emerges as the star with his intense *St George and the Dragon* and frescoes; also some visiting artists like Giotto, the Vivarini brothers and Cima da Conegliano of Venice, and a fine collection of works from the Ferrara school (Costa, Cossa, and fresco fragments by Ercole de' Roberti, especially the tearful *Magdalene*). Later Bolognese paintings are by Francesco Francia, Aspertini and Tibaldi. Raphael's *S. Cecilia in Estasi* was moved here from a local church; near it are pictures by Perugino, Giulio Romano, and Parmigianino. Beyond them are fine works from Bologna's 16th–18th century eclectic revival—the Carracci brothers, Guido Reni, and Guercino.

Via Belle Arti, heading back towards the centre, passes several fine old palaces and ends at the intersection of Via Mentana. Turn left here for **San Martino**, which was remodelled in the 15th century. Paolo Uccello painted a fresco here at that time which was believed completely lost until 1981, when a delightful fragment was discovered. The church also contains fine works by Francia and Costa.

---

## North and West of Piazza Maggiore

The Via dell'Indipendenza is the main thoroughfare linking the Piazza Maggiore to the station. In its northern reaches is the attractive **Montagnola Public Garden** and the bustling **Piazza VIII Agosto**, site of a busy popular food, clothes and second-hand goods market on Fridays and Saturdays. The 10th-century **Duomo di San Pietro**, on Via dell'Indipendenza near Piazza Nettuno, was remodelled in the Baroque style, and like Venice's old cathedral, was the local symbol of the Vatican's authority as opposed to that of the municipality, embodied in the basilica of the city's patron saint. And as such it received little affection, and is not very interesting, unless you are a devotee of St Anne, whose skull is the chief treasure, a gift of Henry VI of England. The Romanesque campanile is a survivor of the original structure, and it's worthwhile strolling down Via Altabella and its adjacent lanes for a view of medieval Bologna, with its ancient towers.

Opposite the cathedral, Via Manzoni leads to the Palazzo Fava, site of the **Museo Civico Medioevale e del Rinascimento** (*open 9am–2pm Mon, Wed–Fri; 9–1, 3.30–5, Sat, Sun; closed Tues; adm*), with an interesting collection of armour, ceramics, Majolica plates, the carved tombs of medieval scholars, ivory works, glass, and a 13th-century English Cope. In addition, several rooms of the old palazzo have recently been opened to the public, with wall decorations by Annibale Carracci and other Bolognese painters showing scenes from the *Aeneid* and classical mythology.

Via Ugo Bassi, the westerly section of the Via Aemilia, leads to the narrow and lively **Piazza Malpighi**, with one of Bologna's old city gates, the 13th-century **Tombs of the Glossatori**, and the lovely Gothic **San Francesco**, with its fine old towers and beautiful 14th-century marble altar screen sculpted by Pier Paolo dalle Masegne. Back towards the centre, Via C. Battisti runs south from Via Ugo Bassi to the 17th-century **San Salvatore**, with a striking Mannerist *Marriage of St Catherine* (1534) by Girolamo da Carpi, a work generally acclaimed as his masterpiece.

## South of Piazza Maggiore

From the Archiginnasio, continue south down Via Garibaldi to **San Domenico**, built in 1251 to house the relics of St Dominic, founder of the Order of Preaching Friars. Dominic built a convent on this site and died here in 1221, and though the exterior and interior of his church have been frequently remodelled, it's well worth a visit for his tomb, the *Arca di San Domenico*. Many hands contributed to it, including Nicolò Pisano and his school, who executed the beautiful reliefs of the saint's life; Nicolò dell'Arca, who gained his name because of this work, added the cover of the sarcophagus and the fine statues on top; and a 20-year-old Michelangelo, who sculpted SS. Petronius and Proculus and an angel. Among the other works, look for a bust of St Dominic by Nicola dell'Arca and the beautiful wooden inlaid choir stalls.

From San Domenico, Via Marsili leads to Via D'Azeglio, with the **Palazzo Bevilacqua**, a 15th-century Tuscan-style palace where the Council of Trent took refuge from a plague in Trent in 1547. Just north of here, at Via Val D'Aposa 6, is the lovely brick and terracotta façade of **Spirito Santo**. Via Marsili, now Via Urbana, continues to the **Collegio di Spagna**, the Spanish college founded in 1365 by Cardinal Albornoz for Spanish students. In the Middle Ages Bologna had many such colleges, but this one (an official corner of Spanish territory) is the only one to survive. Cervantes studied here, as did St Ignatius.

From here Via Saragozza wends down to the **Porta Saragozza**, from where begins the portico to beat all porticoes—winding 4km up the hill to the **Sanctuary of the Madonna di San Luca**. The church was built to house an icon attributed to St Luke, and the 666 arch portico was added between 1674 and 1793. There are fantastic views from the sanctuary of the Apennines (if you can't face the whole hike, bus 37 from Piazza Maggiore covers some of the route). Other famous viewpoints in the hills south of Bologna are from **San Michele in Bosco,** a hospital in a former Olivetan convent (bus 30) and from the **Villa Aldini** (bus 52), built on the site where Napoleon admired the panorama of the city skyline. From this villa you can walk down towards the Porta San Mamolo and the fine 15th-century church of the **Annunziata**.

## Shopping

The Via Rizzoli and Via dell'Independenza are the main centres for fashion shops and other chic outlets. Probably Bologna's most interesting buys, though, are the wonderful food products of the surrounding countryside, which can be found in abundance at the city's bustling **food markets** at the Mercato delle Erbe, Via Ugo Bassi 2, and Via Clavature, just off the Piazza Maggiore. Both are open every morning, Monday to Saturday. There's also a market selling just about everything on Fridays and Saturdays in Piazza VIII Agosto (*see* above). As an alternative to the market stalls are Bologna's general **food stores**, whose windows present a dazzling array of delicacies; there is a string of them in the streets around the Piazza Maggiore, particularly towards the Two Towers.

Every April Bologna hosts the **International Children's Book Fair**; otherwise look in at **Feltrinelli**, Via dei Giudei 6/c, for books in English.

## Sports and Activities

Bologna has 15 **swimming pools**, but the most central are **Stadia**, Via Andrea Costa 174, ✆ 6179055 (bus 14), and **Sterlino**, Via Murri 113, ✆ 6237034 (bus 13). Both are open all year, but ring first, because they're often fully booked by school groups.

*Bologna ✆ (051–)*

## Where to Stay

### very expensive

The ★★★★★**Royal Hotel Carlton**, Via Montebello 8, ✆ 554141, is an ultra-modern palace in the centre of Bologna, with six floors of deluxe, flamboyant designer rooms. The lobby and bar are striking, and there's a spacious underground garage. All rooms are carpeted, air-conditioned, and equipped with TV and minibar. So embedded in Bologna's history as to be almost a monument (Morandi's paintings were first exhibited here, in 1914) and right in the centre is the ★★★★**Grand Hotel Baglioni**, Via Independenza 8, ✆ 510242, ✇ 234840, with frescoed ceilings and luxurious, if ancient, rooms, plus an underground garage and baby-sitting service. ★★★★**Grand Hotel Elite**, Via Aurelio Saffi 36, ✆ 437417, ✇ 424968, on the western side of the city outside Porta S. Felice, is a grim, concrete structure that nevertheless houses an elegant and very comfortable hotel, air-conditioned with TVs and minibars in all rooms. It is the proud possessor of one of Bologna's best restaurants, the Cordon Bleu (*see* below).

### expensive

For a swimming pool, you'll have to venture outside the city walls to the ★★★★**Holiday Inn**, Piazza della Costituzione, ✆ 372172, ✇ 357662.

### moderate

A minute from the Piazza Maggiore, ★★★**Hotel Roma**, Via D'Azeglio 9, ✆ 226322, ✇ 239909, is a fine choice in medieval Bologna, offering large, if slightly eccentric, air-conditioned rooms with good beds; another charming feature is its roof garden bar. Occupying an aged palazzo in a pleasant square beside San Petronio, ★★★**Orologio**, Via IV Novembre 10, ☎ 231253, @ 260552, has cosy rooms with good views of the city's streets.

Tucked away in the university quarter, ★★**Rossini**, Via Bibiena 11, ☎ 237716, offers clean, comfortable rooms, and very friendly management.

### inexpensive

Cheaper accommodation is thin on the ground in Bologna, but what exists is mostly centrally located. Just off Piazza Maggiore, in a nest of shopping streets, is the ★**Apollo**, Via Drapperie 5, ☎ 223955; the rooms are small, and the market outside starts up early, but you couldn't be better placed. Two other good choices, both central, clean, and friendly, are ★**Panorama**, Via Livraghi 1, ☎ 221802 (which only has rooms without baths), and ★**Marconi**, Via Marconi 22, ☎ 262832.

There are two **youth hostels**, both inconveniently located 6km east of the city centre at Via Viadagola 5, ☎ 501810, and Via Viadagola 14, ☎ 519202. To get there, take bus 93 from Via Irnerio. IYHF cards are required and there is an 11.30pm curfew.

---

*Bologna* ☎ *(051–)*          ***Eating Out***

In Italy's gastronomic capital, eating out is a pleasure, whether you plump for a meal at a star restaurant or head for one of the city's traditional late-night inns or *osterie*. Locally they call it *cucina petroniana*, and it gave Italy its tagliatelle, tortellini, and lasagne, which the Bolognese like to tint green with spinach. *Alla bolognese* means with a meat and tomato sauce that only Bologna knows how to prepare *just so*. The city is known for the best pâtés in Italy, its veal dishes, and, of late, for its innovations in the kitchen. Colli Bolognesi wines are produced in the hills just to the south of the city, and for an authentic Bolognese repast, order a fruity amber-coloured Albana, white Trebbiano, or dry Sauvignon to accompany your antipasti; a Bianco dei Colli with your tagliatelle, or a heartier Barbera Bolognese for pasta dishes from the oven; with veal dishes, a Merlot dei Colli, and if you order seafood, an energetic Pignoletto from the Colli, which is also good with cheese.

### very expensive

One of Bologna's most innovative and unusual restaurants is the **Cordon Bleu** in the Grand Hotel Elite (*see* above)—innovative in that the chef's speciality is the revival of recipes from the Renaissance. Many dishes feature exciting combinations of meat or fish with fruit, served with unusual wines from all over Italy. (*Closed Sat midday, Sun, 25 July–25 Aug.*) Near the cathedral, **Notai**, Via dei Pignattari 1, ☎ 228694 , is a Bolognese classic, with a piano bar upstairs and an elegant Victorian dining room below, with delicious and unusual pasta dishes and unorthodox but succulent variations on local favourites on the monthly changing menu. It also has Bologna's best wine list. (*Closed Sun.*)

Bologna's most celebrated restaurant, **Pappagallo**, in the pretty Piazza della Mercanzia 3, ✆ 232807, has an enchanting dining room formerly frequented by such notables as Alfred Hitchcock and Albert Einstein. The *menu degustazione* is firmly rooted in local tradition, with *tortellini in brodo* or *tagliatelle al ragù bolognese* as fixtures. (*Closed Sun, Mon midday.*)

On the north side of the city centre, **Il Tartufo**, Via del Porto 34, ✆ 252662, features both traditional Emilian dishes and delightful new creations like rabbit with black truffles or lamb in balsamic vinegar. (*Closed Sun.*)

**Le Tre Frecce** is located in the medieval Casa Isolani at Strada Maggiore 19, ✆ 231200; complementing the beautiful Gothic décor are dishes like tagliatelle with asparagus tips and breast of pheasant with white grapes, rich desserts and fine Trebbiano wine. (*Closed Sun evenings, Mon, Aug.*)

Another favourite, **Franco Rossi**, Via delle Donzelle 1/a, off Via dell'Independenza, ✆ 238818, has a very pleasant and friendly ambience, and specialities based in Bolognese traditions—tagliatelle and good risotto, duck with green peppercorns or devilled scampi. (*Closed Sun, July.*)

**Da Bertino**, Via Lame 55, ✆ 522230, offers properly prepared and very tasty Bolognese cuisine without frills. (*Closed Sun.*)

**Boni**, an old-timer on Via Saragozza 88, ✆ 585060, will please with tortelli in cream, roast meats, and omelettes with balsamic vinegar. (*Closed Fri evenings, Sat.*)

To the south, just off Via S. Stefano, **Trattoria Sale e Pepe**, Via de' Coltelli 1/12, ✆ 228532, has innovative specialities cooked to a T with a Neopolitan touch, and great desserts and wine; there's also a good cheap lunch menu every day.

There is a large number of budget-priced restaurants in the university area, particularly around Piazza Verdi and the Via Belle Arti. Such is the strength of the local food cult that even cheaper restaurants generally maintain a very high standard.

The **Osteria del Matusél**, Via Bertolini 2/2, near the university, offers hearty, filling meals: expect thick soup, macaroni, and hunks of meat. (*Open till 12.45am; closed Sun.*) As an alternative to traditional fare, the **Centro Naturista**, Via Albari 6, ✆ 235643, has vegetarian and wholefoods, and an interesting crowd.

The lively **Osteria la Botte**, Via Sant'Isaia 30, has a fine list of wines, accompanied by a small but delicious choice of daily dishes.

Just off Piazza Maggiore, **Osteria del Sole**, Vicolo Ranocchi, which is only open until 9pm on weekdays, has long wooden tables where you can eat your own food bought at the surrounding market, and excellent wine. Also *see* the listings under *osterie*, below.

Not surprisingly, a thousand-year-old university city like Bologna stays up later than most other Italian cities. People here eat late—often around 10pm—and there are plenty of bars and cafés open till 3am. During college terms, you have only to take a look at the student bars around the university and the posters in their windows to find out about concerts, films, exhibitions, performances and clubs; alternatively, check out the listings in Bologna's oddly named local paper, *Il Resto del Carlino* (which does not mean 'the remains of little Charles' as many foreigners suspect, but the change from an old coin called a Carlino—instead of change you could have a newspaper). The local fortnightly magazine *La Mongolfiera* usually has better listings on more youth-orientated events, concerts and so on, and interesting articles if you can read Italian.

One reflection of Bologna's progressive open-mindedness is that it contains the headquarters of Italy's largest **gay organization**, **Arci-Gay**, and is the only city in the country to have a municipally supported gay centre, the **Cassero**, in Porta Saragozza, ✆ 433395, which sponsors films and discussions during the week and discos at weekends. There are several **women's organisations** in the city; **Ufficio Progetto Donna**, Via Oberdan 24, ✆ 204767, issues lists.

### opera, classical music, theatre and cinema

The **drama** season at the Teatro Duse runs from November to May, while **operas** are performed at the Teatro Comunale from December to May. During the winter **films** are also shown in their original language on Wednesdays at **Tiffany**, Piazza di Porta Saragozza 5, and on Mondays at **Adriano**, Via S. Felice 52. In addition, throughout the year the **Cinema Lumière**, Via Pietralata 55, shows mainly arthouse movies, many of which have never been dubbed into Italian in the first place.

In June especially, but also in July and August, dance performances and concerts are presented in the Piazza Maggiore. As an alternative to the usual Italian mid-summer shutdown Bologna's enterprising local authorities also organise the *Bologna Sogna* festival throughout July and August, featuring concerts, theatre, and open-air cinema.

### cafés, bars and osterie

No visitor should leave Bologna without drinking in one of the city's traditional *osterie*; most serve food, many have live music, and they nearly always stay open late into the night. Three of the many are **Osteria dell'Orsa**, near the university at Via Mentana 1, with live jazz and good food; **Bentivoglio**, Via Mascarella 4, a huge, smart cellar for live music, with snacks or full meals, and an endless wine list; and the great, lively **Osteria del Montesino**, Via del Pratello 74, which serves good *crostini* and stays open till 2am, or 4am on Fri and Sat. (*Closed Tues.*)

Bologna also has its stock of sleeker and more modern bars, such as **Bar Rosa Rose**, Via Clavature 18, a popular early-evening meeting point just off the Piazza Maggiore, and **C'entro**, Via dell'Indipendenza 45. **Stranamore**, Via del Pratello 44, is a very trendy hangout for the local intelligentsia. For fine-quality *gelati*, try **Moline**, Via delle Moline 6, near the university, or, more central **Frulé**, Via Clavature.

### clubs and discos

As often happens in Italy, many of the bigger clubs are outside the city centre. One of the best-established is **Bestial Market**, Via delle Scale 21, outside the Porta San Felice on the edge of the central area, a very student-oriented venue that offers a wide mix of techno and other dance music, and occasional live gigs. **Porta di Mare**, Via Sampieri, near the Two Towers, is a rare centrally located lively music and dance venue. **Candilejas**, Via Bentini 20, is a funky sometimes Latin-oriented club in the suburb of Corticella (nightbus 62 from Piazza Nettuno). Also, in summer the ever-generous Bologna city council sponsors cheap, open-air **raves**, usually in the city outskirts; check posters and the local press for any coming up.

## East of Bologna

Between Bologna and the Adriatic are a hotchpotch of attractions—Italy's most important trotting course and the Imola motor-racing course, the fine medieval town of Brisighella, Faenza, Italy's most important ceramics town, and Forlì, decorated by Mussolini.

### Getting Around

Between Bologna and Rimini **trains** are fast, frequent, and occasionally packed, particularly in August. A slow local train runs from Faenza to Florence and stops at Brisighella; to continue to Florence you may have to change at Borgo San Lorenzo. Bagno di Romagna and other towns near the Tuscan frontier can be reached by **bus** from Forlì or Florence.

**Driving** between Bologna and the coast you have a choice between *autostrada* A14 to Rimini (from which the A14 dir branches off near Imola for Ravenna) or the some-times nerve-racking SS9/Via Emilia. The main road south into the Apennines and to Florence is the SS67 from Forlì. The E45 leads from Cesena to Bagno di Romagna and other points further east.

### Tourist Information

The main tourist office for **Forlì** province is at Corso della Repubblica 23, Forlì, ✆ (0543) 25532, @ 25026. There are also offices in **Faenza**, at Piazza del Popolo 1, ✆ (0546) 25231, and **Bagno di Romagna**, Via Lungo Savio 14, ✆ (0543) 911046, @ 911026.

## Imola

Nearest to Bologna, **Imola** is best known for the 'San Marino Gran Prix', held on the race track here, and for a restaurant, the San Domenico, a pilgrimage shrine for grand gourmets. As in Roman days the Via Aemilia divides the town in two. In the 18th-century cathedral you can pay your respects at the tomb of Imola's patron saint Cassian, a schoolteacher whose martyrdom was particularly unpleasant: he was stabbed with the pens of his students. **Imola Castle** to the south of the Via Emilia was defended by Caterina Sforza, widow of the Lord of Imola, until its capture by Cesare Borgia in 1500. In the nearby village of **Dozza**, a few kilometres back towards Bologna, the castle houses the **Enoteca Regionale Emilia-Romagna**, © (0542) 678089, @ 678073 (*open April–Oct 10–12, 3–6, Mon–Sat; 10–12, 3–7, Sun, holidays; Nov–Mar 2–5pm Mon–Sat; 2–6pm Sun, holidays*), a treasure-trove where you can sample 450 of the region's wines

## Faenza

'Faience ware' was born in the 16th century in Faenza, with the invention of a new style of majolica: a piece was given a solid white glaze, then rapidly, almost impressionistically, decorated with two tones of yellow and blue. It caused a sensation, and was in such demand throughout Europe that Faenza became a household word.

Today Faenza has regained much of its 16th-century renown as a ceramics centre. There are 500 students enrolled in its *Istituto d'Arte per la Ceramica* and experimental laboratory, as well as some 60 artists from around the world who run workshops in the town. The **Associati Ente Ceramica**, Voltone Molinella 2, © (0546) 25110, issues a list of studios that you may visit and buy from: particularly worth seeing are Carlo Zauli, on Via della Croce 6, © (0546) 22123; Ivo Sassi, Via S. Filippo Neri 3 © (0546) 663069; and Goffredo Gaeta, Via Ceonia, © (0546) 22816. Among several buildings and palaces adorned with majolica, the most splendid is the Liberty-style **Palazzo Matteucci** in Corso Mazzini. Every year, in September–October, Faenza hosts an international ceramics exhibition; the theme is contemporary in odd years, and antique in even.

Faenza Ceramics

The **Museo Internazionale delle Ceramiche**, Viale Baccarini 19 (*open April–Oct 9am–7pm Tues–Sat; 9.30am–1pm Sun; Nov–Mar 9.30am–2pm Tues–Sat; 9.30am–1pm Sun; adm exp—If you're carrying on to Ravenna, it's worth buying the biglietto cumulativo, which includes the major monuments there*), was founded in 1908 and restored after its bombing in the War. It houses a magnificent collection of ceramics, centred on 16th- and 17th-century Italian works; pieces from Faenza adorned with giraffe-necked Renaissance ladies were typical nuptial gifts. There are fine Liberty-style pieces by Domenico Baccarini and Francesco Nonni, and downstairs an excellent collection of international ceramic art, including pieces by Picasso,

Matisse, Chagall, and Rouault. Faenza's unfinished Renaissance **Duomo**, in the central Piazza della Libertà, has some good Renaissance sculpture inside; the town **Museum**, on Via Severoli (*closed for restoration; inquire at the tourist office*) contains a good collection of paintings by Romagna artists, sculpture by Alfonso Lombardi, and some works formerly attributed to Donatello .

## Brisighella

Some 12km south of Faenza on the Florence road, Brisighella is a charming village and thermal spa in the Lamone Valley. The sharp cliffs overhead are crowned by the splendid towers of the 12th-century **Rocca** and the **Torre dell'Orologio**, the latter originally a respectable guard tower with a clock slapped on its front in the 18th century. Brisighella traditionally produced much of the clay fired in Faenza's kilns—next to the village you can see the gashes left in the hills by the old quarries. So precious was this cargo borne by the village's mule caravans that a protected, elevated passageway, the **Via degli Asini** (Mule Road), was built through the centre of town which, in case of attack, could be sealed up at either end. In the Rocca you can visit the **Museo del Lavoro Contadino** (*open 15 April–15 Oct 10–12, 3.30–5.30, Tues–Sun; Oct–April 2.30–4.30pm Sat; 10–12, 2.30–4.30, Sun; adm*), with a collection devoted to the region's traditional peasant culture, life and work. On the edge of town there's an ancient Romanesque church, the **Pieve del Thò**. Several ceramics workshops still operate in Brisighella; from the end of June to the first week of July the city also hosts an elaborate **Medieval Festival**, with music, games, feasts, plays, and more.

---

## Forlì

The *Forum Livii* on the Via Aemilia was elided over the years into Forlì, a city split between an attractive old town and the architectural legacy of Mussolini, who was born in nearby Predappio. The centrepiece of old Forlì is the striking 12th-century **Basilica di San Mercurio**, with a good campanile, a fine 13th-century lunette of the Magi by the school of Antelami, and an interesting interior. The **Duomo** on Corso Garibaldi has a temple façade; note the painting inside of 15th-century firemen. On Corso della Repubblica, the worthy **Museo Archeologico e Pinacoteca Saffi** (*open 9am–2pm Mon–Fri; 10am–1pm Sun*), contains works by local artist Marco Palmezzano, Fra Angelico, and others, as well as Flemish tapestries, ethnographic exhibits, and ceramics. The nearby **Santa Maria dei Servi** merits a stop for the finely sculpted tomb of Luffo Namai (1502). Further south Forlì's castle, the picturesque 15th-century **Rocca di Ravaldino**, was another possession of Caterina Sforza, and the birthplace in 1498 of her son Giovanni de' Medici (better known as 'Giovanni delle Bande Nere', a famous condottiere and father of Cosimo I, first Duke of Tuscany). It now serves as a prison.

## The Local Palio

 Siena's Palio may be the most famous, but it's neither unique in Italy, nor the only one to claim the longest history. However, whereas Siena's has continued virtually uninterrupted for centuries, the others, particularly in Emilia-Romagna, have resurrected themselves over the past few decades, and so lack the pomp, vast crowds, and deep emotional response of that gallop around the Piazza del Campo. The Palio in Montagnana, Ferrara, or Forlimpopoli may be less vital, violent, cosmopolitan, and crooked, but they do have other charms: no tourists, few police, small crowds, and a chance to see an Italian community expressing its self-love. Older traditions do remain (the tug of war to decide placings at the race's start), but the lack of formality and crowds allow a relaxed atmosphere; kids clothed in medieval finery will spend the afternoon tearing round the streets, beating on drums.

Siena provides the framework, which lesser palios copy. The day begins with a procession in medieval costume, probably led by the town's standard, followed by a delegation from each district: 'landowners' on horseback, young married couples holding hands, a matron in the middle of a crowd of urchins, a criminal in the stocks, massed ranks of young men clasping spears and pushing a catapult, a cart piled with geese, and troupes of teenage *sbandierati*, twirling long, silken flags from one hand to the other, between their legs and behind their back, tossing them into the air, and, as they unfurl, catching them again.

By comparison the race itself is chaotic. Bales of hay line wooden barriers which shield the crowds from the thundering horses. Each bareback rider carries a *nerbo*, a whip with which he may hit any horse or opponent, and wears a small coat named *giacchetto*, from which we derive the English word 'jockey'. The horses, fired up, take several minutes to form a regular starting-line. The race is brief and furious. Its aftermath depends where you are: in Montagnana, near Rovigo (see p.549), a small town competing against surrounding villages, the victor will be carried home for a beer and barbecue. In Siena, supporters will try to kill the losers for having lost and the victor for having won; the entire city weeps, for joy or shame at the outcome; casks of wine are splintered open on the pavement, and goblets handed out to any passer-by.

## Into the Apennines

South of Forlì there are three principal routes into Tuscany, each passing through pretty mountain scenery. Some of the best is in the Montone Valley, the main route to Florence, along the SS67. On the way there is the Renaissance planned village of **Terra del Sole**, begun in 1564 in the form of a perfect rectangle, not far from the small spa of **Castrocaro Terme**. Ruined medieval castles haunt the next towns of **Dovadola** and **Rocca San Casciano**. Dante's beloved Beatrice spent several summers in the old medieval town of **Portico di Romagna**; the Portinari house where she stayed can still be seen in the main street. Near the Tuscan frontier, the 9th-century abbey in **San Benedetto in Alpe** sheltered Dante after his unsuccessful bid to return to Florence from exile (*Inferno*, Canto XVI, 94–105). In San Benedetto you can hire horses to explore the region's valleys, especially the lovely **Valle dell'Acquacheta** with its bucolic, stepped waterfall. The rapid Brusia river is popular with canoeists and kayakers.

The narrow alternative route just to the east (SS9 ter) passes through the Sangiovese wine country around **Predappio**, where Mussolini was born in 1883, the son of a socialist blacksmith, and where his remains were re-buried in the local cemetery in 1957, near those of his

wife Rachele. Mussolini made his home village the seat of the local *comune*, and embellished it with public buildings, leaving the old *comune*, **Predappio Alta**, alone beneath its
overgrown castle. In Predappio Alta, the **Cà de Sanvès** is the place to taste the local ruby-
red 'blood of Jove' (*open 10–12, 3–12 midnight; closed Tues*).

From Forlimpopoli, with its well-preserved medieval castle on the Via Emilia, another road
heads south for **Bertinoro**, an old town famous for its wine and hospitality. And such were
the squabbles over guests in old Bertinoro that a column was erected in front of the 14th-
century **Palazzo Comunale** and hung with rings, one belonging to each family. Whichever
ring a stranger tethered his horse to decided which family would be his host. Nearby
**Polenta** has a fine 9th-century Byzantine-Romanesque temple. The main SS310 road from
Forlì continues into the scenic Upper Bidenta valley, where the **Ridracoli dam** and
Romagna Aqueduct, in the midst of a heavily forested region, have only been completed in
the last few years (*open weekends only*). There are ski facilities in the valley at Monte
Campigna, near the old Tuscan town of **Santa Sofia**. Much further south, near **Balze**,
there's more skiing at Monte Fumaiolo, on whose slopes the river Tiber (Tevere) begins its
418km journey to Rome. **San Piero in Bagno** and **Bagno di Romagna**, with thermal and
mud baths, are popular summer resorts in the region.

## Cesena and the Rubicon

Cesena, site of the European Trotting Championships in August, was, in the 14th–15th
centuries, one of the jewels of the Malatesta clan. Their castle still dominates the town,
while a 1452 basilica built for Domenico Malatesta Novello is the main sight, housing the
**Biblioteca Malatestiana** (*open 8am–1pm Mon–Sat*), with a priceless collection of manuscripts. Between Cesena and Rimini at **Savignano**, the road crosses a poor excuse for a
stream that most authorities accept as the shadowy Rubicon, which in those days divided
what was then Gaul from what was then Roman Italy, and which Julius Caesar crossed with
his army, thereby defying the Senate and declaring his intention to take over the Roman
state. Today it separates respectable Emilia-Romagna from the international bikini beach
boogaroo at Rimini.

---

### Activities

Faenza and Forlimpopoli both have a traditional *palio* each summer—Faenza's takes
place on the last two Sundays in July. Tourist offices have details of these and other
traditional events in the region.

---

### Where to Stay
### expensive/moderate

### Faenza

In central Faenza, the ★★★★**Albergo Vittoria**, Corso Garibaldi 23,
© (0546) 21508, ✆ 29136 (expensive) is an attractive hotel with 19th-
century furnishings and a dining room with a fine frescoed ceiling. If
you're driving, ★★★★**Cavallino** (moderate) is outside Faenza at Via
Forlivese 185, © (0546) 30226, ✆ 30852, and has a garage, garden

and restaurant. Beside the railway station is **★★Torricelli**, Piazzale Cesare Battisti 7, ✆ (0546) 22287 (inexpensive) with rather stark rooms, with or without baths.

## Forli

**★★★★Principe**, just outside the centre at Viale Bologna 153, ✆ (0543) 701570, ✉ 702270 (moderate) has air-conditioned, comfortable modern rooms; the restaurant serves good land- and seafood, like salmon tarragon.

## Bagno di Romagna

**★★★★Hotel Tosco Romagnolo**, Piazza Dante Aligheri 2, ✆ (0543) 911260, ✉ 911014 (expensive/moderate) is a charming place to stay, relax, and dine in one of Italy's most enchanting dining rooms, where the food is based on Tuscan and Romagna country traditions—delicious pâtés, crêpes, rack of lamb, and wines. (*Open Easter–15th Nov.*)

It is also possible to stay in farmhouses in the region (*agriturismo*), particularly around Faenza and Brisighella; inquire at tourist offices for details.

---

*Eating Out*

## Faenza

Beside the Duomo, the **Enoteca Astorre**, Piazza Libertà 16, ✆ (0546) 681407 (moderate) offers interesting wines, accompanied by *bruschette* or full meals. (*Closed Sun midday, Mon.*) **Le Volte**, Corso Mazzini 54, ✆ (0546) 661600 (moderate) is hidden in the basement of an arcade, the Galleria Gessi. Surrounded by antique furniture, you can eat green gnocchi with ricotta, aubergine risotto, lamb with mushrooms or veal in a sauce of various cheeses. (*Closed Sun.*)

**Osteria Il Coccio**, Corso Garibaldi 2 (inexpensive) is Faenza's most typical eating place in atmosphere and menu, serving tasty and well-prepared pasta, pizza and meats.

## Imola

**Ristorante San Domenico**, Via G. Sacchi 1, ✆ (0542) 29000 (very expensive) is a place of veneration for gastronomes from around the world. Consistently rated in the top five in the country, this holy temple of Italian culinary traditions offers a constantly changing menu of the day, sublimely prepared with the lightest and most delicate of touches. The dining room is as beautiful as the desserts, and the wine list is exquisite enough to shatter a plastic credit card. (*Closed Mon, most of Aug.*) Breathing on San Domenico's sacred heels is a much newer establishment, **Naldi**, Via Santerno 13, ✆ (0542) 29581 (expensive), which offers tempting and innovative variations on Emilia-Romagna recipes—pâtés with black truffles, tortellini in walnut cream, or stuffed chicken breasts—in a charming setting.

## Forli

Within 10km of Forlì are two more gourmet restaurants. Outside Forlimpopoli in Selbagnone is **Al Maneggio**, ✆ (0543) 742042 (very expensive), located in a villa next to a delightful garden. The kitchen's specialities are based in an elegant simplicity—superb risotto, *gamberoni*, desserts, and wines. (*Closed Sun evenings, Mon.*) At Castrocaro Terme is **La Frasca**, Via Matteotti 38, ✆ (0543) 767471 (very expensive), which offers wonderful local cuisine including specialities such as white bean and mushroom soup, lamb with truffles, red mullet with coriander, and hundreds of cheeses. (*Closed Mon, two weeks Jan, two weeks Aug.*)

## Brisighella

At **Gigiolè**, Piazza Carducci 5, ✆ (0546) 81209 (moderate), the chef has done detailed research into Romagna's medieval culinary traditions—ravioli stuffed with rabbit and mint, veal with wild fennel, mulberry pudding, and more. (*Closed Mon.*) If you're too stuffed to move afterwards, there's an *albergo* upstairs. **La Grotta Osteria con Uso di Cucina**, Via Metelli 2, ✆ (0546) 81829 (moderate) offers three daily menus—the bargain, the regional, and the *degustazione*. It's rated one of the best restaurants in Emilia-Romagna, and the prices are amazing. (*Closed Tues.*)

## Ferrara

There's been a certain mystique attached to Ferrara ever since Jacob Burckhardt called it 'the first modern city in Europe' in his classic *Civilization of the Renaissance in Italy*. Whether or not Burckhardt was right can be debated endlessly; it is certain that the famous 'additions' to the medieval city in the Renaissance were far too ambitious. Ferrara, even in the most brilliant days of the Court of the Este family, never had more than 30,000 citizens—not enough to fill the long, straight, rational streets laid out within the 9km circuit of the walls.

But what was a failure in the Renaissance is a happy success today; if Italian art cities can be said to come and go in fashion, Ferrara is definitely in, popularized by a well-received international campaign to save its uniquely well-preserved walls. Thanks to the rather tyrannical Este, the charming city they enclose was one of the brightest stars of the Renaissance, with its own fine school of art, led by the great Cosmè Tura, Ercole de' Roberti, Lorenza Costa, and Francesco del Cossa. Poets patronized by the Este produced three of the Italian Renaissance's greatest epic poems—Boiardo's *Orlando Innamorato* (1483), Ariosto's better known continuation of the same story, *Orlando Furioso* (1532), and Tasso's *Gerusalemme Liberata* (1581), all of which praise the ducal family.

## History

Ferrara grew up on a formerly navigable branch of the Po, and until the 17th century based its economy on river tolls, the salt pans of the Comacchio, and the rich agricultural land of the Delta. It was always ruled by one or other of the powerful local dynasties, but it was the rise of the Este family in 1250 that made Ferrara a great Guelph city, an outpost of papal power in the north. The Este clan produced and married some of the most interesting characters of the Renaissance: there was Nicolò II (1361–88), the friend of Petrarch; Alberto

(1388–93) who founded the University of Ferrara; Nicolò III (1393–1441), reputedly the father of hundreds of children on both banks of the Po, and the villain who perpetrated one of the tragic love stories of his day—he found that his young wife Parisina and his son by another woman were lovers, and had both of them executed. The other sons of Nicolò III, Leonello, Borso and Ercole I (1471–1505), met happier fates, and were responsible for the city's great cultural flowering. Ercole I had the first addition to the city (known as the Herculean Addition) designed by his architect Rossetti; his offspring, Isabella (wife of Francesco Gonzaga), Beatrice (married to Lodovico Sforza, *Il Moro*), and Cardinal Ippolito were among the most cultured and influential people of their day. His heir Alfonso I (1505–34) married the beautiful and unjustly maligned Lucrezia Borgia, who ran a brilliant and fashionable court, patronizing Ariosto and Titian, while her husband spent his days casting huge cannons. Their son, Ercole II (1534–59) married Renée, daughter of Louis XII of France and a Calvinist, who even sheltered John Calvin in Ferrara under an assumed name; eventually relations with Rome became so touchy that she had to be sent away.

The last Este Duke, Alfonso II (1559–97), patron of the unstable and unruly Tasso, was considered the best-educated and most courtly ruler of his day—at the expense of his people. When he died without issue, Ferrara was glad to see the last of the family, and was ruled thereafter by a papal legate (though a branch of the Este family continued to rule as dukes of Modena and Reggio until the time of Napoleon). Without the largesse of the Este, Ferrara became an artistic backwater for several centuries, and even its population declined considerably. In this century, however, the modern 'Metaphysical School' of painting (De Chirico, Carrà, De Pises, Morandi, and others) had its origins in the city, inspired at least in part by the great frescoes in the Palazzo Schifanoia.

## Getting Around

Ferrara's **railway station** is just outside the city walls, a 15-minute walk west of the centre along the Viale Cavour (or take local buses 1, 2 or 9). There are frequent rail connections to Bologna, Venice, and Ravenna. The **bus station** is near the corner of the Rampari di San Paolo and the Corso Isonzo, ✆ 40679, information ✆ 771302; a fine network of lines serves the coast, Bologna, Modena, Ravenna, Rovigo, and other local destinations.

The main **road** to Ferrara is the *autostrada* A13 from Bologna to Padua, which passes just west of the city. Alternately, the SS64 leads from Bologna and the SS16 from Ravenna and on northwards to Rovigo. South of Ferrara a new, motorway-standard road cuts eastward off the A13 and SS64 for Comacchio and the Delta.

Almost completely flat, Ferrara apparently has the second-largest ratio of **bicycles** to humans in Europe (after Copenhagen). Plans are afoot for a municipally run hire scheme, but this is taking decades to set up. Until then, try **Bicincittà**, Via Kennedy, just off Piazza Travaglio, ✆ (0532) 628072.

## Tourist Information

The tourist office is in the heart of town at Piazza Municipio 19, ✆ (0532) 209370, ✉ 210844.

## The Castle and the Cathedral

At the very centre of Ferrara towers the imposing **Castello Estense** (*open 9–1, 2.30–6, Mon–Fri; 9am–8pm Sat, Sun; adm, not necessary for the drawbridge and courtyard*), which would look like a Victorian factory building, were it not for the moat and drawbridges. It was begun in 1385 by Nicolò II after a local revolt, though later the Este transformed it into their chief residence, its crenellations replaced by white marble balustrades, and its great halls adorned with art. A few decorated rooms survive: the *Salone* and *Saletta dei Giochi* (the games room, the latter belonging to the children) and the fine *Sala dell'Aurora* (the dukes' bedroom) and *Camerina dei Baccanali* are the most interesting. The tour includes Renée's Calvinist chapel, the dungeon where Ugo and Parisina languished before their beheading, and the prison where Giulio and Ferrante, brothers of Alfonso I, spent their lives after attempting a conspiracy. Even the life of a cultured duke wasn't all peaches and cream.

From the Castello the Corso dei Martiri leads first to the **Palazzo Comunale**, built in 1243 and adorned with statues of Nicolò III and Borso; next to it in the Piazza della Repubblica stands a statue of Savonarola, a native of Ferrara. Opposite the palazzo is the pretty rose-coloured **Duomo**, begun in 1135 by Wiligelmo, and finished a century later. Its glory is a marble portico, carved with a magnificent 13th-century scene of the *Last Judgement* by an unknown sculptor; a certain Maestro Nicolò executed the bas-reliefs of *St George* in the lunette over the door. The lovely candy-striped campanile is from the 15th century; the arcade on the north side retains its original twisted columns. The interior was remodelled in the 17th century and contains many fine pieces of art, although the best are in the **Cathedral Museum** (*open 10–12, 3–5, Mon–Sat*), including the lovely marble *Madonna of the Pomegranate* by Jacopo della Quercia, two fine painted organ shutters by Cosmè Tura, featuring an *Annunciation* and a *St George*, and a relief of the months that once adorned the cathedral exterior. The picturesque market portico flanking the cathedral in the Piazza Trento e Trieste was erected in 1473.

## Renaissance Palaces

From behind the cathedral in Via Voltapaletto, Via Savonarola will take you to the **Casa Romei** (*open 10am–5pm Tues–Sun; adm*), a fine example of the typical Renaissance palace, built for a banker who married an Este in 1445. As well as its charming frescoes, fireplaces and elegant courtyards, there are some expressive detached frescoes moved here from Sant'Andrea and other disused churches. Further down the Via Praisolo, behind the church of San Girolamo, is the **Corpus Domini** (*open 9.30–12, 3–5, Sun–Fri; closed Sat, holidays*), containing the austere tombs of Alfonso I, Alfonso II and Lucrezia Borgia.

Nearby, a short walk up Via Ugo Bassi, is the late-Renaissance **Palazzina di Marfisa d'Este** (*open 9–12.30, 3–6, daily; adm, free 2nd Sun and 2nd Mon of each month*), in a garden at Corso della Giovecca 170. It once formed part of a larger complex of buildings, now unfortunately lost. Marfisa, a friend of Tasso, was beautiful and eccentric, and the subject of several ghost stories; it seems that she enjoyed post-mortem rides through the city at midnight in a wolf-drawn carriage. The interior of her little palace, with its unusual *grotteschi* frescoes on the ceiling, has been admirably restored and fitted with period furnishings.

## Palazzo Schifanoia

Ferrara's most famous palace, the 1385 **Palazzo Schifanoia** (*open 7am–7pm daily; adm, free 2nd Sun and 2nd Mon of each month*), is a couple of streets away at Via Scandiana 23 (follow Via Ugo Bassi to Via Madama). Schifanoia translates as 'disgust with boredom', and it would be hard to stay bored in the delightful **Salone dei Mesi**, a secular masterpiece painted for Borso d'Este by Cosmè Tura, Ercole de' Roberti and Francesco del Cossa. The scenes of mythological and allegorical subjects peopled by charming 15th-century aristocrats are believed to have been inspired by Petrarch's *Triumphs*—in each month a different god is seen to 'triumph', most famously Venus in the month of April, with a rare scene of a Renaissance kiss. The palace has several other rooms with beautiful ceilings, and houses an eclectic collection of medieval (note the alabaster *Passion of Christ* from Nottingham) and ancient art.

## Palazzo di Lodovico il Moro

Turn right at the walls at the end of Via Scandiana and continue to Via XX Settembre. At No 124 stands the elegant **Palazzo di Lodovico il Moro** designed by Biagio Rossetti and erroneously named after Beatrice d'Este's Milanese husband, though it never belonged to him. It has frescoes on the ground floor by Raphael's pupil, Garofalo, and upstairs houses an excellent **Museo Archeologico Nazionale** (closed for restoration at time of writing), with a collection of finds from the ancient necropolis in the Graeco-Etruscan seaport of Spina (near Comacchio), including Attic vases, a splendid gold diadem and two pirogues (canoes) carved from tree trunks in the later Roman period. Just outside the walls (through the Porta Romana) **San Giorgio** was Ferrara's cathedral until the 12th century, and is worth a look for the sumptuous 1475 **Tomb of Lorenzo Roverella**, Pope Julius II's physician. Back within the walls, near the Palazzo di Lodovico il Moro and just off the Via Beatrice d'Este, is the convent of **Sant'Antonio in Polèsine**, with some fine frescoes dating back to the 13th century and inlaid choir stalls.

On the way back towards the centre from here, on the Via delle Scienze, is the 13th-century **Palazzo Paradiso**, former seat of the university, and site of the Ariosto library, with the complete manuscript of *Orlando Furioso* and Ariosto's tomb.

## The Herculean Addition

North of the Castello Estense stretches the Herculean Addition, laid out by Biagio Rossetti for Ercole I, which more than doubled the size of 15th-century Ferrara. Not long after the fall of the Este dynasty, travellers noted that many of the streets here were abandoned and overgrown, and even today they feel somewhat melancholy and quiet. Rossetti's showpiece **Palazzo dei Diamanti**, in the very centre of the Addition, takes its name from the 8,500 pointed, diamond-shaped stones that stud the façade—diamonds being the emblem of the Este. It houses the **Pinacoteca Nazionale** (*open 9am–2pm Tues–Sat; 9am–1pm Sun, holidays; adm*), a collection mainly of works by the Ferrara school—Tura, Cossa, Costa, Roberti, the sweet Raphaelesque Garofalo (a favourite of the 18th century), and Dossi, as well as detached frescoes from old churches and palaces. There's also a Carpaccio, *Death of the Virgin*, and 19th- and 20th-century art on the ground floor.

The Diamond palace lies at the junction of two main streets; down one, Corso Biagio Rossetti, Via Ariosto leads off to the right to the **Casa di Ariosto** (*closed for restoration*), which the poet built for himself. 'Small,' he described it modestly, 'but suited to me'. To the east of the Diamond Palace, on Corso Porta Mare 9, the **Palazzo Massari** (*open 9.30–1, 3.30–7, Tues–Sun; adm, free 1st Sun, 1st Mon of each month*), houses the **Civic Museum of Modern Art** and the **Documentario della Metafisica**, a collection of slides and reproductions of major works by the Metaphysical School, covering the origins of the movement in Ferrara. Pass through it to reach the **Palazzina dei Cavalieri di Malta**, seat of the Knights of Malta from 1826–34, which contains a collection of 19th-century and Liberty-style art.

From the Palazzo Massari, Via Borso leads to the **Certosa**, founded by Borso d'Este in 1452, and now the city cemetery. Its church of **San Cristoforo** is embellished with a huge luck-giving St Christopher. The **Cimitero Israelitico**, along the walls by Via Porta Mare, was founded in the 17th century, when Ferrara had a considerable Jewish population, many of them refugees from Spain; strewn with wild flowers, it is one of the prettiest spots in the city.

## The Walls

Ferrara's well-preserved 9km circuit of red-brick walls is most easily seen by bicycle. They date from the 15th and 16th centuries, and the best stretch is between the Porta Mare and the former Porta degli Angeli, built by Rossetti, on the north side of the city. Cycle paths run along their length, linking with routes into the city and out to the Po.

## Around Ferrara

Most of the region around Ferrara is flat and somewhat dreary. **Argenta**, on the river Reno to the southeast of the city, is mainly visited for a much-praised restaurant (*see* below). Its attractive quattrocento church of **San Domenico** now houses a small art gallery, with works by Garofalo and others. Between Ferrara and Modena, **Cento**, under its 14th-century castle, was the birthplace of the Baroque painter Guercino (1591–1666) and of some of the ancestors of Disraeli; a representative collection of the former's paintings is in the **Pinacoteca Civica**, at Via Matteotti 10.

Ferrara has its own *Palio* or traditional horse race, every year on the last Sunday in May. It isn't remotely as well known as the one in Siena, but can be more fun (*see* p.544–5).

*Ferrara* ✆ *(0532–)* **Where to Stay**

*expensive*

The ★★★★**Ripagrande**, Via Ripagrande 23, ✆ 765250, ✉ 764377, housed in the Renaissance Beccari-Freguglia palace in the medieval quarter of town, offers the most memorable accommodation in Ferrara. Its ground floor retains its Renaissance décor and heavy-beamed ceiling, and there's a fine restaurant as well. The 40 rooms upstairs are very modern, all equipped with kitchenettes and sitting rooms, air-conditioning, and TV. There are also pleasant courtyards at the back, parking, and bicycles to rent available for guests. The ★★★★**Astra**, Viale Cavour 55, ✆ 206088, ✉ 247002, on the main street to the station, is a sturdy, long-established and well-furnished hotel, recently renovated and under new management. It, too, has a fine restaurant. If you want to escape from urban life while remaining within reach of it, try the beautiful ★★★★**Villa Regina**, Via Comacchio 402, ✆ 740222, ✉ 761085, outside the city in a converted villa set amid luxurious parkland.

*moderate*

Right beside the castle is the modern, slick ★★★**Touring**, Viale Cavour 11, ✆ 206200, which has an underground car park to complement its air-conditioned rooms. Also in the medieval city, ★★★**Europa**, Corso Giovecca 49, ✆ 33460, is a fine old hotel in a 17th-century palace, with parking, and rooms with or without baths.

*inexpensive*

★★**San Paolo**, Via Baluardi 9, ✆ 762040, ✉ 762040, is pleasantly situated near the city walls beside Piazza Travaglio, with rooms and service beyond what one would expect for its price. The best of the cheapest options is ★**Casa Degli Artisti**, Via Vittoria 66, ✆ 761038, which is right in the centre of town near the Duomo.

*Ferrara* ✆ *(0532–)* **Eating Out**

Ferrara's most famous dish (the favourite of Lucrezia Borgia) is *salama da sugo*—a sausage that is cured for a year, then gently boiled and eaten with a spoon. The bakers of Ferrara are famous for their X-shaped bread *ciupèta*; little caps of pasta, *cappelletti*, often filled with pumpkin, are another local speciality. When Renée of France came to Ferrara she brought her own vines, the origin of the local viticulture and the delicious *Vino di Bosco*.

A restaurant all locals rave about is in Argenta, the **Trigabolo**, Piazza Garibaldi 4/5, ✆ 804121, another gourmet enclave in an unlikely spot. In its elegant dining room you can feast on delicious first courses like ravioli stuffed with artichokes with basil sauce, cannoli with turbot in clam sauce, ravioli with guinea fowl, *zuppa di pesce*, and more, according to season, while for seconds there are delicacies like goose liver with pears or veal with lettuce, cream and almonds. Naturally, there's a great wine list and rich desserts to top it all off. (*Closed Tues, first three weeks July.*)

### *expensive*

Back in the city the **Aldobrando**, Corso Porta Mare 45, ✆ 752648, bases its menu solidly on Ferrara's cuisine, especially *salama da sugo*. (*Closed Sun.*)

In a side-street behind the Palazzo Comunale is **Centrale**, Via Boccaleone 8, ✆ 206735, which offers an interesting variety of tortelloni, beef with truffles, and desserts made on the premises. (*Closed Mon.*)

### *moderate*

**Le Grazie**, Via Vignatagliata 61, ✆ 761052, is a small, intimate trattoria with specialities such as fresh artichokes, breast of duck with apple sauce, and good seafood, like marinated salmon and scampi. (*Closed Tues, July.*)

At **La Provvidenza**, flanked by trees at Corso Ercole d'Este 92, ✆ 205187, the menu always features fish on Thursday and Friday, or you'll have to make do with *salama da sugo* and meats cooked over a charcoal grill. (*Closed Mon.*)

### *inexpensive*

In a tiny medieval street, one of the oldest in Ferrara, is the **Osteria Degli Angeli**, Via Volte 4, ✆ 764376, with innovative varities of panini, like *Piadina* and *Crescione* (fried bread with various toppings), or full meals. (*Closed Mon.*)

Slightly outside the centre is **Tenuta S. Teresa**, Via Gramicia 83, ✆ 750337 , run by a family who produce hearty home-cooking, with a bustling atmosphere, and an open fire in the winter. (*Closed Mon.*)

---

### *Entertainment and Nightlife*

A university town, Ferrara is quite lively at night. Listings of forthcoming programmes in cinema, theatre and so on can be found in the local newspaper, *La Nuova Ferrara*. Ferrara has a unique place to drink: **Al Brindisi**, Via degli Adelardi 11, near the cathedral. It occupies the same locale as the ancient Taverna da Chiucchiolino, opened in 1435, and although the furnishings are much newer, the atmosphere is often just as jovial as it was in the 15th century. For coffee and delicious pastries, try the **Caffè Europa**, at Via della Giovecca 51. To find the hip young things of Ferrara, go to **Bar Ariosto**, in Piazza Ariostea.

For most people the main attractions along this coast are the Po Delta and magnificent Romanesque abbey of Poimposa, though there are pleanty of Italian family lidos in the vicinity if you're tempted to join the summer ice cream, pizza and parasol brigades.

## Getting Around

**Buses** from Ferrara radiate to the flatlands of the coast. If you have a **car**, a new fast road now leads directly from just south of Ferrara to the beaches past Comacchio. There it meets the coast road, the SS309, between Chioggia and Ravenna. Another, slower, road also runs from Ferrara to the coast, the SS495, which passes the abbey at Pomposa.

## Tourist Information

There are tourist information offices in **Comacchio**, at Via Buonafede 12, © (0533) 312844, @ 312880; **Lidi di Comacchio**, at Lido degli Estensi, Viale Carducci 31, © (0533) 87464; and **Pomposa** (summer only), © (0533) 710000.

## The Southern Po Delta

Alfonso II d'Este was the first to start draining the marshes south of the Po Delta. Much of the land was planted with rice; a large part of the rest now belongs to the **Parco del Delta del Po**, one of Italy's most important wetlands and a birdwatcher's paradise. Part of the primordial coastal pine forest survives intact in the **Bosco di Mésola**, now a nature reserve; visitors are admitted on Sundays and holidays only from 8am to sunset. Not far to the west, near Italba, this varied and ever-changing coastline offers something completely different—a marooned 100-acre patch of dunes, once part of the coast, called the 'Moraro'. Excursion boats plying the small, narrow canals between the reeds explore the mouth of the Po di Goro and the Valle di Gorino, departing from the picturesque fishing hamlets of Gorino, Goro, or Mésola; for information, contact **Freccia del Delta**, © (0533) 999817, or **Principessa**, © (0533) 999815, both in Gorino; in Goro, try **Delta Express**, © (0533) 996577.

## The Abbey of Pomposa

The main coast road from the north, the SS309, follows the old Roman coastal road, the Via Romea. Just south of the Po di Goro it passes through **Mésola**, with an old hunting lodge, the 'Delizia Estense' of Alfonso I d'Este, then continues down to the haunting and serene **Abbey of Pomposa**, an 8th-century Benedictine foundation, formerly on its own islet; in this atmosphere of total tranquility the monk Guido d'Arezzo invented the modern musical scale in the early 11th century. Uninhabited since the 17th century, the abbey is dwarfed by its great **campanile**, adorned with a unique series of mullioned windows which progress tier by tier from a narrow slit on the bottom to a grand *quadrifore* (four arches) on top. The **Church** (7th–11th centuries) has a lovely Byzantine atrium and an interior embellished with colourful 14th-century frescoes, many by the charming Vitale da Bologna; there are other good frescoes by his school in the monks' Chapter House. The abbot governed from the beautifully austere 11th-century **Palazzo della Ragione**. A **museum** contains items relating to the monastery (*the entire complex is open 7–12, 2–7, daily*).

The resorts along the sandy **Lidi di Comacchio** begin at the **Lido di Volano** on the other side of the wetlands of the Valle Bertuzzi, where the setting sun ignites the waters in a thousand colours. Of the resorts the **Lido delle Nazioni** and **Porto Garibaldi** are the most interesting and best equipped. The name of the latter recalls that the defeated hero attempted to escape from here after the collapse of the Roman Republic in 1849, in a desperate guerrilla movement that cost the life of his pregnant wife Anita.

The most important town in the area is **Comacchio**, with its famous monumental triple bridge, the **Trepponti**, spanning three of the town's many canals. Comacchio is famed for its eels, farmed in the Valli di Comacchio—if you're in the area between September and December, you can watch the fishermen scoop them up on their way to the sea. Just west of Comacchio stood the ancient Graeco-Etruscan port of **Spina** (now miles from the sea); its rich necropolis produced the exhibits in Ferrara's archaeology museum.

## Ravenna

Innocently tucked away among the art towns of Emilia-Romagna there is one famous city that has nothing to do with Renaissance popes and potentates, Guelphs or Ghibellines, sports cars or socialists. Little, in fact, has been heard from Ravenna in the last thousand years. Before that time, however, this little city's career was simply astounding—heir to Rome itself, and the leading city of western Europe for centuries. For anyone interested in Italy's shadowy progress through the Dark Ages, this is the place to visit.

There's a certain magic in three-digit years; history guards their secrets closely, giving us only occasional glimpses of battling barbarians, careful monks 'keeping alive the flame of knowledge' and local Byzantine dukes and counts doing their best to hold things together. In Italy, the Dark Ages were never quite so dark, never the vacuum most people think. This can be seen in Rome, but much more clearly here, in the only Italian city that not only survived but prospered all through those troubled times. In Ravenna's churches, adorned with the finest mosaics ever made, such an interruption as the Dark Ages seems to disappear, and you experience the development of Italian history and art from ancient to medieval times as a continuous and logical process.

## History

Ravenna first became a prominent Roman town during the reign of Augustus. With its port of Classis, the city lay on an important route to Dalmatia and the Danube. With their nearly impregnable setting, surrounded by broad marshes, the military advantage was clear, and Classis became Rome's biggest naval base on the Adriatic. As conditions in Italy became unsettled in the 5th century, the relative safety of Ravenna began to look very inviting to frightened emperors. Honorius moved the capital of the Western Empire here in 402—just in time, with Alaric's sack of Rome coming eight years later. Honorius' sister, a Roman lady named Galla Placidia, ruled the city in the emperor's absence, and began to embellish it with churches and monuments befitting its new status. When the Visigoths attacked Ravenna,

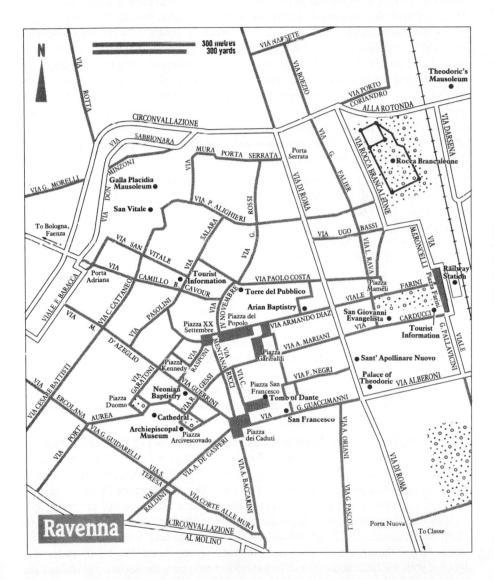

N

300 metres
300 yards

VIA NAPSETE

Theodoric's
Mausoleum ●

VIA ROTTA

VIA BOEZIO

VIA PORTO
CORIANDRO
ALLA ROTONDA

VIA DARSENA

CIRCONVALLAZIONE

VIA SABBIONARA

MURA  PORTA  SERRATA

Porta
Serrata

VIA ROCCA BRANCALEONE

VIA G. FALIER

● Rocca Brancaleone

VIA DON MINZONI

Galla Placidia
Mausoleum ●

VIA P. ALIGHIERI

VIA DI ROMA

VIA G. MORELLI

San Vitale ●

VIA G. ROSSI

SALARA

To Bologna,
Faenza

VIA SAN VITALE

VIA UGO  BASSI

VIA L. RAVA

MARONCELLI

Railway
Station ●

Porta
Adriana

CAMILLO B. CAVOUR

VIA C. CATTANEO

Tourist
Information ●

VIA PAOLO COSTA

● Torre del Pubblico

Piazza
Mameli

FARINI

VIALE

Piazza Farini

G. PALLAVICINI

VIA E. BARACCA

VIALE

PASOLINI

IV NOVEMBRE

Arian Baptistry ●

San Giovanni
Evangelista ●

CARDUCCI

VIA

M.

VIA

D'AZEGLIO

Piazza XX
Settembre

Piazza del
Popolo

VIA ARMANDO DIAZ

VIA

Tourist
Information

VIA A. MARIANI

Sant' Apollinare Nuovo ●

VIA CESARE BATTISTI

VIA GARATONI

Piazza
Kennedy

RASPONI

MENTANA

ARCI

VIA I. C.

Piazza
Garibaldi

VIA F. NEGRI

Palace of
Theodoric ●

VIA ALBERONI

ERCOLANA

Piazza
Duomo

Neonian
Baptistry ●

VIA GUERRINI

Piazza San
Francesco

● Tomb of Dante

G. GUACCIMANNI

VIA PORT'

VIA G. GUIDARELLI

AUREA

● Cathedral .

Archiepiscopal ●
Museum

Piazza
Arcivescovado

Piazza
dei Caduti

San Francesco ●

VIA A. ORIANI

VIA DI ROMA

VIA S.
TERESA

VIA A. DE GASPERI

VIA A. BACCARINI

VIA G. PASCOLI

VIA
BALDINI

CIRCONVALLAZIONE
AL MOLINO

VIA CORTE ALLE MURA

Porta Nuova

To Classe

**Ravenna**

Galla Placidia was taken hostage, and later married the Visigothic king Ataulf. They got on well together in Toulouse, and before his assassination she rode at his side everywhere, even in battle. She returned eventually to Ravenna, and ruled it until her death in 450.

By the 6th century, with sheep grazing in the Roman Forum and cooling off in the ruins of Diocletian's baths, Ravenna had become accepted as the metropolis of Italy. Odoacer and Theodoric made it their capital; during the reign of the latter the last flowering of Latin letters took place, under the influence of the Ostrogothic king's three famous councillors: Boethius, Symmachus, and Cassiodorus. Boethius, one of the Fathers of the Church, wrote his *Consolation of Philosophy* in Theodoric's dungeon, where the king had consigned him after suspecting the philosopher of intrigues with Constantinople. The terrible wars between the Ostrogoths and the Eastern Emperor for control of Italy were beginning. Ravenna was spared the destruction the Byzantine generals Belisarius and Narses spread through the rest of Italy; after their victory, the city became the seat of the *exarchs*, the Byzantine viceroys who were to rule increasingly smaller bits of Italy over the next 500 years. It was this period that would see the city's golden age.

The Greek exarchs, never popular among their new subjects, performed the occasional service of obtaining Constantinople's aid in keeping the Lombards at bay throughout their period of rule. While tolerating the exarch's presence, the people of Ravenna were coming to rely increasingly on their own resources; when help from the east failed to appear it was their own citizen militia that defended the city against invaders. So, in the worst times, the city survived as a sort of cultural time capsule, protected by its own efforts—and its surrounding swamps—still maintaining trade and cultural relations with the east, and carrying on the best traditions of classical culture single-handedly.

In 751 the Lombards finally succeeded in taking Ravenna, chasing out the last exarch and erasing Constantinople's last sure foothold in Italy. Only six years later, however, Pepin the Short's Frankish army snatched it back, and the city was placed under the rule of the popes. Ravenna declined slowly and gracefully in the following centuries. Venice took over its role as leading port of the Adriatic as Classis silted up and was abandoned. The newer cities of the Romagna, such as Ferrara and Faenza, assumed a larger role in the region's economy, and even Ravenna's ancient school of Roman law was transferred to Bologna, there to become the foundation of Europe's first university.

Despite its declining fortunes, Ravenna still managed to rouse itself in 1177, becoming a free *comune* like so many other towns in the Romagna. During the 13th century, government fell into the hands of the Da Polenta family, famous for offering refuge to Dante when a change in Florentine politics made the poet an exile. Dante finished the *Divine Comedy* in Ravenna, and died here in 1321. In 1441, Ravenna came under the rule of Venice, and enjoyed a brief period of renewed prosperity, which lasted until the popes came back in 1509; the economic decadence brought by papal rule has been reversed only since the 1940s. Parts of the city were heavily damaged in the Second World War, but in the last few decades, with the construction of a ship channel and new port, the discovery of offshore gas deposits and the introduction of large chemical industries, Ravenna has become a booming modern city—just coincidentally one with a medieval centre full of Byzantine mosaics.

# The Mosaics

*Either light was born here,*
*Or reigns here imprisoned.*

Latin inscription, Sant'Andrea chapel

 In Byzantine times, the greatest gift an emperor could bestow on any dependent town was a few tons of gold and enamel *tesserae* and an artist. Before Christianity, mosaics were a favourite Roman medium, but not always taken too seriously. They were usually reserved for the decoration of villas. Some reached the level of fine art (examples are in the Naples museum, or the great villa at Piazza Armerina, Sicily), but more often the productions were on the level of the famous 'Beware of the dog' mosaic in Pompeii, or prophylactic images of Priapus. It was the early Christians, with a desire to build for the ages and a body of scriptures that could best be related pictorially, who made mosaics the new medium of public art in the 6th century. Mostly it was an affair of the Greeks, who still had the talent and the resources for it; we cannot say with absolute certainty, but it's most likely that Greek artists from the court of Constantinople created the celebrated mosaics in the churches and baptistries of Ravenna.

Western Christian art was born here, developing from the simple images—the Good Shepherd and the Cross and Stars—to the iconic Christ in Sant'Apollinare Nuovo and the beautiful scriptural scenes in San Vitale. Never, though, did the early mosaicists turn their back on the idea of art; with the ideals of the ancient world still in their minds, they naturally thought of art and religion as going hand in hand, and found no problem in serving the cause of both. Using a new vocabulary of images, and the new techniques of mosaic art, they strove to duplicate, and surpass, the sense of awe and mystery still half-remembered from the interiors of the pagan temples. Try to imagine a church like San Vitale in its original state, with candles—lots of candles—fickering below the gold ground and gorgeous colours. You may see that same light that enchanted the Byzantines—the light of the Gospels, the light from beyond the stars.

---

## Getting Around

 Ravenna is not on the main Adriatic **railway** line, but there are several trains a day from Florence, Venice, Ancona and Bologna (change at Faenza or Ferrara from other cities). The station is in Piazza Farini, on the eastern edge of the old town next to the ship channel, and a short walk from the centre. The **bus station** is nearby, across the tracks from the train station. City buses from the train station or from Piazza del Popolo will take you to Classe or any of Ravenna's nearby lidos. The no.2 bus from the train station goes past Theodoric's Mausoleum, otherwise a half-hour walk from the centre on a busy highway.

The main **road** to Ravenna from Bologna and central Italy, the *autostrada* A14 dir, comes to an end just west of the city, where it meets the SS16, between Rimini and

Ravenna: Getting Around   559

Ferrara, which skirts round Ravenna. Drivers approaching from the north and west normally come into the city centre along the Via Roma, its modern main thoroughfare, which crosses the *circonvallazione* or inner ring road.

## Tourist Information

The main local APT office is at Via Salaria 8, ✆ (0544) 35404, ✉ 35094; there is also an information office outside the railway station, where you can hire **bicycles**. Ravenna's monuments are centrally administered, and the summer opening-times for all of them operate from mid-March to mid-October. As well as individual tickets for each place, single block tickets (a *biglietto cumulativo*) are available that cover several of the local sites. The ticket that includes San Vitale, S. Apollinare, and the Battistero Neoniano, with their attendant bits and pieces, is worth buying if you're going to all of them, and the comprehensive ticket which also includes Faenza's ceramics museum is a real bargain.

## San Vitale

*Open summer 9am–7pm daily; winter 9am–4.30pm daily.*

At first this dark old church may not seem like much, but as soon as the now-automatic lights come on (a large bag of coins is no longer an essential requirement), the 1400-year-old mosaics ignite into an explosion of colour. The mosaics of San Vitale, Ravenna's best, are one of the last great works of art of the ancient world, and one of Christianity's first. The octagonal church, begun in 525 during the reign of Theodoric, is itself a fine example of the surprisingly sophisticated architecture from that troubled age. By the time it was finished, in 548, the city was in the hands of Belisarius' Byzantine army; the famous mosaic portraits of Justinian and Theodora can be taken as the traditional imperial style of political propaganda.

Outside Ravenna, nothing like this church was built, or could have been built, in the 6th century. Far from being the sorry recapitulation of old building forms and styles you might expect, San Vitale was a breathtakingly original departure in architecture—not the last work of the Romans, but the first of the Romanesque. Take some time to admire the interior, with its beautiful interplay of octagons, arches, gables, and exedrae, pure proportional geometry done in plain solid brick. Inside, the curious double capitals on the columns are no design conceit, but an important 5th-century invention; the trapezoidal *impost block* on top is a capital specially designed to support the weight of arches. Holding up the second-floor galleries and large octagonal cupola was an unusual design problem; these capitals and the eight stout piers around the dome were the solution. We do not know the name of San Vitale's architects, or whether they were Latins or Greeks, but the year after it was begun, work commenced on the very similar church of SS. Sergius and Bacchus in Constantinople, the prototype for the Hagia Sophia 10 years later.

In its structure, the great dome in Constantinople owes everything to the little dome of Ravenna: the innovation of the galleries, for example, in which the women were segregated during services, and the elongated apse cleverly combining the central plan favoured by eastern Christians with the basilica form needed for a court's religious ceremonies. Nowhere in Constantinople, however, or anywhere else in the east will you find anything as brilliant as San Vitale's **mosaics**. Much of the best was undoubtedly lost during the iconoclastic troubles of the 8th century; though iconoclasm was fiercely resisted in Italy—it was one of the first causes of the rupture between the Roman and Greek churches—and most of Ravenna's art was fortunately left in peace.

The colours are startling. Almost all the other surviving Byzantine mosaics, in Sicily, Greece and Turkey, are simple figures on a bright gold ground, dazzling at first but somewhat monotonous. There is plenty of gold on the walls of San Vitale, but the best mosaics, in the **choir**, have deep blue skies and rich green meadows for backgrounds, highlighted by brightly coloured birds and flowers. (The usual nomenclature is misleading; the 'choir' was and is the site of the main altar, while the clergy actually sat on the bench around the apse.) The two **lunettes** over the arches flanking the choir, each a masterpiece, show the hospitality of Abraham and the sacrifice of Isaac, and the offerings of Abel and Melchisedek, set under fiery clouds with hands of benediction extended from Heaven. These sacrifices are the two events in the Old Testament that prefigure the Transfiguration of Christ. Around the two lunettes are scenes of Moses and Jeremiah; note, above the lunettes, the delicately posed pairs of angels holding golden crosses—almost identical to the fanciful figures from earlier Roman art displaying the civic crown of the Caesars. At the front of the choir, the **triumphal arch** has excellent mosaic portraits of the Apostles supported by a pair of dolphins. Look up at the galleries, and you will see more fine portraits of the four evangelists.

The **apse** is dominated by portraits of Justinian and Theodora—mostly, of course, of Theodora, the Constantinople dancing girl who used her many talents to become an empress, eventually coming to wear poor Justinian like a charm on her bracelet. Here she is wearing a rich crown, with long strings of fat diamonds and real pearls. Justinian, like Theodora, appears among his retinue offering a gift to the new church; here he has the air of a hung-over saxophone player, badly in need of a shave and a cup of coffee. His cute daisy slipper steps on the foot (a convention of Byzantine art to show who's boss) of his General Belisarius, to his left. The likenesses are good—very like those in Constantinople, suggesting that the artist may have come from there, or at least have copied closely imperial portraits on display at Ravenna.

It can easily be imagined how expensive it was in the 5th century to make mosaics like these. It is said that the Hagia Sophia in Constantinople originally had over 2 hectares of them, and even the treasury of Justinian and Theodora was not bottomless; consequently most of San Vitale remained undecorated until the 17th-century bishops did the dome and the other parts in a not-too-discordant Baroque. Recently, the new floor they laid has been pulled up to reveal the original, an inlaid marble pavement in floral and geometric patterns that is a direct ancestor of medieval pavements in the churches of Tuscany and the south.

## Mausoleum of Galla Placidia

This small chapel, set in the grounds of San Vitale and originally attached to the neighbouring church of Santa Croce, never really held the tomb of Ravenna's great patroness—she is buried near St Peter's in Rome. Nobody has peeked into the three huge stone sarcophagi, traditionally the resting places of Galla Placidia and two emperors, her second husband Constantius III and her son Valentinian, and it's anyone's guess who is really inside. Galla Placidia did construct the chapel, a small, gabled and cross-shaped building that is almost 2m shorter than when it was built; the ground level has risen that much in 1400 years (*same hours and adm as S. Vitale*).

The simplicity of the brick exterior, as in San Vitale, makes the brilliant mosaics within that much more of a surprise. Save some coins for the light box; the only natural light inside comes from a few tiny slits of windows, made of thin sheets of alabaster that probably came from Egypt. The two important mosaics, on lunettes at opposite ends of the chapel, are coloured as richly as San Vitale. One represents St Lawrence, with his flaming grid-iron; the other is a beautiful and typical early Christian portrait of Jesus as the Good Shepherd, a beardless, classical-looking figure in a fine cloak and sandals, stroking one of the flock. On the lunettes of the cross-axis, pairs of stags come to drink at the fountain of life; around all four lunettes, floral arabesques and maze patterns in bright colours cover the arches and ceilings. Everything in the design betrays as much of the classical Roman style as the nascent Christian, and the unusual figures on the arches holding up the central vault seem hardly out of place. They are SS. Peter and Paul, dressed in togas and standing with outstretched hands in the conventional pose of Roman senators.

The vault itself, a deep blue firmament glowing with hundreds of dazzling golden stars set in concentric circles, is the mausoleum's most remarkable feature. In the centre, at the top of the vault, a golden cross represents the unimaginable, transcendent God above the heavens. At the corners, symbols of the four evangelists provide an insight into the origins of Christian iconography.

*Galla Placida Mosaic*

Mark's lion, Luke's ox, and Matthew's man occupy the places in this sky where you would expect the constellations of the lion, the bull, and Aquarius, 90 degrees apart along the zodiac. For the fourth corner, instead of the objectionable scorpion (or serpent, as it often appeared in ancient times) the early Christians substituted the eagle of St John.

## The National Museum

The medieval and Baroque cloisters attached to San Vitale now house this large collection of antiquities found in Ravenna and Classis (*summer 8.30am–7.30pm daily; winter 8.30am–1.30pm daily; adm*). There's a little bit of everything: lead pipes and other bits of good Roman plumbing, a boy's linen shirt that has somehow survived from the 6th century, and no end of coins and broken pots. The detailed and well-labelled coin collection is interesting, even to the non-specialist, providing a picture history of Italy from Classical times into the early Middle Ages. This is a museum worth spending some time in, for exceptional works of art like the beautiful 6th-century Byzantine carved screens, and a possibly unique sculpture of Hercules capturing the Cerynean hind. This, too, is from the 6th century, perhaps the last piece of art made in ancient times with a classical subject, possibly a copy of an earlier Greek work. Not all of the exhibits are ancient; lovely, intricately carved ivory chests and plaques from the Middle Ages and Renaissance fill an entire room. Most are from France, with charming tableaux of medieval scenes such as tournaments and banquets. Cinquecento Italy is represented by a lavishly fancy intarsia cabinet. To understand Ravenna and its buildings better, be sure to see the fascinating architectural models of the Neonian baptistry (*see* below), the work of a modern Ravenna architect named Raffaello Trinci. Glass cross-sections elaborate the proportions and geometrical theory behind the Byzantines' new architecture of the 6th century, a recasting of ancient sacred geometry that was to have a great influence on the cathedral builders of the Middle Ages.

## Ravenna's Centre

The **Piazza del Popolo**, at the centre of Ravenna, has a Venetian feel to it; the Venetians built it during their brief period of rule, and added the twin columns bearing statues of Ravenna's two patrons, San Vitale and Sant'Apollinare. A little way south, off the colonnaded **Piazza San Francesco**, a modest neoclassical pavilion was built in the 18th century over the **Tomb of Dante**. Ravenna is especially proud of having sheltered the storm-tossed poet in his last years, and the city will gently remind you of it in its street names, its tourist brochures, its Teatro Alighieri, and its frequent artistic competitions based on themes from the *Divina Commedia*. Coming here may help explain just what Dante means to Italy; in all the country's more recent wars, for example, groups of soldiers have come here for little rituals to 'dedicate their sacrifice' to the poet's memory. Today there are always wreaths or bouquets from organizations of all kinds and private citizens from all over Italy. Beside the tomb is the **Museo Dantesco** (*open 9–12, 3–6, daily; adm, free on Sun*), with a collection of paintings, sculptures and books connected with the poet.

The church of **San Francesco**, behind the tomb, was founded in the 5th century, but rebuilt in the 11th and then thoroughly 'Baroqued' in the 1700s. Greek marble columns and a fine 4th-century altar survive, and in the church itself and the adjacent 'Braccioforte' oratory (behind the iron gate, next to Dante's tomb) there are some fine early-Christian sarcophagi, one familiarly called the 'Tomb of Elijah'.

North of Piazza del Popolo, Ravenna has a fine example of a medieval leaning tower, the tall, 12th-century **Torre Pubblica**. This one seems good evidence for those who believe such things to be intentional. The tower leans more than Pisa's, but the windows near the top were built perfectly level. Byron lived for a time in a house in the nearby Via Cavour, during his affair with Countess Teresa Guiccioli. His home now houses the Carabinieri.

In a little square between Via Paolo Costa and Via Armando Diaz, the **Arian Baptistry** (*open summer 8.30am–7.30pm daily; winter 8.30–12, 2.30–dusk, daily; adm*) recalls church struggles of the 6th century. Theodoric and his Ostrogoths, like most of the Germanic peoples, adhered to the Arian heresy, a doctrine that mixed in elements of pagan religion and was condemned by more orthodox Christians as denying the absolute divinity of Christ. Like all heresies, this one is really the story of a political struggle, between the Gothic kings and the emperor in Constantinople. Unlike Justinian, a great persecutor, the Goths seemed to tolerate both faiths; the baptistry belonged to the adjacent Santo Spirito church (rebuilt in the 16th century), once the Arians' cathedral, while the Athenasians (orthodox) worshipped at what is now the cathedral of Ravenna. The Arian baptistry preserves a fine mosaic ceiling, with the 12 Apostles arranged around a scene of the baptism of Jesus. The old man with the palm branch, across from John the Baptist, represents the River Jordan.

There is another leaning tower—an even tipsier one—nearby on Viale Farini, two streets up from the railway station. It is the 12th-century campanile of **San Giovanni Evangelista**, a much-altered church that was begun by Galla Placidia in 425. Bombings in the last War destroyed the apse with its original mosaics, but some parts of the 13th-century mosaic floor, with scenes of the Fourth Crusade and some fantastical monsters, can be seen in the aisles.

## Sant'Apollinare Nuovo

*Open summer 9am–7pm daily; winter 9.30am–4.30pm daily; adm.*

After those of San Vitale, the mosaics of this 6th-century church are the finest in Ravenna. Theodoric built it, and after the Byzantine conquest and the suppression of Arianism it was re-dedicated to St Martin, another famous persecutor of heretics. The present name comes from the 9th century, when the remains of Sant'Apollinare were moved here from the old Sant'Apollinare in Classe. The tall, cylindrical campanile, a style that is a trademark of Ravenna's churches, was added in the 10th century.

Unlike San Vitale, Sant'Apollinare was built in the basilica form, with a long nave and side aisles. The two rows of Greek marble columns were probably recycled from an ancient temple. Above them are the mosaics on panels that stretch the length of the church. On the left, by the door, you see the city of Classe, with ships in the protected harbour between twin beacons, and the monuments of the city rearing up behind its walls. On the right, among the monuments of Ravenna, is the Palatium, Theodoric's royal palace. The curtains in the archways of the palace cover painted-over Gothic notables and probably Theodoric himself, effaced by the Byzantines. Beyond these two urban scenes are processions of martyrs bearing crowns: 22 ladies on the left side, 26 men on the right. The female procession is led by colourful, remarkable portraits of the Magi (officially enrolled as Saints of the Church, according to the inscription above), offering their gifts to the enthroned Virgin Mary. Above these panels, more mosaics on both sides portray Old Testament prophets and doctors of the Church, as well as a series of scenes from the life of Jesus. These mosaics, smaller and not as well executed, are from Theodoric's time.

Next to Sant'Apollinare are the remains of the 6th-century building traditionally called the **Palace of Theodoric** (*open July–Sept only 8.30am–1.30pm*). More likely this was a later governmental building of some sort; it may have been the palace of the Byzantine exarchs. Inside its tower there is a display of mosaics discovered while excavating the area.

## The Neonian Baptistry and the Archiepiscopal Museum

*Open summer 9am–7pm daily; winter 9.30am–4.30pm daily; adm.*

An earthquake in 1733 wrecked Ravenna's **cathedral**, west of the Piazza del Popolo, and there's little to see in the replacement but another round medieval tower. Somehow the disaster spared the 'Orthodox' or **Neonian Baptistry**, named after the 5th-century bishop Neon who commissioned its splendid mosaics. Unlike the Arian baptistery, here almost the entire decoration has survived: a scene of the Baptism of Jesus and fine portraits of the 12 Apostles on the ceiling under the dome, while below, the eight walls bear four altars and four empty thrones. The *etimasia*, the preparing of the Throne for Jesus for the Last Judgement, is an odd bit of Byzantine mysticism; interestingly enough, classical Greek art often depicts an empty throne as a symbol for Zeus, only with a pair of thunderbolts instead of a cross.

In the 1500 years since its construction, the ground level here has risen over 3m—so has the baptistry's floor, and recent excavations have uncovered marble supporting columns down to the bottom. In the side niches are a 6th-century Byzantine altar and a huge, thoroughly pagan marble vase. The marble font, big enough for immersion baptisms of adults, is from the 13th century.

The **Archiepiscopal Museum**, behind the Cathedral, comes as a real surprise, and receives few visitors. Its little-known treasures include the ivory throne of Bishop Maximian, a masterpiece of 6th-century sculpture thought to have been a gift from Emperor Justinian, and an 11th-century reliquary, the silver 'Cross of Sant' Agnello'. Among the fragments of sculpture and mosaics are works saved from the original cathedral. The large marble disc by the wall, divided into 19 sections, is an episcopal calendar, regulated to the 19-year Julian cycle to allow Ravenna's medieval bishops to calculate the date of Easter and other holy days.

The biggest surprise, however, is finding that the nondescript Archbishop's Palace, in which the museum is located, is in parts as old as anything in Ravenna. A little door at the back leads to a small chapel called the **Oratorio di Sant'Andrea**, built around 500 during the reign of Theodoric. The mosaics on the vaults are among Ravenna's best: in the antechamber a fanciful scene of multicoloured birds and flowers, and an unusual warrior Christ, in full Roman armour and wielding the cross like a sword, treading a lion and snake underfoot. In the chapel itself, four angels and the four evangelists' symbols surround Christ's monogram on the dome, and the apse bears a beautiful starry sky around a golden cross, like the one at the Galla Placidia mausoleum. The best mosaics, however, are the excellent portraits of saints decorating the arches. Early Christian representations of the saints are often much stronger than the pale, conventional figures of later art. Such portraits as these betray a fascination with the personalities and the psychology of saints; such figures as St Felicitas or St Ursicinus may be forgotten now, but to the early Christians they were not mere holy myths, but near-contemporaries, the spiritual heroes and heroines responsible for the miraculous growth of Christianity, the exemplars of a new age and a new way of life.

## Theodoric's Mausoleum

*Open summer 8.30am–7.30pm daily, winter 8.30am–1.30pm daily; adm.*

For the real flavour of the days of the Roman twilight, nothing can beat this compellingly strange, sophisticated yet half-barbaric building outside the old city. To reach it, walk north from the railway station, past the new port and the Venetian fortress called the **Rocca di Brancaleone**, which now has a city park inside. Theodoric's tomb is in another small park on Via Cimitero, near the industrial zone. Perhaps the only regular 10-sided building in Italy, the Mausoleum has two floors. Downstairs, there is a cross-shaped chamber of unknown purpose. The second story, also decagonal though slightly smaller, contains the porphyry sarcophagus, now empty. It is a comment on the times that scholars believe this originally to have been a recycled bathtub from a Roman palace. Theodoric was hardly broke, though; he could afford to bring the stone for his tomb over from Istria—and note the roof, a single slab of stone weighing over 300 tons. No one has yet explained how the Goths brought it here and raised it—or why.

## Classe

If you have the time, there is another important monument to Ravenna's golden age to be seen at the ruins of **Classe**, 5km from town; any local train towards Rimini or the regular bus service can take you there. **Sant'Apollinare in Classe**, in fact, is literally all that remains of what was once the leading port of the northern Adriatic. The little River Uniti began to silt up Classe's harbour in classical times; when the port ceased to be a Roman military base and the funds for yearly dredging were no longer there, the city's fate was sealed. By the 9th century Classe was abandoned. The people of Ravenna presumably carted away most of its stone, and encroaching forests and swamps erased the last traces. Today the former port is good farmland, 6km from the sea.

Sant'Apollinare (*open 8–12, 2–6, daily*), a huge basilica-form church completed in 549, survives only because of its importance as the burial place of Ravenna's patron. The exterior, in plain brick, is another finely proportioned example of Ravenna's pre-Romanesque, with another tall cylindrical campanile. Inside it's almost empty, with only a few early-Christian sarcophagi lining the walls. The beautiful Greek marble columns have well-carved capitals in a unique style. Above them are 18th-century portraits of all Ravenna's bishops—important to this city, where for centuries the bishops defended local autonomy against emperors, exarchs, and popes. The real attraction, however, is the mosaics in the apse, an impressive green-and-gold ground allegorical vision of the **Transfiguration of Christ**, with Sant'Apollinare in attendance and three sheep, in a flower-strewn Mediterranean landscape, that represent Peter, James, and John, who were with Christ on Mount Tabor. As at San Vitale, there are scenes of the sacrifices of Abel, Melchizedek, and Abraham, opposite a mosaic of the Byzantine Emperor Constantine IV bestowing privileges on Ravenna's independent church. Archangels Gabriel and Michael appear in Byzantine court dress, under a pair of palm trees, the 'tree of life'.

Elsewhere around Classe, there's little to see; bits of Roman road, pine groves, some foundations. Excavations began only in 1961, and continue today. Sant'Apollinare is near the centre of an immense necropolis with some half-million burials. Some interesting things could turn up here in coming years (*visiting hours at the excavations, daily 9am–dusk*).

---

### Ravenna ✆ (0544–)

**Where to Stay**

*expensive*

At the top of the list, on a quiet street near San Vitale, is the ★★★★**Bisanzio**, Via Salaria 30, ✆ 217111, ✆ 32539, which is modern, luxurious and serene, with only 36 rooms, all air-conditioned.

*moderate*

★★★**Diana**, Via G. Rossi, ✆ 39164, ✆ 30001, has been recently refurbished, and now has all modern facilities, such as air-conditioning and TV in every room.

An older favourite, ageing gracefully just off the Piazza del Popolo, is the ★★★**Centrale Byron**, Via IV Novembre 14, ✆ 33479, ✆ 551070—also air-conditioned, with some very nice rooms and some very plain ones. Despite appearances Byron never lived here (*see* above, 'Ravenna's Centre').

If you wish to loll on the beach after a day perusing the mosaics, there is one good bargain along the Lido at Classe: the ★★★**Adler**, Viale Caboto 121, ✆ 939216, ✆ 939222, with a pool and private beach. Marina Romea, more to the north and a little further from the city, is, though, a more attractive place: the ★★★**Columbia**, Viale Italia 70, ✆ 446038, ✆ 447202, is a beautiful modern hotel—but like all the places here it's a 10-minute walk from the beach.

*inexpensive*

Ravenna has plenty of budget accommodation, but much of it is around the port, a long walk from the centre, along Via delle Industrie. In a more convenient, if not particularly pleasant, location is ★★**Roma**, Via Candiano 26, ✆ 421515, ✆ 420505, on the other side of the tracks from the railway station.

A nicer option is ★**Al Giaciglio**, at Via Rocca Brancaleone 42, ✆ 39403. Both have rooms with or without baths. In all the various *Lidi* around Ravenna there is an infinity of hotels in the L40–70,000 range.

There is also a **youth hostel**, at Via Nicolodi 12, ✆ 420405 , which is, again, on the east side of the railway tracks, a 10-minute walk down the Via Candiano from the station. (*Open Mar–Oct only.*)

Ravenna lacks excitement after dark, but does shelter some interesting restaurants. One not to be missed is **Tre Spade**, Via Faentina 136, ✆ 500522 , in the suburbs west of the centre, where they like to innovate and never misstep. Most of Ravenna comes here for the seafood, but you can be adventurous and try the vegetable/pastry concoctions, stuffed pigeon or some pasta combinations never seen before on this planet. (*Closed Sun evenings, Mon, Aug.*)

*moderate*

**La Gardella**, Via Ponte Marino 3, ✆ 217147, is a small, air-conditioned restaurant in the centre of Ravenna, which makes its own tortelloni; follow it with scaloppine al Madera, and sample their large collection of grappas. (*Closed Thurs.*) In the same area, in a beautiful building with painted ceilings, **Ca' de Ven**, Via Corrado Ricci 24, is an enoteca with a huge selection of Emilia-Romagna wines and snacks using local cheeses, hams and sausages. Suitably calm and dark, it's a great local favourite, the perfect place to kiss off an afternoon after a morning with the Byzantines.

*inexpensive*

**Renato Guidarello**, with entrances at both Via Mentana 33 and Via Gessi 9, ✆ 213684, has a pleasant, traditional atmosphere and local cuisine, with fish still the main item every Friday. The restaurant of the Albergo Al Giaciglio (*see* above) also has good home cooking, and a policy of using only fresh ingredients. There is a cheap lunch menu that changes daily. For a light lunch, try the elegant **Caffè del Teatro**, Via Mariani 1. (*Closed Sun.*)

# The Adriatic Riviera

From Ravenna and Classe, the long stretch of small resorts that began at Comacchio straggles on towards the beach-Babylon of Rimini. The various tiny lidos are slow-paced, if packed with Bolognese families in the summer. Those nearest Ravenna suffer somewhat from industrial pollution, but there has been a big effort to keep the beaches clean. **Marina Romea**, a spit of land with a broad beach and a pine forest behind it, is perhaps the nicest. None is a really good choice for a long stay, though quite convenient for a day on the beach if you're passing through; any of them would be an easy day's outing from Ravenna. The first big centre on the coast is **Cervia-Milano Marittima**, the next, **Cesenatico**, built around a pretty, canal-like harbour designed for Cesare Borgia in 1502 by Leonardo da Vinci. The **Museo della Mariniera** in the harbour itself is a floating maritime museum, a display of the traditional types of fishing and trading boats used in the northern Adriatic.

## Rimini

At first glance, Italy's biggest resort may strike you as strictly cold potatoes, a full 15km of peeling skin and pizza, serenaded by the portable radios of ten thousand teenagers and the eternal whines and giggles of their little brothers and sisters. To many Italians, however, Rimini means pure sweaty-palmed excitement. In the sixties, following the grand old Italian pastime of *caccia alle svedesi*, a staple of the national film industry was the Rimini holiday seduction movie, in which a bumbling protagonist with glasses was swept off his feet by some incredible Nordic goddess, who was as bouncy as she was adventurous. After many complications, embarrassing both for the audience and the actors, it could all lead to true love. For the bumbling protagonists of real life, whether from Milan or Munich, all this may only be wishful thinking, but they still come in their millions each year. As a resort, Rimini has its advantages. Noisy as it is, it's a respectable, family place, relatively cheap for northern Italy, convenient and well organized. Also, tucked away behind the beachfront is a genuine old city, dishevelled, much damaged in the Second World War, but inviting, and offering one first-rate Renaissance attraction.

## Getting Around

On this stretch of coast, the FS Adriatic **rail** line works almost like a tram service, with lots of trains and stops near the beaches in all the resorts. In summer, there are regular flights from Milan and lots of foreign charters to Rimini's little **airport**, behind the beaches at Miramare. Rimini city **buses** run regularly in summer, carrying holiday-makers up and down the long beach strip. As well as individual tickets a 24 hour 'Orange Ticket' is available, giving unlimited travel within Rimini and the whole area between Bellaria and Riccione. From the railway station in Rimini, on Piazzale Cesare Battisti, there are also buses to most nearby towns, and 10 buses a day to San Marino—14 in summer. For **taxis**, © (0541) 50020. Cultural day trippers who shudder at the thought of Rimini's beach madness can dip in easily—the Tempio Malatesta is only a 10-minute walk from the station.

## Tourist Information

In summer, at least, it's positively difficult to remain uninformed, as Rimini and its suburbs have as many information offices as ice-cream stands. The main local tourist office is at Piazzale C. Battisti, next to the station, © (0541) 51331), and there is another large office on the beach at Parco dell'Independenza 3, © (0541) 51101, @ 26566. Next to both these offices there are offices of the **Promozione Alberghiera**, the local hotel association and accommodation service (see below). There are five more information desks along the 15km beach, and in the Municipio, on Piazza Cavour, there is a city information office with information on entertainment and forthcoming cultural events. Next door to the Piazzale C. Battisti tourist office is an information office for San Marino, © (0541) 56333.

Outside Rimini itself there are more offices in **Cesenatico**, Via Roma 112, © (0547) 80091; **Gatteo a Mare**, Piazza della Libertà 5, © (0547) 85393; **Bellaria**, Via Leonardo da Vinci 10, © (0541) 344574, @ 345491; **Riccione**, Piazzale Ceccarini 10, © (0541) 693302, @ 605752; **Misano Adriatico**, Via Platani 22, © (0541) 615520, @ 613295; and **Cattolica**, Piazza Nettuno 1, © (0541) 963341, @ 963344.

# The Malatesta Temple

Sigismondo Malatesta ('Headache'), tyrant of Rimini, went into the books as one bad hombre. According to Jakob Burckhardt, 'the verdict of history...convicts him of murder, rape, adultery, incest, sacrilege, perjury, and treason, committed not once, but often'. The historian adds that his frequent attempts on the virtue of his chilardren, both male and female, may have resulted from 'some astrological superstition'. Pope Pius II, in 1462, accorded him a unique honour—a canonization to Hell. The Pope, who was behind most of the accusations, can be excused a little exaggeration. He wanted Sigismondo's land, and resorted to invoking supernatural aid when he couldn't beat him at war.

Modern historians give Sigismondo better reviews, finding him on the whole no more pagan and perverse than the average Renaissance duke, and less so than many popes. The family had ruled at Rimini since the 1300s—ironically it was a pope who first put them in business. Early dukes, like Malatesta 'Guastafamiglia' ('Destroyer of Families') were hard men, and good role models for Sigismondo, but they succeeded for a time in spreading their rule as far as Cesena and Fano. By Sigismondo's time, money and allies were suddenly lacking, and the family was deposed by the unspeakable Alexander VI in 1500.

The shortage of funds was also responsible for the abandonment in 1461 of Sigismondo's personal monument, the eclectic and thoroughly mysterious work that has come to be known as the **Malatesta Temple** (*open summer 7–12, 3.30–7, daily; winter closes at 6pm*). Whatever Sigismondo's personal habits, he was a learned man and a good judge of art. To transform this unfinished 13th-century Franciscan church into his Temple, he called in Leon Battista Alberti to redesign the exterior and Agostino di Duccio for the reliefs inside. Scholars have been puzzling for centuries over Sigismondo's intentions. Though the temple has been Rimini's cathedral since 1809, it is hardly a Christian building, full of undecipherable sculptural allegories with everywhere the entwined monograms of Sigismondo and his wife Isotta degli Atti; in part it seems a tribute to this famous lady, who is buried here along with Sigismondo.

Alberti's unfinished exterior, grafting Roman arcades and pilasters onto the plain Franciscan building, grievously feels the lack of the planned cupola that might have tied the composition together. The big arches on the sides were meant to hold sarcophagi of Rimini's notable men; only a few were ever used. Inside these arches, four pairs of chapels hold the Temple's major feature, the **sculptural reliefs** made by Agostino, among the greatest works of the Renaissance. These low reliefs, on blue backgrounds like a della Robbia cameo, depict angels and child musicians, the Arts and the Sciences, St Michael, various putti, Sigismondo himself, and the Triumph of Scipio. Some of the best are the allegorical panels of the planets and signs of the zodiac; note especially the enchanting *Moon*, Cynthia in her silver car, and a scene of 14th-century Rimini beneath the claws of the Crab.

Among the other works in the Temple are a fresco by Piero della Francesca of Sigismondo and his patron, St Sigismund of Burgundy, and a painted crucifix by Giotto. The tombs of Sigismondo and Isotta, with their strange device (the omnipresent monograms S and I together like a dollar sign) and elephants (the Malatesta heraldic symbol) are also fine works.

Old Rimini was the home town of the late Federico Fellini, and you may recognize some of the street scenes from *Amarcord.* Some ruins survive as reminders of Roman *Arminium*, a thriving Adriatic port and a rival to Classe: the foundation of an amphitheatre near the southern walls, and the well-preserved **Arch of Augustus** in the southern gate near the post office. This arch marked the meeting of the Via Aemilia and the Via Flaminia. The Roman high street, the *cardo*, is now called Corso di Augusto; from here it passes through the central **Piazza Tre Martiri**—which retains some arcades in the shop fronts from the days when it was the Roman forum and continues on to the north gate and the five-arched **Bridge of Tiberius** of AD 21, a fine work badly patched up after damage in the Greek-Gothic wars. A few streets further over the bridge, the church of **San Giuliano** contains a painting of that saint's martyrdom, the last work of Paolo Veronese. From here towards the sea, along the riverbank, stretches Rimini's colourful fishing port. Back at the centre, on Piazza Cavour, the **Palazzo del'Arengo** has been Rimini's town hall since 1207; it faces the bulky castle of the Malatestas, the **Rocca Sigismondo**, which now houses the **Museo delle Culture Extraeuropee** (*open 8am–1pm Mon–Sat; adm*), with ancient and folk art from Africa, Asia and the Americas. Two streets away at Via Gambalunga 27, the **Museo Comunale** (*open 8am–1pm Mon–Sat; 4-6pm Sun, holidays; adm*) has Roman mosaics and earlier archaeological items, and paintings by Ghirlandaio and Giovanni Bellini.

## Some Beach Statistics

*Rimini is not the place for those who want to be alone.*

tourist brochure

The subject makes Rimini's holiday barons and the hotel consortium mildly uneasy. 'There's room for everybody,' they say, and in a way they're right. The resort has 15km of broad beaches, and about 1600 hotels with some 55,000 rooms. At the usual resort ratio, that means about 85,000 beds. It could be a problem in the really busy season. If all the beds are full—plus another 25,000 day-trippers, campers, and holiday apartment tenants—that makes 110,000 souls, or 7333 per kilometre of beach front. There's plenty of other things to do in Rimini, fortunately, but with only 13.6cm of shore per bum, if everyone tries to hit the water at the same time the results could be catastrophic.

This really need never happen. Many of these people at any given time will be in Rimini's 751 bars, 343 restaurants, 70 dance halls and discos, 49 cinemas, or three miniature golf courses. There's something for everybody—plenty of sailing schools and wind-surfing schools, and a dolphin show (on the beach near the port). Other attractions include **Fiabilandia**, an amusement park for the little ones with a Mississippi riverboat, a Fort Apache, coloured fountains, and the genuine King Kong (on SS16 south of Rimini; buses 8 and 9 go there). North of town there's **Italia in Miniatura**, which besides mouse-sized cathedrals and castles, offers you performing bears, go-carts, and 'bumper boats' (on the coast road, towards Viserba), and there are long water-slides to be found at Riccione.

## More Beaches

Holiday madness continues in a big way through the string of resorts south of Rimini. **Riccione, Misano Adriatico, Cattolica**, and **Gabicce Mare** are all huge places, and in the summer they can be as crowded and intense as Rimini itself. None of them have any particular charm, and it's hard to tell one from another—they're really more or less suburban extensions of Rimini, and there's no great reason to go out of your way to see them. The Adriatic Riviera begins to fade when the wide beaches of the Romagna give way to the more rugged coast of the Marches, but soon picks up again when the hills recede (to continue this route, *see* p.577).

---

*Rimini* ✆ *(0541–)*                                                    ***Where to Stay***

A holiday in Rimini usually means a standard package, and it's unlikely there will be any surprises, good or bad. Expect a modern room with a balcony, pleasant enough but rather unimaginatively furnished; in the high-season you'll probably have to take half-board, which is unfortunate. You may as well take pot luck by calling on the **Promozione Alberghiera**, Piazza Tripoli, ✆ 390530, or in the railway station, ✆ 51194, the local hoteliers' association, and let them find you a vacancy. They also have four other well-marked offices around town, as well as one in Bellaria, ✆ 340060, and Riccione, ✆ 600381. People do not come to Rimini for scenery, charming inns or fine cuisine, but to join the crowd and seek out the endless possibilites for fun that go with it. If that sounds good, make sure to get a place in the centre where the action is—don't let the PA stick you out in Torre Pedrera or Miramare. Tell them precisely what you want, and they'll find it for you. They do not, though, cover all hotels, and those mentioned below are not on their list, but are close to both the beach and the town.

***luxury***

An old-fashioned Grand Hotel might seem terribly out of place in Rimini, but that's exactly what you'll find right in the centre, on Parco dell'Indipendenza at Marina Centro—the ★★★★★**Grand Hotel**, Via Ramusio 1, ✆ 56000, ✆ 56866. This imposing turn-of-the-century palace helped make Rimini what it is today. The place hasn't slipped at all, with rooms that are almost indecently luxurious, all the brass well-polished, and the enormous crystal chandeliers well-dusted. It's the only hotel in Rimini with its own dance orchestra, as well as a pool and private beach, and nice gardens.

The ★★★★**Ambasciatori**, just back from the sea at Viale Amerigo Vespucci 22, ✆ 55561, ✉ 23790, is a splashy modern building designed to attract a youngish crowd, with air-conditioning and TVs, and a private beach.

### *moderate*

Where Viale Vespucci changes its name to Via Regina Elena, you will find the ★★★**Admiral**, Via R. Elena 67, ✆ 381771, ✉ 389562, another sharp ultra-modern palace, with a rooftop terrace and spacious balconies for most rooms. ★★★**Apogeo**, Via Oriani 10, ✆ 381366, has a small swimming pool.

### *inexpensive*

Of the hundreds, two in a good position with comfortable rooms are ★★**Primavera**, Viale Lagomaggio 113, ✆ 380206, and ★★**Pensione Primula**, Viale Trento 12, ✆ 23712.

The **youth hostel** is at Via Flaminia 300, ✆ 373216 , which is south of Rimini in Miramare (bus no.9). IYHF cards are required and reservations are virtually always necessary. (*Open May–Sept only.*)

---

*Rimini ✆ (0541–)*  **Eating Out**

### *expensive*

There's nothing to complain about as regards Rimini's restaurants (this is still Emilia-Romagna, after all). **Lo Squero**, Lungomare Tintori 7, ✆ 27676, near the Grand Hotel, has an outdoor terrace overlooking the beach: shellfish are a speciality. The **Taverna degli Artisti**, Viale Vespucci 1, ✆ 28519, with its colourful menu, is also best known for its seafood, along with some imaginative light pasta openers and something unexpected—a little *degustazione* of whisky; they have almost every brand from around the world.

### *moderate*

In the old town, **Dallo Zio**, Via S. Chiara 16, ✆ 786160, is an excellent seafood palace, offering marine lasagna, fishy vol-au-vent and other surprises, that's very popular with locals and tourists alike. (*Closed Wed.*) Near the market and Piazza Malatesta there's the **Osteria di Santa Colomba**, Via Agostino di Duccio 2, ✆ 780048, an old favourite (they say Napoleon slept here), with simple traditional fare—the best possible antidote to the cosmopolitanism of beach Rimini may be a plate of pasta with chickpeas. (*Closed Sat midday.*) Just over the Ponte Tiberio, and therefore off the tourist route, is **Colombo**, Via Tiberio 7, ✆ 51512, with excellent seafood; try the steaming bowls of mussels.

### *inexpensive*

The **Ristorante Pic-Nic**, Via Tempio Malatestiano 30, ✆ 21916, owes everything to cosmopolitanism, with a completely eclectic range of pizza—*noisy pizza, atomic* *pizza*, or perhaps pizza with radishes, not to mention roast beef (*all'Inglese*), and goulash. (*Closed Mon.*) Along the seafront, several thousand more pizzerias will try and tempt you to sit down or take-away; try **Rimini Key**, Piazzale B. Croce, for good-value pizza and set menus.

## Entertainment and Nightlife

### music, theatre and cinema

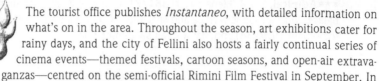

The tourist office publishes *Instantaneo*, with detailed information on what's on in the area. Throughout the season, art exhibitions cater for rainy days, and the city of Fellini also hosts a fairly continual series of cinema events—themed festivals, cartoon seasons, and open-air extravaganzas—centred on the semi-official Rimini Film Festival in September. In late summer and autumn, Rimini stages the **Sagra Musicale Malatestina**, a festival of classical music (information, ✆ 0541 26239). The nearby town of Santarcangelo holds an annual **theatre festival** in July, packed with dynamic, innovative work (information, ✆ 0541 626185).

### clubs and discos

Rimini and its perhaps-even-more-in-vogue neighbour Riccione make up the undisputed clubland capital of Italy, a magnet for ravers from all over Italy and abroad. On summer weekends crowds descend from all the cities within a 200km radius, and on mornings-after the road back to Bologna is often scattered with the battered cars of partygoers who didn't make it home.

For listings and information on clubs, one-nighters and anything else coming up, check *Il Resto del Carlino* and the magazine *Chiamami Città*, or search for posters. The main place for cruising the clubs is along the seafront, from about 10pm onwards, though there's also another little knot of activity in Rimini away from the beach in Covignano. If you get fed up with walking, a night bus runs along the whole length of the seafront between Riccione and Bellaria, and to Covignano.

Of the Riviera's best-established and most popular clubs, **Pascià**, Via Sardegna 30, Riccione, is a large, stylish venue offering a bouncy mix of house, techno and other Euro-dance sounds. The most fashionable club of all is **Paradiso**, Via Covignano 260, with a regular diet of Euro-dance but also special events every week involving visiting DJs, performances, and the gamut of musical styles. Also in Covignano an open-air rave, **Bandiera Gialla**, is held every weekend in summer.

## San Marino

As a perfect counterpart to the sand-strewn fun fair of Rimini, just 23km inland you may visit the world's only sovereign and independent roadside attraction. Before Rimini became the Italian Miami Beach, the 50,000 citizens of San Marino had to make a living peddling postage stamps. Now, with their medieval streets crowded with day-trippers, the San Marinese have been unable to resist the temptation to order some bright medieval costumes, polish up their picturesque mountain villages, and open up some souvenir stands and 'duty free' shops. Their famous stamps, though nothing like the engraved numbers of 40 years ago, are still prized by collectors, and recently the country has begun to mint its own coins again after a lapse of 39 years; nevertheless, the citizens of San Marino, who may just have the highest average income in Europe, still make their living almost entirely from tourism.

## Getting Around

There are frequent buses to San Marino from Rimini. The road into the Republic is the SS72, also from Rimini.

## Tourist Information

The main tourist office is in San Marino town at Contrado Omagnano 20, ℭ (0549) 882412, ✉ 990388. There are also information desks in most of the villages that make up the rest of the republic.

# The World's Smallest Republic

Also the oldest republic. According to legend, San Marino was founded as a Christian settlement on the easily defensible slopes of Monte Titano by a stonecutter named Marinus, fleeing from the persecutions of Diocletian in the early 4th century. 'Overlooked', as the San Marinese charmingly put it, by the empire and various states that followed it, the little community had the peace and quiet to evolve its medieval democratic institutions; its constitution in its present form dates from 1243, when the first pair of 'consuls' was elected by a popular assembly. The consuls are now called Captains Regent, but little else has changed in 700 years. Twice, in 1503 and 1739, the Republic was invaded by papal forces, and independence was preserved only by a little good luck. Napoleon, passing through in 1797, found San Marino amusing, and half-seriously offered to enlarge its boundaries, a proposal that was politely declined. Garibaldi, fleeing from Rome after the end of the nationalist revolt of 1849, sought refuge here, and was allowed in, though the Republic, jittery at the approach of an Austrian army, kicked him out before dawn the next morning. It redeemed itself by becoming an island of peace and taking in thousands of refugees in the Second World War.

Entering San Marino from Rimini at the hamlet called Dogana (though there are no border formalities now), you pass through a string of villages in a green and pretty countryside. San Marino, no midget like the Vatican City, is all of 12km long at its widest extent. At the foot of Monte Titano, rising dramatically above the plain, is **Borgomaggiore**, the largest town, with a cable car up to the capital and citadel of the republic, also called **San Marino**. Here, among medieval streets and squares, are wonderful views over Rimini and the coast. Nothing is really as old as it looks; the **Palazzo del Governo**, full of Ruritanian guardsmen in brass buttons and epaulets, is a reconstruction of 1894. Here the Grand Council meets, and the Captains Regent have their offices. Some new museums have been conjured up for the tourists—a Stamp and Coin Museum, Garibaldi Museum, a Museum of Weaponry, and a wax museum complete with instruments of torture—but the best thing to do is walk the paths through Monte Titano's forests to the three (rebuilt) medieval **tower fortresses** on the three peaks that give San Marino its famous silhouette; famous to philatelists anyhow, and long the symbol of the republic.

Two other mountain towns near the borders of San Marino are most easily visited from Rimini: **Verucchio**, a pleasant medieval village that retains some of its gates and churches, as well as a 10th-century fortress that became the stronghold of the tyrants of Rimini, the **Rocca Malatesta**. There is a small **Archaeology Museum** at the lower end of town, with unusual ceramics from the 1400 BC Villanova culture. **San Leo**, on the western side of San Marino in the Marches, was according to legend founded by a companion of Marinus, but lost its independence long ago. The rough-walled, 9th-century church called the **Pieve** is worth a look, but San Leo's real attraction is the **castle**, built for the Montefeltro dukes of Urbino in the 15th century. Like their palace at Urbino itself, this fortress is a perfect representative building of the Renaissance, balanced, finely proportioned in its lines, a building of intelligence and style. Also it is impregnable, hung on a breathtakingly sheer cliff. Once this mountain held a temple of Jupiter; as *Mons Feretrius* (referring to Jove's lightning) it gave its name to the Montefeltro family. A later fortress on this site was briefly 'capital of Italy' in the 960s, during the reign of King Berengar II. Now there is a small picture gallery in the castle—which is a stiff climb if you don't have a car.

---

*San Marino ℂ (0549–)*                                         **Where to Stay**

San Marino has become accustomed to entertaining tourists in the last 20 years, and being so close to Rimini has turned out to be an unexpected windfall. Italian currency is valid everywhere, but make sure you don't get too many San Marino coins in change; they are only good for souvenirs once you get back to Italy. It isn't a bad place to stop over if you can resist the charms of the Rimini lido.

On San Marino's citadel, in the middle of the old town, is the ★★★★**Titano**, at Contrada del Collegio 21, ℂ 991375, ✉ 991006, a restored century-old building where half the rooms have great views over the countryside. Not far away, ★★★**La Rocca**, on Salita alla Rocca, ℂ 991166, has a TV in each of its 10 rooms, a pool, and balconies with a view. Both hotels are in the moderate price range. You won't find anything much cheaper—price-fixing is an old tradition of the republic.

---

*San Marino ℂ (0549–)*                                               **Eating Out**

*moderate*

The best restaurant in the centre, and a very pretty place it is, can be found at Piazzetta Placito Feretrano, snuggling up to the Hotel Titano. **Buca San Francesco**, ℂ 991462, has nothing out of the ordinary, but its soups, tortellini, and *scallopine alla sanmarinese* are good. Of the many cheaper restaurants in the town, the best is probably the **Trattoria Panoramica** on Salita alla Rocca, ℂ 992305, with an outdoor terrace overlooking San Marino and the surrounding hills.

---

# The Marches

A *march*, or *mark*, in the Middle Ages meant a border province of the Holy Roman Empire, usually an unsettled frontier held by one of the Emperor's fighting barons. With no better name than that, one might expect this Italian region to be somewhat lacking in personality. In fact, this has always been the odd bit of central Italy. In ancient times it was also a border zone, shared by Umbrians, Piceni, Gauls and Sabines. Today, the Marchegiani still have a little identity problem, but it doesn't keep them awake at night. Their land, tucked between the Apennines and the Adriatic, is one of the greenest, prettiest and most civilized corners of Italy, with two lovely Renaissance art towns in Urbino and Ascoli Piceno, lots of beaches and scores of fine old towns in the valleys that lead up to the impressive snowy peaks of the Sibelline Mountains, one of the highest sections of the Apennines.

## Itineraries

You can shoot through the Marches in two hours, or get lost for weeks exploring its mountain valleys. The only good roads across it, from north to south, are the A14 *autostrada* and parallel SS16, which run all along the coast through Ancona and a few dozen resorts (168km), and the best way to escape them is the SS76, the only major road over the Apennines north of Ascoli Piceno (92km from Falconara, near Ancona, over the Umbrian border to Perugia). Along the coast, overbuilt beach resorts are everywhere, but the only places recommended for a stay are **Pesaro, Faro**, and **Senigallia**, pleasant old towns in their own right, or the beautiful but little-known strip called the **Cónero Riviera**.

**Urbino** most people probably know of, and it must be considered the Marches' major artistic attraction, along with a surprise, lovely medieval **Ascoli Piceno**, and the Renaissance pilgrimage town of **Loreto**. Since the roads inland generally follow parallel mountain valleys from the Adriatic, you'll need to make a special effort to see more than a few of the hill towns. **Jesi** and **Fabriano**, with the nearby **Caves of Frasassi**, are most worth the trouble, as well as being on the best road over to Umbria.

## Pesaro and Urbino

Just across the border from Emilia-Romagna on the coastal road from Rimini the impressive castle of **Gradara** appears, looming over the A14. Built in the 11th century, this castle is, according to tradition, the scene of the story of Francesca da Rimini and Paolo Malatesta, tragic lovers consigned to hell by the heartless Dante in the fifth canto of the *Inferno*. Much of the castle was rebuilt in the 1400s, and it has a beautiful little chapel that can be visited, with a ceramic altarpiece by Luca della Robbia. From there, the road quickly arrives at the provincial capital of Pesaro.

### Getting Around

Pesaro's **railway station** (all trains stop) is on the southern edge of town at Viale Roma, about ½km from the centre. Don't waste time waiting for one of the infrequent local trains to Urbino (via Fano and Fermignano),

The Marches

to Bologna

RIMINI

SAN MARINO

San Leo
Tavoleto

Gradara

Pesaro

Sassocorvaro

Piandimeleto

Fano

Sant'
Angelo in Vado

Urbino

Mercatello
Urbania  Fermignano

Fossombrone

Mondavio

Senigallia

Acqualagna

Gola di
Furlo

M  A  R  C  H  E  S

Falconara

Cagli

Ancona

Portonovo

Arcevia

Jesi

Monte Conero

Sirolo

Sassoferrato

Osimo

Numana

to Città di
Castello

Genga

Gola di
Rossa

Filottrano

Castelfidardo

to Greece

Fabriano

Recanati

Porto Recanati

Montecassiano

Loreto

to Arezzo

Helvia Recina

Matelica

San Severino
Marche

Macerata

Civitanova
Marche

PERUGIA

Chiascio

Assisi

Camerino

Tolentino

Corridonia

Porto Sant'
Elpidio

Chiaravalle
di Fiastra

Porto
San Giorgio

San
Ginesio

Fermo

Tevere

Foligno

Pedaso

to Terni

Sarnano

Grottammare

N

Monti Sibillini

Ascoli
Piceno

San Benedetto
del Tronto

2476m

M. Vettore

to Pescara

Arquata
del Tronto

Land over 200 metres

to Rieti

25km
15 miles

as there aren't many, and the FS has been trying to close the line for years. At least 10 **buses** a day go to Urbino, also via Faro and (usually) Fermignano. There are different companies, and conflicting schedules posted, but most leave from the bus station in the Piazza Matteotti, and all leave from or stop at the Pesaro train station. In Urbino, the bus depot is in Piazzale Mercatale, at the town's southern gate, with connections to most of the inland villages and towns in Pesaro province. All arrivals and departures are listed on a board under the loggia in Piazza della Repubblica.

There is a choice of two routes by **road** from Pesaro to Urbino: the main SS3 (Via Flaminia) via Fano, and the more direct but narrower and sometimes slower SS423.

---

### Tourist Information

**Pesaro** has tourist offices at Via Mazzolari 4, ✆ (0721) 30258, and Viale Trieste 164, ✆ (0721) 69341. There's also a desk at the train station. The **Urbino** tourist office is at Piazza Rinascimento 1, ✆ (0722) 2613, near the Palazzo Ducale.

---

## Pesaro

In the Middle Ages, the five big ports of the central Adriatic were known as the Pentapolis—Rimini, Fano, Senigallia, Ancona and Pesaro. Pesaro, like Rimini, has developed into a large resort, but a much tidier and more pleasant one. Pesaro is proud to be the home town of Gioacchino Rossini; you can visit his **birthplace** at Via Rossini 34 (*opening hours vary; inquire at the tourist office*) near the cathedral, see his piano and manuscripts at the **conservatory** he founded, on Piazza Olivieri, or take in one of his operas at Pesaro's unusually grand house, the **Teatro Rossini**, during the Rossini festival in late summer.

The Sforzas of Milan ruled Pesaro for a time, and they sold it to the della Rovere, the family of Julius II, in 1512. The big **Palazzo Ducale** in the centre of town was completed in 1510. In those years Pesaro rivalled Faenza as a producer of fine ceramics; you can see examples at the **Museo Civico**, Via Toschi Mosca (*open April–Sept 9am–8pm Tues–Sat; 9–1 Sun; Oct–Mar 8.30–1.30 Tues–Sat; 9.30–12.30 Sun; adm*). Besides the majolica plates there are a few good pictures—and one very great one, a *Coronation of the Virgin* by Giovanni Bellini. Another museum, the **Museo Oliveriano** (*open Sept–July 9.30–12.30 Mon–Sat; August only 9.30–12.30, 4–7, Mon–Sat; if closed call at library next door*), has a collection of archaeological finds left by the Romans and the various tribes who lived in the Marches before them.

Though it doesn't have many exceptional monuments, Pesaro is nonetheless a lovely town to walk through, both in its older quarters and in the newer streets by the beach. They are full of trees and little villas from the turn of the century—many in the Liberty style, including one small but outrageous house right on the centre of the beach front in the Piazzale della Libertà, with its cornice supported by terracotta lobsters, designed by an architect named Oreste Ruggiero in 1907. Pesaro's castle, the **Rocca Costanza** near the sea, was built by Luciano Laurana, the designer of the palace at nearby Urbino.

## Urbino

From Pesaro—and from almost nowhere else—it is easy to reach the isolated mountain town of Urbino. With its celebrated ducal palace, and the memory of the honourable and refined Duke Federico who built it, Urbino is one of the great monuments of the Italian Renaissance. Today its boosters go perhaps too far—'the ideal city of the Renaissance' and 'most beautiful palace in the world', and so on and on, a lack of modesty that would probably have disappointed Federico da Montefeltro. Even so, Urbino does represent more clearly than any Italian town a certain facet of the Renaissance: elegance, learning, and intelligent patronage combined in a small place. Urbino's golden age may not have long outlasted the reign of Duke Federico, but, as an example of what a community can be, it exerts a fascination even today.

## The Court of Duke Federico

 Throughout the Middle Ages, Urbino's fortunes were attached to those of the house of Montefeltro, mountain warlords from around San Leo who gradually extended their influence in the northern Marches. Most of them were *condottieri* working throughout Italy, serving various masters. In 1443, Oddantonio da Montefeltro earned the title of Duke for his services. His halfbrother and successor, Federico (reigned 1444–82), was the most successful of all the family *condottieri*, a crafty and respected warrior who earned the money for his famous palace serving the cause of the Pope and Alfonso of Naples. In his later days, with more of a chance to stay at home, Federico became one of the quattrocento's great patrons, as well as a slow but close student of the Classics and the new humanities; he learned Greek and Latin, and the library he assembled was one of the best in Europe. Much of the legend of Urbino in Federico's time comes from Baldassare Castiglione, in whose book *The Courtier* Urbino's court was idealized as the height of civilized existence.

Federico ruled Urbino paternally and well, always liberal to those of his subjects in need, peering into every detail of his little state's economy and social life, and educating the sons of the poor. It is also said that he banished gambling and cursing, and made the people of Urbino exert themselves mightily to keep the place clean. His admirable wife, Battista Sforza, was a duchess beloved of her subjects, a lady capable of delivering an impromptu speech in impeccable Latin to welcome any surprise visitor. Their son, Guidobaldo I, was as enlightened a ruler as his father, and clever enough to survive and prevail after an occupation by Cesare Borgia's Papal army in 1497. However, when Guidobaldo died without an heir, the duchy fell to a nephew of Pope Julius II, a member of the della Rovere family, one of the great clans of the papal aristocracy.

Urbino's time as an independent state lasted less than two hundred years. The last of the della Rovere dukes willed the town and its territories to the popes in 1626, and it was left as a quiet backwater, ruled with the same lazy neglect as the rest of the Papal States for most of the following centuries. Urbino had, though, a moment of high drama in 1944. Many of the works of art of central Italy had been taken there for safekeeping as the war had spread to the Italian mainland. During the German retreat in August, one of their commanders planted enough explosives under the town walls to blow the whole place to kingdom come. Only a small number went off, and the remainder were defused by the British after the liberation—a job that took over a week.

## The Palazzo Ducale

So many architects helped Federico build his dream house, it is difficult to divide the credit. Alberti may have been an original adviser, and the Dalmatian Luciano Laurana is generally given credit for most of the work, but the finest part of it, the twin-turreted façade, is by Ambrogio Barocchi, and no one is quite sure who did the elegant arcaded courtyard. That every Italian schoolchild should know this to be 'the most beautiful palace in the world' is an interesting reflection both on the Italians and on the quattrocento. Federico's palace is not finished, not symmetrical, and not really even very grand; its aesthetic is utterly foreign to the tastes of the centuries that followed.

For all that, it is a great building, and a test of one's faith in the genuine Renaissance—the 15th-century high noon of life and art, as opposed to the cinquecento of Spaniardism, surrender, and neurotic excess. Many critics have regarded it, though unfinished, as the culmination of Renaissance architecture, not yet entirely enslaved to perspectivism or imitation of the ancients, but a creation of freedom and delight. The palace was comfortable for the Montefeltri to live in, and an exquisite decoration for the city of Urbino.

The palace **façade**, overlooking the hills on the edge of town, consists of three levels of balconies between two slender towers; the decorative trim is done in a fine Dalmatian limestone that eventually hardened to look like marble. To enter the palace today, you have to go round the back through the courtyard, called the **Cortile d'Onore**, a prototype for so many other palace courtyards around the western Mediterranean. Inside, much of the palace is occupied by the **Galleria Nazionale delle Marche**, a splendid collection whose finest works were originally the property of Duke Federico (*open April–Sept 9am–7pm Mon–Sat, 9–1 Sun; Oct–Mar 9–2 Mon–Sat, 9–1 Sun; adm exp*).

Piero della Francesca's amazing *Flagellation* is perhaps the best-known work in Urbino, an endlessly disturbing image that has troubled art scholars for centuries. Standing before a pavilion of fantasy classical architecture, three gentlemen in contemporary dress hold a serious discussion, indifferent to the scourging of Christ going on behind them—a bloodless scourging, for that matter. Piero had already written one of the great Renaissance treatises on theoretical perspective; a complex system of foreshortening is here the major feature of the work. The combination of a surreal, dream-like scene and a drily scientific visual presentation gives the painting its enigmatic quality—as critics have often noted, this is one of the places where art crosses the line into sorcery. Almost as strange a display of perspectivist wizardry is another work, often attributed to Piero or Laurana, the *Ideal City*. The scene is a broad, paved square, lined with buildings in the new style, dominated by a large circular temple in the centre. Here again, perspective is the star of the work. Disturbingly, there are no people present—no living things at all save a few potted plants on the balconies.

Not to be outdone by Piero, Paolo Uccello offers a similarly mysterious *Miracle of the Profaned Host*, and Luca Signorelli is represented by two inspired paintings, the *Crucifixion* and *Pentecost*. Other paintings not to miss: a *Crucifixion* by Antonio Alberti de Ferrara, taking care to show off contemporary fashions, in armour as well as court dress; the *Annunciation* of Vicenzo Pagani (and a pagan-looking work it is, too); *La Muta*, a portrait of a lady by Raphael; also fine works by Luca della Robbia, Giovanni Santi, Crivelli, Verrocchio and the Venetian Alvise Vivarini. The Spanish artist Pedro Berruguete contributes the famous *Portrait of Duke Federico*: the tough old warrior, with his broken nose, symbolically still wears armour as he pores over a heavy book, with his little son Guidobaldo at his knee; note the badge of the Order of the Garter, conferred on Federico by King Edward IV of England.

Some of the surviving interior decoration of the palace is wonderful too—carved mantel-pieces and window frames in many rooms, and, above all, the intarsia (inlaid wood) **study** of Duke Federico. Some of the designs are said to be by Botticelli, and they portray the 'Life of a Scholar' with many interesting *trompe l'œil* effects. The paintings above, representing philosophers and illustrious men, are by Berruguete. Nearby, reached by a spiral staircase inside one of the façade's towers, are the **Cappella del Perdono**, with an ornate ceiling of hundreds of angel heads in stucco, and an equally fancy chamber called the **Tempietto delle Muse**. The palace's upper floor has rooms full of 16th- and 17th-century paintings, and many portraits of the poor Italians dressed in black like their Spanish overlords. Some chiaroscuros of the *Life of St Paul* by Claudio Ridolfi, colourful 18th-century ceramics, and surprisingly good woodcuts by a Marchegiano artist of the 1900s named Adolfo di Carolia, make the climb upstairs worth while. The palace's basement houses a display on the difficult job of restoration of the palace undertaken after the vandalism and neglect of papal rule. Among the exhibits are bits of the duke's plumbing and cooking pots, with other curiosities found during the restoration, such as the sundial-birdbath from the roof garden (sadly, long destroyed), and a big book with a conspicuous dedication to *James III, Re di Gran Bretagna*. The Old Pretender was a guest here twice in the 1700s.

## The Town and the Walls

Urbino today is above all a university town, and despite its small size is a lively place full of students from many countries. Though its streets and roads are often steep, the town and its surrounding hills make an enchanting spot for walks. Adjacent to the ducal palace, the **Cathedral** is a work of the 1790s, completely rebuilt after an earthquake that caused the collapse of its dome; there is a small collection of religious art and artefacts in the **Museo Diocesano Albani** (*open April–Sept 9–12, 3–6, daily; Oct–Mar by request,* © *0722 2892*). On Via Barocci, off Via Mazzini, the street that leads up from Urbino's main gate, the little **Oratorio di San Giovanni** (*open 10–12, 3–5, daily; adm*) has strikingly colourful frescoes by the brothers Jacopo and Lorenzo Salimbeni (1416), artists from the town of San Severino Marche, near Macerata, who showed a distinctive approach to early Renaissance painting, still heavily under the influence of Giotto. Their work includes a *Crucifixion*, an enthroned *Madonna*, and a cycle on the life of John the Baptist. On the same street, the **Oratorio di San Giuseppe** has a carved *presepio* (crib) by another Urbino artist, Federico Brandani. The town's most famous son, though, was undoubtedly Raphael (Raffaello Sanzio), born here in

1483, and his birthplace is now restored as a museum. The **Casa di Raffaello** (*open 9am–2pm Tue–Sat; 9am–1pm Sun; adm*) has works by other artists, some pieces of furniture, and a *Madonna* attributed to Raphael himself, but nothing major by the artist.

All of Urbino's 16th-century walls are still intact, and the garden enclosed by one of the corner bastions, the **Fortezza Albornoz**, has a fine view of the palace and town. A pleasant half-hour walk out from the western end of town will take you to the pretty church of **San Bernardino**, attributed by some to Bramante, another son of the Urbino area; inside are the simple but impressive black marble tombs of the Montefeltro dukes.

### *Where to Stay*

At first sight Pesaro looks to be a refined, perhaps exclusive, resort; it comes as a pleasant surprise to find that prices are on a level with Rimini, and often a little lower. Hotels in Urbino can be extremely crowded in the summer, and even springtime. There aren't many of them, and it's always wise to book ahead. Even so, this isn't a town where you can spend many lire, even if you try. Much of the civilized air of Duke Federico's time seems to have survived into our own—it's notable for its clean, attractive, inexpensive hotels and restaurants, with disarmingly friendly proprietors, and you may end up staying longer than you planned.

### Pesaro

There's only one fine old establishment at the top of the list—the ★★★★**Vittoria**, Piazzale della Libertà 2, ✆ (0721) 34343, @ 65204 (expensive), a renovated century-old villa in the centre of the beach strip. All its rooms have TV and air-conditioning.

Pesaro's speciality is the modern, understated three-star hotel, all of which seem to cost (high season) around L65–90,000 for a decent double room. It's difficult to recommend one over the other: the ★★★**Principe**, Viale Trieste 180, ✆ (0721) 30222, @ 31636 (moderate), quite a distance from the centre, has a very good and popular restaurant. Just outside the town is the ★★★**Villa Serena**, Via San Nicola 6, ✆ (0721) 55211 (moderate), a 17th-century palace with fireplaces in every room and antique furniture, and remarkably reasonable prices. There is also a wide selection of one- and two-star places, many around the L50,000 range, both along the beach and in the side streets behind it; try the ★★**Liana**, Viale Trieste 102, ✆ (0721) 68330 (inexpensive).

### Urbino

Perched next to Urbino's city walls, the most luxurious place in town short of the palace itself is the ★★★★**Bonconte**, Via delle Mura 28, ✆ (0722) 2463, @ 4782 (expensive). A very good (centrally located hotel is the ★★**Italia**, Corso Garibaldi 32, ✆ (0722) 2701 (inexpensive), a few steps away from the ducal palace; another is the ★★**San Giovanni**, Via Barocci 13, ✆ (0722) 2827 (inexpensive), in an old *palazzo* with a good restaurant. Both have rooms with or without baths.

## Pesaro

In the centre of the old town of Pesaro, **Lo Scudiero**, Via Baldassini 2. ✆ (0721) 64107 (expensive), occupies the cellar of a 17th-century palace. Specialities include some imaginative dishes with seafood and pasta—ravioli with sole, or *tagliatelle marine*. Roast lamb is another dish they do well.

**Da Alceo**, Via Panoramica Ardizio 101, ✆ (0721) 51360 (expensive), right on the sea, offers great fresh fish dishes and home made pasta and desserts, and has a good friendly atmosphere, with tables outside. (*Closed Mon.*) Also on the seafront, **Teresa**, Viale Trieste 180, ✆ (0721) 30222 (expensive) has exceptional specialities such as a risotto made with locally picked wild herbs and fried calamari with sage. Away from central Pesaro the **Villa Serena** hotel (*see* above; expensive) also has a very pleasant restaurant.

For a fine fish dinner there's **Nuovo Carlo**, Viale Zara 54, ✆ (0721) 68984 (moderate)—often crowded, and not without reason. **Daniela e Umberto**, at Loc. S. Veneranda, Pesaro, ✆ (0721) 452325 (moderate) offers hearty local dishes—gnocchi in duck sauce, rabbit and *porchetta*, as well as creations with frogs, snails, and pigeon. (*Closed Wed.*) For modest but delicious home cooking try **Bibo e Biba**, Via G. Bruno 37 (moderate), behind the post office. For under L30,000 you can enjoy dishes such as *polenta con funghi* or *farfalle al salmone*, and there's also pizza.

## Urbino

In a fancy restored granary in Urbino is the **Vecchia Urbino**, Via dei Vasari 3, ✆ (0722) 4447 (expensive). Specialities include tagliatelle with sole or truffles and a savoury *millefoglie ducale*, and there's a good list of local wines. (*Closed Tues.*) A good and excellent-value traditional restaurant is the **Trattoria Leone**, ✆ (0722) 329894 (moderate), right in Piazza della Repubblica, with surprise specialities like *coniglio al porchetto* on the menu. **Da Franco**, Via del Poggio 1 (moderate), is a large restaurant that also serves regional dishes. (*Closed Sun.*) **Il Cortegiano**, Via Puccinotti 13 (moderate), near the cathedral, may look more pricy, but in fact offers local food and roasts, like other Urbino restaurants, for about L35,000 for a full meal.

# Urbino to Ancona

### Tourist Information

There are local tourist offices in the beach resorts of **Fano**, Viale Cesare Battisti 10, ✆ (0721) 803534, and **Senigallia**, Piazza Morandi 2, ✆ (071) 7922725. Both concern themselves mostly with helping you find a hotel in the summer. There are no tourist offices further inland, except in **Urbino**.

## Towns and Villages Around Urbino

If you have the time, Urbino can be used as a base for excursions to a number of interesting towns and villages in the rolling hills and mountains of the northern Marches—towns as serene and lovely as those in Tuscany, though much less known. **Fermignano**, where Bramante may have been born (that honour is also claimed by Urbania), is one of the most attractive and most conveniently placed, about 9km south of Urbino. At its centre, under a graceful medieval tower and bridge, there is a little waterfall on the Metauro river. From Fermignano, you can follow the Metauro valley eastwards to a scenic rocky canyon called the **Gola del Furio**, and beyond to **Fossombrone**, a small town with a small museum and a collection of simple Renaissance palaces and churches. Fossombrone was a Roman foundation, and takes its name, *Forum Sempronii*, from the famous reformer Sempronius Gracchus.

To the west, the Metauro valley will take you to **Urbania**, a sometime residence of the Montefeltro dukes; originally called Castel Durante, it was renamed after Pope Urban VIII. Urbania retains a smaller **Ducal Palace** with a museum, a picture gallery, and the remains of Duke Federico's famous library, with many antique globes and maps.

Beyond Urbania, all roads lead towards the summits of the Apennines, and villagers dream of the truffles they will find in the autumn, just like their counterparts across the mountains in Umbria. The *Sagra del Tartufo* in October is the big event of the year in **Sant'Angelo in Vado**, another exceptionally pretty town on the Metauro; from here the road begins the climb over the mountains to Arezzo and Perugia. To the north, **Piandimeleto**, **Sassocorvaro**, and **Tavoleto** are three villages built around rather genteel Renaissance castle-palaces; Sassocorvaro's is an unusual round one, built by Francesco di Giorgio Martini, with a small museum. For **San Leo**, in the northernmost corner of the Marches, *see* p.576.

## The Valle dell'Esino

The mountain valleys, stretching in parallel down to the sea, neatly divide the Marches' geography. South of the Metauro, the Esino is the next important valley, most easily reached from Ancona and Falconara, or Perugia. From Ancona, the first town is **Jesi**, once the Roman *Aesis*, set on a narrow ridge between crumbling, picturesque Renaissance walls with houses built on and over their tops. Jesi was the birthplace of none other than the Emperor Frederick II, and on the entrance of the **Palazzo del Comune** is engraved the text of a letter from Frederick confirming the town's ancient privileges.

Adjacent to it, the 16th-century **Palazzo Ricci** has an odd waffle-iron façade like the Gesù Nuovo in Naples. Two streets over to the west, the **Palazzo della Signoria** is another fine building of the same period, with a small museum of paintings and archaeological finds. Jesi's real treasure, however, is a set of excellent paintings by Lorenzo Lotto, including the strange *Annunciation* in the **Pinoteca Comunale**, located in the Palazzo Pianetti on Via XX Settembre (*open 9–12.30, 4–7, Tues–Sat; 10–12.30 Sun; adm*). Outside the walls, the church of **San Marco** has some fine 14th-century frescoes in the manner of Giotto.

Further up river, after another limestone gorge, the **Gola di Rossa**, a road off to the right leads to the village of **Genga** and the recently explored series of caves called the **Grotte di**

**Frasassi** (*open 8am–8pm daily; guided tours every 90min, every 10min Sun; adm*). One of them, already a popular attraction, is the 'cave of the winds', with a spectacular display of glistening pastel stalactites and calcareous pools that go on for over a kilometre. Another cave, called the **Grotto del Santuario,** has an octagonal 18th-century chapel built inside it. Recently a whole new stretch of the caves has been opened to the public. Nearby, close to the Genga railway station, is the 10th-century church of **San Vittore delle Chiese**. Another rather difficult 17km past Genga takes you to the lovely hill village of **Arcevia**, where there is an altarpiece by Luca Signorelli in the church of San Medardo.

**Fabriano**, near the border with Umbria and a stop on the Rome–Ancona railway, was famous in Renaissance times as a centre of paper-making (the watermark was invented here), and as the home of a school of painting, influenced by Gentile da Fabriano, one of the major figures of the early quattrocento. Some of his work and of that by other Fabriano artists can be seen in the gallery in the **Pinacoteca Civica** on Piazza Umberto di Savoia, along with a good collection of other late medieval and Renaissance works (*open April–Sept 10–12.30, 4–7, Tues–Sat; 10–12.30 Sun; Oct–Mar 9.30–12.30 Tues–Sat; 10–12.30 Sun*). The centre of town is a fine arcaded square, the **Piazza del Comune**, with a Palazzo del Comune and fountain very reminiscent of those in Perugia. Nearby **San Domenico**, Fabriano's most important church, has interesting frescoes by local artists of the 14th century, most notably those in the Chapel of S. Orsola. San Domenico's convent has been restored to hold the **Museum of Papermaking** (*open 9–12, 3–6, Tues–Sat; 9am–12.30pm Sun; adm*). In a way that's very typical of the tenacity of craftwork in many Italian towns, Fabriano still makes its living from paper, using modern methods as well as the old-fashioned way. The most important use for speciality paper is, of course, banknotes; besides supplying the Italian treasury, Fabriano paper changes hands every day from Kashmir to the Congo. At the museum much of the equipment of the old craft has been assembled, and demonstrations are given of how it's done.

For a real detour off the beaten track, press on south to **Matelica**, with another fine town square and a picture gallery, the **Museo Piersanti** (*open 10am–12 midday daily*), with an exceptional triptych by Antonio da Fabriano and some saints by Giovanni Bellini. **Cerreto d'Esi** nearby has remains of a Byzantine gate and a leaning tower, said to have been built in the time of Justinian.

### Back on the Coast: Fano and Senigallia

South of Pesaro, the string of Adriatic resorts continues through these two towns. Fano and

Frasassi
Caves

Senigallia are not just resorts, however, but fine old towns, both members of the medieval Pentapolis. Older even than the Romans, **Fano** takes its name—once *Fanum Fortunae*—from a famous temple to the goddess Fortuna. Under Roman rule it became the most important of the Marches' coastal cities, the terminus of the Via Flaminia from Rome. Today, in the central Piazza XX Settembre, a statue of Fortune from the 1500s decorates the **Fontana della Fortuna**. The elegant loggia behind it belongs to the **Corte Malatestiano** (*open July–Sept 8.30–12.30, 5–7, Tues–Sat; 9–12 Sun; Oct–June 8.30–12.30 Tues–Sat; 9–12 Sun; adm*), a palace built in the 1420s and enlarged in 1544, when Fano was ruled by the tyrants of Rimini. In the picture gallery inside the best works are by Giovanni Santi and Mattia Preti.

In the church of **Santa Maria Nuova**, two blocks south on Via dei Pili, there are altarpieces by Giovanni Santi and Perugino, with a small predella panel attributed to the young Raphael. From Roman days, Fano preserves a stately gate built in the year AD 2, the **Arco di Augusto**. San Michele Church, to the right of the gate, has a relief carved on its façade showing how the arch looked before it was heavily damaged in 1463. The eventually successful besieger who bombarded it was none other than Duke Federico of Urbino, working at that time for the pope; the defender—Sigismundo Malatesta of Rimini.

Fano's **Lido**, modern and a little overbuilt, is typical of the resorts on the Adriatic, but the long broad beach continues down the coast for miles, through the resort suburbs of Torrette and Marotta, and there's room for all. **Senigallia**, the next town on the coast, was the site of an important trade fair in the Middle Ages. Besides its long 'velvet beach', one of the nicest on the Adriatic, its main landmark is an elegant though serviceable fortress, built by the della Rovere in 1480, the **Rocca Roveresca** (*open April–Sept only 9–1, 3–7, Tues–Sat; 9am–1pm Sun; Aug only also open 5–10pm Sun; adm*).

### Where to Stay

There aren't any special choices in Fano or Senigallia—most of what the towns have to offer consists of pretty standard beach hotels, all less than 30 years old. Senigallia, though, has the largest choice of modern hotels and, unlike Fano, has its seafront divided up into private beaches, owned by individual hotels. All the hotels listed here are in the moderate price bracket.

In Fano the **★★★Excelsior**, Lungomare Simonetti 21, © (0721) 803558, is pleasant and centrally located. The **★★★Piccolo**, Viale Cairoli 1, © (0721) 800626, ✆ 8305(all rooms with baths), and the **★★Astoria**, Viale Cairoli 86, © (0721) 803474, are, similarly, in the middle of the seafront area. In Senigallia **★★★La Vela**, Piazza N. Bixio 35, © (071) 60135, is a nice place with a garden and tennis courts; its biggest advantage, though, is that it's the furthest hotel from the railway line.

Fano also has a **youth hostel**, the **Ardizio**, © (0721) 55798 (inexpensive), near the beach north of the town towards Pesaro. (*Open mid-May–Sept only.*) In both Fano and Senigallia and in fact all along the coast there are also innumerable well-established **campsites**.

*Eating Out*

In Fano there are several good restaurants, such as **Augustus**, Via Puccini 2, *©* (0721) 809781 (moderate), which serves creative dishes that do not only feature fish. (*Closed Mon.*) There is also a little place on the beach where you can put away an enormous pile of little fishes for under L25,000— **Pesce Azzurro**, on Lungomare Sarsonia (inexpensive). *Pesce azzurro*—'blue fish'—is something you'll see all along the Adriatic, and refers not to one specific variety, but many kinds of (very tasty) small fish that were once common in these waters. The deterioration in the condition of the Adriatic makes them harder to find each year, so appreciate them while you can.

An excellent restaurant in Senigallia is **Riccardone's**, Via Rieti 69, *©* (071) 647762 (expensive), with tables outside and local dishes made from the freshest ingredients. It's best to let the chef direct you on the menu, featuring such delicacies as squid with artichokes or a wonderful mixed grill of fresh fish. (*Closed Mon.*)

# Ancona

Just before the city, the mountains once more reach the sea, giving the mid-Adriatic's biggest port a splendid setting, a crescent-shaped harbour under the steep promontory of Monte Guasco; here colonists from Syracuse founded the city in the 5th century BC. It was the furthest north the Greeks ever went in the Adriatic, and the colony was never a great success until Roman emperors, especially Trajan, built it up. Ancona recovered from the centuries of decay to become the leading city of the Pentapolis in the 12th century, and lived on quietly thereafter, coming under papal rule in 1532. Our own century, however, has been murderous to Ancona. The Austrians bombarded it in 1915, and the British and Americans did a much more thorough job in 1944. Then came a major flood, a serious earthquake, in 1972, and after that a landslide that caused parts of the old town to be abandoned. For all its troubles, Ancona has come up smiling. The port is prospering, and even though most of the population now live in newer districts to the south and west, the city is finally devoting its attention to the restoration of the historic centre.

*Getting Around*

*by air*

Ancona's two **air terminals** are both near the railway station, **ATI**, at Corso Stamira 80, *©* (071) 31801, for flights to Bari, Tàranto, and Venice, and **Italia**, Piazza Roma, *©* (071) 53696, for Bologna, Crotone, Fóggia, Genoa, Milan, Pescara, Turin, and Rome. Raffaello Sanzio **Airport** is 5km outside the city at Falconara.

*by sea*

There are plenty of **ferry** services from Ancona to different points in Greece. In former times there were also regular sailings to ports along the coast of ex-Yugoslavia—now in Croatia—but when these services will be fully restored is impossible to say. If you're heading to Greece from Rome or anywhere further north, taking the ferry from here is a moderately better bet than making the long trip down to Brindisi, Bari, or Otranto. Fares are only slightly higher, and in both cases it will be an overnight trip. To Greece fares range from L75,000–345,000, depending on the standard of accommodation on board and the season.

All ferries leave from the **Stazione Marittima**, which is in the centre of the port 2km north of the railway station. The lines that operate to Greece are **Minoan Lines**, Via XXIX Settembre 4, ✆ (071) 201708, which has the best boats and most comprehensive services (to Corfu, Igoumenitsa, Patras, Piraeus, Crete and some other destinations) but is slightly more expensive; **Anec Lines**, Via XXIX Settembre 2/a, ✆ (071) 202033; **Mar Lines**, Via XXIX Settembre 8/a, ✆ (071) 202566; and **Strintzis Lines**, Via Buozzi 8, ✆ (071) 286431. The last three mainly run only to Corfu, Igoumenitsa and Patras. The tourist office in the port has all the information on these lines and on connections to Turkey, Cyprus and Israel, but in summer especially it's necessary to book tickets in advance before arriving in Ancona.

### by rail

Ancona lies at the intersection of two major railway lines—the Adriatic coast route and Ancona-Rome, with no long waits for trains in either direction. The **FS station** is west of the port at Piazza Roselli (buses nos.1 or 3 to or from Piazza Repubblica by the port). Some trains, but not many, continue to Ancona Marittima station on the port itself.

### by bus

Buses to Portonovo and the Cónero Riviera, to other towns in the province and to Bologna, Rome and other long-distance destinations all leave from the **bus station** at Piazza Stamira, just west of Piazza Cavour, ✆ (071) 41836. Many buses also stop at the railway station. Ancona's few sights are not far from each other, but they are uphill—If you're not up to making the long climb up to the cathedral, the no. 11 bus from Piazza Cavour or Piazza Repubblica will save you the trouble.

### by road

The A14 and the SS16 continue more or less in parallel along the coast, slightly inland from Ancona. Ferry passengers can drive directly to the Stazione Marittima without having to go through the old town, though the port traffic itself is often very heavy. Just north of the city at Falconara the SS76, the main road inland to Perugia and points west, turns off the A14 and SS16.

---

### Tourist Information

**Ancona**'s main tourist office is in Via Thaon de Revel 4, ✆ (071) 33249, 🖶 31966, and there are branch offices in the railway station, ✆ (071) 41703, and in the Palazzo Provincia on Corso Stamira, ✆ (071) 29882. In **Falconara Marittima** the local office is at Via Cavour 3, ✆ (071) 910458.

In summer only there's also a booth in the port, ✆ (071) 201183, and offices in the Cónero resorts of **Numana**, Piazza Santuario, ✆ (071) 936142, and **Sirolo**, Piazza Vittorio Veneto, ✆ (071) 936141.

# Around the Port

It's surprising anything is left at all, but most of Ancona's monuments have survived the recent misfortunes, even if many are a little the worse for wear. The business centre has gravitated a few streets inland, around the broad **Piazza Cavour**; from here Corso Garibaldi leads down to the sea. At its western end, the long curve of the port is anchored by the **Mole Vanvitelliana**, a pentagonal building that resembles a fortress, but really served as Ancona's *lazaretto* or quarantine hospital in the 18th century. At the other end, the tall, graceful **Arch of Trajan** was built in AD 115, in honour of Ancona's imperial benefactor; even though the sculptural reliefs have disappeared, it is one of the better preserved Roman arches in Italy. Nearby, the 18th-century Pope Clement XII imitated Roman glory by having an arch put up to himself; the **Arco Clementino**, like the lazaretto, was the work of Vanvitelli, the court architect of the Bourbons at Naples, best known for his palace at Caserta. At the centre of the port, the 15th-century Venetian Gothic **Loggia dei Mercanti**, the merchants' exchange, is the best souvenir of Ancona's heyday as a free maritime city.

To see the oldest quarters of Ancona you'll have to climb a little, starting up Via Gramsci and passing under the Renaissance decorative arch of the **Piazza del Governo**. Off in a little square to the left, the church of **Santa Maria della Piazza** has a fine late Romanesque façade with figures of musicians, soldiers and odd animals carved by a 'Master Phillippus'. Another two cross-streets up take you to **San Francesco delle Scale**, with another Gothic portal, and a late Renaissance palace that houses a small collection in the **Pinacoteca Comunale** (*open 10–7 Tues Sat; 9–1 Sun; adm*). It contains a masterpiece by the eccentric but endearing Carlo Crivelli, tidiest of all Renaissance painters—a *Madonna col Bambino*, complete with Crivelli's trademark apples and cucumbers hanging overhead. There is also a good *Madonna* by Lotto, formerly in the Santa Maria church, and yet another by Titian, floating smugly on a cloud.

# On Monte Guasco

Further up, the street changes its name to Via del Guasco, in an area where bits of decorative brickwork from Roman Ancona's theatre peek out in between and under the buildings. This was the area hardest hit by the earthquake and landslide, and restoration work is going on everywhere. One building that may never be completely finished is the one on Via Ferretti that houses the **Museo Nazionale delle Marche** (*open 8.30am–1.30pm Tues–Sun; adm*), an important archaeological collection with some exceptional Greek vases, sculpture, and metalwork. The wartime bombings blew up its first home, and the second was jolted severely in the earthquake and closed entirely to visitors for many years, though it has now partially reopened. Also damaged in 1972 was the 13th-century **Palazzo del Senato**, around the corner, Ancona's capital when it was a self-governing *comune*.

Ancona's **Cathedral** crowns Monte Guasco, a site that in antiquity held a famous temple of Venus. To reach it, you either climb a long stairway flanked by gardens, the **Scalone Nappi**, or drive up from the port, where an ugly new road has replaced the neighbourhoods lost in the landslide. Unusually for a church this far north, the 11th-century cathedral shows a strong influence of the Apulian Romanesque, and but for the long, rounded transepts the building would not look out of place in any of the cathedral towns around Bari. The sculpted portals and detached campanile were both added about 1200. Inside, there isn't much to see; the marble columns came originally from the Temple of Venus, and there is an unusual carved altar screen from the 12th century. The cathedral is dedicated to St Cyriacus, an early bishop and martyr—not a real martyr, but a clever piece of propaganda from the time of the virtuous but non-Christian Emperor Julian the Apostate.

## The Cónero Riviera

The same arm of the Apennines that stretches down to shelter Ancona's port also creates a short but uniquely beautiful stretch of Adriatic coast. South of Ancona, the cliffs of Monte Cónero plunge steeply into the sea, forcing the railway and coastal highway to bend inland, and isolating a number of beautiful beaches and coves only a few kilometres from the centre of Ancona, and now a national park.

The little resort town of **Portonovo**, on the northern slopes of Cónero, can be reached by bus from Ancona in half an hour. There is a small beach, and a church of the 1030s in the same style as Ancona cathedral. **Santa Maria di Portonovo**, with the same blind arcading around the roofline and a distinctive cupola in the centre, is one of the better Romanesque churches in the north. Dante mentioned it, as 'the House of Our Lady on the Adriatic Coast' in the 21st canto of the *Paradiso*.

The southern end of Cónero is marked by the often very crowded, but attractive, resorts of **Sirolo** and **Numana**. Both Sirolo and Numana have beaches nearby, but the best in the area are in places that can only be reached by small boat, like the beach of **Due Sorelle** or the stretch of jagged white cliffs called **Sassi Bianchi**.

℗ (071–)            ***Where to Stay***

## Ancona

With all the ferry passengers passing through, Ancona has a wide choice of accommodation. The finest place in the city is the ★★★★**Grand Hotel Palace**, Lungomare Vanvitelli 24, ℗ 201813, ✉ 2064832 (very expensive), by the port near Trajan's Arch. It's a small, but very comfortable hotel with a good restaurant, and a roof garden with views over the port.

For a little tranquillity and reasonable prices the ★★**Viale**, Viale della Vittoria 23, ℗ 201861 (moderate), is a good choice, nearly a kilometre from the centre. Near the railway station, the recently upgraded ★★★**Rosa**, Piazza Fratelli Rosselli 3, ℗ 41388 (moderate), also has good-standard rooms, with baths. Another alternative is ★★**Gino**, Via Flaminia 4, ℗ 43333 (moderate), with rooms with or without baths.

There are quite a number of pretty uninspiring budget-range hotels in Ancona around the railway station, mostly used by people caught in between ferries and trains, and so not offering much in the way of comfort. A basic but cheap, clean and reasonably comfortable hotel in the city centre is the ★**Centrale**, Via Marsala 10, ℗ 54388 (inexpensive).

## Monte Cónero

The ★★★**Monte Cónero**, Via Monte Cónero 27, ☎ 9330592, ✉ 9330365 (moderate), is a pleasant hotel in a relaxed setting on the lush green headland.

## Portonovo

★★★★**Fortino Napoleonico**, Via Poggio 60, ☎ 801124, ✉ 801314 (expensive), as its name implies, incorporates part of a fortress built during the Napoleonic Wars. Nevertheless, it's quiet and modern, and has its own beach and a pool. Suites are available in addition to well-equipped double rooms.

Two kilometres outside Portonovo is the ★★★**Emilia**, Via Poggio 149/a, ☎ 801145 (expensive), a pretty modern place with a swimming pool and tennis courts. The owners invite artists to stay free in exchange for a painting, and so the hotel is covered with pictures, including one by Graham Sutherland.

## Numana

How the hotel-keepers in Numana get away with charging what they do is a mystery — sometimes L70–120,000 for some pretty dismal spots thrown up in the recent building boom. One that's worth the bill is the ★★★**Gigli Eden**, Via Morelli 11, ☎ 933 0652 (moderate), which offers nice rooms with a view, two pools, tennis, and acres of grounds with plenty of trees. There's also a secluded private beach, though it's a bit of a climb to get back up from it. Another good choice in Numana is ★★**Teresa a Mare**, Via del Golfo 26, ☎ 9330623 (moderate).

---

☎ *(071–)*

*Eating Out*

*very expensive*

## Ancona

**Passetto**, on Piazza IV Novembre, ☎ 33214 (expensive) is an excellent seafood restaurant, claimed by some to be the best in Italy—*zuppa di balleri*, made from a kind of mussel that only lives around the Cónero coast, is the speciality. (*Closed Wed.*)

**La Moretta**, Piazza del Plebiscito 52, ☎ 2075382 (expensive), has long been a favourite with locals for its excellent *stoccafisso all'anconetana* (wind-dried cod) and *spaghetti agli scampi*. (*Closed Sun.*) Like any self-respecting port, Ancona has dozens of trattorie where you can put away some less grandiose marine delights at inconceivably low prices.

The **Osteria del Pozzo**, on Via Bonda, ☎ 50396 (inexpensive), in the centre of the port, is one that offers a fine mixed seafood grill for about L20,000. **La Cantineta**, around the corner on Via Gramsci, ☎ 201107 (inexpensive), is another, and offers ferry-travellers a foretaste of Greece, complete with Greek seamen fingering worry-beads. It's one of the most popular places in town, with delicious *stoccafisso*, and, oddly enough, lemon sorbet.

## Torrette

In Torrette, between Ancona and Falconara, **Da Carloni**, Via Flaminia 247, © 888239 (moderate) is another spot that's greatly admired locally for its seafood, though the restaurant sits right next to the railway tracks, so that your mussels rattle when trains pass.

## Portonovo

Portonovo's **Fortino Napoleonico** (*see* above; very expensive) is one of the finest places to dine in the region, with two beautiful dining rooms and immaculate service. Their *menu degustazione* will indulge you with eight superb courses, including stuffed olives and scampi, sole stuffed with spinach, cream and smoked salmon, shrimps with fennel and orange, gnocchi with caviare, and more delights.

If your budget won't stretch to the Fortino, just around the corner on the beach is the **Emilia**, © 801109 (expensive), with a sea terrace and pleasant views, if you ignore the colour of the water. The menu is all fish, with a very good seafood risotto.

**Da Anna**, right on the beach, © 801343 (inexpensive) is a restaurant not to be missed if you're anywhere near the Cónero. The proprietor goes out daily to catch the fish, and his wife does the cooking. The atmosphere and the cuisine couldn't be better, and the prices could be much worse. (*Open Easter–end Oct.*)

# The Southern Marches: Down the Coast

After Monte Cónero, the Adriatic won't show you another stretch of beautiful coastline until the Gargano peninsula in Apulia. All through the southern Marches, the seaside is dotted with humble but growing resort towns, all pleasant enough but nothing special: **Porto Recanati**, **Civitanova Marche**, **Porto Sant'Elpidio**, **Porto San Giorgio** and **Pedaso**. If you're looking for a chance to dip inland, the best places would be, for Catholics, the pilgrimage shrine of **Loreto**, and otherwise **Fermo**, a fine old town 6km west of Porto San Giorgio.

---

### Getting Around

There are frequent **trains** up and down the coast between Ancona and Pescara. Loreto is also on this line—the station is outside the town, but there is a regular connecting bus. There is also a line that cuts inland from Civitanova Marche to Macerata, and meets the Ancona–Rome line near Fabriano. The best way to explore the inland towns is by car, but there are **buses** to most destinations from Ancona, Macerata or Ascoli Piceno. The **road** to Osimo and Castelfidardo is the SS16, then turn right onto the SS361. Loreto is just off the SS16, and for Fermo follow the SS16 to Porto San Giorgio, then take the SS210.

Tourist offices can be found in **Loreto**, at Via Solari 3, ✆ (071) 970276; **Porto San Giorgio**, Via Oberdan 8, ✆ (0734) 678461; and **Fermo**, in the Piazza del Popolo, ✆ (0734) 228738.

## Sweet Music: Castelfidardo and Osimo

Many of the inland towns of the Marches can provide object lessons in the growth and strength of Italy's 'new model' small-scale economy. Just where you least expect it, you'll find a modest, often family-run plant, producing goods that are among the best in their trade. Fermo, for example, and the villages around it produce a quarter of all the shoes made in Italy.

South of Ancona, the town of **Castelfidardo** lives almost entirely on the manufacture of accordions. It is claimed locally that this least academic of musical instruments was invented here in the 1870s (there is more than one alternative theory), and there is an **Accordion Museum** (*open 10.30am–12.30pm Mon; 10.30–12.30, 3.30–7.30, Tues–Sun; adm*), in the Via Mordini, to fill in any gaps in your accordion knowledge.

**Osimo**, 3km up the road, likes to be more up-to-date; the town makes most of Italy's electric guitars and keyboards. Its neighbours aren't impressed; they call people from Osimo '*senza teste*' because of the twelve headless Roman statues that decorate the town hall. Osimo has a small **museum** (*open 4–6pm; closed Wed*) in its Palazzo Campana, with a polyptych by the Vivarini brothers of Venice. Another museum is attached to the 13th-century **cathedral**, with some surprising paintings by little-known local Renaissance artists (*open on request*).

## Loreto

The inventor of the accordion, the story goes, got his inspiration when an Austrian pilgrim on his way to Loreto left behind a button concertina as a gift after staying for the night. The town of Loreto puts up billboards all over Italy inviting us to visit, but few foreigners apart from the devout ever take the hint. That is a pity, for, like Urbino, Loreto is a small but concentrated dose of fine art from the Renaissance.

Its story is a mystery of the faith. During the 13th century, the Church found itself threatened on all sides by heretical movements (the Albigensians, most famously) and free-thinkers. The popes responded with violent repression, but also tried in various more subtle ways to assimilate and control these movements; creating the Franciscans was one such method, and the encouragement of the cult of the Virgin Mary was another. Conveniently enough, a legend of a miracle in the Marches gained wide currency. Mary's house in Nazareth, after being divinely transported to a hill in Istria, decided to fly off again in 1294, this time landing in these laurel woods (*loreti*) south of Ancona. Supposedly the house had bestirred itself in protest over Moslem reoccupation of the Holy Land; the popes were thumping the tub for a new Crusade, and Loreto was just coincidentally located on the route to the Crusader ports on the Adriatic.

# Loreto's Santuario della Santa Casa

Beginning in the 1460s, the simple church originally built to house the *Santa Casa* was reconstructed and embellished in a massive building programme that took well over a century to complete. Corso Boccalini, lined with the inevitable souvenir stands, leads from the town centre up to the Sanctuary—which comes as a very sudden surprise, when you turn the corner and enter the enclosed **Piazza della Madonna**, with the church, a great fountain by Carlo Maderno, one of the architects of St Peter's, and an elegant **loggia** by Bramante, enclosing the square. The sanctuary's understated façade is typical early Roman Baroque, though a little ahead of its time (1587). No one is perfectly sure whom it should be ascribed to, since so many architects had a hand in the work. Giuliano da Sangallo built the cupola (almost a copy of Brunelleschi's great dome in Florence), Bramante did the side chapels, and Sansovino and Sangallo the Younger also contributed. One of the best features is the circle of radiating brick **apses** on the east end, turreted like a Renaissance castle; be sure to walk around for a look. The only unfortunate element in the ensemble is the ungainly neoclassical **campanile**, added by Vanvitelli in the 1750s. Don't blame the architect; the tower had to be squat and strong to hold the 15-ton bell, one that has little trouble making itself heard for miles around once it gets going.

Chapels line the walls inside, embellished by the faithful from nations around the world; two of the more recent are those of the USA and Mexico. The sedate Spanish chapel is one of the better ones, and the English chapel holds a memory of the lyric poet Richard Crashaw, a refugee from Protestantism who served as canon here until his death in the 1640s. A good deal of Loreto's art was pilfered by Napoleon, and consequently most of the paintings in the interior are from the last two centuries; the two **sacristies** in the right aisle have fresco cycles by Melozzo da Forlì and Luca Signorelli. Under the dome you'll see the object of the pilgrims' attention, the **Santa Casa**. A simple brick building with traces of medieval frescoes inside, it was sheathed in marble by Bramante, and its decoration includes beautiful reliefs by Sansovino, Sangallo, della Porta, and others, showing scenes from the *Life of Mary*.

Next to the sanctuary there is a small **museum** (*open April–Oct 9–1, 3–6, Tues–Sat; 9–1 Sun; Nov–Mar 9–1 Tues–Sun; adm*), with a number of works by Lorenzo Lotto.

---

# Fermo

The Sabine town of *Firmum*, later a close ally of Rome, has gained importance and lost it several times; during the 10th century it was the capital of a duchy that included all the southern Marches, and later it was the seat of a university. A singular relic of Roman times can be visited under the Via degli Aceti: the **Piscina Epuratoria**, an enormous underground reservoir of 30 chambers built in AD 140–160 and designed to both hold and clarify rain- and spring-water. The 15th-century façade of the **Palazzo Comunale** is adorned with a mildly eerie statue of Pope Sixtus V, once Fermo's bishop, inviting you in to a fine collection of art in the **Pinacoteca Civica** (*open April–Oct 9–12.30, 5–8, Tues–Sat; 5–8pm Sun; Nov–Mar 10–12, 4–7, Tues–Sat; 4–7pm Sun; adm*), including a moving and intense *Nativity* by Rubens; local records recall a Fermo priest commissioning it in 1608 for the grand sum of 1700 *scudi*. In the museum of the 14th-century **Cathedral**, they'll show you a chasuble of

Moorish silk that belonged to St Thomas à Becket—though they can't really explain how they got it.

### Castelfidardo

****Del Parco**, Via Donizetti 2, ✆ (071) 7821605, 🖷 2820309 (expensive) has most modern comforts, but no pool. Castelfidardo has the ****Piccolo Ranch**, Via Adriatica 22, ✆ (071) 7820385 (moderate), which has a pleasant restaurant.

### Loreto

Hotels in Loreto are invariably clean, quiet, and respectable, with a crucifix above every bed. A good many of them are run by religious orders—Ursulines, Franciscan Sisters, the Holy Family Institute of Piedmont—as accommodation for pilgrims. ***Casa del Clero Madonna di Loreto**, ✆ (071) 970298, 🖷 970102 (moderate), is a typical example, with 32 rooms, all with baths. For a slightly more secular atmosphere, try the ****Centrale** Via Solari 7, ✆ (071) 970173.

### Fermo

If you're stopping in Fermo, there is a comfortable hotel in the town's lovely historic centre, facing the cathedral, the ***Casina delle Rose** on Piazzale Girfalco 16, ✆/🖷 (0734) 228932 (moderate). Another attractive choice is the ****Regina Mundi**, ✆ (0734) 226700 (moderate), outside the centre at S. Petronilla.

### Loreto

It might be worth a stay in Loreto in order to have dinner at the town's one outstanding restaurant, **Orlando Barabani**, Via Villa Constantina 89, at Loreto Archi, ✆ (071) 977696 (moderate). You won't see a humdrum Italian menu; roast small game—quail, pigeon, and thrushes—are a speciality, along with snails or *coniglio con porchetta*. (*Closed Wed.*)

### Fermo

**Da Nasò**, Via G.B. di Crollalanza 45, ✆ (0734) 229661 (moderate), run by a genial proprietor who doesn't mind being called 'big nose', is the place for dinner, with good wine, local food and lots of it. (*Closed Mon.*)

## The Pocket Province of Macerata

You won't find a more out-of-the-way corner in central Italy. Although this hilly enclave lacks great attractions, all of its towns put up a good front, with stout medieval walls or a pretty Romanesque tower to lure you in for a short stop. Many of its villages and towns also have fine works of art in their little museums.

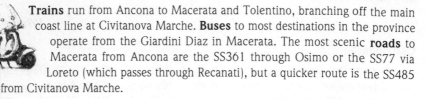

**Trains** run from Ancona to Macerata and Tolentino, branching off the main coast line at Civitanova Marche. **Buses** to most destinations in the province operate from the Giardini Diaz in Macerata. The most scenic **roads** to Macerata from Ancona are the SS361 through Osimo or the SS77 via Loreto (which passes through Recanati), but a quicker route is the SS485 from Civitanova Marche.

## Tourist Information

The main provincial tourist office is at Via Garibaldi 87, **Macerata**, ✆ (0733) 231547, and there are also offices in **Tolentino**, at Piazza Libertà 19, ✆ (0733) 973002, and **Camerino**, Piazza Cavour 9, ✆ (0733) 2534. During the summer there are also information desks in most of the coastal resorts.

## Macerata and Recanati

Macerata, the modest provincial capital, is a pleasant medieval-looking town of 45,000. About one-sixth of them could fit into the town's major landmark, a huge colonnaded hemicycle and outdoor theatre called the **Arena Sferisterio**, built in the 1820s—maybe the grandest setting for opera south of Verona. Macerata makes good use of it in their opera festival, one of the most popular summer music events in Italy (*see* below). On Piazza Vittorio Veneto, the **Pinacoteca Civica** (*open 5–7.30pm Mon; 9–1, 5–7.30, Tues–Sat; 9am–12 midday Sun*) complex houses a *Madonna* by Crivelli (no cucumbers, but a lovely work just the same), archaeological finds from a nearby Roman town called *Helvia Ricina*, and a museum of carriages (*open 9–12.30, 4–6, daily*). If you're fond of *presepi* (Italian Christmas cribs) and can't make it to Naples, Macerata has a little private museum of them too, the **Museo Tipologico del Presepio**. It's on Via Maffeo Pantaleoni; call Cavaliere Cassese on ✆ (0733) 49035 for an appointment.

**Recanati**, on the road between Macerata and Loreto, was the birthplace of Italy's greatest modern poet, Giacomo Leopardi. They have made a discreet cottage industry out of him, and you can visit his birthplace in the **Palazzo Leopardi** (*open 9–12, 3–6, Tues–Sun; adm*), along with a small museum and library. The town's **Pinacoteca** (*open 9–12, 4–6, Mon–Sat*) is full of relics of another favourite son, the great tenor Beniamino Gigli; there is also an altarpiece and three other works by Lorenzo Lotto as well. Recanati is high up on a hill, and there are wonderful views as far as Loreto and the Adriatic from the town and the surrounding area.

South of Macerata the valley of the Chienti carries you deeper into the province, towards the Monti Sibillini. At **Corridonia**, just southwest of Macerata, there is an interesting Byzantine church, **San Claudio al Chienti**, from the 6th century, with a pair of round campaniles like those of the churches in Ravenna. **Tolentino**, further up the valley of the Chienti on the SS77, is one of the larger towns, prosperous and modern and not much to look at until you reach the medieval centre, with the 13th-century **Devil's Bridge** leading to the **Basilica of**

**San Nicola**, from the 1300s. A local artist known only as the 'Maestro di Tolentino' left a beautiful series of frescoes in the **Cappellone Gotico**; intense, inspired work that bears comparison with the best trecento painting in Tuscany. Around the garden cloister, there is a small **museum** of silverwork and ceramics (*open 8.30–12, 3–6.30, daily; adm*). Tolentino has a fascinating **clock tower**, next to the church of San Francesco in the Piazza della Libertà, one that will tell you the phases of the moon, the canonical hour, and the day, among other things. For something different, Tolentino has also opened the world's first **Museum of Caricatures** (*open April–Sept 9–12.30, 3–6, Mon–Sat; Oct–Mar 9–12.30 Mon–Sat; adm*) in the Palazzo Bezzi, with hundreds of cartoons from around the world.

## Camerino and the Monti Sibillini

**Camerino**, up-river, passed the time during the Middle Ages in endless fighting with arch-enemy Fabriano just to the north. Today a mere shadow of the proud and thriving town of those times, Camerino has two good picture galleries, the **Museo Diocesano** and the **Museo Civico**; in both the best works are from a local quattrocento painter named Girolamo di Giovanni. The ruined castle east of town is the **Rocca Varano**, from the 13th century. Beyond Camerino there are only narrow mountain roads over the Apennines to Foligno and Spoleto in Umbria.

Further south, in the southern corner of the Marches, the mountains grow higher, reaching a climax in the dark, dramatic range called the **Monti Sibillini**, with the second highest peak in the Apennines, **Monte Vettore** (2476m), which often has snow until June. Around these there are popular skiing areas at **Ussita** and **Arquata del Tronto**, both with a wide choice of long runs. Arquata del Tronto, a lovely village beneath a hilltop castle, lies along the surest route over the mountains, the SS396, an often spectacular, twisting road that leaves the SS4 from Ascoli Piceno to pass through a 1500m pass, the **Forca Canapine**, before descending to Norcia in Umbria. The route provides a balcony over all the southern Apennines, and is full of wild flowers in the spring. No one is sure how the 'Mountains of the Sibyls' got their name. Ancient writers record no such oracular priestesses in these parts (the closest were at Cumae, near Naples, and at Tivoli). Italy, though, is full of stories about them, and supposedly these mountains gave birth to the legend of Venusberg in Wagner's *Tannhäuser*.

---

## *Where to Stay*

### *expensive*

In Macerata the ★★★★ **Motel AGIP**, Via Roma 149, ☎ (0733) 34246, is an unexceptional but reliable hotel with the usual trimmings, but no pool. For something really special, though, it's worth driving 9km north of town to Montecassiano and the ★★★★**Villa Quiete**, Località Valle Cascia, outside Montecassiano, ☎ (0733) 599559, an 18th-century country house in beautiful grounds with a pool, and rooms furnished with antiques and decorated with a masterful eye. If they could pick it up and move it to Tuscany, it could easily be three or four times more expensive. There's also a fine restaurant.

A perfectly fine place to stop over for the night or during the opera festival in Macerata is the ★★★**Da Rosa**, Via Armaroli 94, ℂ (0733) 232670. Another alternative in Montecassiano is the ★★★★**Roganti**, Località Valle Cascia, km97 on the SS77, ℂ (071) 598639, with comfortable rooms and a garden.

### inexpensive

Accommodation is scarce in Macerata, and there are no real budget hotels. Probably the most reasonably priced is the ★★**San Giorgio**, Via Lauri 6, ℂ (0733) 232376.

---

### Eating Out

Macerata is the place to try *vincisgrassi*, a dish with many variations, a more refined version of lasagna, sometimes with béchamel sauce. Before you get out your Latin dictionary, know that the name comes from the 19th-century Austrian General Windischgrätz, who must have liked it a lot.

Macerata's best restaurant is **Da Secondo**, Via Pescheria Vecchia, ℂ (0733) 44912 (moderate), where besides *vincisgrassi* you can order the famous *fritto misto* of lamb and vegetables—do book, as it's always crowded. For cheaper fare, **Da Silvano**, Piaggia della Torre (inexpensive), offers excellent pizza and some other more local dishes.

---

### Entertainment and Nightlife

Macerata's **opera** festival, the most important such open-air festival in Italy after the season in Verona, is held in the Arena Sferisterio every July. In recent years the programme has featured many major international names, and it's often necessary to book in advance; the tourist office can provide details.

## Ascoli Piceno

Urbino, at the northern end of the Marches, and Ascoli, at the southern, compete for your attention as almost polar opposites. Urbino gets most of the praise, and partisans of Ascoli may find that somewhat unfair. Unlike the northern town, paternalistically led by its enlightened, aesthetic dukes, Ascoli with its long heritage as a free *comune* has always had to do for itself. The difference shows; Ascoli is a beautiful city, but in a gritty, workaday manner, like Florence. It has taken some hard knocks in its 2500 years, which have helped make it a city of character.

## History

For the Piceni, a powerful tribe that lived in the southern Marches and had the woodpecker as its totem beast, Ascoli probably served as the centre of their confederation. To the Romans, *Asculum Picenum* was an early ally, but later a major headache. Asculum fought Rome in the Samnite Wars, and actually initiated the pan-Italian revolt of the Social Wars.

The Romans took the city in 89 BC, and razed it to the ground, soon afterwards refounding it with a colony of veterans. The street plan of Ascoli today has hardly changed since then; it is one of the most perfect examples in Italy of a rectilinear Roman *castrum*. In the Dark Ages, Ascoli's naturally defensible position between steep ravines helped avert trouble. Its citizens, too, showed admirable determination, defeating Odoacer's Goths on one occasion, and the Byzantines and Saracens on several others. Despite periods under the rule of others—Lombards, Franks, Normans, and various feudal lords—Ascoli emerged by the 1100s as a strong free *comune*. Reminders of this most glorious period of the city's history are everywhere, in the 13th-century Palazzo del Popolo, the clutch of tall, noble towers like those of San Gimignano, and in Ascoli's famous festival, the **Quintana**, a jousting contest that happens the first weekend in August, according to rules laid down in 1378. Ascoli lost its freedom immediately, and its prosperity gradually, with the coming of papal rule in the 15th century, only recovering some of its wealth and importance in the last 100 years.

## Getting Around

Ascoli is not the easiest place to reach without a car. The only **train** service is a dead-end branch off the Adriatic coast line, from San Benedetto del Tronto and Porto d'Ascoli. The station (several trains a day), is on Viale Marconi, in the new town. **Buses**, for Pesaro, Ancona, Rome and destinations within the province leave from Viale Alcide di Gasperi, behind the Cathedral; information on both trains and buses can be obtained from the Brumozzi Travel Agency on Corso Trieste, near Piazza del Popolo. For the Rome bus, see the Cameli Agency, Via Dino Angelini 127, west of the Cathedral.

The main **road** to Ascoli has for about 2000 years been the ancient Via Salaria from the Adriatic coast to Rome, now the SS4, which turns off the coast road at Porto d'Ascoli, a short way south of San Benedetto del Tronto. It is now flanked by a motorway-standard road until just west of Ascoli, which enables long-distance traffic to bypass the city.

## Tourist Information

The provincial tourist office is in the middle of **Ascoli** at Piazza del Popolo 1, ✆ (0736) 257288. There is also an office in **San Benedetto del Tronto**, Via delle Tamerici 5, ✆ (0735) 592237, and an information desk in summer in **Porto d'Ascoli**.

## Piazza del Popolo

Like Rome, Ascoli is built of travertine. Also like Rome, it has more traffic than it can handle, and consequently the first impression will be of a grey, sooty town that shows its age. It's all the more a wonder, then, that the central **Piazza del Popolo** can be so nonchalantly, so effortlessly one of the most beautiful squares in all Italy. This is no grand architectural ensemble, not monumental, nor even symmetrical. But the travertine paving shines almost like marble, and the low arcades that surround it give the square architectural unity and provide a fit setting for two fine buildings. The first, the 13th-century **Palazzo del Popolo**, was begun in the 1200s and redone in the late 16th century, with a façade by Ascoli's best-known artist, Cola dell'Amatrice. At the narrow end of the Piazza, the church of **San Francesco** (*c.* 1260) turns its back on the square—not really an insult, since the apse and transepts are the best part of the building, a classic, austere ascent of Gothic bays and towers under a low dome added in the late 15th century. Over the south door is a statue of Pope Julius II. The façade, around the corner, isn't much to look at; a strange, flat square of travertine decorated with a tiny plain rose window, like a wall with an electrical outlet on it. It does have a good sculpted portal, guarded by a pair of sarcastic-looking lions. Inside, there are only grand and simple Gothic vaults to look at. Outside, the southern end of the façade adjoins the **Loggia dei Mercanti**, built by the Wool Corporation—a typical medieval-style manufacturers' cooperative guild—in the early 1500s.

On the northern side, the old Franciscan cloister has become Ascoli's busy and colourful **market**. The street running in front of San Francesco is the centre of activity in Ascoli, the **Via del Trivio**; follow it northwards to Ascoli's oldest and prettiest neighbourhoods, on the cliffs above the River Tronto. Most of the city's surviving **towers** are here. Ascoli has as many of these medieval family-fortresses as San Gimignano in Tuscany, though they are not as well known; the tallest is the **Torre di Ercolani** on Via Soderini. Piazza Ventidio Basso, the medieval commercial centre, has two interesting churches: **SS. Vicenzo ed Anastasio**, with an unfinished Renaissance façade with Romanesque carvings around the portal, and the Gothic **San Pietro Martire**. The former is famous for a miraculous well in the crypt (a cure for leprosy). At the northern tip of Ascoli, a doughty single-arched Roman bridge, the 1st-century **Ponte di Solesta**, still carries traffic across to the northern suburbs without a creak or a groan. If you cross it, and walk along the riverbank to the east, you will see signs for the church of **Sant' Emidio della Grotta**, on the street of the same name, an elegant 1623 Baroque façade that closes off the front of a cave; here San Emidio, Ascoli's patron, was martyred, and the site became the city's earliest place of Christian worship.

All around the northern edge of Ascoli, the lovely valley of the Tronto makes a perfect picnic spot. Parts of Ascoli's walls, still visible in many places, still show the characteristic diamond-shaped brickwork of Roman construction, and at the western entrance to town, on Corso Mazzini, a Roman gate survives, the **Porta Gemina**.

## Piazza Arringo

Ascoli's **Cathedral**, dedicated to Sant'Emidio, is a 12th-century building similar to San Francesco, but with a new façade from the 1530s, also by Cola dell'Amatrice. In a chapel on the south side you can see the inevitable cucumber in an altarpiece by Carlo Crivelli, badly in need of restoration but still one of his finest works. The 10th-century octagonal **baptistry**, off to the side of the cathedral, stands resolutely in the middle of Ascoli's busiest street. Facing the cathedral, behind the fierce dragons in the twin Renaissance fountains, is the **Palazzo Comunale**, the Baroque façade of which hides the original 13th-century town hall. Inside in the **Pinacoteca** (*open April–Oct 9–1, 4.30–7, Mon–Fri; 9–1 Sat; 4–8 Sun; Nov–Mar 9–1 Mon–Sat; 9.30–12.30 Sun; adm*) there are works by Cola dell'Amatrice and other local artists, as well as by Simone de Magistris, Titian, Guido Reni, Van Dyck and, of course, Crivelli, and collections of ceramics and musical instruments. Across the square, the **Museo**

San Benedetto

**Archeologico** (*open 9am–1pm Tues–Fri; 3.30–5.30 Sat; 9.30–1.30 Sun*) has some good bronzes and Roman mosaics, and a plan of the city in Roman times.

A walk through the streets north of Piazza Arringo will take you past some of the palaces of medieval Ascoli, with many curious carvings and inscriptions on the old houses; one, the **Palazzo Bonaparte** on Via Bonaparte, was built by a prominent family of the 1500s that local legend claims as the ancestors of the famous Bonapartes. Napoleon himself said he didn't know if it was true or not. The **Palazzo Malaspina** on Corso Mazzini is one of the more elaborate buildings.

## The Ascoli Coast

As in the provinces further north, the coast is lined with small resorts, but the centre of activity is about 30 kilometers from Ascoli Piceno at **San Benedetto del Tronto**, one of the most popular resorts on the whole Adriatic riviera, which began life as a Benedictine monastery and is now a modern resort where you can find beaches, discos, restaurants and hotels galore. It also has a smarter, more chic ambience than most of the beach towns in this area. **Grottamare** is a slightly cheaper version, a little further up the coast.

*Where to Stay*

### Ascoli

One of Ascoli's attractions is that it is largely undiscovered, but that also means accommodation is scarce. One thoroughly pleasant hotel, on the edge of the old town of Ascoli near the cathedral, is the ★★★**Gioli**, Via Alcide De Gasperi 14, ✆ (0736) 255550 (moderate), with parking—a real blessing in this crowded town—and a small garden. ★★**Pavoni**, Via Navicella 135, ✆ (0736) 247501 (inexpensive), has ten simple but comfortable rooms. Ascoli also has a very individual, and very friendly, **youth hostel**—the **Ostello de' Longobardi**, Via Guiderocchi 5, ✆ (0736) 259007 (inexpensive) located in the Palazetto Longobardi, the tallest of the medieval towers on the northern edge of town.

## San Benedetto

San Benedetto has a vast choice of hotels, mostly in the moderate price range. There is the ★★★★**Ambassador** Via Cimarosa 5, ✆ (0735) 659443 (expensive), with a swimming pool, tennis courts, air-conditioning and sea views.

## Grottamare

The cheapest hotel in Grottamare is ★**Parco**, Lungomare della Repubblica 48, ✆ (0735) 631015 (inexpensive), with good doubles going for exceptionally low prices. San Benedetto, again, has a large selection of cheap hotels. One of the better ones is the ★★**Miami**, Viale Europa 40, ✆ (0735) 82115 (inexpensive).

---

*Eating Out*

## Ascoli

Forget about jousting and Crivelli madonnas—to most Italians Ascoli means one thing, *olivi ripieni.* These breaded and fried stuffed olives are wonderful, but one of the most tedious dishes imaginable to prepare, and you won't find them often outside Ascoli. The best place to try them is the **Cantina Al Pennile** on Via Spalvieri, ✆ (0736) 42504 (moderate), in the eastern suburbs, a long-time Ascoli institution, and a real bargain. Closer to the centre, olives and other specialities *all'Ascolana* await you at **Tornasacco**, Piazza del Popolo 36, off Piazza Arringo, ✆ (0736) 254151 (moderate), such as tagliatelle with lamb sauce, and very good local cheeses and charcuterie. (*Closed Fri.*)

**Kursal**, Corso Mazzini 221, ✆ (0736) 253140 (moderate), in the centre, has a variety of risotto dishes—with asparagus, salmon and caviare, or truffles—as well as other local specialities. Ascoli is also a fine town for inexpensive family-run trattorie. You can pick one out at random, or seek out **Da Giovanna** on Rua Marcolini, a block west of Piazza Arringo (inexpensive), a typical place where you can have an agreeably satisfying dinner for under L25,000.

## San Benedetto

In San Benedetto **Messer Chichibio**, Via Bezzecca 19, ✆ (0735) 4001 (moderate), is one of the few quality restaurants left in this tourist haven, offering fresh fish dishes and regional food at reasonable prices. Also a good place to stop for fish in San Benedetto without breaking the bank is **Al Gambero**, Via Galilei 3, ✆ (0735) 5184 (moderate). Try the *brodetto di San Benedetto* and *rigatoni al sugo di pesce.*

## Grottamare

In Grottamare the **Osteria dell'Arancio**, Piazza Pareti, ✆ (0735) 631059 (inexpensive) has excellent food, and tables outdoors.

# Abruzzo and Molise

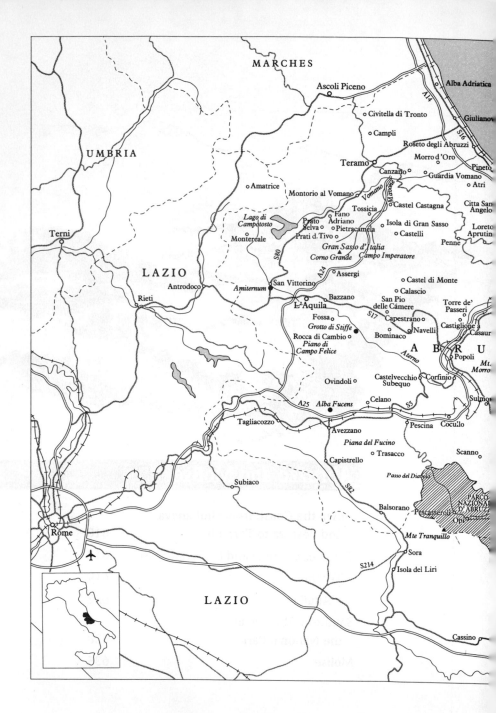

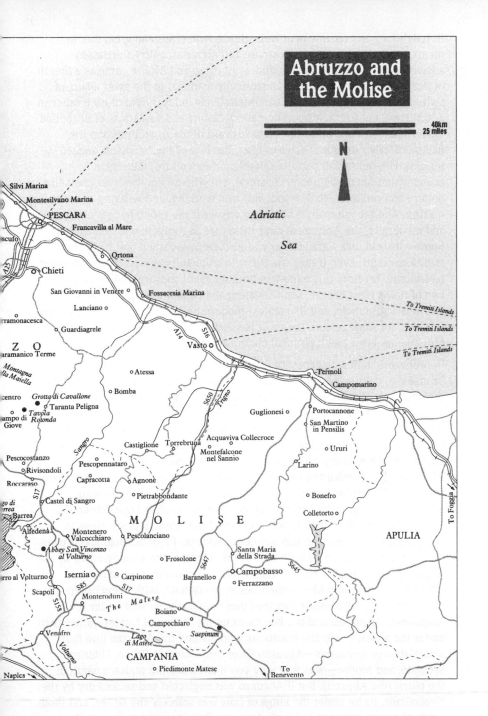

# Abruzzo and
# the Molise

40km
25 miles

N

Silvi Marina
Montesilvano Marina
**PESCARA**
Francavilla al Mare
scufo
Ortona

*Adriatic*

*Sea*

Chieti
San Giovanni in Venere
Lanciano
ramonacesca
Guardiagrele

To Tremiti Islands

Z O
aramanico Terme
Vasto

To Tremiti Islands

Montagna
lla Maiella
Atessa
Termoli

To Tremiti Islands

centro   Grotta di Cavallone
Bomba
Campomarino

Taranta Peligna
Tavola
ampo di   Rotonda
Giove

Guglionesi
Portocannone
San Martino
in Pensilis

Pescocostanzo
Castiglione   Torrebruna   Acquaviva Collecroce
Ururi

Rivisondoli
Pescopennataro
Montefalcone
nel Sannio

Roccaraso
Capracotta   Agnone
Larino

o di
rrea
Pietrabbondante
Bonefro

Barrea
Castel di Sangro
Colletorto

M   O   L   I   S   E

Alfedena
Montenero
Valcocchiaro
Pescolanciano

**APULIA**

Abbey San Vincenzo
al Volturno
Frosolone
Santa Maria
della Strada

rro al Volturno
Isernia
Carpinone   Baranello
Campobasso

Scapoli
Ferrazzano
Monteroduni

The   Matese

Boiano
Venafro
Campochiaro

Lago
di Matese
Saepinum

**CAMPANIA**
Piedimonte Matese

To
Benevento

Naples

In Italy's long and narrow peninsula, dense with cities and great monuments, artworks and ruins, autostrade and pizzerias, sultry sunglassed signorinas and Vespa-wrangling dudes, Abruzzo and Molise come as a breath of fresh air. Sparsely populated, historically marginal to the great affairs of state, these two regions (made administratively independent of each other in 1963) stand out for their majestic natural beauty and vast tracts of unspoiled wilderness that encompass the highest peaks of the Apennines and the habitat of Italy's unique species of bear. Because of the harsh and rugged terrain, with only small pockets suitable for agriculture, the region's economy has been traditionally pastoral, but with an emphasis on crafts like pottery and ceramics, gold, wood, and iron-working, and weaving and lace-making. And though many Abruzzo towns wear the proud badges of progress and modernity, the Abruzzese have little care to compete with Milan and Rome—instead, like Candide, they tend their own garden and hone their traditional skills, even if they use them to tailor suits as well as to embroider tablecloths. Yet from this mountain-bound land of country tradition came two of Italy's most urbane, sophisticated, and passionate poets, Ovid and Gabriele d'Annunzio, and its greatest modern philosopher, Benedetto Croce. It is also, for some reason, the most passionately enthusiastic about rugby— L'Aquila has been Italy's national champion several times.

In prehistoric times, the coast of Abruzzo formed part of a little-known Bronze Age culture, sometimes known as the Middle Adriatic, that produced the enigmatic Warrior in Chieti's archaeology museums. Culture was less advanced up in the hills, but the different Italic tribes who gathered here— the Praetutii, the Vestini, the Paeligni, and others, of whom almost nothing is known beyond their names—formed a formidable challenge to Roman expansion before being overwhelmed by the legions in the Social Wars of 91–82 BC. The Lombards gave what is now Abruzzo to the Duchy of Spoleto, and the Molise to the Duchy of Benevento. The Normans, under King William I of Sicily, picked up the region from the English Pope Adrian IV, and the Emperor Frederick II, who inherited the Norman possessions in Italy, made the Abruzzo an independent province. Frederick had grand plans for the region, which died with him as the Abruzzo was swallowed up by the Angevins, then kings of Naples. Like Umbria, Lazio and most of the Marches, Abruzzo and Molise then began to stagnate, with a few exceptions—the only difference being that these regions stagnated under the Aragonese, Spaniards, and the Bourbons on the throne of Naples, rather than under the popes. It was the Bourbons who divided the Abruzzo into four administrative territories—Abruzzo Citeriore, Ulteriore Primo, Ulteriore Secondo, and Molise—which is why you'll often see the region's name in the plural (the Abruzzi). But if Abruzzo was neglected and sucked dry by the Neapolitans, its lot under the kings of Italy was scarcely any better, and thousands of people migrated to North America, Britain, and other parts of

Europe—among them the father of Dante Gabriel Rossetti, and the ancestors of Madonna. Only after the Second World War, with the small boom of its compact seaside resorts, the development of small-scale industries and the building of new roads, financed by the Cassa per il Mezzogiorno, and the growing interest in the unsullied charms of its landscape, has the tide of emigration been stemmed.

Belted with mountains, Molise is an atavistic and introspective *banlleu*, designated its own region not so much for historical as for cultural reasons, though it formed a county of its own back in the 13th century, which is when its name, of unknown derivation, was first used. This rather charming patch of the Abruzzi that got away has its own customs and dialect—a direct result of its impossible geography, and the large settlements established there in the 15th and 16th century by Slavs and Albanians. Molise is one of the last regions in Italy where women still don their traditional costumes to please themselves and not the shutter-happy hordes.

## Itineraries

The coast, like that of the Marches, is mostly cold toast, though there are some fine sandy beaches and pretty hills here and there. **Pescara**, the region's biggest resort, has started to take on the international charter market with its recently expanded airport. Since the opening of the tunnel through the Gran Sasso, it's possible to drive by *autostrada* from Rome to the northern Abruzzo coast (A24) or Pescara (A25) in an hour and a half. **Termoli** in Molise is another big resort. Inland, mountains and magnificent scenery provide the main attractions, in the famous **Gran Sasso** and lesser-known **Maiella** and **Matese** ranges, and in the **National Park of the Abruzzo**—all paradises for hiking and climbing, and boasting the best downhill and cross-country skiing in Central Italy.

Of the towns, there is pretty, old **L'Aquila**, the regional capital (and best base for visiting the Gran Sasso) and the ceramics town of **Castelli** just under the Gran Sasso; medieval **Sulmona** and **Scanno** near the National Park; **Penne** and **Atri** near the coast, and medieval **Tagliacozzo** and the Roman ruins of **Alba Fucens** on the road to Rome. Molise has an exceptional Roman town, **Saepinum**, and lovely, unspoiled mountain villages like **Boiano** in the Matese, bell-casting **Agnone** and the highest town on the peninsula, **Capracotta**. Artistically, Abruzzo preserves enough **Romanesque monuments** to warm the cockles of any anachronistic heart, several of which are superlative: **San Giovanni in Venere** on the coast, **Santa Maria di Collemaggio** in L'Aquila, the two churches of **Bominaco**, and **San Clemente in Casauria**, on the Via Valeria.

## Food and Wines in Abruzzo and Molise

 Abruzzo pasta is sold all over Italy, but the great local speciality is *maccheroni alla chitarra*, so called because it is cut with an implement shaped a little like a guitar, which you will see on many restaurant menus. Inland Abruzzo is mountainous, and well suited to sheep rearing; lamb dishes (especially grilled or roasted) are popular here, while the local variant of *pecorino* cheese, made from sheep's milk, is often served with pasta. Pork also often features on Abruzzo menus.

Along the coast, of course, fish and seafood become important. Like all coastal areas of Italy, the Abruzzo has its own squid speciality—squid stuffed with anchovies, breadcrumbs and garlic. The food of the Molise uses many of the same basic ingredients as Abruzzo cooking, except that here you're likely to come across a lot more offal, and virtually everything tends to be flavoured with little, hot red peppers, called *diavolini* ('little devils') by the Molisani.

The local **wines**, white and red, make excellent accompaniments both to the local hearty stews and to the more delicate fish dishes of the coast. Montepulciano d'Abruzzo is the best-known wine of the area. It's a smooth, dry red, which, like many Italian wines, is best drunk within three years. Trebbiano is the best Abruzzo white, while in Molise the Biferno and Pentro wines both come in red, white or rosé. They're not quite as good as the Abruzzo wines, but are excellent with the simple local dishes.

## Down the Coast: from Giulianova and Pescara to Termoli

Small inexpensive seaside resorts, jam-packed with Italian families in the summer, and some beautiful artworks and churches of the Romanesque era are the main attractions along the Adriatic coast and its immediate hinterland. If you're not into Italian-style seaside holidays, though—where you pay for a beach chair, umbrella, and changing facilities in neat little rows, in order to have the privilege of watching everyone else watching every one else do the same thing—you may have difficulty finding undeveloped stretches of beach where you can just sit on the sands under the pines.

### *Getting Around*

Pescara's **airport** now has a weekly flight to and from London Gatwick, in addition to regular scheduled flights to Milan and charter connections with other European destinations. Also there used to be frequent ferries between Pescara and the coast of former Yugoslavia, but this service has been suspended indefinitely. During the summer season domestic **boats and hydrofoils** link Ortona to Vasto, and Vasto to points further south— Termoli, the Tremiti Islands and Rodi Garganico in Apulia. Termoli is the main port for the Tremiti (*see* p.1032, **Apulia**), with hydrofoils (40 minutes) and motorboats (1½ hours) daily.

Services by both train and bus are better and more frequent between the various towns along the coast than to just about any of the inland destinations in the region. There is a direct **rail** line from Rome to Chieti and Pescara, via Sulmona (4 hours), while the length of the coast is served by the north-south line between Bologna and Lecce. There are at least two direct ARPA **buses** a day from Rome to Chieti and Pescara, departing from the Piazza della Repubblica (2½ hours). ARPA, the Abruzzo bus company, also has lines inland from the coast to local destinations, most of them originating from Pescara.

The main coast **roads** are the SS16 and the A14. At Giulianova the SS80 turns off inland for Teramo, where it meets the A24 *autostrada* for L'Aquila and Rome. From Pescara another *autostrada*, the A25, also turns off the A14 for Rome, via Chieti and Avezzano. Alongside it for most of the way runs another of the ancient Roman consular roads, the Via Tiburtina/Via Valeria, now the SS5. Away from the main routes roads in the region tend to be circuitous and pretty slow.

---

### Tourist Information

The main tourist office in **Pescara** is at Via Fabrizi 173, ✆ (085) 4211707, ✉ 298246. There are also offices along the coast in **Giulianova**, Via Galilei 18, ✆ (085) 8003013; **Pineto**, at Viale G. D'Annunzio 123, ✆ (085) 9491745; **Chieti**, Via B. Spaventa 29, Palazzo INAIL, ✆ (0871) 65231, ✉ 65232; **Ortona**, Piazza Municipio, ✆ (085) 9063841; **Vasto**, Rotonda Lungomare Dalmazia, ✆ (0873) 801751; and **Termoli**, Via M. Bega, ✆ (0875) 706754, and in summer there are also additional offices in some other beach resorts.

---

## Giulianova, Roseto, and the Lower Vomano Valley

Between the Marches and Pescara, the Adriatic is lined with the same kind of small, Italian family beach resorts that began south of Ancona; places like Alba Adriatica, Giulianova, Roseto degli Abruzzi, Silvi, and Pineto all offer big beaches, modern hotels, amuseument arcades, and playgrounds. The most interesting of the resorts is Giulianova, with its medieval old town set back behind the beachfront sprawl. It was known in Roman times as *Castrum Novum*, and within the old walls you can see the town's best monument, the Romanesque **Santa Maria a Mare**, with unusual bas-reliefs on its façade, and the Renaissance **Cathedral**. The SS80 road turns inland here for Teramo (*see* below).

**Roseto degli Abruzzi**, another resort out of the same mould, lies near the mouth of the Vomano, one of the principal rivers coming down from the Gran Sasso, and has fine views up the valley to the naked limestone peaks of the Corno Grande . From Roseto you can head up the valley (on the SS150) to see two Romanesque gems. One is the 11th-century **San Clemente a Guardia Vomano** near Notaresco, whose builders made good use of Roman ruins lying about, fitting them in here and there like a jigsaw. The church houses an unusual and lovely 12th-century ciborium. The other is the church and abbey of **Santa Maria di Propezzano**, near Morro d'Oro, where the Abruzzese fondness for simple forms has created a handsome asymmetrical façade and a charming two-storey cloister. The church walls are embellished with 12th- and 13th-century frescoes, the cloister with scriptural scenes by the 17th-century Polish artist Sebastiano Majewski. A side road to the north leads to **Canzano**, locally known as the 'Castle of King Turkey' after a popular Abruzzese dish.

## Pineto and Atri

Pineto, another little resort, with a pretty pine-lined beach, has for its landmark the **Torre di Cerrano**, built by Charles V against the Ottoman threat, and now a merchant marine research station. Pineto is an easy starting point for visiting Atri (10km inland), by car or bus—though buses also reach Atri from Pescara and Teramo, if you're coming from further afield. Atri stands on the site of the ancient Sabine city and Roman colony of *Hatriaticum*, founded under the sign of the woodpecker, the bird of Mars. Atri disputes with Adria in the Veneto the honour of having lent its name to the Adriatic sea, a controversy that raged among ancient scholars like Pliny, Livy and Strabo; Atri tried to boost its claim by engraving the fact on its singular coins—the heaviest ever minted in western Europe, guaranteed to put a hole in the pocket of any toga.

The Roman sites that have been excavated in the town include the remains of some ancient baths, in the crypt of Atri's majestic 13th-century **cathedral**. The building itself has an austerely elegant square façade and matching campanile, and in the choir there are excellent quattrocento frescoes by Andrea de Litio, the Piero della Francesca of the Abruzzo, who gave his scenes on *The Life of the Virgin* surreal landscapes of knobby hills and imaginary towers. Other fine artworks include a 1503 tabernacle, and in the cathedral **museum** (*open 10–12, 4–8, daily; adm*) there are ivories, polyptychs and statues, majolicas by Grue of Castelli (see below, 'Teramo, L'Aquila and the Gran Sasso'), and some interesting mosaics and architectural fragments from the 9th-century church that preceded the cathedral. During the Middle Ages and Renaissance Atri was controlled, off and on, by the Acquaviva dukes, whose frowning 14th-century **Palazzo Ducale** (now the town hall and post office), contains a cheerful courtyard. The outskirts of Atri boast some strange geology: once-inhabited caves, eroded rock formations (*calanques*), and 'Danteesque pits'.

South of Pineto, the SS16bis heads inland from Montesilvano Marina, a satellite resort of Silvi, towards a clutch of interesting villages. In **Loreto Aprutino**, the church of **Santa Maria in Piano** contains 14th–15th-century frescoes—the *Life of St Thomas Aquinas* and one called *The Particular Judgement*, portraying Heaven's elect marching to the pearly gates on a bridge the width of a hair. Loreto also has the **Museo Civico della Civiltà Contadina** (*open 5–8pm Tues, Thurs, Sat, Sun*), a collection of agricultural implements, traditional craft work and rather naïve tableaux of peasant life. The pale-pink town of **Penne**, further west, was an important town of the Vestini, and today preserves a rare if eclectic urban harmony, its narrow winding streets dotted with Renaissance mansions. Its sights include the ancient crypt of the **cathedral**, itself destroyed in the Second World War and rebuilt, and the church of **Santa Maria in Colleromano**, a 15-minute walk from the centre, with good 14th–15th-century statues. In **Moscufo**, further south, **Santa Maria del Lago** merits a visit for its unique 12th-century pulpit adorned with painted reliefs.

## Pescara

Pescara is both Abruzzo's biggest resort and most prosperous town, a fishing port and provincial capital. In ancient times it was an important port, shared by several Italic tribes and later by the Romans, who made it the terminus of their Via Tibartina–Via Valeria (the modern SS5). In 1864 Gabriele D'Annunzio was born in the city, the son of a minor local merchant, and his birthplace or **Casa Natale** on Corso Manthonè (*open 9am–1pm Tues–Sat*), with its charming little courtyard, has been carefully preserved. Pescara also has an outdoor theatre built in D'Annunzio's honour, which is worth a visit each July when the Pescara Jazz Festival is held there. Another thing to see in the town is the regional folk museum, the **Museo delle Genti d'Abruzzo** (*open 9am–12 midday Tues–Sun; adm*), on Via delle

Caserme, a comprehensive and recently modernized collection, reopened in 1991, dedicated to everyday life and popular traditions in the Abruzzo over the ages.

Pescara's golden egg, though, is its 16km-long sandy beach, almost solid with hotels, cafés and fish restaurants between the Pescara River and Montesilvano; whatever old buildings it had were decimated in the fierce fighting that took place along the coast in the Second World War. Still, this is no Rimini; families bake together in the day, and stroll about eating ice cream in the evening. If you need some excitement, there are riding stables, go-kart tracks, tennis courts, fishing, and for some real thrills, the **Fish Museum** in Pescara's bustling fish market on Lungofiume Paolucci (*open April–Oct 8.30–1, 3.30–7, Mon–Sat; Nov–Mar 8.30am–1pm, Mon–Sat*).

## Chieti

For something a bit heavier than gills and beachballs, head up to **Chieti**, about 13km up the Pescara river. Another provincial capital, Chieti was the Roman *Theate Marrucinorum*, a name that its bishop, Pietro Carafa, made use of when founding the Theatine Order, in 1524. Bishop Carafa went on to become Paul IV, the most vicious and intolerant of popes, but it's no reflection on Chieti, that avoids such extremes.

The **Museo Nazionale Archeologico di Antichità** (*open April–Oct 9–1.30, 3.30–7.30, daily; Nov–Mar 9am–1.30pm daily; adm*), in the Villa Comunale, is Chieti's star attraction, and one of the region's most important museums. The main building is the chief repository of pre-Roman and Roman artworks unearthed in the Abruzzo, including the shapely *Warrior of Capestrano* from the 6th century BC, dressed like a Mexican bandit and accompanied by an as yet untranslated inscription—the language of the mysterious Middle Adriatic Bronze Age culture. There is a room of other items found in Bronze Age tombs, and others containing good Hellenistic and Roman sculptures, tombs, portraits, coins, jewellery, bronze figurines, vases and votive offerings, many of them discovered in Alba Fucens, in the Abruzzo National Park, and Amiternum, near L'Aquila (for both, *see* below). A neighbouring building concentrates on the documentation of material from Abruzzo's many Upper Palaeolithic caves, ancient ceramics, and artefacts from Italic necropolises, all more or less in chronological order.

Out of doors, Chieti retains a couple of traces of *Theate Marrucinorum*—the remains of three little temples on Via Spaventa, near the post office, while in the eastern residential quarters you can visit the **Terme Romane**, or baths, of which a mighty cistern is the most impressive feature. Best of all are the lovely views, stretching from the sea to the Gran Sasso and Maiella mountains. From Chieti the Via Valeria (which later becomes the Via Tiburtina), the *autostrada*, and the railway cross the peninsula to Rome.

## Ortona and Lanciano

South of Pescara, beyond the pleasant resort of **Francavilla al Mare**, lies Abruzzo's largest port, **Ortona**. Over the years Ortona has taken more than its share of damage, earthquakes, and major battle wounds, particularly in the Second World War; in the autumn of 1943, the Germans were well entrenched along a line north of the river Sangro, and thousands of lives were lost in the six-week Battle of the Sangro and Moro Rivers before they were rooted out and Ortona was taken at the end of December. There are two large British military cemeteries in the vicinity, one near the river Moro, about 3km south of Ortona, and the other just south of Torino di Sangro Marina, between Ortona and Vasto.

From Ortona, you can take a narrow-gauge local train for an inland loop (although admittedly the bus is much faster), taking in Guardiagrele and Lanciano on the way. **Guardiagrele** was a famous goldsmiths' centre in the Renaissance, the birthplace of the renowned Nicola da Guardiagrele, who produced some of the 15th century's finest works, including the silver crucifix in the treasure of the church of **Santa Maria Maggiore** (*open mid-July–Aug 10–12.30, 4–7.30, daily; at other times call ahead, © 0871 82117*). This church was also famed for its huge exterior fresco of St Christopher by Andrea de Lito, which was believed to bring good luck to any traveller who saw it. Its portico, however, was destroyed in 1943.

**Lanciano**, a medieval market town that once attracted merchants from all over the Mediterranean to its wool and cloth fairs, retains several grey stone monuments from its golden days: **Porta San Biagio**, the only medieval gate to survive; **Santa Maria Maggiore**, with a refined Gothic portal with stone stitches like an embroidery sampler, and, within, Lanciano's chief treasure, a crucifix by Nicola da Guardiagrele; and the **cathedral**, uniquely sited on a Roman bridge, which was restored in the 11th century to support the church. The church of **San Francesco** is a place of pilgrimage for its relics of an 8th-century miracle—some drops of blood and a little piece of human heart—when the bread and wine of the Mass supposedly really did turn into flesh and blood, to quiet the doubts of a sceptical monk. Above the church is the 11th-century fortress of the **Torri Montanare**, from which there are great views of the surrounding hills and the mountains further inland. Lanciano is also the starting point for one of the most spectacular drives in the Abruzzo—the SS84 to Roccaraso, near the Abruzzo National Park.

## San Giovanni in Venere and Vasto

Back on the coast, above the railway station of the small resort of **Fossacesia Marina**, stands one of Abruzzo's most remarkable monuments—**San Giovanni in Venere**. 'Venere' refers to the goddess Venus, over whose temple this church was erected; temples to Venus were very often placed in similar spots, high over the sea. Begun as early as the 8th century, the church was rebuilt in 1015, and converted into a Cistercian abbey in 1165, and there are several Apulian-Sicilian touches in the church—in the decoration of the narrow windows, the robust figures of the bas-reliefs, and the name and design of the magnificent *Portale della Luna*, the marble 'Portal of the Moon' (1230)—that suggest the not-always-orthodox influence of Emperor Frederick II. Be sure to walk around the church to see the beautiful apses; inside the ceiling is supported by cruciform piers, and there are some old if not very interesting frescoes dating back to the 12th century. The large crypt, entered from the aisles, contains ancient columns from the temple of Venus.

Further south, salty old **Vasto**, hometown of the father of Dante Gabriel and Christina Rossetti, stands on a low natural terrace above its beach and port, the former attracting large numbers of French as well as Italian tourists. Its narrow streets end at the weathered but very distinctive 13th-century **castle**, with a cylindrical tower. Vasto is proud of its local painter, Filippo Palizzi (1818–99), whose works can be seen in the church of **San Pietro**, and, when it reopens after restoration, in the local **Museo Civico**.

## Termoli

Crossing over the river Trigno, you enter Molise, which is, in the main, even more rural and unspoiled than Abruzzo, although this may not be immediately apparent from the busy beaches along the coast. **Termoli** gets top billing here, a bright little fishing town with a long sandy beach, palms and oleanders. The austerity of its pale stone buildings is akin to Apulia, if not to the sunny shores of North Africa.

The diva of the old town, or at least the part that survived a Turkish raid in 1566, is the 13th-century **cathedral**, its façade undulating with blind Apulian-style arcades, but it also boasts a **castle** and walls from the same period, both built by the Emperor Frederick II. After enjoying the view from the castle there's nothing more demanding to do than relax on the beach and try to decide which seafood restaurant to try in the evening. If Termoli's too crowded, there's another modest resort down the coast, **Campomarino**. A little further south, and the road enters Apulia (*see* p.1021).

### *Where to Stay*

Hotels in this area mostly date from the past couple of decades. In many cases their prices have skyrocketed in the last few years, but on the whole they are still a bargain compared to the rest of Italy. On the coast, moreover, the seafood is as tempting as the beach.

### Giulianova

The ★★★★**Gran Hotel Don Juan**, Lungomare Zara 97, ✆ (085) 8008341, ✉ 8004805 (expensive) is perhaps the smartest hotel on this stretch of coast, with contemporary Mediterranean styling. Located right on its own beach, it has a pool, tennis courts, and garden, and comfortable air-conditioned rooms, including some with wheelchair access. (*Closed Oct–April.*)

Also in Giulianova, the smaller ★★★**Promenade**, Lungomare Zara 119, ✆ (085) 8003338, ✉ 8005983 (moderate) has some of the same amenities without the style, or the air-conditioning, of the Don Juan. (*Closed Oct–mid-May.*)

### Pineto

Close to the beach and very pleasant is ★**Maria**, Via Morandi, Pineto, ✆ (085) 9492065 (inexpensive).

### Atri

There are plenty of budget-range hotels all along the coast, though many are pretty characterless. One slightly more interesting cheap alternative, in the historic centre of Atri, is the ★**San Francesco**, Corso Adriano 38, ✆ (085) 87473 (inexpensive).

## Montesilvano Marina

In Pescara's adjacent resort suburb of Montesilvano Marina there's the large, modern and comfortable ★★★★**Serena Majestic**, Viale Kennedy 12, ✆ (085) 83699, 📧 8369859 (moderate), on the beach and offering gardens, tennis courts and a pool.

★★**Piccolo Mondo**, Via Marinelli 86, ✆ (085) 4452647 (inexpensive) is one of the best-value hotels on the coast. With only 20 rooms, with and without baths, a garden, and its own beach facilities, it is a pleasant choice for a family holiday.

## Pescara

Pescara has by far the most hotels and restaurants on the coast, but be aware that tranquillity is one of its rarest commodities in the summer, and full pension is bound to be required in July and August. The top hotel, the ★★★★**Carlton**, Viale Riviera 35, ✆ (085) 373125, 📧 4213922 (moderate) is a very comfortable resort palace on the sea—though still in the moderate price range—with a private beach and gardens that almost absorb the racket, and you can also shut the window and bask in the quiet air-conditioning.

★★★**Bellariva**, Viale Riviera 213, ✆ (085) 4712641 (moderate) is a medium-sized, pleasant, and unpretentious place that's good for families. All its 33 rooms have private baths. In the centre of Pescara, but still only a short walk from the *Lungomare* and the beach, is the ★**Bristol**, Via Trento 122, ✆ (085) 374126 (inexpensive) which has good standard rooms with or without baths.

## Chieti

In Chieti, the best place both to stay and eat is ★★★★**Dangio'**, Strada Solferino 20, ✆ (0871) 347356, 📧 (0871) 346984 (moderate) which offers good, comfortable rooms, all with baths, and also has a gourmet restaurant, **La Regine**, attached (*see* below).

## Termoli

★★★★**Corona**, Via M. Milano 2, ✆/📧 (0875) 84041 (moderate) is a medium-sized traditional hotel located in the centre of town. All its rooms have private baths, minibar, and TVs, and there's a good restaurant with a Liberty-style dining room.

A good budget hotel is the nine-room ★★★**Cian**, Lungomare Colombo 48, ✆ (0875) 704436 (inexpensive) located on a rock above the coast, with fine views. All rooms have showers.

---

*Eating Out*

## Giulianova

Giulianova's—and indeed, all of the Abruzzo's—most celebrated seafood restaurant is **Beccaceci**, Via Zola 28, ✆ (085) 8003550 (expensive) where the menu features its own long-established seafood and pasta inventions, so good they've been copied elsewhere—try the *linguine alla giuliese*, or the squid stuffed with prawns. (*Open Sept–May, closed Tues.*) For traditional regional cuisine in Giulianova, **Il Gabbiano**, Via Marsala 20, ✆ (085) 8004930 (moderate) is one of the best restaurants in town, with outstanding pasta and seafood. (*Open Sept–May, closed Tues.*)

### Atri

In the old centre of Atri is **Alla Campana d'Oro**, Piazza Duomo 23, ✆ (085) 870177 (inexpensive) an enjoyable and good-value trattoria-pizzeria where the speciality is a sweet pizza with cream and liqueur. (*Closed Mon.*)

### Pescara

Since Pescara is a working town as well as a resort, it has good restaurants that are not attached to hotels. **Guerino**, Viale della Riviera 4, ✆ (085) 4212065 (expensive) is the city's best seafood choice, elegant and serving the tasty Adriatic speciality of fillets of John Dory with prosciutto, which go down especially well in fine weather out on the restaurant's seafront terrace. (*Open Sept–April, closed Tues.*) **Duilio**, Via Regina Margherita 11, ✆ (085) 378278 (moderate) is a pleasant place that features seafood in nearly every delicately prepared dish. (*Closed Sun evenings, Mon.*)

One of Pescara's best restaurants, though, **La Terrazza Verde**, Largo Madonna 6, ✆ (085) 413239 (moderate) doesn't serve fish at all (except on Fridays). In a panoramic setting with a beautiful garden terrace high up in the hills behind the city, it offers a menu that features delicious gnocchi, and duck, a popular dish in Abruzzo, prepared in a variety of ways. A good place to find hearty Abruzzese cooking in Pescara is the **Osteria Romana**, tucked away off Via Trento, ✆ (085) 295374 (inexpensive). It's very popular with locals, and the menu changes daily, though there's always at least one good fish choice. (*Closed Mon.*)

### Chieti

In Chieti the restaurant of the **Dangio'** hotel (for details, *see* above), **La Regine** (expensive) serves a famous *zuppa di cozze* (mussels) and many other dishes, all prepared with refinement. (*Closed Mon.*)

### San Giovanni in Venere

Next to the abbey of San Giovanni in Venere, **Priori**, Via San Giovanni in Venere 41, ✆ (0872) 608171, is located in a well-restored 18th-century villa, and serves lovely seafood, including fine lobster (prices vary substantially according to the type of fish you order).

### Lanciano

**Taverna Ranieri**, Via Luigi de Crecchio 42, ✆ (0872) 710602 (moderate) serves unusual, lightly prepared dishes, as well as rich Abruzzese desserts. (*Closed Mon.*)

## Guardiagrele

**Villa Majella**, Via Sette Dolori 30, ℘ (0871) 83202 (inexpensive). This imaginative newcomer to the Abruzzo restaurant scene is enthusiastically run and has excellent food, though full meals can still cost less than L30,000. (*Closed Mon.*)

## Vasto

Vasto is a bit of a gastronomic capital on the coast: for the best *risotto di pesce* around, head up to the old town to **Jeannot**, Loggia Amblingh, ℘ (0873) 365000 (moderate) an elegant place that also specializes in seafood for *secondi.* (*Closed Mon.*) Excellent sea and land food are both served at Vasto's **Lo Scudo**, Via Garibaldi 39, ℘ (0873) 2782 (moderate) followed by delicious desserts.

## Termoli

Termoli is endowed with an excellent restaurant, **Lo Squalo Blu**, Via De Gaspari 49, ℘ (0875) 83203 (moderate) where the fare includes exquisitely cooked (and also raw) molluscs and crustaceans as well as duck, followed by a delicious variety of local Molise cheeses. Five kilometres north from the centre of Termoli, on the Adriatica Highway, **Torre Saracena**, ℘ (0875) 3318 (moderate) is located in an ancient watchtower on the beach, and features the freshest of fish, prepared in some surprising ways. (*Closed Mon.*)

# Teramo, L'Aquila and the Gran Sasso

Two provincial capitals—metropolises by Abruzzo standards—Teramo and L'Aquila, stand on either side of the Gran Sasso range, each providing access to the peaks' trails and ski slopes. L'Aquila, which also reigns as regional capital, is an intriguing town in its own right, and for many visitors makes an ideal base for travelling around the rest of the Abruzzo.

### *Getting Around*

Teramo is fairly easily reached by **train**, on a spur from the coastal line at Giulianova. Trains also connect L'Aquila (with no great hurry or frequency) to Rieti in Lazio and Terni in Umbria, as well as to Pescara by way of Sulmona, the main junction for rail routes in the central Abruzzo.

**Buses** on both the *autostrada* and local roads also link Teramo quickly to the coast, to Ascoli Piceno, and to L'Aquila. L'Aquila itself is easily reached by bus from Rome, on either the ARPA or OGNIVIA lines, with 18 departures on weekdays (a 2-hour trip), and from Pescara (9 times a day, 2 hours by autostrada, otherwise 3 hours). To get to smaller towns and villages in the region you really need a car, or a lot of patience to wait for the regular, but infrequent, bus services from Teramo or L'Aquila. The bus station in L'Aquila is in the Piazza Battaglione Alpini, just below the Castello.

If you have a **car** the A24 *autostrada* will now take you quickly between the coast, Teramo and L'Aquila, via the Gran Sasso tunnel, and carries on to Rome. The alternative is the old main thoroughfare between the two towns, the much more scenic SS80, which runs across the top of the Gran Sasso through the Val di Vomano.

## Tourist Information

Away from the coast there are tourist offices only in the provincial capitals, at Teramo, Via del Castello 10, ✆ (0861) 244222, and L'Aquila, Piazza Santa Maria di Paganica 5, ✆ (0862) 410808, ✆ 65442. For information on sights, hiking, winter sports and other outdoor activities in the region's mountains you can also consult the **Centro Turistico di Gran Sasso**, Corso Vittorio Emanuele, L'Aquila, ✆ (0862) 22146, and the local office of the Club Alpino Italiano (*see* below, p.625).

## Teramo

From Giulianova the SS80 heads 20km inland to Teramo, midway between the coast and the Gran Sasso. Originally a Roman city, Teramo knew its happiest days in the 14th century under the Angevins, and even though it wears mostly 20th-century fashions today, it retains several fine monuments. The **cathedral** stands out with its remarkable Cosmati-decorated portal and Romanesque statues of saints; around them a miscellany of lions, collected from here and there, lend feline elegance to the façade, which is simple, square and ungabled, as is typical of the Abruzzo. The cathedral's Ghibelline (swallowtail) crenellations recall the days when Teramo was the fief of its bishop, who still possesses the title of 'Prince of Teramo', though he no longer makes much use of a special papal dispensation from more rough and ready days that allowed him to wear armour under his robes and keep his sword handy by the altar. The pretty campanile is from the 15th century; inside there is a silver altar frontal with 30 scenes from the Bible, a masterpiece by Nicola da Guardiagrele (1448), who also made the silver statues of Mary and Gabriel by the main door. The 15th-century polyptych is by the Venetian Jacobello del Fiore.

Near the cathedral lie the ruins of the **Roman Theatre** and, a short distance further on, the original cathedral, **Santa Maria Aprutiensis** (6th–12th century) which has recently been restored—its name reminds us of the Italic tribe of the Praetutii, who once lived here, and gave their name to *Aprutium* (and hence to Abruzzo). Santa Maria (also called Sant'Anna), which was built incorporating some bits of Roman columns and other ancient fragments, is Teramo's attic of odds and ends—Lombard carvings, a 6th-century triforium, and ancient angelic frescoes. Another block or so east is a well-preserved house built in the 14th century during the Angevin era, the **Casa dei Melatini**. In the Franciscan church of **Maria Santissima delle Grazie,** to the east by the Piazza della Libertà, is a painted wooden statue of the *Madonna and Child* by one of the Abruzzo's best sculptors, Silvestro dall'Aquila (15th century). More 15th-century Abruzzese works of art are on display in the **Museo Civico** (*open May–Sept 9.30am–7pm Tues–Sat; 9.30am–12.30pm Sun; Oct–April 9.30am –1.30pm Tues–Sat; 9.30am–12.30pm Sun; adm*), located in the Villa Comunale. If you're driving, take the road to the **Osservatorio Astrofisico** for good views of the Gran Sasso.

## The Virtù of Teramo

 Teramo has its own particular culinary speciality, a powerful stew called *virtù* that's customarily cooked at the beginning of May. Judging from its ingredients, it began as a way of using up whatever was left of the winter stocks and adding the first of the new season's goodies—traditionally, local women each contributed an ingredient. It's really a cross between a soup and a stew—a type of minestrone, in fact—based on a stock, to which are added twelve different kinds of dried peas, beans and lentils, along with celery, sausage and different bits and pieces of pig, such as trotters and ears, all well salted and seasoned with herbs.

## Around Teramo

Heading north from Teramo towards Ascoli Piceno on the SS81, the road passes **Camplì** just to the east, a small town with several good Romanesque and Gothic monuments. The rather formidable **Palazzo del Comune** was built in the 14th century, but much altered in 1520. The Romanesque church of **San Francesco** is a fine embodiment of the Abruzzese ideal that less is more; inside are some good 14th-century frescoes. Its former convent now houses an **Archaeology Museum** (*open June–Dec 8.30–1.30, 3–7.30, Tues–Sun; Jan–May 8.30am–1.30pm Tues–Sun* ), containing artefacts from the 6th–3rd century BC Italic necropolis at Campovalano, a kilometre away back on the main road. In Campovalano, the excavations aren't much to look at, but nearby there's the interesting ancient abbey and church of **San Pietro**, founded in the 8th century and rebuilt in the 13th century; the frescoed figures on the piers inside were designed to be part of the congregation. Part of an early Christian sarcophagus may be seen along the wall.

A few kilometres north of Camplì rises the superbly positioned Renaissance town of **Civitella del Tronto**, crowned by an impregnable castle that the Bourbons managed to hold right to the bitter end in 1861. First built around the year 1000, it has a travertine walled terrace a half-kilometre in length, lending Civitella its distinctive crew-cut skyline.

## Eastern Approaches to the Gran Sasso

South of Teramo the SS150 runs inland from Roseto degli Abruzzi along the Val di Vomano, and near the beginning of the *autostrada* divides into two arms embracing the Gran Sasso—the main road that joins up with the SS80 from Teramo and continues up the increasingly narrow Val di Vomano to the north, and another that follows the higher **Valle di Mavone** to the south. The latter (the SS491) is an excellent approach to the mountains, with the highest peak of the Apennines, the **Corno Grande** (2912m) looming ahead.

Several curiosities along the way offer tempting detours—near Castelcastagna there's **Santa Maria di Ronzano**, an ancient three-nave church embellished with frescoes dated 1181, among the finest examples of Lombard art in Central Italy; another attraction is panoramic views of the Corno Grande. Between Montorio al Vomano and Isola del Gran Sasso on the SS491 road you can take in the village of **Tossicia**, with a pretty medieval nucleus lying between two mountain streams; the tiny church of **Sant'Antonio Abate** has a grand 1471

Renaissance portal by the Venetian Antonio Lombardo. Works by one of Italy's best known *naif* painters, Annunziata Scipione, may be seen in nearby **Azzinano**.

The scenery is stunning as the road reaches **Isola del Gran Sasso**, a fine stone village and a good base for hikes up to the **Campo Imperatore** (see below, 'L'Aquila'); it has another Romanesque church, **San Giovanni ad Insulam**, as well as a very much more recent shrine to the modern patron saint of Abruzzo-Molise, San Gabriele dell'Addolorata, a young Franciscan monk from Assisi who died in the monastery here in 1862. His relics draw pilgrims by the bus-load, who are processed through a huge, disconcerting steel-and-concrete basilica designed in shopping mall moderne.

To the southeast, dramatically positioned at the foot of the great wall of Monte Camica, is **Castelli**, another good mountain base and a village worth visiting in its own right. Castelli is the great centre in the Abruzzo for ceramics, a local industry that achieved art and glory in the 17th-century workshops of the Grue and Gentilli families. The ceramic tradition is still continued in various workshops in the town, and in the August ceramics fair, where part of the fun is tossing reject plates over the river. Castelli's **Chiesa Madre** contains an unusual majolica *pala* by Francesco Grue, as well as 12th-century wooden statues. More of the Grues' work as well as that of other local craftsmen may be seen in the **Museo della Ceramica Abruzzese** (*open April–Sept 10–1, 3–7, daily; Oct–Mar 10am–1pm Tues–Sat; adm*). Most splendiferous of all, however, is the rural church of **San Donato**, which Carlo Levi has rightfully dubbed 'The Sistine Chapel of Italian Majolica' for its ceiling of a thousand ceramic tiles—the only ceiling like it in Italy, an impressive 33.4 square metres covered with a colourful patchwork of different folk motifs—plenty of rabbits, skulls, portraits, notices of various kinds, geometric patterns, and so on—and made in 1615–17. Also on the outskirts is the derelict Romanesque church of **San Salvatore**, with a charming medieval pulpit.

## The Upper Vomano Valley Towards L'Aquila

At **Montorio al Vomano** the SS150 joins the main SS80, the scenic road which, like the more efficent but less panoramic *autostrada*, links Teramo with L'Aquila. Montorio, topped by its grand but never-completed Spanish castle, has an eclectic church, the **Collegiata di**

Amiternum

**San Rocco**, with a façade that has been added to whenever funds were handy; within, the carved wooden Baroque altar and tapestries are the main attraction.

Further up the valley, the twin, blunt, snow-shrouded peaks of the Due Corni del Gran Sasso look over the shoulder of **Fano Adriano**, an old town that's now a small winter and summer resort, with skiing and hiking at **Pratoselva**. The village's name translates as 'Hadrian's Temple', although none of this remains; the 12th-century **San Pietro** is modern Fano's finest church, with a Renaissance façade from 1550. **Pietracamela**, even higher up in the lap of the Gran Sasso (1005m), is a base for hikes over the Sella dei Due Corni to the Campo Imperatore, and for skiing at the Gran Sasso's biggest resort, the **Prati di Tivo**, a fine lofty meadow of beech forests. During the peak season a helicopter takes expert skiers up to otherwise inaccessible runs.

The SS80 towards L'Aquila continues past the **Lago di Campotosto**, an irregular, man-made lake richly stocked with fish, and with the Gran Sasso for a striking backdrop, and then winds around the western flank of the Gran Sasso. About 10km before L'Aquila it comes to **Amiternum**, the ruins of a Sabine city mentioned in the *Aeneid*, and later a Roman colony that was the birthplace of the poet Sallust. A small theatre, amphitheatre, houses with mosaics and frescoes, and other relics were brought to light in 1978 (*open 9am–1.30pm daily; adm*). Nearby medieval **San Vittorino** has, underneath its 12th–16th century church of **San Michele**, something out of the ordinary in this part of the world: catacombs, although unlike the great ones in Rome, these have been embellished with 15th-century frescoes. A procession is held through them on the last Sunday of every May; at other times, you may have to ask at the church to be able to see the catacombs. The church itself is singularly split into two sections by a wall.

---

*Teramo* © *(0861–)* · **Where to Stay and Eat**

Teramo has a handful of hotels, the most attractive of which is the **★★★★Sporting**, Via De Gasperi 41, © 414723, @ 210285 (expensive) because of its pool and garden, although it's located on the outskirts of town. A cheap, basic but adequate choice is the **★Castello**, Via del Castello 62, © 247582 (inexpensive). Only three of its 17 rooms have private baths. Up in Prati di Tivo, above Pietracamela between Teramo and L'Aquila, the **★★★★Miramonti**, Via Prati di Tivo, © 959621, @ 959649 (moderate) , is a comfortable, modern, resort hotel, with a garden, pool, and tennis courts. All rooms have private baths. (*Open 20 Dec–10 April, 20 June–10 Sept only.*) Local specialities are served up throughout the year at **Il Duomo**, Via Stazio 9, © 241774 (expensive), with specialities such as *maccheroni alla chitarra* (so named because it is cut with an instrument shaped like a guitar), and fine meat dishes.

## L'Aquila

L'Aquila in Italian means 'the eagle', the symbol of empire, and it's not surprising to learn that the city was founded by Emperor Frederick II in 1240 as a bulwark against the Popes, who were trying to infringe on his territory. L'Aquila is one of the few cities in Italy of any importance not to have ancient precedents; instead, to populate his new town, Frederick relocated the inhabitants of surrounding castles and hamlets—99 of them in all, according to tradition, who supposedly each built their own church in the new town. But what made L'Aquila especially prosperous was its loyalty in 1423 to Queen Giovanna II, when the city was besieged for over a year by the Aragonese. The queen thanked the city for its steadfastness by granting it numerous privileges that helped it to become, for several centuries, the second city in the Kingdom of Naples, with its own coins, a chief wool and livestock market town, and a producer of silk and saffron. Its success attracted Adamo di Rottweil, a student of Gutenburg, who founded a printing press here in 1482, one of the first in Italy.

L'Aquila's good fortune made it cocky, and in 1529 it rose up against its rulers in Naples. The Spanish viceroy quickly put an end to its pretensions and punished the Aquilani by forcing them to pay for a huge new citadel to discourage any further revolts. Much of what the Spaniards didn't destroy in their reprisal fell in the earthquake of 1703. And yet, despite its vicissitudes, L'Aquila has managed to keep a considerable portion of its labyrinthine old quarter, its walls, and even some of its exceptional 13th-century monuments.

## A 99-headed Fountain

L'Aquila's most famous monument, the venerable **Fontana delle 99 Cannelle**, built in 1272, stands in a corner of the city walls near the Porta Rivera, not far from the railway station on the western side of the old city. The fountain's water flows through the mouths of 93 mouldering grotesque heads (and six unadorned spouts), each said to symbolize one of the 99 hamlets that were brought together to form the city of L'Aquila. The fountain has three sides (the one to the left is a more recent addition, built in the 16th century), and the whole is sheltered in a pretty pink-and-white chequered courtyard. While you're there, try to figure out how the two sundials work on the facade of the little church opposite.

From the fountain the Via San Jacopo ascends to join Via XX Settembre, the main entry-point into the city if you're approaching from Rome. If you follow Via XX Settembre straight into a small piazza laid out as a park, turn right at the next street and then left onto the Viale di Collemaggio to reach L'Aquila's greatest Romanesque church, **Santa Maria di Collemaggio**, founded in 1270 by the hermit Pietro Morrone. The church has one of the most sumptuous and attractive façades of any in Abruzzo, its three rounded portals decorated with spiral mouldings and niches for saints, who have mostly vanished. Above the portals runs a pretty ribbon-like frieze, and above that are three rose windows of different patterns, the large centre one in particular a masterpiece of the stonecarver's art. The elegant interior has been stripped of its centuries' accumulation of art and debris, leaving the fancy Renaissance tomb of Celestine V as its chief decoration, though the church also contains some 15th-century frescoes, on the left-hand side of the the nave, and some later ones by a pupil of Perugino on the right. The hermit Pietro Morrone, who founded the church, was an utterly holy man, but rather naïve, and in 1294, to his surprise, was crowned pope here by cardinals who hoped to use him as their instrument. After a few months it became evident to the powers in the Church that the new Pope Celestine V wasn't quite turning out the way they had hoped, and he was subtly 'encouraged' in Naples' Egg Castle (*see* p.944) to resign St Peter's throne—the only pope ever to do so voluntarily. Soon after his death, however, one of his successors canonized him, and here he rests as St Peter Celestine. He gained an additional, somewhat embarrassing claim to fame in 1988, when his saintly remains were stolen and held up to ransom, only for them to be returned without further ado when it became clear to the 'kidnappers' that Celestine would not win for them the amount they had hoped for. A privilege Celestine V granted the church during his brief office is a Holy Door, an uncommon feature, which is opened annually on 28 August for the faithful to pass through and receive the still-distributed papal indulgence.

## Around Piazza Duomo

From Via XX Settembre and the park, Corso Federico II leads into the Piazza Duomo. L'Aquila is one town where the **Cathedral** is the least interesting building, frequently shattered by earthquakes and now dressed in a dull neoclassical façade. On the south side of the square, however, next to the post office, is the much more original 18th-century Baroque façade of the **Santuario del Suffragio**, with opulent curves and a death's head above the entrance. The large piazza itself is also lively, having been L'Aquila's main market square ever since 1304, when Charles of Anjou granted the town the right to hold one here—you'll find produce and vegetables, and a variety of handicrafts on sale here daily from dawn to 1pm. The neighbourhood around the Piazza del Duomo is one of L'Aquila's most attractive. On Via Santa Giusta, the portal and rose window of the 13th-century church of **Santa Giusta** are worth a look, the rose window embellished with 12 droll figures, while all around it the streets are full of Baroque palaces. On Via Sassa, the church of **San Giuseppe** contains a 15th-century equestrian tomb by Ludovico d'Alemagna, while the **Palazzo Franchi**, at No.56, contains a lovely Renaissance courtyard with a double loggia.

From the Piazza Duomo, Corso Vittorio Emanuele leads to the **Quattro Cantoni**, the 'Four Corners', one of the city's main crossroads. To the left, on Corso Umberto, lies the Piazza del Palazzo, the palazzo in question being the **Palazzo di Giustizia**, from where Margherita of Austria, a daughter of Charles V born on the wrong side of the blanket, ruled as Governess of Abruzzo. The bell in the palace's tower sounds 99 strokes every day at dusk, in memory, once again, of the city's origins.

## San Bernardino

On the other side of the Quattro Cantoni, Via San Bernardino leads to the masterpiece of Abruzzese Renaissance art, the **Church of San Bernardino**. We are fortunate that its restoration and cleaning has recently been completed, and it now shines out magnificently among the more modern buildings around it. The great Franciscan revivalist preacher, San Bernardino da Siena, spent several years in the Franciscan convent in L'Aquila before he died, whereupon one of his chief disciples in Abruzzo, St John of Capestrano, founded this church as his memorial. Work began in 1452, but the perfectly balanced, elegant façade was only finished by Cola d'Amatrice in 1542. It is best seen from the bottom of the stair in front of the church; we are in Abruzzo, so the roof is gable-less. The 1703 earthquake smashed the vast interior, which was rebuilt à la Grand Baroque; the magnificent gilt wood ceiling, incorporating San Bernardino's IHS monogram, is by Ferdinando Mosca. San Bernardino's mausoleum and the *Tomb of Maria Periera* are both works by Silvestro d'Aquila, the master of Abruzzo sculpture and pupil of Donatello. The second chapel on the right contains a *pala* by Andrea della Robbia, grandson of the more famous Luca.

## The Castello

To the north the Corso Vittorio Emanuele runs out into the shady Parco del Castello and, above it, the grand, moated **Castello**, built in 1535 by Pier Luigi Sacrivà, a showpiece of military architecture unwillingly financed by the citizens of L'Aquila. From outside the main entrance there are fine views over L'Aquila and the surrounding mountains. Within the grand doorway, crowned by Charles V's two-headed eagle, the castle no longer contains Neapolitans and Spaniards, but the **Museo Nazionale d'Abruzzo** (*open April–Sept 9–2, 3–7.30, Tues–Sat; 9am–1pm Sun; Oct–Mar 9am–2pm Tues–Sat; 9am–1pm Sun; adm*), the region's finest, with a well arranged collection of archaeological treasures and artworks salvaged from abandoned local churches. The biggest exhibit is on the ground floor, to the right of the entrance: the *Elephas Meridionalis*, a mighty reconstructed prehistoric pachyderm, discovered by accident near L'Aquila in 1954. The ground floor also contains an archaeological section, with Roman portraits, statues, tombs, several fine tympanums, reliefs, tools, and so on; upstairs on the first floor is the medieval section, with a vast collection of religious art, among the highlights of which are its polychrome wooden statues, including a *St Sebastian* and a *Madonna and Child* by Silvestro d'Aquila, and a fine 15th-century panel painting of *St John of Capestrano*. There are many other fine triptychs, several showing Sienese-Umbrian influence. On the next floor up there are later works by Neapolitan painters like Mattia Preti and Andrea Vaccaro, as well as by Abruzzesi artists like Pompeo Cesari. The third and final floor contains 20th-century works, mainly by local artists, many of them depicting scenes of local life. Concerts are held regularly in the castle's auditorium.

## The Gran Sasso d'Italia

'The Big Rock of Italy' offers alpine grandeur only an hour on the motorway from Rome, and as such is an immensely popular ski and hiking resort. There are plans to designate the Gran Sasso a nature park, but until it becomes official, environmentalists and developers will continue to disagree on its future. If you plan to do any hiking, pick up a map, either from the tourist office or from the Italian Alpine Club (CAI) in L'Aquila, at Via XX Settembre 17, © (0862) 24342 (*open 7–8pm daily*).

To reach the Gran Sasso from L'Aquila, catch the bus from Corso Vittorio Emanuele to the Funicular at **Fonte Cerreto**, near **Assergi**, the village at the mouth of the Gran Sasso Tunnel—alternatively, if you have a car and the roads are clear, drive up the SS17bis by way of **Bazzano** (site of an interesting 12th-century church, **Santa Giusta**). Both the funicular and the road will take you to the **Campo Imperatore** (2126m), a beautiful, gentle upland basin, filled with flowers in the late spring and ski bunnies in the winter.

## Mussolini's Least Favourite Hotel

Near the upper funicular station stands the *Albergo di Campo Imperatore*, which once sheltered a real would-be emperor. After the ad hoc Italian government of Marshal Badoglio had deposed Mussolini and begun to seek peace with the Allies in 1943, there remained the delicate question of what to do with the former *Duce*. After being shuttled off to a Tyrrhenian island, he was brought here, to this hotel, at the time inaccessible by road—which set the stage for the SS Commando Otto Skorzeny's rescue on 12 September 1943. German paratroopers slipped in and out by flying in a Fieseler Storch—an aeroplane the size of the average bedroom—into which Skorzeny somehow managed to squeeze the portly Mussolini before escaping. Hitler then set up a new headquarters for his associate on Lake Garda, the capital of the ill-fated Italian Social Republic. This episode fooled the Allies, and has fooled historians for decades. Only recently has it been established that Skorzeny's exploit wasn't necessary at all—the Germans might have picked him up in a car. It was all a publicity stunt, part of Hitler's campaign to glorify the SS at the expense of regular German army, which was getting beaten ion all fronts, and whose political loyalty was already suspect.

Many of the trails through the Gran Sasso begin at the hotel, including one up past the Duca d'Abruzzi refuge to the **Corno Grande** (2912m)—a spectacular eight-hour walk. There are also three ski lifts in the Campo Imperatore, and four nearby at Monte Cristo, with runs suitable for both novice and expert. South of L'Aquila there is more good skiing as well as bobsledding at **Campo Felice**, above the picturesque village of **Rocca di Cambio**, the highest in Abruzzo at 1433m.

## From L'Aquila to Popoli

The SS17 runs southeast from L'Aquila along the southern flanks of the Gran Sasso, passing turn-offs—most of them on to the SS17bis for several rarely touristy villages, like **Calascio**, with its impressive ruined citadel 1,500m up, or further up still, **Castel del Monte**, with an interesting medieval core. On the other (southwestern) side of SS17, **Fossa** has 12th-century frescoes of the *Day of Judgement* in its church of **Santa Maria ad Cryptas** that are said to have inspired Dante.

Tiny **Bominaco** (near Caporciano) is the site of the most celebrated monuments in this corner of Abruzzo, two churches that formerly belonged to a fortified Benedictine Abbey. The monastery dates from some shadowy three-digit year; the lower church, **San Pellegrino**, is said to have been founded by Charlemagne, though it was rebuilt in 1263. The interior, rectangular in shape, with an ogival vault, is covered with an excellent example of the colourful, stylized frescoes of the period; some of the upper pictures represent a calendar of the months and the major feast days, while others represent scenes from the New Testament, saints, and geometrical patterns. The sanctuary is set apart from the nave by a marble transenna carved with a griffon with a cup, and another with a fearsome dragon—not ordinary subject matter for a Christian temple. The saint is buried under the sanctuary, and it is said that you can hear his heart beating through a hole next to the altar. The upper church, **Santa Maria Assunta**, has none of the ancient strangeness of San Pellegrino, but is a 12th-century gem, beautifully endowed with carved doors, windows, capitals, and a pulpit. Just to the west of Bominaco are the caves of the **Grotte di Stiffe**, (*guided tours on the hour, July–Aug 9am–3pm daily; Sept–June 9am–3pm Mon–Fri; 9am–1pm Sat, Sun; adm*) where about half a kilometre of illuminated walkway takes you along an underground river beneath an eerie assortment of stalactites.

From Navelli the road makes a dramatic writhing descent to Popoli (*see* below), on the Via Valeria and the Rome-Pescara *autostrada*, or you can turn eastwards to **Capestrano**, birthplace of San Bernardino's saintly follower, St John Capestrano (1386–1456); unlike its name-sake in California, however, it has to get by without any swallows.

---

*L'Aquila* ✆ *(0862–)*　　　　　　　　　　　　　　　　　　　　　　**Where to Stay**

As elsewhere in the Abruzzo, prices are notably low compared to the Italian norm, and even the more expensive hotels are at the lower end of their price ranges.

L'Aquila offers the widest choice of accommodation in the area. The ★★★**Castello**, across from the castle in Piazza Battaglione Alpini, ✆ 419147 (moderate) is an attractive, quite classy hotel of 44 rooms, all with baths. Down at the foot of town, near the fountain and train station, is ★★★**Le Cannelle**, Borgo Riviera, ✆ 41194 (moderate) which has 125 modern furnished rooms, all with baths, as well as a pool and tennis court. The ★★★**Sole**, Largo Silvestro dell'Aquila, ✆ 24041 (moderate) is a prettily decorated and peaceful hotel, with rooms with and without baths. The ★★**Italia**, Corso Vittorio Emanuele 79, ✆ 413566 (inexpensive) is centrally located and has reasonable rooms with and without baths. Unusually, it also has wheelchair access.

Up on the Gran Sasso, Mussolini's least favourite hotel, at the top of the cable car route, the hotel-refuge ★★★★**Albergo di Campo Imperatore**, ✆ 400002, ✆ 400004 (expensive) has recently reopened after extensive renovation, and now has very comfortable facilities. Another hotel that was used to hold Mussolini in 1943, the little ★★**La Villetta**, by the lower funicular station at Fonte Cerreto, ✆ 606171 (moderate) is now a pretty, friendly hotel that makes a good base for visiting the mountains.

---

*L'Aquila* ✆ *(0862–)*　　　　　　　　　　　　　　　　　　　　　　**Eating Out**

The region's eating establishments are more original than its hotels, especially if you come in May when the locals are cooking up pots of *virtù* (see above).

Traditional Abruzzese cuisine is a speciality at **Tre Marie**, Via Tre Marie 3, ✆ 413191 (expensive). The tasty regional *salumi*, dishes featuring truf-fles or saffron, and roast lamb and kid offered by the menu go down easily amid a charming décor of panelling and paintings. (*Closed Sun evenings, Mon; booking advisable.*) **Aquila da Remo**, Via San Flaviano 9, ✆ 22010 (moderate) has good solid cooking in a simple setting, providing you don't mind the sometimes less than charming service of the long-established family owners. Slightly cheaper, **Trattoria del Giaguaro**, Piazza Santa Maria Paganica 4, ✆ 24001 (moderate) is conveniently placed, and offers good local cuisine. (*Closed Mon evenings, Tues.*) A trattoria that's worth a detour—with wonderful homemade pasta—is **Dei Gemelli**, near the Duomo at Via Guelfaglione 27, ✆ 27574 (inexpen-sive; *closed Mon*). The town is also home to the eccentric but pretty restaurant **Minestra, Baccalà e Gnocchi**, Via Fortebraccio 49, which serves exactly (and only) what its name says.

For many people the highlight of the Abruzzo is its National Park, the second-largest in Italy and one of special interest for its rare fauna and flora. For mountain-lovers, there's also the Montagna della Maiella, a range nearly as impressive as the Gran Sasso and considerably less touristy. Man-made sights there are, too: *Alba Fucens*, Abruzzo's best archaeological sight, and intriguing old towns like Sulmona, Scanno, Pescocostanzo and Tagliacozzo.

## Getting Around

As a major **rail** junction, and with **bus** services to most of the area, Sulmona, located near Abruzzo's main east–west and north–south arteries, is the best base for exploring the works of nature and man. You should be aware, however, that although there are bus or train connections to most destinations in the region they are often very infrequent, so visitors have to be very well organized if they are depending on public transport. Buses run fairly frequently from L'Aquila to Avezzano, and from there to Pescasséroli, the administrative centre of the Abruzzo National Park. In the summer months there are direct buses every day between Pescasséroli and Rome.

The main **roads** through the region are, as on the coast, the east–west Via Tiburtina/Via Valeria (SS5) and the *autostrada* A25 from Pescara, which joins the A24 a little way past Avezzano. The main north–south road is the SS17 through Sulmona. There are several spectacular drives in the region: the SS5bis from L'Aquila to Celano, the SS84 from Lanciano to Roccaraso, and the SS83 from Pescina, near Celano, through the National Park.

## Tourist Information

There are tourist offices in **Tagliacozzo**, at Piazza Argoli, ✆ (0863) 610318; **Sulmona**, at Via Roma 21, ✆ (0864) 53276; and in the valleys south of Sulmona at **Scanno**, Piazza Santa Maria della Valle, ✆ (0864) 74317, and in the resorts of **Pescocostanzo**, **Rivisondoli** and **Roccaraso**. The office in **Pescasséroli**, at Via Piave, ✆ (0863) 910461, provides full information on hiking routes and other features of the Abruzzo National Park, and there are also information centres at various points around the park.

## The Via Valeria: Pescara to Rome

Inland from Chieti, the old Roman Via Valeria/Via Tiburtina accompanies the A25 up the Pescara valley. Near the village of **Torre de' Passeri**, more Romanesque awaits at **San Clemente in Casauria**, founded by Emperor Louis II, Charlemagne's great-grandson, in 871. The Cistercians took San Clemente over and rebuilt the church in the 12th century, endowing it with a magnificent three-arched porch and intricately carved capitals, and a stunning portal with well-executed reliefs that form a fitting frame for the bronze doors, with ornate panels of geometric patterns, which also date from the 12th century. The same sculptors of the porch and door may also have carved the baldacchino and pulpit in the

Romanesque interior; Louis II's original crypt was preserved in the reconstruction of the church, and may be reached by steps from the aisles.

**Popoli** stands at the confluence of the Aterno and the Sagittario, where they meet to form the River Pescara. The town's largest church, **San Francesco**, boasting an elegant Romanesque façade, is topped with statues and an unusual rose window. The 14th-century **Taverna Ducale**, decorated with a row of escutcheons, was not where Popoli's Cantelmi dukes drank, but where they stored the tithes from their subjects. It has survived in better shape than their ruined castle, looming over Popoli. **Corfinio**, next to the west, was called *Pentima* until renamed by Mussolini as part of his campaign to restore geographical names from antiquity—for here stood the Paeligni capital *Corfinium*, famous in history as the united headquarters of the rebellious Italic tribes in the Social Wars of the 1st century BC. They renamed the city *Italica*, the first time the name was used in history to signify a union of the peninsula's peoples, and hoped it would soon take over from Rome as capital. Its ruins are not much; there's a small archaeology museum in the convent of **Sant'Alessandro** (*for admission, inquire at the church*). The most important monument in Corfinio is the large 13th-century **Basilica di San Pelino**, with fine architectural details.

Near Corfinio, the SS17 leaves the Via Valeria to continue south to Sulmona (*see* below), while the *autostrada* veers south to avoid the scenic gorges of the Aterno river and the lofty pass at Forca Caruso. Back on the old Roman road, **Celano** is a pretty hilltown spread out beneath the skirts of its four-square **Piccolomini Castle**. Celano is best known as the birthplace of the Blessed Tommaso da Celano, a disciple of St Francis and his first biographer; he also composed the 'Dies Irae', the eerie medieval hymn of the dead most often heard these days in the finale of Berlioz' *Symphonie Fantastique*. Nearby you can visit the stunningly steep and narrow gorge, the **Gole di Celano**, or head north on the scenic SS5bis towards L'Aquila, by way of the mountain resort town of **Ovindoli** and Rocca di Cambio.

## Avezzano and Alba Fucens

The region south of Celano is known as the Marsica, after its ancient inhabitants, the Marsi, who lived on the shores of Lake Fucino. The modern capital of the Marsica, **Avezzano**, has little to commend it, having been toppled by an earthquake in 1915 and bombed during the Second World War. Its one surviving monument, the **Castello Orsini**, has a portal with a relief celebrating the Victory of Lepanto. In the **Palazzo Comunale** there's a small museum of inscriptions and architectural fragments from the cities of the Marsica (*open 10–1, 4–6, Mon–Sat*).

If the ancient Marsi were to return to their homeland today, they would be amazed to find their lake—once the largest in Central Italy—replaced by the fertile basin called the **Piana del Fucino**. But they would be the first to tell you that their *Lacus Fucinus* had an inadequate outlet and was prone to disastrous flooding. To drain it, Emperor Claudius in the year AD 54 ordered what became the greatest underground engineering work of antiquity—the 6km-long tunnel intended to spill the lake's waters into the River Liri. However, for all the amazing skill that went into the work, the tunnel didn't work very well and was eventually blocked up. In 1240 Frederick II tried to have it unblocked, but the project was not brought to a successful conclusion until 1875, when British, Italian, French and Swiss engineers finally drained the lake, reclaiming thousands of hectares. It's particularly hard to imagine what the Marsi would make of the huge satellite dishes of Italy's biggest telecommunications centre, looming out of the west end of the basin.

Of all the ancient cities of the Marsica, the only one to leave behind considerable traces is *Alba Fucens*, near the modern village of **Albe**, completely rebuilt after the 1915 earthquake, 8km from Avezzano. Buses run regularly to the site from Avezzano. Alba was founded as a Roman colony in 300 BC, to keep an eye on the area's tribes—as can be seen from its mighty walls. Ancient Alba occupies three hills, and its ruins intermingle with the ruins of medieval Alba. Much has been excavated, including the amphitheatre, the forum, the basilica, the weedy theatre, the baths, and a long section of the original Via Valeria. Near the amphitheatre is the well-preserved Romanesque church of **San Pietro**, adorned with Cosmati work.

Avezzano is a main departure point for the Abruzzo National Park (*see* below).

## Tagliacozzo

Named after Thalia, the Muse of Theatre, Tagliacozzo is a pretty, ancient town on the slopes of Monte Bove. Historically it is known for the battle that took place nearby on 12 August 1268, which ended the reign of the Swabians and heirs of Frederick II. As Dante described it, the Germans under Conradin were caught unawares and disarmed by the clever plans and intrigues of the Angevins, led by William di Villehardouin. The site of the battle is marked by the ruined church of **Santa Maria della Vittoria**, at Scurcola Marsicana, which is east of Tagliacozzo. In the town itself, the simple church of **San Francesco**, with a fine rose window and portal, contains the relics of Tommaso da Celano. Tagliacozzo's secular architecture is, however, more interesting than its churches, beginning with the 14th-century **Palazzo Ducale**, a grand building on a grand piazza; the loggia on the first floor shelters fine though damaged frescoes by Lorenzo da Viterbo. The quarter around the genteel old **Piazza dell'Obelisco**, with its Renaissance obelisk, has many picturesque houses and peeling palaces from the 14th and 15th centuries.

The town's theatrical connections do not lie only in its name, as near the Palazzo Ducale it has a small theatre, the **Teatro Thalia**, and an open-air festival of theatre, music and dance is held there each summer, usually in July. Buses run from Tagliacozzo to Tivoli and Rome, only a one-hour journey on the *autostrada*.

---

## Sulmona

South of the Via Valeria, Sulmona, beautifully located in a green basin surrounded by mountains, was the ancient capital of another obscure Italic tribe, the Paeligni. It is best remembered, though, as the birthplace of Ovid (43 BC–AD17 ), who is now commemorated with a large 20th-century statue in the Piazza XX Settembre. Much later Sulmona became a capital of its own province, created by Frederick II. As such it became a minor centre of learning and religion, home of the main abbey of the Celestine Order, and of Pietro Angeleri, who lived in the hermitage of Monte Morrone (and was also known as Pietro Morrone), before being brought down to L'Aquila to be crowned Pope Celestine V. In the early Renaissance its craftsmen were celebrated for their gold-work, although since then they have learned a sweeter skill—what the Italians call *confetti*.

## Confetti Nuts

 To Italians *confetti* means the sweets covered in sugar of all kinds of colours that are given out to the guests at a wedding. They have been a speciality of the Abruzzo since the Middle Ages, and, though the original *confetti* were sugared almonds, today you can buy them with a variety of fillings that include chocolate or hazelnuts. The acknowledged capital of *confetti*-making is Sulmona, where there any number of shops in the historic centre that sell ornate confectionery concoctions made up to look like flowers or gold and silver ornaments, and have lavish window displays to match. William di Carlo, which has its factory and showroom near the station, reckons that they are the oldest *confetti* manufacturer in the town, but you'll soon find that all of them make some claim to fame.

The main street, Corso Ovidio, holds Sulmona's loveliest monument, the church and palace of **Santa Maria Annunziata**, a Gothic and Renaissance ensemble first begun in 1320. Although the three portals on the palace's façade were done at different periods, the result is as harmonically sweet as *confetti*: here is a finely carved, floridly Gothic left portal, crowned by a statue of St Michael, while the middle portal is pure symmetrical Renaissance in form; the comparatively plain portal on the right was the last built, in 1522. Figures of Doctors of the Church and saints stand sentry along the façade, while above them runs an intricate ribbon frieze, and above that there are three lacy Gothic windows. The first floor contains a small **museum** (*open 8.30am–12.30pm Tues–Sat; 9.30am–12.30pm Sun*) where you can see some of the work of the goldsmiths of Renaissance Sulmona. The church's sombre Baroque façade was rebuilt after the 1703 earthquake, yet it still complements the adjacent palace. Concerts are held in the palace courtyard each summer.

Running through the centre of Sulmona is an unusual Gothic **aqueduct** (built in 1256), which supplied water to the towns and its mills; a good place to see it is the huge Piazza Garibaldi, site of the 1474 **Fontana del Vecchio**, so-called because of the bust of a jovial old man on top. Across the road from the fountain stands the lovely carved Romanesque portal of **San Francesco della Scarpa** ('with shoes' because here the Franciscans wore shoes instead of sandals), but it's a portal and nothing more, the rest having tumbled in one of Sulmona's earthquakes. Outside town, towards Monte Morrone, are some Roman ruins (steps, platform, a mosaic pavement and a stretch of road), part of a **Temple of Hercules**, that locals have for centuries referred to as 'Ovid's villa', though any connection with the poet has now been disproved.

## Around Sulmona

There are several picturesque hill towns in the vicinity of Sulmona, like **Pacentro**, 9km to the east, its lanes winding around the battlemented towers of the ruined Cantelmo Castle. Beyond Pacentro the road, the SS487, heads up in a serious way into the rugged Maiella mountains, and a few winding kilometres further east, near Passo San Leonardo, reaches a T-junction where you can turn north towards **Caramanico Terme** (a pretty hill town and sulphur-water spa) and the Via Valeria, or south past the **Campo di Giove**, a winter sports centre with a cable car up the slopes of a mountain called the Round Table (2404m), towards the dramatic SS84 road and the Sangro valley. This area is well endowed with winter and mountain sports facilities, in **Pescocostanzo, Rivisondoli**, and especially **Roccoraso**, further south on the SS17 (all of them stops on the Sulmona-Isernia railway). Pescocostanzo, which once owed allegiance to Vittorio Colonna, poet and friend of Michelangelo, is a charming little town, formerly more famous for its lace than as a ski resort, and ornamented with the lovely **Collegiata di Santa Maria del Colle**, its interior adorned with excellent wood carvings, the oldest ones dating back to the 11th century.

On the SS84 between Roccaraso and Lanciano (and accessible by bus from either end), is **Taranta Peligna**, which has a new cable car that rises up to what must be the most spectacular cave in Central Italy, the **Grotta del Cavallone** (1425m) (*open April–Sept; guided visits last an hour and a half; to make sure it's open, call ahead, © (0872) 910236*), used as a setting in D'Annunzio's play *La figlia di Jorio*. The cave's name, the 'Big Horse' comes from the profile carved by nature on the wall at the grandiose entrance of the grotto: other rooms are adorned with stone flowers or lace, alabaster streaks that remind Italians of ham (in the 'Sala del Prosciutto'), and fairies, while the 'Sala del Pantheon' is full of curious stalagmite monsters and deities.

South of Roccaraso near the western entrance into the National Park is **Castel di Sangro**, badly damaged in the Second World War, though still preserving its ruined citadel, reached by a steep mule path. The modern *municipio* contains a collection of ancient statues and bronzes found in the vicinity (*open 8–2, 3–6, Mon–Fri*), and in the upper part of the town stands the fine Baroque church of **Santa Maria Assunta**, which retains its Renaissance plan and paintings by De Matteis and Vaccaro. The SS17 continues south through Isernia towards Naples; for centuries this was the kingdom's busy 'Via degli Abruzzi'.

To the west of Sulmona lies **Cocullo**, famous for its bizarre 'Procession of Serpents', held on the first Thursday of every May. Live snakes are draped over a statue of Cocullo's patron, San Domenico, as well as over the more inspired locals, who thus form a procession through the streets, uncannily coiling and writhing. There is a story that St Dominic rid the area of poisonous snakes, but scholars have a sneaking suspicion that the festival is a living folk memory of the cult of the goddess Angizia, the enchantress of snakes.

## Scanno

From Cocullo (or Anversa degli Abruzzi) the SS479 road ascends the lovely **Valle del Sagittario**, passing through the steep Gorge of the Sagittario and alongside the pretty trout-filled Lago di Scanno. Perched high above the lake, the village of **Scanno** is one of the most popular destinations in the Abruzzo, a picturesque place that fascinated 18th-century travellers who wondered at its customs and costumes, more reminiscent of Asia Minor than Italy. Even today the women of Scanno still sometimes wear their traditional dress, with their turban-like head-dresses, as much an attraction as the beautiful old village itself. All the women of the town put on traditional dress during Scanno's main festival in mid-August, which celebrates the very unusual traditional local marriage customs. On a different note, a classical music festival is also held during the same month, with concerts in the town's squares. For magnificent views of the sunset over the lake and mountains, drive up the zigzagging road from here to **Frattura**, or take the chair lift up to Monte Rotondo, Scanno's small winter resort.

## The Abruzzo National Park

West of Cocullo lies **Pescina**, the birthplace of Cardinal Mazarin, and the SS83 road for the **Abruzzo National Park**. Founded in 1923 and enlarged in 1976, the park is Italy's second largest, covering 400 square kilometres of some of the loveliest scenery in the Apennine range, a little paradise of flowery meadows and forests of beech, pine, oak, ash, maple, and yew, that are the last home of *ursus arctos marsicanus*, the brown Abruzzo bear, and the Abruzzo chamois; here too are Apennine lynxes, boars, wolves, badgers, red squirrels, eagles, falcons, woodpeckers, owls, and many unusual species of songbirds, all protected by law from the enthusiastic Italian hunter. After passing through the beautiful **Passo del Diavolo**, the road reaches **Pescassèroli**, the largest village within the confines of the park. The main Park Visitors' Centre is

here, where you can pick up trail maps and information on where to find the flora and fauna, although some of the fauna is easiest to see near the centre, in the small **zoo and park museum** (*open 10–12, 3–6, daily; adm*). If you want to camp in the park, apply to the Ufficio di Zona del Parco, Via Consultore 1, ☎ (0863) 91955, or stay in one of the nearby campsites listed below. Pescassèroli was the birthplace of Benedetto Croce (1866–1952), the greatest Italian philosopher of the past two centuries, and is a pleasant town in its own right. A pleasant excursion from here even for non-committed hikers is the not very difficult two-hour walk up to the **Valico di Monte Tranquillo**. In the height of summer and in winter you can also ride Pescassèroli's cable car up to the summit of Monte Vitelle. Further south, **Opi** and **Barrea** are other pretty villages in the park, near the Lago di Barrea and the Camosciara, where most of the park's graceful chamois live.

Just outside of the park the fine scenery continues around the village of **Alfedena**, built on the site of the ancient Samnite town of *Aufidena*—across the river from the modern village you can see the ancient walls and necropolis. A 3km dirt track also leads up from here to the lake of Montagna Spaccata. The SS83, meanwhile, follows the river Sangro to the main SS17, the crossroads for Sulmona and Molise.

### Where to Stay

This area is reasonably well served with hotels, but many are seasonal, open only in the summer and winter. Although not very attractive, Avezzano has the largest choice of hotels and fairly nondescript restaurants, many of them along the SS5.

## Pescassèroli

The **★★★★Hotel del Parco**, ℰ (0863) 912745, ⊜ 912749 (expensive) is the grandest hotel in the area, enjoying a beautiful setting, with a garden and heated pool as well to keep its guests contented. (*Open Christmas–Mar, 15 June–Sept.*)

A good choice here in the National Park is 'the penguin', **★★★Il Pinguino**, VIII Traversa Collacchi, ℰ (0863) 912580, ⊜ 910449 (inexpensive), with rooms that are far too snug for a real Antarctican, but still at very accessible prices.

## Tagliacozzo

One nice hotel open all year is the **★★★Miramonti**, ℰ (0863) 6581, ⊜ 6582 (moderate), with 21 comfortable rooms all with baths, garden and tennis courts.

## Sulmona

Sulmona's largest and most comfortable hotel is the **★★★Europa Park**, on SS17 just north of town, ℰ (0864) 251260, ⊜ 251317 (moderate). All the rooms have private baths (and some have disabled facilities), and there's also a tennis court, bar, and a good restaurant on the premises.

The **★Italia**, Piazza San Tommaso 3, ℰ (0864) 52308 (inexpensive) is a cheap but nevertheless atmospheric and comfortable hotel, with pleasant rooms with or without baths.

## Rivisondoli

**★★★Cinquemiglia**, up at Piano Cinquemiglia, SS17 Km 134, ℰ (0864) 69281 (moderate) is a largish, cosy resort hotel, with a pool and tennis courts. (*Open all year.*)

## Roccaroso

In nearby Roccaraso, the most developed resort in the area, the **★★★Excelsior**, Via Roma 28, ℰ (0864) 602351 (moderate) , is one of the classier choices, with well-equipped rooms all fitted with private baths. (*Open mid-Dec–mid-Jan, April–Aug.*)

The **★★★Motel AGIP**, SS17, ℰ (0864) 62443, ⊜ (0864) 10030 (moderate) is even more comfortable, if only really convenient for drivers. It does, though, have an excellent restaurant as well.

## Scanno

**★★★Del Lago**, ℰ/⊜ (0864) 74343 (moderate), is a small, tranquil hotel with a garden and a lovely setting on the lake. There are private baths in all rooms. (*Open mid-Dec–mid-Jan, Mar–Oct.*)

Scanno is slightly more expensive than the surrounding area, but the **★★Margherita**, Via D. Tanturri 100, ℰ (0864) 74353 (inexpensive) is a good-value hotel with simple rooms, all with baths.

## Avezzano

A good, reasonably priced restaurant in Avezzano is the **Aquila**, Corso della Libertà 26, ✆ (0863) 3413152 (moderate), with local specialities, including particularly fine pasta and lamb dishes. (*Closed Mon.*)

## Sulmona

Sulmona's best restaurant, **Italia** on Piazza XX Settembre, ✆ (0864) 33070 (moderate) offers interesting and finely prepared variations on traditional local cuisine, with delicious homemade pasta and lamb with rosemary. The **Stella** on Via Mazaro, ✆ (0864) 52653, is a *trattoria* specializing in minestrone and, among its pasta dishes, *penne*. In the same town, **Al Quadrivio**, Via Mazzara 38, is an excellent place to sample local specialities at very reasonable prices.

## Scanno

**Gli Archetti**, Via Silla 8, ✆ (0864) 74645 (moderate) is the top restaurant, serving dishes made from home-grown ingredients; try the grilled lamb with pears if it's on the menu. The ambience is all refined old elegance, but the bill is still likely to be on the borders of the inexpensive price range.

# Molise

Isolated, mountainous, and even more sparsely populated than Abruzzo, Molise is one of the least-known regions of Italy. It belonged to the tenacious Samnites of old, and Italians still sometimes call it *Sanno*; at some point in the murky early Middle Ages it became the county of Molise, and then like the other *Abruzzi* it was joined to the Kingdom of Naples. In the 14th and 15th centuries Slav and Albanian refugees from the Turkish invasion found new homes in Molise; their languages contributed to the great variety of regional dialects, and there are still cases today of neighbouring villages unable to understand one another.

Although an improved network of roads and even a *superstrada* has ended most of Molise's isolation, the rugged, mountainous terrain makes the going slow no matter how you travel. But it's just as well, for it is a region to drink in slowly, to sip instead of gulp down. This is very much backwoods Italy; the biggest events in the region are village rodeos, and the most famous attractions are ancient remains. However, unlike so much of Italy, the constant glare of flashbulbs has not made Molise fade into a picture of itself; you will not recognize much, if any, of it. In its freshness it is one of Italy's last frontiers.

### *Getting Around*

Isernia is linked by **train** with Naples, Rome, Sulmona, Pescara, and Campobasso; other trains from Naples to Campobasso pass through Benevento, then continue on to the coast at Termoli, via Larino. **Buses—**

from Naples, Rome, Cassino and Vasto to Campobasso and Isernia—are on the whole much quicker, and less aggravating. The bus service for outlying villages is fair, and invariably departs from the provincial capitals of Isernia or Campobasso.

Apart from the SS16 and A14 along the coast, the region has just three main roads: the SS650 inland from San Salvo, near Vasto, to Isernia; the SS647 and SS647dB., also inland between Termoli and Campobasso, and the SS17/SS87, which runs across the south of the region through Isernia.

---

### Tourist Information

Apart from one on the coast in **Termoli** (see above), there are tourist offices only in the provincial capitals, in **Isernia** at Via Farinacci 9, ✆ (0865) 3992, and in **Campobasso** at Piazza della Vittoria 14, ✆ (0874) 415662.

---

## Isernia

Heading down the SS17 from Sulmona and Castel di Sangro you enter Italy's newest province, Pentria (or Isernia), created in 1970. The dismal little capital **Isernia** was the Samnite town of *Aesernium*, where the Italic tribes either first united against Rome, or fled after the Romans captured their capital of Corfinium in the Social Wars—at any rate Isernia modestly puts forth a claim of being 'the first capital of Italy', although even that boast pales before the fame of its onions (fêted every 28–29 June) and its lace. Over the centuries Isernia has been severely damaged by earthquakes—the last of them only in 1984—and was also badly bombed in 1943, so there is little to see of its old town, other than the 14th-century **Fontana Fraterna**, which has somehow managed to survive. It was built using bits of Roman masonry, and bears an inscription that reads *AE PONT*—which led to a popular belief that Aesernium gave the world Pontius Pilate.

Today, though, the town's main attraction is a Palaeolithic village that was accidently uncovered in 1979, during the building of a new main road. At one million years old this is the most ancient evidence of human life yet discovered in Europe. There are no human remains on the site, but a variety of other relics such as weapons, fireplaces, face paint and so on, and plenty of remains of the huge ancestors of the elephant, deer, rhinoceros, bison, bear, and hippopotamus. They are well presented, accompanied by reconstructions of life in the prehistoric villages and, very unusually, multi-lingual explanations and computerized displays, in the **Museo Nazionale della Pentria ed Isernia** (*open 9am–1pm Tues–Sun*), on Piazza Santa Maria.

## North of Isernia

The *comuni* in the high altitudes north of Isernia have been compared to the isolated villages of Tibet, each perched on its lonely hilltop. Highest in all the Apennines at 1421m is **Capracotta**, a village immersed in woods and mountain pastures, often buried under banks of snow in the winter, so much so that there are tales of the residents having to use their upper-floor windows as doors—and so a fitting place for the first Italian ski club, founded in 1914. Nearby **Agnone**, the 'Athens of the Samnites', has been known for the past thousand years for its bells. One factory, the **Marinelli Pontifical Foundry**, still survives, the oldest in

Italy, supplier to the Vatican and nearly every country in the world. Bells in the foundry are still made according to the ancient formula; while the molten bronze is being poured into the mould a priest is on hand to chant the medieval litanies that have always guaranteed a successful, clear-toned bell. You can see the foundry at work and visit its small museum on any weekday, at Via d'Onofrio 14, though with admirable reserve the company does not allow the taking of any photos. Besides bells, Agnone is known for its coppersmiths, whose workshops line the main streets of town, selling every imaginable utensil; also be sure to note the fine Romanesque portal on the cathedral of **Sant'Emidio**.

South of Agnone, **Pietrabbondante** has some of the most extensive Samnite ruins yet discovered. The site, excavated in the 19th century, was a religious sanctuary, and includes a well-preserved Greek theatre and a couple of temples, all built in the 2nd century BC. The ruins are located in a green field filled with flowers, making them especially attractive. **Pescolanciano**, on the way back towards Isernia, is dominated by its picturesque **Castello d'Alessandro**, founded in the 13th century and topped in later years by a pretty arcade. Even closer to Isernia (8km) is the old village and 14th-century castle of **Carpinone**.

## West of Isernia

Spaghetti Western fans in Molise in the middle of August can whoop it up at an Italian 'rodeo' at **Montenero Val Cocchiara**, northwest of Isernia; as usual in Italy, food is as much of an attraction as the events, and in this case it's barbeques. In the pre-cowboy days of the Lombards, the Benedictines built the abbey of **San Vincenzo al Volturno** to the south near **Castel San Vicenzo**, and close to a small lake of the same name. Often altered, damaged and rebuilt, the abbey was last restored in the 1950s; the nearby **Crypt of San Lorenzo** managed to escape the assorted disasters that befell the abbey, and preserves some interesting 11th-century frescoes. Note, however, that the abbey is rarely open, so it's advisable to check with the Isernia tourist office before going out there.

The most impressive castle in Molise, **Cerro al Volturno**, was originally built by the Benedictines in the 10th century, but was rebuilt at the end of the 15th century. Appearing to grow organically out of a massive rock over the town, the castle is inaccessible except by a narrow path; in the 1920s the supporting cement bulwarks on the hill were added, all impressive enough to star on a L200 stamp. There aren't many souvenirs to buy in Cerro, but further south in **Scapoli**, at the end of July, you can visit the bagpipe (*zampogna*) display-market, and choose your goat-bellied instrument from among the olive and cherry-wood models on display. The bagpipe has a long (and still living) tradition among the shepherds of the Molise; shepherds still take them down to play in the streets of Rome and Naples for Christmas. The market also features pipes from Scotland, Sardinia, Hungary and other regions and countries.

On the road south towards Campania, **Venafro** was made famous by Horace for its olive oil. Although now more than a little run down, it is also one of the most interesting towns in Molise. Cyclopean walls run along the road leading into town, and in the Middle Ages the Roman **amphitheatre** was turned into an oval piazza, in which the arcades have been incorporated into the front doors of the houses. Portable remains of Roman *Venafrum* are now in the **Museo Nazionale** (*open 9am–1pm Tues–Sun; adm*) in the former convent of Santa

Chiara. Of the churches the most interesting are the 15th-century **cathedral** and the **Annunziata**, a church that has preserved its Romanesque interior if not exterior, and contains in one of its chapels a series of 15th-century English alabasters. Venafro's derelict **castle** (14th–16th centuries) and the 15th-century fortified ducal **Palazzo Caracciolo** are waiting for funds to be restored and opened to the public.

---

© *(0865–)*  **Where to Stay**

The few hotels that grace Molise tend to be either recently built and sterile, or old and worn-in at the heels—but their prices are low.

## Isernia

★★★★**La Tequila** is just outside the centre at San Lazzaro 69, ©/@ 412345 (moderate). All its rooms have baths and TV, and there's a pool surrounded by young trees.

## Capracotta

Up in the mountains, the ★**Montecampo**, Corso da Santa Lucia, © 949128 (inexpensive) is a basic but pleasant 13-room hotel in an out-of-the-way setting.

## Agnone

★★★**Sammartino**, Largo P. Micca 44, © 78239 (inexpensive) is a medium-sized, comfortable hotel with baths in all rooms, and also an excellent restaurant (*see* below). Another solid choice in the same town, both for sleeping and eating, is the ★★★**San Salvador**, Viale Marconi 28, © 78591 (inexpensive) which likewise possesses a fine traditional restaurant (*see* below).

---

© *(0865–)*  **Eating Out**

If their hotels tend to be new and bland, the Molisani at table are a solidly old-fashioned and often spicy crew, favouring dishes like stuffed lamb heads (*testine d'agnello*), kid tripe, a kind of hillbilly pizza topped with greens and boiled pork (*pizza con le foglie*), smelly mountain cheese, and polenta with red beans, olive oil, hot peppers, and garlic (*polenta maritata*).

## Isernia

You can dip your fork into these and tamer dishes at the **Taverna Maresca**, Corso Marcelli 186, © 3976 (moderate), a fine old restaurant in the old quarter.

## Agnone

There are two more excellent moderate-price restaurants offering local cuisine to the north in Agnone, in the hotels **Sammartino**, where you can dine on the succulent lamb of Molise prepared in traditional and innovative styles (*restaurant closed Mon, Oct*), and the **San Salvador**, which has some of the best traditional food in the region—try their pasta (particularly the *spaghetti alla San Salvador*) and the meat and fish specialities (for details of both hotels, *see* above).

#### Venafro

There is nowhere to stay in Venafro, but there is a good restaurant, **Il Quadrifoglio**, Via Flacco 6, ℂ 909886 (moderate) with a surprise—the freshest of seafood (Venafro is a stop for the seafood trucks from the Adriatic to Rome), as well as lamb and other Molise dishes.

## The Matese

South of Isernia and Campobasso is a lovely curve of snow-swept peaks and forests called the Matese, of which the southern half lies in Campania. Few Italians, much less foreigners, penetrate its quiet villages, where women in traditional dress sit out in the streets over their round *tomboli* making delicate lace. The lakes of the Matese are full of waterfowl, its streams brim with fish, and its forests are home to squirrels, wildcats, wolves, and other creatures seldom seen in the rest of Italy; its glens produce *porcini* mushrooms by the ton.

The scenery is spectacular, especially around the largest of the district's several lakes, the **Lago del Matese**, with its resort of **Piedimonte Matese**, both in Campania. The road back to Molise (the SS158dir) runs through the Passo del Prete Morto ('dead priest pass'); the northern slopes of the Matese are equally lovely, with a wonderful quality of light that gives **Campochiaro** its name. This medieval village still retains its walls and tower; recently a huge Samnite temple complex was unearthed in the vicinity. Just to the west is the lofty little town of **Boiano**, the former Samnite stronghold of *Bovianum*. The upper part of town, called *Città*, retains Megalithic-era walls and the ruins of a Lombard castle. The views are great, but become fabulous if you're up to a rather stiff two-hour climb to the summit of **Monte la Gallinola** (1923m)—on a clear day you can see as far as the Bay of Naples. In winter, there's skiing nearby at **Campitello Matese**, southwest of Boiano in the very centre of the Matese mountains.

### Saepinum

In 295 BC, the Samnite city of *Saipins* was laid waste by the Romans. The few inhabitants who were neither killed nor taken into slavery went on to found a new town for themselves, a Roman colony called *Saepinum*. As a quiet provincial town, it managed to avoid most of history until the 9th century, when the Saracens destroyed it. Later in the Middle Ages, when times were surer, the site was resettled, only higher up (now modern **Sepino**), and old Saepinum was slowly covered by the dust of the ages, and quarried here and there for its stone. Dilettantes began excavating the ancient town in the 18th century, and nowadays groups of archaeologists come to uncover more of it every summer. To get there by public transport, take a bus from Campobasso to Sepino or, better still, Altilia, next to the site itself—though you'll find that the latter service is very infrequent.

The charm of Saepinum comes partly from its remote and lovely setting in the Matese; its isolation has preserved it well, making it one of the most evocative Roman sites in all Italy—the best example there is of a small provincial city. In Saepinum there is very little marble, no plush villas as in Pompeii and Heraculaneum, but neither are there any modern intrusions beyond a few farmhouses, making use of a column here, an architrave there; it is an ancient

Anytown in the empire, in its layout and amenities a miniature version of nearly every colony founded by Rome.

The defensive **walls** encompassing Saepinum, built in the diamond patterns of *opus reticulatum*, are over 1km long and defended by 27 bastions—the best preserved of which, over 11m high, stands near the theatre. Four gates lead into the central axis of the city; from the car park at Porta di Terravecchia you pass through the walls on the *cardus maximus*. This street retains its original paving stones along the stretch closest to the heart of the town, as you approach the central crossroads with the *decumanus*, the main street of every Roman town. Here, as usual, you'll find the **Forum** and civic buildings. The slender Ionic columns on one corner belonged to the **Basilica**, the main meeting place and courts of a Roman city, with its podium for orators and lawyers. Just off it is an octagonal atrium, surrounded by the foundations of shop counters—Saepinum's central market. Across from the forum itself on the *decumanus* are, first, on the corner, the elections office (*Comitium*), the *Curia* (town hall), a temple, believed to have been dedicated to the cult of an emperor, and then the *Terme* (baths) and the well-preserved Griffon fountain.

The *decumanus* continues past a house called the **Casa dell'Impluvio Sannitico**, its atrium containing a fountain and Samnite-style *impluvium* (container to collect rain water) with an inscription in Oscan, the pre-Roman language of the region, to the Porta di Benevento, marked by a figure of Mars. Beyond the gate stands the funeral monument, with its inscriptions lauding the virtues of the deceased Caius Ennius Marso, one of the town's leading citizens. A **museum** near here (*open 9am–2pm Tues–Sat; 9am–1pm Sun; adm*) documents the excavations of the site.

In the opposite direction, the *decumanus* passes through Saepinum's main commercial district, lined with shops, taverns, and private residences. It ends at the most complete surviving gate, the impressive **Porta Boiano**, with steps to the top which you can ascend for an excellent view of the excavations. Figures of prisoners (or slaves?) stand on plinths on either side, and its inscription informs us that Tiberius and his brother Drusas paid for the fortifications. Beyond this gate is a monumental **mausoleum** of Numisio Ligure. Along the walls there are remains of a private bath complex; beyond is the well-preserved **theatre**, with a crescent of medieval farmhouses that were built into the upper cavea; in its heyday the theatre could seat 3,000 spectators. The stage is now occupied by another farmhouse, which contains another interesting **museum** of items such as funerary sculpture found during the digs, as well as plans and maps (*same hours as above*).

## Campobasso

The regional capital from the days of the County of Molise, Campobasso was once best known for its engraved cutlery—its knives, scissors and razors are still highly regarded in Italy today—and wolfmen, but is now better known as the site of the National School for Carabinieri (which has managed to keep the wolfmen under control) and its June procession, the *Sagra dei Misteri di Corpus Domini*. In the 17th century, Campobasso's old Corpus Domini processions were banned by the bishop for making spectators laugh instead of increasing their faith; and they stayed banned until 1740, when a local sculptor named Di

Zinno came up with the idea of building metal contraptions to support real people in the soaring Baroque postures of the angels and saints he carved for churches. The bishop accepted these as faith-augmenters, and indeed they are, for it seems as if faith alone is holding up the bevy of six-year-old angels and saints suspended on the 13 floats or 'Mysteries' that are solemnly paraded through the streets to the accompaniment of the local bands.

Apart from the festival Campobasso doesn't have much to offer except Carabinieri cadets. The older, upper part of town has a couple of Romanesque churches, **San Giorgio** and **San Leonardo**, and the **Castello Monforte**, on top. A long-planned museum of Samnite antiquities is yet to be opened. From Campobasso, however, buses head out to some of the scenic villages nearby, like **Ferrazzano** with a castle and belvedere, and **Baranello**, an ancient town, the heir of the Samnite *Vairanum*.

Baranello has a little **Museo Civico** (*call in advance to find out when it will be open,* ✆ *(0874) 460406*) containing Samnite artefacts, 17th- and 18th-century Neapolitan kitsch paintings, Chinese porcelains, and other objets d'art donated by a collector. Nearby, on the river Biferno, you can watch a still-functioning waterwheel grind some of the grains that go into Molise's folksy cuisine. The most striking church in the area is the hilltop Romanesque **Santa Maria della Strada**, just off the SS87 road north to Larino.

## Larino

Between Campobasso and Termoli on the coast the main attraction is the small town of **Larino**, the Samnite *Larinum*, prettily located amid hills of olive groves. The most important monument here is the **Cathedral**, built in 1319 and embellished with an ornate portal in its Apulian-style façade; the nearby church of **San Francesco** has some good 18th-century frescoes. Near the Cathedral take a look too inside the museum of the **Palazzo Comunale** (*open 9am–1pm Mon–Fri*), the local repository of art and artefacts, the most important of which is the *Ara Frentana*, a cylindrical Roman altar. It used to stand by the road leading to the train station, in the area that was once the centre of the ancient Samnite town.

Near the station there are also the remains of a large **amphitheatre** and some fragments of the ancient town walls. In late May Larino holds a 10-day folklore festival, centred on the celebration of the *Sagra di San Pardo*, with a procession of finely decorated Roman-style ox carts.

## Albanian and Slavic Villages

In the district around Larino there are several diehard communities of Albanians and Slavs, who still maintain their language, traditions, and festivals. **Ururi**, west of Larino, is an Albanian town, as is **Portocannone**, which conserves in its Romanesque parish church an icon of the *Madonna of Constantinople*, brought over by settlers, as well as a baronial palace. The most interesting of the Slavic villages is **Acquaviva Collecroce**, where a dialect called 'Stokavo' is spoken. In the campanile of the church of **Santa Maria Esther** there is a medieval curiosity: a stone carved with the palindromic magic square of the words SATOR TENET AREPO, an ancient charm.

## Boiano

Boiano has a few hotels, among them ★★★**Mary**, Via Barcellona 21, © 778375 (inexpensive), with unpretentious rooms, nearly all of which have baths.

## Campochiaro

The little ★**La Stella del Matese**, Via Roma 16, © 789122 (inexpensive) is a good, clean, simple hotel with very low prices.

## Campobasso

There are several hotels in Campobasso, led by the ★★★★**Hotel Roxy**, Piazza Savoia 7, © 411542 (moderate), a plush, newly modernized place. Its rooms are air-conditioned, and fitted out with minibars, private baths and TV—and there's even a discotheque for wild Campobassani nights. The ★★★**Hotel Skanderberg**, Via Novelli 3, © 413341 (moderate) is another good choice, offering modern comforts with touches of Molise tradition. All rooms have baths. The ★★**Hotel Tricolore**, Via San Giovanni in Golfo 10, © 63190 (inexpensive) is a little family-run hotel in one of the prettier parts of town, with rooms with or without baths.

## Larino

There is not much in the way of hotels or restaurants in Larino, but the ★★★**Campitelli**, Via Mazzini 16 (near the amphitheatre), © 822666 (inexpensive) is modern and functional, and has a good restaurant.

Campobasso has several good restaurants, all in the moderate range, beginning with **Aciniello**, Via Torino 4, © 94001 , which is simple but genuine in its atmosphere and cuisine, and offers dishes like pizza rustica and rabbit. (*Closed Tues, Aug.*) **Il Potestà**, Via Persichillo 3, © 311101, serves good traditional dishes and some that are bizarre, like *penne alla vodka*, which sane people should avoid. (*Closed Sun, Aug.*) The good wine list includes some of the finest local Molise labels.

One of the best restaurants in the region is outside Campobasso in the pretty village of Ferrazzano—**Da Emilio**, Piazza Spensieri 21, © 978376 (moderate) where you can dine out on the terrace on meals with a delightful Emilia-Romagna touch. Try the tasty kid cooked over embers, and especially the pasta and desserts.

# Tuscany

No region could be more essentially Italian. Its Renaissance culture and art became Italy's in common, and its dialect, as refined by Dante, cast a hundred others into the shadows to become the Italian language. Nevertheless, Tuscany seems to stand a bit aloof from the rest of the nation; it keeps its own counsels, never changes its ways, and faces the world with a Mona Lisa smile that has proved irresistible to northerners since the days of Shelley and Browning. Today, Britons, Dutchmen, Germans, and Americans jostle each year for the privilege of paying two or three million lire for a month in a classic Tuscan farmhouse, with a view over a charmed, civilized landscape of cypresses and parasol pines, orderly rows of vines and olives, and a chapel on the hill with a quattrocento fresco. In Florence and the other cities, they stand in queues like refugees, waiting to enter the churches and museums that are the shrines of Tuscan art.

For a province that has contributed so much to western civilization since the Middle Ages, Tuscany's career remains slightly mysterious. Some have attempted to credit its cultural prominence to an inheritance from the ancient Etruscans, but most of modern Tuscany was never more than provincial throughout Etruscan and Roman times. Out of the Dark Ages, inexplicably, new centres of learning and art appeared, first in Pisa and Florence, and then in a dozen other towns, inaugurating a cultural Renaissance that really began as early as the 1100s.

As abruptly as it began, this brilliant age was extinguished in the 16th century, but it left behind a new province of Europe, finished, solid, and well -formed. Tuscany can be excused for a little complacency. Though prosperous and enlightened, fully a part of modern Italy today, the region for centuries has seemed perfectly content to let the currents of culture and innovation flow elsewhere. There's no sense in painting when anything new would have to hang next to Da Vincis and Botticellis, no incentive to build in a city full of churches and palaces by the medieval masters. After the surprising wave of bad taste that brought the Renaissance to a close, Tuscany was shamed into an introspectiveness and cultural conservatism of almost Chinese proportions.

Of course these centuries, during which Tuscany has quietly cultivated its own garden, have not been without some advantages. Its cities and their art treasures have been preserved with loving care. So has the countryside; if anything the last few hundred years have emphasized the frugal, hardworking side of the Tuscan character, the side that longs for the rural life, counts its pennies, and finds tripe with chickpeas a perfectly satisfying repast. All this at times makes a striking contrast with the motorways, the new industry around the cities, and the hordes of tourists descending on Florence, Pisa, and Siena.

## Tuscan Itineraries

If you are coming for the first time, you will probably be chiefly interested in the three great art cities: **Pisa**, with its Field of Miracles and memories of its exotic career as an early medieval power; **Siena**, where the Middle Ages begin to look disconcertingly attractive, and most of all, the Renaissance city of **Florence**. If there's time for more, you may consider picture-pretty **Lucca**, **Pistoia**, **Arezzo**, or some of the wonderful hill towns in the south, places like **San Gimignano** or **Montepulciano**, which offer small doses of the best of Tuscan culture in a lovely setting.

There's little to see on Tuscany's lonely coastline, and if you're passing through on the way to Rome or Umbria the inland routes will be the best bet. All the approaches over the Apennines from Emilia-Romagna offer delightful scenic drives—and plenty of curves and climbs. The best is the SS12 from Modena over to Lucca (161km), with a branch off on the SS66 to Pistoia (147km) and Florence. From Genoa, if you have the time, consider the roundabout routes through the Apuan Alps and Serchio valley to Lucca (107km from La Spezia, as opposed to 76km on the coastal *autostrada*).

To continue on to Rome, head towards San Gimignano (SS2 from Florence, 39km; or SS67 then SS429 from Pisa, 83km), and continue the 22km to Siena, which will give you time for a detour at San Gimignano or Colle di Val d'Elsa. After Siena, stay on the SS2 (the old Roman Via Cassia) for another 32km to San Quirico d'Orcia and the turning east onto the SS146, a pleasant 35km drive through the southern hills that passes the interesting towns of Pienza and Montepulciano before meeting the A1 *autostrada* to Orvieto and Rome.

## Florence

Venice, they say, moves one to dream a bit; Rome to contemplate the endless panorama of popes and Caesars; Naples convinces you that all is vanity. Florence (Firenze), on the other hand, a town long famed for good common sense and healthy scepticism, is different. It will not tempt you to easy conclusions; it is as romantic as a reference library. Florence, they say, moves one to *argue*.

So let's begin. Most writers have always assumed a certain point of view. You may think Florence is a museum city, they'll tell you, but you'll be wrong. Florence on the contrary is a thriving, progressive town that refuses to live in the past, insisting on earning its own way in the 20th century. Once it made Galileo's telescope, and today it still exports precision optical instruments. In the 1400s, it led Europe in fashion as well as art; today its busy seamstresses on back streets do much of the work for the designers in Milan. This argument is nice, but unfortunately untrue; despite its noise, ice cream, light industry, and horrendous traffic, Florence *is* a museum city, and if you don't care to look at pictures, you'd do better just to stay on the train.

But what a museum town it is! Florence's collections easily surpass those of any other Italian city, and just from the odd bits in the back rooms its curators are able to mount a score of blockbuster special exhibitions each year. Most impressive of all is the fact that nearly all the art in them was made by the Florentines themselves, testimony to the city's position during two centuries as the great innovator of western culture.

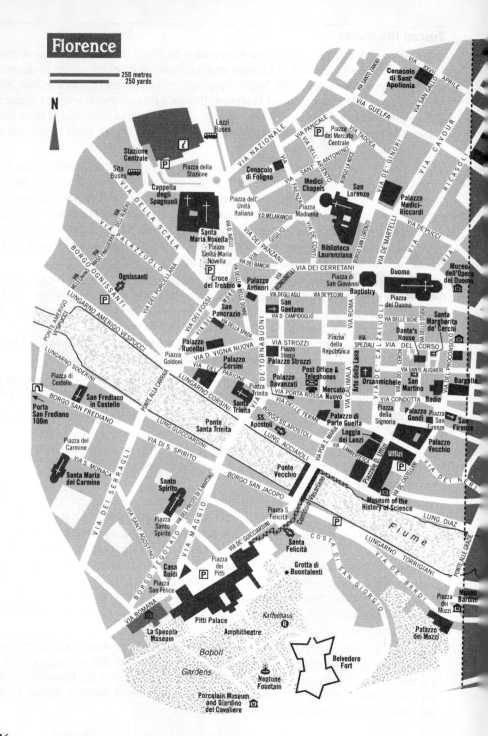

# Florence

250 metres
250 yards

N

Lazzi Buses

Stazione Centrale

Sita Buses

Piazza della Stazione

Cappella degli Spagnuoli

Santa Maria Novella

Piazza Santa Maria Novella

VIA DELLA SCALA

VIA DEL MELARANCIO

BORGO OGNISSANTI

VIA DEL PORCELLANA

VIA DELLA SPADA

Ognissanti

Croce del Trebbio

Palazzo Antinori

LUNGARNO AMERIGO VESPUCCI

PONTE AMERIGO VESPUCCI

LUNGARNO SODERINI

San Pancrazio

Palazzo Rucellai

Piazza Goldoni

Palazzo Corsini

VIA D. VIGNA NUOVA

Piazza di Cestello

San Frediano in Castello

Porta San Frediano 100m

BORGO SAN FREDIANO

PONTE ALLA CARRAIA

LUNGARNO CORSINI

Santa Trinita

VIA DEL PARIONE

Piazza S. Trinita

Palazzo Davanzati

Ponte Santa Trinita

SS. Apostoli

BORGO SS. APOSTOLI

VIA DE' SERRAGLI

VIA S. MONACA

VIA S. AGOSTINO

Santa Maria del Carmine

Piazza del Carmine

VIA DI S. SPIRITO

LUNG. GUICCIARDINI

PONTE ALLA CARRAIA

Santo Spirito

Piazza Santo Spirito

VIA MAGGIO

VIA DEL PRESTO DI S. MARTINO

BORGO SAN JACOPO

Ponte Vecchio

Piazza S. Felicità

Corridoio Vasariano

VIA DE' GUICCIARDINI

Santa Felicità

VIA DE' BARDI

BORGO TEGOLAIO

Casa Guidi

Piazza San Felice

VIA ROMANA

Piazza dei Pitti

Pitti Palace

La Specola Museum

Amphitheatre

Grotta di Buontalenti

Kaffeehaus

COSTA DI SAN GIORGIO

Boboli Gardens

Neptune Fountain

Belvedere Fort

Porcelain Museum and Giardino del Cavaliere

VIA NAZIONALE

VIA PANICALE

VIA TADDEA

VIA GUELFA

Cenacolo di Sant' Apollonia

VIA SANTA ZANOBI

VIA XXVII APRILE

VIA SAN GALLO

VIA SAN ZANOBI

Piazza del Mercato Centrale

VIA DELL' ARIENTO

VIA SANT' ANTONINO

Cenacolo di Foligno

VIA FAENZA

BORGO LA NOCE

Medici Chapels

San Lorenzo

Piazza Madonna

Piazza dell' Unità Italiana

V.D. MELARANCIO

GIGLIO

VIA DE' PANZANI

VIA DE' CONTI

Biblioteca Laurenziana

BORGO SAN LORENZO

VIA DE' CERRETANI

VIA DE' GINORI

VIA CAVOUR

Palazzo Medici-Riccardi

VIA DE' MARTELLI

VIA DE' PUCCI

VIA RICASOLI

VIA DEI BANCHI

San Gaetano

Piazza di San Giovanni

Baptistry

Duomo

Piazza del Duomo

Museo dell'Opera del Duomo

Santa Margherita de' Cerchi

VIA DEGLI AGLI

VIA DE' PECORI

VIA DELLE OCHE

VIA DELLO STUDIO

VIA ROMA

VIA D. CAMPIDOGLIO

Piazza della Repubblica

VIA SPEZIALI

Dante's House

VIA DEL CORSO

VIA DANTE ALIGHIERI

VIA DE' CERCHI

Bargello

VIA DE' CALZAIUOLI

Orsanmichele

San Martino

Badia

VIA DEI NERI

VIA STROZZI

Piazza Strozzi

Palazzo Strozzi

Post Office & Telephones

Mercato Nuovo

Arte della Lana

VIA CALIMALA

VIA PORTA ROSSA

VIA DELLE TERME

VIA POR S. MARIA

Palazzo di Parte Guelfa

Piazza della Signoria

Palazzo Gondi

VIA DE' GONDI

Piazza S. Firenze

San Firenze

Palazzo Vecchio

Loggia dei Lanzi

VIA LAMBERTESCA

Piazzale degli Uffizi

Uffizi

VIA DE' CASTELLANI

Museum of the History of Science

LUNG. DIAZ

Fiume

LUNGARNO TORRIGIANI

VIA DE' BARDI

PONTE ALLE GRAZIE

Museo Bardini

Piazza dei Mozzi

Palazzo dei Mozzi

LUNG. ACCIAIOLI

VIA DETORNABUONI

MORO

VIA DEL FOSSI

VIA DELLE BELLE DONNE

VIA DEI RONDINELLI

VIA DELLA VIGNA

Palazzo di

646

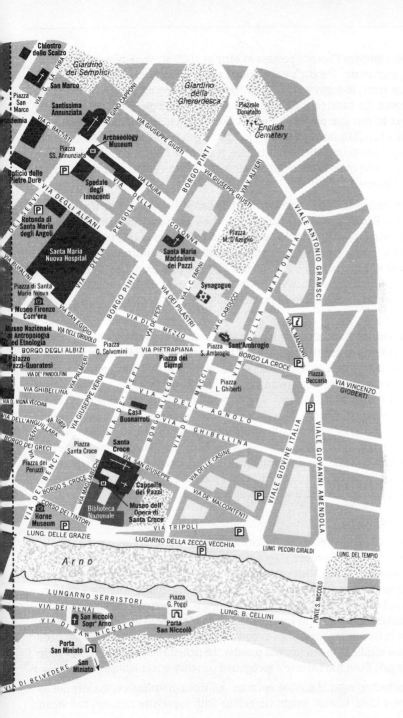

# History

The Etruscans, who founded Florence perhaps as early as 1000 BC, were typically coy about providing any further details; the city's early history remains a puzzle. Like so many cities, however, Florence seems to begin with a bridge. Dante and many other writers commonly invoke the *marzocco*, the battered ancient icon that sat in the middle of the Ponte Vecchio and any number of bridges that preceded it until a flood swept it away in the 14th century. Often pictured as a lion (like the replacement for the original made by Donatello, now on display in the Bargello museum), the marzocco may really have been a mounted cult image of the god Mars. Nothing could be more fitting, for in the centuries of its greatness Florence was a town full of trouble.

The city's apprenticeship in strife came during the endless Italian wars of the 4th–2nd centuries BC, when Rome was consolidating its hold on the peninsula. Florence seems usually to have chosen the wrong side. Sulla razed it to the ground during the Social Wars, and the town seems to have struggled back only gradually. Julius Caesar helped it along by planting a colony of veterans here in 59 BC. Roman Florence prospered, trading throughout the whole Empire. Its street plan survives in the neat rectangle of straight streets at the city's core. The town had an impressive forum right in the middle, at what is now Piazza della Repubblica.

If almost nothing remains from Roman times, it is only because Florence has been continuously occupied ever since, its centre constantly replanned and rebuilt. There were some hard times, especially during the Greek–Gothic wars of the 6th century and the Lombard occupation, but the city regained importance with the coming of Charlemagne, becoming for a while the seat of the 'march' of Tuscany. Here, in what must have been one of the most fascinating eras of the city's history, once again we are left without much information. Florence, for whatever reason, was one of the first inland cities to regain its balance after the fall of the Empire. During the Dark Ages the city was already beginning to develop the free institutions of the later republic, and establishing the trading connections that were later to make it the merchant capital of Europe. About 1115, upon the death of the famous Countess Matilda of Tuscany, Florence became a self-governing *comune*.

## The Florentine Republic

From the beginning, circumstances forced the city into an aggressive posture against enemies within and outside its walls. Florence waged constant war against the extortionist petty nobles of the hinterlands, razing their castles and forcing them to live in the city. As an important Guelph stronghold, Florence constantly got itself into trouble with the Emperors, as well as with Ghibelline Pisa, Pistoia, and Siena, towns that were to become its sworn enemies. In its darkest hour, after the crushing defeat at Montaperti in 1260, the Sienese almost succeeded in convincing their allies to bury Florence. A good sack would have been fun; Florence by the middle 13th century was possibly the richest banking and trading centre anywhere, and its gold florin had become a recognized currency across Europe.

In truth, Florence had no need of outside enemies. All through its history, the city did its level best to destroy itself. Guelph fought Ghibelline with impressive rancour, and when there were no Ghibellines left the Guelphs split into factions called the Blacks and Whites and began murdering each other. In a different dimension, the city found different causes of civil strife in the class struggles between the *popolari grossi*—the 'fat commons' or wealthy merchant class—and the members of the poorer guilds. Playing one side against the other was the newly urbanized nobility. They brought their gangster habits to town with them, turning Florence into a forest of tall brick tower-fortresses and carrying on bloody feuds in the streets that the city officials were helpless to stop. No historian has ever been able to explain how medieval Florence avoided committing suicide altogether. But despite all the troubles, this was the era of Dante (d. 1321, in political exile in Ravenna) and Giotto (d. 1337), the beginning of Florence's cultural golden age. Banking and the manufacture of wool (the leading commodity in the pre-industrial economy) were booming, and the florins kept rolling in no matter which faction was on top.

In 1282, and again in 1293, Florence tried to clean up its violent and corrupt government by a series of reforms; the *Ordinamenti della Giustizia* in 1293 finally excluded the nobles from politics. It didn't work for long. Political strife continued throughout the 14th century, along with eternal wars with Lucca, Pisa, and Siena, and some novel catastrophes. In 1339 Edward III of England repudiated his enormous foreign debt, and Florence's two largest banks, the Bardi and Peruzzi, went bust. Plagues and famines dominated the 1340s; the plague of 1348, the Black Death, killed three-fifths of the population (and provided the frame story for Boccaccio's *Decameron*). The nobles and merchants then took advantage of the situation to establish tight boss rule. You can still see their Guelph Party building on Via Porta Rossa, where the spoils were divided—the original Tammany Hall. A genuine revolution in 1378 among the *ciompi*, the wool trade proletariat, might have succeeded if its leaders had been half as devious and ruthless as their opponents.

Florence's continuing good luck again saw it through, however, and prosperity gradually returned after 1400. In 1406, Pisa was finally conquered, giving Florence a seaport. Florentine armies bested the Visconti of Milan twice, and once (1410) even occupied Rome. At the dawn of the Renaissance, not only Florence's artists, scholars, and scientists were making innovations—the city government in the 1420s and '30s invented the progressive income tax and the national debt.

## The Rise of the Medici

Although they are said to have begun as pharmacists (*medici*), by 1400 the House of Medici was the biggest merchant concern in Florence. With the resources of the Medici Bank behind him, Cosimo de' Medici installed himself as the city's political godfather, coercing or buying off the various interests and factions. In 1449 his son Lorenzo inherited the job, presiding over the greatest days of the Renaissance and a sustained stretch of peace and prosperity. Opposition, squashed originally by Cosimo, stayed squashed under Lorenzo. His military campaigns proved successful on the whole, and his impressive propaganda machine gave him an exaggerated reputation as a philosopher-king and patron of the arts. Lorenzo almost ruined the Medici Bank through neglect, but then made up his losses from public funds. His personal tastes in art seem to have been limited to knick knacks, big jewels and antique bronzes, but his real hobby was nepotism. His son Giovanni, later to be made Pope Leo X at the age of 38, became a cardinal at 14.

Two years after Lorenzo's death in 1494, the wealthy classes of Florence finally succeeded in ending Medici rule when they exiled Lorenzo's weak son and successor, Piero. The republic was restored, but soon came under the influence of a remarkable Dominican demagogue, Girolamo Savonarola. Thundering out a fierce fundamentalist line, his preaching resulted in in the famous 1497 'Bonfire of Vanities' on the Piazza della Signoria, when the people collected their paintings, fancy clothes, carnival masks, and books and put them to the flame (a Venetian merchant offered instead to buy the whole lot from them, but the Florentines hurriedly sketched a portrait of him too, and threw it on the pyre). But Savonarola was more than a ridiculous prude. His idealistic republicanism resulted in some real democratic reforms for the new government, and his emphasis on morals provided a much needed purgative after the reigning depravity of the last 200 years. The friar reserved his strongest blasts, however, for the corruption of the church; not a bad idea in the time of Alexander VI, the Borgia pope. When Savonarola's opponents, the *Arrabbiati* ('infuriated') beat his supporters, the *Piagnoni* ('snivellers') in the 1498 elections, the way was clear for Alexander to order the friar's execution. Savonarola burned on 22 May 1498, on the same spot where the 'Bonfire of Vanities' had been held, and his ashes were thrown in the Arno.

The Medici returned in 1512, thanks to Pope Julius II and his Spanish troops. The Spaniards' exemplary sack of Prato, with remarkable atrocities, was intended as a lesson to the Florentines. It had the desired effect, and Lorenzo's nephew Giuliano de' Medici was able to re-enter the city. When Giuliano was elected Pope Clement VII in 1523 he attempted to continue running the city at a distance, but yet another Medici expulsion would take place after his humiliation in the sack of Rome in 1527, followed by the founding of the last Florentine republic. By now Florentine politics had become a death struggle between an entire city and a single family; in the end the Medici would prove to have the stronger will. The last republic lived nervously in an atmosphere of revolutionary apocalypse; meanwhile Clement intrigued with the Spaniards for his return. An Imperial army arrived in 1530 to besiege the city, and despite heroic, last-ditch resistance Florence had to capitulate when its commander sold out to the Pope and turned his guns on the city itself. In 1532, the Medici broke the terms of the surrender agreement by abolishing all self-government, obtaining the title of Grand Dukes of Tuscany from Emperor Charles V.

To all intents and purposes Florentine history ends here. Cosimo I Medici (d. 1574) ruled over a state that declined rapidly into a provincial backwater. When the last Medici, fat Gian Gastone, died in 1737, the powers of Europe gave the duchy to the House of Lorraine. With the rest of Tuscany, Florence was annexed to Piedmont-Sardinia in 1859, and from 1865 to 1870 it served as the capital of united Italy.

Today, despite repeated attempts to diversify the local economy through the creation of new industrial areas on the outskirts, Florence largely lives on the sheer weight of its past creativity. It suffered badly in the Second World War, when the retreating German army blew up all the bridges over the Arno except the Ponte Vecchio, and destroyed many medieval buildings along the river's' edge. Still worse damage was caused by the great floods of November 1966, which left several dead and many buildings and artworks in need of restoration work that is still continuing today. The most recent damage to be inflicted on the city came in May 1993, when a bomb—who planted it, and with what objective, remains

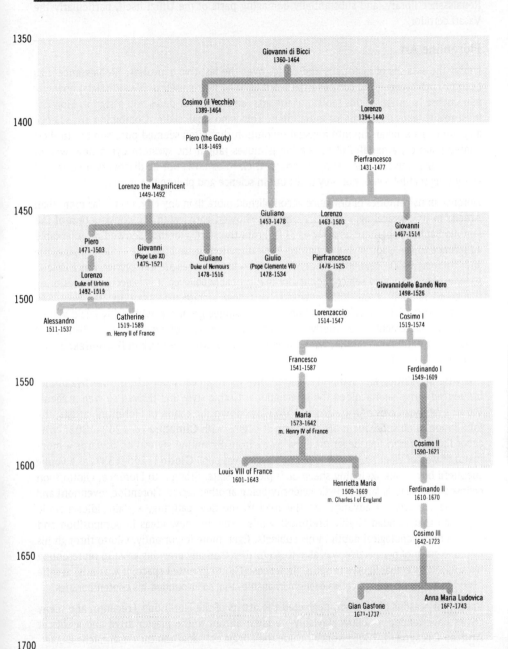

1350

1400

1450

1500

1550

1600

1650

1700

Giovanni di Bicci
1360-1464

Cosimo (il Vecchio)
1389-1464

Lorenzo
1394-1440

Piero (the Gouty)
1418-1469

Pierfrancesco
1431-1477

Lorenzo the Magnificent
1449-1492

Giuliano
1453-1478

Lorenzo
1463-1503

Giovanni
1467-1514

Piero
1471-1503

Giovanni
(Pope Leo XI)
1475-1521

Giuliano
Duke of Nemours
1478-1516

Giulio
(Pope Clemente VII)
1478-1534

Pierfrancesco
1478-1525

Lorenzo
Duke of Urbino
1492-1519

Giovanni delle Bande Nere
1498-1526

Alessandro
1511-1537

Catherine
1519-1589
m. Henry II of France

Lorenzaccio
1514-1547

Cosimo I
1519-1574

Francesco
1541-1587

Ferdinando I
1549-1609

Maria
1573-1642
m. Henry IV of France

Cosimo II
1590-1621

Louis VIII of France
1601-1643

Henrietta Maria
1509-1669
m. Charles I of England

Ferdinando II
1610-1670

Cosimo III
1642-1723

Gian Gastone
1671-1737

Anna Maria Ludovica
1667-1743

651

unexplained—exploded near the Uffizi, killing the family of a caretaker, destroying a Renaissance library, and substantially damaging parts of the Uffizi itself, particularly the Vasari corridor.

## Florentine Art

Under the assaults of historians and critics over the last two centuries, 'Renaissance' has become such a vague and controversial word as to be nearly useless. Nevertheless, however you choose to interpret this rebirth of the arts, and whatever dates you assign it, Florence inescapably takes the credit for initiating it. This is no small claim. Combining art, science and humanist scholarship into a visual revolution that often seemed pure sorcery to their contemporaries, a handful of Florentine geniuses taught the western eye a new way of seeing. Perspective seems a simple enough trick to us now, but its discovery determined everything that followed, not only in art but in science and philosophy as well.

Florence in its centuries of brilliance accomplished more than any city, ever—far more than Athens in its classical age. The city's talents showed early, with the construction of the famous Baptistry, perhaps as early as 700. From the start, Florence showed a remarkable adherence to the traditions of antiquity. New directions in architecture—the Romanesque after the year 1000—had little effect; what passed for Romanesque in Florence was a unique style, evolved by a very self-confident city that probably believed it was accurately restoring the grand manner of the Roman world. This new architecture (*see* the Baptistry, San Miniato, Santa Maria Novella), based on elegantly simple geometry, with richly inlaid marble façades and pavements, was utterly unlike even the creations of nearby Pisa and Siena, and began a continuity of style that would reach its climax with the work of **Brunelleschi** and **Alberti** in the 1400s.

Likewise in painting and sculpture, Florentines made an early departure from Byzantine-influenced forms, and avoided the International Gothic style that thrived so well in Siena. Vasari's famous *Lives of the Artists* (1547) lays down the canon of Florentine artists, the foundation of all subsequent art criticism. It begins with **Cimabue** (*c.* 1240–1302), who according to Vasari first began to draw away from Byzantine stylization towards a more 'natural' way of painting. Cimabue found his greatest pupil **Giotto** (1266–1337) as a young shepherd boy, chalk-sketching sheep on a piece of slate. Brought to Florence, Giotto soon eclipsed his master's fame (artistic celebrity being another recent Florentine invention) and achieved the greatest advances on the road to the new painting, a plain, idiosyncratic approach that avoided Gothic prettiness while exploring new ideas in composition and expressing psychological depth in his subjects. Even more importantly, Giotto through his intuitive grasp of perspective was able to go further than any previous artist in representing his subjects as actual figures in space. In a sense Giotto invented space; it was this, despite his often awkward and graceless draughtsmanship, that so astounded his contemporaries.

Vasari, for reasons of his own, neglected the artists of the Florentine Trecento, and many critics have tended to follow slavishly—a great affront to the master artist and architect **Andrea Orcagna** (d. 1368; works include the Loggia dei Lanzi and the Orsanmichele tabernacle) and others including **Taddeo and Agnolo Gaddi** (d. 1366 and 1396) whose frescoes can be compared to Giotto's at Santa Croce.

# Masters and Students: the Progress of the Renaissance

*The purpose of this chart is to show who learned from whom, an insight into some 300 years of artistic continuity*

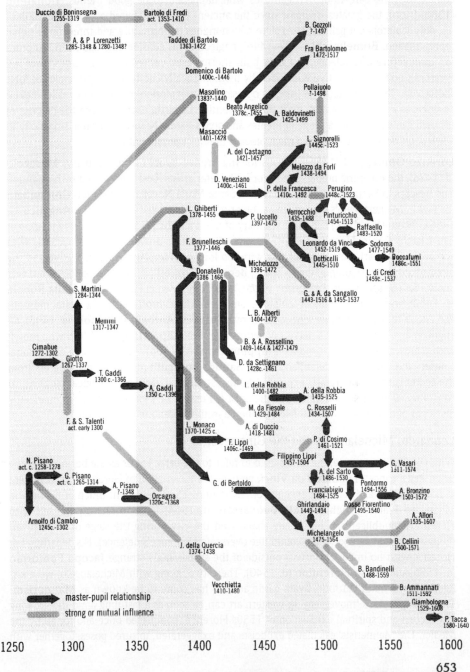

**Duccio di Boninsegna** 1255-1319
**Bartolo di Fredi** act. 1353-1410
**A. & P. Lorenzetti** 1285-1348 & 1280-1348?
**Taddeo di Bartolo** 1363-1422
**B. Gozzoli** ?-1497
**Domenico di Bartolo** 1400c.-1446
**Fra Bartolomeo** 1472-1517
**Masolino** 1383?-1440
**Pollaiuolo** ?-1498
**Beato Angelico** 1378c.-1455
**A. Baldovinetti** 1425-1499
**Masaccio** 1401-1428
**A. del Castagno** 1421-1457
**L. Signorelli** 1445c.-1523
**Melozzo da Forlí** 1438-1494
**D. Veneziano** 1400c.-1461
**P. della Francesca** 1410c.-1492
**Perugino** 1448c.-1523
**L. Ghiberti** 1378-1455
**P. Uccello** 1397-1475
**Verrocchio** 1435-1488
**Pinturicchio** 1454-1513
**Raffaello** 1483-1520
**F. Brunelleschi** 1377-1446
**Leonardo da Vinci** 1452-1519
**Sodoma** 1477-1549
**Michelozzo** 1396-1472
**Botticelli** 1445-1510
**Boccafumi** 1486c.-1551
**Donatello** 1386-1466
**L. di Credi** 1459c.-1537
**S. Martini** 1284-1344
**G. & A. da Sangallo** 1443-1516 & 1455-1537
**L. B. Alberti** 1404-1472
**Memmi** 1317-1347
**B. & A. Rossellino** 1409-1464 & 1427-1479
**Cimabue** 1272-1302
**D. da Settignano** 1428c.-1461
**Giotto** 1267-1337
**T. Gaddi** 1300 c.-1366
**I. della Robbia** 1400-1482
**A. della Robbia** 1435-1525
**A. Gaddi** 1350 c.-1396
**M. da Fiesole** 1429-1484
**C. Rosselli** 1434-1507
**F. & S. Talenti** act. early 1300
**L. Monaco** 1370-1425 c.
**A. di Duccio** 1418-1481
**P. di Cosimo** 1461-1521
**N. Pisano** act. c. 1258-1278
**F. Lippi** 1406c.-1469
**Filippino Lippi** 1457-1504
**G. Vasari** 1511-1574
**G. Pisano** act. c. 1265-1314
**A. Pisano** ?-1348
**G. di Bertoldo** ?
**A. del Sarto** 1486-1530
**Pontormo** 1494-1556
**A. Bronzino** 1503-1572
**Orcagna** 1320c.-1368
**Franciabigio** 1484-1525
**Arnolfo di Cambio** 1245c.-1302
**Ghirlandaio** 1449-1494
**Rosso Fiorentino** 1495-1540
**A. Allori** 1535-1607
**Michelangelo** 1475-1564
**B. Cellini** 1500-1571
**J. della Quercia** 1374-1438
**B. Bandinelli** 1488-1559
**Vecchietta** 1410-1480
**B. Ammannati** 1511-1592
**Giambologna** 1529-1608
**P. Tacca** 1580-1640

→ master-pupil relationship

→ strong or mutual influence

1250  1300  1350  1400  1450  1500  1550  1600

653

# The Quattrocento

The next turn in the story, what scholars self-assuredly used to call the 'Early Renaissance', comes with the careers of two geniuses who happened to be good friends. **Donatello** (1386–1466), the greatest sculptor since the ancient Greeks, inspired a new generation of not only sculptors but painters to explore new horizons in portraiture and three-dimensional representation. **Brunelleschi** (1377–1446), neglecting his considerable talents in sculpture for architecture and science, not only built the majestic cathedral dome, but threw the Pandora's box of perspective wide open by mathematically codifying the principles of fore-shortening. The new science of painting occasioned an explosion of talent unequalled before or since, as a score of masters, most them Florentine by birth, each followed the dictates of his own genius to create a range of themes and styles hardly believable for one single city in a few short decades of its life. To mention only the most prominent:

**Lorenzo Ghiberti** (d. 1455), famous for the bronze doors of the Baptistry; **Masaccio** (d. 1428), the eccentric prodigy much copied by later artists, best represented by his natural-istic frescoes in Santa Maria del Carmine and Santa Maria Novella; **Domenico Ghirlandaio** (d. 1494), Michelangelo's teacher and another master of detailed frescoes; **Fra Angelico** (d. 1455), the most spiritual, and most visionary of them all, the painter of the *Annunciation* at San Marco; **Paolo Uccello** (d. 1475), one of the most provocative of all artists, who according to Vasari drove himself bats with too long contemplation of perspective and the newly discovered vacuum of empty space; **Benozzo Gozzoli** (d. 1497), a happier soul, best known for the springtime *Procession of the Magi* in the Medici Palace; **Luca Della Robbia** (d. 1482), greatest of a family of sculptors, famous for the *cantoria* of the Cathedral museum and exquisite blue and white terracottas all over Tuscany; **Antonio Pollaiuolo** (d. 1498), an engraver and sculptor with a nervously perfect line; **Fra Filippo Lippi** (d. 1469) who ran off with a brown-eyed nun to produce **Filippino Lippi** (d. 1504)—both of them exceptional painters and sticklers for detail; and finally **Sandro Botticelli** (d. 1510); his progress from the secret garden of pure art, expressed in his astounding early mythological pictures, to conventional holy pictures, done after the artist fell under the sway of Savonarola, marks the first signs of trouble and the first failure of nerve in the Florentine imagination.

## Leonardo, Michelangelo and the Cinquecento

With equal self-assurance, the critics used to refer to the early 1500s as the beginning of the 'High Renaissance'. **Leonardo da Vinci**, perhaps the incarnation of Florentine achievement in both painting and scientific speculation, lived until 1519, but spent much of his time in Milan and France. **Michelangelo Buonarroti** (d. 1564) liked to identify himself with Florentine republicanism, but finally abandoned the city during the siege of 1530 (even though he was a member of the committee overseeing Florence's defence). His departure left Florence with no important artists outside of the surpassingly strange **Jacopo Pontormo** (d. 1556) and **Rosso Fiorentino** (d. 1540). These two, along with Michelangelo, were key figures in the bold, neurotic, avant-garde art that has come to be known as **Mannerism**. This first conscious 'movement' in western art can be seen as a last fling amid the growing intellectual and spiritual exhaustion of 1530s Florence, conquered once and for all by the Medici. The Mannerists' calculated exoticism and exaggerated, tortured poses, together with the brooding self-absorption of Michelangelo and many others, are the prelude to Florentine art's remarkably abrupt downturn into decadence, and prophesy its final extinction.

There was another strain to Mannerism in Florence, following the cold classicism of Raphael of Urbino, less disturbed, less intense and challenging than Michelangelo or Pontormo. With artists like **Agnolo Bronzino** (d. 1572), the sculptor **Bartolomeo Ammannati** (d. 1592), **Andrea del Sarto** (d. 1531), and **Giorgio Vasari** himself (d. 1574), Florentine art loses almost all imaginative and intellectual content, becoming a virtuoso style of interior decoration perfectly adaptable to saccharine holy pictures, portraits of newly enthroned dukes, or absurd mythological fountains and ballroom ceilings. In the cinquecento, with plenty of money to spend and a long Medici tradition of patronage to uphold, this tendency soon got out of hand. Under the reign of Cosimo I, indefatigable collector of *pietra dura* tables, silver and gold gimcracks, and exotic stuffed animals, Florence gave birth to the artistic phenomenon modern critics call kitsch.

In the cinquecento, Florence taught vulgarity to the Romans, degeneracy to the Venetians, and preciosity to the French. Oddly enough, the city had as great an influence in its age of decay as in its age of greatness. The cute, well-educated Florentine pranced across Europe, finding himself praised as the paragon of culture and refinement. Even in England—though that honest nation soon found him out:

> *A little Apish hatte, couched fast to the Pate, like an Oyster,*
> *French Camarick Ruffes, deepe with a witnesse, starched to the purpose,*
> *Delicate in speach, queynte in arraye: conceited in all poyntes:*
> *In Courtly guyles, a passing singular odde man…*

Mirror of Tuscanism, Gabriel Harvey, 1580

It's almost disconcerting to learn that Florence gave us not only much of the best of our civilization, but even a lot of the worst. Somehow the later world of powdered wigs and chubby winged *putti* is unthinkable without 1500s Florence. Then again, so is all the last 500 years of art unthinkable without Florence, not to mention modern medicine (the careful anatomical studies of the artists did much to help set it on its way) or technology (from the endless speculations and gadgets of Leonardo) or political science (from Machiavelli). The Florentines of course found the time to invent opera too, and give music a poke into the modern world. And without that little discovery of the painters, so simple though perhaps so very hard for us in the 20th century to comprehend—the invention of space—Copernicus, Newton, Descartes, and all who followed them would never have discovered anything.

But Florence soon tired of the whole business. The city withdrew into itself, made a modest living, polished its manners and its conceit, and generally avoided trouble. Not a peep has been heard out of it since 1600.

## The Best of Florence

No city in Italy has such a wealth of art—perhaps only Venice comes close. If you wanted to see everything worth seeing, it would take at least two weeks, and museum admissions alone would set you back some L300,000.

For an abbreviated tour, be sure to see the **Cathedral, Baptistry,** and **Cathedral Museum,** and Florence's two great museums, the **Uffizi** and the **Bargello,** leaving time for a walk around the Ponte Vecchio and the old streets and alleys of Florence's centre, and a stop at **Orsanmichele.** Around the edges of the old centre, the churches of **Santa Croce, Santa Maria Novella, Santa Maria del Carmine** and the monastery of **San Marco** contain some of the best of Florentine painting. Finally, try to make it up to **San Miniato,** both for the beautiful medieval church and the view over the city.

Those with more time to spend can consider the florid 16th-century art in the **Palazzo Vecchio** and **Pitti Palace,** Gozzoli's frescoes in the **Medici Palace,** the very good **Archaeology Museum** and **Museum of Science,** and Brunelleschi's **Santo Spirito.** And for devotees of the Michelangelo cult, there's the real David in the **Accademia,** the **Medici Chapels** at San Lorenzo, and the **Casa Buonarroti.**

---

### Getting to and from Florence

#### by air

A very few international flights, and services from Rome and Milan, use Florence's own little **Peretola airport,** 5km northwest of the city (information, ✆ 371498), but the principal airport for the area is the Galileo Galilei at **Pisa** (*see* below). There are frequent rail connections direct from Pisa airport station to Florence, and the journey takes one hour.

#### by rail

The central station is **Santa Maria Novella** (information, ✆ 278785), which the state railways often refers to as Firenze S.M.N. It is right in the centre of Florence, and the piazza it faces, Piazza della Stazione, and adjacent Piazza Santa Maria Novella; are also a major terminus for local bus routes. Some trains also stop at **Campo di Marte,** on the eastern side of the city.

#### by long-distance bus

Several lines run services to towns in the province and around Tuscany. **SITA,** Via S. Caterina di Siena 15 (near the train station, ✆ 214721) operates to Firenzuola, Greve, and the Mugello valley, and also to Siena, Pisa, and Perugia; **Lazzi,** Piazza Stazione 4 (✆ 2398840) goes to Empoli, Incisa Valdarno, Prato, Pistoia, Lucca, and also to other European countries; and **COPIT,** Piazza Santa Maria Novella (✆ 215451) has services to Vinci.

#### by road

The north-south autostrada A1 skirts round to the west of Florence, though the A11 from Lucca and Pistoia comes further into the city from the northwest. From the A1 the main roads into Florence are the Firenze-Sud interchange, from the southeast, the SS2, the Via Senese, from the south; and the Via Etruria from the west. All roads into the city meet up with an inner ring of roads, the *Viali,* which go around the historic centre, much of which is closed to traffic. Driving in Florence is difficult, and it's advisable to leave your vehicle in a car park as soon as you can and get a bus into town. There are large car parks all around the *Viali,* particularly around the **Fortezza**

**da Basso**, which are quite expensive, though still not as much as the ones that are actually within the centre itself. For unrestricted free parking it's necessary to leave your car near one of the access roads, and catch a bus from there.

## Getting Around

Large areas of Florence's *centro storico* are closed to traffic, but many of its great sights are close enough to each other to make walking, the simplest way of getting round. Elsewhere Florence is a very businesslike town of dusty streets (admittedly, occasionally punctuated by lovely buildings), with one of the grimmest traffic problems in Italy. Noise and dirt make walking down the busiest traffic corridors unpleasant, especially in summer. When you do need to get directly from A to B, the city has an efficient local **bus** service. Most of the more useful routes for visitors start from the main railway station: Bus no.7 goes to San Marco and then all the way to Fiesole; no.10, to the Duomo, San Marco, and the Campo di Marte station; no.13, to Piazzale Michelangelo and the Belvedere—especially useful if you want to avoid that long climb. no.37 goes to Galluzzo and the Certosa.

For a radio **taxi**, call 4798 or 4390. The really adventurous can **rent a bicycle** from Ciao & Basta, Via Alamanni, ✆ 263985, near the station, or Alinari, Via Guelfa 85/r, ✆ 280500 (spring and summer only), or a **scooter**, also from Alinari or from Motorent, Via San Zanobi 9/r, ✆ 490113.

Just to make life difficult, Florence has two sets of address numbers on every street—red ones for business, blue for residences; your hotel might be either one.

## Tourist Information

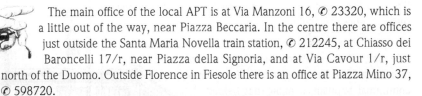

The main office of the local APT is at Via Manzoni 16, ✆ 23320, which is a little out of the way, near Piazza Beccaria. In the centre there are offices just outside the Santa Maria Novella train station, ✆ 212245, at Chiasso dei Baroncelli 17/r, near Piazza della Signoria, and at Via Cavour 1/r, just north of the Duomo. Outside Florence in Fiesole there is an office at Piazza Mino 37, ✆ 598720.

There is no end of local agencies able to help you find a hotel (*see* below, 'Where to Stay') but the tourist offices do not have accommodation services. However, they will provide you with a list of hotels and prices.

The phone area code for Florence is **055**.

**Fire**, ✆ 115.
**Police emergencies**, ✆ 113.
**Police**, Via Zara 2, ✆ 49771.
**Ambulance**, ✆ 113.

**Hospital: Ospedale Santa Maria Nuova**, Piazza Santa Maria Nuova, ✆ 27581. There is also a private **Tourist Medical Service**, Via Lorenzo il Magnifico 59, ✆ 475411, which has English-speaking doctors available 24 hours.

**24-hour pharmacies: Comunale della Stazione**, at the main railway station, and **Molteni**, Via Calzaiuoli 7/r, are both open 24 hours daily. In addition, every pharmacy has a list outside indicating those in the city on night duty each day. For information ✆ 110.

Places that exchange money outside normal banking hours include **American Express**, Via Guicciardini 49/r, ✆ 278751, in Oltrarno, open 9am–6pm Mon–Fri, 9am–1pm Sat; and **CIT**, Via Cavour 56, ✆ 294306, and Piazza della Stazione, ✆ 284145, both open 9–12.30, 3.30–7.30, Mon–Fri, 9am–12 midday Sat.

The **main post office** is at Via Pellicceria 8, near the Piazza della Repubblica, and is open 8.15am–7pm Mon–Fri, 8.15am–12 midday Sat. Alongside it and at the railway station there are 24-hour phone centres.

## Piazza del Duomo

## The Baptistry

This ancient, mysterious building, the egg from which Florence's golden age was hatched, makes as good a place to start as any. Medieval Florentines were always too busy to look back, and now and then they lost track of themselves. The men of the quattrocento believed their baptistry to have been originally a Roman building, a Temple of Mars. After all the research that has gone into the question in the last few centuries, the best guesses put the actual building in the 9th century—but maybe as far back as the 7th. The distinctive black and white marble facing, the tidily classical pattern of arches and rectangles that deceived Brunelleschi and Alberti, was probably added in the 10th or 11th century. The masters who built it remain unknown, but their strikingly original exercise in geometry provided the model for all Florence's great church façades. When it was new, there was nothing remotely like it in Europe; to visitors from outside the city it must have seemed almost miraculous.

Every 21 March, New Year's Day on the old Florentine calendar, all the children born over the last 12 months would be brought here for a great communal baptism, a habit that helped make the baptistry not merely a religious monument but also a civic symbol, in fact the oldest and fondest symbol of the republic. As such, the Florentines never finished embellishing it. Under the octagonal cupola, the 13th- and 14th-century gold-ground mosaics show a strong Byzantine influence, though some (*The Life of John the Baptist*) may be the work of Cimabue. To match them, there is a beautiful inlaid marble floor, decorated with signs of the zodiac. Even more than

the exterior, the patterned black and white marble of the interior walls is remarkable, combining influences from the ancient world and modern inspiration for something entirely new, a perfect source that the architects of the Middle Ages and Renaissance would ever strive to match. It isn't cluttered inside; only a 13th-century Pisan-style baptismal font and the tomb of Anti-pope John XXIII, by Donatello and Michelozzo, stand out.

Historians used to date the coming of the 'Renaissance' as 1401, with the famous competition for the baptistry's **bronze doors**, when Lorenzo Ghiberti defeated Brunelleschi and others for the commission. The south door had already been completed by Andrea Pisano, with scenes from the life of John the Baptist in Gothic quatrefoil frames, and in his north door Ghiberti attempted no new departures. After 1425, however, he began the great east doors (the ones with tourists piled up in front) which were to occupy much of his time for the next 27 years. These are the doors Michelangelo is said to have called the 'Gates of Paradise', and undoubtedly they made a tremendous impression on all the artists of the quattrocento, using the same advances in composition and perspective, and the same wealth of detail as the painters. Unfortunately, the panels currently displayed are replicas, as the originals are being restored (four are now exhibited in the **Museo dell'Opera del Duomo**, *see* below), but you can still appreciate the richness of the original design. The Old Testament scenes begin with the creation of Adam and Eve in the upper left corner, finishing with Solomon and Sheba in the Temple on the lower right-hand panel. On the frames, busts of contemporary Florentine artists peer out from tiny circles. It is a typical exhibition of Florentine pride that Ghiberti should put his friends among the prophets and sibyls that adorn the rest of the frames. Near the centre, the balding figure with arched eyebrows is Ghiberti himself.

## The Duomo

For all its importance and prosperity, Florence was one of the last cities to plan a great cathedral. Work began in the 1290s, with the sculptor Arnolfo di Cambio in charge, and the Florentines from the beginning attempted to make up for their delay with audacity and size. Arnolfo laid the foundations for an octagonal crossing 44.5m in diameter, then died before working out a way to cover it, leaving future architects with the job of designing the biggest dome in the world. Surprisingly, the Duomo shows little interest in contemporary innovations and styles; a visitor from France or England in the 1400s would certainly have found it somewhat drab and architecturally primitive. Visitors today often do not know what to think; they circle confusedly around its grimy, ponderous bulk (this is one of very few cathedrals in Italy that you can walk completely around). Instead of the striped bravura of Siena or the elegant colonnades of Pisa, they behold an astonishingly eccentric pattern of marble rectangles and flowers—like Victorian wallpaper, or as one critic better expressed it, a 'cathedral wearing pyjamas'.

The west front cannot be blamed on Arnolfo; his original design, only one-quarter completed, was taken down in the late 16th century in a Medici rebuilding programme that never got off the ground. The Duomo turned a blank face to the world until 1888, when the present neo-Gothic extravaganza was added. After this façade, the austerity of the interior is almost startling. There is plenty of room; contemporary writers mention 10,000 souls packed inside to hear the brimstone and hell-fire sermons of Savonarola. Even with that in mind, the Duomo hardly seems a religious building—more of a *Florentine* building, with simple arches and the counterpoint of grey stone and white plaster, full of old familiar Florentine things. Near the entrance, there are busts of Brunelleschi and Giotto along the right side. For building the great dome, Brunelleschi was accorded a great honour—he is the only Florentine to be buried in the cathedral. On the left wall, posed inconspicuously, you will see the two most conspicuous monuments to private individuals ever commissioned by the Florentine republic. The older one, on the right, is to Sir John Hawkwood, the famous English condottiere whose name the Italians mangled to Giovanni Acuto, a legendary commander who served Florence for many years. All along, he had the promise of the Florentines to build him an equestrian monument after his death; it was a typical Florentine trick to cheat a dead man—but still they hired the greatest master of perspective, Paolo Uccello, to make a picture that looked like a statue. Twenty years later, they pulled the same trick again, commissioning another great illusionist, Andrea del Castagno, to paint the non-existent equestrian statue of another condottiere named Nicolò da Tolentino. A little further down, near the entrance to Brunelleschi's dome, Florence commemorates its own secular scripture with a fresco of Dante by Michelino, a vision of the poet and his *Paradiso*. Two singular icons of Florence's fascination with science stand at opposite ends of the building: behind the west front, a bizarre clock, also painted by Uccello, and in the pavement of the left apse, a gnomon fixed by the astronomer Toscanelli in 1475. A beam of sunlight strikes it every year on the day of the summer solstice.

There is suprisingly little religious art. Luca della Robbia contributed terra-cotta lunettes above the doors to the sacristies; the scene of the Resurrection over the north sacristy is one of his earliest and best works. He also did the bronze doors beneath it, with tiny portraits on the handles of Lorenzo il Magnifico and his brother Giuliano de' Medici, targets of the Pazzi conspiracy in 1478. In this ill-fated attempt to dispose of the Medici, Giuliano was stabbed during Mass, but Lorenzo managed to escape, taking refuge in this sacristy. In the middle apse, there is a beautiful bronze urn by Ghiberti containing relics of the Florentine St Zenobius. The only really conventional religious decorations are the frescoes in the dome, high overhead, mostly the work of Vasari, and currently covered over for restoration.

### Brunelleschi's Dome

*Open 9.30am–12 midday, 2.30–5pm, Mon–Sat; adm.*

Losing the competition for the baptistry doors was a bitter disappointment to Brunelleschi, but a good piece of luck for Florence. His reaction was typically Florentine: not content with being the second-best sculptor, he began to devote all his talents to a field where he thought no one could beat him. He launched himself into an intense study of architecture and engineering, visiting Rome and probably Ravenna to snatch secrets from the ancients. When proposals were solicited for the cathedral's dome, he was ready with a brilliant tour de force. Not only would he build the biggest dome of that era, and the most beautiful, but he would do it without any need for expensive supports while work was in progress, making use of a cantilevered system of bricks that could support itself while it ascended. Even today, architects marvel at Brunelleschi's systematic way of tackling the job. Problems with weather and air pressure were foreseen and managed; hooks were inserted to hold up scaffolding for future cleaning or repairs.

Not only had Brunelleschi recaptured the technique of the ancients, he had surpassed them, with a system simpler and better than that of the Pantheon or Hagia Sophia. To the Florentines, a people who could have invented the slogan 'Form follows function' for their own tastes in building, it must have come as a revelation; the most logical way of covering the space turned out to be a work of perfect beauty. Brunelleschi, in building his dome, put a crown on the achievements of Florence, after five hundred years still the city's pride and its symbol. To climb it, take the door on the left aisle near the Dante fresco; the complex network of stairs and walks between the inner and outer domes provides a thorough lesson on how Brunelleschi did it, and the views from the top are priceless.

## Giotto's Campanile

*Open April–Sept 9–7.30pm daily; Oct–Mar 9am–5.30 daily; adm.*

There's no doubt; the dome steals the show on Piazza del Duomo, putting one of Italy's most beautiful bell towers in the shade both figuratively and literally. The dome's great size—111.6m to the gold ball atop the lantern—makes the campanile look small, though 85.4m is not exactly tiny. Giotto was made director of the cathedral works in 1334, and his basic design was completed after his death (1337) by Andrea Pisano and Francesco Talenti. It is difficult to say whether they were entirely faithful to the plan. Giotto was an artist, not an engineer; after he died his successors realized the thing was about to topple, a problem they overcame by doubling the thickness of the walls.

Besides its lovely form, the campanile's major fame

Giotto's campanile

rests with Pisano and Talenti's sculptural relief—a veritable encyclopedia of the medieval world view with prophets, saints and sibyls, allegories of the planets, virtues, and sacraments, the liberal arts and industries (the artist's craft is fittingly symbolized by a figure of Daedalus). All these are copies; the originals can be seen in the cathedral museum (*see* below). If, after climbing the dome, you can take another 400 steps or so, the terrace on top offers a slightly different view of Florence. Some lesser-known monuments line the southern edge of the Piazza del Duomo. The **Loggia del Bigallo**, headquarters of one of Florence's still operating charitable confraternities, was the place where mothers dropped off children they couldn't support. Inside there is a small museum of works commissioned by the confraternity in the 1400s (open by request, *©* 215440). A little way to the east, **Dante's Seat** is the ancient stone bench where, according to local legend, the poet would take the air, observing his fellow citizens and the building of the Duomo.

## Museo dell'Opera del Duomo

*Open April–Sept 9am–8pm Mon–Sat, 10–1 Sun; Oct–Mar 9–6 Mon–Sat, 10–1 Sun; adm.*

Relatively few tourists find their way to the cathedral museum, hidden away in an inconspicuous building behind the central apse, but it contains some of the finest works of art in Florence, along with fascinating relics of the Duomo's past: brick moulds, tools, and a block and tackle from the original construction; models of the dome, and even Brunelleschi's death mask. Arnolfo di Cambio's sculpture from the original façade is here, along with drawings that show how it would have looked. There are a dozen big models of proposed reconstructions from the 1580s in various hack Mannerist styles—the façade could have been much, much worse. Florentines were never enthusiastic about the worship of relics, and long ago they shipped San Girolamo's jawbone, John the Baptist's index finger and St Philip's arm across the street to this museum.

In the 1430s, Donatello and Luca della Robbia were commissioned to create a matching pair of *cantorie*, marble choir balconies, with exquisite low reliefs. Both works rank among the Renaissance's greatest productions: Donatello's features dancing *putti* in a setting of quattrocento decorative motifs, and della Robbia's a delightful horde of children dancing, singing, and playing instruments, a truly angelic choir; one imagines the artist enjoying himself thoroughly making them, dragging in all the children of the neighbourhood for models. From the campanile, besides the reliefs of Pisano, there are some fine Old Testament figures by Donatello, as well as his gruesome wood statue of Mary Magdalen, something the Florentines no longer wished to see in their Baptistry.

In the 1980s Michelangelo's last *Pietà* also joined the company, a strange, unfinished work that so exasperated the artist that he finally took a hammer to it, breaking Christ's left arm and leg. The tall, hooded figure supporting Christ, Nicodemus, dominates the composition; according to Vasari its face is that of Michelangelo himself. The finished, polished sections of the work, Mary Magdalen and part of the body of Jesus, are not Michelangelo's work at all, but that of a student, who also did his best to patch the arm. The most recent additions to the museum are some of Ghiberti's original bronze panels from the 'Gates of Paradise' of the Baptistry, newly restored.

# Orsanmichele

Florence likes things neat and in their place. To balance Piazza del Duomo, the religious centre, there is Piazza della Signoria, the civic centre, with an equally formidable array of architecture and art, directly to the south at the other end of Via dei Calzaiuoli, long the city's main artery. On your way there, through the crowds navigating past the Via's fashionable jewellery shops and street knick-knack sellers, you pass the very unusual church of **Orsanmichele**. This stately square building, built up to the street, is easy to miss; it doesn't look anything like a church, and in fact began its life as a grain market, with an open loggia at street level and emergency storehouses above where grain was kept against a siege. In 1304 when the market was relocated, the building was left to the city's powerful guilds, the *Arti*, as a trade and meeting hall. In 1380, Simone Talenti was hired to close in the arches of the loggia and make the 'Oratory of St Michael' (as the building was familiarly known because of the ancient chapel that had preceded it) into a church, although throughout the following century it continued to be closely associated with the guilds, the leaders of each of which strove to outdo the other by commissioning sculptures from the finest artists of the day.

All around the exterior, the guilds erected statues of their patron saints: a remarkable collection, including Donatello's famed *St George* (now a copy; the original is in the Bargello) and *St Mark*, a work much admired by Michelangelo. *Saints Stephen* and *Matthew* are by Ghiberti. *Doubting Thomas* is by Verrocchio. The dim interior, full of stained glass and painted vaults, is ornate and cosy, with more of the air of a guildhall than a church. It makes a picturebook medieval setting for the wonderful **Tabernacle**, a free-standing chapel with fine reliefs and sculpted angels by Andrea Orcagna (1350), precious stones and metalwork (every guild contributed something if it could), and a *Madonna* by Bernardo Daddi.

---

## Piazza della Signoria

Now that the city has finally chased the cars out of this big medieval piazza, it serves as a great corral for tourists, sitting on the loggia steps, endlessly snapping pictures of the Palazzo Vecchio, or strutting in circles like pigeons. In the old days, it would be full of Florentines, the stage set for the tempestuous life of their republic. The public assemblies met here, and at times of danger the bells would ring and the piazza quickly fill with citizen militia, assembling under the banners of their quarters and guilds. Savonarola held his Bonfire of Vanities here, and only a few years later the disenchanted Florentines ignited their Bonfire of Savonarola on the same spot. (You can see a painting of the event at San Marco). Today the piazza is still the favoured spot for political rallies, and each St John's Day they keep up the good medieval custom of the *Calcio in Costume*, a free-for-all football game that has its origins in the exercises of the citizen militias.

Next to the Palazzo Vecchio, the three graceful arches of the **Loggia dei Lanzi** were the reviewing stand for city officials during assemblies and celebrations. Florentines often call it the *Loggia dell'Orcagna*, after the architect who designed it in the 1370s. In its simple classicism, the Loggia anticipates the architecture of Brunelleschi and all those who came after him. The city has made it an outdoor sculpture gallery, with some of the best-known works in Florence: Cellini's triumphant *Perseus* and Giambologna's *Rape of the Sabines*, other works by Giambologna, and a chorus of Roman-era Vestal Virgins along the back wall. The

*Perseus* was commissioned by Duke Cosimo I in the 1540s, and it contains a rather blunt political message for the Florentines—the end of their republic and the final victory of the Medici. Cosimo himself stands imperiously at the centre of the piazza, a bronze equestrian statue also by Giambologna.

All the statues in the piazza are dear to the Florentines for one reason or another. Some are fine works of art; others have only historical associations. Michelangelo's *David*, a copy of which stands in front of the Palazzo near the spot the artist intended for it, was meant as a symbol of republican virtue and Florentine excellence. At the opposite extreme, Florentines are taught almost from birth to ridicule the **Neptune Fountain**, a pompous monstrosity with a giant marble figure of the god. The sculptor, Ammannati, thought he would upstage Michelangelo, though the result is derisively known to all Florence as *Il Biancone* ('Big Whitey'). Bandinelli's statue of *Hercules and Cacus* is almost as big and just as awful; according to Cellini, it looks like a 'sack of melons'.

## Palazzo Vecchio

*Open 9am–7pm Mon–Fri; 8am–1pm Sun; closed Sat; adm.*

Florence's republican government was never perfect. In the better times chronic factionalism was barely kept in check, usually by the utter destruction or exile of one side or the other. Typically, however, the Florentines managed to give their aspirations a perfect symbol. The proud republic would accept nothing less than the most imposing 'Palazzo del Popolo' (as it was originally called) and Arnolfo di Cambio was able to give it to them. Even though the 94m tower was for a long time Florence's tallest, Arnolfo avoided the sort of theatrical façade he was planning for the Duomo. The **Palazzo Vecchio** is part council hall, part fortress, and part prison, and looks to fit all three roles well. Its rugged façade, copied in so many Florentine palaces, is not quite as frank and plain as it looks; all its proportions are based on the Golden Section of the ancient Greeks, rediscovered by medieval mathematicians. You may also accuse it of politically playing both sides—with square Guelph crenellations on the cornice, and the swallowtail Ghibelline style on the tower.

The palace is often called the Palazzo della Signoria, the name it had under the rule of the Medici. After the final consolidation of their new government, the Duchy of Tuscany, the Medici turned the Palazzo Vecchio upside down. The house where Guelphs and Ghibellines once brawled in the council hall, and where lions were kept in the basement as a totem animal for the state, now became a florid Mannerist bower fit for a duke. Cosimo de' Medici's pet architect, Giorgio Vasari, oversaw the work in the 1550s and 1560s. Though the Medici did not reside there for long, the Palazzo was always used for state functions.

Today, the Palazzo has somewhat recovered its old purpose. It serves as Florence's city hall, and the council holds its meetings in the **Salone dei Cinquecento**, built by the republic in 1495. At that time, Leonardo da Vinci and Michelangelo were commissioned to fresco the two longer sides, a contest of talents that everyone in Florence looked forward to. For a number of reasons, it never came off; only a small part of Leonardo's fresco was ever completed, and Vasari painted it over sixty years later. Even the designs for both men's concepts have been lost. However, Michelangelo's statue of *Victory*, originally intended for the tomb of Pope Julius II in San Pietro in Vincoli in Rome, does stand in this room, installed here by Vasari in the 1560s.

Despite the Palazzo's functional role as a base for the city administration, nearly all of the more historic rooms are open to the public. Without even buying a ticket you can look round the ferociously overdecorated **Cortile**, or courtyard, redone by Vasari. Inside, and upstairs on the first floor there is the fascinating **Studiolo di Francesco I**, a little retreat created for Duke Cosimo's son, who liked to dabble in poisons, where Vasari and his assistants created a vast allegory of mythology, science, and alchemy; more Vasari in the Chambers of Leo X and Clement VII (including a famous scene of the 1527 siege); and even more Vasari in the 'Quartiere degli Elementi'. Vasari's workshop was perhaps the fastest and most reliable fresco machine in history—he never turned down a request from the dukes. Rooms with frescoes glorifying the Medici go on and on, but try not to miss the rooms of Eleanor of Toledo (Cosimo I's consort), done by Bronzino, or the **Sala del Giglio**, with a fine ceiling by the da Maiano brothers and the recently restored *Judith and Holofernes* by Donatello.

---

## Bargello

*Open 9am–2pm Tues–Sat; 9am–1pm Sun; adm.*

For hundreds of years, this medieval fortress-palace on the Via del Proconsolo behind the Palazzo Vecchio served as Florence's prison; today the inmates are men of marble—Italy's finest collection of sculpture, a fitting complement to the paintings in the Uffizi. When it was begun, about 1250, the Bargello was the Palazzo del Popolo, though by 1271 it was home to the foreign *podestà* installed by Charles of Anjou. When the Republic was reconstructed under the *Ordinamenti*, the decision was made to erect a bigger and grander seat of government—the Palazzo Vecchio. Just as that structure served as the model for so many Florentine palaces, so the Bargello was the model for the Palazzo, a rugged, austere work with a solid air of civic virtue about it. The Medici made a jail of it, but a thorough—and perhaps somewhat imaginative—restoration of the interior in the 19th century got it ready for its current job of housing the **Museo Nazionale**.

After the plain façade, the delightful arcaded courtyard comes as a surprise, full of interesting architectural fragments, plaques, and coats of arms in a wild vocabulary of symbols. In the first-floor galleries, there are some early works of Michelangelo, including the *Bacchus*, and also Giambologna's *Mercury*—a work so popular it has entered everyone's consciousness as the way Mercury should look. There are too a number of works by Cellini, including his preliminary model for *Perseus* and his bust of *Cosimo I*. Upstairs, passing through the **Loggia**, now converted into an 'aviary' for Giambologna's charming bronze birds, you come to the **Salone del Consiglio**. This 14th-century hall contains many of the greatest works of Donatello: the fascinatingly androgynous *David*, the *St George* from Orsanmichele, and the enigmatic Cupid or *Amor Atys*. These three alone make up a powerful case for considering Donatello the greatest of Renaissance sculptors. The alert watchfulness of *St George* created new possibilities in expressing movement, emotion, and depth of character in stone, a revolution in art that was obvious even to Donatello's contemporaries. The *David*, obviously from a different planet from Michelangelo's *David*, explores depths of the Florentine psyche the Florentines probably didn't know they had. The same could be said of the dangerous-looking little boy Cupid. No one knows for whom Donatello made it, or who it is really meant to represent. With its poppies, serpents, and winged sandals, it could easily be the ancient idol people in the 18th century mistook it for. Like Botticelli's mythological paintings, it reflects the artistic and intellectual undercurrents of the quattrocento, full of pagan philosophy and eroticism, a possibility rooted out in the terror of the Counter-Reformation and quite forgotten soon after.

Among the other artists represented in the hall are Luca della Robbia, Verrocchio, Bernini, Michelozzo and di Duccio. The two bronze panels made by Brunelleschi and Ghiberti for the Baptistry doors competition are preserved here; judge for yourself which is the better. Above, on the second floor, the collection continues with works mainly by Antonio Pollaiuolo and Verrocchio. The Bargello also houses an important collection of the decorative arts—rooms full of pretty bric-a-brac such as combs, mirrors, jewel caskets, reliquaries, Turkish helmets, vases and silks, wax anatomical figures, and majolica from Urbino. Some of the most beautiful pieces are in a collection of medieval French ivory—intricately carved scenes like the 'Assault on the Castle of Love' and other medieval fancies. The Bargello's **Chapel** has frescoes by an unknown follower of Giotto.

## Dante's Florence

Dante would contemplate his Beatrice, the story goes, at Mass in the **Badia Fiorentina**, a Benedictine church on Via del Proconsolo across from the Bargello, with a lovely Gothic spire to grace this corner of the Florentine skyline. The church has undergone many rebuildings since Willa, widow of a Margrave of Tuscany, began it in around 990, but there is still a monument to Ugo, the 'Good Margrave' mentioned in Dante, and a painting of the *Madonna Appearing to St Bernard* by Filippino Lippi.

Between the Badia and Via dei Calzaiuoli, a little corner of medieval Florence has survived the changes of centuries. In these quiet, narrow streets, you can visit the poet's birthplace, the **Casa di Dante** (*open 9.30–12.30, 3.30–6.30, Mon, Tues, Thurs–Sat; 9.30–12.30 Sun; closed Wed*), restored in this century as a museum to the poet, although now with the sad air of an after thought.. Nearby, the stoutly medieval **Torre del Castagna** is the last extant part of the original Palazzo del Popolo, predecessor to the Bargello and Palazzo Vecchio. After giving up on Beatrice, Dante married his second choice, Gemma Donati, in the **Santa Margherita** church on the same block. Another church nearby, **San Martino del Vescovo**, has a fine set of frescoes from the workshop of Ghirlandaio—worth a look inside if it's open.

## Florence As It Was

If, tramping the long and tired streets of this city, you still haven't discovered the Florence you came to find, stop in at the **Museo di Firenze Com'Era** (Museum of Florence As It Was), north of the Bargello and not far from the Duomo at Via dell'Oriuolo 24 (*open 9am–2pm Mon–Wed, Fri, Sat; 9am–1pm Sun; closed Thurs; adm*). In the first room, almost covering the entire wall, is the *Pianta della Catena*, most famous and most beautiful of the early views of Florence. Made in 1490 by an unknown artist (the handsome fellow pictured in the lower right-hand corner), it is really a copy of the original, lost during the Second World War in a Berlin museum. This fascinating painting captures Florence at the height of the Renaissance. Not much has changed; the great churches are without their façades, the Uffizi and Medici chapels have not yet appeared, and the Medici and Pitti palaces are shown without their later extensions. Most old views and paintings, like this one, show the city's buildings in bright colours—white, pink, and tan. If this really was the case, this exotic bloom of a city—as it was in the quattrocento—somehow becomes easier to imagine.

This museum is not large—at present it has only a number of plans and maps, as well as a collection of amateurish watercolours of Florence's sights from the last century. One surprising fact that becomes clear from a visit here is that today's fussy and staid Florentines are much less interested in Renaissance Florence than in the city of their grandparents. For some further evidence, check around the corner on Via Sant' Egidio, where some recent remodelling has uncovered posters from 1925 announcing plans for paying the war debt and a forthcoming visit of the Folies Bergère. The Florentines have restored them and put them under glass.

## The Uffizi Gallery

*Open 9am–7pm Tues–Sat; 9am–1pm Sun; adm exp.*

Poor Giorgio Vasari. His roosterish boastfulness and conviction that his was the best of all possible artistic worlds, set next to his very modest talents, have made him almost a comic figure in some art criticism. Even the Florentines don't like him. On one of the rare occasions when he tried his hand as an architect, though, he gave Florence something to be proud of. The Uffizi ('offices'), were meant as Cosimo's secretariat, incorporating the old mint and archive buildings, with plenty of room for the bureaucrats needed to run the efficient, modern state Cosimo was building. Vasari's plan, a matched pair of arcaded buildings with restrained, elegant façades, conceals a revolutionary but little-known innovation. Iron reinforcements inside the façades make the huge amount of window area possible, and keep the building stable on the soft ground below; it was a trick that would be almost forgotten until the building of the Crystal Palace and the first American skyscrapers.

The architects of the Renaissance in Florence were astoundingly indifferent to matters of urban design. They thought like painters, and gave as little attention to streets and squares as a painter would to the design of a museum gallery. The Uffizi is the noble exception, an intelligent conception that unites the Piazza della Signoria with the Arno. Almost from the start, the Medici began to store their huge art collections in parts of the Uffizi. The last of the Medici, Duchess Anna Maria Lodovica, willed the entire hoard to the people of Florence in

1737. Give yourself a day or two to spend on the most important picture gallery in Italy, and come early in the day, especially in summer, when queues sometimes stretch around the arcades and beyond by 11am.

## The British in Italy

'A man who has not been in Italy is always conscious of an inferiority, for his not having seen what is expected of a man to see.' So intoned Dr Johnson, but the plain fact is that Italy can be dangerous to your health, especially if you're of the British persuasion. For centuries its dishevelled natural beauty, its acres of great art, its easy opportunities (now sadly extinct) for love, lust, and assorted other vices, especially during endless bacchanalian carnivals, played with people's minds, often turning perfectly coherent brains into plates of mushy polenta. This is a known historical fact, because thousands of travellers (especially British) have felt compelled to commit their breathless impressions to paper. Many of these earnest souls have compared Italy to Circe, the lovely sorceress who transformed men into pigs, and indeed, the country does have the peculiar power to delude any number of good secretaries and accountants into believing that they are really poets, sculptors, or artists. Those who are already poets and artists, on the other hand, tend to suffer adverse effects once they cross the frontier. Even those who refused to talk to Italians, like Robert Browning, disintegrated in the country's enervating humours. 'Open my heart and you will see/Graven inside of it, Italy' he wrote, and the Venetians, with wicked smiles, have engraved it into the wall of his palazzo on the Grand Canal.

One of the most chronic and ultimately incurable cases of Italophilism infected Stendhal, author of the *Charterhouse of Parma* and a freight load of such dubious slop as '…in this beautiful country one must only make love; other pleasures of the soul are cramped here. Love here is delicious. Anywhere else it is only a bad copy.' As silly as it may seem, this is no joke. Every year, especially in Florence, hospitals receive dozens of cases—almost always British tourists—who have been so dazzled and overwhelmed by art and Italy that they become giddy, their hearts flutter, they collapse. They are victims of what Italian medical books call 'the Stendhal Syndrome'.

The size of the collection in the Uffizi is not overwhelming, but every work is choice. All the Florentine masters are represented, and the Medici even deigned to purchase a few foreigners. Here is a brief list of the works most worth seeing: near the entrance, amid halls of Medici clutter, the series of *Illustrious Men* (which includes the Cumean sibyl!) in the dry precise style of Andrea del Castagno, then some fine trecento works by Duccio di Boninsegna and Cimabue. If you can't make it to Siena this trip, be sure to see the works of that city's school, especially the Lorenzetti brothers and Simone Martini. From the early quattrocento Florentine painters, there is Uccello's *Battle of San Romano*; even with only one third of the original present, this is one of the most provocative of all paintings, a surreal vision of war with pink, white, and blue toy horses. Piero della Francesca contributes a *Portrait of Federico di Montefeltro* with his famous nose (*see* 'Urbino', p.581); among the works by Filippo and

Filippino Lippi there is a powerful grey *St Jerome*. Botticelli gets one big room to himself, in which are displayed his uncanny, erotic masterpieces including *The Birth of Venus*, *Primavera*, and *Pallas and the Centaur* (another subtle allegory of the Medici triumph—the rings on Athena's gown were a family symbol), as well as some of his religious paintings and the disturbing *Calumny*, an introduction to the dark side of the quattrocento psyche.

Be sure to visit Room 15 and Leonardo's *Annunciation*, an intellectual rather than divine revelation that is one of the foremost achievements of Florentine art. Nearby are works by Verrocchio (Leonardo's teacher) and Luca Signorelli, and a formidable sea monster in Piero di Cosimo's *Perseus and Andromeda*. In the Tribuna, a gaudy chamber designed by Bernardo Buontalenti, the Medici kept a valuable collection of Hellenistic and Roman sculpture, as well as portraits of *Cosimo* and *Eleanor of Toledo* by Bronzino. There's a surprising amount of German and Flemish painting, including Dürer's *Adoration of the Magi* and *Adam and Eve*, both looking as much like Italian painting as he could make them—and for a still bigger surprise, Cranach's *Portraits of Luther and Melanchthon*, spying on the Catholics. Venetians aren't as well represented, but there is the *Judgement of Solomon* by Giorgione and a *Sacred Allegory* by Giovanni Bellini.

Michelangelo always maintained that sculpture and fresco were the only arts fit for a man; oil painting he disdained, and just coincidentally he wasn't very good at it. The *Sacra Famiglia* here is the only canvas he ever finished. Next come some portraits by Raphael, Rosso Fiorentino and Pontormo. Those of Andrea del Sarto have been been singled out for restoration—they will light up the room when the bright original colours are revealed. Titian's overdressed Spaniards and well-upholstered girls get a room to themselves. The collections continue through painters of the 17th and 18th centuries—works of Rembrandt (two self-portraits), Rubens, Van Dyck, even Goya; the one exceptional picture here is the *Boy Playing at Cards* by Chardin.

In May 1993 the gallery became a victim of Italy's ongoing political drama when a mysterious bomb exploded in one of the streets outside. The blast affected various parts of the structure, and—although the restoration of the Uffizi is being carried on with much more alacrity than the routine 'restoration' work in Italian museums—for the next few years you will find more rooms than usual closed for restoration, and some pictures withdrawn from show. Thankfully, no major works of art were lost, and the most important paintings and sculpture from the rooms that are closed have in the meantime all been relocated to undamaged areas of the gallery. However, the one section of the Uffizi that was seriously damaged was the fascinating *Corridoio Vasariano*, or Vasari Corridor. Vasari built it at the request of Cosimo I, who wanted to pass from the Palazzo Vecchio and the Uffizi to his new home across the river in the Pitti Palace without rubbing elbows with his subjects—from the bottom end of the Uffizi, facing the Arno, a covered passageway up above street level leads along the river, then over the top of the Ponte Vecchio, through the rooftops on the other side and into the Pitti. The corridor contains a unique collection of artists' self-portraits, by Vasari himself, Velasquez, Rubens, Hogarth, and many French artists, most of which are still unharmed. Admission to the corridor was always restricted (with a tour, by previous appointment only), but when it will again be possible to see it even on these terms is, at time of writing, impossible to say.

## The Museum of the History of Science

*Open 9.30–1, 2–5, Mon, Wed, Fri; 9.30am–1pm Tues, Thurs, Sat; adm exp.*

Given the amount that Florence and the rest of Tuscany contributed to the birth of science, it is only fitting to have such a museum in the heart of the city, in the Via Castellani just behind the Uffizi. Even in the dark centuries, Florence never abandoned its scientific interests; this museum's collections began with an institute founded by the Medici in the 1730s. It was called the Accademia del Cimento, whose motto was 'Try and try again'. Pride of place goes to Galileo's instruments, including his first telescope, in addition to a large number of astrolobes, early microscopes, models of the planets, and armillary spheres, many of which are beautiful works of art in their own right. The last rooms conrain wax anatomical models, a 15th-century Medici fetish.

## Ponte Vecchio and Ponte S. Trinità

The 'Old Bridge' is to Florence what Tower Bridge is to London. No one knows how long the Arno has been spanned at this point. The present bridge, built in 1345, replaced a wooden construction from the 970s, which in turn was the successor to a span that may have gone back to the Romans. Like medieval bridges in London and many other European cities, the new 14th-century bridge had shops and houses built all along it. By the 1500s it had become the street of the butchers; after Vasari built Cosimo's secret passage over the top, the duke evicted the butchers (he didn't like the pong) and gave their places to the gold-smiths. They have kept their spot ever since, and hordes of shoppers from around the world descend on it each year to scrutinize the Florentine talent for jewellery. This is the most pres-tigious shopping location in Florence, and the jewellers are happy to stay—they could not be deterred even by the 1966 flood, when a fortune in gold was washed down the Arno.

In the summer of 1944, the river briefly became a German defensive line during the slow painful retreat across central Italy. Before they left Florence, the Germans blew up every one of the city's bridges, saving only the Ponte Vecchio. Somehow the city managed to talk them out of it, and instead, buildings on both sides were destroyed, and the rubble piled up to block the approaches. Florence's most beautiful span, the **Ponte Santa Trinità**, had to go,

*Ponte Vecchio*

however. The Florentines like their city just as it is, and immediately after the war they set about replacing the bridges exactly as they were. In the case of Santa Trinità it was quite a task. Old quarries had to be reopened to duplicate the stone, and old methods used to cut it (modern power saws would have done it too cleanly). The graceful curve of the three arches was a problem; they cannot be constructed geometrically, and considerable speculation went on over how the architect (Ammannati, in 1567) had done it. Finally, remembering that Michelangelo had advised Ammannati on the project, someone discovered that the same form of arch could be seen on the decoration of Michelangelo's Medici Chapels, constructed most likely not by mathematics and common engineering, but by pure artistic imagination. Fortune lent a hand in the reconstruction; of the original statues of the 'Four Seasons', almost all the pieces were fished out of the Arno and reconstructed. Spring's head was missing, however, and controversy raged for a decade over whether to replace it or leave it as it was, until some divers found it, completely by accident, in 1961.

## Around Piazza della Repubblica

On the map, it is easy to pick out the small rectangle of narrow, straight streets at the heart of Florence; these remain unchanged from the little *castrum* of Roman days. At its centre, the old forum deteriorated through the Dark Ages into a shabby market square, surrounded by the Jewish ghetto. So it remained, until Florence in a fit of post-Risorgimento ambition decided to make it a symbol of the city's reawakening. The square was given a new design and a thorough facelift, and a grand arch was built, with a big inscription: THE ANCIENT CITY CENTRE RESTORED TO NEW LIFE FROM THE SQUALOR OF CENTURIES. Unfortunately the results were the same as in the new façade for the Duomo; Piazza della Repubblica is one of the ghastliest squares in Italy. Just the same, it is a popular place with tourists and natives alike, full of cafés with outside tables, and something of an oasis among the severe, unwelcoming streets of old Florence.

Those streets are worth walking. Dreary as they look at first sight, they are part of the soul of Florence. Also they are full of surprises; walk down Calimala, an important shopping street south of the Piazza, and you will encounter the **Arte della Lana**, behind Orsanmichele and connected to it by an overhead passageway. The 'Wool Corporation', richest of the guilds save that of the bankers, was really a sort of manufacturers' cooperative; its headquarters, built in 1308, was restored in 1905 in a delightful William Morris style of medieval picturesque. Nearby, further towards the river, is one of Florence's oldest marketplaces, covered by a beautiful loggia built in the 1500s. The **Mercato Nuovo**, where vendors hawk purses, toys, and every sort of trinket, was in medieval times a merchants' exchange; it was also the place where the *carroccio*, the decorated wagon that served as a rallying point for the citizen armies during battles, was kept in time of peace. Florentines often call this the *Loggia del Porcellino*, after the drooling bronze boar put up as a decoration in 1612, a copy of a Greek sculpture in the Uffizi.

On the corner of Via delle Terme and Via Porta Rossa, the 14th-century Palazzo Davanzati has been restored (also with a touch of the William Morris, it seems) to recreate the atmosphere of a wealthy merchant's house of the 1400s as the **Museo della Casa**. Though some of the furnishings are from a century or two later, the late medieval atmosphere is certainly present and if historically accurate, a tribute to the taste of the honest burghers of the time. Two fine rooms, called the 'Room of the Parrot' and the 'Room of the Peacocks' have murals, tapestries, furniture (especially wedding chests), and ceramics, and even 14th-century high-heeled shoes are part of the furnishings; the dumb-waiter and bathrooms were luxurious at the time. **Museo della Casa Fiorentina Antica**, Via Porta Rossa 13 (*open 9am–2pm Tues–Sat; 9am–12.45pm Sun; adm*). Some of Florence's oldest and most typical town houses lie between here and the river. Off Via Pellicceria, behind the Mercato Nuovo, is the 14th-century Guelph Party Building, often the real seat of power in the city, built with money confiscated from exiled Ghibellines.

Closer to the Arno stands the **Church of SS. Apostoli**, with a tabernacle by Andrea della Robbia; in the narrow streets around it you'll find the Piazzetta del Limbo, where unbaptized babies were buried in the Middle Ages. Further down along the river **Santa Trinità** is a Gothic church with a dull façade added in the 1590s. One of the chapels has colourful frescoes by Lorenzo Monaco, who also did the altarpiece; another, the Sassetti Chapel, was decorated by Ghirlandaio. Francesco Sassetti, a banker and friend of the Medici, commissioned the work, and though ostensibly a series on the life of St Francis, scholars always comment on it as a document of Florence's social history. All the Medici, Sassetti, and their friends are present in finely detailed portraits, arranged to show in a subtle way the new hierarchy of political and economic power in the city.

For more Ghirlandaio, continue on to the 13th-century **Ognissanti** (All Saints' Church), with another heavy façade added later. The man who named a convinent, Amerigo Vespucci, is buried by the second altar on the right. Botticelli and Ghirlandaio both contributed versions of St Jerome for the cloister (*open 9–12:45 daily*), and the latter's *Cenacolo* in the refectory is one of his better known works, a Last Supper that is more a garden party, with lemon trees and exotic birds, as well as a sulky Judas, third from the right.

## Conspicuous Consumption *alla Fiorentina*

The streets west of Piazza della Repubblica have always been the choicest district of Florence. Via Tornabuoni, the fanciest shopping street, is as well known in fashion as Via Montenapoleone in Milan or Via dei Condotti in Rome. In the 15th century, this was the area most of the new merchant élite chose for their palaces. Today's bankers build great skyscrapers for the firm and settle for modest mansions themselves; in medieval Florence, things were reversed. The bankers and wool tycoons really owned their businesses, and in absolute terms probably had more money than anyone had ever had before. While their places of business were usually quite simple, for themselves they constructed imposing city palaces; all in the same conservative style, and competing with each other in size like some Millionaire's Row of Victorian-era America.

The style, derived from the Palazzo Vecchio, began at the **Rucellai Palace** on Via della Vigna Nuova, a building designed by Alberti in 1446 for a prominent manufacturer and patron of learning. Much has been made of this building as a turning point in architecture; its only real innovation, though, is a consistent and skilful use of the classical 'orders', the system of proportion learned from Vitruvius. Of many other palaces in the neighbourhood north of Piazza S. Trinità, two stand out—the 1465 **Palazzo Antinori** at the northern end of Tornabuoni, and the **Palazzo Strozzi**, two streets south. The Strozzi is the daddy of them all, the accustomed design blown up to heroic proportions; though three storeys like the rest, here each floor is as tall as three or four normal ones. Filippo Strozzi, head of a family of bankers who often felt strong enough to challenge the leadership of the Medici, built it in 1489 at the height of the clan's fortunes. Fifty years later his grandchildren were all exiles, bankers and advisers to the king of France. Both the Antinori and Strozzi palaces were the work of Benedetto da Maiano; for their use of classical proportions, the Florentines counted them among their highest achievements, surpassing the architecture of the ancients. The Strozzi houses a large library, and often hosts art exhibitions.

## Santa Maria Novella

The broad piazza in front of this church bears two fat obelisks set on bronze turtles and placed like the monuments in a Roman circus. They served the same purpose; in the 1600s the wealthy families of the neighbourhood would hold an annual carriage race around them. But Santa Maria Novella, begun by the Dominicans in 1246, was always associated with the great families. Between them they bestowed so much money to embellish it, that by the 1500s the church had become a museum in itself, with important works of many late medieval and Renaissance artists.

The brilliant black-and-white patterned façade, badly in need of a cleaning but still the finest in Florence, shows the continuity of the city's style from medieval times. The lower half is

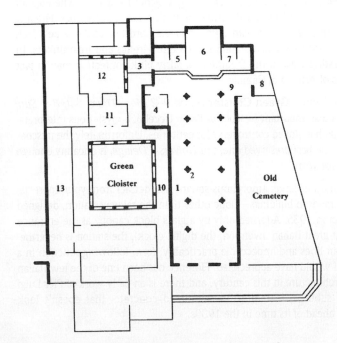

### Santa Maria Novella

1  Mascio's 'Trinity'
2  Brunelleschi's Pulpit
3  Cappèlla Strozzi
4  Sacristy
5  Cappèlla Gondi
6  Sanctuary
7  Filippo Strozzi Chapel
8  Ruccellai Chapel
9  Gothic Tombs
10  Universal Deluge
11  Spanish Chapel
12  Chiostrino dei Morti
13  Refectory

part of the original work, finished before 1360, but the rest had to wait for one of the Rucellai family to commission Alberti to finish the job. It's his best work in Florence, a synthesis of classical architecture and medieval Florentine tradition, with volutes and arabesques that seem already to prefigure the Baroque. An odd touch is the image of the sun at the apex, the only image or symbol of any kind in Alberti's plan. Lower down, Cosimo I added the two unusual sundials over the left- and right-hand arches.

Inside, above the portal, there is a recently restored *Nativity* by Botticelli. From there, proceeding clockwise around the church: a pulpit with reliefs by Brunelleschi, and Massaccio's *Trinità* fresco, perhaps one of the earliest works with the temerity to depict God the Father, and then a *Resurrection* by Vasari. In the left transept, the Gondi Chapel has Brunelleschi's only wood sculpture, a crucifix—Vasari tells the story of how he made it to show Donatello a Christ with proper dignity, after complaining that his friend's crucifix (now in Santa Croce) made the Redeemer 'look like a peasant'. A great series of frescoes of the *Lives of St John and the Virgin* by Ghirlandaio surrounds the main altar. All his students helped him complete it—little Michelangelo included. Some equally fine frescoes by Filippino Lippi adorn the Filippo Strozzi Chapel in the right transept, where Strozzi is buried; the architect who designed his palace, da Maiano, also carved his tomb. Another tomb nearby belongs to a Patriarch of Constantinople who accompanied the Byzantine emperor to Italy in 1440 seeking last-minute aid against the Turks.

There's little of interest in the right-hand chapels, but just outside the left transept are some of the best parts of this surprisingly large monastic complex. Another Strozzi Chapel, this one from the 1360s, has a fine early fresco series of the *Last Judgement* by Nardo di Cione, brother of Orcagna. The Spanish Chapel, commissioned by Cosimo I's Spanish wife Eleanor of Toledo, offers a chilling touch of Counter-Reformation with a series of frescoes detailing the history of the Dominicans: the *domini canes* ('dogs of the Lord') sit at the pope's feet, symbolizing the order that ran the Inquisition and sniffed out heretics and freethinkers. In the background, an interesting view of the Duomo as a fairly pink confection may in fact represent the original plans of Arnolfo di Cambio.

Best of all, however, is the famous **Green Cloister** (*open 9–2 Mon–Thurs, Sat; 8–1 Sun; adm*), decorated with the most important frescoes of Paolo Uccello, a mysterious interpretation of the story of Noah that has stoked controversy for centuries. Unfortunately the frescoes are much deteriorated, but the best preserved one, the *Universal Deluge*, is uncanny enough to haunt your imagination for years.

Just behind Santa Maria, another large, amorphous square will detract from your appreciation of one of Italy's finest modern buildings—none other than the railway station, designed by the architect Michelucci in 1935. Adorned only by a glass block canopy at the entrance (and an early model of that great Italian invention, the digital clock), the station is nevertheless remarkable for its clean lines and impeccable practicality; form following function in a way that even Brunelleschi would have appreciated. Florence has been one of the few Italian cities to encourage good architecture in this century, and there is an early work of Pier Luigi Nervi out in the eastern suburbs, a stadium in reinforced concrete, that doesn't look anything now, but was far ahead of its time in the 1930s.

# San Lorenzo

Around the railway station beats the true heart of tourist Florence, dozens of streets around the Via Nazionale packed with hotels, restaurants, and bars. There's an almost Neapolitan air about the boisterous street market that surrounds the **Mercato Centrale**, built in the 1890s to replace the old market evicted from the Piazza della Repubblica. The market *bancarelle* extend all the way to **San Lorenzo**, a church always associated with the Medici and a shrine to the art of Brunelleschi and Michelangelo. Brunelleschi built it in the 1420s; Michelangelo designed a façade that was never realized, leaving the odd shaped church as charming as a huge dreadnought docked in the piazza. The interior, however, is essential Brunelleschi, a contemplative repetition of arches and columns in grey and white, while nothing else in Florence prepares you for the two pulpits in the nave, the last violent, near-impressionistic works of Donatello. Off the left transept, the **Old Sacristy** is a beautiful vaulted chamber with calmer sculptural decoration by Donatello.

The real interest is outside the church; a separate entrance on Piazza Madonna degli Aldobrandini leads to the famous **Medici Chapels** (*open 9–2 Tues–Sat; 9–1 Sun; adm*), and their celebrated sculptures by Michelangelo. First, however, you will have to pass through the Prince's Chapel, under a huge eight-sided dome that dwarfs the rest of San Lorenzo, begun in 1604 following a design by a dilettante architect member of the Medici family. Several of the Medici dukes are buried in this dreary, trashy rotunda, the true monument of the ducal period and a sobering demonstration of just how soon Florence's great age of art declined into provincialism and preciosity. It certainly cost enough—the entire lower walls and floor are done in *pietra dura* with rich marbles from around the world, a job not completed until this century.

From here, a corridor to the left leads to the **New Sacristy**, designed by Michelangelo in a severe style to match the Old Sacristy on the other side. The two tombs, of Giuliano Medici, Duke of Nemours, and Lorenzo, Duke of Urbino, the ruler to whom Machiavelli dedicated *The Prince*, are decorated with an allegorical sculptural scheme that has caused much discussion over the centuries. Giuliano is portrayed as a soldier representing the Active Life, with figures representing Day and Night reclining on his sarcophagus below. Lorenzo, as the Contemplative Life, sits and contemplates, overlooking figures of Dawn and Dusk (true to life in one respect; the passive Lorenzo was a disappointment to Machiavelli and everyone else). The male figures, at least, are among Michelangelo's triumphs. The women, Dawn and Night, come off less well. Michelangelo never had much use for the ladies—he wouldn't even use female models—and whatever role they played in his personal mythology he portrays them here as imperfect men, male forms with flabbier musculature and breasts stuck on like superfluous appendages.

In front of San Lorenzo, a separate entrance leads to the **Laurentian Library** (open 9am–1pm Mon–Sat), designed for the Medici by Michelangelo, an important landmark in architecture: it was Michelangelo's first commission (along with the Medici chapels), and one of the first steps on the slippery slope to Mannerism.

## Palazzo Medici

San Lorenzo became the Medici's church because it stood just round the corner from the family palace—a huge, stately building on Via Cavour constructed by Alberti and Michelozzo about the same time as the Rucellai Palace. The family's coat-of-arms, which you've probably already noticed everywhere in Florence, is prominently displayed in the corners. The seven, sometimes six, red boluses probably come from the family's origin as pharmacists (*medici*), and opponents called them 'the pills'. Medici supporters, however, made them their battle cry in street battles: 'Balls! Balls!'.

The main reason for visiting is one of Florence's hidden delights, the **Chapel** (*open 9–12.30, 3–5, Mon, Tues, Thurs–Sat; 9–12 Sun; closed Wed*) with extravagantly colourful frescoes by Benozzo Gozzoli. The *Procession of the Magi* is hardly a religious painting, a merry scene full of portraits of the Medici and others among the crowd following the Three Kings. The artist included himself, with his name on his hat. In the foreground of one of the panels, note the black man carrying a bow. Blacks (also Turks, Circassians, Tartars, and other non-Europeans) were common enough in Renaissance Florence. Though originally brought as slaves, by the 1400s not all were still servants. Contemporary writers mention them as artisans, fencing masters, soldiers and, in one famous case, as an archery instructor, who may be the man pictured here. For an extraordinary contrast, pop into the **gallery** (up the second set of stairs) with its 17th-century ceiling by Neopolitan Luca Giordano, showing the last, unspeakable Medici floating around in marshmallow clouds.

## Fra Angelico's San Marco

*Open 9am–2pm Tues–Sat; 9am–1pm Sun; adm.*

Despite all the others who contributed to this Dominican monastery and church, it has always been best known for the work of its most famous resident. Fra Angelico lived here from 1436 until his death in 1455, spending the time turning Michelozzo's simple **cloister** into a complete exposition of his own deep faith, expressed in bright playroom colours and angelic pastels. Fra Angelico painted the frescoes in the corners of the cloister, and on the first floor there is a small museum of his work, collected from various Florentine churches, as well as a number of early 15th-century portraits by Fra Bartolomeo, capturing some of the most sincere spirituality of that age. The *Last Supper* in the refectory is by Ghirlandaio. Other Fra Angelico works include the series of the *Life of Christ*, telling the story sweetly and succinctly, and a serenely confident *Last Judgement* in which all the saved are well-dressed Italians, holding hands. They get to keep their clothes in heaven, while the bad (mostly princes and prelates) are stripped to receive their interesting tortures.

Climbing the stairs to the monk's dormitory, right at the top your eyes meet the Angelic Friar's masterpiece, a miraculous *Annunciation* that offers an intriguing comparison to Leonardo's *Annunciation* in the Uffizi. The subject was a favourite with Florentine artists, not only because it was a severe test—expressing a divine revelation with a composition of strict economy—but because the Annunciation, falling near the spring equinox, was New Year's Day for Florence until the Medici adopted the Pope's calendar in the 17th century. In each of the monks' cells, Fra Angelico and students painted scenes of the Crucifixion, all the same but for some slight differences in pose; walking down the corridor and glancing in the cells successively gives the impression of a cartoon. One of the cells belonged to Savonarola, who was the prior here during his period of dominance in Florence; it has simple furniture of the period and a portrait of Savonarola by Fra Bartolomeo. In a nearby corridor, you can see an anonymous painting of the monk and two of his followers being led to the stake on Piazza della Signoria. Michelozzo's Library, off the main corridor, is as light and airy as the cloisters below; in it is displayed a collection of choir books, one illuminated by Fra Angelico.

If you liked Andrea del Castagno's work in the Uffizi, just around the corner from San Marco is a work many consider to be his best, the *Last Supper*, in the **Cenacolo di Sant' Apollonia**, Via XXVII Aprile 1 (*open 9–2 Tues–Sat; 9–1 Sun*).

## Piazza Santissima Annunziata

This square, really the only Renaissance attempt at a unified ensemble in Florence, is surrounded by arcades on three sides. The earliest of its buildings, one of Brunelleschi's most famous works, is also a monument to Renaissance Italy's long, hard and ultimately unsuccessful struggle towards some kind of social consciousness. Even in the best times, Florence's poor were treated like dirt; if any enlightened soul had been so bold as to propose even a modern conservative 'trickle down' theory to the Medici and the banking élite, their first thought would have been how to stop the leaks. Babies, at least, had it a little better. The **Spedale degli Innocenti** (*open 9–2 Mon, Tues, Thurs–Sat; 9–1 Sun; closed Wed; adm*), built in the 1440s, was Italy's first foundling hospital (in most Italian cities unwanted children were commonly abandoned in alleyways), and still functions as an orphanage today. Brunelleschi's beautiful arcade, decorated with the famous *tondi* of infants in swaddling clothes by Luca della Robbia, was one of the early classicizing experiments in architecture. There's a small picture gallery containing Ghirlandaio's *Adoration of the Magi* and several other works.

To complement Brunelleschi's arches, the old church of **Santissima Annunziata** was rebuilt and given a broad arcaded portico by Michelozzo facing the street. Behind the portico the architect added the *Chiostrino dei Voti*, a porch decorated with a collection of early 16th-century frescoes, including two by Andrea del Sarto. The best of these, faded as it is, is a finely detailed *Nativity* by Alessio Baldovinetti, one of the quattrocento's underappreciated masters. The church itself is the gaudiest in Florence; its freshly gilded elliptical dome, its unusual polygonal tribune around the sanctuary and megatons of *pietra dura* have helped it become the city's high-society parish, where even funerals are major social events. The huge candlelit chapel in the rear is the Tempietta, also by Michelozzo, sheltering a miraculous painting of *The Annunciation*.

## The Accademia

*Open 9am–2pm Tues–Sat; 9am–1pm Sun; adm exp.*

It may not be Florence's most interesting museum, but in summer the queues at the Accademia, just off the Piazza Santissima Annunziata, are often as long as those at the Uffizi. What they are most anxious to get a look at is of course Michelangelo's *David*. Just over a hundred years ago Florence decided to take this precocious symbol of republican liberty in out of the rain. The artist completed it for the city in 1501, when he was 26, and it was this work that established the overwhelming reputation he had in his own time. Looking entirely contented with his own perfection, he stands in a classical exedra built just for him. As the political symbol the republic commissioned, he may be excessive—the irony of a David the size of Goliath is disconcerting—but as a symbol of the artistic and intellectual aspirations of the Renaissance, he is unsurpassed. Other works by Michelangelo include the famous *non finiti*: the *Prisoners*, and *St Matthew*, tortured forms still waiting for Michelangelo to come back and finish liberating them from the stone; also one of his three versions of the *Pietà*.

There is plenty of indifferent painting in the Accademia, but persevere for such works as the *Deposition from the Cross* by Perugino, the sweet and small *Madonna del Mare* by Botticelli, and Uccello's very dirty *Thebaid*. Some of the best works are in a room of lesser-known masters of the quattrocento, especially Mariotto di Cristoforo and the 'Maestro del Casione Adimare', the latter known only for the painted chest here, a delightful scene of a marriage in Florence in the 1450s that has been reproduced in half the books ever written about the Renaissance.

# The Archaeology Museum

*Open 9am–2pm Tues–Sat; 9am–1pm Sun; adm.*

One of the most devious tricks of the Florentine museum torture is to keep your interest by changing the subject; just when you can't take another transcendent Renaissance painting, they politely offer a chance to see the greatest collection of Etruscan art in Tuscany. Nor is that all; the Egyptian and pre-historic collections in the **Museo Archeologico**, at Via della Colonna 36, are also exceptional. Again, the Medici are responsible; the museum began with purchases by Cosimo and Lorenzo il Magnifico. The Etruscans fill room after room, but the star attractions are two exquisite bronzes; the *Arringatore*, or Orator, a civic-minded and civilized-looking gentleman whom the inscription tells us was named Aurus Metellus, and the *Chimera*, a remarkable beast with the three heads of a lion, goat, and snake. This 5th-century BC Etruscan work, dug up near Arezzo in 1555 and immediately snatched by the Medici, had a great influence on the Mannerist artists. There is no Mannerist fancy about its origins, though; like all such composite monsters, it is a religious icon, a calendar beast symbolizing the three seasons of the ancient Mediterranean agricultural year.

Greek art is also represented; Etruscan and Roman noble families were wont to buy up all they could afford. There is an excellent *kouros*, a young man in the archaic style from 6th-century BC Sicily, an almost complete ancient chariot, some good vases, and an unusual recent find, a 4th-century BC silver urn called the *Baratti Amphora*, made in Antioch and covered with scores of small medallions showing mythological figures. Scholars believe that images and their arrangement may encode an entire system of belief, the secret teaching of one of the mystic-philosophical cults common in Hellenistic times, and they hope some day to decipher it.

# Santa Croce

Santa Maria Novella was the Dominicans' church, and so naturally the Franciscans had to have one just as big and grand. The original church, said to have been founded by St Francis himself, went by the board in Florence's colossal building programme of the 1290s. Arnolfo di Cambio planned its successor, largely completed by the 1450s, but a job of 'restoration' by Vasari in the 1560s ruined much of the original interior. The façade, in the accustomed Florentine black and white marble, nevertheless has something of the Victorian Gothic about it—just as it should, since it was only added in the 1850s, a gift from Sir Francis Sloane. Of all the modern façades on Italy's churches, built to atone finally for the chronic Renaissance inability ever to finish anything, this one may be the best. No one has yet succeeded in doing anything with the vast, hideous piazza in front of it; at present there is a large chunk of rock there, posing as contemporary sculpture.

The interior is a different story; like Santa Maria Novella it is a museum in itself. Starting clockwise from the left side: near the door is the tomb of Galileo, whose remains were moved here only after the Church grudgingly consented to allow him a Christian burial in 1737. For a while it was the custom to bury great Italians here, as a sort of Tuscan Westminster Abbey, and you'll see plenty of tombs along both sides, mostly of thoroughly forgotten men of the 19th century. Two chapels down, the *Monument to Carlo Marsuppini*

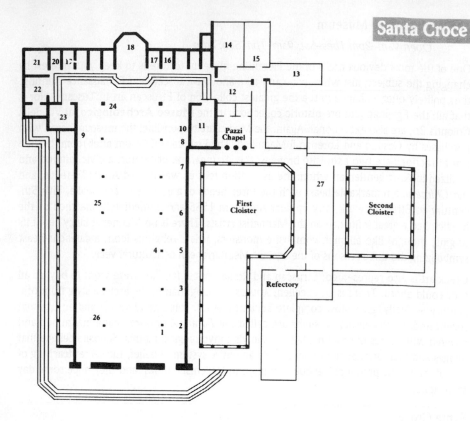

1 Madonna del Latte

2 Tomb of Michelangelo

3 Monument to Dante

4 Benedetto da Maiano's Pulpit

5 Vittorio Alfieri's Tomb

6 Tomb of Machaivelli

7 Donatello's *Annunciation*

8 Tomb of Leonardo Bruni

9 Tomb of Carlo Marsuppini

10 Tomb of Rossini

11 Castellani Chapel

12 Baroncelli Chapel

13 Medici Chapel

14 Sacristy

15 Rinuccini Chapel

16 Peruzzi Chapel

17 Bardi Chapel

18 Sanctuary

19 Bardi di Libertà Chapel

20 Bardi di Vernio Chapel

21 Niccolini Chapel

22 Bardi Chapel

23 Salviati Chapel

24 Monument to Alberti

25 Tomb of Lorenzo Ghiberti

26 Galileo's Tomb

27 Museo dell'Opera di S. Croce

is a mine of good quattrocento sculpture, mostly by Verrocchio and Desiderio da Settignano. Look in the Bardi Chapel in the left transept for the *Crucifix* by Donatello (the one Brunelleschi said looked like a peasant). Many of the small vaulted chapels that flank the high altar contain important late (1330s) works by Giotto, his assistants, and his followers. In the second **Bardi Chapel** is a series of frescoes on the *Life of St Francis* that can be compared with the more famous ones at Assisi.

The Peruzzi Chapel frescoes detail the *Lives of St John the Evangelist and St John the Baptist*. These works had a tremendous influence on all the later Florentine artists, but by the 18th century they were considered eyesores and whitewashed for 150 years—hence their fragmentary state. Two of Giotto's immediate artistic heirs, the Gaddi, also contributed much to Santa Croce. Agnolo Gaddi did the stained glass around the high altar, as well as the fascinating series of frescoes on the *Legend of the Cross*—how Seth received a branch from St Michael and planted it over Adam's grave, how the tree that grew from it was shaped into a beam for a bridge, then buried by Solomon when his guest the Queen of Sheba prophesied that it would someday bring about the end of the Jews. The beam was dug up and shaped into Christ's Cross, later found by St Helena, Constantine's mother, and then stolen by a Persian king and eventually recovered by the Emperor Heraclius. In the **Sacristy**, off to the right, there are more fine frescoes by Agnolo Gaddi's father Taddeo, and yet more Gaddis in the Castellani Chapel (Agnolo) and Baroncelli Chapel (Taddeo).

Back down the right side of the church, Donatello's Tabernacle has a beautiful relief of the *Annunciation*. Then some more tombs: Rossini, Machiavelli, Michelangelo, and Dante. Michelangelo's is the work of Vasari, who thought himself just the fellow for the job. Vasari's vandalism ruined most of the chapels on this side, once embellished with frescoes by Orcagna and other great trecento painters. His replacements, like his tomb for Michelangelo, are misfortunes. Dante isn't buried here at all. The Florentines always thought they would eventually get his body back from Ravenna; once they even bribed a pope to order the Ravennese to give it up, whereupon the body mysteriously disappeared for a decade or two until the affair was forgotten.

## The Pazzi Chapel

*Open April–Sept 10–12.30, 2–6.30; Oct–Mar 10–12.30, 3–5; closed Wed; adm, one charge for both Pazzi Chapel and museum.*

One of Santa Croce's chapels carries an entrance fee, but it's well worth it. Brunelleschi, who could excel on the monumental scale of the cathedral dome, saved some of his best work for small places. Without knowing the architect, and something about the austere religious tendencies of the Florentines, the Pazzi Chapel is inexplicable, a Protestant reformation in architecture, unlike anything ever built before. The 'vocabulary' is essential Brunelleschi: simple pilasters, arches, and rosettes in grey stone and white plaster. The only decoration is a set of modest terracotta apostles by Luca della Robbia, coloured roundels of the Evangelists by Donatello, and a small stained-glass window by Alessio Baldovinetti. Even so, this is enough. The contemplative repetition of elements makes for an aesthetic that posed a direct challenge to the international Gothic of the time.

Across the broad cloister, the monks' refectory and several adjoining rooms now house the **Museo dell'Opera di Santa Croce**, with more works by della Robbia, bits from a large fresco by Orcagna wrecked by Vasari's remodelling, one of Donatello's statues from Orsanmichele, the gilded bronze *St Louis of Toulouse*, and a famous, mournful *Crucifix* by Cimabue, one of the early landmarks of Florentine painting, but only partially restored after damage in the 1966 flood. Yet another fresco of the *Tree of the Cross*, by Taddeo Gaddi, adorns one wall of the refectory.

## Around Santa Croce

The east end of Florence, a rambling district packed with artisans and small manufacturers, was the artists' quarter in Renaissance times. Close to the river, it suffered grievously in the 1966 floods, and to some extent has never quite recovered; but a few artists of sorts still lodge in the upper storeys hoping to breathe inspiration from the very stones where Michelangelo walked and it's a good, lively place to observe the workaday Florence behind the glossy façade. Few things around this district are very old, but just west of Piazza Santa Croce you will see a series of streets—Via Bentacorti, Via Torta, and Piazza Peruzzi—making an almost complete ellipse. These mark the course of the inner arcade of Roman Florence's amphitheatre, some stones of which can still be seen among the foundations of the old palaces. To the south, on Via dei Benci near the Arno, is a collection that a turn-of-the-century English art historian and Florentinophile named Herbert Horne bequeathed to Italy as the **Horne Museum** (*open 9am–1pm Mon–Sat; adm*), with tons of odds and ends, ceramics, and works by Giotto, Gozzoli, and Desiderio da Settignano.

Michelangelo never actually lived in the **Casa Buonarroti**, at Via Ghibellina 70 (*open 9.30am–1.30pm; closed Tues; adm exp*). The artist's continuing fascination with real estate has given critics since Vasari something to gossip about; he picked this property up for some of his relatives, and later generations made it into a Michelangelo museum. Besides some drawings and models, the collection contains some of the artist's early works, the *Battle of the Centaurs*, and a beautiful bas-relief called the *Madonna of the Stairs*. Also present is the wooden model he made for the projected façade of San Lorenzo. From here, three blocks north along Via Buonar'oti will take you to the city's most colourful corner, the Sant'Ambrogio market and the *mercatino* in **Piazza dei Ciompi**. This is Florence's famous flea market, where dozens of vendors wait to sell you endearing junk in all shapes and sizes behind the typically Florentine 'Fish Loggia', designed by Vasari and moved here when the old market in Piazza della Repubblica was demolished. Just to the east is **Sant'Ambrogio Church**, which has been thoroughly Baroqued inside, but you can seek out good frescoes by Orcagna and Baldovinetti.

## Across the Arno—the Pitti Palace

Once across the Ponte Vecchio, a different Florence reveals itself—not too different, but at least a more pleasant place to walk around, greener, quieter, and less burdened with traffic. The **Oltrarno**, as it is called, is not a large district. A chain of hills squeezes it against the river, and their summits afford the best views over the city. Across the bridge, the Medici's catwalk passes almost over the top of **Santa Felicità** church, best known as a monument to the quirky Mannerist painter Jacopo Pontormo. This artist, a recluse who lived atop a tower he built for himself, often pulling up the ladder to keep his friends at bay, frequently got himself into trouble with his neighbours for keeping the place full of dead animals and even human bodies, from which he studied form and anatomy. His work in Santa Felicità includes his acknowledged masterpiece, the *Deposition*, with its luminous, distorted figures and exaggerated expressions, as well as frescoes of the Annunciation and the Evangelists.

As the Medicis consolidated their power in Florence, they made a point of buying up all the important properties of their former rivals, especially their proud family palaces. The most spectacular example of this ducal eminent domain was the acquisition by Cosimo I of the **Pitti Palace**, built in 1457 by a powerful banker named Luca Pitti who seems to have had vague ambitions of toppling the Medici and becoming the big boss himself. The palace and its extensive grounds, now the **Boboli Gardens**, were purchased by Cosimo in the 1540s; he and his wife Eleanor of Toledo liked it much better than the medieval Palazzo Vecchio, and soon moved in for good, and the palace remained the residence of the Medici, and later the House of Lorraine, until 1868. The original building, said to have been designed by Brunelleschi, was only as wide as the seven central windows of the façade. Succeeding generations of Medici and Lorraines found it too small for their burgeoning collections of bric-à-brac, and added several stages of symmetrical additions, resulting in a long bulky profile, resembling some sort of Stalinist ministry on its bleak asphalt piazza. The grand dukes kept it better landscaped. Piazza Pitti was a prized address in the old days—the greatest of all Florence fans, the Brownings, kept house across from the palace, and so for a time did Dostoevsky.

## Galleria Palatina

Altogether there are no less than eight separate museums in the Pitti complex, including collections dedicated to clothes, ceramics, and carriages—a tribute to Medici acquisitiveness in the centuries of decadence, a period from which, in the words of Mary McCarthy, '...flowed a torrent of bad taste that has not yet dried up...if there had been Toby jugs and Swiss weather clocks available, the grand dukes would certainly have collected them.' Their picture collection, the **Galleria Palatina** (*open 9am–2pm Tues–Sat; 9am–1pm Sun; adm exp*), will hold a place in your memory not so much for its Titians and Raphaels as for the thick gilt frames around them and the berserk opulence of the frescoed ceilings overhead. There are plenty of bad pictures, but also some fine portraits by Titian, Van Dyck, and

Raphael, as well as some of the later religious works by Botticelli. Plenty of Medici portraits appear, the whole line from Cosimo I to the dilapidated Gian Gastone. For a surprise, there are contemporary portraits of Queen Elizabeth I and Oliver Cromwell, both looking a little ill-at-ease in such surroundings. Near the entrance to the galleries, the *Tavola delle Muse* makes a good introduction to the Florentine 'decorative arts'; the table, a masterpiece of *pietra dura*, the painstaking process of making pictures with varicoloured inlaid marble, was done in the 1870s.

While Florence was briefly the capital of Italy in the 1860s, the Savoy kings installed themselves in the Pitti, leaving behind a set of garish chambers inexplicably restored, and usually open to the public. The **State Apartments** are worth a look for connoisseurs of 19th-century French tapestries and furnishings (*at time of writing only the Winter Apartments are open to visitors, by appointment only, © 287096; at other times, hours and ticket are the same as for the Galleria Palatina*). Those serious about trinkets will find a wonderland at the Pitti: the **Museo degli Argenti**, a surprisingly vast collection of gold and silver work, engraved precious stones, cameos, ivory and crystal (*same hours as the Galleria Palatina; adm also valid for the costume and carriage museums*); the **Museo delle Carrozze**, with the fancy carriages of the Medici and the Lorraines; and a **Museum of Porcelain**, out in the Boboli Gardens, in a little palace called the Casino del Cavaliere. Also in this corner of the Pitti, the **Museum of Modern Art** has the best collection extant of the 19th-century school called *Macchiaieli* ('Splatterers' might be the best translation)—Tuscan painters who tried to revive moribund Italian art by transplanting Impressionism from France (*same hours as Galleria Palatina; separate adm exp*).

Finally, the hardest part of the Pitti to get into may be worth the trouble if you're fond of Spanish painting. Until it finds a permanent home, the **Contini Bonacossi Collection** resides in the Meridiana pavilion. This recent bequest includes works of Cimabue, Duccio, and Giovanni Bellini, some sculpture and china, and also paintings by El Greco, Goya, and Velasquez—the last represented by a very exceptional work, *The Water Carrier of Seville* (*open by appointment only, © 2388652*).

## Boboli Gardens

*Open April–Oct 9am–7.30pm daily; Nov–Mar 9am–4.30pm daily; adm.*

It is the loveliest park in the centre of Florence, the only park in the centre of Florence, and if you're visiting in the summer, the sooner you become acquainted with it the better. The Boboli is the only escape from the sun, humidity and crowds of July and August. Cosimo I began the planning and landscaping in the 1550s. The tone for what was to be the first Mannerist park was set early on by the incredible **Grotta del Buontalenti**, near the entrance behind the Pitti Palace. The Florentines do not seem to like this artificial cavern. In Rome or Venice, cities where decadence is properly valued and honoured, it would be one of the biggest tourist attractions; here in Florence it is forgotten and allowed to deteriorate. The Grotto is sheer madness, Gaudiesque dripping stone with peculiar creatures seeming to grow out of it. Inside are fantastic painted landscapes, surrounded by leopards, bears, satyrs, and others harder to define.

The groves and walks of the Boboli are haunted by platoons of statuary, some Roman and some absurd Mannerist work, like the fat baby Bacchus riding a turtle. There's a genuine obelisk, in the centre of a miniature Roman circus, and a fountain from the Baths of Caracalla. Some of the best parts of the gardens are the furthest away, shady paths and flower beds towards the south, near Florence's southern gate, the Porta Romana.

## Santo Spirito

The centre of the Oltrarno district, Piazza Santo Spirito usually has a small market going under the plane trees, as well as restaurants and a quiet café or two. The church, **Santo Spirito**, shows a severe 18th-century façade that conceals one of Brunelleschi's triumphs, a characteristic, contemplative interior of grey and white surrounded by ranks of semi-circular chapels. Even though later architects tinkered grievously with the plan after Brunelleschi's death, many consider this to be one of his best churches. Among the paintings in the chapels are works by Filippino Lippi (south transept, a *Madonna and Child*) and Orcagna (a fresco of the Crucifixion, in the refectory of the adjacent monastery).

## Santa Maria del Carmine

With its walls of rough stone—the projected façade was never completed—**Santa Maria del Carmine** looks more like a country farmhouse than a church. Most of it was destroyed in a fire and reconstructed in the 1700s, but the **Brancacci Chapel** (*open 7–12, 3.30–7, adm*), another of the landmarks of Florentine art, somehow survived, and has been recently restored. Three artists worked on the chapel frescoes: Masolino, beginning in 1424, his pupil Masaccio, working alone from 1428, and Filippino Lippi, who completed the work in the 1480s. Scholars never tire of disputing the attributions of the various scenes, especially those that could be either Masolino's or Masaccio's. It doesn't matter; 'Little Tom' and 'Shabby Tom' both contributed greatly to the visual revolution of quattrocento painting. Both were revolutionary in their understanding of light and space, though art historians these days make more of a fuss over the precocious, eccentric Shabby Tom, who died at the age of 27 shortly after his work here. Some of the scenes, the *Expulsion of Adam and Eve*, the *Tribute Money*, and scenes from the life of St Peter, are among Masaccio's masterpieces. Almost every artist of the later 1400s and 1500s came here to do sketches and study how Shabby Tom did it; some of Michelangelo's sketches after Masaccio still survive.

## The Belvedere Fort

For the best views over Florence, and the best chance to get away from the city's dust and noise, you can climb up to the heights around Oltrarno. It's a pleasant walk whether you do it the short way, up Costa San Giorgio and through the old city walls, or the longer route towards Piazzale Michelangelo. This leads through an interesting , little-known corner of the city around Via dei Bardi and Via San Niccolò, two fine old streets with a scattering of Renaissance palazzi, and good frescoes by Alessandro Baldovinetti in the church of **San Niccolò sopò'Arno**. At the top of a winding road and a long set of steps, Piazzale Michelangelo is a popular lookout point adorned with yet another full-size copy of the *David*. Beneath it, Via del Belvedere leads up between the walls and some country villas to the **Belvedere Fort** (*open 8am–8pm*), from 1590, dominating the city's defences along the southern heights. This fort and adjacent walls replaced the earlier ones (those Michelangelo helped design) that survived the siege of 1529. The central bulding of the Belvedere has been restored to hold special art exhibitions, as well as bits of frescoes rescued from some of the lesser-known churches. Even if nothing is on, the view makes the climb worthwhile.

## San Miniato

Despite the fact that the lovely Romanesque façade of this church can be glimpsed from almost anywhere in Florence, few visitors are ever moved to see it up close. As a result, you may have one of Florence's best churches all to yourself. Built in 1015 over an earlier church on the spot where the head of obscure St Minias bounced after the Romans decapitated him, the exterior echoes the black and white geometric style of the baptistry. The playful patterns are continued inside, framing a richly coloured 13th-century mosaic of Christ Pantocrator in the apse.

Despite its distance from the city centre, this has always been a church dear to the hearts of the Florentines. At the top of the façade, you'll notice the gold eagle symbol of the Calimala, the medieval cloth merchants' guild. These rich businessmen had the church in their care, and over the centuries they bestowed on it many lovely things. Inside, be sure to see the wonderful inlaid marble floor, with signs of the zodiac and fantastical animals; also the **Cappella del Crocifisso**, a joint effort by Michelozzo and Luca della Robbia. The fine pulpit and choir screen date from the early 1200s, and the Chapel of the Cardinal of Portugal contains work by Baldovinetti (who also restored the apse mosaic), della Robbia, Pollaiuolo, and Rossellino.

## Peripheral Attractions

Most of these, inevitably, are museums. If it is possible that somehow, somewhere, there lives an indefatigable culture-tourist capable of taking on the major sites of Florence and still asking for more, the city will be glad to oblige.

First and foremost, there is the utterly peculiar **Villa Stibbert** at Via Stibbert 26, north of the centre off Via Vittorio Emanuele (*open 9–1 Mon–Wed, Fri, Sat; 9–12.30 Sun; adm, free on Sun; guided tours on the hour; at other times you may wander around freely*). To get there, take bus no.31 from the station. The life's vocation of an eccentric English collector (d. 1906) who fought with Garibaldi and later settled here, the villa, inside and out, is a sumptuous Victorian version of how the Florentine medieval style ought to have looked, populated by scores of mannequins parading in arms and armour of all nations and periods—from Portugal to Indonesia. Besides tin suits, Stibbert's taste in collectables tended towards large bulky footfaraws, lace, snuff boxes, and plenty of what a local guide intriguingly describes as 'brass and silver basins, used daily by Stibbert'.

Fans of Andrea del Sarto, Browning's 'Perfect Painter', can go a little out of their way to see two of his best works, a *Last Supper* in the **Cenacolo of San Salvi** at Via San Salvi 16 (*open 9am–2pm Tues–Sat; 9am–1pm Sun; adm*), and a set of chiaroscuro frescoes on the life of St John at the **Chiostro dello Scalzo**, Via Cavour 69 (same hours as San Salvi; free). There are more architectural fragments, bric-à-brac, della Robbias, musical instruments—and also some beautiful medieval paintings and sculpture—at another former private collection, the **Museo Bardini**, Piazza de' Mazzi 1, in the Oltrarno near Via dei Bardi (*open 9–2 Mon, Tues, Thurs–Sat; 8–1 Sun; closed Wed; adm*).

As for science museums, Florence has more than any city in Italy. Many are gathered in the complex at Via la Pina 4, including a **Botanical Garden**, a **Mineralogy and Lithology Museum**, and a **Botanical Museum** full of wax flowers. All of these have collections that began with the ever-inquisitive Medici grand dukes. They were also behind one of Florence's real curiosities, the stuffed hippopotamus in the **La Specola Zoological Museum** (*open 9–12 Tues, Sun only*).

## Fiesole

No ordinary suburb, **Fiesole** can claim to be the mother city of Florence itself. In fact the town is of Etruscan origin, the northernmost member of the federation of city-states called the Dodecapolis. *Faesulum* dwindled in the heyday of Roman-era Florence, but in the Dark Ages its secure hilltop site ensured its survival. When times became a little bit safer its families began moving back down to the Arno to rebuild Florence. For centuries now, Fiesole has played the role of Florence's aristocratic suburb; its cool breezes and belvedere views make it the perfect retreat from the torrid Florentine summers. There's no escaping the tourists, however; we foreigners have been tramping up and down Fiesole's hill since the days of Shelley. They're used to us by now, and a day trip here is for many an obligatory part of a stay in Florence. The no.7 city bus from the Piazza della Stazione will have you there in less than half an hour, stopping in Piazza Mino da Fiesole, the town centre.

Mino da Fiesole is a favourite son, a quattrocento sculptor whose best work can be seen in the early 11th-century **Duomo** on the piazza; the tomb of Bishop Salutati off the right aisle contains his altarpiece with the Madonna and saints. Behind the cathedral on Via Dupré is the **Bandini Museum** (*open April–Sept 9.30–1, 3–7; Oct–Mar 10–1, 3–6; closed Tues; adm*), a must for anybody who loves the iridescent della Robbia terracottas on Tuscany's churches and would like a chance to see some up close. The museum has an entire roomful, along with a collection of 14th- and 15th-century Tuscan paintings.

Not much is left of Etruscan or Roman Fiesole, but you can visit the small **Roman Theatre**, excavated in 1911 and often used for plays and concerts in the summer; the archaeological area, on the hillside near the Bandini Museum on Via Partigiani, also includes scanty remains of baths and temples and a small museum (*open April–Sept 9–7; Oct–Mar 10–4; closed*

*Tues; adm*). Perhaps the best sights Fiesole has to offer, though, are the perfect views over Florence and the surrounding area from old streets like Via Francesco on the edge of town. Walks around the outskirts reveal some lovely countryside and a few surprises; the **Church of San Domenico** at San Domenico di Fiesole, a couple of kilometres from town, has three paintings by Fra Angelico, who lived for a while in the adjoining monastery. Nearby on Via di Badia, the **Badia Fiesolana**, Fiesole's original cathedral, has an unfinished geometric façade (11th century) like that of Florence's San Miniato or Santa Maria Novella, and an interior in the manner of Brunelleschi.

---

## Shopping

Florence can no longer be called an important **fashion** centre—the lack of a full-sized airport has been one of the many factors that have caused what was left of the business to trickle to Milan over the last two decades. Today the range of fashion items you'll see is the same as in any other large Italian city; all the big names of the 1960s and 1970s, now grown into the fashion chains of the 1990s, are well represented along Via Tornabuoni and the surrounding streets, but there is little new and exciting, and very few bargains. Fortunately for all those who come to Florence itching to spend some cash, there are a few exceptions: **jewellery**, surprisingly, heads the list. The shops that line the Ponte Vecchio are forced by the nature of their location into competition, and good prices for Florentine brushed gold, cameos, and antique jewellery (much of it actually made in Arezzo these days) are more common than you might think. They do not set up shop here just to exploit tourists—they've been on the bridge for over 300 years. Near the Oltrarno end, there's also one shop that specializes in fascinating antique telescopes and other instruments.
**Leather goods** are also still something

Via Tornabuoni

Florence is known for; you can have a look in a number of choice shops around Via della Vigna Nuova and Via del Parione, and less expensively at an unusual institution called the **Leather School**, which occupies part of Santa Croce's cloister and has a showroom on the square in front.

For bargains and surprises, try Florence's famous and boisterous **street markets**, usually open every day. The big San Lorenzo market, which has spread all over the neighbourhood around San Lorenzo church, is where ordinary Florentines actually probably buy most of their clothes. In this little bit of Naples transplanted to Tuscany, the range of choice is equal to three department stores; you'll see plenty of fake designer labels, and even some real ones. Further west in Santa Croce, in the Piazza dei Ciompi, the *mercato delle pulci* (flea market) carries on daily, with a wide array of desirable junk, beneath Vasari's Fish Loggia; the shopkeepers, being Florentines, are a little smug and not inclined to bargain. At both locations there are also lavishly stocked **food markets**, where you should find what you're looking for, whether you want to stock up for a train journey or find local specialities, like *stracchino* cheese, to take home. More serious **antique** shops, and Florence has plenty of them, tend to cluster in the streets between Via Tornabuoni and the Ognissanti Church. The **Mercato Nuovo**, or *Mercato del Porcellino*, right in the centre of town, still performs its age-old function of selling Florentine straw goods—hats and bags—though tourist trinkets have taken over most of the stalls. There is also a small market in Piazza Santo Spirito in the Oltrarno (mornings) and a larger one in the Cascine Park (Tuesday mornings). Some of the real finds are in the towns around Florence: **glassware** in the shops of Empoli, and **ceramics** (including the inevitable della Robbia reproductions) in Impruneta, and especially in Montelupo.

---

*Florence ✆ (055–)*          **Where to Stay**

Hotels in Florence tend to be expensive, and the problems of finding a room become chronic in the frenetic tourist rush of July and August. But don't be discouraged; the Florentines are old pros in the tourist business, and even if you're daft enough to drop in during August without booking, you'll find plenty of help in locating a bed. There are several hotel consortiums that can find you something with one of their members; most have some rooms in all price ranges. The first night's room fee or a similar amount will usually have to be paid at the office when booking as a deposit, and will then be deducted from your final bill.

**ITA**, in Santa Maria Novella station, ✆ 282893 (*open 9am–8.30 pm daily*), and in the AGIP service station at Peretola, to the west of Florence on the A11, ✆ 4211800; Mar–Nov only there are also offices in the Chianti-Est service area on the A1, and in the Fortezza da Basso, by the car park, ✆ 471960. No bookings can be made over the telephone. This is the largest of the local hotel agencies, and queues at their offices are often huge.

**Florence Promhotels**, Viale A. Volta 72, ✆ 570481.
**Toscana Hotels 80**, Viale Gramsci 9, ✆ 2478543.

An alternative to staying actually in Florence is to look for a hotel in Fiesole, which is cooler, and quieter at night, when you can appreciate the wonderful views over the city far below, twinkling like a mass of fairy lights. In addition, anywhere within half an hour of Florence you will find fine old villas and monasteries that have been turned into quiet, luxury hotels; though often in the most unlikely places, they are very popular with those in need of fresh air and tranquillity (*see* also below, 'From Florence to Pisa').

### luxury

★★★★★ **Excelsior**, Piazza Ognissanti 3, ✆ 264201, ✉ 210278. In Florence itself the leader in luxury is the former Florentine address of Napoleon's sister Caroline. Neoclassically plush, with lots of marble, and lush and green with plants, it's immaculately staffed, and has a smart roof garden with views down the Arno and decadently luxurious bedrooms; not even Gian Gastone de' Medici had heated towel racks. A stylish bar and first-quality restaurant are added amenities.

★★★★★ **Regency**, Piazza d'Azeglio 3, ✆/✉ 245247. In a more tranquil spot, on Florence's plane-tree shaded 'London square', this charming and intimate hotel has only 29 air-conditioned rooms, and an elegant town garden between its two wings. The public rooms are beautifully panelled, and the fare in the restaurant is superb. It also has full garage parking.

★★★★★ **Villa San Michele**, in a breathtaking location just below Fiesole at Via Doccia 4, ✆ 59451, ✉ 598734. If money is really no object, the best choice in the area must be this superb hotel with a façade and loggia reputedly designed by Michelangelo himself. Originally a monastery in the 14th century, it has been carefully reconstructed after bomb damage in the Second World War to become one of the most beautiful hotels in Italy, set in a lovely Tuscan garden, complete with a pool. The prices are seriously astronomical, but the food is wonderful, and the reasons to go down to Florence begin to seem insignificant. (*Closed mid-Nov–mid-Mar.*)

★★★★★ **Villa La Massa**, Via La Massa 6, ✆ 666141. Another lovely choice, a bit further from the city and just slightly less expensive, located up the Arno some 6km from Florence at Candeli. The former 15th-century villa of the Counts Giraldi, the hotel retains the old dungeon (now one of two restaurants), the family chapel (now a bar), and other early Renaissance amenities, combined with 20th-century features like tennis courts, a pool and air-conditioning.

### very expensive

★★★★ **Mona Lisa**, Borgo Pinti 27, ✆ 2479751, ✉ 2479755, is one of the most charming small hotels in Florence, a Renaissance palace now owned by the descendants of sculptor Giovanni Dupre, hiding behind a stern façade. The *palazzo* is well preserved, and the furnishings are family heirlooms, as are the many works of art. Try to reserve one of the tranquil rooms that overlook the garden; all are air-conditioned and have minibars. There is no restaurant, but breakfast is available, and it also has private parking.

**★★★★** **Atlantic Palace**, Via Nazionale 12, ✆ 294234, ✉ 268353. Near the train station, one of the most attractive hotels with large, striking bedrooms built in the framework of a 17th-century convent, luxuriously furnished and air-conditioned.

**★★★★** **Anglo-American**, Via Garibaldi 9, ✆ 282114, ✉ 268513, near the Cascine park, a large but attractive hotel in an older palace, decorated in a light, airy, garden style that makes a pleasant retreat after pounding the pavements; the rooms are air-conditioned, and there's parking nearby.

*expensive*

**★★★** **Loggiato dei Serviti**, Piazza SS. Annunziata 3, ✆ 289592. The most delightful choice in this category was designed for the Servite fathers by Antonio da Sangallo the Elder, who added a loggia to match Brunelleschi's Spedale degli Innocenti across the square. It has since been redone with the best of Florentine taste and refinement, with Italian and English antiques; all rooms have minibars, and air-conditioning and colour TVs are available as well; parking is possible in a nearby garage. The lovely garden is a blessing in the middle of Florence.

**★★★** **Beacci Tornabuoni**, Via Tornabuoni 3, ✆ 212645. Another excellent small hotel that puts you in the centre of fashionable Florence, on the top three floors of an elegant Renaissance palace. The rooms are comfortable, air-conditioned and equipped with minibars, though it's more fun to sit over your drink on the panoramic roof terrace.

**★★★** **Annalena**, Via Romana 34, ✆ 222402, a 15th-century palace in the Oltrarno, is a grand and famous old *pensione*, with high ceilings, antiques, and works of art. Its rooms are large and comfortable, all with private baths, and the atmosphere is friendly. The large garden at the back is also a boon.

**★★★** **Hermitage**, very near the Ponte Vecchio in Vicolo Marzio 1, ✆ 287216. One of the best places to stay in ther very heart of Florence; reserve well in advance to get one of its 14 cosy old rooms, and even further in advance to get one overlooking the Arno. There are rooms with and without baths.

*moderate*

**★★★** **Porta Rossa** at Via Porta Rossa 19, ✆ 287551. Right in the middle of Florence, on a narrow lane off Piazza della Signoria, this the noisy, ageing, dimly lit hotel isn't for everyone, but there are plenty of visitors to Florence who swear they wouldn't stay anywhere else. Rooms are available with and without baths.

**★★★** **Pensione Bencista**, Via B. da Maiano 4, ✆ 59163, located in a sprawling villa dating back to the 14th century, in San Domenico di Fiesole, just below Fiesole itself. The hotel has recently been revamped to push it up a category, many of its rooms are furnished with antiques, and there's a garden and fine views. On the no.7 bus route.

**★★** **Splendor**, Via San Gallo 30 (off Via Guelfa), ✆ 483427. Most of the city's moderate range hotels are found around the station. Although convenient if you arrive by train, few of them will brighten your stay in Florence; grouchy owners who lock the door at midnight tend to be the norm. This noteworthy exception is on the fringe of the zone, near Piazza San Marco, and has old frescoes and antiques that hint of past splendour, and some bedrooms that are almost palatial; others are not so interesting, but there's an attractive terrace.

★★ **La Scaletta**, Via Guicciardini 13, ✆ 283028. Not many people travelling on the cheap make it over to the Oltrarno, making it less frenetic. This hotel has a fairly central, busy location, near the Ponte Vecchio, and offers good rooms and a great roof terrace.

★★ **Pensione Alessandra**, Borgo SS. Apostoli 17, ✆ 283438, ✆ 210619. A 1507 palazzo designed by Baccio d'Agnolo, again near the Ponte Vecchio.

★ **Tony's Inn**, Via Faenza 77, ✆ 217975, another solid recommendation in the area, is run by a friendly Italian-Canadian couple, and has pleasant rooms, most with private baths.

*inexpensive*

Again, most of Florence's budget (or at least budget-ish) hotels are grouped together around the railway station. Most of them send touts to the station to pick up wandering bed-less backpackers, and if you're getting stuck it's worth at least checking the prices they are offering. Except in very high season it's usually possible to bargain.

★ **La Mia Casa**, Piazza Santa Maria Novella 20, ✆ 213061, across from the station, offers simple rooms, inexpensive breakfasts, free showers and a free film in English every night.

★ **Maxim**, Via de' Medici 4, just off Via Calzaiuoli, ✆ 217474, has nice, quiet rooms that go for L80,000 or less.

★ **Firenze**, Piazza dei Donati, ✆ 214203. Near the Duomo, this is the classiest inexpensive hotel in Florence. It's worthwhile asking for one of the newer rooms, and booking in advance.

Besides hotels, a number of **institutions and private homes** let rooms—there's a complete list in the back of the annual provincial hotel book (*Elenco degli Alberghi*), available from tourist offices. There are two main **youth hostels** in Florence: the **Ostello Europa Villa Camerata**, Viale A. Righi 2/4, ✆ 601451 (bus 17B from the station), and the **Ostello Santa Monaca**, Via S. Monaca 6, ✆ 268338, in Oltrarno.

---

*Florence ✆ (055–)*          **Eating Out**

For better or worse, the real Florentine specialities rarely turn up on many restaurant menus, and you'll probably finish your stay without ever learning what a Florentine cook can do with cocks' combs, calves' foot, and tripe. Florence in its loftier moods likes to call itself the 'birthplace of international *haute cuisine*', but in fact the city's contribution to the Italian kitchen is minimal; everyone knows its only really popular dish, *bistecca alla Fiorentina*—thick grilled steaks seasoned with salt and pepper. Nevertheless, like any sophisticated city with lots of visitors, Florence has plenty of fine restaurants; even in the cheaper places, standards are high, and if you don't care for anything fancier there will be lots of good red Chianti to wash it down.

Florence is blessed with one of the finest gourmet restaurants in Italy, the **Enoteca Pinchiorri**, Via Ghibellina 87, ✆ 242777, near the Casa Buonarroti. The owners inherited the building, a wine shop, some 10 years ago, and have converted it into a beautifully appointed restaurant, with meals served in a garden court in the summer; they've also expanded what was already in the cellars to an astonishing collection of some 80,000 bottles of the best Italy and France have to offer. The cooking, a mixture of *nouvelle cuisine* and traditional Tuscan recipes, wins prizes every year. Be warned that you can leave behind as much as L150,000 per person here. (*Closed Sun, Mon midday, Aug.*)

**Relais le Jardin**, the restaurant in the Regency hotel in Piazza d'Azeglio (for details *see* above; closed Sun), is rapidly establishing itself as one of Florence's best; the setting is lovely and refined, and dishes like delicate crêpes filled with courgette blossoms, artichoke hearts, or asparagus and medallions of veal with rhubarb are bringing Florentines and visitors back for more.

## *expensive*

One of the most Florentine of Florentine restaurants, **Cibreo** overlooks the market of Sant'Ambrogio at Via dei Macci 118/r, ✆ 2341100. The décor is simple—food is the main concern here, and all of it is market-fresh. You can go native here and order tripe antipasto, pumpkin soup, and cocks' combs and kidneys, or play it safe with prosciutto from the Casentino, a fragrant soup (no pasta here) of tomatoes, mussels, or peppers, and leg of lamb stuffed with artichokes or duck stuffed with sultanas and pine nuts. Also near the Piazza dei Ciompi, and a bit cheaper, **La Vie en Rose**, Borgo Allegri 68/r, ✆ 245860, is another popular place, serving delights like fresh green pasta with clams and saffron, and duck with prunes. (*Closed Sun, Mon, Easter, mid-July–mid-Sept.*)

**Buca Lapi**, Via del Trebbio 1/r, ✆ 213768, is another traditional Florentine restaurant, located since 1800 in the old wine cellar of the lovely Palazzo Antinori. Experiment with *pappardelle al cinghiale* (broad pasta with wild boar), which tastes better than it sounds; the *bistecca fiorentina con fagioli* here is hard to beat, downed with one of many Tuscan wines. **Sabatini**, Via Panzani 9/a, ✆ 282802, behind S. Maria Novella, the only Florence restaurant with a branch in Tokyo, has been a favourite with tourists and locals for decades. (*Closed Mon, first 2 weeks July.*)

## *moderate*

If *cucina nuova fiorentina* sounds intriguing, try the fare at **Caffè Concerto**, Lungarno C. Colombo 7, ✆ 677377, served on a fine veranda overlooking the Arno. Unlike most restaurants it remains open late, for light midnight suppers. (*Closed Sun.*) **Taverna del Bronzino**, Via delle Ruote 25/r, ✆ 495220, has a pleasant, spacious atmosphere, and is a good place to try *ossobuco alla Fiorentina*. (*Closed Sun, 3 weeks Aug.*)

At a slightly lower price level, but still in the moderate category, in the Oltrarno you can descend into a subterranean wine cellar, **Il Cantinone**, Via S. Spirito 5,

© 218898, that specializes in Chianti Classico and country cooking—*pappa al pomodoro* (thick tomato soup), polenta with boar, or beans and sausage; one room is devoted to wine tasting and antipasti. **Angiolino**, Via S. Spirito 57/r, © 2398976, is, though, probably the most characteristic place this side of the river, with a stove in the centre of the room and the kitchen in full view; the food is typical and of good quality (especially the tasty vegetable *antipasti*). (*Closed Sun evenings, Mon.*)

Back on the north side of the river, **Il Latini**, Via dei Palchetti 6/r, © 210916, near Santa Maria Novella, is noisy, chaotic and great fun. Huge hams hang from the ceiling, and you share the long tables with fellow eaters; the food is good local fare and the prices are modest, on the borders of the moderate/inexpensive ranges. You cannot book, so come early to avoid the queues. Slightly more upmarket, **Garga**, Via del Moro 48/r, © 239898, is a charming if slightly cramped place run by a Florentine and his Canadian wife, serving mouthwatering homemade pasta, and delicately prepared meat and fish dishes. (*Closed Mon.*)

### inexpensive

Central Florence, by popular demand, is full of *tavole calde*, pizzerias, cafeterias, and snack bars, where you can grab a sandwich or a salad instead of a full sit-down meal (one of the best pizza-by-the-slice places is just across from the Medici Chapels). This may change. Lately the city has been trying to banish 'fast food' from the centre, in a bizarre attempt to upscale its tourism—they would prefer that we bought fewer hamburgers and more jewellery. In the meantime, a good place for a sit-down snack or a full meal is **Benvenuto**, situated just behind the Uffizi, in Via dei Neri.

An excellent but low-cost traditional restuarant is **La Casalinga**, Via Michelozzo 9/r, just by Piazza Santo Spirito in Oltrarno. Serving hearty Tuscan food, it's particularly popular with students and young tourists, despite the cranky waiting staff. A similar, not quite as cheap but sometimes friendlier little restaurant near the railway station is **Da Mario**, Via Rosina 2/r. Large queues build up outside every lunchtime, so get there early.

The cheapest meal in Florence, though, will almost certainly be found at the lunch counter, the **Tavola Calda**, in the Sant'Ambrogio market, where once you've fought your way through the crowds of market traders you can get a full three courses for around L20,000, served with a complete absence of the usual restaurant courtesies.

---

## Entertainment and Nightlife
### opera, classical music, theatre

Florence is not renowned for its nightlife, but it does have plenty of theatre and music. The main **opera** season runs only from November to February, but the city's main cultural festival, the **Maggio Musicale**, combining opera and classical concerts, begins in April and lasts into June, with events at a variety of venues, including open-air performances in the Boboli Gardens. For festival information inquire at tourist offices or call © 2779236. There is also a festival in Fiesole each summer, the **Estate**

**Fiesolana**, featuring concerts—particularly chamber music—film screenings and theatre. In addition, at almost any time of the year there is a busy concert calendar in Florence including many of the world's best-known musicians.

The city also takes **theatre** seriously, and at any given time you are likely to find the likes of Pirandello, Shakespeare, Brecht—even Niccolò Machiavelli—playing along with contemporary works. *Firenze Spettacolo* and the bilingual handout *Florence Today*, available from the city tourist office, has full listings of upcoming events. The **Cinema Astro**, on Piazza San Simone near Santa Croce, has movies in English every night except Monday.

### cafés and bars

 Florence has plenty of stylish and pretty expensive bars, most of all around the main shopping and tourist streets such as the Via Tornabuoni. A more relaxed atmosphere—and lower prices will more likely be found around San Marco, the main student area, or in Oltrarno.

The city's most classic and elegant *gran caffè is* **Rivoire**, on the Piazza Signoria, a fine place to watch the milling throng once you've got over the prices. Also elegant and a traditionally fashionable venue for fine-quality snacks is **Procacci** at Via Tornabuoni 64, bizarrely an Italian bar that doesn't serve coffee.

For a livelier, younger clientèle, the long-established main meeting-point in San Marco is the **Gran Caffè San Marco**, on the Piazza of the same name. Nearby, **La Mescita**, Via degli Alfani 70, is a good-value snacks and wine bar. For ice cream, Florence's most lavish range of varieties is on offer at **Festival del Gelato**, Via del Corso 75.

### clubs and discos

Although Florence after dark isn't exactly humming, in the last few years a number of new clubs, discos and late-night music bars have opened up. The best way to find out about what's going on is to buy *Firenze Spettacolo*, available from new-stands, look out for posters, particularly in the San Marco area, or inquire at one of the many English pubs.

A permanent venue with regular live jazz and rock sessions, and occasional cabaret, is **Amadeus**, Via degli Alfani 26, in San Marco. A funky time can also usually be had at **Stonehenge**, Via dell'Amorino 16, which also has live acts frequently, and is open till 4am every night except Mondays. Two of Florence's most regularly packed discos are **Space Electronic**, Via Palazzuolo 37, and the very centrally located **Yab Yum**, Via Sassetti 5. The liveliest gay club in town is the **Flamingo**, Via Pandolfi 26.

### traditional festivals

Florence's major celebration is the **Gioco di Calcio Storico** or traditional football game—which Mussolini claimed to be *the* origin of soccer worldwide—played four times in the days immediately following the feast of St John the Baptist, on 24 June. Four teams, representing the city's four *quartiere* and suitably fitted out in medieval costume, battle it out, usually in the Piazza Santa Croce, in a game with few rules and a great deal of knockabout violence. Tickets for the stands are usually sold out weeks in advance.

## Florentine Excursions

The countryside around Fiesole presents a lovely, thoroughly civilized landscape of villas and gardens, cypresses and parasol pines. Outside **Settignano**, back towards Florence, you'll pass the Villa Poggio Gherardo, which the Florentines like to say was the rendezvous for the genteel storytellers of the *Decameron*, and also the interesting church of **San Martino a Mensola**, with some parts as old as the 9th century, and paintings by Agnolo and Taddeo Gaddi inside. Settignano has fine views over Florence and its valley. In recent times the area was best known as the home of the art historian and legendary Florentinophile Bernard Berenson; his **Villa I Tatti** now belongs to Harvard University. North of Fiesole, near the village of Pratolino, Duke Francesco I kept a country house now known as the **Villa Demidoff** (*open May–Sept 10–7 Fri, Sat, Sun only*). It was rich in bizarre gardens and statuary under the Medici, including a famous menagerie, but all that's left now is a strange colossal statue by Giambologna called the 'Apennine'.

South of Florence is one of the typically grand fortress-monasteries of the Carthusian order, begun in the 1340s. The **Certosa di Galluzzo**, near the SS2 highway to Siena, contains works by the della Robbias and Pontormo. A few monks—Cistercians now—look after the place, and they keep up the tradition of cooking up bottles of potent chartreuse; they will be glad to sell you one in their old pharmacy.

Like their Bourbon cousins in France, the Medici dukes liked to pass the time by building new palaces for themselves. In their case, however, the reason was less self-exaltation than pure and simple real estate speculation; the Medici always thought generations ahead. As a result the countryside around Florence is littered with Medici villas, most privately owned but some open to the public. **Villa della Petraia** (*villa open 9–1 Tues–Sun; gardens usually open 9–5.30-6 Tues–Sun*) in the northern suburbs near the Via Gramsci, has beautiful gardens and a fountain statue of Venus of Giambologna. More lovely gardens, typical of late Renaissance landscaping, can also be seen in the same area, the suburb of Castello, at the **Villa di Castello**. Here the attraction is a fascinating example of the Medici's penchant for the offbeat and excessive, an artificial cavern called the **Grotta degli Animali**, filled by Ammannati and Giambologna with statues of every animal and fish known to man, along with mosaics made of seashells. Kitsch, perhaps, but truly great kitsch in the best Medici tradition. You may have to climb a fence, as they don't seem to want anyone seeing it. (Also *see* **Poggio a Caiano**, p.702). (*Gardens only open 9–4.30 Tues–Sun; closes later in spring and summer.*)

Further out, at Quinto Fiorentino, you can visit two unusual 7th-century BC Etruscan tombs. **La Montagnola**, Via Flli. Rosselli 95, and **La Mula**, Via della Mula 2, have no artworks, but the chambers under their 8-metre artificial hills bear an odd relationship to much older cultures elsewhere in the Mediterranean—domed tholos tombs as in Mycenaean Greece, corbelled passages like the navetas of Mallorca, and entrances that look like the sacred wells of Sardinia. (*La Mula open April–Sept 10am–12 midday Tues, 10–12, 3–6.30, Sat;*

Oct–Mar 10am–12 midday Sat
only. La Montagnola open April–Sept
10am–1pm Tues, Thurs, 10–1, 5–7, Sat,
Sun; Oct–Mar 10am–1pm Sat, Sun only.)

From Florence through Prato and beyond, the towns strung along the *Autostrada del Sole*
make up an almost continuous conurbation, full of power lines and industrial landscapes that
blast your sensibility out of its quattrocento daydream and leave it somewhere in New
Jersey. At **Sesto Fiorentino**, the famous 250-year-old Richard Ginori china and porcelain
firm has a big collection of work dating back to 1737, including some special pieces made for
Medici and such—the **Doccia Museum**, at Via Pratese 31 (*open 9.30–1, 3.30–6.30, Tues,
Thurs, Sat; adm.*)

## The Plonk That Made Firenze Famous

Before the days of rampant wine-consciousness, Chianti was just the stuff in the straw-clad
bottles, the inevitable accompaniment in Italian restaurants across the English-speaking
world. Today, even if everybody knows what remarkably good, honest wine it is, some of it
ranking among Italy's best, Chianti doesn't let the praise go to its head. It is still cheap,
unpretentious, and a way of life in much of Tuscany. Actually, Chianti is grown from around
Pistola all the way to Chiusi, but the best, Chianti Classico, has its home in the original
Chianti region between Florence and Siena.

## The Wine of the Iron Baron

Wine has been produced in the hills south of Florence since the cows came
home, but what we know as Chianti was born in the 19th century, of a
husband's jealousy. The 'Iron Baron' Bettino Ricasoli was extremely wealthy
but not very good-looking. After serving as the second prime minister of
unified Italy, he married and took his lovely bride to a ball in Florence. A
young man asked her to dance. The Baron at once ordered her into their
carriage and drove straight to the ancient family seat in Brolio in the

Monti dei Chianti—an isolated castle that the poor woman would rarely leave for the rest of her life. To pass the time the Baron experimented in his vineyards, and over the years evolved a joyful, pleasing blend of Sangiovese and Caniolo grapes, with a touch of Malvasia, twice fermented in the old Tuscan manner. At the same time the famous dark green flask clad in straw (the *strapeso*) was invented. The Baron's Chianti and its distinctive bottle took the Paris Exposition of 1878 by storm. As imitators flooded the market, the boundaries of Chianti Classico were drawn in 1924, and the black cockerel, symbol of the Lega dei Chianti in 1385, was made its trademark, distinguishing it from Tuscany's six other Chianti-growing districts. If you take the Via Chiantigiana (SS222) between Florence and Siena you'll find many vineyards to explore and to wine-taste, especially at Greve, midway down the SS222, or at the Castello di Brolio itself, 10km south of Gaiole on the N484. (*9am–12 midday, 3pm–sunset daily.*)

The gateway to the Chianti from Florence, **Impruneta**, prefers making bricks and terracotta to growing grapes, but it's worth a stop for the **Basilica di Santa Maria**, with beautiful works by Michelozzo and Andrea della Robbia in two of its chapels. Up in the mountains to the east, the area around San Polo is famous for the cultivation of irises. **Greve**, the unofficial capital of the Chianti, has an unusual arcaded triangular piazza, and attracts big crowds for the Chianti Classico Market Show in September.

## North of Florence

The lush green valley of the **Mugello** and the hills around it border on four different provinces; it is a corner of Tuscany not well known, even though its villages get their share of summer foreigners in holiday homes. **Vicchio** is a humble town, though the birthplace of both Giotto and Fra Angelico; there is a small collection of medieval art in the town museum (*for admission, ask at the* Comune.) To the west, past Borgo San Lorenzo, **San Piero a Sieve** sits beneath the huge, mouldering pentagonal San Martino fortress, built by Michelozzo for the Medici; the village church has a lovely baptismal font by Andrea della Robbia. Michelozzo also designed another Medici villa, a pretty building on the squat foundations of an earlier fortress at nearby **Caffagiolo** (1451).

Up in the mountains to the north, **Scarperia**'s interesting Palazzo Pretoria was a governors' palace built by the Florentines in the early 14th century, its façade covered with the coats of arms of all the town's many governors. The **Madonna dei Terremoti** (Our Lady of the Earthquakes) church has frescoes attributed to Filippo Lippi. **Firenzuola**, with its narrow, arcaded streets, is a lovely town, a good place to stop if you're on your way to Bologna and the north.

## From Florence to Pisa

There are two routes to choose from, whether you're going by train or car. Surprisingly, the valley of the Arno is the less populated and less busy route, and always has been. Trade and traffic prefer to follow a northern route through the large towns of Prato, Pistoia, and Lucca.

## Getting Around

The fastest **train** line between Florence and Pisa is via Empoli, but there is also a frequent service through Prato, Pistoia and Lucca and then to Pisa or Viareggio. In Pistoia the railway station, with connections to Florence, Pisa, and occasionally Bologna, is on the southern edge of town, two blocks from the town walls on Via XX Settembre. Most **buses** to other Tuscan cities leave Pistoia from Piazza San Francesco, at the west end of town, inside the walls off Corso Gramsci.

The busiest **road** from Florence to Pisa is the A11 *autostrada*, which leaves Florence near the airport (take Via delle Porte Nuove from the Viale). Alongside it through Prato, Pisoia, Montecatini and Lucca runs the SS435. For the new superstrada to Pisa by the southern route, via Empoli, take the Via Pisana and Via Talenti from the Viale in Florence.

## Tourist Information

There are two information offices in **Prato**, at Via L.Muzzi 51, © (0574) 35141, near the Duomo, and at Via Cairoli 48/52, © (0574) 24112. In **Pistoia** the tourist office is in Piazza Duomo, in the Bishop's Palace, © (0573) 21622, and there is also an office in **Montecatini Terme**, Viale Verdi 66, © (0572) 772244.

## Empoli and the Arno Valley

**Montelupo**, with a castle overlooking the Arno, is a pretty town given to the manufacture of delicately painted ceramics, famous throughout Tuscany. Further down the valley comes **Empoli**, a fair-sized city that like Prato makes its living from textiles. Empoli's landmark is the **Chiesa Collegiata** on the central Piazza Farinata degli Uberti, with a façade in the best medieval Florentine style of black and white geometry. The lower half bears a strong resemblance to Santa Maria Novella, but the upper was added only in the 18th century. The adjacent **Collegiata Museum** (*open 10am–12 midday Tues–Sun; adm*) has one of the better art collections in Tuscany outside Florence, with a famous *Pietà* of Masolino, a pair of saints by Pontormo, works by Lippi, Rossellino, della Robbia, and a baptismal font by the circle of Donatello. There is a pair of possible detours from Empoli: south to **Castelfiorentino** up in the hills, with its crumbling castle and a Pinacoteca in the Santa Verdiana Church (many good paintings on the life of St Francis); or north to **Vinci**, where fans of Leonardo can visit his birthplace, and lovers of gadgets in general can have a good time with the intricate models of the master's inventions in the **Museo Leonardiano** (*open 9.30–12, 2.30–6, daily; adm*)—like the bicycle, tank and helicopter, and dozens of other things he never had the chance to try, but left detailed plans for in his notebooks. The museum is housed in the 13th-century Guidi Castle, which also has a small art collection.

Closer to the main Pisa and Livorno road, **San Miniato**, home of the national kite flying festival (first Sunday after Easter), is a fine town set in some of the fairest and most typically Tuscan countryside. It has yet another good picture gallery, in the **Museo Diocesano** (*open*

*April–Sept 9–12.30, 4–7, Tues–Sun; Oct–Mar 9–12, 3.30–5, Sat, Sun only; adm*). San Miniato's half-ruined fortifications were built by the town's great benefactor, Frederick II. **Cascina**, further down the road to Pisa, is an old spa they say is good for your rheumatism.

## Prato

Living in Florence's shadow for a thousand years has not dampened Prato's spirit as much as you would expect. A town of almost 200,000, with a textile industry that has been impor- tant in Europe for 600 years, Prato could certainly express some weariness at having seen its wealth and talent constantly drained off to glorify its imperious neighbour. Florence usually controlled Prato in the Middle Ages. Twice the city was conquered, and on one occasion the Florentines simply bought it. Twice, in 1470 and 1512, the Pratese rebelled, but were crushed each time. The gruesome sack of the city in 1514, an atrocity with which the Spaniards and the Medici Pope Leo X meant to intimidate all Italy, quietened Prato down considerably. Now, almost 500 years later, Prato's industries are thriving once more, and the town makes a point of showing that it, too, has some culture. On entering the city by rail (the station, with its park and bridges over the Bisenzio, makes perhaps the most blissful introduction to any Italian city) one of the first things you'll see is a roundabout decorated with a great puffy sculpture by Henry Moore.

### Santa Maria delle Carceri

Entering old Prato by Viale Piave, the defiantly Ghibelline swallowtail crenellations of the **Castello dell'Imperatore** mark a strange interlude in Prato's past. Frederick II (*see* p.1025, **Apulia**) built it in 1237, his only such castle in Northern Italy. Like the Emperor's Apulian castles, this one was meant to impress his subjects as much by design as by its strength—its clear lines must have seemed very sharp and modern in the 13th century—but the castle's location inside the walls hints that the purpose was less to protect Prato from the Florentines than to protect mperial officials from the Pratese. There isn't much inside, but the city often uses its halls for special exhibitions.

Behind the castle stands the unfinished black and white marble façade of **Santa Maria delle Carceri**, begun in 1485 by Giuliano Sangallo. Brunelleschian architecture was always a fragile blossom, as shown clearly by the failure of this sole serious attempt to transplant it outside the walls of Florence. Santa Maria always rates a mention in architectural histories. It was an audacious enterprise; Sangallo, a furiously diligent student of Vitruvius and Alberti, attempted a building based entirely on philosophical principles. Order, simplicity, and correct proportion, as in Brunelleschi's churches, were to be manifest, with no frills allowed. Sangallo, the favourite of Lorenzo the Magnificent, proved unfortunately a better theorist than architect. Santa Maria came out tedious and clumsy, a tombstone for the theoretical architecture that was a fad in the quattrocento, more often expressed in paintings than actual buildings. The interior is better than the outside, a plain Greek cross very much in the Brunelleschi manner with a decorative frieze and tondos of the four Evangelists by Andrea della Robbia. The name of the church—*carceri* means prisons—refers to a miracle, a speaking image of the Virgin painted on a nearby prison wall, that occasioned the building of the church.

# The Duomo

North of the church, Via Pugliesi and Via Garibaldi pass several medieval towers on their way to the Piazza del Duomo. Prato's **Cathedral of St Stephen**, in flagrant green and white stripes like the Duomo at Siena, was begun in the 13th century and finished in bits and pieces over the next 200 years. Its best features are an exotic, almost Moorish-looking campanile, a della Robbia lunette of the Madonna with St Stephen over the door, a big clock that makes you smile when you notice it sitting where the rose window ought to be, and above all the **Pulpit of the Sacred Girdle**. Perhaps no church in Italy has such a perfectly felicitous ornament, something beautiful and special that the Pratese can look at every day when they walk through the piazza. Michelozzo designed it (1428) and Donatello added the delightful reliefs of dancing children, along the lines of his *cantoria* in the cathedral museum in Florence. Mary's girdle came to Prato during the First Crusade; the circular pulpit hung on the right corner of the cathedral façade was built so that it could be displayed to the people, five times a year on major church holidays.

In the cathedral, the prime attraction is in the choir: two series of lucent, precise **frescoes** by Filippo Lippi illustrating the stories of St Stephen and John the Baptist (the nun who would later run off with Lippi is said to be the model for Salome). A separate entrance on the side of the building leads to the **Museo dell'Opera del Duomo** (*open 9.30–12.30, 3–6.30, Mon, Wed–Sat; 9.30am–12.30pm Sun; closed Tues; adm*), where you can see the original Donatello reliefs from the pulpit—of course they had copies made to face the weather outside—in addition to works by Filippino Lippi, an early painting by Uccello, and a sophisticated *Madonna* by the quattrocento 'Master of the Nativity of Castello'. Outside the museum, stop for a look at the cathedral's Romanesque cloister, done in patterns of the same green and white stone as the exterior.

## More Museums

On the sleepy streets of old Prato, you'll find only a few reminders of the city's businesslike past. **Piazza Mercatale**, by the river, is an attractive, huge, very Tuscan square, full of peeling yellow paint and flowers. Near the centre of town, off Piazza San Francesco on Via Rinaldesca, you'll pass the house of Renaissance Prato's most flamboyant tycoon, Francesco di Marco Datini. If there were an accountants' hall of fame, Datini would surely be one of the stars. He helped invent that dismal science, and also gets credit, according to the Pratese, for the 'invention of the promissory note'. Datini put his talents to good use, piling up an indecent fortune, fooling in politics, and dropping huge sums for charity. His **Palazzo Datini** (*c.* 1350) shows bits of the frescoes that once covered the entire façade—scenes from the merchant-accountant's own life.

Two streets to the north, the rugged, four-square **Palazzo Pretorio** was Prato's seat of government in the days of independence, and now serves as home to the **Galleria Comunale** (*open 9.30–12.30, 3–6.30, Mon, Wed–Sat; 9–1 Sun; closed Tues; adm*), a rich collection containing works by the Lippis, Bernardo Daddi, and many lesser-known Renaissance artists. From there, Via C. Guasti takes you four blocks to the big 13th-century church of San Domenico. Its cloister houses the grandiosely named **Museum of Mural Painting** (*open 9–12; closed Tues; if not open call © 31208*)—really only a small collection of frescoes taken from local churches and palazzi, but well worth a visit for the unusual Palazzo Vaj graffiti, etched mythological and court scenes by an unknown hand that are exquisite examples of quattrocento drawing. There is also a *sinopia*, believed to be the work of Uccello.

## Around Prato

**Carmignano**, like Prato, was an ancient *comune* that lost its freedom to the Florentines. The town isn't much, but at the church of **San Michele** you can spend a long time looking at the masterpiece of crazy Jacopo Pontormo, *The Visitation*. The soulful, ethereal women, their feet barely touching the ground, make up perhaps the most unforgettable image of 16th-century Florentine painting. You can see more Pontormo, in a sunnier vein, along with other frescoes by Andrea del Sarto and Filippino Lippi, just east of town at the 1479 Medici villa of **Poggio a Caiano** (*open for guided tours 9–1.30 Tues–Sat; 9–12.30 Sun; adm*), built by Giuliano da Sangallo for Lorenzo il Magnifico, a stately, almost Palladian villa with a big clock on top—as if the Medici ever cared what time it was. Besides the art, the villa has lovely woods and gardens all around.

## Pistoia

Many have found it a gloomy town. Pistoia does seem to get more than its share of fog and clouds, and laughter in its plain, narrow streets seems a bit out of place. Pistoia has been around since it was *Pistoria* in Roman times, and it has usually been bad luck for somebody. The Catiline conspiracy, the famous attempted coup against the Roman Republic in 62 BC, ended when the legions tracked down the escaped Catiline and his henchmen near Pistoia. In the Middle Ages Pistoia had a dark reputation among its neighbours for violence and treachery. The Black versus White Guelph struggles that obsessed Florence for so long actually began here. Dante, himself a victim of that feud, never let a chance go by in the *Divine Comedy* to curse and condemn the fateful city. In 1329 Florence captured Pistoia once and for all. The city carried on, living well off its old speciality, iron-working. True to its reputation, Pistoia supplied the warriors and conspirators of Europe with fine daggers. Later, keeping up with technology, the city gave its name to that new invention, the pistol.

Today Pistoia, the centre of a plain full of gardens and greenhouses, is better known for its flowers. Its people laugh at their odd history; bring it up and they'll be ready to blame it all on those obnoxious Florentines. Pistoia's somnolence over the last 600 years has left it with a historic centre almost entirely intact, many fine buildings, and a wealth of art. Tucked as it is between Florence and Pisa, few people visit, which is a pity.

## Piazza del Duomo

Old Pistoia is almost perfectly diamond-shaped, surrounded by 16th-century walls with the old moats preserved on the northern and eastern sides. Right in the middle you'll find one of the finest squares in Italy, and a lesson in the subtle medieval aesthetic of urban design, something lost with the endless theorizing and compulsive regularity of the Renaissance. The arrangements of the buildings around the L-shaped **Piazza del Duomo** seems haphazard at first. The design is something meant to be experienced from street level; walk into the piazza from a few of the surrounding streets, and you'll see how from each approach the monuments reveal themselves in a different order and pattern, like the shaking of a kaleidoscope. Much of old Pistoia is like this, shaped by centuries of anonymous builders into a work of art, a half-forgotten art that appeals not only to the eye but the brain. Once you learn how to see it, you may find the symmetry of the Renaissance and Baroque art looking a little wearisome.

The façade of the **Duomo**, with its Pisan arcades and stripes, over some Florentine rectangular patterns and a tympanum by Andrea della Robbia, makes an uneasy balance between the two architectural traditions. The tall, impressive campanile tips the balance towards Pisa, with a touch of the exotic in its Moorish-inspired arches. Inside, there is a wealth of painting and sculpture in the chapels, but the real attraction is the enormous **Altar of St James**, about a ton of solid silver, begun in 1287 and added to over the next two centuries (the sacristan opens the chapel for L2000). Some of the earliest sculptural fragments from the Duomo have been taken down to the dim and ancient crypt.

Directly across from the cathedral is the striped, octagonal **Baptistry** (1350), credited to Andrea Pisano, one of the outstanding Gothic buildings of Tuscany, with especially fine sculptural trim on the exterior and an unusual conical dome under the roof, visible from inside. The 12th-century Palazzo dei Vescovi, recently restored, contains a small **Archaeological Museum** (*open mornings Fri only*) and the collection of the cathedral Treasure, including some medieval painting and a *Madonna* by Pollaiuolo.

On the façade of the **Palazzo del Comune**, a head in black marble is set into the wall, the face of a Moorish king captured on a freebooting expedition to Mallorca. Besides the town council and offices, it houses the **Museo Civico** (*open 9–1, 3–7, Tues–Sat; 9–1 Sun; adm*), which provides you with an introduction to the 13th- and 14th-century 'Pistoian School' and much else; don't miss the hallucinatory battle scenes by Francesco Graziani.

From behind the cathedral, Via F. Pacini takes you north to another Pistoian surprise, the refined, arcaded façade of the **Ospedale del Ceppo**, done in the manner of the famous Ospedale degli Innocenti in Florence. As in Florence, the della Robbias were called upon to provide the decoration, but besides the simple terracotta medallions there is a unique terracotta frieze across the entire façade—and not just blue and white, but resplendent Renaissance technicolor. The frieze, by Giovanni della Robbia and later artists in the 1510s and 1580s, portrays the works of the hospital and some allegorical virtues. A little way to the east, the 12th-century **Sant'Andrea** contains a real treasure, an exquisite pulpit by Giovanni Pisano, lifted on columns over figures of the four Evangelists and surrounded with reliefs full of intricately carved figures: a fitting introduction to the more famous works of the Pisano family in Pisa.

Two other churches on the northern side of Pistoia are worth a look. **San Francesco al Prato**, on the piazza of the same name, has an exceptional collection of 14th-century frescoes, and the **Madonna dell'Umiltà**, on the central Via della Madonna, is a curious, octagonal High Renaissance building. Giorgio Vasari didn't only make mischief in Florence. In the 1460s, called upon to complete this long-unfinished church, he added a dome so heavy that the church has been threatening to collapse ever since. More work to shore it up is currently under way.

## More Stripes

From Piazza del Duomo, one block south and another east will put you in Piazza San Leone; the stubby tower here once belonged to perhaps the rottenest of all the Pistoians, a 13th-century noble thug and sworn enemy of the Church named Vanni Fucci; Dante found him in one of the lower circles of Hell, cursing and making obscene gestures up at God. Around the corner of Via Cavour, **San Giovanni Fuoricivitas** claims the honour of being the stripiest church in Christendom. Turning its side to the street, bristling with lozenge windows and blind arches, the 12th-century work looks more Pisan than anything in Pisa. Inside (if anyone ever opens it) there will be another fine pulpit, by a pupil of Pisano, and a della Robbia plaque of the *Visitation*.

**San Domenico**, nearby on Corso Silvano, is less flamboyant on the outside, but the church and adjacent convent have some good frescoes, as does the **Cappella del Tau** across the street. Some of the pictures here, scenes from the story of Adam and Eve, are little-known works by Masolino. There is another good Gothic façade on **San Pietro**, another street over to the east.

The best stripes of all, however, may be on the zebras in the **Pistoia Zoo** (*open April–Sept 9–7; Oct–Mar 9–5; adm exp*), 4km west of town on Via Pieve a Calle. Italians don't usually care for zoos (though the Medici always kept big menageries) and this one may be the best in the country, even though it's only 20 years old. Polar bears, kangaroos, rhinos, giant turtles and all the other zoo favourites are in attendance.

## Montecatini Terme

Only 15 km west of Pistoia, this is perhaps Italy's best-known spa, a party centre for crowned heads and their sycophants in the 1890s and popular ever since. The waters, good for just about anything according to Montecatini's boosters, are the town's sole reason for being. To please its elevated clientele, Montecatini in the 19th century built itself into quite an elegant place, with a large park at the centre and imposing establishments such as the Versailles-like **Tettuccio**, where string quartets once serenaded those who came to take the waters. Many of the other establishments are almost as good and, even if you prefer stronger stuff than mineral water for your cures, you can come for the florid 1890s architecture and genteel atmosphere. The other favourite recreation of Montecatini visitors is taking the **cable car** up to the pretty village of Montecatini Alto.

Further west towards Lucca, **Pescia** is another garden centre, with a famous wholesale flower market. The church of San Francesco there has a painting of St Francis done shortly after his death—believed to be an accurate portrayal by an artist who knew him. In **Collodi** you'll see a monument to Pinocchio; his creator, Carlo Collodi, took his pen name from his family's native town.

### *Where to Stay*

When you come to Tuscany for the first time, stay in Florence long enough to see it well. On the second trip, however, you might consider spending some time in one of the outlying towns: Prato, only a few minutes from Florence on the train, is a tranquil place to spend your evenings when the Tuscan capital is jam-packed with rubbernecks and gawkers. In Pistoia you have a Tuscan city that is an attraction in its own right and, even in the summer, chances are you'll have it all to yourself when the day-trippers go home. In both cities, you'll find little more than simple, practical accommodation.

There is a large concentration of hotel space, much of it upper-range and on the way to it, in Montecatini Terme. If you don't care to take the waters, the scores of hotels here ensure that you can find a room in a pinch. Italy's choicest spa has no fewer than six hotels that claim the title of 'Grand' and half a dozen others that only decline to for discretion's sake.

## Prato

The ★★★**San Marco**, Piazza San Marco 48, ✆ (0574) 21321 (moderate) is a pleasant place, with rooms with and without baths. For something more modern there's ★★★**Flora**, Via Cairoli 31, near S. Maria dei Carceri, ✆ (0574) 20021 (moderate) with air-conditioned rooms, all with baths. The ★★**Stella d'Italia**, Piazza Duomo 8, ✆ (0574) 27910 (inexpensive) is Prato's old-fashioned, once actually grand hotel, looking on to the cathedral, and with slightly faded rooms with and without baths. On a quiet square near the Stazione Porta al Serraglio, the ★★**Toscana**, Piazza Ciardi 3, ✆ (0574) 28096 (inexpensive) is the best of the budget choice, with air-conditioning in some rooms.

## Carmignano

Near Carmignano, the ★★★★**Paggeria Medicea**, Viale Papa Giovanni XXIII 3, ✆ (055) 8718081, ✉ 8718080 (expensive) is a villa with some unusual amenities— a hunting reserve and a lake stocked with fish, also a pool and tennis court, and pleasant modern rooms, many with balconies, all air-conditioned.

## Pistoia

A pleasant hotel near Pistoia is ★★★**Il Convento**, Via S. Quirico 33, ✆ (0573) 452651, 5km east of the centre of town at Pontenuovo (moderate). It's a former convent, preserving its exterior if not all of its interior, in a quiet setting with views over Pistoia; there's also a pool and one of the city's better restaurants. In Pistoia itself, there's the older (as a hotel) but comfortable ★★★**Leon Bianco**, Via Panciatichi 2, ✆ (0573) 26675 (moderate) with views over the campanile. Inexpensive accommodation is rare in Pistoia; the ★★**Appenino**, near the station at Via XX Settembre 21, ✆ (0573) 32243 (inexpensive) has simple but adequate rooms, most with baths, though rates are much cheaper for rooms without them. Alternatively try ★★**Firenze**, a skip away from Piazza del Duomo at Via Curtatone e Montanara 42, ✆ (0573) 23141 (inexpensive) with clean, quiet rooms.

## Montecatini Terme

One of the grandest of Montecatini's hotels, the ★★★★★**Grand Hotel Bellavista**, Viale Fedeli, ✆ (0572) 78122, ✉ 73352 (very expensive) offers golf, tennis, indoor pool, luxurious rooms, sauna, a health club, and an infinite number of opportunities for self-indulgence. But for genuine Belle Epoque charm the *****Grand Hotel & La Pace, Viale della Torretta 1, ✆ (0572) 75801, @ 78451 (very expensive) is renowned throughout Europe, with a similarly impressive array of luxuries, and a very elegant restaurant. (*Open April–Oct only.*)

There are any number of middle-range hotels in Montecatini Terme, which seem to be uniformly good, if expensive for their range. In Montecatini most one-star hotels are expensive even by Italian standards. One that is good value, up in Montecatini Alto, is the *Belsoggiorno, Viale Cavallotti, ✆ (0572) 78859 (inexpensive) which has rooms overlooking a garden, with or without baths.

---

### Eating Out

One reason for staying in Prato is its restaurants, which are as good as those in Florence. Pistoia, however, really has no interesting restaurants—traditionally it never has—and in the centre you'll be limited to simple trattorias and pizzerias.

## Prato

Prato's **Il Pirana**, Via Valentini 110, ✆ (0574) 25746, south of Viale Veneto, the main street between the central station and Piazza San Marco (very expensive) has an entirely justified reputation as one of the best seafood restaurants in inland Tuscany; try the scampi. Opposite the Metastasio theatre, **Osvaldo Baroncelli**, Via Fra Bartolomeo 13, ✆ (0574) 23810 (expensive) is an unpretentious, small establishment with an innovative chef who turns out dishes like tagliatelle with artichokes, veal *scaloppa* with truffles or stuffed celery and duck stuffed with its own kidney, as well as more traditional Tuscan favourites. (*Closed Sun, Wed evenings.*) A good and reasonably priced local restaurant in Prato is the **Trattoria Lapo**, Piazza Mercatale 141, ✆ (0574) 23745 (inexpensive), which is unspectacular, but usually crowded.

## Pistoia

Just outside Pistoia is the **Locanda degli Elfi**, in Loc. San Felice, ✆ (0573) 41490 (expensive), in a beautiful 18th-century villa, and offering fine fish and traditional local dishes. Perhaps the best restaurant in Pistoia is **Leon Rosso**, Via Panciatichi 4, ✆ (0573) 29230 (moderate). The food served comes from the owner's farm in the mountains, and you should try their *maccheroncini* with pigeon sauce and wild boar steaks. (*Closed Sun.*) **Rafanelli**, Via Sant'Agostino 47, ✆ (0573) 5329460 (moderate), just outside the town at Sant'Agostino, offers Tuscan home cooking (*maccheroni* with duck, game dishes, or lamb) served in a country villa setting. (*Closed Sun evenings, Mon, Aug.*) For good pizza and basic local cooking in Pistoia, try **Le Chiavi d'Oro**, Via Pacini 17–19 (inexpensive).

## Montecatini Terme

In Montecatini Terme, at **Pierangelo**, Viale IV Novembre 99 ✆ (0572) 771552 (very expensive), a husband and wife team prepare creative and traditional dishes—

sample the rabbit salad and the stuffed *caramelle* in sauce. (*Closed Sun, Mon midday.*) **Enoteca da Giovanni**, Via Garibaldi 25, ✆ (0572) 71695 (expensive) is a unique and much-honoured place where game dishes—hare, venison, wild duck—turn into impeccably *haute cuisine* surprises at the hands of a genuine master chef; you won't even notice the price.

## Lucca

The famous walls—'much like the walls of Berwick-on-Tweed', the Lucchese for some reason like to say—do not seem very formidable, more like a garden wall than something that would keep the Florentines at bay. Behind them, you can see only pine trees and neat stucco buildings with the inevitable green shutters. The walls and the surrounding areas, once the outworks of the fortifications, are now full of lawns and trees, making a sort of green belt for the little city. The Lucchese ride their bikes and walk their dogs around the ramparts, and often stop to admire the view. Lucca at first glance may seem too bijou and tidy to be true. It is a dream city—not like Venice, but in a quiet, very domestic sort of way. After its long and brave history it has certainly earned the right to a little quiet. The annual hordes of Tuscan tourists leave Lucca alone for the most part, though there seems to be a small number of discreet visitors who come back every year. They don't spread the word, apparently trying to keep one of Italy's most beautiful cities to themselves.

Lucca's rigid grid of streets betrays its Roman origins. The town survived continuously through the bad centuries, and emerged in the age of the *comuni* as one of the leading trading towns of Tuscany, specializing in the production of silk. Guelphs and Ghibellines, Blacks and Whites, made nuisances of themselves as they did everywhere else, and Lucca often found itself pressed to maintain its independence from Pisa, and later Florence. In the early 1300s, perhaps the height of the city's wealth and power, a remarkable adventurer named Castruccio Castracani appeared in the spotlight. Castracani, who for years had lived in exile—part of it in England—returned in 1314 when Pisan and Ghibelline troops captured Lucca. Within a year he chased the Pisans out and seized power for himself, and by

Lucca Walls

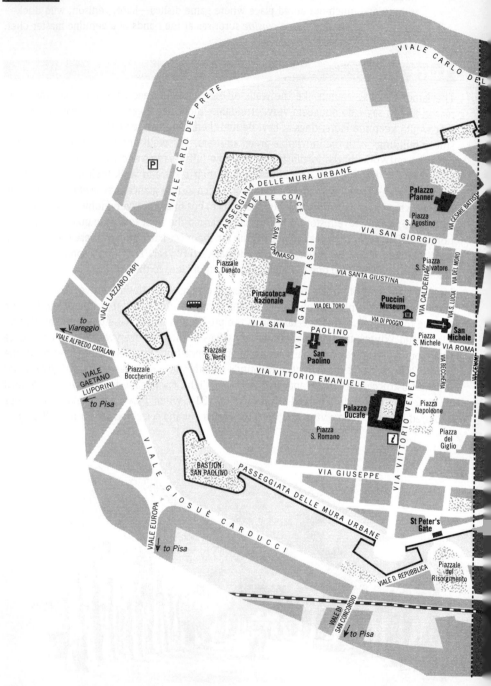

VIALE CARLO DEL

VIA CESARE BATTISTI

VIA CARLO DEL PRETE

PASSEGGIATA DELLE MURA URBANE

VIA DELLE CON

**Palazzo Pfanner**

Piazza S. Agostino

VIA SAN GIORGIO

VIA CALDERIA

VIA DEL MORO

VIA S. LUCIA

VIA SAN TOMMASO

VIA GALLI TASSI

Piazzale S. Donato

VIA SANTA GIUSTINA

Piazza S. Salvatore

**Pinacoteca Nazionale**

VIA DEL TORO

**Puccini Museum**

VIA DI POGGIO

VIA SAN

PAOLINO

**San Michele**

Piazza S. Michele

VIA ROMA

VIA CALDERIA

P

VIA CARLO DEL PRETE

VIA LAZZARO PAPI

to Viareggio

VIALE ALFREDO CATALANI

Piazzale G. Verdi

**San Paolino**

VIALE GAETANO LUPORINI

Piazzale Boccherini

to Pisa

VIA VITTORIO EMANUELE

VIA BECCHERIA

**Palazzo Ducale**

Piazza Napoleone

Piazza S. Romano

Piazza del Giglio

i

BASTION SAN PAOLINO

PASSEGGIATA DELLE MURA URBANE

VIA GIUSEPPE

VIA VITTORIO VENETO

VIALE GIOSUE CARDUCCI

VIALE EUROPA

to Pisa

**St Peter's Gate**

Piazzale del Risorgimento

VIALE D. REPUBBLICA

VIALE DI SAN CONCORDIO

to Pisa

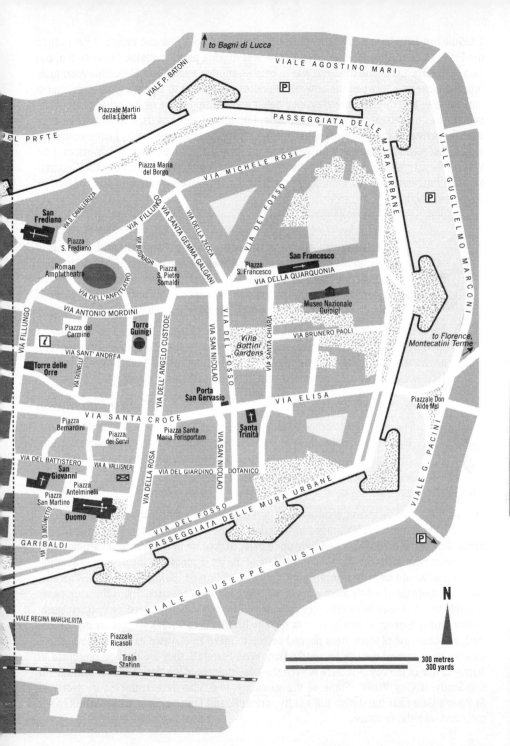

to Bagni di Lucca

VIALE AGOSTINO MARI

VIALE P. BATONI

Piazzale Martiri
della Libertà

PASSEGGIATA DELLE MURA URBANE

DEL PRFTE

Piazza Maria
del Borgo

VIA MICHELE ROSI

VIALE GUGLIELMO MARCONI

San
Frediano

VIA D. CAVALLERIZZA

VIA FILLUNGO

VIA SANTA GEMMA GALGANI

VIA DELLA ZECCA

VIA DEL FOSSO

Piazza
S. Frediano

VIA BUSDRAGHI

Piazza
S. Pietro
Somaldi

Piazza
S. Francesco

San Francesco

Roman
Amphitheatre

VIA DELL'ANFITEATRO

VIA DELLA QUARQUONIA

Museo Nazionale
Guinigi

VIA ANTONIO MORDINI

VIA FILLUNGO

Piazza del
Carmine

Torre
Guinigi

VIA DELL'ANGELO CUSTODE

VIA DEL FOSSO

VIA SAN NICOLAO

Villa
Bottini
Gardens

VIA SANTA CHIARA

VIA BRUNERO PAOLI

to Florence,
Montecatini Terme

i

VIA SANT' ANDREA

VIA FATINELLI

Torre delle
Ore

Porta
San Gervasio

VIA ELISA

Piazzale Don
Aldo Mei

VIA SANTA CROCE

Piazza
Bernardini

Piazza
dei Servi

Piazza Santa
Maria Forisportam

VIA SAN NICOLAO

Santa
Trinità

VIALE G. PACINI

VIA DELLA ROSA

VIA DEL BATTISTERO

VIA A. VALLISNERI

VIA DEL GIARDINO

BOTANICO

San
Giovanni

Piazza
Antelminelli

VIA D. MOLINETTO

Piazza
San Martino

Duomo

VIA DEL FOSSO

PASSEGGIATA DELLE MURA URBANE

GARIBALDI

PASSEGGIATA GIUSEPPE GIUSTI

VIALE REGINA MARGHERITA

Piazzale
Ricasoli

Train
Station

N

300 metres
300 yards

1325 he had built for Lucca a little empire that included both Pisa and Pistoia. After routing the Florentines at Altopascio in that year, he was making plans to snatch Florence too, but died of malaria just before the siege was to begin—another example of Florentine good luck. Internal bickering between the powerful families put an end to Lucca's glory days almost immediately, and the city barely escaped being gobbled up by one or the other of its neighbours. As a competently functioning republic, Lucca used tact and tenacity to survive even after the arrival of the Spaniards. After the Treaty of Chateau-Cambresis, Lucca amazingly found itself standing together with Venice as the only truly independent Italian states. Like Venice, the city was an island of relative tolerance and enlightenment during the Counter-Reformation, and it shared Venice's fate in 1805 when Napoleon arrived, and ordered its political extinction.

## Getting Around

The **railway** station is just south of the walls on Piazza Ricasoli, with lots of trains on the Pisa-Florence line. **Buses** leave from Piazzale G. Verdi, just inside the walls at the western end of the city: LAZZI buses run to Florence, Pistoia, Pisa, Prato, or Viareggio, and CLAP buses to towns in Lucca province, including the upper Serchio valley in the Apuan Alps.

Lucca is a crossroads for two main **roads**, the SS435 from Florence to Viareggio and the SS12 to Pisq and, to the north, to Modena. Just south of Lucca the A11 autostrada divides: the A11 continues west, meeting the A12 on the coast north of Pisa, while the A11/12 runs north and joins the A12 above Viareggio.

## Tourist Information

The city tourist office is at Vecchia Porta San Donato, in Piazzale Verdi, © (0583) 419689, near the bus station. It has **bicycles** available for hire in summer.

## The Walls

Lucca's walls owe their considerable charm to Renaissance advances in military technology. The city began them in 1500, urged to the effort by the beginning of the Wars of Italy. The councillors wanted fortifictions entirely up to date, to counter new advances in artillery, and their (unknown) architects gave them the state of the art, a model for the new style of fortification that would soon be transforming the cities of Europe. Being Renaissance Tuscans, they also made them a little more elegant than perhaps was necessary. The walls were never severely tested. Today, with the outer ravelins, fosses, and salients cleared away (such earthworks usually took up as much space as the city itself), Lucca's walls are just for decoration, with a double row of shade trees planted on top to make an elevated garden boulevard that extends clear around the city for nearly 4km. With Ferrara's, they are the best preserved in Italy—in one of the bastions there is even the headquarters of the 'International Institute for the Study of City Walls'. Some of the gates are fine, elaborate 16th-century works— St Peter's Gate near the station still has its portcullis, and Lucca's proud motto LIBERTAS is inscribed over the entrance.

# St Martin's Cathedral

Lucca's **Duomo**, perhaps the outstanding work of the Pisan style outside Pisa itself, was begun in the 11th century and completed only in the 15th. A porch with three arches, each a different size, makes the façade somewhat unusual. Above is a typical Pisan design of three levels of colonnades, and behind the arch are exquisite 12th- and 13th-century reliefs and sculpture—the best work Lucca has to offer. See especially the *Adoration of the Magi* by Nicola Pisano, and a host of fantastical animals and hunting scenes, the 12 months and their occupations, even *Roland at Roncevalles*, all by unknown masters. It's worth the trouble to walk around the back, where there's a small park. The apse and transepts, if not as ornate as the front, are still splendid medieval architecture.

Inside, a large marble tabernacle in the left aisle contains the *Volto Santo* ('Holy Image'), a painted wooden crucifix brought from Byzantium to Italy in 782 during the Iconoclast movement. According to legend, the crucifix was carved by Nicodemus, and accurately represents the face of Jesus. Long an object of pilgrimage, the image goes out for a night on the town in a candlelight procession each 13 September. In the transept, there is a fine work by the sculptor Jacopo della Quercia, the **tomb of Ilaria del Carretto**, a tranquil effigy complete with family dog that is his acknowledged masterpiece. Opposite the cathedral is the newly opened **Museo della Cattedrale** (*open 10–6.30 Mon–Fri; 10–7 Sat, Sun; adm*) with a second work by della Quercia, *St John the Evangelist*, as well as other treasures from the cathedral and the adjoining church of San Giovanni.

From the cathedral, in a quiet corner of town near the southern wall, Via Duomo takes you to twin piazzas full of trees, the focus of Lucca's evening *passeggiata*, **Piazza del Giglio** and **Piazza Napoleone**. After Napoleon seized Lucca, he gave it to his sister Elisa Baciocchi. This queen for a day occupied the old seat of the republican council, and after Waterloo, when Lucca was given to a branch of the Bourbons, the 16th-century building became the **Ducal Palace**, the name it still has today.

## San Michele

Many people mistake this church, set on a piazza right in the centre of Lucca, for the cathedral. Built about the same time, and with a similar Pisan façade, it is almost as impressive. The full name, **San Michele in Foro**, comes from its location on what was Roman Lucca's forum. The ambitious façade rises high above the level of the roof, like the false fronts on buildings in Wild West towns of the 1880s. Every column in the Pisan arcading is different; some doubled, some twisted like corkscrews, inlaid with mosaic Cosmati work, or carved into medieval monsters. The graceful, rectangular campanile is Lucca's tallest and best.

West of San Michele, in a neighbourhood perfumed by the big tobacco factory near Porta Vittorio Emanuele, the 17th-century Palazzo Mansi contains the **Pinacoteca Nazionale** (*open 9–2 Tues–Sat; 9–1 Sun; adm*), with mostly 16th–17th century paintings, works by the Medici court painters Bronzino and Sustermans, and also Andrea del Sarto, Pontormo, and Tintoretto. East of the church, **Via Fillungo** and its surrounding streets make up the busy shopping area of Lucca, a tidy nest of straight and narrow alleys where the contented cheerfulness that distinguishes Lucca from many of its neighbouring cities seems somehow magnified. Near Via Fillungo's northern end, the 12th-century church of **San Frediano** stands out, thanks to the big mosaic panel on its façade, showing Christ and the Apostles in an elegant, flowing style. Inside is a beautiful covered baptismal font with a terracotta of the *Annunciation* by Andrea della Robbia.

Across Via Fillungo, narrow arches lead to something most visitors miss, the **Roman Amphitheatre**. Not a stone of it remains— the marble was probably carted off for San Michele and the cathedral—but Lucca is a city that changes so gradually and organically that the outline of the amphitheatre was perfectly preserved. Where the grand-

*San Frediano*

stands were, you now see a complete ellipse of medieval houses, with a piazza where the gladiators once slugged it out.

Many of the streets in this part of Lucca have scarcely changed at all in 500 years. Down Via S. Andrea, you'll pass a number of resolutely medieval palaces, including that of the Guinigi family; long the leading power-brokers of Lucca, the Guinigi once even went so far as to imitate the Visconti and Medici and seize power for themselves. The reign of Signor Paolo Guinigi lasted only from 1400 to 1430. Their stronghold, the **Torre Guinigi** (*open April–Sept 9–7 daily; Oct–Mar 10–4.30 daily; adm*), next to the palace, is one of Lucca's landmarks, the best example of the odd Italian fancy of towers with big trees growing out of the top. One of the most elaborate of the medieval family fortresses, the tower has recently been restored; it's worth the climb up for the view over the city and the Apuan Alps .

Continuing eastwards, you pass the Via del Fosso; the canal running down the middle was the moat (*fosso*) of Lucca's oldest fortifications. Another Guinigi house, a suburban villa before the extension of the walls, contains the **Museo Guinigi** (*open 9–2 Tues–Sat; 9–1 Sun; adm*), with a good selection of painting and sculpture from this side of Tuscany. Sculptures from the 9th to the 15th century show the logical development of the Pisan-Luccan style, along with some original columns from the façade of San Michele, and an inspired *Annunciation* and other works by a sculptor named Matteo Civitoli, who deserves to be better known. Lucchese Renaissance painting, with a fond reluctance to give up the Middle Ages, is also well represented.

North of the city there are two showy but refined 17th-century villas, usually open to the public: **Villa Mansi** at Segronugo, and the **Villa Torregiani**, nearby at Marfia, the country home of Elisa Bonaparte Baciocchi during her reign. Both have extensive grounds with English gardens.

---

*Lucca ☏ (0583–)*

**Where to Stay**

*very expensive*

There are no very special hotels in Lucca, but outside the city at Massa Pisana, on the Pisa road, you can stay in Castruccio Castracani's own palace, built for the great Lucchese *generalissimo* in 1321. The

\*\*\*\*\***Principessa Elisa**, ℭ 379737, ℗ 379019, often rebuilt since, currently wears the façade of a stately Rococo mansion, surrounded by acres of 18th-century gardens and a pool. Thoroughly modern inside, its amenities include air-conditioning, TV, and minibars in all rooms. (*Open Mar–Nov only.*)

*moderate*

In Lucca you cannot do better than the slightly frayed, green-shuttered and thoroughly delightful \*\*\***Universo**, Piazza del Giglio, ℭ 493678, right in the centre of the old town's life; Ruskin and nearly everyone else who followed him to Lucca has slept here. Note that some rooms are much nicer than others. \*\***Villa Casanova**, in Via Casanova, ℭ 548429, just outside the city at Balbano (city bus 5), has simple rooms but a pleasant garden, tennis courts, and a swimming-pool to lounge by.

*inexpensive*

The less expensive places in Lucca can be great bargains; witness the friendly, well-run \*\***Diana** near the Cathedral on Via del Molinetto, ℭ 42202, with some of the nicest rooms in this price range in Italy. The modern, comfortable, and rarely crowded **youth hostel** is 2km north of town on Via del Brennero, ℭ 341811 (*open 10 Mar–10 Oct*), in Salicchi (bus 7 from the station). IYHF cards are required.

*Lucca* ℭ *(0583–)* **Eating Out**

In Lucca, wherever you eat, you may be fortunate enough to find a dry white wine called *Montecarlo*, produced only in a small area east of the city; it's one of Tuscany's best.

*expensive*

Duck with truffles, wild boar, and grilled seafood are a few of the treats on the extensive menu at **Solferino**, 6km west of Lucca on the Viareggio road in San Macario in Piano, Via delle Gavine 50, ℭ (0583) 59118. It's been run by the same family for four generations, and famous throughout Tuscany for almost as long. Simple Tuscan country specialities are also in evidence, but this is one place where you might want to splurge.

*moderate*

In the centre of Lucca, across from the Hotel Universo on Piazza del Giglio, **Il Giglio**, ℭ 494058, is Lucca's best seafood palace—river trout is a speciality as well—with prices between the moderate and expensive ranges. Another Lucca restaurant with a high reputation is **Il Buca di Sant'Antonio**, Via della Cervia 1, ℭ 55881, which has been an inn since 1782, and offers old recipes like smoked herring and kid on a spit, and newer dishes like ravioli with ricotta and sage.

*inexpensive*

For good cheap food, seek out Via Conce, in the northwest corner within the walls, where you can enjoy some surprising dishes at rock-bottom prices at **Da Giulio in Pelleria**, ℭ 55948, which is popular enough to warrant reservations, with top-quality 'peasant' fare. (*Closed Sun, Mon.*) **Canaleia**, Via Canaleia, ℭ 47470, is situated near the amphitheatre in a medieval workshop, and serves local food with some surprises, and usually a choice of vegetarian dishes. (*Closed Sat, Sun.*)

## The Apuan Alps and the Serchio Valley

All across northern Tuscany, the mountains have never been very far away. In the region's northwest corner, they stretch to the very edge of the sea itself. These are no piddling foothills; two peaks within 45km of Lucca are 2000m high. Not many tourists find their way up the Serchio—it may be the only truly worthwhile corner of Tuscany that hasn't been overrun. But if you simply can't look at another cathedral or picture gallery, and would like a spell in some striking yet civilized mountain scenery, this is the place.

### Getting Around

The most convenient way to get into these mountains is by **road** from Lucca, on the SS12 to Fornoli, and then northwest on to the SS445, which follows the river Serchio up a narrow valley between the Apennines proper and the Apuan Alps, the rugged patch of marble peaks along the coast. **Buses** also run to most destinations in the valley from Lucca, but some services are very slow.

### Tourist Information

There is a permanent tourist office in **Bagni di Lucca** at Piazza Municipio 101, ✆ (0583) 87946. In **Barga** there is an office at Piazza Angelio, ✆ (0583) 73499, open April–Sept only.

## Lucca to Bagni di Lucca

North of Lucca you quickly arrive at **Diecimo**, a name that has survived from Roman times—10 Roman miles from the city. Its fine Renaissance campanile stands out starkly among the surrounding hills. Next, **Borgo a Mozzano** is famous for its beautiful little hogback bridge, the **Ponte Maddalena**, with arches in five different sizes, and a legend attached to it of how the devil built it in one night. The credit really goes to Countess Matilda of Tuscany, who besides the bridge endowed the villages around Borgo with a set of solid Romanesque churches. Just beyond the town is the main turn-off left for the SS445 and the Serchio valley.

A little further up river beyond the turn, still on the main SS12 road, **Bagni di Lucca** has another interesting bridge, an early 19th-century suspension bridge of 1840 hung on iron chains, the *Ponte alle Catene*. Bagni is a town worth visiting, a spa that enjoyed a brief spell of high society's favour in the 19th century and then was quietly forgotten. It has elegant old establishments to take the waters (one like a miniature Roman Pantheon), a pretty site along the river, charming villas and gardens, and even a Victorian-Gothic-Alhambresque Anglican church; among the many English visitors in the old days were Shelley, Byron, and Browning. Bagni's casino (1837) invented the roulette to clean them out.

Up in the mountains above Bagni, **San Cassiano** has another picturesque medieval bridge and a 13th-century Pisan style church, with a delicate carved façade; in its isolated setting few people ever see it. From Bagni, you have a choice of continuing along the SS12 towards **Abetone**, Tuscany's only big ski resort, under Monte Cimone, the highest peak in the area, or else turning back to head up the Serchio, into the region called the Garfagnana.

## The Garfagnana and the Lunigiana

**Barga**, the main town along the Serchio valley, is a little mountain *comune* that managed to keep its independence until 1341. It has an unusual 13th-century **cathedral**, begun in the year 1000 and set high on a terrace, with a plain, squarish façade that makes it look more like a medieval Palazzo del Popolo. Be sure to step in and see the 13th-century **pulpit**, by a Como sculptor named Guido Bigorelli. The pillars that support it, resting on a pair of lions devouring some poor fellows, are in the Pisan style, but the reliefs around the pulpit itself are unique, startling naïve-sophisticated versions of familiar scriptural scenes. From Barga, you can detour 17km to the **Grotta del Vento** ( *open April–Sept, guided tours from 10am daily; Oct–Mar Sun and holidays only* ), up in the mountains, a long cavern hung with fat stalactites and set in a barren, eerie landscape of eroded limestone. The castle at **Castelnuovo Garfagnana**, further up the valley, properly decorative in the best 14th-century manner, was once commanded by the poet Ariosto, then in the service of the Estes of Ferrara. The Apuan mountains around Castelnuovo are full of lakes, one with a romantic tiny village tucked on an island: the **Isola Santa**.

Further north, past **Piazza al Serchio**, the road leaves the Serchio behind and crosses over a pass into a region called the Lunigiana, the mountain hinterlands of the long-disappeared Roman port town of **Luni**. This rugged territory covered with chestnut forests has often given its governors fits; at the turn of the century it was a stronghold of rural anarchy, and in 1944 the partisans made it one of the bigger free zones in the north. It must always have been like this, for these mountains are jammed full of castles; **Monti, Fivizzano, Bagnone**, and **Fosidinovo** have the best ones, and on the back roads of the region you'll find a number of tiny mountain lakes and Romanesque country churches. This hidden corner conceals a genuine prehistoric mystery. Up in **Pontrémoli**, the northernmost town in Tuscany, the stout grey 14th-century **Piagnaro Castle** has been restored as a museum to hold over a score of large, carved 'statue-steles' of an unknown culture that flourished in Lunigiana about 1500–100 BC. The steles, sort of menhirs with personality, include some shaped into stylized warriors with daggers or axes; others are women with little knobby breasts. Dozens have been discovered in the Lunigiana, all in isolated areas. Many others probably still remain. Similar things turn up in southern Corsica and other places around the Mediterranean. They undoubtedly served some religious function, though perhaps not exactly the hero-fertility goddess cliché of the anthropologists. Interestingly, the records say Christianity only began to make headway here after 700 AD. Most of the steles at Pontrémoli have their heads knocked off, a sure sign that at some time the Pope's missionaries were at work.

---

© *(0583–)*                                               ***Where to Stay***

If you are passing through these mountains, either Bagni di Lucca or Barga makes a pleasant place to stop—or even stay a few days, to recharge your batteries in the country air.

## Bagni di Lucca

Bagni di Lucca has some quiet, modest old hotels like ★★★**Silvania**, at Lugliano, ✆ 87586 (moderate), which is very tranquil with nice rooms, all with bath, or the ★★**Svizzero**, Via Casalini 30, ✆ 87114 (moderate), ineffably Tuscan, a strange place where the clock has stopped at about 1840, and so has the owner. Toscanini stayed in Bagni di Lucca's small ★**Roma**, Via Umberto I 110, ✆ 87278 (inexpensive), with a shady little garden at the back, and rooms with and without baths.

## Barga

Outside Barga, there's a huge 234-room resort hotel, ★★★★**Il Ciocco**, 6km north in Castelvecchio Pascoli, ✆ (0583) 7191, @ 723197 (expensive), with an indoor pool, tennis courts, air-conditioning, and, in short, the works. In the town itself, ★★★**Villa Libano**, Via del Sasso 6, ✆ (0583) 73059 (moderate), is a lovely place in a courtyard, set next to the town's park; there's a pleasant restaurant, with tables out in the garden.

---

### Eating Out

In Bagni, **Da Vinicio**, Via del Casino, ✆ (0583) 87250 (moderate), is a chaotic and popular pizzeria that also serves good roast pigeon and seafood. Anything more than a simple trattoria is hard to come by in the Serchio valley, but if you make it as far north as Pontrémoli, try the town's special pasta *testaroli* and the roast meats, stuffed vegetables and other local dishes at **Da Bussé**, Piazza Duomo 9, ✆ (0585) 831371 (moderate).

## The Tuscan Coast

The ancient Etruscans weren't shy; these early free traders happily accepted goods, art, and ideas from all over the Mediterranean world. For the last thousand years, however, for all its accomplishments, modern Tuscany has been a moody, introspective region, and usually a little dismissive towards what goes on in the rest of the world. The Tuscan coastline somehow reflects this; there is one big port, and a few little resorts, but on the whole Tuscany turns a blank face to the sea.

---

### Getting Around

The main Rome–Genoa **rail** line runs a few kilometres inland all along the coast, making communications very easy. **Buses** to most of the smaller destinations without a train station run from Massa or Viareggio. As in Liguria, the main roads serving the coast towns are the A12 *autostrada* and the SS1, the Via Aurelia.

---

### Tourist Information

There are information offices in **Carrara**, Viale XX Settembre, ✆ (0585) 70668, and in among the beach resorts at **Marina di Carrara**, Piazza

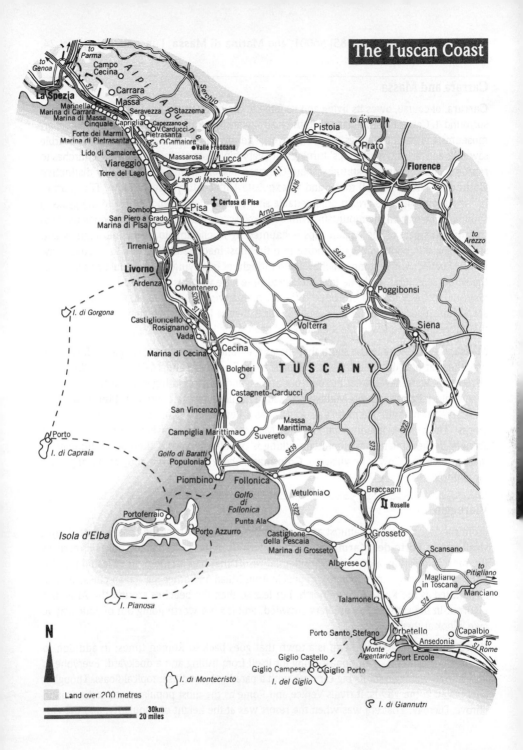

The Tuscan Coast

Menconi 6/b, ✆ (0585) 56001, and **Marina di Massa**, Lungomare Vespucci 24, ✆ (0585) 243630.

## Carrara and Massa

**Carrara**, of course, owes its living and its fame to the marble masses of the Apuan Alps that surround it. Carrara marble has added the lustre to ancient Rome, Renaissance Rome, and art museums and bank buildings the world over. The town is still busy, with scores of marble sawmills and 'artistic workshops' turning out everything from sculptures for new churches to reproductions of famous statues. Some Carraran marble went into the city's distinctive **Cathedral**, with a tall bell tower and an exquisite 13th-century rose window. The quarries in the surrounding hills are an unforgettable site; usually they extend almost to the peaks, a shining white scar on the mountains with a narrow access road zigzagging perpendicularly to the top. This part of the Apuan Alps is haunted by Michelangelo, in his old clothes and smelly goatskin boots, taking his horse into the most inaccessible corners to discover new veins of perfect white stone. Michelangelo thought of quarrying as an art just as serious as the actual sculptural work; he loved to spend time here with his rock, and he claimed with his usual modesty to have 'introduced the art of quarrying' into the area. Carrara's quarries are in no danger of running out; you wonder if they're joking when they gravely mention that there are only a few cubic kilometres of good stone left.

**Massa**, the small city to the south that shares the honour of provincial capital with Carrara, was the seat of a duchy during the Renaissance. The Cybo and Malaspina families who governed it were never great builders or patrons, and the only thing in town to see is their 17th-century **Palazzo Cybo-Malaspina**, with a beautiful ornate courtyard. **Pietrasanta**, an attractive town about 10km further south, has a Renaissance cathedral and many marble works. The villages inland from Carrara, Massa and Pietrasanta have some of the best scenery in the Apuan Alps; mountain hiking is popular here, and there are a number of marked trails to follow. The village of **Colonnata**, above Carrara, is a popular starting point for walkers.

## Viareggio

From the Ligurian border almost as far as the mouth of the Arno, the coast is dotted with small resorts. **Forte dei Marmi**, built under a fortress of the Tuscan grand dukes, is perhaps the most interesting, a once-posh residential resort that had its moment of fashion in the 1860s. The others, very popular with people from Milan and other big Italian cities, are just as polluted as the Riviera to the north, but less so than the beaches around the Arno and Livorno. In the summer, all are very crowded, and it's not worth going out of your way to take a look at them.

**Viareggio**, the largest of them, is a town that goes back to Roman times; in addition to tourism it tries to make an honest living for itself from fishing and a dockyard. Everyone in Italy knows Viareggio for its big carnival, with a parade of grandiose, topical floats. Though it only began in the 1890s, it rivals Venice and Rome as the most popular place to be around Shrove Tuesday. That era was when the resort was at the height of popularity, and the Gay

Nineties bequeathed to Viareggio a number of Art Nouveau hotels and beachfront pavilions. These, plus the two beautiful shore promenades and the large pine groves that surround the town, make it one of the more pleasant resorts on the Tyrrhenian sea.

A few kilometres to the south, **Torre del Lago Puccini** is a beauty spot built around a small lake, and you can visit the **Villa Puccini**, the home where the composer (of whom they're so fond that they renamed the town) wrote most of his operas (*open April–Sept 10–12, 4–7, Tues–Sun; Oct–Mar 10–12, 3–6, Tues–Sun; adm*). Every summer there's also a small-scale **Festival Pucciniano**, with opera performances in an open-air theatre. Most of the free beach area on this resort strip is between Viareggio and Torre del Lago.

## *Where to Stay*

### Carrara

In Carrara, the best hotel is called, naturally, ★★★**Michelangelo**, Corso F.lli Rosselli 3, ✆ (0585) 777161 (moderate), and has modern rooms, all with baths, and garage parking.

### Forte dei Marmi

Forte dei Marmi lacks Viareggio's bustle and cosmopolitan air, but many Italians prefer its calmer atmosphere and less crowded beaches. Hotels here are more modern than in Viareggio, and the cruel rule of fashion is making prices higher all the time. Try ★★★★**Raffaeli Park**, Via Mazzini 37, ✆ (0584) 787294, 787115 (expensive), which has ample facilities including a private beach, pool, garden and air-conditioning in all rooms. The ★★★**Raffaeli Villa Angela**, Via Mazzini 64, ✆ (0584) 787472, ✆ 787115 (moderate) has very good facilities for a moderate-range hotel, including a private beach and a pool.

### Viareggio

Viareggio isn't quite the smart resort it once was, but still retains some of its posh 19th-century places—often with unfortunate modernizations. One of the most extravagant is the ★★★★**Grand Hotel Excelsior**, Viale Carducci 88, ✆ (0584) 50726, ✆ 50729 (very expensive), built in 1923. The original décor of the public rooms is well preserved. (*Open 20 May–20 Oct only.*) Very close to the Excelsior in Viareggio, but rather more moderate in price, the ★★★★**Grand Hotel & Royal**, Viale Carducci 44, ✆ (0584) 45151, ✆31438 (expensive), was built in a kind of neo-Renaissance eclectic style, with an impressive lobby, and has an indoor pool. (*Open April–Oct only.*) There are scores of one- and two-star hotels all along the miles of beachfront. Viareggio's ageing ★★**Villa Argentina**, Via Fratti 400, ✆ (0584) 962474 (inexpensive) opened in 1926, is one of the very few cheaper-range hotels that stay open all year.

There's also a **youth hostel** at Marina di Massa, the **Ostello Apuano**, Viale delle Pinete 89, ✆ (0585) 240288. (*Open mid-Mar–Sept.*)

## Carrara

There are also quite a few good restaurants in Carrara—if you're lucky you may find a bottle of Candia, the white wine eked from Carrara's mountain terraces. Try **Soldaini**, Via Mazzini 11, ℂ (0585) 71928 (expensive), which offers simple dishes from other Italian regions, exquisitely prepared.

## Viareggio

One might suspect that the hordes of Italians who descend on Viareggio every summer do so mainly to eat; the resort has a disproportionate number of good restaurants. Heading the list, **L'Oca Bianca**, Via Aurelia 312, ℂ (0584) 67205 (very expensive), north of the centre, is the place to go for Mediterranean lobster (*aragosta*), all kinds of fish, and elaborately prepared and served gourmet concoctions. Try the *menu degustazione*, for L90,000—you could spend considerably more à la carte. (*Closed Wed.*)

**Burrasca**, Via Garibaldi 122, ℂ (0584) 31402 (expensive) offers a real surprise—Sardinian dishes, not often seen outside the island; not only *mallorredus* (nasty-looking Sard pasta), but great seafood antipasti and stews.

Near Camaiore, the resort just north of Viareggio, **Emilio e Bona**, Località Candalla, Via Lombrici 22, ℂ (0584) 989289 (moderate), offer excellent food, particularly their duck breast with herbs and steak with almonds. (*Closed Mon.*) In Viareggio itself, if you want seafood with few pretensions and reasonable prices, head for **Giorgio**, Via IV Novembre, ℂ (0584) 44493 (moderate), a lively and warm place decorated with the works of local artists.

# Pisa

Unless you spend all your time around the raucous narrow streets around the market and the university, Pisa may strike you as an uncannily quiet, almost empty place. But this is no museum city; Pisa has a hundred thousand reasonably active and noisy people who do not choose just to live in the past. Still, the city itself seems somehow too big for them. There are no ruins, but definitely an air of unfulfilled ambitions, of a past greatness nipped in the bud.

Change the scene to about 1100, when, according to the chroniclers, Pisa, the 'city of marvels', the 'city of ten thousand towers', had a population of some 300,000. If you believe those numbers, we have some fine stories about Prester John and the Sultans of Cathay to tell you, too—but the medieval writers are to be excused for their extravagance. Excepting Venice, of course, nothing like this enormous, exotically cosmopolitan city had been seen in Christian Europe since the fall of Rome. Its merchants made themselves at home in every corner of the Mediterranean, bringing back new ideas and new styles in art in addition to their fat bags of profit. Pisa in the early Middle Ages made good use of these cultural exchanges, contributing as much as any city to the rebirth of western culture.

# History

In the Middle Ages, Pisa liked to claim that it began as a Greek city, founded by colonists from Elis. Most historians, however, won't give them credit for anything earlier than about 100 BC, when a Roman veterans' colony was settled here. Records on what followed are scarce, but Pisa, like Amalfi and Venice, must have had an early start building a navy and establishing trade connections. By the 11th century, the effort had blossomed into opulence; Pisa had built itself a small empire, including Corsica, Sardinia, and for a while the Balearics. About 1060, work was begun on the great cathedral complex and many other buildings, inaugurating the Pisan Romanesque.

In 1135 Pisa captured and sacked its greatest rival in the Western Mediterranean, Amalfi. The First Crusade, when Pisa's Archbishop led the entire fleet in support of the Christian Knights, turned out to be an economic windfall for the city. Unlike Amalfi, from the start Pisa had adopted a policy of combat with the states of the Moslem world, less from religious bigotry than a clear eye on the main chance. When the Pisans weren't battling the Moslems of Spain and Africa, they were learning from them. Influences from the mosques of Andalucia turn up in almost all the Pisan Romanesque work, and a steady exchange of ideas brought much of medieval Arab science and philosophy into Europe through Pisa's port. Pisa's architecture, the highest development of the Romanesque in Italy, saw its influence spread from Sardinia to Apulia; in addition, when Gothic arrived in Italy Pisa was among the few cities to take it seriously, and the city's accomplishments in that style rank with Siena's. In science, Pisa contributed a great though somewhat shadowy figure, that most excellent mathematician Nicolo Fibonacci, who either rediscovered the principle of the Golden Section or learned it from the Arabs, and also introduced Arabic numerals to Europe. Pisa's scholarly tradition over the centuries would be crowned in the 1600s by its most famous son, Galileo Galilei.

Pisa was always a Ghibelline city, the greatest ally of the Emperors in Tuscany if only for expediency's sake. When a real threat came, however, it was not from Florence or any of the other Tuscan cities, but the rising mercantile port of Genoa. After years of constant struggle, the Genoese devastated the Pisan navy at the Battle of Meloria (an islet off Livorno) in 1284. It meant the end of Pisan supremacy, but all chance of recovery was quashed by an even more implacable enemy: the Arno. Pisa's port was gradually silting up, and when the cost of dredging became greater than the traffic could bear, the city's fate was sealed. The Visconti of Milan seized the economically enfeebled city in 1396, and nine years later Florence snatched it from them. Excepting the period 1494–1505, when the city rebelled and kept the Florentines out despite an almost constant siege of 15 years, Pisa's history was ended. The Medici dukes did the city one big favour, supporting the University and even removing Florence's own university to Pisa. In the last 500 years of Pisa's long, pleasant twilight, this institution has helped the city stay alive and vital, and in touch with the modern world.

## Getting Around

Pisa's **Galileo Galilei airport** is the main regional airport for Tuscany, and has its own railway station with direct connections to Florence and other cities. Most trains from there also stop at Pisa-Centrale station in the

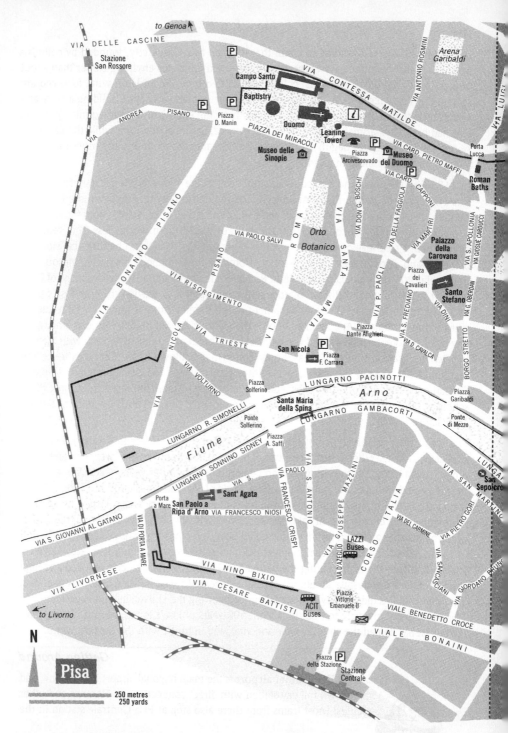

to Genoa

VIA DELLE CASCINE

Stazione
San Rossore

Campo Santo

VIA CONTESSA MATILDE

Arena
Garibaldi

VIA ANTONIO ROSMINI

VIA LUIGI

Baptistry

Piazza
D. Manin

ANDREA    PISANO

Duomo

PIAZZA DEI MIRACOLI

Leaning
Tower

Museo delle
Sinopie

Piazza
Arcivescovado

Museo
del Duomo

VIA CARD. PIETRO MAFFI

Porta
Lucca

Roman
Baths

VIA CARD. CAPPONI

VIA
BONANNO    PISANO

VIA PAOLO SALVI

Orto
Botanico

VIA    ROMA

VIA DON G. BOSCHI

VIA SANTA

VIA DELLA FAGGIOLA

VIA MARTIRI

Palazzo
della
Carovana

VIA S. APOLLONIA

VIA GIOSUÈ CARDUCCI

VIA    RISORGIMENTO

VIA    PISANO

VIA    SANTA    MARIA

Piazza
dei
Cavalieri

Santo
Stefano

VIA DINI

VIA G. OBERDAN

VIA    NICOLA

VIA    TRIESTE

VIA    VOLTURNO

San Nicola

Piazza
F. Carrara

Piazza
Dante Alighieri

VIA P. PAOLI

VIA S. FREDIANO

VIA D. CAVALCA

BORGO STRETTO

Piazza
Solferino

LUNGARNO PACINOTTI

Piazza
Garibaldi

Arno

Santa Maria
della Spina

LUNGARNO GAMBACORTI

Ponte
di Mezzo

LUNGARNO R. SIMONELLI

Fiume

Ponte
Solferino

Piazza
A. Saffi

LUNGARNO SONNINO SIDNEY

VIA S.

VIA PAOLO

VIA S. ANTONIO

VIA SAN MARTINO

LUNGAR

San
Sepolcro

Sant' Agata

Porta
a Mare

San Paolo a
Ripa d' Arno

VIA FRANCESCO NIOSI

VIA FRANCESCO CRISPI

VIA D'AZEGLIO GIUSEPPE MAZZINI

CORSO    ITALIA

VIA DEL CARMINE

VIA PIETRO GORI

VIA GIORDANO BRUN

VIA S. GIOVANNI AL GATANO

VIA DI PORTA A MARE

VIA NINO BIXIO

LAZZI
Buses

VIA SANCASCIANI

VIA LIVORNESE

to Livorno

VIA CESARE BATTISTI

ACIT Buses

Piazza
Vittorio
Emanuele II

VIALE BENEDETTO CROCE

VIALE    BONAINI

N

Pisa

250 metres
250 yards

Piazza
della Stazione

Stazione
Centrale

722

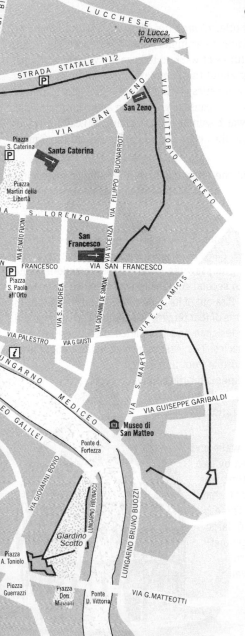

town, about a 10-minute journey. For airport information call ✆ (050) 28088.

**Pisa-Centrale station** is south of the Arno, on Piazza della Stazione (information, ✆ (050) 28546). It is about a 20-minute walk from the centre; alternatively, take city bus no.1 from outside the station, which will take you directly to the Field of Miracles and the city centre. Many trains (Florence–Pisa or Genoa–Rome lines) also stop at Stazione San Rossore; if you're making Pisa a day trip you may wish to get off there, as it's only a short distance from the Cathedral and the Leaning Tower.

All intercity **buses** leave from near Piazza Vittorio Emanuele, the big roundabout just north of the Central station: APT buses for Volterra, Livorno, and the coastal resorts (to the left on Via Nino Bixio, ✆ (050) 501038) and LAZZI to Florence, Lucca and La Spezia (on Via d'Azeglio, ✆ (050) 42688). Many long-distance and local buses also stop at Piazza Manin, just outside the walls by the cathedral and the Leaning Tower.

Pisa is a relatively quiet town, so it is one of the few cities in this part of the world where it's possible to get around in a **car**, and actually park—though it's still hardly worth it, given the distances involved.

## Tourist Information

The main office is right near the cathedral, at the east end of Piazza del Duomo, ☎ (050) 560464. There are also offices at the Central station and at Via Benedetto Croce 26, ☎ (050) 40903.

## The Field of Miracles

Almost from the time of its conception, this title, *Campo dei Miracoli*, was the nickname given to medieval Italy's most ambitious building programme. As with Florence's cathedral, too many changes were made over two centuries of work to tell exactly what the original intentions were. But of all the unique things about this complex, the location strikes one first. Whether their reasons had to do with aesthetics or land values—probably a little of both—the Pisans built their cathedral on a broad expanse of green lawn at the northern edge of town, just inside the walls. The cathedral was begun in 1063, the famous Leaning Tower and the Baptistry in the middle 12th century, at the height of Pisa's fortunes, and the Campo Santo in 1278.

If you plan to visit all three monuments and the museums here, the reduced-price joint ticket, the *biglietto cumulativo*, for L12,000, is worthwhile rather than paying separately.

## The Baptistry

The biggest of its kind in Italy; those of many other cities would fit neatly inside it (*open April–Sept 8am–sunset, Oct–Mar 9am–sunset, daily; adm*). The original architect, with the felicitous name of Master Diotisalvi ('God save you') saw the lower half of the building done in the typical stripes-and-arcades Pisan style. A second colonnade was intended to go over the first, but as the Genoese gradually muscled Pisa out of its trade routes, funds ran short. In the 1260s, Nicolà and Giovanni Pisano, members of that remarkable family of artists who did so much to re-establish sculpture in Italy, redesigned and completed the upper half in a harmonious Gothic crown of gables and pinnacles. The Pisanos also added the dome over the original prismatic dome of Diotisalvi, still visible from the inside. Both of these domes were impressive achievements for their time, among the largest attempted in the Middle Ages. The distinctive red tile roof has been taken down for restoration; it's been missing for years now.

Inside, the austerity of the simple, striped walls and heavy columns of grey Elban granite is broken by two superb works of art. The great **baptismal font** was the work of Guido Bargarelli, the 13th-century Como sculptor who made the crazy pulpit in Barga. There is little figurative sculpture on it, but the 16 large marble panels are finely carved in floral and geometrical patterns of inlaid stones, a northern variation on the Cosmati work of medieval Rome and Campania. Nicolà Pisano's **pulpit**, made about 1260, was one of the first of that family's masterpieces, and established the form for their later pulpits, the columns resting on fierce lions,

Baptistry

the relief panels crowded with intricately carved figures in impassioned New Testament episodes, a style that seems to owe much to the reliefs on old Roman triumphal arches and columns. The baptistry is famous for its uncanny acoustics; if you have the place to yourself, try singing a few notes from the centre of the floor. If there's a crowd, the guards will be just waiting for someone to bribe them to do it.

## The Cathedral

One of the first and finest works of the Pisan Romanesque, the cathedral façade, with four levels of colonnades, came out a little more ornate than Buscheto, the architect, planned back in 1063. These columns, with the similar colonnades around the apse and the Gothic frills later added around the unique elliptical dome, are the only showy features on the calm, restrained exterior. On the south transept, the late 12th-century **Porte San Ranieri** has a fine pair of bronze doors by Bonanno, one of the architects of the Leaning Tower. The biblical scenes are enacted under real palms and acacia trees; naturally, the well-travelled Pisans would have known what such things looked like.

In the interior (*open April–Sept 7.45–12.45, 3–7, daily; Oct–Mar 7.45–12.45, 3–5, daily*), little of the original art survived a fire in 1595. The roof went, as well as the Cosmati pavement, of which a few spots still remain. A coffered Baroque roof and lots of bad painting were contributed during the reconstruction, but some fine work survives. The great mosaic of Christ Pantocrator in the apse is a work of Cimabue, and there are portraits of saints by Andrea del Sarto in the choir. The **pulpit**, done about 1300 by Giovanni Pisano, is the acknowledged masterpiece of that family. The men of 1595 used the fire as an opportunity to get rid of this nasty old medieval relic, and the greatest achievement of Pisan sculpture sat disassembled in crates, quite forgotten until this century. Works of genuine inspiration often prove profoundly disturbing to ages of certainty and good taste. Pisano's pulpit is startling, mixing classical and Christian elements with a fluency never seen before his time. St Michael, as a *telamone*, shares the honour of supporting the pulpit with Hercules and the Fates, while prophets, saints, and sibyls look on from their appointed places. The relief panels, jammed with expressive faces, diffuse an electric immediacy equal to the best work of the Renaissance. Notice particularly the Nativity, the Massacre of the Innocents, the Flight into Egypt, and the Last Judgement.

## The Leaning Tower

Most likely, the stories claiming the tilt was accidental were pure fabrications, desperate tales woven by the Pisans to account for what, before mass tourism, must have seemed a great civic embarrassment. The argument isn't very convincing. That the tower would start to lean when only 10m tall seems hard to believe; half the weight would still be in the foundations. Even less credible would be that they doggedly kept building it after the lean commenced. The architects who measured the stones in the last century to get to the bottom of the mystery concluded that the tower's odd state was absolutely intentional. Trying to tell that to someone from Pisa, however, will be received as if you had suggested lunacy is a problem in his family.

But the leaning campanile is hardly the only strange thing in the Field of Miracles. The more time you spend here, the more you will notice: little monster-griffins, dragons, and such, peeking out of every corner of the oldest sculptural work, skilfully hidden where you have to look twice to see them; or the big bronze griffin sitting on a column atop of the apse (a copy), the Moslem arabesques in the Camposanto, or the perfect classical Corinthian capitals in the cathedral nave, next to the pagan images on the pulpit. The elliptical cathedral dome, in its time the only one in Europe, shows that the Pisans not only had audacity but the mathematical skills to back it up. You may have noticed that the baptistry too is leaning—about 1.5m in the opposite direction. And the cathedral façade leans outwards about 40cm, hard to notice but disconcerting if you see it from the right angle. This could hardly be accidental. So much in the Field of Miracles gives evidence of a very sophisticated, strangely modern taste for the outlandish, it may have been that the medieval master masons in charge here simply thought that plain perpendicular buildings were becoming just a little trite.

Whatever, the campanile is a beautiful building and something unique in the world—also a very expensive bit of whimsy, with some 190 marble and granite columns. For the past few decades, it has proved particularly expensive to the local and national governments, as they have struggled to shore up the tower. During the eighties, the angle of its lean, which had been changing by minute amounts for years, began to increase at an unprecedented rate, and in 1990 the tower was closed to visitors—amid howls of protest from local businesses, who thought their tourist trade would be utterly destroyed—while scientists and experts from around the world put forward a whole series of proposals for stabilizing the monument. Tens of billions of lire have already been spent on trying to save what has become one of Italy's most universally recognized landmarks, and at the beginning of 1994 it was announced that one of the systems used to shore up the foundations was proving almost unexpectedly successful. It has even been promised that within the next two years it should be possible to reopen the tower to the public but, this being Italy, don't hold your breath.

## The Camposanto

*Open April–Sept 8am–8pm daily; Oct–Mar 9am–5pm daily; adm.*

If one more marvel in the Campo dei Miracoli is not excessive, there is this remarkable cloister, a cemetery, as unique in its way as the Leaning Tower. Essentially this cemetery is a rectangle of gleaming white marble, unadorned save for the blind arcading around the façade and the beautiful Gothic tabernacle of the enthroned Virgin Mary over the entrance. With its uncluttered, simple lines, the Camposanto seems more like a work of our own century than of the 13th. The cemetery began, according to legend, when the battling Archbishop Lanfranchi, who led the Pisan fleet into the Crusades, came back with boatloads of soil from the Holy Land, in which the prominent citizens of the town could be given extra-blessed burials. The building around the site was built about a century later, in the 1270s. Over the centuries an exceptional hoard of painting and sculpture accumulated here. Much of it, however, went up in flames on a terrible night in July 1944, when an Allied incendiary bomb hit the roof and set it on fire. Many priceless works of art were destroyed and others, including most of the frescoes, damaged beyond hope of ever being perfectly restored. The biggest loss, perhaps, was the set of frescoes by Benozzo Gozzoli—the *Tower of Babel, Solomon and Sheba, Life of Moses*, the *Grape Harvest* and others; in their original state they must have been as fresh and colourful as his famous frescoes in Florence's Medici Palace.

Even better known, and somewhat better preserved, are two 14th-century frescoes of the *Triumph of Death* and the *Last Judgement* by an unknown artist (perhaps Andrea Orcagna of Florence) whose failure to leave his name unfortunately put him down to posterity as the 'Master of the Triumph of Death'. In this memento of the century of plagues and trouble, the damned are variously cooked, wrapped up in snakes, poked, disembowelled, banged up and chewed on; still, they are some of the best paintings of the trecento, and somehow seem less gruesome and paranoid than similar works of centuries to come (though good enough to have inspired that pop classic, Lizst's *Totentanz*).

For another curiosity, there is the **Cosmography** of Piero di Puccio, a diagram of the 22 spheres of the planets and stars, angels, archangels, thrones and dominations, cherubim and seraphim, and so on; in the centre, the small circle trisected by a T-shape was a common medieval map pattern for the known earth. The three sides represent Asia, Europe, and Africa, and the three lines the Mediterranean, the Black Sea, and the Nile. Among the sculpture in the Campo Santo, there is a group with Emperor Henry VII sitting among his court like some exotic oriental potentate, taken from what survived of his tomb, and also some ancient relics, including a famous Hellenistic marble vase and sarcophagi.

## Museo del Duomo

*Open April–Sept 8am–7.40pm daily; Oct–Mar 9am–4.20pm daily; adm.*

The collection of the cathedral museum is exhibited in the chapter house, in the southeast corner of the Campo dei Miracoli near the Leaning Tower. The first rooms contain the oldest works, including two strange Islamic pieces, the strange 11th-century **Griffin** originally on the top of the cathedral, believed to have first come from Egypt, and a bronze basin. Most of the statues by the Pisanos exhibited here were bought in from the elements only when they were so worn and bleached as to be barely recognizable, and resemble a convention of mummies. However, in room 5 there is Giovanni Pisano's superb *Madonna del Colloquio*, one of the finest of the family's sculptures, and in room 10 his lovely ivory *Madonna and Child.* The museum continues upstairs with two large angels used as candle sticks, intarsia, Roman and Etruscan odds and ends, some rare illuminated scrolls, and the *Pisan Cross*, carried by the Pisan soldiers on the First Crusade.

## The Museo delle Sinopie

*Open April–Sept 9.30am–12.40pm, 3–6.40pm; Oct–Mar 9.30am–12.40pm, 3–5.30pm; adm.*

Many of the damaged frescoes from the Campo Santo were moved to this building, across the Piazza from the Cathedral, after the war, along with the *sinopie* discovered underneath when they were removed from the walls. Many of these simple sketches are works of art in their own right, and together with drawings and photos made before the bombing they help to give an idea how the frescoes once looked.

---

## North Pisa

With the cathedral off on the edge of town, Pisa has no real centre. Still, the Pisans are very conscious of the division made by the Arno; every year on 27 June the two sides fight it out on the Ponte di Mezzo in the *Gioco del Ponte*, a sort of medieval tug-of-war where the opponents try to push a big decorated cart over each other.

From the Field of Miracles, Via Cardinale Maffi leads east to some ruins of **Roman baths** near the Lucca gate; two interesting churches in the neighbourhood are **San Zeno**, in a corner of the walls, with some parts as old as the 5th century, and **Santa Caterina**, a Dominican church with a beautiful, typically Pisan façade. Inside there is an *Annunciation* and a sculpted tomb by Nino Pisano, as well as a large painting from the 1340s of the *Apotheosis of St Thomas Aquinas*, with Plato and Aristotle in attendance and defeated infidel philosopher Averroes below.

Santo Stefano

There is a long street that begins near the Campo dei Miracoli as Via Carducci and changes its name along its route, becoming the old, arcaded **Borgo Largo** and **Borgo Stretto**. This is Pisa's traditional main artery, the most fashionable shopping street and the centre for the evening *passeggiata*. The twisting alleys of the lively market area are just off to the west, along with the **University**, still one of Italy's most important, and the **Piazza dei Cavalieri**. Duke Cosimo I, in 1562, started what was probably the last crusading order of knights, the Cavalieri di Santo Stefano, in 1562. The crusading urge had ended long before, but the Duke found this a useful tool for placating the anachronistic fantasies of the Tuscan nobility—most of them newly titled bankers—and for licensing out freebooting expeditions against the Turks. Cosimo had Vasari build the **Palazzo della Carovana** for the order, conveniently demolishing the old Palazzo del Popolo, the symbol of Pisa's lost independence. Vasari gave the Palazzo an outlandishly ornate *graffito* façade (currently under restoration); the building now holds a college of the university. Next to it, the **Palazzo dell'Orologio** was built around the 'Hunger Tower' (left of the big clock), famous from Dante's story in the *Inferno* of Ugolino della Gherardesca, the Pisan commander who was walled in here with his two young sons after his fickle city began to suspect him of intrigues with the Genoese. **Santo Stefano**, the order's church, is also by Vasari, though the façade is by a young dilettante of the Medici family; inside are some long, fantastical war pennants the order's pirates captured from the Moslems in North Africa.

## Museo di San Michele

*Open 9am–2pm Tues–Sun; 9am–1pm Sun; adm.*

Much of the best Pisan art from the Middle Ages and Renaissance has been collected here, in an old convent that also once served as a prison. Most came from Pisan churches, and so there is a predominance of straightforward religious subjects. The Pisano family is, of course, well represented, including one magically beautiful *Madonna* in medieval Pisan dress, a wooden sculpture by Andrea Pisano. Besides the Pisan statues, reliefs, ivory work, and sarcophagi, there are paintings by such artists as Masaccio (*St Paul*), Fra Angelico, Ghirlandaio, Simone Martini, Gozzoli, and Brueghel

## South of the Arno

Pisa's stretch of Arno is an exercise in Tuscan gravity, two mirror-image lines of blank-faced yellow and tan buildings all the same height. Only one landmark breaks the monotony, but it is something special. Near the Solferino Bridge, **Santa Maria della Spina** sits on the bank like a precious, tiny Gothic jewel box. Though one of the few outstanding achievements of Italian Gothic, originally it wasn't Gothic at all. Partially rebuilt in 1323, its new architect—perhaps one of the Pisanos—turned it into an extravaganza of pointy gables and blooming pinnacles. All of the sculptural work is first class, especially the figures of Christ and the Apostles in the 13 niches facing the streets. The chapel takes its name from a thorn of Christ's crown of thorns, a relic brought back from the Crusades.

Not far to the west, near the walls where the famous 'Golden Gate'—Pisa's door to the sea—once stood, remains of the old Citadel and Arsenal are still visible across the river. On the southern side, **San Paolo a Ripa del Arno** has an interesting 12th-century façade similar to the Cathedral. San Paolo stands in a small park, and interestingly it is believed to have been built over the site of Pisa's original cathedral; perhaps building cathedrals in open fields was an old custom. Behind it, the unusual and very small 12th-century chapel of **Sant'Agata** has eight sides and an eight-sided prismatic roof. A similar building can be seen at the other end of South Pisa, the octagonal **San Sepolcro** off Lungarno Galilei, built originally for the Knights Templar.

## Around Pisa

Just outside Pisa there are good Romanesque Pisan churches in the villages of Calci, Vicopisano, and San Casciano. The **Certosa di Pisa** (*open April–Sept 9am–6pm Tues–Sun; Oct–Mar 9am–4pm Tues–Sat, 9am–12 midday Sun; adm*), a typically lavish 18th-century Charterhouse, has a prominent site north of the Arno and a huge low building in some sort of 1920s Spanish-Californian exhibition style. West of the city at **Gombo** is a small beach where in 1822 Percy Shelley was brought ashore after being drowned, in the company of a British lieutenant, when a storm struck their small boat on the way to Livorno. His body was burned here too, as Trelawney, Leigh Hunt and Byron looked on.

Most of Pisa's beaches are south of the Arno, a strip through **Marina di Pisa** and **Tirrenia** that is often plagued by pollution—though there are many pleasant pine woods nearby.

*Pisa ☎ (050–)*

*Where to Stay*

*expensive*

The best hotel in Pisa, very close to the Campo dei Miracoli, is the ★★★★**Grand Hotel Duomo**, Via S. Maria 94, ☎ 561894, ℡ 560418, a modern but richly appointed luxury hotel with a roof garden and a garage; all the rooms are air-conditioned.

Right in the centre on Lungarno Pacinotti, the ★★★**Royal Victoria**, ✆ 502130, is a tasteful and modern hotel, with rooms overlooking the Arno and its own garage. Many of the middle-range hotels are in the streets around the train station, south of the Arno, like the ★★★**Terminus e Plaza**, Via Colombo 45, ✆ 500303. If you're driving, you may want to stay just north of the city on the SS12r at the ★★★**California Park Hotel** in San Giuliano Terme, ✆ 890726, a large hotel in a park with a pool. (*Open Mar–Oct only.*)

### inexpensive

Inexpensive places are spread around town, and most of them are usually full of local students; it's always best to call first, or else go up to the Campo di Miracoli and try the ★**Gronchi** on Piazza Archivescovado, ✆ 561823; the friendly ★**Helvetia**, Via Don Boschi 31, ✆ 553084; ★**Di Stefano** Via Sant'Apollonia 35, off Via Carducci, ✆ 553559; or ★**Albergo Giardino**, Piazza Manin, just outside the walls, ✆ 563101. All are relatively convivial places with plenty of rooms within easy walking distance of the cathedral.

---

## Pisa ✆ (050–)                                      Eating Out

In Pisa, walks on the wild side of the Tuscan kitchen seem more common than in other towns—eels and squid, baccalà, brains, tripe, wild mushrooms, 'twice-boiled soup' and some dishes that cannot be found in the fattest dictionaries, and that waiters cannot satisfactorily explain. Don't be intimidated; there's always more common fare present on the menu, and occasionally the more outlandish items turn into surprisingly refined treats.

### very expensive

**Ristorante Sergio**, ✆ 48245, a highly regarded temple of Pisan cuisine, is in a medieval setting on the Lungarno Pacinotti near the Royal Victoria hotel. The menu changes according to what's available and fresh, and although standards sometimes vary, you will most likely have a truly superb meal. There's a *menu degustazione* for L90,000, where you can sample the best dishes of the day; à la carte can be considerably more. (*Closed Sun, Mon midday.*)

### expensive

Eels from Lake Massaciuccoli and other fresh seafood delicacies hold pride of place at **Lo Schiaccianoci**, Via Vespucci 104, ✆ 21024, east of the station.

### moderate

**Da Bruno**, Via Luigi Bianchi, ✆ 560818, outside the walls a few streets east of the Campo dei Miracoli, is a good place to see how well you like simple Pisan cooking—things like polenta with mushrooms and *baccalà* (salt cod).

In the centre of the city, near the Piazza dei Cavalieri, **Cateni**, Via della Faggiola 1, ✆ 552725, is an excellent, comfortable and very friendly family-run traditional restaurant, with wonderful gnocchi and fish.

Pisa is well endowed with unpretentious trattorias, many of them near the centre around the university. **Osteria dei Cavalieri**, Via San Frediano 16, ✆ 49008, has good game dishes such as rabbit with thyme. (*Closed Sat midday, Sun.*) **Da Gino**, Piazza Vittorio Emanuele 19, ✆ 23437, has cheaper prices and simple trattoria decor. **La Mescita**, Via Cavalca 2, ✆ 544292, is another alternative with varied, good quality food for cheap prices. (*Closed Sat midday, Sun.*)

# Livorno and the Islands

## Getting Around

Livorno's **train** station is about 2km from the port, but there are regular city **buses** from there to the port and Piazza Grande in the centre. **Ferries** go from Livorno to the islands of Elba, Gorgona, and Capraia (**Toremar**—a very well-run line—usually at least twice daily, ✆ 0586 22772, to Bastia in Corsica (**Corsica Ferries**, ✆ 0586 34723, and to Olbia in Sardinia (**Trans Tirreno Express**, ✆ 0586 31002). All offices are in the **Stazione Marittima** in the port. Ferries to Elba are very heavily booked up in advance in mid-summer and it can be easier to get the boat from Piombino, closer to Elba (*see* below).

## Tourist Information

In **Livorno** the main office is at Piazza Cavour 6, ✆ (0586) 33111, and there are also portside offices open in the summer, at Porto Mediceo and Terminal Calata Carrara. On **Elba** there is a tourist office in the main town, Portoferraio, at Calata Italia 26, ✆ (0565) 914671.

Further south in **Grosseto** there is a main office at Via Monterosa 206, ✆ (0564) 22534, and in summer another at Corso Carducci, just beside the Duomo, ✆ (0564) 488207. Also in **Porto Santo Stefano**, at Corso Umberto 55, ✆ (0564) 814208.

## Livorno

A few kilometres out to sea beyond Livorno's harbour, a medieval stone tower marks the tiny islet of Meloria, the place where the Genoese navy put an end to Pisa's importance as a Mediterranean power in 1284. And when the silting up of its river harbour put an end to Pisa as a great port, fate had this spot in mind to replace her. Livorno was founded in 1571 by Cosimo di Medici; over the next 200 years, while nearly all the rest of peninsular Italy was in economic decline, Livorno thrived as the nation's third port, after Genoa and Naples. It was an interesting town; after Duke Ferdinand decreed religious liberty for it, persecuted Jews, Greeks, English Catholics, and even Spanish Moors settled here, along with political refugees from all over Europe. From the beginning, there was a strong connection with England; an English engineer, son of the Duke of Leicester, designed the port, and trade connections were strong. Englishmen became so familiar with Livorno in the 17th century that they bestowed on it the bizarre anglicization of Leghorn.

Livorno, though the home town of the artist Modigliani, hasn't much to show for its 400 years, but its modern, ambitious outlook has earned it an important role in seagoing container traffic and a position as Tuscany's second city. There isn't much to see, but the city has plenty of ferries to jump on, and a reputation for seafood that is entirely deserved.

While you're waiting at the port, have a look at Livorno's landmark, the **Ferdinand I Monument**, better known as the 'Quattro Mori' for the four bronze Moors in chains around the pedestal, exceptional sculptures by a 17th-century artist named Pietro Tacca (four Moors' heads are the symbol of Sardinia). The best part of Livorno is the 'Venice' neighbourhood near the port, sliced through by small canals; also striking, and near the waterfront, is the **Piazzale Mascagni**, a grandiose terrace overlooking the sea. Otherwise the city wears a strangely blank look, pure north-Tuscan taciturnity undiluted by medieval or Renaissance charm. It's pleasant enough, and the people are on the whole good cheerful Communists, but even when the streets are crowded Livorno can seem like a city seen in a dream.

## The Tuscan Archipelago

Mostly this means **Elba**, one of Italy's number one holiday playgrounds, though there are also six smaller islands, tracing a broad arc along the coast from Livorno to Orbetello. Some of them might also be desirable holiday destinations, but for the Italian government's bad habit of using them as prisons.

Elba, reached by ferry from Piombino or Livorno, attracts over two million visitors each year, to unspectacular, family-style holidays on its miles of beaches. The scenery, reminiscent of nearby Corsica, is often impressive; pink granite, green *macchia* and forests, and a severely mountainous coast. In ancient times Elba was best known for its iron ore, and more recently for the brief sojourn of Napoleon in 1814–15. Everyone visits his thoroughly depressing palace in the otherwise lovely island capital of **Portoferraio**. Other sights are few, but you can enjoy the mountains and beaches and wash down a fish dinner with Elban *Aleatico* or *Moscato*, two of Tuscany's best wines.

As for the other islands, from north to south: **Gorgona** and, south of Elba, **Pianosa** once had villas of wealthy Romans, but are now only gloomy prison camps. The larger **Capraia**, only recently opened to tourists, has one small town, some ruins, and plenty of rocks, in addition to a penal colony; an exotic, out-of-the-way place for confirmed island addicts to explore. Below Elba come **Montecristo**, a beautiful, uninhabited nature reserve, accessible only for day trips from Elba, and **Giglio**, the only real resort island, which boasts superb scenery and bird life, several hotels, three little villages, one of them medieval, Giglio Castello, and fine small beaches. Finally, **Giannutri**, a pretty, tiny island just big enough to hold some villas and one holiday village.

Gorgona and Capraia can be reached by a regular ferry service from Livorno and Elba; Giglio and Giannutri from Porto Santo Stefano, near Orbetello.

## South of Livorno

The rugged coast south of Livorno is dotted with small beaches that can become tremendously crowded all through the summer: around **Castiglioncello**, a pretty spot when things are slow, then Rosignano Solvay, Marina di Cecina, San Vicenzo, Follonica and Punta Ala, all along the coastal plain. There are Etruscan tombs, not especially interesting, at **Populonia**, one of the big Etruscan cities of which few traces remain. It stands on a mountainous promontory, at the other end of which is **Piombino**, a town full of steel works that is also the most convenient ferry port for Elba.

**Grosseto**, today a fair-sized provincial capital, has no ancient memories—of course it doesn't, having been underwater until late Roman times. Grosseto does have a Medici fortress and a small archaeological museum (currently closed for restoration), but is otherwise one of the most characterless of Italian provincial capitals. Its plain, now reclaimed from swamps and made into rich farmland, marks the beginning of the **Maremma**, a low-lying region that extends almost as far as Rome. Once one of the centres of Etruscan civilization, malaria and Roman misrule led to its almost complete abandonment. For centuries the Maremma remained a ghostly, disease-ridden marsh, though modern drainage and reclamation projects much like those in the Pontine Marshes to the south have made good farmland of it once more. Parts have been maintained in their original state as wildlife reserves— notably at the **Monti dell'Uccellina**, a range of ragged hills set among parasol pine forests on the coast south of Grosseto. This is a favourite rest stop for migratory birds going to and from Africa—hence the name. There are no roads, but you can explore this stretch of coast by boat from **Talamone**, a little fishing port at its southern tip.

**Monte Argentario**, near the end of Tuscany's coast, this curiosity of the Tuscan coast with its genuine Mediterranean feel, makes an odd bit of geography. Once, perhaps thousands of years ago, Argentario was an island, the member of the Tuscan archipelago closest to the shore. It gradually became joined to the mainland by three narrow sand bars, now solid and covered with trees. There's a story that sailors gave the Argentario its name in classical times, noticing the flashes of silver from the olive leaves that still cover the mountain slopes. The placid lagoons between the sand bars make up another renowned nature and bird reserve, and those who are prepared to use their feet and walk out along the southernmost strip are also rewarded by the discovery of remarkably unspoilt beaches. **Orbetello**, on the central strip, was once a fashionable resort, though today this charming town must make way for trendy **Porto Ercole** and **Porto Santo Stefano**, two pretty fishing villages that in summer are a bit overburdened with Florentines and Romans on holiday. The mount itself is the greatest attraction, a rugged green island girt by a scenic road some 24km long.

---

*Where to Stay*

## Livorno

Some of the rooms at the ★★★**Gran Duca**, Piazza Micheli 16, ✆ (0586) 891024 (moderate), Livorno's most interesting hotel, look out over the Quattro Mori and the busy port; though modern inside, the Gran Duca is built into a surviving section of the walls. Livorno, being a port town, has an abundance of less expensive hotels. Many can be  found across the wide piazza from the train station, though none is especially distinguished. A good one is the old-fashioned ★★**Corsica**, Corso Mazzini 148, ✆ (0586) 882280 (inexpensive).

## Elba

There are quite a few hotels on Elba, mostly in Portoferraio, but they still get very heavily booked up in summer. One good middle-range option is the **★★Touring**, Via Roma 13, © (0565) 915851 (moderate). It's a good idea to consult the tourist office, who have lists not just of hotels but also of **private rooms and apartments** to rent, a major industry on Elba.

## Monte Argentario

If you're planning a stay of a few days or more in the Monte Argentario area, there's a hotel-residence hidden away on the western tip of the peninsula, the **★★★★Torre di Calapiccola**, Località Carla Piccola, © (0564) 825133, ✆ 825235 (expensive), an apartment complex in a great setting, with a beach and plenty of activities, or peace and quiet if that's what you're looking for.

## Ortobello

The **★Piccolo Parigi** on Corso Italia 169, © (0586) 867233 (inexpensive) is a delightful, friendly and very Mediterranean establishment, in the middle of town.

## Porto Ercole

In Porto Ercole, the preferred hotel stands on the cliffs behind the town, with a garden and views over the sea; **★★★★★Il Pellicano**, Cala dei Santi, © (0564) 833801, ✆ 833418 (luxury). With its own beach below it in a little cove just outside Porto Ercole, it has all imaginable amenities, including a pool and possibilities for windsurfing and every other water sport, and tennis—not to mention the presence of a first-class restaurant. Prices for the best rooms are close to L600,000, but rates are notably lower off-season.

## Porto Santo Stefano

Porto Santo Stefano's most pleasant hotel is the **★★★Filippo II**, © (0564) 812640 (moderate), with air-conditioning, and close to the beaches at Poggio Calvella.

---

*Eating Out*

## Livorno

If you're stuck in Livorno, you can pass the time amenably eating fish; the Livornese have their own ways of preparing it, much copied now throughout Tuscany, and restaurants usually prove easier on your budget than those elsewhere. Besides lobster and grilled fish, pasta dishes with seafood figure on all the local menus.

Probably the best restaurant in Livorno is **La Chiave**, Scali della Cantine 52, © (0586) 888609 (expensive)—try their *tagliolini* with octopus and basil. (*Closed Wed.*) Another good place to sample Livornese fish dishes is **L'Antico Moro**, Via di Franco 59, © (0586) 884659 (expensive). At Viale Carducci 63, towards the train station, **La Barcarola**, © (0586) 402367 (expensive) is a very big and very noisy place, where *zuppa di pesce*, penne with scampi, and everything else good from the Tyrrhenian is cooked in traditional Livornese style. (*Closed Sun, Aug.*) Some of the best restaurants in the Livorno area are to the south of the city in the seaside suburb of Ardenza. **Da Oscar**, Via Franchini 78, © (0586) 501258 (moderate) has been a favourite for decades; there is a good selection of wines to go with the *linguine* and clams, excellent risottos and grilled *triglie* and *orate*. (*Closed Mon.*) The wine bar **Cantina Nardi**, Via L. Cambini 6, © (0586) 808006 (inexpensive), has a pleasant surprise at lunchtime, when a few tables are laid and excellent food is to be had. You can eat for under L30,000, surrounded by hundreds of wine bottles. (*Closed Sun.*)

## Piombino

In Piombino, while you're waiting for the ferry to Elba, you should try lunch at the **Ristorante Terrazza**, above the bar in the port area (moderate); besides the *spaghetti alla vongole*, there's an unforgettable panoramic view of Piombino's steel mills out of the picture windows.

## Elba

An excellent restaurant is **Il Chiasso**, Via Sauro (moderate), in the village of Capoliveri, on the eastern side of the island.

## Porto Ercole

**La Lampara**, Lungomare Andrea Doria 67, © (0564) 833024 (moderate) is an outstanding restaurant with tables outdoors on the port, where the cooking is more or less Neapolitan—so of course there's pizza, too, as well as excellent grilled fish.

## Porto Santo Stefano

The popular and lively **Orlando**, Via Breschi 3, © (0564) 81278 (moderate) is one of the few genuine traditional restaurants left in this busy resort. (*Closed Thurs.*)

# Siena

Understanding Florence, Siena's arch-enemy and artistic rival over the centuries, requires some work—a few bulky tomes of history and art criticism for starters, and an effort of the imagination beyond that. For Siena, on the other hand, you need only come to the city and look around. Draped on its hills, Siena reveals itself as a flamboyant ensemble of medieval buildings in honest brown (*siena*-coloured) brick; on the lower slopes, gardens and olive groves fill almost half the space within the old city wall, and above it all Tuscany's tallest tower and its gayest, most dazzling cathedral compete like beauties at the fair. Medieval Siena created beauty almost effortlessly, and its fierce civic pride tolerated nothing less than the building of a city that in itself is a single great work of art.

## History

Why Siena should have been so prominent for so long, instead of just another sleepy south-Tuscan hill town, no historian attempts to explain. The location, though defensible and wonderfully picturesque, is not promising, and there were never any great resources at hand. Just the same, early in the age of the *comuni* the city emerges as one of the leading powers of central Italy, achieving its total independence in 1125. Like Florence, Siena lived on wool and banking; the clothing industry was never very large, but the bankers managed to make themselves indispensable to kings and princes all over Europe.

Ghibelline by convenience, Siena found itself almost constantly at war with Guelph Florence. The greatest moment in its history came in 1260, when news arrived of a huge army raised by Florence and other Tuscan cities coming to demand Siena's surrender. The city militias—reinforced by about 5000 Florentine political exiles—marched out and met the Florentines at Montaperti, beating them so badly that Florence was entirely at their mercy; only the attitude of the Florentine exiles prevented the Sienese from razing Florence to the ground, a famous story told by Dante in the *Inferno*. Nevertheless, as Florence's military and economic equal, Siena enjoyed a golden age that ended in 1348, when the Black Death carried off a third of the population. Political infighting as violent as Florence's, together with a steady decline of its banking business, made recovery impossible, but with difficulty Siena held on to its independence. Only once, in 1399, when Gian Galeazzo Visconti of Milan occupied the city, did it lose its liberty, but Visconti rule lasted only until 1404.

In art, if the quattrocento was the high noon of Florence's Renaissance, the 13th and 14th centuries belonged to Siena. With palaces, churches, and public buildings far grander than those of Florence at this time, Siena also led in painting. Giorgio Vasari, because he was a Florentine, gave all the credit for advances in painting to Cimabue and Giotto, but Sienese artists such as Duccio di Buoninsegna, Simone Martini, Matteo di Giovanni, and Pietro and Ambrogio Lorenzetti often surpassed their Florentine counterparts in many ways—less innovative, perhaps, but they brought the 'International Gothic' style of art to its highest form in Italy. Even as its economic decline continued, Siena remained an important artistic centre.

Throughout the 15th century factionalism kept Siena paralysed. Like Florence, the city eventually found some peace with the accession of a powerful political boss, Pandolfo Petrucci, called 'il Magnifico' like Lorenzo de' Medici. He and his family successors ruled the city from 1487 to 1524. By that time, Siena was only a pawn in Italian politics. In a nine years' war, starting with a popular revolt against Charles V's garrison in the city in 1552, combined Florentine and Spanish forces conquered the republic, eventually starving the city into submission in a protracted siege.

---

### Getting Around

The face of Siena has changed little since the 14th century. From the centre, the famous piazza called simply the **Campo**, the city unfolds like a three-petalled flower along three ridges—a natural division since medieval times, with the quarter called the **Terzo di Città**, including the cathedral, to the southwest; the **Terzo di San Martino** to the southeast; and the **Terzo di Camollia** to the north. **Cars** are banned from most of the centre. As amiable as the city is for walking, the topography makes it seem larger than it really is—don't expect any short cuts between the three hills.

Not many **trains** pass through; Siena is only on a branch line from Empoli (on the Pisa–Florence line) to Chiusi (on the Florence–Rome line). The station is on the Via Mazzini, about 2km north of the old city. However, most city **bus** routes from the station run to the Piazza Matteotti, the main local bus terminus a short walk north of the Campo. To save a trip to the station, all rail information and tickets are available at the **SETA** agency, no.56 on the Campo. They know all about the buses, too.

A short distance from Piazza Matteotti, on the little square in front of San Domenico and along the Viale dei Mille, are the stops for **buses** to towns and villages in the province and also for long-distance destinations. The TRA-IN (*sic*) and Lazzi lines have several buses a day to Florence, Volterra, San Gimignano, Montalcino and smaller local destinations.

The main road from Florence, the *Autostradale*, loops around Siena to the west, enabling drivers to avoid the old city completely. South of Siena there is a complicated clover-leaf junction where the road divides into the SS73 eastwards for Arezzo and Perugia, the SS2 (Via Cassia) for Montalcino and Montepulciano (and Rome, if you have time to take this leisurely road), and the SS223 for Grosseto. On the north side of town there is also a turn eastwrads for the SS222, the Chiantigiana, the main road for the Chianto wine district. If you wish to drive into Siena, Via Mazzini will take you in directly from the *Autostradale*, connecting up with the Viale around the *centro storico*. The largest concentration of car parks is around the Fortezza, on the Viale, but even here it's often difficult to find a space.

### Tourist Information

The local APT has offices at Piazza del Campo 55, ✆ (0577) 280551, and Via di Città 43, ✆ (0577) 42209. The Siena hoteliers' co-operative also has its own bookings office (*see* below).

## The Campo and the Corsa del Palio

It is hard to imagine a lovelier square, or one more beloved by the people who live and work around it. Laid out in the 1100s on the site of the Roman forum of *Sena Julia*, the original settlement here, the unique, semicircular Campo was paved in brick as early as the 1340s. Today, lined with pavement cafés all along its steep northern arc, it is still the centre of the town's life.

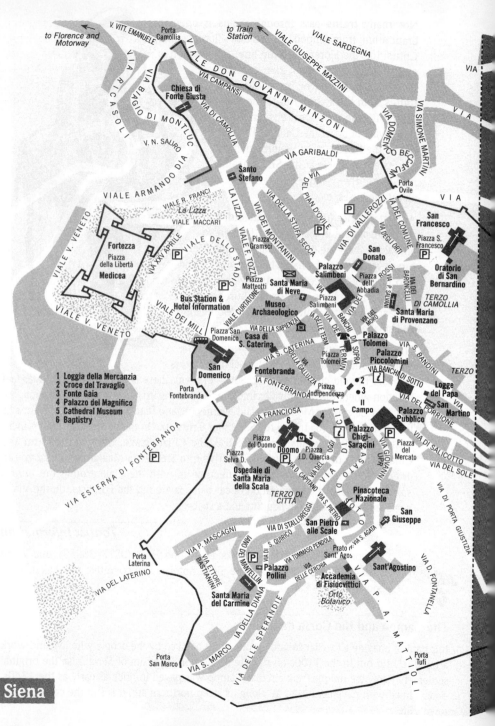

Siena

Twice each year, on 2 July and 16 August, Siena puts on the noisiest medieval blowout in Italy, the horse race around the Campo called the **Palio**. Though its origins go back to the days of the *comune*, the Palio in its present form began in the 1600s; riders from 10 of the city's 17 quarters (each *contrada* known by its totem animal: elephant, snail, unicorn, giraffe, owl, caterpillar, etc.) career recklessly around the edge of the piazza while thousands jam the centre and any available open space to watch.

The riders mean business; losers have a year of insults and rotten tomatoes to look forward to in their home district. With no rules (not even against bribery!), they crowd and push frantically. Especially at the two right angles they must navigate, the sight of not only jockeys but horses flying through the air is not uncommon. Often less then half actually finish, and the deaths of several horses in the last few years' races has led to controversy over the increasing use of near-thoroughbred racehorses more susceptible to injury on the square's cobbles— rather than the sturdy local nags that the *contrade* made do with for several centuries.

The post-Palio carousing, while not up to medieval standards, is still impressive; in the winning *contrada* the parties go on for days. Siena's tranquil beauty today conceals its true character. In addition to the Palio, there was once also a festival called *Gioca del Pugno*—a general fistfight in the Campo with 300 on each side (for more information on lesser-known traditional *palios*, see p.745).

In the centre of the curved north end of the Campo, the **Fonte Gaia** is a large rectangular fountain decorated with mythological reliefs by Jacopo della Quercia (all copies; the originals are in the Palazzo Publico, *see* below). In the 14th century, the Sienese dug up a beautiful Greek statue of Venus by Lysippus and built a pedestal for her atop the fountain. After the plague, the priests succeeded in convincing the people that the pagan statue had called down God's wrath. The statue was smashed to bits, and a band of Sienese dressed as peasants smuggled the pieces over the border with Florence and buried them, to transfer the bad luck to their enemies.

SIMONE MARTINI

DUCCIO DI BONINSEGNA

BALDASSARRE PERUZZI

DI SAN MARTINO

Santo Spirito

V. DELL'OLIVERA
DEI
SASSO
DI PANTANETO
V. A. S. MARTINO
VIA S. MARTINO
V. DELL'ORO

PISPINI
Porta Pispini

to Arezzo and Motorway

Palazzo di San Galagno

VIA ROMA

VIA DEI SERVI
VIA CANTINE

Piazza A. Manzoni

VIA VAL DI MONTONE

Basilica di Santa Maria dei Servi

VIA GIROLAMO GIGLI

Porta Romana

VIA E.S. PICCOLOMINI

# Palazzo Pubblico

*Open Mar–Nov 9.30am–7.45pm Mon–Sat; 9am–1pm Sun; Dec–Feb 9.30am –1.45pm daily; adm exp.*

This is the civic pride of Siena expressed in brick and marble, a huge building that still serves as the seat of the city council, as well as being the repository of much of the best Sienese art (). Above it rises the tallest secular tower of medieval Italy, the graceful, needle-like construction that Henry James called Siena's 'Declaration of Independence'. The **Torre del Mangia** takes its odd name from a legendary glutton (and relative of the artist Duccio) whose job it was to ring the bell—there's a little statue of him in one of the courtyards. At the foot of the tower, the equally graceful marble loggia leads to the 'Cappella di Piazza', built to give thanks for Siena's deliverance from the Black Death.

Most of the Palazzo was built in the early 14th century. At the top, you'll notice the familiar Christian symbol of the letters IHS inside a radiant sun. This was the mark of the 14th-century religious reformer San Bernardino of Siena, who preached often before huge crowds in the Campo. San Bernardino wanted to persuade the constantly warring nobles to replace their own heraldic devices with this holy sign—completely without success. Around the façade are other devices from Siena's history: the city's black and white coat of arms, the wolf (according to legend Siena was founded by a son of Remus), and the balls of the Medici dukes. Inside, the ground floor is all city offices, and you'll need to climb the long stairs to see the rooms open to the public.

Among the old municipal chambers are the **Sala di Risorgimento**, with florid 1890s frescoes of Garibaldi and Vittorio Emanuele II in action, and an 'allegory of Italian liberty'; a **Council Room** with Gobelin tapestries and figures of political virtue from antiquity by an interesting 15th-century Sienese painter named Beccafumi; and more of the same—classical gods, Caesar, Pompey, and Judas Maccabaeus—around the pretty **chapel**, frescoed with a giant St Christopher (before setting out on a journey it was good luck to glimpse this saint, and in Italy and Spain he is often painted as large as possible so no one could miss him).

The **Sala del Mappamondo**, named after a lost cosmographical fresco, has a number of 13th-century frescoes, including the famous scene of the resolute condottiere **Guidoriccio da Fogliano**, off to besiege a castle. It has traditionally been attributed to Simone Martini (*c.* 1330), the greatest of Sienese fresco artists, but controversy has been stirred up of late with a theory (put forward by some non-Italian art historians, based on the style of the castles in the background) that it must have been painted at a later date, and so could not be by Martini. Unquestionably his is the fabulous *Maestà*, in the same room, a dignified Madonna surrounded by saints, believed to be his earliest work. A multilingual computerised display is now on hand to explain the many figures in the picture.

The Palazzo's greatest treasure, however, is the unique series of frescoes by Ambrogio Lorenzetti in the **Sala della Pace**, the *Effects of Good and Bad Government*. Here medieval allegory is applied to politics; two rival princes sit in state, one with Justice, Wisdom and Compassion for his counsellors, the other with such characters as Pride, Wrath, and Avarice. On the long walls of the chamber two mirror-image cities are portrayed, the well-governed one (with Siena's cathedral discreetly painted in) is clean, orderly, and happy, with smiling shopkeepers who look to be making nice profits. The other—urban blight, crime, oppression, corruption, housing problems and slipshod municipal services, the very picture of a 1300s South Bronx.

For views over Siena, you may climb more stairs up to the **Loggia**, where the original reliefs from the Fonte Gaia are kept—or more stairs than you have ever seen, up the 100-metre Mangia Tower (*open Mar–Nov 10–6.30; Dec–Feb 10–1.30*), for a view that is absolutely, positively worth the slight risk of cardiac arrest.

Behind the Palazzo, steps lead down to the **Piazza del Mercato**, Siena's cheerful market-place. At the opposite end of the Campo, narrow stairs under arches lead up to the **Croce del Travaglio**, the meeting place for the main streets from the three corners of the city. Here stands the 15th-century arcade known as the **Loggia della Mercanzia**, where guilds transacted business and Italy's most respected commercial tribunal once sat in judgement.

## Terzo di Città and the Cathedral

From Via di Città, winding behind the Campo, a narrow street off to the right called Via dei Pellegrini leads to what seems at first a huge striped bastion in the wall. Siena's glorious Cathedral sits atop the highest point in the city, a hill not quite large enough to hold it. The apse spills down the slope, its crypt at the street level of the rest of the city. Perhaps to save space and money, the architects tucked their **baptistry** under here. It contains some of the best art in Siena, though dim and hard to see even when the lighting machine is working. The **baptismal font**, one of Siena's crown jewels, has relief panels by Donatello (Herod's banquet), Ghiberti (Baptism of Christ), and Jacopo della Quercia (Birth of John the Baptist). Donatello also contributed the six bronze angels and some of the other statuary. Across the street from the Baptistry, the **Palazzo del Magnifico** was home to Siena's 15th-century power brokers, the Petrucci.

A flight of steps leads up to the Piazza del Duomo, but at the top you must first pass through a portal in a huge, free-standing wall of striped marble arches. Siena's cathedral, 88m long, might have seemed big enough, but the news that Florence was beginning a bigger one came as an insult to the city's pride. In 1339, the Council adopted an incredible plan to rebuild the cathedral; the old one was to be preserved, but only as a transept, and a new nave, almost double the length of the old one, would be built out from the southern end. Had it ever been

Battistero

completed, it would have surpassed even St Peter's in Rome, the biggest in the world. Only nine years later, however, the Black Death struck, and Siena soon found itself without the means to continue. In addition, one wall that had already been built was found to be unsound and had to be demolished. The northern wall and façade still stand, however, their arches bricked in and incorporated into other buildings. What was to be a cathedral nave is now a piazza, and a symbol for the end of a city's ambitions.

Even after all the other grand Tuscan cathedrals, Siena's comes as a revelation. It may not be a transcendent expression of faith, and it may not be an important landmark in architecture, but it certainly is one of the most delightful ornaments in Christendom. One suspects even sober-minded art critics are tempted to buy one of the illuminated plastic models in the souvenir shops, to take home and put on top of their television sets. The tall campanile stands striped like an ice cream parfait—stripes darker and bolder than in Pisa or Lucca. The façade, even more confectionery-like, was largely the work of Giovanni Pisano, who added many of the statues of saints, prophets and pagan philosophers on the three great portals. The upper half was completed later, in the 1390s, and the glittering mosaics in the gables were added by artists from Venice only in the last century.

Inside, one hardly knows where to look first. Above the striped columns and walls, the ornate Gothic vaulting is painted as a blue firmament with golden stars and angels—note the long rows of finely detailed heads of saints, running all along the nave. The most spectacular feature, however, is under your feet. Beginning in the 1360s, and continuing over the next two centuries, Siena's finest artists were commissioned to create inlaid marble scenes for the **pavement**, nearly an acre of them covering the entire cathedral floor. The subjects are fascinating. Entering from the west door, for example, you might not expect to see a portrait of Hermes Trismegistus, the legendary patron of alchemists whose 'works', brought from Byzantium, caused such a stir in medieval Europe. Further down come the 10 Sibyls of antiquity, and a few images straight out of a deck of tarot cards: snakes and newts, a wheel of fortune, Socrates and Crates, and other symbols too arcane to think about. Many of the best have become somewhat fragile, and are only uncovered 15 August–15 September.

The **stained glass**, some of it from designs by Duccio, is also not to be missed, along with a **pulpit** by Nicola Pisano with reliefs of philosophers and allegories of the Liberal Arts. Also, in the left aisle, there is the **Piccolomini Chapel**, with an altar with some early work by Michelangelo (the statues of four saints on the lower level) and in the transept on the same side of the church there are two beautiful Renaissance sculptural ensembles, that of Bishop Giovanni Pecci, by Donatello, and another, of a cardinal, by Tino di Camaino.

## The Piccolomini Library

*Open Mar–Nov 9am–7.30pm; Dec–Feb 10am–1pm, 2.30–5pm, Mon–Sat; 9am–1pm Sun; adm.*

The Piccolomini family, prominent in Siena for centuries, eventually attained European renown. Some were famous generals for the emperor in the Thirty Years' War (Schiller wrote a trilogy of plays about them), and during the Renaissance two of them made it to the Vatican—Popes Pius II and Pius III. The latter, in 1495, created this chamber, just off the left aisle of the cathedral, to hold the library of the former, who was his uncle. Pius II, Aeneas Silvius Piccolomini, was a genuine Renaissance man, a poet, diplomat, historian, antiquarian, religious reformer, and great geographer; Columbus studied his works closely. In an exercise that was to be a great artistic success, though perhaps somewhat lacking in Christian humility, Pius III hired Pinturicchio to cover the library walls with frescoes of his famous uncle's life. We see Aeneas Silvius in the courts of James II of Scotland and Emperor Frederick III, proclaiming a crusade and canonizing Catherine of Siena, among others. Like Gozzoli's famous frescoes in Florence's Medici Palace, these are less great art than the most elevated interior decoration of all time.

Pinturicchio's frescoes are spectacularly colourful, incorporating dozens of careful portraits of the famous and not-so-famous of the age, with loving attention to current court fashions in dress and coiffure. No better image of *la dolce vita* at the height of the Renaissance could be imagined.

Aeneas Silvius' books have been carted off somewhere, but one of his favourite things still holds pride of place in the centre of the library: a beautiful marble vase with the Three Graces, a Roman copy of a work by Praxiteles that was studied closely by a good number of Renaissance artists.

## Museo dell'Opera del Duomo

*Open Mar–Nov 9am–6.30pm daily; Dec–Feb 9am–1.30pm daily; adm.*

For a close-up look at the façade of the Cathedral, the only place to go is the Cathedral Museum, where most of the original sculptural work has been preserved. Some of these rank among the best Italian Gothic and Renaissance sculpture, especially statues of saints by Nicola Pisano and Jacopo della Quercia, remarkable for their kinetic possibilities—they seem ready to hop down from their pedestals and start declaiming if they suspect for a minute you've been skipping Sunday mass. Besides them, there are some original bits of the Cathedral's pavement that had to be replaced, as well as some leftover pinnacles and other architectural details.

Upstairs, the collection of Sienese paintings includes Duccio di Buoninsegna's masterpiece, the former cathedral altarpiece called the *Maestà*, with an enthroned Virgin on one side and scenes from the Passion on the other. Duccio's animated composition and expressive faces here clearly surpass the work of his more celebrated contemporary, Giotto.

The Cathedral Treasure contains lavish golden monstrances and reliquaries, and in one corner a simple, exquisite bouquet of gold flowers—the kind of gift popes would send along with their ambassadors in the 13th and 14th centuries. Part of the museum is actually built into the unfinished 14th-century cathedral. From the top floor you can climb up to the **Facciatone** ('big façade') for a view over the cathedral and the city.

At time of writing a new museum, the **Museo Archeologico**, containing a collection of Etruscan relics, is being set up in its new location in the Spedale Santa Maria della Scala, in Piazza Duomo. For information call © (0577) 49153.

## Near the Cathedral: the Pinacoteca

*Open April–Sept 8.30am–7pm Tues–Sun; Oct–Mar 8.30am–2pm Tues–Sat; 8.30am–1pm Sun; adm exp.*

The neighbourhood around the cathedral is rhinoceros country. To be specific, you're in the neighbourhood of the *Selva* (forest); that beast is its symbol, and if you take the little stairs just west of the cathedral you'll find yourself in the **Piazza della Selva**, where a bronze rhinoceros commemorates some past Palio victory. South of the cathedral on Via San Pietro, Siena's **Pinacoteca** occupies the restored 14th-century Palazzo Buonsignori, and has an excellent collection of Sienese art from its beginnings to the 17th century. The earliest works, on the top floor, include fine pieces by Guido di Siena, often called the founder of Sienese painting, and his followers. Most were brought here from churches around the city. As always, the works of Pietro and Ambrogio Lorenzetti stand out, for their dramatic faces and poses, and for their original approach to colour.

On the other floors, Madonnas and saints line up in room after room. Very few are without interest, though; the serious spirituality of all its painters, paradoxically expressed in rich settings and gorgeous colours, is a constant feature of the Siena school. Something else readily apparent is Sienese civic pride; almost all the painters have a fondness for painting their town in the background, even in a Nativity. Among later Sienese painters, Beccafumi is well represented, along with Il Sodoma, who initiated the Mannerist tradition in Siena, as well as acquiring his name from a still-popular vice.

More Sodoma (an *Epiphany*) and some other fine paintings can be seen in the Piccolomini Chapel of **Sant'Agostino**, a 13th-century church two blocks south of the Pinacoteca on Via della Cerchia.

## Terzo di San Martino

Beginning again at the Loggia di Mercanzia, Via Banchi di Sotto leads down into the southeast 'third' of Siena, through the quarters of the Unicorn and the Elephant. Just off the Campo, the 1460 **Palazzo Piccolomini** has for centuries been the home of Siena's archives. The old documents and letters are interesting relics, but the surprise attraction here is old Siena's **account books**. From the 1200s, it became a tradition to have the city's best artists paint the covers—fascinating scenes of such prosaic subjects as medieval citizens coming to pay their tax, city workers receiving their pay, and honest monks at their tables trying to make the figures square.

Another elegant loggia, the **Logge del Papa** built by Aeneas Silvius (Pius II), stands on the next small piazza on the Banchi di Sotto. In the narrow streets down to the Piazza del Mercato, there is another Palio victory statuette—an elephant, for the Torre district in the pretty Piazzetta Franchi on Via Salicotto. The **Basilica Servi di Maria** is this *terzo*'s biggest church, with good frescoes in the right transept by Pietro Lorenzetti.

## Terzo di Camollia

The biggest and busiest of the *terzi*, this one runs northwards along Via Banchi di Sopra, Siena's fashionable shopping street and, for centuries, the town's main drag, where the entire population appears to make an evening *passeggiata* down to the Campo and back. Along it there are some of the palaces of the great medieval banking families. **Palazzo Tolomei** (1200–50) is the oldest, but much larger is the **Palazzo Salimbeni**, around a small piazza of the same name further up the street. The latter is the head office of Siena's bank, the *Monte dei Paschi di Siena*, founded in 1472, and now one of the most powerful in Italy, and by some way the town's most important employer. At the bottom of the hill behind it is the large church of **San Francesco**, with more frescoes by the Lorenzettis.

The quarter of the Goose, west of Banchi di Sopra, is a warren of narrow streets associated with the life of St Catherine of Siena, co-patron of Italy and one of medieval Italy's great mystics and religious reformers. Caterina Benincasa, born in 1347, 24th of 25 children in a poor family, began having visions at an early age, and like St Francis she received the stigmata. Besides her devotional writings, for which she was recently proclaimed a Doctor of the Church, she kept a busy interest in the affairs of her day; as a woman she was able constantly to insult the popes over the crooked Church they ran without coming to any harm.

**Saint Catherine's House** (*open 9–12.30, 3.30–6, daily*) still stands, on Costa Sant'Antonio just below San Domenico, and has been restored as a shrine and museum. **San Domenico** itself, a lofty 13th-century church at the end of Viale Curtatone, has her head in a golden reliquary, along with wonderfully hysterical frescoes of her life by the aforementioned Sodoma. San Domenico may seem a plain church from the outside, but you'll have a good view of its Sienese Gothic subtleties from below, at the **Fonte Branda**, a medieval fountain that once was the city's only source of water.

On the western edge of the city, the triumphant Duke Cosimo I of Florence built a fortress in 1560 to keep watch over the conquered city. The **Fortezza Medicea**, however, has nothing threatening about it; this most genteel of fortifications seems less a military work than a nobleman's villa and garden. The Sienese, who have long memories, have nevertheless turned the grounds into a park called Piazza della Libertà. The old munitions cellars, fittingly enough, are now the **Enoteca Italica**, a permanent exhibition where you can have a taste of just about any fine wine produced in Italy, and particularly the best of Tuscan production.

## Sienese Pastimes

If you have more time to spend in Siena, there are plenty of ways to do it enjoyably. Just walking around the city is a treat. Nearly any old church you find open will be worth a look inside; more than most cities, Siena has preserved its medieval interiors and their art intact. South of the Cathedral, you can take a walk in the country without leaving town, in the valleys between the *terzi*. Most of the medieval walls, and eight of the gates, survive, and there are plenty of picnic spots close to the city in the lovely surrounding countryside.

If you want to learn more about the *contrade* and the Palio, each of the 17 neighbourhood organizations (which are really legally chartered communities, a fascinating survival of the 'tribes' into which Roman and pre-Roman cities were organized) maintains its own museum. They are happy to show you around with some advance warning; the tourist office can give you a list of addresses and phone numbers, and will sometimes arrange visits for you.

Just outside the city, with fine views over Siena and its countryside, the monastery of **L'Osservanza** was founded by San Bernardino in the 1420s. Severely damaged in 1944, the church and cloister have been lovingly restored according to the original plans; there are works inside by Sano di Pietro and other Sienese painters, as well as Andrea della Robbia.

---

*Siena ⓒ (0577–)*                                                **Where to Stay**

The city's hotels run an **information and reservations booth** in Piazza San Domenico, ⓒ 288084, where all the long-distance buses stop. If you arrive by train without a reservation, take the local bus up to Piazza Matteotti, and then walk down the steps on one side of the piazza and along Via Curtatone to reach the booth.

### luxury

Most of Siena's best hotels are outside the walls, where the views and rural charm more than compensate for the slight inconvenience. At the top of the list is one of Italy's most remarkable establishments, built in the 14th century on a hill south of Siena. At ★★★★**La Certosa di Maggiano**, Via di Certosa 82, ⓒ 288180, ✉ 288189, the emphasis is on surprise luxuries—a heated pool, air-conditioning that works, a quiet chapel and cloister, a salon for games, tennis courts, an excellent restaurant, and a library that would be an antiquarian's dream. The cloister and the rest of this medieval complex are intact, and contain a bar and a restaurant open only to hotel guests. Of course, all this doesn't come cheap.

### very expensive

For a second choice, there are sunset views over Siena from the ★★★★**Villa Scacciapensieri**, 3km north of the city at Strada Scacciapensieri 10, ⓒ 41441, ✉ 270854. This is a quiet country house divided into 29 spacious rooms; besides the view, it also has a pool and a fine restaurant, with tables on an outdoor terrace.

### expensive

Just inside the walls, the ★★★**Palazzo Ravizza**, ⓒ 280462, and its 30 rooms occupy an old town house on Pian dei Mantellini, below the Duomo near the Porta Laterana; the restaurant isn't anything special, but the rooms are cosy, and there is a pretty terrace.

### moderate

There are a number of reasonable choices near the centre, including the ★★★**Duomo**, south of the Duomo on Via Stalloreggi 34, ⓒ 289088, and the ★★**Canon d'Oro**, a well-run establishment at Via Montanini 28, ⓒ 44321, near the Piazza Matteotti.

The ★★**Piccolo Hotel il Palio** is a little way from the centre, at Piazza del Sale 19, ⓒ 281131, just off the Via Garibaldi, but has the advantages of a quiet location and a friendly, English-speaking proprietress.

Genuinely inexpensive places are a little hard to find—especially at the start of the university terms, when they're full of students looking for a permanent place. Highly recommended in readers' letters is **★★Il Giardino**, Via Baldassare Peruzzi 43, ✆ 220090, situated near the Porta Pispini, with good views and a swimming pool. The very centrally located **★Tre Donzelle**, Via delle Donzelle, ✆ 280358, is also pleasant, with good, clean rooms.

The city of Siena also runs its own **youth hostel**, the **Ostello della Gioventù Guidoriccio**, Via Fiorentina 89, ✆ 52212, in Lo Stellino, 2km north of the city centre. Buses 3, 10 and 15 run there from Piazza Matteotti. IYHF cards are required.

---

*Siena ✆ (0577–)*                        **Eating Out**

Quite a few visitors to Siena find they have no room for lunch or dinner, after spending the day sneaking into pastry shops for slices of *panforte*, an alarmingly heavy concoction laced with fruits, nuts, and secret Sienese ingredients. The chief producer by a long way is **Nannini**, who have several café-shops along the Banchi di Sopra. Anything in Siena's pastry shops is worth trying, for that matter. They are all artists—this is one of the cities where you will see gargantuan creations of cake and crystallized fruit in the shop windows, as colourful as a Lorenzetti fresco, set out for all Siena to admire before they are carted off to some wedding party.

*expensive*

If you've survived the wine and the pastry shops, you'll appreciate the succulent risottos and pasta dishes at **Osteria le Logge**, just off the Campo at Via del Porrione 33, ✆ 48013, as well as the exotic second courses like stuffed guinea-fowl (*faraona*) and a fine wine list, all served in attractive traditional surroundings. (*Closed Sun.*)

At Via del Castoro 3, just off the Piazza del Duomo, **Al Marsili**, ✆ 47154, is another of Siena's best, in a singularly elegant setting—not very traditional, with dishes like gnocchi in duck sauce, but it's hard to complain. (*Closed Mon.*)

*moderate*

**Tullio ai Tre Cristi**, ✆ 280608, has been on Vicolo Provenzano, near San Francesco, since about 1830; perhaps the most authentic of Sienese restaurants, its menu includes things like *ribollita*, tripe with sausages, and roast boar from the Maremma. (*Closed Mon.*)

Just outside Siena on the road to Gaiole (SS408) is **Antica Botteganova**, Strada Chiantigiana 29, ✆ 284 230, offering earthy Sienese cooking, such as veal cooked in Chianti Classico, at reasonable prices. (*Closed Sun.*)

*inexpensive*

There are a few American-style hamburger joints in conspicuous places, plenty of pizzerias and some cheap trattorias, many of them a little way away from the Campo.

Not far from the Palazzo Pubblico, however, is **Da Marino**, Via Salicotto 137, ℰ 42249, which is always busy, offering good-value Sienese home cooking. Nearby, **La Torre**, Via Salicotto 17, is another fun, lively place, popular with students.

**Il Cavallino Bianco**, Via di Città 20, ℰ 44258, serves regional food and pizza, but its main bonus is that it stays open until late. (*Closed Wed.*) Also a pleasant pizzeria is the **Malborghetto**, Via Porta Giustizia 6, ℰ 289258, on the Piazza del Mercato, with tables outside for a fine view of the rear of the Palazzo Pubblico.

## The Southern Hill Towns

Southern Tuscany may not be exactly what you think. There will still be plenty of typical, carefully tended Tuscan farmland, arranged as if by an artist with every garden, orchard, wood, and vineyard in its proper place, but among the variety of landscapes in this small corner of Italy you will find marshland and rugged hills, and even lonely, deserted corners like the half-eroded heaths the Tuscans call the *Crete*. Some of the hill towns in this region go back to the Etruscans, and many can show you fine buildings and works of art from the age of the *comuni* or the Renaissance. Any number of them would make memorable day-trips from Siena on the way to Rome or the coast.

## West of Siena

### Getting Around

**Buses** run to most villages in the region from Piazza San Domenico in Siena (*see* above). To get to San Gimignano it's possible to take a **train** to Poggibonsi (on the Empoli–Siena line) and then a bus from there, but it can be quicker just to take a bus direct from Siena. There is no rail service to Volterra, but an infrequent branch line service runs from Cecina on the coast to nearby Saline di Volterra. However, there are frequent bus services to Florence, Pisa, Siena, and Massa Marittima, all from Piazza XX Settembre in Volterra.

Having a **car**, of course, naturally gives you much more flexibility. From Siena the best road to the area is the SS2 to Colle di Val d'Elsa, from where several minor roads lead to San Gimignano and the SS68 heads directly west to Volterra. At Saline di Volterra the very scenic SS439 road heads south to Massa Maritima.

**Parking** is difficult in most of these towns, but in most cases, as in San Gimignano, there are large car parks on the perimeter roads around the *centro storico*, and it's best to walk in from there.

### Tourist Information

There is a local tourist office in **San Gimignano**, at Piazza del Duomo 1, ℰ (0577) 940008, and another in **Volterra**, at Via G. Turazza 2, ℰ (0588) 86150, behind the Duomo.

## Colle di Val d'Elsa

This lovely village, set along a steep ridge, makes a perfect introduction to the hill towns. Though it has scarcely more than 10,000 people, Colle di Val d'Elsa boasts a wall, with a grand Renaissance gate on the road to Volterra, a **cathedral** (16th-century) and three little museums, including the **Museo d'Arte Sacra** (due to reopen summer 1994, © 0577 920180) in the old bishop's palace, with a few Sienese and Florentine works in addition to the frescoes commissioned by some jolly 14th-century bishop—no martyrs or crucifixions, but scenes of the hunt. Colle di Val d'Elsa was the birthplace of Arnolfo di Cambio, the master architect of Florence; his house is marked with a plaque. On the way to the town from Siena, the *Autostradale* passes **Monteriggioni**, an old Sienese castle with huge towers mentioned by Dante, and the nearby **Abbadia a Isola** up in the hills, with frescoes from the late 15th century.

## San Gimignano

In many of the smaller towns of Italy, you can sense a false start, a free, self-reliant *comune* of the Middle Ages that could build a wall and defend itself, yet eventually found itself lacking either the money or the will to turn itself into a Florence or a Siena. When they ceased to grow, many crystallized into their medieval form and never changed. None did this more completely than San Gimignano. Approaching the town, the startling skyline can be seen poking out from the surrounding hills from miles away: a dozen, lofty square towers, some over 45m tall, haphazardly arranged like the boxy skyscrapers of a Dallas or Calgary.

The main museums and attractions of San Gimignano (Museo Civico and the tower of the Palazzo del Popolo, Chapel of Santa Fina, Museo d'Arte Sacra e Museo Etrusco, and the Ornithological Museum) offer a *biglietto cumulativo* giving admission to all of them for

*San Giminiano*

L15,000. They also all operate the same opening times (*open April–Sept 9.30am–7.30pm daily; Mar, Oct 9.30am–5.30pm Tues–Sun; Nov–Feb 9.30–12.30, 2.30–5.30, Tues–Sun*).

## The Palazzo del Popolo

Unlike its 20th-century imitators, San Gimignano is an utterly charming town. Since the Middle Ages its population has dwindled to less than 9000, and those that are left are kept busy feeding day-trippers from Florence. Its medieval beauty and serenity have made San Gimignano perhaps the trendiest tourist destination in Tuscany (seven hotels, all three-star) but it wears its strange fate well.

The usual entrance is the southern **Porta San Giovanni**, at Piazza Martiri di Montemaggio, where you can park your car. Going up through the walls into the old town, Via San Giovanni leads you past another ancient gate, the Arco dei Bacci, to the church of San Giovanni, a Pisan-style building constructed for the Knights Templar, and then to the triangular Piazza della Cisterna, with the town's well and a few of its medieval towers. If you can imagine it, San Gimignano in the 13th century was said to have had 76 of these family fortresses. Pisa's and Florence's numbered in the hundreds. Most cities eventually made regulations against them, or demolished them. For whatever reason, San Gimignano was a special case; even in the 1400s it was known as the 'city of towers'.

By city ordinance, none could be taller than the 50m **Torre della Rognosa**, part of the **Palazzo del Podestà** on the adjacent Piazza del Duomo. This was a Ghibelline tower; Frederick II built it and the Palazzo as the seat of the imperial officials. Civic pride, however, dictated an even taller one be built for the **Palazzo del Popolo**, designed perhaps by Arnolfo di Cambio about 1300. The tower remains San Gimignano's tallest, and the only one you may climb; the Palazzo also has a beautiful, rustic-looking courtyard with bits of frescoes surviving around its walls, and upstairs the **Museo Civico**, with an *Annunciation* by Filippo Lippi and other works by Florentine and Sienese artists. Other rooms of the Palazzo have interesting frescoes, including the Sala di Dante, an audience hall so called because Dante once spoke here, as a Florentine ambassador attempting to talk the citizens into joining the Guelph League. Dante wasn't the only Florentine to pay a call; in the quattrocento San Gimignano seems to have been almost a kind of resort for the big city; besides the artists who left behind so many fine works, Savonarola, Machiavelli, and others all spent time here.

## The Collegiata

This is the name of San Gimignano's biggest church (1466–70), plain on the outside but a delightful, smaller version of Siena's cathedral within: the same striped arches, starry vaults, and a superlative collection of frescoes on its walls, including a *Crucifixion* by Barna di Siena full of angels, devils, evil Romans and fainting women, among other New and Old Testament scenes, and a *Last Judgement* by Taddeo di Bartolo. A ticket from the Museo Civico will get you into the **Chapel of Santa Fina**, with an introduction to what is surely the most moronic saint story in all Italy. There are many competitors for this honour, but consider little Fina going to the well for water, and accepting an orange from a young swain. When she returned home, her mother told her how wicked she was to take it, and the poor girl became so mortified over her great sin that she lay down on the table and prayed for forgiveness without ceasing for five years. After this, St Gregory appeared to call her soul to heaven, and the table burst into bloom with violets. Domenico Ghirlandaio got the commission to paint all this; he pocketed the money and did a splendid job, with sweet faces and springtime colours. Note San Gimignano's famous towers in the background.

In a courtyard to the left of the Collegiata, the **Baptistry** has another work of Ghirlandaio, an *Annunciation*. The **Museo d'Arte Sacra e Museo Etrusco** occupy two sides of the court-yard—one with more 13th–15th-century sculpture, painting, and illuminated choir books, and the other with finds from Etruscan tombs excavated in the area. Behind the Collegiata, you can walk around the half-ruined fortress, the **Rocca**, or else continue northwards to Piazza Sant'Agostino and **Sant'Agostino**, famous for a series of frescoes by Benozzo Gozzoli on the life of St Augustine. The merriest of all Renaissance painters has a good time with this one, as shown in the charming panel where the master of grammar comes to drag sullen little Augustine off to school. Lastly, another museum included in the *biglietto cumulativo* is the **Ornithological Museum**, a fairly fusty collection of stuffed birds bequeathed to the town by a local aristocrat in 1919, and housed in the **Oratory of St Francis**, with some 16th-century frescoes by Lorenzo Ciardi, in Via Queccerchio below the Rocca.

---

## Volterra

Volterra has a talent for making visitors a bit uneasy. Its situation, among bleak, windy hills, could be the scene for some medieval Tuscan Wuthering Heights. The city itself seems taciturn and grey, brooding on its ancient memories. *Velathri* was a powerful city, the northwestern corner of the Etruscan Dodecapolis. Its 5.5km circuit of walls encloses an area three times the size of the present town.

Volterra's periphery is as interesting as the town itself; besides the **Etruscan walls**, traceable for most of their length, there are the *balze*, the barren, eroded ravines that probably began as Etruscan mining cuts. Already the *balze* have swallowed up medieval churches and exposed some ancient ruins, and they are still growing. It was this erosion that led to the discovery of the Etruscan necropoli around Volterra. Not many substantial ruins have survived, but you can see the remains of a **Roman theatre** and **baths** just outside the northern wall by the Porta Fiorentina, and also some ruins in the 'archaeological park' near the **Fortezza Medicea**, a big castle of the 1470s built on what was the Etruscan acropolis. Just to the north of the fortress, on Via Don Minzoni, the **Museo Etrusco Guarnacci** (*open April–Sept 9–1, 3–6.30, daily; Oct–Mar 9am–2pm; adm; as in San Gimignano, there is a reduced-price joint museum ticket*) has a huge collection of funerary urns found in the *balze* tombs since the 1700s. Most of them, with the familiar reclining figures of the deceased on top, are carved with battle scenes or images from Greek mythology.

Volterra's most conspicuous ancient relic, however, is the **Etruscan arch** in the southern wall, over Via Porta all'Arco. Much rebuilt in Roman times—like the one in Perugia—the gate has three black stone protuberances, once probably images of the Etruscan versions of Jupiter, Juno, and Minerva, now completely worn away. Near the other end of Via Porta all'Arco, Piazza dei Priori is the medieval centre, with the 1208 **Palazzo dei Priori**, the oldest town hall in Tuscany. The imperial **Palazzo Pretorio** is nearly as old; around the corner on Via Sarti, the **Pinacoteca Comunale** (*open 10–1, 3–6, daily; adm*) has a small collection of very fine 15th-century paintings, including a great *Annunciation* by Luca Signorelli, though the prize of the collection is the precise, intense and unforgettable *Deposition* (1521) by Rosso Fiorentino, a seminal work on the threshold between the Renaissance and Mannerism.

Behind Piazza dei Priori is the 15th-century **cathedral** standing behind a large octagonal Baptistry from the 1280s; have a look inside the Duomo for the fresco of the Three Kings by Gozzoli, in a chapel off the left aisle, and the tabernacle over the high altar by Mino da Fiesole. In the **Museo d'Arte Sacra** (*open April–Sept 9.30–1, 2.30–4.30, Tues–Sun; Oct–Mar 9.30am–1pm Tues–Sun; adm*), you can see a della Robbia bust of Volterra's patron, San Lino (Linus), successor to Peter as bishop of Rome—the first pope.

Etruscan and Roman Volterra made its living by mining; one of the most important resources was alabaster, still one of the mainstays of the local economy. Volterra is full of workshops where artists turn this luminous stone into vases and figurines—some of the work is very good. You can seek out the shops yourself (they are everywhere; just look for the coating of fine white dust on the buildings) or stop at the permanent display by the artists' co-operative on Via Turazza.

## Massa Marittima and San Galgano

South of Volterra, along the SS439 road, you'll pass over one of the loneliest and least-known corners of Italy. The **Colline Metallifere**, as the name implies, have been attractive to miners and nobody else since Etruscan times. The iron the Etruscans found here and in nearby Elba made them rich; today the ore is mostly worked out, but there is still plenty of borax and other minerals. After the pass called **Ala dei Diavoli**, the 'Devil's wing', you can detour west on to the SS398 to see the real kingdom of borax at **Lago Boracifero**, near Monterotondo Marittimo. It's a bizarre landscape, and it smells bad too; miniature geysers and steamy pits bubble up boric salts amid grey and yellow slag piles. Lately it's been looking even stranger. In places the ground has become covered with webs of steampipes, ever since the *comune* discovered its geothermal resources could power everything in town almost free.

Across the metal hills, **Massa Marittima** is nowhere near Massa, and over 20km from the sea. Its odd name recalls the Romans, who thought of the entire coastal zone as the 'Maremma' or Marittima. Massa is the unlikely setting for one of Tuscany's finest **cathedrals**, a big 13th-century Pisan Romanesque building set on a stepped pedestal at the end of a broad piazza. There is a beautiful altarpiece in one of the chapels, a *Madonna della Grazie* attributed to Duccio; the tomb of San Cerbone, Massa's patron, is down in the crypt, with 14th-century reliefs of the saint's life. Massa has three museums: the well-organised but not especially interesting **Museo Archeologico** and the small **Pinacoteca** are both situated in the 1230 **Palazzo del Podestà**. The art gallery has another notable Madonna, by Ambrogio Lorenzetti. The same ticket is also valid for the **Mining Museum**, in an old quarry on the edge of town (*all three museums open April–Sept 10–12.30, 3.30–7, Tues–Sun; Oct–Mar 9–1, 3–5, Tues–Sun; adm*).

If you take the SS441/SS73 road between Massa Marittima and Siena, be sure not to miss the ruined abbey of **San Galgano**, about halfway in between, near the village of Monticiano. A Cistercian community from France settled here in the 1100s, and work commenced in 1218 on what must have been the grandest purely French Gothic building in Italy. The monastery was dissolved in the 1600s, and since then the roof and the marble façade have gone, leaving as romantic a ruin as you could ask for: beautiful pointed arches and stone columns with grass for a pavement and the sky for a roof. Parts of the vaulting remain, and besides the romanticism San Galgano affords a rare opportunity to look at the bare structure of a Gothic building; it will increase your appreciation of the 13th century.

## The Sword in the Stone

 On some of the altarpieces in churches and museums in Siena you may have noticed the odd figure of a saint in what appears to be a scene from the *Morte d'Arthur*. This is San Galgano, a dissolute young soldier who received a vision of St Michael and thrust his sword into a stone, leaving his old ways to become a holy hermit. As Michael directed, after Galgano's death a circular chapel was built around the sword. This is the **Cappella di Montesiepi**, on a hill above San Galgano abbey, and here you will find the sword still in its stone, sticking up from the pavement in the centre of the chapel. Whatever role this legend had in someone's religious secret agenda, like all the sites associated with St Michael it is exceedingly strange, a relic from the great age of western mysticism. There are some frescoes by Ambrogio Lorenzetti on the saint's life, but note also the strange shallow dome, done in 22 concentric stripes of brick and stone and probably representing the heavenly spheres of the medieval cosmology, as in the famous fresco in Pisa's Campo Santo.

*Where to Stay*
*moderate*

### San Gimignano

An excellent hotel on the Piazza della Cisterna in San Gimignano is the ★★★**Leon Bianco**, ✆ (0577) 941294 (moderate). If you would prefer the tranquillity of this very lovely patch of Tuscan countryside, there is ★★★**Le Renaie** north of town at Pancole, about 7km towards Certaldo, ✆ (0577) 955044 (moderate). The attractive modern building has a garden, pool, and tennis court.

Though prices in San Gimignano tend to be high, the friendly **Locanda Il Pino**, Via Cellolese 4, ✆ (0577) 940415 (inexpensive), above a restaurant of the same name, has very comfortable, high-quality rooms with baths still just within this bracket.

There are two **youth hostels** in the area, in San Gimignano at Via delle Fonti 1, ✆ (0577) 941991, and the **Ostello Volterra** in Volterra, in Via del Pozzetto, ✆ (0588) 85577, near the Porta a Selci. Another alternative in San Gimignano is to stay at the **Convento di Sant'Agostino**, in the Piazza Sant'Agostino, ✆ (0577)

940383 (inexpensive), a religious house that rents out basic but atmospheric rooms (to men and women, including couples) subject to certain restrictions, such as an evening curfew.

## Volterra

Volterra sees fewer tourists than San Gimignano, but has similar prices. **★★★Nencini**, ✆ (0588) 86386 (moderate) is a 16th-century villa with lovely views, just north of the city centre on Borgo S. Stefano.

Within the walls, the **★★★★San Lino**, Via San Lino 26, near Porta San Francesco, ✆ (0588) 85250 (moderate) stands out only for being the only place with parking, with quite simple accommodation despite its star rating.

Closer to the centre, the **★★★Etruria** Via Matteotti 32, ✆ (0588) 87377 (moderate) has the attraction of one of Volterra's best restaurants—offering roast boar and game dishes in season.

## Massa

Massa is increasingly popular as a place to stay—especially with Germans and Swiss—and its few hotels, all of which are quite cheap, are often full. The **★★Duca del Mare**, Via D. Alighieri 1, ✆ (0566) 901905 (inexpensive), and the **★★Girafalco** on Via Massentana, ✆ (0566) 902177 (inexpensive) are both just below the town centre, with gardens and fine views over the surrounding countryside, and in fact are nearly impossible to tell apart.

In town, on Via degli Albizzeschi, the **★Cris**, ✆ (0566) 903830 (inexpensive) is a bit cheaper, and adequate enough.

---

### *Eating Out*

Virtually all restaurants in the region feature exclusively Tuscan cuisine, accompanied by a fine selection of *Vernaccia*, San Gimignano's delicious, crisp, light white wine.

## San Gimignano

With all the visitors it entertains, it should come as no surprise that San Gimignano has plenty of good restaurants. One of the most popular is **Le Terrazze** in the Hotel La Cisterna, Piazza Cisterna, ✆ (0577) 940328 (expensive). The *medaglione al Vinsanto* is a surprise treat, or else try the *osso buco 'alla Toscana'*, following old house specialities like *zuppa sangimignese* and *pappardelle alla lepre* (broad pasta with hare sauce). Altogether it makes for a memorable dinner. (*Closed Tues evenings, Wed midday.*) **Il Pino**, Via San Matteo 102, ✆ (0577) 940415 (moderate) offers traditional Tuscan food, with the usual emphasis on game and fairly heavy dishes, in comfortable surroundings.

A simple but enjoyable pizzeria in San Gimignano is the **Taverna Paradiso**, Via San Giovanni 6, ✆ (0577) 940302 (inexpensive; *closed Fri.*). Don't miss an ice cream from the **Gelateria di Piazza**, in Piazza Cisterna (inexpensive), an award-winning establishment whose luscious concoctions are among the best in Italy.

## Volterra

Most restaurants in Volterra specialize in roast boar and the like, good medieval Tuscan cuisine entirely in keeping with the spirit of the place. The menu at **Il Porcellino**, Vicolo delle Prigioni 8, ✆ (0588) 86392 (moderate) combines seafood and familiar Tuscan favourites with local treats like roast pigeon and boar with olives, and, given the price, represents a real bargain. (*Closed Tues.*) You can also try more creative Tuscan cooking in Volterra, at **Trattoria del Sacco Fiorentino**, Piazza XX Settembre, ✆ (0588) 88537 (moderate).

## Massa

Try the **Ricca**, Via Colombo, ✆ (0566) 201070 (moderate), with excellent fresh fish and grilled meats, following a delicious plate of penne with scampi and porcini mushrooms. Another good choice is the **Taverna del Vecchio Borgo**, Via Butigni 12, ✆ (0566) 903950 (moderate), which has been highly recommended by readers, not only for its food but also for its extensive list of *grappas*.

Nearby in Località Ghirlanda **Da Bracali** ✆ (0566) 902063 (moderate) offers variations on the local cooking, and some seafood dishes. (*Closed Mon evenings, Tues.*)

# South of Siena

### Getting Around

There are regular **buses** from Siena to most destinations in the area. The only town directly accessible by **train** is Chiusi, on the Florence–Rome line, which also has good bus connections to Chianciano and Montepulciano. There is a rail station called Montepulciano, but it is 10km northeast of the town, and is a stop only for very local trains.

By **road** the area's main artery is the SS2, the Via Cassia, which runs south from Siena. At San Quirico d'Orcia the SS146, a winding but attractive road, turns off eastwards for Montepulciano, Chianciano and Chiusi.

### Tourist Information

South of Siena there are tourist offices only in **Chianciano**, Via Sabatini 7, ✆ (0578) 63538, and **Abbadia San Salvatore**, Via Mentana 95, ✆ (0577) 778608, but many of the towns have information offices attached to their town halls.

## Monte Oliveto Maggiore and Montalcino

As the SS2 rolls towards Rome it passes through another empty region, a landscape of chalk hills and cliffs called the *Crete*. East of the highway, **Asciano** is a medieval walled village with another small collection of Sienese artists in its **Museo d'Arte Sacra** (*entrance on request, ℗ 0577 718207*), next to the Collegiata church. Some 9km to the south, the **Monte Oliveto Maggiore** monastery complex was founded by Giovanni Tolomei, a member of one of Siena's leading families who abandoned banking and civic strife for the life of a hermit.

With such backing, it comes as no surprise that Monte Oliveto became one of the most elegant retreats in Tuscany. A few fortunate monks, artisans who specialize in the restoration of old books, still keep the place going. Set in a striking grove of cypresses, something of an oasis among the bare chalk hills, the monastery has a lovely fortress-gate decorated with della Robbia terracottas, a simple but exceptionally well-proportioned church from the early 15th century, and a library with some skilful wooden *intarsia* pictures by Giovanni da Verona.

The real prize, though, is the **Great Cloister** (*open April–Sept 9–12.45, 3–7, daily; Oct–Mar 9–12.45, 3–5.30, daily*), with a cycle of over 40 frescoes from the life of St Benedict, whose monastic rule Giovanni Tolomei and his new Olivetan order were attempting to restore in all its purity. Nine are by Luca Signorelli; although somewhat deteriorated, they show the artist's usual perfection of line and characteristic colouring. The rest are the work of Sodoma, seemingly attempting to work in the style of Signorelli, but with a Mannerist tendency to more excited poses and expressions, extravagant architectural backgrounds, and the inclusion of his badger and other pets in the scenes.

South of the monastery, **Montalcino**, an easy day trip from Siena by bus, has a strong castle, the **Rocca**, that was the last word in 14th-century military architecture. It defended the town well. After the siege of Siena in 1552, a party of bitter-enders escaped here to found the 'Republic of Siena at Montalcino'—perhaps the first ever republican government-in-exile. With the help of the Rocca, they held out for several years against the minions of Spain and the Medici, one of the last strongholds of Italian liberty. Today the town is better known for its red wines, the dark, pungent *Brunello* and the slightly less prestigious but also very good *Rosso di Montalcino*, some of Tuscany's best, which can be sampled and bought in the official **Enoteca** in the Rocca, as well as at many other private establishments around the town.

There are also two more good collections of Sienese painting in Montalcino, in the **Museo Civico** (*open April–Sept 9.30–1, 3.30–7, Tues–Sun; Oct–Mar 10–1, 3–5, Tues–Sun; adm*) in Piazza Cavour, and the **Museo Diocesano** (same times, combined ticket available), and just south of the town another abandoned monastery, the 12th-century **Abbazia di Sant'Antimo**. It has left behind an especially beautiful Romanesque church, with a luminous interior partially done in alabaster. Another good Romanesque church, from the 1080s, can be seen in the nearby village of **San Quirico**, back on the main road.

## Pienza

Italians like to carry on, more perhaps than is necessary, about Pienza, a small town in the sheep country east of Montalcino that became one of the most characteristic early Renaissance experiments in architecture and design. Before 1460 it was only the humble little village of Corsignano, but in that year Pope Pius II (Aeneas Sylvius Piccolomini) decreed that the town of his birth was to be glorified into a city of art, which he modestly renamed after himself. The new city got off to a flying start with Pius' commissioning of Bernardo

Rossellino to design a cathedral, palace, and central piazza.

Though mannerly and decorous, Rossellino's work makes a lacklustre ensemble, a reminder that alongside the triumphs of the imagination in the Renaissance there were also some losses. The **cathedral** has a simple three-arched entrance, decorated only with the Piccolomini arms and the keys of St Peter; ironically the best features are pure Gothic in inspiration, high pointed vaulting and some pretty traceried windows. They chose a bad spot for it; the cathedral has been settling and threatening

to collapse since it was built, and occasionally sulphur fumes seep out of the floor. Around the cathedral square (Piazza Pio II), Rossellino's **Palazzo Piccolomini** (*open April–Sept 10–12.30, 3–6, daily; Oct–Mar 10–12.30, 2–4, daily; adm*) is nearly a copy of Alberti's design for the Rucellai palace in Florence, which Rossellino helped build.

The best part is around the back, a three-storey loggia and a garden with a pleasant view. The Piccolomini had large estates around Pienza; Aeneas Silvius was born here only because the family had temporarily exiled itself from Siena, after a revolt that excluded nobles from public office. Several other palaces went up in the wake of the Piccolomini, including the **Palazzo dei Canonici**, with a small museum (*open 10–1, 2–5; closed Tues; adm*). Pienza, however, never fulfilled the ambitions of its founder; today it is just another Tuscan farming village known for its piazza and also for its *cacio*; the self-proclaimed 'Capital of Sheep Cheese' has been making it at least since the days of the Etruscans.

---

## Montepulciano

Inhabitants of this town, the Roman *Mons Politianus*, are called *Poliziani*, and that is the name by which we know its most famous son. Angelo Ambrogini, as Poliziano, was a favourite at the court of Lorenzo the Magnificent and one of the greatest classical scholars of his day, as well as a playwright and poet (Botticelli's mythological paintings may have been inspired by his *Stanze per la Giostra*). Like Pienza, Montepulciano has its share of Renaissance monuments, most notably Antonio da Sangallo's church of **San Biagio** (1518), 1km south of the town in the countryside. This superb, though unfinished building captures some of the highest aspirations of Renaissance architecture. The graceful loggia of the adjacent **Canonica** (parish house), also by Sangallo, makes a fitting architectural complement.

In the town, the also unfinished **Duomo** has a beautiful altarpiece by Taddeo di Bartolo and other works by both Florentine and Sienese artists. The two cities fought over Montepulciano for centuries. Florence finally prevailed in both politics and art; the **Palazzo Comunale** (begun *c.* 1360) facing the Duomo, is a smaller copy of Florence's Palazzo Vecchio, with a façade by the Florentine Michelozzo, who also contributed a fine Renaissance façade for the **Sant'Agostino Church** on Via Sangallo.

In the 16th century the town become something like Florence's southern outpost, and was equipped by the city's favoured architects Sangallo the Younger and Vignola with a set of walls, public buildings and palazzi that today, exuding faded grandeur, seem quite out of proportion for a small town. There are several good palaces, several by Sangallo, along the main street, the Corso. Note his **Palazzo Bucelli** at No.73, with a foundation made entirely of carved Etruscan burial urns, filled with cement and stacked like bricks. Montepulciano is also much-visited today for its unusual, very powerful red wine, *Vino Nobile di Montepulciano*, which is on sale at any number of any *enoteche* run by the producers themselves all around the town.

South of Montepulciano, **Chianciano Terme** is a large, bright and busy spa, whose motto *Chianciano—fegato sano* (Chianciano for a healthy liver) draws in many an imbiding Tuscan for an annual flush. It's not only the perfect cure for too much *Vino Nobile*, but usually has overnight accommodation in a pinch.

## Chiusi

If anyone ever read you Lord Macaulay's rouser about Horatio at the Bridge when you were a child you will remember the fateful name Lars Porsena of Clusium, leading the Etruscan confederation to besiege Rome in the brave days of old. Thanks to Horatio, of course, Rome survived and made a name for itself; you can come here to see what happened to Clusium—or *Camars* as the Etruscans actually called it. Modern Chiusi isn't much, but it has a first-class archaeological museum, the **Museo Nazionale Etrusco** (*open 9am–1.40pm Tues–Fri; 9–12.40 Sat; adm*), with lots of burial urns—many with scenes from Homer—and examples of the black pottery called *bucchero* that was an Etruscan speciality. Several tombs can be visited off the road to Chianciano Terme; the **Tombe delle Scimmie**, with some wall paintings, is the most interesting.

From Chiusi, the SS478 road will take you back south-westwards to the southern end of Siena province, passing **Radicofani**, a startling sight with its tall castle perched atop a weirdly eroded barren hill. Further south comes the region of **Monte Amiata**, Tuscany's highest peak (1738m), with Europe's second largest mercury mine; Amiata is an extinct volcano, and full of unusual minerals. There is a small ski resort at **Abbadia San Salvatore**, as well as the remains of a 12th-century Cistercian abbey that was the predecessor to San Galgano. The southernmost corner of Tuscany is a strange and empty quarter, thriving in the days of the Etruscans but at no time since. Ruins of Etruscan tombs and walls can be seen at the grim villages of **Saturnia** and **Pitigliano**. **Sorano**, north of Pitigliano, is the natural conclusion to this somewhat disturbing region; it is almost a ghost town, most of it abandoned after landslides in the 1920s.

Just outside Montalcino ★★★**Al Brunello**, ✆ (0577) 849304, in Loc. Bellaria, is an attractive place in a garden setting. In Pienza, there is only one hotel as such, the simple but comfortable ★★★**Corsignano**, Via della Madonnina, ✆ (0578) 748501, but rooms are also available at the **Ristorante dal Falco**, Piazza Dante, ✆ (0578) 748551. Montepulciano has a few hotels: the rather elegant 19th-century ★★**Il Marzocco**, ✆ (0578) 757262, near the centre, is the best. All the hotels mentioned here are in the moderate price bracket.

Don't despair, though, if you are looking for a place to stay in this southern hill country, and if your expectations are not too great. Almost every town has rooms to rent, in private homes or above bars or restaurants; ask around (even ask the local cops) and you'll probably find something before dark. And, at another point on the scale, Chianciano Terme has a number of large, fairly stuffy spa hotels.

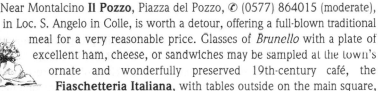

Near Montalcino **Il Pozzo**, Piazza del Pozzo, ✆ (0577) 864015 (moderate), in Loc. S. Angelo in Colle, is worth a detour, offering a full-blown traditional meal for a very reasonable price. Glasses of *Brunello* with a plate of excellent ham, cheese, or sandwiches may be sampled at the town's ornate and wonderfully preserved 19th-century café, the **Fiaschetteria Italiana**, with tables outside on the main square, the Piazza del Popolo.

Two good restaurants in Montepulciano are the **Cittino**, on Vicola Via Nuova, ✆ (0578) 757335 (moderate), and the **Trattoria Diva**, Via Gracciano nel Corso 92, ✆ (0578) 716951 (moderate/inexpensive). For a snack and a drink in comfortable surroundings Montepulciano also has a very enjoyable café, the **Caffè Poliziano**, Via Voltaia nel Corso 27–29, not quite as historic as Montalcino's but maybe more attractive, with towering views over the surrounding countryside from the windows and the outside terrace at the back.

Chiusi makes a good stop for lunch if you're travelling between Florence and Rome; at **Zaira**, Via Arunte 12, ✆ (0578) 20260 (moderate); rabbit, duck, and game dishes are on the menu, accompanied by a good wine list. (*Closed Mon.*)

## From Florence to Arezzo

Like all the northern part of Arezzo province, the routes along the Arno are lined with typically Tuscan small towns that managed not to be left behind in the Middle Ages. On the contrary, it is a highly industrialized region; lignite and felt hats are important, but new factories and power lines seem to be going up all the time. At **Incisa Val d'Arno** the cliffs close in towards the river; from here you have the choice of the fast route, the A1 *autostrada* direct to Arezzo, or dallying through the pretty villages in the hills above either bank of the Arno along the SS69. **San Giovanni Valdarno**, the birthplace of Masaccio and a long-time Florentine fortress on the border with hostile Arezzo, is the largest and perhaps most interesting town in this area, with its arcaded piazza around the Palazzo Comunale, a building thought to be the work of Florence's Arnolfo di Cambio. The loggias that surround it are covered with the coats of arms of its Florentine governors. In the 15th-century **Basilica di Santa Maria delle Grazie** there is a priceless *Annunciation* by Fra Angelico, an early work that seems like a study for his famous Annunciation at San Marco in Florence.

In **Montevarchi**, there is a little museum where you can see a mastadon skeleton, a relic of the area's prehistory. **Terranuova Bracciolini** is an old Aretine fortress town, its walls still standing. In the hills north of the Arno, **Loro Ciuffena** and **Castiglion Fibbochi** are two more typical, pretty towns where little has changed—save the industry around the outskirts—since the 16th century. **Grópina**, near Loro Ciuffena, has a Romanesque church with a truly bizarre relic of the Dark Ages, a stone pulpit carved with wolves, eagles and unusual patterns; it may be from the time of the Lombards or even earlier.

## Arezzo

Compared to the other cities of Tuscany, Arezzo looks a little down-at-heel and rustic, as if the art and sophistication of the Renaissance had somehow passed it by. The medieval air is part of its charm, and easily explainable; Arezzo lost its prosperity along with its independence when Florence annexed it in 1384. The lack of fine buildings, however, conceals a mildly glorious past. Arezzo was one of the richest cities of the Etruscan Dodecapolis; the famous bronze chimaera in the Florence archaeology museum was found here. The long list of famous Aretini begins in Roman times with Maecenas, the fabulously wealthy friend of Augustus and patron of Horace and Virgil. In the Middle Ages, Arezzo was a typical free *comune*, a rival to Florence and a city of great cultural distinction. Guido d'Arezzo, the inventor of musical notation and the scale, was born here, as was Petrarch. Later came Giorgio Vasari and Pietro Aretino, the uninhibited writer and poet whose celebrated poison pen allowed him to make a fortune by *not* writing about contemporary princes and popes—the most genteel extortionist of all time. In the game of Tuscan power politics, Arezzo was at its strongest in the early 14th century, under the rule of a remarkable series of warrior-bishops, of whom the best remembered is the fierce Guido Tarlati (d. 1327).

Today, Arezzo is a very prosperous place. It should be, having perhaps the biggest jewellery industry in Europe, with hundreds of small firms stamping out chains and rings, and bank vaults full of gold ingots. The old centre, however, hasn't really shared in this prosperity. Most people have moved out, and more and more shop fronts are given over to the city's other industry—antiques. Arezzo has become a curiosity shop for all Italy; especially during the **Antiques Fairs,** held on the first weekend of every month in Piazza Grande, you'll see cars with plates from every province crowding Arezzo's narrow streets.

---

### Getting Around

From Florence, Perugia, and Cortona, the **train** is the easiest way to reach Arezzo; the station is at the southern end of town, where Via Guido Monaco crosses Viale Piero della Francesca and the old city walls.

Many smaller towns, such as San Giovanni Valdarno, Poppi, Bibbiena, Sansepolcro, and Castiglion Fiorentino can also be easily reached by train. **Buses** for Cortona and other towns in Arezzo province, as well as for Siena, leave from the bus station, directly opposite the railway station on Viale Piero della Francesca, ✆ (0575) 382169. Schedules are posted for all lines.

By road, the a1 passes 10km to the west of Arezzo, and you must leave it and take one of the three main access roads into the town. As in Siena, the main road, the SS71, makes a large loop around the old town, enabling through traffic to continue on to the SS71 south for Cortona and Lake Trasimeno, or the SS73 east to Sansepolcro and Urbino. Again, in Arezzo it's advisable to use one of the large car parks outside the *centro storico*, and walk in from there.

## The Piazza Grande

The medieval-looking houses around **Piazza Grande** make a perfect setting for Arezzo's annual medieval festival, the *Giostra del Saracino* in early September, where the colourful old costumes are dusted off and the town sports tilt at a wooden figure called the 'King of the Indies'. The antique fairs are also held here, on the first Sunday of each month. Giorgio Vasari built the long **Loggia** in the manner of an ancient Greek stoa, and contributed the clock tower to the **Palazzo della Fraternità dei Laici**, an odd building, half-Gothic and half by Bernardo Rossellino. If you thought this was the town hall, you've been fooled. The palazzo is really the home of a layman's brotherhood founded in the 1200s, and Arezzo's old Palazzo del Popolo exists only in ruins, behind Vasari's Loggia on Via dei Pileati. Like Pisa's, it was destroyed by the Florentines after they captured the city.

Also on Via dei Pileati, **Petrarch's House** is a replacement for the original, destroyed during the Second World War; it stands near the 14th-century **Palazzo Pretorio**, decked with the coats of arms of imperial and Florentine governors. One block south, you'll see the singular façade of Arezzo's finest church, **Santa Maria della Pieve**. This church turns its back on Piazza Grande, showing only a graceful arched apse. In the front, a distinctive irregular campanile and four levels of columns make a unique mountaineer's version of the Pisan-Luccan Romanesque style, done in rough-hewn stone with hardly any two columns or capitals alike. Under the arch at the front portal, note the interesting early medieval reliefs of the 12 months: April with its flowers, February with his pruning hook, and the pagan two-headed god Janus for January. The interior is dim and stark, but there is a good altarpiece by Piero Lorenzetti, with a Madonna and saints modelling Tuscan fashions of the 14th century.

## The Cathedral and Art Museum

Narrow streets from Piazza Grande lead up to the **Passeggio del Prato**, a big, English-style park with lawns and monuments. All of Arezzo slopes gradually upwards from the railway station, ending abruptly here; from the cliffs on the edge of the Prato there is a memorable view over the mountains, extending towards Florence and Urbino. Overlooking the park is a half-ruined Medici fortress of the 16th century; at the other end, you'll see the back of the **Cathedral** with a lovely Gothic bell tower (less than a hundred years old). This Duomo, built in bits and pieces over the centuries, is worth a look inside for the 16th-century stained glass windows, done by a French master named Guillaume de Marcillat, whose work resembles illuminated frescoes by a Gozzoli or Luca Signorelli. In the north aisle, the 1327 **tomb of Bishop Guido Tarlati** is a fascinating early predecessor of the heroic sculptural tombs of the Renaissance, perhaps designed by Giotto; 16 relief panels tell the story of his life, his battles, and his good works—all under a big Ghibelline eagle, like a party badge. The Duomo also has terracottas by Andrea della Robbia and a fresco by Piero della Francesca.

From here, Via Ricasoli leads west towards the **National Museum of Medieval and Modern Art** (*open 9am–6.30pm Tues–Sat; 9am–1pm Sun; adm*), where you can get to know some good local artists not often seen elsewhere, such as Spinello Aretino, his son, Parri di Spinello, and Bartolomeo della Gatta. Renaissance ceramics from Urbino, Deruta and Montelupo are also well represented. Around the corner on Via XX Settembre, you can swallow a heavy load of Mannerist excess at the **Casa Museo Giorgio Vasari**. In the frescoes for his own house, the indefatigable Vasari and his workshop went far beyond anything they ever did for Duke Cosimo (*open 9–7 Mon–Sat; 9–1 Sun; ring bell*).

## San Francesco

For many, the real allure of Arezzo is behind the doors of this dowdy, barnlike, typically Franciscan church (*open 7–12, 2.30–7, daily*). Beginning in 1452, Piero della Francesca created here one of the greatest of all Renaissance fresco cycles, the *Legend of the Cross*. As with Giotto's cycle at Santa Croce in Florence, the story is taken from Jacopo da Voraigne's *Golden Legend*. Though faded, and damaged in many places, the work still shows Piero's use of glowing colours and complex perspectives, especially in such virtuoso achievements, still novel in his day, as night scenes (the *Annunciation* and *Constantine's Dream*) and grimly lifelike portrayals of battles. Even the philistine Vasari was impressed, though the best compliment he can manage in the *Lives of the Artists* is that Piero's drawing of horses was 'almost too excellent for those times'. The frescoes have been undergoing large-scale restoration work, and at time of writing many parts are still under covers.

Out on the southern edge of Arezzo, near the station on Via Margaritone, are the remains of a **Roman amphitheatre**, made into a quiet park. A former monastery, built on a curve over the amphitheatre's foundations, has been restored to house the **Archaeological Museum** (*open 9am–1.30pm Tues–Sat; 9am–12.30pm Sun; adm*). Not much has survived from the thriving Etruscan and Roman city of *Arretium*, but there are some mosaics and sarcophagi, Greek vases and Etruscan funerary urns. Finally, you can take a pleasant 15-minute walk from Via Mecanate out through Arezzo's southern suburbs to see a simple but exceptionally pretty Renaissance church. **Santa Maria delle Grazie**, built by Benedetto di Marano in 1470, has a Florentine-style loggia for a porch in front, and a della Robbia tabernacle.

No hotels in Arezzo really stand out; unlike some of Tuscany's art cities, the forces of tourism have yet to convert old villas into modern accommodation. What the city does have is clean, comfortable, and up-to-date, but nothing to tempt you into lingering.

### moderate

If you're travelling by car, ★★★**Minerva**, Via Fiorentina 4, ✆ 27891, may be the most convenient; it's a few streets west of the city walls, but besides pleasant rooms, all with baths, TV, and air-conditioning, it can offer you a parking place. It also has an excellent, unpretentious restaurant. In town, most of the rooms available are close to the station.

You may enjoy contemplating the towers and red rooftops from the roof terrace of the ★★★**Continentale**, a fine, older hotel in Piazza Guido Monaco 7, ✆ 20251. Its competitor, ★★★**Europa**, Via Spinello 43, ✆ 357701, is just across from the station, and is similarly modern and plain, but many of its rooms are air-conditioned. ★★★**Truciolini**, Via Pacinotti 6, ✆ 984104, also has parking, air-conditioning, and baths in all rooms.

### inexpensive

Budget hotels are a bit cheaper than elsewhere in Tuscany. Near the station, ★**Michelangelo**, Viale Michelangelo 26, ✆ 20 673, is one of the best, friendly and well-kept. There's also a new **youth hostel**, at Via Francesco Redi 16, ✆ 29047.

---

Arezzo isn't going to blind you with science in the kitchen, though while you wait for a train you can enjoy Tuscany's best railway cuisine in the station bar.

### moderate

One restaurant that tries hard (it even has a piano bar, which may seem a little incongruous after a day in medieval Arezzo) is **Le Tastevin**, Via de' Cenci 9, ✆ 28304; specialities include a fine *carpaccio*, and good *penne* with pepper sauce, and its cellar features wines from around the world.

Tourists favour the **Buca di San Francesco**, opposite Piero's frescoes in Via S. Francesco 1, ✆ 23271, but don't let that discourage you—the Buca has an honest-to-goodness medieval atmosphere and tasty Tuscan cooking to match, though slightly adapted for the uninitiated.

For a meal in the country, one of the best restaurants near Arezzo is the **Osteria La Capannaccia**, Loc. Campriano 51/c, ✆ 361759, where the specialities are those of the Aretine countryside—simple dishes like *minestra di pane*, roast meats, and wines from the Colli Aretini—at very reasonable prices.

A good, if very basic local trattoria is **La Scaletta**, Piazza del Popolo 1, right in the centre of Arezzo. **Il Ruspante**, Via Roma 34, is an enjoyable, good-quality pizzeria with a wood oven.

## Around Arezzo

### Getting Around

**Trains** from Arezzo run north up the Arno valley, via Bibbiena, and south to Cortona. There are also regular **buses** from Arezzo to most local destinations (*see* above). The road that links both areas of the province is the SS71, from Emilia-Romagna (and ultimately Ravenna) in the north to Cortona and points further south.

### Tourist Information

Provincial APT tourist offices are located in **Bibbiena**, at Via Berni 29, © 593098, and **Cortona**, Via Nazionale 72, © 603056. Many of the smaller towns also have local, municipally-run information desks.

## North of Arezzo: the Casentino and the Valtiberina

If you are going to or coming from Florence by car, the SS70 and SS7171 make an attractive alternative route to the *autostrada* up the Arno valley. This route, ironically, follows the Arno too, up to its source and then over the Consuma pass to Florence. The region it traverses is called the **Casentino**, a hard-working, backwoods corner of Tuscany full of grapes, olives, small family businesses, chestnut groves, cattle, and monasteries.

Starting from Arezzo, the first important town is **Bibbiena**, a typical hill town from which you can make a detour to **Chiusi della Verna**, up in a range of hills that bravely calls itself the 'Alpe di Catenaia'. St Francis lived here for many years, as a hermit on the wooded slopes of Monte Penna, and it was here in 1224 that he received the stigmata, an event recorded in the frescoes of the basilica at Assisi and scores of other churches around Italy. **La Verna**, an unusual rocky outcrop 3km above Chiusi della Verna, was the site of his hermitage; a Franciscan sanctuary still occupies the rock. They are always happy to receive visitors; in the Chiesa Maggiore and two smaller chapels you can see one of the largest collections of Andrea della Robbia terracottas—some of his best work, including a brilliant *Annunciation*. From the monastery it is an easy walk through pine groves up to the summit of Monte Penna.

North of Bibbiena the valley road divides. The SS71 north-eastwards will take you to another famous monastic retreat, **Camaldoli**, set in thick forests over 1100m up the mountains, the home of an order founded by San Romualdo in the early 11th century. The monks still live in separate cottages, sworn to complete isolation. The narrower SS70 carries on up the Arno valley. **Poppi**, 8km up from Bibbiena, is the real attraction of this route, a beautiful little town of arcaded streets and squares with a stalwart, erect **Palazzo Pretorio** modelled after the Palazzo Vecchio in Florence. Further north, you can take another detour to Pratovecchio and then another mile into the mountains to the locality of **Romena**, where there is a fine Romanesque church and a **castle**; this was once the home of the Giudi family, benefactors of Dante who once controlled all of the Casentino. Beyond, the road continues climbing towards Florence.

From Bibbiena, the road past Chiusi della Verna leads east over the mountains to the next valley, that of the Tiber. Both the Tiber and Arno are near their sources here, and in places they flow less than 15km apart. A few bumpy kilometres south of Chiusi della Verna, **Caprese Michelangelo** does not let any opportunity go by to remind you of its famous son. Besides changing its name, the tiny hamlet has restored the artist's purported birth-place, the old town hall where his father was a Florentine governor. Now a **museum** (*open on request*), it has full-size reproductions of Michelangelo's works, Michelangelo memorabilia, and questionable tributes from modern sculptors.

Further down the Tiber valley, **Sansepolcro**, similarly, lives on as a shrine to *its* favourite son, Piero della Francesca, with two of his most famous paintings in the town hall's **Museo Civico** (*open 9.30–1, 2.30–6, daily; adm*). The *Resurrection*, an intense, almost eerie depiction of the triumphant Christ rising over his tomb and the sleeping soldiers guarding it, shares pride of place with the *Misericordia Polyptych*, a gold-background altar-piece dominated by a giant-sized Madonna, sheltering under her cloak members of the confraternity (note the black hood on one) who commissioned the picture. Other works present are from Luca Signorelli, Pontormo, and Matteo di Giovanni; more Renaissance painting, by both Sienese and Florentine artists, can be seen in Sansepolcro's Romanesque **Duomo**. For yet another Piero della Francesca, stop at the cemetery chapel on the SS221 just west of **Monterchi**, south of Sansepolcro near the border with Umbria: his *Madonna del Parto*, a rare portrayal of a weary, pregnant Virgin, is a popular icon for expectant mothers.

## South of Arezzo: the Valdichiana

Much of this area is a broad plain called the Valdichiana, all swamps and lakes before a 19th-century reclamation plan, and now full of prosperous farms. On both sides, you'll find some of the most beautiful villages in this part of Tuscany—none with much history of their own, but comfortable, essentially Tuscan towns worth a stop and a walk around if you're on your way to Rome or Perugia. **Monte San Savino**, the hometown of the archi-tect Sansovino, is one of these; he designed the market loggia and other buildings around the town. Nearby **Lucignano** will run you in circles—ellipses really; the village has a unique plan of concentric ellipses, with four picturesque piazzas in the centre. The **Palazzo Comunale** has a number of interesting frescoes, and now houses a small museum (*open April–Sept 9.30–1, 3–7.30, Tues–Sun; Oct–Mar 9.30–1, 3–6.30, Tues–Sun; adm*).

Just as distinctive is **Marciano della Chiana**, an old fortress town of gates and towers. Across the Valdichiana, **Castiglion Fiorentino** was known as Castiglion Aretino until the Florentines snatched it in 1384. It, too, has a museum in its **Palazzo Comunale**, with 15th- and 16th-century art, and some good frescoes in the Collegiata church. The town takes its name from the big castle of **Montecchio** on the opposite hill, a landmark visible all over the Valdichiana, now abandoned. For a while in the 1400s it was the stronghold of the condottiere Sir John Hawkwood, he of the famous 'monument' in Florence cathedral.

# Cortona

Cortona may not be entirely undiscovered, but it is still one of the real jewels among the hill towns. Set among terraced slopes covered with olives and vines, almost a kilometre above sea level, it's a web of crooked streets that climb precipitously to the old fortress—even halfway up, if there's a space between the houses, you will be able to see Lake Trasimeno below. Cortona was an Etruscan city, one of the Dodecapolis, and ragged, monolithic Etruscan stonework can still be seen at the foundations of its wall. As a medieval *comune*, it held its own against Siena, Arezzo, and Perugia until 1490, when King Ladislas of Naples captured the city and sold it at a good price to the Florentines.

As in Arezzo, Florentine rule meant a long decline for Cortona, and consequently much that is genuinely medieval has survived. Some old streets, like Via del Gesù, have brick or stuccoed houses with the upper floors propped out over the street on timbers—the very picture of an old Italian town from any quattrocento painting. Cortona also retains one superb medieval square, the **Piazza della Repubblica**, an asymmetrical masterpiece of urban design in a very small space. The building with the clock is the 13th-century **Palazzo Comunale**. Directly behind it, facing the adjacent Piazza Signorelli, the **Palazzo Pretorio** has been restored to house the fascinating little **Museum of the Etruscan Academy** (*open April–Sept 10–1, 4–7, Tues–Sun; Oct–Mar 9–1, 3–5, Tues–Sun; adm*). Not everything here is Etruscan, but the fine Greek vases and Egyptian artefacts testify to the city's wealth and trade contacts long ago. There is even a genuine mummy in an ornate sarcophagus—but that came only in the last century. Among the Etruscan art, the star exhibit is an odd bronze lamp that looks for all the world like an Aztec calendar stone. In the museum's picture collection, expect works by Lorenzetti of Siena, Pinturicchio, and Luca Signorelli, born in Cortona.

Behind the Academy, yet another tiny piazza leads to the **Duomo**, rebuilt to an uninteresting design in the 1560s. The **Museo Diocesano** (*open April–Sept 9–1, 3–6.30, Tues–Sun; Oct–Mar 9–1, 3–5, Tues–Sun; adm*), however, has excellent paintings, including an *Annunciation* by Fra Angelico, who spent 10 years in Cortona, as well as a famous *Deposition* and other works by Luca Signorelli: also some Duccio di Buoninsegna and Pietro Lorenzetti, and a Roman sarcophagus with reliefs of the Battle of Lapiths and Centaurs that was closely studied by Donatello and Brunelleschi .

## Up and Down Cortona

If you have the urge to do some climbing, you can visit the 1240 **Church of San Francesco**, where both Luca Signorelli and Brother Elias, St Francis' businesslike successor, are buried. The town's four gates, like those of many Etruscan and Roman cities, are set at the four points of the compass. The northern **Porte Colonia** has an Etruscan-Roman arch; the southern, on Via Nazionale, has a little terrace with the best view over Lake Trasimeno. Climb higher, to an area within the walls devoted to olives and vegetable gardens, and there will be even better views from the 19th-century **Basilica Santa Margherita** and the overgrown **Medici Fortress** at the top of Cortona's hill, built on the site of the ancient Etruscan acropolis, and a great place for a picnic.

Outside Cortona, down on the plain near the city's modern suburb of Camucia, be sure to stop to see the church of **Santa Maria del Calcinaio**, done in elegant Renaissance symmetry by Giorgio Martini in 1485, on a simple central plan with an octagonal drum and dome. The stained glass is by Guillaume de Marcillat, the same artist who worked at Arezzo Cathedral. Nearby there are some Etruscan tombs: the intriguingly named, circular **Tanella of Pythagoras** and the **Tanella Angori**.

---

© *(0575–)* ***Where to Stay***

## Sansepolcro

In Sansepolcro, ★★★★**La Balestra**, Via del Montefeltro 29, © 735151, ✆ 740282 (moderate), has modern, comfortable rooms and parking, plus an excellent restaurant (*see* below).

A basic but clean and reasonable hotel in Sansepolcro is the ★★**Orfeo**, Viale Diaz 12, © 742287 (inexpensive), on the main road around the town walls.

## Monte San Savino

South of Arezzo, or on the way to Siena, you might wish to plan ahead for a short stay at the ★★★★**Castello di Gargonza**, 7km west of Monte San Savino off the SS73, © 847021, ✆ 847054 (moderate), an entire walled village converted into a hotel, with 20 rooms in restored houses, a pool, and forests all around; the restaurant, with local specialities, is also very good.

## Cortona

In Cortona, the accommodation available has yet to catch up with demand, particularly since the town receives a great many art and language students on study programmes from the University of Georgia, USA. ★★★**San Luca**, Piazza Garibaldi 2, © 603787 (moderate), is simple but comfortable, and many of the rooms enjoy wonderful views. ★★★★**San Michele**, Via Guelfa 15, © 604348, ✆ 630 147 (moderate), is another comfortable hotel, on a medieval street, with rooms with and without baths. ★★★ **Portale**, Via Umbro Cortonese 39, © 691008 (moderate), has good-quality doubles, with a pleasant restaurant attached (*see* below). The ★**Athens** (named after Athens, Georgia, not Greece), Via S. Antonio, © 603008 (inexpensive) is a good budget choice with spacious rooms, with and without baths, and is often packed. The **youth hostel**, Ostello San Marco, Via Maffei 57, © 601392, is one of Italy's more pleasant ones, and a good option if all is full. IYHF cards are required. (*Open Mar–Oct only; inexpensive meals available.*)

---

© *(0575–)* ***Eating Out***

## Sansepolcro

**Paola e Marco Mercati dell'Oroscopo**, Loc. Pieve Vecchia, © 34875 (expensive), mixing traditional with more creative cooking, such as their flamed king prawns in garlic sauce and a chocolate tart with zabaglione and mascarpone. They also have a small, moderately priced hotel, with 12 rooms. (*Open evenings only; closed Sun.*) The restaurant in **La Balestra** hotel (*see* above for details; moderate) offers fine local cooking, with delicious homemade pasta; for seconds try the lamb chops with zucchini flowers. An enjoyable and excellent-value local restaurant in Sansepolcro is the **Fiorentino**, Via Pacioli 60, © 740350 (inexpensive), also a hotel.

## Cortona

Cortona's restaurants are not fancy, but make a point of using local ingredients—homemade pasta, *salumeria* and beefsteaks from the Valdichiana, mushrooms and truffles in season. **La Logetta**, Piazza Pescheria, © 630575 (moderate) is a pretty little restaurant where you can try some of these delicacies prepared *alla Cortonese*. **Portale**, also a hotel (*see* above for details; moderate) is a good place for steaks.

For good, well-prepared, but cheap, local fare in Cortona try the **Trattoria dell'Amico**, Via Dardano 12, © 604192 (inexpensive). More basic, but lively, is the **Spaghetteria Fluflons**, Via Ghibellina 3 (inexpensive).

# Umbria

The Umbrians tell it this way: in the centre of the world there is a sea, in the centre of the sea lies a peninsula, in the centre of the peninsula there is a region, in the centre of the region there is a town, in the centre of the town there is a bar, in the centre of the bar stands a billiard table, in the centre of the billiard table there are four markers, and in the centre of these markers lies the centre of all creation.

The town is Foligno, and the Umbrians, as unabashedly parochial as only Italians can be, are only partly in jest. Their rural little city-region, the 'Green Heart of Italy' is also her introspective soul, scarcely touched by the onrush of contemporary events. Umbria is rarely in the news; it bowed out of time long ago, a medieval backwater that stagnated for centuries under papal rule. As Americans say of North Carolina, it is 'a vale of humility between two mountains of conceit', and Tuscany and Rome are veritable Everests of conceit, casting long shadows even back in the days of the Umbrii, an Italic tribe that gave the region its name. The Umbrii were best known for their pacifism in a peninsula of aggressive peoples. Rather than fight the Etruscans, they assimilated their ways, and used their alphabet whenever they had something to say (which, as far as anybody knows, was only once). Later, in the Etruscan twilight, the Umbrii were one of the few tribes passive (or smart) enough to accept the inevitable Romans without spilling buckets of blood.

Mild-tempered, isolated from outside influences—Umbria is the only Italian region that neither touches the sea nor shares a frontier with another country—the Umbrians tend to be complacent in their cocoon and conservative in their ways, refusing even to improve the recipe for the medieval paving stones they insist on calling bread. But for many this basic lack of interest in the outside world, combined with Umbria's gentle beauty, makes the region an ideal retreat for the spirit. St Francis of Assisi's doctrine of mystical love for all creation seems to come out of the soft bluish-green hills of Umbria, which has proved a fertile land for saints, producing a bumper crop, not only St Francis and St Clare, but St Benedict, the founder of monasticism; St Rita, the saint of impossibilities; and St Valentine, the patron of lovers. Umbrians go to visit their relics the way we would call on a fond uncle or aunt.

Umbria is lush and green, even in the middle of its blistering summer. Its medieval towns, hilltop tiaras of pinkish-grey stone, are evocative and lovely, and their churches and museums contain artworks that rival those of big sister Tuscany. But perhaps the greatest gift Umbria has to offer to the modern visitor is its stillness. You can see it in the soulful, introspective works of the Umbrian school of painting, in early Peruginos and gilded Pinturicchios—but especially in the paintings of Piero della Francesca, born on the Tuscan-Umbrian frontier, whose figures, having achieved

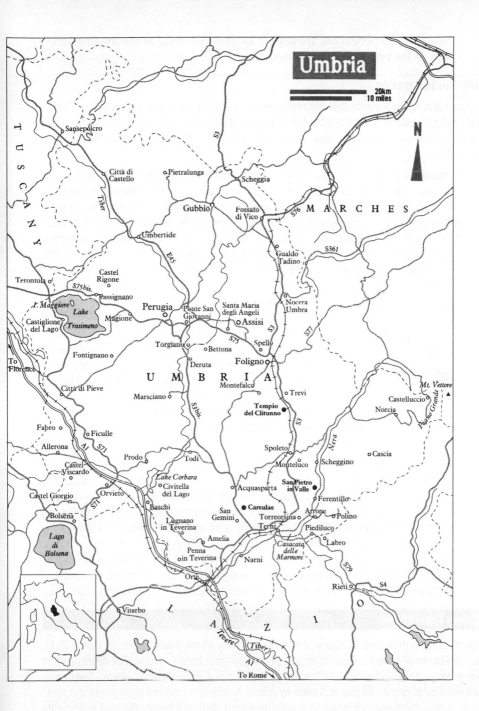

# Umbria

20km
10 miles

N

TUSCANY

Sansepolcro

Città di
Castello

Pietralunga

Scheggia

Tiber

Gubbio

Fossato
di Vico

MARCHES

Umbertide

Gualdo
Tadino

S361

E45

Castel
Rigone

Terontola

S75bis.

Passignano

L. Maggiore

Lake
Trasimeno

Castiglione
del Lago

Magione

Perugia

Ponte San
Giovanni

Santa Maria
degli Angeli

Nocera
Umbra

Assisi

S3

S77

To
Florence

Fontignano

Torgiano

S75

Spello

Bettona

Città di Pieve

Marsciano

Deruta

Foligno

UMBRIA

Montefalco

Trevi

Castelluccio

Mt. Vettore

Piano Grande

Fabro

Ficulle

Tempio
del Clitunno

Norcia

Allerona

A1

S71

Prodo

Todi

S3bis.

Spoleto

Nera

Cascia

Castel
Viscardo

Lake Corbara

Civitella
del Lago

Monteluco

Scheggino

San Pietro
in Valle

Castel Giorgio

Orvieto

Baschi

Acquasparta

Ferentillo

Bolsena

Lugnano
in Teverina

San
Gemini

Carsulae

Torreorsina

Arrone

Polino

Lago
di
Bolsena

Penna
in Teverina

Amelia

Terni

Piediluco

Labro

Narni

Casacata
delle
Marmore

Orte

LAZIO

Tevere (Tiber)

Rieti

S4

S79

Viterbo

A1

To Rome

771

mathematical perfection, are beyond all time. 'Umbria,' as the friendly nun said on the bus, 'speaks in silences.'

## Umbrian Itineraries

Compact and full of interest, but not really on the way to or from anywhere, Umbria's best sights can be easily visited in a loop. Every tourist office in Umbria distributes an excellent free map showing every one-horse town and backroad in the region—just pick one up and explore.

The big medieval art five—Perugia, Assisi, Orvieto, Gubbio, and Spoleto—are Umbria's top attractions, but the smaller hill towns like Todi, Narni, Deruta, and Bettona are charming destinations as well. Each little town seems to have its art treasure—in lovely Spello there are frescoes by Pinturicchio; Città della Pieve has its Peruginos, and Montefalco a magnificent fresco cycle by Gozzoli. The Romans endowed Umbria with a lovely waterfall, the Cascata delle Marmore; an ancient spa at Clitunno, and an evocative ruined city, Carsulae. What the region lacks in coast is compensated for with two lovely lakes, Trasimeno and Piediluco.

### Getting Around

Main **road** routes into Umbria include the SS71/SS75 from Florence and Arezzo to Perugia, and the A1 *autostrada*, which between Florence and Rome passes by way of Orvieto. The Roman Via Flaminia (now the SS3) links Fano, on the Marches' coast, with Nocera Umbra, Foligno, Spoleto, Terni and ultimately Rome; the SS3bis, another road laid out by the Romans, and now upgraded into the *autostrada*-standard E45 for much of its length, also begins near Terni and follows the Tiber from Todi through Perugia up towards Cesena and Ravenna in Emilia-Romagna.

Besides the FS state **railways**, Umbria has its own private line, the FCU (*Ferrovia Centrale Umbria*). This humblest of railroads runs from Sansepolcro in Tuscany to Città di Castello, Umbertide, Perugia, Todi, and Terni. The FS's Rome–Ancona main line reaches Terni, Spoleto, and Foligno; at Foligno you can change trains for the branch line to Perugia. From Terni trains head south for Rieti and L'Aquila, in Abruzzo. Trains between Rome and Florence stop at Orte (where you can change for Terni), at Orvieto, and at Terontola (the junction for Perugia). Towns not reached by train, like Gubbio, are served by buses, though service isn't frequent, especially at weekends. This is one region where you should seriously consider hiring a car.

## Lake Trasimeno

Approaching Umbria from Tuscany, this section begins where that one left off (*see* p.761), near the banks of Lake Trasimeno, easily reached by train from Cortona. The fourth-largest lake in Italy after Lombardy's big three, Trasimeno has a subtle charm, sleepy, placid and shallow, almost marshy in places, kissed by gently rolling hills covered with olives and vineyards. Special flat-bottomed boats skim over its waters, fishing for eels; the lake is doing its darnedest to become a peat bog. In 217 BC the peace of Trasimeno's shores was shattered by the thundering and trumpeting of Carthaginian elephants and the clashing of Roman spears, a battle that ended with the dismal destruction of two legions of the SPQR. It is said 15,000 legionaries perished—their rivers of blood are commemorated in the name of the hamlet **Sanguineto** (from *sangue*, Italian for blood), and their whitened bones in **Ossaia** (from *ossa*, bones). After Trasimeno the Roman military machine grimly threw even more legions to their death against Hannibal at Cannae, before giving the Carthaginians the run of the peninsula, defeating them by refusing to fight.

More recently, Trasimeno has become an area much favoured by English expatriates, searching for new pastures away from crowded Chiantishire. There are several British colonies around the lake's shores.

---

## Getting Around

Lake Trasimeno lies 37km south of Arezzo, 69km east of Siena, and 30km west of Perugia. By **road**, approaching by the A1 from the north, take the Val di Chiana exit for the spur of the *autostrada* that skirts the north shore *en route* to Perugia; from the south, the Chiusi exit will bring you onto the SS71 to Castiglione del Lago on the lake, or Città della Pieve to the south.

**Rail** travel can be awkward: Castiglione del Lago is a stop on the main Florence-Rome line, but only on slower trains, so check before setting out. On the same line is Terontola, the junction for Perugia and the north-shore towns of Tuoro and Passignano; from Siena, change at Chiusi for Castiglione or Città della Pieve.

Perugia is the main **bus** terminus for the area, with fairly frequent services around the northern and southern shores of the lake. Connections from Cortona and Siena are less frequent. Contact tourist offices for timetables.

On the lake itself there is a regular **boat** service linking the ports of Castiglione, Tuoro, and Passignano with each other and with Isola Maggiore. Connections are frequent in summer, but there are only one or two boats a day in winter. For sailing times, contact ✆ (075) 827157.

---

## Tourist Information

There are tourist offices on either side of the lake, in **Castiglione del Lago**, at Piazza Mazzini 10, ✆ (075) 9652484, @ 9652763, and on the north shore in **Passignano sul Trasimeno**, Via Roma 36, ✆ (075) 827635.

---

## The Lake Towns

The west bank of Trasimeno is dominated by the picturesque promontory of **Castiglione del Lago**, the lake's biggest resort, with a castle and beaches. Boats sail from here to pretty **Isola Maggiore**, the largest of the islands, with one little fishing hamlet, and lacemaking women-folk. In 1211 St Francis visited the island, and made a lasting impression by throwing back a pike a fisherman had given him, only to be followed across the lake by his grateful 'brother

## Città delle Pieve

fish' until the saint blessed him—events commemorated in the island's church of San Michele. A pretty path encircles the island, offering good picnicking sites on the way.

Castiglione is also a good base for visiting the Etruscan sights and tombs of Chiusi in Tuscany and **Città della Pieve**, the latter famous as the home town of Pietro Vannucci (1446–1523), better known as *Il Perugino* because of the years he spent working in Perugia. He did leave several paintings in his home town: a lovely fresco of *The Adoration of the Magi* in Santa Maria dei Bianchi (*ring the doorbell marked* custode *to visit*) and some paintings in the Duomo (*open 8–12, 3.30–6, daily*). Perugino is a disturbing character, and you will find his art in Umbria and elsewhere sometimes beautiful, but perhaps more often unsatisfying. Although a forerunner of the High Renaissance, the teacher of Raphael and a master of technique, Perugino was perhaps the most bitter Renaissance artist. Born into a desperately poor family, once successful he became an untrusting miser, and would ride out from Città della Pieve from job to job with his saddlebags full of money. About midpoint in his career he became an atheist; even so, he mechanically cranked out two more decades of richly rewarded but vacuous Madonnas and religious scenes before dying, stubbornly unconfessed and unabsolved on his deathbed (extremely rare in the 16th century), rejecting any future with the sweet-faced angels he depicted for others.

On the north shore of Lake Trasimeno, **Passignano** enjoys a favoured location on its own promontory, and has boats out to Isola Maggiore. A quiet resort with a beach, its oldest quarter is still defended by its walls. From here a road ascends to **Castel Rigone**, a restful little town with a fine Renaissance church called the Tricine. Going by road from Trasimeno to Perugia, if you can snub the fast company of the *autostrada*, you can take in a castle built in 1420 by the Knights of Malta at **Magione**.

---

### Where to Stay

#### Castiglione

Hotels in Castiglione are quite simple, but the **★★Trasimeno**, Via Roma 174, ℂ (075) 829355, ✉ 829267 (moderate) has just what you need if you want to take a swim—a pool—plus a bar and TV in some rooms.

## Isola Maggiore

The most unusual option around Trasimeno is out on Isola Maggiore—the best place in Umbria to get really away from it all; the island's only hotel is the **Sauro**, Via Guglielmi, ✆ (075) 826168, ✆ 825130 (moderate), a gracious, uncomplicated place (only 12 rooms), and a real bargain, with a brilliant restaurant that naturally specializes in fish from the lake: eels, carp and such, along with more traditional Umbrian dishes. All rooms have baths.

## Città della Pieve

North of Città della Pieve, at Po Bandino, *Villa Maraska, ✆ (0578) 20524 (inexpensive) has seven quiet rooms in a garden setting.

## Passignano

**La Vela**, Via Rinascita 2, ✆ 827221 (moderate), offers clean modern rooms for modest prices. The ***Lido**, Via Roma 1, ✆ 827219, ✆ 827251 (moderate) offers slightly more sophistication, at higher, but still reasonable, prices. Up above Passignano in dramatically poised Castel Rigone, with spectacular views over the lake, the **** **Relais La Fattoria**, Via Rigone 1, Castel Rigone, ✆ (075) 845322, ✆ 845197 (moderate) is a pretty hotel, converted from a cluster of 17th-century buildings, with a pool, well-furnished rooms and a good restaurant serving local specialities such as *filetto di persico* (fillets of perch) and *spaghetti al sugo di Trasimeno* (spaghetti with a sauce of mixed lake fish).

## Magione

In San Feliciano, a lakeside village 7km south of Magione, *Da Settimio, Via Lungolago 1, ✆ (075) 849104 (inexpensive), is a small charmer, with peaceful rooms and a simple but good fish restaurant.

An increasingly popular alternative in this area is to stay in local farmhouses. For information, contact: **Agriturismo Azienda La Dogana**, Via Dogana 107, Tuoro del Trasimeno 06100, ✆ (075) 230158, ✆ 8230252; the **Azienda Agraria I Cucchi**, Voc. I Cucchi, Petrignano del Lago, ✆ (075) 9528116, ✆ 5003101; or the **Locanda del Galluzzo**, Via Case Sparse 12/a, Loc. Trecine, ✆ (075) 845352.

---

### *Eating Out*

Medieval Perugians were so fond of fish from Trasimeno that Nicola Pisano jokingly sculpted some on his famous fountain in front of the city's cathedral. Today the catch isn't really big enough to send too much outside the lake area, but you can still try some at the little restaurants around the lake.

## Castiglione

**La Cantina**, Via Vittorio Emanuele 89/a, ✆ (075) 9652463 (moderate) makes good pasta dishes with a *ragù* of fish or eels; their other speciality is game dishes like pheasant and quails, when in season. (*Closed Mon.*)

## Città della Pieve

Away from the lake in Città della Pieve, **Le Cantine del Vescovo,** Via Pietro Vannucci 37, ✆ (0578) 299200 (moderate) turns out more creative versions of the usual Umbrian fare. (*Closed Mon.*) Further down the same street, the **Trattoria Da Bruno,** Via Pietro Vannucci 90, ✆ (0578) 298108 (moderate/inexpensive) serves unpretentious home-cooking, as does the **Trattoria Serenella,** Via Fiorenzuola 28, ✆ (0578) 299683 (moderate).

## Passignano

The **Fischio del Merlo,** Via A. Gramsci 14, ✆ (075) 829283 (moderate) is an attractive trattoria, serving good lake fish. So too is the **Trattoria del Pescatore,** Via San Bernadino 5, ✆ (075) 827165 (moderate). The **Cacciatori,** Via Nazionale 14, ✆ (075) 827210 (expensive), is a lakeside restaurant with slightly higher pretensions—the fish is excellent here, but prices can be steep.

# Perugia

Balanced on a commanding hill high above the Tiber, Perugia is a fascinating medieval acrobat adroitly able to juggle several roles at the same time: those of an ancient hill town, a magnificent *città d'arte*, and a slick, cosmopolitan modern city, famous for its two universities and its chocolates. It is a fit capital for Umbria, with splendid monuments from the Etruscan era to the Late Renaissance, artistically stacked side by side; its gallery contains the region's finest paintings, but in its medieval alleyways cats sleep undisturbed. It daydreams, and yet it sparkles with the enthusiasm and youth of thousands of students, and with the industriousness of the Perugini themselves. It also has the most connections by bus or train to other towns in the region, making it an excellent base if you're using public transport.

## History

An ancient Umbrian centre, conquered or assimilated by the Etruscans relatively late (around 500 BC), *Peiresa* grew to become one of the 12 cities of the Etruscan Federation, and was peacefully integrated into the Roman world in 310 BC. It had the misfortune to be the refuge of Mark Anthony's brother in one of the civil wars, and was subsequently besieged and accidently burned to the ground by one of its own residents when it finally surrendered to Augustus' forces. Augustus had the city rebuilt and renamed *Augusta Perusia*.

Early in the Middle Ages Perugia became an autonomous and rather rascally city that liked nothing better than a punch-up with its neighbours. Strife, external and internal, was to be a constant until the 19th century, and if the city was well fortified against assaults, the towers and palaces of its citizens were equally well fortified against one another. The most prominent family from the 13th century on, the Baglioni, were prevented from taking power by their chief rivals, the Oddi. Their feud was interrupted by the great condottiere Braccio Fortebraccio ('Arm Strongarm', the Popeye of his day, judging by his name and the spinach in a helmet portrayed on his escutcheon), who took the city in 1414 with the pope's army, and ruled it well.

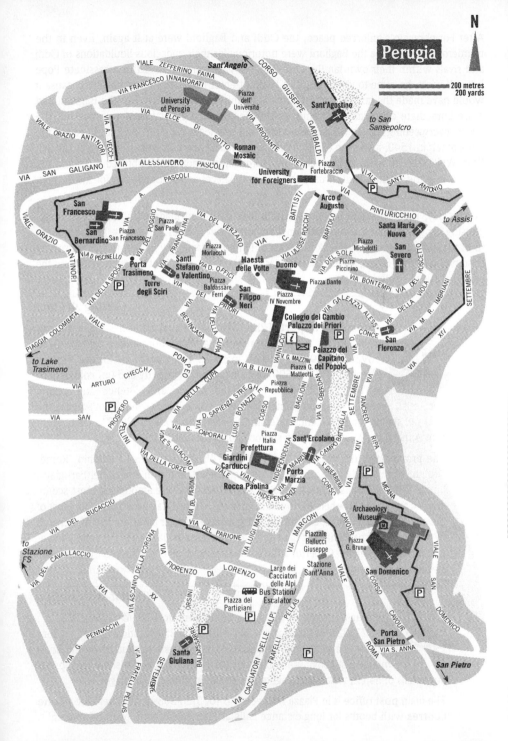

After Fortebraccio's enforced peace, the Oddi and Baglioni were at it again. Even in the murderous Renaissance the Baglioni were notorious for their audacious liquidations of Oddi and rivals within their own family. One Baglioni gangster even tried to assassinate Pope Julius II when he came to visit Perugia, a failed attempt regretted by Machiavelli because it would have made the family immortal, for its iniquity if nothing else. But the Baglioni had more immediate concerns than fame; as the Renaissance papacy became powerful, the popes' overweening legates were eroding their old privileges. When Pope Paul III raised the price of salt in 1540, it was the excuse Perugia needed to revolt in what is known as the Salt War. While the city vainly awaited aid from Florence, the papal army captured it. To add still more salt to the wound, Paul III used the Baglioni palaces as the foundation for his fortress, the Rocca Paolina.

To this day, Perugians, and indeed all Umbrians, eat bread made without salt, an unappetising hangover from the salt rebellion (they often swear it tastes better!). From then on, until the Risorgimento, Perugia, like the rest of Umbria, was firmly held in the unnourishing bosom of the Papal States, states that were, as Goethe remarked, kept 'alive only because the earth refuses to swallow them'.

### Getting Around

Perugia has an **airport**, 12km west of the city, but it has flights only to Milan and, in summer, to Sardinia. For information, call ✆ (075) 6929447/5928017. The main FS **rail** station in Piazza Vittorio Veneto, ✆ (075) 5001091, is just below the city and has connections to Terontola (for Lake Trasimeno, Arezzo, and Florence) and Foligno (for Assisi, Spoleto, Terni, and Rome). Halfway up the hill, Stazione Sant'Anna is the FCU rail station for Todi, Umbertide, and Sansepolcro, ✆ (075) 29121. Trains from Sant'Anna also stop at a suburban station, Ponte San Giovanni.

The provincial **bus** terminus, ✆ (075) 751145, has services to Gubbio, Rome, Urbino, Norcia and other destinations in the region, and is in Piazza dei Partigiani, linked to Piazza Italia by escalators (*scala mobile*) that are among the most scenographic anywhere (*see* below). If you're **driving**, parking can be a headache; most of the city is closed to traffic, and surrounding garages and car parks are few and charge by the hour. Car parks nearest the centre are in Piazza Italia, Piazza Piccinino, and at Piazza Pellini, Mercato Coperto, and Piazza Partigiani, all connected to the centre by elevator or escalator.

### Tourist Information

Perugia has tourist offices at Corso Vannucci 30, ✆ (075) 5723327, 🖷 5723327, at Via Mazzini 21, ✆ (075) 5725431, and at the FS station. There is also a computerised information system, situated on the *scala mobile* just above the Piazza dei Partigiani, which, if it's working, prints out details of hotels, restaurants, sights and so on, in different languages.

The main **post office** is in Piazza Matteotti, ✆ (075) 5720395, and there are **phone centres** with booths for long-distance calls at Piazza Matteotti, open till midnight, and Via Marconi 21, open till 9.30pm. Unless otherwise noted, all **churches** in Perugia are open from 8am–12 midday and 4pm–sunset.

## Up to Piazza Italia

Most people, whether arriving by train, bus, or car ascend into Perugia from the west on Via XX Settembre. Between the FS and Sant'Anna stations, the Largo Cacciatori delle Alpi gives onto Piazza dei Partigiani, from where elevators ascend to the Piazza Italia, fully inside the city. On the way, you can stroll through a surreal, shadowy medieval quarter—all located underground. These streets were vaulted over to support the **Rocca Paolina**, the popes' fortress, designed after the Salt War by Sangallo and a much-hated symbol of papal authority that was joyfully ripped apart in 1860, when Perugia joined the new Italian Kingdom. Only a bulwark remains of the handsome but useless structure, pierced by the beautiful Etruscan gate called the **Porta Marzia**, dating from the 3rd century BC, and originally located in the way of Sangallo's works; he took it apart and reconstructed it here. Porta Marzia leads into Via Baglioni Sotteranea, the main underground street, reopened in 1965. By literally burying the Baglioni palaces, Pope Paul III effectively put a halt to that murderous family's influence; today, this silent, sunless land of good medieval brick is their memorial (*Via Baglioni Sotteranea open 9–1, 4–7, daily; other sections always open*).

On top of the Baglioni palaces lie the **Giardini Carducci**, a terraced public garden with an excellent view of the Umbrian countryside. Next to the gardens stand the dignified public buildings and hotels of **Piazza Italia** that replaced the Rocca Paolina; the proud griffon, emblazoned on the **Prefettura**, is the symbol of both the old and new *comune*.

## Corso Vannucci

Two of Perugia's principal streets radiate from Piazza Italia; Via Baglioni and the stately, pedestrian-only **Corso Vannucci**, a splendid curve lined with the fortified palaces of Perugia's no-account nobility. Their forbidding residences are now elegant cafés and shops; their street has been renamed after Perugino (Pietro Vannucci) who in 1499 was commissioned to fresco the hall and chapel of the **Collegio del Cambio**, or Bankers' Guild (*open Mar–Oct 9–12.30, 2.30–5.30, Tues–Sat, 9–12.30 Sun; Nov–Feb 8–2 Tues–Sun; adm*), a task he performed with a bevy of assistants. The hall is adorned with allegorical figures, fashionably clothed in early 16th-century garb. Perugino painted a self-portrait in the middle of the left wall, and his most famous pupil, Raphael, then a mere pup of 17, painted the figure of Fortitude. The frescoes in the chapel are by another of Perugino's pupils, Giannicola di Paolo. The same ticket is also good for the **Collegio della Mercanzia**, decorated with almost Moorish style 15th-century carvings and inlays, located at the far end of the Palazzo dei Priori.

## Palazzo dei Priori

Next to the Collegio del Cambio, this huge, magnificent complex, crowned with toothlike crenellations and pierced by narrow mullioned windows, has been the civic centre of Perugia since 1297. The façade on the Corso was added in 1443, and wears a lovely portal; enter here for the elevator to the third-floor **Galleria Nazionale dell'Umbria**, the finest and largest ensemble of Umbrian paintings anywhere, with many Florentines to keep them company (*open 9–1.45, 3–7, Tues–Sat; 9–1 Sun; adm exp*).

The pious Umbrians never painted anything secular, and the gallery's multitude of Madonnas and saints may give you holy vertigo after a while. If you feel it coming on, save your eyes for the masterpieces: a serene, 13th-century wood sculpture, *Deposition from the Cross*; Fra Angelico's triptych of the *Dominicans*; a *Madonna* by Gozzoli; and Piero della Francesca's *Madonna With Angels and Saints* polyptych, with an unusual Annunciation at the top, in which Piero, as he so often does, creates an eerie stillness with his mathematical purity—on either side of the angel and Virgin rows of arches recede into a blank wall. Giovanni Boccati's *Madonna dell'Orchestra* is a lovely, musical work. There are a number of paintings by Perugino and Pinturicchio, who both worked on the *Miracles of San Bernardino of Siena*. At his best Perugino eschews drama and tension, preferring simplicity, gentle lines, and rather static compositions often filled with a 'sweetness' that Raphael mastered, and which gives sugar-shock to people who cut their teeth on Michelangelo. You may find Perugian native Pinturicchio (Bernardino di Betto, 1454–1513) more palatable. His nickname, 'rich painter', derived from his use of gold and gorgeous colours. Although Pinturicchio stubbornly refused to participate in the High Renaissance, his most interesting works here are the small experiments in perspective. Near the end of the gallery are some good 16th-century views of Perugia, bristling with now mostly vanished towers; other scenes of the city, by Bonfigli, are in the chapel.

## Piazza Quattro Novembre

Harmonious Corso Vannucci attains melodic rapture at its climax in this lovely square, a fine example of the subtle art of medieval town planning. Built long ago over a 1st-century AD Roman reservoir, the sloping piazza is adorned with the most beautiful Gothic fountain in Italy, the circular **Fontana Maggiore**, designed by Fra Bevignate in 1280, with bas-relief panels executed by the great masters Nicola and Giovanni Pisano. The 50 panels on the lower basin show the scenes of the months, sciences, Aesop's fables, and Roman history; the upper basin has 24 saints; on the topmost basin pose three water-nymphs.

Facing the fountain is the 13th-century façade of the Palazzo dei Priori, with stairs leading up to its main door. Above the portal are Perugia's original griffon (perhaps crafted from an Etruscan creature) and the lion of the Guelph party, hung with chains and bolts from the gate of Siena, captured by the Perugini in 1358. Not a few of the wars of central Italy seem like college football rivalries, one club making off with the other's mascot, or even door-knobs, which seem to be the equivalent of Perugia's proud trophy. The door below leads to the **Sala dei Notari**, a monumental vaulted council hall covered with fine 13th-century frescoes by an anonymous painter (*open 9–1, 3–7, Tues–Sun*).

Across the piazza stands the **Cathedral of San Lorenzo**, a 15th-century Gothic church, its best exterior feature the **Loggia di Braccio Fortebraccio**, added by the condottiere in 1423. The typical, stylized bronze pope in front is Julius III, while the pulpit behind him was especially constructed for charismatic revivalist San Bernardino of Siena to preach to the crowd in the piazza. The vast, sombre interior contains a far greater trophy than Siena's links of chain—the 'wedding ring' of the Virgin, which the Perugini pinched from Chiusi and now keep in the **Cappello del Santo Anello**. The ring, made of onyx and uncomfortably large, is kept in a reliquary with 15 locks (in case the Chiusini try to steal it back), and only displayed on 30 July. On the same side of the church look for the good bas-reliefs by Agostino di Duccio. Much of the cathedral's other art is in the **Museo dell'Opera** (*closed for restoration at time of writing*), including a good *Madonna* by Signorelli, illuminated manuscripts, and a gonfalon painted with a fine portrait of the towered city, in thanksgiving for the end of the plague of 1526.

The cathedral cloisters are unusual, built like a balcony over the arch and narrow lane. A sign nearby points the way to the **Pozzo Etrusco**, the well that supplied the Etruscan city, 35m deep and supported by huge travertine beams, now within the Palazzo Ranieri de Sorbello (*open Mar–Oct 10.30–6 Tues–Sun; Nov–Feb 10–12.30, 2.30–4.30, Tues–Sun; adm*).

## Oratorio di San Bernardino

Flanking the Palazzo dei Priori, attractive medieval Via dei Priori leads down past Perugia's only surviving tower, the 13th-century **Torre degli Sciri** (the others were destroyed in the city's internal warfare), and an Etruscan arch remodelled as the **Porta di San Luca** in the Middle Ages. Turn at the Renaissance church of **Madonna della Luce** for Piazza San Francesco. Perugia was never a lucky city for St Francis: as a young rake he spent a year in prison after a Perugian raid on Assisi, and became ill (events, however, that led directly to his conversion); and his 13th-century church on the piazza, **San Francesco al Prato**, with its lovely Cosmatesque work, was partly ruined in a landslide. Next to it, however, stands a gem of the Renaissance, the **Oratorio di San Bernardino** (1461), its façade rich with colourful marbles and Agostino di Duccio's exquisite bas-reliefs. They are in the same almost Art Deco spirit as his more famous ones in Rimini, with especially good angels that wouldn't look too out of place in Rockefeller Center. If it's open, go in to see the 3rd-century AD sarcophagus used as the altar.

An alternative route back to Piazza IV Novembre, by Via del Poggio, Via Tartuga and Via Aquilone, will take you past the **Teatro Morlacchi**, Perugia's most beautiful theatre, designed in 1788 by Alessio Lerenzini. After Piazza Cavallotti, you can walk through a medieval architectural triumph of interwoven arches and asymmetrical vaults, **Via Maestà delle Volte**.

---

## North Perugia

From Piazza Dante, next to the cathedral, Via del Sole leads up to the fine old **Piazza Michelotti**, the highest point in the city, with good views. Just below the piazza, Via dell'Aquila descends to **San Severo**, an ancient church 'Baroqued' in the 18th century, but preserving intact a Renaissance chapel containing Raphael's first important commission, a fresco of *The Holy Trinity* painted in 1505 (*open Mar–Oct 10.30–6 Tues–Sun; Nov–Feb 10–12.30, 2.30–4.30, Tues–Sun; adm*).

Via Ulisse Rocchi, also beginning in Piazza Dante, heads down to what has become Perugia's symbol, the **Arco di Augusto**, a magnificent gate built over a span of 2000 years—the lowest section by the Etruscans, and the upper part by the Romans after the siege by Augustus (whose new name for the city *Augusta Perusia* is still legible over the arch), while on top of all is a pretty loggia added in the 16th century. Beyond the gate lies Piazza Fortebraccio and the 18th-century Palazzo Gallenga Stuart, home of the **University for Foreigners** (*Università Italiana per Stranieri*), founded in 1921 as a centre for studies in Italian language and culture and attended by students from all over the world. Behind the university, steps lead down to Via Sant'Elisabetta and the Istituto di Chimica, built around a beautiful **Roman mosaic** of the 2nd century AD, portraying the myth of Orpheus (*open 8am–8pm Mon–Fri, 8–1 Sat*). To the north, in a former Olivetan monastery is the main **University of Perugia**, founded in 1307.

At the northernmost edge of Perugia (take Via Garibaldi or Via Z. Faina) stands a tower built by Fortebraccio and the remarkable, 5th-century round church of **Sant'Angelo**, dedicated to St Michael and standing on the site of an ancient temple, of which 24 columns were re-used in the church. Another church at the other end of Via Garibaldi, **Sant'Agostino**, contains some good art, especially its inlaid choir-stalls by Baccio d'Agnolo and frescoes from the 14th–16th centuries.

## South Perugia

Perugia's second main street, Via Baglioni, widens just below Piazza IV Novembre to form Piazza Matteotti, built over the Etruscan walls and lined with early Renaissance palaces. From here, Via Oberdan descends to Perugia's oddest church, **Sant'Ercolano** (1297–1326), a tall, octagonal church with a railway station clock over the door and lace curtains in the upstairs window. The Porta Marzia (*see* above) is nearby, while Corso Cavour descends to Piazza G. Bruno and the huge **Church of San Domenico**, founded in 1305 and rebuilt in Baroque style in 1632, but retaining an immense 15th-century stained-glass window, equal to any of the great windows in Milan cathedral, as well as the beautiful 14th-century **tomb of Pope Benedict XI** and some terracottas by Agostino di Duccio.

The monastery alongside the church contains the **Museo Archeologico Nazionale dell'Umbria** (*open 9–1.45, 3–7, Mon–Sat; 9–1 Sun; adm exp*), with an excellent collection of material from prehistoric Umbria, especially from the Iron Age settlement at Belverde sul Monte Cetona. The Etruscan and Roman sections were founded in 1790. A large part of the collection comes from the Etruscan cemeteries around Perugia—a lovely 3rd-century BC incised bronze mirror (an Etruscan speciality), intricate gold filigree jewellery, sarcophagi, a famous stone slab called the *Cippus Perusinus*, with one of the longest Etruscan inscriptions ever found, funerary urns, vases (one showing a hero who looks just like a dentist about to examine a monster's teeth), bronzes, armour and weapons, and a *kottabos*, thought to have been used in Etruscan party games. The Romans contribute busts, statues, and tombs.

Further down, Corso Cavour passes through **Porta San Pietro**, a 15th-century gate by Agostino di Duccio, then, with a change of name to Borgo XX Giugno, continues to **San Pietro**—begun by the monks of Montecassino in 926, and remodelled since, but maintaining its ancient basilican form in the interior. It contains numerous works of art, with a rich, colourful ceiling and works by Perugino (in the nave and sacristy), beautiful inlaid choir-stalls and stone pulpits; a lovely inlaid door leads out to a terrace with a stunning view towards Assisi. Across the street you can take a breather in the 18th-century gardens, the **Giardini del Frontone**.

## Around Perugia

Near Ponte San Giovanni, just east of Perugia, signs lead to Perugia's finest Etruscan tomb, the **Ipogeo dei Volumni**, sheltered by a modern yellow building (*open 9.30–12.30, 3–5, Mon–Sat; 9.30–12.30 Sun; adm; visits are limited to a maximum of 5 people at a time and for up to 5 minutes only*). Dating from the 2nd century BC, the hypogeum is shaped like an Etruscan house, with an underground 'atrium' (under a high gabled roof carved in the rock), and surrounded by small rooms, the main one holding the travertine urns containing the ashes of four generations of the family. The oldest one, that of Arnth, is a typical Etruscan tomb with a representation of the deceased on the lid, while that of his descendant, the 1st-century AD Publius Voluminius, demonstrates Perugia's rapid Romanization. Unlike most other Etruscan tombs, the Volumni has no paintings, but unusual high-reliefs in stucco.

## Deruta

About 10km south of Perugia, Deruta is Umbria's most famous ceramics centre, having produced its colourful majolica since the Middle Ages. Shops in the streets are adorned with contemporary examples of the art, while pieces from the past may be seen in the **Pinacoteca Comunale and Museo delle Maioliche**, in the Piazza dei Consoli (*open 9.30–12.30, 3–6, Tues–Sun; adm*), along with some lovely detached frescoes from local churches.

---

### Activities

If you're travelling with children, Perugia has a large, brightly lit **fun-fair** and Umbria's modest but sincerely meant 'Disneyland', the **Città della Domenica**, just west of the city, with a miniature Africa, a serpentarium, bumper cars, and more (*© 075 754941, open April–Sept, Oct–Mar Sat, Sun only*).

---

*Perugia © (075–)*                                    ### Where to Stay

#### very expensive

The ★★★★★**Brufani**, Piazza Italia 12, © 62541, @ 5720210, is a renovated, traditional 19th-century hotel with fine views over the countryside and an attractive central courtyard. It has a garage, and each of the very comfortable rooms has TV, minibar and air-conditioning.

#### expensive

Also in Piazza Italia, ★★★★**La Rosetta**, Piazza Italia 19, ©/@ 5720841, is another older hotel, deservedly popular, with a wide variety of rooms from various periods and remodellings. It has a celebrated restaurant, with tables in the garden in summer, and the rooms are cosy and quiet.

When Goethe passed through Perugia he checked in at the ★★★★**Della Posta**, Corso Vannucci 97, © 5722413, @ 5728925, the oldest hotel in town, with an ornate exterior and pleasant, renovated rooms. It also has a garage, and minibar and radio in each room.

There are a couple of special places outside the city. Between Perugia and Deruta in Torgiano is a Relais et Châteaux inn called ★★★★★**Le Tre Vaselle**, Via Garibaldi 48,

© 9880147, © 9880214. A lovely villa set in the Lungarotti family vineyards, it's an exquisite place, often frequented by conferences and symposiums, offering lovely comfortable rooms with air-conditioning and minibar, baby-sitting service and other facilities. Further attractions include a magnificent wine museum, run by the wife of the owner and open for visits (*open 9–12, 3–8; adm*), and one of the finest gourmet restaurants in Umbria, serving the villa's own-label wine with its delicious meals.

Corciano, between Perugia and Lake Trasimeno, is the site of the ★★★★**Colle della Trinità**, Loc. Fontana, © 5172048, © 5171197, a pretty hotel in a fine setting, with a garden and tennis courts, and TV and minibar in each room.

### *moderate*

Enjoying a good location just off Corso Vannucci, the ★★★★**Fortuna**, Via Bonazzi 19, © 5722845, © 65040, has more comfort than charm; all rooms have bath and TV, and there's a garage. Further from the centre, but worth the extra few minutes' drive, is the memorable ★★★★**Giò Arte e Vini**, Via Ruggero d'Andreotto 19, ©/© 5731100, a hotel dedicated to the noble art of wine drinking. Each room is furnished with rustic Umbrian furniture, including a display case filled with bottles of wine. Guests are encouraged to taste them and purchase from the amply stocked cellars on departure. The restaurant is another treat for grape fans. Every evening, the *sommelier* chooses three different wines and, for a surprisingly modest fee, diners can quaff to their hearts' content.

### *inexpensive*

The friendly and convenient ★★**Aurora**, Viale Indipendenza 21, © 5724819, is only a minute's walk from Piazza Italia, on the main road up from the station. Rooms are rather spartan, but comfortable enough for a short stay. ★**Etruria**, Via della Luna 21, © 5723730, is a simple place just off Corso Vannucci. Rooms are without baths. The local youth hostel is the **Centro Internazionale Accoglienza per Giovani**, Via Bontempi 13, ©/© 5722880, near San Severo, with bunk beds and a midnight curfew. IYHF membership is not required.

---

*Perugia © (075–)* | **Eating Out**

### *expensive*

Besides the restaurant in the Hotel La Rosetta and the renowned dining room of the Hotel Brufani (both moderate to expensive), Perugia has several fine places to eat. **Sommella e Parisi**, Via Baldeschi 5, © 65819, is run by a Neapolitan, hence the excellent seafood, especially shrimps and oysters. In fact, you'll find no meat at all here, but there are also tempting desserts. (*Closed Sun, Mon.*) For a taste of old Umbria, try the **Osteria del Bartolo**, Via Bartolo 30, © 61461, where inventive and beautifully prepared dishes have been re-created from ancient recipes. (*Closed Sun.*)

### *moderate*

On 'Witch Street', Via delle Streghe, in the medieval quarter west of Corso Vannucci, **La Taverna**, at No.8, © 61028, has an atmosphere matching its surroundings, and simple dishes from Umbria and the rest of Italy like succulent roast lamb and game, and a wide variety of pasta dishes with truffles and mushrooms. (*Closed Mon.*) Another fine old inn is **Falchetto**, Via Bartolo 20, © 61875, near the cathedral. The kitchen features Umbrian specialities—salumeria, *crostini* (pâté on toast), tagliatelle with truffles, *pasta e fagioli* (pasta with beans), grilled lamb and trout—all well prepared and followed by tasty desserts.(*Closed Mon.*) **La Lanterna**, Via Ulisse Rocchi 6, © 5736064, is a pretty trattoria, furnished in wood and terracotta and turning out good game dishes such as *cinghiale al ginepro* (wild boar with juniper berries) and *capriolo ai mirtilli* (venison with bilberries). (*Closed Wed.*)

At **Ubu Re**, Via Baldeschi 17, © 5735461, close to the cathedral, the chef has a lighter touch, but here too there are good variations on the usual Umbrian theme, including an excellent *coscio di agnello alle olive* (leg of lamb cooked with olives) and a well-stocked wine cellar. (*Closed Mon, Sat, Sun midday.*) **Il Cantinone**, Via Ritorto 6, © 5734430, also near the cathedral, offers mostly simple things: *spaghetti all'amatriciana*, beans and sausage, and *filetto tartufato*—fillet of steak smothered with a black truffle sauce. (*Closed Tues.*)

### *inexpensive*

Just off Piazza Italia on Via Cesare Caporali, **Trattoria Calzoni** (no phone) is run by a kindly grandmother, and will take old-time travellers to Italy back with its plastic tablecloths and holy pictures, and simple, tasty meals for little money. (*Closed Sun.*) A noisy student atmosphere can be found at **Fratelli Brizi**, Via Fabretti (no phone), near the Arco Augusto. (*Closed Sun.*)

If you're not that hungry, you can go for a beer and banana break at the stands on Corso Matteotti, or go a-wine-tasting of Umbrian vintages at the **Enoteca Provinciale**, Ulisse Rocchi 16, © 24824, behind the cathedral. **Pasticceria Sandri**, on Corso Vannucci, may be the fanciest pastry shop in Italy, with a pretty frescoed ceiling and divinely artistic confections; their window has more colours than the Pinacoteca across the street.

---

## Entertainment and Nightlife

The principal Perugian occupation in the evening is the *passeggiata* down Corso Vannucci, with a stop for a tantalizing bite at the Bar Ferrari, perhaps, before hanging out in Piazza IV Novembre. Other activities include July's **Umbria Jazz** festival, which draws lights like Wynton Marsalis to Perugia's stadium. There are also drama performances in the city's cloisters and squares in the **Teatro in Piazza** festival in July and August.

In September the **Sacra Musicale Umbra** features sacred music in Perugia's churches. At other times the large student population brings in numerous concerts, films and other performances, advertised on posters and bulletin boards around the universities. Summer **courses** in painting and sculpture are offered by the Accademia di Belle Arti Pietro Vannucci, Piazza S. Francesco al Prato 5, © 5730631, or you can take Italian in the summer at the University for Foreigners; write ahead for details (Palazzo Gallenga, Piazza Fortebraccio 4, © 64344).

Rome may be the Eternal City, capital of an empire, and Whore of Babylon; Florence the birthplace of the Renaissance, of modern western culture and the Italian language; and Foligno's billiard table the centre of the cosmos; but Assisi is the gentle soul of Italy, imbued with the spirit of the country's patron saint, and known affectionately as *Il Poverello*, the Little Poor One. The importance of St Francis (1182–1226) in the history of Christianity cannot be overestimated; he was the first to crack the strict hierarchy of the established Church; a democrat who preached a natural, popular, everyday religion of love, and who had a simple, humble faith without dogma that had such a deep, mass appeal that the Church quickly institutionalized his teachings. Francis' own life, as an imitation of Christ, became part of the new iconography of the great religious revival he initiated, a life illustrated by Giotto and the other great artists of the trecento. Born to a wealthy cloth merchant named Pietro Bernardone, he was baptized Giovanni, but always called Francesco by his francophile father. Francis grew up speaking Provençal, the language of his Occitan mother, and spent a merry, wild youth as a troubadour. He was captured in Assisi's war against Perugia, and spent a year in prison reflecting on the vanity of the world. When released, he gave everything he owned to the poor, tended lepers, and preached his message of poverty, humility and joy, attracting a band of followers, or 'brethren', who lived with him in Porziuncola. Although Francis refused to take priestly orders, he received authorization for his community from Innocent III in 1209.

Francis spent much of his career preaching and wandering, travelling through Spain to Morocco, accompanying the Crusaders to Egypt and the Holy Land. His songs and canticles, drawing on his troubadour days, were among the first vernacular verses composed in Italy, and the foundation for a 13th-century literary movement, of which the most famous work was the *Fioretti*, 'The Little Flowers', believed to be in part written by Francis himself. In 1221 the Franciscan Rule of poverty, chastity and obedience was sanctioned by Honorius III. Francis later received the stigmata, and died two years later.

Assisi

More than any other saint, Francis crosses ecumenical boundaries; in 1987, when Pope John Paul II invited representatives of all the world's religions to pray together, he chose Assisi as the host city. But Assisi is not only Italy's greatest pilgrimage shrine after Rome, it's a beautiful medieval town as well, built high on a spur of Monte Subasio, overlooking the velvet green Umbrian countryside. Don't become too distracted by the crowds or garish souvenir shops peddling ceramics, toy monks, lace, child-size crossbows and other baubles (admittedly, no shrine would seem right without them); but for a taste of the Assisi that Saints Francesco and Chiara would recognise, stroll through the city's steep, dimly lit lanes at midnight, when all is silent and still.

There are two periods when Assisi is anything but silent, or still. Easter week, when its processions and mystery plays bring thousands of people to the city, as does the *Calendimaggio* (first ten days in May), a medieval May Day celebration that commemorates Francis's troubadour past with songs, dances, torchlit processions, competitions between Upper and Lower Assisi, and beautiful costumes.

### Getting Around

Assisi is a 30-minute **train** ride from Perugia or Foligno, where you'll have to change if you've come from Rome or Ancona. The station (☎ (075) 8040272), however, is 5km from the centre, in the suburb of Santa Maria degli Angeli; connecting buses will take you up to Piazzale Unità d'Italia, just below the basilica. Assisi is also linked by **bus** from Piazza Santa Chiara and Piazza Matteotti with Perugia, Foligno, and Ascoli Piceno.

The main **road** into Assisi is the SS147, which leads off the SS75 road between Perugia and Foligno. There are three large car parks around the fringes of the old city, most of which is closed to traffic: in the Piazzale Unità d'Italia, below the basilica; near the Porta Nuova, below Santa Chiara, off the Foligno road; and at Piazza Matteotti, within the walls, below the Duomo.

### Tourist Information

The Assisi tourist office is at Piazza del Comune 12, ☎ (075) 812534/812450, ✉ 813727. The post office and telephone office are nearby in the same square. Unless otherwise stated, all **churches** in Assisi are open 7am–12 midday, and 2am–sunset, daily.

## The Basilica di San Francesco

Before Francis died, he asked to be buried with the criminals on 'Infernal Hill' outside the city walls. His lieutenant and vicar of the order, Brother Elia, was not about to go against his wishes, but he waited until Francis was canonized in April 1228, and the next day began work on an ambitious two-storey basilica on the hill, now re-christened the Hill of Paradise, that would serve as a proper memorial to the new saint. Not all of the order agreed that such a project was fitting for a holy man wedded to poverty, but brother Elia and Pope Gregory IX, who laid the cornerstone, won the day, creating not only the chief Franciscan memorial, but a rare work of art as well.

The two churches that make up the basilica are believed to have been designed by Brother Elia himself, who created here what was to become a model for numerous other Franciscan churches, especially in the lines of the simple Gothic upper church. The **Lower Church** (*open April–Oct 7am–sunset daily; Nov–Mar 7–12, 2–sunset; closed Sun mornings during services*) much resembles a crypt with its low dark vaults, although once your eyes adjust to the dim light you can see that they are covered with beautiful frescoes by the masters of the 13th and 14th centuries (bring plenty of 100-lire coins to illuminate them). In the first chapel to the left there are relics of the saint—an autographed letter, his humble habit and sandals, and Honorius III's Papal Bull authorizing the Franciscan Rule. The first chapel to the left of the frescoed nave contains magnificent frescoes on the *Life of St Martin* by the Sienese Simone Martini, painted around 1322, while the third chapel on the right contains frescoes on the *Life of Mary Magdalen*, attributed to Giotto (1314). All of the frescoes attributed to Giotto in Assisi, dating from around 1295, constitute one of the most furious and longest-raging controversies in art history. The Italian faction is convinced that the frescoes in the lower and upper churches are the climax of Giotto's early career, while most foreign scholars believe Giotto didn't paint them at all. Whatever the case, Martini's 'International Gothic style' poses a serious artistic challenge to the great precursor of the Renaissance. Giotto is also credited with the four beautiful allegorical frescoes over the high altar, depicting Poverty, Chastity, Obedience, and the Glory of St Francis. In the left transept are fine works by Pietro Lorenzetti of Siena, among the best in the basilica, especially the lovely *Madonna della Tramontana*, with *St Francis and St John*, a *Crucifixion* and a *Descent from the Cross*. In the right transept is Cimabue's *Madonna and Saints*, with a famous portrait of St Francis (1280), believed to be an accurate likeness; a female saint nearby, by Simone Martini, is believed to be St Clare.

In the **Crypt** lie the tombs of Francis and four of his closest followers, discovered in 1818 after having been secretly sealed off in the 15th century to protect the remains from Assisi's devious, relic-snatching arch enemy, Perugia. From the transepts stairs lead up to a terrace and the **Museo-Tesoro della Basilica** (*open April–Oct only 9.30–12, 2–6, Mon–Sat; adm*) containing whatever wasn't pillaged from the treasury over the centuries—a beautiful Venetian cross, a French ivory Madonna from the 13th century, a Flemish tapestry with St Francis, and more.

In comparison with the lower church, the **Upper Church**, facing its emerald-green lawn, is strikingly bright and airy, and dazzles with its colour. Here, under the azure, star-spangled ceilings are two major series of medieval frescoes, the lower set on the *Life of St Francis*, by Giotto or his school, and the upper, with Old and New Testament scenes, attributed to Pietro Cavallini. What makes most Italian scholars attribute the St Francis frescoes to Giotto is the artist's mastery of composition; Giotto amazed his contemporaries by his ability to illus-trate the physical and spiritual essentials of a scene with simplicity and drama, cutting directly to the core. The scenes begin with the young *St Francis Honoured by a Simple Man*, who lays down his cloak and foretells his destiny; he returns his clothes to his father, who in his anger and disappointment has to be restrained; Pope Innocent III has a dream of Francis supporting the falling Lateran; the demons are expelled from Arezzo by Brother Sylvester; Francis meets the Sultan of Egypt, creates the first Christmas crib, or *presepio*, at Greccio; he preaches to the attentive birds, then to Pope Honorius III; he appears in two places at the same time, and next, receives the stigmata from a six-winged Christ. He dies, bewailed by the Poor Clares, and is canonized.

The transepts were painted by Giotto's master, Cimabue, though these works have deteriorated into mere shadows or negatives of their former selves. Look especially at the *Crucifixion* on the left, a faded masterpiece still radiating some of its original drama and feeling. Behind the basilica, propped up on huge arches, the enormous convent is now used as a missionary college.

## To the Piazza del Comune

From the Basilica, Via San Francesco leads up past many fine medieval houses to the centre of Assisi. On the way there are several buildings of note: no.14, the Mason's Guild, or **Casa dei Maestri Comacini** (since most of those who built the basilica came from Como); at no.11, the pretty, frescoed **Oratorio dei Pellegrini**, a 15th-century gem surviving from a hospice built for pilgrims; and at no. 3, the **Monte Frumentario**, a 13th-century hospital, converted into a granary. Next to it is a 16th-century fountain, still bearing the warning that the penalty for washing clothes here is one *scudo* and confiscation of the laundry. Near the entrance to the piazza is the **Museo Romano** (*open 9.30–1, 3–7, daily*), located in the crypt of a now-vanished church, with a small collection of Etruscan urns. A passageway from the museum leads into the ancient Roman forum, which lies directly under the piazza. Currently work is going on to excavate the forum completely, underground—leaving the square above intact.

This square, the long, attractive **Piazza del Comune**, was built up after the barbarians destroyed the forum. It has always been the main axis of Assisi, and is embellished with the 13th-century buildings of the old *comune* (the **Torre and Palazzo del Comune** and the **Palazzo del Capitano del Popolo**), and what at first looks like a decrepit bank building with a classical façade, but is in reality a Roman **Temple of Minerva**, its Corinthian columns and travertine steps incorporated into what is now the church of Santa Maria. When Herr 'Anti-Middle Ages' Goethe came to Assisi it was to see this façade—and nothing else. The Palazzo del Comune also contains the **Pinacoteca Civica** (*open 9.30–1, 3–7, daily; adm*), with a collection of Umbrian Renaissance art. To the left of the Palazzo, the **Chiesa Nuova** was built by Philip III of Spain on property owned by St Francis' father; the **Oratorio di San Francesco Piccolino** (of 'Little baby St Francis') is believed to mark the saint's birthplace.

## Upper Assisi: the Cathedral and the Castle

From the Piazza, Via San Rufino leads up to the **Cattedrale di San Rufino**. This has a huge campanile and a beautiful Romanesque façade, designed by Giovanni da Gubbio in 1140 and adorned with three fine rose windows and the kind of robust medieval carvings of animals and saints that Goethe disdained. The interior was redone in the 16th century and is of little interest, but you can see the porphyry font where Saints Francis and Clare were baptized, as well as Emperor Frederick II, who was born in Jesi in the Marches. It is an amazing coincidence that the two leading figures of the 13th century should have been baptized in the same place; the holy water must have had a special Moslem essence to it, for both Francis and Frederick (*see* 'Lucera' and 'Castel di Monte' in **Apulia**, pp.1025 and 1036) were influenced by Eastern thought: Francis and his Order of Minor Brethren had much in common with a Sufi order of 'Greater Brethren' founded by Najmuddin Kubra, who also had an amazing influence over animals. Francis, before finding religion, had been a Provençal-speaking troubador, a vocation that had its roots in Moorish singers in Spain, and when he left Italy it was to go to Spain, Egypt, and the Holy Land, journeys his biographers found hard to explain, though it may be that he went to learn about the ancient roots of the troubadors; Egypt's Sultan Malik el-Kamil welcomed him warmly when he came to visit and when Francis returned to the camp of the Crusaders he tried to persuade them not to attack. The themes of Francis' poetry, especially the canticles, are very similar to those of Rumi, the great love poet and founder of the Whirling Dervishes.

From the cathedral a stepped lane leads up further to the **Rocca Maggiore** (*open April–Oct 9am–sunset; Nov–Mar 10am–sunset; adm*), Assisi's well-preserved castle, built in 1174 and used by Corrado di Lutzen (who cared for the little orphan Emperor Frederick II), then afterwards destroyed and rebuilt on several occasions. It offers excellent views of Assisi and the countryside. From the Rocca you can visit more of Roman *Asisium*—the remains of the **amphitheatre** in the public gardens, and the **theatre** in Via del Torrione. The **Porta Perlici** near the amphitheatre dates from 1199, and there are some well-preserved 13th-century houses on the Via del Comune Vecchio.

## Basilica di Santa Chiara

When Santa Chiara (St Clare, 1193–1253) was 17 she ran away from her wealthy and noble family to become a disciple of St Francis, and head of the Franciscan Order for women, the Poor Clares. Gentle, humble and well-loved, she once had a vision of a Christmas service in the Basilica of St Francis while at the monastery of San Damiano, over a kilometre away, a feat that brought Pope Pius XII in 1958 to declare her the patroness of television. (Unfortunately the plastic, reception-guaranteeing statues of St Clare, with two holes in the back for your TV antennae, are now hard to find among the countless trinkets of Assisi).

Her basilica, below the Piazza del Comune (by way of Corso Mazzini), is a pink and white striped beauty with a lovely rose window, made memorable by the huge flying buttresses that support its outward side, masterpieces of medieval abstract art that seem unnecessary, but create a memorable space below. The basilica was built on the site of old San Giorgio, where Francis attended school and where his body lay for two years before being moved to his own basilica. The interior of Santa Chiara is decorated with fine frescoes by followers of Giotto, though unfortunately only fragments of many of them now remain. The main chapel on the right contains the famous *Crucifix of San Damiano* that spoke to St Francis, commanding him to 'Rebuild my Church', while the adjacent chapel, of the Holy Sacrament, has fine Sienese frescoes; these two chapels were part of the original church of San Giorgio. The nearby portrait of St Clare, with scenes from her life, is by the Byzantine-ish, 13th-century Maestro di Santa Chiara, while St Clare's body, darkened with age, lies like Sleeping Beauty in a crystal coffin in the neo-Gothic crypt.

From Santa Chiara, Via Sant'Agnese leads to the very simple 1163 church of **Santa Maria Maggiore**, built on the site of the Roman Temple of Apollo, traces of which are still visible in the crypt. Near here was discovered the house of Sextus Propertius, the Roman poet of love (46 BC–AD 14), complete with wall paintings, but it has not yet been made possible for the public to see it. Between here and the Piazzale Unità d'Italia, stroll along Via Cristofani and Via Fontebella, the latter adorned with wrought-iron dragons and another old fountain.

## On the Outskirts of Assisi

The seminal events of Francis' life all took place in the countryside around Assisi, all easily visited by car, though **San Damiano** is a gentle 1km walk down from Santa Chiara. San Damiano is a small, simple, asymmetrical church, where Francis heard the voice of the crucifix that changed his life. While staying here he composed his masterful *Canticle of All Things Created*. He brought Clare here to live with her sisters in frugal contemplation. Once, when they were interrupted by the Saracen army of Frederick II about to attack Assisi, St Clare, holding the Sacrament, drove the infidels away and kept the city free from harm, an event celebrated every 22 June.

Another Franciscan shrine, one more in the spirit of the saint than the great art-filled basilicas, the peaceful **Eremo delle Carceri**, lies along the scenic road up Monte Subasio, a pleasant walk or drive 4km east of Assisi. This was Francis' forest hermitage, where he would retreat to walk through the woods, and where he preached to the birds from a simple stone altar; here you can see his humble bed hollowed from the rock. The handful of Franciscans here live a traditional Franciscan existence, off the alms they receive.

**Santa Maria degli Angeli**, near the railway station, is a large unwieldy nutshell of a basilica built in 1569 to protect a sacred kernel—the tiny **Porziuncola**, an ancient chapel belonging to the Benedictines in the 6th century, where angels were wont to appear. The chapel was given by the Benedictines to St Francis, in return for a yearly basket of carp from the river Tescio, still faithfully paid by the Franciscans. St Francis founded his first monastery here, the remains of which have been partially excavated under the high altar; here St Clare took her vows of poverty as the spiritual daughter of Francis; here Francis died, 'naked on the bare earth' in the convent's infirmary, now the **Cappella del Transito**, with a statue of St Francis by Andrea della Robbia. The garden contains the roses that St Francis threw himself on while wrestling with a severe temptation, staining their leaves red with blood, only to find that they lost their thorns on contact with his body. Still thornless, they bloom every May. Francis' cave has been covered with the frescoed Cappella del Roseto, and there's an old pharmacy and museum (*open April–Oct only 9–12, 2.30–4.30, daily; adm*), with a portrait of St Francis by an unknown 13th-century master, another sometimes attributed to Cimabue, a *Crucifix* by Giunta Pisano, and items relating to Franciscan missionary work. The big feast day in the basilica, the *Festa del Perdono*, was initiated by Francis, after he had a vision of Christ at the Porziuncola, who asked what would be most helpful for the soul. Francis asked for forgiveness for any who crossed the threshold; and indulgences are still given out every 1–2 August.

## Towns Around Assisi: Bettona and Spello

There are a couple of pretty towns easily reached from Assisi. **Bettona**, a small hill town to the southwest, still retains a considerable portion of its Etruscan walls intact, and in its stern

Palazzetto Podestarile a small **Pinacoteca**, unfortunately robbed a few years ago of its two Peruginos, but still containing works by Dono Doni, Fiorenzo di Lorenzo and Andrea della Robbia. The key is now kept in the police station.

**Spello**, an outstanding medieval hill town towards Foligno, was the Roman *Hispellum* and still retains from that period its main gate, the republican-era **Porta Consolare**. But Spello's special claims to fame are its frescoes by Pinturicchio (1501) in the Cappella Baglioni in the Romanesque church of **Santa Maria Maggiore** (*open 8–12.30, 2.30–6, daily*), painted with the same brilliant palette that he used in Siena's Piccolomini Library, and restored during the eighties to their original hues; the *Annunciation* is especially lovely. Even the floor, made of Deruta majolica tiles, is bright and colourful. Other works there by Pinturicchio include an angel and *Madonna*. He also painted the altarpiece in **Sant'Andrea**, a church located up the street, that's also famous for its 13th-century Umbrian *Crucifix*. Further up, there are excellent views from the **Torre Belvedere**, near the scant remains of the Roman acropolis and the medieval castle. Around Spello there are two other Roman gates in the walls: the **Porta Venere** and **Porta Urbica**, near the pretty 12th-century church of **San Claudio**.

*Assisi Ⓒ (075–)*

### Where to Stay

Tourists have been coming to Assisi for longer than to any town in Umbria, and it does its best to please. There are plenty of rooms, but still not enough for Calendimaggio, Easter, and in July and August, when you should definitely book.

### expensive

Two hotels compete for top billing. The traditional, formal ★★★★**Subasio**, Via Frate Elia 2, Ⓒ 812206, ⊕ 816691, is linked to the Basilica of St Francis by the portico. Many of the rooms have views over the famous mystical countryside from vine-shaded terraces, and it has a private garage and an attractive medieval vaulted restaurant. St Francis never slept here, but the King of Belgium and Charlie Chaplin did. ★★★★**Hotel Fontebella**, Via Fontebella 25, Ⓒ 816456, ⊕ 812941, is a bit nearer the centre, housed in a 17th-century *palazzo*. The bedrooms are comfortable, and the public rooms elegant; a garden and garage are added attractions. ★★★★**Giotto**, Via Fontebella 41, Ⓒ 812209, ⊕ 816479, is another hotel with very pleasant, modern rooms near the Basilica, as well as a garage and garden terraces.

### moderate

The ★★★**Umbra**, Via degli Archi 6, Ⓒ 812240, ⊕ 813653, near Piazza del Comune at the end of a narrow alley, is a real charmer, a little family-run inn; quiet, sunny and friendly with a walled garden in front. Rooms can be a bit small, but serendipitous, and many have balconies overlooking the countryside. The Umbra's restaurant (also moderately priced) deserves special mention as one of the most attractive in Assisi, with the best of regional cuisine (like *risotto* with white truffles from Gubbio) and an excellent wine cellar; in summer, meals are served in the garden. Parking can be a minor problem, though there is a car park not far away.

The ★★★**Hotel dei Priori**, Corso Mazzini 15, ⓒ 812237, ⓪ 816804, is housed in a gracious old palazzo, well-restored and very conveniently placed, just off Assisi's main piazza. The ★★★**Hermitage**, Via del Pozzo 1, ⓒ 812764, ⓪ 816691, is a comfortable, reasonably priced hotel in a good central position, a short walk from the Basilica. Nearly a kilometre away—a 10-minute walk from the west gate of Assisi—in a pretty country setting, the old stone ★★**Country House**, S. Pietro Campagna 178, ⓒ/⓪ 816363, has lovely rooms furnished with items from the owner's ground-floor antiques shop.

Still further afield, at Ospedalicchio di Bastia (SS147 towards Perugia), the very friendly ★★★**Lo Spedalicchio**, Piazza B. Buozzi 3, ⓒ/⓪ 8010323, is a hotel converted from a medieval fortified house, nicely restored and preserving many of its original features, but with added creature comforts like private baths, phones and TV; there's also a garden and an excellent restaurant. Northwest of Assisi (12km) at San Gregorio, ★★★**Castel San Gregorio**, Via S. Gregorio 16, ⓒ 8038009, ⓪ 8038904, offers 12 rooms in a restored 13th-century castle, set in a pretty garden. A local *Agriturismo* agency, Le Silve, at Armenzano, ⓒ 8019000, has a listing of cottages and farmhouses to rent in the whole of the Assisi area.

There are five moderate hotels in Spello, of which ★★★**La Bastiglia**, Via dei Molini, ⓒ/⓪ (0742) 651277, stands out, not only for its pleasant rooms but for its beautiful terrace and views; all rooms have baths. The ★★★**Altavilla**, Via Mancinelli 2, ⓒ (0742) 301515, ⓪ 651258, run by the Prioetti family, also has a pleasant terrace and 24 well-furnished rooms.

### inexpensive

Near the amphitheatre, the ★★**Ideale per Turisti**, Piazza Matteotti 1, ⓒ 813570, ⓪ 813020, has a name that says it all: a fine, small hotel with a garden, views, and a bath for every room. ★**Anfiteatro Romano**, Via Anfiteatro 4, ⓒ 813025, ⓪ 815110, is a good quiet choice near Piazza Matteotti, with only seven rooms, some with private bath. American nuns run **S. Antonio's Guest House**, Via G. Alessi 10, ⓒ 812542, in a 12th-century villa, with pleasant rooms. Guests who arrive in the morning can also have a good cheap lunch here, but no dinner. Beware the early curfew. If everything is full, try the large pilgrimage houses in Santa Maria degli Angeli, especially the ★★**Cenacolo Francescano**, Via Piazza d'Italia 70, ⓒ 8041083, ⓪ 8040552, with 130 adequate rooms, all with private bath, a short walk from the train station, or go to the tourist office for a list of smaller religious houses and rooms in private houses, of which there are dozens in Assisi.

There is a **youth hostel** at Rivotorto, 3km south of Assisi—**Victor**, loc. Rivotorto di Assisi, ⓒ/⓪ 8065562.

*Assisi* ⓒ *(075–)*

Besides the Umbra, mentioned above, Assisi has the well-known **Buca di San Francesco**, Via Brizi 1, ⓒ 812204, below street level in a cavernous medieval cellar. Served here are delicious cannelloni, home-made pasta with meat and porcini mushrooms, pigeon cooked Assisi-style, or *filet al Rubesco* (fillet of steak cooked in red Umbrian wine). There is a good selection of wines from Umbria and other regions. (*Closed Mon, Jan, Feb, most of July.*)

Another venerable choice, **Il Medioevo**, Via dell' Arco dei Priori 4, © 813068, has an elegant medieval atmosphere and tasty antipasti with Umbrian prosciutto, pasta with truffles, and *faraona all'uva* (guinea-fowl cooked with grapes). (*Closed Wed, most of Jan, mid-July.*)

*moderate*

**La Fortezza**, Via della Fortezza, © 812418, near the Piazza del Comune, has delicious *cappelletti al tartufo nero o funghi* (truffle- or mushroom-filled pasta caps), roast guinea-fowl (*faraona alla Fortezza*), or rabbit in asparagus sauce. (*Closed Thurs.*) The **Taverna dei Consoli**, Via della Fortezza 1, © 812516, is a meat-lover's dream, with a wide range of Umbrian salami, pasta courses such as *penne alla norcina* (with sausage) and *secondi* of *agnello scottadito* (tiny tender lamb chops) or *cinghiale alla griglia* (grilled wild boar). (*Closed Wed, Jan, Feb, Nov.*)

A lovely stop on the road up to the breathtaking sanctuary of Eremo delle Carceri is **La Stalla**, Via Eremo delle Carceri, © 812317, a typical country trattoria, converted, as its name suggests, from an old barn. Good hearty fare is served here at very reasonable prices, washed down with jugs of local wine. (*Closed Mon.*)

In central Spello there is fine, mellow dining under the vaulted ceiling at **Il Molino**, Piazza Matteotti, © (0742) 651305—try the homemade pasta or traditional Umbrian meats cooked over the flames with a few glasses of Spello's own wines (*Closed Tues.*) Or for beautifully prepared game try the **Trattoria del Cacciatore** Via Giulia, © (0742) 651141, a popular local eating spot with excellent food and decent prices. (*Closed Mon.*) At **La Cantina**, Via Cavour 2, © (0742) 651775, the menu changes according to the season, but depending on when you go, you may be offered *oca al sagrantino e castagne* (goose braised with chestnuts in *sagrantino* wine), *agnello al limone* (lamb cooked with lemon) or, in summer, lighter dishes such as fresh grilled trout. (*Closed Wed.*)

*inexpensive*

For pizza in Assisi, try the popular **Il Pozzo Romano**, Via Sant'Agnese near Santa Chiara, © 813057, which also stocks imported beers. For a treat, try one of the rich strudels or chocolate-and-nut breads in the speciality bakery in Piazza del Comune, near the Temple of Minerva, or at the Santa Monica, Via Portica 4.

# North of Perugia

The two main attractions north of Perugia are artsy Città di Castello and medieval Gubbio, the former linked by train with Perugia, the latter by bus. There are also buses from Città di Castello and Umbertide to Gubbio, and from Fossato di Vico, the nearest railway station. There is little worth stopping for in between—typical rural Umbrian countryside, low hills and valleys, tobacco fields, small farms and flocks of sheep.

Città di Castello is on the FCU local **rail** line from Perugia. There are no trains to Gubbio, but some 10 **buses** a day along the beautiful SS298 from Perugia (40km, about a one-hour journey), stopping at the central Piazza Quaranta Martiri in Gubbio, where schedules are posted. There are also buses from here to the closest train station on the Rome–Foligno–Ancona line, 20km south at Fossato di Vico, and to Città di Castello, Arezzo, Florence and Rome. There is a bus and train information office in Gubbio at Via della Repubblica 13, ✆ (075) 9220918.

The main **roads** from Perugia are the SS3bis, flanked by the E45 *superstrada*, for the Upper Tiber valley and Città di Castello, and the SS298, for Gubbio. The best route from one area to the other is the SS219, which cuts west from the SS3bis towards Gubbio just south of Umbertide, at Civitella Ranieri.

### Tourist Information

In **Città di Castello** the tourist office is at Via Raffaele di Cesare 2/b, ✆ (075) 8554817/8554922, ✉ 8552100. The **Gubbio** office is at Piazza Oderisi, ✆ (075) 9220693/9220790, ✉ 9273409. The Gubbio post office is at Via Cairoli 11, ✆ (075) 9273925.

## Città di Castello

An ancient Umbrian town on the Upper Tiber, Città di Castello is now one of Italy's major tobacco towns, though one that preserves some of its old civic monuments from the 14th century (the **Palazzo del Governo** and **Palazzo Comunale**, with its lofty vaulted hall). Nearby, the part-Romanesque, part-Renaissance **Duomo** has a tilted Ravenna-style campanile, a Rosso Fiorentino, a 6th-century treasury and a lovely 12th-century silver altar-piece in its museum (*open 10.30–1, 3–5, Mon–Sat; 10.30–1 Sun; adm*). Another church, **San Domenico**, has ruined frescoes and a copy of Raphael's *Crucifixion* (the original is now in the National Gallery in London). Città di Castello's best pictures, however, are now in the **Pinacoteca** of the Palazzo Vitelli on Via della Cannoniera 22 (*open 10–1, 3–6.30, Tues–Sun; adm*), a harmonious Renaissance palace by the younger Antonio da Sangallo, with exterior graffiti by Vasari. The gallery includes a fine collection of Renaissance works, with civic standards by Luca Signorelli and Raphael, Ghirlandaio, the della Robbia family and Ghiberti. Another museum, in the Palazzo Albizzini, has paintings by local contemporary painter Alberto Burri (*open 10–12, 3–5, Tues–Sun; adm*).

## Gubbio

It's hard to think of any other Italian town as resolutely medieval as good grey Gubbio, the sombre stone 'City of Silence,' with its orderly Roman street plan draped over the steep, lower slopes of Monte Ingino. As one of Umbria's most-visited hill towns, its dark magic has become grist for the tourist mill, but you'd have to be very particular to think Gubbio is spoiled. Like many other towns in the area, it is a ceramics centre, inheriting the tradition if not the secrets of the 16th-century Mastro Giorgio, who discovered a beautiful ruby lustre to give to his majolica. Mastro Giorgio's secret died with him, but Gubbio's potters still make fine ware, black like that of the Etruscans, or in lovely muted colours.

Gubbio was an important town of the ancient Umbrii, known as *Eugubium*. Long an independent *comune*, it was plagued in the Middle Ages by wolves, one of which in particular ravaged the countryside and terrorized the populace. St Francis heard of it while in town, and, ignoring the townspeople's pleas for his safety, went out and had a word with the wolf, brought it to the town, and made a public agreement that it would stop terrorizing Gubbio in exchange for regular meals, an agreement sealed with a shake of the paw. The wolf kept its part of the bargain, and is immortalized in a bas-relief over the door of a little church in Via Mastro Giorgio.

In 1384 Gubbio was captured by Urbino's Montefeltro duke, and from that time on its fortunes followed those of the Marches. It has retained two exceedingly medieval festivals, however, which fill Gubbio's solemn streets with colour and exuberance, most tumultuously the famous festival of the *Ceri*, held every 15 May in honour of San Ubaldo, Gubbio's patron, who persuaded Frederick Barbarossa not to attack the town in 1155; the festa itself is first documented a couple of years later, although it seemingly was adapted from an ancient pagan celebration. The *ceri* (or 'candles') are three very tall, wooden, and rather phallic towers, each topped by a wax saint—San Ubaldo, San Giorgio, and Sant'Antonio Abate, each representing a clan. The *ceri* are baptized with a jug of water, and then carried on supports by teams of ten men. The climax of the day is when the teams race pell-mell through the crowds up to the mountaintop church of San Ubaldo, a steep race that San Ubaldo invariably wins. On the last Sunday in May crossbowmen from Sansepolcro come to compete in the *Palio dei Balestrieri*, a contest dating back to 1461.

## Gubbio, from the Bottom Up

Approaching Gubbio from the west, the first thing you see is the large, well-preserved 1st-century AD **Roman amphitheatre**, used these days by Gubbio for summer performances of ancient Greek and Roman plays and Shakespeare. Lower Gubbio proper is entered by way of the green **Piazza dei Quaranta Martiri**, the most important square of the lower town, named in memory of the 40 citizens executed on this spot by the Nazis in reprisals for partisan activities in the vicinity. To the right, the church of **San Francesco** has a fine triple apse and some good frescoes, especially the 15th-century series on the Madonna in the left apse, by Gubbio's own Ottaviano Nelli. Lining the other side of the piazza is the **Tiratoio**, or Weavers' Loggia, a 14th-century arcade under which newly woven textiles could be stretched to shrink evenly—one of the few such loggias to survive.

From the piazza the streets ascend past picturesque medieval lanes on the banks of the rushing Camignano. Many of the houses and modest palazzi date back to the 13th century, here and there adorned with carved doors or windows, or secondary doorways called the *Porta del Morto*, used solely to remove the dead—an ancient superstition. The main street, Via dei Consoli, passes by one of Gubbio's finest buildings, the 13th-century **Bargello**, the combined police station and governor's office; its fountain used to be Gubbio's main water source. Further up, the street widens to form the magnificent **Piazza della Signoria**, occupying a ledge of the hill, its belvedere hovering over a steep drop and a stunning view of the town below.

*Gubbio amphitheatre*

The king of the piazza is the beautiful **Palazzo dei Consoli**, a lofty, graceful 14th-century town hall attributed to Gubbio's best architect of the period, Gattapone. Supported on the hill by a mighty substructure of arches, the palazzo is graced with an elegant loggia, a slender campanile, square Guelph crenellations, and asymmetrically arranged windows and arches. Inside are two museums (*open April–Oct 9–12.30, 3.30–6; Nov–Mar 9–1, 3–5.30; adm*): the **Museo Civico**, with archaeological odds and ends and a unique treasure, the bronze *Eugubian Tablets*, discovered in the 15th century beside the Roman theatre. These are the only extant records ever found in the Umbrian language, five written in Etruscan characters, the other two in Latin letters—they concern priestly rites and auguries. A stiff climb up the stairs leads to the painting gallery, with some of Gubbio's ceramics, and an interesting collection of art spanning the centuries. Most memorable, however, is the grand view from the loggia. Sharing the piazza is the present *municipio*, in the 14th-century **Palazzo Pretorio**.

Further up, at the top of the town, stands Gubbio's simple **Duomo**, built in the 13th century and most notable for the pattern of its stone vaulting and its 12th-century stained glass windows. There are several good paintings in its chapel, but its chief work of art is in the museum: a beautiful 16th-century Flemish cope, magnificently embroidered and presented to the cathedral by Pope Marcellus II, a native of Gubbio. The **Palazzo Ducale** (*open 9am–2pm Tues–Sun; adm*), facing the cathedral, was designed for Federico da Montefeltro by Luciano Laurana, as a more compact version of the ducal palace in Urbino. The courtyard is well worth a look.

From the cathedral you can make the stiff climb up Monte Ingino to the church of **San Ubaldo**, but it's much easier to take the funicular up from the Porta Romana on the southeast side of town. In San Ubaldo you can examine the three *Ceri*, and see that it's no wonder that the Gubbites need a considerable amount of Dutch courage to run up the mountain lugging these towers on their shoulders. There's a café where you can while away the afternoon, or walk a bit further up for even more spectacular views from the **Rocca** (888m).

Two churches near Porta Romana, near the lower funicular station, contain some of the finest works by Gubbio's Ottaviano Nelli. In **Santa Maria Nuova** is the lovely and joyous *Madonna del Belvedere*, Nelli's masterpiece, from 1403 (*if the church is closed, knock on* *the door marked* custode *in Via Dante for the key*). The 13th-century **Sant'Agostino**, just outside the gate, has some fine frescoes by Nelli and his students in the apse.

---

© *(075–)*                                           ***Where to Stay***

Though not yet in the same league as Assisi, Gubbio gets its share of visitors, and reservations are essential in July and August.

## Città di Castello

The central ★★★★**Tiferno**, Piazza R. Sanzio 13, © 8550331 (expensive) is the best place both to stay and dine, with good comfortable rooms, a garage, and one of the best restaurants in the area, with dishes like ravioli with shrimps in orange sauce, or pigeon with white grapes. ★★★**Hotel delle Terme**, Via delle Terme, Loc. Fontecchio, © 8559440, @ 8557236 (moderate), at Fontecchio, a natural spa just outside Città di Castello, is a pleasant place to stay even if you don't take advantage of the treatments on offer. Pliny the Younger used to come here to take the waters, but you may be content with the fine open-air pool. (*Open April–Nov only.*) Cheaper choices in Città di Castello, all good, clean, if uninspiring hotels, include the ★★**Europa**, Via V. E. Orlando 2, © 8550551 (inexpensive), and the ★★**Umbria**, Via dei Galanti, © 8554925 (inexpensive). Further down the Tiber valley in Umbertide, there is a simple central hotel with an equally simple restaurant, the ★★**Capponi**, Piazza 25 Aprile 19, © 932256 (inexpensive).

## Gubbio

If you feel like seeing Gubbio in grand style, *the* place to stay is the ★★★★**Park Hotel ai Cappuccini**, Via Tifernate, © 9234, @ 9220323 (expensive), a beautifully restored Franciscan monastery, 3km out of town, set in its own grounds with a pool and, inside, a sauna and fitness centre. The ★★★**Bosone**, Via XX Settembre 22, © 9220688, @ 9220552 (moderate) is conveniently located in a picturesque setting. Rooms are comfortable, though not brilliant, and there's a private garage for your car. ★★★**San Marco**, Via Perugina 5, © 9220234, @ 9273716 (moderate) has modern comforts and a pretty garden terrace at the back. All rooms have baths, and there's parking nearby.

★★**Dei Consoli**, Via dei Consoli 59, © 9273335 (inexpensive), near the Piazza della Signoria, is small and simple, but enjoys an excellent location. It also has a good restaurant in a medieval cellar, with tasty *spiedini* (meat on a spit). ★★**Gattapone**, Via G. Ansidei 6, © 9272489, @ 9271269 (inexpensive) is another pleasant hotel in the central medieval zone. All rooms have private baths, and there's a small garden at the back. ★**Locanda Galletti**, Via Ambrogio Piccardi 1, © 9274247 (inexpensive), overlooking the river, has simple rooms, some with private bath. There's also a restaurant, with outdoor tables in a beautiful setting—roast duck and lamb for moderate prices. If you don't mind its monastic flavour, the **Casa Beniamino Ubaldi**, Via Perugina 74, © 9277773, is a modern seminarians' college just outside the city walls, which rents out spotlessly clean rooms, all with bath, representing probably the best deal in town—and there's a bar!

# Gubbio

Gubbio has no good wines, but there are local poisons like *Amaro Iguvium* and *Liquore Ingeno* to top off a meal. For a taste of tradition, dine at the **Fornace di Mastro Giorgio**, Via della Fornace di Mastro Giorgio, © 9275740 (expensive), in the workshop where the master ceramicist once created his famous ruby glaze. The cuisine combines the best traditions of Apulia and Umbria, with seafood (rare in Umbria) on Thursday and Friday, and pungent delicacies like *tagliolini alle alici* (with anchovies) or Umbrian pigeon with olives, topped off by delicious desserts. (*Closed Mon, Sun evenings.*) Another classic eatery recalls the legend of St Francis: the **Taverna del Lupo**, Via Ansidei 21/a, © 9274368 (expensive), a beautifully medieval place, where you can dine on such traditional fare as boar sausage, game, in the autumn, and *risotto dei tartufi* (Gubbio, like Piedmont, is a land of white truffles, which are even more expensive than the black truffles of the Valnerina in southern Umbria), as well as delicious pasta dishes like lasagne with prosciutto and truffles and *Frico*, a local speciality of mixed meats with cress. (*Closed Mon.*)

On a clear day, the restaurant **Funivia**, on Monte Ingino above Gubbio, © 9273464 (moderate) is an exceptional dining experience, offering fabulous views as well as delicious pasta with truffles or *porcini* mushrooms, and tasty *secondi* like grilled lamb or stuffed pigeon, good desserts, and local wines. (*Closed Wed.*) Inside Gubbio itself, **La Balestra**, Via della Repubblica 41, © 9273810 (moderate) features unusual antipasti, including herring (*aringa*) and dishes like *fondutina con tartufo*, home-made pasta, and a good selection of meats. (*Closed Tues.*)

**Ristorante Pizzeria S. Francesco e Il Lupo**, Via Cairoli 24, © 9272344 (inexpensive), features local products, including prosciutto, porcini mushrooms, and truffles, or you can just order pizza. **Del Bargello**, Via dei Consoli 37, at Largo Bargello, © (075) 9273724, is another ristorante-pizzeria, offering good choices with polenta (quite popular in this corner of Umbria), *agnolotti*, *agnello scottadito* (burn-your-fingers lamb) and other grilled meats. (*Closed Sun.*)

# Città di Castello

**Il Bersaglio**, Via E. Orlando 14, © 8555534 (moderate), just outside the city walls of Città di Castello, offers a wealth of pasta dishes, well-prepared meat and game and especially good truffles and wild mushrooms, many of them gathered by the restaurant owner himself, Luigi Manfroni. Tucked down one of the town centre's small alleyways, **Amici Miei**, Via del Monte 2, © 8559904 (moderate), is a welcoming trattoria serving good honest Umbrian food with typical pasta dishes and a tempting array of home-made desserts. (*Closed Wed.*)

For anyone with a car, a 10km drive from Città di Castello east along the SS257 (the Adriatica) road to the village of Fraccano will take you to a small trattoria of the kind fast disappearing in Italy. You choose from a limited but excellent menu of the day—usually a good pasta dish followed by meat grilled in front of you—and have a pleasant surprise when it comes to the bill. **SS Adriatica**, loc. Fraccano, ✆ 8553870.

## Via Flaminia: Gualdo Tadino to Spoleto

Whether you're travelling by car, bus or train, the eastern Umbrian towns along the ancient Via Flaminia (SS3) offer both lovely scenery and interesting monuments, including some unexpected artistic treasures. Admittedly most people don't know about Foligno's cosmic billiard table, but many have heard of Spoleto's renowned **Festival of the Two Worlds**, the concept of which has given birth to a twin Spoleto festival in Charleston, North Carolina. Spoleto is also one of Umbria's loveliest hill towns, while Nocera Umbra, Trevi, Montefalco and Clitunno are small but worthy destinations in between.

### Getting Around

The Rome-Ancona **railway** follows the Via Flaminia up from Spoleto all the way up to Gualdo Tadino, before veering east towards Jesi and Ancona. There are also **buses** from Perugia, Città di Castello and Gubbio to Gualdo. The Via Flaminia itself continues further north, towards Urbino and Fano. During the Due Mondi festival, there are special trains and buses between Rome and Spoleto to accommodate the crowds of festival-goers from the capital.

The main SS3 **road**, the Via Flaminia, links all the main towns. For Bevagna and Montefalco, take the SS316 from Foligno.

### Tourist Information

There are tourist offices in the area at **Foligno**, Porta Romana, ✆ (0742) 354459, and Piazza Garibaldi 12, ✆ (0742) 350439, ✉ 340545; **Montefalco**, at Corso Mameli 68, in the Palazzo Comunale, ✆ (0742) 79122; and in **Spoleto**, in Piazza della Libertà, ✆ (0743) 220311, ✉ 46241, which has a phone centre attached. The post office in Spoleto is at Piazza della Libertà 12, ✆ (0743) 40231.

## Gualdo Tadino and Nocera Umbra

Gualdo Tadino is a lofty little town where the Byzantine eunuch general Narses defeated the Goths in 552, a battle essential in preserving the Marches for the Eastern Church. It has a handful of good paintings in its **Pinacoteca**, housed in the church of San Francesco; some are by 15th-century native Matteo da Gualdo.

From Gualdo the road descends the Valle del Topino ('Mousey') to **Nocera Umbra**, the region's most important spa and bottler of mineral water, a pretty, green little place, the Roman *Nuceria Camellaria*. Another former church of San Francesco houses the local painting collection, with works mainly by Umbrian painters, especially an excellent *Nativity* by L'Alunno, the master of Foligno.

# Foligno

Foligno is an ancient and important town, the Roman *Fulginia*, and it was one of the earliest printing centres in Italy, producing its first book in 1470. Unfortunately much of the town was bombed to smithereens in the war, although some of the old quarter has survived, especially the central Piazza della Repubblica.

The 14th-century Palazzo dei Signori, the Trinci, is now used as a **Pinacoteca** (*under restoration at time of writing*); in the chapel, however, you can see more works by Gubbio's Ottaviano Nelli. The nearby **Duomo** has retained an impressive south front of 1201, which rates as one of the most unorthodox in Italy. Among the zodiac and monsters is a portrait of Emperor Frederick II, arch enemy of the popes, and even a little Islamic star and crescent. The oldest thing in Foligno is the Romanesque **Santa Maria Infraportas**, with 12th-century frescoes in the Byzantine style.

More interesting than Foligno itself are the sites that surround it, all linked to the city by bus, with the exception of the 13th-century **Abbazia di Sassovivo** (*open 9am–sunset daily*), with its magnificent and serene cloister, an hour's walk to the east. To the southwest lie three charming hill towns: **Bevagna**, with two Romanesque churches; tiny medieval **Gualdo Cattaneo**, and the old town of **Montefalco**, called the 'Balcony Rail (*Ringhiera*) of Umbria' because of its lofty, commanding position.

The pride of Montefalco is its rich 15th-century fresco cycle on the *Life of St Francis* by the great Sienese Benozzo Gozzoli, painted in the apse of the church-museum of **San Francesco** (*open 10–1, 3–6, Tues–Sun; adm*); other works include good frescoes by Umbrian and other artists. Above the church, the attractive, round **Piazza della Repubblica** affords excellent views of the countryside from the tower of the Palazzo Comunale. Most of Montefalco's other churches contain good frescoes as well, especially **Sant'Agostino**, near the frescoed main gate the **Porta Sant'Agostino**, and **San Fortunato**, beyond the Porta Spoleto, which boasts a few Gozzolis of its own.

**Trevi**, just on the eastern side of the main road, is another charming hill town, wrapped in olive groves that produce Umbria's rich green oil (buses link the train station with the town up above). Its name, like that of the famous fountain in Rome, derived from *Tre Via*, or Three Roads. Its tight, narrow streets contain some good medieval buildings and the 15th-century church of **Madonna delle Lacrime**, sheltering a good *Adoration of the Magi* by a sceptical 76-year-old Perugino, and other Umbrian frescoes. One of them is by Lo Spagna, who is also on exhibit in Trevi's little *pinacoteca* in the medieval **Municipio** (*closed for restoration at time of writing*).

Further south, just off the Via Flaminia, the **Fonti di Clitunno**, ancient *Clitumnus*, is famous for its snow-cold clear spring and pool. Romans were fond of building villas on the surrounding hillside, and bred pure white oxen on its dark green banks; they built a temple here to the river god over a now-dry second spring. In the 4th or 5th century the temple was converted into a church, the delightful **Tempietto di Clitunno** (1km further), with simple frescoes from the 7th century (*open 9–12, 4–7, Tues–Sun; ring the bell*). From here buses continue to Spoleto.

# Spoleto

Set among thickly wooded hills, ancient Spoleto is one of the most attractive towns in Italy, one that provides, in its numerous well-preserved monuments, a nearly complete history of the peninsula. At night, when its chief landmarks are illuminated and the city lights twinkle, it becomes a magical place, a fit setting for the dynamic **Festival dei Due Mondi** (Festival of Two Worlds), founded by composer Giancarlo Menotti and the late Thomas Schippers in 1958, and now Italy's most important performing arts festival. The annual influx of international culture has left a noticeable mark on this once drowsy hill town: monuments have been restored, art galleries and trendy crafts shops line the medieval streets, and prices, during the three weeks of the festival (some time between mid-June and mid-July) get knocked way out of line. The ancient Umbrian *Spoletium* was settled by the Romans in 242 BC, a few decades before an over-confident Hannibal came knocking at the gates, expecting an easy victory after his rout over the legions at Lake Trasimeno. But Spoletium held firm and repulsed him, and Hannibal, who intended to move on to Rome from there, took his elephants to graze in the Marches instead. The Goths under Totila wrecked the city, while the Lombards, slowly piecing it back together, made it a powerful duchy, so powerful that in 890 Duke Guido III made an armed play for the imperial crown against the heirs of Charlemagne; later the duchy became a fief of Countess Matilda of Tuscany, the Guelphiest of Guelphs, and then in the 13th century it was incorporated into the Papal States. In 1499 was briefly ruled by Lucrezia Borgia, a 19-year-old recently married to the second of her three husbands by her intriguing father. By all accounts, Lucrezia ruled well, but was sent off two years later to marry Alfonso d'Este of Ferrara.

If you arrive in Spoleto by train, you are greeted, not by an Umbrian hill town, but by a huge iron sculpture by Alexander Calder, a relic of the 1962 festival now used to shade a taxi stand. Buses every 10 minutes link the station to the central **Piazza della Libertà**, with the tourist office and the nearby **Roman theatre**, some 122m in diameter, built in the 1st century AD and recently restored for festival performances. The stage structure was removed in the Middle Ages, and replaced by the pleasant Convent of Sant'Agata.

More Roman memories are nearby, beyond the Piazza Fontana: the **Arco di Druso**, built in the year AD 23 to celebrate a victory over the barbarians. This once marked the entrance to the Roman forum, now the Piazza del Mercato, but before arriving, take the steps down to the 12th-century **Crypt of San Isacco**, with curiously primitive frescoes. The church above, **Sant'Ansano**, was built into a Roman temple, remains of which may be seen near the altar. In Piazza del Mercato the landmark is an 18th-century fountain by Carlo Fiaschetti.

The next square, the pretty Piazza Municipio, contains a **Roman house** believed to have once been the address of Emperor Vespasian's mother, with an atrium, bedrooms, and baths, some with surviving mosaics. The house can be visited together with the **Pinacoteca Comunale**, in the nearby Palazzo Comunale (*open 10–1, 3–6, Tues–Sun; adm*), with works by native son Giovanni di Pietro (known as Lo Spagna), L'Alunno and other Umbriani.

## The Rocca and Ponte delle Torri

From the Piazza del Municipio, Via Saffi climbs up to the Piazza Campello, with a 17th-century fountain called the **Mascherone** after its grotesque face. Above this looms the

**Rocca**, the impressive, six-towered castle built by Gattapone for the 14th-century papal legate, Cardinal Albornoz. It is built of third-hand stone, first used in the Roman amphitheatre and later cannibalized by the Goth Totila for his fortress. The Rocca was a popular papal country resort, frequented by Julius II, accompanied on occasion by Michelangelo, who loved the peace of the surrounding hills. Until 1983 it was used as a prison, but is currently closed for restoration as the new home for Spoleto's Pinacoteca. For now, the best thing to do is stroll along the garden walk that encircles the Rocca, with great views of Spoleto below.

The **Porta della Rocca** leads down to Master Gattapone's unique masterpiece, and one of the greatest engineering works of the trecento, the **Ponte delle Torri**, a bridge and aqueduct of 10 towering arches linking Spoleto with the slopes of Monteluco, spanning an 80m-deep ravine and the Tessino river far below. Gattapone built the bridge on a Roman foundation; it leads to the towers that gave it its name, and to the road for San Pietro and San Francesco (*see* below).

## Sant'Eufemia and the Duomo

Below the Rocca on Via Saffi stands the pure and lovely 12th-century church of **Sant'Eufemia** (*open April–Oct 8am–8pm; Nov–Mar 8–6*), with a dignified façade and beautiful blond Romanesque interior of ancient capitals and columns, a *matroneum* (women's gallery), and picturesque vaults. Sant'Eufemia is next to the dramatic **Via dell'Arringo**, a grand, shallow stairway descending to the **Piazza del Duomo**. One can't help thinking that it was this stairway that sold Menotti on Spoleto when he travelled about Italy, seeking a venue for the Two Worlds Festival; it doubles perfectly as an outdoor auditorium for the concerts held in the piazza below, with the cathedral and Umbrian hills as a backdrop. Thomas Schippers, co-founder of the festival, was so fond of the concerts and piazza that he asked to be buried in the square when he died, in 1977.

The elegant **Duomo** was consecrated in 1198 by the most powerful of medieval popes, Innocent III, and rebuilt after Emperor Frederick Barbarossa, the greatest of papal enemies, had razed its predecessor. It has several unusual features: eight rose windows of varying sizes, like buttons, adorn its horizontally divided façade, surrounding a gold-ground Byzantine-style mosaic of 1207. Its campanile is built out of Roman odds and ends, and very un-Italian flying buttresses help to hold it up. Although the interior was unfortunately redone in the 17th century, it contains several treasures, most piously the *Santissimo Icone*, with a picture of the Madonna, believed to have been brought to Spoleto from Constantinople. Pinturicchio painted the frescoes in the first chapel, the **Eroli**, and in the apse there are the richly coloured frescoes on the *Life of the Virgin* by Fra Filippo Lippi, who portrayed himself and his assistant among the mourners in the scene of the Virgin's death. The fun-loving monk from Florence died in Spoleto while working on the project, and it was finished by his chief helper, Fra Diamanti; when Lorenzo de' Medici asked that Lippi's body be returned to Florence, the Spoletini refused, and Lorenzo had to be content with ordering a fine Florentine tomb for him, now in the right transept.

Sharing the square with the cathedral is Spoleto's **Museo Civico** (*open 9.30–12.30, 3–6, Mon, Wed–Sun; closed Tues; adm*), housed in a Renaissance palace, with an interesting collection of sculpture extending up to the 14th century, as well as the **Teatro Caio Melisso**, also used for festival events.

## Lower Spoleto

On the opposite side of town (Via del Duomo to Via Filitteria) there's another grand theatre, the **Teatro Nuovo**, used both for the festival and for the even older September Festival of Experimental Opera. Nearby, the colourful church of **San Domenico** was built in the 13th century, and contains some interesting if fragmentary 13th–15th-century frescoes. From San Domenico walk down to the tall-towered 13th-century **Porta Fuga**, and then along Via Cecili, where you can take in an excellent stretch of Spoleto's **walls**, an intriguing record of the town's history, beginning at their 6th-century BC 'Cyclopean' base of huge polygonal rough blocks built by the ancient Umbrii, and going all the way up to the 15th-century additions on the top. The street ends at Piazza Cairoli; from here Via dell'Anfiteatro descends past the ruined **amphitheatre**, now part of a military barracks, to Piazza Garibaldi, with the fine 12th-century church of **San Gregorio** and the Roman **Ponte Sanguinario** ('bloody bridge'), so called because of all the Christians who were martyred here.

From the bridge, signs point the way to the cemetery church of **San Salvatore**, a 15-minute walk away. San Salvatore is Spoleto's most ancient church, built in the 4th century. It has an unusual façade, and preserves much of its original vertical lines and simplicity despite subsequent rebuildings. The elegant, fluted Corinthian columns in the interior were incorporated from a Roman temple.

## Monteluco

Beautiful, forested Monteluco is Spoleto's holy mountain, lying just to the east of town, connected by bus from the Piazza della Libertà, or by walking from the Ponte delle Torri. If you're walking, take the right-hand fork in the road for the great Romanesque church of **San Pietro**, only a few minutes away, with a romp of a façade dating back to the days of the dukes of Spoleto; if you've visited the medieval cathedrals of the north, you'll recognize the vigorous animals, real and imaginary, that the Lombards delighted in portraying: here is a fox playing dead to capture some too-curious chickens, battles with lions, oxen, eagles, a wolf in monk's clothing, and the rest, along with a relief of St Michael slaying the dragon.

The other (left) fork in the road demands some vigorous walking through beautiful holm oak forests to reach the 12th-century church of **San Giuliano**, with a façade incorporating some 6th-century elements of its predecessor. In the 7th century anchorites and hermits, refugees from the wars in the Holy Land, settled here and set up early monasteries; in the 13th century St Francis and San Bernardino of Siena came to meditate here, at the tiny monastery of **San Francesco** near the summit of Monteluco, a serene spot enjoying a lovely view of the surrounding countryside. Monteluco now has more summer villas and hotels than hermitages, but it's still a cool and tranquil place to spend an afternoon, and a good place to look for accommodation when Spoleto itself is jammed solid.

### *Where to Stay*

During the Festival of the Two Worlds accommodation is tight in Spoleto and in the surrounding area from Foligno to Terni, so reserve months in advance. The tourist office in Spoleto has a list of private rooms to rent, but again, don't count on finding one on the spot: plan ahead.

## Foligno

***Villa Roncalli**, Via Roma 25, ℰ (0742) 670291 (moderate) is a fashionable, central villa-hotel in a shady garden, with garage, and comfortable rooms. Other safe bets are the ***Villa Fiorita**, Via del Lago 9, loc. Colfiorito, ℰ (0742) 681125, ✆ 681579 (moderate), some kilometres to the east of the town along the SS77 road, but with the advantage of a pool, or alternatively the centrally placed ****Umbria**, Via C. Battisti 1, ℰ/✆ (0742) 352821 (moderate), with 48 good-sized clean rooms.

To the east of Foligno the *Lieta Sosta**, Via Adriatica 228/a, loc. Colfiorito, ℰ/✆ (0742) 681321 (inexpensive), up in the hills near the Villa Fiorita (*see* above) has 7 clean rooms, all with bath, a fine restaurant, and even an outdoor pool. Foligno is also the site of the region's modest youth hostel, the **Ostello Fulginium**, Piazza San Giacomo 11, ℰ (0742) 352882 (inexpensive). To get there, take bus no.1 from the train station. (*Open Mar–Sept only.*)

## Montefalco

****Villa Pambuffetti**, Via della Vittoria 20, ℰ (0742) 79417, ✆ 79245 (expensive) is a delightful 19th-century villa owned by a local noble family who now run it as a beautifully kept inn, with 15 rooms, all decorated differently, some with family antiques. The villa is set in a lovely park with an outdoor pool. A cheap but comfortable choice is the **Ringhiera Umbra**, Via G. Mameli, ℰ (0742) 378413, ✆ 79166 (inexpensive), a pretty *pensione* that has been recently refurbished. Some rooms have baths, and there is a good restaurant.

## Trevi

**Del Pescatore**, Via Chiesa Tonda 50, ℰ/✆ (0742) 78483 (inexpensive) is a good *pensione*, with nine pleasant rooms all with baths, and a good restaurant attached (*see* below).

## Clitunno

Besides its own virtues, Clitunno is a quiet alternative to Spoleto if you've come for the festival. **Le Fontanelle**, Via d'Elci 1, ℰ (0742) 521091 (moderate) is a lovely hotel and restaurant surrounded by refreshing greenery. Rooms are comfortable, and all equipped with baths; the restaurant serves Umbrian specialities like country prosciutto, *strangozzi* (home-made pasta) and platters of tender lamb, chicken, pigeon, and game. At the Fonti di Clitunno, **Ravale**, Via Virgilio, ℰ (0742) 521320 (moderate) has simple rooms, all with baths, as well as a modestly priced ristorante-pizzeria.

## Spoleto

Spoleto itself has several fine hotels, of which the most spectacular is the tiny ****Gattapone**, Via del Ponte 6, ℰ (0743) 223447, ✆ 223448 (expensive), located in a stone house clinging to the slope near the Rocca and the Ponte delle Torri, with fabulous views; even during the festival rush it remains serene. Its eight rooms are spacious and finely furnished; another house next door contains the restaurant. Another very comfortable choice, ★★★★**Dei Duchi**, Viale Matteotti 4, ✆ (0743) 44541, ✉ 44543 (expensive), is centrally located near the Piazza della Libertà, yet enjoys fine views over Spoleto. Popular among visiting artists and performers, it is a well-designed contemporary hotel. The ★★★**Nuovo Clitunno**, Piazza Sordini 6, ✆ (0743) 223340, ✉ 222663 (moderate), is a good, fairly central hotel, all rooms with baths. The ★★★**Charleston**, Piazza Collicola 10, ✆ (0743) 220052, ✉ 222010 (moderate), is in a pretty 17th-century palazzo, with 18 comfortably furnished rooms in the *centro storico*. Run by the same family, the ★★★**Clarici** Piazza della Vittoria 32, ✆ (0743) 223311, ✉ 222010 (moderate) is more modern, in the lower part of town, but still decorated with taste and style. ★★**Dell'Angelo**, Via Arco di Druso 25, ✆ (0743) 222385 (inexpensive) offers seven good double rooms near the centre of the action.

About 12km south of Spoleto on the SS3 road towards Terni is the **Pecoraro**, frazione Strettura, ✆ (0743) 54431 (inexpensive), a very pretty and above all welcoming *pensione* where guests are treated like members of the family by owners Sandro and Illy Montefalchesi. There is also a small outdoor pool, a luxury in these parts, and very good home-cooking and home-made grappas make this a memorable place to stay or eat.

### Monteluco

Outside Spoleto in more tranquil Monteluco, the ★★★**Parco Ipost**, ✆ (0743) 223441, ✉ 223443 (moderate) is a pleasant resort hotel, with a garden, tennis courts, pool, great views and peace and quiet. The ★★**Ferretti** , Loc. Monteluco 20, ✆ (0743) 49849, ✉ 222344 (inexpensive) is a *pensione* with plenty of charm, and some rooms with balconies looking out on to the pretty tree-shaded piazza.

---

### Eating Out

Montefalco is perhaps best known for a couple of red wines, Sagrantino and Rosso di Montefalco. Sagrantino is quite special, with a delicate aroma of blackberries; both are sold in many shops around town.

### Foligno

Foligno's **Da Remo**, Viale C. Battisti 11, ✆ (0742) 340679 (moderate) serves a tasty *strangozzi* (fat, homemade spaghetti) and roast kid cooked in Sagrantino wine. (*Closed Sun evenings, Mon.*) While up in the mountains to the east at Colfiorito, the **Lieta Sosta** hotel (*see* above for details; moderate) offers fine country dining Umbrian style, with grilled lamb and *strangozzi* with truffles.

### Bevagna

Bevagna offers an attractive lunch stop: **Da Nina**, Piazza Garibaldi, ✆ (0742) 360 161 (moderate), has truffles, and good pasta dishes with porcini mushrooms—fancy dining for these parts. (*Closed Tues.*) Mario Siena is the smiling host at **El Rancho**, Via Flaminia 53, ✆ (0742) 360105 (inexpensive), serving a tempting array of local dishes and products at down-to-earth prices. (*Closed Mon.*)

## Montefalco

**Coccorone**, Vicolo Fabbri, ℂ (0742) 79535 (moderate), off the central square, is an elegant, quiet and understated place with tempting crêpes and *tagliatelle al tartufo* for *primo* and dishes like *faraona ai salmi* (braised guinea-fowl) and grilled pigeon for seconds. (*Closed Wed.*) For a similar price, **Il Falisco**, Via XX Settembre, ℂ (0742) 79185 (moderate), offers well-cooked local specialities such as *filetto al sagrantino* (beef fillet cooked in Sagrantino wine). (*Closed Mon.*)

## Trevi

In Trevi, the **Taverna del Pescatore**, ℂ (0742) 780920 (moderate), beneath the Del Pescatore hotel and run by another branch of the same family, is an excellent restaurant with an interesting range of menu choices based on meat or fish, both very good value and beautifully prepared. (*Closed Wed.*) **La Cerquetta**, Via Flaminia km 144, loc. Parrano, ℂ (0742) 78366 (inexpensive), also turns out reliable Umbrian food for very honest prices. (*Closed Sun.*)

## Clitunno

In Poreta di Spoleto, 3km from Campello sul Clitunno, **Casaline**, ℂ (0742) 521113, ℂ 275099 (moderate) is a good, old-fashioned Umbrian inn in the country, specializing in game and truffle dishes in season, wild asparagus in the spring, and delicious pasta all year round. (*Closed Mon.*)

## Spoleto

In one of Spoleto's main squares, good Umbrian truffle dishes are the speciality at **Il Tartufo**, Piazza Garibaldi 24, ℂ (0743) 40236 (expensive), utilizing the black truffles of the Valnerina in various combinations of pasta and eggs; other dishes include grilled lamb and kid, and veal. Prices depend on whether or not you indulge in the tasty tuber. (*Closed Wed.*) Outside Spoleto, on the SS3 to Terni, the **Madrigale**, ℂ (0743) 54144 (expensive) offers a gourmet *menu degustazione* of Umbrian specialities; just sit down and a tasty array of pasta and meat courses will arrive at your table. (*Closed Tues.*)

Spoleto is, as one would expect, well supplied with restaurants. **Sabatini**, Corso Mazzini 54, ℂ (0743) 221831 (moderate) has good traditional Umbrian fare, served indoors and out. (*Closed Mon.*) At **Il Panciolle**, Via Duomo 3, ℂ (0743) 45598 (moderate), diners feast on truffles and meat grilled over the open fire. There are also seven nicely decorated rooms for rent, all with bath. (*Closed Wed.*) In the heart of Spoleto, the **Trattoria del Festival**, Via Brignone 8, ℂ (0743) 220993 (moderate) has a pretty dining room with arched ceilings, and a blazing fireplace in winter. As well as truffle dishes of every kind, the chef has a winning way with desserts. Regulars are given a membership card which guarantees them a 10 per cent discount off the already very reasonable prices. (*Closed Fri.*)

For a good glass of wine and tasty snacks and spaghetti in Spoleto, try **La Cantina**, Via Filitteria 10/a, ℂ (0743) 44475 (moderate; *closed Mon.*)

### Monteluco

Up on Monteluco, near the church of San Giuliano, **Trattoria S. Giuliano**, © (0743) 47797 (moderate) is a lovely place overlooking Spoleto, with seasonal Umbrian dishes like *bruschetto*, *strangozzi*, asparagus omelettes, mushrooms, and game dishes. (*Closed Wed.*)

---

## Entertainment and Nightlife

The Two Worlds Festival is the one great event on Spoleto's calendar, and dominates the life of the town in June and July. Major international music, dance and theatre companies, ensembles and performers are featured, alongside many lesser-known names, and the festival has had a high reputation for launching new talent. It is also a major social event, particularly for Romans, and the audiences for the major performances are correspondingly sharply dressed, and prices very high. In the last few years, though, in response to criticism that the festival had become too top-heavy, the programme has sought to give greater prominence to more avant-garde work, and there are plenty of fringe shows alongside the official programme. For information and tickets to festival events, write well in advance to the **Associazione Festival dei Due Mondi**, Teatro Olimpico, Piazza Gentile da Fabbriano 15, Rome, © (06) 393304/3962635. In Spoleto, information, programmes and tickets can be obtained by writing, phoning or visiting the festival headquarters, **Associazione Festival dei Due Mondi**, Piazza Del Duomo 9, © (0743) 40396.

## The Valnerina

The River Nera, one of the main tributaries of the Tiber, flows from the slopes of the mighty Monti Sibillini of the Marches along the southern edge of Umbria. Many of its sights are still Italian secrets; its black truffles, waterfalls and saints enjoy a national reputation, but the rest is touristically *terra incognita*.

---

## Getting Around

Terni and Narni are the only towns in this area served by **rail**. Both are on the Rome–Ancona line, and from Terni there are also trains to Rieti and L'Aquila in Abruzzo. From Spoleto's Piazza della Repubblica **buses** depart frequently for Cascia and Norcia; others go to Scheggino, where you can catch a Terni provincial bus down the rest of the valley to Terni, Narni, or Orvieto.

For **drivers** the SS209 from Terni to Visso is the main thoroughfare through the Valnerina; for Norcia and Cascia, turn off at either Sant'Anatolia di Narco (the slowest route) or Triponzo. From Norcia a new highway is under construction to Ascoli Piceno, but for spectacular, almost alpine scenery, the old road through the Forca Canapine can't be beaten; a branch leads off through the lovely Piano Grande to Castelluccio.

South of Terni the SS3, the Via Flaminia, is the main road to Narni, from where the SS205 leads to Amelia.

---

### Tourist Information

There are several local tourist offices in the valley, in **Norcia**, at Piazza San Benedetto, ✆ (0743) 816701; **Cascia**, Via G. da Chiavano 2, ✆ (0743) 71401, ✆ 76630; in **Terni**, at Viale C. Battisti 7/a, ✆ (0744) 43047, ✆ 427259; and in **Amelia**, at Via Orvieto 1, ✆ (0744) 981453, ✆ 981566.

---

## Norcia

Little Norcia gave the world St Benedict (480–543), the father of monasticism, and his twin sister St Scholastica. It has also been known at times for witches, surgeons (who, it was claimed in the 16th century, were the only ones capable of properly castrating a boy with operatic potential), cheeses and bristling boar hams. An ancient place, mentioned by Virgil, it looks more Spanish than Italian, and although earthquakes have slapped it around, Norcia retains several of its historic monuments, most of them in the central Piazza San Benedetto. It has a stern statue of St Benedict for a centrepiece, the 14th-century church of **San Benedetto**, built over the late Roman house where the famous twins were born, and the handsome **Palazzo Comunale**, with a 13th-century campanile and door, next to the gastronomic speciality shops. The other side of the square is occupied by the **castle**, designed in 1554 by Vignola for Pope Julius III, now housing a modest museum of Umbrian art.

Above Norcia lies the beautiful **Piano Grande**, an unusual flat meadow measuring 16 square kilometres and surrounded by rolling hills and mountains that seem covered with huge swathes of coloured velvet in May and June. It is a rarefied landscape (used by Franco Zeffirelli in his 'Franciscan film' *Brother Sun, Sister Moon*) where herds graze and fields produce the famous minute lentils of **Castelluccio**, the old village in an upper corner of the plain. Castelluccio had 700 inhabitants in 1951, and now has around 40; winter conditions are so bad that the village is often cut off. From the summit of Monte Vettore (2476m), the tallest peak in the area, you can see both the Adriatic and Tyrrhenian seas on clear days. In the winter there's skiing at Forca Canapine, on the south side of Piano Grande.

**Cascia**, in the Corno valley south of Norcia, has an even more popular pilgrimage destination, the shrine of Santa Rita, the 'Saint of Impossibilities', who was born near here in 1381, and suffered a rotten husband (hence all the tired Italian housewives you see) and a smelly wound in the middle of her forehead, but had to wait until the Fascist era to get a sanctuary.

---

## Down the Valnerina: Crayfish and Mummies

Back in the main valley on the SS209, **Scheggino** is a small but pretty town on the river Nera, laced with tiny canals full of trout and a rare species of crayfish (*gamberettini*) imported from Turkey. It is also the fief of Italy's truffle tycoons, the Urbani family. Further down the valley a sign indicates the turn-off for the **Abbey of San Pietro in Valle** (*open 10.30–1, 2.30–5, daily*), founded in the 8th century by Faroaldo II, Duke of Spoleto. Set far up above the road, with views across the valley to an abandoned citadel, the church has a lovely 12th-century campanile embedded with Roman bits, and a two-storey cloister, with a

Roman sacrificial altar in the centre. Inside, the nave is covered with frescoes of Old and New Testament scenes from 1190, an unusual example of the Italian response to the Byzantine style. The altar is a rare example of Lombard work, sculpted on both the front and back; one of their early saints is interred to the right in a lovely 3rd-century Roman sarcophagus. On either side of the altar are good 13th-century frescoes by the school of Giotto, with a pretty Madonna. In the back there's a cylindrical Etruscan altar, now used for monetary rather than animal offerings. Among the stone fragments arranged on the wall there's a real rarity—a bas-relief of a monk with oriental features, believed to depict one of two Syrian monks who set up a hermitage here in the 7th century.

The abbey is in the *comune* of **Ferentillo**, defended by two 14th-century fortresses that rise up like matching bookends. In **Precetto**, the oldest section of town, the crypt of **Santo Stefano** (*open 10–12.30, 2.30–5, daily; knock on door marked* custode *opposite church*) contains something most people don't expect to find in Umbria: **mummies**. Accidentally preserved by the soil and ventilation, you can see the poor mummified Chinese newlyweds who came here in the last century for a honeymoon and got cholera instead, two gruesome French prisoners who were hanged in the Napoleonic era, and a grinning pyramid of skulls; a desiccated vulture mummy points the way inside with its wing. Sad to relate, the mummies have recently been imprisoned in glass display cases, ruining much of their charm.

Picturesque **Arrone**, spilling over its rock, was once run by feudal lordlings, the bitter enemies of the abbots of Ferentillo. Their tower, sprouting a tree, is the local landmark. From Arrone, the road leads up to Piediluco and **Polino**, also endowed with a feudal tower and a monumental fountain; above Polino the Colle Bertone affords panoramic picnicking sites.

## Cascate delle Marmore and Lake Piediluco

Between Arrone and Terni the road passes below another pretty hill townlet, **Torreorsini**, before reaching the 126m-high, green and misty **Cascata delle Marmore**, one of Europe's tallest and most photographed waterfalls—when it's running. Surprisingly, the Cascata is an artificial creation; in 271 BC Curius Dentatus, best known as the conqueror of the Sabines, first dug the channel to drain the marshlands of Rieti, diverting the river Velino into the Nera. Although the falls are usually swallowed up by hydroelectric turbines, the thundering waters are let down on the following schedule (after dark they are brilliantly illuminated)— from *Nov–15 Mar, 3–4pm, Sun and holidays; from 16 March–April and Sept–Oct, 6–9pm Sat, 10am–12 noon, 3–9pm Sun; May–15 July, 5–10pm Sat, 10am–1pm, 3–11pm Sun; 15 July–31 Aug, 5–6.30pm Mon–Fri; 5–10pm Sat, 10am–1pm, 3–11pm Sun.*

There are two places from which to view the falls—from down below on the SS209, or from the belvedere on top, in the village of Marmore. A path through the woods connects the two, though it's steep, prone to be muddy in the off season, and much nicer to walk down than up (the path at the bottom begins 100m downstream from the falls). There are some pleasant places to swim near the bottom, but you can't use them when the falls are on. A siren goes off 15 minutes before the falls are turned on to warn swimmers not to linger. Both places are easily reached by bus from Terni, 6km away.

Above Marmore, the lake of Piediluco zigzags in and out of the wooded hills, one of which is crowned by a 14th-century fortress. There are a couple of beaches, but unfortunately the lake is better to look at than swim in—the water is cold and dangerous. Perched high above the east shore of the lake is the pale old village of **Labro**, former nest of noblemen on the run, now almost completely taken over by Belgians, who have bought up and restored most of the houses. Just below the lake, the Arrone road passes by **Villalago** which has an outdoor theatre used during the Umbria Jazz Festival and other summertime events, and lovely gardens for picnicking.

# Terni

By some quirk of fate, the first bishop and patron saint of Terni, San Valentino, became the special patron of lovers and the greeting card industry. Curiously, the stodgy Terni-ites themselves have only recently picked up on the notoriety of their old bishop, and at the St Valentine's Market you may even see a pink heart or two as you go to pay your respects to his headless body in the basilica (some lovesick sinner stole his head in 1986 which was found, three years later, wrapped in newspaper under a park bench at the Cascate delle Marmore). Terni has little else to offer, besides trains and buses to other places, and shots of viper juice (or *Viparo*, the local *aperitivo* that has all the qualities of flat rum and Coke); as one of Italy's chief steel and armaments manufacturers—the gun that shot Kennedy was made in Terni—the city was condensed into rubble by air raids during the Second World War. It was during the original building of the steelworks that bulldozers uncovered one of the largest and richest Etruscan necropoli, although all the finds have been carted off to Rome's Villa Giulia museum. The ancient Romans called it *Interamna Nahars*—a real mouthful that was traditionally considered the birthplace of the historian Tacitus, although scholars now quibble that Terni actually produced a more meagre Tacitus, Claudius Tacitus, emperor for a day. Of Roman Terni only part of the **amphitheatre** remains, now employed as a pensioners' *bocce* court in the city's prettiest area, off the main Corso del Popolo. Visible from the Corso and Piazza Europa, the tiny round church of **San Salvatore**, locally known as the Sun Temple, was built in the 5th century, with a nave added in the 12th. Nearby stands the **Palazzo Spada** (1546) by Antonio da Sangallo the Younger, the best of Terni's surviving palaces. Across Via Garibaldi from the Manassei is the Palazzo Manassei, which houses the **Pinacoteca Comunale** (*open 10–1, 4–7, Tues–Sun; adm*), with Umbrian paintings, a *Marriage of St Catherine* by Gozzoli and, best of all, a large collection of works by Terni's own Orneore Metelli (1872–1938), a shoemaker and great naïve artist.

There are a couple of other churches worthy of note: the Knights of Malta's 12th-century church of **Sant'Alò**, off Via Cavour, and the 13th-century **San Francesco**, on the other side of Via Cavour. Its landmark 14th-century bell tower is by Angelo da Orvieto, and inside, to the right of the altar, is a 15th-century fresco based on the *Divine Comedy*.

**San Gemini**, 13km north of Terni, is known for its mineral springs, located in a pretty park of old oaks. Four kilometres further on lie the evocative ruins of the Roman city of **Carsulae**, destroyed by the Goths and never rebuilt. Lying unfenced out in the open, Carsulae is made lovely by its pretty environs: here you can see a section of the original Via Flaminia, and the ruins of a theatre, amphitheatre, a mausoleum, temples, and an arch dedicated to Trajan. Further north, **Acquasparta**, within its medieval walls, has more locally famous curative waters, and a small zoo; in the summer it hosts a German *lieder*-singing contest.

## Narni

Narni, on a cliff over the Nera, is a picturesque hill town, tumbling in a jumble under its well-preserved castle, built in the 14th century by the ubiquitous Cardinal Albornoz. It was a Roman colony, and birthplace of Emperor Nerva, who lasted somewhat longer than Terni's emperor. Narni has several gems—in its **Duomo**, founded in the 12th century but remodelled several times since, there's a lovely early medieval screen of marble and Cosmati work. In the attractive 13th-century **Palazzo del Podestà** (*open 8am–2pm Mon–Sat*) hang a Ghirlandaio, a Gozzoli, and a collection of other paintings; with the nearby **Loggia dei Priori** by Gattapone, it forms a fine setting for Narni's springtime medieval pageant, the *Corso dell'Anello*, the Tournament of the Ring, in which the various quarters of the town compete in a festival traditionally held on the second Sunday in May, one of the most spectacular and evocative festas in Umbria.

Narni has several other interesting churches, the pretty 12th-century **Santa Maria in Pensole**, the 14th-century **San Francesco** built over one of St Francis' huts, and the 15th-century **Sant'Agostino** on the other side of town. Down by the river and Narni's railway station are the romantic ruins of the **Ponte d'Augusto**, the 1st-century bridge that carried the Via Flaminia over the Nera.

## Amelia

North of Narni, halfway between the Nera and the Tiber, lies the ancient agricultural town of Amelia. Both Cato and Pliny wrote that *Ameria* was centuries older than Rome, and as towering evidence of the fact stand its ancient **Pelasgian-Umbrian Walls**, dating back to the 5th century BC, built of massive polygonal blocks, 3m thick and 7m high. The **Duomo**, founded in 1050, with its original campanile, contains two Turkish banners captured at the Battle of Lepanto. There are several places of interest near Amelia and the Tiber. **Lugnano in Teverina** has a 12th-century church, **Santa Maria Assunta**, a Romanesque gem with a curious porch and bas-reliefs, topped by an eagle instead of a cross; inside there's a good triptych by L'Alunno. **Penna in Teverina**, near Orte, is an old fortified town with a castle much disputed by Rome's eternal Punch and Judy factions, the Colonna and Orsini families, until the Colonna simply sold it to the Orsini. Some members of the family liked the area so much that they constructed a **Palazzo Orsini** with a fine 18th-century Italian garden attached. Other relics of that century are the *Mammalocchi*, allegorical figures in travertine standing at the entrance to another estate. A picturesque wine festa is held in this town on the first Sunday of October each year, when wine is miraculously made to pour from the fountains.

### Where to Stay

Terni is dull, but can be a good base for visiting the Valnerina if you're dependent on public transport; it's also a good place to look for lodgings if Spoleto is filled up for the Two Worlds festival.

## Norcia

In Norcia the **★★★Posta**, Via C. Battisti 10, ✆ (0743) 816274, ✉ 817434 (moderate) is a fine hotel and restaurant (*see* below), where the pleasant rooms all have baths. **★★★Grotta Azzurra**, Via Alfieri, ✆ and ✉ (0743) 816513 (moderate) is Norcia's other hotel of any size, and offers equally good rooms with showers, and also a very enjoyable restaurant (*see* below). In Cascia, the top place to stay and eat is the **★★★Cursula**, Via Cavour 3, ✆ (0743) 76206, ✉ 76207 (moderate), with extremely pleasant rooms, all with baths, and good Umbrian specialities in the restaurant.

Up above Norcia in Castelluccio you can spend a rural medieval interlude at the only hotel in town, the **★Sibilla**, ✆ (0743) 870113 (inexpensive), which also boasts the sole restaurant. Its 11 rooms each have private showers. (*Restaurant closed Tues.*)

In Cascia, as its name suggests, the **★★Centrale**, Piazza Garibaldi 36, ✆ (0743) 76736 (inexpensive) is in a handy location, while the **★★Mini Hotel**, Via Palombi, ✆ (0743) 71387 (inexpensive), is a family-run establishment, with eight clean comfortable rooms, all with bath.

## Scheggino

Quiet Scheggino has one hotel, the charming little **★★Del Ponte**, Via Borgo 15, ✆ (075) 61131 (moderate), right on the Nera river, offering 12 rooms with baths, and in the restaurant, delicious meals based on Scheggino's two specialities, crayfish and truffles. For a trip to Umbrian heaven, try the fettuccine with a sauce that combines both ingredients. (*Closed Mon.*)

## Ferentillo

On the SS209 south of Ferentillo, near Montefranco, **★★★Fontegaia**, ✆ (0744) 388621, ✉ 388623 (moderate) is the hotel with most pretensions in the Valnerina; its rooms are very comfortable, there's a playground for children, and beautiful gardens for dining *al fresco*; the restaurant is a favourite for locals going out for a special occasion, if a bit heavy-handed with cream sauces.

## Arrone

Near Arrone on the SS209, **★★Rossi**, ✆ (0744) 788372, ✉ 788305 (inexpensive) has 16 modern rooms, all with bath, and one of the best restaurants in the area (*see* below).

## Terni

Terni's best hotel is in the centre, the **★★★★Valentino**, Via Plinio il Giovane 3, ✆ (0744) 55246, ✉ 55240 (expensive), with very comfortable modern rooms, all air-conditioned (an important consideration here in summer) and furnished with private bath, minibar, and TV. Near the *superstrada* exit, the contemporary **★★★★Garden**, Via Bramante 6, ✆ (0744) 300041, ✉ 300414 (expensive) is Terni's prettiest hotel, with plant-filled balconies and a pool; the comfortable rooms come equipped with private baths, minibars, and TVs.

A short distance from the station, **★★★Hotel de Paris**, Viale Stazione 52, ✆ (0744) 58040, ✉ 58047 (moderate) is nondescript but convenient, and air-conditioned, too. Outside the town up at Lake Piediluco, the posh place to stay is **★★★Casalago**,

℃ (0744) 38421 (moderate), a largish hotel with a garden overlooking the water, but still moderate-range prices. **★Brenta II**, Via Montegrappa 51, ℃ (0744) 283007 (inexpensive), near the Nera and the Corso del Popolo, has nice modern rooms, all with baths, in one of Terni's shady, but anonymous neighbourhoods.

## Narni

Most of the hotels are down by the river and the station, at Narni Scalo. The finest is **★★★★Dei Priori**, Vicolo del Comune 4, ℃ (0744) 726843, ✆ 717259 (moderate), located in a medieval palace in a lane, with very comfortable rooms, and a high-quality restaurant (*see* below). For something on the outskirts, with a touch of the Arabian Nights, try the **★★★Minareto**, Via Cappuccini Nuovi 32, ℃ (0744) 726343, ✆ 726143 (moderate), which has eight pretty rooms near a tiny lake and garden.

## Lugnano in Teverina

In Lugnano in Teverina the best (and only) place to stay and eat is **★★La Rocca**, Via Cavour 60, ℃ (0744) 902129 (inexpensive), a small, pleasant inn in the centre, with parking. All rooms have private baths, and there's good home-style cooking in the restaurant.

---

*Eating Out*

## Norcia

Norcia's **Dal Francese**, Via Riguardati 16, ℃ (0743) 816290 (expensive) is the ideal place for a bumper meal in this corner of Umbria, where the truffle is king. Try the smoked turkey and home-made salami for antipasto, followed by a pasta medley of *tris al tartufo*, *gnocchi al tartufo* or *tortellini con crema di tordi* (thrushes) *e tartufi*; for a main course choose between trout dishes, tender grilled lamb or the unusual *braciola in agrodolce con tartufi* (chop in sweet-and-sour sauce with truffles). There's also a good wine list. (*Closed Fri.*)

After the Dal Francese, the best places to eat in Norcia are the hotels. In the **Posta** (moderate) they serve the famous, hearty, robust local fare of Castelluccio lentils, boar salami, *tortellini alla norcina* (with ricotta and sausage), and lamb with truffles, topped off, if you dare, by a tumbler of Norcia's nasty grappa flavoured with black truffles. The **Grotta Azzurra** (moderate) has a different approach to local culinary traditions in its restaurant: a lighter touch, perhaps, its mandatory truffled dishes competing with a tasty risotto with crayfish from the Nera, or fettuccine with trout, or delicious grilled mushrooms. In Cascia the **Mini Hotel** (moderate) also has a very good restaurant, serving well-cooked local dishes based on wild mushrooms, salame, trout and lamb. (*Closed Tues.*) For details of all three, *see* above.

## Arrone

In the main Valnerina, the small **Rossi** hotel near Arrone (*see* above; moderate) also has one of the best restaurants in the area, with excellent *crostini*, spaghetti with truffles, the usual grilled meats and a wide variety of trout dishes, served in a pretty garden in summer. (*Closed Fri.*) On the small Polino road out of Arrone to the east, keep your eyes peeled for the **Rema**, ℗ (0744) 78292 (inexpensive), a little trattoria with outdoor picnic tables and an outdoor grill, serving the usual Umbrian fare with a flair and prices that cheapskates like; try the *ciriole* (home-made spaghetti) with mushrooms, the grilled lamb, or the *Desirée farcita.* (*Closed Mon.*)

### Terni

The Valentino hotel (*see* above; expensive) also has one of the city's classiest restaurants, the **Fontanello**, with a menu featuring fresh, natural ingredients in tasty and imaginative dishes. The **Tacitus**, Piazza Tacito, ℗ (0744) 425147 (moderate), in the main piazza, offers good local cooking for reasonable prices. (*Closed Mon.*) For more adventurous dining, try the **Gulliver**, Via Sant'Alò 10, ℗ (0744) 425225 (moderate), owned by four young locals, determined to wake Terni out of its stultifying provincialism with dishes as daring as sturgeon stuffed with saffron and courgettes, and spinach with quails' eggs served in a fondue sauce. (*Closed Wed.*)

It's easy to eat cheaply in Terni, where the pizza-by-the-slice and snack competition is fierce. Try the **Old America**, Via P. Braccini 4, ℗ (0744) 59767 (inexpensive), a pizzeria which is less garish than most. (*Closed Mon.*)

### Narni

In Narni, the restaurant of the **Dei Priori** hotel (*see* above), **La Loggia** ℗ (0744) 722744 (moderate) actually predates the hotel, and has long been on the maps of visiting gourmets, featuring an amazing variety of country fare and local specialities, with unusual surprises that nevertheless don't cost a bomb. (*Closed Mon.*)

## Todi and Orvieto

Two of Umbria's best-known hill towns are easily accessible from Rome; Orvieto especially, with its stupendous cathedral and renowned wine, is a popular destination for trippers. Todi is a bit further and a bit more sombre, more mysteriously Umbrian, a good foil to Orvieto. For a memorable dose of beauty and culture, take in both towns and the lovely scenery that separates them, with a stop at Baschi for an amazing meal at one of the jewels in Italy's gastronomic crown.

---

### Getting Around

Todi is linked by **bus** with Terni, Perugia, and Rome, and by the FCU's little choochoo **trains** with Perugia and Terni. Trains arrive at the Stazione Ponte Rio, ℗ (075) 8942092. Orvieto is on the main railway line between Florence and Rome, and is also linked by bus with Terni. In both towns municipal buses make the trip up the hill; in Orvieto, there is also a **funicular** from the station to the top of the town. Unfortunately only one bus a day runs between Todi and Orvieto, passing through the lovely scenery above the Tiber valley.

If you're **driving**, Todi is just off the SS3bis and the E45, and Orvieto an exit on the main A1 *autostrada*. The SS71 is a less hectic route from Orvieto to Lake Bolsena, Viterbo, and Rome. Of the two roads connecting Todi and Orvieto, the SS79bis is the more dramatically scenic, but Baschi and Lake Corbara are along the wider and more southerly SS448.

## Todi

Despite a name that suggests an Italian *Wind in the Willows*, Todi is a serious-minded place, perched atop its high and lonely hill, with more affinity to eagles than amphibians; it was the former who showed the ancient Umbrians where to build the city they called *Tuter*, high atop what is now the Rocca. Later the Etruscans built their city lower down, around the Piazza del Popolo, and according to legend, one day slaughtered many of their Umbrian neighbours and made the rest slaves. In Todi's plump and prosperous Middle Ages the eagle struck again, this time swooping down on Amelia and Terni (symbolized by the two eaglets on Todi's coat of arms); yet at the same time it produced one of Italy's great uncanonized saints, Jacopone dei Benedetti (1228–1306), the master of the *laudesi*, or medieval Franciscan poets, who, like St Francis, sang songs of praise to cheer the people. Jacopone, before becoming 'Christ's clown' was a wealthy lawyer, married to a noble lady. Like any true Italian he loved to see her dressed up to the nines, and although she gently protested, she let him have his way. Then came the day, at a public festival, when the platform she stood on collapsed; as she lay there, Jacopone ripped aside her garments to examine her injuries, only to discover that under her silks she wore a rough hair shirt. She died, and he became a convert—but such an eccentric one that the Franciscans at first refused him admission. In the end, however, he found his niche with the Spirituals, the most unworldly branch of the order, living in a monastery at Collazzone, near Perugia, where he is believed to have composed the famous Latin *Stabat Mater Dolorosa* and the *Stabat Mater Speciosa*.

Modern Todi is a sophisticated little place, famous for its carpentry and woodworking. In the past few years it has, believe it or not, consistently been voted the world's most livable town by the University of Kentucky, an accolade which has brought American tycoons rushing to buy up its villas and castles and turn them into holiday retreats. Inevitably, this has had an effect on prices in the shops and restaurants. In April Todi hosts one of Italy's major antique fairs, and in August and September the *Mostra Nazionale dell'Artigianato*, a national crafts fair. There is also a cooking school in Todi, that offers courses in regional cuisine; contact the tourist office for information.

### Tourist Information

The Todi tourist office is at Piazza del Popolo 38, © (075) 8942526.

## Tempio della Consolazione

The best way to approach Todi is from the southwest, where the road, winding its way to the clouds, passes by way of one of the most perfect of Renaissance churches, the ivory-coloured **Tempio della Consolazione**, designed by Cola da Caprorola in 1508, and completed 99 years later. Its serene purity of form, geometrically harmonious lines, and lovely proportions are the hallmarks of Bramante, who may well have had a hand in the design. The Tempio's setting, alone amid the wooded hills and farmlands, lends it a special charm, best viewed from Todi's citadel; its fine dome and four half-domes are a graceful note of divinity. The equally white classical interior, in the symmetrical form of a Greek cross, contains good Baroque statues of the 12 apostles.

## Piazza del Popolo

Todi's streets all converge on its magnificent 13th–15th century Piazza del Popolo, the centre of civic life since the days of the Etruscans. The piazza is a medieval pageant in grey stone, though now its great palazzi glare down with haughty contempt on the rows of parked Fiats jammed onto their noble doorsteps. Sternest of them all, the **Palazzo dei Priori** (1293–1337) has square battlements with a chunky tower, while the **Palazzo del Popolo** (1213, with the swallowtail crenellations) and its adjacent **Palazzo del Capitano** (1290) manage to drum up more charm with a grand Gothic stairway and attractive mullioned windows. Up on the fourth floor, there's a small **Museo Etrusco-Romano** and **Pinacoteca** that you can take in if it decides to rain, and an impressive Gothic hall with frescoes (*normally open 8am–2pm Tues–Sat; 9–1 Sun; adm; at time of writing they were closed for restoration, so check with the tourist office before visiting*).

On the far side of the piazza, the squarish **Duomo** is enthroned atop a distinguished flight of steps. Begun in the 12th century, the façade has a fine rose window and delicately decorated portal, while the interior is embellished with good Gothic capitals and a Gothic arcade with a 14th-century altarpiece; parishioners who turned around to gossip during Mass were confronted by a not-too-terrifying 16th-century vision of the *Last Judgement*, painted by Farraù da Faenza. You can also visit the crypt for its cryptic charm. Before leaving the piazza, be sure to take a look from its belvedere.

## San Fortunato and the Rocca

Todi's medieval lanes invite aimless roaming, but if you're pressed for time, head straight for the Franciscan church of **San Fortunato**, built in 1292 (take Via Mazzini), located in a prominent position atop a broad stairway. A bronze statue of Jacopone stands near the foot of the steps; his locally revered tomb is in San Fortunato's crypt. The church's unfinished façade has three recessed Romanesque portals, the central one especially lovely with its carvings of acanthus leaves and human figures. Through Romanesque doors awaits a Gothic interior, notable for its airiness. It contains Todi's greatest work of art, a fresco by Masolino of the *Madonna and Child*.

Above San Fortunato, at the top of the town, the **Rocca** is Todi's ruined 14th-century citadel, public park, and magnificent belvedere, offering an unforgettable view of the valley of the Tiber and the Tempio della Consolazione.

---

Todi © (075–)

**Where to Stay**

*very expensive*

If money is no problem, the loveliest hotel in Todi is the **★★★★★San Valentino**, Frazione Fiore, © 8944103, @ 8948695, actually just outside town on the road to Perugia. In this gracious villa, set in its own grounds, there are just 12 rooms, each beautifully furnished, mostly with antiques. There is also a tennis court and swimming pool.

*expensive*

The ★★★★**Bramante**, Via Orvietana 48, ℭ 8948074, ℗ 8948381, is a former 13th-century convent, also located just outside the town. Rooms have air-conditioning, baths, and minibars, but although the setting is lovely, service and decor have tended to become a bit run-down in recent years.

*moderate*

★★★**Villa Luisa**, Via A. Cortesi 147, ℭ 8948571, ℗ 8948472, is a pleasant place near the centre, with parking and a garden; most rooms have TV, and all have private baths.

*inexpensive*

★★**Zodiaco**, Via del Crocefisso 23, ℭ 8942625, ℗ 8944107, is as inexpensive as you can find in Todi, with 29 clean rooms, most with bath.

---

*Todi ℭ (075–)*                                                             ***Eating Out***

In Todi, the local specialities in the kitchen include the usual pigeon, lamb, and *porchetta*, though here the home-made fat spaghetti is called *ombricelli*, served by preference *alla boscaiola* (with tomatoes, piquant black olives, and hot peppers); the wine to look for, dating back to the days of the Roman Republic, is the dry white *Grechetto di Todi*.

For fine Umbrian cuisine with an enchanting Umbrian view, eat at—where else?—the **Umbria**, Via S. Bonaventura 13, ℭ 8942390 (expensive) under the stone arches just off the Piazza del Popolo. Meals begin with a delicious selection of antipasti, followed perhaps by *spaghetti alla tudertina*, and succulent grilled *secondi*, ranging from trout to boar. (*Closed Tues.*) **Lucaroni**, Viale Cortesi 57, ℭ 8942694 (expensive) offers more sophisticated dishes, such as a delicious risotto with pigeon, black truffles and port and an excellent linguine with crab—a refreshing change after so many Umbrian meat dishes. (*Closed Tues.*)

Otherwise, try **Jacopone**, Piazza Jacopone, ℭ 8942366 (moderate), with traditional Umbrian specialities, served in an attractive dining room by friendly staff. (*Closed Mon.*) Tucked away down a narrow alley off the main piazza, the **Italia**, Via del Monte 27, ℭ (075) 882643 (moderate) is an unpretentious but welcoming trattoria, with cheerful red tablecloths and a rustic feel. The kitchen offers the usual fare, plus a few specialities, most notably the *capriccio*, a pasta dish cooked in the oven, a bit like lasagne. (*Closed Mon.*)

## Orvieto

Orvieto owes much of its success to an ancient volcano. First, it created the city's magnificent pedestal—a 325m sheer crag of tufa, resembling a mesa in the American southwest. The same volcano then enriched the hillsides below with a special mixture of minerals that are part of a secret alchemy that results in Orvieto's famous white wine. Although new buildings crowd the outskirts of Orvieto's unique hill, the medieval town on top, crowned by its stupendous cathedral, looks much the same as it has for the last 500 years. The scaffolding you see around the cliffs, however, is part of a recent effort to shore it up; human progress isn't as much of a threat to the old centre as are such natural forces as erosion and landslides.

Attracted by Orvieto's incomparable defensive position, the Etruscans settled it early and named it *Volsinii*. It was one of the 12 cities of the Etruscan confederation, and one that fought frequently with the Roman upstarts until those same upstarts laid it waste in 280 BC. The Etruscans departed in a huff and founded a new *Volsinii* on the shores of Lake Bolseno, leaving behind their old city (*Urbs Vetus*, hence 'Orvieto'). Like Viterbo, Orvieto in the Middle Ages was an important stronghold of the Papal States—important primarily for popes who could take refuge here when their polls were down in Rome.

---

### Tourist Information

Orvieto's tourist office is at Piazza Duomo 24, © (0763) 41772, @ 44433.

---

## The Cathedral

It was during one of Orvieto's papal visitations, in the 1260s (Urban IV), that the Miracle of Bolsena occurred. A Bohemian priest named Peter, passing through on his way to Rome, was asked to celebrate Mass in the town of Bolsena. Father Peter had long been secretly sceptical about the doctrine of transubstantiation (that the Host in truth becomes the body of Christ), but during this Mass the Host itself answered his doubts by dripping blood on the altar linen. Marvelling, Peter took the linen to the pope in Orvieto, who declared it a miracle and instituted the feast of Corpus Christi. Thomas Aquinas, also in Orvieto at the time, was instructed to compose a suitable office for the new holy day, while the pope promised Orvieto (and not poor Bolsena!) a magnificent new cathedral to enshrine the blood-stained relic.

The cornerstone was laid in 1290, and though begun in the Romanesque style, its plan was transformed into the new-fangled Gothic by master architect Lorenzo Maitani of Siena in 1310. Subsequent master architects included such luminaries as Andrea Pisano, Orcagna, and Sanmicheli, but even then the mighty edifice, visible for miles around, wasn't completed until the 17th century.

The end result is one of Italy's greatest cathedrals, with a stunning, sumptuous façade resembling a giant triptych. This is Maitani's masterpiece, a creation that earned the church the nickname the 'Golden Lily of Cathedrals'. As you approach, you are struck first by the dazzling, technicolor hues of its mosaics, then by the elaborate prickly spires and tracery, and then by the richness and beauty of the sculptural detail. It is said that 152 sculptors worked on the cathedral, but it was Maitani himself who contributed some of the best work—the remarkable design and execution of the celebrated **bas-reliefs** on the lower pilasters that recount the Christian story from the Creation to the Last Judgement, a Bible in stone that captures the essence of the stories with vivid drama and detail. Maitani's *Last Judgement*, in particular, is enough to make the fresco in Todi Cathedral look as dire as a soft touch card. Maitani also cast the four bronze figures of the Evangelists' symbols, the ox, eagle, man, and

*Orvieto's duomo*

winged lion, all ready to step right off the façade, and did the angels in the lunette over the central portal, who pay homage to a *Madonna* by Andrea Pisano. The great rose window is by Orcagna, and the controversial bronze doors, portraying *Works of Mercy* are by Emilio Greco, finished in 1965.

In contrast with the soaring verticality of the façade, the sides and interior are banded with horizontal zebra stripes, a handsome contrast. In the muted light of the **interior**, filtered through alabaster windows, the stripes merge into shadows. The lack of clutter does much to reveal the cathedral's fine proportions and the sense of height. The columns of the nave support rounded arches, and above them runs a pretty clerestory. Among the artworks in the nave, the most notable are Gentile da Fabriano's 1426 fresco of the *Madonna*, near the baptismal font, and the 1579 *Pietà* by Ippolito Scalza, a native of Orvieto.

The greatest treasures, however, are in the chapels, especially the **Cappella della Madonna di San Brizio**, embellished with one of the finest fresco cycles of the Renaissance. The project was begun in 1447 by Fra Angelico, with the assistance of Benozzo Gozzoli. The Angelic One finished two sections—the serene *Christ in Judgement*, with the prophets, while Gozzoli contributed the hierarchies of angels. Before he could finish, however, Fra Angelico was summoned to Rome. Orvieto then commissioned Perugino to complete the work, but he never got around to it, and finally, in 1499, the city hired Luca Signorelli, who finished the vaults according to Fra Angelico's design. The walls, however, are Signorelli's own masterpiece; his breathtaking and awesome compositions of the *Last Judgement*, the *Preaching of the Antichrist* (a most unusual subject), and the *Resurrection of the Dead* are generally acclaimed to be the forerunners of Michelangelo's *Last Judgement* in the Sistine Chapel. Yet it is hard to say that Michelangelo surpassed them; Signorelli's remarkable foreshortening skills, draughtsmanship, and ability to simplify nature and architecture into their essential geometrical forms, give the frescoes tremendous power. To the left of the figure of the preaching Antichrist, Signorelli has portrayed himself and Fra Angelico, both listening solemnly, as does Dante standing amid the crowd, while in the background chaos and catastrophe are busy at work. Then the world ends, a darkened sky is shot with streaks of fire, the earth shakes, and in literal detail the dead re-emerge from the earth, skeletons pulling themselves out of the ground forming new coats of flesh. Some are met by Charon, who rows them across to a Renaissance Hell, to keep company with Signorelli's faithless mistress. Below the frescoes Signorelli painted medallions of the great poets and the pre-Socratic philosopher Empedocles, and some scenes from the *Divine Comedy*.

To the left, the **Chapel of the Corporale** (of the blood-stained linen cloth) is frescoed with scenes of the *Miracle of Bolsena* by Ugolino of Siena (1360s) and the 1339 *Madonna dei Raccomandati* by Lippo Memmi. The magnificent colourful silver and enamel *Reliquary of the Corporale* on the altar is by another Sienese, Ugolino di Vieri; the cloth it holds is shown only on major religious holidays, and is taken around Orvieto in procession during the feast of Corpus Christi.

## The Piazza del Duomo

The cathedral square is a fitting setting for the Golden Lily. On one side a row of old houses includes a couple of wine bars where you can try Orvieto's vintages and salumeria, while on top of the square clock tower a 14th-century figure named Maurizio strikes the hours. Across from the cathedral, in the Palazzo Faina, is the **Museo Civico** (*closed for restoration until further notice*), containing Orvieto's excellent Etruscan collection, excavated from local tombs. The top floor of the palace enjoys one of the best views of the cathedral. On the south side of the cathedral, the **Palazzo dei Papi**, or Popes' Palace, built by Urban IV and finished in 1304, contains the **Museo dell'Opera del Duomo** (*closed for restoration at time of writing*), with art that once filled the cathedral—statues by grand masters like Arnulfo di Cambio and the Pisanos, and grand statues by little-known hands, especially the colossal *Apostles*. The best work—if one can get to see it—is a lovely, richly coloured polyptych by Simone Martini.

## Smaller Churches

In contrast to its heavenly cathedral (even Pope John XXIII said that on Judgement Day the angels would bear it up to paradise), the rest of Orvieto is unpretentious and worldly, a solid, bourgeois, medieval town. On Via del Duomo stands the **Torre del Moro**, another medieval tower, and further on, the pretty 12th-century **Palazzo del Popolo**, a tufa palace with mullioned windows and arches; the little piazza in front is the site of a colourful vegetable market. From here, Via della Pace leads back to the narrow church of **San Domenico**, built in 1233, just after St Dominic's canonization—the first church ever dedicated to him. The most scholarly Dominican of them all, St Thomas Aquinas, taught here at the former monastery. Inside, the most beautiful thing is a Cardinal's tomb by the great Florentine Arnulfo di Cambio (1281).

From Via del Duomo, Orvieto's main drag, Corso Cavour, continues west to the city's main square, Piazza della Repubblica. On the corner, the historic 12th-century church of **Sant'Andrea** has an extremely unusual 12-sided campanile, pierced by mullioned windows and topped by bellicose crenellations. The ruins of a 6th-century church were discovered underneath Sant'Andrea, and, in turn, beneath this palaeo-Christian church were found an Etruscan street and buildings (*the sacristan has the key to the excavations*). Sant'Andrea, with 14th-century frescoes, basks in the memory of great events that took place within its walls: here Innocent III proclaimed the Fourth Crusade, and here, in 1281, Charles of Anjou and his glittering retinue attended the coronation of Pope Martin IV. Beyond Piazza della Repubblica lie some of Orvieto's most ancient streets, lined with tufa houses; follow them back to the northwesternmost corner of town, site of the church of **San Giovenale**, begun in 1009 and crammed full of frescoes from the 12th to the 15th centuries.

Orvieto claims one other noteworthy church, **San Lorenzo**, reached by Via Maitani from the Piazza Duomo, or on Via Scalza from Corso Cavour. Built in the 14th century, San Lorenzo shelters a cylindrical Etruscan altar under its Christian high altar, both of which are protected by a lovely 12th-century stone canopy. Byzantine-style frescoes cover the walls, with elongated figures and staring eyes; one set depicts the life of St Lawrence, who retained his sense of humour even while being literally grilled.

## Pozzo di San Patrizio

Orvieto's northeastern end (near the upper station of the funicular) is dominated by a citadel built in 1364 by the great papal legate, Cardinal Albornoz. Only the walls, a gate, and a tower survive, encompassing a pretty little garden of parasol pines. There are lovely views from the ramparts, stretching from the shallow Paglia river all the way to the Tiber Valley.

Next to the citadel lie the foundations of an **Etruscan temple** and the **Pozzo di San Patrizio** or St Patrick's Well (*open April–Oct 9.30–7; Nov–Mar 10–6 ; adm*), designed in the 1530s by Antonio da Sangallo the Younger on the orders of the calamitous Pope Clement VII. It is a unique work of engineering, meant to supply Orvieto in times of siege; to reach the spring below, Sangallo had to dig down the equivalent of seven storeys, and to haul the water to the surface he designed two spiral stairs of 248 steps, which never cross—one for the water-carriers and their donkeys going down, another for going up. Clement, having just fled the Sack of Rome, was perhaps justified in the paranoia that made him desire such a monumental drinking hole, but in the end it was never really needed. The stairs are dimly lit by windows onto the central shaft, but beware if you descend; you have to get back up again under your own steam.

Down below Orvieto's northern cliffs, along the road that leads to the railway station, there are several **Etruscan tombs**, nothing special as Etruscan tombs go, but worth a look if you don't have a chance to see any of the more elaborate models. The most impressive is the 4th-century BC **Necropoli del Crocefisso** (*open 8am–sunset daily*).

## The Vine of Life

**Orvieto Classico**, Umbria's most famous wine, comes from 16 designated areas in Terni and Viterbo provinces, and consists of a careful mixture of several different grapes, with Tuscan Trebbiano and Verdello dominant. The resulting wine, either dry (Orvieto *secco*) or moderately sweet *abboccato* (often served with dessert), is a delicious, light straw-coloured wine; there are plenty of places in Orvieto to try it,  beginning with the wine shops and bars around the cathedral; the Antinori label is one of the best, but don't neglect the others. They can be tasted and bought at *cantine* around town, including the following: **Di Mario**, Via della Pace 26, (0763) ✆ 42527; **Foresi**, Piazza Duomo 2, ✆ (0763) 41611; **La Bottega del Buon Vino**, Via della Cava 26, ✆ (0763) 42373; **Vinovino**, Via Loggia dei Mercanti 21, ✆ (0763) 44308. All are closed on Tuesdays.

## Villages around Orvieto

Between Orvieto and Todi, **Baschi** is a harmonious hill town above the Tiber Valley, near where the river widens to form the **Lago di Corbara**; the area is a popular centre for *agriturismo*, for those who dream of staying in a farmhouse amid the vineyards. **Porano**, south of Orvieto, is a pretty town with a castle, set in the rolling hills. Nearby there's a painted Etruscan tomb, the **Eskanas Tomb**: to see it, inquire at the *Comune* (town hall).

Little **Castel Giorgio**, west of Orvieto on SS74 road into Lazio, is a relatively new town, but one that has taken peculiarly well to American football, having constructed one of the finest stadiums in Europe. **Ficulle**, north of Orvieto on SS71, was the birthplace of Rome's tragic hero of the Middle Ages, Cola di Rienzo, and its castle of the Marchese Antinori produces some of Orvieto's finest wine. Near **Fabro**, further north, you can visit **Salci**, a tiny hamlet scarcely aware that it's in the 20th century.

### Where to Stay

#### expensive

Orvieto's hotels have more character than is often the case, most stunningly ★★★★**La Badia**, located in the hills 5km south on the road towards Bagnoregio, ✆ (0763) 90359, ✉ 92796, with views up to a tufa-crowned citadel. A 12th-century abbey, renovated in the 19th century, it preserves much of its original ambience; the rooms are lovely and comfortable, and in the grounds there's a pool and tennis court, although it doesn't come cheaply. Up in Orvieto itself, ★★★★**Maitani**, Via Maitani 5, ✆ (0763) 42011, ✉ 42012, is a fine hotel just opposite the cathedral, where the comfortable rooms all have baths, air-conditioning, and TV, and there's parking too.

#### moderate

The ★★★**Grand Hotel Reale**, Piazza del Popolo 25, ✆ and ✉ (0763) 41247, was one of the town's first hotels, an old dear full of personality and atmosphere, if not modern amenities, and offering fine accommodation for its price range. The ★★★★**Aquila Bianca**, Via Garibaldi 13, ✆ (0763) 41246, ✉ 42273, is another old-fashioned hotel that's not particularly luxurious, but has a good central position, a garage, and a wine cellar for the all-important business of tasting Orvieto. The ★★★**Virgilio**, Piazza Duomo 5/6, ✆ (0763) 41882, also has an excellent location, across from the Duomo, and 13 pleasant rooms, all with bath.

About 12km outside Orvieto, on the shores of Lake Corbara near Baschi, the ★★★★**Villa Bellago**, Strada SS448 Baschi, ✆ (0744) 950521, ✉ 950524, is a lovely waterfront hotel, converted from three farmhouses and set in its own grounds with a pool, tennis court and pretty terrace restaurant. Run by former New York restaurateur George Harpootlian and his wife Davida Shear, it makes a very pleasant base for exploring the Orvieto and Todi area, and is one of the best deals around.

#### inexpensive

Many of Orvieto's cheaper hotels are outside the old city, in the area around the train station. Two that are within the city walls are the ★**Duomo**, Via Maurizio 7,

© (0763) 41887, and the **Posta**, Via Signorelli 18, © (0763) 41909. Both are basic, but clean and comfortable.

## Eating Out

### very expensive

Southeast of Orvieto at Baschi, 13km from the town on Lake Corbara, you can splurge at a restaurant that gourmets rank as one of the five best in Italy: **Vissani**, on SS448, © (0744) 950396. In this almost religiously passionate inner sanctum of *altissima cucina*, you may dip your fork (but only if you've diligently reserved a table in advance) into such marvels as oysters with roast onions and thyme sauce, suckling pig with bilberries, or lobster in broccoli leaves; each dish is accompanied by a specially prepared bread. A fabulous array of Italian and French cheeses and exquisite wines will help make your meal unforgettable, though so too will the bill; the restaurant is also one of the most expensive in Italy. (*Closed Wed, Sun evenings.*)

### expensive

If the prices at Vissani might ruin your appetite, you can also eat very well nearby at **Il Padrino**, run by Gianfranco Vissani's parents, in the same building on the lake on the SS448, © (0744) 950206. The pasta with seafood or asparagus in season is lovely, and the *secondi* are classics rarely seen (or prepared very well) in Italy, like Chateaubriand, scampi Newburg, *coq-au-vin*, and sole Colbert. (*Closed Wed.*)

### moderate

Orvieto often sees bus-loads of day-trippers from Rome, who help keep its mediocre and often expensive restaurants in business. A triad of real choices among the pretenders are: **Le Grotte del Funaro**, Via Ripa Serancia 41, © (0763) 43276, located in one of Orvieto's prettier corners. This elegant restaurant occupies a set of tufa caves, and dishes up good, solid Umbrian cuisine with especially good pasta and mixed grilled meats. (*Closed Mon.*)

**Del Pino da Checco**, Via di Piazza del Popolo 15, © (0763) 42661, has a lovely terrace with views over the oldest part of town, where you can also enjoy appetizing specialities like *cannelloni alla Ducale* or tagliatelle with artichokes, or *bistecca in intingolo* (beef in a savoury sauce), accompanied by the delicious dry wines of Orvieto. More inspired pasta dishes can be had at **Maurizio**, Via Duomo 78, © (0763) 43212. (*Closed Tues.*)

Outside Orvieto, again by the side of Lake Corbara on the SS448, the restaurant of the hotel **Villa Bellago** (*see above*) is worth a stop for the imaginative pasta courses and particularly good meat dishes, especially the giant *Fiorentina* steaks.

### inexpensive

**La Grotta**, Via Signorelli 5 (no phone) is a welcoming, good-value local restaurant, offering hearty traditional cooking.

Via Appia Antica

# Lazio

On a Saturday night variety show, the television host discusses the founding of Rome with two comedians dressed up as Romulus and Remus; turning to Remus, the sillier-looking of the pair, he asks: 'What did you ever do?' Remus gets a big laugh from the audience by proudly claiming, 'Well, I founded Lazio'.

Despite being the location of the capital city, Lazio does not get much respect from the average Italian, who thinks of it as a sort of vacuum, half swamps and half poor mountain villages that need to be crossed to get to Rome. Northerners often lump it in with Campania and Calabria as part of the backward south. To an extent it is, though great changes have come in the last 60 years with land reclamation and new industry. Lazio's problem is a simple one: Rome, that most parasitic of all cities. Before there was a Rome, this was probably the wealthiest and most densely populated part of non-Greek Italy, the homeland of the Etruscans as well as the rapidly civilizing nations of Sabines, Aequi, Hernici, Volsci, and the Latins themselves, from whom Lazio (*Latium*) takes its name.

After the Roman triumph, the Etruscan and the Italic cities shrivelled and died; those Romans who proved such good governors elsewhere caused utter ruin to their own backyard. A revival came in the Middle Ages, when Rome was only one of a score of squabbling feudal towns, but once again, when the popes restored Rome, Lazio's fortunes declined. To finance their grandiose building projects, Renaissance popes literally taxed Lazio into extinction; whole villages and large stretches of countryside were abandoned and given over to bandits, and land drained in medieval times reverted to malarial swamps. Modern Rome, at least since Mussolini's day, has begun to mend its ways; the government still considers Lazio a development area, and pumps a lot of money into it.

## What to See

Many of Lazio's attractions are easily seen as day-trips from Rome—Tivoli, Ostia, and a garland of interesting hill towns. These towns are detailed in a special section following that on Rome itself. Northern Lazio contains no fewer than 28 excavated **Etruscan sites**, and if these ancient charmers interest you, there will be plenty of opportunities for Etruscan detours, whether you approach Rome along the SS2 (Via Cassia) from Orvieto, or the A12 and SS1 (Via Aurelia) along the coast—including the spectacular painted tombs of **Cerveteri**. Northern Lazio also offers the fine old city of **Viterbo**, and a string of large **lakes** in a pretty landscape of jumbled hills.

In southern Lazio, you'll see new land and new towns: the reclaimed Pontine Marshes, with Mussolini-founded towns like Aprilia and Latina, and others with a completely modern look only because they had to be rebuilt from the bottom up after the Second World War. Others, like **Alatri** and **Cori** with their impressive cyclopean walls, are among the oldest towns in Europe. Early monastic centres make up most of the religious sights, with **Montecassino**

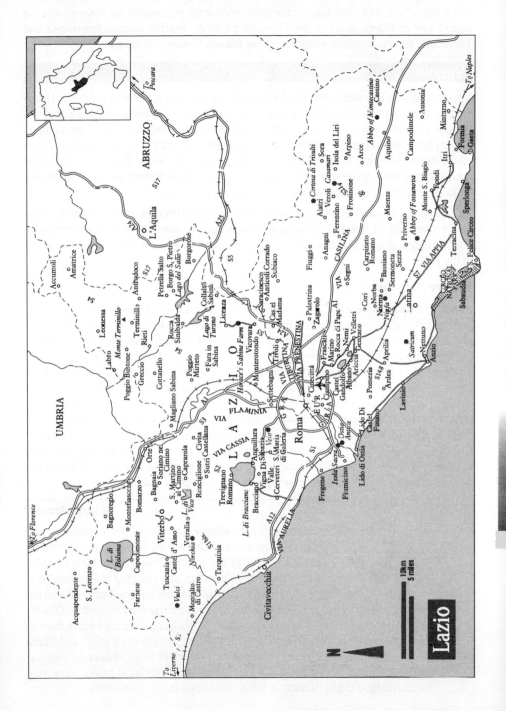

Lazio

N

10 km
5 miles

first among them. The coast is generally plain, with some noteworthy exceptions—the old walled port of **Gaeta**, some of the Tyrrhenian's nicest beaches around **Sperlonga** and **Terracina**, and the wetlands wilderness of the **Monte Circeo** national park.

## Viterbo

Viterbo ought to be visited. Where else in Italy can one rest a while in a café on Death Square, or stroll over to the Piazza of the Fallen to pay one's respects to Our Lady of the Plague? Surrounded by grey, forbidding walls and the ghastly modern districts beyond them, the city is actually rather cute inside, full of grand churches and palaces, and well-preserved medieval streets brightened everywhere with fountains and flowers. The population seems evenly divided between teenagers on scooters, as bejewelled and trendy as their counterparts in Rome, and blasé young soldiers from Italy's biggest army base.

Like the rest of Lazio, Viterbo has had more than its share of troubles, most of them traceable to the proximity of Rome. That geographical necessity, however, also gave Viterbo its greatest period of glory. For much of the 13th century, Viterbo, and not Rome, was the seat of the popes.

## History

Although a small city in both Etruscan and Roman times, Viterbo's modern history begins with its fortification by the Lombards in the 8th century. By 1100, it was a free *comune*, one of the few cities in this part of Italy strong and energetic enough to manage it. Viterbo was usually an enemy of Rome, and when Arnold of Brescia's revolution made Pope Eugenius III a refugee in 1145, he sought refuge here. Emperor Frederick Barbarossa soon restored the popes to Rome, but again in 1257, Martin V found Viterban hospitality gratifying when the Guelph-Ghibelline wars made Rome too hot for him. In this most confusing period of Italian history, over a dozen popes were crowned, died, or at least spent time here, in short stays on their way to or from France, Tivoli—and sometimes even Rome. In 1309, when the 'Babylonian Captivity' began and the papacy was carted off to Avignon, Viterbo could only decline, and when the popes came back to Rome once more, the city that had once been Rome's strongest rival found itself a mere provincial town of the Papal State.

### Getting Around

Viterbo actually has three **railway** stations, all just outside the city walls. Regular FS trains north to Orvieto and Florence stop at Stazione Porta Fiorentina, north of the walls on Viale Trento. Most trains for Rome usually leave from here too, also stopping at Stazione Porta Romana, on Viale Raniero Capocci, the big boulevard east of the walls. In addition there is a local line run by the Lazio transport authority COTRAL, often called the Ferrovie Roma-Nord, which rattles along a separate route from its station next door to Porta Fiorentina, via Bagnaia, Soriano del Cimino and Città Castellana, to Piazzale Flaminio (Roma-Nord) station in Rome. **Buses** for Rome as well as Tarquinia, Bolsena, Civitavecchia, and other provincial towns leave from Piazza Martiri d'Ungheria, next to Piazza dei Caduti in the town centre.

The main north–south **road** through Viterbo is the SS2, the Via Cassia. South of Viterbo at Vetralla the SS1bis turns off to the right for the coast. In addition there is now a new *superstrada* which runs east from Viterbo to connect with the A1.

## Tourist Information

Viterbo has three tourist information desks, at Piazza dei Caduti 16, ✆ (0761) 234795, Piazza Verdi 4, ✆ (0761) 226666; and Piazza della Morte, 18, ✆ (0761) 345229 (*open April–Sept only*).

## Piazza del Plebiscito

In Viterbo's centre, two not-so-fierce looking lions, the city's ancient symbol, gaze out over the 13th-century **Palazzo del Podestà** with its clock tower, and the **Palazzo Comunale** of the 1460s, the typical pair of buildings representing the often conflicting imperial and local powers. The politicians won't mind you looking around the town hall and its fine Renaissance courtyard; if you ask, they'll let you see the Council Chamber, the **Sala Regia**, decorated with fanciful Mannerist frescoes on the history of Viterbo from Etruscan times. Across the square is **Sant'Angelo**, the façade of which has for centuries incorporated a Roman sarcophagus (presently removed for restoration, and replaced by nothing more than a photograph) containing the body of a medieval lady of incomparable virtue named Galiena; accounts of her fatal charm and sad demise vary from one Viterban to another.

There's any number of directions you can take from here. Via Ascenzi, under the arch, leads to the Piazza dei Caduti and the **Madonna delle Peste**, an octagonal Renaissance church next to the tourist office. Beyond that, by the walls, the **Rocca** was built by Cardinal Albornoz in 1354 to keep watch on the Viterbans when the pope returned to Rome. This squat palace-fortress is being restored to hold the small collection of the **Museo Archeologico**, though at time of writing only three ground floor rooms had been opened (*open April–Sept 9am–7pm Tues–Sun; Oct–Mar 9am–1.30pm; adm*). Two of Viterbo's 13th-century popes are buried in the 13th-century **San Francesco** church, near Porta Murata at the northern end of the walls. Nearby, off Piazza Verdi, the late 19th-century church of **Santa Rosa** houses the considerable remains of Viterbo's 13th-century patroness, too holy to decompose and usually on display for all to see. Santa Rosa's preaching helped the Viterbans defeat a siege by the heretical Emperor Frederick II in 1243. To commemorate her, each year on 3 September the men of the town carry a 30m illuminated wooden steeple called the *macchina*—which is always in danger of toppling—through the streets, surmounted by an image of the saint. Local artists create a new *macchina* every five years (the present one, good until 1998, is a genuine work of art). The festival is similar to the 'Dance of the Lilies' in Nola and other towns down in Campania.

East from Piazza del Plebiscito, Via Cavour takes you to the **Casa Poscia**, an interesting 13th-century house on a stairway to the left, and then the **Fontana Grande**, the best of Viterbo's many fountains. Via Garibaldi leads on further east to the Roman Gate and **San Sisto**, a church in parts as old as the 9th century, with an altar made from ancient sculptural fragments. Outside the walls and across Viale Capocci, **Santa Maria della Verità** from the 13th century suffered terrible vandalism at the hands of 18th-century redecorators; the frills and plaster frosting are gone now, but only a few fragments have survived of the Renaissance frescoes by Melozzo di Forli. The Cappella Mazzatosta, behind an iron grille, has good frescoes of the *Marriage of the Virgin* by Renaissance artist Lorenzo of Viterbo. In the adjacent cloisters there are fine works from the 14th century, and the **Museo Civico** (*closed for restoration*), with a small archaeological section and a picture gallery.

## The Popes' Palace

From Piazza del Plebiscito, the best route of all is down Via San Lorenzo, into the heart of Viterbo's oldest quarter. Three streets down and off to the left, **Santa Maria Nuova** is the best-preserved of the city's medieval churches. On the façade, there is an ancient image of Jupiter set into the portal, and a small outdoor pulpit in the corner where St Thomas Aquinas once preached. On the other side of Via San Lorenzo, Viterbo's old market square faces the church of the **Gesù** (11th century), a medieval tower-fortress, one of several left in the city, and a palazzo that long ago was the town hall. To the south, trailing down from the aforementioned **Piazza della Morte**—ironically one of the lovelier squares in Viterbo—the **San Pellegrino** quarter hangs its web of alleys, arches, and stairs along Via San Pellegrino with a romantic and thoroughly medieval air, though in fact few of the buildings are quite that old. At Via San Pellegrino 60 is the **Museo della Macchina di Santa Rosa** (*open 10–12, 4–7, Sat, Sun only*), which chronicles Viterbo's most traditional *festa*.

In the opposite direction from San Pellegrino, a bridge on Roman and Etruscan foundations called the **Ponte del Duomo**, carries over to Piazza San Lorenzo and the **Papal Palace**, begun in 1266. This squarish, battlemented building, very much in the style of a medieval city hall or private palace, is a finer building than the pope's present address in Rome, though admittedly much smaller. On the best part, the open Gothic loggia, you will see in the decoration lions (for Viterbo), interspersed with the striped coat of arms of the French pope Clement V, who completed the building. Three popes were elected at conclaves in the palace's Great Hall.

Popes and cardinals did not always have a easy time in Viterbo. When Clement IV died—two weeks after he arrived—arguments between the French and Italian factions led to a two-year deadlock among the cardinals. The exasperated people of Viterbo finally tried to speed up the conclave, by locking the cardinals in the palace, and then by tearing off the roof; somehow, according to the story, the churchmen got around this by making tents in the Great Hall. Finally the Viterbans decided to starve them out, and before long the Church was blessed with the rather undistinguished compromise choice of Gregory X. He had the roof fixed, but should have repaired the floor as well, since it collapsed six years later, killing his successor, John XXI. He is buried next door in Viterbo's plain Romanesque **cathedral**.

## Around Viterbo: Hot Mud and Tombs

West of the city, some of the Etruscans' and Romans' favourite thermal springs still carry on doing whatever it is they do that makes Italians so happy. At the ancient **Springs of Bullicame** you can stop by the roadside for a dip in a sulphurous pool, check into a hotel spa, or visit the municipally run baths for an aerosol inhalation to help your sinuses, and a frosting with hot mineral mud to calm your nerves. The city also runs a naturally heated outdoor pool, where swimming in January is quite fashionable.

Further west, **Tuscania** stands alone at the centre of one of the emptiest, eeriest corners of Italy, a region of low green hills where you will find Etruscan ruins, old castles and religious shrines, but no people. Tuscania was a leading Etruscan city around the 4th century BC, and regained its importance for a short while in the early Middle Ages. Today, the city is still recovering from a bad earthquake in 1971. Etruscan sarcophagi from the nearby necropolis are on display at the **Museo Archeologico** in the former Santa Maria del Riposo convent (*open April–Sept 9–7 Tues–Sun; Oct–Mar 9–6 Tues–Sun; adm*). They are nothing special, but Tuscania is worth a short stop for two unique early churches east of the town. **San Pietro** and **Santa Maria Maggiore** were both begun in the 8th century, with additions in the 11th and 12th centuries. Besides their carved altars, pulpits, and bits of painting from the 8th–14th centuries, both churches' best features are their unusual sculpted façades—San Pietro's especially, with colourful Cosmati work, fragments of ancient sculpture, and outlandish carved grotesques. Perhaps some of the churches of Rome looked like this before their Renaissance and Baroque rebuildings.

Another road west from Viterbo—this one an 8km dead end—leads to the site of **Ferento**, a rival city that Viterbo destroyed in the Middle Ages. Little is left, really, save a very well-preserved **Roman Theatre**, where concerts are sometimes held in the summer (*open April–Sept 9–7 Tues–Sun; Oct–Mar 9–1.30 Tues–Sun*).

East of Viterbo, the road for Orte enters the old suburb of La Quercia, passing in front of a landmark of late Renaissance architecture: **Santa Maria della Quercia**, built in the late 1470s. The distinctive 1509 façade has a carved oak tree (*quercia*) and lions, and lunettes by Andrea della Robbia over the doors. Inside, the beautiful marble tabernacle contains a miraculous painting of the Virgin, and there is also a fine Gothic cloister; ask the custodian to let you in to the **Museo degli Ex-Voto**, a collection of some 200 devotional plaques brought to this shrine over the centuries, painted with fascinating scenes of miracles attributed to the Madonna. Six kilometres further east is **Bagnaia**, an old hill village expanded by wealthy Viterban bishops into a residence town. In the 1570s Cardinal de Gambera commissioned the architect Vignola to create the **Villa Lante** (*gardens open 9am–one hour before sunset daily. Guided tours of the gardens and villa every half-hour; adm*), with one of the most striking of all Renaissance gardens. Besides the two villas there is a large public park and a classic 'Italian garden', geometrically arranged and full of groves and statuary; water rises from a number of fountains, then cascades back down decorative stairs and terraces—an impressive sight, when they feel like turning it on.

This road continues into the beech forests of the Cimino hills, meeting the town of **Soriano nel Cimino**, with a medieval castle and an extinct volcano, Monte Cimino, for a neighbour. South of Viterbo, if you're heading for Lake Vico (*see* below), you'll pass through the lovely town of **San Martino al Cimino**, built around a fine 13th-century Cistercian abbey, done in the French Gothic style; the town itself is an unusual example of Baroque planning, full of trees and half-surrounded by a single curving lane of terraced houses.

## The Monster Park at Bomarzo

Some of the same sculptors who worked on St Peter's in Rome made this shabby little nightmare, hidden away in the Lazio hills. The two works seem somehow related, opposite sides of the coin that may help in explaining the tragic, neurotic atmosphere of late 16th-century Italy. One of the Orsini, that ancient and powerful Roman family, commissioned this collection of huge, strange sculptures; he called it his *Sacro Bosco*—Sacred Wood—and in its present state it is impossible to tell whether it was the complex allegory it pretends to be, or just a joke.

The **Parco dei Mostri** (*open 9am–one hour before sunset daily; adm exp*)—one of the most popular sights in Lazio—lies just outside **Bomarzo**, one of the most woebegone little towns in this part of Italy. The setting adds to its charm, as does the habit of the present owners of running it like some Alabama roadside attraction, complete with tame deer for your children to pet, an albino peacock, miniature goats, and plenty of souvenirs. Near the entrance, you come upon the impressive though dilapidated **Tempietto**, a domed temple of unknown purpose attributed to Vignola. From there, you wander the ill-kept grounds, encountering at every turn colossal monuments and eroded illegible inscriptions: a 6m tall screaming face, where you can walk inside the mouth, under an inscription that reads 'every thought flees', and find a small table and benches, apparently waiting for a dinner party; a life-size elephant, perhaps one of Hannibal's, crushing a terrified Roman soldier in its trunk; a giant wrestler, in the act of ripping a defeated opponent in two from the legs; and a leaning tower, just for fun. In every corner decayed Madonnas, mermaids, sphinxes, nymphs, and harpies wait to spook you. All are done in a distorted, almost primitive style. It would be almost too easy to read too much into these images: a cry of pain from the degraded, humiliated Italy of the 1560s, half pretending madness as the only way to be safe from the Spanish and the Inquisition, an exaggerated expression of the over-heated mentality of Mannerism—or perhaps merely a symbol for the loss of mental balance that followed too many centuries of high culture and over-stimulation. Whatever, the Monster Park will make you feel yourself an archaeologist, discovering some peculiar lost civilization. Perhaps the Italians understand it too well; it may be the only important monument of the 16th century that neither the government nor anyone else is interested in preserving.

---

*Viterbo ✆ (0761–)*             ***Where to Stay***

 Viterbo doesn't have a lot of choices, but for a good place to stay you need look no further than Via della Cava, where there are hotels covering different price ranges: the ★★★**Leon d'Oro**, at no.36, ✆/🖷 344444 (moderate), quiet and a little staid, with baths in all rooms. Almost next door is the slightly cheaper ★★**Roma**, Via della Cava 26, ✆ 227274 (moderate). Both of these hotels have garages. The ★**Milano**, Via della Cava 54, ✆ 345180 (inexpensive) has doubles with baths, some with TV—and cheaper rooms still without baths.

Getting in and out of Viterbo can be a little hectic, and if you're just passing through on the way to or from Rome, you might consider stopping at one of the smaller towns in the region instead. Near the woods in Soriano nel Cimino, ★★★**La Bastia Residence**, Via Giovanni XXIII, ✆, 🌐 745062 (moderate; inexpensive rooms without baths), has attractive terrace-style apartments with air-conditioning.

---

*Viterbo* ✆ *(0761–)* **Eating Out**

Restaurants in these parts are often very good, with a determined adherence to traditional Viterban dishes: slender fettucine called *fieno*, roast baby lamb, eels and fish from the lakes: *lattarini*, *coregone* (whitefish) or *persico* (perch). In Viterbo, do not by any means miss a dinner at **Il Richiastro**, Via della Marrocca 18, ✆ 223609 (*open Thurs–Sun only*), occupying the well-restored courtyard and cellars of a medieval palace near Piazza Dante. At bargain prices (moderate) you can dine on smoked trout, roast lamb, polenta, and some unusual homemade desserts, with everything fresh according to the season, and prepared with pride and care.

The **Scaletta**, Via Marconi 45, ✆ 340003 (moderate) is another old favourite, with traditional cooking, and also pizza if you don't feel like a big dinner; and the **Tre Re**, Via Macel Gattesco, ✆ 234619 (inexpensive), a few streets north of Piazza del Plebiscito, serves excellent dinners at inexpensive prices. If you make it out to Bagnaia and the Villa Lante, stop off at La Quercia for a meal at **Aquilanti**, Località La Quercia, Via del Santuraio 4, ✆ 341701 (expensive), an ex-trattoria offering an unusual and adventurous menu, though this time not at bottom-range prices.

## Three Lakes

All of the lakes of northern Lazio, surrounded by circular ranges of hills, are the craters of long-dead volcanoes; long ago they must have been like the famous Phlegraean Fields outside Naples. They are also the most ingratiating features in the Lazio landscape, with a few sleepy beaches here and there; not exactly off the main tourist tracks, and popular enough with the Romans. For swimming and watersports they are often more pleasant than any of the coastal beach resorts within easy reach of Rome.

---

**Getting Around**

Bracciano town is on the main FS **rail** line between Rome and Viterbo. The main way to get to the lakes by public transport, though, is by **bus**. There are frequent services from Lepanto and Saxa Rubra termini in Rome to Bracciano and Vico, and from Viterbo to the towns around Lake Bolsena.

By **road** all three lakes can be reached from turnings off the SS2. To get to Lake Bracciano from Rome take the SS2 out of the city and turn left onto the SS493 shortly after La Giustiniana.

# Lake Bolsena

The largest and northernmost of the three, it has **Bolsena** town at one end, with the medieval **Castello Mondaleschi** that holds a small archaeological collection; the 15th-century church of **Santa Cristina**, with small Christian catacombs underneath; and narrow beaches. At the southern end, **Capodimonte** on its small promontory offers more beaches and small boat excursions (© (0761) 98213) to the lake's two islands: the pretty rock of **Martana**, with steep granite cliffs and woods above, and the **Isola Bisentina**. This was a favoured retreat of the Farnese in the 1500s, when the family was just beginning its spectacular career. They commissioned Antonio da Sangallo the Younger to build them a palace and a large domed church, SS. Giacomo e Cristoforo, now in decay. The island's hill also has a string of Calvary Chapels.

Towns in the region around Lake Bolsena include **Bagnoregio**, with its adjacent medieval core, the 'Civitá' intact but almost a ghost town; **Acquapendente**, at the northernmost extremity of Lazio, with an ancient church crypt under its cathedral, built as a copy of the Holy Sepulchre in Jerusalem, and a nature reserve on nearby Monte Rufeno; and **Montefiascone**, just south of the lake, famous for its *Est! Est! Est!* wine since a German Renaissance bishop did himself in by drinking too much of it. His tomb is in the 12th-century church of **San Flaviano**, just outside town. Montefiascone makes a good living from its wine, and the embroidered legend that goes with it.

# Lake Vico and Caprarola

The smallest and perhaps loveliest of the lakes, Vico is ringed by rugged hills; parts of the shore are unspoiled marshes, a favourite stop for migratory birds that is now protected as a wildlife reserve. At the northern edge, this ancient crater has a younger volcano (also extinct) poking up inside it: **Monte Venere**. Also, just over the hills from the lake, you should definitely not pass up a chance to see one of Italy's most arrogantly ambitious late Renaissance palaces, the **Villa Farnese** in Caprarola (*open Nov–Feb 9–3:30, Oct 9–5.30, Mar, Apr, Sep 9–6.30, May–Aug 9–7, daily. To visit the garden there are guided tours at 10, 11.30, 3, and May–Aug also 5pm, Mon–Sat; adm*).

When Alessandro Farnese, member of an obscure Lazio noble family, set his sister Giulia up as mistress to Pope Alexander VI, his fortune was made; Alessandro later became Pope Paul III, a great pope who called the Council of Trent, rebuilt Rome, and kept Michelangelo busy—also a rotten pope, who oppressed his people, reinvigorated the Inquisition, and became the most successful grafter in papal history. Before long the Farnese family ruled Parma, Piacenza, and most of northern Lazio. With the fantastic wealth Alessandro accumulated, his grandson, also named Alessandro, built this family headquarters; Vignola, the family architect, turned the entire town of Caprarola into a setting for the palace, ploughing a new avenue through the town as an axis that led to a grand stairway, then a set of gardens (now disappeared), and then another stairway up to the huge pentagonal villa, built over the the massive foundations of an earlier, uncompleted fortress. The palace is empty today; the Farnese lost everything in later papal intrigues, and someone, some time, probably had to sell the furniture.

Nevertheless, it is still an impressive place; some of the highlights of the guided tour include Vignola's elegant central courtyard, a room with uncanny acoustical tricks that the guides love to demonstrate, frescoes of the *Labours of Hercules*, another with a wonderful ceiling painted with the figures of the constellations, and an incredible **spiral staircase** of stone columns and neo-classical frescoes, Vignola's decorative masterpiece. The best part, however, is the 'secret garden' in the rear, an extensive park full of azaleas and rhododendrons leading up to a sculpture garden of grotesques and fantastical *telemones* that recall the Monster Park (there is a connection, as one of the Orsini of Bomarzo was Alessandro Farnese's secretary), and finally a delightful, smaller villa, the **Palazzina del Piacere**.

The hills between Lake Vico and the coast conceal no less than 12 minor Etruscan sites; all you'll see of these vanished cities, however, are the usual rock-cut tombs, some with temple-like carved façades, as at **Blera** and **Norchia**. Also at Norchia is a strange 365.5m avenue, cut deeply into the easily worked tufa.

## Lake Bracciano

This broad sheet of water, still beautiful despite the summer crowds, is one of Rome's most popular swimming holes, and yet remains remarkably clean. There is little of great monumental interest around the lake—but a good view of it can be gained from the grim 1470s castle of the Orsini family called the **Odescalchi Castle** (*open 9am–12.30, 3 5.30, Tues–Sun, guided tours only; adm*), in the town of Bracciano. Boats run from there around the lake in summer. Trevignano and Anguillara are two more pretty lakeside villages, with medieval centres and many places to eat.

*© (0761–)*                                        ***Where to Stay and Eating Out***

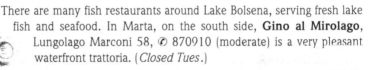

There are many fish restaurants around Lake Bolsena, serving fresh lake fish and seafood. In Marta, on the south side, **Gino al Mirolago**, Lungolago Marconi 58, © 870910 (moderate) is a very pleasant waterfront trattoria. (*Closed Tues.*)

At Lago di Vico, the ★★★**Bella Venere**, Loc. Lago di Vico, © 612342, © 612344 (moderate), on the eastern shore of the lake towards Caprarola, is a rare find, a lovely small hotel on the lake with gardens, a beach, tennis courts and a restaurant. Moreover, its 14 double rooms with baths are still remarkable value. Another choice around the same lake is the ★★★**Sans Soucis sul Lago**, © 612052, © 612053 (moderate), at Punta del Lago near the road to Ronciglione, also with a beach and garden, and views over the lake from a roof terrace.

Towards Caprarola, you can sample mushrooms in every conceivable form, and also big Florentine steaks, at the **Autorifugio Cimino**, © 646121 (moderate), on the Via Cassia Cimino near Caprarola, again at very reasonable prices.

## Rieti and its Province

This comes as something of a digression, but this strip of land reaching over the Apennines to touch the borders of the Marches is also a part of Lazio. Before the Roman conquest in 290 BC, it was the land of the Sabines, sometime allies but often fierce enemies of Rome. The

Romans pushed their Via Salaria through here on its way to the Adriatic, generally following the route of the modern SS4 to Ascoli Piceno, and made it an important staging post.

### Getting Around

Rieti is on the **rail** line between Terni and L'Aquila, but this is not a frequent service. There are several **buses** each day to Rome, Terni and L'Aquila. The main **road** into town is, as it has always been, the Via Salaria, the SS4. From Rieti the SS4bis leads up into the mountains to Terminillo, and the SS79 runs to Lake Piediluco and Terni.

### Tourist Information

**Rieti** has a tourist office at Via Cintia 87, ✆ (0746) 41146, ✉ 270446, and there is also an office in the ski resort at **Terminillo**, Pian de' Valli, ✆ (0746) 61121.

## Lazio's Least-known Towns

**Rieti**, the capital, has a 12th-century cathedral and a small picture collection in its Museo Civico, as well as about a kilometre of well-preserved and very medieval-looking walls. The territory around it, once mostly swamps, was drained by the Romans when they built the Marmore Falls in Terni; now it's a fertile plain with views of some of the highest peaks of the Apennines—the Gran Sasso is just over the border in the Abruzzo.

There is plenty of lovely scenery and good walking country in the province, most of it in rather remote areas. South of Rieti, there are the hills around the artificial lakes of **Salto** and **Turano**; on the way to the latter you will see an impressive medieval castle called the **Rocca Sinibalda**. North of the city, **Monte Terminillo** has a modest ski resort on the slopes of its 2132m peak; in summer the road around it makes a panoramic drive to **Leonessa**, an attractive medieval town that is one of the quietest, most out-of-the-way places in Italy. St Francis spent much time in these mountains; among the several humble sanctuaries where he preached, **Greccio**, on its lovely mountain-top site, west of Rieti, is said to be the place where the saint made the first Christmas crib.

### *Rieti (0746–)*                           *Where to Stay and Eating Out*

In Rieti there is an elegant hotel, the ★★★★**Quattro Stagioni**, Piazza C. Battisti 14, ✆, ✉ 271 090, which offers fine quality accommodation for moderate-range prices, and there is also good food to be had close by at **Il Grottino**, Piazza C. Battisti, ✆ 497683, offering traditional local dishes (moderate). Another fine restaurant is **La Fontanella**, Via San Francesco 36, ✆ 46585, with wonderful *tagliatelle al tartufo*—tagliatelle in truffle sauce.

## The North Coast: Tarquinia and Cerveteri

It will seem hard to believe, but this bare stretch of coast north of Rome was the richest and most heavily populated part of Etruria, including the only two sites worth visiting for those not enchanted with archaeology: the museums and necropoli at Tarquinia and Cerveteri.

There are a few **trains** on the Rome–Genoa line that stop at Cerveteri-Ladispoli (6km from the excavations) and Tarquinia. There are more frequent **buses** from Lepanto terminus in Rome. By **road** both Cerveteri and Tarquinia are close to the SS1, the Via Aurelia (flanked by the A12 *autostrada* as far as Civitavecchia. To get to Vulci turn inland off the SS1 on a minor road just north of Montalto di Castro.

## Vulci and Tarquinia

Beginning from the Lazio–Tuscany border on the coastal highway (the Roman Via Aurelia), truly dedicated Etruscophiles may wish to detour into the hills to **Vulci**, an important town in the 9th–1st centuries BC, and a renowned centre of bronze-working and art. There are scanty ruins of the city, a small museum in modern Vulci's 13th-century **Castello dell'Abbadia**, and a possibly interesting necropolis, closed at present while excavations are under way.

After the turn-off for Vulci, continuing southwards, you won't see anything until the next Etruscan site at the large, modern town of **Tarquinia**, of interest in its own right, with a Cosmatesque 12th-century church and a Roman aqueduct, rebuilt in the Middle Ages and still in use. In the 15th-century Palazzo Vitelleschi, many of the finest discoveries from the Etruscan city and its necropolis have been assembled for the **Museo Nazionale di Tarquinia** (*museum and necropolis open Jul–Sep 9–7 Tues–Sun; Oct–May 9–2 Tues–Sat, 9–1 Sun; evening tours Jul, Aug at 9.30pm Tues, Fri, book in advance by phoning tourist office (0766) 856384; adm ticket is valid for both sites*).

Undoubtedly the stars of the collection are the famous winged horses from the 'Altar of the Queen' temple on the acropolis; beautiful beasts, but made of clay like most Etruscan temple decorations—which explains why so few have survived. Well-carved sarcophagi are present in abundance, and there is a collection of Greek vases by some of the greatest 6th–5th century BC Attic painters. The Etruscans were talented at ceramics, too, as seen by the large amount of fine *bucchero* ware: their black pottery incised or painted with the usual puzzling Etruscan images. Some of the paintings from the tombs have been relocated here for their protection, including scenes of chariot riding and athletics—almost any subject is likely to turn up on Etruscan tomb walls.

There is not enough staff to keep all the hundreds of tombs open at Tarquinia's **necropolis**, all that remains of the city that dominated southern Etruria for centuries and enforced on Rome its early dynasty of Etruscan kings. The few you can see on any given day, however, rank among the finest productions of Etruscan art. Tombs like that of 'the Lionesses', with their beautiful 'Ionic style' paintings, seem remarkably close to the art of the ancient Minoans. These paintings began to appear in the 6th century BC, and only in the tombs of the richest Etruscans; more typical of the rest is the 'Tomb of the Warrior', carved simply out of the tufa and hung with arms and trophies.

Further down the coast, on the way to Cerveteri, you'll pass the not-so-old-looking city of **Civitavecchia**, a port for Rome and the gateway for ferries to Sardinia. The big fortress overlooking the harbour was designed by Michelangelo for the popes, but there's little else to detain you. Unless, that is, you feel a sudden desire to bolt for the island of *nuraghi* and *mallorredus*, in which case repair to the offices of the Tirrenia Line or the FS, the two ferry concessionaries, both at the harbour near the docks.

## Cerveteri

Cerveteri, down the coast, was originally known as *Caere*, and was the richest if not the strongest of the Etruscan cities, and the one with the closest cultural ties to Greece. According to Herodotus it was the only non-Greek city with a sanctuary at Delphi. Cerveteri, like Tarquinia, has extensive **necropoli** (*open May–Sept 9–7 Tues–Sun; Oct–April 9–4 Tues–Sun; adm*), laid out in the form of a town, with streets and squares. The site is quite large, and you may wish to purchase the map on sale at the entrance.

The most striking section is called the Banditaccia Necropolis, where the heavy stone domes, set low to the ground, look more like some sort of defence bunkers than tombs. In them you see the forerunners of all the round tombs in Rome, such as the Mausolea of Augustus and Hadrian. Be sure to see the 'Tomb of the Capitals', carved from tufa to resemble the interior of an Etruscan house (the Etruscans built all their homes, public buildings and even temples of wood, plaster and terracotta, which explains why only tombs are left). The 'Tomb of Shields and Chairs' has unusual military decoration; another, even stranger, is covered with stone reliefs of cooking utensils and other household objects.

---

### Where to Stay and Eating Out

★★★**Al Gallo** in Tuscania, Via del Gallo 22, ✆ (0761) 443388, (moderate) is a convenient place to stay in Etruscan Lazio, and has a good restaurant attached. In Tarquinia, Cerveteri and Civitavecchia there are many cheaper and duller places to stay; Tarquinia's ★★**San Marco**, Piazza Cavour 20 (moderate) is one of the better ones, a small, well-run hotel with pleasant double rooms.

Near Cerveteri at Ceri you can eat well and cheaply at **Sora Lella**, Piazza Alessandrina 1 (no phone; inexpensive). A slightly pricier option is the **Antico Giudizi** in Tarquinia, Piazza Cavour 18/20, ✆ (0766) 855061 (moderate), which serves local food and especially good wild game and roast boar.

## Rome

To know what Rome is, you might pay a visit to the little church of San Clemente, unobtrusively hidden away on the back streets behind the Colosseum. The Baroque façade conceals a 12th-century basilica with a beautiful marble choir screen 600 years older. Underneath the church, a cardinal from Boston in 1857 discovered the original church of 313, one of the first great Christian basilicas. And beneath that have been discovered the remains of two ancient buildings and a Temple of Mithras from the time of Augustus; from it you can walk out into a Roman alley that looks exactly as it did 2000 years ago, now some 9m below ground level. There are commemorative plaques in San Clemente, placed there by a Medici duke, a bishop of New York, and the last chairman of the Bulgarian Communist Party.

You are not going to get to the bottom of this city, or even begin to understand it, whether your stay is for three days or a month. With its legions of headless statues, acres of paintings, 913 churches and megatons of artistic sediment, this metropolis of aching feet will wear down even the most resolute of travellers (and travel writers). The name Rome passed out of the plane of reality into legend some 2200 years ago, when princes as far away as China first began to hear of the faraway city and its invincible armies building an empire in the west. At the same time, the Romans were cooking up a personified goddess, the Divine Rome, and beginning the strange myth of their city's destiny to conquer and pacify the world, a myth that would still haunt Europe a thousand years later.

In our prosaic times, though, you may find it requires a considerable effort of the imagination to break through to the past Romes of the Caesars and popes. All of them may be found if sought, but first you will need to peel away the increasingly thick veneer of the 'Third Rome', the burgeoning, thoroughly up-to-date creation of post-Reunification Italy. Ancient Rome at the height of its glory had perhaps a million and a half people; today there are four million, and at any given time at least half of them will be pushing their way into the Metro train while you are trying to get off. The popes, for all their centuries of experience in spectacle and ceremony, cannot often steal the show in this new Rome, and have to share the stage with a deplorable overabundance of preposterous politicians, with *Cinecittà* and the rest of the cultural apparatus of a great nation, and of course with the tourists, who sometimes put on the best show in town.

The old guard Romani, now a minority in a city swollen with new arrivals, often bewail the loss of old Rome's slow and easy pace, its vintage brand of *dolce vita* that once impressed other Italians, let alone foreigners. Lots of money, lots of traffic, and an endless caravan of tour buses have a way of compromising even the most beautiful cities. Don't concern yourself; the present is only one snapshot from a 2600-year history, and no one has ever left Rome disappointed.

## History

The beginnings of Rome are obscure enough. Historians believe the settlement of the Tiber Valley began some time about 1000 BC, when an outbreak of volcanic eruptions in the Alban hills to the south forced the Latin tribes down into the lowlands. Beyond that there are not many clues for the archaeologists to follow. But remembering that every ancient legend conceals a kernel of truth— perhaps more a poetic than a scientific truth—it would be best to follow the accounts of Virgil, the poet of the empire, and Livy, the great 1st-century Roman chronicler and mythographer.

When Virgil wrote, in the reign of Augustus, Greek culture was an irresistible force in all the recently civilized lands of the Mediterranean. For Rome, Virgil concocted the story of Aeneas, fleeing from Troy after the Homeric sack and finding his way over the sea to Latium. Descent from the Trojans, however specious, connected Rome to the Greek world and made it seem less of an upstart in its imperial age. As Virgil tells it, Aeneas' son Ascanius founded Alba Longa, a city that by the 800s was leader of the Latin Confederation. Livy takes up the tale with Numitor, a descendant of Ascanius and rightful king of Alba Longa, tossed off the throne by his usurping brother Amulius. In order that Numitor should have no heirs,

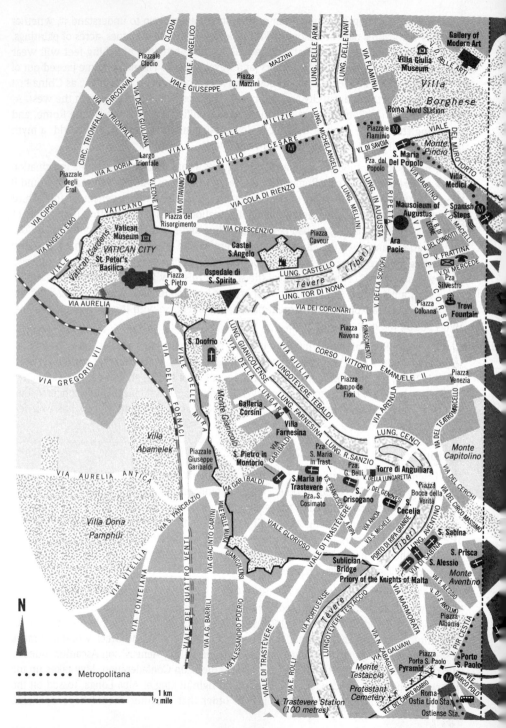

N

•••••• Metropolitana

1 km
½ mile

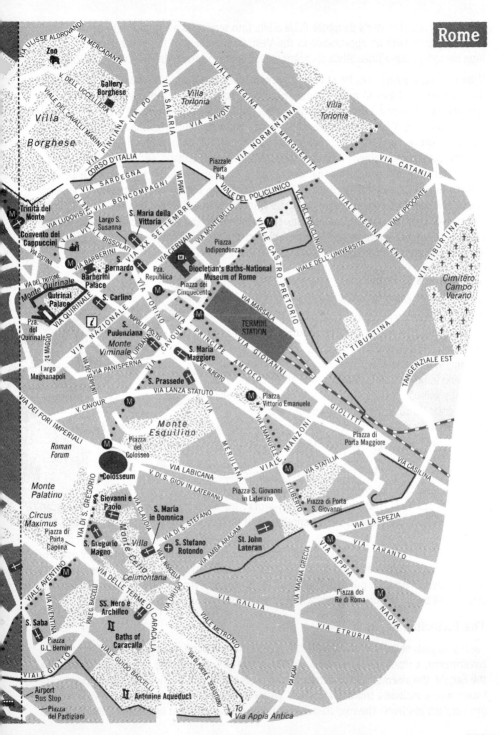

Amulius forced Numitor's daughter Rhea Silvia into service as a Vestal Virgin. Here Rome's destiny begins, with an appearance in the Vestals' chambers of the god Mars, staying just long enough to leave Rhea Silvia pregnant with the precocious twins Romulus and Remus.

When Amulius found out, he of course packed them away in a little boat, which the gods directed up the Tiber to a spot somewhere near today's Piazza Bocca della Verità. The famous she-wolf then looked after the babies, until they were found by a shepherd, who brought them up. When Mars revealed to the grown twins their origin, they returned to Alba Longa to sort out Amulius, and then returned home (in 753 BC, traditionally) to found the city the gods had ordained. Romulus soon found himself constrained to kill Remus, who would not believe the auguries that declared his brother should be king, and this sets the pattern for the bloody millennium of Rome's history to come. The legends portray early Rome as a glorified pirates' camp, and the historians are only too glad to agree. Finding themselves short of women, the Romans stole some from the Sabines. Not especially interested in farming or learning a trade, they adopted the hobby of subjugating their neighbours and soon polished it to an art.

## Seven Kings of Rome

Romulus was the first, followed by Numa Pompilius, who by divine inspiration laid down the forms for Rome's cults and priesthoods, its auguries and its College of Vestals. Tullius Hostilius, the next, made Rome ruler of all Latium, and Ancus Martius founded the port of Ostia. The next king, Tarquinius Priscus, was an Etruscan, and probably gained his throne thanks to a conquest by one of the great Etruscan city-states. Tarquin made a city of Rome, building the first real temples, the Cloaca Maxima or Great Drain, and the first Circus Maximus. His successor, Servius Tullius, restored Latin rule, inaugurated the division of the citizens between patricians (the senatorial class) and plebeians, and built a great wall to keep the Etruscans out. It apparently did not work, for as next king we find the Etruscan Tarquinius Superbus (about 534 BC), another great builder. His misfortune was to have a hotheaded son like Tarquinius Sextus, who imposed himself on a noble and virtuous Roman maiden named Lucretia (cf. Shakespeare's *Rape of Lucrece*). She committed public suicide in the morning, and the enraged Roman patricians, under the leadership of Lucius Junius Brutus, then chased out proud Tarquin and the Etruscan dynasty forever. The republic was established before the day was out, with Brutus as first consul, or chief magistrate.

## The Invincible Republic

Taking an oath never to allow another king in Rome, the patricians designed a novel form of government, a republic (*res publica*—public thing) governed by the two consuls elected by the Senate, the assembly of the patricians themselves; later innovations in the Roman constitution would include a tribune, an official with inviolable powers elected by the Plebeians to protect their interests. The two classes fought like cats and dogs at home, but combined with impressive resolve in their foreign wars. Etruscans, Aequi, Hernici, Volscii, Samnites and Sabines, all powerful nations, were defeated by Rome's citizen armies. Some of Livy's best stories come from this period, such as the taking of Rome by marauding Gauls in 390, when the cackling of geese awakened the Romans and saved the citadel on the Capitoline Hill.

By 270 BC, Rome had eliminated all its rivals to become master of Italy. It had taken about 200 years, and in the next 200 Roman rule would be established from Spain to Egypt. The first stage had proved more difficult. In Rome's final victory over the other Italians, the city digested its rivals; whole cities and tribes simply disappeared, their peoples joining the mushrooming population of Rome. After 270 it was much the same story, but on a wider scale. In the three Punic Wars against Carthage (264–146 BC), Rome gained almost all the western Mediterranean; Greece, North Africa, and Asia Minor were absorbed in small bites over the next 100 years. Rome's history was now the history of the western world.

## Imperial Rome

The old pirates' nest had never really changed its ways. Rome, like old Assyria, makes a fine example of that species of carnivore that can only live by continuous conquest. When the Romans took Greece, they first met Culture, and it had the effect on them that puberty has on little boys. After some bizarre behaviour, evidenced in the continuous civil wars (Sulla, Marius, Pompey, Julius Caesar), the Romans began tarting up their city in the worst way, vacuuming all the gold, paintings, statues, cooks, poets, and architects out of the civilized East. Beginning perhaps with Pompey, every contender for control of the now constitutionally deranged republic added some great work to the city centre: Pompey's theatre, the Julian Basilica, and something from almost every emperor up to Constantine. Julius Caesar and Augustus were perhaps Rome's greatest benefactors, initiating every sort of progressive legislation, turning dirt lanes into paved streets, and erecting new forums, temples, and the vast network of aqueducts. In their time Rome's population probably reached the million mark, surpassing Antioch and Alexandria as the largest city in the western world.

It was Augustus who effectively ended the Republic in 27 BC, by firmly establishing his personal rule and reducing the old constitution to a mere series of formalities. During the imperial era that followed his reign, Rome's position as administrative and judicial centre of the empire kept it growing, creating a new cosmopolitan population as provincials from throughout the empire—from Britain to Mesopotamia—crowded in. The city also became the unquestioned capital of banking and the financial markets—and also of religion; Rome's policy was always to induct everyone's local god as an honorary Roman, and every important cult image and relic was abducted to the Capitoline Temple. The emperor himself was *Pontifex Maximus*, head priest of Rome, whose title derives from the early Roman veneration of bridges (*pontifex* means keeper of bridges; crossing running water for many ancient religions was a slightly sacred business). St Peter, of course, arrived, and was duly martyred in AD 67. His successor, Linus, became the first pope—or *pontiff*—first in the long line of hierophants who would inherit Rome's longstanding religious tradition.

For all its glitter, Rome was still the complete economic predator, producing nothing and consuming everything. No one with any spare *denarii* would be foolish enough to go into business with them, when the only real money was to be made from government, speculation or real estate. At times almost half the population of Roman citizens (as opposed to slaves) was on the public dole. Naturally, when things went sour they really went sour. Uncertain times made Aurelian give Rome a real defensive wall in 275. By 330 the necessity of staying near the armies at the front led the western emperors to spend most of their time at army headquarters in Milan. Rome became a bloated backwater, and after three sacks of the city (Alaric the Goth in 410, Geiseric the Vandal in 455, and Odoacer the Goth in 476), there was no reason to stay. The sources disagree: perhaps 100,000 inhabitants were left by the year 500, perhaps as few as 10,000.

## Rome in the Shadows

Contrary to what most people think, Rome did not ever quite go down the drain in the Dark Ages. Its lowest point in prestige undoubtedly came in the 14th century, when the popes were at Avignon. The Dark Ages were never entirely dark; the number of important churches built (most, unfortunately, 'Baroqued' later) and the mosaics that embellished them, equal in number if not in quality to those of Ravenna, testify to the city's continuing importance. There was certainly enough to attract a few more sacks (Goths and Greeks in the 6th-century wars, Saracens from Africa in 746).

As in many other western cities, but on a larger scale, the bishops of Rome—the popes—picked up some of the pieces when civil administration disintegrated, and extended their power to temporal offices. Chroniclers report fights between them and the local barons, self-proclaimed heirs of the Roman Senate, as early as 741. It must have been a fascinating place, much too big for its population though still, thanks to the popes, thinking of itself as the centre of the western world. The forum was mostly abandoned, as were the gigantic baths, rendered useless as the aqueducts decayed and no one had the means to repair them. Almost all of the temples and basilicas survived, converted to Christian churches. Hadrian's massive tomb on the banks of the Tiber was converted into a fortress, the Castel Sant'Angelo, an impregnable haven of safety for the popes in times of trouble.

The popes deserve credit for keeping Rome alive, but the tithe money trickling in from across Europe confirmed the city in its parasitical behaviour. With two outrageous forgeries, the 'Donation of Constantine' and the 'Donation of Pepin', the popes staked their claim to temporal power in Italy. Charlemagne visited the city after driving the Lombards out in 800; during a prayer vigil in St Peter's on Christmas Eve, Pope Leo III sneaked up behind the Frankish king and set an imperial crown on his head. The surprise coronation, which the outraged Charlemagne could not or would not undo, established the precedent of Holy Roman Emperors having to cross over the Alps to receive their crown from the pope; for centuries to come Rome was able to keep its hand in the political struggles of all Europe.

## Arnold of Brescia and Rienzo

Not that Rome ever spoke with one voice; over the next 500 years it was only the idea of Rome, as the spiritual centre of the universal Christian community, that kept the actual city of Rome from disappearing altogether. Down to some 20–30,000 people in this era, Rome evolved a sort of stable anarchy, in which the major contenders for power were the popes and various noble families. First among the latter were the Orsini and the Colonna, racketeer clans who built fortresses for themselves among the ancient ruins and fought over the city like gangs in 1920s Chicago. Very often, outsiders would get into the game. A remarkable woman of obscure birth named Theodora was able to seize the Castel Sant'Angelo in the 880s; with the title of Senatrix she and her daughter Marozia ruled Rome for decades. Various German emperors seized the city, but were never able to hold it. In the 10th century, things got even more complicated as the Roman people began to assert themselves. Caught between the people and the barons, nine of the 24 popes in that century managed to get themselves murdered. The 1140s was a characteristic period of this convoluted history. A Jewish family, the Pierleoni, held power, and a Jewish antipope sat enthroned in St Peter's. Mighty Rome occupied itself with a series of wars against its neighbouring village of Tivoli, and usually lost. A sincere monkish reformer appeared, the Christian and democrat Arnold of Brescia; he recreated the Senate and almost succeeded in establishing Rome as a free *comune*, but somehow in 1155 he fell into the hands of the German emperor Frederick Barbarossa, who sold him to the English pope (Adrian IV) for hanging.

Too many centuries of this made Rome uncomfortable for the popes, who frequently removed themselves to Viterbo during the 13th century. The final indignity came when, under French pressure, the papacy decamped entirely to Avignon in 1309. Pulling strings from a distance, the papacy only made life more complicated for the Romans left behind. Into the vacuum they created stepped one of the noblest Romans of them all, later to be the subject of Wagner's first opera. Cola di Rienzo was the son of an innkeeper, but he had a good enough education to read the Latin inscriptions that lay on ruins all around him, and the works of Livy, Cicero, and Tacitus wherever he could find them. Obsessed by the idea of re-establishing Roman glory, he talked and talked at the bewildered inhabitants until they caught the fever too. With Rienzo as Tribune of the People, the Roman Republic was reborn in May of 1347.

Power does corrupt, however, in Rome more than any spot on the globe, and an increasingly fat and ridiculous Rienzo was hustled out of Rome by the united nobles before the year was out. His return to power, in 1354, ended with his murder by a mob after only two months. Rome was now at its lowest ebb, with only some 15,000 people, and prosperity and influence were not to be completely restored until the reign of Pope Nicholas V after 1447.

## The New Rome

The old papacy, before Avignon, had largely been a tool of the Roman nobles; periods when it was able to achieve real independence were the exception rather than the rule. In the more settled conditions of the 15th century, a new papacy emerged, richer and more sophisticated. Political power, as a guarantee of stability, was always its goal, and a series of talented Renaissance popes saw their best hopes for achieving this by rebuilding Rome. By the 1500s this process was in full swing. Under Julius II (1503–13), the papal domains for the first time were run like a modern state; Julius also laid plans for the rebuilding of St Peter's, beginning the great building programme that was to transform the city. New streets were laid out, especially the Via Giulia and the grand avenues radiating from the Piazza del Popolo; Julius' main architect, Bramante, knocked down medieval Rome with such gay abandon that Raphael nicknamed him 'Ruinante'.

Over the next two centuries, the work continued at a frenetic pace. Besides St Peter's, hundreds of churches were either built or rebuilt, and cardinals and noble families lined the streets with new palaces, imposing if not always beautiful. A new departure in urban design was developed in the 1580s, under Sixtus V, recreating some of the monumentality of ancient Rome. Piazzas were cleared in front of the major religious sites, each with its Egyptian obelisk, linked by a network of straight boulevards. The New Rome, symbol of the Counter-Reformation and the majesty of the popes, was however bought at a terrible price. Besides the destruction of Bramante, buildings that had survived substantially intact for 1500 years were cannibalized for their marble; the popes wantonly destroyed more of ancient Rome than Goths or Saracens had ever managed. Also, to pay for their programme, they taxed the economy of the Papal States out of existence. Areas of Lazio that had been relatively prosperous even in the Dark Ages turned into wastelands as exasperated farmers simply abandoned them, and the other cities of Lazio and Umbria were set back centuries in their development. The New Rome was proving as voracious a predator as the old.

Worst of all, the new papacy in the 16th century instituted terror as an instrument of public policy. In the course of the previous century the last vestiges of Roman liberty had been gradually extinguished. The popes tried to extend their power by playing a game of high-stakes diplomacy between Emperor Charles V of Spain and King Francis I of France, but reaped a bitter harvest in the 1527 sack of Rome. An out-of-control imperial army occupied the city for almost a year, causing tremendous destruction, while the disastrous Pope Clement VII looked on helplessly from the Castel Sant'Angelo. Afterwards, the popes were happy to become part of the Imperial-Spanish system. Political repression was fiercer than anywhere else in Italy; the Inquisition was refounded in 1542 by Paul III, and book burnings, torture of freethinkers, and executions became even more common than in Spain itself.

## The End of Papal Rule

By about 1610, there was no Roman foolish enough to get burned at the stake; at the same time workmen were adding the last stones to the cupola of St Peter's. It was the end of an era, but the building continued. A thick accretion of Baroque, like coral, collected over Rome. Bernini did his Piazza Navona fountain in 1650, and the Colonnade for St Peter's 15 years later. The political importance of the popes, however, disappeared with surprising finality. As Joseph Stalin was later to note, the popes had plenty of Bulls, but few army divisions, and they drifted into irrelevance in the power politics of modern Europe during the Thirty Years War and after.

Rome was left to enjoy a decadent but rather pleasant twilight. A brief interruption came when revolutionaries in 1798 once again proclaimed the Roman Republic, and a French army sent the pope packing. Rome later became part of Napoleon's empire, but papal rule was restored in 1815. Another republic appeared in 1848, on the crest of that romantic year's revolutionary wave, but this time a French army besieged the city and had the pope propped back on his throne by July 1849. Garibaldi, the republic's military commander, barely escaped with his life.

For twenty years Napoleon III maintained a garrison in Rome to look after the pope, and consequently Rome became the last part of Italy to join the new Italian kingdom. After the French defeat in the war of 1870, Italian troops blew a hole in the old Aurelian wall near the Porta Pia and marched in. Pius IX, who ironically had decreed papal infallibility just the year before, locked himself in the Vatican and pouted; the popes were to be 'prisoners' until Mussolini's Concordat of 1929, by which they agreed to recognize the Italian state.

As capital of the new state, Rome underwent another building boom; new streets like Via del Tritone, Via Vittorio Veneto, and Via Nazionale made circulation a little easier around the seven hills; villas and gardens disappeared under endless blocks of speculative building (everything around Termini Station, for example); long-needed projects like the Tiber embankments were built; and, at the same time, the kingdom strove mightily to impress the world with gigantic, absurd public buildings and monuments, such as the Altar of the Nation and the Finance Ministry on Via XX Settembre, as big as two Colosseums. Growth has been steady; from some 200,000 people in 1879, Rome has since increased twentyfold.

## The Twentieth Century

In 1922 the city was the objective of Mussolini's 'March on Rome', when the Fascist leader used his blackshirt squads to demand, and win, complete power in the Italian government, though he himself famously made the journey into town by train, and in his best suit. Mussolini was one more figure who wanted to revive the greatness of ancient Rome, and to create a 'New Roman Empire' for Italy. For twenty years, the Piazza Venezia was the chosen theatre for his oratorical performances. He also had big ideas for the city itself: it was under Fascism that many of the relics of ancient Rome were first opened up as public monuments, in order to remind Italians of their great heritage, and the Via dei Fori Imperiali was driven past the Forum, destroying some of the archaeological sites in the process. His greatest legacy to Rome, however, was the EUR suburb to the south, the projected site of a world exhibition for 1942, and a huge showcase of his preferred Fascist-classical architecture. At the end of the war it was only half built, but the Italians, not wishing to waste anything, decided to finish the project, and it now houses many of Rome's museums and sports venues (see below).

Since the war Rome has continued to grow fat as the capital of the often ramshackle, notoriously corrupt, never-changing political system thrown up by the Italian Republic, and the headquarters of the smug *classe politica* that ran it. Rome has been accused by Lombard regionalists of drawing off wealth from the productive areas of Italy in much the same way that it once demanded to be fed by the Empire; nevertheless, Romans have joined in Italy's 'Moral Revolution' of the last few years, abusing the old-style political bosses like the rest of the country, despite the fact that a great many in this city of civil servants themselves benefited from the system. At the end of 1993 Romans surprised most observers by electing as mayor the ecologist Francesco Rutelli at the head of a Green/PDS alliance, with the promise of dramatic reforms in the local administration—and such measures as the pedestrianization of more major streets, in an effort to prise Romans away from their fanatical devotion to their cars. Just what effect this will have, or whether it will fall down before the proverbial Roman cynicism, remains to be seen.

## A Little Orientation

*'There's three things I want to see in Rome:*
*the Colosseum, St Peter's and the Acropolis.'*

a big-time tourist from Texas

## Two Walls

Of Rome's earliest wall, built by King Servius Tullius before the republic was founded, little remains; you can see one of the last surviving bits right outside Termini Station. The second, built by Aurelian in 275 AD, is one of the wonders of Rome, though taken for granted. With its 19km length and 383 towers, it is one of the largest ever built in Europe—and certainly the best-preserved of antiquity. In several places you can see almost perfectly preserved bastions and monumental gates.

## Three Romes

Historians and Romans often think of the city in this way. Classical Rome began on the Palatine Hill, and all through its history its business and administrative centre stayed nearby, in the original Forum and the great Imperial Fora built around it. Many of the busiest parts of the city lay to the south, where now you see only green on the tourist office's map. After Rome's fall, these areas were never really rebuilt, and even now substantial ruins like Trajan's Baths remain unexcavated. The Second Rome, that of the popes, had its centre in the Campus Martius, the plain west and north of the Capitoline Hill, later expanding to include the 'Leonine City' around St Peter's, and the new Baroque district around Piazza del Popolo and the Spanish Steps. The Third Rome, capital of United Italy, has expanded in all directions; the closest it has to a centre is the long, straight Via del Corso.

## Seven Hills

Originally they were much higher; centuries of building, rebuilding and river flooding have made the ground level in the valleys much higher, and at various times emperors and popes shaved bits off their tops in building programmes. The **Capitoline Hill**, smallest but most important, now has Rome's City Hall, the Campidoglio, roughly on the site of ancient Rome's greatest temple, that of Jupiter Greatest and Best. The **Palatine**, adjacent to it, was originally the most fashionable district, and eventually got entirely covered by the palaces of the emperors—the heart of the Roman Empire. The usually plebeian **Aventine** lies to the south of it, across from the Circus Maximus. Between the Colosseum and the Termini Station, the **Esquiline** (Colle Oppio), the **Viminal** and the **Quirinal** stand three in a row. The Quirinal was long the residence of the popes, and later of the Italian kings. Finally, there is the **Caelian Hill** south of the Colosseum, now a charming oasis of parkland and ancient churches in the centre of Rome. Rome of course has other hills not included in the canonical seven: **Monte Vaticano**, from which the Vatican takes its name, **Monte Pincio**, including the Villa Borghese, Rome's biggest park, and the **Gianicolo**, the long ridge above Trastevere the ancients called the Janiculum.

## Fourteen Regions

Ancient Rome had neither street lights nor street signs; drunks trying to find their way home had a job on their hands. Modern Rome has plenty of both. Being Rome, of course the street signs are of marble. In the corner, you will notice a small number in Roman numerals; this refers to the *rione*, or ward. In the Middle Ages, there were 14 of these, descendants of the 14 *regii* of the ancient city; even after the fall of Rome they maintained their organization and offered protection to their people in the worst of times. With the growth of the city in the last 100 years there are now many more *rione*, but on a few older buildings you will still see the heraldic devices of the originals at the *rione* boundaries.

## Passing the Time of Day in Ancient Rome

 Recreating some of the atmosphere of the old days is not hard; a score of books have been written on the subject, of which one of the best is *Daily Life in Ancient Rome* by Jerome Carcopino (available in Penguin). Roman poets such as Horace, Martial and especially Juvenal also have plenty to say about it. Life in Rome at the height of empire was an imperial pain: ridiculously high rents, high taxes, street crime, noise around the clock, and neighbours from Baetica or Rhaetia with peculiar habits—but naturally everyone in the empire dreamed of someday moving there. The most significant difference between the way they lived then and our times was the sharp contrast between the quality of life in public versus private places. The average Roman citizen, usually unemployed or underemployed, could loll about magnificent baths and forums all day; only with reluctance did he drag himself home to his nasty fourth-floor flat at night.

### Public Rome

The Roman *forum*, developed from the Greek *agora*, usually took the form of an open space surrounded by temples, basilicas and colonnades. In the centre, the original Roman Forum and the Fora of Augustus and Trajan made up a single vast complex, the public stage of Roman life. A typical Roman citizen would be there in the morning, to transact business, meet friends, watch the cosmopolitan crowd go by, or indulge in the favourite pastime of watching court proceedings in the basilica. Often they would have their own actions running; the Romans were easily the most litigious nation in all history. Always, surrounding the fora would be the market-places of the city, some of them imposing buildings like the five-storey Market of Trajan (which can be visited today, but to get a living idea of what one was like you should see the Covered Market in Istanbul).

For all their skill at plumbing, the Romans never managed to bring running water into most of their homes. The baths, therefore, were a daily spot on any respectable Roman's agenda. He could have stayed all day, for these great establishments were a stage for public life as much as the forum. Every neighbourhood had some, and counting the big ones built by the emperors they covered almost 10 per cent of Rome. The biggest ones, with bathing halls bigger than the present St Peter's, also included parks, museums, libraries, lunch counters, and of course the *palaestrae*—athletic grounds for the Romans' favourite ball games, and wrestling. No civilization, perhaps, ever conceived a more useful institution for its citizens to spend their leisure time. The baths were cheap and accessible to even the poorest Roman; many of the emperors frequented them, too. There were other places to pursue the classical *dolce vita*—the emperors' extensive gardens, usually open to the public, the temples, which in an irreligious age were really glorified art museums, and the taverns—one on every block, usually with a few prostitutes upstairs and gambling in the back room. Romans were terrible gamblers; even the virtuous Augustus would regularly present his children, slaves and dinner guests with bags of *sestertii* to wager against him. Finally, there were the races and games in the Colosseum or the Circus Maximus, all of them extraordinarily brutal and bloody, which occupied something on the average of 90–100 days a year. These were free, though you needed a ticket just to remind you of the imperial largesse that made it all possible. You also needed a toga, unless you were in the plebeian cheap seats, for these were among this informal city's few dress-up occasions.

## Private Rome

Over 90 per cent of Romans lived in flats, in pretty but generally poorly built insulae up to 10 storeys in height. From the outside, they looked much the same as some of the older Roman apartment blocks today, only with more imaginative façades of brick, stucco, and patterned timbers. Many had balconies, and every part of these balconies and windows that received any sun would be full of climbing vines and flowers. Unfortunately, most of the streets were less than 4m across. Rich and poor Romans lived mixed together in every *regio* or ward; the very rich in walled houses of their own (like those at Pompeii), set perhaps next to a four-storey block with wine and oil shops, taverns, and ironmongers on the ground floor, middle-class bureaucrats and clients of the rich on the first (with perhaps three or four slaves in the household), and the very poor above them. These would have the furthest to climb, and they could be certain of doom in case of fire or collapse. Both of these were constant worries. Crassus, who ruled Rome in the second Triumvirate with Caesar and Pompey, got his start as a weasling building contractor, following the fire squads.

People who lived in flats did not use them much for entertaining, or even for cooking. Flats may have had paid water-carriers, but no heating except braziers, no glass windows, and little furniture. The shops that filled the ground floors of almost every building always spilled out into the narrow streets, occupying them along with the market barrows and the grammar school classes, which rented space under shop awnings or in porticoes—learning to live with distractions was a part of any Roman's education. Traffic problems were probably Rome's biggest headache after the 2nd century BC; Julius Caesar decreed an end to chariots and carriages (the rich had to get by with slave-borne litters) and banished wagons during daylight hours.

---

*Getting There*

*by air*

It's a little confusing; the main airport, **Leonardo da Vinci**, will usually be referred to as **Fiumicino**. Officially the first name (℗ 60121) means the part of this sprawling complex that handles international flights, and Fiumicino (℗ 65951/65954252) is the domestic terminal (most Romans don't know this, either). Taking a taxi from there into Rome should cost about L60,000, including airport and luggage supplements. There are two rail services from the airport to the city: the main service runs from there to Trastevere, Ostiense, Tuscolana and Tiburtina stations in Rome, leaving about every 20 minutes and costing L7000. Ostiense and Tiburtina are both on the Metro system. There is now also a faster *aerotreno* direct from Fiumicino to Rome's main rail station, the Stazione Termini, which costs L12,000. Trains do not run between 10.20pm and 7am, at which times the only way to go is the COTRAL bus, hourly through the night between a stop outside the Arrivals hall and Piazzale dei Partigiani, near Piramide Metro station in Rome. The bus costs L6000. The train will take about 40 minutes from Tiburtina to Fiumicino; allow at least 50 minutes for the bus.

A secondary airport, **Ciampino** (✆ 794941) is the base for most charters, and also takes some scheduled flights. A COTRAL bus runs from here 6.15am–10.20pm daily to the Anagnina stop at the southern end of the Metro A line, from where it's about 20 minutes to Termini Station.

Almost all the foreign airlines have their offices on Via Barberini or Via Bissolati, just off Via Vittorio Veneto.

### *by rail*

Almost all long-distance trains arrive at and depart from the huge **Stazione Termini**, which is chaotic but modern and efficiently run. The rail information booth is usually terribly crowded, but you can try to find your destination on one of the clever, multi-lingual computer screens the FS has installed in the lobby (to phone for information, ✆ 4775, though this line is nearly always engaged). Keep an eye out for predatory gypsies. There is a taxi stand right in front, along with city buses to most points in Rome, and the main Metro station is in the basement.

There are plenty of other stations in Rome: **Tiburtina** (Ⓜ Tiburtina), on the eastern edge of town, and **Ostiense** (Ⓜ Piramide) south of the Aventine Hill serve some long distance north–south lines that stop in Rome. During the night, from 12 midnight to 5am, Termini station is shut and trains stop at the other city stations. A few trains to Tuscany and Umbria do start from **Ostiense** and stop at **Trastevere**, on Viale Trastevere.

The Lazio transport authority COTRAL also operates its own little rail network with three lines, the **Roma-Nord** line to Viterbo from their own station on Piazzale Flaminio, just north of Piazza del Popolo, a line to Frascati and the Castelli Romani from the Stazione Laziale, alongside Termini, and a line to Ostia and the Lido, from Porta San Paolo (next to the main Ostiense FS station) and Magliana.

### *by bus*

Long distance bus services to Rome are run by several different companies, with no central bus station or information service. Most, however, now arrive at the Tiburtina FS and Metro station, on the eastern side of Rome.

Buses to almost every town in Lazio are run by COTRAL. They leave from different locations around the edge of the city, depending on the destination. Buses heading north and northwest leave from Saxa Rubra (on the Roma-Nord rail line) and Lepanto (Ⓜ Lepanto); for the south, southwest and east buses leave from Anagnina,

EUR Fermi and Tiburtina metro stops. The COTRAL head office is at Via Ostiense 131 (© 57531/5915551).

### by road

All the *autostrade* converging on Rome—the A1 from Florence and the north, the A24 from the Adriatic, the A2 from Naples and the A12 from Civitavecchia—run into the city's giant ring road, the *Grande Raccordo Anulare* or *GRA*. From there, good routes into the city are the Via Aurelia, SS1, from the west, the local SS201 *autostrada* from the airport, in the southwest, and the A24, from the east.

Rome is, as it has been for 2000 years, the hub of a network of ancient routes serving every direction, now transmogrified into state roads (SS) but retaining their old names, and they still provide the most direct means of getting out of the city.

---

## Getting Around

 Looking at the map, Rome seems to be a city made for getting around on foot. This may be so in the *centro storico* around Piazza Navona, but elsewhere it's deceptive—city blocks in the newer areas are huge, and it will always take you longer than you think to walk anywhere. The hills, the outsize scale, and the traffic and noise also make Rome a very tiring place, but there is some pleasant strolling to be had in the old districts west of the Corso, around the Tiber Island, in the old parts of Trastevere, and around the Caelian hill.

### by Metro

Rome's underground system is efficient, but often indecently crowded and inconvenient. There are only two lines, and very few stops near the oldest parts of the city; imagine trying to dig any sort of hole in Rome, with legions of archaeologists ready to pounce when you hit something interesting, and it will become clear why progress has been so slow. The two lines, A and B, cross at Termini Station; one or the other will take you to the Colosseum, around the Aventine Hill, to Piazza di Spagna, St John Lateran, St Paul's outside the walls, Piazza del Popolo, or within eight blocks of St Peter's, but outside these areas the Metropolitana's usefulness is very limited. Single tickets cost L1000, but not every station sells them; buy them beforehand at nearby tobacco shops, bars, or newspaper kiosks.

### by bus and tram

By far the best way to get around, although the complexity of the route system intimidates most visitors. First thing to do, if you are planning to stay a while in Rome, is to buy a L1000 route map from the ATAC (city bus company) information booth outside Termini Station. Tickets are sold there (L1200 for a single ticket), as well as in tobacco shops, news-stands and some bars. They cannot be bought on the buses themselves, but must be cancelled in the machines at the back of the bus. There are also special-price full-day tickets (which also include the Metro) and weekly tickets for tourists. Most routes run quite frequently, and are of course often crowded. In the outer districts there are also some cute, rickety tram routes, which more or less make a ring around the city. They use the same tickets as the buses.

## Some Useful Bus Routes

**19**    (tram) Piazza Risorgimento (near the Vatican)–Viale delle Milizie–Villa Borghese–Viale Regina Margherita– Porta Maggiore–San Lorenzo and down the Via Prenestina.

**23**    Vatican Museums–Castel Sant'Angelo–along the Tiber–Porta San Paolo-St Paul's Basilica.

**27**    Termini–Via Cavour–Colosseum–Porta San Paolo.

**30b**    (tram) Villa Borghese–Viale Regina Margherita–San Lorenzo–Santa Croce in Gerusalemme–St John Lateran–Colosseum–Viale Aventino–Porta San Paolo–Viale Trastevere (a fun trip, taking in many of the city's most important sights).

**36**    Termini–Via Nomentana (Sant'Agnese Church).

**46**    Piazza Venezia–Corso Vittorio Emanuele–Vatican.

**56**    Piazza Sonnino (Trastevere)–Largo Argentina–Via del Corso–Via Tritone–Via Vittorio Veneto.

**64**    Termini–Via Nazionale–Corso Vittorio Emanuele–Vatican (the main bus route from the *centro storico* to the Vatican).

**118**    St John Lateran–Colosseum–Caracalla's Baths–Via Appia Antica (passing all the catacombs and tombs).

**119**    Augustus' Mausoleum–Pantheon–Via del Tritone–Piazza di Spagna–Piazza del Popolo–Augustus' mausoleum (a circular minibus service around the *centro storico*).

### by taxi

Taxis, painted yellow or, less commonly, white, are in plentiful supply, though it's normally easier to get one waiting at a rank than to flag one down in the street. There are ranks in most of the main piazzas, such as Largo Argentina, Piazza Venezia, Piazza di Spagna and so on. They are quite expensive, with sizeable added surcharges for luggage, on Sundays and after 10.30 at night. Don't expect to find one when it's raining.

To phone for a taxi, call © 88177 or © 4994.

### by car

Absolutely not recommended! Rome isn't as chaotic as Naples, but nearly so. Parking is expensive, and street parking difficult to find; so many areas in the centre are closed to traffic (and the signs for them so hard to spot) you can easily make a mistake that will earn you a ticket. Rome and its cars are mortal enemies; sooner or later one or the other will have to succumb.

### Tourist Information

The big main office is the **EPT**, at Via Parigi 5, © 4871270, just behind Diocletian's Baths and three blocks north of Termini Station; they have plenty of things in English to hand out, including a book called *Here Rome* (sic),

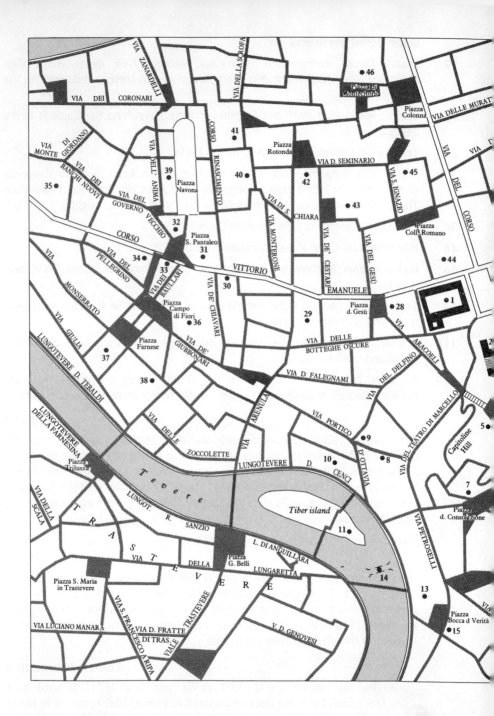

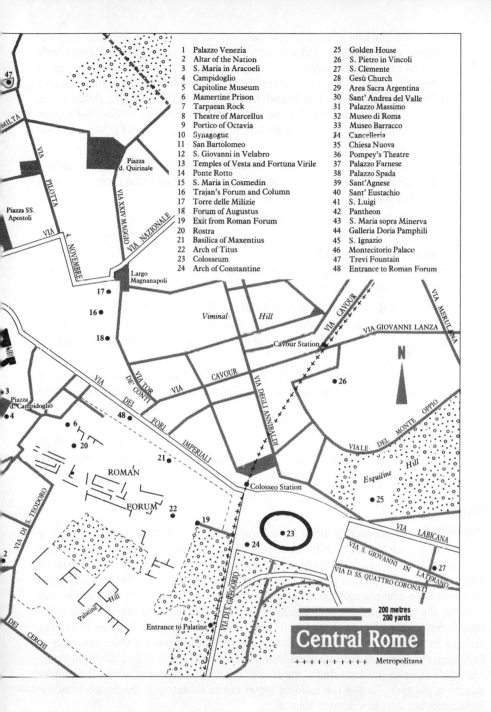

| | | | |
|---|---|---|---|
| 1 | Palazzo Venezia | 25 | Golden House |
| 2 | Altar of the Nation | 26 | S. Pietro in Vincoli |
| 3 | S. Maria in Aracoeli | 27 | S. Clemente |
| 4 | Campidoglio | 28 | Gesù Church |
| 5 | Capitoline Museum | 29 | Area Sacra Argentina |
| 6 | Mamertine Prison | 30 | Sant' Andrea del Valle |
| 7 | Tarpaean Rock | 31 | Palazzo Massimo |
| 8 | Theatre of Marcellus | 32 | Museo di Roma |
| 9 | Portico of Octavia | 33 | Museo Barracco |
| 10 | Synagogue | 34 | Cancelleria |
| 11 | San Bartolomeo | 35 | Chiesa Nuova |
| 12 | S. Giovanni in Velabro | 36 | Pompey's Theatre |
| 13 | Temples of Vesta and Fortuna Virile | 37 | Palazzo Farnese |
| 14 | Ponte Rotto | 38 | Palazzo Spada |
| 15 | S. Maria in Cosmedin | 39 | Sant'Agnese |
| 16 | Trajan's Forum and Column | 40 | Sant' Eustachio |
| 17 | Torre delle Milizie | 41 | S. Luigi |
| 18 | Forum of Augustus | 42 | Pantheon |
| 19 | Exit from Roman Forum | 43 | S. Maria sopra Minerva |
| 20 | Rostra | 44 | Galleria Doria Pamphili |
| 21 | Basilica of Maxentius | 45 | S. Ignazio |
| 22 | Arch of Titus | 46 | Montecitorio Palace |
| 23 | Colosseum | 47 | Trevi Fountain |
| 24 | Arch of Constantine | 48 | Entrance to Roman Forum |

Central Rome

200 metres
200 yards

+ + + + + + + + + + +  Metropolitana

with lots of practical information, *Musei e monumenti* with the opening times and prices of all the museums, and a monthly list of events called *Carnet di Roma*, with colourful stories and sidelights about the city and 'A year in Rome and its Province', a calendar of events. There is also a very competent branch office inside the track area at **Termini Station**, and at **Fiumicino Airport**. An alternative, privately run English-speaking agency offering the same services as EPT but without the queues (and often more efficiently) is **Enjoy Rome**, Via Varese, 39, ✆ 4451843, also near Termini Station.

The best local source of information on what's on in Rome in the arts, culture and entertainment is *Trovaroma*, a weekly listings supplement that comes free with Thursday's edition of *La Repubblica* newspaper.

The phone code for Rome from elsewhere in Italy is **06**.

**Fire, ✆ 115.**

**Police emergencies, 113.**

**Police**, Questura Centrale, Via San Vitale 15, ✆ 4886.

**Ambulance, ✆ 113 or 5510.**

**Hospital: Ospedale Santo Spirito**, Lungotevere in Sassia 1, ✆ 68351.

**24-hour pharmacies: Spinedi**, Via Arenula 73, ✆ 68803278, near Largo Argentina. Open 24 hours daily. Lists of duty pharmacists are also posted outside all other pharmacies.

Outside banking hours money can be exchanged at **American Express**, Piazza di Spagna 38, ✆ 67641, open 9–5.30 Mon–Fri, 9–12.30 Sat; **Casa del Turista**, Via Giolitti 97, ✆ 44633470, open 9–1, 3–6, Mon–Sat; and **Thomas Cook**, Via della Conciliazione 23–25, ✆ 68300435, open 8.30–6 Mon–Sat, 9–5.30 Sun.

The **main post office** is in the Piazza San Silvestro, ✆ 6771, and is open 8.30am –7.40pm Mon–Fri, 8.30–12 Sat. There is also a post office at Termini Station. There are phone centres in Piazza San Silvestro, at Termini and at Fiumicino airport.

## Piazza Venezia

This traffic-crazed, thoroughly awful piazza may be a poor introduction to Rome, but it makes a good place to start, with the ruins of old Rome on one side and the boutiques and bureaucracies of the new city on the other. The piazza takes its name from the **Palazzo Venezia**, built for Pope Paul II in 1455, but long the Embassy of the Venetian Republic. Mussolini made it his residence, leaving a light on all night to make the Italians think he was working. His famous balcony, from which he would declaim to the 'oceanic' crowds in the square (renamed the Forum of the Fascist Empire in those days) still holds its prominent place, a bad memory for the Italians. Nowadays the Palazzo holds a small **museum** of Renaissance and Baroque decorative arts (*open 9–1.30 Tues–Sat; 9–1 Sun; adm expensive*). The palace complex was built around the ancient church of **San Marco**, with a 9th-century mosaic in the apse. Parts of the building are as old as AD 400, and the façade is by the Renaissance architect Benedetto di Maiano.

Long ago the southern edge of this piazza had approaches up to the Capitoline Hill. The hill is still there, though you can't see it, it being entirely blocked out by the mammoth white bulk of the **Altar of the Nation** (also known as the *Vittoriano*, the Vittorio Emanuele Monument, or, less respectfully, the 'Wedding Cake' or the 'Typewriter'), Risorgimento Italy's own self-inflicted satire and one of the world's apotheoses of kitsch. Its size, and its solid marble walls, are explained by the 1880s prime minister who commissioned it; he happened to have a marble quarry back in his home district of Brescia. Recounting the sculptural allegory of the scheme would take pages—but of the two big bronze imperial-style *quadrigae* on top, one represents Italian Liberty and the other Italian Unity. In the centre, under the colonnades, the modest virtues of Vittorio Emanuele II have earned him a 12m bronze equestrian statue, perhaps the world's largest. Beneath him, Italy's Unknown Soldier sleeps peacefully with a round-the-clock guard. Built into the monument on the left-hand side you can see the remains of the republican Roman tomb of C. Publius Bibulus.

## The Capitoline Hill

Behind the Vittoriano, two stairways lead to the top of the hill. This is a fateful spot; in 121 BC the great reformer Tiberius Gracchus was murdered here by what today would be called a 'right-wing death squad'. Almost a millennium and a half later, Cola di Rienzo was trying to escape Rome in disguise when the enraged mob recognized him by the rings on his fingers and tore him to pieces. Rienzo built the left-hand staircase, and was the first to climb it. It leads to the church of **Santa Maria in Aracoeli**, begun in the 7th century over the temple of Juno Moneta—the ancient Roman Mint was adjacent to it. The Aracoeli, which in Rienzo's time served as a sort of council hall for the Romans, is one of the most revered of Roman churches; legend has it that one of the ancient sibyls, that of Tivoli, prophesied the coming of Jesus and told Augustus to build a temple here to the 'first born of God'. Inside, you can seek out frescoes by Pinturicchio (*San Bernardino of Siena*) and Gozzoli (*St Anthony of Padua*), and also a small tombstone by Donatello, near the entrance.

Aracoeli

The second stairway takes you to the real heart of Rome, Michelangelo's **Piazza del Campidoglio**, passing on the way a rather flattering statue of Rienzo set on a bronze pedestal. At the top, bordering the piazza, a formidable cast of statues includes the Dioscuri, who come from Pompey's Theatre, and Marforio (in the Capitoline Museum courtyard), a river god once employed as one of the 'talking statues' of Rome, decorated with graffiti and placards commenting on current events. Someone is missing, however, namely **Marcus**

**Aurelius,** the great 2nd-century AD bronze equestrian statue of the benign and philosophical emperor that stood on the plinth in the middle of the piazza from the 16th century until 1981, when he was taken down for essential restoration work. He is now, finally, on show once again after re-gilding, but in the security of the Capitoline Museums. Fortunately enough, since it was an old Roman saying that the world would end when all the original gold flaked off. The Christians of old only refrained from melting him down for cash because they believed he was not Marcus Aurelius, but Constantine.

## The Capitoline Museums

Michelangelo's original plans may have been adapted and tinkered with by later architects, but nevertheless his plan for the Campidoglio has come out as one of the triumphs of Renaissance design. The centrepiece, the **Palazzo Senatorio**, Rome's city hall, with its distinctive stairway and bell tower, is built over the ruins of the Roman *tabularium*, the state archive. At the base of the stair note the statue of Minerva, in her aspect as the allegorical goddess Roma.

Flanking it, Michelangelo's **Palazzo dei Conservatori** has been incorporated into the **Capitoline Museums** together with its opposite number, the later **Palazzo Nuovo** across the square. Founded by Pope Clement XII in 1734, and so the oldest true museum in the world, the Capitoline is one of the most interesting of Roman museums (*open 9–1.30, 5–8pm, Tues, Thurs; 9–1.30 Wed, Fri; 8.30pm–11pm Sat; 9am–1pm Sun; adm exp*). Its exhibits display both the heights and depths of ancient society and culture. For the heights, there are the reliefs from the triumphal arch of Marcus Aurelius—first-class work in scenes of the emperor's clemency and piety, and his triumphal receptions in Rome. Marcus always looks a little worried in these, perhaps considering his good-for-nothing son Commodus and the empire he would inherit, sinking into corruption and excess. What was to come is well illustrated by the degenerate art of the 4th century, like the colossal bronze head, hand and foot of Constantine, parts of a colossal statue in the Basilica of Maxentius (now on display in the courtyard).

In between these extremes come roomfuls of statuary, including the famous *Capitoline She-Wolf*, the very symbol of Rome; statues of most of the emperors, busts of Homer, Sophocles, Pythagoras and other lights; the voluptuous *Capitoline Venus*; a big baby Hercules (who may have inspired Donatello's famous *Amor* in Florence); and the *Muse Polyhymnia*, one of the most delightful and beautiful statues of antiquity. Later works include lots of papal paraphernalia, a statue of Charles of Anjou by Florence's Arnolfo di Cambio, and a small **Pinacoteca**, in the Palazzo dei Conservatori, with some dignified Velázquez gentlemen looking scornfully at the other paintings, and two major works by Caravaggio, the *Fortune Teller* and *John the Baptist.* There are also some lovely, though at times silly, 18th-century porcelains—orchestras of monkeys in powdered wigs, and such.

From behind the Palazzo Senatorio, a stairway leads down, offering the best overview of the Roman Forum; the entrance is a little further down Via dei Fori Imperiali. On the way, beneath the church of San Giuseppe Falegnami, you can visit the **Mamertine Prison** (*open April–Sept 9–12.30, 2.30–6 daily; Oct–Mar 9–12, 2–5 daily*), the small calaboose used by the ancient Romans for their most important prisoners—the Cataline conspirators,

Vercingetorix, the Gaulish chief captured by Caesar, and finally St Peter. Because of this, the prison is now a revered shrine to the saint. You will see his symbol, an upside-down cross; this, according to legend, is how they crucified him. The southern end of the Capitol, one of the quietest corners of Rome, was the site of Jupiter Greatest and Best, a temple built originally by the Etruscan kings. At the time it was the largest in Italy, testimony to Rome's importance as far back as 450 BC. Along the southern edge of the hill, the cliffs you see are the somewhat reduced remains of the **Tarpeian Rock**, from which traitors and other malefactors were thrown in Rome's early days.

## Along the Tiber

The early emperors did their best to import classical Greek drama to Rome, and for a while, with the poets of the Latin New Comedy, it seemed the Romans would carry on the tradition. Great theatres were built in Rome, like the **Theatre of Marcellus** at the foot of the Capitoline, begun by Caesar and completed by Augustus. By the second century AD, however, theatre had already begun to degenerate into music hall shows, lewd performances with naked actresses and grisly murders (condemned prisoners were sometimes butchered on stage), and shows by celebrity actors probably much like some unseemly spectacles of our own time. Marcellus' theatre (Augustus named it after his favourite nephew) survived into the Middle Ages, when the Orsini family converted it into their palace-fortress, the strongest in Rome after the Castel Sant'Angelo. Today it presents one of Rome's more curious sights, the tall arches of the circumference surmounted by the rough medieval walls of the Orsini. Behind it, the **Portico of Octavia** stands battered but erect; Augustus built it as a decoration and place of rest amid the shops and markets that once covered this area.

The streets to the west contain a mix of some of Rome's oldest houses with new buildings; the latter have replaced the old walled **ghetto**, demolished only a century ago. Jews have formed a sizeable community in Rome since Pompey and Titus first brought them as slaves. They helped finance the career of Julius Caesar, who would prove to be their greatest benefactor. For centuries they lived near this bend in the river and in Trastevere. Paul IV took time off from burning books and heretics to wall them into the tiny ghetto in 1555; at the same time he forced them to wear orange hats, attend Mass on Sunday, and limited them to the rag and old iron trades. Tearing down the ghetto walls was one of the first acts of the Italian kingdom after the entry into Rome in 1870. The exotic, eclectic main **synagogue** was built in 1874, after the last of the ghetto was demolished. Inside, there is a small museum, the **Permanent Exhibition of the Jewish Community in Rome** (*open 9.30–2, 3–5, Mon–Thurs; 9.30–2 Fri; 9.30–12 Sun; adm. Ask at the Centre for Jewish Culture, Via del Tempio 4, just around the corner, for tours of the ghetto and the Jewish catacombs*).

Opposite the synagogue, the **Tiber Island** is joined to both sides of the river by surviving ancient bridges. In imperial times, the island was sacred to Aesculapius, god of healing; a legend records how some serpents brought from the god's shrine in Greece escaped and swam to the spot, choosing the site by divine guidance. Now, as in ancient times, most of the lovely island is taken up by a hospital, the Ospedale Fatebenefratelli; in place of the Temple of Asculapius, there is the church of **San Bartolomeo**, most recently rebuilt in the 1690s.

The **Velabrum**, in the earliest days of Rome, was a cattle market (interestingly, when Rome reverted to a small town in the Middle Ages, the Roman Forum itself was used for the same purpose). In this area, east of the Tiber Island, is another church, **San Giorgio in Velabro**, in parts as old as the 7th century; there is a good Cosmatesque altar and canopy, and interesting early-Christian fragments inside on the left wall. Unfortunately a still-unattributed bomb attack in 1993 destroyed the lovely portico, and consequently the church is now closed for restoration. Of the two ancient arches outside, the **Arch of the Argentarii** was erected by the moneychangers in honour of Septimius Severus. The larger, the unfinished, four-sided **Janus Quadrifons**, dates from the time of Constantine.

## Piazza Bocca della Verità

Tourists almost always overlook this beautiful corner along the Tiber, but here you can see two well-preserved Roman temples. Both have probably been conventionally misnamed, the round **Temple of Vesta**, used as an Armenian church in the Middle Ages, and the **Temple of Fortuna Virilis**—it now seems almost certain that they were actually dedicated to Hercules Victor and Portunus, the god of harbours, respectively. Some bits of an exotic, ornate Roman cornice are built into the brick building opposite, part of the **Palace of the Crescenzi**, a powerful family in the 9th century, descended from Theodora Senatrix. Look over the side of the Tiber embankment here, and you can see the outlet of the **Cloaca Maxima**, the great ancient sewer begun by King Tarquin. Big enough to drive two carriages through, it is still in use today. Just upstream, past the Palatine Bridge, a single arch decorated with dragons in the middle of the river is all that remains of the ancient *Pons Aemilius*. Originally built in the 2nd century BC, it collapsed twice and was last restored in 1575 by Gregory XIII, only to fall down once again 20 years later. Now it is familiarly known as the 'broken bridge', or **Ponte Rotto**.

Across from the temples, the handsome medieval church with the lofty campanile is **Santa Maria in Cosmedin**, built over an altar of Hercules in the 6th century and given to Byzantine Greeks escaping from the Iconoclast heretic emperors in the 8th. The name (like 'cosmetic') means 'decorated', but little of the original art has survived; most of what you see is from the 12th century, including some fine Cosmatesque work inside. In the portico, an ancient, ghostly image in stone built into the walls has come down in legend as the Bocca della Verità—the Mouth of Truth. Medieval Romans would swear oaths and close business deals here; if you tell a lie with your hand in the image's mouth, he will most assuredly bite your fingers off. Try it.

## The Heart of Ancient Rome

In the 1930s, Mussolini built a grand boulevard between the Vittoriano and the Colosseum to ease traffic congestion and show off the ancient sites, the **Via dei Fori Imperiali**. However, it covers part of ancient Rome's heart, the great, completely ruined **Imperial Fora** of Augustus and Trajan, themselves built to relieve congestion in the original Roman Forum. **Trajan's Forum**, built with the spoils of his conquest of Dacia (modern Romania) was perhaps the grandest architectural and planning conception ever built in Rome, a broad square surrounded by colonnades, with a huge basilica flanked by two libraries and a covered market outside. A large part of **Trajan's Market** still stands, with the entrance on Via IV Novembre (*open 9–1 Tues, Wed, Fri; 9–6 Thurs, Sat; 9–12.30 Sun; adm*).

Behind it, you can see Rome's own leaning tower, built in the 12th century and called the **Torre delle Milizie**. All that remains of Trajan's great square is some paving and its centre-piece, the **Trajan Column**. The spiralling bands of sculptural reliefs, illustrating the Dacian Wars, reach to the top, some 30m high. They rank with the greatest works of Roman art, and have only recently been finally revealed after lengthy restoration work. Next to it, the church of **Santa Maria di Loreto** is a somewhat garish High Renaissance bauble, built by Bramante and Antonio da Sangallo the Younger, starting in 1501. The Romans liked it so much they built another one just like it next door, the **Santissimo Nome di Maria**, from the 1730s. Scanty remains of the **Forum of Caesar** and the **Forum of Augustus** can be seen along the boulevard to the south.

## The Roman Forum

*i fori romani.*

For a place that was once the centre of the Mediterranean world, there is surprisingly little to see; centuries of use as a quarry have seen to that. The word *forum* originally meant 'outside' (like the Italian *fuori*), a market-place outside the original Rome that became the centre of both government and business as the city expanded around it. The entrance is on the Via dei Fori Imperiali (*open 9am–one hour before sunset Mon–Sat; 9–1 Sun; adm exp, includes Palatine Hill*).

The **Via Sacra**, ancient Rome's most important street, runs the length of the Forum. At the end of it beneath the Capitol, you will be facing the **Arch of Septimius Severus**, of AD 203, with reliefs of some rather trivial victories over the Arabs and Parthians; conservative Romans of the time must have strongly resented this upstart African emperor planting his monument in such an important spot. The arch also commemorated Septimius' two sons, Geta and Caracalla; when the nasty Caracalla did his brother in, he had his name effaced from it. In front of it, the **Lapis Niger**, a mysterious stone with an underground chamber beneath it, is the legendary tomb of Romulus. The inscription down below, a threat against the profaning of this sacred spot, is one of the oldest ever found in the Latin language. The famous Golden Milestone also stood here, the 'umbilicus' of Rome and the point from which all distances in the Empire were measured. To the right is the **Curia**, the Senate House, restored after centuries' use as a church (the good Baroque church behind it is **SS. Luca e Martina**, built by Pietro di Cortona in the 1660s). To the left of the arch, the remains of a raised stone area

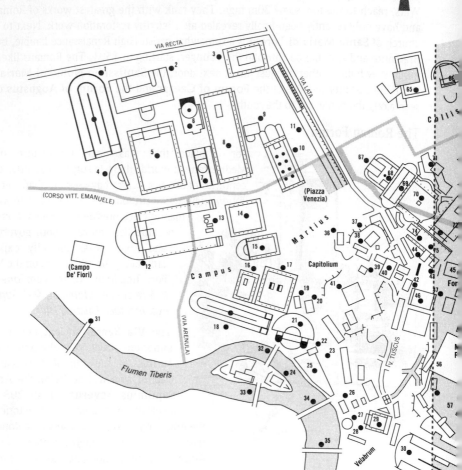

N

VIA RECTA

VIA LATA

(CORSO VITT. EMANUELE)

(Piazza
Venezia)

Martius

Capitolium

(Campo
De' Fiori)

Campus

(VIA ARENULA)

Flumen Tiberis

Velabrum

For

Callis

862

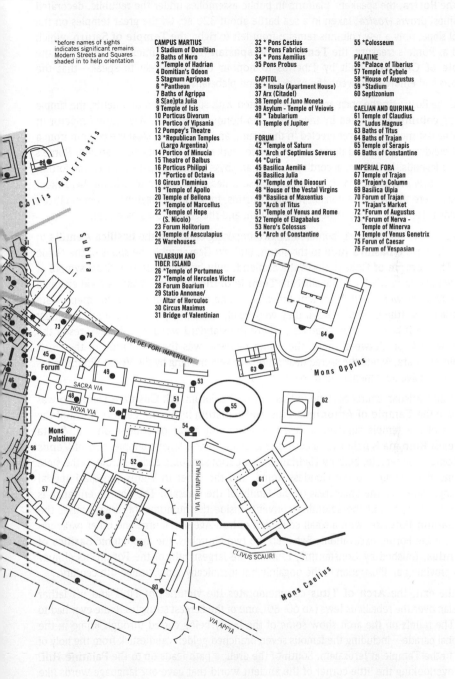

**CAMPUS MARTIUS**
1 Stadium of Domitian
2 Baths of Nero
3 *Temple of Hadrian
4 Domitian's Odeon
5 Stagnum Agrippae
6 *Pantheon
7 Baths of Agrippa
8 S[ae]pta Julia
9 Temple of Isis
10 Porticus Divorum
11 Portico of Vipsania
12 Pompey's Theatre
13 *Republican Temples
   (Largo Argentina)
14 Portico of Minucia
15 Theatre of Balbus
16 Porticus Philippi
17 *Portico of Octavia
18 Circus Flaminius
19 *Temple of Apollo
20 Temple of Bellona
21 *Temple of Marcellus
22 *Temple of Hope
   (S. Nicolo)
23 Forum Holitorium
24 Temple of Aesculapius
25 Warehouses

**VELABRUM AND
TIBER ISLAND**
26 *Temple of Portumnus
27 *Temple of Hercules Victor
28 Forum Boarium
29 Statio Annonae/
   Altar of Hercules
30 Circus Maximus
31 Bridge of Valentinian

32 * Pons Cestius
33 * Pons Fabricius
34 * Pons Aemilius
35 Pons Probus

**CAPITOL**
36 * Insula (Apartment House)
37 Arx (Citadel)
38 Temple of Juno Moneta
39 Asylum - Temple of Veiovis
40 * Tabularium
41 Temple of Jupiter

**FORUM**
42 *Temple of Saturn
43 *Arch of Septimius Severus
44 *Curia
45 Basilica Aemilia
46 Basilica Julia
47 *Temple of the Dioscuri
48 *House of the Vestal Virgins
49 *Basilica of Maxentius
50 *Arch of Titus
51 *Temple of Venus and Rome
52 Temple of Elagabalus
53 Nero's Colossus
54 *Arch of Constantine

55 *Colosseum

**PALATINE**
56 *Palace of Tiberius
57 Temple of Cybele
58 *House of Augustus
59 *Stadium
60 Septizonium

**CAELIAN AND QUIRINAL**
61 Temple of Claudius
62 *Ludus Magnus
63 Baths of Titus
64 Baths of Trajan
65 Temple of Serapis
66 Baths of Constantine

**IMPERIAL FORA**
67 Temple of Trajan
68 *Trajan's Column
69 Basilica Ulpia
70 Forum of Trajan
71 *Trajan's Market
72 *Forum of Augustus
73 *Forum of Nerva -
   Temple of Minerva
74 Temple of Venus Genetrix
75 Forun of Caesar
76 Forum of Vespasian

were the **Rostra**, the speakers' platform in public assemblies under the republic, decorated with ships' prows (*rostra*) taken in a sea battle about 320 BC. Of the great temples on the Capitol slope, only a few columns remain; from left to right, the **Temple of Saturn**, which served as Rome's treasury, the **Temple of Vespasian** (three columns standing), and the **Temple of Concord**, built by Tiberius to honour the peace—so to speak—that the emperors had enforced between the patricians and plebeians.

Behind the Rostra, in the open area once decorated with statues and monuments, the simple standing **column** was placed by the Romans in honour of Phocas, Byzantine Emperor in 608—the last monument ever erected in the forum, and they had to steal the column from a ruined building. Just behind it, a small pool once marked the spot of one of ancient Rome's favourite legends. In 362 BC, according to Livy, an abyss suddenly opened across the forum, and the sibyls predicted that it would not close unless the 'things that Rome held most precious' were thrown in. A consul, Mettius Curtius, took this as meaning a Roman citizen and soldier. He leapt in fully armed, horse and all, and the crack closed over him.

This section of the forum was bordered by two imposing buildings, the **Basilica Aemilia** to the north and the **Basilica Julia** to the south, built by Caesar with the spoils of the Gallic Wars. The **Temple of Caesar** closes the east end, built by Augustus as a visual symbol of the new imperial mythology. The adjacent **Temple of the Dioscuri** makes a good example of how temples were used in ancient times. This one was a meeting hall for men of the equestrian class (the knights, though they were really more likely to be businessmen); they had safe-deposit boxes in the basement, where the standard weights and measures of the empire were kept. Between them, the round pedestal was the foundation of the small **Temple of Vesta**, where the sacred hearth fire was kept burning by the Vestal Virgins; ruins of their extensive apartments can be seen next door.

Two more Christian churches stand in this part of the Forum. **SS. Cosma e Damiano** was built onto the **Temple of Antoninus Pius and Faustina** in the 6th century; most of the columns of the temple survive, with a fine sculptural frieze of griffons on top. **Santa Francesca Romana** is built over a corner of ancient Rome's largest temple, that of **Venus and Rome**. The temple, built by Hadrian, was a curious, double-ended shrine to the state cult; one side devoted to the Goddess Roma, and the other to Venus—in the imperial mythology, she was the ancestress of the family of the Caesars. The church entrance is outside the Forum, but the adjoining convent, inside the monumental area, houses the **Antiquarium Forense**, with a small collection of Iron Age burial urns and other paraphernalia from the Forum excavations. Between the two churches, the mastodonic **Basilica of Maxentius**, finished by Constantine, remains the largest ruin of the Forum, its clumsy arches providing an illustration of the ungainly but technically sophisticated 4th century.

Near the exit, the **Arch of Titus** commemorates the victories of Titus and his father Vespasian over the rebellious Jews (AD 60–80), one of the fiercest struggles Rome ever had to fight. The reliefs on the arch show some of the booty being carted through Rome in the triumphal parade—including the famous seven-branched golden candlestick from the holy of holies in the Temple at Jerusalem. South of the arch, a path leads up to the **Palatine Hill**. Here, overlooking the little corner of the ancient world that gave our language words like *senate, committee, rostrum, republic, plebiscite* and *magistrate*, you can leave democracy behind and visit the etymological birthplace of *palace*. The ruins of the imperial *Palatium* once covered the entire hill. As with the forum, almost all the stone has been cannibalized, and there's little to see of what was once a palace complex three-quarters of a kilometre long, to which a dozen of the emperors contributed. There are good views across the Circus Maximus from the gardens planted by the Farnese family; these lie over what were the imperial servants' quarters. This southern face of the Palatine also had a big portico from which the emperor could watch the races at the Circus Maximus.

## The Colosseum

Its real name was the Flavian Amphitheatre, after the family of emperors who built it, beginning with Vespasian in AD 72; Colosseum refers to the *Colossus*, a huge gilded statue of Nero (erected by himself, of course) that had formerly stood in the square in front. There doesn't seem to be much evidence that Christians were literally thrown to lions here—there were other places for that—but what did go on was perhaps the grossest and best-organized perversity in all history. Gladiatorial contests began under the republic, designed to make Romans better soldiers by rendering them indifferent to the sight of death. Later emperors introduced new displays to relieve the monotony—men versus animals, lions versus elephants, women versus dwarfs, sea-battles (the arena could be flooded at a moment's notice), public tortures of condemned criminals, and even genuine athletics, a Greek import the Romans never much cared for. In one memorable day of games, 5000 animals were slaughtered, about one every 10 seconds. The native elephant and lion of North Africa and Arabia are extinct thanks to such shenanigans.

However hideous its purpose, the Colosseum ranks with the greatest works of Roman architecture and engineering; all modern stadiums have copied most of its general plan. One surprising feature was a removable awning that covered the stands. A detachment of sailors from Cape Misenum was kept to operate it; they also manned the galleys in the mock sea-battles. Originally there were statues in all of the arches, and a ring of bronze shields all around the cornice. The concrete stands have eroded away, showing the brick structure underneath. Renaissance and Baroque popes hauled away half the travertine exterior—enough to build the Palazzo Venezia, the Palazzo Barberini, a few other palaces and bridges and part of St Peter's. Almost all of the construction work, under Vespasian and Titus, was performed by Jewish slaves, brought here for the purpose after the suppression of their revolt (*open 9am–2 hours before sunset Mon, Tues, Thurs–Sat; 9am-1pm Wed, Sun; adm to upper level; ground floor free*).

Just outside the Colosseum, the **Arch of Constantine** marks the end of the ancient Triumphal Way (now Via San Gregorio) where victorious emperors and their troops would parade their captives and booty. The arch, with a coy inscription mentioning Constantine's 'divine inspiration' (the Romans weren't sure whether it was yet respectable to mention Christianity), is covered with reliefs stolen from older arches and public buildings—a sad commentary on the state of art in Constantine's day.

### Domus Aurea and the Esquiline Hill

When Nero decided he needed a new palace, money was no object. Taking advantage of the great fire of AD 64 (which he apparently did *not* start), he had a huge section of Rome (temporarily renamed Neropolis) cleared to make him a rural estate right in the middle of town. The **Golden House** was probably the most sumptuous palace ever built in Rome, decorated in an age when Roman art was at its height. Nero never lived to see it finished, as he committed suicide during an army coup by Spanish legions. When the dust settled, the new Emperor Vespasian realized that this flagrant symbol of imperial decadence had to go. He demolished it, and Titus and Trajan later erected great bath complexes on its foundations; Nero's gardens and fishponds became the site of the Colosseum. In the 1500s, some beautifully decorated rooms of the Domus Aurea were discovered underground, saved for use as the basement of Titus' baths. Raphael and other artists studied them closely, and incorporated some of the spirit of the fresco decoration into the grand manner of the High Renaissance (our word 'grotesque', originally referring to the leering faces and floral designs of this time, comes from the finds in this 'grotto'). The rooms are at present closed for restoration, which may take years.

The **Esquiline Hill** is better known today as the *Colle Oppio*. Much of it is covered with parks; besides the Domus Aurea there are very substantial ruins of the **Baths of Trajan**, still unexcavated. On the northern slope of the hill, **San Pietro in Vincoli** takes its name from relics supposed to be the chains Peter was locked in before Nero had him crucified. They are kept over the main altar, though the real attraction of this church for non-Catholics is the famous, ill-fated **Tomb of Julius II** which tortured Michelangelo for so many years. Of the original project, planned as a sort of tabernacle with 40 individual statues, the artist completed only the powerful figure of *Moses*, perhaps the closest anyone has ever come to capturing prophetic vision in stone. It has irreverently been claimed that this Moses bears a resemblance to Charlton Heston, and it does. All the other statues on the tomb are the work of Michelangelo's students.

## San Clemente

This church, a little way to the east of the Colosseum on Via San Giovanni in Laterano, is one of the more fascinating remnants of Rome's many-layered history. One of the first substantial building projects of the Christians in Rome, the original basilica of *c.*375 burned along with the rest of the quarter during a sacking by the Normans in 1084. It was rebuilt soon afterwards with a new Cosmatesque pavement, and the 6th-century choir screen—a rare example of sculpture from that ungifted time— saved from the original church. The 12th-century mosaic in the apse represents the *Triumph of the Cross*, and the chapel at the entrance contains a beautiful series of quattrocento frescoes by Masolino, partly uncovered after restoration. From a vestibule, nuns sell tickets to the **Lower Church** (*open 9–12, 3.30–6.30, Mon–Sat; 10–12, 3.30–6.30, Sun; adm*). This is the lower half of the original San Clemente, and there are remarkable, though deteriorated, frescoes from the 900s and the 12th century, some of the oldest medieval paintings to have survived anywhere in Italy. The plaque from Bulgaria, mentioned in the introduction, commemorates SS. Cyril and Methodius, who went from this church to spread the Gospel among the Slavs; they translated the Bible into Old Slavonic, and invented the first Slavic alphabet (Cyrillic) to do it.

From here, steps lead down to the lowest stratum, 1st and 2nd century AD buildings divided by an alley; this includes the **Mithraeum**, the best-preserved such temple after the one in Capua. The larger, neighbouring building was filled with rubble to serve as a foundation for the basilica, and the apse was later added over the Mithraeum. Father Mulhooly of Boston started excavating in the 1860s, and later excavations have revealed a Mithraic antechamber with a fine stuccoed ceiling, the Mithraic school with an early fresco, and the temple proper, a small cavern-like hall with benches for the initiates to share a ritual supper.

Mithraism was a mystery religion, full of secrets closely held by the initiates (all male, and largely soldiers) and it is difficult to say what else went on down here. Two altars were found, each with the usual image of the Persian-import god Mithras despatching a white bull, including a snake, a scorpion and a crow, and astrological symbolism in the decorative scheme. Underneath all this, there is yet a fourth building level, some foundations from the republican era. At the end of the 1st-century building you can look down into an ancient sewer or underground stream, one of a thousand entrances to the surreal sub-Roma of endless subterranean caves, buildings, rivers and lakes, mostly unexplored and unexplorable. A century ago a schoolboy fell in the water here; they found him, barely alive, in open country several kilometres from the city.

## Along Corso Vittorio Emanuele

This street, chopped through the medieval centre of Rome in the 1880s, still hasn't quite been assimilated into its surroundings; nevertheless, this ragged, smoky traffic tunnel will come in handy when you find yourself lost in the tortuous, meandering streets of Rome's oldest quarter. Starting west from Piazza Venezia, the church of the **Gesù** (1568–84) was a landmark for a new era and the new aesthetic of cinquecento Rome. The transitional, pre-Baroque fashion was often referred to as the 'Jesuit style', and here in the Jesuits' head church architects Vignola and della Porta first laid down Baroque's cardinal principle: an intimation of paradise for the impressionable through decorative excess. It hasn't aged well, though at the time it must have seemed to most Romans a perfect marriage of Renaissance art and a reformed, revitalized faith. St Ignatius, the Jesuits' founder, is buried in the left transept right under the altar, Spanish-style; the globe incorporated in the sculpted Trinity overhead is the biggest piece of lapis lazuli in the world.

A little way further west, the street opens into a ghastly square called Largo Argentina. Remains of several republican-era temples, unearthed far below ground level, can be seen in the square's centre. Next comes another grand Baroque church, **Sant'Andrea della Valle**, with the city's second-tallest dome. Maderno, one of the architects of St Peter's, did most of the work. The curving façade across the street belongs to the **Palazzo Massimo**, the masterpiece of the Renaissance architect Baldassare Peruzzi: he transplanted something of the Florentine style of monumental palaces, adding some light-hearted proto-Baroque decoration; have a look at the adjacent church of **SS. Pantaleone e Josepho**, with its outlandish sculptural frieze of shields, trays, and popes' hats piled like a rubbish heap. The Palazzo Braschi next door houses the small **Museo di Roma**, closed almost permanently for restoration, though the ground-floor rooms are used for occasional temporary art exhibitions.

One of the earliest and best of the palaces on Corso Vittorio Emanuele, the delicate **Piccola Farnesina** by Antonio da Sangallo the Younger, houses another little museum, a collection of ancient sculpture called the **Museo Barracco** (*open 9–1, 5–8, Tues, Thur; 9–1 Wed, Fri, Sat; 9–2 Sun; adm*). A third museum—not a well-known one—is just around the corner from Sant'Andrea on Via Sudario. The **Burcardo Theatre Museum** is a collection of fascinating old relics from the Roman theatrical tradition—but alas, another victim of restoration.

The biggest palace on the street, attributed to Bramante, is the **Palazzo della Cancelleria**, once the seat of the papal municipal government. St Philip Neri, the gifted, irascible holy man who is patron saint of Rome, built the **Chiesa Nuova** near the eastern end of the Corso (1584). Philip was quite a character, with something of the Zen Buddhist in him. He forbade his followers any sort of philosophical speculation or dialectic, but made them sing and recite poetry; two of his favourite pastimes were insulting popes and embarrassing new initiates— making them walk through Rome with a foxtail sewn to the back of their coat to learn humility. As was common in those times, sincere faith and humility were eventually translated into flagrant Baroque. The Chiesa Nuova is one of the larger and fancier of the species. Its altarpiece is a *Madonna with Angels* by Rubens. Even more flagrant, outside the church you can see the curved arch-Baroque façade of the **Philippine Oratory** by Borromini. The form of music called the *oratorio* takes its name from this chapel, a tribute to St Philip's role in promoting sacred music.

## South of Corso Vittorio Emanuele: the Campo de' Fiori

Few cities anywhere can put on such a variety of faces to beguile the visitor; depending on where you spend your time in Rome, you may come away with the impression of a city that is one great Baroque stage set, or all grimy early 1900s palazzi and bad traffic, or a city full of nothing but ruins and parks. Around **Campo de' Fiori**, one of the spots dearest to the hearts of Romans themselves, you may think yourself in the middle of some scruffy south Italian village. Rome's market square, disorderly, cramped and chaotic, is easily the liveliest corner of the city, full of market barrows, buskers, teenage Bohemians, and the folkloresque types who have lived here all their lives—the least decorous and worst-dressed crowd in Rome. During papal rule, the old square was also used for executions—most notoriously the burning of Giordano Bruno in 1600. This well-travelled philosopher was the first to take Copernican astronomy to its logical extremes—an infinite universe with no centre, no room for Heaven, and nothing eternal but change. The Church had few enemies more dangerous. Italy never forgot him; the statue of Bruno in Campo de Fiori went up only a few years after the end of papal rule.

Just east of the square, the heap of buildings around Piazzetta di Grottapinta is built over the cavea of **Pompey's Theatre**, ancient Rome's biggest. This complex included a *curia*, where Julius Caesar was assassinated in 44 BC. Walk south from Campo de' Fiori, and you will be thrown back from cosy medievalism into the High Renaissance with the **Palazzo Farnese**, one of the definitive works of that Olympian style. The younger Sangallo began it in 1514, and Michelangelo contributed to the façades and interiors. The building now serves as the French Embassy, and it isn't easy to get in to see it. Most of the palaces that fill up this neighbourhood have one thing in common—they were made possible by someone's accession to the papacy, the biggest jackpot available to any aspiring Italian family. Built on the pennies of the faithful, they provide the most outrageous illustration of Church corruption at the dawn of the Reformation. Alessandro Farnese, who as Pope Paul III was a clever and effective pope though perhaps the greatest nepotist ever to decorate St Peter's throne (*see* 'Caprarola',

p.834), managed to build this palace 20 years before his election—with the income from his 16 absentee bishoprics.

**Palazzo Spada**, just to the east along Via Capo di Ferro, was the home of a mere cardinal, but its florid stucco façade (1540) almost upstages the Farnese. Inside, the **Galleria Spada** (*open 9–7 Tues–Sat; 9–1 Sun; adm*) is one of Rome's great collections of 16th- and 17th-century painting. Guido Reni, Guercino and the other favourites of the age are well represented. To the south, close to the Tiber, **Via Giulia** was laid out by Pope Julius II, a famous and pretty thoroughfare lined with churches and palazzi from that time. Many artists (successful ones) have lived here, including Raphael.

## Piazza Navona

In 1477, the area now covered by one of Rome's most beautiful piazzas was a half-forgotten field full of huts and vineyards, tucked inside the still-imposing ruins of the Stadium of Domitian. A redevelopment of the area covered the long grandstands with new houses, but the decoration had to wait for the Age of Baroque. In 1644, with the election of Innocent X, it was the Pamphili family that won the papal sweepstakes. Innocent, a great grafter and such a villainous pope that when he died no one—not even his newly wealthy relatives—would pay for a proper burial, built the ornate **Palazzo Pamphili** (now the Brazilian Embassy) and hired Borromini to complete the gaudy church of **Sant'Agnese in Agone**, begun by Carlo and Girolamo Rainaldi.

Borromini's arch-rival, Bernini, got the commission for the piazza's famous fountains; the Romans still tell stories of how the two artists carried on. All the figures in Bernini's great **Fountain of the Four Rivers** seem to be expressing shock at the church across the street—one even has his head veiled. Supposedly Borromini started a rumour that the tall obelisk atop the fountain was about to topple; when the alarmed papal commissioners arrived to confront Bernini with the news, he tied a piece of twine around it, secured the other end to a lamppost, and laughed all the way home. The fountain is Bernini's masterpiece, Baroque at its flashiest and most likeable. Among the travertine grottoes and fantastical flora and fauna under the obelisk, the four colossal figures represent the Ganges, Danube, Rio de la Plata, and Nile (with the veiled head because its source was unknown). Bernini also designed the smaller fountain, the **Fontana del Moro**, at the southern end. The third fountain, that of *Neptune*, was an empty basin until the nineteenth century, when the statues, by Giacomo della Porta, were added to make the square seem more symmetrical. Off the southern end of

Pza Navona —
fontana del Nettuno

the piazza, at the back of Palazzo Braschi, **Pasquino** is the original Roman 'talking statue', embellished with placards and graffiti ('pasquinades') since the 1500s—one of his favourite subjects in those days was the insatiable pigginess of families like the Farnese; serious religious issues were usually too hot to touch, even for a statue.

Piazza Navona seems mildly schizoid these days, unable to become entirely part of high-fashion, tourist-itinerary Rome, yet no longer as comfortable and unpretentious as the rest of the neighbourhood. One symptom will be readily apparent should you step into any of the old cosy-looking cafés and restaurants around the piazza; they're as expensive as in any part of Rome. The best time to come to Piazza Navona is at night, when the fountain is illuminated—or if you can, for the noisy, traditional toy fair of the **Befana**, set up between just before Christmas and Epiphany (6 January). Some of the churches in the neighbourhood are interesting, such as **Santa Maria della Pace**, with Raphael's famous series of *Sibyls and Prophets* on the vaulting and a cloister by Bramante, his first work in Rome. **San Luigi dei Francesi**, the French church in Rome, is worth a stop for the great paintings on the *Life of St Matthew* by Caravaggio, in a chapel on the left aisle. Towards the Pantheon, **Sant'Ivo alla Sapienza** once served the English community in Rome. Borromini built them one of his most singular buildings (1660), with its dome and spiralling cupola (*open 10–12 Sun only*).

## The Pantheon

When we consider the fate of so many other great buildings of ancient Rome, we begin to understand what a slim chance it was that allowed this one to come down to us. The first Pantheon was built in 27 BC by Agrippa, Emperor Augustus' son-in-law and right-hand man, but was demolished and replaced by the present temple in 119–128 by the Emperor Hadrian, though, curiously, retaining Agrippa's original inscription on the pediment. Its history has been precarious ever since. In 609 the empty Pantheon was consecrated to Christianity as 'St Mary of the Martyrs'. Becoming a church is probably what saved it, though the Byzantines hauled away the gilded bronze roof tiles soon after, and for a while in the Middle Ages the portico saw use as a fish market. The Pantheon's greatest enemy, however, was Gian Lorenzo Bernini. He not only 'improved' it with a pair of Baroque belfries over the porch (demolished in 1887), but he had Pope Urban VIII take down the bronze covering on the inside of the dome, to use the metal for his baldacchino over the altar at St Peter's. Supposedly there was enough left over to make the pope 60 cannons. (Urban was of the Barberini family, and Pasquino's comment about this act was, 'What the barbarians didn't do, the Barberini did').

Looking at the outside, you may notice the building seems perilously unsound. There is no way a simple vertical wall can support such a heavy, shallow dome (steep domes push downwards, shallow ones outwards). Obviously the walls will tumble at any moment. That is a little joke the Roman architects are playing on us, for here they are showing off their engineering virtuosity as shamelessly as in the Colosseum, or the aqueduct with four storeys of arches that used to run up to the Palatine Hill. The wall that looks so fragile is really 7.6m thick, and the dome on top isn't a dome at all; the real, hemispherical dome lies underneath, resting easily on the walls inside. The ridges you see on the upper dome are courses of cantilevered bricks, effectively almost weightless.

The real surprise, however, lies behind the enormous original bronze doors, an interior of precious marbles and finely sculpted details, the grandest and best-preserved building to have survived from the ancient world (*open 9–5 Mon–Sat; 9–1 Sun*). The movie directors who made all those Roman epics in the 1950s and '60s certainly took much of their settings from this High Imperial creation of Hadrian's time, just as architects from the early Middle Ages onwards have tried to equal it. Brunelleschi learned enough from it to build his dome in Florence, and a visit here will show you at a glance what Michelangelo and his contemporaries were trying so hard to outdo. The coffered dome, the biggest cast concrete construction ever made before the 20th century, is the crowning audacity, even without its bronze plate. At 42.6m in diameter, it is probably the largest in the world (a little-known fact—but St Peter's dome is almost 2m less, though much taller). Standing in the centre and looking at the clouds through the 9m *oculus*, the hole at the top, is an odd sensation you can experience nowhere else.

Inside, the niches and recesses around the perimeter were devoted to statues of the Pantheon's 12 gods, plus those of Augustus and Hadrian; in the centre, illuminated by a direct sunbeam at midsummer noon, stood Jove. All these are gone, of course, and the interior decoration is limited to an *Annunciation*, to the right of the door, attributed to Melozzo da Forlì, and the tombs of eminent Italians such as kings Vittorio Emanuele II and Umberto I, as well as those of Raphael and other artists. Hardly ever used for church services, the Pantheon simply stands open, with no admission charges, probably fulfilling the same purpose as in Hadrian's day—no purpose at all, save that of an unequalled monument to art and the builder's skill. The Cult of the Twelve Gods, a Greek import from Augustus' time, never attracted many followers in Rome—even though many of the individual gods were present in Roman religion from the earliest times.

Just behind the Pantheon, the big church of **Santa Maria Sopra Minerva** is interesting for being one of the few important medieval churches of Rome (*c.* 1280) to escape the Baroque treatment; its Gothic was preserved in restoration work in the 1840s. Two Medici popes, Leo X and Clement VII, are buried here, as is Fra Angelico. Santa Maria's Florentine connection began with the Dominican monks who designed it; they also did Florence's Santa Maria Novella. A work of Michelangelo, *Christ with the Cross*, can be seen near the high altar; the Carafa Chapel off the right aisle, where you can pay your respects to Pope Paul IV, has an earlier (1489) series of frescoes on the *Life of St Thomas* by Filippino Lippi, his best work outside Florence.

# Via del Corso

The Campus Martius, the open plain between Rome's hills and the Tiber, was the training ground for soldiers in the early days of the republic. Eventually the city swallowed it up, and the old path towards the Via Flaminia became one of the most important thoroughfares, *Via Lata* (Broad Street). Not entirely by coincidence, the popes of the 14th and 15th centuries laid out a new grand boulevard almost in the same place. **Via del Corso**, or simply the Corso, has been the main axis of Roman society ever since. Goethe recorded a fascinating account of the Carnival festivities held here in Rome's benignly decadent 18th century; the horse races that were held as the climax of the Carnival gave the street its name. Much of its length is taken up by the overdone palaces of the age, such as the Palazzo Doria (1780), where the **Galleria Doria Pamphili** (*open 10–1 Tues, Fri–Sun; adm*), still wholly owned by the Pamphili, has a fine painting collection with Velásquez' *Portrait of Innocent X*, Caravaggio's *Flight into Egypt*, and works by Rubens, Titian, Brueghel, and more.

Continuing northwards, the palaces have come down in the world somewhat, tired-looking blocks that now house banks and offices. Look on the side-streets for some hidden attractions: **Sant'Ignazio**, on Via del Seminario, is another spectacular Jesuit church with tricky *trompe-l'œil* frescoes on the ceiling; a block north, columns of the ancient **Temple of Hadrian** are incorporated into the north side of the Roman Stock Exchange. **Piazza Colonna** takes its name from the column of Marcus Aurelius, forlorn without the gold statue of the emperor that once stood atop it. The obelisk in adjacent Piazza di Montecitorio once marked the hours on a gigantic sundial in Emperor Augustus' garden; the **Palazzo Montecitorio**, begun by Bernini, now houses the Italian Chamber of Deputies.

A little way east of Piazza Colonna is where you can throw your coins into the **Trevi Fountain**, to guarantee your return trip to Rome. You may also scoop everyone else's coins out to help pay for it, if the police let you get near it. The fountain, completed in 1762, was originally planned to commemorate the restoration of Agrippa's aqueduct by Nicholas V in 1453. The source was called the 'Virgin Water' after Virgo, a young girl who had showed thirsty Roman soldiers the hidden spring. It makes a grand sight—enough to make you want to come back; not many fountains have an entire palace (the Palazzo Poli) for a stage backdrop. The big fellow in the centre is Oceanus, drawn by horses and tritons through cascades of travertine and blue water. Across from the fountain, the little church of **SS. Vicenzo and Anastasio** has the distinction of caring for the pickled hearts and entrails of several dozen popes; an odd custom. They're kept down in the crypt.

Further north, the Corso reaches close to the Tiber and the pathetically sad **Mausoleum of Augustus**, a cylinder of shabby brick once covered in marble and golden statues. All the Julian emperors except Nero were interred here, in the middle of what were Augustus' enormous gardens. After the centuries had despoiled the tomb of its riches, the Colonna family turned the hulk into one of its fortresses. Still further indignities were in store. Until 1823, when the pope forbade them, bullfights were extremely popular in Rome; a certain Spanish entrepreneur found the circular enclosure perfect for the toreros. After that, the tomb was used as a theatre and a circus, before Mussolini, wishing to afford the founders of Imperial Rome due respect (and perhaps intending to be buried there himself) declared it a national monument, and had trees planted around it. Even so, no one quite seems to know what to do with it, and it usually sits locked and empty, and is open with individual permission only.

Across the street, Augustus' **Ara Pacis** (Altar of Peace) has had a better fate. Bits and pieces of the beautiful sculpted reliefs, dug up in 1937, were joined with casts of others from museums around Europe to recreate the small building almost in its entirety. One of antiquity's noblest (and least pretentious) conceptions now sits protected under an attractive glass pavilion; among the mythological reliefs, note the side facing the river, with the emperor and his family dedicating a sacrifice (*open April–Sept 9–1.30, 4–7, Tues, Sat; 9–1.30 Wed, Thurs, Fri; 9–1 Sun; Oct–Mar 9–1.30 Tues–Sat; 9–1 Sun; adm*).

## Piazza di Spagna

The shuffling crowds of tourists who congregate here at all hours of the day are not a recent phenomenon; this irregular but supremely sophisticated piazza has been a favourite with foreigners ever since it was laid out in the early 16th century. The Spaniards came first, as their embassy to the popes was established here in 1646, giving the square and the steps their name. Later, the English Romantic poets made it their headquarters in Italy; typical Romantic mementoes—locks of hair, fond remembrances, mortal remains, death masks—are awaiting your inspired contemplation at the **Keats-Shelley Memorial House** at no.26 (*open April–Sept 3–6pm, Mon–Fri; Oct–Mar 9–1, 2.30–5, Mon–Fri; adm*). Almost every artist, writer or musician of the last century spent some time in the neigbourhood, but today the piazza often finds itself bursting at the seams with refreshingly Philistine gawkers and wayward youth from all over Europe, America and Japan, caught between the charms of the gargantuan, controversial new McDonald's (the first one built in Rome, seating 700) and the fancy shops on and around nearby Via Condotti.

All these visitors need somewhere to sit, and the popes obliged them in 1725 with the construction of the **Spanish Steps**, an exceptionally beautiful and exceptionally Baroque ornament about which it is hard to be cynical. The youth of today who loll about here are taking the place of the hopeful artists' models of the more picturesque centuries, who once crowded the steps, striking poses of antique heroes and Madonnas, waiting for some easy money. At the top of the stairs, the simple but equally effective church of **Trinità dei Monti** by Carlo Maderno (early 16th century) was paid for by the King of France. At the southern end of Piazza di Spagna, a Borromini palace housed the papal office called the *Propaganda Fide*, whose job was just what the name implies. The column in front (1856) celebrates the proclamation of the

Pza di Spagna

Dogma of the Immaculate Conception, one of their hardest tasks. Via del Babuino, a street named after a siren on a fountain so ugly that Romans called her the 'baboon', connects Piazza di Spagna with the Piazza del Popolo. Besides its very impressive and equally expensive antique shops, the street carries on the English connection, with All Saints' Church, a sleepy neo-pub just off it, and an English bookshop.

## Piazza del Popolo

If you have a choice of how you enter Rome, this is the way to do it, through the gate in the old Aurelian wall and into one of the most successful of all Roman piazzas, copied on a smaller scale all over Italy. No city has a better introduction, and the three diverging boulevards direct you with thoughtful efficiency towards your destination. Valadier, the pope's architect after the Napoleonic occupation, gave the piazza the form it has today, but the big obelisk of Pharaoh Ramses II punctuating the view down the boulevards arrived in the 1580s. It is 3200 years old, but like all obelisks it looks mysteriously brand-new; Augustus brought it to Rome from Heliopolis and planted it in the Circus Maximus, and it was transferred here by Pope Sixtus V. The two domed churches designed by Rainaldi, set like bookends at the entrance to the three boulevards, are from the 1670s, part of the original plan for the piazza to which Bernini and Fontana may have contributed.

Emperor Nero's ashes were interred in a mausoleum here, at the foot of the Pincio Hill. The site was planted with walnut trees, and soon everyone in Rome knew the stories of how Nero's ghost haunted the grove, sending out demons—in the forms of flocks of ravens that nested there—to perform deeds of evil. About 1100, Pope Paschal II destroyed the grove and scattered the ashes; to complete the exorcism he built a church on the site, **Santa Maria del Popolo**. Rebuilt in the 1470s, it contains some of the best painting in Rome: Caravaggio's stunning *Crucifixion of St Peter* and *Paul on the Road to Damascus* (in the left transept), and frescoes by Pinturicchio around the altar. Raphael designed the Chigi Chapel, off the left aisle, and contributed the designs for its mosaics.

## Villa Borghese

From the Piazza del Popolo, a winding ramp leads up to Rome's great complex of parks. Just by coincidence, this was mostly parkland in ancient times. The hill of the **Pincio** formed part of Augustus' imperial gardens, and the adjacent **Villa Medici** occupies the site of the Villa of Lucullus, the 2nd-century BC philosopher and general who conquered northern Anatolia and first brought cherries to Europe. Now the home of the French Academy, the Villa Medici was a posh jail of sorts for Galileo during his Inquisitorial trials. The Pincio, a lovely formal garden designed by Valadier, offers rare views over Rome. It is separated from the **Villa Borghese** proper by the Aurelian wall and the modern sunken highway that borders it; its name, Viale del Muro Torto, means crooked wall, and refers to a section of the Roman wall that collapsed in the 6th century, and was left as it was because it was believed to be protected by St Peter.

Villa Borghese has its charms, mitigated somewhat by the ubiquitous squads of Carabinieri trying gamely to keep the place respectable. Exploring its vast spaces, you will come across charming vales, woods, and a pond (rowing boats for rent), an imitation Roman temple or two, rococo avenues where the bewigged dandies and powdered tarts of the 1700s came to promenade, bits of ancient aqueduct, and the small but pleasant **Zoological Garden** (*open*

*Il Pincio*

8am–2 hours before sunset daily; adm). On the northern edge, late 19th-century Rome created a ponderous boulevard called **Viale delle Belle Arti** as a setting for new museums and foreign 'academies', where, for example, really jaded visitors can assault their senses with exhibits of post-Modernist art from Romania. The **National Gallery of Modern Art** (*open 9–7 Tues–Sat; 9–1 Sun; adm exp*) makes its home in one of Rome's biggest and most inexcusable buildings (1913), but the collection includes some of the best works of Modigliani and the Futurists, as well as a fair sampling of 19th- and 20th-century artists from the rest of Europe. From there, gingerly skirting the Romanian Academy, you come to the **Villa Giulia Museum** (*open 9–7 Tues–Sun; adm exp*).

If you cannot make it to Tarquinia, this is the best place to get to know the Etruscans. Some of their best art has been collected here, as well as laboriously reconstructed terracotta façades to give you some idea of how an Etruscan temple looked. As usual, the compelling attraction of the art here is the Etruscans' effortless, endearing talent for portraiture: expressive faces that help bridge the gap between the centuries can be seen in terracotta ex-votos (some of children), sarcophagi, and even architectural decoration. Serious art is often more stylized; fine examples are the charming couple on the *Sarcophago dei Sposi* from Cerveteri, and the roof statues from the Temple of Portonaccio at Veii—these by Vulca, the only Etruscan artist whose name has survived along with his work. The museum building and its courts and gardens are attractions in themselves; Julius III had Vignola and Ammannati build this quirky Mannerist villa in 1553, and Vasari and Michelangelo may also have helped.

The Borghese family, an important ecclesiastical dynasty of the 17th century, collected an impressive hoard of ancient and modern art. Much of it was shipped off to the Louvre in the 1800s, when the head of the family made a gift of it to please his brother-in-law, Napoleon. Later generations did their best to rebuild the collection, and the **Galleria Borghese** (*open 9–7 Tues–Sat; 9–1 Sun; adm*) today offers an intriguing mix of great art and Roman preciosity. Often the two go hand in hand, as with the sensuously charged showpieces of Bernini: *Apollo and Daphne*, *The Rape of Proserpina*, and especially his *David*, which the artist modestly chiselled in his own image. Canova, the hot item among sculptors in Napoleon's day, contributes a titillatingly languorous statue of Princess Borghese (Napoleon's ardent sister, Pauline) as the *Conquering Venus*. Even the ancient world joins in the fun, with such works as the famous Hellenistic *Sleeping Hermaphrodite*.

Due to sudden land subsidence the Villa seemed on the verge of collapsing in 1985, and was completely closed for restoration for several years. The sculpture collection has now been returned to its original home, but, apart from some Caravaggio canvases, all the Borghese paintings have been moved to a temporary site near Porta Portese in Trastevere, the **San Michele a Ripa** complex, Via San Michele a Ripa 22 (*open 9–7 Tues–Sun; adm*). The many paintings on show here—exhibited in very unsatisfactory conditions, and all jumbled together—include more fine Caravaggios, *Allegories of Love* by Titian, two Bernini self-portraits, and Rubens' *Deposition*, perhaps one of the weakest paintings of all time with its pink, chubby Jesus and a crowd of bored-looking attendants.

## Via Veneto and the Quirinal

Once this chain of gardens was much bigger, but at the end of the last century, many of the old villas that hemmed in Rome were lost to the inevitable expansion of the city. Perhaps the greatest loss was the Villa Ludovisi, praised by many as the most beautiful of all Rome's parks. Now the choice 'Ludovisi' quarter, it has given the city one of its most famous streets, Via Vittorio Veneto, the long winding boulevard of grand hotels, cafés and embassies that stretches down from Villa Borghese to the Piazza Barberini. A promenade for the smart set in the 1950s, it wears something of the forlorn air of a jilted beau now that fashion has moved on, though the new local authorities' attempts to pedestrianize it have led to a certain revival in its popularity. Pull yourself away from the passing show on the boulevard to take in the unique spectacle provided by the **Convento dei Cappuccini** at the southern end of the street, around the corner from Piazza Barberini (*entrance halfway up the stairs of Santa Maria della Concezione church; open 9–12, 3–6, daily*). Unique, that is, outside Palermo, for, much like the Capuchin convent there, the Roman brethren have created a loving tribute to our friend Death. In the cellars, 4000 dead monks team up for an unforgettable *Danse Macabre* of bones and grinning skulls, carefully arranged by serious-minded Capuchins long ago to remind us of something we know only too well.

On the other side of Piazza Barberini, down a gloomy Baroque avenue called Via delle Quattro Fontane, you'll find the Palazzo Barberini, one of the showier places in Rome, decorated everywhere with the bees from the family arms. Maderno, Borromini and Bernini all worked on it, with financing made possible by the election of a Barberini as Pope Urban VIII in 1623. Currently it houses the **National Museum of Ancient Art** (*open 9–7 Tues–Sun; adm*)—a misleading title, since this is a gallery devoted to Italian works of the 12th–18th centuries. Often the original decoration steals the show from the pictures: Bernini's Great Hall, for example, with a ceiling fresco by Pietro da Cortona, the *Triumph of Divine Providence*, or the ceiling in Room 7, with a fresco by Andrea Sacchi where the enthroned Virgin looking down on the round earth seems like a Baroque attempt to create a new Catholic astronomy. Works present include a Bernini self-portrait, Raphael's famous portrait of his beloved mistress *La Fornarina*, the 'baker's girl', more portraits by the Genoese artist Di Baciccio, lots of Caravaggios and Lippi's *Madonna*, and two rather sedate pictures by El Greco, among the few by that artist ever to find their way to Italy. A large section of 15th-century artists not from Tuscany proves that not all the action in the quattrocento was happening in Florence.

**San Carlino**, on the corner of Via delle Quattro Fontane and Via Quirinale, is one of Borromini's best works—and his first one (1638), a purposely eccentric little flight of fancy built exactly the size of one of the four massive pillars that hold up the dome in St Peter's. Follow **Via Quirinale** and you'll reach the summit of that hill, covered with villas and gardens in ancient times, and abandoned in the Middle Ages. Then even the name Quirinale had been forgotten, and the Romans called the place 'Montecavallo' after the two big horses' heads projecting above the ground. During the reign of Sixtus V, they were excavated to reveal monumental Roman statues of the **Dioscuri** (Castor and Pollux), probably copied from Phidias or Praxiteles. Together with a huge basin found in the Forum, they make a centrepiece for Piazza di Quirinale. Behind it, stretching for a dreary half-kilometre along the street is the **Quirinale Palace**, built in 1574 to symbolize the political domination of the popes, later occupied by the kings of Italy, and now the residence of the country's presidents.

## Around Termini Station: Diocletian's Baths

Even though Rome's great big station truly is the terminus for all Italy, its name in fact comes from the *termini* or **Baths of Diocletian** on the other side of Piazza Cinquecento. Until the popes dismantled it for building stone, this was by far Rome's biggest ruin; its outer wall followed the present-day lines of Via XX Settembre, Via Volturno, and Piazza Cinquecento, and the big semi-circular **Piazza della Repubblica**, with its mouldering, grandiose 1890s palazzi and huge fountain, occupies the sites of the baths' exercise ground, or *palaestra*. All together the complex covered some 11 hectares. The surviving portions were converted into a monastery in the 1560s.

Michelangelo, not on one of his better days, gave it a broad new cloister and converted a section of the lofty, vaulted central bathhouse into the church of **SS. Maria degli Angeli**, conserving some of the building's original form. The cloister and adjacent building now house the **National Museum of Rome** (*open 9–2 Tues–Sat; 9–1 Sun; adm*), the greatest Italian collection of antiquities after the museum in Naples—and like Naples' it is very badly run and usually half-closed; you'll be lucky if they let you see more than a few of the treasures inside. These include a unique, incredible collection of the finest Greek and Hellenistic era sculpture, much of it in the rooms of the Ludovisi Collection: the famous **Ludovisi Throne**, with reliefs of the *Birth of Venus*, statues of Hermes, and the *Resting Ares*. Some fine Roman works are here, too—skilful copies like the *Discus Thrower* after Myron, and an unusual image of the pope's great predecessor, Emperor Augustus, in the dress of a Pontifex Maximus. Hundreds of other statues fill up several halls and all four sides of Michelangelo's cloister. Upstairs there are more rooms of mosaics and fragmentary frescoes, including an entire room moved here from the Villa of Livia on the Palatine, painted to look like an open courtyard.

A block north of the baths, Piazza San Bernardo marks the beginning of Via Barberini, an ugly modern street with most of Rome's travel and airline offices. The Piazza itself has two interesting churches. **San Bernardo**, built out of a circular library that once occupied a corner of the baths' walls, and **Santa Maria della Vittoria**, home to one of the essential works of Baroque sculpture, the disconcertingly erotic *St Teresa in Ecstasy* by Bernini (in a chapel off the left aisle).

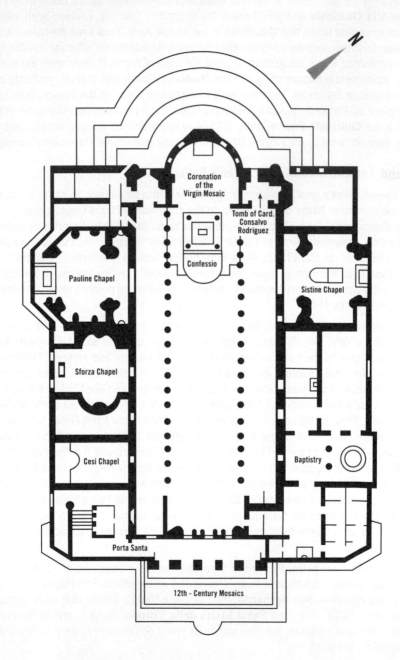

# Santa Maria Maggiore

Coronation
of the
Virgin Mosaic

Tomb of Card.
Consalvo
Rodriguez

Confessio

Pauline Chapel

Sistine Chapel

Sforza Chapel

Cesi Chapel

Baptistry

Porta Santa

12th - Century Mosaics

# The Patriarchal Basilicas: Santa Maria Maggiore

Besides St Peter's, there are three Patriarchal Basilicas, ancient and revered churches under the care of the pope that have always been a part of the Roman Pilgrimage. Santa Maria Maggiore, St Paul's outside the Walls, and St John Lateran are all on the edges of the city, away from the political and commercial centre; by the Middle Ages they stood in open countryside, and only recently has the city grown outwards to swallow them once more.

**Santa Maria Maggiore**, at the end of the Esquiline Hill, was probably begun about 352, when a rich Christian saw a vision of the Virgin Mary directing him to build a church; Pope Liberius had received the same vision at the same time, and the two supposedly found the site marked out for them by a miraculous August snowfall. With various rebuildings over the centuries, the church took its current form in the 1740s, with a perfectly elegant façade by Fernando Fuga and an equally impressive rear elevation by other architects; the obelisk behind it came from the Mausoleum of Augustus. Above everything rises the tallest and fairest **campanile** in Rome, an incongruous survival from the 1380s. Inside, the most conspicuous feature is the coffered ceiling by Renaissance architect Giuliano da Sangallo, gilded with the first gold brought back from the New World by Columbus, a gift from King Ferdinand and Queen Isabella of Spain. In the apse, there are splendid but faded mosaics from 1295 of the *Coronation of the Virgin*. Mosaics from the 5th century can be seen in the nave and in the 'triumphal arch' in front of the apse. Santa Maria has a prize relic—nothing less than the genuine manger from Bethlehem, preserved in a sunken shrine in front of the altar; in front, kneeling in prayer, is a colossal, rather grotesque statue of Pope Pius IV added in the 1880s.

Two little churches in the streets around Santa Maria Maggiore commemorate two sisters, early Christian martyrs of the 1st century; both of them have fascinating mosaic decorations that are among the oldest and best in Rome. In **Santa Pudenziana**, on Via Urbana, there is a mosaic of *Christ and the Apostles* from the 4th century, a thoroughly classical work from the very beginnings of Christian art. At **Santa Prassede**, on Via Santa Prassede, the mosaics reveal a different world; the shadowy Rome of the not-entirely Dark Ages. In 822, two decades after Charlemagne visited the city, Pope Paschal II found the money and the talent to build works he hoped would be compared to the magnificent ruins that lay on every side. The churches he had rebuilt were not large, but they were a start, and to embellish them he imported Byzantine artists who originated a rebirth of mosaic work and painting in Rome. The jewel of Santa Prassede is the small **San Zeno Chapel**, which Paschal intended as a mausoleum for his mother. The square vaulted chamber is entirely covered with gold-ground mosaics of Christ Pantocrator, saints, and some very dignified, classical angels who look as if they never heard anything about the fall of Rome. The 9th-century mosaics around the altar are even better, though not as lavishly gilded.

## St John Lateran

Where is Rome's cathedral? It isn't St Peter's, and never has been. The true seat of the Bishop of Rome, and the end of a Roman Pilgrimage, is here in the shadow of the Aurelian wall, a church believed to have been established by Constantine himself. The family of Plautius Lateranus, according to ancient records, had their property here confiscated after a failed coup against Nero in AD 66. It eventually became part of the imperial real estate, and Constantine and his wife Fausta (whom he later executed) once kept house in the Lateran Palace. Later he donated it to Pope Miltiades, as a cult centre for the Christians of Rome. Almost nothing remains of the original basilica; the sacks of the Vandals and Normans, two earthquakes and several fires have resulted in a building with some bits and pieces left from each of the last 16 centuries.

Like Santa Maria Maggiore, this church has an 18th-century exterior that is almost miraculously good, considering other Italian buildings from that age, with a west front by Alessandro Galilei (1736) that confidently and competently reuses the High Renaissance architectural vernacular. The equally fine north façade is earlier, done by Domenico Fontana in 1586, incorporating the twin medieval bell towers into the design. Entering at the west front, you pass an ancient statue of Constantine, found at the baths he built on the Quirinal; the bronze doors in the central portal once graced the entrance to the Senate House in the forum. Inside, the nave is dominated by giant, impressive statues of the Apostles (c. 1720), glaring down like Roman emperors of old. There is some carefree and glorious Baroque work in the side chapels—also remains of a fresco by Giotto, behind the first column on the right. Near the apse, decorated with 13th-century mosaics (of a reindeer worshipping the cross, an odd conceit probably adapted from older mosaics in Ravenna), the Papal Altar supposedly contains the heads of Peter and Paul. Below floor level is the tomb of Pope Martin V; for some reason pilgrims drop flowers and telephone tokens on him for good luck.

Rome in the later Middle Ages had evolved an architectural style entirely its own, strangely uninterested in Gothic or reviving classicism, or, for that matter, anything else that was going on in the rest of Italy. Sadly, almost all of it disappeared in the Renaissance and Baroque rebuildings. The towers of Santa Maria in Cosmedin and Santa Maria Maggiore are good examples of it, as well as the expressive mosaics of Pietro Cavallini and his school and the intricate, geometrical Cosmatesque pavements in this church and so many others. Perhaps the most striking survival of this lost chapter in art is the Lateran **Cloister**, with its pairs of spiral columns and 13th-century Cosmatesque mosaics; it completely upstages everything else in the church. All around the cloister walls, fragments from the earlier incarnations of the basilica have been assembled, a hoard of broken pretty things that includes an interesting tomb of a 13th-century bishop, which may be the work of Arnolfo di Cambio.

The Lateran's **Baptistry** is no ordinary baptistry—nothing less than the first one in Christendom, converted from an older temple by Constantine; its octagonal form has been copied in other baptistries all over Italy. Unfortunately, this is another of Rome's treasures that was damaged by mysterious terrorist bombs in 1993, and now may be closed for restoration. Inside there are unusual pairs of bronze doors on either side: one from 1196 with scenes of how the Lateran basilica appeared at that time, and the other from the Baths of Caracalla, 'singing' doors that make a low, harmonic sound when you open them slowly. Built around the baptistry are three venerable chapels with more mosaics from the early Middle Ages. The entrance to the baptistry is in Piazza San Giovanni in Laterano, behind the **Lateran Palace**, rebuilt in 1588 over the original building that had served as home of the popes for 1000 years (4th–14th centuries). In the piazza, besides the obligatory obelisk, you will see the **Scala Santa**, supposedly the stairs of Pilate's palace in Jerusalem, ascended by Christ on his way to Judgement and brought to Rome by Constantine's mother, St Helena.

The more serious pilgrims ascend them on their knees. The Chapel of San Lorenzo at the top, a part of the medieval Papal Palace, contains two miraculous portraits of Jesus, painted by angels, but it is hardly ever open.

While you're here, you have a good opportunity to explore the Aurelian wall. The stretch of it behind the Lateran probably looks much as it did originally, and the nearby **Porta Asinara** (next to Porta San Giovanni) is one of the best-preserved monumental ancient gateways.

## The Caelian Hill

South of the Colosseum you can see nothing but trees, but on every inch of this vast tract of parkland, almost 2.5 square kilometres in extent, the ruins of ancient neighbourhoods wait just a few feet beneath the surface. Modern Rome never expanded in this direction, and almost the whole of it has been preserved as open space. It's a fascinating place to walk around, if you can avoid the traffic thundering down the big boulevards towards the southern suburbs. The Caelian Hill is only a small part of it, but it is one of the least known and most delightful corners of Rome. Have a picnic in the big park called the **Villa Celimontana**, and you may find some squirrels keeping you company.

Some of Rome's most ancient churches repose in quiet settings here, all worth a look inside if they are open: **Santo Stefano Rotondo**, the oldest circular church in Italy, was built around 470 over the ruins of a market-place of Nero's time; across the street, more mosaics from the age of Paschal I (c. 820) can be seen in **Santa Maria in Dominica**, standing in **Piazza della Navicella**, with a fountain made in the form of an ancient Roman ship. This piazza is also the main entrance to the Villa Celimontana. Heading downhill from here you arrive at **SS. Giovanni e Paolo**, built in the 4th century in the top floor of three Roman houses, which could be visited were they not closed for restoration. Down the western slope, you reach **San Gregorio Magno**, begun by Pope Gregory the Great in 590. St Augustine lived here before being sent by Gregory to convert the Angles and Saxons of Britain.

## Circus Maximus and Caracalla's Baths

Piazza Porta Capena, at the foot of the Caelian hill, has an odd decoration, an obelisk erected by Mussolini to commemorate his conquest of Ethiopia—he stole it from the Ethiopian city of Axum. The piazza itself is a vortex of Mussolinian pretensions; the dictator built himself a new Triumphal Way (now Via San Gregorio) along the route of the original one, to celebrate his piddling triumphs in proper Roman style. Behind the obelisk an unfinished building that was to be the Ministry of Africa found a more agreeable use after the war—it is now the home of the United Nations Food and Agricultural Organisation, the FAO. To the west, a broad green lawn is all that's left of the great **Circus Maximus**. Archaeologists have estimated that as many as 300,000 Romans could squeeze in here and place their bets for the frequent chariot races. Founded by King Tarquin and completed in its final form by Trajan, the stadium proved simply too convenient a quarry; the banked, horseshoe-shaped depression, however, still follows closely the line of the ancient grandstands.

The **Baths of Caracalla** (206–220 AD), in a large park south of Porta Capena, rank with those of Diocletian as the largest and most lavish of the type. Roughly 305m square, with excellent libraries and spacious exercise courts, the baths probably boasted more gold, marble and precious artworks than any building complex in Rome; here the Farnese family dug up such masterpieces as the *Hercules* and the *Farnese Bull*, now in the Naples museum. In the 1700s these baths were one of the obligatory sights of the Grand Tour; their lofty, broken arches and vaults appealed to the Romantic love of ruins like no others. Much of the central building survives, with its hot and cold rooms, great hall and swimming pool, all decorated with colourful mosaics. A large tunnel connects the baths with the area around Palazzo Venezia, over a kilometre away; its purpose was to transport the vast amounts of wood needed to keep the baths hot. Mussolini initiated the custom (now under threat due to the frailty of the ruins) of holding summer operas here; he liked to drive his roadster through the tunnel and pop out dramatically on stage at the beginning of the festivities.

Behind the baths a stretch of the **Antonine Aqueduct** that supplied it can still be seen. On the other side, facing Via Terme di Caracalla, **SS. Nereo e Achilleo** has more mosaics from the time of Leo III (*c.* 800), a Cosmatesque floor and choir, and some gruesome 16th-century frescoes of the martydoms of the saints.

## The Appian Way: Rome's Catacombs

Rome's 'Queen of Roads', the path of trade and conquest to Campania, Brindisi, and the East, was begun in 312 BC by Consul Appius Claudius. Like most of the consular roads outside Rome, over the centuries it became lined with cemeteries and the elaborate mausolea of the wealthy; ancient Roman practice, inherited from the Etruscans, prohibited any burials within the *pomerium*, the sacred ground of the city itself. Later, the early Christian community built some of its most extensive catacombs here—the word itself comes from the location, *ad catacumbas*, referring to the dip in the Appian Way near the suburban Circus of Maxentius. The road, now Via Appia Antica to distinguish it from the modern Via Appia Nuova to the east, makes a pleasant excursion outside the city; take the no.118 bus from the Colosseum to Cecilia Metella, and then walk on or walk back.

The road passes under the Aurelian wall at **Porta San Sebastiano**, one of the best-preserved of the old gates. It houses the **Museum of the Walls** (*open 9–1.30, 4–7, Tues, Thurs, Sat; 9–1.30 Wed, Fri; 9–1 Sun; adm*), a very thorough exhibition on the history of Rome's walls, admission to which also gives you access to a well-preserved section of the 4th-century wall alongside it. Continuing along the road, after about ½km, with some ruins of tombs along the way, there is the famous church of **Domine Quo Vadis**, on the spot where Peter, fleeing from the dangers of Rome, met Christ coming the other way. 'Where goest thou, Lord?' Peter asked. 'I am going to be crucified once more,' was the reply. As the vision departed the shamed Apostle turned back, soon to face his own crucifixion in Rome.

Another kilometre or so takes you to the **Catacombs of St Calixtus**, off on a side road to the right (*open 8.30–12, 2.30–5, Mon, Tues, Thurs–Sun; open April–Sept till 5.30pm; closed Wed; guided tours; adm*). Here the biggest attraction is the 'Crypt of the Popes', burial places of 3rd- and 4th-century pontiffs with some well-executed frescoes and inscriptions. A word about catacombs: popular romance and modern cinema notwithstanding, these were never places of refuge from persecution or anything else, but simply burial grounds. The word catacombs was only used after the 5th century; before that the Christians preferred simply to call them 'cemeteries'. The burrowing instinct is harder to explain. Few other Mediterranean cities have catacombs (Naples, Syracuse, Malta, and the Greek island of Milos are among them). One of the requirements for catacombs seems to be tufa, or some other stone that can be easily excavated. Even so, the work involved was tremendous, and not explainable by any reasons of necessity. Christians were still digging them after they had become a power in Rome, in Constantine's time. No one knows for certain what sort of funeral rites were celebrated in them, just as no one knows much about any of the prayers or rituals of the early Christians; we can only suspect that a Christian of the 4th century and one of the 16th would have had considerable difficulty recognizing each other as brothers in the faith.

Most catacombs began small, as private family cemeteries; over generations some grew into enormous termitaries extending for miles beneath the surface. Inside, most of the tombs you will see will be simple *loculi*, walled-up niches with only a symbol or short inscription scratched in to identify the deceased. Others, especially the tombs of popes or the wealthy, may have paintings of scriptural scenes, usually very poor work that reflects more on the dire state of the late Roman imagination than on the Christians.

You can detour from here another ½km west to the **Catacombs of Domatilla** (*open 8.30–12, 2.30–5, Mon, Wed–Sun; open April–Sept till 5.30pm; closed Tues; guided tours; adm*). She was a member of a senatorial family, and interestingly the catacombs seem to incorporate parts of earlier pagan *hypogea*, including a cemetery of the Imperial Flavian family; the paintings include an unusual *Last Supper* scene, portraying a young and beardless Jesus and Apostles in Roman dress. There is an adjacent basilica, built about the tombs of SS. Nereus and Achilleus, on Via delle Sette Chiese. Not far away is a monument to martyrs of a very different sort, the **Mausoleum of the Fosse Ardeatine**, dedicated to the three hundred Romans massacred on this spot in 1944 after a Resistance uprising. Back on the Via Appia Antica, there are several catacombs near the corner of Via Appia Pignatelli, including a Jewish one, but the largest, and the only ones that may be visited, are the **Catacombs of San Sebastiano** (*open 8.30–12, 2.30–5, Mon–Wed, Fri–Sun; open April–Sept till 5.30pm; closed Thurs; guided tours; adm*). This complex, too, began as a pagan cemetery. It is one of the largest, with intriguing paintings and incised symbols throughout. The place had some special significance for the early Christians, and it has been conjectured that Peter and Paul were originally buried here, before their removal to the city basilicas in Constantine's time.

Further south, by now in fairly open country, there are the ruins of the Circus of Maxentius, built in the early 4th century, and then the imposing, cylindrical **tomb of Cecilia Metella**, from the time of Augustus. In the Middle Ages the Caetani family turned the tomb into a family fortress, guarding the road to the south; at other times, before and since, it was a famous rendezvous for *banditti*. The road continues, flanked by tombs and with stretches of the original paving, for 16km from the walls of Rome.

## The Aventine Hill

Every now and then, whenever left-wing parties walk out on negotiations or talks to establish a government coalition, Italian newspapers may call it an 'Aventine Secession', an off-the-cuff reference to events in Rome 2500 years ago. Under the Roman Republic, the

Aventine Hill was the most solidly plebeian quarter of the city. On several occasions, when legislation proposed by the senate and consuls seriously threatened the rights or interests of the people, they retired *en masse* to the Aventine and stayed there until the plan was dropped. Rome's unionists today often keep the city tied up in knots, but most are probably unaware that their ancestors had the honour of inventing the general strike.

The Aventine had another distinction in those times. In its uninhabited regions, the steep, cave-ridden slopes and parks towards the south, Greek immigrants and returning soldiers introduced the midnight rituals of Dionysus and Bacchus. Though secret, such goings-on soon came to the attention of the senate, which saw the orgies quite rightly as a danger to the state and banned them in 146 BC. They must not have died out completely, however, and in the Middle Ages the Aventine had a reputation as a haunt of witches. The early Christian community also prospered here, and some of their churches are the oldest relics on the Aventine today. Coming up from the Circus Maximus along Via Santa Sabina, the **Santa Sabina** church is a simple, rare example of a 5th-century basilica, with an atrium at its entrance like a Roman secular basilica, and an original door of cypress carved with scriptural scenes. This has been the head church of the Dominicans ever since a 13th-century pope gave it to St Dominic. Both Santa Sabina and the church of **Sant'Alessio e Bonifacio** down the street have good Cosmatesque cloisters.

At the end of this street, one of the oddities only Rome can offer stands on its quiet square, oblivious of the centuries, the **Priory of the Sovereign Order of Malta,** a fancy Rococo complex designed by Giambattista Piranesi. The Knights of Malta—or more properly, the Knights Hospitallers of St John—no longer wait for the popes to unleash them against Saracen and Turk. Mostly this social club for old nobles bestirs itself to assist hospitals, its original job during the Crusades. The headquarters is presently at a fancier address in Rome, but the order's ambassadors to Italy and the Vatican live here.

Elsewhere on the Aventine, **Santa Prisca** has beginnings typical of an early Roman church; its crypt, the original church, was allegedly converted from the house of the martyr Prisca, host to St Peter; the Apostle must have often presided over Mass here. **San Saba**, another member of that first Roman Christian community, has her church on Via San Saba, founded in the 7th century by monks fleeing the Arabs in Jordan and Syria, is on a 1205 rebuilding, including some Cosmatesque details, a superb mosaic floor and a crypt with 7th–11th-century frescoes.

## Rome's Pyramid and Monte Testaccio

**Porta San Paolo** stands among one of the most perfectly preserved sections of the Aurelian wall. The gate itself looks just as it did 1700 years ago, when it was the *Porta Ostiense*; its change of name came about because Paul passed through it on the way to his execution. Built into the wall near the gate is a unique site: the **Pyramid of Caius Cestius Poplicius** may seem a strange self-tribute for a Roman, but Cestius, an official who had served in Egypt, at least paid for it himself. The tomb was built in 12 AD, and is 28m tall.

Behind it, following the inside of the walls, the lovely **Protestant Cemetery** is a popular point of Romantic pilgrimage. The graves of Shelley and Keats are there, recently joined by 400 British soldiers who died during the march on Rome in 1944. Just to the west, you can climb the youngest and certainly the oddest of Rome's hills. **Monte Testaccio** is made entirely of pot-shards. In ancient times, wine, oil, olives, grain and nearly everything else was shipped in big *amphorae*; here, in part of what was Rome's port warehouse district, all the broken, discarded ones accumulated in one place. The hill, now grassed over, is 35m at its highest point—there is a big cross on top—and it covers a large area. The vast cellars the Romans left beneath it are now used as workshops, wine cellars and nightclubs that make Testaccio a swinging area after dark.

## St Paul's Outside the Walls

Paul was beheaded on a spot near the Ostia road; according to an old legend, the head bounced three times, and at each place where it hit a fountain sprung up. The Abbazia delle Tre Fontane, near EUR, occupies the site today. Later, Constantine would build a basilica alongside the road as a fitting resting place for the saint. Of the five patriarchal basilicas, this one has had the worst luck. Today it sits in the middle of the unprepossessing neighbour-hood of Ostiense, full of factories, gasworks and concrete flats. Once it was the grandest of them all; 9th-century chroniclers speak of the separate walled city of 'Giovannipolis' that had grown up around St Paul's, connected to the Aurelian wall by a 1½km-long colonnade built by Pope John VIII in the 870s.

The Norman sack of 1084, a few good earthquakes, and finally a catastrophic fire in 1823 wiped Giovannipolis off the map, and left us with a St Paul's that for the most part is barely more than a century old. Still, the façade of golden mosaics and sturdy Corinthian columns is pleasant to look at, and some older features survive—the 11th-century door made in Constantinople, a Gothic baldachin over Paul's tomb by Arnolfo di Cambio, a beautiful 13th-century Cosmatesque cloister, almost a double of the one in the Lateran, and 5th-century mosaics over the 'Triumphal Arch' in front of the apse, the restored remains of the original mosaics from the façade, contributed by Empress Galla Placidia (*see* 'Ravenna'). Art Deco is not what you would expect from those times, but Americans at least will have a hard time believing these mosaics were not done by President Roosevelt's WPA. The apse itself has some more conventional mosaics from the 13th-century Roman school, and the nave is lined with the portraits of all 265 popes. According to Roman tradition, when the remaining eight spaces are filled, the world will end.

## EUR

By the late 1930s, Mussolini was proud enough of his accomplishments to plan a great world's fair. Its theme was to be the Progress of Civilization, measured no doubt from the invention of the wheel up to the invention of the Corporate State. A vast area south of Rome was cleared and transformed into a grid of wide boulevards broken by parks and lagoons. Huge Mussolini-style pavilions and colonnades were begun, and a design was accepted for a tremendous aluminium arch—forerunner of the famous one in St Louis but many times bigger—that would overspread the entire fairgrounds. War intervening, the arch never appeared, and the Esposizione Universale di Roma never came off. After 1945 the Italians tried to make the best of it, turning EUR into a model satellite city and trade centre on the lines of La Défense in Paris. The result will derange your senses as much as it does the average Roman's, a chilly nightmare of modernism with street names like the Boulevard of

Humanism, Boulevard of Electronics, and the Boulevard of Social Security. All these are immensely wide speedways, where the few foolish pedestrians are mowed down like ducks in a shooting gallery, lined with glass skyscrapers that make the crumbling old Mussolini buildings look positively cosy and cheerful.

Still, for those who can appreciate the well-landscaped macabre, EUR can be fun. Some of the older corners reveal giant fascist mosaics of heroic miners, soldiers, assembly-line workers, and mothers, and at the end of the Boulevard of Civilization and Labour you can have a look at the modest masterpiece of Mussolini architecture, a small, elegantly proportioned building called the **Palazzo della Civiltà del Lavoro**. Liberal, post-war Italy has rarely, if ever, been able to conceive anything with such a sure sense of design and a feeling for history (of course some Roman malcontents call it the 'Square Colosseum').

The only serious reason to come to EUR is for the sports arenas and the museums, especially the **Museo della Civiltà Romana**, Piazza G. Agnelli 10 (*open 9–1.30, 4–7, Tues, Thurs; 9am–1.30pm Wed, Fri, Sat; 9am–1pm Sun; adm*), a collection of antiques and exhibits including a huge scale-model of ancient Rome with every building present, a great place to seed your imagination with visions of the old city's splendour. Other museums in the area include the **Prehistorical and Ethnographic Museum** nearby in Piazza Marconi (*open 9–1.30 Mon–Sat; 9–1 Sun; adm*), covering civilizations before classical Rome, and the **Museum of the Late Middle Ages** on Viale Lincoln (*open 9–1.30 Mon–Sat; 9–12.30 Sun; adm*).

## Trastevere

So often, just being on the wrong side of the river encourages a city district to cultivate its differences and its eccentricities. Trastevere isn't really a Left Bank—more of a pocket-sized Brooklyn, and as in Brooklyn those differences and eccentricities often turn out to be the old habits of the whole city, distilled and preserved in an out-of-the-way corner. The people of Trastevere are more Roman than the Romans. Indeed, they claim to be the real descendants of the Romans of old; one story traces their ancestry back to the sailors who worked the great awning and choreographed the mock sea-battles at the Colosseum. Such places have a hard time surviving these days, especially when they are as trendy and popular as Trastevere is right now. But even though such things as Trastevere's famous school of dialect poets may be mostly a memory, the quarter remains the liveliest and most entertaining in Rome. The young crowd that Trastevere attracts now provides much of the local colour, dressed in colourful trendy clothes that somehow seem a perfect match for the medieval alleys and jumbles of flats.

If you cross over on the **Sublician Bridge** under the Aventine Hill, the successor to Rome's first bridge (the one Horatio defended), you'll arrive at Porta Portese and Rome's big **flea market**. From there, Via San Michele a Ripa takes you to the church of **Santa Cecilia in Trastevere**, founded over the house of the 2nd-century martyr whom centuries of hagiography have turned into one of the most agreeable of saints, the inventor of the organ and patroness of music. Cecilia was disinterred in 1599, apparently out of curiosity, and her body was found entirely uncorrupted. Clement VIII commissioned Maderno to sculpt an exact copy from sketches made before her body dissolved into thin air; this charming work can be seen near the altar, beneath an altarpiece by Giuliano Romano. Nearby there is a *Tabernacle* by Arnolfo di Cambio similar to the one in St Paul's, and some 9th-century mosaics in the apse. The church has any number of other treasures: Renaissance tombs, including one of a 14th-century cardinal from Hertford named Adam Easton; frescoes by the school of Pinturicchio in a chapel on the right, and a crypt built in the underlying Roman constructions, thought to be Cecilia's home (*adm*). Up in the singing gallery (*open 10.30–11.30 Tues, Fri only; adm*) are the remains of the original church wall decoration—a wonderful fresco of the *Last Judgement* by Pietro Cavallini, one of the masters of the Roman 13th-century school, more famous for his mosaics in Santa Maria in Trastevere. There is also a 12th-century cloister, though it is rarely open.

Across Viale Trastevere, an intrusive modern boulevard that slices the district in two, lies the heart of old Trastevere, around **Piazza Santa Maria in Trastevere** and the church of the same name. Most of this building dates from the 1140s, though the original church, begun perhaps in 222, may be the first anywhere dedicated to the Virgin Mary. The medieval building is a treasure-house of Roman mosaics, starting with the frieze with the Virgin breast-feeding Christ flanked by ten female figures on the façade, and continuing with the remarkable series from the *Life of Mary* by Cavallini in the apse and on the apse wall, a bit of the early Renaissance 100 years ahead of schedule (*c.* 1290). Above them there are earlier, more glittering mosaics from the 1140s. The piazza, and the streets around it, have been for decades one of the most popular spots in Rome for restaurants; tables are spread out wherever there's room, and there will always be a crowd in the evening hours. Down Via della Lungaretta, Piazza Sidney Sonnino faces Ponte Garibaldi, Trastevere's front door. The **Torre degli Anguillara** is an uncommon survival of the defence towers that loomed threateningly over medieval Rome, and the 12th-century church of **San Crisogono** has more mosaics by Cavallini. Near the bridge, the dapper statue in the top hat is Giuseppe Gioacchino Belli, one of Trastevere's 19th-century dialect poets.

## Two Roads to St Peter's

One is broad and straight, the route of the many; the other is tortuous and narrow, and after it but few inquire. **Via della Lungara**, the route of the slothful from Trastevere, takes you past the **Villa Farnesina** (*open 9–1 Tues–Sun*), an early 1500s palace built for the Chigi family. Inside is some of the best fresco painting in Rome: the *Galatea* by Raphael and the *Cupid and Psyche gallery*, designed by Raphael and carried out by his pupils; a prospect of the constellations and a room of false perspectives by Baldassare Peruzzi, who also designed the building; and works of Sodoma. Across the street, the **Palazzo Corsini** (*open 9–7 Tues–Sat; 9–1 Sun; adm*), contains an exceptional collection of 16th- and 17th-century art, including works by Caravaggio, Van Dyck, Guido Reni, Salvatore Rosa and many others—it's out of the way, but this may be the best of all Rome's many small state picture galleries.

The other road may be more difficult to find, but repays the effort with lovely gardens and some of the best views over Rome from the Gianicolo, the ancient *Janiculum.* First find Via Garibaldi, in the back streets behind Ponte Sisto, and it will carry you up to the Renaissance church of **San Pietro in Montorio**, once erroneously believed to be the spot of St Peter's upside-down crucifixion. There's a fair amount of earnest 16th- and 17th-century painting inside, but the true reason for stopping is in the adjacent courtyard, the now half-forgotten **Tempietto** of Bramante. In so many Renaissance paintings—Perugino's *Donation of the Keys* in the Sistine Chapel, or Raphael's well-known *Betrothal of the Virgin* in Milan, the characters in the foreground take second place in interest to an ethereal, round temple centred at the perspectival vanishing point. These constructions, seemingly built not of vulgar stone but of pure intelligence and light, could stand as a symbol for the aspirations of the Renaissance. Bramante was the first to try actually to build one; his perfect little Tempietto (1502), the first building to re-use the ancient Doric order in all of its proportions, probably inspired Raphael's painting two years later.

A little further up the Janiculum, you'll come to the giant fountain of the Acqua Paola, where you should turn right along the Passeggiata del Gianicolo. The Garibaldi Monument stands at the summit, overlooking the Botanical Gardens and the rest of Rome. At the other end of the hill, going towards the Vatican, the road curves downwards, passing the Renaissance church of **Sant'Onofrio**, with frescoes by Peruzzi in the apse. After descending the Passeggiata del Gianicolo, cross the wide modern Piazza della Rovere into the Borgo district. On your right is the venerable hospital of Santo Spirito and the church of **Santo Spirito in Sassia**. This name may ring a bell for antiquarians. 'Sassia' refers to the Saxons of England, who immediately upon their conversion became among the most devoted servants of the Church. English princes founded this hospital sometime in the 8th century—astounding enough when you think about it. The Angles and Saxons who settled in Rome made up almost a small village into themselves at this bend of the Tiber, and their 'burgh' gave its name to the big neighbourhood called the Borgo today.

## Castel Sant'Angelo

Though intended as a resting place for a most serene emperor, this building has seen more blood, treachery and turmoil than any in Rome. Hadrian, it seems, designed his own mausoleum three years before his death in 138, on an eccentric plan consisting of a huge marble cylinder, surmounted by a conical hill planted with cypresses. The marble, the obelisks, the gold and

Castel St. Angelo

bronze decorations did not survive the 5th-century sacks, but in about 590, during a plague, Pope Gregory the Great saw a vision of St Michael over the mausoleum, ostensibly announcing the end of the plague, but perhaps also mentioning discreetly that here, if anyone cared to use it, was the most valuable fortress in Europe.

There would be no papacy, perhaps, without this castle—at least not in its present form. Hadrian's great cylinder is high, steep, and almost solid—impregnable even after the invention of artillery. With rebellions of some sort occurring on average every two years before 1400, the popes often had recourse to this place of safety. It last saw action in the sack of 1527, when the miserable Clement VII withstood a siege of several months while his city went up in flames around him. The popes also used Castel Sant'Angelo as a prison; famous inmates included Giordano Bruno, Benvenuto Cellini and Beatrice Cenci (better known to the English than the Italians, thanks to Shelley's verse drama). Tosca tosses herself off the top at the end of Puccini's opera.

Inside the castle (*open 9–6 daily, closed the second and fourth Monday of each month; adm*) many of the rooms and the original spiral ramp are unfortunately closed for restoration, but some of the more spectacular chambers can be seen. A medieval ramp leads up to the **Papal Apartments**, decorated as lavishly by 16th-century artists as anything in the Vatican. The **Sala Paolina** has frescoes by Perin del Vaga depicting events in the history of Rome, and the **Sala di Apollo** is frescoed with grotesques attempting to reproduce the wall decorations of the ancient palaces, perhaps like Nero's Golden House. Above everything, a mighty statue of Michael commemorates Pope Gregory's vision. Just below the castle, the three central arches of the **Ponte Sant'Angelo** were built by Hadrian, although the statues added in 1688 steal the show; at once dubbed Bernini's Breezy Maniacs, they battle a never-ending Baroque hurricane to display the symbols of Christ's Passion.

## St Peter's

Along Borgo Sant'Angelo, leading towards the Vatican, you can see the famous **covered passageway**, used by the popes since 1277 to escape to the castle when things became dangerous. The customary route, however, leads up **Via della Concilazione**, a broad boulevard laid out under Mussolini over a tangled web of medieval streets. Critics have said it spoils the surprise, but no arrangement of streets and buildings could really prepare you for Bernini's Brobdingnagian **Piazza San Pietro**. Someone has calculated there is room for about 300,000 people in the piazza, with no crowding. Few have ever noticed Bernini's little joke on antiquity; the open space almost exactly meets the size and dimensions of the Colosseum. Bernini's **Colonnade** (1656), with 284 massive columns and statues of 140 saints, stretches around it like 'the arms of the Church embracing the world'—perhaps the biggest cliché in Christendom by now, but exactly what Bernini had in mind. Stand on either of the two dark stones at the foci of the elliptical piazza, and you will see Bernini's forest of columns resolve into neat rows, a subtly impressive optical effect like the hole in the top of the Pantheon. Flanked by two lovely fountains, the work of Maderno and Fontana, the Vatican **obelisk** seems nothing special as obelisks go, but is actually one of the most fantastical relics in all Rome. This obelisk comes from Heliopolis, the Egyptian city founded as a capital and cult centre by Akhnaton, the half-legendary Pharaoh and religious reformer who, according to Sigmund Freud and others, founded the first monotheistic religion, influencing Moses and all that came after. Caligula brought it over to Rome in 37 AD to decorate the now-disappeared Circus Vaticanus (later referred to as the Circus of Nero) where it would have overlooked Peter's martyrdom. In the Middle Ages it was placed to the side of the basilica, but Sixtus V moved it to where it now stands in 1586.

It may be irreverent to say so, but the original St Peter's, begun over the Apostle's tomb by Constantine in 324, may well have been a more interesting building, a richly decorated basilica full of gold and mosaics with a vast porch of marble and bronze in front and a lofty campanile, topped by the famous golden cockerel that everyone believed would some day crow to announce the end of the world. This St Peter's, where Charlemagne and Frederick II received their imperial crowns, was falling to pieces by the 1400s, conveniently in time for the popes and artists of the Renaissance to plan a replacement. NicholasV, in about 1450, conceived an almost Neronian building programme for the Vatican, ten times as large as anything his ancestors could have contemplated. It was not until the time of Julius II, however, that Bramante was commissioned to demolish the old church and begin the new. His original plan called for a great dome over a centralized Greek cross. Michelangelo, who took over the work in 1546, basically agreed, and if he had had his way St Peter's might indeed have become the crowning achievement of Renaissance art that everyone hoped it would be.

Unfortunately, over the 120 years of construction too many popes and too many artists got their hand in—Rossellino, Giuliano da Sangallo, Raphael, Antonio da Sangallo, Vignola, Ligorio, della Porta, Fontana, Bernini and Maderno all contributed something to the tremendous hodgepodge we see today. The most substantial tinkering came in the early 17th century, when a committee of cardinals decided that a Latin cross was desired, resulting in the huge extension of the nave that blocks the view of Michelangelo's dome from the piazza. Baroque architects, mistaking size and virtuosity for art, found perfect patrons in the Baroque popes, less interested in faith than the power and majesty of the papacy. Passing though Maderno's gigantic façade seems like entering a Grand Central Station full of stone saints and angels, keeping an eye on the big clocks overhead as they wait for trains to Paradise. All along the nave, markers showing the length of other proud cathedrals prove how each fails miserably to measure up to the Biggest Church in the World. This being Rome, not even the markers are honest—Milan's cathedral is actually 20m longer.

The best is on the right: Michelangelo's *Pietà*, now restored and kept behind glass to protect it from future madmen. This work, done when he was only 25, helped make Michelangelo's reputation. Its smooth and elegant figures, with the realities of death and grief sublimated onto some ethereal plane known only to saints and artists, were a turning point in religious art. From here the beautiful, unreal art of the religious Baroque was the logical next step. Note how Michelangelo has carved his name in small letters on the band around the Virgin's garment; he added this after overhearing a group of tourists from Milan who thought the *Pietà* the work of a fellow Milanese. Not much else in St Peter's really stands out. In its vast spaces scores of popes and saints are remembered in assembly-line Baroque, and the paintings over most of the altars have been replaced by mosaic copies. The famous bronze statute of St Peter, its foot worn away by the touch of millions of pilgrims, is by the right front pier.

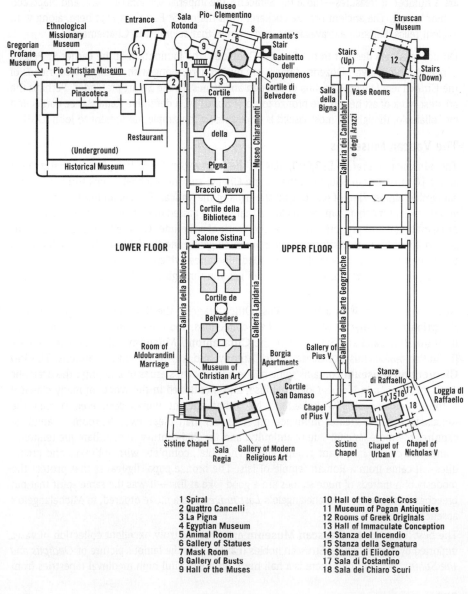

1 Spiral
2 Quattro Cancelli
3 La Pigna
4 Egyptian Museum
5 Animal Room
6 Gallery of Statues
7 Mask Room
8 Gallery of Busts
9 Hall of the Muses

10 Hall of the Greek Cross
11 Museum of Pagan Antiquities
12 Rooms of Greek Originals
13 Hall of Immaculate Conception
14 Stanza del Incendio
15 Stanza della Segnatura
16 Stanza di Eliodoro
17 Sala di Costantino
18 Sala dei Chiaro Scuri

Stealing the show, just as he knew it would, is Bernini's great, garish **baldacchino** over the high altar, cast out of bronze looted from the Pantheon roof.

Many visitors head straight for Michelangelo's **dome** (*open April–Sept 8–6 daily; Oct–Mar 8–5 daily; adm, plus additional fare for the lift halfway to the top*). To be in the middle of such a spectacular construction is worth the climb itself. You can walk out on the roof for a view over Rome, but even more startling is the chance to look down from the interior balcony over the vast church 76m below. In the **Sacristy**, built in the 18th century, there are a number of treasures—those the Saracens, the imperial soldiers of 1527, and Napoleon couldn't steal. The ancient bronze cockerel from the old St Peter's is kept here, along with ancient relics, Baroque extravaganzas, and a gown that belonged to Charlemagne.

Do not pass up a descent to the **Sacred Grottoes**, the foundation of the earlier St Peter's converted into a crypt. Dozens of popes are buried here, along with distinguished friends of the Church like Queen Christina of Sweden and James III, the Stuart pretender. Perhaps the greatest work of art here is the bronze tomb of Sixtus IV, a definitive Renaissance confection by Pollaiuolo, though the most visited is undoubtedly the simple monument to John XXIII.

## The Vatican Museums

The admission (currently L13,000) may be the most expensive in Italy, but for that you get about 10 museums in one, with the Sistine Chapel and the Raphael rooms thrown in free. Altogether almost 7km of exhibits fill the halls of the Vatican Palace, and unfortunately for you there isn't much dull museum clutter that can be passed over lightly. Seeing this infinite, exasperating hoard properly would be the work of a lifetime. On the bright side, the pope sees to it that his museum is managed more intelligently and thoughtfully than anything run by the Italian state. A choice of colour-coded itineraries, which you may follow according to the amount of time you have to spend, will get you through the labyrinth in 90 minutes, or five hours.

Near the entrance (with a Vatican Post Office branch), the first big challenge is a large **Egyptian Museum**, one of Europe's best collections, and then some rooms of antiquities from the Holy Land and Syria, before the **Chiaramonti Museum**, full of Roman statuary (including famous busts of Caesar, Mark Antony, and Augustus) and inscriptions. The **Pio Clementino Museum** contains some of the best-known statues of antiquity; the dramatic *Laocoön*, dug up in Nero's Golden House, and mentioned in the works of many classical authors, and the *Apollo Belvedere*. No other ancient works recovered during the Renaissance had a greater influence on sculptors than these two. A 'room of animals' captures the more fanciful side of antiquity, and the 2nd-century Roman Baroque tendency comes out clearly in a giant group called 'The Nile', complete with sphinxes and crocodiles—it came from a Roman temple of Isis. The bronze papal fig-leaves that protect the modesty of hundreds of nude statues are a good joke at first—it was the same spirit that put breeches on the saints in Michelangelo's *Last Judgement*, a move ordered, in Michelangelo's absence, by Pius IV.

The best things in the **Etruscan Museum** are Greek, a truly excellent collection of vases imported by discriminating Etruscan nobles that includes the famous picture of *Oedipus and the Sphinx*. Beyond that, there is a hall hung with beautiful high medieval tapestries from

Tournai (15th century), and the long, long **Map Room**, lined with carefully painted town views and maps of every corner of Italy; note the long scene of the 1566 Great Siege of Malta at the entrance. Anywhere else, with no Michelangelos to offer competition, Raphael's celebrated frescoes in the **Stanze della Segnatura** would have been the prime destination on anyone's itinerary. The *School of Athens* is too well known to require much of an introduction, but here is a guide to some of the figures: on Aristotle's side, Archimedes and Euclid surrounded by their disciples (Euclid, drawing plane figures on a slate, is supposedly a portrait of Bramante); off to the right, Ptolemy and Zoroaster hold the terrestrial and celestial globes. Raphael includes himself among the Aristotelians, standing between Zoroaster and the painter Il Sodoma. Behind Plato stand Socrates and Alcibiades, among others, and to the left, Zeno and Epicurus. In the foreground, a crouching Pythagoras writes while Empedocles and the Arab Averroes look on. Diogenes sprawls philosophically on the steps, while isolated near the front is Heraclitus—really Michelangelo, according to legend; Raphael put him in at the last minute after seeing the work in progress on the Sistine Chapel.

Across from this apotheosis of philosophy, Raphael painted a Triumph of Theology to keep the clerics happy, the *Dispute of the Holy Sacrament*. The other frescoes include the *Parnassus*, a vision of the ancient Greek and Latin poets, the *Miracle of Bolsena*, the *Expulsion of Heliodorus*, an allegory of the triumphs of the Counter-Reformation papacy, the *Meeting of Leo I and Attila*, and best of all, the solemn, spectacularly lit *Liberation of St Peter*. Nearby, there is the **Loggia** of Bramante, also with decoration designed by Raphael, though executed by other artists (*only visitable with written permission*), and the **Chapel of Nicholas V**, with frescoes by Fra Angelico. The **Borgia Apartments**, a luxurious suite built for Pope Alexander VI, have walls decorated with saints, myths and sibyls by Pinturicchio. These run into the **Gallery of Modern Religious Art**, a game attempt by the Vatican to prove that such a thing really exists.

## The Sistine Chapel

To the sophisticated Sixtus IV, building this ungainly barn of a chapel may have seemed a mistake in the first place. When the pushy, despotic Julius II sent Michelangelo, against his will, up to paint the vast ceiling, it might have turned out to be a project as hopeless as the tomb Julius had already commissioned. Michelangelo spent four years on his back to get it done. No one can say what drove him to turn his surly patron's whim into a masterpiece: the fear of wasting those years, the challenge of an impossible task, or maybe just to spite

*Musei Vaticani*

Julius—he exasperated the pope by making him wait, and refused all demands that he hire some assistants. Everywhere on the Sistine ceilings you will note the austere blankness of the backgrounds. Michelangelo always eschewed stage props; one of the tenets of his art was that complex ideas could be expressed in the portrayal of the human body alone. With sculpture, that takes time. Perhaps the inspiration that kept Michelangelo on the ceiling so long was the chance of distilling out of the Book of Genesis and his own genius an entirely new vocabulary of images, Christian and intellectual. Like most Renaissance patrons, Julius had asked for nothing more than virtuoso interior decoration. What he got was nothing like simple illustrations from Scripture; this is the way the Old Testament looks in the deepest recesses of the imagination.

The fascination of the Sistine ceiling, and the equally compelling **Last Judgement** on the rear wall, done much later (1534–41), is that while we may recognize the individual figures we still have not captured their secret meanings. Hordes of tourists stare up at the heroic Adam, the mysterious *ignudi* in the corners, the Russian masseuse sibyls with their longshoremen's arms, the six-toed prophets, the strange vision of Noah's deluge. They wonder what they're looking at, a question that would take years of inspired wondering to answer. Mostly they direct their attention to the all too famous scene of the Creation, with perhaps the only representation of God the Father ever painted that escapes being merely ridiculous. One might suspect that the figure is really some ageing Florentine artist, and that Michelangelo only forgot to paint the brush in his hand.

The ceiling restorations are finished, and the Last Judgement has now been unveiled. Despite a chorus of protest from some fashionable American artists, there seems to be a consensus that the work, paid for by a Japanese television network, is accurately revealing Michelangelo's true colours—jarring, surprise colours that no interior decorator would ever choose, plenty of sea-green, with splashes of yellow and purple and dramatic shadows. No new paint is being applied, only solvents to clear off the grime. Most visitors overlook the earlier frescoes on the lower walls, great works of art that would have made the Sistine Chapel famous by themselves: scenes from the *Exodus* by Botticelli, Perugino's *Donation of the Keys*, and Signorelli's *Moses Consigning his Staff to Joshua*.

## More Miles in the Big Museum

There's still the **Vatican Library** to go, with its endless halls and precious manuscripts tucked neatly away in cabinets. The brightly painted rooms contain every sort of oddity: thousands of reliquaries and an entire wall of monstrances, a memorable collection of medieval ivories, gold-glass medallions from the catacombs, every sort of globe, orrery and astronomical instrument. If you survive this, the next hurdle is the new and beautifully laid out **Museo Gregoriano**, with a hoard of excellent classical statuary, mosaics and inscriptions collected by Pope Gregory XVI. Then comes a **Carriage Museum**, the **Pius Christian Museum** of early Christian art, and finally one of the most interesting of all, though no one has time for it: the **Ethnological Museum**, with wonderful art from peoples of every continent, brought home by Catholic missionaries over the centuries.

By itself, the Vatican **Pinacoteca** would be by far the finest picture gallery in Rome, a representative sampling of Renaissance art from its beginnings, with some fine works of Giotto

(*Il Redentore* and the *Martyrdoms of Peter and Paul*) and contemporary Sienese painters, as well as Gentile da Fabbriano, Sano di Pietro, and Filippo Lippi. Don't overlook the tiny but electrically surreal masterpiece of Fra Angelico, the *Story of St Nicolas at Bari*, or the *Angelic Musicians* of Melozzo da Forli, set next to Melozzo's famous painting of Platina being nominated by Sixtus IV to head the Vatican Library—a rare snapshot of Renaissance humanism. Venetian artists are not well represented, but there is a *Pietà* by Bellini and a *Madonna* by the fastidious Carlo Crivelli. Perhaps the best-known paintings are the recently restored *Transfiguration of Christ*, Raphael's last work, and the *St Jerome* of Da Vinci.

## Vatican Practicalities

The **museums** are open 8.45am–2pm (last admission at 1pm) daily for most of the year, and 8.45–5 Mon–Fri, 8.45–2 Sat during Easter and the months of July, August, and September. They are closed on Sundays, except the last Sunday of each month (9am–2pm) when admission is free. The entrance is rather far from St Peter's Square, to the north on Viale Vaticano—a shuttle bus makes the trip every half-hour. **St Peter's** is open 7am–6pm daily, and till 7pm Oct–Mar; there may be a Mass going on somewhere in the vast church, but visitors are never excluded. The papal gendarmes, however, will certainly give you the bum's rush if you don't meet the dress code—no shorts, short skirts, or sleeveless dresses.

The **Vatican Information Office**, © (06) 69884466, in St Peter's Square is very helpful, and there are Vatican Post Offices on both sides of the square for distinctive postcards home. The Information Office arranges 3hr-long morning tours of the **Vatican Gardens**, easily Rome's most beautiful park, with a remarkable Renaissance jewel of a villa inside, the **Casino of Pius IV** by Pietro Ligorio and Peruzzi (1558–62). Underneath the crypt of St Peter's, archaeologists in the 1940s discovered a **street of Roman tombs**, perfectly preserved with many beautiful paintings and mosaics. Tours can be arranged through the Uffizio degli Scavi, just to the left of St Peter's; in the summer, book early, as fragile conditions permit only 15 people at a time in the necropolis. The rest of the Vatican is strictly off limits, patrolled by genuine Swiss Guards (still recruited from the three Catholic Swiss Cantons, though now usually lacking the fancy uniforms Michelangelo or some say Raphael—designed for them).

Michelangelo also designed the **defensive wall** that since 1929 has marked the Vatican boundaries. Behind them are things most of us will never see: several small old churches, a printing press, the headquarters of *L'Osservatore Romano* and Vatican Radio (run, of course, by the Jesuits), a motor garage, a 'Palazzo di Giustizia', and even a big shop—everything the world's smallest nation could ever need. Modern popes, in glaring contrast to their predecessors, do not take up much space. The current Papal Apartments are in a corner of the Vatican Palace overlooking Piazza San Pietro; John Paul II usually appears to say a few electrically amplified words from his window at noon on Sundays. For tickets to **papal audiences**, apply at the Papal Prefecture—through the bronze door in the right-hand colonnade of Piazza San Pietro (*open 9–1 Tues–Wed*). These large affairs are relatively easy to get in to; private audiences are of course much harder.

# Peripheral Attractions of Rome

There are plenty of interesting things on the city's outskirts—here is a brief review, tracing a clockwise circle around Rome from the north. Near the Tiber, the **Foro Italico** was certainly Mussolini's most blatant monument to himself; he left his mark everywhere, on a giant obelisk, in the paving stones, and around the kitschy grandiose **Marble Stadium**, chiselled too deep ever to be worn away. The adjacent sports complex housed the 1960 Olympics. Across the Tiber, on Via Salaria, **Villa Ada** once served as the hunting reserve of Vittorio Emanuele III; now a huge city park (though one section serves as the Egyptian Embassy), it contains the entrance to the **Catacombs of Priscilla** with 2nd-century frescoes and the tombs of many early popes and martyrs (*open 8.30–12, 2.30–5, Tues–Sun; open April–Sept till 5.30pm; adm*).

Via XX Settembre, the important thoroughfare coming off the Quirinal Hill, passes the Aurelian Wall at **Porta Pia**, redesigned by Michelangelo. Here it changes its name to Via Nomentana, a chic boulevard where many of the old villas have not yet been swallowed by creeping urbanization. A kilometre or so east, you can make a stop at the thoroughly charming complex of **Sant'Agnese Outside the Walls**, including a 4th-century church with a beautiful early mosaic of St Agnes in the apse and 15 ancient marble columns. Along the stairway descending to the church, Early-Christian reliefs and inscriptions have been arranged as in a museum; inside the church is the entrance to the small, aristocratic **catacombs** (3rd century), absorbing parts of earlier pagan catacombs (*guided tours arranged daily, except Tues*). Around the back, through gardens where the neighbourhood children play, stands one of Rome's least known but most remarkable churches. **Santa Costanza** was built as a mausoleum for Constantia, the daughter of Emperor Constantine. In this domed, circular building, one of the finest late Roman works, more than anywhere else you can see the great religious turning point of the 4th century come alive; among the exquisite mosaics (regrettably not all have survived) are scenes of a grape harvest and motifs that would be familiar to any ancient devotee of Dionysus or Bacchus. In the two side chapels are later mosaics of Christ and the Apostles.

At the end of Viale Regina Elena, tucked between the University City and the enormous Verano Cemetery, **San Lorenzo** is another of the seven churches on a Roman pilgrim's itinerary. The original building, begun under Constantine, was reconstructed in the early 13th century and contains some fine work of the Cosmati family around the altar. From here you can re-enter the city through the impressive **Porta Maggiore**, built under Emperor Claudius; note how this section of the wall carries one of the ancient aqueducts on top. In the neighbourhood you can also see the **Temple of Minerva** on Via Giolitti, a round brick ruin from the 3rd century AD, and **Santa Croce in Gerusalemme**, another of the 'Seven Churches', founded by Constantine but now thoroughly Baroqued. The real attraction, however, lies almost directly under the tracks going into Termini Station. The **Underground Basilica**, discovered only in 1916 near Porta Maggiore, was not covered up by the centuries like so many other Roman relics—it was built that way for a secret, possibly illegal, religious sect in the 1st century AD. Its stucco reliefs are fascinating and strange; scholars can't guess anything about the cult's beliefs, but venture to call it 'neo-Pythagorian' (*not open to the public at* *present, but you can write to the Soprintendenza Archeologica di Roma, Piazza Santa Maria Nova 53, © 6990110, for permission to visit).*

Jumping all the way over to the western edge of Rome, behind the Janiculum, **Villa Doria Pamphili** is an enormous old estate, bought by the city relatively recently, with beautiful parks that have been opened to the public.

## Shopping

Rome on the whole isn't as exciting for big-game shoppers as Milan, though the Roman shops are as well designed, just as enticing, and quite expensive. Rome is also the capital of Italian *haute couture*, made-to-order clothes designed for a tiny proportion of the buying public. It is, too, a good city for **antiques**, and it's easy enough to have a look at what's available because all the shops are clustered together between the Tiber and Piazza Navona; look especially off Via Monserrato, Via dei Coronari, and Via dell'Anima—for old prints, generally inexpensive, try **Casali**, Piazza Rotonda 81A; for antique jewellery, **Manasse**, Via di Campo Marzio 44; **L'Art Nouveau**, Via dei Coronari 221, offers just what its name implies. Antiques also show up in Rome's large and celebrated Sunday flea market at **Porta Portese**, as well as anything else you can imagine, all lumped together in often surreal displays. It lasts from dawn and closes gradually around 2pm; beware the pickpockets.

The most **fashionable shopping** is in the former 'English ghetto', around Piazza di Spagna. You'll find the chic and elegant boutiques of Italy's traditional and trendy designers along Vias Condotti, Frattina, Vite and Borgognona, and up at the top of the steps around Via Sistina and Via dei Barbieri. Some special items: **Massoni**, Largo Goldoni 48, near Via Condotti, much frequented by film stars, sells some of Rome's finest jewellery; for menswear, **Testa,** Via Frattini 104, or **Valentino**, Via Mario de' Fiori 22, or for custom tailoring, **Battistoni**, Via Condotti 57 and 61; for womenswear try **La Mendola**, Piazza Trinità dei Monti (near Via Sistina), or Rome's outlets of the great designers like **Missoni**, Via del Babuino 96, **Giorgio Armani**, Via del Babuino 102, or the Rome-based **Fendi**, Via Borgognona nos.8, 10, 12 and 39. For leather, exceptional **Gucci** outlets are at Via Condotti 18 and Via Borgognona 25.

Discounted designer fashion may be had at **Il Discount dell'Alto Moda** on Via Gesù e Maria 16a; for high-fashion shoes, try **Barrilà**, Via Condotti 29, and for Borsalino hats **Troncarelli**, Via della Cuccugna 15, near Piazza Navona. For smart children's clothes there's **Tablò**, Via della Croce 84 and Piazza di Spagna 96, and **Il Palloncino Rosso**, Via dei Pettinari 49.

For a special bottle of **wine**, try **Enoteca Constantini**, Piazza Cavour 16, for a wide selection. If you wish to stock up on Italian **coffee**, **Tazza d'Oro**, Via degli Orfani 84, has special bags of the city's best, the 'Aroma di Roma'. Alternatively, if you need a good read in Rome, try the **Anglo-American Book Co.**, Via della Vite 57, the **Lion Bookshop**, Via del Babuino 181, or the **Economy Book Center**, Via Torino 136, near Via Nazionale. For an amazing selection of kitsch kitchen gear, there's **Art'e'**, Piazza Rondanini; **Lunadicarta**, Vicolo dell'Atleta 10–11 sells imaginative designs in paper; and **De Ritis**, Via de'Cestari 1 has all the latest ecclesiastical fashions, along with Madonnas, crucifixes and chalices.

## Sports and Activities

Much of monumental Rome is illuminated at night, and strolling through the city then is a unique pleasure. For even bigger, brightly lit thrills, particularly if you have children in tow, head out to the Luna Park fun-fair in EUR (Metro Magliana), with its thrilling rickety roller-coaster, huge Ferris wheel and over 100 attractions. More bright lights attract visiting moths in the fountains and gardens of Tivoli's Villa d'Este (*see* below, 'Day Trips from Rome'), which are lit four nights a week 8.30–11.30pm from May to September.

Rome's main public swimming pool is also in EUR, the Piscina delle Rose, Viale America 20, © 5926717 (Metro EUR Fermi). There is also an attractive private pool off the Via Appia Antica, the Oasi della Pace, Via degli Eugeni 2, © 7184550.

Rome's two first-division football clubs, AS Roma and Lazio, both play at the Stadio Olimpico, Via dei Gladiatori, ticket office © 3237333, in the Foro Italico, during the September–May season. Matches are usually on Sundays at 3pm. Ticket prices for non-club members usually begin at around L20,000.

---

*Rome © (06–)*                                                    ## Where to Stay

For a city that has been entertaining crowds of visitors for the last 2000 years, Rome does not seem to have acquired any special flair for accommodating them. Hotels here are neither better or worse than anywhere else in Italy; from Belle Epoque palaces on Via Veneto to grimy hovels on the wrong side of Termini Station, there will be something for you to come home to after a hard day's sight-seeing although places with a history, a famous view, or quiet gardens to shut out the city noise are rare. Exceptions exist, of course, but all things considered this is not the place to make the big splurge. Check into some modest, comfortable spot in the area that suits your fancy, and save your hotel money for Venice or the Amalfi Drive.

In the 1890s, when the Termini station district was the newest and choicest part of Rome, the streets around the station spawned hundreds of hotels, some quite elegant. Today a great part of the city's accommodation is still here. Unfortunately, it has gone the way of all such 19th-century toadstool neighbourhoods: overbuilt, dingy and down-at-heel, and not at all the place to savour the real Rome. It's also inconvenient for most of the sights.

Any of the city tourist offices or **Enjoy Rome** (*see* 'Tourist Information' pp.853–6), will help you find a place, and even make the call. It's kind of them to do it, but in the summer months, when tourists are queuing up to the door and beyond, you may prefer to try your own luck. Hotel prices, understandably, are a little higher than elsewhere in central Italy—about the same as in Florence.

★★★★★ **Hassler-Villa Medici**, Piazza Trinità dei Monti 6, ✆ 6782651, ◉ 6789991. The area around the Piazza di Spagna has been a favoured spot since the 18th century, especially with the British. One of Rome's best hotels has a fine location at the top of the steps, with wonderful views over the city for the fortunate ones who book far enough in advance. Around for over a century, it seems to have regained its position as the élite hotel of Rome; it offers a garage and a beautiful garden courtyard, deferential service, and large wood-panelled rooms. Naturally, it is also one of the city's most expensive.

★★★★★ **Excelsior**, Via V. Veneto 125, ✆ 4708, ◉ 4826205. The surroundings of the Via Veneto is also a choice area, though lacking the aura of glamour it had in the 1950s. Still, if you can spare up to L620,000 for a good night's sleep, this will prove an experience. The reception areas have thicker carpets, bigger chandeliers and more gilded plaster than anywhere in Italy, and most of the rooms are just as good—don't let them give you one of the modernized ones. There are saunas, boutiques, a famous bar, and as much personal attention as you could ask for.

*very expensive*

★★★★ **D'Inghilterra**, Via Bocca di Leone 14, ✆ 672161, ◉ 6840828. Another favourite in the Piazza di Spagna area, convenient for the de luxe shopping around Via Condotti. Parts of this building date from the 15th century, when it served as a prince's guest house; in its career as a hotel, since 1850, it has played host to most of the literati and artists of Europe and America. Recent restorations have left it looking more palatial than ever.

★★★★ **Forum**, Via Tor de' Conti 25, ✆6792446, ◉ 6786479. Anyone serious about experiencing the city at its best should consider spending some time in its oldest and most convivial neighbourhoods; unfortunately, there is not a wide choice of hotels. The only real luxury establishment near the ancient Forum is this dignified and some what old-fashioned hotel, with a unique view over the ruins from the rooftop bar and restaurant, and discreetly elegant rooms with air-conditioning and TV.

*expensive*

★★★★ **Cardinal**, Via Giulia 62, ✆ 68802719. In the heart of the *centro storico*, this is perhaps the best place to experience Renaissance Rome in style—in a building attributed to Bramante, though completely restored inside (air-conditioning and TV in all rooms, which doesn't really spoil the atmosphere).

★★★ **Carriage**, Via delle Carrozze 36, ✆ 6990124, ◉ 6788279. Almost at the foot of the Spanish Steps, this is a sleepy but well-run place, with air-conditioning.

★★★ **La Residenza**, Via Emilia 22, ✆ 4880789. Near the Via Veneto, this hotel stands out as a very pleasant base for a visit to Rome, with beautifully appointed rooms in an old town house, and some luxuries more common in the most expensive hotels.

★★★ **Teatro di Pompeo**, Largo del Pallaro 8, ✆ 6872566, ◉ 6545531 For some peace and quiet in the middle of Rome, this is a pleasant, small place built over Pompey's Theatre, just off Campo de' Fiori, with its own garage.

★★★ **Columbus**, Via della Conciliazione 33, ✆ 6865435, ✉ 6864874. Surprisingly, there isn't a wide choice of hotels around the Vatican. This somewhat staid but reliable place has nice rooms, and views over St Peter's from some of them, though prices are a bit high for the standard of the hotel.

★★★ **Villa Florence**, Via Nomentana 28, ✆ 4403036. Near the Porta Pia and the British Embassy, this 19th-century villa (with a garden) has been thoroughly restored inside, and is now a very well run and friendly hotel.

★★★ **Villa del Parco**, Via Nomentana 110, ✆ 8554115. Similar, only slightly more expensive, this has air-conditioning in all rooms, and parking space.

*moderate*

★★★ **Gregoriana**, Via Gregoriana 18, ✆ 6794269, ✉ 6784258. Close to the Spanish Steps but reasonably priced, this small, tasteful and gratifyingly friendly place has accumulated a devoted regular clientele—there are only 19 rooms, so book early. Rooms have air-conditioning.

★★★ **Fontana**, Piazza di Trevi 96, ✆ 6786113, ✉ 6786113 would be a good hotel anywhere, but its unique amenity is a location right across the street from the Trevi Fountain—something to look at out of your window that will guarantee nice dreams.

★★★ **Hotel Sant'Anselmo**, Piazza Sant'Anselmo 2, ✆ 5783214, ✉ 5783604. Up on the Aventine hill; a very peaceful hotel with garden and comfortable rooms.

★★★ **Villa San Pio**, Via Sant'Anselmo 19, ✆ 5745231, ✉ 5743547. Run by the same management as the Sant'Anselmo, and just as peaceful. Prices are very reasonable for this quality of accommodation.

★★ **Margutta** at Via Laurina 34, ✆ 6798440, in a quiet street off Via del Babuino, has simple accommodation at lower-moderate rates, depending on the room.

★★ **Campo de' Fiori**, Via del Biscione 6, ✆ 68806865, ✉ 6876003. A good, cheap alternative with small but comfortable rooms and a roof terrace overlooking Campo de' Fiori.

★★ **Rinascimento**, Via dei Pellegrino 122, ✆ 6874813, ✉ 6833518, just west of Campo de' Fiori, has some very nice rooms.

★★ **Sole**, Via del Biscione 76, ✆ 68806873, ✉ 6893787. A large old hotel with lots of character, just off the market-place. It has rooms with and without baths.

*inexpensive*

★★ **Abruzzi**, Piazza della Rotonda 69, ✆ 6792021. Campo de' Fiori is usually the best area to look for inexpensive rooms if you want to escape staying around Termini Station. The Abruzzi has a view of the Pantheon right across the square.

★ **Primavera**, Via San Pantaleo, ✆ 68803109. A slightly cheaper hotel just west of Piazza Navona.

★ **Campo Marzio**, Piazza Campo Marzio 7, ✆ 68801486, just north of the Pantheon, has rooms without private baths, and is even cheaper than the above two.

The Termini area is good for the really inexpensive hotels; there is such a wide choice that you'll be able to find a place even when the city is at its most crowded. They range from plain, family-run establishments, often quite comfortable and friendly, to bizarre dives with exposed plumbing run by Sudanese and Sri Lankans for the benefit of visiting countrymen. Opinion is divided over the accommodation service provided by the tourist office in Termini Station, but they do seem to make an effort to find you something respectable. Otherwise, **Via Principe Amedeo** is a good place to look, particularly at no.76, a big building with a pretty courtyard that houses about eight old *pensioni*.

★ **Licia**, Via Principe Amedeo 76, ✆ 4825293 (rooms without baths), is one possibility in the building just described, though any of the others will be acceptable.

★ **Tony**, Via Principe Amedeo 79, ✆ 4466887. Other blocks with a choice of places are nos.62, 82, and 79, and this last includes this friendly and above-average quality budget hotel, with rooms with and without baths.

★ **Gexim**, Via Palestro 34, ✆ 4441311. on the east side of the station, also offers a number of cheap hotels. This one is simple and clean, offering rooms with and without baths.

---

*Rome* ✆ *(06–)*                                                        ***Eating Out***

Unlike many other Italians, the Romans aren't afraid to try something new. Lately, for example, Chinese restaurants have been appearing in numbers that culinary conservatives find alarming, not to mention Arab, Korean and macrobiotic places and the occasional hamburger stand. This should not be taken as a reflection on local cooking. Rome attracts talented chefs from all over Italy, and every region is represented by a typical restaurant somewhere in town, giving a microcosm of Italian cuisine you'll find nowhere else.

Of course, there is also a grand old tradition of Roman cooking, with such specialities as *saltimbocca* (literally, 'jump in the mouth'), tender veal *scalope* cooked with ham, *stracciatella* (a soup with eggs, parmesan cheese and parsley), fried artichokes called *carciofi alla giudea*, and veal *involtini*. On a genuine Roman menu in the less expensive places, you are likely to encounter such favourites as *baccalà* (salt cod), *spaghetti alla matriciana* (with bacon) or *alla carbonara*, tripe, and *gnocchi*. Unless you ask for something different, the wine will probably come from the Castelli Romani—light, fruity whites of which the best come from Frascati and Velletri.

Though you can drop as much as L120,000 in a Roman restaurant if you follow the politicians and the TV crowd, prices somehow manage to keep close to the Italian average—Rome is certainly much more reasonable than Milan. Watch out for tourist traps—most places near a major sight with a 'tourist menu', for example. Rome also has some quite expensive joints that could best be described as parodies of old, famous establishments; they advertise heavily, and aren't hard to smell out. Hotel restaurants, those in the de luxe class, can often be quite good but ridiculously expensive. You can always do better dining out.

Along with the most basic trattorias, many of the city's best are found in the old city. At the top of the list, perhaps, is **Papa Giovanni**, Via dei Sediari 4, ℗6865308, just east of Piazza Navona. This old favourite serves typical Roman cuisine at its best, and the collection of lesser-known fine Italian wines is just as excellent. Altogether a complete experience. Many have acclaimed **Chez Albert**, Vicolo della Vaccarella 11, off Via della Scrofa, ℗ 6865549, as Rome's best French restaurant; most dishes come from the south, like the famous *bouillabaisse Marseillaise*, but the cook's talent extends to specialities from around the Western Mediterranean—even paella and couscous.

There is no better place to try *carciofi alla giudea* than right on the edge of the old ghetto at **Piperno**, Via Monte de' Cenci 9, ℗ 68806629, Rome's most famous purveyor of Roman-Jewish cooking—simple dishes on the whole, but prepared and served with refinement. Across the river in Trastevere, **Sabatini**, on Piazza Santa Maria in Trastevere, ℗ 5818307, has been a Roman tradition for many long years, as much for the cuisine (again, lots of seafood) as for the tables outside, which face the lovely piazza and its church (strolling musicians may sound trite, but it's always fun at the time).

The quarters just outside the Aurelian wall and north and east of the Villa Borghese are more good places to look for restaurants. **Club 56**, Via Basento 56, ℗ 8440196, between Via Salaria and Viale Regina Margherita, may be the most beautiful restaurant in Rome, decorated with an Art Nouveau lavishness that makes the unusual combination of French and Neapolitan cooking seem even better.

If you find yourself anywhere around Porta San Paolo and the Testaccio district at dinnertime, don't pass up a chance to dine at the acknowledged temple of old Roman cooking: **Checchino dal 1887**, Via di Monte Testaccio 30, ℗ 5746318, which has been owned by the same family for 107 years—the longest family record in Rome. Both the fancy and humble sides of Roman food are well represented, with plenty of the powerful offal dishes that Romans have been eating since ancient times, and the setting is unique—on the edge of Monte Testaccio.

### *expensive*

For something just a little bit different, you can come to terms with *malloreddus* (perhaps the weirdest shape ever invented for pasta) and *carta di musica* (country-style crisp, very thin bread) at **Il Drappo**, Vicolo del Malpasso,9, off Via Giulia, ℗ 6877365, featuring the delights of one of Italy's least-known and most distinctive regional cuisines, that of Sardinia. Fish are a speciality on the impressive menu. Notice how the best places are always hardest to find, tucked away in alleys where you can build up an appetite searching for them. Yet another devotes its efforts to meats of all kinds—especially *bistecca alla fiorentina* and veal with truffles. **Il Bistecchiere**, Via dei Gigli d'Oro, ℗ 68808104, is also one of the smartest modern restaurants in old Rome. The street is north of Piazza Navona, off the little Piazza Sant'Apollinare. Around the Forum and Piazza Venezia, there isn't much choice, but **Vecchia Roma**, Piazza Campitelli, ✆ 6864604, provides good food, an imaginative seasonal menu, and a lovely quiet setting, with tables outdoors.

Only in Rome would you find a good French restaurant run by a Catholic lay missionary society—*sole meunière* and onion soup in the well-scrubbed and righteous atmosphere of **L'Eau Vive**, Via Monterone 85, ✆ 68801095, between Piazza Navona and the Pantheon. Don't be put off; besides offering a serendipitous experience this is also one of the best and trendiest places in Rome.

The Piazza di Spagna area is not as promising for restaurants as it is for hotels, but there are a few, of which the best, perhaps, is a renowned fishy pantheon—offering swordfish, aragosta, scampi, octopus, fried fish, fish in pastry, in stews, in soufflés, whatever you like—done up as imaginatively as anywhere in Italy. **Porto di Ripetta**, Via di Ripetta 250, ✆ 3612376, near Piazza del Popolo, is quite expensive, but there is a special lower-price *menu degustazione* at lunchtime.

Trastevere, with its attractive piazzas with space for tables outside, has long been one of the most popular corners of the city for dining. Many of its restaurants specialize in fish, most notably **Alberto Ciarla**, Piazza San Cosimato 40, ✆ 5818668, some way south of Santa Maria in Trastevere. The French-trained owner, proud enough to put his name on the sign, sees to it that everything is delicately and perfectly done, and graciously served: oysters, seafood ravioli, and quite a few adventurous styles of *pesce crudo* (raw fish) are among the most asked for, though you may find the lamb and game dishes will tempt you away from the seafood. It can be very expensive, but the set lunch menus make it more digestible. Not far away, but more towards the lower end of this price bracket, at **Paris**, Piazza San Calisto, ✆ 5815378, just beyond Piazza Santa Maria in Trastevere, you get classic Roman-Jewish cuisine; particularly good is the *minestra di arzilla*, skate soup.

A hotel restaurant, in the **Massimo D'Azeglio**, Via Cavour 16, ✆ 4814101, near Termini, used to be the place to find statesmen and diplomats in the early days of United Italy. Power and fashion may have left the neighbourhood, but the same family still runs this establishment, and they keep up standards very well. Good wines and exceptional antipasti, and portraits of old Italian premiers staring down from the walls wishing they could still be there to enjoy it.

If you don't feel like really pushing the boat out at Checchino (*see* above), a slightly cheaper version is **Cannavota**, Piazza San Giovanni in Laterano 20, ✆ 77205007, across the piazza from St John Lateran, another thoroughly Roman trattoria with especially good seafood antipasti and pasta dishes.

### *moderate*

Less expensive places are not hard to find in the *centro storico*. The most remarkable thing about **Da Pancrazio**, Piazza del Biscione, ✆ 6861246, is its setting, built over the ruins of Pompey's Theatre; the fish is good and always fresh, sharing space on the menus with typical Roman dishes. The **Grappolo d'Oro**, Piazza della Cancelleria 80, ✆ 6864118, near Campo de' Fiori, offers exceptionally good value traditional Roman cooking. **Da Giovanni** in the northeast corner of the Piazza Farnese (no phone) has good *stracetti con rughetta*, also at very reasonable prices.

Fashionable Rome can seem a world away if you stop in at the **Birreria Viennese**, Via della Croce 21, ✆ 6795569, near the Piazza di Spagna and the Via Condotti, a venerable, unchangeable place where you can forget all about the Baroque while hoisting a few with your plate of kraut and wurst. Down the same street, you can re-cross the Italian border for dinner at **Beltramme**, Via della Croce 39, (no phone), a simple but excellent traditional *vini e cucina*, officially now a historical monument, that offers simple Roman food grilled over charcoal. One more restaurant worth a mention in the same area is the **Margutta**, Via Margutta 119, ✆ 6786033, an airy, delightful and unpretentious vegetarian place. Vegetarian cooking raised to Italian standards could prove a revelation to you.

In Trastevere there's a small family trattoria, **Da Lucia**, Vicolo del Mattonato, ✆ 5803601, two street north of Piazza Santa Maria, that offers excellent local cooking at prices only just inside the moderate bracket. If you are near the Vatican, an area with little more than forgettable tourist restaurants, venture a little way north to **Il Matriciano**, Via dei Gracchi 55, ✆ 3212327, a smart yet simple place with some outdoor tables, and good ravioli and roast lamb (*abbacchio al forno*).

### inexpensive

One of the best places for cheap eats in the centre is the pizzeria **Da Baffetto**, Via del Governo Vecchio 11, ✆ 6861617, not far to the west of Piazza Navona, possibly the best-known pizzeria in the whole of Rome. Like most traditional pizzerias, it only opens in the evenings, and get there early, as queues soon build up. An excellent budget trattoria nearby is **Gino in Vicolo Rosini**, Vicolo Rosini 4, off Piazza del Parlamento, ✆ 6873434, near the parliament building, and so often crammed with civil servants and the occasional deputy.

There are many pizzerias in Trastevere which are cheap, bustly and fun. **Ivo**, Via San Francesco a Ripa 158, ✆ 5817082, is large and always crowded; and the smaller Neapolitan-run pizzeria, **Da Vittorio**, Via di San Cosimato 14/a, ✆ 5800353, offers the thicker Neapolitan style pizza. Both have outside tables.

There is another beer garden north of Porta Pia, near the Piazza Fiume. The ambience at **Birreria Peroni**, Via Brescia 24, is genuine Milwaukee Teutonic, but the typical beer-hall cuisine comes with an Italian twist. It is located in the century-old Peroni brewery, a Rome landmark, and as well as beer provides dinner for less than L30,000.

Among the vast array of unexciting restaurants that cram the streets around Termini there are also several African places, opened in recent years. **Africa**, Via Gaeta 46, ✆ 4941077, is an Ethiopian/Eritrean restaurant that offers spicy meals at very low prices, and is open all day long; the similar but still cheaper **Aduliss** is at Via Milazzo 1/c, ✆ 4451695. Every street in this area has a few little trattorias, pizzerias and tavola caldas. None seems to be especially good or especially awful—but at least they give you a chance to avoid the depressing Termini Station self-service. For better budget food head to the student area of San Lorenzo, east of the station, where there is a much better assortment of trattorie and pizzerie, and even an Indian restaurant.

The best entertainment in Rome is often in the passing cosmopolitan spectacle of its streets; as nightlife goes, the capital can be a real snoozer compared with other European cities, though if you don't expect too much, you'll have a good time. Like most Italians, many Romans have most of their fun with families and a close-knit circle of friends, and teenagers will spend hours simply hanging out in or outside bars, meeting and chatting, before heading off to a club or back home. If you're determined, the back-streets around the smart Piazza Navona or the funkier Campo de' Fiori swarm with people in the evenings, and these are the places to come to plan your night ahead, as leaflets and free tickets are always being handed out. Often these are to the new places that have opened, offering a long-awaited alternative to the ulta-chic posturing by glamorous Romans in the 'in' spots of the hour.

In July and August, as tourists flock in, Romans themselves close everything down, including most theatres, clubs or music venues, which usually either shut or decamp to the beach (*see* below) However, in the summer there are also many outdoor events that take place all around Rome, along the Tiber, in the gardens around Castel Sant'Angelo, and at Foro Italico. Ask at the tourist office for information, and keep an eye out for posters. A far older Roman party is the traditional **Festa dei Noantri** in Trastevere (16–31 July), where you may well find a gust of old Roman spontaneity along with music from all across the spectrum, acrobats, dancing, and stalls upon stalls extending down Viale Trastevere and into the quarter's piazzas.

To keep up with any area of entertainment in Rome, you would do well to buy a copy of *La Repubblica* on Thursdays, for the weekly city listings supplement *Trovaroma*. The tourist offices put out a monthly calendar as well. Other sources for listings are the English-language local papers *Wanted in Rome* and *Metropolitan*, available at the English bookshops and some newspaper stands.

### opera, classical music, theatre and film

From November until May you can take in a performance at the **Teatro dell'Opera di Roma**, Piazza Beniamino Gigli, © 44881755. Tickets officially go on sale two days before each performance but they are often very difficult to get. Classical music, John Cage, ballet, Sunday concerts, etc. are presented at the opera company's second house, the **Teatro dell'Opera Brancaccio**. Other concerts and chamber music are performed at and by the **Accademia Nazionale di Santa Cecilia** in the auditorium on Via della Conciliazione 4, © 6780742, and by the **Filarmonica Romana** at the **Teatro Olimpico**, Piazza Gentile da Fabriano, © 3234936. Medieval music, Baroque music, chamber music and choral music are frequently performed at the **Oratorio del Gonfalone**, Via del Gonfalone 32/a, © 6875952.

Rome has traditionally seen a high level of musical activity of all kinds throughout the year, and during the summer there has been a range of special seasons, often featuring open-air performances. Lately, though, the city has become noticeably sluggish in organizing summer programmes. There are evening concerts held outside

Teatro di Marcello from July to 3rd October (☎ 4814800), and a series of concerts are performed by the Accademia di Santa Cecilia and visiting international orchestras during July at Villa Giulia (☎ 6786428). One major annual summer event has been the sometimes Cecil B. De Millesque **summer opera** performances in the Baths of Caracalla, in July and August. However, a concerted campaign has been carried on, with increasing support on Rome city council, to stop these shows because of the damage they do to the Roman ruins, and it is never certain from one year to the next whether the season will go on or if an alternative venue can be found. Tourist offices will have full information on the situation. Another, more stable annual event is the **RomaEuropa** festival, featuring theatre groups, dancers and musicians from all over Europe, and held every July (information ☎ 48904024, ✉ 48904030).

If you want to go to any concerts in Rome, try to get tickets as soon as possible to avoid disappointment. The procedures for acquiring tickets are often unnecessarily complicated, and agencies can often be very useful in resolving problems. **Orbis**, Piazza Esquilino 37, ☎ 4827403, is a reliable concert and theatre ticket agency.

In recent years more and more cinemas are showing films in the original language, usually on a Monday. The **Alcazar**, Via Cardinal Merry del Val 14, the **Nuova Sacher**, Largo Ascianghi, 1, and the **Majestic**, Via SS. Apostoli 20, regularly screen films in *versione originale*. Check for details under *VO* in the daily newspapers. **Pasquino**, on Vicolo del Piede, near Piazza Santa Maria in Trastevere, ☎ 5803622), is a fully English-language cinema, showing a different film every few days.

### cafés and bars

When you're tired of window-shopping you can rest your legs at Rome's oldest café, the **Antico Caffè Greco**, Via Condotti 86, founded 1760, and fantasize that you are sitting perhaps in the very place where Keats or Casanova was wont to do. The headquarters for visiting poets in the Romantic era, the Greco is now the average tourist's cheapest chance for a 20-minute dose of *ancien régime* luxury in Rome. Another of the city's *grand cafés* is the **Cafe Rosati**, in Piazza del Popolo, an elegant place founded in 1922, and traditionally popular with the Roman intelligentsia, no doubt attracted by its extravagant ice creams. Other cafés can be dignified, historic, or crazily expensive—for example, the 150-year-old **Babington's Tea Rooms** on Piazza di Spagna, for scones and tea or a full lunch in the proper Victorian atmosphere. Aficionados agree, though, that the best *cappuccino* in Italy is made at **Sant'Eustachio**, Piazza Sant'Eustachio, near Piazza Navona, but tell them to mind the sugar.

Another kind of Roman bar is represented by the ultra-hip **Bar della Pace**, Via della Pace 3, supposedly much frequented by celebrities, and a place for serious posing. A more funky and friendly atmosphere can be found most evenings at **La Vineria**, Campo de' Fiori 15, a relaxed traditional wine bar/shop with tables outside.

At least once, every visitor has to stop in for what is claimed to be the best ice cream in Italy, at the celebrated, elegant **Giolitti**, Via degli Uffici del Vicario 40 (by the Pantheon), or try the competition at **Tre Scalini**, on Piazza Navona. In the ghetto, you can sample some unusual sweets at the no-name Jewish bakery at the west end of Via del Portico d'Ottavia (note the incredible building it's in, a recycled ancient structure covered with reliefs and inscriptions).

### rock, jazz and clubs

Rome has a select band of clubs with live music almost every night—*Trovaroma* will have details of current programmes at the (naturally) folk-oriented **Folkstudio**, Via Frangipane 42, © 4871063, the mainly-rock venues such as **Big Mama**, Vicolo San Francesca a Ripa 18, in Trastevere, © 5812551, a blues club, **Alpheus**, Via del Commercio, 36-38, in Ostiense, © 5749826, and **Palladium**, Piazza B. Romano 8, in Garbatella, © 5110203, both of the last two well outside the usual tourist round of central Rome. Also for jazz venues—which have a strong Roman following—like the suave **Alexanderplatz**, Via Ostia 9, in Prati, © 3729398, and the **Saint Louis Music City**, Via del Cardello 13/a, near the Colosseum, © 4745076. All of them feature foreign as well as Italian performers, and are fairly eclectic. Medium-sized rock and jazz concerts are often staged at the permanent tent near EUR, the **Tendastrisce**, Via Cristoforo Colombo 393, © 5415521.

For serious dancing, try **Alien**, Via Velletri 13, in Nomentana, © 8412212, **Castello**, Via di Porto Castello 44, near the Vatican, © 6868328, or **Radio Londra**, Via di Monte Testaccio 57 (no phone). All are what Italians call *di tendenza*, meaning they keep up with current UK and US musical trends. Most indoor clubs and music venues close down completely in late July and August. This is the time, though, when **beach discos** along the coast at Ostia, Fregene and points further afield are hugely popular. **Lido**, Piazzale Fregene 5, © 6464496, is generally one of the liveliest near to Rome.

In July, too, look out in Rome for the **Jazz Festival**, held outdoors, usually in the Tennis stadium in Foro Italico, and often featuring some of the biggest names in jazz. For other summer music, you may want to do as the Romans do and head out to Umbria for the **Spoleto Festival** or the **Umbria Jazz** festival (*see* **Umbria** for both), or fight it out for a ticket to one of the big-name rock concerts at Stadio Flaminio or Palaeur (EUR's Palazzo dello Sport), neither of which win any blue ribbons.

## Day Trips from Rome

### *Getting Around*

 There are frequent **trains** to Ostia and Ostia Lido on the COTRAL line from Porta San Paolo in Rome. For Tivoli, the best way to get there is by COTRAL **bus**, from Rebibbia terminal. There are trains to Tivoli on the FS line to Avezzano, but they are much slower than the bus. To get to Tivoli by **car** from Rome, take the A24 or the Via Tiburtina, the SS5.

For the Castelli Romani, there are **trains** on a very picturesque COTRAL line from Laziali station, alongside Termini in Rome (entrance in the Via Giolitti). There are also frequent COTRAL **buses** from Anagnina, on Metro line A. By **car**, take the Via Appia, SS7, or Via Tuscolana, SS215, out of Rome.

There are tourist offices in **Tivoli**, Largo Garibaldi, ✆ (0774) 293522, and in **Frascati**, at Piazza Marconi 1, ✆ (06) 9420331.

## Ostia

According to the archaeologists, Rome's port was founded only in the 4th century BC, 400 years after Rome itself. But in the centuries of conquest, Ostia grew into a major city in its own right, with a population of perhaps 100,000 and nearly 2km of *horrea* (warehouses) near the mouth of the Tiber. In the 4th century, when the flow of trade and tribute slowed, and even the grain supply from Africa was diverted to Constantinople, Ostia lost its reason for being. Malaria increased as the coast declined, and by 800 AD the site was totally abandoned. In the centuries since, Old Father Tiber obliged future archaeologists by covering Ostia in sand and mud, thus preserving it better than most ancient cities. Mussolini shovelled it out in the 1930s, recovering an ancient attraction that many visitors overlook. It's easy to reach by train: get off at the Ostia Antica stop (*site open April–Sept 9–6.30 Tues–Sun; Mar–Oct 9–4.30 Tues–Sun; adm exp*).

As in Pompeii, you can walk along the streets and imagine the life of the big city; the temples, frescoed houses, baths, barracks and warehouses are amazingly intact. Ostia had a **forum**, with some re-erected columns of temples, and a little hill rather wistfully called the 'Capitol'. All the buildings are labelled: the baths, a small, restored **theatre** with an interesting **Mithraeum** nearby, like the one under Rome's San Clemente; also the police station (*Caserna dei Vigili*), homes, warehouses, and the oldest **synagogue** ever discovered in Italy. One vast square called the 'Piazzale delle Corporazione' preserves mosaics symbolizing the various trades and businesses. On a floor mosaic in **Fortunatus' Tavern** you can see what may be the earliest known specimen of advertising: 'Fortunatus says: if you're thirsty, have a bowl of wine'. Near the ruins, you can spare a few minutes for the sleepy, pretty hamlet of **Ostia Antica**, also called the 'Borgo', founded as a fortress town in 830 by Pope Gregory IV; it wasn't enough to keep the Saracens out when they sacked Rome 19 years later. There is a small Renaissance church dedicated to **Sant'Aurea**, a 3rd-century Ostian martyr, and the almost startlingly elegant **Castello**, erected in 1483 by Julius II (still only a cardinal), who at the time was worried about the Turks.

## Tivoli and the Villa Adriana

Ancient *Tibur*, set in a cliff with a beautiful view over the Roman Campagna, became a sort of garden suburb for the senatorial class in the early days of the Empire. But a place with a view is also usually easily defensible, and by the early Middle Ages, despite all the dirty work of Goths and Huns, Tibur had changed its name to Tivoli and managed a successful transition from posh resort to feisty, independent hill town. Once, in its struggles with Rome, it even defeated its big bossy neighbour in battle and captured a pope. Wealth returned in the late Renaissance in the form of moneybags cardinals; one in particular, Ippolito d'Este, son of Duke Ercole I of Ferrara, created perhaps the most fantastically worldly villa and gardens Italy has ever seen.

That is no small statement, but the **Villa d'Este** (*open 9am–1½ hours before sunset Tues–Sun; adm currently half-price, as only some of the fountains are working. Also opens on certain summer evenings for son et lumière shows. Check at the Rome tourist office for schedules*) still has charms enough to attract hordes of day-trippers from Rome year-round. The buildings themselves, designed by Pietro Ligorio and decorated with Mannerist frescoes, are completely upstaged by the symmetrical Italian gardens, set on a series of terraces on the slopes below the town centre. Among palms and cypresses, flowers and lawns, every corner turned will expose some incredible confectionary fountain: the 'Fountain of Glass' by Bernini, the 'Grotto of Diana', the 'Fountain of Dragons'—dozens in all, along with artificial waterfalls and pools. The cardinal's water organ and mechanical birds may no longer be working, and fountains aren't always turned on, but you won't regret you came.

Tivoli has a gaudy 17th-century **cathedral**, and the interesting Romanesque church of **San Silvestro** on Via del Colle, with early medieval frescoes, which you will pass on the way to another Renaissance cardinal's fantasy, the **Villa Gregoriana** (*open 9am–one hour before sunset Tues–Sun; adm*). Built in a dramatic natural chasm, the shady paths and gardens are irresistible to visitors, who trip gaily down to the bottom— then realize they face a climb of well over 60m to get back to ground level. It's worth the trip, if you're up to it, for the spectacular natural waterfall on the River Aniene, and a smaller, artificial one designed by Bernini. On the edge of the abyss, you'll notice two small, remarkably well preserved Roman temples, one circular and the other a rectangle, called the **Temples of the Sibyl and Vesta**. There was indeed a college of sibyls in Tibur, as at Cumae near Naples (you can see pictures of them in the Baptistry of Florence, in Siena Cathedral, and on Michelangelo's Sistine Chapel ceiling), and they may possibly have kept one of these temples. Wherever, the presence of these oracular ladies, cousins to the oracle at Delphi, show the influence of Greek thought and religion in Latium from the earliest times.

On the highway towards Rome, the Via Tiburtina, you'll see everywhere the travertine quarries that have helped Tivoli to make a living since ancient times. Almost all of Rome is built of this solemn grey stone. One variety went into the Colosseum, the city gates, and most of the other ruins. The other, streaked with beige and black, is the material Mussolini used for the scores of railway stations he built all over Italy. Nowadays demand is still great, and Tivoli ships travertine all over the world.

Just outside the town, signs direct you to the quiet residential neighbourhood that has grown up around **Hadrian's Villa**, the grandest palace complex ever built in Italy (*open 9am–1½ hours before sunset daily; adm exp*). To get some idea of the scale on which a 2nd-century emperor could build, stop first at the room-sized model of the villa near the entrance. All marble and travertine, and about the same size as the monumental centre of Rome—the imperial fora included—Hadrian's dream house will clearly show the excess that even the most intelligent and useful of emperors was capable of. Archaeologists have found features that would surprise even the Californians—a heated beach, for example, with steam pipes under the sand. Hadrian fancied himself an architect, and in his villa he helped to create reproductions of many famous buildings he had admired on his travels: the Canopic Temple of Alexandria, the Platonic Academy and Stoa Poikile of Athens, and others, set among huge baths, libraries, a Praetorian barracks, temples, theatres, and a little palace on an island, built on an artificial lagoon, that may have been the emperor's private retreat. Many of the greatest statues in the Vatican and other museums were found here; occasionally some nice things still turn up when new excavations are under way.

Even by public transport, Tivoli makes an easy day-trip. To see any of the hill towns to the east and south, however, you'll need a car. Quite a few interesting little villages have managed so far to escape modern tourism: lovely **Anticoli Corrado** on its steep cliff, and **Saracinesco**, founded on a nearly inaccessible crag by Saracen raiders in the 9th century; the present townspeople are their direct descendants. Few towns can claim as glorious a past as **Subiaco**, where St Benedict retired in the troubled late 5th century to write his *Rule* and set Christian monasticism on its way. All through the dark centuries his monasteries (originally Subiaco had 12) provided a haven for learning and piety. In the 1460s, the first printed books in Italy were made here by two monks from Germany. Today the oldest surviving buildings are in the **Convent of Santa Scholastica** (*open 9–12, 4–6, Mon–Sat; 9–10.30, 4–6, Sun*), Benedict's twin sister, with cloisters from the 6th and 11th centuries, and a medieval church decorated by the Cosmati. Two churches with a number of fine late medieval and Sienese quattrocento frescoes are all that remain of **St Benedict's Monastery**, a 15-minute walk from the town. Nearby, in the gorge of the Aniene, there is a beautiful little lake with a waterfall; it may have been constructed by Nero, who had a villa at Subiaco.

South of Tivoli, **Zagarolo** is a town full of Baroque churches, with a medieval citadel and one thoroughly strange Baroque gate, perhaps the work of Vignola. Nearby **Palestrina**, the ancient *Praeneste* and birthplace of the great 16th-century composer, has some unusual relics, in particular the **Temple of Fortuna Primigenia**, an oracle of the Latin tribes. Of the complex, rebuilt in the 1st century BC, the lower sanctuary survives, with a number of mosaics and some mysterious tablets involved in the decoding of the oracle's responses. Part of the upper sanctuary was employed as a foundation for the 17th-century Colonna—Barberini Palace, which now houses the **Praeneste Museum** (*open 9am–1 hour before sunset Tues–Sun; adm*); here the star attraction is a beautiful mosaic with scenes of Egypt, showing the flooding of the Nile. These two towns can be reached by COTRAL bus (from Rome's metro stop Anagnina) and by train on the Laziale line.

## The Castelli Romani

Before there was a Rome, these towns around the Alban Hills were some of the strongest members of the Latin Confederation. Since being pounded into submission some 2200 years ago, their role has been reduced to that of providing the capital with wine, flowers, and a place to spend summer weekends. The countryside is beautiful, even though some of the nearer 'Castelli' are being enveloped by the Roman suburbs. All these towns can be reached by COTRAL bus, from the depot at the Anagnina station, on the Metro A-line (✆ 57531)

**Frascati**, the nearest of the Castelli and one of the most popular, was a medieval replacement for the ancient Latin city of Tusculum, destroyed in 1191. Frascati itself took some hard knocks during the Second World War, but it is still lovely, with an elegant park in the grounds of the 17th-century **Villa Aldobrandini** (*open 9am–12 midday daily; ask at the tourist office on Piazza Marconi for details*). Nearby **Grottaferrata** was built around the

11th-century **abbey**, founded by SS.Nilus and Bartholomew and still in business, under the care of Greek Catholic monks; its church of Santa Maria has some medieval frescoes and some by the 17th-century artist Domenichino, as well as a fine columned campanile from the 1200s (*the abbey, with a small museum, is open 9–12, 4.15–7, Tues–Sun*). **Marino**, like Frascati, is famed for its wine; the town fountains flow with the stuff during the merry grape festival on the first Sunday of October. From here a panoramic route called the Via dei Laghi passes **Lago Albano** on the way to Velletri and the south. After the lake, there is a turn-off to **Rocca di Papa**, a dramatically sited town with a picturesque medieval citadel called the *Quartiere dei Bavaresi*, from the Bavarian troops of Emperor Ludwig stationed here in the 1320s. From the town you can drive up to the highest of all the Alban Hills, **Monte Cavo** (948m), passing a spot where, according to local legend, Hannibal and his elephants camped during the Punic Wars.

From Rome, the Via Appia Antica passes on the other side of Lago Albano in a dead straight line, as far as **Castel Gandolfo**, the well-known enclave of the Vatican City where popes take their summer holidays (three months in the old days, but John Paul II doesn't spend much time here). After that comes the **Albano Laziale**, the ancient Alba Longa, mother city of Rome. Bits and snatches of the distant past abound, including a 3rd-century cistern, still in use, and the strange 'Tomb of the Horatii and Curiatii' on the road to **Ariccia**. Anyone familiar with Sir James Frazier's *The Golden Bough* (the foundation work of modern anthropology) will remember the priest of Diana who once ruled the Arician Grove, the 'King of the Wood', and how as late as Roman times any man who cared to could cut a piece of mistletoe from one of the sacred oaks, then kill the king and take his place. There are still oak groves around Ariccia, and 'Diana's Mirror', the beautiful **Lake Nemi**, is still an enchanted spot, a deep blue oval surrounded by wooded hills and villas. The town of Nemi itself, a pretty place known for violets and strawberries, is also worth a detour.

Beyond Nemi, **Velletri** is the last of the Castelli, also famous for wine, with a Baroque cathedral, a small museum, and an odd, 45m striped tower of 1353 called the Torre del Trivio. With a car, you can press on further, into the Monte Lepini and some charming old hill towns well off the beaten track. **Cori**, like Rome and so many other Latin towns, liked to trace its founding to Trojan refugees. It may well be 3000 years old; that, at least, is the date archaeologists assign to its 'cyclopean' walls, built of huge, neatly fitted polygonal chunks of rock, still visible in many places. There are also many Roman ruins, including an intact bridge and the **Temple of Hercules** (really a temple of Jupiter), a small Doric building complete except for its roof. Nearby **Ninfa** has been called the 'medieval Pompeii', a town abandoned in the 17th century because of malaria, where many of the buildings survive in an exceptionally beautiful setting with small streams and lakes, overgrown with wildflowers and trees (*open on the first Saturday and Sunday of each month*). **Norma**, built on the edges of a steep, curving cliff, seems almost like a city hanging in air. Nearby are more cyclopean walls around the ruins of **Norba**, once capital of Rome's bitter enemies, the Volscians. It was besieged and destroyed by the legions during the Social Wars in 89 BC, never to be rebuilt.

As well as all these, there are other possible day-trips from Rome towards the north: Viterbo and the lakes of Northern Lazio (*see above, p.828–35*) and one very popular excursion, to the Etruscan necropolises at Tarquinia and Cerveteri (p.836).

All the towns around Rome have some accommodation to offer, though increasingly the trend is towards driver-orientated places along the highways. And, popular as these towns are with both Romans and tourists, there are plenty of restaurants.

## Ostia Antica

For lunch, try the grilled fish at **Al Monumento**, ✆ (06) 5650021 (moderate), near the castle.

## Tivoli

A good place to stay is the ★★★**Padovano**, Via Tiburtina 160, Tiburtina,✆ (0774) 530807, ✆ 531382, a bargain at L45,000 for a double with bath, or, even cheaper, the ★**Del Giglio** in Località Acquoria, a simple place just out of town with comfortable rooms at knockdown price. The **Sibilla** restaurant, Via della Sibilla, ✆ (0774) 20281 (moderate) is famous above all else for its location, incorporating the famous 'Temple of the Sibyls' right in its building. The place makes a living off tourists, but the food is still good (grilled trout, for example) and the price is right.

## Frascati

Frascati makes a good place to stop for dinner, with restaurants like the **Domino**, Via Tuscolana 20, (06) 9426043, with a picturesque panorama, local cooking and good Frascati wine all for a moderate price.

## Nemi

If you have a car, the area around Nemi and the lakes is a nice place to stay, at ★**Al Refugio**, ✆ (06) 9368075, just outside Nemi (inexpensive), or the ★★★**Culla del Lago**, ✆ (06) 9360047 (moderate), in Castel Gandolfo, on the shore of Lake Albano. Outside Nemi, try the restaurant **Da Baffone**, Via dei Laghi, ✆ (06) 9633892 (expensive), if you like dishes done with wild mushrooms, as well as good roast meats and exceptional house wine, or the **Capriccio sul Lago**, also on Via dei Laghi, ✆ (06) 9368120 (moderate), with *pappardelle alle lepre* (pasta in hare sauce), and year-round wild strawberries.

## Velletri

**Da Benito**, Via Lata 83 ✆ (06) 9632220 (moderate) is one of the few places in the area to get good fresh seafood.

# Southern Lazio: Along the Coast

### Getting Around

The main Rome–Naples **rail** line runs parallel to the coast a few kilometres inland. For Terracina and Sabaudia, get off at Priverno; for Sperlonga, at Fondi; and for Gaeta, at Formia, and take local buses. There are regular

COTRAL **buses** to all destinations from EUR Fermi terminus (Metro Line B) in Rome.

The main **road** to all points along the coast has traditionally been the Via Appia, the SS7. A quicker alternative is the Via Pontina, SS148, which runs closer to the coast, and directly to Latina and Terracina.

---

### Tourist Information

There is a tourist information office in **Latina**, at Via Duca del Mare 19, ✆ (0773) 498711. There are also smaller offices in many of the towns along the coast.

---

## The Pontine Marshes

*'...nowhere else has the creative power of Fascism left a deeper mark. The immense works can be summed up in the lapidary phrase of Il Duce: "You redeem the land, you found some cities."'*

from a 1939 Italian guidebook

You wouldn't be travelling this way 60 years ago, when the broad plain of the Pontine Marshes was the biggest no man's land in Italy, wracked by malaria and healthy only for the water-buffalo. Under the Romans, canals were dug to reclaim the swamps, but they became blocked up in the Dark Ages when no one had the money to keep them cleared. Once again, during the 13th century, some of the marshes were drained, but a few centuries of papal rule had the area back to its pristine emptiness when Mussolini decided to make it one of the showpieces of his regime. Today, except for the small corner preserved as a park and wildlife refuge, the Pontine Marshes no longer exist, and brand-new towns like Aprilia, Pomezia, Pontinia, and Sabaudia sit amid miles of prosperous farms as curious monuments to the brighter side of fascism. So does **Latina**, largest of the Pontine towns and Italy's youngest provincial capital, founded in 1932, a bright and busy place built on a radial plan with plenty of trees and chunky Mussolini palazzi.

If you drive along the coast, you'll pass plenty of beaches, including those of the small resort of **Anzio**, ancient *Antium*, popular with the Romans. In January 1944, the British and American forces found its beaches an ideal spot for a landing; that bloody but successful end run forced the Germans to abandon their Gustav Line and opened the way for the liberation of Rome. Large military cemeteries surround the town. Between Anzio and Cape Circeo, the coast is almost a solid stretch of beaches and dunes. At the end, **Monte Circeo** was an island in ancient times, one of many candidates around the Mediterranean for Homer's Isle of Circe from the *Odyssey*. **San Felice Circeo** on its slopes is a growing resort, offering boat trips around the big rock and its many caves. Since 1934, much of this area has been included in the **Circeo National Park**, a beautiful and unspoiled expanse of watery landscape on the Italian peninsula. Migratory birds of all kinds stop here twice a year, and besides a wealth of wild flowers and primeval forests you may see woodpeckers, buzzards, peregrine falcons, and herons—maybe even that most overdressed of sea birds, the *Cavaliere d'Italia*.

Further down the coast, the Ausonian Mountains crowd against the sea at **Terracina**, once the Volscian port of *Anxur*; stop here for a look at the lovely hodge podge of a **cathedral**, with Baroque and neo-classical elements on the façade and a Moorish-looking 14th-century campanile. Inside, besides the remains of the Temple of Roma and Augustus that the cathedral replaced, there are medieval mosaics in the apse and on the floor. To the east, Emperor Trajan cut a deep passage through the mountains, the 'Pisco Montano', to allow the Appian Way to continue along the coast. If you can stay a while, take the Strada Panoramica up to the top of Monte Sant'Angelo, with ruins of the **Temple of Jupiter Anxurus**, built on a mighty stone platform that survives intact, some of Terracina's medieval walls, and a wonderful view for miles along the coast.

From Terracina there are some possible detours into the mountains: to **Fondi**, an old town that has stuck to its rectilinear Roman street plan almost without change; or to **Fossanova** and its 12th-century Cistercian abbey. French monks came down in the 1130s to show the Italians how to make a proper Gothic building; the Italians weren't interested, of course, and Fossanova survives along with San Galgano in Tuscany, San Martino nel Cimino near Viterbo and a few others as a rare example of the northern style on this side of the Alps. The **Abbey Church**, of cathedral proportions, is a fine, sedate Burgundian Gothic work with a beautiful rose window. Not much is left to look at inside, except the stately rows of piers and pointed arches. Fossanova was a great centre of learning in its day (St Thomas Aquinas spent some time here), but after the 1400s both wealth and talent deserted it. After centuries of decadence, the monastery was expropriated in 1873, and its treasures dispersed.

## Sperlonga and Gaeta

Continuing towards Naples, **Sperlonga** is one of the most pleasant small resorts on the Tyrrhenian coast, with a medieval quarter on its steep promontory and miles of fine beaches to either side. About 3km beyond it, you may inspect the pretty sea cave called the **Grotto of Tiberius**, once fitted out as a sort of pleasure dome for that thoroughly hedonistic emperor. Some excellent classical sculpture has been excavated here, including one large composition related to the *Laocoön* in the Vatican. A small **museum** further down the road has been built for them.

At the end of this scenic stretch of coast, **Gaeta** stands behind its medieval walls on a narrow peninsula, the grandest sight between Monte Argentario and the Bay of Naples. For a while in the early Middle Ages, this town was an important Mediterranean trading centre, a rival to Amalfi and Pisa. Its naturally defensible site made it a valued stronghold for centuries after; in 1861, it was briefly the last redoubt of the House of Bourbon, when the King of Naples and his palace guard withstood a siege from the army of the new Italy, hoping for help from France that never came. The town has a quiet medieval atmosphere, with a much rebuilt **cathedral**, a 13th-century castle, and evocative, crumbling old streets and alleys around the harbour. On the hill above Gaeta, you can make the difficult climb to see the rich and well-preserved tomb of a Roman general named Munatius Planctus, the founder of Lyons, France.

Nearby **Formia**, the major base for ferries to the Pontine islands, enjoyed a blessed past as one of the gilded resorts of Imperial Rome, like Capri or Baiae. Mark Antony's men caught up with the virtuous but capitally tedious orator Cicero here, after the assassination of Caesar, and knifed him in the baths of his villa. Little of ancient Formia survived through the Dark Ages, and the little city that replaced it suffered grievously in 1944. Today Formia is entirely new, a happy and growing place that seems to have a bright future ahead of it. Before you reach Campania, the last town along the coast is **Minturno**, a medieval replacement for ancient *Minturnae*, the ruins of which, closer to the coast, include a restored theatre, slight remains of temples, and an aqueduct.

## Ponza and the Pontine Islands

An ancient volcano gave birth to the five small islands of the Pontine archipelago, and to it they owe much of their charm and eccentricities. Two are inhabited: **Ponza**, the larger and more visited, is stunningly beautiful and shaped like a crescent moon. The curve of its fishing harbour, with its oddly shaped sea rocks, arches, and coves, shelters a charming pastel-tinted town and small tower. On the other side of the island, but within walking distance, is the island's famous 'moonlit' beach, the **Chiaia di Luna** a crescent-shaped beach beneath the steep pale cliffs. Wandering (or, far better, sailing) along its long, jagged shores, you'll discover such wonders as a volcanically created swimming pool and the glaringly white Infernal Cove, both near **Le Forna** (the only other real settlement on Ponza). The **Grotte di Pilato**, only accessible by boat, are made up of three grottoes connnected by tunnels built in Republican times as part of a luxury villa, and were used to store live fish. Motor launches are available for hire at Ponza and Santa Maria.

The other inhabited island, tiny **Ventotene**, is a table of reddish tufa sitting on the surface of the sea; Augustus' daughter Julia found it the perfect place to build a grand villa to receive her many lovers far from the wagging tongues of Rome—although her scandalous behaviour eventually caught up with her, and Ventotene became her rock of exile instead of a bower of bliss. Later Julians found it a usefully isolated place to do their dirty work, too; Caligula's mother starved herself to death here, and Nero had his young, unwanted wife Octavia murdered in Ventotene's baths. The meagre ruins of her villa stand evocative and lonely on windswept Punta Eolo. The town of **Porto Ventotene** is piled over the old Porto Romano, carved out of tufa. There is a small museum in the Municipio, open in the mornings, displaying items found from Julia's villa, the scarce remains of which can be seen beyond the rocky beach of Cala Rossano. You can stroll around the island in less than an hour, past little fields of lentils. Here and there you will find little paths winding towards the sea, the cliffs and beaches.

Formia is the main year-round port for both islands, with departures daily; in the summer you can also catch a hydrofoil and ferry from Anzio or Terracina.

## The Ciociaria

If you're in a hurry to get to Naples, the quickest route is the *Autostrade del Sole*, following the route of the Roman Via Casalina behind the coastal mountains. After Velletri, in the Castelli Romani, however, there are still some possible detours to delay you. This humble corner of Lazio is known as the **Ciociaria**, after the *ciocie*, or bark sandals, worn by the countrymen not so long ago, when this was one of the backwaters of Italy.

**Anagni**, small as it is, held centre stage in European politics on several occasions during the Middle Ages. Four 14th-century popes were born here, and several others made it their summer home. Greatest among them was Boniface VIII, a nasty intriguer who had the poor timing to proclaim loudly the temporal supremacy of the popes long after anyone else took the idea seriously. Captured in Anagni by the Colonna family and the forces of the King of France, Boniface received a resounding slap in the face from Sciarra Colonna that put a temporary end to papal dreams of world domination. Parts of his palace can still be seen, along with the stout and squarish **cathedral**, one of the finest in central Italy, sharing a little of the genius of the Tuscan and Apulian churches of the same period. Outside, it is 11th-century Romanesque; a rebuilding in the 1300s left it tentatively Gothic within. There is a Cosmatesque pavement, and a wonderful 13th-century stone baldachin over the altar. Be sure to see the crypt, with blue and gold Byzantine frescoes from the 13th century that are among the best of their kind in Italy. Take some time for a walk around Anagni, a medieval time-capsule with its walls, towers, and palaces like the **Casa Barnekow** that have changed little in 600 years.

Up in the mountains above Anagni, **Fiuggi** has been a popular spa for centuries; Michelangelo came here to take the waters after the strain of working on the Sistine Chapel. **Alatri**, 2400 years ago, was one of the main cities of the Hernici, an Italic tribe that differed from its neighbours mainly by being a firm ally of Rome, a wise policy that spared Alatri the destruction that befell many of the other ancient cities of Lazio. Consequently, Alatri remains the best example we have of a pre-Roman Italian town, with almost a complete circuit of 'cyclopean' walls from about the 6th century BC. Besides the defending walls, there is another set at the top of Alatri's hill that marked the boundaries of the **acropolis**, where today the cathedral and the Bishop's Palace stand over the temples of the long-forgotten Hernici. Just outside the town there is an early Carthusian monastery, the **Certosa di Trisulti**, with buildings as old as 1210.

Along the old Via Casalina, little **Frosinone** serves as provincial capital for the Ciociaria, and the centre for all bus lines in the region. A side road from here (SS214) will take you on a delightful detour to the **Abbey of Casamari**, a little-known 13th-century French Cistercian complex with a church much like the one at Fossanova, and then to **Isola del Liri**, a pretty town with a dramatic waterfall in the middle, which hosts a blues festival each July. Further down the Via Casilina, **Aquino** is full of Roman-era ruins, including a small decorative arch near the village church.

For something really out of the way, you might venture up into the highest and least-visited corner of Lazio, the Valley of the Comino on the borders of the Abruzzo National Park. In this mountainous region, there are beautiful **lakes** at Posta Fibreno and Biagio Saracinesco, and ruins of a 12th-century castle at **Vicalvi**. **Atina** is the most important town in this district, and has been since the days of the Samnites; relics from its past are preserved in the Municipal Museum.

## Montecassino

If divine guidance led St Benedict from Subiaco to found a monastery here, as the old legend states, perhaps God just wasn't thinking clearly that day. Montecassino may be the most famous monastery in Italy, and it certainly owns the most dramatic site, high on a mountaintop over the Garigliano valley, but that very location has caused the honest monks nothing but trouble over the centuries. They were essential in keeping alive the traditions of letters and scholarship through the Dark Ages, all the more remarkable when you consider that Montecassino has been utterly destroyed five times. Benedict came in 529, but the Lombards wrecked the place only 60 years later. The Saracens and the Normans repeated the scene in the 9th and 11th centuries, and an earthquake finished off what must have been one of Italy's treasures of medieval architecture in 1348. Each time the place has been rebuilt, but the reason why Montecassino attracts so much strife was demonstrated again during the Italian Campaign of 1944. The rock happens to be the most strategically important spot in central Italy, the key to either Rome or Naples, depending on which way your army is walking.

In 1944, the Germans made it the western bastion of their Gustav Line, and it held up the Allied advance for four months. Enough bombs were dropped to destroy the monastery once more, without seriously disconcerting the defenders, and typically for the polyglot Italian Front, New Zealanders, Indians, Brazilians, and French participated in unsuccessful attacks between January and May. It was the Poles who finally beat their way in, losing over 1000 men on the way up; their cemetery can be seen near the hill. Already the Benedictines have finished the rebuilding, and while not up to the artistic level of its predecessors, it's still a popular place to visit (*open 9.30–12, 3.30–half an hour before sunset, daily*), most especially for the wonderful views around southern Lazio.

---

### Where to Stay and Eating Out

The stretch of coast between Terracina and Formia makes a great place to rest if you are passing along the coast between Rome and Naples.

### Sperlonga

Sperlonga has some nice spots around the beaches: ***La Playa**, outside town at Località Fiorelle, © (0771) 549496, @ 54106 (moderate) is modern, with pool, tennis courts, and a bit of a beach, and there's also the slightly less expensive ***Parkotel Fiorelle**, ©, @ (0771) 54092 (moderate), very close by. There are plenty of relatively inexpensive fish restaurants around the beaches; try **Al Fortino**, © (0771) 54337 (moderate), on the main route, Via Flacca, in Sperlonga.

### Gaeta

Near Gaeta, on the coastal Via Flacca, the ***Summit**, © (0771) 741741 (moderate), is a fine modern resort hotel in a good location, but a bit large, and only open from April–Sept. All rooms have TV and air-conditioning.

The *****Amyclae**, Via C. Colombo 77, © (0771) 54051 (moderate) has very cheap doubles with balconies overlooking the sea. **La Scarpetta** restaurant, Piazza Conca 1, © (0771) 462142, has good local food as well as other, more experimental dishes.

## Formia

If you want to splurge on this part of the coast, the best place must be the ★★★★**Grande Albergo Miramare**, ✆/✉ (0771) 267181 (expensive), on the Via Appia on the southern edge of the town, a beautiful old villa with extensive gardens on the shore, beach and pool, and modernized but pleasant rooms, as well as an elegant restaurant in a little pavilion.

Another good restaurant in Formia, in fact an excellent one, is **Italo**, on the central Viale Unità d'Italia, ✆ (0771) 21529 (moderate). More seafood, like fish cooked *in cartoccio* (in paper), and a surprisingly large choice of what comes out of this part of the Tyrrhenian, but also memorable *primo piatti*.

## Pontine Islands

The most picturesque place to stay on Ponza is ★★**La Torre dei Borboni**, Via Madonna, ✆ (0771) 80109, with a third of its rooms and apartments in an 18th-century castle with wonderful views, an excellent restaurant and a private beach. Prices are still in the moderate category.

In the same price range is the ★★★**Bella Vista**, Via Parata, ✆ (0771) 80036 (moderate), which sits in its own secluded bay. Alternatively, on Ventotene there is the cheaper and simpler **Il Cacciatore**, località Montagnozzo, ✆ (0771) 85055.

The culinary specialities of Ponza include *lenticchie alla ponzese* (lentil soup), *coniglio alla cacciatore* (rabbit with onions, tomatoes, and so on) and lobster dishes. The best place to eat is **L'Antico Murenaio**, Spiaggia di S. Maria, ✆ (0771) 809948, offering of course excellent fish and wonderful home-made puddings at moderate-to-expensive prices. For something more economical, try the family-run **La Lanterna**, Corso Carlo Pisacane (inexpensive), with simple good local food.

## Campania

The Italian south—the *Mezzogiorno*, the Noonday—is one of the extremities of Europe, poised in a calm sea between the Balkans and the Sahara. The contrasts within the south are greater than in the other two-thirds of Italy; from the dreamy coastline of Amalfi and Positano it is only an afternoon's drive to the grimmest deforested wastelands of the Basilicata. Some sections of the south are prosperous and forward-looking, and not too distant from their northern counterparts, while others lag astonishingly behind, despite all the efforts of the government and the *Cassa per il Mezzogiorno*. Some areas are surprising, others surprisingly empty.

In Roman times, to distinguish the *Campania* around Naples from parts further north (the present Roman *Campagna*), the southern section acquired the name of *Campania Felix*. A happy land it was, the richest and most civilized province in Italy, with a mix of Greek and Etruscan culture superimposed on the native Samnites and Ausones, not to mention the merry Oscans and their perfumed city of Capua. Campania's charm, then as now, starts with one of the most captivating stretches of coastline in Italy— the Amalfi Drive—Capri and Ischia, Sorrento, Vesuvius, the Phlegraean Fields around Pozzuoli, and the beautiful but lesser-known Cilento coast at the southern tip of the region. Roman emperors and senators spent as much time here as business would allow, and even today it is said that the dream of every Italian is to have a villa at Capri or Sorrento overlooking the sea.

In the middle of all this, of course, sprawls Italy's third-largest city, Naples— a place that may well be either your favourite or least favourite Italian city—or both at the same time. Campania shares fully in all the complexes and problems of the Italian south as a whole. It has large new industries, ambitious planning schemes to attract still more, and substantial difficulties with pollution, poverty, soaring unemployment, corruption and crime. Though the potential certainly exists, there is a long way to go before the region can reclaim the position it had in the days of the Caesars.

## Campanian Itineraries

Campania and the three other southern regions have almost half of Italy's coastline, though most of it is flat and not too exciting. If you are looking for classic Mediterranean scenery and a spot on the beach, the first, really obvious place to send you is the spectacular **Amalfi coast** and the **islands** around the Bay of Naples. If these long-established fleshpots are too overripe for your tastes, or simply too crowded, you'll need to press on further into the region. Try the small resorts of the **Cilento** (*see* p.997) or **Maratea** in the Basilicata (p.1006), both well south of Naples.

Those interested in the ancient Greeks and Romans must first visit **Pompeii**, **Herculaneum**, the splendid temples at **Paestum** and then **Capua**, though the best relics from all these sites are in the great **museum** at Naples. From the Middle Ages, there is exotic Arab-Norman architecture in **Amalfi**, **Salerno** and **Ravello**. Inland, queer old **Benevento** is another fascinating place to visit.

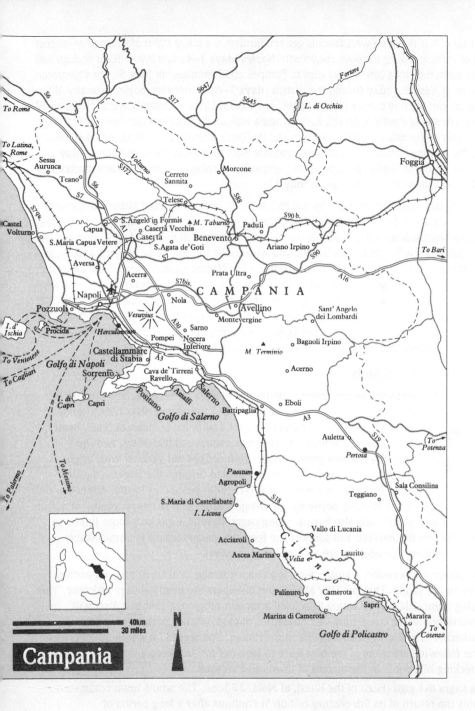

To Rome

To Latina,
Rome

Castel
Volturno

Sessa
Aurunca
Teano

Capua

S.Maria Capua Vetere

Aversa

Acerra

Napoli

Pozzuoli

I. d'
Ischia

Procida

To Ventotene

To Cagliari

Golfo di Napoli

Sorrento

I. di
Capri

Capri

To Palermo

To Messina

S6

S17

S372

Volturno

Cerreto
Sannita

Telese

S.Angelo in Formis
Caserta Vecchia
Caserta
S.Agata de' Goti

S7

S7

S6

▲ M. Taburno

Paduli

Benevento

Prata Ultra

C A M P A N I A

Nola

Vesuvius

Herculaneum

Pompei

Castellammare
di Stabia

Cava de' Tirreni
Ravello

Amalfi

Positano

Golfo di Salerno

S647

Fortore

L. di Occhito

Morcone

S645

S88

S90 b.

S90

Avellino

Montevergine

Sarno

Nocera
Inferiore

A3

Salerno

Battipaglia

Paestum

Agropoli

S.Maria di Castellabate

I. Licosa

Acciaroli

Ascea Marina

Palinuro

Marina di Camerota

Foggia

To Bari

Sant' Angelo
dei Lombardi

▲
M. Terminio

Bagnoli Irpino

Acerno

Eboli

A3

Auletta

Pertosa

Sala Consilina

Teggiano

Vallo di Lucania

Velia

Laurito

Camerota

Sapri

Golfo di Policastro

C
i
l
e
n
t
o

S19

To
Potenza

S18

Maratea

To
Cosenzo

Ariano Irpino

A16

A1

A30

S7bis.

S1

Prata Ultra

Montevergine

To
Cosenzo

40km
30 miles

N

Campania

A tour of less than two weeks should get you through the major sights of Campania—almost all of them are along the coast. Begin with Naples (**days 1–4**), and if you like it enough you can make the city a base for day-trips to Pompeii and Herculaneum (**day 5**), the Phlegraean Fields or Vesuvius (**day 6**), and the islands (**days 7–8**). Otherwise, Sorrento or any of the islands can provide a more pleasant base. The Amalfi Drive is certainly worth two days (**9 and 10**; seeing Positano, Amalfi, Ravello, and a look at old Salerno when you finish) though you may never want to leave. Paestum and its Greek temples come next (**day 11**), and, if you're heading further south, you can continue from here along the Cilento coast (**day 12**), or else return to Naples through inland Campania, stopping at Benevento (**alternative day 12**) then visiting Capua and Caserta (**day 13**).

A seven-day excursion through classical antiquity: for ancient sites and museums, Campania is the equal of Sicily and even Rome itself. Again, start with Naples and its great Archaeological Museum, and a walk through the Spaccanapoli district (**day 1**). Pompeii and Herculaneum will each require a day if you wish to see them in detail (**days 2 and 3**), and another day can be spent exploring the sites west of Naples: Cumae, Baiae, Cape Misenum, Pozzuoli, and so on (**day 4**). Be sure to make at least a day-trip to Benevento to see the Arch of Trajan and the odd Egyptian relics around town (**day 5**). Capua, with its unique *mithraeum* and amphitheatre, comes next (**day 6**). Depending on what direction your travels are taking you, you may either begin or end this itinerary with mainland Italy's best-preserved Greek temples, plus an interesting museum, at Paestum (**day 7**).

## The *Feste* of Campania

In Campania, any excuse will do for throwing a party, especially if it can be combined with having a day off work, and the region plays host to some of Italy's most spectacular and colourful traditional festivals or *feste*. Most of the festivities are linked to religious events and feast days, and the Madonna features prominently, often decked out garishly with bright fairy-lights and gaudy flowers and hauled through the streets atop tiny Fiats hastily covered with red velvet (with peepholes for the driver), or on platforms stoically borne by the village's fittest and strongest young men. But many of the celebrations also have a strong pagan flavour, especially those linked to the land and the harvest, and some of the feast-day paraphernalia is unmistakably phallic (towers and obelisks are an obvious give-away).

Whatever the occasion, a village *festa* is a chance to see local traditions and ancient rites in full swing. They are jolly affairs, and outsiders are nearly always welcome. This being Campania, where eating is in itself a second religion, a visit to a *festa* will invariably involve consuming vast quantities of food, often superbly cooked in makeshift kitchens organized by the local women, and served for knock-down prices. The following are some of the best *feste* to look out for, but keep a watch for others by checking billboards in the piazzas of towns and villages.

**La sagra dei gigli** (Feast of the lilies), at Nola, 27 June. The whole town commemorates the return of its 5th-century bishop St Paulinus after a long period of imprisonment in Africa. The original Nolesi welcomed him home with bunches of lilies. Today, the townspeople recall this reunion by hauling 80-foot tall wooden tower 'lilies' through the streets.

**Festa di Sant'Anna** (Feast of St Anne), at Ischia, 26 July. A dazzling torchlight procession of hundreds of boats, transformed into floats, to honour the island's patron saint.

**Festa dell'obelisco di paglia** (Feast of the straw obelisk), at Fontanarosa, near Avellino, 14 August. A harvest thanksgiving ritual, with a giant 100ft-high spire of plaited straw, around which villagers dance and sing.

**La sagra del grano** (The wheat feast), at Foglianise, near Benevento, 14 August. A striking display of allegorical floats depicting famous churches and monuments, all of them made out of straw and corn-stalks.

**Festa dell'Assunta** (Feast of the Assumption), at Positano, 15 August. An ancient celebration in honour of the Virgin, which also recreates the landing—and the defeat—of the hated Saracens. Local townspeople dress up in costumes and stage a parade of decorated boats before the grand finale, a dramatic firework display over the sea. In neighbouring Montepertuso there is another attractive *festa* two weeks later, the **Sagra del Fagiolo** or 'Feast of the Bean' (*see* below).

**Festa di San Gennaro** (Feast of St Gennaro), in Naples, 19 September. This major event commemorates Naples' patron saint, with a service held in the cathedral to witness the miracle of the liquefaction of his blood (for further details of this most Neapolitan of festas, *see* p.939). Afterwards, relieved citizens (the miracle always works) take to the streets to watch the silver statue of the saint being paraded through the streets. Needless to say, no one goes to work that day.

**Festa dell'Immacolata** (Feast of the Immaculate Conception), at Torre del Greco, 8 December. More than 100 local men carry a huge triumphal float, topped by the Madonna, through the streets, to commemorate the town's lucky escape from the 1861 eruption of Vesuvius.

# Naples

For many, Naples is the true homeland of a particular Italian fantasy, the last bastion of singing waiters and red checked tablecloths, operatic passion and colourful poverty, balanced precariously between Love's own coastline and the menace of Vesuvius. But mention Naples or the Neapolitans to any modern, respectable north Italian, and as they gesticulate and roll their eyes to heaven you will get a first-hand lesson in the dynamics of Italy's 'Problem of the South'. Many Italians simply cannot accept that such an outlandish place can be in the same country with them, a sentiment that probably contains as much envy as contempt. Naples, the city that has given the world Enrico Caruso, Sophia Loren, pizza, and syphilis (the disease appeared here in 1495, and was immediately blamed on the French garrison) may also be the first city to make social disorder into an art form.

## Degradation, Italian Style

On Naples' Piazza Garibaldi you can buy a boiled pigs' organ on a stick, served with a slice of lemon, and watch eight-year-old *scugnizzi*—street children—puff on contraband Marlboros while casually tossing firecrackers into traffic. Fireworks, along with slamming doors, impromptu arias, screams, ambulance sirens and howling cats, are an essential part of the Neapolitan ambience. This anarchic symphony is harder to catch these days, unfortunately, drowned as it is under the roar of Italy's worst traffic problem. In central Naples, three-quarters of a million rude drivers chase each other around a street plan that hasn't changed much since Roman times. Meanwhile, the nation's worst air pollution keeps the hospitals full, in spite of occasional half-hearted attempts to solve the problem by only allowing drivers to take their cars out on alternate days, and every few weeks some old lady on a back street burns to a crisp while the firemen, just down the block, push illegally parked cars out of their way.

Another chronic problem is housing, enough of a nightmare even before the earthquake of 1980; on the outskirts of the city, you may see Napoletani living in stolen ship cargo containers, with windows cut in the sides, in shacks made of sheet metal and old doors, or in abandoned buses. In the city centre, thousands of earthquake refugees are still camping in hotels. One bizarre side-effect of this housing shortage—found all over Italy, but particularly visible here—is the 'quivering car' phenomenon. You'll see them everywhere, especially up on Posillipo hill, cars parked nose to tail, their windows blacked out with newspaper, turned into temporary bedrooms by courting couples or even married couples who have no privacy at home. A cruel but popular prank with Neapolitan kids is to sneak up on the cars and set fire to the newspaper.

No hope for reform seems yet in sight. Even if Naples' notorious city government should some day miraculously turn competent and honest, it would still first have to deal with the spectre of the *Camorra*, a loose term for the

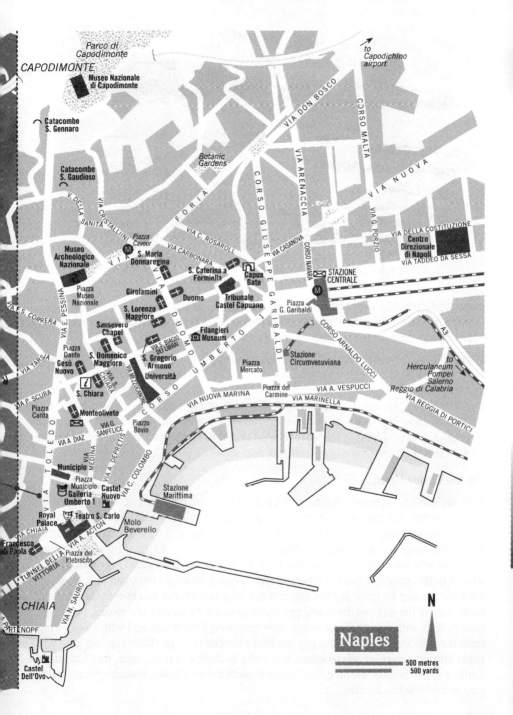

*Porto di Napoli*

crime syndicates that keep Naples as securely strung up as any mountain village in Sicily. Crime is so well organized here, to give one example, that seagoing smugglers have formed a trade union to protect their interests against the police.

In the 18th century, when the city and its spectacular setting were a highlight of the Grand Tour, the saying was 'See Naples and die...'. Nowadays you usually can't see much of anything through the smog, and you'll probably survive if you're careful crossing streets. Don't let Naples' current degradation spoil your visit, though; you haven't seen Italy—no, you haven't seen the Mediterranean—until you have spent some time in this fascinating metropolis. The only thing subtle about Naples is its charm, and the city will probably win your heart at the same time as it is deranging your senses.

## On the Other Hand...

If Naples immediately repels you, however, it means you are probably a sticky sort, and will miss all the fun. The city has an incomparable setting, and much of it is still admittedly beautiful, but its real attraction is a priceless insight into humanity, at the hands of a population of 2.2 million dangerous anarchists. The Napoletani may be numbered among the few peoples of Europe who realize they are alive, and try to enjoy it as best they can. Their history being what it is, this manifests itself in diverse ways. The Napoletani do not stand in lines, or fill out forms, or stop for traffic signals; they will talk your ears off, run you over in their ancient Fiats, criticize the way you dress, whisper alarming propositions, give you sweets, try to pick your pockets with engaging artlessness, offer surprising kindnesses, and with a reassuring smile they will always, always give you the wrong directions. In an official capacity, they will either break the rules for you or invent new ones; in shops and restaurants, they will either charge you too much or too little. The former is much more common, though whichever it is they will do it with a flourish.

If the accounts of long-ago travellers are to be believed, Naples has always been like this. Too much sunshine, and living under such a large and ill-mannered volcano, must contribute much to the effect. It would be somewhat harder to explain some of Naples' ancient distinctions. First and foremost, Naples is Italy's city of philosophers. Her greatest, Giambattista Vico, was a Neapolitan, and others, such as St Thomas Aquinas and Benedetto Croce, spent much of their time here.

Naples can also claim to be first in music. Among native composers are Gesualdo, Scarlatti, and Leoncavallo, and the conservatory is claimed to be the oldest in Europe. Even today, members of the opera company at San Carlo look down on their colleagues at Milan's La Scala as a band of promising upstarts who could stand to take their jobs a little more seriously. Neapolitan popular song, expressive and intense, is an unchained Italian stereotype; the Napoletani maintain its traditions as jealously as they do their impenetrable dialect, one of the most widely spoken and robust in modern Italy.

## History

Naples' rise to become the metropolis of Campania was largely the result of the lucky elimination of her rivals over the centuries. Capua, Cumae, and Benevento rose and fell, and Pompeii and Herculaneum disappeared under volcanic ash, but fortune has always seemed to protect Naples from the really big disasters. As a Greek colony founded by Cumae in 750 BC, the city began with the name Neapolis, and prospered moderately throughout the periods of Greek, Samnite, and Roman rule. Belisarius, Justinian's famous general, seized the region for Byzantium in 536, after invasions of the Goths and Vandals, but a Duke of Naples declared the city independent in 763, acknowledging only the authority of the pope.

The chronicles are understandably slim for this period; early medieval Naples offers us more fairy-tales than facts. Many of its early legends deal with none other than the poet Virgil; somehow, folklore in the dark ages had transformed the greatest Latin poet into Master Virgil, a mighty magician who was given credit for many of the unexplainable engineering feats of the ancient Romans. Naples claimed him for its founder, and its legends told of how he built the Castel dell'Ovo, balancing it on an egg at the bottom of the harbour. Master Virgil also built a talking statue that warned the city of enemies, earthquakes, or plagues, and medieval chroniclers mention the bronze horses and bronze fly he built over two of the city's gates, still to be seen in those days, and said to be magical charms on which the fortune of the city depended.

Naples lost its independence to the Normans in 1139, later passing under the rule of the Hohenstaufen emperors along with the rest of southern Italy. Charles of Anjou took over in 1266, and lopped off the head of the last Hohenstaufen, Conradin, in what is now Naples' Piazza del Mercato. Under the Angevins, Naples for the first time assumed the status and architectural embellishments of a capital. The Angevin Kings of Naples, however, did little to develop their new realm, expending most of their energy in futile attempts to recapture Sicily, lost to them after the Sicilian Vespers revolution of 1282. After their line expired in 1435 with the death of Giovanni II, the kingdom fell to Alfonso V of Aragon—a fateful event, marking Spain's first foothold on the Italian mainland.

## Habsburgs and Bourbons

Aragonese rule seemed promising at first, under the enlightened Alfonso. In later decades, though, it became clear that the Spaniards were mainly interested in milking Italy for taxes with which to finance further conquests. The city itself, as the seat of the viceregal court, prospered greatly; by 1600 its population of 280,000 made it perhaps the largest city on the Mediterranean. The long period of Spanish control did much to give Naples its distinct character, especially during the 17th and 18th centuries, when the city participated almost joyfully in the decadence and decay of the Spanish Empire. This period saw the construction of the scores of frilly, gloomy Baroque churches—now half-abandoned, with bushes growing out of the cornices—that add so much to the Neapolitan scene. In manners especially, the Imperial Spanish influence was felt; 'Nothing', in the words of one observer, 'is cheaper here than human life'.

In 1707, during the War of the Spanish Succession, Naples passed under the rule of Archduke Charles of Austria. Prince Charles of Bourbon, however, snatched it away from him in 1734, and mouldering, picturesque Naples for the next century and a half made the perfect backdrop for the rococo shenanigans of the new Bourbon kingdom. The new rulers were little improvement over the Spaniards, but immigrants from all over the south poured into the city, chasing the thousands of ducats dropped by a free-spending court. Naples became the most densely populated city in Europe, a distinction it still holds today, and crime and epidemics became widespread.

Nevertheless, this was the Naples that became a major attraction for thousands of northern aesthetes doing the Grand Tour in the 18th and 19th centuries. Goethe flirted with *contessas* here, while the English poets were flirting with dread diseases and Lord Nelson was making eyes at Lady Hamilton. The Neapolitans are frank about it; Naples owed its prominence on the Grand Tour less to Vesuvius and the ruins of Pompeii than to good old-fashioned sex. Naples at the time was incontestably the easiest place in Europe to find some, and everyone knew it—saving Goethe and the rest the trouble of ever mentioning the subject in their travel accounts and letters home.

Garibaldi's army entered Naples in February, 1861. As the new Italy's biggest basket case, the city has since received considerable assistance with its planning and social problems—though not nearly enough to make up for the centuries of neglect. The Second World War didn't help; for four days in late September 1944, the city staged a heroic though unsuccessful revolt against the Germans. Even more damage was done by Allied bombing, and the destruction of the city's port and utilities by the retreating Nazis.

While the post-War period saw considerable rebuilding, it also brought new calamities. Illegal and speculative building projects grabbed most of the already crowded city's open space (you'll notice the almost total absence of parks), and turned the fringe areas and much of the once-beautiful Bay of Naples shore into a nightmare of human detritus, one of the eeriest industrial wastelands of Europe. At the moment, there seems to be a common realization that Naples has reached a point of no return, and it will soon have either to clean itself up or perish; discussions of the city's problems in the press are often conducted in alarmingly apocalyptic tones. Leave some room for exaggeration—the Napoletani probably couldn't enjoy life properly without a permanent state of crisis.

In the political turmoil that has taken over Italy since the beginning of the nineties, with the collapse of the old parties, Naples has become one of the major bases of support for the neo-Fascist MSI party, in yet another twist to the city's history. It has, though, marked up one genuine accomplishment in the books in the last few years, though not one that will have much effect on the most serious problems—the *Centro Direzionale*, a huge modernistic development built over the wastelands around Corso Malta, north of the Central Station. In spite of a few hiccups, most notably when the new palace of justice was mysteriously burnt to the ground (no prizes for guessing by whom), the project is currently nearing completion, its aim being to provide a new centre for the regional economy.

## Getting There

### by air

Naples' **Capodichino airport** is on the north side of the city, relatively close to the centre. It has frequent direct services to and from all major Italian destinations, as well as to the islands of Pantelleria and Lampedusa in the summer, and to many foreign cities, including London (several flights daily). For airport information, call ✆ 7092815. From 6am to midnight there is a half-hourly bus service (city bus no.14), between the airport and the Stazione Centrale in central Naples. The journey takes 20–45min, depending on the time of day. As on all city buses, tickets should be bought at a news-stand or ticket booth before boarding.

If you opt for a taxi, remember that on top of the fare on the meter you will officially be charged extra supplements for the airport trip and for luggage—plus, very possibly, additional unexplained 'extras' (*see* below). If in doubt, ask to see the list of prices, which should be displayed in the cab, or try to agree on the fare to your destination before getting into the cab. If traffic is not too heavy—and this is a big if—the fare to the centre should not exceed L40,000.

### by sea

Naples' port has more ship and hydrofoil connections than anywhere else in the Mediterranean, so you can choose to arrive by sea from—or flee to—a wide variety of places, among them the islands in the Bay of Naples, Sicily, Sardinia, Reggio Calabria, the Aeolian Islands or points further afield such as Corsica or Malta. Generally, ferries are cheaper than hydrofoils, but take approximately twice as long. One of the loveliest of the possible sea excursions is the night ferry to the Aeolian Islands, which arrives as the sun is rising over Vulcano.

Ferries and hydrofoils leave from three different points in Naples, but most longer-distance ferries operate from the **Stazione Marittima**, in the centre of the port near the Castel Nuovo. Consult the individual companies for timetables, or look in the daily newspaper *Il Mattino*. The main companies operating from the Stazione Marittima are **Tirrenia**, ✆ 7613688, for Palermo, Cagliari, Reggio Calabria and Malta; **Siremar**, ✆ 7613688, for the Aeolian Islands; and **Lauro**, ✆ 5513352, for Corsica. In addition, one company, **SNAV**, ✆ 7612348, operates a long-distance hydrofoil service from Mergellina quay to the Aeolian Islands.

For more information on all boat services from Naples and hydrofoil services to the islands and ports around the bay, *see* below, 'Around the Bay: from Baia to Sorrento', p.953.

### by rail

Most visitors arrive by train, at the modern **Stazione Centrale** (for information, call ✆ 5534188), on Piazza Garibaldi, which is convenient since this is also a junction for city buses and the local *Circumvesuviana* railway. Trains along the coast towards Rome or Reggio Calabria pass through every half hour on average. In addition, many trains also stop at **Napoli Mergellina** and **Napoli Campi Flegrei**, on the western side of the city, and at some other local stations. Trains from Rome to Naples take 2–2½ hours, depending on the type of train. Travellers arriving in Italy at Rome's Fiumicino Airport can take a direct train from there to Naples, thus avoiding going into Rome itself. There are also good rail connections from Naples to Palermo (4–8 hours, depending on the train) via Messina.

As well as the state FS lines, there are three local railway lines serving the Bay of Naples area. One, the **Ferrovia Circumvesuviana** (information ✆ 7792444), runs trains to Herculaneum, Pompeii and Sorrento from the **Stazione Circumvesuviana** in Corso Garibaldi, and from the Stazione Centrale. Another separate line, the **Ferrovia Cumana**, ✆ 5513328, runs regular trains to the Campi Flegrei area, including Pozzuoli and Baia, from the station at Piazza Montesanto. A third line, the **Ferrovia Circumflegrea**, also ✆ 5513328, runs from the same station at Piazza Montesanto to points west, including Licola and Cuma. For more information on the regional rail lines *see* below, p.953.

### by long-distance bus

Most services to destinations within the province and the Campania region operate from the Piazza Garibaldi, in front of the FS Stazione Centrale. An exception is the bus service to Salerno along the coast, which runs from Via Pisanelli, near Piazza Municipio (*see* p.953).

### by road

The A2 *autostrada* from Rome approaches Naples from due north, Via Caserta, and in the outskirts of the city, just east of Capodichino airport, meets up with a series of massive road junctions: the A16 turns off east for Avellino, Bari and the Adriatic, and then two roads head off to the west, the P1 for the coast and the Naples inner ring road, the *tangenziale*, which leads around the back of the city towards Pozzuoli and the Campi Flegrei. Using the *tangenziale* makes it possible to reach most areas of the city without going through the centre. Traffic going further south should stay on the A2 until it meets the A3, so avoiding the city entirely.

Once you arrive at wherever you are staying in Naples, you are categorically advised to park your car in a safe place (such as a hotel garage) and not attempt to use it anywhere within the city (*see* below).

## Tourist Information

The best place to go for information about Naples itself is the well-run and friendly information booth run by the city's **Azienda Autonoma di Soggiorno** on Piazza Gesù Nuovo, ✆ 5523328/5512701, in the old town (open 9am–7pm Mon–Sat; 9am–3pm Sun). Their main office is in the Royal Palace, ✆ 418744, ✆ 418619. In summer they open offices in the Castel dell'Ovo, ✆ 764 5688, on the harbour at Mergellina, ✆ 7614585, and in a trailer in Piazza Garibaldi, in front of the Stazione Centrale. Information about excursions outside the city and so on is only available from the less helpful provincial **EPT**, Piazza dei Martiri 58, ✆ 405311. The EPT also has another, intermittently manned office at the Stazione Centrale, which, if anyone is around, may be some help in finding a hotel. Look out for the free monthly handbook *Qui Napoli*, available at tourist offices and some hotels, which carries a great deal of useful information, timetables, listings and calendars of events.

**Fire,** ✆ 115.
**Police emergencies,** ✆ 112.
**Police** (stolen cars), ✆ 7941435.
**Ambulance,** ✆ 7520696, 24 hours; daytime only 7520850.
**Hospital: Policlinico,** Via Sergio Pansini, ✆ 7461111. There is also a public health service **doctor** on call 24 hours on ✆ 7513177.
**24-hour pharmacy: Carducci,** Via Carducci 21–23, ✆ 417283.

Outside normal banking hours, you can change money at the post office (*see* below), in most good hotels, and at travel agents, such as **Ashiba**, Piazza Municipio 1, ✆ 5512366; **CIT**, Piazza Municipio 70, ✆ 5525426; and **Partenotour**, Piazza dei Martiri 23, ✆ 7643415.

The **main post office** is in Piazza Matteotti, ✆ 5511456, near Via Toledo, and is open 8am–8pm Mon–Fri, 8am–12 midday Sat. You can also send faxes and telegrams from here. There are **phone centres** at the Stazione Centrale, at Via Depretis 40, and in the Galleria Umberto I.

The telephone area code for Naples is **081**.

## Getting Around

Travelling around the city is a fascinating subject. Such is the state of most public transport and so impenetrable is the traffic that walking is often by far the most practical way of getting anywhere, apart from up to the heights by the funicolari.

Orientation is a little difficult. If you arrive by sea—the only proper way to do it— you'll get a good idea of the layout. Naples' dominant landmarks, visible from almost anywhere in town, are Castel Sant'Elmo and the huge, fortress-like monastery of San Martino. They are neighbours on the steep hill that slopes down to the sea near the port, neatly dividing the city into its old and new quarters.

Modern Naples is on the western side, the busy, pleasant districts of Mergellina, Vomero and Fuorigrotta, to which middle-class Napoletani escape from the city centre each night on their creaking old funicular railways. To the east, towards Vesuvius, lies the centre, along Via Toledo, and beyond it the oldest neighbourhoods, tall tenements jammed into a grid of narrow streets, reaching a climax in the oriental bazaar atmosphere of the Piazza Mercato and the Piazza Garibaldi.

For more on travel by train or bus to destinations outside the city, around the Bay of Naples or further into Campania, *see* below, p.987.

### by bus

Given the problems involved in using their own cars and even taxis in Naples, visitors often find themselves left with the local buses, which is small cheer, since the city indisputably has the worst bus system in Italy. Buses will be slow and usually indecently crowded. There are no schedules, no maps, and nowhere you can get accurate information; even the drivers usually do not have the faintest idea what is happening. The ultimate Neapolitan experience is waiting an hour for a bus after being misinformed by line employees, and then finding out the right bus is the one marked 'out of service'. Most lines start at either Piazza Garibaldi or Piazza del Plebiscito. Some that might be useful are:

**1** and **4** trolleys, from Piazza Garibaldi to Corso Umberto, Piazza Plebiscito, Riviera di Chiaia, and Mergellina.

**24**, from Piazza Plebiscito up Via Toledo to Capodimonte.

**120, 127**, from Piazza Garibaldi to Piazza Cavour and Capodimonte.

**150, 152**, to Pozzuoli.

### by Metro and funicolare

Naples also has a sort of underground. The **Metropolitana**, a single line from Piazza Garibaldi (basement of the Stazione Centrale) to Fuorigrotta, is really a part of the state railway, and uses the same underground tracks as the long-distance trains. The FS runs it as anarchically as the buses, but it will be helpful for reaching the station, the archaeological museum, and points in Vomero and Fuorigrotta. As on the buses, few people ever buy tickets.

A much more agreeable way to travel, though you can't go very far, is on the three **funicolari**, or inclined railways, up to Vomero. The longest—one of the longest in the world, in fact—is the **Funicolare Centrale**, from Via Toledo, just behind the Galleria, up to Via Cimarosa. The **Funicolare di Chiaia** also ends nearby in the same street, having started from Piazza Amedeo in Chiaia. Finally, the **Funicolare di Montesanto** travels up to Via Morghen from Montesanto Station, the start of the suburban Circumflegrea and Cumana rail-lines. All three bring you out near the San Martino Museum and the Castel Sant'Elmo. All run until about 7pm daily.

### by taxi

Neapolitan taxi drivers are uniformly dishonest, and try out any number of scams involving fixed meters, turning the meter on before you get in the car, imaginary 'surcharges' and so on. Also, the traffic is frequently so thick that relatively short journeys can take so long (and cost so much) that they're really not worth it. If you want to take a taxi to a specific destination, always try to agree on the fare in advance, whether there is a meter or not.

*by car*

The first thing to get straight is simply—*leave your car elsewhere*. Cars disappear in Naples with alarming frequency, and foreign number plates are especially prized. Even if you get to keep your wheels, you'll be sorry. Driving in Naples is a unique experience. Motorists studiously disregard all traffic signals and warnings, and the city has given up trying to coerce them. There are no rules, except to get there first, and fatalities are common. Even if this sounds exciting, note that the novelty soon wears off, even for the most boorish motorhead. For scant sympathy about stolen cars, call the city police on © 313131.

Several **car hire** firms have offices in Naples, mainly on Via Partenope (near the port), at the airport, and/or at the Stazione Centrale: **Avis**, © 7645600; **Europcar**, © 7645859; **Hertz**, © 7645533; **InterRent**, © 7646364. Be warned though that as car theft is so rife in Naples some companies will not rent certain models in the city, so you may find your choice restricted.

## Piazza del Plebiscito—the Parking Lot of Naples

It's a shame this immense and elegant square, the centre of modern Naples, should suffer such a fate, but for the present there seems to be little hope of improvement. The huge domed church, embracing the piazza in its curving colonnades as does St Peter's in Rome, is **San Francesco di Paola**. King Ferdinand IV, after the British restored him to power in 1815, made a vow to construct it; the great dome and classical portico were modelled after the Pantheon in Rome. There's little to see in the austere interior, and anyone with a little understanding of Naples will not be surprised to find the colonnades given over to light manufacturing and warehouse space.

Across the square rises the equally imposing bulk of the **Royal Palace** (*Palazzo Reale*), begun by the Spanish viceroys in 1600, expanded by the Bourbons and finished by the kings of Italy (*open 9–1.30, 4.30–7.30, daily; adm*). Umberto I, a good friend of the Neapolitans, added the eight giant figures on the façade, representing the eight houses that have ruled at Naples. It seems the 19th-century sculptors had trouble taking some of them seriously; note the preposterous figures of Charles of Anjou, whom the Neapolitans never liked, and Vittorio Emanuele II, the latter probably an accurate portrayal. There are Ruritanian stone sentry boxes and stone peacocks in the courtyard to recall the Bourbons, and a number of rooms inside that can be visited—the ones that escaped the bombings in the Second World War, including a suitably grand staircase, a theatre, and several chambers in 18th-century style. The palace's theatre saw the premières of many of the works of Alessandro Scarlatti. The rear of the palace, now the home of Naples' important **Biblioteca Nazionale**, faces a pretty, little visited garden across from the Castel Nuovo.

The Bourbons were great opera buffs, and they built Italy's largest opera house, the **San Carlo**, right next to their palace. Begun in 1737, making it older than La Scala, the theatre was sumptuously restored after a fire in 1816, during the period when Naples was the unquestioned capital of opera; so important was the theatre to the people of Naples that King Ferdinand made sure the the workmen got the job done in record time—300 days. Today the San Carlo is still among the most prestigious in the world (the Neapolitans of course would place it first), and its productions are certainly among the most polished and professional, and occasionally among the most adventurous. Also, each season at least one lesser-known Neapolitan opera is performed. Tickets are as expensive as anywhere (up to L400,000 on an opening night), but you can take a brief tour of the theatre for considerably less (© 7972111; tours 9am–2pm Mon–Fri; 9am–1pm Sun; adm).

Opposite the San Carlo is the grandest interior of Southern Italy, the **Galleria Umberto I**. This great glass-roofed arcade, perhaps the largest in the world, was begun in 1887, nine years after the Galleria Vittorio Emanuele in Milan. The arcade is cross-shaped, with a mosaic of the zodiac on the floor at the centre, and its dome is 56m tall; surprisingly, the Neapolitans do not seem to like it as much as much as they once did; even at high noon, you are likely to find its vast spaces deserted but for a few small clouds of grey-suited men arguing politics around the entrances.

## Castel Nuovo

The port of Naples has been protected by this odd, beautiful castle, looming over the harbour behind the Royal Palace and San Carlo, for some 700 years now. Charles of Anjou built it in 1279; many Napoletani still call it by the curious name of *Maschio* (male) *Angioino*. Most of what you see today, however, including the eccentric, ponderous round towers, is the work of Guillermo Sagrera, the great Catalan architect who built the famous Exchange in Palma de Mallorca. Between two of these towers at the entrance, the conquering Aragonese hired the finest sculptors from all over Italy to build Alfonso's **Triumphal Arch**, a unique masterpiece of Renaissance sculpture and design inspired by the triumphal arches of the ancient Romans. The symbolism, as in the Roman arches, may be a little confusing. The figure at the top is Saint Michael; below him are a matched pair of sea gods, and further down, allegorical virtues and relief panels portraying Alfonso's victories and wise governance.

*Castel Nuovo*

Inside, the castle currently houses parts of the Naples city administration and some cultural societies. If you come during office hours (*8am–1pm Mon–Fri*), someone will probably be around to show you the **Sala dei Baroni**, where the city council meets; it has a cupola with an unusual Moorish vaulting, an eight-pointed star made of interlocking arches. King Ferrante used this as his dining hall, and it takes its name from the evening when he invited a score of the kingdom's leading barons to a ball, and then arrested the lot. There are also two museums (*open 9am–2pm Mon–Fri; 9am–1.30pm Sat; adm*). One, housed in the Gothic **Cappella Palatina**, next to the council hall, contains 14th and 15th-century frescoes; the other, in the south wing, has paintings, and a good collection of silver and bronzes, from the 15th century to the present day.

## Via Toledo

From the landward side of Piazza del Plebiscito and the Palace, Naples' most imposing street, the Via Toledo, runs northwards past the Galleria. Its name commemorates its builder, Don Pedro de Toledo, the Spanish viceroy at the beginning of the 16th century, and a great benefactor of Naples. Stendhal, in 1817, rightly called this 'the most populous and gayest street in the world', and it is still the city's main business and shopping street, leading up to Capodimonte and the northern suburbs (many Neapolitans still call it by its Mussolini-era name, Via Roma). Don Pedro's elegant Renaissance tomb, among others, can be seen in the little church of **San Giacomo degli Spagnuoli**, now swallowed up by the 19th-century Palazzo Municipale complex, originally a home for the Bourbon royal bureaucracy.

Going north along Via Toledo, any street on your left can be the entrance to the dense, crumbling, slightly sinister inner sanctum of the Neapolitan soul, the vast slum called the Quartieri Spagnuoli. It can be a fascinating place to walk around, in daytime at least. Lately though, thanks to battling factions of the Camorra, the Quartieri have achieved even more than their accustomed share of notoriety; for a while the hoods were bumping each other off at a rate of one per week. Though the Quartieri cover almost all the area sloping up to San Martino and Vomero, the most populous and colourful part is that immediately adjoining Via Toledo, a strict grid of narrow streets laid out by Don Pedro de Toledo and now called the Tavoliere, or chessboard.

To the right of Via Toledo, the confusion of Naples' half-crumbling, half-modern business centre conceals a few buildings worth a look. The **Palazzo Gravina**, on Via Monteoliveto, is a fine palace in the northern Renaissance style, built between 1513 and 1549. Almost directly across the street, the church of **Monteoliveto** is a little treasure house of late Renaissance sculpture and painting, with tombs and altars in the various chapels by southern artists like Giovanni da Nola and Antonio Rosellino, as well as some frescoes by Vasari.

## Spaccanapoli

This street's familiar name means 'Split-Naples', and that is exactly what it has done for the last 2600 years. On the map, it changes its name with alarming frequency—Via Benedetto Croce and Via San Biagio dei Librai are two of the most prominent—but in Roman times you would have found it by asking for the *decumanus inferior*, the name for the second east–west street in any planned Roman city. No large city in all the lands conquered by Rome has maintained its ancient street plan as completely as Naples (the Greeks laid out these streets, of course, but the Romans learned their planning from them). It is easier here to imagine the atmosphere of a big ancient city than in Rome itself, or even in Pompeii. The narrow, straight streets and tall *insulae* cannot have changed much; only the forum and temples are missing.

This is the heart of old Naples—and what a street it is, lined with grocery barrows and scholarly bookshops, shops that sell old violins, plaster saints, pizza, or used clothes pegs. Drama is supplied by the arch-Neapolitan characters who live here, haunting the street-corners and entertaining wan hopes of dodging the manic motorists; the colour comes from the district's laundry—down any of the long alleys of impossibly tall tenements you may see as many as a hundred clothes-lines, swelling bravely in the breeze and hoping for a glint of southern sun. It has always been a poor neighbourhood, though even now it is not a desperate one. As always, its people live much of their life on the streets, carrying on whatever is their business from makeshift benches on the kerbs. The visitor will probably find that claustrophobia is right around the corner, but anyone born and raised here would never feel at home anywhere else.

## Santa Chiara and the Gesù Nuovo

Your introduction to this world, just off Via Toledo, is the cramped, disorderly, most characteristic of Neapolitan squares: the **Piazza Gesù Nuovo**, decorated by the gaudiest and most random of Neapolitan decorations, the **Guglia della Immacolata**. A *guglia* (pinnacle), in Naples, is a kind of rococo obelisk, dripping with frills, saints and *putti*, of which there are three, all in this area. The unsightly, unfinished façade behind the Guglia, covered with pyramidal extrusions in dark basalt, belongs to the Church of **Gesù Nuovo**. As strange as it is, the façade, originally part of a late 15th-century palace, has become one of the landmarks of Naples. The interior is typically lavish Neapolitan Baroque, gloriously overdone in acres of coloured marbles and frescoes, some by the Spanish artist Ribera and some by Solimena.

**Santa Chiara**, just across the piazza, dates from the early 14th century, though it once had a Baroque interior as good as the Gesù; Allied bombers remodelled it to suit modern tastes in 1943, and only a few of the original Angevin tombs have survived. To get some idea of what the interior must have been like, stop in and see the adjacent **Cloister of the Clarisse**, nothing less than the loveliest and most peaceful spot in Naples—especially in contrast to the neighbourhood outside. So much in Naples shows the Spanish influence—like the use of the title 'Don', now largely limited to Camorra bosses—and here someone in the 1740s transplanted the Andalucian love of pictures done in painted *azulejo* tiles, turning a simple monkish cloister into a little fairyland of gaily coloured arbours, benches and columns, shaded by the only trees in the whole district.

Recently, during the restoration of a vestibule off the cloister, it was discovered that underneath the indifferent 18th-century frescoes there were some earlier, highly original paintings of the Last Judgement. They have since been uncovered and restored, revealing an inspired 16th-century vision of the event, in a style utterly unlike the slick virtuosity of the time, with plenty of novel tortures for the damned and angels welcoming some cute naked nuns among the elect.

# The Sansevero Chapel

A few streets further down Via Benedetto Croce is tiny Piazza San Domenico, which has monuments from Naples' three most creative periods. **San Domenico Maggiore**, built in 1289, was the Dominican church in Naples. St Thomas Aquinas lived in the adjacent monastery. Later this became the favourite church of the Spanish, and it contains some interesting Renaissance funerary monuments; a better one, though, is across the Piazza in the church of **Sant'Angelo a Nilo**—the tomb of Cardinal Brancaccio, designed by Michelozzo, with a relief of the *Assumption of the Virgin* by Donatello. The second of the Baroque pinnacles decorates the Piazza, the **Guglia di San Domenico**, a work of Cosimo Fanzago, who also designed the church. Best of all, just around the corner on Via F. De Sanctis, you can inspect Neapolitan Rococo at its very queerest in the **Sansevero Chapel** (*open 10–1, 5–7, Mon, Wed–Sat; 10am–1pm Tues, Sun; adm*). Prince Raimondo di Sangro (b.1701), who was responsible for the final form of this, his family's private chapel, was a strange bird, a sort of aristocratic dilettante mystic. Supposedly there is a grand allegorical scheme behind the arrangement of the sculptures and frescoes he commissioned, but a work like this, only 200 years old, seems as foreign to our sensibilities and understanding as some Mayan temple. The sculptures, by little-known Neapolitan artists like Giuseppe Sammartino and Antonio Corradini, are inscrutable allegories in themselves, often executed with a breathtakingly showy virtuosity. Francesco Queirolo's *Il Disinganno* (disillusion) is an extreme case; nobody else, perhaps, has ever tried to carve a fishing-net, or the turning pages of a book, out of marble. Others, such as Sammartino's *Cristo Velato*, display a remarkable illusion of figures under transparent veils. There are a dozen or so of these large sculptural groups, all under a crazy heavenly vortex in the ceiling fresco, by Francesco Mario Russo. Down in the crypt are two complete human cardiovascular systems, removed from the bodies and preserved by Prince Raimondo in his alchemical experiments. Ask to see them (if you care to).

Near San Domenico, a block south of the Spacca, is Naples' **University**, one of Europe's oldest and most distinguished. The Emperor Frederick founded it in 1224, as a 'Ghibelline' university to counter the pope's 'Guelph' university at Bologna, as well as to provide scholars and trained officials for the new state he was trying to build. It still occupies its ancient, woefully overcrowded quarters around Via Mezzocannone.

## Around the Piazza del Duomo

Continuing down the Spaccanapoli (now Via San Biagio ai Librai), just around the corner on Via San Gregorio is the **San Gregorio Armeno** church, with another gaudy Baroque interior. In December, this street and others around it become Naples' famous Christmas Market, where everyone comes to buy figurines of the Holy Family, the Three Kings and all the other accessories required for their Christmas *presepi*, or manger scenes, one of the most devotedly followed of local traditions. For several weeks, hundreds of stands fill up the neighbourhood's narrow streets.

## The *Presepi*

It would not be easy to explain why the genius of Naples should have chosen Christmas cribs as a subject to elevate to an art form. After philosophy, pizza and music, it's what this city does best. Churches and private homes have always had a little competitive edge on when they begin their displays (some time in November, if not earlier). The most extreme cases have been assembled inside the Museo Nazionale di San Martino. One is as big as a bus, and must have taken someone a lifetime; another is fitted inside an eggshell—still with over a hundred figures in it. The best parts are the large, finely carved individual wooden or ceramic figures. Most represent Neapolitans of two or three centuries ago, from every walk of life; with their painstakingly detailed and wonderfully expressive faces, each is a genuine portrait. To have them all here in one place is like old Bourbon Naples appearing before your eyes. For do-it-yourself, modern cribs, Via San Gregorio is the place to go. At Christmas time, the whole street is taken over by the stalls of artisans who make and sell figurines for the crib scene, as well as little trees, sheep, donkeys, amphorae, cooking pots, Turks, salamis, dogs, chickens, angels, cheese wheels, and all the other items without which no Neapolitan *presepe* would be complete.

Convention requires that, quite apart from the Holy Family, certain things be present in every crib. Besides the usual angels, shepherds, and animals, a **Roman ruin** is absolutely necessary, as are several **Turks** in Ottoman Empire dress (which come in handy if one of the Three Kings gets lost). A **band of musicians** is also expected, and all the better if they too are Turks. **Beggars and dwarfs** earn envy for the crib-maker—there is a whole display of figures called the 'deformities'—but above all there must be **tons of food** everywhere there is room for it. The best cribs have the busiest cooks and the most bulging pantries, with tiny wooden roast pigs, sausages, eggs, plates of macaroni, cheeses and fancy cakes—even a pizza or two. Look out for the giant *presepe* in the Galleria Umberto at Christmas time, and watch Neapolitans throw money at it to pay for its upkeep for another year.

A little further north up Via San Gregorio is **San Lorenzo Maggiore** (*c*. 1330), one of Naples' finest medieval churches; Petrarch lived for a while in the adjacent monastery. In addition, recent excavations have also uncovered some interesting Greek and Roman remains on the site. **San Paolo**, across the street, isn't much to see now, but before an earthquake wrecked it in the 17th century, its façade was the portico of an ancient Roman temple to Castor and Pollux. Andrea Palladio studied it closely, and it provided much of the inspiration for his classical palaces in the Veneto.

After Spaccanapoli, **Via dei Tribunali** (the *decumanus major*) is the busiest street of old Naples, and has been for a long time. The arcades that line the street in places, a sort of continuous covered market, are a thousand years old or more. Here, at the otherwise unremarkable **Girolamini Church**, you may see the modest tomb of Naples's greatest philosopher, Giambattista Vico). Since his death in 1744, Vico's philosophy of historical cyles and the poetic origins of each new civilization has been a dark undercurrent in Western thought and literature; Joyce's *Finnegan's Wake* is based on it. Vico lived all his life in this neighbourhood, and had a wonderfully Neapolitan funeral: at the procession, his confraternity got into an argument with his University colleagues over who would carry the coffin. This somehow degenerated into a general neighbourhood brawl, and the corpse, abandoned and forgotten, spent the day and night in the middle of Via dei Tribunali.

Northwest of the Girolamini, around Via dell'Anticaglia, you'll find a few crooked streets, the only ones in old Naples that do not stick to the rectilinear Roman plan. These follow the outline of the **Roman Theatre**, much of which still survives, hidden among the tenements. A few arches are all that is visible from the street.

## The Cathedral of San Gennaro

The wide **Via del Duomo** is a breath of fresh air in this crowded district—exactly what the city intended, when they ploughed it through Old Naples after the cholera epidemic of 1884. The **Duomo** itself is another fine medieval building, though it is hidden behind an awful pseudo-Gothic façade pasted on in 1905. The best things are inside: the Renaissance **Capella Minùtolo**, the tomb of Charles of Anjou and the **Capella San Gennaro**, glittering with the gold and silver of the Cathedral treasure, and with frescoes by Domenichino and Lanfranco, the latter a swirling *Paradiso* in the dome (1643).

The **Basilica Santa Restituta**, a sizeable church in its own right, is tacked onto the side of the cathedral. Its columns are thought to be from the temple of Apollo that once occupied the site. Begun in 324, though often rebuilt, this is the oldest building in Naples. The ceiling frescoes are by Luca Giordano. Just off the basilica, the 5th-century **baptistry** contains a good Byzantine-style mosaic by the 14th-century artist Lello di Roma; the baptismal font itself probably comes from an ancient temple of Dionysus. The last and most elaborate of the *guglie*, the **Guglia San Gennaro**, can be seen just outside the south transept.

If the sacristan is around, you can visit the **Crypt of San Gennaro**, patron of Naples, with elaborate marble decoration from the Renaissance, and the tomb of Pope Innocent IV. Whoever is really buried here, San Gennaro (Januarius) is a rather doubtful character; most likely he is a Christian assimilation of the Roman god Janus. The saint's head is kept upstairs in the chapel named after him, along with two phials of his blood that miraculously liquefy and 'boil' three times each year—the first Sunday in May, 19th September, and 16th December—so as to prove that San Gennaro is still looking out for the Napoletani. The only time the miracle has ever failed, during the Napoleonic occupation, the people of the city became enormously excited and seemed ready to revolt. At this the French commander, a true son of the Enlightenment, announced that San Gennaro had 10 minutes to come through—or else he'd shoot the Archbishop. Somehow, just in time, the miracle occurred.

On a small piazza a block north of the Duomo, **Santa Maria Donnaregina** offers more over-done Baroque, but off to the side of this 17th-century work is the smaller, original church, built in 1307 by Queen Mary of Hungary (who was none other than the wife of Charles of Anjou; her title only reflects a claim to the throne). Her elaborate tomb, and some good contemporary frescoes, are the sights of the church.

South of the cathedral in the Via del Duomo is the **Filangieri Museum** (*open 9–2 Mon–Sat; 9–1 Sun; adm*), housed in the 15th-century Palazzo Cuomo, a small collection of china, armour, and curiosities. Its picture collection includes works by some of Naples' favourite artists, Luca Giordano, Mattia Preti, Ribera and others. Almost all the collection was gathered in the last forty years. Count Filangieri's original collection was larger, but the Nazis torched it before they left in 1944.

## Piazza Garibaldi

In Italian, the word for a market stand is *bancarella*. In Naples they are as much a part of everyday life as they must have been in the Middle Ages; the city probably has as many of them as all the rest of Italy put together. The greatest concentration can be found in the Forcella market district, in the narrow streets east of the Via del Duomo, selling everything from stereos to light bulbs. According to the government's economists, at least one-third of Naples' economy is underground—outright illegal, or at the least not paying taxes or subject to any regulation.

Bootleg cassette tapes are one example; Naples is one of the world leaders in this thriving industry, and you'll have your choice of thousands of titles along these streets, though it might be a good idea to get them to play your tape before you part with any money. Hundreds of tired-looking folks sit in front of little tables, selling contraband American cigarettes. This is one of the easiest means for Naples' poor to make a living, and it is all controlled by the Camorra. As in New York, whenever it rains, shady characters crawl out of the woodwork selling umbrellas. You will see plenty of designer labels on the *bancarelle*—if they're real, don't ask where they came from.

**Piazza Mercato**, one of the nodes of the Neapolitan bazaar, has been a market square perhaps since Roman times. In the old days this was always the site of major executions, most notably that of 16 year-old Conradin, the rightful heir to the throne, by Charles of Anjou in 1268, an act that shocked all Europe. Charles ordered him buried underneath the Piazza— he couldn't be laid in consecrated ground, since he had just been excommunicated for political reasons by Charles's ally the pope.

In 1647, Masaniello's Revolt started here, during the festival of Our Lady of Mount Carmel; Masaniello (Tommaso Aniello), a young fisherman of Amalfi, had been chosen by his fellow conspirators to step up in the middle of the ceremonies and proclaim to the people and the viceroy that the new tax the viceroy had introduced 'no longer existed'. As the plotters had hoped, a spontaneous rising followed, and for a week Masaniello ruled Naples while the frightened viceroy locked himself up in Castel Sant'Elmo. In Naples, unfortunately, such risings can burn out as quickly as a match; the viceroy's spies first secretly drugged Masaniello, so that he appeared drunk or mad to the people, and then in an unguarded moment they murdered him and sent his head to the viceroy. That was the end for Naples, but the incident touched off a wave of revolts across the south that it took the Spaniards three years to stamp out.

The incredible **Piazza Garibaldi** is the other main centre of the Forcella area. For rail travellers, it is an unforgettable introduction to Naples; they walk out of the incongruously modern Stazione Centrale into the vast square, paved with asphalt that melts in the hot sun and sticks to their shoes, and enter a world unlike anything else in Italy—bums, addicts and crazies draped picturesquely along the pavement, solid ranks of *bancarelle* wherever there's room, eternal crowds of odd characters from every nation of the world, Italy's worst hotels and its ugliest whores. Most of the piazza is really one gigantic parking lot; traffic whistles through it on lanes marked with yellow paint. Neapolitans don't mind the Piazza Garibaldi; tourists often come to like it. Sailors generally avoid it, as do the police.

## The Capua Gate

Northwest of the Piazza Garibaldi, some of Naples' shabbiest streets lead towards the Piazza Enrico di Nicola, once the city's main gate. The **Porta Capuana**, built in 1492, seems a smaller version of the Castel Nuovo's triumphal arch, crowded in by the same squat round towers. The **Castel Capuano**, next to it, began its life as a castle-residence for the Hohenstaufen kings. Since its construction in the 13th century it has been reshaped so many times it doesn't even look like a castle any more; for four centuries it has served as Naples' law courts. If anything makes wandering into this unlikely district worthwhile, though, it is **Santa Caterina a Formiella**, facing the Porta Capuana, a neglected, almost abandoned church by the obscure architect Romolo Balsimelli, one of the masterpieces of 16th-century Italian architecture. Completed in 1517, the church's squarish form was a Renaissance eccentricity, but an important stepping-stone towards the Baroque. Today, Santa Caterina is hardly ever open, and its dome tilts at a more precarious angle with each passing year.

## The Archaeological Museum, the Catacombs and Capodimonte

Back on the western side of the old city, Via Toledo, after passing Spaccanapoli and changing its name to Via Pessina, continues northwards through the **Piazza Dante**, one of the most delightful and animated corners of the city; beyond this, in an area of oversized tenements and busy streets, it opens to display the crumbling red palazzo that contains the **Museo Archeologico Nazionale** (*open 9am–7pm daily; adm*).

Naples has the most important collection of Roman-era art and antiquities in the world, due partly to Vesuvius, for burying Pompeii and Herculaneum, and partly to the sharp eyes and deep pockets of the Farnese family—many of the best works here come from the collection they built up over 300 years. Unfortunately, the place is run by Neapolitans; at any given time, half of the collections will be closed for 'restorations' that never seem to happen, and what they condescend to let you see may well be the worst-exhibited and worst-labelled major museum in Europe.

On the first floor, room after room is filled with ancient sculpture. Many of the pieces on view are the best existing Roman-era copies of lost Greek statues, including some by Phidias and Praxiteles; some are masterpieces in their own right, such as the huge, dramatic ensemble called the *Farnese Bull*, the *Tyrannicides* (with other statues' heads stuck on them), and the truly heroic *Farnese Hercules* that once decorated the Baths of Caracalla. Several provocative Aphrodites compete for your attention, along with a platoon of formidable Athenas. Also the famous *Doryphorus* (spear-bearer), and enough Greek and Roman busts to populate a Colosseum.

Upstairs, most of the rooms are given over to finds from Pompeii. The collection of **Roman mosaics**, mostly from Pompeii and Herculaneum, is one of the two best anywhere

Tom Farnese

(the other is in Antalya, Turkey); the insight it provides into the life and thought of the ancients is priceless. One feature it betrays clearly is a certain fond silliness—plenty of chickens, ducks and grinning cats, the famous *Cave canem* (beware of the dog) mosaic from the front of a house, comic scenes from the theatre, and especially one wonderful panel of crocodiles and hippopotami along the Nile. Some of the mosaics are very consciously 'art': a detailed scene of the Battle of Issus, where Alexander the Great defeated the Persian king Darius, and a view of the Academy of Athens that includes a portrait of Plato. A recently opened addition is a section devoted entirely to the Temple of Isis at Pompeii. Five rooms display sculptures, frescoes and paintings taken from the temple, which was first dicovered in 1765.

Besides the mosaics, nowhere in the world will you find a larger collection of **Roman mural painting**, and much of it is fascinatingly modern in theme and execution. Many of the walls of Pompeiian villas were decorated with architectural fantasias that seem strangely like those of the Renaissance. Other works show an almost Baroque lack of respect for the gods—see the *Wedding of Zeus and Hera*. Scholars in fact do denote a period of 'Roman Baroque', beginning about the 2nd century. From it come paintings graced by genuine winged *putti*, called *amoretti* in Roman days. Among the most famous pictures are *The Astragal Players*— young girls shooting craps—and the beautiful *Portrait of an Unknown Woman*, a thoughtful lady holding her pen to her lips who is now one of the best-known images from Roman art.

Other attractions of the museum include large collections of jewellery, coins, fancy gladia- tors' armour, the famous *sezione pornografica* that you may get to see if you ask politely, Greek vases, decorative bronzes and a highly detailed, room-sized **scale model** of the entire city of Pompeii (lovingly restored since the memorable assault on it by the authors' baby boy, back in 1980). The Egyptian collection is not a large one, but it is fun, with a dog-headed Anubis in a Roman toga, some ancient feet under glass, and a mummified crocodile.

## Capodimonte

North of the museum, the neighbourhoods along Via Toledo—briefly named Via Santa Teresa degli Scalzi—begin to lose some of their Neapolitan intensity as they climb to the suburban heights. On the way, after changing its name again to Corso Amedeo di Savoia, the street passes an area that was full of cemeteries in Roman times. Three Christian under- ground burial vaults have been discovered here, with a total area of over 100,000 square metres, only part of which have been completely explored. Two may be visited: the **Catacombe di San Gennaro** (*entrance off the northern end of the Corso; look for the yellow signs. Tours at 9.30, 10.15, 11.00, 11.45am, Fri, Sat, Sun only; adm*) is the more interesting, with extensive early Christian mosaics and carvings, some as early as the 2nd century. The **Catacombe di San Gaudioso** (*tours at 9.45, 11.45am, daily; adm*), which include the 5th-century tomb of the saint of the same name, a martyred African bishop, were discovered under the Baroque church of **Santa Maria della Sanità**, on Via Sanità.

The **Parco di Capodimonte**, a well-kept and exotically tropical park, began as a hunting preserve of the Bourbons in the 18th century. Charles III built a Royal Palace here in 1738 that now houses Naples' picture gallery, the **Museo Nazionale di Capodimonte** (*open 2–7.30pm Mon; 9–7.30 Tues–Sat; 9–2 Sun; adm*). The collection is the best in the south of

Italy, and especially rich in works of the late Renaissance. Some of the works you shouldn't miss: an *Annunciation* by Filippino Lippi; a Botticelli *Madonna*; the mystical portrait of the mathematician *Fra Luca Pacioli*, by an unknown quattrocento artist; two wry homilies by the elder Brueghel, *The Misanthrope* and *The Blind*; works by Masaccio and Mantegna, and a hilarious picture of *St Peter Martyr* by Lotto, showing that famous anti-Semitic rabble-rouser conversing nonchalantly with the Virgin Mary—with a hatchet sticking out of his head.

Five big, beautifully restored Caravaggios take up one room; others are devoted to important works by Titian. One entire wing of the museum is filled with delightfully frivolous 18th-century **porcelain figurines**; the Bourbons maintained a royal factory for making such things at Capodimonte, which is still in operation today. In another hall, there are scores of 19th-century watercolour scenes of Naples and the Campanian countryside (the best of them by Giacinto Gigante). Here, for the first time, you will see the Naples that so struck the 18th-century travellers. Not much has changed, really; if only all the traffic could magically disappear, it would still be almost the same spectacular city today.

The museum's collections are mostly up on the second floor; the first, the old *piano nobile* (royal apartments), is still much the way the Bourbons left it. Persevere through the score of overdecorated chambers; the *Salotto di porcellana*, a little room entirely lined with Capodimonte porcelain, makes the whole thing worthwhile.

## The Certosa di San Martino

Up on the highest point overlooking Naples, the 17th-century **Castel Sant'Elmo** (*open 9am–7.30pm Mon–Fri; 9–2 Sat; adm*) is an impressive enough Baroque fortification, partly built of the tufa rock on which it stands (the city now uses it to park the cars the police tow away). Next to it, hogging the best view in Naples, the Carthusians built their original, modest, monastery of **San Martino**, some time in the early 14th century. Two centuries later, like most Carthusian branch offices, they were rolling embarrassingly in lucre; building the poshest monastery in all Italy was the only thing to do. The rebuilt **Certosa** (charterhouse) is only marginally smaller than Fort St Elmo. Built on the slope of the mountain, it is supported by a gargantuan platform, visible for miles out to sea and probably containing enough stone to construct a small pyramid.

Nobody knows exactly what is in the **Museo Nazionale di San Martino** (*open 9–2 Tues–Sat; 9–1 Sun; adm*), which now occupies the monastery. Intended as a museum specifically of Naples, its history, art and traditions, San Martino suffers from the same mismanagement as the Archaeological Museum; only parts are ever open, and the Grand Cloister, at time of writing, has become a wilderness of weeds and scaffolding. Not that this should discourage you from taking the long ride up the Montesanto Funicular. The views and the architecture are marvellous, and at least they always keep open the collection of *presepi*—what the Neapolitans come here to see (*see* pp.937–8).

Upon entering the complex, the first attraction is the **church**, another of the glories of Neapolitan Baroque, with an excess of lovely coloured inlaid marble to complement the overabundance of painting. The work over the altar, the *Descent from the Cross*, is one of the finest of José Ribera. This tormented artist, often called *Lo Spagnuolo* in Italy, has paintings all over Naples. His popularity does not owe everything to his artistic talent; apparently he formed a little cartel with two local artists, and cornered the market by hiring a gang of thugs to harry all the other painters out of town.

The cloister, the **Chiostro Grande**, even in its present state, is a masterpiece of Baroque, elegantly proportioned and gloriously original in its decoration. Also, thanks to a sculptural scheme by a pious, mad artist named Cosimo Fanzago, it is the creepiest cloister east of Seville. Fanzago (who was also one of the architects of San Martino) gives us eight figures of saints that seem more like vampires in priestly robes and mitres, a perfect background for his little enclosed garden, its wall topped with rows of gleaming marble skulls. Most of the collections are in the halls surrounding the Chiostro Grande—costume, painting, ship models and every sort of curiosity; at the corners are **belvederes** from which to look over Naples (outside the complex, a series of lovely terraced gardens offer a similar view). The *presepi* take up a few large rooms near the entrance.

## West of the Piazza del Plebiscito

The hill called Pizzofalcone rises directly behind the Piazza del Plebiscito; around it was the site of Parthenope, the Greek town that antedated Neapolis and was eventually swallowed up by it (though Neapolitans still like to refer to themselves as Parthenopeans). Parthenope had a little harbour, formed by an island that is now almost completely covered by the ancient, strangely-shaped fortress of the **Castel dell'Ovo**—the one Master Virgil is said to have built balanced on an egg, hence the name. Most of it was really built by Frederick II, and expanded by the Angevins.

There isn't much to see today—though the chapel was once covered with murals by Giotto, of which nothing remains—and most of it is closed to the public, but the Egg Castle has been the scene of many unusual events in Italian history. Long before there was a castle, the island may have been part of the original Greek settlement of Parthenope. Later it contained the villa of the Roman general and philosopher Lucullus, victor over Mithradates in the Pontic Wars; Lucullus curried favour with the people by making his sumptuous gardens, and his famous library, open to the public. In the 5th century AD the villa became a home in exile for Romulus Augustulus, last of the western Roman emperors. The Goths spared him only because of his youth and simple-mindedness, and pensioned him off here. Columns from Lucullus' villa are still to be seen among the castle's famous dungeons.

## Modern Naples: the Villa Comunale

Once past the Egg Castle, a handsome sweep of coastline opens up the districts of **Chiaia** and **Mergellina**, the most pleasant parts of the new city. Here the long, pretty **Villa Comunale**, central Naples' only park, follows the shore. In it, there is an **Aquarium** (*open 9–5 daily; adm*), built by the German naturalist Dr Anton Dohrn in the 1870s, and perhaps the oldest in the world. All the wide variety of fish, octopuses and other marine delicacies here are from the Bay of Naples; depending on the hour of day, you will find them fascinating, or else overwhelmingly appetizing. When the Allied armies marched into town in 1943, the Neapolitans put on a big party for the officers. There being practically nothing decent to eat anywhere in Naples, they cleaned out the aquarium and managed an all-seafood menu. General Mark Clark, the commander, is said to have got the aquarium's prize specimen, a baby manatee, though how they prepared it is not recorded.

Behind the park, on the Riviera di Chiaia, the **Museo Principe di Aragona Pignatelli Cortes** (*open 9–2 Tues–Sat; 9–1 Sun; adm*) will show you more of the same kind of decorative porcelain as at Capodimonte, along with a score of 18th- and 19th-century noble carriages, furniture and art.

If you're still not tired of little smiling figurines, you can plunge deeper into Chiaia to see the greatest collection of all at the Museo Nazionale della Ceramica, also known as the Duca di Martina Museum, but familiar to Neapolitans only as the **Villa Floridiana** (*open 9–2 Tues–Sat; 9–1 Sun; adm*), after the tasteful 18th-century estate it occupies, with one of the loveliest gardens in Naples and one of Italy's great hoards of bric-à-brac. The museum is on Via Cimarosa, near the Funicolare di Chiaia.

## Virgil's Tomb

Beginning a few streets beyond the western end of the Villa Comunale, **Mergellina** is one of the brightest and most popular quarters of Naples, a good place for dinner or a *passeggiata* around the busy Piazza Sannazzaro. Its centre is the **Marina**, where besides small craft there are hydrofoils to Sorrento and the islands in the summer months, and excursion boats which do daily tours of the shore between the Egg Castle and Point Posillipo. From the harbour, Mergellina rises steeply up the surrounding hills; there is a funicular up to the top. On the hillside, between the railway bridge and the tunnel that leads under the hill to Fuorigrotta, there is a Roman funerary monument that tradition has always held to be the **Tomb of Virgil** (*open 9–1 daily*). The poet died in Brindisi in 19 BC, on his way back from a trip to Greece, but Neapolis was a city dear to him—he wrote most of the *Aeneid* here—and the legend may well be true.

Just below it lies the entrance to one of the little-known wonders of the ancient world. The **Crypta Neapolitana**, unfortunately closed at present, is a 606m road tunnel built during the reign of Augustus, to connect Neapolis with Pozzuoli and Baiae, the longest such work the Romans ever attempted.

---

### Shopping

Surprisingly, no one ever thinks of Naples as one of the prime shopping destinations of Italy; this is a mistake, as there are as many pretty and unusual things to be bought here as anywhere else, and usually at lower prices. The back streets around Spaccanapoli and other old sections are still full of artisan workshops of all kinds. The Royal Factory at Capodimonte, founded by the Bourbons, still makes what may be the most beautiful **porcelain and ceramic figures** in Europe, sold at the fancier shops in the city centre. Another old Naples tradition is the making of **cameos** in various materials; you'll see them everywhere, but the shops outside the San Martino monastery have a good selection at relatively low prices.

Via San Biagio dei Librai, the middle of the Spaccanapoli, is as its name implies a street of **booksellers**—some of the best old book dealers in Italy, conveniently near the University—but the street is also full of many more odd surprises for shoppers as well. Many of the religious goods shops have surprisingly good works in terracotta; the **Doll Hospital** at No.81, © 203067, is one of the most charming shops in Naples.

All around the back streets there are antique and junk shops that won't overcharge you unless you let them. The city has an immense twice-monthly antiques market, the **Fiera dell'Antiquariato,** held on alternate Saturday and Sunday mornings in the gardens of the Villa Comunale. You can buy lovely old prints of Naples and beyond at **Bowinkel,** at Piazza dei Martiri 24, ✆ 7644344, and beautiful candles, including some sculpted to depict well-known Italian political and showbusiness personalities, from the **Antica Cereria** at Via C. Doria 6–8, ✆ 5499745. Finally, for the once-in-a-lifetime souvenir, the 150-year-old **Fonderia Chiurazzi,** Via Ponti Rossi 271, ✆ 7512685, makes artistic bronzes, specializing in reproductions of works in the Museo Archeologico; if you have billions of lire to spare, they'll do them life-size, or even bigger.

## Sports and Activities

The best sources of information on forthcoming events of all kinds are the local newspaper *Il Mattino* and the free multi-lingual monthly guide *Qui Napoli.* Many of the city's permanent attractions are concentrated in the Fuorigrotta district, west of Mergellina. **Edenlandia** is the big amusement park there, on Viale Kennedy in the Mostra d'Oltremare, Naples' big trade fair site. There is also a **dog-racing** track and a small but fun **zoo** in the same area.

Nearby on Via Fuorigrotta, just past the tunnel, there's **jai-alai** (Basque Pelota) every night at 8pm. Anything a Neapolitan can bet on flourishes here; the **racetrack,** the *Ippodromo di Agnano,* with both Thoroughbred and trotting races throughout most of the year, is out west in Agnano, 10km from the city centre along the *tangenziale.* And of course there's always **football.** With the help of Diego Armando Maradona, Napoli won its first-ever league title in 1987; since his departure the club has fallen on harder times, but every significant victory still calls forth a spontaneous celebration all over town that seems like Carnival in Rio de Janeiro, and any match is likely to prove an unforgettable experience with the Neapolitans to make up the crowd. Matches are played at the **Stadio San Paolo,** Piazzale Vincenzo Tecchio, ✆ 615623. To get there, take the Ferrovia Cumana to Mostra.

However tempting the sea off Naples might look on a scorching summer day, it's worth waiting until you get to one of the islands before taking a plunge. There is a public **swimming pool,** the **Piscina Scandone,** also in the Fuorigrotta area of town, at Via Giochi del Mediterraneo, ✆ 5709154. **Tennis** can be played at the **Tennis Club Napoli,** Viale Dohrn, ✆ 7614656, in the Villa Comunale, the **Tennis Club Vomero,** Via Rossini 8, ✆ 688912, and the **Sporting Club Virgilio,** Via Tito Lucrezio Caro, ✆ 7695261.

*Naples ✆ (081–)*                                      ## Where to Stay

Naples does have less than its share of top-quality hotels; the Germans, inexplicably, blew up a few of them before their retreat in 1944. Most of the best hotels are along Via Partenope, near the Castel dell'Ovo, a location where the views over the bay more than compensate for the traffic noise below.

★★★★★ **Excelsior**, Via Partenope 48, © 7640111, @ 411743. Visiting sheiks, kings and rock stars favour Naples' finest hotel, with beautiful suites and a tradition of perfect service since 1909, though some of the rooms could do with a bit of sprucing up.

*expensive*

★★★★ **Santa Lucia**, Via Partenope 46, © 7640666, @ 419044. A dozen or so other hotels cluster in the Excelsior's shadow on Via Partenope. Of these, this is the nicest, a beautifully restored 18th-century *palazzo*, with antique paintings and furniture.

★★★★ **Vesuvio**, Via Partenope 45, © 7640044, @ 407520, is another gracious hotel, with an attractive mix of old and new and a lovely roof garden for dining, with a view over the bay of Naples.

★★★★ **Miramare**, Via N. Sauro, © 427388, @ 416775. Still on the seafront, this is a smaller, more intimate hotel, with 31 pleasantly decorated rooms.

★★★★ **Paradiso**, Via Catullo 11, © 7614161, @ 663527, also has stunning views over the bay—make sure you book a sea-facing room.

★★★★ **Parker**, Corso Vittorio Emanuele 135, © 7612474, @ 663527, has a more old-fashioned atmosphere, but further inland—ample charm, with plenty of polished wood, chandeliers and comfortable furniture.

*moderate*

★★★★ **Angioino**, Via De Pretis 123, © 5529500, @ 5529509. One of the most recent arrivals in Naples, owned by the French Mercure hotel chain, offering 86 good-sized rooms in a central location, with efficient service that makes it popular with the business crowd.

★★★ **Rex**, Via Palepoli 12, © 7649227, @ 7649227, is a clean, well-run hotel, also convenient for the centre, with the advantage—essential for drivers—of a garage.

★★★ **Cavour**, Piazza Garibaldi 32, © 283122, @ 287488. In the hotel-packed Piazza Garibaldi area by the station—not the most pleasant place to stay, if you can find somewhere better, such as near the seafront—a reasonable, decent hotel.

★★★ **Canada**, Via Mergellina 43, © 680952, @ 681595, is a good choice near the harbour-side, with 12 rooms, well located in an attractive area near the pretty Mergellina esplanade.

*inexpensive*

★★ **Ausonia**, Via Caracciolo 11, © 682278, is a clean, comfortable *pensione*, with 20 rooms, all with bath, and an excellent position right on the seafront in Mergellina.

★★ **Bella Napoli**, Via Caracciolo 10, © 680200, for a modest walk-up that won't ruin your holiday.

★★ **Fontane al Mare**, Via N. Tommaseo 14, © 7643811, has 21 rooms, some with bath, for similar prices.

★★ **Muller**, Piazza Mergellina 7, © 669056, is slightly set back from the sea, but still a good deal, with 10 rooms, six of them with baths.

★★    **Eden**, Corso Novara 9, ✆ 285344. There are thousands of cheap hotel rooms around the Piazza Garibaldi, but most of them are in horrible dives. This is not the best place to make your base, but if you do desire to stay close to the station this is one reasonably comfortable but still cheap place, with decent though not Edenic rooms, a sleepy bar, and a garage. To find it, turn right as you leave the station, and it's one block up.

★    **Fiore**, Via Milano 109, ✆ 5538798. Among the very cheap places, this Polish-Italian hotel, rumoured to have Naples' fattest cat, is barely acceptable, but good for the area.

★    **Zara**, Via Firenze 81, ✆ 287125, is a bit better, with 10 rooms, six with baths.

Another place to look for cheap accommodation is Via Mezzocannone, south of Spaccanapoli. This street borders the university, and many of the most pleasant cheap lodgings in Naples can be found here—though with so many students it may be hard to find a vacancy. Naples' **youth hostel** is the **Ostello Mergellina**, Salita della Grotta 23, ✆ 7612346, near the Mergellina Metropolitana station. IYHF cards are required.

---

*Naples* ✆ *(081–)*                                                       **Eating Out**

*'Now, everyone thinks of China as a ponderous, elephantine country; Naples, on the other hand we think of as something exciting, stimulating. Perhaps the Chinese invented slow, pacific fat macaronis, not the spaghetti that moves like the waves of the sea . . .'*

Domenico Rea

This local savant, writing in the pages of *Qui Napoli*, is carrying on one of Naples' grand old causes. Forget those old legends about Marco Polo—just imagine anyone brazen enough to say spaghetti doesn't originally come from Naples! This capital of cooking, this citadel of *Italianità*, can already claim pizza, and probably many other Italian specialities as well. Neapolitans spend as much time worrying about what's for dinner as any people in the world, but like most other Italians they have a perfectly healthy attitude towards the subject. Neapolitan cuisine is simple—one of the most celebrated dishes is *spaghetti alle vongole*—and even in some of the more pretentious places you will see favourites of the Neapolitan *cucina povera* sneaking onto the menu, like *pasta e fagioli*. There are very few bad restaurants or tourist restaurants in the city, but an infinity of tiny, family-run *trattorie* or *pizzerie*; you will depart from most of them serene and satisfied.

For famous Neapolitan pizza, look for the genuine Neapolitan pizza oven, a built-in, bell-shaped affair made of stone with a broad, clean tile floor; the fire (only certain kinds of wood will do), is at the back, close to the pizza, not hidden underneath. Watch out in restaurants for the house wines; in cheaper places this is likely to be Gragnano from nearby Monte Faito—detestable rough stuff. On the other hand you can find some real surprises from Campania; a dry white called Greco di Tufo, and

Taurasi, a distinguished red—as well as Falerno, the descendant of the far-famed ancient *Falernian* that Latin poets never tired of praising. Some restaurants in Naples, you will find, are the cheapest in all Italy—as they cheat on their taxes. Others can be alarmingly expensive, especially if you order fish.

### *expensive*

Restaurants in all price ranges are spread pretty evenly around central Naples. **La Cantinella**, Via Nazario Sauro 23, © 404884, near the Castel dell'Ovo, is believed by many to be Naples' finest—also the place to be seen for the Parthenopeans, with a telephone on each table. Known for its four different kinds of risotto, and a dessert called *Millefoglie con Zuppa Inglese*, it certainly isn't cheap, but you can easily spend more in other establishments. At **Ciro**, Via Santa Brigida 71, © 5524072, near the Castel Nuovo, go ahead and order *pasta e fagioli* or any other humble pasta dish; that's what the place is famous for, typical Naples cuisine at its best, and they have been a local favourite for decades. (*Closed Sun.*) **La Sacrestia**, Via Orazio 116, © 641186, run for generations by the Ponsiglione family, is another temple of Neapolitan gastronomy, in a superb location overlooking the Bay of Naples. Try the risotto with baby squid (*risotto con neonati di seppietta*). (*Closed Wed.*)

**Giuseppone a Mare**, Via Ferdinando Russo 13, © 7696002, overlooking Cape Posillipo, is one of Naples' institutions, especially popular with wedding parties. The fish is excellent, the setting memorable, and you probably won't forget the bill either. (*Closed Sun.*) **Don Salvatore**, Via Mergellina 5, © 681817, similarly, has been around for more than 40 years, during which time it has built up a well-deserved reputation for turning out consistently fine Neapolitan dishes, accompanied by some of the area's best wines. There are set menus for those who want an introduction to Naples' best, and pizza for those who want to keep the bill down. (*Closed Wed.*) At **Mimi alla Ferrovia**, Via Alfonso d'Aragona 21, © 5538525, again, you'll find no new-fangled concoctions, just honest-to-goodness dishes based on the freshest ingredients and recipes handed down for generations. For a real blow-out, let the waiters choose for you. You'll be rewarded with a table-groaning succession of antipasti, pasta and *secondi*, all cooked to perfection. (*Closed Sun.*)

### *moderate*

**La Cantina di Triunfo**, Riviera di Chiaia 64, © 668101, offers Neapolitan *cucina povera* raised to an art form—wintry soups of chestnuts and lentils, or lighter versions of broad beans and fresh peas in spring, *polpette di baccalà*—small balls of minced salt-cod, fried or served in a fresh tomato sauce—and mouth-watering pasta dishes, all of which change according to the season. The wine list is also exceptional, and the grappas home-made. Be sure to book, as space is very limited. (*Closed Sun.*) Lively and friendly, **Da Peppino**, Via Palipoli, © 7649582, offers dining in the Santa Lucia area at a fraction of the price charged by some of the smarter restaurants. Don't expect anything too refined, but the pizza, in all its many forms, is a real treat here. (*Closed Sun.*)

The **Osteria Canterbury**, Via Ascensione a Chiaia 6, © 413584, is tastefully decorated, with a warm welcoming atmosphere and a kitchen that turns out consistently good food, especially pasta dishes, including a house speciality, which combines mozzarella, aubergines and *ragù* sauce. At lunchtime, the office crowd comes here for the excellent value set menu. Book for dinner. (*Closed Sun.*) At the **Taverna e Zi Carmela**, Via Niccolò Tommaseo 112, © 7643581, Aunt Carmela runs a busy and well-kept ship, with excellent home cooking, much of it done by herself, and other members of the family waiting at table. (*Closed Sun.*) **O Sole Mio**, Via Tommaso Campanella 7, © 7612323, is run by a fisherman's family, and though you will find some meat on the menu, you will be better advised to go straight for the seafood, in all its many forms. Try the wonderfully tasty *cassuola di pesce*—fish casserole—but tuck your napkin into your collar, Neapolitan-style, before you start! (*Closed Tues.*)

## Pizza Paradise

Its origins are almost certainly Arab. Some people maintain the word may be derived from *pitta*, the unleavened bread eaten throughout Greece, Turkey and the Middle East. But wherever it hails from, pizza as we know it is an invention of Naples. Neapolitans are fiercely proud of this versatile dish, and haughtily disdainful of imitations and the variations made by others on the formula—the thin-crusted affair served in Roman *pizzerie* is enough to make a Neapolitan cry. And as for the deep-pan version invented in Chicago and served up in many British and American pizza parlours—the less said the better.

For Neapolitans, a real pizza must have an uneven base and be cooked in a real wood-fired oven. Some say the secret is in the flour, others in the water. But all agree the technique for flattening the dough is crucial. Not for the Neapolitans the pedantic practice of stretching out the dough with a rolling pin. In Naples, the *pizzaiolo* is a flamboyant character, flinging the dough up into the air, smashing it down on the marble table and swinging it round his head until it reaches the required shape and thickness. The best *pizzaioli* are much in demand, and take home very respectable salaries. As for the topping, the most authentic is *pomodoro fresco*—fresh tomatoes chopped over a bed of mozzarella, sprinkled with fresh basil and liberally doused with olive oil. Another Neapolitan favourite is the *ripieno*, a gut-buster of a pizza folded in two, and stuffed with fresh ricotta, mozzarella, pieces of salami and cooked ham.

However you order it, pizza should really be eaten with beer rather than wine. Many pizzerias only serve fizzy, bottled wine, which is much more expensive and best left alone. Pizza is usually eaten as a meal in itself, sometimes for lunch but more often in the evening, preceded by an antipasto of *bruschetta*—slices of thick toasted bread soused in olive oil and garlic and topped with tomatoes and basil, or fried bite-sized chunks of mozzarella and vegetables. For anyone on a tight budget—Neapolitans and tourists alike—the pizzeria is a lifeline. The bill for a pizza and a beer comes to about half that of a normal restaurant. In Naples, particularly good pizzerias are rewarded by a *vera pizza* (real pizza) emblem to hang up outside. Some of the best are the **Brandi**, the **Lombardi a Santa Chiara** and the exceptional **Da Pasqualino**, now in its fourth generation (for details *see* below).

Pizza is always the best friend of the budget-minded tourist (*see* above), and you can get two superb pizzas and lots of wine for the price of a plate of pasta in some smarter places at **Da Pasqualino**, Piazza Sannazzaro 78/9, © 681524, in Mergellina. If you need cigarettes, shout 'Gennaro!' to the balconies above and they will appear. Don't miss the old granny in the corner, whose job it is to make the superb but calorie-laden *crocchette*—potato croquettes spiked with mozzarella cheese, with which the locals invariably start their meal. (*Closed Tues.*) Nearby, on Via Mergellina, **Tonino il Ragno** is another deservedly popular pizzeria, as is the **Pizzeria Port'Alba**, Via Port'Alba 18, © 459713, where in addition you can get full dinners, including the house speciality, *linguine al cartoccio*—seafood pasta made into a foil parcel and baked in the oven, for a reasonable sum.

Slightly more upmarket, but only slightly, the **Lombardi a Santa Chiara**, Via Benedetto Croce 59, © 5520780, offers memorable *antipasti* of fried courgettes, baby mozzarella and artichokes, before you ever get to eat your pizza, wonderfully cooked in the classic wood oven. Noisy but friendly, this place fills up quickly, so book ahead or be prepared to wait. (*Closed Sun.*) At the **Bellini**, Via Santa Maria di Costantinopoli 80, © 459774, you'll find good pizza and pasta dishes, with a few outdoor tables for summer dining. (*Closed Sun.*) **Brandi**, Salita Sant'Anna di Palazzo 1/2, © 416928, a pretty, lively pizzeria, claims to have invented the *Margherita*, Naples' most famous pizza, with mozzarella, tomatoes and fresh basil, in honour of the Bourbon queen whose favourite dish it apparently was. Whether or not you believe it, the food is always first-class. At **Da Michele**, Via C. Sersale 1, © 5539204, you'll probably find yourself sharing a marble-topped table with a noisy Neapolitan family. This is a decidedly no-frills place, with rough and ready service, but the atmosphere is great fun, the pizza sublime and the prices downright miraculous. (*Closed Sun.*)

Many of the cheapest and homeliest places in Naples can be found on or around Via Speranzella, a block west of Via Toledo in the *Tavoliere*, where few tourists ever penetrate. As for the area around the railway station, restaurants here, more than elsewhere in Naples, have succumbed to opportunity and necessity; Piazza Garibaldi isn't nearly as much fun as it was a few years ago, and its hundreds of restaurants are neither keeping standards up nor prices down. But this area, and also Piazza Mercato, is an open bazaar, and you can get fat and happy just snacking from the bars and stands—slices of pizza, heavy *arancini*, and the flaky pastries called *sfogliatelle*, another Naples speciality.

Finally, we offer you an honest breakfast—bacon and eggs, if you like—at the **Ristorante California**, Via Santa Lucia 101, © 7649752, Italy's greatest rendezvous for homesick Americans and a longtime Naples landmark. For dinner, the menu is split between Italian and Gringo dishes, and the roast turkey isn't bad.

### *cafés and gelaterie*

As well as the inventors of the pizza, Neapolitans are, it is generally recognized, Italy's most dedicated and punctilious coffee consumers, and the city accordingly has its crop of elegant, now often fadedly ornate 19th-century *gran caffè*, mostly not too far from the Galleria and the Piazza del Plebiscito (*see* below). Other fine places to take coffee can be found along the waterfront, particularly out towards Mergellina. Naples also, naturally, produces some great ice cream and pastries. Gelaterie can be found all over town, but Scimmia, Piazza della Carità 4, just off the Via Toledo not far from Spaccanapoli, has for long been regarded as one of the city's best.

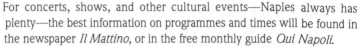

## Entertainment and Nightlife

For concerts, shows, and other cultural events—Naples always has plenty—the best information on programmes and times will be found in the newspaper *Il Mattino*, or in the free monthly guide *Qui Napoli*.

### opera, classical music and theatre

For opera lovers one of the ultimate experiences is a night at the **San Carlo** (box office ✆ 7972370/7972111), but tickets are extremely hard to come by, and very pricey. Hotels may be able to get them most easily. If you do manage to get a ticket, be sure to dress your best.

You may have more luck catching a **concert** at the **Auditorium RAI-TV**, Via Guglielmo Marconi, ✆ 610122, at the **Conservatorio di Musica**, Via San Pietro a Maiella, ✆ 459255, or at the **Associazione Alessandro Scarlatti**, Piazza dei Martiri 58, ✆ 406011. Check with the tourist office or in *Qui Napoli* for programmes, and don't forget also that many, often free concerts are staged in the city's churches. Look out for street billboards with details of coming events.

Unless your Italian is fluent, **theatre** will probably be a frustrating experience, and if you go for one of the superbly executed dialect plays, especially by the **Gruppo Repertorio di Eduardo de Filippo**, Piazza Teatro S. Ferdinando, ✆ 444500, you may not understand a word. If that doesn't put you off, the best theatres are the **Politeama**, Via Monte di Dio, ✆ 7645016, the **Cilea**, Via S. Domenico, ✆ 646830, the **Bracco**, Via Tarsia, ✆ 5495904 and the **Sannazaro**, Via Chiaia 157, ✆ 411723.

### clubs, bars and discos

Neapolitans are night-owls, probably thanks to their Spanish heritage, and many, especially in summer, don't even think about going out to dinner until 10pm. That doesn't leave too much time for partying, once the 2–3-hour eating ritual is over, but there are some reasonable clubs and late-night bars (as well as some terrible ones). The thing to remember is that some areas are best left alone after midnight, most notably the Piazza Garibaldi area near the station, and the so-called *quartieri*, the narrow side streets that run off the Via Toledo. And if the vampish hookers to be seen at every street corner after dark should take your fancy, remember to take a second look—those girls could well be boys. Naples is famous even in drag-obsessed Italy for its transvestites, and some of them are positively remarkable. The genuine female prostitutes tend to be the crones on the other side of the street.

**KGB**, Salita Scudillo, ✆ 7435206, is a discotheque which also puts on live bands, some of them quite good. (*Open 11pm–3am Thurs–Sat only*.) **The Jam Club**, Via

G. Martucci 85/7, ℰ 7614864, is aimed at a 30-plus age group, which makes it a pleasant place for a late-night drink. (*Open 8.30pm–4.30am; closed Mon.*) The barman is a dab hand with cocktails, there is live music played every night, and on Fridays pasta is offered on the house. The **Kiss Kiss**, Via Sgambati 47, ℰ 5466566, Naples' biggest disco, is an institution, with different theme nights every night of the week, and an affluent young crowd. **My Way**, Via Cappella Vecchia 30/c, ℰ 7644735, is another popular nightspot, where Neapolitans have been dancing into the small hours for as long as anyone can remember. (*Open 10pm–4am Fri–Sun only.*)

At the **Otto Club**, Piazzetta Cariati 24, ℰ 666262, you'll get **jazz** and plenty of it, including some very talented local musicians. It also serves plates of pasta and light meals, and has a well-stocked bar, but don't take too much cash with you, as this otherwise very pleasant club is in a pretty hard area, and when you leave it's best to get a taxi rather than walk around much outside. (*Closed Mon.*) The **Virgilio Sporting Club**, Via Tito Lucrezio Caro 6, ℰ 7695261 (*open midnight–4am Fri–Sun only*), up on Posillipo hill, is a much more tranquil nightclub, set in its own parkland, with tables outside in fine weather.

## Around the Bay: from Baia to Sorrento

Naples' hinterlands share fully in the peculiarities and sharp contrasts of the big city. Creation left nothing half-done or poorly done; against any other part of the monotonous Italian coastline, the Campanian shore seems almost indecently blessed, possessing the kind of irresistibly distracting beauty that seduces history off the path of duty and virtue. Today, for all the troubles that come seeping out of Naples, this coast is still one of the capitals of Mediterranean languor.

In Roman days, it was nothing less than the California of the ancient world: fantastically prosperous, lined with glittering resort towns full of refugees from the Roman rat-race, as favoured by artists and poets as it was by rich patricians. Like California, though, the perfume was mixed with a little whiff of insecurity. Vesuvius would be enough, but even outside of the regularly scheduled eruptions and earthquakes, the region is Vulcan's own curiosity shop. West of Naples especially, there are eternally rising and sinking landscapes, sulphurous pools, thermal springs and even a baby volcano—altogether, perhaps the most unstable corner of the broad earth's crust.

### Getting Around the Bay of Naples

Naples, of course, is the hub for all transport throughout the area; buses, ferries and local commuter rail lines lead out from the city to all points.

#### by boat to the islands

In summer, there are as many as six ferries and 20 hydrofoils a day from Naples to Capri, and as many to Ischia. There are also regular departures to Procida. In addition, there are a few ferries and hydrofoils daily from Sorrento to Capri, from Pozzuoli to Procida and between the islands of Ischia and Procida. All are very short rides. For more information on long-distance ferry services from Naples, see above, under 'Naples', p.929.

Local and longer-distance ferries and hydrofoils from Naples leave from three different points along the harbourside—**Molo Beverello** and the **Stazione Marittima**, both in the centre of the port, and **Mergellina**, further to the west. Be sure to check you know the right dock for your ticket and destination. Listed here are the principal ferry and hydrofoil operators; check with them for timetables, or look in the daily newspaper *Il Mattino*.

From **Molo Beverello: Caremar**, ✆ 5513882, for Capri, Ischia and Procida; **Navigazione Libera del Golfo**, ✆ 5527209, for Capri; **Linee Lauro**, ✆ 5522838, for Ischia; and **Alilauro**, ✆ 5522838, for Sorrento.

From the **Stazione Marittima** (used by ferries only): **Tirrenia**, ✆ 7613688, for Palermo, Cagliari, Reggio Calabria and Malta; **Siremar**, ✆ 7613688, for the Aeolian Islands; and **Lauro**, ✆ 5513352, for Corsica.

From **Mergellina** (hydrofoils): **Alilauro**, ✆ 7611004, for Ischia and Sorrento; and **SNAV**, ✆ 7612348, for Capri, Ischia, Procida, and the Aeolian Islands.

In addition, from Salerno there is a boat called the *Faraglione* that offers a different way of seeing the Amalfi coast, a daily ferry that hugs the shore to Capri, stopping at Amalfi and Positano along the way. It leaves Salerno at 7.30pm each day from Molo Manfredi, at the western end of town, and does not run between 15th October and 6th January.

### by rail

Regular FS trains aren't much help here, except for a fast trip between Naples and Salerno. Fortunately, there are the other, local, lines, of which the most important is the refreshingly clean and efficient **Circumvesuviana**, the best way to reach Pompeii, Herculaneum and Sorrento. This line has its own ultramodern station, on Corso Garibaldi just south of the Piazza Garibaldi (✆ 7792444), but all of its trains also make a stop at the Stazione Centrale itself before proceeding east. At Centrale their station is underground, sharing space with that of the Naples Metropolitana; this can be confusing, since there are no schedules posted and the ticket windows aren't marked—you need to ask someone to make sure you are heading for the right train. The main lines run east through Ercolano (the stop for Herculaneum) and Torre del Greco, and then diverge near Torre Annunziata, one line heading for Sarno, out in the farm country east of Vesuvius, and the other for Sorrento. Both pass Pompeii, though on opposite sides. The Sorrento train leaves you near the main entrance; on the other line the stop at Villa dei Misteri is closest. The Circumvesuviana terminal in Sorrento is two streets east from Piazza Tasso, the town centre. Circumvesuviana trains usually run every half-hour between 5am and 10.45pm. On a *direttissima*, of which there are several daily, the Naples–Sorrento trip takes an hour—locals are considerably slower. An additional Circumvesuviana line has infrequent trains north of Vesuvius to Nola and Baiano.

For the west bay, Naples' own **Metropolitana** goes as far as Pozzuoli-Solfatara. The two other regional lines both have trains about every half-hour from Piazza

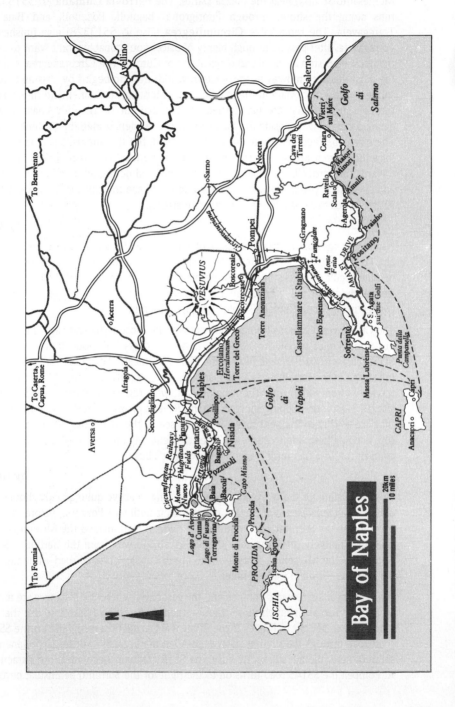

Bay of Naples

Montesanto Station, near the Piazza Dante. The **Ferrovia Cumana** (© 5513328) runs along the shore, through Fuorigrotta, Bagnoli, Pozzuoli, and Baia to Torregaveta. The remarkable **Circumflegrea** (also © 5513328) also finishes at Torregaveta, after passing through plenty of places you probably won't want to visit, though it does stop at the archaeological site of Cumae. The Circumflegrea is easily the most macabre railway in the western world; the trip begins by passing a neon shrine to the Virgin Mary in the middle of the Montesanto Tunnel, and then passes through stations that are metal sheds or bombed-out ruins, with smashed and derailed cars lying alongside the tracks to give passengers something to think about. There are no schedules printed or even imagined, but the line usually closes down for a long lunch break. The station at Cumae is gutted and abandoned; head up towards the acropolis, through the thorn bushes and dense, adder-haunted forests, and eventually you'll sneak in the back and get to see the ruins of Cumae for free (there's a bus from Baia to the front gate for sissies).

### by bus

Naples city bus no.152, from Piazza Garibaldi and Via Mergellina, travels to Solfatara and Pozzuoli. Other buses run by the local transport authorities of Baia and Bacoli operate regular services from these towns along the coast road to Naples. All stop frequently along the way. From the bus stop in the centre of Baia, there are connecting buses to Cumae, Bacoli, and Cape Misenum.

The Circumvesuviana makes buses unnecessary for most of the east bay. The express bus from Naples to Salerno, which usually runs every half hour, leaves from the **SITA** office on Via Pisanelli, just off the Piazza Municipio (© 5522176), and arrives in Salerno at the terminal at Corso Garibaldi 117, © (089) 226604. SITA also runs the buses from Salerno for the Amalfi coast, with regular departures for Sorrento (Piazza Tasso), or stopping short at Amalfi, Ravello or other towns along the route; they are usually so frequent that it is easy to see all the main coast towns on a day-trip, hopping from one to the next. Buses are definitely the best way to do it; driving yourself can be a hair-raising experience when it's busy.

### by road

Drivers heading for the west bay area and wishing to arrive quite quickly should get onto the *tangenziale* out of Naples and stay on it until past Pozzuoli, before turning off onto the (by then) more tranquil SS7qu, which runs around the Miseno peninsula. Alternatively, they can take the SS7qu all the way from the harbourside in Naples, via the Mergellina tunnel, or the pretty but slow coastal road—initially the Via Posillipo—around Cape Posillipo.

If you are heading towards Pompeii and the east bay—where the distances are much greater, and so a car much more useful—then, again, it's advisable to use the A3 *autostrada* to get out of Naples if you don't want to spend a long time on the SS18 coast road through the suburbs. Leave the A3 at the Ercolano exit for Herculaneum; south of here, though still pretty busy, the SS18 gradually becomes more attractive. At Pompeii the SS145 road turns off to the right for the Sorrento peninsula; beyond

Sorrento it becomes the famous, or infamous, **Amalfi drive**. This spectacular road—at its most extreme, no more than a winding ledge of hairpins half way up a sheer cliff—is unquestionably worth seeing, but drivers should be aware of what is ahead of them, and avoid it at night or in bad weather. For some idea of the difficulties of the road, consider that it takes the express bus almost three hours to navigate the 66km from Salerno to Sorrento.

## Shopping around the Bay of Naples

The town of **Torre del Greco** has for centuries been making fine jewellery out of the coral its fishermen bring home from the bay. You'll see it everywhere in Naples, but at the shops around the harbour in Torre del Greco itself it is much cheaper. **Amalfi**'s specialities are fine stationery (papermaking was already an art, and an important industry, here in the Middle Ages), and ceramics—mostly tourist bric-à-brac, but some of it very well done. You can tour one of the workshops: **Giovanni Fusco**, on Via della Cantiere behind the cliffs at the edge of town.

Every conceivable luxury item Italy makes is sold in the shops of **Sorrento**—but make sure you come in the off-season (December or January are best) when you'll find some outstanding bargains in fashions, Murano glass and other trinkets. Sorrento's own speciality is *intarsia*, inlaid wood scenes on tables or trays, or simply framed for hanging. They are exquisite things, and prices are often reasonable: from L25,000 in the off-season. **Da Nicola** on Strada Tasso has some of the best work, with **Ferdinando Corcione** on Piazza Gargiulo not far behind.

# West from Naples: Pozzuoli and the Phlegraean Fields

The very pretty coastal road leaving the city, with views of Vesuvius all through the suburb of Posillipo, passes the little island of Nisida; this was a favoured spot in ancient times, and legend has it that Brutus and Cassius planned Caesar's murder here in the villa of one of their fellow conspirators. Naples' suburbs continue through **Agnano**, a town of spas and hot springs set around a mile-wide extinct crater, and stretch as far as **Pozzuoli**.

Pozzuoli today is a modest little city, with only its ruins to remind it of the time when Roman *Puteoli*, and not Naples, was the metropolis of the bay. The **amphitheatre**, on Via Domiziana, near the railway station, was the third-largest in the Roman world (after those in Rome itself, and Capua), with 60 gates for letting the beasts in, and pipes to flood it for mock naval battles. Pozzuoli's other important ruin is a little embarrassment to the town; for centuries people here were showing off the ancient **serapeum**—temple to the popular Egyptian god Serapis—until some killjoy archaeologist proved the thing to be an unusually lavish *macellum*, or market. Only the foundations remain, in a park near Pozzuoli's small harbour, and they are usually underwater, but it was an important tourist sight in the days of the Grand Tour, before the Bourbons stole all the columns for their dreary palace at Caserta.

For all ancient Puteoli's size and wealth, little else remains. There is a reason, and Pozzuoli would like to introduce a new word to your vocabulary to explain it: *bradyseism* is a rare seismic phenomenon that afflicts this town and other spots around the bay. It manifests itself in the form of 'slow' earthquakes; no one notices them, but the level of the land can rise or fall several feet in a few months. Mostly, it has been falling, and all of Puteoli that hasn't been gently shaken to pieces over the centuries is now underwater. Roman moles and docks can still sometimes be made out beneath the surface.

## Solfatara

What's troubling Pozzuoli can be seen more clearly just outside the town at **Solfatara**, the storm centre of what the Greeks called the Phlegraean (fiery) Fields, in Italian the *Campi Flegrei*. To the Romans, it was the *Forum Vulcani*, and a major attraction of the Campanian coast. It hasn't changed much since. Solfatara (*open 9am–sunset daily; adm*) is another crater of a collapsed volcano, but one that just can't be still; sulphur gas vents, bubbling mud pits and whistling superheated steam fumaroles decorate the eerie landscape. Guides are around to keep you away from the dangerous spots. Their favourite trick is to hold a flame to one of the gas vents—making a dozen others nearby go off at the same time. Solfatara is perfectly safe, even though the ground underneath feels hot and sounds strangely hollow. It is; scientists keep a close watch on the huge plug of cooled lava that underlies the whole of the area about Pozzuoli, and they say the pressure on it from below is only one-third as much as it was under Vesuvius in AD 79.

We promised you a baby volcano, and you'll see it near the coast west of Pozzuoli. **Monte Nuovo** has been quiet for some time (inexplicably passing up the opportunity to celebrate its 450th birthday, on 29th September 1988). The same earthquake in 1538 that wrecked much of Pozzuoli gave birth to this little cone. It's only about 140m tall, and so it's an easy climb up to the crater. Its percolation from the bowels of Campania filled up half of the **Lago di Lucrino**, separated from the sea by a narrow strip of land. Since antiquity, it has been renowned for its oysters.

## Cape Misenum

**Baia**, the next town along the coast, was the greatest pleasure dome of classical antiquity. Anybody who was anybody in the Roman world had a villa here, with a view of the sea, beach access, and a few hundred slaves to dust the statues and clean up after the orgies. You'll find little hint of that today; Goths, malaria and earthquakes have done a thorough job of wrecking the place. Most of ancient *Baiae* is now underwater, a victim of the same brady-seism that afflicts Pozzuoli. Modern Baia is a pleasant small town, but its lovely bay has been consigned to use as a graveyard for dead freighters. Nevertheless, the humble remains of the imperial villa can be visited at the **Parco Archeologico** (*open 9–7 Tues–Sun; adm*).

At Baia, the coast curves southwards towards Bacoli and **Cape Misenum** (*Capo Miseno*), a beautiful spot that for centuries was the greatest naval base of the Roman Empire. As at Baia, foundations and bits of columns and cornices are everywhere, though nothing of any real interest has survived intact. Nearby Lake Miseno, also called the 'Dead Sea', was once a part of the base, joined to the sea by a canal.

Two other lakes, both created as a by-product of volcanic action, lie north of Cape Misenum; one, the **Lago di Fusaro**, is a large, shallow oyster farm, cut off from the sea by a sand bar near the woebegone fishing village of Torregaveta, the terminus of the Circumflegrea and Cumana railways. The decaying rococo palace on an island in the centre is the Casino, built in 1782 by the Bourbon kings' favourite architect, Luigi Vanvitelli. **Lago d'Averno**—Lake

Avernus—may ring a bell from your school days; it's the mouth of Hell, according to the ancient Greeks, who believed any passing bird would be suffocated by the infernal fumes rising from it. Agrippa, Augustus' great general, hadn't much respect for mythology, and turned the lake into a part of the naval base by cutting another canal. Among the ruins that surround it are the remains of a domed building, perhaps a sort of spa, originally as big as the Pantheon in Rome.

## Cumae

As the story has it, King Tarquin of Rome came here, to the most venerable and respected oracle in all the western Mediterranean, with the intention of purchasing nine prophetic books from the Cumaean Sibyl. Unwisely, he said they were too dear, whereupon the Sibyl threw three of the books into the fire and offered him the remaining six at the same price. Again he complained, and the Sibyl put three more in the flames; finally Tarquin gave up, and took the last three at the original price. It was a good bargain. The Sibylline Books guided Rome's destiny until they too were burned up in the great fire of 82 BC.

Cumae had other distinctions. As the first Greek foundation in Italy, the city was the mother colony for Naples and many other cities of Magna Graecia. In 421 BC, Cumae lost its independence to the Samnites, and declined steadily from then on; Arab raiders, who did so much damage everywhere else around Campania, finally wiped the city off the map in the 9th century AD. They did a good job of it, and there is little to see at the site (*open 9–7 Tues–Sun; adm*), only the foundations of a few temples on the high **acropolis**, worth the climb for the views around Cape Misenum.

Just below the summit, you may visit the **Cave of the Cumaean Sibyl** itself, discovered by accident in 1932. This is a place of mystery, a long series of strange, trapezoidal galleries cut out of solid rock—impressive enough, even stripped of the sumptuous decoration they must once have had (all ancient oracles were marvellously profitable). Nobody has a clear idea how old it is; Cumae may well have been a religious centre long before the Greek colonists arrived. By classical times, it took the form of an oracle quite like the one at Delphi. At the far end of the cave, a plain alcove with two benches marks the spot where the Sibyls would inhale fumes over the sacred tripod, chew laurel leaves, and go into their trance.

---

### *Eating Out*

Nobody has made the western side of the bay a base for their holiday since the 4th century AD. But, if you're out looking over the ruins at Pozzuoli, Baia and Cumae, there are a few good places to have lunch.

#### Pozzuoli

On the harbour in Pozzuoli, the **Martusciello**, Via Emporio 24, © 5261702 (moderate) is one of the best places for fish you'll find anywhere—*zuppa di pesce, risotto al pescatore* and grilled sea bass are all excellent. **Del Capitano**, Via Lungomare C. Colombo 10, © 5262283 (moderate) is another good rendezvous for fish-lovers. Slightly more expensive, but worth the extra, is **La Lanterna**, Via C. Colombo 20, © 5263081 (moderate/expensive), a small ristorante on the port, especially attractive in the evening, where chef Giancarlo Schettini produces more refined variations on the usual seafood theme. The menu changes regularly, according to season (*Closed Mon.*)

At **La Granzeola**, Via Terracciano 1, ✆ 5262777 (expensive), owner-chef Carmine Russo turns fish bought directly off the local boats into a dazzling array of unusual and tasty dishes, especially with pasta. Try the *rigatoni con ragù di cozze*—short pasta with a delicious mussel sauce. (*Closed Sun.*) **Il Tempio**, Via Serapide 13, ✆ 8665179 (moderate), overlooking the ruined temple in Pozzuoli's main square, is justly famous for its antipasti. Leave it to the waiter and he will bring you plate after plate, mostly fish-based, including octopus, fried squid, baby red mullet, clams and giant prawns, until you tell him to stop. Many people call it a day after this, and few ever get beyond the *primi*. (*Closed Wed.*)

### Baia and Bacoli

At Baia's **L'Altro Cucchiaro**, Via Lucullo 13, ✆ 8687196 (expensive) you can dine on divine concoctions of seafood and pasta, and superb fish. (*Closed Sun evenings, Mon, 3 weeks Aug.*) Another member of the same family runs the nearby **Franco Cucchiaro**, Via Lucullo 6, ✆ 8687673 (moderate), where you can feast on a fabulous *linguine alle zucchine*, and not just fish, but also fine lamb, rabbit and veal dishes as well. At **La Ninfea**, Via Lago Lucrino, ✆ 8661326 (expensive) you can bask on the lakeside terrace as you dine on fish and grilled meats.

In Bacoli, two good fish restaurants are the **Giardino degli Aranci**, Via Cuma 75, ✆ 8543120, and the **Villa Chiara**, Via Torre di Cappella 8, ✆ 8687139 (both moderate).

### Torregaveta

Restaurants in shabbyish Torregaveta are cheaper than in the towns inside the bay. The **Pizzeria Ristorante Al Pontile**, Via Stiagi 123, ✆ 8689180 (inexpensive) has pizzas and full dinners for reasonable prices. So too does the **Anfiteatro Cumano**, ✆ 854 3119 (inexpensive), with a nice seafront terrace, in nearby Lido Fusaro. (*Open summer only.*)

## East of Naples: Mount Vesuvius and Pompeii

Despite its fearsome reputation, and its formidable appearance looming over Naples, **Mount Vesuvius** is a midget as volcanoes go—only 1281m. No one suspected it even was a volcano, in fact, until it surprised the people of Pompeii, Herculaneum, and Stabiae on 24 August, AD 79. That titanic eruption did not include much lava, but it buried Herculaneum under mud and the other two cities under cinders and ash, while coating most of Italy with a thin layer of dust. Over a hundred eruptions since have destroyed various towns and villages, some more than once. But just as at Mount Etna in Sicily, people just can't stay away from Vesuvius' slopes. Volcanic soil grows grapes and olives in abundance, though the novelty of it often makes the Italians exaggerate their quality. The AD 79 explosion hasn't been equalled since; it blew the top of the mountain clean off, leaving two peaks, with the main fissure in between. The lower one is called Monte Somma, or *nasone*—'big nose'—by the Neapolitans; the higher, parallel peak is Vesuvius proper.

Vesuvius was last heard from in 1944. The final eruption left the lava flows you'll see on the upper slopes; it also sealed the main fissure, putting an end to the permanent plume of smoke that once was such a familiar landmark. You can bet the scientists are watching Vesuvius. Despite the long hiatus, they say there is no reason to expect another eruption soon, though if it were to explode now, they warn, it would cause a catastrophe—the area around the volcano has become one of the most densely populated in all Italy. To visit the main crater (between the two peaks), take the Vesuvius bus from the Circumvesuviana stop in Ercolano; then you have a choice of a stiff, one-hour climb over rough stones and ash, or a ride on the cable car (*cars run April–Sept 10–5.30 daily; Oct 10–4 daily; Dec–Mar 10.30–3.30 daily; closed Nov; tickets cost L7,600 for round trip, and guide at the top*).

*Il Vesuvo*

### Tourist Information

There is a well-organized tourist office in Pompei town, at Via Sacra 1, ✆ (081) 8507255, ✉ 8632401, which has a branch office near the Porta Marina entrance to the old Pompeii site.

## Herculaneum

Naples' discouraging industrial sprawl spreads eastwards as far as Torre del Greco without a break. The drab suburb of **Ercolano** is a part of it, built over the mass of rock that imprisons ancient **Herculaneum**, a smaller and less famous sight than Pompeii but just as much worth visiting (*open 9am–one hour before sunset daily; adm*). Some people like it even better than its more famous sister site.

Unlike Pompeii, an important commercial centre, Herculaneum seems to have been a wealthy resort, only about one-third the size. Also, Vesuvius destroyed them in different ways. Pompeii was buried under layers of ash, while Herculaneum, much closer to the volcano, drowned under a sea of mud. Over time the mud hardened to a soft stone, preserving the city and nearly everything in it as a sort of fossil—furniture, clothing and even some of the goods in the shops have survived.

Like Pompeii, Herculaneum was discovered by accident. In the early 1700s, a Bourbon officer named Prince Elbeuf had a well dug here; not too far down, the workmen struck a stone pavement the stage of the city's theatre. The Bourbon government began some old-fashioned destructive excavation, but serious archaeological work began only under

Mussolini. Only about eight blocks of shops and villas, some quite fashionable, have been excavated. The rest is covered not only by tens of metres of rock, but also a dense modern neighbourhood; bringing more of Herculaneum to light is a fantastically slow and expensive operation, but new digs are still going on.

At any given time, most of the buildings will be locked, but the guards wandering about have all the keys and will show you almost any of them upon request (they are not supposed to accept tips, though you'll find they often seem to expect them). Many of the most interesting houses can be found along Cardo IV, the street in the centre of the excavated area; on the corner of the Decumanus Inferior, the **House of the Wooden Partition** may be the best example we have of the façade of a Roman house. Next door, the **Trellis House** was a much more modest dwelling, with a built-in workshop; the **House of the Mosaic Atrium**, down the street, is another luxurious villa, built with a mind to the sea view from the bedrooms upstairs. On the other side of the Decumanus, Cardo IV passes the **Samnite House** (so named because of its architectural style), and further up a column with police notices painted on it stands near the **House of the Neptune**, with a lovely mythological mosaic in the atrium.

Other buildings worth a visit are the **House of the Deer**, with its infamous statue of a drunken Hercules relieving himself; the well-preserved **Baths**; and the **Palaestra**, or gym, with its unusual serpent fountain and elegant, cross-shaped swimming pool.

Beyond Ercolano, the coastal road passes through three sorry towns. The men of **Torre del Greco** have long been famous for gathering and working coral, a business now threatened by pollution. These days, much of the coral is imported from Asia, though it is still worked locally. Torre del Greco has recently become more famous for organized crime and gangland killings, though the population still turn out en masse to express their devotion to the Madonna in the procession for the Immaculate Conception, on 8 December, when the town gives thanks for having been spared in one the last century's eruptions of Vesuvius (*see* also above, 'The *Feste* of Campania', p.922). In **Torre Annunziata** they make lots of pasta, and in **Castellammare di Stabia**, beneath a 12th-century Hohenstaufen castle, are the modern shipyards of the Italian Navy. Roman *Stabiae* was the port of Pompeii, and the other big town destroyed by Vesuvius, but it has never been excavated. From Castellammare, you can take a short ride on the funicular railway up to **Monte Faito**, a broad, heavily forested mountain that may well be the last really tranquil spot on the Bay—though a few hotels have already appeared.

## Pompeii

Herculaneum may have been better preserved, but to see an entire ancient city come to life, the only place on earth you can go is this magic time capsule, left to us by the good graces of Mount Vesuvius. Pompeii is no mere ruin; walking down the old Roman high street, you can peek into the shops, read the graffiti on the walls, then wander off down the back streets to explore the homes of the inhabitants and appraise their taste in painting—they won't mind a bit if you do. Almost everything we know for sure concerning the daily life of the ancients was learned here, and the huge mass of artefacts and art dug up over 200 years is still helping scholars to re-evaluate the Roman world.

Though a fair-sized city by Roman standards, with a population of some 20,000, Pompeii was probably only the third or fourth city of Campania, a trading and manufacturing centre of no special distinction. Founded perhaps in the 7th century BC, the city came under the Roman sphere of influence around 200; by the fateful year of AD 79, it was still a cosmopolitan place, culturally more Greek than Roman. Vesuvius' rumblings, and the tall, sinister-looking cloud that began to form above it, gave those Pompeiians with any presence of mind a chance to leave. Only about 10 per cent of the population perished.

After the city was buried under the stones and ash of the eruption, the upper floors still stuck out; these were looted, and gradually cleared by farmers, and eventually the city was forgotten altogether. Engineers found it while digging an aqueduct in 1600, and the first excavations began in 1748—a four-star attraction for northern Europeans on the Grand Tour. The early digs were far from scientific; archaeologists today sniff that they did more damage than Vesuvius. Resurrected Pompeii has had other problems: theft of artworks, a good dose of bombs in the Second World War, and most recently the earthquake of 1980. The damage from that is still being repaired today, though almost all the buildings are once more open to visitors (*site open 9am–one hour before sunset Tues–Sun; adm*).

There are two ways to see Pompeii; spend two or three hours on the main sights, or devote the day to scrutinizing details, for a total immersion in the ancient world you won't find anywhere else like it (the detailed guidebooks sold in the stands outside will help you with this). The arrangement is the same as at Herculaneum, and you'll need to ask the guards (or follow a tour group) to get into most of the buildings. Guards will discreetly extort large or small sums from you; this is Naples, after all.

Pompeii isn't quite a perfect time capsule; a little background will help to complete the picture. The site today is all too serene, with a small-town air. Remember that almost every building was two or three storeys high, and that most streets of a Roman town were permanent market-places. As long as daylight lasted, Pompeii's would have been crowded with improvised *bancarelle*; any chariot or wagon driver who wished to pass would need all manner of creative cursing. At least the streets are well-paved—better than Rome itself in fact; Campania's cities, the richest in western Europe, could well afford such luxuries. All the pavements were much more smooth and even than you see them now. The purpose of the flat stones laid across the streets should not be hard to guess. They were places to cross when it rained—streets here were also drains—and the slots in them allowed wagon wheels to pass.

*Pompeii*

The shops, open to the street in the day, would be sealed up behind shutters at night, just as they are in the old parts of Mediterranean cities today. Houses, on the other hand, turn a completely blank wall to the street; they got their light and air from skylights in the *atrium*, the roofed court around which the rooms were arranged. Later, fancier villas will have a second, open court directly behind the first, designed after the Greek *peristyle*. As in Rome, no part of town was necessarily the fashionable district; elegant villas will be found anywhere, often between two simple workmen's flats. And don't take the street names too seriously. They were bestowed by the archaeologists, often, as with the Via di Mercurio (Mercury Street), after mythological subjects depicted on the street fountains.

## Around the Forum

Past the throng of hawkers and refreshment stands, the main entrance to the site takes you through the walls at the **Porta Marina**. Just inside the gate, the **Antiquarium** displays some of the artworks that haven't been spirited off to the Naples museum, as well as some truly gruesome casts of fossilized victims of the eruption, caught in their death poses. Two blocks beyond the Antiquarium and you're in the **Forum**, orientated towards a view of Vesuvius. Unfortunately this is the worst-preserved part of town. Here you can see the tribune from which orators addressed public meetings, and the pedestals that held statues of heroes and civic benefactors, as well as the once-imposing **Basilica** (the law courts), temples to Apollo and Jupiter, and, among other buildings, a public latrine and a **Macellum**, or market, decorated with frescoes.

## Down Mercury Street

Heading for Pompeii's old East End, there are several interesting houses along the Via di Mercurio, including a **Temple of Fortune** on the corner of Via di Nola. The real attractions in this part of town, though, are a few lavish villas off on the side streets: the enormous **House of Pansa**; the **House of the Faun**, with the oldest known welcome mat (set in the pavement, really); and the wonderful **House of the Vetii**, owned by a pair of wealthy brothers who were oil and wine merchants. Here are several rooms of excellent, well-preserved paintings of mythological scenes, but the guards will be whispering in your ear (if you are male) to show you the little niche off the entrance with the picture of Priapus. This over-endowed sport, in legend the son of Venus and Adonis, together with a couple of wall paintings along the lines of the Kamasutra, has managed to make Pompeii something more than a respectable tourist trap. There are quite a few paintings of Priapus showing it off in the houses of Pompeii, besides the phallic images that adorn bakers' ovens, wine shops, and almost every other establishment in town.

The Pompeiians would be terribly embarrassed, however, if they knew what you are thinking. They were a libidinous lot, like anyone else fortunate enough to live on the Campanian coast during recorded history, but the omnipresent phalluses were never meant as decoration. Almost always they are found close to the entrances, where their job was to ward off the evil eye. This use of phallic symbols against evil probably dates from the earliest times in southern Italy; the horn-shaped amulets that millions of people wear around their necks today are their direct descendants. Even so, not so long ago, women visiting Pompeii were not allowed to set eyes on the various erotic images around the site, and were obliged by the guides to wait chastely outside while their male companions went in for a peek.

The nearby Via di Nola, one of Pompeii's main streets, leads to the north. It passes the **Central Baths**, a new construction that was not yet completed when Vesuvius went off, and the **House of Marcus Fronto**, with more good paintings and a reconstructed roof.

## The 'New Excavations'

Beginning in 1911, the archaeologists cleared a vast area of western Pompeii, around what was probably the most important thoroughfare of the city, now called the Via dell'Abbondanza. Three blocks west of the Forum, this street leads to the Via dei Teatri and the **Triangular Forum**, bordering the southern walls. Two **Theatres** here are worth a visit, a large open one seating 5000, and a smaller, covered one that was used for concerts.

The big quadrangle, originally a lobby for the theatres, seems to have been converted at one point into a gladiators' barracks. This is only one of the disconcerting things you will find on the streets of Pompeii. The ruined temple in the Triangular Forum was already long ruined in AD 79, and scholars who study the art of the city find the last (fourth) period to betray a growing lack of skill and coarseness of spirit—altogether, there are plenty of clues that 1st-century Pompeii had its share of urban problems and cultural malaise.

## The Via dell'Abbondanza

Next to the theatres, a small **Temple of Isis** testifies to the religious diversity of Pompeii; elsewhere around town there is graffiti satirizing that new and troublesome cult, the Christians. Three blocks north, there is a stretch of Via dell'Abbondanza that is one of the most fascinating corners of Pompeii. Among its shops are a smith's, a grocers, a weaver's, a laundry, and a typical Roman tavern with its modest walk-up brothel. The most common are those with built-in tubs facing the street—shops that sold wine, and oil for cooking and for lamps. Notices painted on the walls announce coming games at the amphitheatre, or recommend candidates for public office.

Some of the best-decorated villas in this neighbourhood are to be found along the side streets: the **House of Loreius**, the **House of Amandus**, and an odd underground chamber called the **Cryptoporticus**. Pompeii's two most impressive structures occupy a corner just within the walls: the **Palaestra**, a big colonnaded exercise yard, and the **Amphitheatre**, the best-preserved in Italy, with seats for two-thirds of Pompeii's population.

Not all of Pompeii's attractions are within the walls. If you have the time, it would be worth visiting the tombs and suburban villas around the **Via delle Tombe**. One, the famous **Villa dei Misteri**, is thought to have been used as a place of initiation in the forbidden Bacchic (or Dionysiac) Mysteries, one of the cults most feared by the Roman Senate, and later by the emperors. Scenes from the myth of Dionysus and of the rituals are painted on the walls.

The town of Pompei (the modern town has one 'i'), an important pilgrimage centre, is also worth a visit, if nothing else for a look at the wonderfully overdone church, dedicated to the **Madonna di Pompei**, who holds a special place in the affections of Neapolitan women. You'll probably see some of them, busily saying their rosaries, asking for the Madonna's intercession to help sort out their problems. If they have bare feet, this is not poverty, but devotion—usually the fulfilment of a personal pledge to the Madonna in thanks for a favour received. Neapolitans who ask for the Madonna's help often promise to walk there barefoot from Naples (26km) if their prayers are answered.

## *Ercolano/Pompei* ℰ *(081–)*

One, perhaps chancy place for you to base yourself would be the **★★Eremo**, ℰ 7779749 (inexpensive/moderate), above Ercolano on the very slopes of Vesuvius—an isolated spot, but there is a bar and restaurant on the premises. Out of reach of possible lava flows, the best resort hotel up on Monte Faito is the **★★★★Grand Hotel Monte Faito**, ℰ 8793134, ℰ 8793166 (expensive), with gardens and a pool in a lovely setting close to the funicular; not really Grand, but still a relative bargain.

As a place of pilgrimage, Pompei is well supplied with hotels, mostly inexpensive pensiones on or around Via Roma. A little fancier is the **★★★Rosario**, also on Via Roma, ℰ 8630624 (moderate), a serene, older hotel with a garage and pleasant rooms . Also reasonable is the **★★★Bristol**, Piazza V. Veneto 1/3, ℰ 8503005, ℰ 8631625 (moderate).

## *Ercolano/Pompei* ℰ *(081–)*

Restaurants in Pompei have a captive market in visitors to the ruins, and it is true that some of them see the tourists as easy marks. You can choose for yourself among the ubiquitous multilingual menus, or try one of these if you're in the mood for a treat—**Zi Caterina**, Via Roma 16, ℰ 8507447, with live lobsters in the tank and other seafood dishes, is also a good place to try Lacrima Cristi wine from the nearby slopes of Vesuvius. At **Al Gamberone**, Via Piave 36, ℰ 8638322, close to Pompei's main church, you can feast on prawns doused in cognac and other good fish dishes. (*Closed Fri.*) A little further out is the **Anfiteatro**, Via Roma 125, ℰ 8631245. Here the seafood is more modest—it's one of the few places in Pompei you'll see *baccalà*, salt cod, on the menu, along with truly good *spaghetti alle vongole*.

## Sorrento

There are tourist offices in Sorrento itself, at Via L. de Maio 35, ℰ (081) 8782104, ℰ 8773397, and in Vico Equense, at Via S. Ciro 16, ℰ (081) 8015752.

## Sorrento and its Peninsula

After Pompeii, the coastline swings outwards to meet Capri. At first, there is little intimation that you are entering one of the most beautiful corners of all Italy. The first clue comes when the coast road begins to climb into a corniche at **Vico Equense**, a pretty village that is becoming a small resort, absorbing some of the overflow from Sorrento; there is a nice beach under the cliffs at the back of the town.

**Sorrento** began its career as a resort in the early 19th century, when Naples began to grow too piquant for English tastes. The English, especially, have never forsaken it; Sorrento's secret is a certain perfect cosiness, comfortable like old shoes. Visitors get the reassuring sense that nothing distressing is going to happen to them, and sure enough, nothing ever does. It helps that Sorrento is a lovely, civilized old town. Not many resorts can trace their ancestry back to the Etruscans, or claim a native son like the poet Torquato Tasso. (Today, the Sorrentines are more proud of a songwriter named De Curtio, whose *Come Back to Sorrento*, according to a local brochure, ranks with *O Sole Mio* as one of the 'two most familiar songs in the world'. There's a bust of him in front of the Circumvesuviana station).

Sorrento doesn't flagrantly chase after your money, like many places in Italy, and it lacks the high-density garishness of, say, Rimini. If Sorrento has one big drawback, it is its lack of a decent beach—though at some of the fancier hotels you may enjoy taking a lift down to the sea. There are also several *stabilimenti*—piers jutting out into the sea, kitted out with loungers and beach umbrellas, for which you pay a hire charge. Sorrento is built on a long cliff that follows the shore. A narrow ravine cuts the town in half, between a suburban area of quiet, mostly expensive hotels around Via Correale, and the old town itself, which still preserves its grid of narrow Roman streets. There isn't much of artistic or historical interest; Sorrento was never a large town, though in the Middle Ages it was for a while an important trading post. The Sorrentine recall with pride that their fleet once beat Amalfi in a sea battle (897). Even today the population is only 15,000. It's pleasant to walk the old streets; half the shop windows seem to be displaying *intarsia*—surprisingly fine pictures done in inlaid woods, a local craft for centuries. If you are stuck on a rainy day, you can visit the **Correale Museum,** on Via Correale, a grab-bag of Neapolitan bric-à-brac, art and curiosities (*open 9.30–12.30, 3–5, Mon, Wed–Fri; 9.30am–12.30pm Sat, Sun; closed Tues; adm*).

Around Sorrento, as far as the mountains permit, stretches one of the great garden spots of Campania, a lush plain full of vines and orange groves. Among the excursions that can be made from Sorrento are the visit to the scanty ruins of the Roman **Villa di Pollio**, in a beautiful setting on the cape west of the town, and the short trip to **Massa Lubrense**, an uncrowded fishing village with more fine views as far as Campanella Point, the tip of the peninsula, opposite the rugged outline of Capri. In the old days, a permanent watch was kept on Campanella Point, and it takes its name from the big bell that was hung here and rung to warn the towns around the bay when pirates were sighted.

---

*Sorrento ☎ (081–)*  **Where to Stay**

In Sorrento, some 90 hotels compete for your attention, the best of which are converted villas by the sea—almost indecently elegant, even when they're a bit frayed about the edges. Sorrento isn't the status resort it once was, but it still seems to have more four-star places than anywhere in Italy; most of them are good bargains, too, compared to comparable spots in the north.

### expensive

At the top of the list is the ★★★★**Grand Hotel Ambasciatori**, Via Califano 18, ☎ 8782025, ✆ 8071021, a bit removed from the centre, but with a palatial interior and gardens overlooking the sea. In the same area is the beautifully remodelled **Royal**, Via Correale 42, ☎ 8781920, ✆ 8772905, with a pool and beach access.

In a more central location, set in incredible tropical gardens on Via Vittorio Veneto, the ★★★★**Imperial Tramontana**, ☎ 8782585, ✆ 8072344, is one of the places long favoured by British travellers, as is evident from the club-like décor. There is an elevator down to the private beach, and also a pool. Another villa-hotel, just around the corner on Via Marina Grande, is the ★★★**Bellevue-Syrene**, ☎ 878 1024, ✆ 8783963. This one has lush gardens, beautifully restored rooms and a lift to the beach.

### moderate

In Vico Equense, the best places are a little outside the town centre, notably the ★★★★**Capo La Gala**, ☎ 8015758, ✆ 8798747, on the beach at nearby Scrajo (where there are sulphur springs)—a beautiful modern resort hotel where every room has a private terrace overlooking the beach. There's plenty of sea, and a pool too, but note that full board is usually required.

In Sorrento itself, the ★★★★**President**, Via Nastro Verde, Colle Parise, ☎ 878262, ✆ 8785411, is slightly out of town, set in its own park, with lovely views and a good-sized pool. At the ★★★**Minerva**, Via Capo 30, ☎ 8781011, ✆ 8781949, you'll find 50 nice rooms, some with stunning views over the sea. (*Closed Nov–Mar.*)

### inexpensive

Not all the hotels in Sorrento are luxury villas; one of the charms of the place is that it caters to every budget. A real bargain, in a villa with a private beach and a good restaurant, is the ★★**Pensione La Tonnarella**, Via Capo 31, ☎ 8781153, ✆ 8782169; it's advisable to make reservations here early. Another clean, well-run *pensione* with lovely sea views is the ★★**Loreley et Londres**, Via Califano 2, ☎ 8781508. There are plenty of simple hotels around the town centre, of which the ★**City**, Corso d'Italia 217, ☎ 877221, is one of the nicest.

***very expensive/expensive***

At Nerano, on the road from Vico Equense to Sorrento, **Da Pappone**, © 8081209, specializes in fish fresh out of the sea, and elaborate (but pricy!) *antipasto* surprises.

Sorrento has every kind of restaurant, including the grand and gloriously decorated **Parrucchiano**, Corso Italia 71, © 8781321, by tradition one of Italy's best, with a choice of anything you could imagine. If you are celebrating a social occasion, though, or just in the mood for a very unusual experience, the place to go nowadays is **Don Alfonso**, Piazza Sant'Agata, © 8780026, in Sant'Agata sui Due Golfi, a Michelin-starred restaurant that some food critics reckon to be the best in southern Italy. Food here is an art form, beautifully cooked, and presented on fine china with wine served in delicate crystal glasses. The restaurant, run by husband-and-wife team Alfonso and Livia Iaccarino, is actually 9km outside Sorrento, but the trip is well worth it. (*Open Sept–May closed Sun evenings, Mon.*)

***moderate/inexpensive***

Sorrento can also offer restaurants of a completely different variety, like the honestly named **Boozer Pub**, Via P.R. Giuliani 66, © 8783617, with light dinners, English beer and music nightly. **Ristorante Gioiello**, Via Casarlano 19, © 8072200, where the menu changes daily, is very popular with the Sorrentini themselves. For one of the best deals in town, try the **Trattoria da Emilia**, Via Marina Grande 62, © 8781489, a family-run trattoria with tables on a terrace overlooking the sea, and an excellent-value fixed menu based on fresh local ingredients and classic recipes.

## The Amalfi Drive

When confronted with something generally acclaimed to be the most beautiful stretch of scenery in the entire Mediterranean, the honest writer is at a loss. Few who have been there would argue the point, but describing it properly is another matter. Along this coast, where one mountain after another plunges sheer into the sea, there is a string of towns that not long ago were accessible only by boat. Today, a spectacular corniche road of 'a thousand bends' covers the route, climbing in places to a thousand feet above the sea; necessity makes it so narrow that every oncoming vehicle is an adventure, but everyone except the driver will have the treat of a lifetime. Nature here has created an amazing vertical landscape, a mix of sharp crags and deep green forests; in doing so she inspired the Italians to add three of their most beautiful towns.

This coast has always attracted foreigners, but only relatively recently has it become a major resort area. Places like Positano have become reserves for the wealthy, and swarms of day trippers are likely to descend at any moment. They'll never spoil it, though; all the engineers in Italy couldn't widen the Amalfi road, and the impossible terrain leaves no room at all for new development.

There are tourist offices along the peninsula in **Positano**, at Via Saracino 4, ℂ (089) 875067, ✆ 875766; **Amalfi**, at Corso Roma 19, ℂ (089) 871107, ✆ 872619; **Ravello**, Piazza Vescovado, ℂ (089) 857096, ✆ 857977; and **Maiori**, at Corso Regina, ℂ (089) 877452. In **Salerno** the helpful EPT is at Via Velia 15, ℂ (089) 224322, ✆ 251844. Their excellent *Annuario Alberghi* has, besides a list of hotels throughout the province (which includes the Amalfi coast), a map and just about everything else you may need to know.

## Positano

To complement the vertical landscape, here is Italy's most nearly vertical town. Positano spills down from the corniche like a waterfall of pink, cream and yellow villas. The day trippers may walk down to the sea; only the alpinists among them make it back up (fortunately, there is a regular bus service along the one main street). After the Second World War Positano became a well-known hideaway for artists and writers—many of them American, following the lead given by John Steinbeck—and fashion was not slow to followNow, even though infested with boutiques, Positano reverts to the Positanesi in the off-season, and quiets down considerably. When you get to the bottom, there is a soft, grey beach and the town's church, decorated with a pretty tiled dome like so many others along this coast. A highlight of the town's year is its spectacular *festa* on the Feast of the Assumption, 15 August—the main holiday of the summer throughout Italy—when the local people take their town back in order to stage a performance recreating the Amalfi coast's centuries-long battles with the Saracens (*see* also above, 'The *Feste* of Campania', p.922).

If you have time, take a trip further up to **Montepertuso**, a village perched three kilometres above Positano, and which takes its name (meaning 'hole in the mountain') from an old legend— the devil challenged the Virgin Mary to blow a hole in the mountain, saying the winner could have control of the village. The devil tried, but failed miserably, while the Virgin coolly walked through the mountainside, leaving a hole still visible today. The locals re-enact the scene each 2 July, with much merriment and fireworks. On the last Saturday in August, the village stages another of the best festas in all Italy, the *sagra del fagiolo*—the feast of the

Positano

bean. The streets are decked out with stalls selling beans cooked in every possible way, plus a great many other home-cooked dishes, washed down with local wine served from oak barrels by waiters dressed in traditional costume.

The next town east along the drive from Positano, **Praiano**, could be Positano's little sister: with a similar beach and church, but not quite as scenic and perpendicular, and not quite as beleaguered by tourism. The last part, at least, is changing fast. After Praiano, keep an eye out for the most impressive natural feature along the drive, the steep, impenetrable **Furore Gorge**. On either side are tiny isolated villages along the shore, with beaches—if only you have a way to get to them. Further down the road you'll notice the lift leading down to the **Grotta Smeralda** (*open April–Oct 9.30–5; Nov–Mar 10–6; adm*). The strange green light that is diffused throughout this sea-level cavern gives it its name. Beyond this, **Conca dei Marini** is another vertical village, with a beach and a Norman lookout tower to climb.

---

*Positano ✆ (089–)*  **Where to Stay**

**luxury**

With Positano's new-found status has come some of the highest hotel prices in Italy. If you're feeling self-indulgent—and very rich—you may care to stay at a place many believe to be the finest resort hotel in the country. The ★★★★★**San Pietro**, ✆ 875455, ✆ 811449, 1½km from Positano on the Amalfi drive, is an intimate paradise, 60 rooms with individual terraces, strung down the cliffs next to Positano and connected to the coast road on top by a long elevator. The entrance is hidden behind an old chapel; there are no signs, which is all part of the management's plan to maintain the privacy and tranquillity of its celebrity clientele. It also offers a private beach, tennis courts, and its own excursion boat.

**very expensive**

★★★★★**Le Sirenuse**, Via Cristoforo Colombo 30, ✆ 875066, ✆ 811798, is the former home of a noble Neapolitan family. It became a hotel in 1951, and has since established itself as one of Positano's best. Everything is done with style, from the beautifully decorated drawing room to the swimming pool with its mosaic tiles.

**expensive**

The ★★★★**Palazzo Murat**, Via dei Mulini 23, ✆ 875177, ✆ 811419, in Positano, an 18th-century palazzo which once belonged to Napoleon's brother-in-law Joachim Murat, briefly King of Naples, also has plenty of old-world charm, with antiques in many rooms and a beautiful courtyard where classical concerts are sometimes staged in summer.

**moderate**

On a more modest level, the ★★★**Casa Albertina**, Via Favolozza 4, ✆ 811149, ✆ 875540, is done in a lovely, understated manner, the better to accentuate the views over Positano and the sea. It's a family-run place, with a nice restaurant on the rooftop terrace, a few minutes from the beach, and in the busy season its quietness can be an advantage. A little closer to the water is the ★★★**Ancora**, on Via Columbo,

875318, 811784, a peaceful and professionally run place, though it too is family-owned. A good bargain is the **California**, Via Colombo 141, 875382, with 10 very pleasant rooms, all with bath, and a lovely terrace for breakfast and other meals.

If you have a car, you can expand your horizons to include some of the more secluded spots along the coast. In Praiano, new hotels seem to be opening at least once a month; for the time being, the better choices are just outside the village at Vettica Maggiore, a little way back towards Positano along the Amalfi drive. One exceptional bargain here is the ***Tramonto d'Oro**, Via G. Caprigliona 119, 874008, 874670, which offers tennis courts, a pool, beach access, and great views; the restaurant isn't exceptional, but will do. Further towards Amalfi at Conca dei Marini, the ***Belvedere**, (089) 831282, 831439, is an airy and modern hotel in a delightful setting, with a beach and an old Norman tower in the grounds.

### inexpensive

In Positano the *****Maria Luisa**, Via Fornillo 40, 875023, also has 10 rooms, all with baths, and a friendly family atmosphere. A few very inexpensive *pensioni* can also be found along Via Fornillo and on the other streets leading down to the beach. In Praiano, similarly, there are some cheaper old pensions by the port, but they are usually full to bursting in the summer.

---

*Positano* ( *(081–)* **Eating Out**

In the high season at least, most of the resort hotels along the coast will coerce you into dining with them. Not that that's always bad—some of the better hotels have well-known gourmet restaurants—but there are also some equally good places elsewhere to enjoy if you can escape. Like many of the restaurants on the Costiera, a good number of Positano's eateries close from November till Easter.

### expensive

**La Cambusa**, Spiaggia Grande, 875432, in a lovely position with a terrace looking out onto the beach, is a Positano favourite. The chef serves excellently cooked fresh fish and seafood in as many ways as you can think of, and more, and a house speciality is *penne con gamberetti, rugola e pomodoro*—penne with prawns, rocket and fresh tomatoes. Across the road, the **Buca di Bacco**, Via Rampa Teglia 8, 875699, is another Positano institution, *the* place to stop off for a drink on the way back from the beach. The fish is always well cooked here, and you'd be crazy to go for anything else.

### moderate

Down on Positano's beach, the centre of the action in the summer is **Chez Black**, Via Brigantino, 875036, a slick and sophisticated spot that fortunately turns out to be a good deal cosier—and less expensive—than it looks. Good Neapolitan favourites like *spaghetti alle vongole*—with clams—are done well here, leading up to a vast choice of seafood, and maybe a banana split with *liquore Strega* for dessert.

**O'Caporale**, near the water on Via Regina Giovanna, ✆ 811188, offers much of the same (and who needs anything fancier?)—the swordfish and *zuppa di pesce* are particularly good.

**Lo Guarracino**, Via Positanesi d'America 12, ✆ 875794, is situated in one of Positano's most lovely spots, on a terrace perched over the sea, reached by a ½km walk along a cliff path. Its informal atmosphere and well-cooked local dishes make this a favourite with the Positanesi. Further uptown, the **Grottino Azzurro**, Via Chiesa Nuova, ✆ 875466, is a family-run trattoria, where the *signora* comes to the table to advise you on the catch of the day, and how best you should sample it.

In summer, for a memorable experience, watch out for boats marked **Da Laurito** leaving the jetty at Positano beach. This is a free ferry service to a delightful trattoria around the next bay, set on a small beach, with makeshift tables under a straw canopy. The speciality here is good old-fashioned recipes such as *totani con patate*— squid cooked with potatoes in a wonderful sauce of oil and garlic, all washed down with white wine spiked with fresh peaches. At the end of your meal, they'll ferry you back again as part of the service (✆ 875022).

Just east of Praiano, tucked away in a tiny bay at the foot of Il Furore, is the **Petit Ristorante**, Via Praia 15, ✆ 874706. Diners eat at tables outside, surrounded by gaily painted fishing boats, choosing from a menu that features mainly simple dishes such as fresh grilled fish and salad. (*Closed Oct–Easter.*)

*inexpensive*

Given Positano's fashionable standing genuinely cheap places to eat are hard to find, though there are some pizzerias around Via Fornillo, and some of the restaurants listed above, such as Chez Black, also provide pizzas at less than their main-menu prices. At Montepertuso, above Positano, **Il Ritrovo**, Via Monte 53, ✆ 811336, is a pretty trattoria, with tomatoes strung from its beams and good local dishes including, a rarity for these parts, grilled meats. Also, just outside Praiano, in a dramatic setting in a cave reached by a cliff path, is the prime-spot nightclub for the Amalfi coast, the **Africana**, Via Torre a Mare, Praiano, ✆ 874 042). *Open 10pm–3.30am during the season*, it also offers light meals.

## Amalfi

Sometimes history seems to be kidding us. Can it be true, can this minuscule village once have had a population of 80,000? There is no room among these jagged rocks for even a fraction of that—but then we remember that in Campania anything is possible, and we read how most of the old town simply slid into the sea during a storm and earthquake in 1343. The history is a glorious one. Amalfi was the first Italian city to regain its balance after the Dark Ages, the first to recreate its civic pride and its mercantile daring. As such, she showed the way to Venice, Pisa and Genoa, though she would get to keep few of the prizes.

There is a legend that Amalfi was founded by a party of Roman noblemen, fleeing the barbarians after the fall of the Empire, and carrying on the old Roman spirit and culture in this safe and hidden enclave. The Amalfitan Republic first appears in the 6th century; by the 9th it

*Duomo di Amalfi*

was probably the most important trading port of Italy, with a large colony of merchants at Constantinople and connections with all the Muslim lands. All of this came at a time for which historical records are scarce, but Amalfi's merchant adventurers must have had as romantically exciting a time as those of Venice. Their luck turned sour in the 1130s, with one brief occupation by the Normans, and a sacking at the hands of their mortal enemies, the Pisans, after a fatal sea battle that broke Amalfi's power forever.

The disaster of 1343 ensured that Amalfi's decline would be complete, but what's left of the place today—with its 5000 or so people—is beautiful almost to excess. Over the little square around the harbour, a conspicuous inscription brags: 'The Judgement Day, when the Amalfitani go to heaven, will be a day like any other day'. The square is called **Piazza Flavio Gioia**, after Amalfi's most famous merchant adventurer—they claim he invented the compass in the 12th century.

From here, an arch under the buildings leads to the centre of the town, the **Piazza del Duomo,** with a long flight of steps up to what may be the loveliest **cathedral** in all the south of Italy (9th–12th centuries). Not even in Sicily was the Arab-Norman style ever carried to such a flight of fancy as in this delicate façade, with four levels of interlaced arches in stripes of different-coloured stone. The lace-like open arches on the porch are unique in Italy, though common enough in Muslim Spain, one of the countries with which Amalfi had regular trade relations. The cathedral's greatest treasure is its set of bronze doors, cast with scenes from scripture; they were made in Constantinople in 1066, commissioned by the leader of the Amalfitan colony there. The interior, unfortunately, was restored in the 18th-century Baroque à la Napoletana, with plenty of frills in inlaid coloured marble. Down in the crypt you can see the head of St Andrew, patron of the city; this relic was a part of Amalfi's share of the loot in the sack of Constantinople in 1204.

One of the oldest parts of the cathedral to survive is the **Chiostro del Paradiso**, a white-washed quadrangle of interlaced arches with a decidedly African air. Many of the bits and pieces of old Amalfi that have survived its calamities have been assembled here: there are classical sarcophagi, medieval sculpture and coats-of-arms. Best of all are the fragments of Cosmatesque work, brightly-coloured geometric mosaics that once were parts of pulpits and pillars, a speciality of this part of Campania.

From the centre of Amalfi, you can walk in a few minutes out to the northern edge of the city, the narrow 'Valley of the Mills', set along a stream bed between steep cliffs; some of the mills that made medieval Amalfi famous for paper-making are still in operation, and there is a small **Paper Museum** (*open 9–1, 3–6, Tues–Sun; adm*) in the town. You can also watch paper being made and buy paper products at **Armatruda**, Via Fiume, ✆ (089) 871315, in central Amalfi, near the museum.

---

*Amalfi ✆ (089–)* **Where to Stay**

Unlike Positano, Amalfi has been a resort for a long time, and some of its older establishments are among the most distinctive on the Mediterranean.

### very expensive

The ★★★★★**Santa Caterina**, Via Statale Amálfitano 173, ✆ (089) 871012, ✆ (089) 871351, with perhaps the loveliest gardens of all, is a converted villa with wonderful sea views from most rooms.

### expensive

St Francis himself is said to have founded the ★★★★**Luna**, Via Comite 33, ✆ (089) 871002, ✆ (089) 871333, though the lifts and Hollywood-style pool are a little more recent. This former monastery, above the drive on Amalfi's eastern edge, was already a hotel in the waning days of the Grand Tour—Wagner stayed here while searching for his Garden of Klingsor, and they can show you the room where Ibsen wrote *A Doll's House*. Among other famous guests, the owners claim the Luna to have been a favourite of both Mussolini and Otto von Bismarck; modern-day authoritarians will enjoy the comfortable rooms and attentive service. If Franciscan accommodation isn't to your taste, see what the 12th-century Capuchins could come up with at the ★★★★**Cappuccini Convento**, Via Annunziatella, ✆ 871877, ✆ 871886, built by Emperor Frederick II on a mountainside over the town, with a lift running down through the cliffs to the beach. The monks would have enjoyed seeing the Persian rugs and elegant furnishings in their old digs, though perhaps they might have been dismayed to see their cloister converted into a conference centre. The restaurant is also one of the town's best.

### moderate

Not all of Amalfi's accommodation offers such heights of luxury. Two pleasant hotels that stand out, and which are both conveniently placed for the town and the beach are the ★★★**Miramalfi**, ✆/✆ 871588, and the well kept ★★★**Amalfi** on Via dei Pastai, ✆ 872440, ✆ 872250.

### inexpensive

★★**La Conchiglia**, ✆ 871856, at the end of the Lungomare by Amalfi's little harbour, has 11 nice rooms, all with bath. There is also a fair collection of inexpensive places around the Cathedral. Three particularly good ones are the ★★**Sole** on Largo della Zecca, ✆ 871147, the prettily furnished ★★**Sant'Andrea**, Via Santolo Camera 1, ✆ 871145, and the ★★**Fontana**, Piazza Duomo 7, ✆ 871530.

Amalfi has several fine restaurants, including those in the luxury hotels above.

### expensive

**Da Gemma**, Via Fra Gerardo Sasso 9, ✆ 871345, is one of Amalfi's oldest restaurants, with an attractive terrace for outdoor dining and an excellent fish-based menu. Their *zuppa di pesce* (fish soup) is a wonderfully rich mixture of all sorts of different fish and seafood. Almost directly under the Cathedral, the **Taverna degli Apostoli**, Via Sant'Anna 5, ✆ 872991, also has a fine *risotto marinaio* and other fish dishes.

### moderate

At **Lo Smeraldino**, Piazzale dei Protontini 1, ✆ 871071, at the far end of the port, you'll be offered the house speciality, *scialatiello*, fresh pasta with mixed seafood, and a range of good *secondi*, most notably an excellent *fritto misto*—mixed fried fish. You can also order pizza here. **La Caravella**, Via Matteo Camera 12, ✆ 871029, serves a delicious ravioli stuffed with seafood, and a good range of home-made desserts.

### inexpensive

There's a pretty old-fashioned trattoria-wine shop a little way north of the Cathedral on Via Pietro Capuana, called **La Vinicola**, and though the choice is limited the cooking is good. Close by, the **Tarì**, Via P. Capuana, ✆ 871832, is another pretty, welcoming trattoria with friendly service, and no unpleasant surprises when it's time for the bill.

At the **San Giuseppe**, Via Ruggiero II 4, ✆ 872640, a family-run hostelry, the pizza is sublime—it should be, as the owner is a baker. Good pasta and fish dishes are also available at reasonable prices. In the centre of town, **Da Maria**, Via Lorenzo d'Amalfi 14, ✆ 871880, is a lively trattoria and pizzeria where the waiters are cheerful and helpful, and the food a cut above some of the other less expensive places.

## Villages Inland: Ravello and Scala

As important as it was in its day, the Amalfitan Republic never grew very big. At its greatest extent, it could only claim a small part of this coast, including these two towns up in the mountains; like Amalfi they were once much larger and more prosperous than you see them today. **Ravello** is another beauty, a balcony overlooking the Amalfi coast and a treasure-house of exotic medieval art. As the second city of the Amalfitan Republic, medieval Ravello had a population of 30,000; now it provides an example of that typically Italian phenomenon—a village of 2000 with its own bishop, and a first-rate cathedral to put him in.

Ravello's chief glories are two wonderful gardens: that of the **Villa Cimbrone** (*open 9am–one hour before sunset daily; adm*), laid out by an Englishman in the 1900s, with a priceless view over the Amalfi coast, and that of the **Villa Rùfolo** (*open 9.30am–1pm, 3–7pm daily; adm*)—which, as fans of Wagner will be interested to know, is none other than Klingsor's magic garden. Wagner says so himself, in a note scribbled in the villa's guest book. He really had come here looking for it, for the proper setting in which to imagine the worldly, Faustian enchanter of *Parsifal*. The villa itself is a remarkable 11th-century pleasure palace, a temporary abode of Charles of Anjou, various Norman kings, and Adrian IV, the only English pope (1154–59), who came here fleeing a rebellion in Rome. Even in its present, half-ruined state, it is worth a visit; inside there is a small collection of architectural fragments. The garden, with more fine views, is a small semitropical paradise, full of fountains and flowers in every imaginable colour.

The **cathedral** is named after Ravello's patron San Pantaleone, an obscure early martyr; they have a phial of his blood in one of the side chapels, and it 'boils' like the blood of San Gennaro in Naples whenever the saint is in the mood. Lately he hasn't been, which makes the Ravellans worry. The cathedral has two particular treasures: a pair of bronze doors from the 12th century, inspired by the Greek ones at Amalfi, and an exquisite pair of marble *ambone*, or pulpits, that rank among the outstanding examples of 12th-century Cosmatesque work. Two other Ravello churches where you can see more similar work are **Santa Maria a Gradello** and **San Giovanni del Toro**. From Ravello, it is only a lovely 1½km walk to **Scala**, smallest and oldest of the three Amalfitan towns, with another old cathedral.

Between Amalfi and Ravello, before reaching the turn off inland, the Amalfi Drive passes through **Atrani**, an old village whose cathedral has another tiled dome, and yet another set of bronze doors from Constantinople. Beyond the Ravello turn, next along the way towards Salerno come **Minori** and **Maiori**. Minori is a typical *Costiera* hill-town, with considerable charm. Its bigger sister is somewhat less so, mainly due to a major flood in 1954 which washed away most of the seafront; today, most of the buildings and hotels along the shore are depressingly modern. **Erchie**, a tiny hamlet on the shore far below the road, seems a lovely spot—if you can figure out a way to get down to it. Then, near the end of the drive, there come **Cetara**, with a fine beach behind the mole of the fishing port, and, just before Salerno, **Vietri sul Mare**, a pretty town famous throughout Italy for its beautiful *maiolica* ware. There are ceramics shops everywhere, where you can watch craftsmen hand-painting jugs, vases and tiles, and pick up souvenirs at surprisingly good prices.

---

*Ravello* © *(089–)*  **Where to Stay**

Ravello also has its share of dream hotels: offering no beaches, but unforgettable gardens and views down over the coast. In the shadow of Amalfi and Ravello, the two thoroughly pleasant beach lidos of

Minori and Maiori may seem a little dull, but they can be useful bases, especially if hotels in the better known resorts are full.

### very expensive

Ravello's finest, with an incredible guest book full of the names of the famous over the last 120 years, is the ★★★★★**Palumbo**, Via S. Giovanni del Toro 28, ✆ 857244, 📠 857347. The service is perfect, the 12 rooms are individually decorated with antiques, the restaurant is equally renowned for seafood, local and international dishes, and the excellent house wine really is house wine—made on the premises. Still, lovely as it it, there are no sports facilities, and the room prices may seem hard to justify. There is also a simpler *dipendenza*, with 7 rooms for slightly lower prices.

### expensive

In Ravello the ★★★★**Caruso Belvedere**, Via S. Giovanni del Toro, ✆ 857111, 📠 857372, once popular with the Bloomsbury set and with Greta Garbo (she had room 21), has the quiet elegance of the old patrician villa it was before its present owner's grandfather, a cousin of the famous Neapolitan tenor Enrico Caruso, opened it as a hotel 100 years ago. In the beautifully laid out gardens, there is a belvedere over the sea and mountains, and the well-tended vegetable garden and vineyard on another level provide fresh produce and the hotel's own wine. Guests are encouraged to take half-board, which is no real hardship since the food is superb, and meals are taken on one of the loveliest terraces in Ravello.

With the lushest gardens on the coast, the ★★★**Villa Cimbrone**, Via Santa Chiara 26, ✆ 857459, 📠 858072, is a lovely place to stay: another elegant old villa, once the property of an English duke, set in its own parkland perched dizzyingly high on the cliffs. The rooms are beautifully decorated, and the only drawbacks are the lack of a restaurant and the ten-minute walk needed to get there; cars have to be parked further down in the villlage. It does, though, have a swimming pool.

In Maiori the ★★★★**San Pietro**, Via Nova Chiusi 139, ✆ 877220, 📠 877025, with a pool and tennis courts, is typical of the modern, middle-range resort hotels you'll find in Minori and Maiori. Further along the coast at Vietri sul Mare is the ★★★★★**Raito**, Via Nova, ✆ 210033, 📠 211434, a luxurious hotel, recently restored from top to bottom, with views over the whole coast stretching as far as Paestum.

### moderate

Further down from the Villa Cimbrone is one of the prettiest hotels in Ravello, the delightful ★★★**Villa Maria**, Via Santa Chiara 2, ✆ 857255, 📠 857071, a gracious and tastefully converted villa made all the more attractive by the helpful and friendly owner, Vincenzo Palumbo, known to everyone as *Il Professore*. The vast suite (more expensive than the normal rooms) has one of the most breathtaking terraces in Ravello. Even if you don't stay here, it's worth coming to eat at the very fine-quality but reasonably priced restaurant in the lovely gardens, with a view over the hills.

Under the same ownership, a few minutes' walk away, is the ★★★**Hotel Giordano** (same address and phone numbers as the Villa Maria), which is slightly more modern, but still comfortable and well-run, with the added advantage of a solarium and a heated outdoor pool. Villa Maria guests have equal access to these facilities.

Below Ravello and along the coast in Minori, the ★★★★**Villa Romana**, Corso Vittorio Emmanuele 90, © 877237, ✆ 877302, is a stylish, comfortable modern hotel. On the way to Salerno at Cetara is the ★★★★**Cetus**, SS 163, ©/✆ 261388, another lovely, newer hotel, built into the cliffs and with steps down to a secluded beach.

### inexpensive

A very enjoyable budget choice in Ravello is the ★★**Villa Amore**, Via Santa Chiara 5, © (089) 857135 with 12 clean simple rooms, and a lovely terrace which has the same breathtaking views as the more expensive hotels.

In Maiori, there are several simple hotels near the beaches, such as the ★★**Baia Verde**, Via Arsenale 8, © 877276, and the ★**Vittoria**, Via Cerasuoli 4, © 877652, that offer some of the most convenient budget accommodation on the Amalfi coast. In neighbouring Minori the ★★★**Santa Lucia**, Via Nazionale 44, ©/✆ 877142, is the best in the lower price range.

---

*Ravello © (089–)*                                              **Eating Out**

Unusually, most of the best dining in Ravello is in the hotels, most notably at Villa Maria and at the Caruso (*see* above); non-residents are welcome at all of them for lunch or dinner. By comparison the rest of the restaurants pale into insignificance, but one exception is **Cumpà Cosimo**, Via Roma 44–46, © 857156 (moderate), where owner-cook Signora Netta is always happy to advise diners on her latest concoctions and try out her school English on visitors. Her tour de force is the *piatto misto di primi*, a gargantuan helping of six or seven different pasta dishes on the same ceramic plate.

If you make the trip up to Scala, alongside Ravello, try the wide range of delicious antipasto dishes and desserts at **La Margherita**, Via Torricella, © 857106 (moderate), in the village centre. **Zi'Ntonio**, © 857118 (moderate), further along the same road, serves out well-cooked local dishes on a beautiful covered terrace.

At Maiori, you'll get good fresh fish at **Mammato**, Via Arsenale 6, © 877036 (moderate), and in Minori try **Il Giardinello**, Corso V. Emanuele, © 877050 (inexpensive/moderate), where the house speciality is *risotto al nero di seppia* risotto with squid ink. There are also good pasta dishes, and pizza.

## Salerno

Anywhere else in the south of Italy, a city like Salerno would be an attraction in itself; here it gets lost among the wonders of the Campanian coast—just the big town at the end of the Amalfi drive—and few people ever stop for more than a very brief visit. Nevertheless, Salerno has its modest charms, not least of which is that it is a clean and orderly place; that should endear it to people who hate Naples. Its setting under a backdrop of mountains is memorable. The Italian highway engineers, showing off as usual, have brought a highway to the city on a chain of viaducts, one lofty span after another, an unusual and pleasing ornament for the city; at night the road lights hang on the mountain slopes like strings of fairy-lights on a Christmas tree.

Salerno's ancient distinction was its medical school, the oldest and finest of medieval Europe. Traditionally founded by the legendary 'Four Doctors'—an Italian, a Greek, a Jew and an Arab—the school was of the greatest importance in the transmission of Greek and Muslim science into Europe. Most of us, however, may recognize Salerno better as the site of the Allied invasion in September 1943, one of the biggest and most successful such operations of the Second World War.

Salerno's port is on the outskirts of town, and the shore all through the city centre is graced with a pretty park, the Lungomare Trieste. Parallel with it, and two streets back, the Corso Vittorio Emanuele leads into the old town. Here it changes its name to Via dei Mercanti, most colourful of Salerno's old streets. The **cathedral**, a block to the north on Via del Duomo, is set with its façade behind a courtyard with a fountain at the centre, and a detached campanile—as if it were not a church at all, but a mosque. The Corinthian columns around it come from the ancient city of Paestum, not far down the coast. Robert Guiscard, who built it, spent a lot of time in this city; his wife was a fearsome warrior-princess of Salerno named Sichelgaita. The cathedral was begun in 1086, the year after Guiscard sacked Rome. He brought Pope Gregory VII, ostensibly his ally, to Salerno for safe-keeping, and Gregory, the German Hildebrand who laid down many of the basic traditions of the Catholic church and was perhaps the greatest of the medieval popes, is buried in one of the side chapels. The cathedral's treasures are of the same order as those of the Amalfi coast: another pair of bronze doors from Constantinople, and another beautiful pair of Cosmatesque pulpits. The building itself has been much restored, and many of the best original details have been preserved in the adjacent **Museo del Duomo** (*open 9–1, 4–7*).

From Salerno you can make an easy excursion up into the mountains to the town of **Cava de' Tirreni**. Near it, perched precariously on the slopes of the Val di Bonea, is a little-visited Benedictine monastery called **La Trinità di Cava**—rebuilt, as usual, in tiresome Baroque, but preserving a wealth of 12th–14th-century frescoes, stone-carving and Cosmati work.

---

*Salerno* ✆ *(089–)*

### Where to Stay

#### expensive

Salerno's hotels are fairly modest and utilitarian. The ★★★★★**Jolly Hotel delle Palme**, Lungomare Trieste 1, ✆ 225222, ✆ 237571, is pleasant and reliable, and right on the seafront.

#### moderate

More than acceptable for an overnight stay is the ★★★**Plaza**, Piazza Ferrovia, ✆ 224477, ✆ 237311, right across from the station. Close by, in the pedestrian area, is the recently refurbished ★★★**Montestella**, Corso Vittorio Emanuele, ✆ 225122. Convenient for the beach is the ★★★**Fiorenza**, Via Trento 145, ✆ 338 800, ✆ 337722, a clean, well-run hotel with 30 bedrooms.

Several cheaper hotels are to be found on or around the Corso Vittorio Emanuele. Try the **★★Salerno**, Via G. Vicinanza 42, ✆ 224211—simple but comfortable.

---

*Salerno* ✆ *(089–)*                                                    ***Eating Out***

Despite—or because of—not being a major tourist magnet Salerno has its share of good restaurants, many of them along the shore on Lungomare Trieste.

### expensive

**Nicola dei Principati**, Corso Garibaldi 201, ✆ 225435, in the old centre of Salerno, serves mainly fish dishes, including an excellent *linguine con astice*, long pasta with lobster. At **Il Timone**, Via Generale Clark 29, ✆ 335111, the speciality is *tubetti alla pescatrice*, short pasta served with a delicious fish sauce. The second courses, almost all fish, are equally good.

### moderate

One of the liveliest restaurants in town, right in the *centro storico*, is the **Vicolo della Neve**, Vicolo della Neve 24, ✆ 225705, an attractive place decorated with wall paintings by some of the many artists who have established it as their local. The chef turns out good Campanian favourites such as *melanzane alla parmigiana*, aubergines cooked in layers with mozzarella, parmesan, tomato and basil, and the classic *pasta e fagioli*. You can also order excellent pizza. At **La Lampara**, Lungomare Colombo 333, ✆ 337750, you'll also find pizza on the menu, together with a host of other dishes, mainly fish, including octopus and squid served in a variety of unusual ways. At **Alla Brace**, Lungomare Trieste 13, ✆ (089) 225159, as well as the usual fish dishes, you will be offered a host of delicious local specialities such as stuffed peppers, ravioli filled with ricotta, and a remarkable potato soufflé. There is also a wide range of home-made desserts.

### inexpensive

**Da Sasa** at Via Diaz 42, ✆ 225696, is a good inexpensive trattoria, with traditional home-cooking and especially tasty pasta courses at very accessible prices.

## The Islands of the Bay of Naples

These islands are fully covered in the Cadogan guide to *The Bay of Naples and the Amalfi Coast*, but it would naturally be impossible not to say a few words here about these three little graces. For ships and hydrofoils from Naples and other ports around the bay, *see* p.929.

## Capri

### Getting Around

Arriving in Marina Grande, you can ascend to either Capri or Anacapri by **bus**. They run every 15 minutes 8am–10pm, and every half-hour 10pm–midnight, daily. There is also a **funicular** that runs up to Capri town every 15 minutes from 6.35am–10pm, though in April–September only. The **chairlift** from Anacapri to Monte Solaro (a 12-minute ride) runs continuously from 9am to sunset, also in summer only. There are also buses from Anacapri to the Blue Grotto, Faro and Marina Piccola. From June until September, there are daily **tours** of Capri by motor launch, which leave from Marina Grande, beginning at 9am.

## Tourist Information

The island has tourist offices in **Capri town**, at Piazza Umberto 1, ✆ (081) 8370686, **Marina Grande**, at Banchina del Porto, ✆ (081) 8370634, and in **Anacapri**, at Via G. Orlandi 19/a, ✆ (089) 8371524.

## Italy's Most Visited Island

Capri—pointy rhinestone sunglasses, lime-green stretch pants and all—is still, undeniably, one of the most beautiful islands in the world. An abrupt crag of the Sorrentine peninsula that broke away, Capri is endowed with spectacular limestone cliffs, torn and eroded away into fantastic forms, most famously the incredibly blue **Grotta Azzurra** (boats leave from Capri's port, Marina Grande, when the sea permits, or you can get there by bus and patronize one of the very expensive boatmen closer to the cave). Buses or the funicular (if it's working) will also take you up to flower-bedecked **Capri town**, a charming white village packed to the gills with jewellery shops and designer boutiques, and, in summer, with tourists hailing from anywhere from Berkeley to Baghdad (and 'packed' is no exaggeration).

Capri town is the base for several walks, each more splendid than the last—aim for the famous **Faraglioni**, three towering pinnacles in the sea, or to the **Tragara terrace**, with views over monolithic **Pizzolungo** to the **Arco Naturale**, or to the ruins of Tiberius' pleasure palace, the **Villa Jovis** and the infamous **Salto di Tiberio**, the sheer cliff from which the decadent old Emperor tossed his enemies and the boys that had ceased to entertain him, if you can believe Suetonius.

Capri has some 800 species of flora, many of which you can see in the **Gardens of Augustus**, founded by Caesar himself, which overlook the vertiginous Via Krupp, zigzagging down to the sea. More striking views may be had from Capri's more laid-back second town, **Anacapri**, up on the island's top shelf. There are regular buses connecting it to Marina Grande and Capri town, and a chair lift that goes up even further to the summit of **Monte Solaro**, for a fabulous view of the island and the whole Bay of Naples.

*Capri ✆ (081–)*                                        ## Where to Stay

As one might expect, hotel prices on Capri are well above average for the surrounding area on-shore, and rooms for the summer months are often booked up months in advance.

### very expensive

If money is no object, the **★★★★★Quisiana e Grand Hotel**, Via Camerelle, ✆ 8370788, ✉ 8376080, is the place to stay in Capri town, a luxurious palace of a hotel set in its own grounds and equipped with pool, tennis courts and just about everything else needed for a smart holiday on the island.

Slightly lower down the price-scale, ★★★★**La Palma**, Via V. Emanuele, ✆ 837 0133, 🖂 8376966, is also in a good central location in Capri town, set in its own gardens, with lovely maiolica-tiled floors in the rooms and a pleasant airy feel. ★★★★**La Scalinatella**, Via Tragara 8, ✆ 8370633, 🖂 8378291, is a jewel of a hotel, with 30 beautifully decorated rooms and stunning views. Further up on the way to the panoramic Punta Tragara, the ★★★★**Villa Brunella**, Via Tragara 24, ✆ 8370122, 🖂 8370430, is a pretty hotel looking out over the sea, with a good restaurant and a pool for lazing away hot afternoons.

## *moderate*

Open all year round, the ★★★**Floridiana**, Via Campo di Teste, ✆ 8370166, 🖂 8370434, in Capri town, also has fine panoramas of the sea. The ★★★**Villa Sarah**, Via Tiberio 3, ✆ 8377817, is a gracious old villa, pleasantly converted into a small, well-run hotel.

## *inexpensive*

Book well ahead if you want to stay at the ★★**Villa Krupp**, Viale Matteotti 12, ✆ 8370362, one of the loveliest, and most historic, lower-priced hotels in Capri. Two budget choices, both no-frills establishments, but clean and well-run, are the centrally located ★**Stella Maris**, Via Roma, ✆ 8370452, and ★**La Tosca**, Via D. Birago, ✆ 8370989, both in Capri town.

---

*Capri* ✆ *(081–)*                                              **Eating Out**

## *expensive*

Capri's best restaurant has long been **La Capannina**, Via delle Botteghe 14, ✆ 8370732, set in a secluded garden in Capri town, with delicately prepared shellfish, pasta and fish, and good desserts. A close rival is a relative newcomer, **Al Geranio**, Viale Matteotti 8, ✆ 8370616, where the chef has a magic touch with fish, in particular. Tables overlook the classic Capri panorama.

**I Faraglioni**, Via Camerelle 75, ✆ 8370320, has delectable house specialities like *crêpes al formaggio*, paper-thin pancakes filled with cheese, and *risotto ai frutti di mare*, risotto with all sorts of shellfish.

## *moderate*

At **Da Paolino**, on Via Palazzo a Mare 11, ✆ 8376102, you'll eat in an arbour of lemon trees, tasting dishes mainly inspired by the fruit—as in the pasta, fish and dessert courses, all heavily lemon-influenced. Further down in Capri town, **Da Gemma**, Via Madre Serafina, ✆ 8370461, is one of the few restaurants that stay open all year round. It's as nice in winter as it is in summer, a welcoming trattoria with walls decked with brass pans and ceramic plates, and superbly cooked local dishes including a delicious mozzarella grilled on a lemon leaf. It also serves very good pizza.

In Anacapri, **Da Gelsomina la Migliara**, on Via La Migliara 6, ✆ 8371499, offers not only home-made wine, but true home-cooked island specialities, including mushrooms collected on Monte Solaro.

## Ischia and Procida

### Getting Around

**Ischia** is considerably larger than Capri, with several self-contained communities. Buses to the various towns on the island depart from the square next to Santa Maria di Portosalvo in Ischia Porto, near the beginning of the SS270, which circles the island. An entire circuit of the island takes about 2½ hours. Buses marked CD run clockwise, while those marked CS run anti-clockwise. Cars can be hired relatively cheaply here, from **Davidauto**, Via G. Mazzella 84, ✆ (081) 998043, or **Rentcar Ischia**, Via Alfredo de Luca 59, ✆ (081) 992444. Bikes can be rented from **Autonoleggio-Moto**, Via dello Stadio 16, ✆ (081) 980055. There are frequent ferry and hydrofoil services from both Naples and Ischia to the smallest of the islands, **Procida**. The harbour itself is tiny, and if you want to explore further afield, jump on one of the colourful diesel-powered buggies that serve as taxis. Alternatively, there is a bus service about every half hour between the harbour and the other end of the island at Chiaioella, stopping at many points in between.

### Tourist Information

There are two offices on **Ischia**, both in Ischia Porto, at Corso Vittoria Colonna 116, ✆ (081) 991464, and Via Iasolino, ✆ (081) 991146, near the ferry landing. On **Procida** the tourist office is at Via Rodia, ✆ (081) 8969624, in the Marina Grande (the only substantial town), again near the ferry departure point.

## Ischia

Green, mountainous and volcanic, Ischia comes in a close second to Capri in the beauty and fashion pageant, blessed with something its more famous sister totally lacks—beautiful beaches. Consequently it's one of Italy's biggest resorts, and the main towns, **Ischia Porto** and adjacent **Ischia Ponte** are lively and very

*Ischia*

fashionable, the former boasting curative radioactive hotsprings, the second the storybook **Castello d'Ischia**, home to Michelangelo's great friend, the poetess Vittoria Colonna.

One of the prettiest villages on Ischia is **Sant'Angelo**, a fishing port with a tower-crowned isthmus and fine beach, and hot springs at Cavascura. **Lacco Ameno**, **Barano** and **Casamicciola Terme** are the most important beach resorts/spas. The best viewpoint is atop the extinct volcano **Monte Epomeo** (788m)—there is a mule path to the summit, beginning at Fontana. Like Capri, Ischia is crowded throughout the summer, but one of the peaks of its season is 27 July, the Feast of St Anne, when a spectacular torchlight procession of boats honours the island's patron saint (*see also* above, 'The *Feste* of Campania', p.922).

## Procida

Geologically related to Ischia, little Procida is a real charmer that has slipped through most tour groups' itineraries, mainly because the islanders have always been reluctant to sell their idyllic lifestyle out to tourism. Its main port, overlooked by the ancient village of **Corricella**, is a pastel fantasy with the undulating rhythm of a hundred arches. Perched up on the promontory overhead, the **Terra Murata** is the old walled town, where you can visit the 16th-century **Castello d'Aragona** and the church of **San Michele Arcangelo**. Beyond this minimal urban centre, Procida is an enchanting Ruritania of lemon groves and crumbling old villas—you can walk around it in a day, or take the bus to the south end, where **Chiaioella**, a small fishing port, has a long stretch of sand facing the tiny wooded islet of **Vivara**.

---

© (081–)                                                *Where to Stay*

### Ischia

#### very expensive

The swankiest hotel on Ischia is the ★★★★★**Regina Isabella**, Piazza Santa Restituta, Lacco Ameno, © (081) 994322, @ 986043, right on the waterfront in Lacco Ameno, with a private beach and every kind of spa and gym facility imaginable. Another pricy beauty, but with a very different style, is Forio's ★★★★★**Grand Albergo Mezza Torre**, Via Mezza Torre, Forio, © 986111, @ 987892. This 60-room hotel is housed in a small castle that used to belong to the film director Visconti. Set in its own grounds, it lacks the facilities of the Regina Isabella, but for good old-fashioned luxury it can't be beaten.

#### expensive

The finest hotel in Ischia Porto is the ★★★★**Excelsior Belvedere** at Via Gianturco 19, © 991522, @ 984100. Not only is it quieter than most, but guests can enjoy the fine pool and garden. (*Closed Nov–Mar.*) You can also indulge in luxury at the ★★★★**Mare Blu**, Via Pontano 40, © 982555, @ 982938, which sits in a charming position on the waterfront with a view of the Aragonese Castle.

#### moderate

For those who want to try Ischia's famous thermal treatments, without spending the kind of sums charged in the smarter hotels, the ★★★**Parco Verde**, Via Mazzella 29,

Ischia Porto, © 992282, ✆ 992773, is a good bet. Set in an attractive park, close to the main drag in Ischia Porto, this hotel offers full thermal facilities and trained staff. If you prefer to do without mudbaths, this pleasant hotel also has a pool, and is close to the beach.

In pretty Sant'Angelo, on the south side of the island, the ★★★★**Miramare**, Via Comandante Maddalena 29, © 999219, ✆ 999325, is a lovely hotel, with panoramic views over the small harbour. Further west at Forio is the ★★★**Punta del Sole**, Piazza Maltese, © 998208, ✆ 998209, another hotel that has its own thermal facilities, as well as a pool and garden. In Lacco Ameno, the ★★★**San Montano**, Via Monte Vico, © 994033, ✆ 980242, offers a pool, tennis courts and many other comforts, in addition to thermal baths. Prices tend to be a bit lower in Casamicciola. One pleasant hotel there is the ★★★**Ibsen** at Corso V. Emanuele 10, © 994919, ✆ 994253, which has special facilities for wheelchair users.

### inexpensive

Also in Casamicciola, the ★★**Delle Rose**, Via Casa Mennella 9, © 994082, ✆ 995855, is a very good-value hotel with charm, a swimming pool and 24 nice rooms, all with bath. In Ischia Porto, one of the least expensive places to stay is near the Castello Aragonese, and open all year, ★**Il Monastero**, Via Castello Aragonese, © 992435, which has 14 clean rooms, all with bath. Also a bargain by Ischia standards is the ★★**Bristol**, Via Fundera 72, Lacco Ameno, © 994566, with a small garden and swimming pool.

## Procida

Right on the main harbour front, the ★★★**Crescenzo**, Via Marina Chiaiolella, © 8967255, ✆ 8101260 (moderate), is a landmark in Procida. Its rooms are simply but pleasantly furnished.

The only hotel open all year round on the island is the ★★**Oasi** at Via Elleri 16, © 8967499 (inexpensive), a villa with a restaurant and garden. Another good inexpensive hotel, on the beach at Chiaia, is the ★★**Riviera**, Via Giovanni da Procida 36, © 896 7197 (inexpensive), with 23 rooms, most with bath.

---

© (081–) *Eating Out*

## Ischia

In Ischia, fish features prominently on the menu, but you will also find meat here, and specifically rabbit. For some reason, Ischia is fairly hopping with rabbits, and the locals have dreamed up endless ways of eating them, in stews, roast, or even with pasta.

### expensive

At Ischia Ponte the loveliest place to eat is **Da Ugo Giardini Eden**, Via Nuova Cartaromana 50, © 993909, set right on the sea. You couldn't find fresher fish or lobster anywhere, as they pluck it right out of the water in front of you. Along the port, **Gennaro**, Via Porto 66, © 992917, serves superb giant prawns and much more. Still in Ischia Porto, **Il Damiano**, on the SS270, Ischia Porto, © 983032 (open evenings only), offers diners views over the sea, plus beautifully cooked seafood and fish dishes, most of all the *linguine all'aragosta*, long pasta with a lobster sauce.

*moderate*

On the seafront at Ischia Porto, **Zi Nannina a Mare**, Lungomare Cristoforo Colombo, © 991350, is a delightful family-run trattoria with an outdoor terrace offering well-cooked Ischian specialities, based on either fish or meat. Near Forio, in the open countryside, the **Cavé Gran Diavolo**, Via Bocca 88, Forio, © 989 282, serves more meat than fish, with pride of place going to the famous Ischian dish *bucatini con sugo di coniglio*—fat spaghetti served in rabbit sauce. The rustic feel and good local wine make this a very pleasant place for lunch or dinner. Right on the water's edge at Forio, the **Cava dell'Isola**, Via G. Mazzella, Forio, © 997452, is especially enjoyable at lunchtime, perhaps after a morning spent on the nearby beach. Good local specialities are the mainstay.

At Sant'Angelo the **Conchiglia**, Via Sant'Angelo, © 999270, offers al fresco dining on a tiny but charming terrace, overlooking the harbour. There are also a handful of nice, inexpensive rooms to let above the restaurant.

## Procida

The restaurant of the **★★★Crescenzo**, Via Marina Chiaiolella, © 8967255, ✆ 8101260 (moderate) serves local specialities and pizza in the evening, and is worth a try even if you are not staying here. There are several good restaurants along the port at Marina Grande, like **La Medusa**, © 896 7481 (moderate), serving seafood and meats. **Il Cantino**, Via Nitrodi 6, © 99071 (moderate), serves a very good *fritto misto di pesce* (fresh fried fish), with decent local wine.

# Campania Inland

There's more to the region than just the Bay of Naples. However, the coast and its endless attractions draw off most of the tourists, and it's a rare soul indeed who ever makes it up to old Capua, or the excellent little city of Benevento.

*Getting Around*

The interior of Campania makes up a large territory—the three main towns are all provincial capitals. None are on the main **railway** lines, however, and you will have to scrutinize the schedules in Naples carefully to find your way around. Some Rome–Naples trains pass through Caserta and Capua. **Buses** for Caserta, Capua, Avellino, and Benevento leave Naples from Piazza Garibaldi, in front of the Stazione Centrale. The **ACTP**, © (081) 7005091, runs regular buses to Caserta (one hour).

By far the fastest way to get to the interior of Campania is **by car**, along the A2, which passes between Caserta and Capua, or the A16 Bari *autostrada*, which runs past Avellino. A slower but slightly quieter route to Caserta is along the old SS87 road. To get to it, take the Viale Maddalena to the left of Capodichino airport, and then follow the signs for Caserta.

### Tourist Information

The provincial EPT tourist office is at Caserta, right in the Royal Palace, 81100, © (0823) 322170.

## Capua

This is a double city, consisting of the modern town, founded in the 9th century, and the ancient one, once the second city of Italy, but deserted in the Dark Ages and now modestly reborn as **Santa Maria Capua Vetere**. Capua can trace its founding to the Oscans, blithe folk of ancient Italy who introduced farce to the theatre, and who probably give us the word *obscene*. It is believed that the Oscan farces, banned by all decent Roman emperors, created the prototypes of the *commedia dell'arte* stock characters, including Naples' favourite Pulcinello—Punch. All that should give you some idea of the spirit of old Capua, a city best known for beautiful women and the manufacture of perfume, and as renowned for loose morals in its day as Sybaris. Everyone but the jealous Roman historians liked to give Capua credit for defeating the great Hannibal. The Capuans had always hated those dreary dour Romans, and they eagerly took the Carthaginians' part. Hannibal's men enjoyed Capuan hospitality in the winter of 216 BC; they came out in the spring so dreamy-eyed and dissipated that they never beat the Romans again. Of course there was hell to pay when the Romans came back, but Capua survived, and even flourished for several centuries more as the greatest city of the region. Finally though, some even worse drudges than the Romans arrived—the Arabs, who utterly destroyed the city in about 830. The survivors then refounded Capua on a new site, a few kilometres to the north. Of old Capua, at Santa Maria Capua Vetere, you can see the remains of the second-largest **amphitheatre** in Italy—largest of all before Rome built its Colosseum. Here Spartacus began his gladiators' revolt in 73 BC. Few sections of the stands are still intact, but there is an underground network of tunnels and trap doors much like that in Rome.

While there, ask the attendant to show you something much more interesting—a short walk away is perhaps the best example of a **mithraeum** discovered anywhere in the Mediterranean. The cult of the god Mithras, imported from Persia by the legionaries, was for a while the most widespread of the cults that tried to fill the religious vacuum of the Imperial centuries. Some scholars see in it much in common with Christianity. The resemblance isn't readily apparent; Mithraism was an archaic, gut-level cult, with mystery initiations and lots of bull's blood splashing about. Though it originally took hold in the army, and always remained a men-only affair, as late as the 3rd century AD it could probably claim more adherents than Christianity. The upper classes were never too impressed with it; that is why it lost out to the Christians, and why such well-executed frescoes as these are rare. The *mithraeum* is an underground hall, used in the initiations, and dominated by a large scene of Mithras, a typical Mediterranean solar hero, slaying a white bull with a serpent under its feet; the complementary fresco representing the moon on the opposite wall is less well-preserved.

Also around Santa Maria, there is a crumbling triumphal arch, and some elaborate Roman tombs, off the road to Caserta. The new Capua has all the most interesting finds from the old one at the **Museo Provinciale Campano** (*open 9–1, 2–5, Tues–Sun; adm*). Just north of the town, on the slopes of Mount Tifata, a site once occupied by a temple of Diana now contains the 11th-century basilica of **Sant'Angelo in Formis**. The 12th-century frescoes here are some of the best in the south, oddly archaic figures that would seem much more at home in Constantinople than in Italy. And, more than mere artistry, there is an intense spiritual vision about these paintings—note especially the unearthly, unforgettable face of the enthroned St Michael above the portal.

North of Capua, near the border with Lazio, the last town in Campania along the Via Appia is **Sessa Aurunca**, with a Roman bridge and some other scanty ruins, as well as a 12th-century cathedral, interesting for its surviving ancient and medieval sections.

## Caserta

In one shot, you can see the biggest palace in Italy, and also the most wearisome; both distinctions belong uncontestably to the **Reggia**, or Royal Palace, built here by the Bourbon King of Naples, Charles III (*open 9–1.30 Mon–Sat; 9–12.30 Sun; adm*). His architect, Luigi Vanvitelli (really a Dutchman named Van Wittel) spared no expense; like the Spanish Bourbons, those of Naples were greenly jealous of Versailles, and wanted to show the big Louies back home that they, too, deserved a little respect. The Reggia, begun in 1752, has some 1200 rooms, not much compared to the 2800 of the Bourbon palace in Madrid, but larger than its Spanish cousin just the same (it's also larger than Versailles); the façade is 245m across. Inside, as in Madrid, everything is tasteful, ornate and soberingly expensive; the only good touches from Vanvitelli's heavy hand are the elegant grand staircases. Only the gardens make the trip worthwhile, an amazingly long axis of pools and cascades climbing up to the famous **Diana fountain**, with a lifelike sculptural group of the goddess and her attendants catching Actaeon in the act. There is also an **English garden**, of the sort fashionable in the 18th century. The Reggia was commandeered for use as Allied military headquarters in Italy in 1943, and it was here that the final surrender of the German armies in Italy was accepted two years later.

The village of **San Leucio**, nearly three kilometres north of Caserta, was founded by the Bourbon kings as a paternalistic utopian experiment, and also an establishment for the manufacture of silk. Ferdinand IV, for most of his life, personally saw to every detail of its operation, even christening the children of the workers. The successor of his *Real Fabbrica* is still a centre for silk. Some 9km to the east there is the half-deserted town of **Caserta Vecchia**. The building of the Reggia drew most of the population down to modern Caserta, but the old town still has the 12th-century **cathedral**, with a great octagonal *ciborium* (a cylindrical or prismatic dome) that is one of the glories of Arab-Norman architecture.

---

*Caserta ℭ (0832–)* **Eating Out**

Neither of these towns makes a very attractive base for an overnight stay. Caserta, though, does have some good restaurants.

At **La Castellana**, Via Torre 5, ✆ 371230, in the centre of Caserta Vecchia, you can feast on wild boar or venison, when available, as well as a wonderfully innovative selection of soup and pasta openers.

Outside the town, at the **Ritrovo dei Patriarchi**, Via Conte Landulfo, Località Sommana, ✆ 371510, you'll find game in abundance, including pheasant, venison, partridge and wild boar, depending on the time of year. There are also good hearty soups and vegetable dishes.

*moderate*

Near La Castellana, the **Rocca di Sant'Andrea**, Via Torre 8, ✆ 371232, offers delicious pasta dishes and a variety of *secondi*, many of which are based on meat grilled on the open fire in front of you. There is also a good selection of home-made desserts. **La Massa**, on Via Mazzini 55, ✆ 321268, is a simple and convenient place for lunch near the Reggia.

## Benevento

### Getting Around

Remote Benevento is not well connected with any of Italy's main transport systems. It is on the Naples–Foggia **railway** line, but be careful about Naples–Benevento trains, as some but not all of them are operated by a private railway, and you will need to find out which—ask at the information booth in Naples' Stazione Centrale—to buy the right ticket.

The most frequent public transport connections are by **bus**. The **Consorzio Trasporti Irpini**, ✆ (081) 5534677, has regular services to Avellino (50min) and Benevento (1½ hours) from Piazza Garibaldi in Naples. In Benevento, buses to Naples and a surprising variety of other places (including one daily to Rome) leave from Piazza Pacca, on Corso Dante just west of the cathedral. There are several companies; check at the Benevento EPT for schedules.

To get to Benevento **by road** from Naples take the A2 north and then south of Caserta look for the SS265 eastwards, which joins up with the SS7, the Via Appia, for Benevento. This road is quite slow. An alternative is to take the A16 *autostrada* to Avellino, and then the SS88 north from there to Benevento.

### Tourist Information

Benevento's EPT is east of the city centre at Via Nicola Sala 31, ✆ (0824) 21960. Its information office is at Via Giustiniani 34, ✆ (0824) 25424, @ 312309.

## The Duchy of Benevento

Ever since the Middle Ages, the land around Caserta and Capua has been called the *Terra del Lavoro*—cultivated land—a broad garden plain that is one of the most fertile corners of

Italy. Today its lush landscapes have suffered a bit from creeping industrialism, though it's in the stretch to the south, between Caserta and Naples, where the worst modern depredations can be seen. Nowadays, the Napoletani call the towns around Secondigliano, Afragola and Acerra the 'Triangle of Death', an industrial wasteland of shanties and power lines ruled by the Camorra that has Italy's worst unemployment, and some of its worst social problems.

Go east instead, up into the foothills of the Apennines towards **Benevento**, yet another smallish city that has often played a big role in Italian history. On an old tower in the centre of town, the city fathers have put up maps of southern Italy, showing the boundaries of the two important states of which Benevento was the capital.

At first, as *Malies* or *Maloenton*, it was the leading town of the Samnites, the warlike mountain people who resisted Roman imperialism for so long. The Romans were later to make a big city of it, an important stop along the Appian Way. They Latinized the name to *Maleventum*—ill wind—but after a lucky defeat of Pyrrhus of Epirus here in 275 BC, they thought it might just be a *Beneventum* after all. In 571, the city was captured by the bloodthirsty Lombards, becoming their southern capital. After the Lombards of the north fell to Charlemagne, the Duchy of Benevento carried on as an independent state; at its greatest extent, under relatively enlightened princes like Arechi II (*c.* 800), it ruled almost all of southern Italy. The Normans put an end to it in the 1060s.

Coming to Benevento in the winter, you're bound to think the Romans were crazy to change the name. When people in Salerno are ready to hit the beaches, you'll find the Beneventani shivering on street corners like Muscovites in their fur caps, victims of traditionally the worst weather in southern Italy. It is often claimed this makes them more serious and introspective than people on the coast—certainly coming here from Naples seems metaphorically like a trip of a thousand miles. Benevento has often been the scene of earthquakes, and the city took plenty of hard shots during the battles of 1943, but there are still enough attractions around to make a stop worthwhile.

Benevento's **cathedral** is in the lower town, the part that suffered the most in the bombings. The cathedral itself was almost a total loss; only the odd 13th-century façade remains, built of miscellaneous bits of Roman buildings—inscriptions, reliefs, friezes and pillars—arranged every which way. In the old streets behind the cathedral, you can see a well-preserved **Roman Theatre** (*open daily, 9am–sunset*)—not an amphitheatre, but a place for classical drama, something rare this far north. By the time the Romans conquered them, the culture of the Samnites was almost completely Hellenized. This theatre, built under Hadrian, originally seated 20,000. All through this quarter, called the **Triggio**, you will see bits of Roman brick and medieval masonry—something ancient built into the walls of every house. There is half a Roman bridge over the Sabato (one of Benevento's two rivers), ruins of the baths, remains of a triumphal arch, and plenty of gates and stretches of wall from the fortifications built by the Lombards. On Via Posillipo, a Baroque monument houses the **Bue Apis**, a sacred Egyptian bull sculpture found in Benevento's Temple of Isis.

## Trajan's Arch

Some people claim Benevento's triumphal arch to be better than those of Rome itself; built in AD 117, it is a serious piece of work—over 15m of expensive Parian marble from Greece—

and certainly better preserved than the ones in the capital. It marks the spot where the Appian Way entered Beneventum, (now Via Traiana on the northern edge of the old town) and the skilfully carved reliefs on both faces record significant events in the career of the emperor.

Trajan (AD 98–117), the conqueror of Dacia (modern-day Romania) and Mesopotamia, ranks among the greatest of the emperors, and a little commemoration would not seem out of hand; nevertheless cynics will enjoy the transparent and sometimes heavy-handed political propaganda of ornaments like this. In one of the panels, Trajan (the handsome fellow with the curly beard) is shown distributing gifts to children; in another he presides over the *institutio alimentaria*—the dole. Most of the scenes are about victories: Trajan announcing military reforms, Trajan celebrating a triumph, Jove handing Trajan one of his thunderbolts, and finally the Apotheosis, where the late emperor is received among the gods while the goddess Roma escorts Hadrian to coronation as his divinely ordained successor.

## The Museo Sannio

Corso Garibaldi is Benevento's main street, just south of Trajan's Arch. Near its eastern end stands the city's oldest church, **Santa Sofia**, built in the late 8th century. It is unusual for its plan, an irregular six-pointed star, and was built for the Lombard Duke Gisulfo by an architect thoroughly grounded in the mystic geometry of the early Middle Ages. The vaulting is supported by recycled Roman columns, and other columns have been hollowed out for use as holy water fonts.

The church cloister contains one of the south's more interesting provincial museums, the **Museo Sannio** (*open 9–1, 3–6, Tues–Sun*). *Sannio* refers to Samnium, as Benevento's province is still officially called. The 12th-century cloister is itself well worth a look, with a variety of strange twisted columns under pulvins carved with even stranger scenes: monster-hunting, dancing, fantastical animals, bunnies, and a camel or two. The best things in the museum are in the archaeological section. Almost all the classic vases are Campanian copies of Greek ware—the production of ceramics was the engine that drove *Campania Felix*'s economy in its glory days.

## Some Samnite Curiosities

Two rooms in the museum are filled with objects from the Temple of Isis. Anyone who has read Apuleius' The Golden Ass will remember just how important the cult of the transcendent goddess Isis was throughout the Roman world. This Egyptian import certainly seems to have found a home in Beneventum; nowhere in Europe has so much fine Egyptian statuary been retrieved. The temple had imperial backing. One of the statues is of the founder, Emperor Domitian himself, in Egyptian dress. Other works portray priestesses, sacred boats and sphinxes, another Apis bull, and a porphyry 'cista mistica', carved with a snake. The image of Isis is also there, formidably impressive, even without a head.

Somehow this leads naturally to Benevento's more famous piece of exotica—the witches. In the days of the Lombards, women by the hundreds would dance around a sacred walnut tree on the banks of the River Sabato ('sabbath'). Even after the official conversion to Christianity in 663, the older religion persisted, and Benevento is full of every sort of 'witch' story as a result. The best piece of modern sculpture in the Museo Sannio is a representation of the witches' dance. Of course the city has found ways to put the legend to use. In any bar in Italy, you can pick up a bottle of 'liquore Strega' (strega means witch) and read on the label the proud device: 'Made next to the train station in Benevento, Italy'.

Just a few streets west of the museum on Corso Garibaldi, the dedicatory **obelisk** from the Isis temple stands in front of the town hall. East of the museum, the Corso takes you to the **Rocca de' Rettori**, a fortress built by the popes in the 14th century; for centuries Benevento was a papal enclave surrounded by the Kingdom of Naples. The fortress is now a part of the Museo Sannio. Behind it is a lovely park, the Villa Comunale.

---

### Benevento ℭ (0824–)                            *Where to Stay*

In spite of what it has to offer, Benevento sees few tourists, and accommodation is limited. The ★★★★**Gran Hotel Italiano**, Viale Principe di Napoli 137, ℭ 24923, ✆ 21758 (moderate) is a pleasant, simple place a block from the train station—hardly grand, now or ever, but it will do fine. At the cheap end of the scale, ★**Genova**, down the same street at No.130, ℭ 42926 (inexpensive) has rooms without baths.

---

### Benevento ℭ (0824–)                                *Eating Out*

Dining in Benevento can be interesting; it's another world from the Campanian coast, with seafood replaced on the menu by rabbit, duck, lamb and veal. Samnium makes some good but little-known wines; you might ask for a bottle of stout-hearted Solopaca red with your Samnite repast.

Benevento's favourite restaurant is probably the **Antica Taverna**, at Via Annunziata 41, ℭ 21212 (moderate), not far from the Museo Sannio, where roast kid is one of the more unusual items on the menu. A good traditional restaurant where you can dine for a reasonable price can be found in the back streets around Trajan's Arch, the **Ristorante Palmieri**, at the end of Via Manciotti, ℭ 24947 (moderate). Some of the best food, however, and most of the Beneventani, can be found in the stand-up *tavola calda* on the corner of Corso Dante and Corso Vittorio Emanuele, a block west of the cathedral, which provides really fine pizza.

## Samnium

Samnium is one of Italy's smallest provinces, but there are a few towns and villages of interest; the countryside, full of oak and walnut forests, is often reminiscent of some corner of Umbria. **Morcone**, to the north, has a memorable setting, draped on the curving slope of a hill like a Roman theatre. **Telese**, to the west on the road towards Lazio, lies near a small but pretty lake of the same name, with a popular spa establishment. The nearby ruins of the Samnite Roman town of *Telesia* are remarkable for their perfectly octagonal walls, with gates at the cardinal points.

Best of all, perhaps, is the town of **Sant'Agata dei Goti**, some kilometres north of the Via Appia between Benevento and Caserta, with its long line of buildings like a man-made cliff overhanging a little ravine. Sant'Agata takes its name from the Goths who founded it in the 6th century; it was badly damaged in the 1980 earthquake, and its modest monuments, the **Castello** and the 12th-century **Church of Santa Menna**, are still undergoing restoration.

## Southern Campania

Continuing this broad arc around Naples, south and east of Benevento there are few attractions, but some attractive mountain scenery in a region called **Irpinia**, consisting of most of the province of Avellino. In places, the mountains bear fine forests of oaks and chestnuts, as well as plantations of hazelnut trees; other parts are grim and bare, an introduction to the 19th-century deforestation that ruined so much of southern Italy. Irpinia was the region worst affected by the 1980 earthquake, and you can still see settlements of portacabins which act as homes for hundreds of families. The little provincial capital of **Avellino** itself, an important centre in Norman times, has been wrecked so many times by invaders and earthquakes that today little remains to be seen. Its 17th-century **Palazzo della Dogana** does, though, still retain its façade of ancient statues, and its original clock tower.

The main highway south from Caserta, around the back side of Vesuvius, isn't that much more promising. **Nola**, the biggest town on the route, began as another Oscan foundation. It had a famous early bishop, St Paulinus, a friend of St Augustine and also, it is claimed, the inventor of the bell (bells are *campanelli* in Italian, from their Campanian origin). To celebrate the anniversary of St Paulinus' return from imprisonment at the hands of the Vandals, every 27 June the people of Nola put on one of the more spectacular festivals of the south, the 'Dance of the Lilies', a procession of 15m wooden steeples, elaborately decorated and carried by the men of the town (*see* above, 'The *Feste* of Campania', p.922). Further south, in the hills above the city of **Nocera Inferiore**, an ancient hamlet called **Nocera Superiore** has somehow kept intact its 4th-century church, an unusual round building with a cupola that may have been converted from a pagan sanctuary.

## Paestum and the Cilento

After the Bay and the Amalfi coast—two heavy courses for a holiday banquet—we can offer the Cilento peninsula, as a light, refreshing dessert. The Cilento is a squarish low massif jutting out from the coast between the Gulf of Salerno and the Gulf of Policastro. Its mountain scenery may not be quite as breathtaking as the Amalfi drive, but the Cilento makes up for it by being delightfully wild and unspoilt, and altogether one of the most beguiling out-of-the-way places to spend your time in southern Italy. The interior of the Cilento is not traversed by any easy roads, and the traveller heading south from Salerno will have a choice of two routes: a long, leisurely drive along the coast, past the remarkable ruins of ancient Paestum and a number of small, very casual resorts, or along the present main road, the A3 *Autostrada del Sole*, over the mountains and skirting the eastern edge of the Cilento, a route of often beautiful, wild scenery down the valley of the Tanagro River.

### *Getting Around*

Paestum has a station on the main **railway** line between Naples and Reggio Calabria, but only local trains stop there. More conveniently, there are frequent **buses** from the Piazza Concordia in Salerno (on the shore, by the Porto Turistico). They are run by several companies; some follow the coast route, while others go through Battipaglia. Some of these continue on to various resort towns on the Cilento coast.

All the Cilento towns are connected by **bus** to Salerno's Piazza Concordia; there is a bewildering list of companies, towns and schedules, but fortunately the EPT in Salerno publishes a full list of them in the front of their annual hotel book. The **railway** line only touches the Cilento coast at two points—Ascea and Pisciotta— and, as at Paestum, not too many trains stop.

As we have mentioned, there are only two main **road** routes, the SS18 coast road and the A3 and parallel SS19 further inland. At Agropoli the SS267 leaves the SS18 and runs round the Cilento coast. North of Paestum there is also another turn off the SS18, the SS166 to the east, a long and winding road across the Cilento interior that eventually connects up with the A3.

---

### Tourist Information

**Avellino**'s tourist office is at Via Due Principati 5, ℰ (0825) 35169. The **Salerno** EPT is at Via Velia 15, ℰ (089) 224322, ✉ 251844, and has the most complete information on transport and accommodation in Paestum and the Cilento. There is also the AAST, in the central Piazza Amendola, ℰ (089) 224744, ✉ 752839. There are also information offices in **Paestum**, Via Aquilia, ℰ (0828) 811016, ✉ 722322, and **Palinuro**, in Piazza Virgilio, ℰ (0974) 931147.

## Paestum: A Lost City

Along the coast, the route begins in a fertile plain that meets the Cilento near the ruins of **Paestum**, site of the only well-preserved Greek temples north of Sicily (*site open 9am–two hours before sunset Tues–Sun; museum open 9am–2pm only, Tues–Sun; joint adm for both*). And there is another important player on the Mediterranean stage who needs to be introduced. The anopheles mosquito, as fate would have it, gets the credit for preserving Paestum's ruins so well. By the 9th century or so, this once-great city was breathing its last, a victim of economic decline and Arab raiders. As its people gradually abandoned it for safer settlements in the hills, Paestum was swallowed up by the thick forests of this subtropical corner of Italy.

As usual on a Mediterranean coastal plain, when the people leave the malaria mosquitoes take over. By the Middle Ages, the site of Paestum became utterly uninhabitable—it meant certain death to stay there overnight—and after a while the city's very existence was forgotten. After being hidden away, like the Mayan temples in the Mexican jungle, for almost a thousand years, the city was re-discovered in the 18th century; a crew of Charles III's road builders stumbled onto the huge temples in the midst of the forest.

Originally *Poseidonia*, the city was founded in the 6th century BC by the Sybarites, as a station on the all-important trade route up Italy's west coast. The Romans took over in

273 BC, and the name became Latinized to Paestum. As a steadfast supporter of the Roman cause throughout the Punic Wars, Paestum was a favoured city. Famous around the Mediterranean for its flowers, especially roses, it prospered until the end of the Roman era. Today the forests have been cleared, and the ruins of the city stand in the open on the green and quiet plain. Not only the celebrated temples have survived; much of the 4km circuit of **walls** still stands to some height, along with some of the towers and gates.

Most of Paestum's important buildings were grouped along an axis between the Porta Aurea and the Porta Giustizia, with the forum at its centre. The two grand temples that everyone comes to see are at the southern end: the **Basilica** and the **Temple of Neptune,** two Doric edifices in the finest classical style. The names were just guesses on the part of the early archaeologists; both temples in fact were dedicated to Hera, the tutelary goddess of the city. The 'Neptune' temple, the best preserved, was built about 450 BC. It is about 60m long, and all of the structure survives except the roof and the internal walls. The second temple, the 'Basilica', is a century older, and a little smaller.

The aesthetic may not be quite what you expected—dimensions squat and strong rather than graceful and tall. Still, this is the classic austerity of Greek architecture at its best. There is more to it than meets the eye. If you look closely along the rows of columns, or the lines of the base, you may notice that nothing in either of them is perfectly straight. The edges bulge outwards, as they do in the Parthenon and every other Greek building; this is an architectural trick called *entasis*; it creates an optical illusion, making the lines seem straight at a distance. Greek temples like this are the most sober and serious buildings in western architecture, based on a simple system of perfect proportion. The form may seem austere and academic, but with some imagination you can picture them in their original beauty— covered in a sort of enamel made of gleaming ground marble, setting off the brilliant colours of the polychromed sculptural reliefs on the pediments and frieze.

To the west, some of the streets of the city have been excavated, though very little is left to see. To the north, around the broad Forum—really a simple rectangular space in the manner of a Greek *agora*—are the remains of a theatre, a round *bouleterion*, or council house, and other buildings. Still further north is the third and smallest of the surviving temples, the **Temple of Ceres**.

Paestum's **Museum** holds most of the sculptural fragments and finds from the town. Some of the best reliefs are not from Paestum at all, but from the recently discovered sanctuary of Hera, a few kilometres north at the mouth of the river Sele. This temple, mentioned by many ancient writers, is said to have been founded by Jason and the Argonauts during their wanderings. From tombs excavated just outside the city come some examples of Greek fresco painting—nothing special in themselves, but probably the only ones in existence. Look out for the most famous fresco, *The Diver*, which you have probably seen reproduced innumerable times elsewhere. Even though the Greeks took painting as seriously as they did sculpture, you will not find any similar surviving examples in Greece, or anywhere else.

While you are exploring Paestum, keep an eye out too for the wild flowers. More than one 19th-century traveller claimed to have found descendants of Paestum's famous roses (*bifera rosaria Paestum*) growing wild, and some may still be around.

## The Cilento Coast

For many, one of the attractions of Paestum will be the fine, long beaches that line this part of the coast. South of the ruins, the shore becomes jagged and mountainous, passing groves of pines alternating with rugged cliffs and pocket-sized beaches. Most of the villages along it have become quiet, cosy resorts that cater mostly to Italians. One is usually close to the next, and if you care to stay over, you can keep going until you find one that suits your fancy.

**Agropoli** comes first, then **Santa Maria di Castellabate**, **San Marco**, and **Punta Licosa**, on the westernmost point of the Cilento. From here, you can take a small boat out to an uninhabited islet, also called Licosa, where there are some unidentified ancient ruins. Further down the coast, **Acciaroli** and **Pioppi** are among the nicer resort towns of the Cilento. South of the latter, and just inland from the village of Ascea Marina, you can visit the ruins of another Greek city, **Velia**.

*Sta. Maria Castellabate*

Don't expect any spectacular ruins on the order of Paestum. Velia disappeared gradually, and most of its buildings were carried off for building stone long ago. *Elea*, as it was known back then, was a colony of the Ionian city of Phocaea, and a sister city of another important Phocaean foundation—Marseilles, in France. Elea was never large or important, but its name lives on gloriously in philosophy; the Elean school of philosophers produced some of the most brilliant minds of the ancient world: logical grinds like Parmenides, who proposed the first theory of atoms, and wiseacres like Zeno with his pesky paradoxes. Some of the fortifications survive, including one well-preserved gate, and just enough of the *agora*, baths, and streets are left to enable us to guess at how the city may have looked.

Both **Ascea Marina** and its neighbouring locality of **Casalvelino** have pretty beaches, but the best ones of all can be found in the rugged terrain around **Palinuro**. This town, which has a small museum of archaeological finds, takes its name from Aeneas' pilot Palinurus, who is supposedly buried here—Virgil made the whole story up for the *Aeneid*, but that hasn't stopped it from sticking fast in local legend. Beyond Palinuro, the coast curves back north into the Gulf of Policastro; here two more pleasant beach villages, **Scario** and **Sapri**, mark the southern boundary of Campania (to continue this route, *see* 'Maratea', p.1006).

## The Inland Route: Around the Cilento

South from Salerno, the *autostrada* skirts the back edge of the Cilento on its way to Calabria. Christ may have stopped at **Eboli**, as a local saying goes, but there's no reason why you should—and that goes for **Battipaglia** and **Polla** too. The true delights of this region are subterranean, two first-rate caves on opposite slopes of the Monti Alburni. **Pertosa** (*open 9am–5.30pm Tues–Sun; adm*), near the highway, is the easier and probably the better choice; the pot-holers (spelunkers) suspect it is connected to the other one, at **Castelcivita**, near the village of Controne.

At **Teggiano**, there is a 13th-century castle and cathedral, as well as a little museum. **Padula**, just off the highway, is the unlikely location of the **Certosa di San Lorenzo**, after San Martino in Naples probably the biggest and richest monastery in the south. The Certosa has been closed for over a century, but in its heyday it would have held hundreds of Carthusians, in a complex laid out in the form of a gridiron (recalling the martyrdom of St Lawrence, the same plan used in El Escorial in Spain, also dedicated to the saint). Though it was continuously expanded and rebuilt over 400 years, the best parts are Baroque: an enormous, elegant cloister, some wonderfully garish frescoes and stucco figures in and around the chapel, and eccentric but well-executed decorative details throughout. A small archaeological museum is part of the complex.

---

*Where to Stay*

### Paestum

Most people think of Paestum as a day trip, but there are enough hotels around the site, and on the nearby beaches, to make an overnight stay possible—and very convenient, if you have a car. Some of the best accommodation is at Laura beach, about 5km north of Paestum.

The ★★★★★**Ariston**, Via Laura 13, ✆ (0828) 851333, ✉ 851596 (expensive) is a large hotel that's one of Paestum's best; on the beach, and very well-run. Near Paestum, ★★★★**Le Palme**, Via Stirpinia, ✆ (0828) 851025, ✉ 851507 (moderate), is a modern place with plenty of facilities for sports and recreation as well as its own stretch of beach. The ★★★★**Schumann**, Via Laura Mare 1, ✆ (0828) 851151, ✉ 851183 (moderate) is set in its own gardens, close to the beach, and the ★★★**Clorinda**, Via Laura, ✆ (0828) 851091 (moderate) ✉ 851588, is a recently-built hotel that's well-equipped with sports facilities. Just north of Paestum, the ★★**Laura**, ✆ (0828) 851068 (inexpensive) is a good budget choice, with its own private beach and 13 rooms, all with baths. Near the ruins, close to the Porta Giustizia entrance, the ★★★**Martini**, Via Principe Dipiamonte, ✆ (0828) 811451, ✉ 823717 (inexpensive) is a set of small bungalows set in a wooded area close to the beaches.

### The Cilento Coast

Hotels on the Cilento are on the whole modern and unremarkable, though there are some exceptions. For a stay of three days or more, an alternative to a hotel may be a *villaggio turistico*, of which there are dozens (look out for signs along the coast, or consult the rear section of the hotel guide-book distributed free by the Salerno tourist office). These are Italian-style holiday camps, but are much nicer than they sound, often with small bungalows set in well-landscaped grounds overlooking the sea, and with excellent sports and recreation facilities usually included in the all-in price.

In Castellabate, at San Marco, there is one special resort hotel, the attractive ★★★★**Castelsandra**, Piano Melaino, ✆/✉ (0974) 966021 (expensive), with a pretty setting, pool and tennis courts, a fine restaurant, and TV in many rooms to help your insomnia. A less expensive choice in San Marco is the ★★★★**Approdo**, Via Porto 49, ✆ (0974) 966001, ✉ 966500 (moderate), right on the harbour front. Most of the less expensive hotels around the Castellabate area of the Cilento are found in Santa Maria and Ogliastro—★★**Da Carmine** at the Ogliastro Marina, ✆ (0974) 963023 (inexpensive) has pleasant doubles, all with bath.

Most hotels in Acciaroli are similarly modest, and good bargains too; the best is ★★★**Il Faro**, Via Nicottera 151, ✆ (0974) 904389 (moderate). ★★★**La Vela**, Via Carraciolo 96, ✆ (0974) 905025, ✉ 905140 (inexpensive) right on the beach, is a pleasant family run hotel with prices that won't break the bank.

Towards the southern end of the Cilento coast, Ascea has a small collection of hotels around its marina, but Palinuro has developed into a fully-fledged holiday town. Try the ★★★★**Gabbiano**, Corso Carlo Pisatane, ✆ (0974) 931155, ✉ 931948 (expensive) which has a pool and private beach.

Outside Palinuro, the ★★★★**King's Residence**, Via Piano Farracio, ✆ (0974) 931324, ✉ 931418 (moderate), is in a stunning setting, perched in a crow's nest position high on the cliffs. A pathway runs down to the pretty little private beach, kitted out with a small bar for drinks and light meals. The hotel's own boat takes guests to visit the five grottoes along the coast. ★★★**La Torre**, Via Porto 5, ✆ (0974) 931107/931260, ✉ 931264 (moderate) is another attractive hotel, covered with bougainvillea and close to the beach. In the town of Palinuro, the ★★★**Conchiglia**, Via Indipendenza 52, ✆ (0974) 931018 (moderate) has 25 pleasant rooms, all with baths. The ★**Carminella**, Via Fratelli Capozzoli 28, ✆ (0974) 931237 (inexpensive) close to the King's Residence, is a small *pensione* with eight clean, comfortable rooms, all with baths.

Camerota, near the southeastern point of the Cilento, has a fairly uninspiring bunch of hotels. The ★★★**America**, ✆ (0974) 932131, ✉ 932522 (moderate) is acceptable, though without any particular charm. The ★**Pinguino**, Via S Domenico 26, ✆ (0974) 932115 (inexpensive) is typical of the no-fuss, no-frills accommodation in the region, as is the ★**San Giorgio**, Via Bolivar 113, ✆ (0974) 932468 (inexpensive) on the road going up to Camerota Alta, a small, family-run pension with 13 rooms, all with bath.

### Eating Out

## Paestum

At Paestum there are two good and typical restaurants specializing in seafood in the archaeological zone itself: the excellent **Nettuno**, near Porta Giustizia, ✆ (0828) 811028 (moderate), and the **Museo**, ✆ (0828) 811135 (moderate), at the centre of the site. Both are well worth their prices.

## The Cilento Coast

In the Cilento, most of the restaurants are in the hotels, and in summer the chances are you'll be stuck on full or at least half-board. There is some consolation to be had from the fact that such arrangements are often an excellent deal. Nevertheless, there are some good restaurants to look out for.

In Palinuro, **Da Carmelo**, ✆ (0974) 931138 (moderate), 1km along the road towards Camerota, is a lively trattoria where guests dine well on dishes prepared according to old traditional recipes, often to the strains of Neapolitan songs belted out by a strolling minstrel with a guitar. Two good places to eat near the beach in Palinuro (no phones, no reservations needed) are the **Taverna del Porto** (moderate/inexpensive), with tables a stone's throw from the water's edge, and **O' Guarracino** (moderate/inexpensive), a pretty trattoria with tables under a pleasantly shady canopy.

Camerota has one first-class restaurant, **Da Valentone** on Piazza San Domenico, ✆ (0974) 932004 (moderate), which specializes in freshly caught seafood, and first courses including such local specialities as spaghetti with anchovies.

If you don't mind the wait, the tiny **Reganata e Vasulara**, località S. Vito (no phone), in Camerota Alta (inexpensive) is a delightful spot, one of a kind fast disappearing in Italy. Guests eat cheek by jowl, choosing from a limited but excellent menu based on Neapolitan *cucina povera*—home-made *pizzette*, stuffed tomatoes, aubergines and all sorts of pasta. There is often a queue outside, and once all the food has been eaten, the kitchen closes up.

# Calabria and the Basilicata

Italy may be a country unusually blessed by fortune, but her favours are by no means evenly spread. To balance regions like the Veneto or Campania, with their manifold delights, nature has given Italy its own empty quarter, the adjacent regions of Calabria and the Basilicata. Calabria is the toe of the Italian boot, a gnarled, knobby toe, amply endowed with corns and bunions and pointed accusingly at neighbouring Sicily. Almost all of it is ruggedly mountainous, leaving just enough room at the edges for the longest, broadest, emptiest beaches in Italy. It can claim two natural attractions: a scenic western coast, and the beautifully forested highland region called the Sila, just east of the Calabrian capital, Cosenza. The Basilicata, still better known to many people under its old name of *Lucania*, takes on all comers for the title of Italy's most obscure region.

Anyone coming to Italy for the first time, and wishing to see the best the country has to offer, would not come here. The more experienced traveller, a little jaded with the rest of Italy, may come hoping to find something new and different in these little-known spaces, but great expectations will likely go unrewarded.

## Magna Graecia

It was not always this way. Starting in about 750 BC, the Greeks extensively colonized Southern Italy. *Rhegium*, today's Reggio Calabria, came first, followed in short order by Sybaris, Croton and Locris, among others. These towns, happily situated along the major trade route of the Mediterranean, rapidly became as cultured as those of Greece itself—and far wealthier. It was a brilliant hour, and a brief one. After a time, blessed with a lack of external enemies, the cities of 'greater Greece' took to fighting among themselves, in a series of ghastly, cruel wars over the most trivial of causes, often resulting in the total destruction of a city and the massacre of its inhabitants. Weakened by their own barbarous behaviour, the Greek cities then became pawns between Rome and Carthage in the Punic Wars; the victorious Romans took a terrible vengeance on those such as Taras (Táranto, in modern Apulia) that supported the wrong side. Roman rule meant a slow decline for the survivors, and by the 6th century the beautiful cities of Magna Graecia were abandoned to the mosquitoes.

Don't, however, come to Calabria looking for classical ruins. The great museum at Reggio gives a hint of what these cities were, but at the sites themselves almost nothing remains. Golden Sybaris has only just been found by the archaeologists, and only at Metapontum will you see so much as a few standing columns. Some may call the emptiness a monument to Greek hubris, or perhaps somehow these cities were doomed from the start. Considering Magna Graecia can be profoundly disconcerting; even in the ancient Mediterranean it is strange and rare for so many big cities to disappear so completely.

Nor has this corner of Italy been any more hospitable to civilization in the centuries since. Calabria in particular has suffered more at the hands of history than any region deserves. After the Romans and the malaria mosquito put an end to the brilliant, short-lived civilization of Magna Graecia, Calabria has endured one wrenching earthquake after another, not to mention Arab raiders and Norman bully-boys, Spaniards and Bourbons, the most vicious of

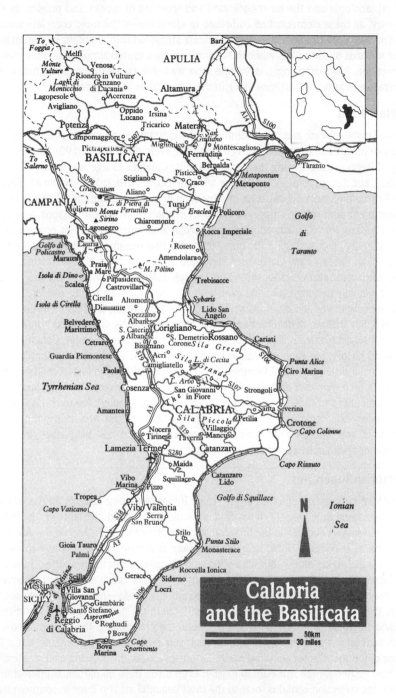

To Foggia

Melfi
Monte Vulture
Venosa
Rionero in Vulture
Laghi di Monticchio
Genzano di Lucania
Lagopesole
Acerenza
Avigliano
Oppido Lucano
Irsina
Potenza
Tricarico
Matera
Campomaggiore
Miglionico
L. San Giuliano
Pietrapertosa
Montescaglioso
BASILICATA
Ferrandina
To Salerno
Bernalda
Táranto
Stigliano
Pisticci
Metapontum
Grumentum
Craco
Metaponto
Aliano
CAMPANIA
Moliterno
L. di Pietra di Pertusillo
Tursi
Monte Sirino
Chiaromonte
Eraclea
Policoro
Lagonegro
Rocca Imperiale
Rivello
Golfo
Lauria
Roseto
di
Golfo di Policastro
Maratea
Amendolara
Taranto
Praia a Mare
M. Pòlino
Isola di Dino
Papasidero
Scalea
Castrovillari
Trebisacce
Isola di Cirella
Cirella
Altomonte
Sybaris
Diamante
Spezzano Albanese
Lido San Angelo
Belvedere Marittimo
S. Caterina Albanese
Corigliano
Cetraro
S. Demetrio Corone
Rossano
Cariati
Guardia Piemontese
Bisignano
Sila Greca
Acri
Sila L. di Cecita
Paola
Camigliatello
Punta Alice
Ciro Marina
Tyrrhenian Sea
Cosenza
L. Arvo
San Giovanni in Fiore
Strongoli
Amantea
CALABRIA
Santa Severina
Sila Piccola
Petilia
Nocera Tirinese
Villaggio Mancuso
Crotone
Taverna
Capo Colonne
Lamezia Terme
Catanzaro
Maida
Capo Rizzuto
Vibo Marina
Squillace
Catanzaro Lido
Tropea
Pizzo
Golfo di Squillace
Capo Vaticano
Vibo Valentia
Ionian
Serra San Bruno
Sea
Stilo
Gioia Tauro
Punta Stilo
Palmi
Monasterace
Roccella Ionica
Gerace
Siderno
Scilla
Messina
Villa San Giovanni
Locri
SICILY
Santo Stefano
Gambàrie
Aspromonte
Reggio di Calabria
Roghudi
Bova
Capo Spartivento
Bova Marina

Ionian Sea

Bari

APULIA

Altamura

# Calabria
# and the Basilicata

50km
30 miles

feudal landlords and the most backward and ignorant of monks and priests. By the 18th century, all these elements had combined to effect one of the most complete social break-downs ever seen in modern Europe. Calabria staggered into anarchy, its mountains given over to bands of cut-throats while the country people endured almost subhuman poverty and oppression. Not surprisingly, everyone who was able chose to emigrate; today there are several times as many Calabresi living in the Americas as in Calabria itself.

## A New Land

While famine, disease and misgovernment were putting an end to old Calabria, natural disasters like the terrible earthquake of 1783, and the even worse one in 1908 that destroyed the city of Reggio, were erasing the last traces of it. Calabria's stage was cleared for a modest rebirth, and the opportunity for it came after the Second World War, when Mr Rockefeller's DDT made the coasts habitable for the first time in over a millennium. Within a few years, a government land reform improved the lives of thousands in both regions, and the *Cassa per il Mezzogiorno*'s roads and industrial projects set out to pull their economies into the 20th century. Today, despite the many problems that remain, it's possible to see the beginnings of an entirely new Calabria. A thousand years or more ago, the Calabrians deserted their once-great port cities for wretched, though defensible villages in the mountains. Now they are finally moving back, and everywhere around Calabria's long and fertile coasts you will see new towns and cities; some, like Locri or Metaponto, are built near the ruins of the Greek cities that are their direct ancestors. Most of this new Calabria isn't much to look at yet; the bigger towns, in fact, can be determinedly ugly (like Crotone). Calabria these days, for all its history, has an unmistakable frontier air about it. The people are simple, straightforward, and a little rough. Unlike other Italians, they seem to have lots of children; they work hard, fix their own cars and tractors, and lay their cement everywhere. So far, the changes have amounted to such a humble revolution that few people have even noticed, and the emigration rate remains enormous. But both these regions are, if anything, a land of survivors, and who is to say they aren't now taking their first baby steps on the road to reclaiming their ancient prosperity and distinction?

---

## Calabrian Itineraries

Most visitors only take at a look at the region if they're passing through on the way to Sicily, and have some time to spare. If so, drivers should take the old coastal road, the SS18, south through Maratea and Paola; the SS585 that connects with it branches off the A3 *Autostrada del Sole* at Lagonegro-Nord, near Maratea, and it is much more scenic a route than the *autostrada*. It takes longer, but it's a good smooth road, and actually shorter. Take as long as you like: Maratea, Praia a Mare, Vibo Valentia, or Gioia Tauro make good stopovers along the way. One detour is via Cosenza into the Sila highlands—no little journey, some 89km from the turn-off at Paola to San Giovanni in Fiore in the heart of the Sila. Another, shorter digression would be from Vibo Valentia, around the peninsula to Tropea and Capo Vaticano. This adds an extra 45km to the trip, through some difficult corniche roads, but it includes some of the south's best coastal scenery. Before you make the crossing over to Messina, take an hour or two for the Museum in Reggio; even if you have no particular interest in archaeology, the collection contains some of the most beautiful art you'll see in southern Italy.

Similarly, travellers en route between Campania and Apulia can with a few detours take in the most interesting parts of eastern Calabria and the Basilicata, such as the cave city of Matera, the dramatic castles built by the Normans and the Emperor Frederick II, and the Greek ruins at Metapontum.

### Getting Around

 Two major **rail** lines pass through these regions: the Rome–Naples–Villa San Giovanni/Reggio Calabria route along the west coast, with 15 trains a day, and the branch that runs from Battaglia in Campania through Potenza and Metaponto on its way to Táranto (6 trains a day). A third line follows the long shore of the Ionian Sea from Reggio to Táranto. Reggio Calabria has two railway stations: the **Stazione Marittima**, from which crossings are made to Messina in Sicily, and the **Stazione Centrale**; if you're just making a quick stop for the museum, the Marittima is closer.

Rail connections to anywhere in the interior are chancy at best: a few trains go through to Cosenza, but you'll usually have to change at Paola or Sibari. There are also regular **buses** from Paola to Cosenza. At Catanzaro it is the same; most trains stop only at Catanzaro Lido, 9km away (though there is a regular local bus to the city centre). In Cosenza, buses leave from Piazza L. Fera, at the northern end of Corso Mazzini, for Catanzaro (several daily) and points around the province, including towns in the Sila. A pleasant way to see the Sila itself is on the old private FCL **narrow-gauge railway** that runs three trains each day between Cosenza and San Giovanni in Fiore. The FCL station in Cosenza is hard to find, as it's behind the now disused FS station inside the town. Near the tip of Calabria there is another attractive local rail line, around the Tropea peninsula between Pizzo and Rosarno.

Matera is served only by another FCL private rail line, which runs 12 trains a day from Bari in Apulia—in fact, a day trip from Bari, only 46km, may be the most convenient way to see Matera. The station there is on Via Nazionale on the western edge of town. There is also a very slow FCL line between Potenza and Bari, via Altamura. FCL and other companies also operate daily bus services from Matera's Piazza Matteotti to Ferrandina, Potenza, Naples and Metaponto.

There are also airports in Calabria at Lamezia-Terme (the main regional airport) on the Plain of Santa Eufemia near the SS280 Catanzaro turn-off from the SS18, which has scheduled flights to most of the major Italian cities, and at Reggio Calabria, just south of the city, with regular services only to Rome and Milan. Car and passenger **ferries** to Sicily leave from Villa San Giovanni—the quickest route, with the most frequent services—and Reggio Calabria. In addition, long-distance **bus** services link all the major towns with the rest of Italy.

**Road** routes around Calabria are simple—the SS18 runs down the western side of the peninsula to Reggio, and the also scenic SS106 goes up the eastern side, both hugging the coast, while the *Autostrada del Sole*, the A3, runs for much of the way through the middle. The main routes across the peninsula are the slow but spectacular SS107 between Paola and Crotone via Cosenza, and the faster SS280 through

Catanzaro. Other, minor roads across are slower. The main road to the Basilicata for drivers coming from the north is the SS407 *superstrada* (currently being upgraded), the Táranto road, which leaves the A3 near Zuppino 25km east of Eboli, and passes Potenza and Metapontum. An interesting route to Matera is the old Roman Via Appia (SS7), which is now only a minor road for most of the stretch from Potenza.

# The West Coast: from Maratea to Reggio di Calabria

*Tourist Information*

The tourist offices along this stretch of coast are in **Maratea** (AAST), Piazza del Gesù 32, ✆ (0973) 876908; **Cosenza**, at Viale Trieste 50, ✆ (0984) 27485; **Vibo Valentia**, Piazza Diaz 8, ✆ (0963) 42008; **Villa San Giovanni**, in the Piazza Stazione, ✆ (0965) 751160; and in **Reggio di Calabria**, Via Tripepi 72, ✆ (0965) 858496. In Reggio there are also offices at the Stazione Centrale and the airport.

## Maratea and the Coast

Just south of Campania's Cilento Peninsula, a little corner of the Basilicata stretches out to touch the Tyrrhenian Sea. The scenery here differs little from the steep cliffs and green slopes of the Cilento, and recent efforts have given the area some excellent beach resorts. The centre of the Basilicata's coast is **Maratea**, a pretty old town of tiny alleys and steps. Maratea has in the last few years become quite sophisticated and expensive, though the atmosphere is still pretty laid-back; besides some of the best coastal scenery in the deep south, you can enjoy relatively uncrowded beaches and modest hotels at Acquafredda, Maratea Marina (where trains on the main Rome–Reggio rail line stop), and several other points along the coast. Maratea itself is up in the hills, under what must be the queerest hilltop Jesus in Italy; all marble, and 20 metres tall. Designed by Bruno Innocenti in 1963 at the start of Maratea's push to become a resort, from a distance it appears to be a perfume bottle with wings.

Some 10 kilometres further down the coast and you're in Calabria, on the outskirts of another, similar resort on a similarly lovely stretch of coast: **Praia a Mare**, where there is a 14th-century castle. From the beach you can rent a boat to visit the 'Blue Grotto' on the **Isola di Dino**, an uninhabited islet just off the shore. Further south along the road are the now pretty much overdeveloped **Scalea** and beyond it **Diamante**, another little holiday town. **Paola**, where the road from Cosenza meets the coast, is a larger, somewhat dishevelled resort, a fitting introduction to the towns of the 'Calabrian Riviera' to the south. Above it stands the 15th-century **Santuario di San Francesco di Paola**, dedicated to the town's most famous son, Calabria's patron saint—not the same Francis as the Saint of Assisi—and the object of pilgrimages from all over southern Italy. The sanctuary is also the focus for the town's lavish annual *festa*, which reaches its climax on the Saint's day, 4 May.

## Cosenza

So far, there hasn't been much reason to leave the coast. **Cosenza** may not be a stellar attraction, but it's the best Calabria can do. The city has been one of Calabria's leading cities throughout most of recorded history; it began as the chief town of the Bruttians, the aboriginal nation from whom today's Calabrians are descended. Medieval Cosenza was a busy place: the Arabs took it twice, Norman freebooters fought over it, and at least one king of France passed through on his way to the Crusades. Today, its most obvious attraction for visitors may be as the chief hub for bus services to the surrounding area.

The river Bucento divides Cosenza neatly, between the flat modern town and the old citadel on the hill. The river is famous, if only because buried somewhere beneath it is no less a personage than Alaric the Goth. Alaric—no drooling barbarian, but just another intriguing Roman general, with a Teutonic accent—came to Cosenza in 410, fresh from his sack of Rome and on his way to conquer Africa. He died of a fever here, and his men temporarily diverted the Bucento and buried him under it, probably along with a fair share of the Roman loot. Archaeologists are still looking for it. For all its history, Cosenza has little left to show; even in Calabria, no place is more prone to earthquakes.

The **cathedral** has survived, a simple Gothic structure built in 1222, during the reign of Frederick II. A museum will, it is officially stated, one day be opened alongside the cathedral in order to display the cathedral treasure, but in the meantime, if you want to see the collection, it's necessary to ring at the door of the nearby Archbishop's Palace, or the marriage office. This little extra effort is worth it, as the real treasure is a little-known masterpiece of medieval art, a Byzantine-style gold and enamel crucifix, made in Sicily in the 12th century and given by Frederick himself on the occasion of the cathedral's consecration. A few blocks south of the cathedral, on Piazza XV Marzo, there is a small **Museo Civico** (*open 9am–1pm Tues–Sat*), with paintings and archaeological finds, and from there you can also climb up to the well-preserved **castle** overlooking the city (*open April–Sept 9–1, 3.30–sunset; Oct–Mar 9am–1pm only*); most of that was built by Frederick too.

## The Sila

Cosenza is the best base from which to see this region, a lovely, peaceful plateau between mountains that offers an unusual experience of Alpine scenery near the southern tip of Italy. Much of the Sila is still covered with trees—beeches, oaks and pines. In summer you can find wild strawberries, and in winter—well, maybe—wolves. Some of Italy's last specimens make their stand in the Sila's wilder corners. Artificial lakes, built since the war as part of Calabria's hydroelectric schemes, add to the scenery, notably **Lake Arvo** and **Lake Cecita**, between Cosenza and the town of San Giovanni in Fiore.

The Sila is the best place in Calabria for motoring or hiking, and maps and information are available from the Cosenza tourist office. Most likely you will see only the largest and prettiest section, the **Sila Grande** in the middle, though more adventurous souls can press on to the barely accessible **Sila Greca** to the north, or south to the **Sila Piccola**, around the little mountain resort of **Villaggio Mancuso**. On the eastern flank of the Sila Piccola, not far from Crotone, is the interesting little town of **Santa Severina**, with a Norman castle and a cathedral with a Byzantine baptistry. Despite the name, the Sila Greca is inhabited not by Greeks, but Albanians of the Greek Orthodox faith. They came to Calabria and Sicily as refugees from the Turks in the 15th century, and today constitute one of Italy's largest ethnic minorities. Albanians can be found all over Calabria, especially here and in the north around Castrovillari; you'll know you've stumbled on one of their villages if you see a Byzantine-domed church or a statue of Skanderbeg, the Albanian national hero.

Back towards the coast south of Cosenza, and just a few kilometres from the main road up in the hills, is the town of **Nocera Terinese**, famous for only one thing—its festival every Easter, when processions of flagellants go around the town, fervently beating themselves into a bloody mess with thorn bushes, in one of the local events that is most regularly deployed to demonstrate Calabria's distance from the modern world. Further south again, the road descends to a dull stretch through the Plain of Santa Eufemia, one of the new agricultural areas reclaimed from the mosquito. The town of **Maida**, site of one of the first French defeats during the Napoleonic Wars, gave its name to London's Maida Vale. **Pizzo**, the largest town in the region, also has its Napoleonic association. The Emperor's great cavalry commander Marshal Murat, whom Bonaparte had made King of Naples, tried after Waterloo to regain his throne by beginning a new revolution in Calabria. When his boat landed here in 1815, instead of the welcome he expected, the crowd almost tore him to pieces. The Bourbons executed him a few days later in the castle, built in the 1480s by Ferdinand of Aragon.

The best part of Calabria's coast begins near Cape Vaticano. **Vibo Valentia**, the largest town in the district, has views overlooking the coast, a 12th-century castle, remains of the fortifications of the ancient Greek city of Hipponion, and a number of overwrought Baroque churches. Finds from the excavations of Hipponion are on view in the museum at the **Palazzo Gagliardi** (*open April–Sept 9–1, 3–5, Tues–Sat; 9am–1pm Sun; Nov–Mar 9–1 Tues–Sun*). Vibo, perched on hills like most old Calabrian towns, has several kilometres below it a growing little industrial port, **Vibo Marina**, from where there is a regular ferry service during the summer season to the Aeolian Islands. South of Vibo the main road cuts inland, but the railway and some back roads head around Cape Vaticano; this is a district of fashionable, pretty beach resorts, and difficult mountains. **Tropea** is a lovely town along the coast; next to it, on a rocky peninsula that was once an island, you can climb up to the romantically ruined Benedictine monastery of **Santa Maria dell'Isola**. Around the cape itself, the road rises to some spectacular views, taking in on a clear day the island volcano of Stromboli and Sicily's northern coast.

Further south, the towns along the coast are more accessible, and some of them have grown into fair-sized holiday spots. Outside **Palmi** there is a recently opened museum and cultural complex, the **Casa di Cultura Leonida Repaci**, that houses among other collections the best folk museum in Calabria, and a modern art gallery with works by De' Chirico and other 20th-century Italian painters (*open 8–2, 3–6, Mon, Wed; 8am–2pm only Tues, Thurs, Fri*). **Scilla**, at the entrance to the straits of Messina, marks the spot where the mythological Scylla, a daughter of Hecate changed into a dog-like sea monster, seized some of Odysseus' crewmen near the end of the *Odyssey*. In classical times, Scylla meant the dangerous rocks of the Calabrian side of the straits, a counterpart to the whirlpool Charybdis towards the Sicilian shore. So many earthquakes have rearranged the topography since then that nothing remains of either. Still, the narrow straits are one of the most dramatic sights in Italy, with

Messina and the Monti Peloritani visible over in Sicily, neatly balancing Reggio and the jumbled peaks of Aspromonte in Calabria. Not far inside the straits is the port of **Villa San Giovanni**, today the major ferry crossing point for Sicily.

## Reggio di Calabria

The last big earthquake came in 1908, when over 100,000 people died here or in Messina across the straits. Both these cities have a remarkable will to survive, considering all the havoc earthquakes have played on them in the last 2000 years. Perhaps the setting is irresistible. Fortune has favoured them unequally in the rebuilding; though both are about the same size, Messina has made of itself a slick, almost beautiful town, while Reggio has chosen to remain swaddled in Calabrian humility. Its plain grid of dusty streets and low buildings, where anyone from a small town in Kansas might feel perfectly at home, was laid out only after the earthquake of 1783, when the destruction was even greater than in 1908 and the city had to be rebuilt from scratch.

The Allies also did a pretty thorough job of bombing Reggio in the Second World War; after all that, it's not surprising that there is little left to see of the city that began its life as Greek *Rhegium* in the 8th century BC. Some bits of Greek wall and Roman baths, and some once-grand 19th-century buildings along the waterfront promenade are almost the only things in the city older than 1908. Part of Reggio's shabbiness is without question due to the corrosive social effect of the local Calabrese mafia, known in dialect as the *'ndrangheta*, which continues to have a hold here stronger even than those that its wealthier partners in crime, the Sicilian Mafia and the Neapolitan Camorra, exert over their own respective backyards. Strangely enough, though, the city does still have one special attraction for the visitor—its **Museo Nazionale della Magna Graecia** (*open 9–1.30, 3.30–7.30, Tues–Sat; 9am–12.30pm Sun; adm*), the finest collection of Greek art between Naples and Sicily.

## The Warriors of Riace

The museum, directly north of the city centre on Corso Garibaldi, is a classic of Mussolini architecture built in chunky travertine. Containing a hoard as precious as anything in Greece itself, the museum would make a trip to Reggio worthwhile just for the **Warriors of Riace**, two bronze masterpieces that rank among the greatest productions of antiquity to have come down to us. If you haven't heard of them, it is because they were only found in 1972, by divers exploring an ancient shipwreck off Riace on Calabria's Ionic coast. Most recently they have been undergoing treatment to protect them from erosion; at time of writing they were due to be put back on display during 1994, but, as with all promised reopenings in Italy, it is possible that they may be under wraps for longer than expected. They are normally kept down in the basement, in a room of their own next to a big exhibition detailing the tremendously complex original restoration job done in the seventies. These fellows, both about six-foot-seven and quite indecently virile, may perhaps have come from a temple at Delphi; no one really knows why they were being shipped to Magna Graecia. One of them has been attributed to the great sculptor Phidias.

The Warriors share the basement with a few other rare works of Greek sculpture, notably the unidentified, 5th-century BC subject called 'the Philosopher', as well as anchors and ship fittings, and amphorae that once held wine or oil—all recovered from the shipwreck, from mud well over a metre deep. The divers are convinced that the dangerous waters around Calabria may hold dozens of such treasures, so some more artefacts may have found their way to the Reggio museum by the time you arrive. And don't neglect the rest of the museum collections. The most beautiful things in it are the terracotta **ex-voto plaques**, recovered from the temples of Magna Graecia. Most of these offerings show goddesses in the magical archaic Greek style—usually Persephone, who had influence over death, being abducted by Hades, receiving propitiatory gifts, or accepting souls into the underworld. Chickens are a recurring motif, not too surprisingly, since to the ancient Greeks a soul rises out of its burial urn the same way a chicken hatches from an egg. Other works help complete the picture of life and art in Magna Graecia: Greek painted ceramics from Locris and from Attica, fragments of architectural decoration from various temples—some still with bits of their original paint—records of city finances on bronze tablets, coins, some treasure recovered from tombs, and a rare early Hellenistic mosaic of a dragon, actually made in Calabria. The museum also has an additional collection of post-classical art and church artefacts dating from the 6th to the 19th centuries.

## Around Aspromonte

All around the toe of Italy, from Palmi as far as Locri, the interior of the peninsula seems utterly impenetrable, a wall of rough peaks tantalizingly close to the narrow coastal plain. In fact all of the toe is really one great round massif, the mountain called **Aspromonte**. Here, the tortuous mountain roads allow few easy opportunities for climbing inland, but from the north end of Reggio a 30-kilometre route, the SS184, will take you up to **Gambarie**, with pine forests and views over the straits and Sicily. In winter Gambarie is Calabria's only ski resort, with just enough snow to get by in an average year; in summer it's a good starting-off point for fairly serious walkers. Aspromonte, with its 22 summits and Greek-speaking villages, was the haunt of the chivalrous 19th-century bandit Musolino, a sort of Calabrian Robin Hood still well remembered in these parts. His well-tended grave is in the cemetery in his birthplace, **Santo Stefano**, a little below Gambarie. Like the Albanians, the Greeks are a Calabrian cultural minority; scholars who have studied their language speculate that they may be descendants of the original Greek population of Magna Graecia, holding on to their cultural identity thanks only to the barely accessible locations of their mountain villages.

On the coastal plain, snow is hardly ever seen. This is one of Italy's gardens, a panorama of lemon and orange groves. Two more exotic crops have also given some fame to the region: jasmine, which grows so well nowhere else in Italy, and bergamot, which refuses to grow anywhere else at all. The bergamot is a small, hard, green orange, discovered and first culti-vated only some 200 years ago. Now it is an indispensable ingredient in the making of the finest perfumes, and a surprisingly important source of income in this area (it's also the stuff used to flavour Earl Grey tea). If it is a clear day, the straits around Reggio can treat you to some of the grandest views in the south; much of the Sicilian coast is visible, and perhaps even Mount Etna will peek out from behind its usual entourage of clouds.

If you are especially lucky, you may be treated to an appearance of the famous *Fata Morgana*, the mirages of islands or many-towered cities that often appear over the straits. The name comes from the enchantress Morgan le Fay. Arthurian romance came to southern Italy with the Normans, and rooted itself deeply in these parts; old Sicilian legends have a lot to say about King Arthur. In one of the tales, Arthur sleeps and awaits his return not up in chilly England, but deep in the smoky bowels of Etna. Roger de Hauteville himself, a close relation of William the Conqueror, is said to have seen the *Fata Morgana*, and his learned men interpreted the vision as a divine invitation to invade Sicily. Roger demurred, thinking it would be better to wait and take Sicily on his own than do it with the aid of sorcery.

## Where to Stay

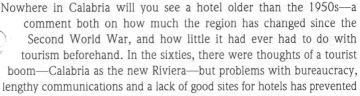

Nowhere in Calabria will you see a hotel older than the 1950s—a comment both on how much the region has changed since the Second World War, and how little it had ever had to do with tourism beforehand. In the sixties, there were thoughts of a tourist boom—Calabria as the new Riviera—but problems with bureaucracy, lengthy communications and a lack of good sites for hotels has prevented this from taking off as much as had been expected. Still, you will find acceptable hotels almost everywhere, whether you are just passing through or planning a week on the beach.

### Maratea

Maratea has become a mature enough resort to have some excellent accommodation. At the top of the tree is the ★★★★★**Santavenere**, Via Santavenere, © (0973) 876910, @ 877654 (very expensive), 1½km north of Porto di Maratea at Fiumicello-Santa Venere, a modern building, though furnished with unusual elegance, in a fine setting on cliffs above the sea. It has a pool and tennis courts, and all rooms are air-conditioned. Less expensive choices are many, with some of the best being a little up the coast at Acquafredda—such as the ★★★★**Villa del Mare**, © (0973) 878007, @ 878102 (moderate), just off the SS18 coastal highway and located up on the cliffs, with a lift down to its private beach. A good cheaper hotel in Maratea itself is the ★★**Villa degli Aranci**, Via Profitti 7, © (0973) 876344 (inexpensive).

Further down the coast in Praia a Mare the beach hotels are generally simple places; the ★★**Calabria** on Via Roma, © (0985) 72350 (moderate) is near the sea, and has its own beach.

### Scalea

Prices tend to be higher here. The best part of the beach is occupied by the ★★★★**De Rose**, Lungo Mare Mediterraneo, © (0985) 20273, @ 920194 (moderate), a typical modern Mediterranean hotel, with air conditioning and TV—both considerations around these parts, where it's always hot, and there can be little to do. You can get many of the same amenities at a slightly better rate at the ★★★**Talao**, Corso Mediterraneo 66, © (0985) 20444 (moderate), also near the beaches.

## Cetraro

Here you'll find an exception to the no pre-1950s rule—a pretty old villa, converted into a hotel to provide a rare island of elegance in homespun Calabria. The ★★★★★ **Grand Hotel San Michele**, ✆ (0982) 91012, ✉ (0982) 91430 (expensive/very expensive, depending on room) is near Cetraro in a location called Bosco—which is no deception, as there are plenty of trees around for shade, as well as a golf course, a beach, and a good restaurant that turns simple local specialities into gourmet treats. The house wine is made in the hotel's own vineyards .

## Cosenza

One place to stay that's comfortable and well-run but very reasonably priced is the ★★**Excelsior**, Piazza Matteotti 14, ✆ (0984) 74383 (inexpensive), in the centre of the historic old town.

## The Sila

San Giovanni in Fiore makes the best base; ★★★**Dino's**, just outside the town in Pirainella, at Viale della Repubblica 166, ✆ (0984) 992090 (inexpensive) is a comfortable enough overnighter. Elsewhere around the Sila, there is very modest accommodation available at Lorica, Bocchigliero and Longobucco, to the north, and Taverna-Vilaggio Mancuso in the Sila Piccola.

## Cape Vaticano

The best places are around Tropea and nearby Parghelia, 3km to the north. Here, on one of the prettiest parts of the coast, is the ★★★★★**Baia Paraelios**, ✆ (0963) 600300, ✉ (0963) 600074 (expensive), a group of well-furnished cottages set on a terraced hill overlooking a beautiful beach. This is one of the few places along this coast where it's usually necessary to reserve some time ahead. The most intense stretch of the 'Calabrian Riviera' begins as you round Cape Vaticano, through resort areas such as Ricadi, Nicotera, Gioia Tauro and Palmi, and as far as Reggio—though there's nothing special here, just very simple family resorts. In Scilla there is a very popular **Youth Hostel**, ✆ (0965) 754033 (inexpensive), atmospherically housed in the castle. (*Open April–Sept only.*)

## Reggio

Most of the hotels are in the north part of town, clustered around the archaeological museum. The poshest is the modern ★★★★**Excelsior**, Via Vittorio Veneto 66, ✆ (0965) 812211, ✉ 893084 (expensive), with fully air-conditioned rooms, but you can get by just as well at the more modest ★★★★**Lido**, Via III Settembre 6, ✆ (0965) 25001, ✉ (0965) 899393 (moderate), just around the corner, or at the ★★**Eremo**, on Via Eremo Botte, ✆ (0965) 22433 (inexpensive), one of the few hotels in the vicinity that has access for wheelchairs.

### *Eating Out*

In ancient Sybaris, the gourmet centre of the Greek Mediterranean, and in the other towns of Magna Graecia, public gastronomical revues rivalled the athletic contests in popularity; good recipes for fish sauces were treated as state secrets, and slaves who happened to be good cooks were worth enormous sums in the open market. Forget all that—Calabrian cooking today is not at all distinctive, except perhaps in a certain fondness for really hot peppers, but with the simple, fresh local ingredients they use, it won't often be disappointing either. The biggest treat may be the best swordfish anywhere, caught fresh from the Straits of Messina in odd little boats with tall lookout towers and equally long booms hanging over the water for the spearmen. Some good wines come from Calabria, though nothing especially distinguished. You're most likely to encounter *Ciro* from the Ionian coast, a strong red wine best drunk in large quantities, or very good golden-coloured varieties from the same area like *Greco di Gerace* or *Kalipea*.

### Maratea

In Maratea Porto, at Via Grotte 2, **Za Mariuccia**, ℰ (0973) 876163 (expensive) is a practically perfect seafood trattoria, with tables overlooking the sea, excellent risottos and pasta dishes that use scampi, lobster and other delights, and the very best of whatever Maratea's fishermen have come up with on that particular day. (*Closed Fri.*) Another treasure is the **Rovita**, Via Rovita 13, ℰ (0973) 876588 (expensive). Here excellent fish is matched with equally good pastas and meat dishes, all making the most of local Basilicata produce—rocket, aubergines and so on. (*Open Sept–April; closed Tues.*) Down on the coast in Praia a Mare is the **Vecchio Frantonio**, on Corso da Viscigliosa (inexpensive), which has a wide selection of grilled fish and seafood served with porcini mushrooms or rocket.

### Scilla

**Alla Pescatora**, on the beach at Marina di Scilla, ℰ (0965) 754147 (inexpensive) offers a wonderful octopus antipasta among its other seafood specialities. (*Open April–Sept only; closed Wed.*)

### Reggio

The **Rodrigo** at Via XXIV Maggio 25, ℰ (0965) 20170 (moderate) serves simple but interesting food, including its speciality *ravioli Rodrigo*, stuffed with fish. (*Closed Sun.*) For something a bit more elegant, there's the **Collina della Scioattolo** on the Via Provinciale, ℰ (0965) 682255 (moderate), just outside town with a view of the Straits, which has first-class swordfish and *aragoste*.(*Closed Wed.*) Or maybe something less elegant—**L'Ancora** at Via Tripepi 126, ℰ (0965) 813274 (inexpensive), not far from the tourist office, offers typical local home cooking. (*Closed Sun.*)

## The Ionian Sea

### Tourist Information

There are tourist offices in **Locri**, Via Matteotti 90, ℰ (0964) 29600, **Crotone**, Via Torino 148, ℰ (0962) 23185, and **Catanzaro**, in the Galleria Mancuso, ℰ (0961) 743901. In addition some of the coastal resorts open local information desks during the summer season.

## Italy's Longest Beach

From Reggio as far as Táranto, the coasts of Calabria and later the Basilicata are one long beach—about 500km of it, broken in only a few places by mountains or patches of industry. All along this route, the pattern will be the same: sleepy new concrete settlements on the shore, within sight of their mother towns, just a few kilometres up in the mountains. If you come in summer, you will see great rivers, like the Amendola, filled not with water but with pebbles; the terrible deforestation of Calabria in the 19th century (committed mostly by northern Europeans with the assistance of corrupt Italian governments) denuded most of Aspromonte's slopes, and made its rivers raging torrents in the spring. Recent governments have worked sincerely to reforest vast tracts of Aspromonte, but wherever you see bare rock on the mountains, there is land that can never be redeemed.

Many of the new villages and towns have become little resorts—two *pensioni* and a pizzeria, on average; none is worth special mention, but you'll never have trouble finding clean water and a kilometre or so of empty beach. About 3km south of **Locri** there are fragmentary ruins of the Greek city of the same name, a few bits of wall and bases of temples. Most of the art excavated from Locri has been taken to the Reggio museum, but enough was left behind to make the **Antiquarium** near the sea worth a visit (*open 9–1, 4–6, Tues–Sat; 9am–1pm Sun*). When pirates and malaria forced the Locrians to abandon their city in the 8th century, they fled to the nearby mountains and founded **Gerace**. Though its population today is only about 2000, Gerace was an important centre in the Middle Ages; it still has Calabria's biggest **cathedral**, an 11th-century Norman Romanesque work supported by columns dragged up from the ruins of Locri. The 13th-century **San Francesco** is the best of a few other Gerace churches that show a strong Arab-Norman influence in their architecture.

**Roccella Ionica**'s hilltop setting and half-ruined castle provide one of the few breaks in the monotony of beach along the coast road. Up in the hills above Monasterace Marina, the Greek village of **Stilo** is famous for its simple 10th-century Byzantine church, **La Cattolica**, with five small domes and remains of medieval frescoes. Further north, there is little out of the ordinary to detain you along the shore of the Gulf of Squillace as far as **Catanzaro**, the Calabrian capital. Catanzaro, really an overgrown village that has straggled gradually down to the sea since the war, is a piquant little city, the kind of place where the young men call you *capo* and ask for a light while they give you the once-over. The city park, called the Villa Trieste, has nice views and a small **museum** (*open 10am–12 midday Thurs, Fri only*), but there is little else in Catanzaro to see.

## Crotone—The City of Pythagoras

Heading into the gulf of Táranto, the ghost cities of Magna Graecia make the only distractions along a lonely coast. **Crotone**, the Greek Croton, is an exception: no ghost, but a dismal middle-sized industrial city. The old Croton was often the most powerful of the Greek cities, though it was more famous in the ancient world as the home of the philosopher Pythagoras. With his scientific discoveries, mathematical mysticism and belief in the transmigration of souls, Pythagoras cast a spell over the Greek world, and particularly over Magna Graecia. He was hardly a disinterested scholar in an ivory tower; around the middle of the 6th century BC, he seems to have led, or merely inspired, a mystic-aristocratic government in

Croton based on his teachings. When a democratic revolution threw him out, he took refuge in Metapontum. Croton had a reputation, too, for other things: its medical school, the success of its athletes at the Olympic games, and especially its aggressive and unyielding attitude towards its neighbours. From all this, nothing is left but the **Museo Archeologico** (*open July–Sept only 9–1, 3.30–7, Tues–Sat; 9am–1pm Sun*), with a large collection of terracotta ex-votos like those at Reggio. On a promontory south of Crotone, a single standing column from a temple of Hera makes a romantic ruin on **Cape Colonna**.

Some 80km further north, from Lido Sant'Angelo, you can dip easily into the mountains at **Rossano**, one of the better-kept Calabrian hill towns. The town's particular treasure, originally in the **cathedral**, is a beautiful 6th-century manuscript called the *Purple Codex*, believed to be the oldest illuminated gospel anywhere, made in Syria and almost certainly brought here by eastern monks fleeing their Moslem invaders. It can now be seen in the **Museo Diocesano** (*open 10–12, 5–7, Mon–Sat; adm*), next to the cathedral. Past Rossano, the mountains recede into the plain of **Sybaris**, named after the Greek city so renowned for luxurious decadence that even today it is echoed in the word *sybarite*.

Sybaris' only misfortune was to have jealous Croton for a neighbour. Croton besieged Sybaris and took it in 510 BC. After razing the city to the ground, the Crotonites diverted the river Crati over the ruins so that it could never be rebuilt. They did such a good job, in fact, that until a few years ago modern archaeologists could not even find the site; some scholars became convinced the whole story of Sybaris was just a myth. Now that they've found it, excavations are feverishly under way, and it is hoped that the richest city of Magna Graecia may yield the archaeologists something worth the trouble it has caused them. The first finds are now on display at the **excavation site** (*open 9–2, 4–7, Mon–Sat*), but so far they consist only of items from the two Roman towns that were later built over the parts of old Sybaris that had not been covered by water.

## Policoro and Metapontum

Nearing the northern boundaries of Calabria, there are castles frowning down over the sea at **Roseto** and **Rocca Imperiale**, the latter built by Frederick II. The Basilicata's share of the Ionian coast offers little change from Calabria. The town of **Policoro** stands near the ancient city of Heraclea, and its **Museo Nazionale** (*open April–Sept 9–1, 3–7.30; Oct–Mar 9–1, 3–6; adm*) has a good collection of Greek vases and terracottas. **Metapontum** was another rich city. It based its prosperity on growing and shipping wheat; today its famous silver coins, always decorated with an ear of wheat, are especially prized by collectors. Metapontum has more ruins to show than any of the other Calabrian sites, but do not expect anything like Paestum. On the banks of the river Bradano there is a small **Antiquarium** (*open 9–1, 3.30–6.30, Tues–Sun; adm*), and a temple to Hera that's called the *Tavole Palatine* by locals. Fifteen of its columns remain. The rest of the city's scanty remains, including the outlines of a horseshoe-shaped classical theatre, are a couple of kilometres' walk to the south.

### Where to Stay

None of the various tiny 'lidos' on Calabria's Ionian shore is particularly inviting for more than a short stopover. One of the more pleasant spots is Marina di Gioiosa Ionica, a little north of Locri, where the **\*\*\*San Giorgio**, Via I Maggio, ℘ (0964) 415064 (moderate) has a nice garden, beach and pool, and pleasant rooms. There is just one hotel, but with an unusual degree of character, in Stilo, also called the **\*\*San Giorgio**, at Via Citarelli 8, ℘ (0964) 731153 (moderate). It occupies a former Cardinal's palace and is furnished partly in period style, as well as having a pool and a terrace with panoramic views.

If you are passing through, there are a few simple hotels in Catanzaro: the modern and attractive **\*\*\*Grand Hotel**, Piazza Matteotti, ℘ (0961) 701256 (moderate), in the centre of town, or the cheaper but still comfortable **\*\*Belvedere** at Via Italia 33, ℘ (0961) 29812 (inexpensive).

### Eating Out

Along the Ionian coast, dining is simple—perhaps a little seafood shack that is only open in the summer, or a small but lively pizzeria with a little terrace and dinners in the L20,000 range. There are some exceptions, such as **Da Annibale** in a pretty spot called Le Castelle on Cape Rizzuto, not far south of Crotone, at Via Duomo 35, ℘ (0962) 795004 (moderate), where the swordfish *involtini* is a rare treat. In Crotone, where you would least expect it, there is one very good restaurant: **Il Girrarosto**, Via Vittorio Veneto 30, ℘ (0962) 22043 (moderate), which specializes in roast lamb and kid, but also knows what to do with swordfish and other seafood. There is a nice terrace, too.

Up in old Catanzaro, there is little choice and little seafood; at **La Corteccia**, Via Indipendenza 30, ℘ (0961) 746130 (inexpensive/moderate), you can eat traditional cuisine for very reasonable prices. The wine shop (with no name; inexpensive) on Vicolo San Rocchello is another, more rough-and-ready place to sample the powerful local specialities.

# The Basilicata Inland

### Tourist Information

There are tourist offices only in the provincial capitals, in **Matera**, at Via Viti de Marco 9, ℘ (0835) 221758, fax 333452, and in **Potenza**, at Via Cavour 15, ℘ (0971) 34594.

## Matera and its Province

The interior of the Basilicata has never been one of the more welcoming regions of Italy. Divided about equally between mountains and rolling hills, the relative isolation of this land has usually allowed it to ignore the major events of Italian history. The territory may be familiar if you have read Carlo Levi's *Christ Stopped at Eboli*, a novel written when the Basilicata was a national scandal, the poorest and most backward corner of all Italy. None of the famous 18th- and 19th-century travellers ever penetrated deeply into the region, and even today it is a part of the country few foreigners ever visit.

Matera

Not that they have been overlooking anything. Of all the towns of the Basilicata, the only one that offers a real reason for stopping is **Matera**, and that only because it is a sort of freak. Matera is the provincial capital for the eastern Basilicata, and it has been an inhabited town since before recorded history in these parts began. Until recently, it had a certain notoriety as the most desperately poor provincial capital in Italy—and the scene of Carlo Levi's chilling book. Times are better now, but Matera has chosen to preserve rather than obliterate its terrible past by turning its poorest sections, the **Sassi**, into a sort of open-air museum, surely one of the most peculiar of tourist attractions. Sassi are the cave neighbourhoods that line the two ravines between which Matera is built. Visitors as recently as 40 years ago reported people living in their cave homes in almost inconceivable poverty, sharing space with pigs and chickens, their children imploring outsiders not for money, but for quinine.

Almost all of the Sassi are abandoned today—Matera and its province have benefited from the good works of the *Cassa per il Mezzogiorno*, as has any part of the south. You may think it somewhat macabre, visiting the scenes of past misery, but the Sassi are indeed fascinating in their own way. Don't be surprised to see a group tour of bewildered foreigners being dragged through the cave neighbourhoods' steps and winding lanes.

There are two Sassi, the *Sasso Barisano*, north of the town centre, and the *Sasso Caveoso*, to the east. If you visit, before long a child or old man of the neighbourhood will come up and approach you with the offer of guide service—worth the trouble and slight expense if you have the time and find the Sassi interesting. They know where the old churches with the Byzantine frescoes are (some as old as the 9th century), and, if you can pick out enough of their southern dialect, they have plenty of stories to tell. Local guides are also probably a better option than the maps and itineraries you can pick up from the tourist office—it's very easy to get lost in the Sassi, or to miss some of the most interesting sights, even with a map.

Don't get the idea that the Sassi are just plain caves. They started that way, but over the centuries they evolved into real neighbourhoods, with quite normal-looking façades, like the cave houses of southern Spain. The predominant stone of the area is tufa, a volcanic rock that is easier to cut and shape than wood; in Matera it was always easier to dig out a house or church than build one. Opposite the Sassi, along the other side of the Gravina ravine, you will see the real caves, many of them with traces of habitation from prehistoric times.

Not all of Matera's sights are in the Sassi; there is also the 13th-century **cathedral**, a fine Romanesque building with some richly decorated side chapels; the churches of **San Francesco** and **San Giovanni Battista**, both with good façades; a 15th-century castle called the **Castello Tramontano**, above the city; an eccentric 18th-century church called the **Purgatorio**, with a leering skull over the main portal; and a first-class local archaeological museum, the **Museo Ridola** (*open 9am–2pm Tues–Sat; 9am–1pm Sun*), housed in the Baroque former convent of Santa Chiara.

The dry, austere countryside around Matera is full of tufa quarries. Across the Gravina ravine from the city, it holds a number of interesting **cave churches**, often with elaborate fronts, even domes, cut out of the tufa, and medieval frescoes. You'll need a map and some help from the provincial tourist office to find them. Among the most interesting are those of **Santa Maria della Palomba** and **Santa Barbara**. There are more of these half-forgotten churches in parts of neighbouring Apulia, but none anywhere else in Italy; indeed, they can only be compared to the similar Greek rock churches of Cappadocia in Turkey.

Among the other places in Matera province that are worth a stop if you are passing through are **Tursi** and **Stigliano**, in the remote south of the province, two otherwise unremarkable villages both with remarkable churches. Tursi's is the sanctuary of **Santa Maria D'Anglona**, out in the country on the road to Policoro, a 13th-century work in an offshoot of the Pisan Romanesque style. In Stigliano, it is the 17th-century church of San Antonio, with an odd waffle-iron façade even better than the one on the Gesù Nuovo in Naples. South of Stigliano, the wild countryside around **Aliano** offers some of the more outlandish scenery in southern Italy. Deforestation and consequent erosion have turned parts of it into a lunar landscape, exposing weirdly twisted rock formations called *calanchi*. Aliano itself is the village where Carlo Levi actually stayed during the time he describes in *Christ Stopped at Eboli*. The house in which he lived is at the bottom of the village, and now houses a **museum** (*open 10.30–12.30, 5–7, Mon–Sat; 9.30–12.30 Sun*), dedicated to the writer and to local folklore, customs and traditional life.

## Monte Vulture and the Castles of Emperor Frederick

Eastern Basilicata is a province to itself, with a capital at **Potenza**, a plain modern, hilltop city regularly rattled to pieces by earthquakes. The northern end of the province, astride the important routes between Naples and Apulia, was a very busy place in the Middle Ages, full of castles and fought over by Normans, Angevins and Holy Roman Emperors. Frederick II, in particular, haunted these bleak hills; he spent his last year at the well-preserved castle of **Lagopésole**, halfway between Potenza and Melfi. Earlier in his reign, the great

Hohenstaufen had spent some time at the castle at **Melfi**, a stronghold that two centuries before had been the first headquarters of the de Hautevilles in Italy, where Robert Guiscard was crowned Duke of Apulia and Calabria. Now the castle holds a small **archaeological museum** (*open 9–2, 3–7.30, Tues–Sat; 9am–1pm Sun; adm*). Melfi itself is a sleepy town, with little but the castle and its 11th-century **cathedral** to remind it of the days when it often occupied the centre stage of European politics.

Looking out from Melfi's castle, the horizon to the south is dominated by the ragged, faintly menacing outline of **Monte Vulture**, a long-extinct volcano with a forest where once it had a smoking crater. Around the back side of the mountain, the Basilicata keeps one of its few beauty spots, the little **Lakes of Monticchio**, with lovely woods and a funicular to the top of the mountain. Out east from Melfi, there is another old castle at **Venosa**, an important town in Roman times and the birthplace of the poet Horace. Just outside the town, on the road to Apulia and near the remains of Venosa's Roman amphitheatre, you can visit what has survived of one of the most ambitious church building projects ever undertaken in the south. The Benedictine **Abbazia della Trinità**, begun in the 1050s, was never completed, but it became the resting place of four of the five famous Norman brothers: William, Drogo, Robert (Guiscard), and Humphrey de Hauteville. Their tombs are in the older, completed church, along with some very fine surviving frescoes and carved capitals; among the heaps of stones tumbled about you may notice some Hebrew inscriptions, ancient and medieval Venosa both had important Jewish communities, and some Jewish catacombs have been discovered outside the town.

### Where to Stay and Eating Out

Despite the relative isolation of the area, you will find simple but good accommodation in all the larger towns, though nothing special.

### Matera

The ★★★**President**, Via Roma 13, ✆ (0835) 335791 (moderate) is a comfortable, air-conditioned hotel in the city centre, with a fair restaurant. Further down the same street, there is a clean and welcoming budget choice, the ★**Roma**, Via Roma 62, ✆ (0835) 333912 (inexpensive).

Matera also has some good restaurants—at **Al Casino del Diavolo**, Via La Martella 48, ✆ (0835) 261986 (inexpensive/ moderate), they lay on lots of *peperoncinis* if you let them, in fearfully hot dishes, one called 'souvenir of Lucania', that explain the restaurant's devilish name. **Il Castello**, Via Castello 1, ✆ (0835) 333752 (moderate), has interesting *orechiette* with mushrooms and sausage, as well as good fish and meat. (*Closed Wed.*).

In Ferrandina, 30km south of Matera, there is only one tiny *locanda*, but the ★★★★**Degli Ulivi**, ✆/✉ (0835) 757020 (moderate), outside the town itself on the SS407, makes a comfortable stopover if you are passing through on the way to Táranto. In Stigliano, where no one ever goes, you can sample the modest charms of the ★**Margariello**, at Corso Umberto 55, ✆ (0835) 561225 (inexpensive), for a rock-bottom price, though you have to accept that there are only two bathrooms to share between the eight bedrooms.

## Potenza

This is the kind of place where you will share a quiet hotel with a small group of government inspectors and travelling salami salesmen. They're all on expense accounts, so there are no bargains. If you do find yourself there, try the straightforward **★★Miramonti**, Via Caserma Lucana 30, ✆ (0971) 22987 (inexpensive), which has rooms with or without baths.

Console yourself perhaps with dinner at Potenza's one exceptionally good restaurant, the **Oraziana**, Via Flacco 2, ✆ (0971) 21851 (expensive), where fine fresh pasta and local produce are used to recreate traditional old local recipes. (*Closed Sun, Aug.*) Alternatively, try the singular, employee-owned **Fuori le Mura** at Via 4 Novembre 34, ✆ (0971) 25409 (moderate), renowned locally for its enormous choice of antipasto treats and good roast pork and lamb. (*Closed Mon.*)

## Melfi

The people who run the hotel **★★★Due Pini**, ✆ (0972) 21301 (inexpensive), outside town at the railway station, work hard to give you a pleasant stay, and some rooms have TV.

For dining, the family-run **Vaddone**, Corso da Sant'Abruzzese, ✆ (0972) 24323 (moderate) offers good regional cuisine washed down with 'ocal Aglianico and Vulture wines. (*Closed Sun evenings, Mon.*)

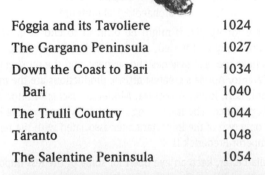

## Apulia

In many ways, this region may well be the best of Italy's south. From the forests and shining limestone cliffs of the beautiful Gargano Peninsula in the north, through the long plain of the Tavoliere to the southernmost tip of Italy's heel, Apulia (Puglia) offers the most variety of any of the southern regions, not only physically, but in its towns and in its art: in Apulia you can see Greek remains at Táranto, a score or so of Norman Romanesque cathedrals, Santa Claus' tomb, the end of the Appian Way, the finest Baroque city in the Mediterranean, and a town of buildings with roofs shaped like oilcans.

Ancient Apulia was home to a number of quiet, modestly cultured and prosperous nations—the Daunii around Fóggia, the Oscans, the Messapians and others. Under Roman rule it was a favoured province, Rome's gateway to the east, and one of the parts of Italy most heavily influenced by the proximity of Greek culture. In the Middle Ages, Apulia was the home of a unique culture influenced by Normans, Arabs and Greeks, fully equal in wealth and artistic talent to the cities of the north.

## Apulian Itineraries

Apulia is a large region—and a long one, all of 405km from the northwestern corner to the tip of the Salentine peninsula. One way of seeing the best it has to offer in little over a week would be to begin with an overnight stay at **Vieste**, on the Gargano. From there, drive south down this beautiful peninsula to **Manfredonia**, stopping on the way at **Monte Sant'Angelo** (55km). Spend a day touring the Apulian cathedral cities or **Castel del Monte** before arriving at **Bari** (112km). Apart from its Romanesque cathedral, Bari has little to detain you, so carry on south through Alberobello and Locorotondo to look at the *trulli* country on the way to the finest city of the south, Baroque **Lecce** (158km in one or two days; **Ostuni** makes a good stop in between). Leave a day or two for the Salentine peninsula before cutting back west to **Táranto**, with its superb archaeological museum.

If you have more time for Apulia, it might be difficult to choose how to spend it—the region's attractions are many and varied, and spread all over the map. The Gargano and Salentine peninsulas have the best beaches and scenery, and the most engaging towns for a stay are Lecce and Táranto. Apulia's greatest artistic productions are the medieval cathedrals and churches of Trani, Bari, Ruvo, Altamura, Molfetta, Bisceglie, Bitonto and Barletta, all close together in Bari province. The fascinating Castel del Monte west of Bari, and the great castle at Lucera, are only two of the important sites associated with the reign of the 'wonder of the world', the Emperor Frederick II.

To get to know Apulia better, keep an eye open for some of the less important sights—pre-classical ruins, dolmens, relics of Greek Italy, religious centres, and especially the unique rural civilization of the *trulli* country. Apulia is not often spectacular, but the depth and meaning of its culture will come as a surprise; it is one of the regions most worth knowing.

## Food in Apulia

*La cucina pugliese* makes use of all the natural resources at its disposal. Bari is particularly famous for fish, while Táranto has excellent mussels, mostly from the Mare

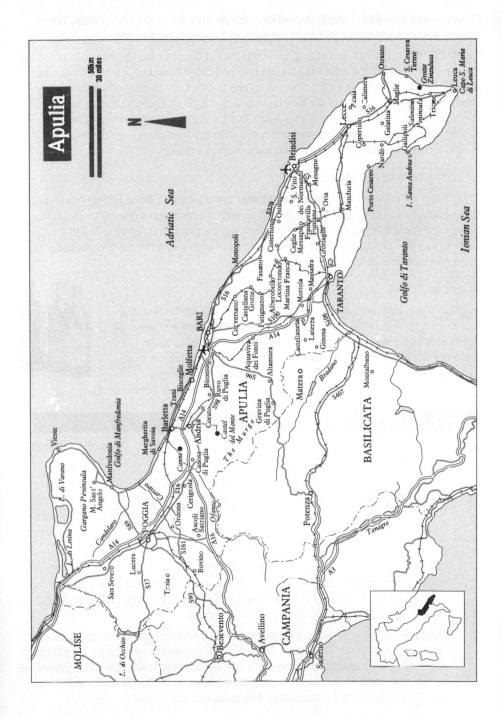

Apulia

50km
30 miles

N

Adriatic Sea

Ionian Sea

Golfo di Taranto

APULIA

BASILICATA

CAMPANIA

MOLISE

Gargano Peninsula

Golfo di Manfredonia

The Murge

Otranto
S. Cesarea Terme
Leuca
Capo S. Maria di Leuca
Grotta Zinzulusa
Tricase
Salentine Peninsula
Maglie
Calimera
Ocaia
Galatina
Nardò
Gallipoli
Copertino
Lecce
S16
S. Vito
Brindisi
Manduria
Porto Cesareo
I. Santa Andrea
Mesagne
Oria
Grottaglie
Fontana
Mesapia dei Normanni
Francavilla
Ceglie
Locorotondo
Martina Franca
Massafra
Mottola
Castellaneta
Laterza
Ginosa
Montalbano
TARANTO
Ostuni
Cisternino
Fasano
Alberobello
Putignano
Castellana Grotte
Corversano
Monopoli
S16
Bitonto
BARI
Molfetta
Bisceglie
Trani
Barletta
Margherita di Savoia
Manfredonia
M. Sant' Angelo
Vieste
L. di Varano
L. di Lesina
Carreno
Candelaro
FOGGIA
San Severo
Lucera
Troia
Bovino
Ascoli Satriano
Cerignola
Canosa di Puglia
Canne
Andria
Corato
Ruvo di Puglia
Acquaviva delle Fonti
Altamura
Gravina di Puglia
Castel del Monte
Matera
Bradano
Potenza
Tanagro
Avellino
Benevento
Salerno
Ofanto
S16
A14
A16
S90
S161
S17
S655
S98
S96
S100
S407
S7
S106
A3
S7
S16
Montalbano

1023

Grande—and called here *mitili*, instead of *cozze* as they are in the rest of Italy. They feature prominently on the menus of virtually all Táranto's restaurants.

The local olive oil is dark and strong, closer to that of Greece than the finer oils of Tuscany and Umbria; the olives too are smaller and fuller flavoured, coming from trees whose roots have to dig deep into the soil to reach water. As in most of southern Italy, sheep make up a great part of the livestock, and the region's sheep's cheeses include the local styles of pecorino and ricotta—look out for the unusually strongly flavoured *ricotta forte*. It goes particularly well in sauces with the local pasta—*orecchiette*, 'little ears'—formed by shaping the uncooked pasta with the thumb.

## Orecchiette with cauliflower

Take 400gr of *orecchiette*, 500gr of cauliflower florets, tomato sauce (either home- or ready-made Italian sauce), and some grated pecorino or parmesan. Wash the cauliflower and stand it in salted water. Begin cooking the pasta, and, when it is half cooked, add the cauliflower. Heat the tomato sauce and, when the pasta is cooked, drain and then mix in the sauce and the cheese.

## Wines in Apulia

Pugliese wine, like the cuisine, tends to be strong and full-bodied, and has had a high reputation since Roman times. Today there are about 24 different wines produced in Apulia, including whites, reds, rosés, sparkling wines and the particularly sweet Muscat. Two that are worth looking out for are the powerful red, *Cacc'emmitte*, from Fóggia province, and the comparatively light, delicate dry white from Locorotondo.

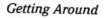

## Fóggia and its Tavoliere

*Getting Around*

Fóggia's **railway station** is on Piazza Veneto, at the end of the central Viale XXIV Maggio (information ✆ 0881 621015). It is an important junction for north–south trains—you may often have to change there—and there will usually not be a long wait for trains to Bari, Naples, Bologna or Rome. Some trains also run from Fóggia to Manfredonia, though it is only a branch off the main east coast line.

Two separate companies operate **buses** to different points around the province, all of which leave from the side of the Piazza Veneto opposite the station, where there is also a bus ticket office. There are several buses a day to Manfredonia, Monte Sant'Angelo and Vieste, and also to Troia and Lucera.

Fóggia is also well connected by **road**, as the A14 Adriatic coast *autostrada* runs just to the north. Around Fóggia there is a ring road, unusually complete for a medium-sized city, that connects up all the roads that run into the town—the SS16, parallel to the A14, the SS89 for Manfredonia and the Gargano, the SS655 for the south and the SS17 to Lucera and Campobasso. For Troia, take the SS546.

The local tourist office is at Via Sen. Emilio Perroni 17, ✆ (0881) 23650. It is quite some distance from the railway station and hard to find, on the second floor of an apartment block.

## Fóggia

Fóggia, after Bari and Táranto the third city of Apulia, was once Frederick's capital, where between campaigns he enjoyed quiet moments with his English wife, his harem, his falcons and his Moslem sorcerers. It must have been quite a place, but old Fóggia has since been obliterated by two of the usual southern plagues: earthquakes have levelled it on several occasions, and the French sacked it in 1528. Allied bombers finished off the remains, and the Foggia you see today is a newborn—homely and awkward as newborns are, but still somehow endearing if you come in the right frame of mind.

Its citizens haven't forgotten Frederick, but these days they seem more proud of a composer of operas named Umberto Giordano, born here in 1867. The municipal theatre is named after him, and there is a big statue of him in the Piazza Giordano in the city centre, among a wonderfully eccentric set of more statues representing characters from his works. Giordano's big hit was *Andrea Chenier*; another of his works, with the intriguing title of *Fedora*, is claimed to be the only opera that calls for bicycles on stage. You'll be able to see one or the other during Fóggia's opera season, in the autumn.

Modern Fóggia shows you broad, planned boulevards and low, earthquake-proof buildings. There's a little left of old Fóggia to see; a charming **cathedral** divided neatly in half, like a layer cake, 12th-century Romanesque on the bottom and Baroque on top. The early medieval door on the north side was rediscovered only during the Second World War, when bombs knocked down the adjacent building that was hiding it. A few twisting streets to the north, on Piazza Nigri, is Fóggia's **Museo Civico** (*open 9am–1pm Mon, Wed–Sun; 9–1, 5–7, Tues*), with a collection devoted to archaeological finds and exhibits on folk life and crafts from around Apulia. The single portal with an inscription incorporated into one side of the building is the last surviving remnant of Frederick's palace. Near the museum, on Piazza Sant'Egidio, the **Chiesa della Croce** (1693–1742), is one of Apulia's more unusual churches: an elegant Baroque gate leads to a long avenue, which passes under five domed chapels that represent stages in the passion of Christ before arriving at the church itself.

## Lucera and Troia

Why does Lucera have a cathedral from the 14th century, while almost all the other Apulian towns built theirs back in the 12th or earlier? Well, sir, there's a story for you. In the 1230s, Emperor Frederick II was hard pressed. Excommunicated by his devious rival, Pope Gregory IX, and at war with all the Guelph towns of Italy, Frederick needed some allies he could trust. At the same time, he had a problem with brigandage in some of the predominantly Moslem mountain areas of Sicily. His solution: induce 20,000 Sicilian Arabs to move to Apulia, with land grants and promises of imperial employment and favours. The almost abandoned town of *Luceria*, once an important Roman colony, was the spot chosen, and before anybody knew it, Frederick had conjured up an entirely Moslem metropolis 290km from

Rome. The Emperor felt right at home in Lucera, and the new city became one of his favourite residences; later it would be the last stronghold of his son Manfred, in the dark days that followed Frederick's death. Charles of Anjou took the city in 1267; attempts at forced Christianization, and the introduction of settlers from Provence, caused a series of revolts among the population, which the Angevins finally settled in 1300 by butchering the lot.

Little remains of Moslem Lucera, or even of the Lucera of the French; most of the Provençals could not take the summer heat, though their descendants still live in the hills to the south. Charles II began the simple, Gothic **cathedral** in 1300, directly after the massacre of the Saracens. This and the equally plain **San Francesco**, a typical barn-like Franciscan church built from recycled Roman ruins, are Lucera's monuments, as well as parts of a gate and an amphitheatre from Roman *Luceria* on the edge of town. Smaller fragments reside at the **Museo Civico** (*open 9am–2pm Tues, Thurs; 9–2, 3–6, Wed, Fri; 9am–1pm Sat, Sun; adm*), just behind the cathedral. Frederick's **castle** (*open 7.30–2.30 Tues–Sun*), one of the largest ever built in Italy, was begun in 1233, the same year as the importation of the Saracens. It is still an impressive sight, with its score of towers and walls nearly a kilometre in circumference, set on a hill looking out over Lucera and the Fóggia plain. Only ruins are left of Frederick's palace inside.

South and west of Fóggia, in the foothills of the Apennines bordering the Molise and the Basilicata, you may consider a side trip to the little village of **Troia**, accessible by bus from Fóggia or Lucera. Its famous **cathedral** is one of the oldest and most beautiful in Apulia, and a good introduction to the glories of the Apulian Romanesque. Troia, once the Roman town of *Aecae*, was refounded in 1017, and prospered from the start. Popes held two small church councils here in the 11th and 12th centuries; the cathedral was begun in 1093, though not finished until the time of Frederick.

Much of the inspiration for the Apulian style came from Pisa, and the Pisan trademark—blind arcades decorated with circle and diamond shapes—is in evidence here. This eclectic building has some surprises though, most especially a set of Byzantine-style decorated bronze doors, similar to those in the churches of Campania, and also perhaps the most beautiful **rose window** in Italy, a small, Arab-inspired fantasy from Frederick's time; the circle is divided into 11 sections, each with a carved screen in a different geometric design. Inside, the cathedral is austere, but strangely asymmetrical, with everything on the right side just slightly out of alignment. If you should be doing any more travelling through the pretty hills south of Fóggia, two more places of interest are **Bovino**, a resolutely medieval-looking village with a 13th-century cathedral and some Roman remains, and **Ascoli Satriano**, where a very well-preserved triple-arched Roman bridge still spans the river Carapelle. You can also see substantial remains of the abandoned Roman town of *Herdonio*, near **Ordona**.

---

### Where to Stay

#### Fóggia

Expect nothing special here; the best is the ★★★★**Cicolella** at Viale XXIV Maggio 60, ✆ (0881) 3890 (expensive), near the station. This old establishment is Victorian on the outside, but remodelled within; the restaurant is also one of the best in town. Two reasonably inexpensive places near the station are the **★Venezia**, Via Piave 40, ✆ (0881) 70903, and the **★Bologna**, Via Monfalcone 53, ✆ (0881) 21341.

## Lucera

The best hotel in Lucera is the characterful **★★Al Passetto**, Piazza del Popolo 26–30, ✆ (0881) 941124 (inexpensive), which also has a very pleasant restaurant. There's also a nice hotel further north in San Severo, the **★★★Milano**, Via Appulo 15, ✆ (0882) 75643, with showers and TV in all rooms, and a lock-up garage (inexpensive/moderate).

---

*Eating Out*

## Fóggia

The same family that runs the **Cicolella Hotel** (*see* above) in Fóggia also operates three fine restaurants; the one in the hotel itself (expensive) is a rare find, and a good place to introduce yourself to Apulian specialities like *orecchiette*, little 'ears' of pasta that lately are becoming fashionable all around Italy. The fish here is very good, and also the roast lamb. (*Restaurant closed Sun.*) A wide range of local and seasonal specialities can also be sampled at **Giordano**, Vicolo al Piano 14, ✆ (0881) 24640 (moderate; *closed Sun.*) For far fewer lire, you won't do better than the anachronistically good, cheap and friendly **Trattoria Santa Lucia**, at Via Trieste 57, which has a fixed price menu at L25,000.

## Lucera

The **Albergo Al Passetto** (*see* above) has a fine but inexpensive restaurant, with average prices of L25,000. (*Closed Mon.*) Even San Severo has a restaurant that can make it worth stopping over. **Le Arcate**, Piazza Cavalotti 28, ✆ (0882) 322146 (moderate), uses lighter variations on rustic cuisine, and offers lamb done in all kinds of interesting ways. (*Closed Mon.*)

# The Gargano Peninsula

It looks a little out of place, being the only stretch of scenic coastline between Venice and the tip of Calabria. The 'spur' of the Italian boot is, in fact, a lost chip of Yugoslavia, left behind when two geological plates separated to form the Adriatic, several million years ago. For a long time, before silt washed down by the rivers gradually joined it to the mainland, the Gargano was an island. It might as well have remained so, for the Gargano is as different from the adjacent lands in attitude as it is in its landscapes.

---

*Getting Around*

The Gargano has a little private **railway**, called the *Ferrovia del Gargano*, that clatters amiably from San Severo, 30km north of Fóggia, up the western edge of the peninsula to Rodi Garganico and Peschici (about six trains a day; information ☎ 0884 707495). Connecting **buses** will take you from Peschici to Vieste along the coast road (SP52). Buses are less frequent between Vieste and Manfredonia and Fóggia. There are several buses a day from Manfredonia to Monte Sant'Angelo, but seeing the Foresta Umbra and the interior of the Gargano will be hard without a car; there is only one bus early in the morning, from Monte Sant'Angelo.

There is also a regular **ferryboat service** around the peninsula from Manfredonia that calls at Vieste, Peschici, Rodi Garganico and the Tremiti islands, with one sailing daily between June and September, and more infrequently in spring and early autumn. It does not operate between October and March.

---

*Tourist Information*

The local tourist offices in **Manfredonia**, at Corso Manfredi 26, ☎ (0884) 21998, **Vieste**, in Piazza Kennedy, ☎ (0884) 708806, and **San Giovanni Rotondo**, Piazza Europa 104, ☎ (0882) 856240; all provide good maps and information on the Gargano area.

---

## Manfredonia

If you are coming from the north, you will enter the Gargano by way of Lesina and the Gargano's two lakes: the **Lago di Lesina** and the **Lago di Varano**, two large lagoons cut off from the sea by broad sand-spits. From Fóggia, the logical base for attacking the Gargano would be **Manfredonia**, a dusty port town with a pretty centre at the southern end of the peninsula. It is the base for ferries to the Tremiti islands and the towns of the Gargano, as well as being a small resort in its own right. As its name implies, this town was founded by Frederick's son Manfred, and it prospered well enough until Dragut's Turkish pirates sacked and razed it in 1620. (One of the hometown girls ended up as the favoured wife of the Sultan). Of old Manfredonia, all that is left is Manfred's **castle**, rebuilt and extended by Charles of Anjou; it now contains a small archaeological museum (*open 9–1, 5–7, Tues–Sun*). The town also has a brash **cathedral**, which dates from the 17th century, although it manages to look much newer, thanks to a recent cleaning.

Along the Fóggia road, about 2 kilometres south of the centre of Manfredonia, you can see the ruins of **Sipontum**, a Roman town that was finally abandoned to the malaria mosquitoes when Manfred moved the population to his healthier new city. The much more recent town of **Siponto**, next to it, is now a popular beach resort. As evidence of how important Sipontum was in the early Middle Ages, there is the impressive 11th-century church of **Santa Maria di Siponto**, in the same style of decoration as the cathedral at Troia, only built on a square, Byzantine-Greek plan. It is built over a much earlier underground, early Christian building, from around the 5th century. Another 11th-century church, very similar to Santa Maria, survives another 9km up the road to Fóggia—**San Leonardo**, an even better work, with finely sculpted portals and a small dome.

---

## Monte Sant'Angelo

The tourists who come to the Gargano for the beaches probably never notice, but this peninsula is holy ground, and has been perhaps since the time of the ancient Daunians.

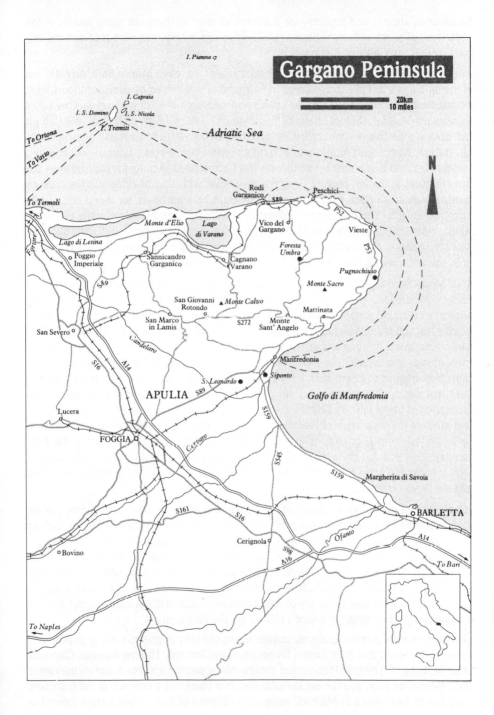

# Gargano Peninsula

20km
10 miles

*I. Pianosa*

*I. Capraia*

*I. S. Domino*    *I. S. Nicola*

*I. Tremiti*

**Adriatic Sea**

To Ortona

To Vasto

To Termoli

Rodi Garganico

Peschici

S89

P52

Monte d'Elio

*Lago di Varano*

Vico del Gargano

Vieste

P53

*Lago di Lesina*

Foresta Umbra

Poggio Imperiale

Sannicandro Garganico

Cagnano Varano

Pugnochiuso

*Frattore*

S89

San Giovanni Rotondo

Monte Sacro

Monte Calvo

San Marco in Lamis

S272

Monte Sant' Angelo

Mattinata

San Severo

*Candelaro*

Manfredonia

S. Leonardo

Siponto

**APULIA**

S89

*Golfo di Manfredonia*

Lucera

S14

A14

S16

S159

FOGGIA

*Cervaro*

S545

Margherita di Savoia

S159

S161

S16

BARLETTA

Cerignola

*Ofunto*

A14

S398

To Bari

Bovino

A16

To Naples

To Naples

N

Sanctuaries, ancient and modern, are scattered all over it; there are many stories of the apparitions of saints and angels, and even 25 years ago, a holy man who received the stigmata lived at San Giovanni Rotondo.

The centre of all this, for the last thousand years at least, has been **Monte Sant'Angelo**, one of the most important pilgrimage towns in Italy (and so well served by public transport, from Manfredonia). Before Christianity, the cavern now dedicated to Saint Michael was the site of a dream oracle; a 5th-century bishop of Sipontum had a vision of the archangel, who left his red cloak as a token and commanded the sanctuary be converted to Christian worship. Early on, the new Monte Sant'Angelo was attracting pilgrims from all over Europe—continuing a tradition that had begun long before the site was Christianized. Among the pilgrims were the first Normans, in the 9th century. They returned home with tales of a rich and fascinatingly civilized Apulia—a place they suspected just might be a pushover for mounted, heavily armoured knights. The first Norman adventurers were not slow in taking up the challenge. All the other sites dedicated to St Michael around the coasts of Europe—including of course Mont St Michel in Normandy—are the spiritual descendants of this one, founded as the cult of St Michael spread across Christendom in the early Middle Ages.

That Monte Sant'Angelo is a special place becomes evident even before you arrive. The trip up from Manfredonia passes through an uncanny landscape: chalky cliffs dotted with caves, ancient agricultural terraces, and a strange clarity in the light and air. The road climbs so quickly that you seem to be looking straight down into Manfredonia, even though it is 14km away. After much twisting and grinding of gears, you arrive at a quiet, whitewashed city, a maze of steps and tunnels. The medieval centre of town, the **Junno**, is one of the most beautiful old quarters in southern Italy, a nonchalant harmony of colour and form that only a few coast towns in Apulia can achieve. Here you will find the **Sanctuary of St Michael**, behind an eight-sided tower built by Charles of Anjou that reproduces the proportions (on one level) and much of the decoration of Frederick's Castel del Monte. The exterior of the sanctuary seems to be a normal church, with a Gothic porch and portals (mostly built in the 19th century; see if you can guess which of the two identical portals is the original 12th-century work). Above the doors is a Latin inscription: 'Terrible is this place; this is the house of God and the Gate of Heaven'.

Inside, instead of the expected church, there is a long series of steps leading down to the cavern, passing a beautiful pair of bronze doors made in Constantinople in 1076, perhaps by the same artists who did the ones at Amalfi Cathedral. In the darkness most of the scenes are difficult to make out, but Jacob's ladder and the expulsion from Eden stand out clearly. Down in the cave, it is chilly and dark; in the old days pilgrims would come down on their knees, shuffling through the puddles to kiss the image of the archangel. The grotto is laid out like a small chapel. There are plenty of bits of medieval sculptural work around, but the best is a wonderful crazy-medieval bishop's chair, from the 12th century.

The town records give us an almost endless list of celebrity pilgrims: a dozen popes, King Ferdinand of Spain, four Holy Roman Emperors, Saints Bernard, Thomas Aquinas, Catherine of Siena, and so on; even St Francis, and they can show you the mark he made on the cavern wall. Behind the altar, you can see the little well that made this a holy site in the first place. Long before there was a St Michael, indigenous religions of Europe had a great interest in springs and underground streams; many scholars believe the idea of dragons began with a primeval fascination with buried streams and accompanying lines of telluric forces beneath the earth's surface; the sleepless 'eye' of the dragon is the fountain, where these forces come to the surface. In the icons of Monte Sant'Angelo, as well as in the endless souvenir figurines hawked outside the sanctuary, Michael is shown dispatching Lucifer in the form of a dragon.

There's more to see in Monte Sant'Angelo, and more oddities. Downhill from the sanctuary, next to the half-ruined church of San Pietro, stands the 12th-century work called the **tomb of Rotari**. The idea that this was the tomb of 'Rotarus', a Lombard chief, stems from a misreading of one of the inscriptions. It is now believed this was intended to be a baptistry— a very large and unusual baptistry, if so; it is hard to make out the original intention, since much of it has been swallowed up into the surrounding buildings. Some of the sculpted detail is extremely odd; note the figure of a woman suckling a serpent—or dragon. In the same Junno district, the town has opened a small museum of the folk arts and culture of the Gargano, the **Museo Tancredi** (*open May–Sept 9.30–12.30, 3.30–7.30, Mon–Sat; Oct–April 9.30am–12.30pm Mon–Sat; adm*). On the top of the town, there is a romantically ruined Norman castle, rebuilt by the Aragonese kings, but left quite alone ever since.

## Padre Pio

From the back of Monte Sant'Angelo, a narrow road leads into the heart of the Gargano, eventually branching off to the 'Forest of Shadows' (*see* below) or **San Giovanni Rotondo**, a little town on the slopes of Monte Calvo. Here, besides the strange round temple that gives the town its name (believed, like the tomb of Rotari, to have been intended as a baptistry), there is a 16th-century monastery that for over 50 years was the home of Padre Pio de Pietralcina, a simple priest who not only received the stigmata, the bleeding wounds of Christ, on his hands, feet and side, but also had the ability to appear before cardinals in Rome while his body was sleeping back in the Gargano. The Church always has its suspicions about phenomena like these, and it did its best, while acknowledging the honesty of Padre Pio's miracles, to keep him a little under wraps lest popular devotion get out of hand. Nevertheless, the town has become a pilgrimage destination in its own right, and before he died in 1968, Padre Pio was able to attract enough donations to build a large modern hospital, the first in the Gargano.

West of San Giovanni, and, like it, an old stop on the pilgrimage route to Monte Sant'Angelo is the town of **San Marco in Lamis**, which has similarly always been a monastic centre. The present, huge Franciscan house dates from the 16th century.

## Vieste

Enough of the holy Gargano. Once past Monte Sacro, on the coast north of Monte Sant'Angelo, you are in the holiday Gargano, on an exceptionally lovely coastline of limestone cliffs, clean blue sea, and good beaches decorated with old watchtowers, or stumps and columns of rock and other curious formations. **Vieste**, at the tip of the peninsula, is in the middle of it, a lively and beautiful white town on white cliffs, surrounded by beaches. So far it has managed to retain its old charm, but Vieste is fast becoming one of the major resorts of the southern Adriatic, and boutiques and tourists are taking over the town centre. On Via Duomo, near the centre of the old town, is the **Chianca Amara** or 'bitter stone', where, it is believed, 5000 of the town's people were beheaded by the Turks when they sacked Vieste in 1554. Nearby are the 11th-century **cathedral**, with 18th-century additions, and, beyond that, another **castle** built by Frederick II, with fine views over the town.

Places of interest along the enchanting coast near Vieste include **San Felice cove**, with a little beach and a natural arch in the cliffs, and the **Grotta Sfondata** ('bottomless lagoon'), one of a few marine grottos and lagoons accessible by boat tours from Vieste. There is also a peculiar early Christian *hypogeum* (cave for burials) on the coast at the site of a long-disappeared town called *Merinum*.

On the Gargano's northern coast, **Peschici** and **Rodi Garganico** are two other pretty fishing villages that are now fast-developing resorts, and particularly crowded in August. Boats call at both of them for the Tremiti islands, and from either village, or from Vieste itself, it is a relatively easy excursion by bus or car up the mountains to the **Foresta Umbra**, the 'forest of shadows', a thick, primeval forest of beeches, oaks, and pines, similar to those that covered most of Apulia in the Middle Ages. A visitors' centre run by the *Corpo Forestale* along the SS528, past the turning for Vico del Gargano, will help you learn more about it.

## The Tremiti Islands

In winter, this minuscule archipelago 40km from the coast has a population of about 50. August, however, finds it crawling with most of the 100,000 holiday-makers who annually spill over from the resorts of the Gargano. The islands have the same well-scoured limestone coasts as the peninsula, though there is only one beach, on the larger island of **San Domino**.

The Tremiti islands enter the history books only as a place of exile—Augustus' daughter and Charlemagne's troublesome Italian father-in-law were both confined here—or as a monkish retreat. Later, beginning in the 18th century, they were used as a penal colony. The only sight, on the smaller island of **San Nicola**, where ferries from the mainland disembark, is a huge, half-ruined fortress monastery begun by Benedictines in the 11th century. Local ferries run from there to San Domino, which has the only hotels. It's a beauty of an island, well forested and surrounded with wonderful coves and lagoons set in a translucent blue-green sea. If you can avoid coming in July or August, when the hordes of day-trippers sail in, the Tremitis can be a perfect spot to let your watch run down.

Ferries serve the islands from Manfredonia, Vieste, Termoli, Vasto, Ortona and some of the other smaller resorts along the coast. There are very few in winter but they are much more frequent in summer, when they are joined by regular hydrofoils from Vieste, Peschici, Rodi Garganico, and Vasto. Detailed information on ferry services is available from regional tourist offices and travel agents.

*Where to Stay*

### Manfredonia

The comfortable, modern **★★Svevo**, Via Vittoria 96, ✆ (0884) 23854 (inexpensive) makes a convenient overnight stop for drivers. In the town centre, places tend to be simpler; the **★San Michele**, Via degli Orti 10, ✆ (0884) 21953 (inexpensive) will do while waiting for a boat.

## Vieste

The best beach hotels are slightly garish places, a little bit of Rimini on the Gargano. The ★★★★**Pizzomunno**, Lungomare Enrico Mattei, ✆ (0884) 708741, ✉ 707325 (expensive; cheaper rooms sometimes available in the *Pizzomunno Residence*), about 1km south of the town centre, is a luxurious place that keeps holiday-makers busy with sailing, sports, a pool, a beautiful beach and a noisy disco, as well as filling them up in an exceptional, highly rated restaurant. Second choice would be the ★★★**Falcone**, Lungomare Enrico Mattei 5, ✆ (0884) 708251 (moderate), with a private beach, and most of the resort amenities at a much better rate. In the centre, a good budget choice is the ★**Pensione San Giorgio** at Via Madonna della Libertà 43, ✆ (0884) 708618 (inexpensive), which also has a good restaurant.

Some good hotels can be found along the coasts around Vieste—usually in lovely spots, but convenient only if you have a car. The ★**Gabbiano Beach**, ✆ (0884) 707038 (inexpensive), 7km north on the road to Peschici, is one of the less expensive, though it has its own beach, pool and sailing facilities. A large selection of hotels similar to those of Vieste—and more of them all the time—will be found in Peschici and Rodi Garganico. The ★★**Peschici**, Via San Maritino 31, ✆ (0884) 764195 (inexpensive) has good views and more facilities and services than most two-star hotels. (*Closed Nov–Mar.*) In the historic centre of Rodi Garganico is the ★★★**Albano**, Via Scalo Marittimo 33, ✆ (0884) 965138 (moderate), another well-appointed and reasonably priced option, with air-conditioning, TV in most rooms, and a good if unexciting restaurant. If you want something cheaper, try the ★★★**Riviera**, at Via Trieste 35, ✆ (0884) 965057 (inexpensive). All rooms have showers, but there's no air-conditioning here.

## Tremiti Islands

There's not a lot of choice, but if you want to stay over it's worth booking in advance at the eight-room ★★**Al Faro**, ✆ (0882) 663072 (inexpensive/moderate), near the central square on San Domino. (*Closed Oct–Easter.*) An alternative is the ★**Gabbiano**, ✆ (0882) 663044 (inexpensive), where it's equally essential to book.

---

*Eating Out*

## Manfredonia

Manfredonia's restaurants are mostly around the port, and most specialize in seafood; **Porto Michele**, Piazza Libertà 3, ✆ (0884) 21800 (moderate) is justifiably proud of its seafood risotto, and the linguine with clam sauce is also a treat. (*Closed Mon.*) There are more treats to be had in the cool modern surroundings of **Il Baracchio**, Corso Roma 38, ✆ (0884) 23874 (moderate), where the octopus salad has to be tasted to be believed. (*Closed Mon.*)

## Monte Sant'Angelo

There is a place where you can get a L50,000 dinner for about half that— **Al Grottino**, at Corso Vittorio Emanuele 179, ✆ (0884) 61132 (inexpensive)—roast lamb and kid, truly elegant antipasti, sweets and cheeses, and one memorable dish called *orecchiette in carozza*. (*Closed Mon.*) A good choice for lunch is the **Garden Paradise** at Via Basilica 51 (inexpensive), with well-prepared seafood and good *involtini*. (*Open Oct–Mar, closed Mon.*)

## Vieste

Not all the good restaurants in Vieste are in hotels; the **Vecchia Vieste**, Via Mafrolla 30, ✆ (0884) 707083 (moderate) offers seafood and specialities like *involtini alla Viestiana* . Many people in Vieste think their finest restaurant is the **San Michele**, Viale XXIV Maggio 72, ✆ (0884) 708143 (moderate), for fish grilled or in soups. (*Closed Mon, Jan, Feb.*) For a similar price you can eat seafood or grilled meats at **Box 19**, Via Santa Maria di Merino 19, ✆ (0884) 705229 (moderate; *open Oct–Mar, closed Mon*). One oɪ Peschici's best restaurants, especially for fish and seafood, although it also has excellent meat dishes too, is **Fra' Stefano**, Via Forno 8, ✆ (0884) 964141 (inexpensive), in the centre of the old town.

## Tremiti Islands

You tend to pay over the odds for food here, but one place where you can find value for money is the **Al Faro** hotel (*see* above), where the restaurant offers home cooking influenced by the food traditions of the San Nicola monastery, washed down with good-quality wines. You even get to choose your own fish out of the fridge.

## Down the Coast to Bari

If you take the main route, a little bit inland, you will be passing through the *Tavoliere*, the long, dull plain that stretches the length of Apulia. Tavoliere means a chessboard; 2000 years ago, when the Romans first sent in surveyors to apportion the land among their Punic War veterans, this flat plain—the only one south of the Po—gave the methodical rectangularity of the Roman mind a chance to express itself. They turned the plain into a grid of neatly squared roads and farms; many of their arrow-straight roads survive, and the many centuries have only succeeded in throwing a few kinks into the rest. If not for the olive groves and vineyards, you might think you were in Iowa.

### Getting Around

Two different **railways** serve this area, and unusually for Apulia you're more likely to find a train than a bus to many destinations. All the coastal towns from Barletta to Monópoli are on the main FS east coast route. From Barletta, there is an FS branch line to the south with infrequent services to Spinazzola and Altamura. In addition, one of the three private regional lines that operate from Bari, the *Ferrovia Bari-Nord* (✆ 213 577), runs a very frequent service through the inland towns such as Andria, Ruvo and Bitonto to Bari. There are also reasonably regular **buses** along the coast road, and to inland destinations from Barletta or Bari. The hardest place to reach is Castel del Monte: the Bari-Nord train from Bari to Andria at 7am will connect you with the only bus to there, but the only return bus the same day leaves a few hours later at 11.15am.

Communications by **car** are very easy, as driving along the straight Roman roads across the flat plain is much faster than on the mountain roads of the neighbouring regions. The main trunk route is the A14, which near Canosa di Apulia is joined by the A16 *autostrada* from Naples and the west coast. Two other roads, the SS16 along the coast and the SS98 through Andria and the inland towns, run roughly in parallel with the A14 into Bari. If you are driving to Castel del Monte from Bari, turn off the SS98 on to the SS170 just west of Ruvo di Apulia. For Altamura and the Murge, take the SS96 south from Bari.

## Tourist Information

There are tourist offices along this stretch of coast in **Barletta**, Via Gabbiani 4, ✆ (0883) 31373, and in **Trani**, at Via Cavour 140, ✆ (0883) 588830.

## Barletta's Colossus

The coastal road, though just as flat, has more to see than the inland route, passing through a string of attractive medieval port towns, each with its contribution to the Apulian Romanesque in the shape of a grand old cathedral. **Barletta**, the first of them coming from the north, is the best introduction. Though quite a prosperous place these days, Barletta has sadly neglected its historical centre. If you pass it by, however, you will miss a unique and astounding sight. On Corso Vittorio Emanuele, beside the church of San Sepolcro, stands the largest bronze statue from antiquity now in existence, locally known as the **Colosso**.

To come upon this 20-foot figure in the middle of a busy city street, wearing an imperial scowl and a pose of conquest, with a cross and a sphere in his hands, is like lapsing into a dream. Scholars have debated for centuries who it might be. Obviously a late Roman emperor, and the guesses have mentioned Valentinian, Heraclius and Marcian; the last is most probable, and especially intriguing, since the triumphal column of Marcian (a rather useless emperor with no real successes to commemorate) still stands in Istanbul, and the statue of the emperor that once stood on top of it was probably carried away by the Venetians after the sack of Constantinople in 1204. A ship full of booty from that sack foundered off Barletta's coast, and the Colosso washed up on a nearby beach; the superstitious citizens let it stay there for decades before they got up enough nerve to bring it into the city. The figure is surpassingly strange, a monument to the onset of the Dark Ages; the costume the emperor wears is only a pale memory of the dress of Marcus Aurelius or Hadrian, with a pair of barbaric-looking leather boots instead of imperial buskins.

**San Sepolcro**, finished in the 13th century, is also interesting in its own right. Above the plain French Gothic vaulting, there is an octagonal dome, recalling the Holy Sepulchre in Jerusalem. Corso Garibaldi leads from here into the heart of old Barletta, passing the **Museo Civico de Nittis** (*open 9am–1pm Tues–Sun*), which has in its collection the only surviving statue of Frederick II—a little the worse for wear, poor fellow—as well as a large collection of works by the local, Impressionist-influenced painter Giuseppe de Nittis (1846–84). Barletta's 12th-century **cathedral** is near the end of Corso Garibaldi. Look on the left-hand wall, between the façade and the campanile, and you will see a cornice supported by thirteen strange figures. If you are clever and have a good eye, you may make out the letters on them that make an acrostic of *Richardus Rex I*—Richard the Lionheart, who contributed to the embellishment of the cathedral on his way to the Crusades.

Nearby is the 13th-century church of **Sant' Andrea**, with another fine façade, the main portal of which, from 1240, was the work of the Dalmatian sculptor Simon di Ragusa. The Third Crusade was launched from Barletta's often-rebuilt **castle**, in a great council of Frederick and his knights. The polygonal bastions you see were added in the 1530s.

## Trani

The next town along the coast, Trani is a sun- and sea-washed old port that still has a large and prosperous fishing fleet. It was an important merchant town in the early Middle Ages— it once fought a war with Venice, and its merchant captains created perhaps the first code of laws of the sea since ancient times. Trani's famous **cathedral** stands in an open piazza on the edge of the sea, another excellent work of the Apulian Romanesque, and a monument to the age of the Crusades. At the centre of the façade is another pair of 12th-century bronze doors, very much like the ones in so many other cities of the south. These ones are special, though, since the artist who did them and several others in the town is a native, Barisano of Trani.

Inside, the most remarkable things are underground. This cathedral is really three buildings stacked on the same site; the lower church, called **Santa Maria della Scala**, is really the earlier, Byzantine cathedral, and below that is the **Crypt of San Leucio**, an unusual early Christian church or catacomb with solid marble columns and bits of medieval frescoes. Some of Trani's other notable buildings are the **Ognissanti**, a typical church of the 12th-century Knights Templar; the **Palazzo Cacetta**, a rare (for southern Italy) example of late Gothic architecture from the 1450s; and two small churches that were once synagogues, **Santa Maria Scuolanove** and **Sant'Anna**, converted after the Spaniards expelled Trani's long-established Jewish community in the 16th century.

From Trani, **Bisceglie** is the next town, with another good Romanesque cathedral. Then comes **Molfetta**, with a cathedral like Trani's on the harbour's edge, the **Duomo Vecchio**. This may be the most peculiar of them all: its plan, subtly asymmetrical like that of Troia, has a wide nave covered by three domes, the central one being elliptical. The west front is almost blank, while the back side has elaborate carved decoration, and a door that leads into the apse. Molfetta also has another cathedral, the Baroque **Duomo Nuovo**, from 1785.

## Castel del Monte

In Enna, the 'navel of Sicily', Emperor Frederick built a mysterious, octagonal structure called the Tower of the Winds. In Apulia, this most esoteric of emperors erected one of the most puzzling palaces of all time. It, too, is a perfect octagon, and if you have been travelling through the region with us, you will have noticed that nearly every town has at least one eight-sided tower, bastion or campanile, and that often enough Frederick was originally behind them. **Castel di Santa Maria del Monte** (*open 9–1, 3–7, Mon–Sat; 9am–1pm Sun; adm*), to give it its original title, was begun by Frederick in the 1240s on a high hill overlooking the Apulian *tavoliere*, south of the town of Andria.

Castel del Monte

At each of the eight corners of Castel del Monte is a slender tower, also octagonal. The building, though 24m tall, has only two storeys; each has eight rooms, almost all interconnected, and each facing the octagonal courtyard. The historians sometimes try to explain the castle as one of Frederick's hunting lodges. This won't do; the rooms each have only one relatively small window, and in spite of the wealth of sculpted stone the castle once had, it would have seemed more like a prison than a forest retreat—and in fact the Emperor's grandsons, the heirs of his son Manfred, were later imprisoned here for thirty years. Neither is it a fortification; there are no ramparts, no slits for archers, and not even a defensible gate. Some writers have suggested that Frederick had an artistic monument in mind. The entrance to the castle, the so-called 'triumphal arch', is a work unique for the 13th century, an elegant classical portal that prefigures the Renaissance. Inside, every room was decorated with columns, friezes and reliefs in Greek marble, porphyry and other precious stones. Almost all of these have disappeared, vandalized by the noblemen who owned the castle over the last five centuries. Only the delicately carved double windows survive, one to each room.

At Castel del Monte, however, it is the things you can't see that are the most interesting. This is nothing less than the Great Pyramid of Italy, and the secrets Frederick built into it have for centuries attracted the attention of cranks and serious scholars alike. Whole books have been written about the measurements and proportions of the castle, finding endless repetitions of the Golden Section, its square and cubic roots, relations to the movements of the planets and the stars, the angles and proportions of the five-pointed star, and so on. The relation of the castle to the ancient surveying of the Apulian plain is a fascinating possibility. Frederick's Tower of the Winds in Sicily has been found to be the centre of an enormous rectilinear network of alignments, uniting scores of ancient temples, towers, and cities in straight lines that run the length and breadth of the island. The tower is believed to be built on the site of some forgotten holy place; the alignments and the vast geometrical temple they form probably predate even the Greeks. No one has yet suggested that Castel del Monte replaced any ancient site, but the particular care of Apulia's ancient surveyors, and the arrangement of the region's holy places, sanctuaries and Frederick's castles suggest that something similarly strange may be hidden here.

# Around the *Tavoliere*

The nearest town to Castel del Monte is **Andria**, a large and thriving centre. Another of the cities associated with Frederick, Andria has an inscription from the Emperor on its St Andrea's Gate, honouring it for its loyalty. Two of Frederick's wives, Yolande of Jerusalem and Isabella of England, daughter of King John, are buried in the crypt of Andria's cathedral.

Back towards the north-west, on the banks of the river Ofanto between Barletta and Canosa di Apulia (SS93 road), you can visit the site of the Battle of Cannae; here, in 216 BC, Hannibal trapped and annihilated four Roman legions in one of the most famous battles of history. Military strategists still study the Carthaginians' brilliant ambush, the only serious defeat Rome was to suffer for centuries. At the time, Hannibal and his elephants had already been in Italy for two years. Cannae was the opportunity they were waiting for, and historians are puzzled why he didn't immediately follow it up with a march on Rome. The chance was missed; Hannibal spent another eight years campaigning fruitlessly in Italy, while the Romans were out conquering Spain and North Africa. Cannae also taught the Romans to be careful, and it could be said that Hannibal's great victory meant the defeat not of Rome, but of Carthage. A small **museum** on the site contains archaeological finds, but at time of writing is unfortunately closed for an indefinite period.

In Roman times, **Canosa di Apulia** was one of the most important towns in the region; the reminders of its former status include three large tombs, excavated in 1843, and a collection of archaeological relics in the **Museo Civico** (*open 8am–2pm Tues–Sun*). The town isn't much today, but its otherwise undistinguished five-domed cathedral has in its courtyard the **tomb of Bohemund**, a striking marble chapel with a small cupola (octagonal, of course) that holds the remains of the doughty Crusader. Bohemund was the son of Robert Guiscard, renowned for valour and chivalry, who seized the main chance when the First Crusade was being preached and ended up Prince of Antioch. The most remarkable feature of his tomb is the pair of bronze doors, signed by an artist named Roger of Melfi. The one on the left, inscribed with geometrical arabesques, is a single slab of bronze. Inside the cathedral, you may notice the early medieval bishop's chair, resting on two weary-looking stone elephants.

## Four Towns, Four More Cathedrals

In this corner of Bari province, there are altogether eight noteworthy cathedrals on a narrow strip of land only some 64km long. They are the only real monuments—nothing has been built ambitiously and well around here since the 14th century—and they stand as the best evidence of Apulia's greatest period of culture and prosperity. One of the best cathedrals in Apulia is at **Ruvo di Apulia**, an ancient settlement that was famous in classical times for pottery—reproducing Greek urns at a lower price, above all between the 5th and the 3rd centuries BC, when the trade was at its most flourishing. A large collection of locally made urns, and some Greek imports too, can be seen at the **Museo Jatta** (*open 9.30–12 Mon–Sat; adm*). The **cathedral** is a tall, almost Gothic work, with a richly decorated façade incorporating a fine rose window. The little arches along the sides of the building are decorated with figures of pagan gods, copied from surviving pieces of ancient Ruvo's pottery.

**Bitonto** has a similar cathedral; here the best features of the exterior are the side galleries and the carvings of fantastical animals and scriptural scenes over the three front portals.

Inside, there is a famous pulpit of 1226 displaying a fierce-looking eagle; on one side a curious, primitive relief shows Emperor Frederick, Isabella of England, and their family.

Apulia's southern borders make up a distinct region, a slightly elevated jumble of plain and rolling hills called **Le Murge**. Here the most important town is **Altamura**, founded by Frederick on the site of an abandoned ancient city. For centuries Altamura was a town of some distinction, even having its own university. Its rather advanced outlook led Altamura to support the French, and the short-lived Parthenopean Republic, during the Napoleonic Wars. As a result, a mob led by a cardinal and egged on by monks, called the Army of the Holy Faith, sacked and burned the city in 1799. The university never recovered, but Altamura still has a beautiful **cathedral,** begun by Frederick in 1232; heavy damage from an earthquake in 1316 accounts for the departures from the Apulian norm. The building retains its exceptional rose window and portal, but the twin towers above were added during the Renaissance. For some reason, in the course of doing so, they turned the cathedral backwards—the old portal and rose window were carefully taken apart, and placed where the apse used to be.

**Gravina in Apulia**, on the road towards Potenza, has the fourth cathedral, but it is only a dull 15th-century replacement for the Norman original. Gravina does have other charms. The town is set above a steep ravine, lined with caves where the inhabitants took refuge from pirates and barbarians during the Dark Ages. One of the town's churches, **San Michele dei Grotti,** is a cave too, with a heap of human bones believed to be those of victims of Arab pirates during the 8th century. It is often closed, and to see the church you may have to ask for the key from the caretaker, if you can track her down. Other churches show somewhat eccentric versions of Renaissance styles, notably the **Madonna delle Grazie**, near the railway station. On Piazza Santomasi there is a **museum** (*open 9am–2pm Mon–Sat; adm*), which contains a full-size reconstruction of another ancient cave church, with fragments of Byzantine frescoes, as well as a more conventional collection of archaeological discoveries.

## Where to Stay

Hotels of all kinds are surprisingly sparse in the whole of Bari province. Barletta is a discouraging place to spend a night, but if you insist, the ★★★★**Artù,** on Piazza Castello, ✆ (0883) 332121, ✉ (0883) 332214 (moderate), between the castle and the cathedral, will do. Trani is a better bet—try the ★★★**Trani**, at Corso Imbriani 137, ✆ (0883) 588010 (moderate), near the sea. All rooms have bath or shower, and most also TV, and there is a good restaurant too. In Molfetta, the ★★★**Molfetta Garden**, Strada Provinciale per Berlizi, ✆ (080) 941722 (inexpensive) is a good-value hotel that has its own tennis courts.

## Eating Out

The province does better for restaurants than hotels, and every town has at least one place to eat worth staying for. In Barletta, it is **Bacco**, Via Sipontina 10, ✆ (0883) 517460 (very expensive), with all kinds of *orecchiette*, seafood antipasti and some exceptional marine concoctions for the second course. (*Closed Sun evenings, Mon, Aug.*) In Trani, the place for fish and shellfish is **La Darsena**, Via Statuti Marittimi, ✆ (0883) 47333 (inexpensive; *closed Mon*), while the **Torrent Antica**, Via Fresco 3, ✆ (0883) 47911 (expensive) uses local produce, both fish and meat, in interesting ways, and has a fine list of the best local wines. (*Closed Sun evenings, Mon, Nov.*) The **Ritrovo degli Amici**, on the Lungomare Cristoforo Colombo, ✆ (0883) 45439 (expensive), serves fish more or less straight from the sea. (*Closed Mon.*)

In Molfetta there are two places worth trying. **Bufi**, at Via Picca 24, ✆ (080) 911597 (expensive) is near the fish market, and presents old and in many cases near-forgotten recipes in innovative ways. (*Closed Mon, Sept.*) Another adventurous but cheaper restaurant is the **Bistrot**, Via Dante 33, ✆ (080) 915812 (moderate), where the specialities include the chef's own *gamberi* and *spaghetti Forza 4.* (*Closed Wed.*)

Andria has the excellent **Fenice**, Via Firenze 35, ✆ (0883) 550260 (expensive) where the Mediterranean and local specialities on offer include sea urchins. (*Closed Sun evenings, Mon, Aug.*) Another of the region's best restaurants is about 3km outside Gravina in Apulia in the Murge, the homely **Villa Coluni** at Via Guardialilo, where the best local, seasonal produce is made use of in deliciously simple recipes (inexpensive).

## Bari

Somehow Bari should be a more interesting place. The second city of the Mezzogiorno is a bustling town full of sailors and fishermen, and also boasts a university and a long heritage of cultural distinction. Bari nonetheless will be a disappointment if you come here expecting Mediterranean charm and medieval romance. If, on the other hand, you'd like to see a southern city that has come close to catching up with the rest of Italy economically, Bari will be just the place. Its newer districts, with their smart shops and numb boulevards jammed with noisy traffic, exhibit a thoroughly northern glitter, and the good burghers who stroll down the Corso Cavour for their evening *passeggiata* are among the most overdressed in Italy. Bari has also become one of the Italian cities most regularly visited by international rock music tours. Be warned, though—and you probably will be, time and again, by people from anywhere else in Italy who hear you're going to Bari—that the city has one of the highest street crime rates in the country, so take care and try to avoid carrying with you anything of particular value, including cameras, above all in the old city and at night.

---

### Getting Around

Bari itself is not a large city, and once there it doesn't take long to get from one side to the other by foot power.

### by air

Bari's **airport**, about 8km west of the city at Palese, has regular connections to Rome, Milan, Turin, Pisa and some other destinations. There is a special bus to the airport which leaves from the Alitalia office at Via Califati 37.

*by sea*

For anyone in Italy discovering a sudden desire to bolt, there are regular ferries from Bari to Corfu, mainland Greece (Igoumenitsa and Patras), Albania and Egypt. All ferries leave from the **Stazione Marittima** (information ✆ 080 5211726), on the Mole San Vito, at the opposite end of the city from the main FS rail station. Car ferry services to Greece are operated by the Ventouris line, with sailings daily from June to September and three times a week during the rest of the year. Services to ports in the former Yugoslavia will presumably be resumed when political circumstances allow.

*by rail*

Bari is an important junction on the main FS east coast line, with many long-distance services, and there is also a busy branch line from Bari to Táranto (Bari FS information ✆ 080 5216801). There are also three private **regional railways** that run from the city. The *Ferrovia Sud-Est* (FSE), ✆ (080) 5832222, runs a line from Bari's central FS station to Lecce, Táranto (in competition with the FS) and towns in the *trulli* country. Just across from the FS station on Piazza Aldo Moro, on the southern side of the town, there is another station that serves two more lines: the FCL, ✆ (080) 5725111, which has 12 trains a day to Altamura and to Matera in the Basilicata, and on the adjacent track the *Ferrovia Bari-Nord*, ✆ (080) 5213577, which runs a kind of commuter service north to Andria and the towns en route.

*by bus*

There are scheduled long-distance bus services from Bari to Rome, Naples and other major Italian cities, most of which also leave from the Piazza Aldo Moro. This square is also the main terminus and junction for most local city bus routes. Some bus services to destinations in the province, though, operate from Piazza Eroi del Mare, on the east side of the port.

*by road*

The A14 *autostrada* reaches the outskirts of Bari, near the town's own ring road, before turning south for Táranto. Given the size of Bari, it's usually quicker and easier to walk or take buses rather than use a car within the city. Moreover, given the city's reputation for street crime, this is one of the places where it's most advisable for drivers to find a hotel with a lock-up garage and leave their car there, and above all not to leave any valuables on view in a car.

*Tourist Information*

 The main provincial EPT office is at Piazza Aldo Moro 53, ✆ (080) 5242244, across from the station. There is also the local AAST, at Corso Vittorio Emanuele 68, ✆ (080) 5235186. The magazine *Ecobari*, available from the tourist offices, has a good map of the city.

## The Town That Stole Santa Claus

Bari can trace its history back to before the Romans, but it began to make a name for itself only in the 10th century. As an important trading city, and seat of a nominally independent

Byzantine governor, Bari was sometimes a rival of Venice, though more often its ally. Robert Guiscard and his Normans, who took the city in 1071, favoured Bari and helped it become the leading town of Apulia.

Sixteen years later, in 1087, a fleet of Barese merchantmen in Antioch got word that some of their Venetian counterparts were planning a little raid on Myra, on what is now the southern coast of Turkey. Their intention was to pinch the mortal remains of St Nicholas, Myra's 4th-century bishop, canonized for his generosity and good deeds. Relic-stealing was a cultural imperative for medieval Italians, and the Barese sneaked in by night and beat the Venetians to their prey, something that did not happen often in those days.

The Greek Christians of Myra were disgusted by the whole affair, but the Baresi had them outmatched, and so St Nicholas went west (his sarcophagus was too heavy to move, and so you can still see it today in the museum at Antalya, Turkey). Every year, on 8 May, the Baresi celebrate their cleverness with a procession of boats in the harbour, and an ancient icon of the saint is held up to receive the homage of the crowds on shore, recreating the scene of Nicholas' arrival 900 years ago.

To provide a fitting home for such an important saint, Bari began almost immediately to construct the **Basilica di San Nicola**, at the centre of the old town. Even though this is one of the monuments of the Apulian Romanesque, it is also a case where the original ambition overreached the ability of succeeding generations to finish the job. The two big towers remain unfinished, and much of the decorative scheme was abandoned, giving the church a dowdy, barn-like appearance. Still, this is the first of the great Apulian churches, the place where the style was first translated from Norman French to southern Italian. Inside, the only surprise is the tomb of Bona Sforza, Queen of Poland and Duchess of Bari. The daughter of a 16th-century Duke of Milan, she inherited Bari on her mother's side and as a teenager was packed off to marry Sigismund, one of Poland's greatest kings. She survived him, and had a brief but memorable career as a dowager queen before retiring to sunny Apulia in her last years. Near the main altar, note the wonderful 11th-century bishop's throne, one of the greatest works of medieval sculpture in Apulia; its legs, carved into the figures of men groaning as if they were supporting some unbearable burden, must have been a good joke on any fat bishop of Bari over the centuries.

Down in the crypt, you can pay your respects to St Nicholas. There will nearly always be somebody down there praying; Nicholas' tomb has always been one of the south's most popular places of pilgrimage, sometimes as much for Orthodox Christians from abroad as for Italian Catholics. Most of the visitors today are local, but an Orthodox chapel has been added to accommodate pilgrims from Greece, and before 1917 the tomb was much visited by Russian Orthodox believers, and now may well be again. The church is also home to a centre for ecumenical studies, as the Baresi try to make amends after nine centuries. One of Nicholas' tricks is to exude gallons of a brownish liquid the faithful call *manna*, to which all sorts of miracles are attributed; half the families in this part of Apulia have a phial of it for good luck. The saint's reputation for helpfulness is certainly still current. The walls of the crypt are literally covered with supplications, written in ballpoint pen, along the lines of 'Dear San Nicola, please let me be married to Alfredo...'

## Around Old Bari

South of San Nicola, you will find the **cathedral**, which is difficult to distinguish from San Nicola, although it was begun almost a century later. The plan is the same, as is the general feeling of austerity broken by small areas of richly detailed carving around some of the doors and windows. Unlike San Nicola, the cathedral still has its original beam ceiling, interrupted only by an octagonal cupola, and much more suited to its Romanesque plainness. Two unusual features are the stone baldachin over the main altar, and the *trullo*, the large round building adjacent to the north wall that once served as the baptistry. Old Bari, as we have said, is a bit drab for a medieval historic centre. There is a reason for this, in that Bari has had more than its share of trouble. The Normans levelled it once after a revolt; more recently, a plague in the 1650s wiped out nearly the entire population, and the port area was heavily bombed in the Second World War. As a result, old Bari in some parts has the air of a new town. The buildings in the old centre may be all rebuilt or restored, but at least the labyrinthine old street plan survives—it's famous, in fact, for being one of the easiest places in all Italy to get lost. There will be no trouble, however, finding the **castle** (*open 9–1, 3–7, Tues–Sat; 9am–1pm Sun; adm*), just across the Piazza Odegitria from the cathedral. The Normans began it, Frederick II completed it, and later centuries added the polygonal bastions to deflect cannonballs. Inside, some sculpted reliefs and windows survive from Frederick's time, along with bits of sculpture and architectural fragments from all over Apulia. Excavations are currently under way on the castle grounds; apparently the centre of Roman Bari lies directly underneath.

## Modern Bari

On your way up towards the railway station, you will be crossing the Corso Vittorio Emanuele—site of both the city hall and Bari's famous fish market, and also the boundary between the old city and the new. When Bari's fortunes began to revive, at the beginning of the 19th century, Joachim Murat's Napoleonic government laid out this broad rectilinear extension to the city. It has the plan of an old Greek or Roman town, only with wider streets, and it fits Bari well; many of the streets have a view open to the sea.

Via Sparano di Bari and Corso Cavour are the choicest shopping streets. Bari's two museums are in the new town. The **Pinacoteca Provinciale** (*open 9–1, 4–8, Tues–Sat; 9am–1pm Sun*) is in the Palazzo della Provincia on Lungomare Nazario Saura, and has a good selection of south Italian art—few Neapolitans are represented, though there is a genuine Neapolitan *presepio* (crib). The **Museo Archeologico** (*open 9am–1pm Tues–Sun*) occupies a corner of Bari University's sprawling, crowded palace on the Piazza Umberto I, near the railway station. As is usual in southern museums, the star exhibits are classical ceramics: painted vases from Attica, including one very beautiful figure of the *Birth of Helen* from Leda's egg, and also several Apulian copies, some of which are as good as the best of the Greeks. Much of the rest of the collection is devoted to the pre-Greek neolithic cultures of Apulia.

---

*Bari* © *(080–)*            *Where to Stay*

Bari makes the most convenient base for seeing the whole region, but be careful; the city is a major business centre, and full of bad hotels at outrageous prices for expense-account travellers. Two unremarkable places that can provide a pleasant night's accommodation are the ★★★**Grand Hotel Moderno** at Via Crisanzio 60, ✆ 5213313 (moderate), and the ★★★**Costa**, at Via Crisanzio 12, ✆ 5219015 (moderate). Both are within a few streets of the railway stations.

There are plenty of cheap hotels around the station area and the Via Calefati, towards the centre, though some of them are pretty awful. If you want to spend as little as possible, one place that's not bad and worth trying is the ★**Bristol**, Via Calefati 15, ✆ (080) 5211503 (inexpensive). There is also a **Youth Hostel**, ✆ 320082, on the beach at Palese, near the airport 8km west of the city.

---

*Bari* ✆ *(080–)*                                                            ***Eating Out***

Bari is a city famous for fish, which, like all the smaller towns around it, still sends its own fishing fleet out each morning. **La Pignata**, Via Melo 9, ✆ 5232481 (expensive) has long been considered by many to be the best restaurant in Apulia, with remarkable seafood risotto, as well as another kind of risotto made with chicken livers called a *sartù*; the chef also likes to innovate, and you shouldn't be surprised to find your fish done up in saffron or mint sauce. (*Closed Wed.*) **Ai Due Ghiottoni**—the 'two gluttons'—at Via Putignani 11, ✆ 5233330 (expensive) is a little more formal than the name might imply, but the food is good and the wine list extensive. (*Closed Sun, Aug.*) Another of Bari's best is the **Executive**, Via Armendola 197, ✆ 339577 (moderate/expensive). At lunchtimes it's usually crowded with business people taking a quick meal, but the food is always good, and in the evening the ambience is more relaxed. (*Closed Fri, Sun evenings.*) For excellent fish in informal surroundings try **Al Pescatore**, Via Frederico II di Sveia 8 (no phone; moderate).

For less expensive places worth the trouble, you'll need to go out along the shore a bit. The **Taverna Verde**, Largo Adua 19, ✆ 540309, near the Molo San Nicola, is a popular place where fish and beer go down together very well, and **Da Tommaso**, ✆ 320038, outside town on the Lungomare Massari at Palese Marina, is another good place for seafood (both inexpensive).

# The Trulli Country

South-west of Bari is a small but especially attractive region of little towns set amid an extraordinary, unique man-made landscape, given its character by one of the oldest forms of building in Italy still in regular use—the strange, whitewashed dome-roofed houses known as *trulli*.

## The Love of *Trulli*

It takes you by surprise. Turning a corner of the road or passing the crest of one of the low hills of the Murge, all at once you meet a kind of landscape you have never seen before. Low stone walls neatly partition the countryside, around acres of vines propped up on arbours, covering the ground like low flat roofs. The houses are the strange part, smooth whitewashed structures in a bewildering variety of shapes and forms, each crowned with one or more tall conical stone roofs. These are the *trulli*, and when there are enough of them in one place, they make a picture that might be at home in Africa, or in a fairy-tale, but certainly nowhere else in Italy.

The *trulli* are still built these days; the dome is easier to raise than it looks, and the form is adaptable to everything from tool sheds to petrol stations. It is anybody's guess as to their origins; some scholars have mentioned the Saracens, others, less probably, the Mycenaean Greeks. None of the *trulli* you see today are more than a century or two old. They are exotically beautiful, but if the form has any other advantage, it would be that the domes give warmer air a chance to rise, making the houses cooler in the broiling Apulian summers. Beyond that one modest tangible contribution, there is no real reason for building *trulli*—only that they are an inseparable part of the lives of the people who live in this part of Apulia. There is no special name for the area around Alberobello where most of the *trulli* are concentrated; people simply call it the '*trulli* district'.

*Trulli* are built of limestone, with thick, whitewashed walls and only a few tiny windows. The domes are limestone too, a single row of narrow slates wound in a gradually decreasing spiral up to the top. Most have some sort of decoration at the point, and a few of the older ones are embellished with some traditional but obscure symbols. *Trulli* seem only to come in one size; when a *trullo*-dweller  needs more room, he simply has another unit added on. In this way, some of the fancier *trullo* palaces come to resemble small castles—Loire châteaux built for hobbits. Grandest of all is the one on Piazza Sacramento in Alberobello, the only specimen with a second floor; they call it the *Sovrano*, or Supreme Trullo.

## Getting Around

One of the best ways to see the area is on the *Ferrovia Sud-Est* **rail** line between Bari and Táranto or Lecce, which stops at most of the *trulli* country towns such as Putignano, Alberobello, Locorotondo and Martina Franca. At Martina Franca the Lecce and Táranto lines divide. The FSE also operates **bus** services to the area from Táranto and Bari. The most attractive **road** route through the district is the SS172—to get on to it from Bari, take the main Táranto road (SS100) south to Casamassima (about 20km), and turn left on to the SS172.

## Tourist Information

The tourist offices in the area are in the larger towns of **Ostuni**, at Piazza della Libertà 63, © (0831) 301268; **Fasano**, at Piazza Ciaia, © (080) 799245; and **Martina Franca**, at Piazza Roma 37, © (080) 705702.

## Alberobello, Locorotondo and Ostuni

The **Valle d'Itria**, between the towns of Putignano and Martina Franca, is the best place for *trullo*-hunting. **Alberobello**, the *trullo* capital, has over a thousand of them (and perhaps as many souvenir stands) in two neighbourhoods called the Rione Monti and the Ala Piccola. Even the church of **Sant'Antonio** is based on the *trullo* design. The *trulli* look prettier out in the countryside, however, and particularly so around **Locorotondo**, a town on a hill with views all around the Itria valley. Locorotondo itself is stunning, a gleaming white town topped not with *trulli*, but tidy rows of distinctive gables. The street plan, from which the town takes its name, is neatly circular, built around an ancient well dedicated to St George.

Not just Locorotondo, but many others of the towns and villages in this district must be counted among the most beautiful in southern Italy. In each of them, white arches and steps climb the hillsides, sometimes punctuated by *trulli* and topped with surprisingly grand Baroque churches. You can spend as much time exploring these little towns as you care to. **Ostuni** is perhaps the loveliest, with an ornate 16th-century cathedral and a handful of other Renaissance and Baroque confections standing out among its white streets—including even a Neapolitan-style *guglia* (spire). Ostuni also has the advantage of being near the sea, at the centre of the long strip of very modest but peaceful beach resorts that line the coast between Monopoli and Brindisi.

**Martina Franca**, the highest town in Apulia, is quite similar to Ostuni, with a garland of Baroque monuments, including the old ducal palace and a cathedral at the top, which towers over the city like a castle. In July and August Martina Franca becomes an important point on the cultural map when it hosts the **Valle d'Itria Festival**, an international music festival that attracts major opera, classical and jazz performers from around the world. The tourist office has information on how to obtain tickets.

## Caves, *Laure*, and a Dolmen

Nor are the attractions of this area limited to *trulli* and white towns. The people around **Castellana Grotte** never tire of bragging that their famous grotto is the most beautiful in Italy. They may be right; the deepest section of the grotto tour, called the *Caverna Bianca*, is a glistening wonderland hung with thousands of bright glassy stalactites (*open April–Sept 8.30–12.15, 2.30–6, daily; Oct–Mar 9–12, 2–5, daily; tours every hour; adm very exp*). Like much of Apulia, this region is what the geologists would call karst topography: built mostly of easily dissolving limestone, the territory is laced with every sort of cave, accompanied by such phenomena as streams and rivers that disappear into the ground, only to pop back up to the surface a few miles away.

In the Middle Ages, the more inviting of the caves filled up with Greek Basilian monks. Here, following their burrowing instinct just as they did in Asia Minor and elsewhere, the Greek hermits turned literally dozens of caves into hidden sanctuaries and chapels. The best are around Táranto, but there are a couple—**Grotto di San Biagio** and **Grotto di San Giovanni**—outside the town of **San Vito dei Normanni,** and some more along the ravines near the town of **Fasano,** where they are called *laure.*

Also near Fasano, just off the Ostuni road at the village of Montealbano, you can visit what may be the most impressive **dolmen** in the south. Apulia's earliest cultures were not often great builders, but they could be counted among the most sophisticated of all the Mediterranean neolithic peoples. Much of their geometric pottery, which you can see scattered among Apulia's museums, is distinctively beautiful. This dolmen, a chamber formed by one huge slab of rock propped horizontally over two others, has acquired an odd local nickname: the **Tavole Palatine,** or Table of the Knights—the Round Table of King Arthur.

## Where to Stay

Because the *trullo* towns are easily accessible by rail from Bari or Táranto, not many people stay over. If that is what you plan to do, however, an ideal place to stop would be Alberobello's ★★★★★**Hotel dei Trulli,** Via Cadore 32, ✆ (080) 9323555, ✉ (080) 9323560 (expensive). This is a group of *trulli* cottages set in a garden and beautifully furnished, each with its own terrace. There is also a pool, and a fair restaurant. A good bargain choice would be the ★★★**Valle d'Itria,** ✆ (080) 9311576 (inexpensive), in Locorotondo, with rooms with and without baths.

Ostuni and its stretch of coast are well equipped with hotels; the pleasant ★★**Tre Torri,** Corso Vittorio Emanuele 298, ✆ (0831) 331114 (inexpensive), is fine for a short stay. Along the shoreline, the sharp modern design of the ★★★★**Hotel Rosa Marina,** ✆/✉ (0831) 970411 (expensive) and its surrounding holiday village stand out at Rosa Marina, on the SS379 north of Ostuni. It's a comfortable place too, with a pool, private beach and all the amenities.

In Martina Franca there is the ★★★**Dell'Erba,** Via dei Cedri 1, ✆ (080) 901055 (moderate/expensive). The hotel has a garden, childminding facilities and TV in each room, as well as an excellent restaurant. In addition, all across this area there are dozens of privately owned *trulli* whose owners rent them out to visitors as part of the local *Agriturismo* programme. You can get more information and a list from tourist information offices or from the Associazione Nazionale per l'Agriturismo, Palazzo Ducale, Martina Franca, ✆ (080) 701096.

## Eating Out

For dinner, Alberobello logically follows the *trullo* hotel with a *trullo* restaurant— too much, you say, but the **Cucina dei Trulli,** part of the hotel (*see* above; moderate), has good home cooking at accessible prices, if you have the fixed-price menu (moderate). A little fancier cuisine obtains at the **Trullo d'Oro**, at Via Cavallotti 27, © (080) 721820 (moderate); try the *spiedini* Apulian style. Alberobello also has another of Apulia's finest restaurants in **Il Poeta Contadino** ('The Peasant Poet'), at Via Indipendenza 21, © (080) 721917 (very expensive). It's not cheap, but the atmosphere is soothing and sophisticated, and both food and wine are among the best you'll find. (*Closed Sun evenings, Mon, Jan.*)

For dinner in Locorotondo, a bottle of Locorotondo wine is mandatory: a pale, dry white made by the local cooperative, much more delicate than most of the strong wines of Apulia. They'll be glad to slip you a bottle with the stuffed peppers or *coniglio al forno* at **Casa Mia**, a fine establishment on Via Cisternino, © (080) 9311218 (inexpensive). At the small, intimate **Centro Storico**, Via Eroi di Dogali 6, © (080) 9315473 (moderate), the owner's love of food is obvious in the care taken with the cooking and presentation. (*Closed Wed.*)

At Castellana Grotte, there's the friendly **Taverna degli Artisti**, at Via Matarrese 23, © (080) 8968234 (inexpensive), where you might try the *canneloni* or the lamb *torcini.*(*Closed Thurs.*) And if you don't mind spending a bit more, the **Fontanina**, on the Alberobello road outside the town, © (080) 8968010, is another welcoming restaurant that serves generous portions of traditional food. (*Closed Mon.*)

## Táranto

According to legend, Táranto was founded by Taras, a son of Poseidon who came riding into the harbour on the back of a dolphin. According to the historians, however, it was only a band of Spartans, shipped here in 708 BC to found a colony. They chose a good spot: probably the best harbour in Italy, and the only good one at all on the Ionian sea. Not surprisingly, their new town of Taras did well. Until the Romans cut it down to size, Taras was the metropolis of Magna Graecia, a town feared in war but more renowned in philosophy. Taras, now Táranto, is still an interesting place, with an exotic old quarter, a good museum, and maybe the best seafood in southern Italy. Nevertheless, the best part of the story is all in the past.

### History: Rotten Shellfish, Sheep With Overcoats

With its harbour, and with the help of a little Spartan know-how on the battlefield, Taras had little trouble acquiring both wealth and political power. By the 4th century BC, the population had reached 300,000. In its palmiest days, Taras' prosperity depended on an unusual variety of luxury goods. Its oysters were a highly prized delicacy, as far away as Rome. Another shellfish, the murex, provided the purple dye—really a deep scarlet—used for the robes of Roman emperors and every other style-conscious ruler across the Mediterranean. This imperial purple, the most expensive stuff of the ancient world, was obtained by allowing masses of the murex to rot in the sun; an enormous heap of the shells, with perhaps the mollusc who coloured Caesar's cloak somewhere near the bottom, was mentioned by travellers only a century ago. For a similarly high price, the Tarantines would have been happy to provide you with the cloth, too. Their sheep were known for the softest and best wool available, and the Tarantine shepherds actually put coats on their flocks to keep it nice.

If contemporary historians are to be believed, Taras managed to avoid most of the terrible inter-city conflicts of Magna Graecia simply by being much larger and more powerful than its neighbours. And it was spared civil troubles by a sound constitution, with a mix of aristocratic and democratic elements. Pythagoras spent part of his life in Taras, an exile from his native Croton, and he helped to set a philosophic tone for the city's affairs. The height of Taras' glory was perhaps the long period of rule under a Pythagorean mathematician and philosopher named Archytas (*c.* 400 BC), a paragon of wisdom and virtue in the ancient world. Plato himself came to visit Archytas, though he never mentions Taras in his writings.

When Taras and Rome went to war in 282 BC, they did so as equals. Taras called in Pyrrhus of Epirus as an ally, but after 10 years of inconclusive Pyrrhic victories, the Romans gained the upper hand and put an end to Taras' independence. Rome graciously refrained from razing the city to the ground after Taras helped Hannibal in the second Punic War; just the same, the Tarantines felt the iron grip of the victors, and their city quickly dwindled both in wealth and importance. Of all the Greek cities of the south, Taras, along with Reggio, proved to be the best survivor. Throughout the Dark Ages the city never quite disappeared, and by the time of the Crusades it was an important port once more.

The modern city, Italianized to Táranto, substantially industrialized and a major base for the Italian navy, has known little of philosophers or well-dressed sheep, but still manages to send its fame around the world in other ways. The city gave its name to the country quick-dance called the *tarantella*, and also to the *tarantula*. Before you change your travel plans, there really are no large hairy poisonous spiders in Apulia, just a few innocent little brown ones. Their bite isn't much, but a little notoriety still clings to them, thanks to the religious pathology of the south Italian. Throughout antiquity and the Middle Ages, various cults of dancing were current around the Mediterranean. Everything from the worship of Dionysus to the medieval Dance of Death touched this region, and when the Catholic church began to frown on such carrying on, the urge took strange forms. People bitten by spiders became convinced they would die, and that their only salvation was to dance the venom out of their system—dance until they dropped, in fact. Sometimes they would dance for four days or more, while musicians played for them, and their friends sought to discover the magic colour—the 'colour' of that particular spider—that would calm the stricken dancer. *Tarantism*, as 19th-century psychologists came to call it, is rarely seen anywhere in the south these days, and for that matter neither is the *tarantella*, a popular style of music that took its name from this bit of folklore, and was in vogue around the beginning of the last century.

---

### Getting Around

There are two **railway** lines, but both use the central station in Táranto, at the far western end of town—between the old town and the steel mills—on Piazzale Duca d'Aosta. Regular FS trains leave for Lecce, Brindisi, Bari and further north, as well as for the horrible endless trip around the Ionian sea to Reggio Calabria (Táranto FS information ℭ 099 411801). On one or another of the FS lines you can get to Massafra, Castellaneta, Grottaglie or Manduria. FSE local trains, which operate from one side of the station, will take you to Locorotondo, Martina Franca, and Alberobello (ℭ 099 28072).

The FSE also operates a large proportion of the province's **bus** services. Several a day for Alberobello, Bari or Lecce leave from Piazza Castello. Their buses for Ostuni and Manduria leave from Via Magnaghi. SITA buses to Matera also leave from Piazza Castello, and there are daily buses to Naples run by the Miccolis company from the Corso Umberto. Buses to Metaponto and Potenza leave outside the train station.

The A14 *autostrada* comes to an end just north of Táranto and all major roads from the north meet up with an outer ring road through the western part of the city, part of the Via Appia (SS7) for Brindisi. The only trunk route that involves crossing over to the older, southern part of Táranto is the SS7*ter*, for Lecce.

---

### Tourist Information

The Táranto EPT is at Corso Umberto 113, © (099) 432392.

---

## The Città Vecchia

Perhaps unique among cities, Táranto has two 'seas' all to itself. Its harbour consists of two large lagoons, the **Mare Grande** and the **Mare Piccolo**. The city is on a narrow strip of land between them, broken into three pieces by a pair of narrow channels. Today, the western-most section, around the railway station, is almost entirely filled up with Italy's biggest steel plant, begun as the showpiece project of the *Cassa per il Mezzogiorno* in the early fifties. This gargantuan complex provides an unexpected and memorable sight if you enter the city by night. Directly below the station along the Via Duca d'Aosta, a bridge takes you over to the old town, a nearly rectangular island that is only four blocks wide, but still does its best to make you lose your way. The ancient Tarantines, lacking any sort of hill, made the island their acropolis—though in those days it was still attached to the mainland. Most of the temples were here, along with a famous gold-plated bronze statue of Zeus that was the second largest piece of sculpture in the world, surpassed only by the Colossus of Rhodes. Today all that remains of ancient Taras are some columns from a **Temple of Poseidon**, which have been re-erected in the main square next to Táranto's **Castello**, built in the 1480s by King Ferdinand of Spain. From the square, a **swinging bridge**, something rare in Italy, connects the old town with the new. The Mare Piccolo, besides being an enormous oyster and mussel farm for the fishermen of Táranto, is also the home of one of Italy's two main naval bases. If you come by very early in the morning when the bridge is open, you may see big warships waiting their turn with little fishing boats to squeeze their way through the narrow channel.

Follow the fishermen home, and you'll end up in the **fish market** on Via Cariati, near the docks at the opposite end of the Città Vecchia. In sometimes slick and up-to-date Italy this is one of the places where you can most truly believe you are in the Mediterranean: a wet and mildly grubby quay awash with the sounds and smells of the sea, where tired fishermen appear each morning at dawn to have coffee, sort out the catch, and bang the life out of octo-puses on the stones. Many of Táranto's best restaurants are here too, hidden behind the most unpretentious of façades, and you can come back in the evening for an exceptional dinner. Of course there are plenty of cats around; true 'aristocats' they are, the descendants of the first cats of Europe. Ancient historians record how the ancient Tarantines imported them from Egypt.

From the fish market, pick your way a short distance across the Città Vecchia to the **cathedral**, built and rebuilt in a hodgepodge of different styles, beginning in the 11th century. Most of the last, florid Baroque remodelling has been cleared away, saving only a curious coffered ceiling, with two golden statues suspended from it. Roman columns and capitals support the arches, and there is a good medieval baptismal font under a baldachin. Some bits of mosaic survive on the floor; mosaics in the Byzantine manner were an important part of all Apulia's medieval churches. Táranto's cathedral is dedicated to St Cataldus, a Munster Irishman who did good works here on his way to the Crusades, and you can see his tomb down in the crypt. The rest of the Città Vecchia's back streets hold few surprises. The area was down at heel and half forgotten for a long time, but with Táranto's new-found prosperity the city is putting a good deal of money into restoring old palaces and other monuments, a process that is already beginning to make a difference.

## The Museum of Magna Graecia

As in Bari, crossing over from the sleepy old town into the hyperactive new centre is a startling contrast. Táranto has nothing to envy Bari these days; its new town is surprisingly bright, busy and sprawling, with as many grey-suited businessmen as blue-clad sailors. There aren't many modern sights here, but the best of Magna Graecia is on display at the **Museo Nazionale** (*open 9–2, 2.30–7.30, Mon, Sat; 9am–2pm Tues–Thurs; 9am–1pm Sun; adm*), on Piazza Archita, just two streets west of the swinging bridge.

With building activity going full-blast around Táranto, new discoveries are being made all the time; already the collection rivals those of Reggio and Naples, and there is always the possibility that some new discovery, like that of the Warriors of Riace, will turn up to broaden our appreciation of the ancient world. There are some fine pieces of sculpture from temples and funeral sites, including the well-preserved 6th-century BC tomb of an athlete, a head of Aphrodite and several other works attributed to the school of Praxiteles, and also a wonderful bronze of the god Poseidon, in the angular, half-oriental Archaic style.

The museum also has what is believed to be the largest collection of Greek terracotta figures in the world. They are fascinating in their thousands, the middle-class *objets d'art* of antiquity. The older ones are more consciously religious images of Dionysus, Demeter or Persephone that served the same purpose as the crucifix on the wall of a modern Italian family. Later examples give every evidence of creeping secularism; the subjects range from ladies at their toilette to grotesque theatre masks, comic dancers, and figures from mythological stories. A few are copies of famous monuments; one figurine reproduces a statue of Nike, or Victory, erected in Taras after one of Pyrrhus' defeats of the Romans—and later moved to the Roman forum after the war went the other way.

Among the fragments from Taras' buildings, there is an entire wall of leering Medusas, protection against the evil eye—as much a preoccupation among the ancient Greeks as it is with southern Italians today. Besides a large collection of delicate jewellery and coins, many minted with the city's own symbol of Taras riding his dolphin, there is also an important selection of Greek ceramics, including fine examples of the earlier, less common black figure-work. They are particularly fascinating to see, with their figures of humans and gods fighting, taking part in sports or revelling. In one room, a rare evocation of Magna Graecia at play is provided by scenes on vases of Athene and contending athletes, near a case full of such odd finds as javelin points, and a genuine ancient discus.

## Towns Around Táranto

**Grottaglie**, just 15 minutes by train to the east of the city, is the ceramics capital of southeast Italy. The town's potters continue to produce plates, vases and pots in enormous quantities today, and attract throngs of visitors on summer weekends, eager to buy their traditional, and sometimes more modern, styles.

## The Potters of Apulia

Ceramics and terracotta have been two of the main products of Apulia since the days of the ancient Greeks. Today the region's pots may be put to different uses from those for which they were originally designed, but their forms and shapes remain much as they have always been. Terracotta production is centred around Bari, but Grottaglie is the capital of Pugliese pottery, boasting an unbroken tradition of working in ceramics since at least the Middle Ages; the thousands of plates and vases stacked on the pavements and rooftops make an arresting sight. As well as producing copies of ancient Greek wine bottles and amphorae (all glazed with flowers and abstract patterns), the town still makes the huge plates that were traditionally used for communal eating on the threshing room floor during harvests, while the giant vases that now make good plant pots or umbrella stands were originally intended to hold soaking laundry before wash day. Grottaglie pottery is found on sale all over Italy, but at its source it's available at almost half the price: a great bargain, especially if you're travelling by car.

Further along the road and rail line towards Brindisi is **Francavilla Fontana**, which takes its title of 'free town' from a favour granted by King Ferdinand IV. The town conserves several 14th–18th-century palaces, including a small one belonging to the 18th-century Bourbon kings, as a reminder of its days as a feudal stronghold. Nearby **Oria** has a history much the same. Frederick II built a strong **castle** here in 1227–33, with three tall round towers, which now resembles a toy fortress. It's one of the few such castles you can visit, and the city has assembled a collection of antiquities and bric-à-brac inside (*open 8–12, 4–6, Tues–Sun; adm*). In the Middle Ages, Oria had an important Jewish community; the ghetto and its buildings are still intact, perhaps the only one in Italy which has survived.

Oria is believed to have been the capital of the ancient Messapians, a quietly civilized people who suffered many indignities at the hands of the Greek colonists, and finally succumbed to the allure of classical culture. **Ceglie Messapico**, south of Ostuni, was another of their cities, and it is here you can see the Messapians' most noteworthy surviving monuments. The *specchie* are tall conical stepped towers; they get their name intriguingly from the Latin *speculum*, a mirror, but no one has the faintest idea what they are or what purpose they served. One is in Ceglie itself, and the other two out in the country. The most impressive, the 11m **Specchia Miano**, is 7km down the road from Ceglie to Francavilla—turn right up the road to *Masseria Bottari* farm and walk through the field on the right.

**Manduria** was another Messapian city, mentioned in the histories as fighting continuous wars with Taras. Ruins of its fortifications can still be seen—three concentric circuits of which the outermost is three miles around—along with caves, necropoli, and a famous well mentioned in Pliny's *Natural History*. To find the well, turn right in front of the church of the Capuccini, on Via Sant'Antonio. The new city has an interesting **cathedral**, with a beautifully carved Renaissance rose window and portals.

## Massafra

West of Táranto, a very short distance back toward Le Murge and Matera, you can visit one of the most unusual cities of Apulia. **Massafra**, even more than Matera, was a city of troglodytes and monks. A steep ravine, the **Gravina di San Marco**, cuts the city in two. The ravine and surrounding valleys are lined with caves, and many of these were expanded into cave-chapels, or *laure*, by Greek monks in the early Middle Ages. Between the caves and the old church crypts, it has been estimated that there are over a hundred medieval frescoes in, around, and under Massafra—some of considerable artistic merit. One of the best is a beautiful Byzantine Virgin called *La Vergine della Scala*, in a sanctuary of the same name, reached from Via del Santuario in the old town of Massafra by a long naif-Baroque set of stairs. The Madonna is shown receiving the homage of two kneeling deer, the subject of an old legend. Adjacent to the sanctuary, some more, this time 13th-century paintings can be seen in the **Cripta della Bona Nova**.

Apart from these well-visited examples, you will have to rely on the locals' considerable goodwill towards strangers to find the rest of the caves, crypts and frescoes. None of the sites is well marked. At the bottom of the ravine is the **Farmacia del Mago Greguro**, a now rather neglected complex of caves that it is believed were used by the monks to store and prepare medicinal herbs.

Other cave churches and frescoes can be seen at **Mottola**, **Palagianello** and **Ginosa**, built like Massafra over a ravine full of caves. **Laterza**, perched on a 200m-deep gorge near the border with the Basilicata, has about 180 caves and *laure*, of which some 30 can be visited. **Castellaneta** also has a ravine, the steepest and wildest of them all, and some cave churches, but this town cares more to be known as the birthplace, in 1895, of Rudolph Valentino. There's a monument to him in the main square, with a life-size ceramic statue of the old matinée idol dressed as the Sheik of Araby.

---

*Táranto ✆ (099–)*     ***Where to Stay***

Most of the better hotels are inconveniently located on the far eastern edge of town. One well-run spot in the centre is the ★★★**Plaza**, facing Piazza Archita at Via d'Aquino 46, ✆ 490775 (moderate). All of the rooms are air-conditioned, and most have a balcony over the square. A cheaper hotel in the same area is the nearby ★★**Imperiale**, Via Pitagora 94, ✆ 433019 (inexpensive), which is basic but clean and quite friendly. The real bargain places are in the old town, in the picturesque environs of the fish market. The ★**Ariston**, Piazza Fontana 15, ✆ 407563 (inexpensive) is a clean and shipshape establishment, and the views over the Mare Piccolo are priceless.

Táranto is a comfortable city in which to spend a few days, and there is little reason to try and find accommodation out in the hinterlands. West of the city, at Castellaneta Marina—Riva dei Tessali, the **\*\*\*\*Golf Hotel**, Riva dei Tesseli, © 6439251, @ 6439255 (expensive), is a resort complex of cottages in a grove near the links—not much of a course, really, but a full 18 holes, and a genuine novelty in these parts. There are no hotels in Massafra—only a locanda or two, while the best-value place in Manduria is the **\*Nuovo Marinelli**, Via Pacelli 19, © 807680 (inexpensive). Note, though, that its rooms do not have baths.

---

*Táranto © (099–)*                                                    **Eating Out**

The fish market in Táranto is naturally the place to go for dinner, and right across the street there are a number of popular places where you can feast on the fruits of the sea and rub elbows with half Táranto at the same time. You can also leave a place like **Posillipo a Mare**, Via Cariati 38, © 411519, with a bill of L25,000 or less. (*Closed Fri.*) For something a little more elegant, there's **Al Gambero**, just across the channel at Vico del Ponte 4, © 4711190 (moderate), a place that has earned a high reputation with its creative dishes involving nearly all the fantastic array of marine delicacies the Ionian sea has to offer. (*Closed Mon, Nov.*) One of the best and newest places to eat in Táranto is the sophisticated **Le Vecchie Cantine**, Corso da Carelli, © 572589 (expensive), where the speciality is swordfish with spaghetti. (*Open Oct–April, closed Wed.*)

All of these places feature prominently the local speciality: mussels, or *mitili*. Another good Táranto seafood restaurant offering such things as roast squid and spaghetti with mussels is the **Rendez Vous**, Viale Virgilio 66, © 339981 (moderate; *closed Fri*). There are many good inexpensive places in the new city: the **Ristorante-Pizzeria Mario** at Via Acclaio 68, © 26008, besides good pizza, has seafood dinners for under L20,000; even better is the **Ristorante Basile**, Via Pitagora 76, © 26240, across from the main city park, which cooks fine dinners at rock-bottom prices. Pass up the *menu turistico* and go for a good fish dinner for L20,000 or so.

Outside Táranto, Francavilla Fontana has a good restaurant, **Al Piccolo Mondo**, Via San Francesco d'Assisi 98, © 943618 (expensive), where fresh pasta, grilled meats and excellent fish are imaginatively prepared and presented. (*Closed Mon, July.*)

# The Salentine Peninsula

It has lovely Lecce and dowdy Brindisi, some flat but unusual countryside, the sun-bleached and sea-washed old towns of Gallipoli and Otranto, lots of caves and neolithic remains. Its coastline, while not as ruggedly beautiful as that of the Gargano, does have its charms, not least of which is that it is relatively uncrowded. Not many tourists, even among the Italians, make their way to this distant Land's End. If you are beachcombing or backpacking, and can resist the temptation presented by the ferries to Greece, this might be a good place to spend a lazy week or so.

Brindisi's Casale **airport** is 4km north of the city and has regular flights to Rome, Milan, Verona and some other destinations. There is a frequent bus service between the airport and the main FS rail station in the city centre.

*by sea*

Brindisi is the most important Italian port for ferries to Greece, and has daily connections almost the year round to Corfu, Patras and Igoumenitsa, with several a day in the busy summer season. All ferries leave from the **Stazione Marittima**, in the centre of the port. Schedules, prices, and even the names of the lines change all the time—as fairly insubstantial companies sometimes set up from one year to the next just for the summer season—but the EPT office should have up-to-date information. That may not be much help in summer—frequently as the boats run, it is a good idea in July and August to book a passage before you get to Brindisi. If you do need to buy a boat ticket here, avoid absolutely the ticket touts clustered around the train station and the Stazione Marittima. There is an enormous number of agencies in Brindisi offering ferry tickets, but many of them too are notoriously unreliable. It is always advisable to look around and to buy tickets from the boat companies themselves or an approved agent. The two most established ferry companies and their main agents in Brindisi are **Adriatica**, Stazione Marittima, ✆ (0831) 523825, and **Hellenic Mediterranean**, Corso Garibaldi 8, ✆ (0831) 528531. They are not as cheap as some ferries, but are reliable.

Between June and September ferries also operate between the little port of Otranto and Corfu and Igoumenitsa. They are faster than many of the Brindisi boats, but more expensive.

*by rail*

Lecce, despite its location, is well served by rail; the city is a terminus for long sleeper runs across Italy to Rome and Milan. All of these trains also pass through Brindisi, and both towns have very frequent trains heading for Bari or Táranto (Lecce FS information ✆ (0832) 301016). In addition, there is always the tired but game FSE, which has services from Lecce to Otranto, Gallipoli and Nardo, as well as some to Bari and Táranto via Manduria (Lecce FSE information ✆ 0832 41931).

*by bus*

In Brindisi, buses to all provincial towns and nearby cities leave from the Viale Porta Pia. In Lecce, most buses to towns in the Salentine, run by the Sud-Est Company, leave from Via Adua near the old western walls. There are also daily long-distance services from Lecce and Brindisi to Rome, Naples and many other Italian cities.

*by road*

The Via Appia (SS7) reaches its end in Brindisi, as it has done for 2000 years. Traffic leaving the port can be very slow in summer, and a more leisurely way to get away from the city can be along the SS16 to San Vito dei Normanni and the *trulli* country, or along the coast road.

---

## Tourist Information

In **Brindisi** the EPT is at Piazza A. Dionisi, ✆ (0831) 521944, and there is another AAST office at Via Rubini 19, ✆ (0831) 521091. On the peninsula there are offices in **Lecce**, in Piazza Sant'Oronzo, ✆ (0832) 304443; **Otranto**, at Via Rondachi 8, ✆ (0836) 81436; and **Santa Cesarea Terme**, at Via Roma 209, ✆ (0836) 944043.

## Brindisi

The word *brindisi* in Italian means a toast. It's just a coincidence; the name comes from the original Greek colony of *Brentesion*, and it isn't likely that anyone has ever proposed a toast to this grey and dusty port. Brindisi today is what it was in Roman times: the gangplank to the boat for Greece. On the Viale Regina Margherita, to the right of the port, a small piazza at the top of a formal stairway holds a magnificent **Roman column**, once topped by the statue of an emperor, that marked the end of the Appian Way (and currently under treatment to protect it from the elements). For six centuries, all of Rome's trade with the East, all its legions heading toward new conquests, and all its trains of triumphant or beaten emperors and generals passed through *Brundisium*. From the 11th century on, the city reassumed its old role when it became one of the most important Crusader ports. A memory of this survives too; if you enter the city from the north or west, you will pass the **Tancredi Fountain**, an Arab-inspired work built by the Norman chief Tancred. Here the Christian knights watered their horses a last time before setting out for the Holy Land.

As a city where people have always been more concerned with coming and going than settling down, Brindisi has not saved up a great store of monuments and art. Travel agents and shipping offices are more in evidence than anything else, helping expedite the hordes of tourists flowing to and from Patras, Corfu, and Igoumenitsa. If you're staying, there are a few things to look at. Alongside the 12th-century **cathedral**, rebuilt in warmed-over Baroque, there is a small exotic-looking portico with striped pointed arches; this is all that remains of the **Temple**, headquarters church of the Knights Templar, and closely related to The Temple in London. Nearby, a small collection of ancient Apulian relics has been assembled at the **Museo Archeologico** (*open 9am–1.30pm daily; adm*). Down Via San Giovanni, a few blocks south, another curious souvenir of the Templars has survived, the round church of **San Giovanni al Sepolcro**, built in the late 11th century, with fanciful carvings of dancers and lions on the portal. Back on the waterfront, on Viale Regina Margherita, there is a small local ferry that runs across the harbour to the 50m-high **Monument to Italian Sailors**, erected by Mussolini in 1933. A lift goes up to the top, from where there are good views of the comings and goings of the port.

### Santa Maria del Casale

The greatest of Brindisi's attractions, however, lies just north of the city, near the sports complex on the way to the airport. **Santa Maria del Casale** is a church unlike any other in

Italy; built in the 1320s, in an austere, almost modern economy of vertical lines and arches, the façade is done in two shades of sandstone, not striped as in so many other Italian churches, but shaped into a variety of simple, exquisite patterns. The church makes use of many of the features of Apulian Romanesque, but defies classification into any period or style; neither is any foreign influence, from the Saracens or Greeks, readily apparent. Santa Maria is a work of pure imagination.

The interior, a simple, barn-like space, is painted with equally noteworthy frescoes in the Byzantine manner. The wall over the entrance is covered with a remarkable visionary **Last Judgement** by an artist named Rinaldo of Táranto, full of brightly coloured angels and apostles, saints and sinners; a river of fire washes the damned into the inferno while above, the fish of the sea disgorge their human prey to be judged. Many of the other frescoes, in the nave and transepts, have become badly faded, though they are still of interest.

---

*Brindisi ℂ (0831–)*                                    ***Where to Stay***

Brindisi's hotel-keepers, accustomed to folks staying just overnight while waiting for the boat to Greece, have not been inspired to exert themselves, and there are no really outstanding places in the city. The best is the ★★★★**Internazionale**, at Lungomare Regina Margherita 26, ℂ 523475, which is very convenient for the ferry docks. This is an older hotel, though very well-kept; you're likely to encounter grandmotherly furnishings, and maybe you'll get one of the rooms with a marble fireplace (moderate). The ★★★**Barsotti**, Via Cavour 1, ℂ 560877, is a plain but acceptable place, near the train station (moderate).

A reasonable quality but inexpensive hotel that's centrally located is the ★★**Europa**, Piazza Cairoli 5, ℂ 528546, on one of the two main squares between the train station and the ferry terminal. Brindisi also has a **Youth Hostel**, at Via Brandi 2, ℂ 413123, which is 2km to the west of the city centre (both inexpensive).

---

*Brindisi ℂ (0831–)*                                         ***Eating Out***

Behind the Appian Way column in Brindisi is the city's most elegant restaurant, which manages to mix traditional and newly invented ways of cooking and presenting meat, seafood and pasta—**La Lanterna**, at Via G. Tarantina 14, ℂ 564026 (expensive; *closed Sun.*) For something simpler, but still good, try **La Camelia**, at Via G. Bruno 11, ℂ (0831) 563071 (inexpensive), for tasty *orecchiette* or seafood risotto. (*Closed Sat.*) Otherwise, if you're waiting for a train or ferry, there are any number of pizzerias and trattorias along the Corso Umberto and Corso Garibaldi where you can find something cheap, filling and quick.

## Lecce

Unfortunately for the traveller, you will have to come a long way, to the furthest corner of Apulia and the last city in this book, to find the most beautiful town in southern Italy. Lecce is worth the trip. Its history, and its tastes, have given it a fate and a look different from any other Italian town. First and foremost, Lecce is a Baroque city—not the chilly, pompous Baroque of Rome, but a sunny, almost frivolous style Lecce created on its own.

Lecce started as a Messapian town, and flourished as the Roman *Lupiae*, but really only came into its own during the Middle Ages, as the centre of a semi-independent county comprising most of the Salentine peninsula. Few buildings are left from this period, but only because Lecce, uniquely among Apulian cities, was prosperous enough to replace them in later centuries when styles changed. Lecce enjoyed royal favour under the Spaniards in the 16th century; with its location near the front lines of the continual wars between Habsburg and Turk, Lecce often found itself the centre of attention even though it was not a port. Somehow, during the Spanish centuries, while every other southern city except the royal seat of Naples was in serious decline, Lecce was enjoying a golden age. In these centuries, the city attained distinction in literature and the arts, giving rise to such unfortunate nicknames as 'The Athens of Apulia'. Lecce also found the wealth virtually to rebuild itself, and took the form we see today with the construction of dozens of palaces, churches and public buildings in the city's own distinctive style.

Even though Lecce was doing well under the Spaniards and Bourbons, it was hardly enjoying the privilege of being ruled by them. On the contrary, perhaps more than any other city in Italy, Lecce's resistance to the new order manifested itself in four serious revolts. First, in 1648, came a popular revolution coinciding with Masaniello's revolt in Naples and, like it, bloodily repressed by Spanish troops. A second rebellion, in 1734, almost succeeded; the rebels were tricked into submitting by the Bourbons, who offered them reforms that were later withdrawn. In the wake of the French revolution, another revolt occurred, and the last came in 1848; the Leccesi worked hard for the unification of Italy, and contributed to the fight both men and ideas.

## Leccese Baroque

One critic has called Baroque the 'most expensive style of architecture ever invented'. Considering all the hours of skilled labour it took to carve all those curlicues and rosettes, this may well be true. Lecce, like southern Sicily, some parts of Spain, and Malta—all places where southern Baroque styles were well developed—was fortunate to have an inexhaustible supply of a perfect stone. *Pietra di Lecce* is a kind of sandstone of a warm golden hue, possessing the additional virtues of being extremely easy to carve, and becoming hard as granite after a few years in the weather. Almost all of Lecce is built of it, giving the city the appearance of one great, delicately crafted architectural ensemble.

The artists and architects who made Lecce's Baroque were almost all local talent, most notably Antonio and Giuseppe Zimbalo, who between them designed many of Lecce's finest buildings in the middle 16th century, and carried the style to its wildest extremes. Leccese Baroque does not involve any new forms or structural innovations. The difference is in the decoration, with an emphasis on vertical lines and planes of rusticated stonework, broken by patches of the most intricate and fanciful stone-carving Baroque ever knew. These churches and palaces, along with the hundreds of complementary little details that adorn almost every street—fountains, gates, balconies and monuments—combine to form an elegant and refined cityscape that paradoxically seems all gravity and restraint. Leccese Baroque owes more than a little to Spanish influences, and the city itself still has an air of Spanish reserve about it. As a king of Spain once described a similar Baroque city—Valetta, in Malta—Lecce is a 'town built for gentlemen'.

## Piazza Sant'Oronzio

A Baroque city, of course, was conceived as a sort of theatre set, its squares as stages on which these decorous gentlemen could promenade. An odd chance has given Lecce's main piazza something even better—a genuine arena right in the middle. In 1901, much to the surprise of the Leccese, workmen digging the basement for a new bank building discovered a **Roman amphitheatre**, with seats for some 15,000, directly under the city centre. In the thirties, the half that lay under the piazza was excavated; occasionally the city uses it for concerts and shows. Only the lower half of the grandstands have survived; the stones of the top levels were probably carted away for other buildings long ago, allowing the rest to become gradually buried and forgotten.

In Brindisi, by the column that marked the end of the Appian Way, you may notice the pedestal of a vanished second column. Lightning toppled that one in 1528, and the Brindisians let it lie until 1661, when the city of Lecce bought it and moved it here, attaching a copper statue of their patron, Sant'Oronzio, or Orontius, the first bishop of Lecce, and supposedly a martyr during the persecutions of Nero. What appears to be a small pavilion in the middle of the square, overlooking the amphitheatre, is the **Sedile**, an elegant early masterpiece of the Leccese style (1596) that once served as the town hall. The lovely portico, now glassed in, serves as the tourist information office. The rest of the square is fairly uninteresting, at least by Lecce standards, as the church of **Santa Maria della Grazia** is one of its few Baroque buildings that has survived. Much of the rest dates from the Fascist era.

## Santa Croce and San Matteo

North of Piazza Sant'Oronzio, the most outrageous Baroque of all awaits along Via Umberto I. **Santa Croce** was begun in 1549, but not completed until 1680, giving Lecce's Baroque berserkers a chance at the façade. The lower half of it is original, done mainly in a sober Renaissance style. The portal, however, and every thing above it, is a fond fancy of Zimbalo and his colleague Cesare Penna. Among the florid cake-icing decoration the rose window stands out, made of concentric choirs of tiny angels. Look carefully at the figures on the corbels supporting the second level: among the various cartoon monsters can be made out Romulus' and Remus' she-wolf, a few dragons, a Turk, an African, and a German. Always have a look inside Lecce's churches if they are open; Santa Croce's interior is one of the best, with beautiful altars in the transept chapels by Penna and Antonio Zimbalo. Giuseppe Zimbalo also designed the **Palazzo del Governo** next door, originally a monastery.

Behind Santa Croce, Lecce's pretty **Giardino Pubblico** and the nearby **castle** built by Emperor Charles V mark old Lecce's eastern edge. The castle is now used for conferences and exhibitions. For another interesting walk through the old town, start from the Piazza Sant'Oronzio down Via Augusto Imperatore (Augustus was in Lecce when he got the news of Julius Caesar's assassination). This street passes another Baroque church, **Santa Chiara**, currently under restoration, and a Salesian convent with a skull and crossbones over the portal—the ultimate Spanish touch. Even better, in a small garden opposite the church there is the most preposterous statue of Vittorio Emanuele in all Italy, surpassing even the bronze colossus on the Altar of the Nation in Rome. This Vittorio is smaller, but the contrast between his ponderous moustaches and jaunty stance leaves him looking half a pirate, half the leader of the firemen's band.

The next Baroque church is the recently cleaned **San Matteo** (1700), architecturally the most adventurous of the lot, with an elliptical nave and a complex façade that is convex on the lower level, and concave above. Continue straight down Via Perroni, and you will come to one of Lecce's fine Baroque town gates, the **Porta San Biagio**. To prove that this city's curiosities are not all Baroque, we can offer the neoclassical **war memorial**, across Piazza Roma near the gate, and off to its right a block of mansions, built around the turn of the century, in a style that perfectly imitates the Alhambra in Spain, complete with pointed arches, minarets and Koranic inscriptions.

## Piazza del Duomo

Leaving Piazza Sant'Oronzio by Via Vittorio Emanuele, you pass the church of **Santa Irene**, a relatively modest Baroque church of the 1720s, with a splendid statue of the saint above the main portal. If you're not careful you may entirely miss the little alley off to the left that leads to the **Piazza del Duomo**, one of the finest Baroque architectural groups anywhere, and, as with many of Lecce's historic buildings, recently restored. It was the plan of the designers to keep this square cut off from the life of the city, making it a sort of tranquil stone park; the alley off Via Vittorio Emanuele is the only entrance.

The **cathedral** is one of the finest works of Giuseppe Zimbalo (1659–70). To make the building stand out in the L-shaped medieval piazza, Zimbalo gave it two façades: one on the west front and a second, more gloriously ornate one facing the open end of the piazza. The angular, unusually tall campanile (68m), with its simple lines and baby obelisks, echoes the Herreran style of imperial Spain. If you can find someone to let you in, the long climb is worth the trouble, with an exceptional view over the city and most of the Salentine peninsula; on a clear day you can see Albania. Adjoining the cathedral are the complementary façades of the **Archbishops' Palace** and the **Seminary**, the latter the work of Giuseppe Cino, a pupil of Zimbalo.

Behind the cathedral, in the back streets off Via Paladini, there is a small but well-preserved **Roman theatre**. In the opposite direction, Via Libertini passes several good churches, including the unique **Rosario** (1691–1728), also known as **San Giovanni Battista**, the last and most unusual work of Giuseppe Zimbalo. Just beyond it, the street leaves the city through the **Porta Rudiae**, the most elaborate of the city's gates, bearing yet another statue of Sant'Oronzio. Leading away to the right from here, Via Adua follows the northwestern face of this diamond-shaped city, passing the remains of the walls Charles V rebuilt to keep out Turkish corsairs; further up, you don't need to read Latin to recognize another relic of Charles' in the **triumphal arch**, erected in 1548. Most destructive and least modest of monarchs, Charles erected monuments like this around the Mediterranean, usually after unsuccessful revolts, to remind the people who was boss. This one, featuring crowned screaming eagles and a huge Spanish coat-of-arms, is a grim reminder of the militaristic, almost totalitarian government with which the Habsburgs tried to conquer Europe.

In a little park in front of the arch, there is an attractive monument to the less grisly, though thoroughly useless King Ferdinand I, called the **Obelisk**. From here, a road off to the right leads off to the city cemetery, behind a quite elegant 19th-century neoclassical gate; next to it stands the church of **SS. Nicolo and Cataldo**. The façade is typical Baroque, but if you look carefully you will notice that the portal and rose window are much older. Behind the 18th-century front hides one of the best Apulian Romanesque churches, and one of the only medieval monuments to survive in Lecce. The nave and the dome are unusually lofty, and the carvings on the portal and elsewhere are especially good.

## The Museo Sigismundo Castromediano

The founder of this collection, now Lecce's city museum, was a duke, and also a famous local patriot who fought against the Bourbons and earned long spells in the Neapolitan dungeons. His prison memoirs shocked Europe in the 1850s, and moved William Gladstone to a few rousing anti-Bourbon speeches. Duke Sigismundo would be happy if he could see his little collection, now become one of the best-arranged and most modern museums in Italy—a corkscrew-shaped ramp through its middle makes it accessible to wheelchair users, and virtually all the exhibits are clearly labelled. The most prized works are several excellent Apulian and Greek vases, found all over the Salentine Peninsula, though there is also a good collection of medieval art and architectural fragments, and a small picture gallery. The museum is on Viale Gallipoli, at the southern end of the old town and not far from the railway station (*open 9–1.30, 2.30–7.30, Mon–Fri; 9am–1.30pm Sun; closed Sat*).

---

*Lecce ✆ (0832–)*  **Where to Stay and Eating Out**

Lecce's hotels are like the town itself: quiet, tasteful and restrained. The best of them is an attractive, gracious, older establishment, the ★★★**Risorgimento**, in the centre at Via Augusto Imperatore 19, ✆ 42125 (moderate). Near the station, the ★★★**Grand Hotel**, Viale Quarta 28, ✆ 29405 (inexpensive/moderate) offers a tiny bit of faded elegance at very reasonable rates.

Although Lecce is an inland city, the sea is not far away, and many of its restaurants have always specialized in fish. One popular place, in the northern part of the old town, is **I Tarocchi**, Via Idomenco 14, ✆ 29212 (moderate), known for its seafood antipasti and crêpes (*Closed Tues.*) Another winner, though a little bit distant from the centre, is **Gino e Gianni**, Via Adriatica, km 2, ✆ 399210 (moderate), with a long list of seafood dishes prepared following the local traditions. (*Closed Wed.*) Near the Charles V monument there is a restaurant named after him, the **Tavola di Carlo V**, Via Palmerie 46, ✆ (0832) 46042 (inexpensive/moderate).

## The Tip of the Salentine

Italy's furthest southeastern corner is one of the quieter parts of the country. It offers a low, rocky coastline, rather like that of the Gargano only without the mountains, a number of towns embellished in the Leccese Baroque style, and a lonely beach or two. One of the most noticeable features of the countryside—and this is true for all of the Salentine Peninsula—is the eccentricity of the rural architecture. There aren't many modern *trulli* here, but a few of their ancient predecessors, low-domed houses of unknown age. Around them, there are little houses with flat roofs curled up at the corners, some recent artistic do-it-yourself experiments in cinder-block, and many tiny pink Baroque palaces, sitting like jewel-boxes in a prairie landscape of olive trees, tobacco, and wildflowers, even in December.

## Flying Saints and Land's End

The towns here show an almost African austerity, excepting perhaps **Nardò**, decorated with a lovely square called the **Piazza Salandra**, in which there is a *guglia* (spire) as frilly as those in Naples. Nardò's much-rebuilt 11th-century **cathedral** retains some medieval frescoes. Near the town walls, on Via Giuseppe Galliano, is a strange, unexplained circular temple called the **Osanna**, built in 1603. Among the other interesting towns and villages around Lecce are **Acaia**, with a romantically ruined Aragonese castle; **Galatina**, with a wonderful set of Renaissance frescoes in the 1392 church of **Santa Caterina**; and **Calimera**, one of the centres of Apulia's Greek community—oddly enough the town's name means 'good morning' in Greek. Very few people anywhere in Apulia actually still speak Greek, though their thick dialect has led many writers into thinking so; the Greeks left are more likely to be descendants of 16th-century refugees from Albania than of the ancient Greek colonists.

Nearby **Copertino**, in the early 17th century, was the home of the original flying monk. St Joseph of Copertino, a carpenter's son born in a stable, was a simple fellow, if his many biographers are to be believed, but he got himself canonized for his nearly effortless talent for levitating. Thousands saw him do it, including the pope's emissaries, a king of Poland, and a Protestant German duke, who immediately converted. Joseph's heart is buried under the altar of the little church named after him. Copertino also has a large Angevin **castle**.

On the Ionian coast, **Porto Cesario** is a peculiar little resort, facing two islets inhabited entirely by rabbits. The larger **Gallipoli**, like its namesake on the Hellespont, was once thought of highly by somebody; the name comes from the Greek *kalli poli*, or 'beautiful city'. The old quarter still has a Greek air about it, with whitewashed houses scoured by the sea air and fishermen folding their nets in the little port. The oldest part, once an island, is now bound to the mainland and dominated by a huge **castle** with squat rounded bastions, parts of which date back to the Byzantines. There is a Baroque **cathedral** that would look right at home in Lecce, but the unexpected attraction is a Greek **nymphaion**, a trough-like fountain decorated with caryatids and badly faded mythological reliefs. In itself it isn't much, but for such a thing to survive the Christians and the barbarians is rare; there are few in Greece itself, and this is the only one in Italy. Gallipoli has the best sort of **museum** (*open April–Sept 9–1, 5–7, daily; Oct–Mar 9–1, 4–6, daily*), on Via De Pace—nothing pretentious, nothing even labelled, but good fun, in a big atrium lined with dusty bookshelves and full of cutlasses, whalebones, old cannonballs, coins, amphorae, and even a crocodile skeleton.

Down the coast, the Salentine's southern tip, not surprisingly, is called Land's End—*Finibus Terrae*. The spot is marked by the church of **Santa Maria di Leuca**, built over the ruins of a temple of Minerva that must have been a familiar landmark to all ancient mariners. The church's altar stone fulfilled the same purpose in the original temple. As in the Land's Ends of Celtic Europe, this corner of the Salentine has quite a few standing stones and dolmens, left from the days of the Messapians or perhaps even earlier. The most important neolithic monument is called the *Centropietre*—'hundred stones'—near the village of **Patù**; it is a small temple of two aisles divided by columns, with flat stone slabs for a roof.

Coming back up the Adriatic side towards Otranto, the coast is lined with caves, many showing evidence of Stone-Age habitation or later religious uses. The **Grotta Zinzulusa**, hung with stalactites, may be the one worth visiting. Just to the north is a thermal spa, **Santa Cesarea Terme**, built around a charming neo-Moorish bath-house.

## Otranto

Readers of Gothic novels might choose to leave **Otranto** out of their itineraries, but there's no reason to be afraid. Horace Walpole, when he was writing his *Castle of Otranto*, knew nothing about the place; he merely picked the name off a map. There really is a **castle**, built by the Aragonese in the 1490s, but it is largely in ruins. Otranto today, (stress on the first syllable, as for most Apulian towns), is probably most familiar as a better option than Brindisi for ferries to Greece.

Although originally a Messapian settlement, the city first entered the Mediterranean consciousness as Greek *Hydruntion*, conquered and probably resettled by Taras, and its proud citizens still refer to themselves as *Idruntini*. It rivalled Brindisi as Rome's window on the east, and reappeared in the 11th century as one of the leading Crusader ports. Otranto's finest hour came in 1480, during Naples' wars with the Turks and their Venetian allies; according to a delicately embroidered legend, Turkish pirates sacked the city, killing some 12,000 or so, and massacred the 800 survivors when they refused, to a man, to forsake Christianity. The place hasn't been the same since; only recently, and thanks to the ferry business, is Otranto beginning to regain some of the importance it had in the Middle Ages.

If you're not bound for Greece, the best reason for visiting will be the **cathedral**, begun in the 11th century by the Normans, and the only one in the south to have conserved an entire medieval **mosaic pavement**. H. V. Morton wrote that coming here felt like 'walking on the Bayeux tapestry'. The vigorous, primitive early medieval figures are the work of a priest named Pantaleone, from about 1165. Three great trees stand at the centre of his composition, supporting small encircled images that encompass all creation: scriptural scenes, animals, heroes, symbols of the months and seasons. If you look carefully, you can find Alexander the Great, and even King Arthur.

*Where to Stay and Eating Out*

### Gallipoli

Most of the available accommodation is along the outlying beaches. There are some fine modern resort hotels at Baia Verde, on the Via Litoranea: the ★★★★**Costa Brada**, ✆ (0833) 22551 (expensive) and ★★★**Le Sireneuse**, ✆ (0833) 22536 (moderate) are both typical white Mediterranean palaces, and both have good restaurants. The coastal areas are well supplied with places to eat: you can choose from a great variety of seafood dishes, as well as trying the local speciality, *orecchiette alla Gallipolina*, at **Il Capriccio**, at Viale Bovio 14, © (0833) 261545 (expensive; *closed Mon, Oct*).

## Otranto

Otranto has several newly opened hotels, including the ★★★**Albania**, Via S. Francesco di Paola 10, © (0836) 801183, with bathrooms in all of its 10 rooms (inexpensive), or, nearer the beaches, the ★★**Miramare**, Viale Lungomare 55, © (0836) 801024 (inexpensive). The inland towns all have only basic accommodation. Otranto's best restaurant is **Da Sergio**, at Corso Garibaldi 7, © (0836) 801408 (moderate), even though the Sergio of the title prides himself on having a local clientele, and is inclined to be patronizing to foreigners. His father is a fisherman, and the restaurant has particularly good fish. (*Closed Wed, Nov, Feb.*)

**Acroterion**: decorative protrusion on the rooftop of an Etruscan, Greek or Roman temple. At the corners of the roof they are called *antefixes*.

**Ambones**: twin pulpits in some southern churches (singular: *ambo*), often elaborately decorated.

**Atrium**: entrance court of a Roman house or early church.

**Badia**: *abbazia*, an abbey or abbey church.

**Baldacchino**: baldachin, a columned stone canopy above the altar of a church.

**Basilica**: a rectangular building, usually divided into three aisles by rows of columns. In Rome this was the common form for law courts and other public buildings, and Roman Christians adapted it for their early churches.

**Borgo**: from the Saxon *burh* of San Spirito in Rome: a suburb.

**Bucchero ware**: black, delicately thin Etruscan ceramics, usually incised or painted.

**Calvary chapels**: a series of outdoor chapels, usually on a hillside, that commemorate the stages of the Passion of Christ.

**Campanile**: a bell-tower.

**Campanilismo**: local patriotism; the Italians' own word for their historic tendency to be more faithful to their home towns than to the abstract idea of 'Italy'.

**Camposanto**: a cemetery.

**Cardo**: transverse street of a Roman *castrum*-shaped city.

**Carroccio**: a wagon carrying the banners of a medieval city and an altar; it served as the rallying point in battles.

**Cartoon**: the preliminary sketch for a fresco or tapestry.

**Caryatid**: supporting pillar or column carved into a standing female form; male versions are called *telamones*.

**Castrum**: a Roman military camp, always neatly

# Architectural, Artistic & Historical Terms

rectangular, with straight streets and gates at the

cardinal points. Later the Romans founded or refounded cities in this form, hundreds of which survive today (Lucca, Aosta, Florence, Pavia, Como, Brescia, Ascoli Piceno, Ancona are clear examples).

**Cavea**: the semicircle of seats in a classical theatre.

**Cenacolo**: fresco of the Last Supper, often on the wall of a monastery refectory.

**Ciborium**: a tabernacle; the word is often used for large freestanding tabernacles, or in the sense of a *baldacchino* (q.v.).

**Comune**: commune, or commonwealth, referring to the governments of the free cities of the Middle Ages. Today it denotes any local government, from the Comune di Roma down to the smallest village.

**Condottiere**: the leader of a band of mercenaries in late medieval and Renaissance times.

**Confraternity**: a religious lay brotherhood, often serving as a neighbourhood mutual-aid and burial society, or following some specific charitable work (Michelangelo, for example, belonged to one that cared for condemned prisoners in Rome).

**Cosmati work**: (or *Cosmatesque*): referring to a distinctive style of inlaid marble or enamel chips used in architectural decoration (pavements, pulpits, paschal candlesticks, etc.) in medieval southern Italy. The Cosmati family of Rome were its greatest practitioners.

**Cupola**: a dome.

**Cyclopean walls**: fortifications built of enormous, irregularly polygonal blocks, as in the pre-Roman cities of Latium.

**Decumanus**: street of a Roman *castrum*-shaped city parallel to the longer axis, the central, main avenue called the Decumanus Major.

**Duomo**: cathedral.

**Forum**: the central square of a Roman town, with its most important temples and public buildings. The word means 'outside', as the original Roman Forum was outside the first city walls.

**Fresco**: wall painting, the most important Italian medium of art since Etruscan times. It isn't easy; first the artist draws the *sinopia* (q.v.) on the wall. This is covered with plaster, but only a little at a time, as the paint must be on the plaster before it dries. Leonardo da

Vinci's endless attempts to find clever short-cuts ensured that little of his work would survive.

**Ghibellines**: one of the two great medieval parties, the supporters of the Holy Roman Emperors.

**Gonfalon**: the banner of a medieval free city; the *gonfaloniere*, or flag bearer, was often the most important public official.

**Grotesques**: carved or painted faces used in Etruscan and later Roman decoration; Raphael and other artists rediscovered them in the 'grotto' of Nero's Golden House in Rome.

**Guelphs**: (see *Ghibellines*). The other great political faction of medieval Italy, supporters of the Pope.

**Hypogeum**: underground burial caverns, usually of pre-Christian religions.

**Intarsia**: work in inlaid wood or marble.

**Laura**: a Greek cave-chapel or monastic cell of southern Apulia, often with frescoes.

**Lozenge**: the diamond shape—like stripes, one of the trademarks of Pisan architecture.

**Narthex**: the enclosed porch of a church.

**Naumachia**: mock naval battles, like those staged in the Colosseum.

**Opus Reticulatum**: Roman masonry consisting of diamond-shaped blocks.

**Palazzo**: not just a palace, but any large, important building (though the word comes from the Imperial *palatium* on Rome's Palatine Hill).

**Palio**: a banner, and the horse race in which city neighbourhoods contend for it in their annual festivals. The most famous is at Siena.

**Pantocrator**: Christ 'ruler of all', a common subject for apse paintings and mosaics in areas influenced by Byzantine art.

**Pietra Dura**: rich inlay work using semi-precious stones, perfected in post-Renaissance Florence.

**Pieve**: a parish church, especially in the north.

**Predella**: smaller paintings on panels below the main subject of a painted altarpiece.

**Presepio**: a Christmas crib.

**Pulvin**: stone, often trapezoidal, that supports or replaces the capital of a column; decoratively carved examples can be seen in many medieval southern cloisters.

**Putti**: flocks of plaster cherubs with rosy cheeks and bums that infested much of Italy in the Baroque era.

**Quadriga**: chariot pulled by four horses.

**Quattrocento**: the 1400s—the Italian way of referring to centuries (*duecento, trecento, quattrocento, cinquecento*, etc.).

**Sinopia**: the layout of a fresco (q.v.), etched by the artist on the wall before the plaster is applied. Often these are works of art in their own right.

**Stigmata**: a miraculous simulation of the bleeding wounds of Christ, appearing in holy men like St Francis in the 12th century, and Padre Pio of Apulia in our own time.

**Telamon**: see *Caryatid*.

**Thermae**: Roman baths.

**Tondo**: round relief, painting or terracotta.

**Transenna**: marble screen separating the altar area from the rest of an early Christian church.

**Travertine**: hard, light-coloured stone, sometimes flecked or pitted with black, sometimes perfect. The most widely used material in ancient and modern Rome.

**Triclinium**: the main hall of a Roman house, used for dining and entertaining.

**Triptych**: a painting, especially an altarpiece, in three sections.

**Trompe l'œil**: art that uses perspective effects to deceive the eye—for example, to create the illusion of depth on a flat surface, or to make columns and arches painted on a wall seem real.

**Tympanum**: the semicircular space, often bearing a painting or relief, above the portal of a church.

BC

# Chronology

| | |
|---|---|
| 305 | Diocletian's reforms turn the Empire into a bureaucratized despotism |
| *306–337* | *Constantine* |
| 312 | Constantine wins Battle of the Milvian Bridge with the Christian cross on his banners |
| 326 | First Basilica of St Peter built |
| 330 | Pagan temples closed by order of Constantine |
| 336 | Final division of the Empire into eastern and western halves |
| *379–95* | *Theodosius* |
| 402–5 | Vandal general Stilicho defends Italy against Gothic invasions |
| 408 | Stilicho murdered at Emperor Honorius' orders |
| 410 | Alaric the Goth sacks Rome |
| *c.* 420 | St Augustine writes *City of God* |
| 452 | Invasion of Attila the Hun |
| 455 | Gaiseric the Vandal sacks Rome |
| 476 | Western Empire ends; last Emperor, Romulus Augustulus, pensioned off to Naples |
| *476–93* | *Odoacer* |
| *493–514* | *Theodoric* |
| 539–53 | Greek–Gothic Wars |
| 546 | Totila the Goth sacks Rome |
| 547 | Belisarius the Byzantine sacks Rome |
| 549 | Totila does it again |
| 553 | Byzantines abolish Roman Senate, found Exarchate of Ravenna |
| 567–8 | Lombards under King Alboin overrun much of Italy |
| *590–604* | *Pope Gregory the Great* |
| *c.* 590 | Lombards convert to Christianity |
| 750s | Campaigns of Frankish King Pepin the Short increase papal power |
| 751 | Lombards finally capture Ravenna |
| 778 | Charlemagne defeats the last Lombard kings |
| *795–816* | *Pope Leo III* |
| 800 | Charlemagne crowned Holy Roman Emperor |
| *c.* 880–896 | Theodora Senatrix and her daughter Marozia rule Rome |
| *936–973* | *Emperor Otto the Great* |

| | |
|---|---|
| **962** | Otto the Great occupies north Italy; is crowned at Rome the same year |
| *987–998* | *Crescenzio rules Rome* |
| **1017** | First Norman mercenaries in Apulia |
| **1060** | Normans undertake conquest of Sicily |
| **1062** | Work begins on Pisa's Cathedral complex |
| *1071–1115* | *Matilda, Countess of Tuscany* |
| *1073–1080* | *Pope Gregory VII (Hildebrand)* |
| *c.* **1070** | Development of the University of Bologna |
| **1075–1122** | Investiture conflict between popes and emperors |
| **1077** | Henry IV's 'penance at Canossa' |
| **1082** | Venice wins Byzantine trade monopoly |
| **1084** | Robert Guiscard's Normans sack Rome while supposedly allied to the Pope |
| **1094** | Rebuilding of St Mark's in Venice |
| **1097** | First Crusade begins |
| *1112–54* | *King Roger II of Sicily* |
| **1135** | Sack of Amalfi by Pisa |
| **1145** | Revolution of Arnold of Brescia in Rome ; Republic temporarily re-established |
| *1152–1190* | *Emperor Frederick I (Barbarossa)* |
| **1161** | Frederick destroys Milan |
| **1167** | Lombard League of cities formed to oppose the emperors |
| *1198–1216* | *Pope Innocent III* |
| **1204** | Venice diverts Fourth Crusade to the Sack of Constantinople |
| *1212–1246* | *Frederick II Emperor and King of Sicily* |
| **1226** | Death of St Francis of Assisi |
| **1252** | Florence mints Europe's first gold coins |
| **1260** | Siena defeats Florence at Battle of Montaperti |
| **??** | Charles of Anjou invades Italy at behest of the Pope |
| **1266** | Charles defeats the last Hohenstaufens |
| **1278** | Papal states chartered in deal with Emperor Rudolf |
| **1282** | Revolt of the 'Sicilian Vespers' |
| **1284** | Battle of Meloria; Genoa replaces Pisa as Tyrrhenian maritime power |

| 1294–1303 | *Pope Boniface VIII* |
| 1298 | Marco Polo returns home to Venice |
| 1309 | French pope Clement V moves papacy to Avignon |
| 1310 | Giotto completes Arena Chapel in Padua |
| 1314 | Dante completes the *Commedia* |
| 1320s | Exploits of Castruccio Castracani, lord of Lucca |
| 1347 | Cola di Rienzo establishes Roman Republic once again |
| 1348–9 | Black Death wipes out one third of the Italians |
| 1354 | Rienzo returns to Rome, is murdered by a mob |
| 1364 | Cardinal Albornoz conquers much of the Marches and Romagna for the pope |
| 1374 | Death of Petrarch |
| 1375 | Death of Boccaccio |
| 1377 | Papacy moves back to Rome once and for all |
| 1378 | *Ciompi* revolt in Florence |
| 1380 | Death of St Catherine of Siena |
| 1379–1402 | *Duke Gian Galeazzo Visconti of Milan* |
| 1379 | Venice defeats Genoa in the Chioggia War |
| 1404–7 | Venice seizes Verona, Vicenza and Padua |
| 1406 | Florence annexes Pisa |
| 1407 | Genoa conquers Corsica |
| 1434 | Cosimo de' Medici seizes power in Florence |
| 1435–58 | *Alfonso the Magnanimous of Naples* |
| 1447–55 | *Pope Nicholas IV* |
| 1447 | Sforza house replaces the Visconti in Milan |
| 1466 | Death of Donatello |
| 1469–92 | *Lorenzo the Magnificent of Florence* |
| 1492–1503 | *Pope Alexander VI (Borgia)* |
| 1494 | Wars of Italy begin with French invasion of Charles VIII |
|  | Battle of Fornovo |
| 1498 | Burning of Savonarola |
| 1500–3 | Wars of Cesare Borgia in central Italy |
| 1503–13 | *Pope Julius II* |

| 1513 | Machiavelli's *The Prince* written |
| *1519–56* | *Emperor Charles V* |
| *1523–34* | *Pope Clement VII* |
| 1525 | Battle of Pavia; Spaniards capture French kng Francis I |
| 1527 | Sack of Rome by Imperial troops |
| 1534 | Founding of the Jesuits |
| *1534–50* | *Pope Paul III* |
| 1540 | Inquisition unleashed on Italy |
| 1559 | Treaty of Chateau-Cambresis confirms Spanish control of Italy |
| 1564 | Death of Michelangelo |
| 1571 | Spanish-Venetian victory over Turks at sea battle of Lepanto |
| 1626 | St Peter's in Rome consecrated |
| 1642 | Death of Galileo |
| 1647 | Masaniello's Revolt in Naples |
| 1700–13 | War of the Spanish Succession |
| 1720 | Piedmont becomes the Kingdom of Piedmont-Sardinia |
| 1737 | Tuscany passes under Austrian rule upon the extinction of the Medici |
| 1755 | Genoa sells Corsica to France |
| 1796 | Napoleon first enters Italy, founds several republics |
| 1808 | French capture Rome for the second time, and exile the Pope |
| 1814 | Overthrow of French Rule |
| 1815 | Venice given to Austrians at Congress of Vienna 1820 |
| | Constitutionalist revolts in Piedmont and Naples |
| 1831 | Mazzini founds *Giovane Italia* |
| 1848 | Revolutions across Italy; Austrians defeat Piedmont at war |
| 1849 | Restoration of Autocratic rule |
| *1849–1878* | *Vittorio Emanuele II* |
| 1852 | Cavour becomes Prime Minister of Piedmont |
| 1854 | Piedmont enters the Crimean War |
| 1859–60 | Piedmont, with French help, annexes most of northern Italy |
| | Garibaldi's 'Thousand' conquer Sicily and Naples |
| 1866 | Venice annexed to Italy |

| 1870 | Italian troops enter Rome; unification completed and Rome becomes capital |
|---|---|
| 1896 | Massacre of Italian troops at Adowa, Ethiopia |
| 1900 | King Umberto I assassinated by anarchist |
| *1900–1945* | *Vittorio Emanuele III* |
| 1902–7 | Era of industrial strikes |
| 1911 | Italy snatches Libya from Turks |
| 1915 | Italy enters First World War |
| 1917 | Military disaster at Caporetto |
| 1918 | Victory in the Veneto |
| 1919 | Fiume seized by Gabriele D'Annunzio; Italian claims generally ignored at Versailles |
| 1922 | Mussolini's March on Rome |
| 1924 | Fascists murder Giacomo Matteotti |
| 1925–6 | Conversion of Italy to a Fascist dictatorship |
| 1935 | War against Ethiopia |
| 1939 | Seizure of Albania |
| 1940 | Italy enters Second World War |
| 1943 | Allies land in Sicily; Mussolini deposed, later rescued by Germans to found puppet government in the north. Provisional government in south surrenders in Sept. |
| 1944 | Anzio landings, liberation of Rome; Vittorio Emanuele abdicates |
| 1946 | National referendum makes Italy a republic |
| 1956 | Italy becomes charter member of the Common Market |
| 1950s–60s | Continuing 'economic miracle' integrates Italy more closely into western Europe. |
| 1966 | Floods in Venice and Florence |
| 1978 | Kidnapping and murder of Premier Aldo Moro |
| 1980 | Earthquake causes severe damage in Campania |
| 1990 | Emergence of Umberto Bossi's Lombard League |
| 1994 | Election of Silvio Berlusconi, Milan's media magnate, as Prime Minister at the head of Forza Italia |

The fathers of modern Italian were Dante, Manzoni, and television. Each had a part in creating a national language from an infinity of regional and local dialects; the Florentine Dante, the first to write in the vernacular, did much to put the Tuscan dialect in the foreground of Italian literature. Manzoni's revolutionary novel, *I Promessi Sposi*, heightened national consciousness by using an everyday language all could understand in the 19th century. Television in the last few decades is performing an even more spectacular linguistic unification; although the majority of Italians still speak a dialect at home, school, and work, their TV idols insist on proper Italian.

Perhaps because they are so busy learning their own beautiful but grammatically complex language, Italians are not especially apt at learning others. English lessons, however, have been the rage for years, and at most hotels and restaurants there will be someone who speaks some English. In small towns and out-of-the-way places, finding an Anglophone may prove more difficult. The words and phrases below should help you out in most situations, but the ideal way to come to Italy is with some Italian under your belt; your visit will be richer, and you're much more likely to make some Italian friends.

Italian words are pronounced phonetically. Every vowel and consonant is sounded. Consonants are the same as in English, except the *c* which, when followed by an 'e' or 'i', is pronounced like the English 'ch' (*cinque* thus becomes cheenquay). Italian *g* is also soft before 'i' or 'e' as in *gira*, or jee-ra. *H* is never sounded; *z* is pronounced like 'ts'. The consonants *sc* before the vowels 'i' or 'e' becomes like the English 'sh' as in *sci*, pronounced shee; *ch* is pronouced like a 'k' as in *Chianti*, kee-an-tee; *gn* as 'ny' in English (*bagno*, pronounced ban-yo; while *gli* is pronounced like the middle of the word million (*Castiglione*, pronounced Ca-stee-lyon-ay).

Vowel pronunciation is: *a* as in English father; *e* when unstressed is pronounced like 'a' in fate as in *mele*, when stressed can be the same or like the 'e' in pet (*bello*); *i* is like the 'i' in machine; *o*, like 'e', has two sounds, 'o' as in hope when unstressed (*tacchino*), and usually 'o' as in rock when stressed (*morte*); *u* is pronounced like the 'u' in June.

The accent usually (but not always!) falls on the penultimate syllable. Also note that in the big northern cities, the informal way of addressing someone as you, *tu*, is widely used; the more formal *lei* or *voi* is commonly used in provincial districts.

## Useful Words and Phrases

| | |
|---|---|
| yes/no/maybe | *si/no/forse* |
| I don't know | *Non lo so* |
| I don't understand (Italian). | *Non capisco (italiano).* |
| Does someone here speak English? | *C'è qualcuno qui che parla inglese?* |
| Speak slowly | *Parla lentamente* |
| Could you assist me? | *Potrebbe aiutarmi?* |
| Help! | *Aiuto!* |
| Please | *Per favore* |
| Thank you (very much) | *(Molte) grazie* |
| You're welcome | *Prego* |
| It doesn't matter | *Non importa* |
| All right | *Va bene* |
| Excuse me | *Scusi* |
| Be careful! | *Attenzione!* |
| Nothing | *Niente* |
| It is urgent! | *È urgente!* |
| How are you? | *Come sta?* |
| Well, and you? | *Bene, e lei?* |
| What is your name? | *Come si chiama?* |
| Hello | *Salve* or *ciao* (both informal) |
| Good morning | *Buongiorno* (formal hello) |
| Good afternoon/evening | *Buona sera* (also formal hello) |
| Goodnight | *Buona notte* |

## Language

| | |
|---|---|
| Goodbye | *Arrivederla* (formal), *arrivederci, ciao* (informal) |
| What do you call this in Italian? | *Come si chiama questo in italiano?* |
| What? | *Che?* |

| | |
|---|---|
| Who? | *Chi?* |
| Where? | *Dove?* |
| When? | *Quando?* |
| Why? | *Perché?* |
| How? | *Come?* |
| How much? | *Quanto?* |
| I am lost | *Mi sono smarrito* |
| I am hungry | *Ho fame* |
| I am thirsty | *Ho sete* |
| I am sorry | *Mi dispiace* |
| I am tired | *Sono stanco* |
| I am sleepy | *Ho sonno* |
| I am ill | *Mi sento male* |
| Leave me alone | *Lasciami in pace* |
| good | *buono/bravo* |
| bad | *male/cattivo* |
| It's all the same | *Fa lo stesso* |
| slow | *piano* |
| fast | *rapido* |
| big | *grande* |
| small | *piccolo* |
| hot | *caldo* |
| cold | *freddo* |
| here | *qui* |
| there | *lì* |

## Shopping, Service, Sightseeing

| | |
|---|---|
| I would like... | *Vorrei...* |
| Where is/are...? | *Dov'è/Dove sono...?* |
| How much is it? | *Quanto viene questo?* |
| open | *aperto* |
| closed | *chiuso* |
| cheap/expensive | *a buon prezzo/caro* |

| bank | banca |
|------|-------|
| beach | spiaggia |
| bed | letto |
| church | chiesa |
| entrance | entrata |
| exit | uscita |
| hospital | ospedale |
| money | soldi |
| museum | museo |
| newspaper (foreign) | giornale (straniero) |
| pharmacy | farmacia |
| police station | commissariato |
| policeman | poliziotto |
| post office | ufficio postale |
| sea | mare |
| shop | negozio |
| telephone | telefono |
| tobacco shop | tabaccaio |
| WC | toilette / bagno |
| men | Signori / Uomini |
| women | Signore / Donne |

## Time

| What time is it? | Che ore sono? |
|------------------|---------------|
| month | mese |
| week | settimana |
| day | giorno |
| morning | mattina |
| afternoon | pomeriggio |
| evening | sera |
| today | oggi |
| yesterday | ieri |
| tomorrow | domani |

| soon | *presto* |
| later | *dopo, più tardi* |
| It is too early | *È troppo presto* |
| It is too late | *È troppo tarde* |

## Days

| Monday | *lunedì* |
| Tuesday | *martedì* |
| Wednesday | *mercoledì* |
| Thursday | *giovedì* |
| Friday | *venerdì* |
| Saturday | *sabato* |
| Sunday | *domenica* |

## Numbers

| one | *uno/una* |
| two | *due* |
| three | *tre* |
| four | *quattri* |
| five | *cinque* |
| six | *sei* |
| seven | *sette* |
| eight | *otto* |
| nine | *nove* |
| ten | *dieci* |
| eleven | *undici* |
| twelve | *dodici* |
| thirteen | *tredici* |
| fourteen | *quattordici* |
| fifteen | *quindici* |
| sixteen | *sedici* |
| seventeen | *diciassette* |

| eighteen | diciotto |
|---|---|
| nineteen | diciannove |
| twenty | venti |
| twenty-one | ventuno |
| twenty-two | ventidue |
| thirty | trenta |
| thirty-one | trentuno |
| forty | quaranta |
| fifty | cinquanta |
| sixty | sessanta |
| seventy | settanta |
| eighty | ottanta |
| ninety | novanta |
| hundred | cento |
| one hundred and one | cento uno |
| two hundred | duecento |
| thousand | mille |
| two thousand | duemila |
| million | milione |
| billion | miliardo |

## Transport

| airport | aeroporto |
|---|---|
| bus stop | fermata |
| bus/coach | autobus/pullman |
| railway station | stazione ferroviaria |
| train | treno |
| track | binario |
| port | porto |
| port station | stazione marittima |
| ship | nave |
| automobile | macchina |
| taxi | tassì |

| | |
|---|---|
| ticket | *biglietto* |
| customs | *dogana* |
| seat (reserved) | *posto (prenotato)* |

## Travel Directions

| | |
|---|---|
| I want to go to... | *Desidero andare a...* |
| How can I get to... ? | *Come posso andare a... ?* |
| Do you stop at... ? | *Ferma a... ?* |
| Where is... ? | *Dov'è... ?* |
| How far is it to... ? | *Quanto siamo lontani da... ?* |
| When does the... leave? | *A che ora parte ... ?* |
| What is the name of this station? | *Come si chiama questa stazione?* |
| When does the next ... leave? | *Quando parte il prossimo... ?* |
| From where does it leave? | *Da dove parte?* |
| How long does the trip take... ? | *Quanto tempo dura il viaggio?* |
| How much is the fare? | *Quant'è il biglietto?* |
| Good trip! | *Buon viaggio!* |
| near | *vicino* |
| far | *lontano* |
| left | *sinistra* |
| right | *destra* |
| straight ahead | *sempre diritto* |
| forward | *avanti* |
| backward | *indietro* |
| north | *nord/settentrione* |
| south | *sud/mezzogiorno* |
| east | *est/oriente* |
| west | *ovest/occidente* |
| around the corner | *dietro l'angolo* |
| crossroads | *bivio* |
| street/road | *strada* |
| square | *piazza* |

## Driving

| | |
|---|---|
| car hire | *noleggio macchina* |
| motorbike/scooter | *motocicletta/Vespa* |
| bicycle | *bicicletta* |
| petrol/diesel | *benzina/gasolio* |
| garage | *garage* |
| This doesn't work | *Questo non funziona* |
| mechanic | *meccanico* |
| map/town plan | *carta/pianta* |
| Where is the road to... ? | *Dov'è la strada per... ?* |
| breakdown | *guasto* or *panne* |
| driver's licence | *patente di guida* |
| driver | *guidatore* |
| speed | *velocità* |
| danger | *pericolo* |
| parking | *parcheggio* |
| no parking | *sosta vietato* |
| narrow | *stretto* |
| bridge | *ponte* |
| toll | *pedaggio* |
| slow down | *rallentare* |

## Italian Menu Vocabulary

### Antipasti

These before-meal treats can include almost anything; among the most common are:

| | |
|---|---|
| *antipasto misto* | mixed antipasto |
| *bruschetta* | garlic toast |
| *carciofi (sott'olio)* | artichokes (in oil) |
| *crostini* | liver paté on toast |
| *frutti di mare* | seafood |

| | |
|---|---|
| *funghi (trifolati)* | mushrooms (with anchovies, garlic, and lemon) |
| *gamberi al fagiolino* | shrimp with white beans |
| *mozzarella (in carrozza)* | buffalo cheese (fried with bread in batter) |
| *olive* | olives |
| *prosciutto (con melone)* | raw ham (with melon) |
| *salame* | cured pork |
| *salsiccia* | dry sausage |

## Minestre e Pasta

These dishes are the principal first courses (*primi*) served throughout Italy.

| | |
|---|---|
| *agnolotti* | ravioli with meat |
| *cacciucco* | spiced fish soup |
| *cannelloni* | meat and cheese rolled in pasta tubes |
| *cappelletti* | small ravioli, often in broth |
| *crespelle* | crêpes |
| *fettuccine* | long strips of pasta |
| *frittata* | omelette |
| *gnocchi* | potato dumplings |
| *lasagne* | sheets of pasta baked with meat and cheese sauce |
| *minestra di verdura* | thick vegetable soup |
| *minestrone* | soup with meat, vegetables, and pasta |
| *orecchiette* | ear-shaped pasta, usually served with turnip greens |
| *panzerotti* | ravioli filled with mozzarella, anchovies and egg |
| *pappardelle alla lepre* | flat pasta ribbons with hare sauce |
| *pasta e fagioli* | soup with beans, bacon, and tomatoes |
| *pastina in brodo* | tiny pasta in broth |
| *penne all'arrabbiata* | quill shaped pasta in hot spicy tomato sauce |
| *polenta* | cake or pudding of corn semolina, prepared with meat or tomato sauce |

| | |
|---|---|
| risotto (alla milanese) | Italian rice (with saffron and wine) |
| spaghetti all'amatriciana | with spicy sauce of bacon, tomatoes, onions, and hot pepper |
| spaghetti alla bolognese | with ground meat, ham, mushrooms, etc. |
| spaghetti alla carbonara | with bacon, eggs, and black pepper |
| spaghetti al pomodoro | with tomato sauce |
| spaghetti al sugo/ragù | with meat sauce |
| spaghetti alle vongole | with clam sauce |
| stracciatella | broth with eggs and cheese |
| tagliatelle | flat egg noodles |
| tortellini al pomodoro/panna/in brodo | pasta caps filled with meat and cheese, served with tomato sauce/cream, or in broth |
| vermicelli | very thin spaghetti |

## Second Courses—Carne (Meat)

| | |
|---|---|
| abbacchio | milk-fed lamb |
| agnello | lamb |
| anatra | duck |
| animelle | sweetbreads |
| arista | pork loin |
| arrosto misto | mixed roat meats |
| bistecca alla fiorentina | Florentine beef steak |
| bocconcini | veal mixed with ham and cheese and fried |
| bollito misto | stew of boiled meats |
| braciola | chop |
| brasato di manzo | braised meat with vegetables |
| bresaola | dried raw meat similar to ham served with lemon, olive oil and parsley |
| capretto | kid |
| capriolo | roe deer |
| carne di castrato/suino | mutton/pork |

| | |
|---|---|
| *carpaccio* | thin slices of raw beef in piquant sauce |
| *cassoeula* | winter stew with pork and cabbage |
| *cervello (al burro nero)* | brains (in black butter sauce) |
| *cervo* | venison |
| *cinghiale* | boar |
| *coniglio* | rabbit |
| *cotoletta (alla milanese/alla bolognese)* | veal cutlet (fried in breadcrumbs/with ham and cheese) |
| *fagiano* | pheasant |
| *faraona (alla creta)* | guinea fowl (in earthenware pot) |
| *fegato alla veneziana* | liver and onions |
| *involtini* | rolled slices of veal with filling |
| *lepre (in salmì)* | hare (marinated in wine) |
| *lombo di maiale* | pork loin |
| *lumache* | snails |
| *maiale (al latte)* | pork (cooked in milk) |
| *manzo* | beef |
| *ossobuco* | braised veal knuckle with herbs |
| *pancetta* | rolled pork |
| *pernice* | partridge |
| *petto di pollo (alla fiorentina/bolognese/sorpresa)* | boned chicken breast (fried in butter/with ham and cheese/stuffed and deep fried) |
| *piccione* | pigeon |
| *pizzaiola* | beef steak with tomato and oregano sauce |
| *pollo (alla cacciatora/alla diavola/alla Marengo)* | chicken (with tomatoes and mushrooms cooked in wine/grilled/ fried with tomatoes, garlic and wine) |
| *polpette* | meatballs |
| *quaglie* | quails |
| *rane* | frogs |
| *rognoni* | kidneys |
| *saltimbocca* | veal scallop with prosciutto and sage, cooked in wine and butter |

| | |
|---|---|
| *scaloppine* | thin slices of veal sautéed in butter |
| *spezzatino* | pieces of beef or veal, usually stewed |
| *spiedino* | meat on a skewer or stick |
| *stufato* | beef braised in white wine with vegetables |
| *tacchino* | turkey |
| *trippa* | tripe |
| *uccelletti* | small birds on a skewer |
| *vitello* | veal |

## Pesce (Fish)

| | |
|---|---|
| *acciughe* or *alici* | anchovies |
| *anguilla* | eel |
| *aragosta* | lobster |
| *aringa* | herring |
| *baccalà* | dried cod |
| *bonito* | small tuna |
| *branzino* | sea bass |
| *calamari* | squid |
| *cappe sante* | scallops |
| *cefalo* | grey mullet |
| *coda di rospo* | angler fish |
| *cozze* | mussels |
| *datteri di mare* | razor (or date) mussels |
| *dentice* | dentex (perch-like fish) |
| *dorato* | gilt head |
| *fritto misto* | mixed fish fry, with squid and shrimp |
| *gamberetto* | shrimp |
| *gamberi (di fiume)* | prawns (crayfish) |
| *granchio* | crab |
| *insalata di mare* | seafood salad |
| *lamprèda* | lamprey |
| *merluzzo* | cod |
| *nasello* | hake |

| | |
|---|---|
| orata | bream |
| ostriche | oysters |
| pescespada | swordfish |
| polipo | octopus |
| pesce azzuro | various types of small fish |
| pesce San Pietro | John Dory |
| rombo | turbot |
| sarde | sardines |
| seppie | cuttlefish |
| sgombro | mackerel |
| sogliola | sole |
| squadro | monkfish |
| tonno | tuna |
| triglia | red mullet (rouget) |
| trota | trout |
| trota salmonata | salmon trout |
| vongole | small clams |
| zuppa di pesce | mixed fish in sauce or stew |

## Contorni (Side Dishes, Vegetables)

| | |
|---|---|
| asparagi (alla fiorentina) | asparagus (with fried eggs) |
| broccoli (calabrese, romana) | broccoli (green, spiral) |
| carciofi (alla giudia) | artichokes (deep fried) |
| cardi | cardoons, thistles |
| carote | carrots |
| cavolfiore | cauliflower |
| cavolo | cabbage |
| ceci | chickpeas |
| cetriolo | cucumber |
| cipolla | onion |
| fagioli | white beans |
| fagiolini | French (green) beans |
| fave | fava beans |

| | |
|---|---|
| *finocchio* | fennel |
| *funghi (porcini)* | mushrooms (boletus) |
| *insalata (mista, verde)* | salad (mixed, green) |
| *lattuga* | lettuce |
| *lenticchie* | lentils |
| *melanzana (al forno)* | aubergine/eggplant (filled and baked) |
| *patate (fritte)* | potatoes (fried) |
| *peperoni* | sweet peppers |
| *peperonata* | stewed peppers, onions and tomatoes etc., similar to ratatouille |
| *piselli (al prosciutto)* | peas (with ham) |
| *pomodoro* | tomato |
| *porri* | leeks |
| *radicchio* | red chicory |
| *radice* | radish |
| *rapa* | turnip |
| *sedano* | celery |
| *spinaci* | spinach |
| *verdure* | greens |
| *zucca* | pumpkin |
| *zucchini* | zucchini (courgettes) |

## Formaggio (Cheese)

| | |
|---|---|
| *bel paese* | a soft white cow's cheese |
| *cacio/caciocavallo* | pale yellow, often sharp cheese |
| *fontina* | rich cow's milk cheese |
| *groviera* | mild cheese |
| *gorgonzola* | soft blue cheese |
| *parmigiano* | Parmesan cheese |
| *pecorino* | sharp sheep's cheese |
| *provolone* | sharp, tangy cheese; *dolce* is more mild |
| *stracchino* | soft white cheese |

## Frutta (Fruit, Nuts)

| | |
|---|---|
| *albicocche* | apricots |
| *ananas* | pineapple |
| *arance* | oranges |
| *banane* | bananas |
| *cachi* | persimmons |
| *ciliegie* | cherries |
| *cocomero* | watermelon |
| *composta di frutta* | stewed fruit |
| *dattero* | date |
| *fichi* | figs |
| *fragole (con panna)* | strawberries (with cream) |
| *frutta di stagione* | fruit in season |
| *lamponi* | raspberries |
| *macedonia di frutta* | fruit salad |
| *mandarino* | tangerine |
| *melagrana* | pomegranate |
| *mele* | apples |
| *melone* | melon |
| *mirtilli* | bilberries |
| *more* | blackberries |
| *nespola* | medlar fruit |
| *nocciole* | hazelnuts |
| *noci* | walnuts |
| *pera* | pear |
| *pesca* | peach |
| *pesca noce* | nectarine |
| *pignoli/pinoli* | pine nuts |
| *pompelmo* | grapefruit |
| *prugna/susina* | plum |
| *uva* | grapes |

## Dolci (Desserts)

| | |
|---|---|
| *amaretti* | macaroons |
| *cannoli* | crisp pastry tubes filled with ricotta, cream, chocolate or fruit |
| *coppa gelato* | assorted ice cream |
| *crema caramella* | caramel-topped custard |
| *crostata* | fruit flan |
| *gelato (produzione propria)* | ice cream (homemade) |
| *granita* | flavoured ice, usually lemon or coffee |
| *Monte Bianco* | chestnut pudding with whipped cream |
| *panettone* | sponge cake with candied fruit and raisins |
| *panforte* | dense cake of chocolate, almonds, and preserved fruit |
| *Saint-Honoré* | meringue cake |
| *semifreddo* | refrigerated cake |
| *sorbetto* | sherbet |
| *spumone* | a soft ice cream |
| *tiramisù* | mascarpone, coffee, chocolate and sponge fingers |
| *torrone* | nougat |
| *torta* | tart |
| *torta millefoglie* | layered custard tart |
| *zabaglione* | whipped eggs, sugar and Marsala wine, served hot |
| *zuppa inglese* | trifle |

## Bevande (Beverages)

| | |
|---|---|
| *acqua minerale con/senza gas* | mineral water with/without fizz |
| *aranciata* | orange soda |
| *birra (alla spina)* | beer (draught) |
| *caffè (freddo)* | coffee (iced) |
| *cioccolata (con panna)* | chocolate (with cream) |

| | |
|---|---|
| *gassosa* | lemon-flavoured soda |
| *latte* | milk |
| *limonata* | lemon soda |
| *succo di frutta* | fruit juice |
| *tè* | tea |
| *vino (rosso, bianco, rosato)* | wine (red, white, rosé) |

## Cooking Terms, Miscellaneous

| | |
|---|---|
| *aceto (balsamico)* | vinegar (balsamic) |
| *affumicato* | smoked |
| *aglio* | garlic |
| *alla brace* | on embers |
| *bicchiere* | glass |
| *burro* | butter |
| *cacciagione* | game |
| *conto* | bill |
| *costoletta/cotoletta* | chop |
| *coltello* | knife |
| *cotto adagio* | braised |
| *cucchaio* | spoon |
| *filetto* | fillet |
| *forchetta* | fork |
| *forno* | oven |
| *fritto* | fried |
| *ghiaccio* | ice |
| *griglia* | grill |
| *limone* | lemon |
| *magro* | lean meat/or pasta without meat |
| *mandorle* | almonds |
| *marmellata* | jam |
| *menta* | mint |
| *miele* | honey |
| *mostarda* | candied mustard sauce |

| | |
|---|---|
| *olio* | oil |
| *pane (tostato)* | bread (toasted) |
| *panini* | sandwiches |
| *panna* | fresh cream |
| *pepe* | pepper |
| *peperoncini* | hot chili peppers |
| *piatto* | plate |
| *prezzemolo* | parsley |
| *ripieno* | stuffed |
| *rosmarino* | rosemary |
| *sale* | salt |
| *salmì* | wine marinade |
| *salsa* | sauce |
| *salvia* | sage |
| *senape* | mustard |
| *tartufi* | truffles |
| *tazza* | cup |
| *tavola* | table |
| *tovagliolo* | napkin |
| *tramezzini* | finger sandwiches |
| *umido* | cooked in sauce |
| *uovo* | egg |
| *zucchero* | sugar |

## General and Travel

**Barzini, Luigi**, *The Italians* (Hamish Hamilton, 1964). A perhaps too clever account of the Italians by an Italian journalist living in London, but one of the classics.

**Douglas, Norman**, *Old Calabria* (Century, 1983). Reprint of a rascally travel classic.

**Goethe, J. W.**, *Italian Journey* (Penguin Classics, 1982). An excellent example of a genius turned to mush by Italy; brilliant insights and big, big mistakes.

**Haycraft, John**, *Italian Labyrinth* (Penguin, 1987). One of the latest attempts to unravel the Italian mess.

**Hutton, Edward**, *Florence, Assisi, and Umbria Revisited, Venice and Venetia, Siena and Southern Tuscany*, and *Naples and Campania Revisited* and *Rome,* (Hollis & Carter).

**Keates, Jonathan**, *Italian Journeys* (Picador, 1991). An argument for re-examining the neglegted charms of northern Italy.

**McCarthy, Mary,** *The Stones of Florence and Venice Observed* (Penguin, 1986). Brilliant evocations of Italy's two great art cities, with an understanding that makes many other works on the subject seem sluggish and pedantic; don't visit them without it.

**Morris, James,** *Venice* (Faber & Faber, 1960). Another classic account of 'the world's most beautiful city'.

**Morton, H. V.**, *A Traveller in Rome, A Traveller in Southern Italy* (Methuen, 1957, 1969). Among the most readable and delightful accounts of the region in print. Morton is a sincere scholar, and a true gentleman. Also a good friend to cats.

**Newby, Eric,** *Love and War in the Apennines* (Picador, 1983). Newby's account of his war days, when Italian villagers hid him from the Nazis.

**Nichols, Peter,** *Italia, Italia* (Macmillan, 1973). An account of modern Italy by an old Italy hand.

## History

**Acton, Harold**, *The Bourbons of Naples* (Methuen, 1956).

**Burckhardt, Jacob**, *The Civilization of the Renaissance in Italy* (Harper & Row, 1975). The classic on the subject (first published 1860), the mark agaist which scholars still level their poison arrows of revisionism.

**Carcopino, Jérome**, *Daily Life in Ancient Rome* (Penguin, 1981). A thorough and lively account of Rome at the height of Empire—guaranteed to evoke empathy from modern city dwellers.

**Ginsborg, Paul**, A *History of Contemporary Italy: Society and Politics 1943–1988* (Penguin, 1990). A good modern account of events up to the fall of Rome.

**Hale, J. R.**, (ed.), *A Concise Encyclopaedia of the Italian Renaissance* (Thames and Hudson, 1981). An excellent reference guide, with many concise, well-written essays.

**Hibbert, Christopher**, *Benito Mussolini, Rise and Fall of the House of Medici* and *Rome* (Penguin, 1965, 1979, 1985).

**Joll, James,** *Gramsci* (Fontana, 1977). A look at the father of modern Italian communism, someone we all should get to know better.

**Masson, Georgina**, *Frederick II of Hohenstaufen* (London, 1957).

**Morris Jan**, *The Venetian Empire* (Faber & Faber, 1980). A fascinating account of the Serenissima's glory days.

**Norwich, John Julius**, *The Normans in the South* (Thames and Hudson, 1967).

**Origo, Iris**, *The Merchant of Prato* (Penguin, 1963). Everyday life in medieval Tuscany with the father of modern accounting, Francesco di Marco Datini.

**Procacci, Giuliano**, *History of the Italian People* (Penguin, 1973). An in-depth view from the year 1000 to the present—also an introduction to the wit and subtlety of the best Italian scholarship.

**Rand, Edward Kennard**, *Founders of the Middle Ages* (Dover reprint, New York), a little-known but incandescently brilliant work that can explain Jerome, Augustine, Boethius and other intellectual currents of the decaying classical world.

---

## Art and Literature

**Boccaccio, Giovanni,** *The Decameron* (Penguin, 1972). The ever-young classic by one of the fathers of Italian literature. Its irreverent worldliness still provides a salutary antidote to whatever dubious ideas persist in your mental baggage.

**Calvino, Italo**, *Invisible Cities, If Upon a Winter's Night a Traveller* (Picador). Provocative fantasies that could only have been written by an Italian. Soething even better is his recent compilation of Italian Folktales, a little bit Brothers grimm and a little bit Fellini.

**Cellini**, *Autobiography of Benvenuto Cellini* (Penguin, trans. by George Bull). Fun reading by a swashbuckling braggart and world-class liar.

**Clark, Kenneth**, *Leonardo da Vinci* (Penguin).

**Dante Alighieri**, *The Divine Comedy* (plenty of equally good translations). Few poems have ever had such a mythical significance for a nation. Anyone serious about understanding Italy and the Italian world view will need more than a passing acquaintance with Dante.

**Gadda, Carlo Emilio**, *That Awful Mess on Via Merulana* (Quartet Books, 1980). Itlay during the Fascist era.

**Gilbert/Linscott**, *Complete Poems and Selected Letters of Michelangelo* (Princeton Press, 1984).

## Further Reading

**Henig, Martin**, (ed.), *A Handbook of Roman Art* (Phaidon, 1983). Essays on all aspects of ancient Roman art.

**Lawrence, D. H.**, *Etruscan Places* (Olive Press).

**Levi, Carlo**, *Christ Stopped at Eboli* (Penguin, 1982). Disturbing post-war realism.

**Levy, Michael**, *Early Renaissance* (1967) and *High Renaissance* (both Penguin, 1975). Old-fashioned accounts of the period, with a breathless reverence for the 1500s— but still full of intriguing interpretations.

**Murray, Linda**, *The High Renaissance* and *The Late Renaissance and Mannerism* (Thames and Hudson, 1977). Excellent introduction to the period; also Peter and Linda Murray, *The Art of the Renaissance* (Thames and Hudson, 1963).

**Pavese, Cesare**, *The Moon and the Bonfire* (Quartet, 1979). Postwar classic.

**Petrarch, Francesco**, *Canzoniere and Other Works* (Oxford, 1985). The most famous poems by the 'First Modern Man'.

**Vasari, Giorgio**, *Lives of the Artists* (Penguin, 1985). Readable, anecdotal accounts of the Renaissance greats by the father of art history, also the first professional Philistine.

**Wittkower, Rudolf**, *Art and Architecture in Italy 1600–1750* (Pelican, 1986). The Bible on Baroque, erudite and full of wit.

Note: Page numbers in *italics* indicate maps. **Bold** entries indicate main references.

Mussolini (*cont'd*)
  and the Esposizione
    Universale di Roma
    885–6, 885–6

Naples 57–8, 59, 61, 62,
    923–53, *924–5*
Naples
  advantages 926–7
  Aquarium 944
  Archaeological Museum
    941–2
  Bay 953–7, *955*
  black marketing 940
  Capua Gate 941
  Castel dell'Ovo (fortress)
    944
  Castel Nuovo 934–5
  catacombs 942
  Certosa di San Martino
    943–4
  drawbacks 923–4, 926–7
  eating out 948–52
  entertainment and nightlife
    952–3
  Gèsu Nuovo (Piazza) 936
  getting around 931–3
  getting to and from 929–30
  history 927–9
  islands 981–7
  Parco di Capodimonte
    (tropical park) 942–3
  Piazza del Duomo 937–9
  Piazza del Plebiscito 933–5
  Piazza Garibaldi 940–1
  *presepi* 937–9
  Roman mosaics 941–2
  San Carlo opera house
    933–4
  San Gennaro Cathedral
    939
  Sansevero Chapel 937
  Santa Chiara church 936
  shopping 945–6

Spaccanapoli street 935–7
  sports and activities 946
  tourist information 931
  tropical park 942
  University 937
  Via Toledo 935
  Villa Comunale 944–5
  Virgil's Tomb 945
  West Fields 957–60
  where to stay 946–8
Narni 812, 814, 815
nature reserve 458
Nemi 912
Nicholas, Saint 1041–2
Nocera Umbra 800–1
Nocino liqueur 516, 524
di Non, Val 464–5
Norcia 809, 812–13, 814
North Coast 836–8
Novara 141, 144, 145
  Duomo 141
  San Gaudenzio church 141
Numana 593
Nuovo, Monte (new volcano)
    958
Nus 127

Oliveto Maggiore, Monte
    755–6
opera 91–4
  Bologna 541
  Busseto 508–9
  Florence 695
  Genoa 195
  Lombardy 287
  Macerata 598, 600
  Modena 527
  Naples 952
  Parma 518
  Pesaro 580
  Reggio Emilia 519
  Rome 905–6

Turin 115
Venice 384
Verona 431, 432
  *see also* La Scala *under*
    Milan
Orta, Lake 269–73
Ortobello 734
Ortona 613–15
Orvieto 815–16, 818–24
  Cathedral 819–22
  churches 821–2
  eating out 824
  getting around 815–16
  Piazza del Duomo 821
  Pozzo di San Patrizio
    (St Patrick's Well) 822
  surrounding villages 823
  tourist information 819
  where to stay 823–4
Osimo 595, 597
Ostia 908
Ostia Antica 912
Ostuni 1046
Otranto 1063, 1064

packing 32–3
Padre Pio de Pietralcina 1031
Padua 398–405, *399*
Padua
  Basilica di Sant'Antonio
    402–3
  Capella degli Scrovegni
    400–2
  eating out 404–5
  Eremitani church 400–2
  getting to and from 398
  North 409–14
  Orto Botanico (botanical
    gardens) 403
  Palazzo della Ragione
    400–1
  palio (horse race) 407
  Piazza del Santo 402–3

1106    Index

'Most literary critics seem to agree that the guides are divine.'

*The Independent*

'Anecdote and the lively conveying of personal experience are what elevate a guidebook to a friend, and Cadogan's writing duo have few equals. Their humour, sensitive discussion of Italian culture and brave attempt at unravelling the country's labyrinthine history, in my opinion, places the Cadogan Guide above its rivals.'

*Weekend Telegraph*

'The characteristic of all these guides is a heady mix of the eminently practical, a stimulating description of the potentially already familiar, and an astonishing quantity of things we'd never thought of, let alone seen.'

*The Art Quarterly*

'Whether you are traveling to this area for the cultural splendors, superb cuisine or natural wonders, this exciting encyclopaedic reference is the only one you will need to consult.'

*US Travel and Leisure*

'*Italy* by Dana Facaros and Michael Pauls is an absolute gem of a travel book, humorous, informed, sympathetic, as irresistible as that land itself.'

*The Sunday Times*

'Dana Facaros and Michael Pauls...give eminently knowledgeable advice... and are not afraid...to give due warning as well as recommendations.'

*The Good Book Guide*

'*Tuscany, Umbria & The Marches* deserves continuing recognition as an important independent traveler's "bible" to the area.'

*The Midwest Book Review*

'Irreverent, unblinkered and hard-eyed, and based on a series of 15 well thought-out walks, each minutely described, the book [*Rome*] throws the city into focus with nothing spared.'

*Sunday Telegraph*

1115

## The Cadogan Guides Series

### Italy Guides by Dana Facaros and Michael Pauls

ITALY: NORTHWEST ITALY

ITALY: NORTHEAST ITALY

ITALY: SOUTH ITALY

FLORENCE, SIENA, PISA & LUCCA

ITALY: THE BAY OF NAPLES &
THE AMALFI COAST

ITALY: LOMBARDY, Milan & the Italian
Lakes

SICILY

ROME

TUSCANY, UMBRIA & THE MARCHES

VENICE & THE VENETO

## Other Titles

### Country Guides

THE CARIBBEAN & THE BAHAMAS

CENTRAL AMERICA

CENTRAL ASIA

ECUADOR, THE GALAPAGOS &
COLOMBIA

EGYPT

FRANCE: THE SOUTH OF FRANCE

FRANCE: SOUTHWEST FRANCE;
Dordogne, Lot & Bordeaux

GERMANY

GERMANY: BAVARIA

GUATEMALA & BELIZE

INDIA

IRELAND

JAPAN

MEXICO

MOROCCO

PORTUGAL

SCOTLAND

SCOTLAND'S HIGHLANDS & ISLANDS

SOUTH AFRICA

SPAIN

SPAIN: SOUTHERN SPAIN

TUNISIA

TURKEY

TURKEY: WESTERN TURKEY

### Island Guides

BALI

THE CARIBBEAN: N. E. CARIBBEAN
The Leeward Islands

THE CARIBBEAN: S. E. CARIBBEAN
The Windward Islands

CYPRUS

GREEK ISLANDS

GREECE: THE CYCLADES

GREECE: THE DODECANESE

GREECE: THE IONIAN ISLANDS

MALTA, COMINO & GOZO

### City Guides

AMSTERDAM

BERLIN

BRUSSELS, BRUGES, GHENT &
ANTWERP

LONDON

MOSCOW & ST PETERSBURG

NEW YORK

PARIS

PRAGUE